CLYMER®

SUZUKI

Katana 600 • 1988-1996
GSX-R750-1100 • 1986-1987

The world's finest publisher of mechanical how-to manuals

PRIMEDIA
Business Magazines & Media

P.O. Box 12901, Overland Park, Kansas 66282-2901

FIRST EDITION
First Printing September, 1989
Second Printing April, 1990

SECOND EDITION
Updated by Ed Scott to include Katana 600 models
First Printing January, 1993
Second Printing August, 1994
Third Printing October, 1995
Fourth Printing August, 1997
Fifth Printing March, 1999

THIRD EDITION
First Printing January, 2001
Second Printing September, 2002
Third Printing June, 2004

Printed in U.S.A.

CLYMER and colophon are registered trademarks of PRIMEDIA Business Magazines & Media Inc.

ISBN: 0-89287-772-3

Library of Congress: 00-111228

MEMBER MOTORCYCLE INDUSTRY COUNCIL, INC.

AUTHOR: Ed Scott.

TECHNICAL PHOTOGRAPHY: Ed Scott, with assistance from David Morgan, Los Angeles, California. Motorcycle courtesy of Victor Boyce, Los Angeles, California.

TECHNICAL ILLUSTRATIONS: Mitzi McCarthy.

TOOLS AND EQUIPMENT: K & L Supply Co. at www.klsupply.com.

COVER: Mark Clifford Photography, Los Angeles, California.

CLYMER®

Publisher Shawn Etheridge

EDITORIAL

Managing Editor
James Grooms

Associate Editor
Jason Beaver
Lee Buell

Technical Writers
Jay Bogart
Michael Morlan
George Parise
Mark Rolling
Ed Scott
Ron Wright

Editorial Production Manager
Dylan Goodwin

Senior Production Editor
Greg Araujo

Production Editors
Holly Messinger
Darin Watson

Associate Production Editor
Susan Hartington
Julie Jantzer
Justin Marciniak

Technical Illustrators
Steve Amos
Errol McCarthy
Mitzi McCarthy
Bob Meyer
Mike Rose

MARKETING/SALES AND ADMINISTRATION

Advertising & Promotions Manager
Elda Starke

Advertising & Promotions Coordinators
Melissa Abbott
Wendy Stringfellow

Art Director
Chris Paxton

Sales Managers
Ted Metzger, Manuals
Dutch Sadler, Marine
Matt Tusken, Motorcycles

Business Manager
Ron Rogers

Customer Service Manager
Terri Cannon

Customer Service Representatives
Shawna Davis
Courtney Hollars
Susan Kohlmeyer
April LeBlond
Jennifer Lassiter
Ernesto Suarez

Warehouse & Inventory Manager
Leah Hicks

PRIMEDIA
Business Magazines & Media
P.O. Box 12901, Overland Park, KS 66282-2901 • 800-262-1954 • 913-967-1719

The following books and guides are published by PRIMEDIA Business Directories & Books.

CLYMER® | CLYMER® PROSERIES | AC-U-KWIK®

I&T SHOP SERVICE™ | PRIMEDIA PRICE DIGESTS Your Valuation & Specification Authority | EC&M Books

More information available at *primediabooks.com*

CONTENTS

QUICK REFERENCE DATA

TIRE INFLATION PRESSURE (COLD)*

Load	Tire Pressure			
	Front		Rear	
	psi	kPa	psi	kPa
Katana 600				
Solo riding	33	225	36	250
Dual riding	33	220	36	250
GSX-R750-1100				
Solo riding	36	250	36	250
Dual riding	36	250	42	290

*Tire inflation pressure for factory equipped tires. Aftermarket tires may require different inflation pressure.

On GSX-R750-1100, the standard tire on this motorcycle is 110/80VR18-240 (250) on the front and 140/70VR18-V240 (250) on the rear. Suzuki states the use of tires other than those originally equipped may cause instability.

ENGINE OIL CAPACITY

Model	Oil change		Oil and filter change		Overhaul	
	Liters	U.S. qt.	Liters	U.S. qt.	Liters	U.S. qt
Katana 600	3.6	3.8	3.8	4.0	5.0	5.3
GSX-R750	3.6	3.8	3.8	4.0	5.0	5.3
GSX-R750R Limited Edition	3.3	3.5	3.51	3.7	4.81	5.1
GSX-R1100	3.4	3.6	3.7	3.9	4.7	5.0

MAINTENANCE AND TUNE UP TORQUE SPECIFICATIONS

Item	N•m	Ft.-lb.
Oil drain plug	20-25	14-18
NEAS unit mounting bolts	6.8-8.0	4.5-6.0
Fork cap bolt (GSX-R5750-1100)	15-30	11-22
Fork drain bolts (Katana 600)	6-9	4.5-6.5
Cylinder head nuts	35-40	25-29
Cylinder head bolts	8-12	6-8.5
Cylinder block nut	7-11	5-8
Cylinder head cover bolts (all)	13-15	9-11
Oil hose fitting Allen bolts	8-12	6-9
Upper fork bridge bolts		
GSX-R750-1100	85-115	61-83
Katana 600		
Upper	15-25	11-18
Lower	25-40	18-29
Handlebar holder (Katana 600)		
Allen bolt nut	24-26	17.5-26
Allen bolt	50-60	36-43.5

FRONT FORK OIL CAPACITY* AND DIMENSION

Year	Capacity cc	Capacity oz.	Distance mm	Distance in.
Katana 600				
1988	416	15.5	134	5.28
1989-on	478	16.1	100	3.93
GSX-R750	456	15.4	107	4.21
GSX-R750R Limited Edition	427	14.4	130	5.21
GSX-R1100	417	14.1	159	6.26

* Each fork leg.

DRIVE CHAIN SLACK AND SERVICE LIMIT LENGTH

Model	Slack	Service limit*
600 cc models	25-35 mm (1.0-1.4 in.)	N.A.**
750 cc models	25-30 mm (1.0-1.2 in.)	319.4 mm (12.6 in.)
1100 cc models	20-25 mm (0.8-1.0 in.)	319.4 mm (12.6 in.)

* Drive chain length between 21 link pins.
** N.A. Information not available from Suzuki.

TUNE-UP SPECIFICATIONS

Valve clearance	
Katana 600	
1988-1991	
Intake and exhaust	0.10-0.15 mm (0.004-0.006 in.)
1992-on	
Intake	0.10-0.20 mm (0.004-0.008 in.)
Exhaust	0.15-0.25 mm (0.006-0.010 in.)
GSX-R750-1100	
Intake and exhaust	0.10-0.15 mm (0.004-0.006 in.)
Spark plug type	
Katana 600	
Standard heat range	NGK DR8ES
All other models	
Standard heat range	
GSX-R750, GSX-R750R Limited Edition	NGK D9EA
GSX-R1100	NGK J9A
Hotter heat range	
GSX-R750, GSX-R750R Limited Edition	NGK D8EA
Colder heat range	
GSX-R1100	NGK J10A
Spark plug gap	0.6-0.7 mm (0.02-0.03 in.)
Idle speed	
Katana 600	1,300 +/-100 rpm
GSX-R750-1100	1,100 +/-100 rpm
Firing order	1, 2, 4, 3
Ignition timing	
Katana 600	13° BTDC below 1,500 rpm
GSX-R750-1100	35° BTDC above 2,350 rpm
	7° BTDC below 1,500 rpm

INTRODUCTION

This detailed, comprehensive manual covers the 1986-1987 Suzuki GSX-R750-1100 cc inline fours. Chapter Thirteen contains all procedures and specifications unique to the 1988-1993 Katana 600.

The expert text gives complete information on maintenance, tune-up, repair and overhaul. Hundreds of photos and drawings guide you through every step. The book includes all you will need to know to keep your Suzuki running right. Throughout this book where differences occur among the models, they are clearly identified.

A shop manual is a reference. You want to be able to find information fast. As in all Clymer books, this one is designed with you in mind. All chapters are thumb tabbed. Important items are extensively indexed at the rear of the book. All procedures, tables, photos, etc., in this manual are for the reader who may be working on the bike for the first time or using this manual for the first time. All the most frequently used specifications and capacities are summarized in the *Quick Reference Data* pages at the front of the book.

Keep the book handy in your tool box. It will help you better understand how your bike runs, lower repair costs and generally improve your satisfaction with the bike.

NOTE: If you own a GSX600F Katana, first refer to Chapter 13 for specific service information.

1

CHAPTER ONE

GENERAL INFORMATION

MANUAL ORGANIZATION

All dimensions and capacities are expressed in English units familiar to U.S. mechanics as well as in metric units. Refer to **Table 1** for decimal and metric equivalents.

This chapter provides general information and discusses equipment and tools useful both for preventive maintenance and troubleshooting.

Chapter Two provides methods and suggestions for quick and accurate diagnosis and repair of problems. Troubleshooting procedures discuss typical symptoms and logical methods to pinpoint the trouble.

Chapter Three explains all periodic lubrication and routine maintenance necessary to keep the Suzuki running well. Chapter Three also includes recommended tune-up procedures, eliminating the need to constantly consult chapters on the various assemblies.

Subsequent chapters describe specific systems such as the engine, clutch, transmission, fuel, exhaust, suspension and brakes. Each chapter provides disassembly, repair and assembly procedures in simple step-by-step form.

If a repair is impractical for a home mechanic, it is so indicated. It is usually faster and less expensive to take such repairs to a dealer or competent repair shop. Specifications concerning a particular system are included at the end of the appropriate chapter.

Some of the procedures in this manual specify special tools. In most cases, the tool is illustrated either in actual use or alone. Well-equipped mechanics may find they can substitute similar tools already on hand or can fabricate their own.

Tables 1-4 are at the end of this chapter.

NOTES, CAUTIONS AND WARNINGS

The terms NOTE, CAUTION and WARNING have specific meanings in this manual. A NOTE provides additional information to make a step or procedure easier or clearer. Disregarding a NOTE could cause inconvenience, but would not cause equipment damage or personal injury.

A CAUTION emphasizes areas where equipment damage could result. Disregarding a CAUTION could cause permanent mechanical damage; however, personal injury is unlikely.

A WARNING emphasizes areas where personal injury or even death could result from negligence. Mechanical damage may also occur. WARNINGS *are to be taken seriously*. In some cases, serious injury or death has resulted from disregarding similar warnings.

Throughout this manual keep in mind these definitions. "Front" refers to the front of the bike. The front of any component, such as the engine, is the end which faces toward the front of the bike.

The "left-" and "right-hand" sides refer to the position of the parts as viewed by a rider sitting on the seat facing forward. For example, the throttle control is on the right-hand side and the clutch lever is on the left-hand side. These rules are simple, but even experienced mechanics occasionally become disoriented.

SAFETY FIRST

Professional mechanics can work for years and never sustain a serious injury. If you observe a few rules of common sense and safety, you can enjoy many hours servicing your own machine. If you ignore these rules you can hurt yourself or damage the bike.

1. *Never* use gasoline as a cleaning solvent.
2. Never smoke or use a torch in the vicinity of flammable liquids such as cleaning solvent in open containers.
3. If welding or brazing is required on the machine, remove the fuel tank to a safe distance, at least 50 feet away.
4. Use the proper sized wrenches to avoid damage to fasteners and injury to yourself.
5. When loosening a tight or stuck nut, think about what would happen if the wrench should slip. Be careful; protect yourself accordingly.
6. Keep your work area clean and uncluttered.
7. Wear safety goggles during all operations involving drilling, grinding or the use of a cold chisel.
8. Never use worn tools.
9. Keep a fire extinguisher handy and be sure it is rated for gasoline and electrical fires.

SERVICE HINTS

Most of the service procedures covered are straightforward and can be performed by anyone reasonably handy with tools. However, you should consider your own capabilities carefully before attempting any operation involving major disassembly of the engine.

Take your time and do the job right. Do not forget that a newly rebuilt engine must be broken in the same as a new one. Keep the rpm within the limits given in your owner's manual when you get back on the road.

1. There are many items available that can be used on your hands before and after working on your bike. A little preparation prior to getting "all greased up" will help when cleaning up later. Before starting out, work Vaseline, soap or a product such as Invisible Glove (**Figure 1**) onto your forearms, into your hands and under your fingernails and cuticles. This will make cleanup a lot easier. For cleanup, use a waterless hand soap such as Sta-Lube and then finish up with powdered Boraxo and a fingernail brush (**Figure 2**).
2. Repairs go much faster and easier if the bike is clean before you begin work. There are special cleaners, such as Gunk or Bel-Ray Degreaser (**Figure 3**) for washing the engine and related parts. Just spray or brush on the cleaning solution, let it stand, then rinse it away with a garden hose. Clean all oily or greasy parts with cleaning solvent as you remove them.

WARNING

***Never** use gasoline as a cleaning agent. It presents an extreme fire hazard. Be sure to work in a well-ventilated area when using cleaning solvent. Keep a fire extinguisher, rated for gasoline fires, handy in any case.*

1

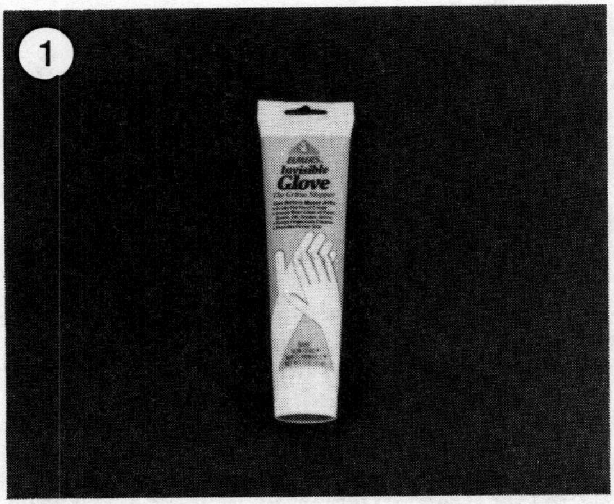

2

3. Special tools are required for some repair procedures. These may be purchased from a Suzuki dealer or motorcycle shop, rented from a tool rental dealer or fabricated by a mechanic or machinist (often at a considerable savings).
4. Much of the labor charged for by mechanics is to remove and disassemble other parts to reach the defective unit. It is usually possible to perform the preliminary operations yourself and then take the defective unit in to the dealer for repair.
5. Once you have decided to tackle the job yourself, read the entire section *completely* while looking at the actual parts before starting the job. Making sure you have identified the proper one. Study the illustrations and text until you have a good idea of what is involved in completing the job satisfactorily. If special tools or replacement parts are required, make arrangements to get them before you start. It is frustrating and time-consuming to get partly into a job and then be unable to complete it.
6. Simple wiring checks can be easily made at home, but knowledge of electronics is almost a necessity for performing tests with complicated electronic testing gear.
7. Whenever servicing the engine or transmission, or when removing a suspension component, the bike should be secured in a safe manner. If the bike is to be parked on the side stand or center stand, check the stand to make sure it is secure and not damaged. Block the front and rear wheels if they remain on the ground. A small hydraulic jack and a block of wood can be used to raise the chassis. If the transmission is not going to be worked on and the drive chain is connected to the rear wheel, shift the transmission into first gear.
8. Disconnect the negative battery cable when working on or near the electrical, clutch, or starter systems and before disconnecting any electrical wires. On most batteries, the negative terminal will be marked with a minus (-) sign and the positive terminal with a plus (+) sign.

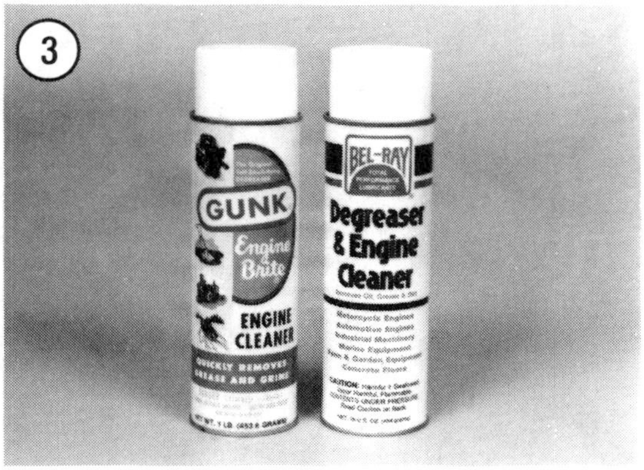

9. During disassembly of parts, keep a few general cautions in mind. Force is rarely needed to get things apart. If parts are a tight fit, such as a bearing in a case, there is usually a tool designed to separate them. Never use a screwdriver to pry parts with machined surfaces such as crankcase halves. You will mar the surfaces and end up with leaks.
10. Make diagrams (or take a Polaroid picture) wherever similar-appearing parts are found. For instance, crankcase bolts are often not the same length. You may think you can remember where everything came from, but mistakes are costly. There is also the possibility you may be sidetracked and not return to work for days or even weeks, in which interval carefully laid out parts may have become disturbed.
11. Tag all similar internal parts for location and mark all mating parts for position. Record the number and thickness of any shims as they are removed. Small parts such as bolts can be identified by placing them in plastic sandwich bags. Seal and label them with masking tape.
12. Wiring should be tagged with masking tape and marked as each wire is removed. Again, do not rely on memory alone.
13. Protect finished surfaces from physical damage or corrosion. Keep gasoline and hydraulic brake fluid off plastic parts and painted and plated surfaces.
14. Frozen or very tight bolts and screws can often be loosened by soaking with penetrating oil, such as WD-40 or Liquid Wrench, then sharply striking the bolt head a few times with a hammer and punch (or screwdriver for screws). Avoid heat unless absolutely necessary, since it may melt, warp or remove the temper from many parts.
15. No parts, except those assembled with a press fit, require unusual force during assembly. If a part is hard to remove or install, find out why before proceeding.
16. Cover all openings after removing parts to keep dirt, small tools, etc., from falling in.
17. Wiring connections and brake components should be kept clean and free of grease and oil.
18. When assembling 2 parts, start all fasteners, then tighten evenly.
19. When assembling parts, be sure all shims and washers are installed exactly as they came out.
20. Whenever a rotating part butts against a stationary part, look for a shim or washer.
21. Use new gaskets if there is any doubt about the condition of the old ones. A thin coat of oil on gaskets may help them seal effectively.

22. Heavy grease can be used to hold small parts in place if they tend to fall out during assembly. However, keep grease and oil away from electrical and brake components.
23. High spots may be sanded off a piston with sandpaper, but fine emery cloth and oil will do a much more professional job.
24. Carbon can be removed from the head, the piston crown and the exhaust port with a dull screwdriver. Do *not* scratch machined surfaces. Wipe off the surface with a clean cloth when finished.
25. The carburetors are best cleaned by disassembling them and cleaning the air and fuel orifices with a spray carburetor cleaner. Never spray gaskets and rubber parts with these cleaners. Soaking the disassembled parts in automotive carburetor cleaner is not recommended since it often does more harm than good. Such methods will remove all paint or protective coating from the exterior of the carburetor body. Also, any sediment in the carburetor cleaner may find its way into an air or fuel passage and plug it. Never use wire to clean out jets and air passages; they are easily damaged. Use compressed air to blow out the carburetor *after* the float has been removed.
26. A baby bottle makes a good measuring device for adding oil to the front forks. Get one that is graduated in fluid ounces and cubic centimeters. After it has been used for this purpose, do *not* let a small child drink out of it as there will always be an oil residue in it.
27. Some operations, for example, require the use of a press. It would be wiser to have these performed by a shop equipped for such work, rather than trying to do the job yourself with makeshift equipment. Other procedures require precise measurements. Unless you have the skills and equipment required, it would be better to have a qualified repair shop make the measurements for you.

SPECIAL TIPS

Because of the extreme demands placed on a bike, several points should be kept in mind when performing service and repair. The following items are general suggestions that may improve the overall life of the machine and help avoid costly failures.

1. Use a locking compound such as Loctite Lock N' Seal No. 242 (blue Loctite) on all bolts and nuts, even if they are secured with lockwashers. This type of Loctite does not harden completely and allows easy removal of the bolt or nut. A screw or bolt lost from an engine cover or bearing retainer could easily cause serious and expensive damage before its loss is noticed. Make sure the threads are clean and free of grease and oil. Clean with contact cleaner before applying the Loctite. When applying Loctite, use a small amount. If too much is used, it can work its way down the threads and stick parts together not meant to be stuck. Keep a tube of Loctite in your tool box. When used properly it is cheap insurance.
2. Use a hammer-driven impact driver tool to remove and install all bolts, particularly engine cover screws. These tools help prevent damage to fastener heads and ensure a tight installation.
3. When replacing missing or broken fasteners (bolts, nuts and screws), especially on the engine or

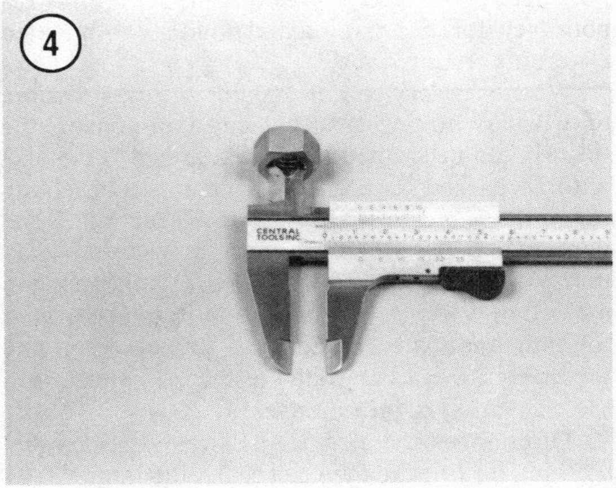

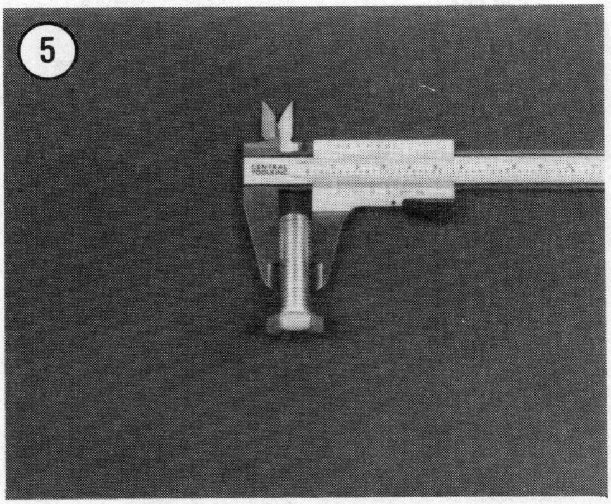

frame components, always use Suzuki replacement parts. They are specially hardened for each application. The wrong fastener could easily cause serious and expensive damage, not to mention rider injury.

4. When installing gaskets in the engine, always use Suzuki replacement gaskets *without* sealer, unless designated. These gaskets are designed to swell when they come in contact with oil. Gasket sealer will prevent the gaskets from swelling as intended, which can result in oil leaks. These Suzuki gaskets are cut from material of the precise thickness needed. Installation of a too thick or too thin gasket in a critical area could cause engine damage.

TORQUE SPECIFICATIONS

Torque specifications throughout this manual are given in Newton meters (N•m) and foot-pounds (ft.-lb.). Newton meters have been adopted in place of meter kilograms (mkg) in accordance with the International Modernized Metric System. Tool manufacturers offer torque wrenches calibrated in both Newton meters and foot-pounds.

Existing torque wrenches calibrated in meter kilograms can be used by performing a simple conversion. All you have to do is move the decimal point one place to the right; for example, 3.5 mkg = 35 N•m. This conversion is accurate enough for mechanical work even though the exact mathematical conversion is 3.5 mkg = 34.3 N•m.

Refer to **Table 2** for standard torque specifications for various size screws, bolts and nuts that may not be listed in the respective chapters. To use the table, first determine the size of the bolt or nut. Use a vernier caliper and measure inside the threaded hole of the nut (**Figure 4**) and across the threads for a bolt (**Figure 5**).

FASTENERS

The materials and designs of the various fasteners used on your Suzuki are not arrived at by chance or accident. Fastener design determines the type of tool required to work the fastener. Fastener material is carefully selected to decrease the possibility of physical failure.

6

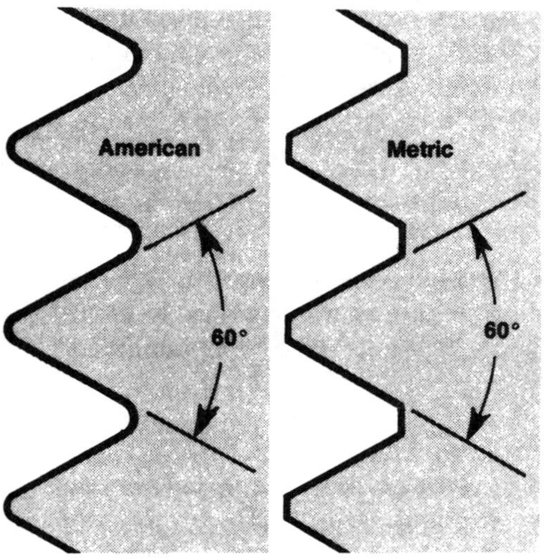

Threads

Nuts, bolts and screws are manufactured in a wide range of thread patterns. To join a nut and bolt, the diameter of the bolt and the diameter of the hole in the nuts must be the same. If is just as important that the threads on both be properly matched.

The best way to tell if the threads on 2 fasteners are matched is to turn the nut on the bolt (or the bolt into the threaded hole in the piece of equipment), with your fingers only. Be sure both pieces are clean. If much force is required, check the thread condition on each fastener. If the thread condition is good but the fastener jams, the threads are not compatible. A thread pitch gauge can also be used to determine pitch. Suzuki motorcycles are manufactured with metric standard fasteners. The threads are cut differently than those of American fasteners (**Figure 6**).

Most threads are cut so that the fastener must be turned *clockwise* to tighten it. These are called right-hand threads. Some fasteners have left-hand threads; they must be turned *counterclockwise* to be tightened.

Left-hand threads are used in locations where normal rotation of the equipment would tend to loosen a right-hand threaded fastener. When left-hand threads are used in this manual they are identified in the text.

Machine Screws

There are many different types of machine screws. **Figure 7** shows a number of screw heads requiring different types of turning tools. Heads are also designed to protrude above the metal (round or hex) or to be slightly recessed in the metal (flat). See **Figure 8**.

Bolts

Commonly called bolts, the technical name for these fasteners is cap screws. Metric bolts are described by the diameter and pitch (or the distance between each thread). For example, an M8—1.25 bolt is one that has a diameter of 8 millimeters and a distance of 1.25 millimeters between each thread. The measurement across 2 flats on the head of the bolt indicates the proper wrench side to be used. Use a vernier caliper and measure across the threads (**Figure 5**) to determine the bolt diameter.

Nuts

Nuts are manufactured in a variety of type and sizes. Most are hexagonal (6-sided) and fit on bolts, screws and studs with the same diameter and pitch.

Figure 9 shows several types of nuts. The common nut is generally used with a lockwasher. Self-locking nuts have a nylon insert which prevents the nut from loosening; no lockwasher is required. Wing nuts are designed for fast removal by hand. Wing nuts are used for convenience in non-critical locations.

To indicate the size of a nut, manufacturer's specify the diameter of the opening and the threads per inch. This is similar to bolt specifications, but without the length dimension. The measurement across 2 flats on the nut indicate the proper wrench side to be used. **Figure 5** shows how to determine bolt diameter.

Self-locking Fasteners

Several types of bolts, screws and nuts incorporate a system that develops an interference

7

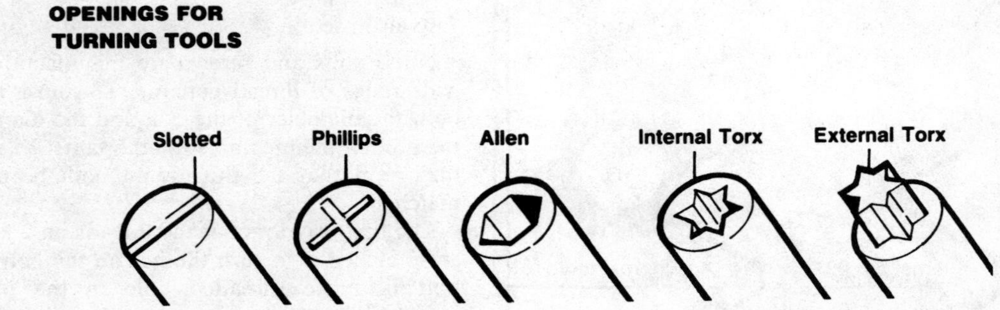

8

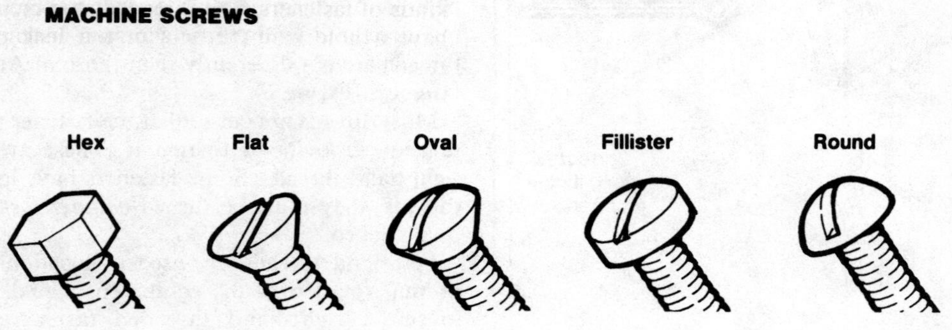

9

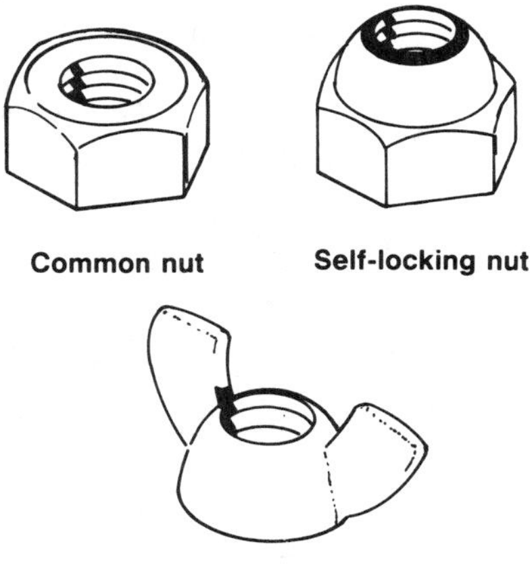

10

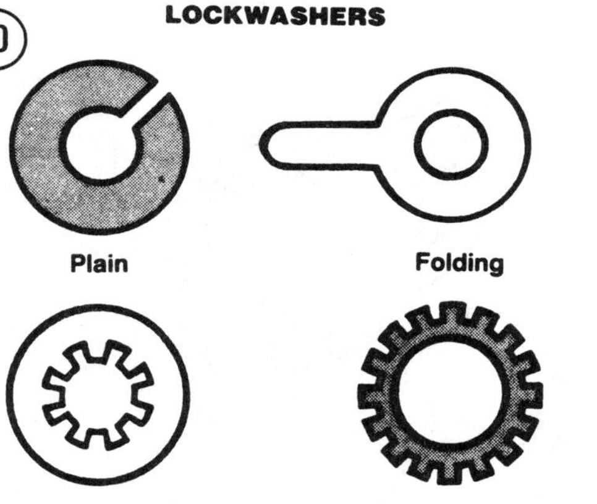

11

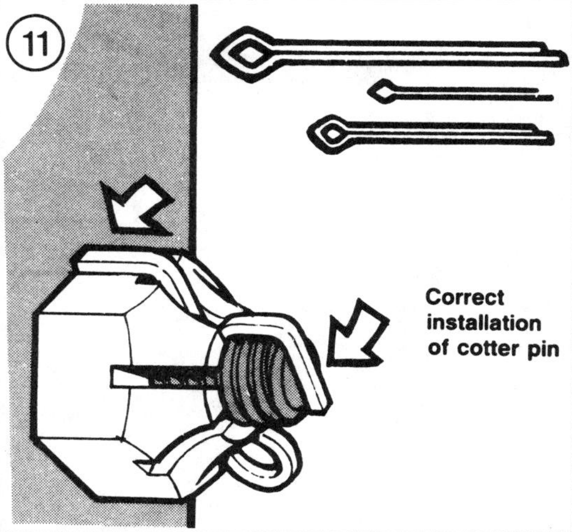

between the bolt, screw, nut or tapped hole threads. Interference is achieved in various ways: by distorting threads, coating threads with dry adhesive or nylon, distorting the top of an all-metal nut, using a nylon insert in the center or at the top of a nut, etc.

Self-locking fasteners offer greater holding strength and better vibration resistance. Some self-locking fasteners can be reused if in good condition. Others, like the nylon insert nut, form an initial locking condition when the nut is first installed; the nylon forms closely to the bolt thread pattern, thus reducing any tendency for the nut to loosen. When the nut is removed, its locking efficiency is greatly reduced. For greatest safety it is recommended that you install new self-locking fasteners whenever they are removed.

Washers

There are 2 basic types of washers: flat washers and lockwashers. Flat washers are simple discs with a hole to fit a screw or bolt. Lockwashers are designed to prevent a fastener from working loose due to vibration, expansion and contraction. **Figure 10** shows several types of washers. Washers are also used in the following functions:

a. As spacers.
b. To prevent galling or damage of the equipment by the fastener.
c. To help distribute fastener load during torquing.
d. As fluid seals (copper, aluminum or laminated washers).

Note that flat washers are often used next to a fastener to provide a smooth bearing surface. This allows the fastener to be turned easily with a tool.

Cotter Pins

Cotter pins (**Figure 11**) are used to secure special kinds of fasteners. The threaded stud or bolt must have a hole in it; the nut or nut lock piece has castellations around its upper edge through which the cotter pin must be inserted. Once fully inserted, the ends of the cotter pin are bent around the outside of the nut to secure it. Cotter pins should not be reused after removal as the ends may break and the cotter pin could then fall out.

Circlips

Circlips (or snap rings) can be internal or external design. They are used to retain items on shafts (external type) or within tubes (internal type). In some applications, circlips of varying thickness are used to control the end play of parts assemblies. These are often called selective fit circlips. Circlips should be replaced during installation, as removal weakens and deforms them.

Two basic types of circlips are available: machined and stamped circlips. Machined circlips can be installed in either direction (shaft or housing) because both faces are machined, thus creating two sharp edges. Stamped circlips (**Figure 12**) are manufactured with one sharp edge and one rounded edge. When installing stamped circlips in a thrust situation (transmission shafts, fork tubes, etc.), the sharp edge must face away from the part producing the thrust, with its ends fully supported (**Figure 13**). When installing circlips, observe the following:

a. Compress or expand the circlip only enough to install or remove them.
b. After the circlip is installed, make sure it is completely seated in its groove.
c. Transmission circlips become worn with use and increase gear side play. For this reason, it is generally better to replace all transmission circlips whenever the transmission is disassembled.

12

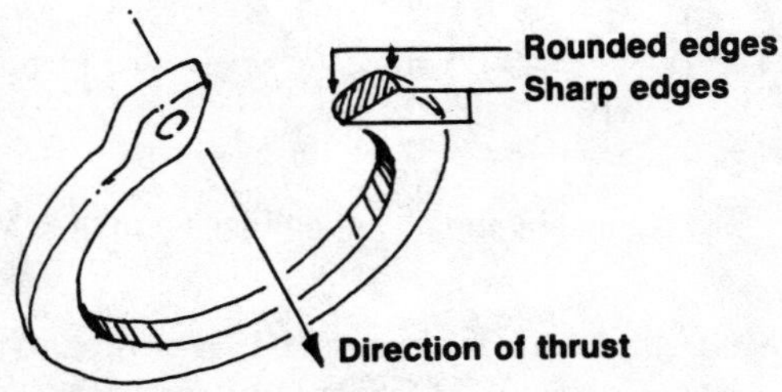

13

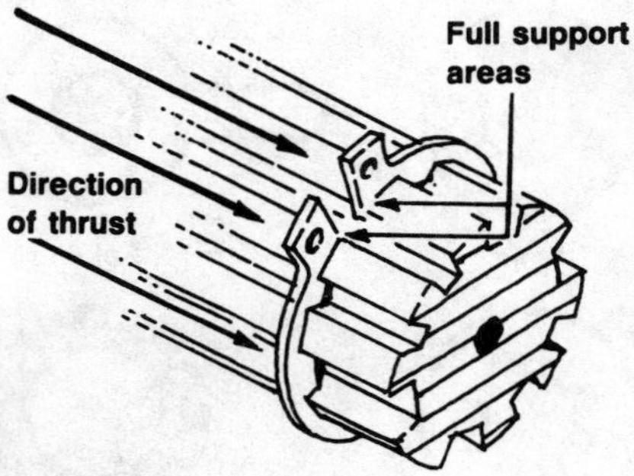

LUBRICANTS

Periodic lubrication assures long life for any type of equipment. The *type* of lubricant used is just as important as the lubrication service itself. The following paragraphs describe the types of lubricants most often used on motorcycle equipment. Be sure to follow the motorcycle manufacturer's recommendations for lubricant types.

Generally, all liquid lubricants are called "oil." They may be mineral-based (including petroleum bases), natural-based (vegetable and animal bases), synthetic-based or emulsions (mixtures). "Grease" is an oil to which a thickening base has been added so that the end product is semi-solid. Grease is often classified by the type of thickener added; lithium soap is commonly used.

Engine Oil

Oil for motorcycle and automotive engines is classified by the American Petroleum Institute (API) and the Society of Automotive Engineers (SAE) in several categories. Oil containers display these classifications on the top of the can or on the bottle label (**Figure 14**).

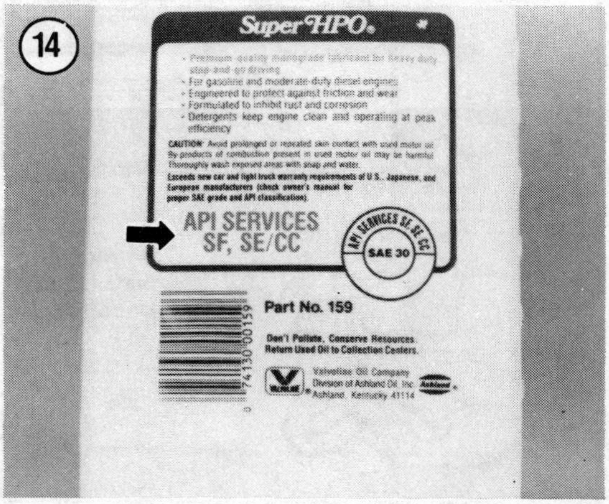

API oil classification is indicated by letters; oils for gasoline engines are identified by an "S." The engines covered in this manual require SE or SF oil.

Viscosity is an indication of the oil's thickness. The SAE uses numbers to indicate viscosity; thin oils have low numbers while thick oils have high numbers. A "W" after the number indicates that the viscosity testing was done at low temperature to simulate cold-weather operation, such as 5W or 10W.

Multi-grade oil (for example 10W-40) can vary its viscosity to suit different temperatures. This allows the oil to perform efficiently across a wide range of engine operating conditions; thin at cold temperatures and thick at hot temperatures. The lower the number, the better the engine will start in cold climates. Higher numbers are usually recommended for engines running in hot weather conditions.

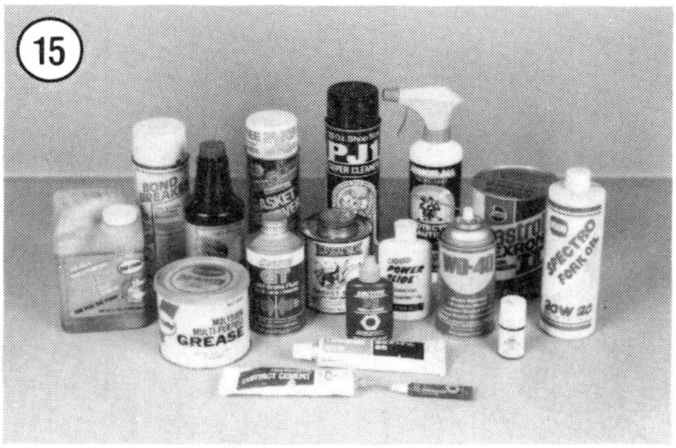

15

16

17

Grease

Greases are graded by the National Lubricating Grease Institute (NLGI). Greases are graded by number according to the consistency of the grease; these range from No. 000 to No. 6, with No. 6 being the most solid. A typical multipurpose grease is NLGI No. 2. For specific applications, equipment manufacturers may require grease with an additive such as molybdenum disulfide (MOS2).

EXPENDABLE SUPPLIES

Certain expendable supplies are required during maintenance and repair work. These include grease, oil, gasket cement, wiping rags and cleaning solvent. Ask your dealer for the special locking compounds, silicone lubricants and other products (**Figure 15**) which make vehicle maintenance simpler and easier. Cleaning solvent or kerosene is available at some service stations or hardware stores.

PARTS REPLACEMENT

Suzuki makes frequent changes during a model year—some minor, some relatively major. When you order parts from the dealer or other parts distributor, always order by engine and frame number. Write the numbers down and carry them with you. Compare new parts to old before purchasing them. If they are not alike, have the parts manager explain the difference to you and be sure they will interchange before leaving the dealer. Most dealers charge a "restocking fee" for parts that are returned.

SERIAL NUMBERS

You must know the model serial number and VIN number for registration purposes and when ordering replacement parts.

The frame serial number is stamped on the right-hand side of the steering head (**Figure 16**). The vehicle identification number (VIN) is on the left-hand side of the frame (**Figure 17**). The engine serial number is located on the top right-hand surface of the crankcase (**Figure 18**). The carburetor identification number is located on the right-hand side of the carburetor body (**Figure 19**).

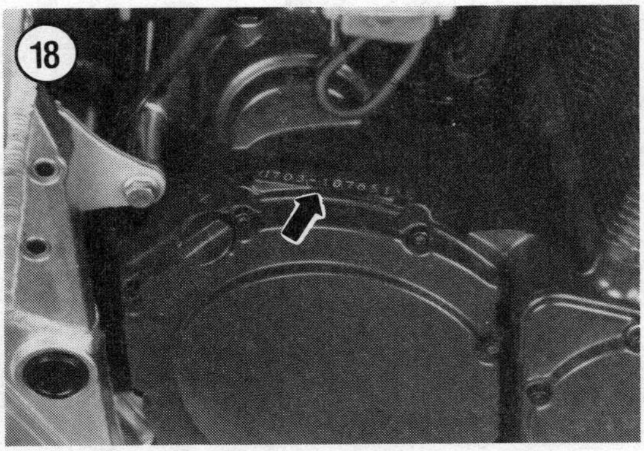

BASIC HAND TOOLS

A number of tools are required to maintain a bike in top riding condition. You may already have some of these tools for home or car repairs. There are also tools made especially for bike repairs; these you will have to purchase. In any case, a wide variety of quality tools will make bike repairs easier and more effective.

Top quality tools are essential; they are also more economical in the long run. If you are now starting to build your tool collection, stay away from the "advertised specials" featured at some parts houses, discount stores and chain drug stores. These are usually a poor grade tool that can be sold cheaply and that is exactly what they are—*cheap*. They are usually made of inferior material and are thick, heavy and clumsy. Their rough finish makes them difficult to clean and they usually don't last very long.

Quality tools are made of alloy steel and are heat treated for greater strength. They are lighter and better balanced than cheap ones. Their surface is smooth, making them a pleasure to work with and easy to clean. The initial cost of good quality tools may be more but it is cheaper in the long run. Don't try to buy everything in all sizes in the beginning; do it a little at a time until you have the necessary tools.

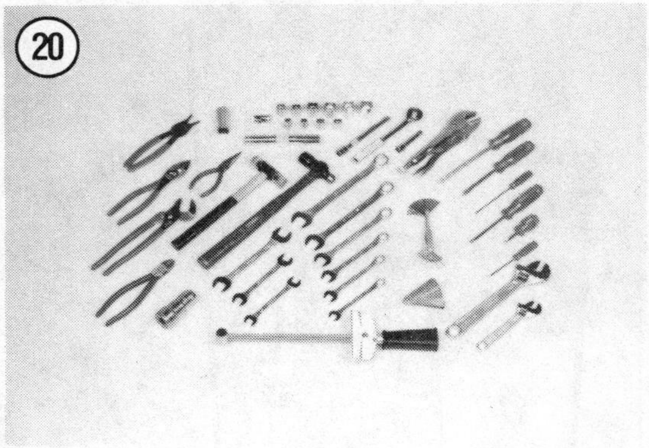

Keep your tools clean and in a tool box. Organize them with the sockets and related drives together and the open end and box wrenches together, etc. After using a tool, wipe off dirt and grease with a clean cloth and place the tool in its correct place. Doing this will save a lot of time you would have spent trying to find a socket buried in a bunch of clutch parts. Also, be careful when lending tools to friends—make sure they return them promptly; if not, your collection will soon disappear.

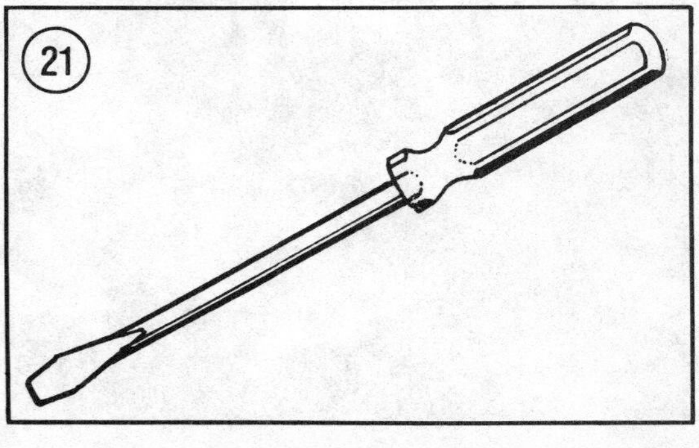

The following tools are required to perform virtually any repair job on a bike. Each tool is described and the recommended size given for starting a tool collection. **Table 3** includes the tools that should be on hand for simple home repairs and/or major overhaul as shown in **Figure 20**. Additional tools and some duplicates may be added as you become more familiar with the bike. Almost all motorcycles (with the exception of the

U.S. built Harley and some English bikes) use metric size bolts and nuts. If you are starting your collection now, buy metric sizes.

Screwdrivers

The screwdriver is a very basic tool, but if used improperly it will do more damage than good. The slot on a screw has a definite dimension and shape. A screwdriver must be selected to conform with that shape. Use a small screwdriver for small screws and a large one for large screws or the screw head will be damaged.

Two basic types of screwdriver are required to repair the bike—common (flat blade) screwdrivers (**Figure 21**) and the Phillips screwdrivers (**Figure 22**).

Screwdrivers are available in sets which often include an assortment of common and Phillips blades. If you buy them individually, buy at least the following:

a. Common screwdriver—5/16×6 in. blade.
b. Common screwdriver—3/8×12 in. blade.
c. Phillips screwdriver—size 2 tip, 6 in. blade.

Use screwdrivers only for driving screws. Never use a screwdriver for prying or chiseling. Do not try to remove a Phillips or Allen head screw with a common screwdriver; you can damage the head so that the proper tool will be unable to remove it.

Keep screwdrivers in the proper condition and they will last longer and perform better. Always keep the tip of a common screwdriver in good condition. **Figure 23** shows how to grind the tip to the proper shape if it becomes damaged. Note the symmetrical sides of the tip.

22

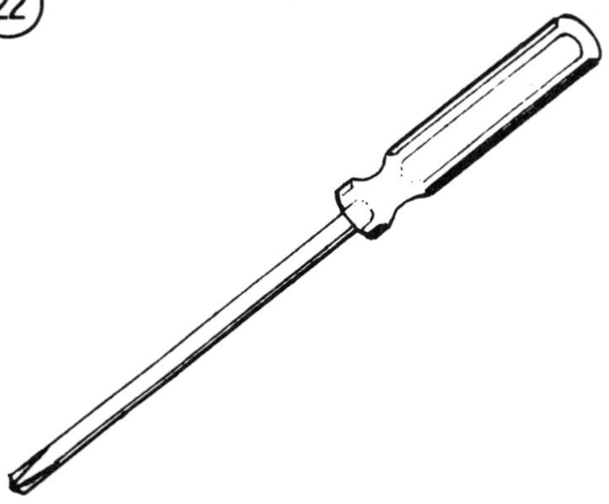

23

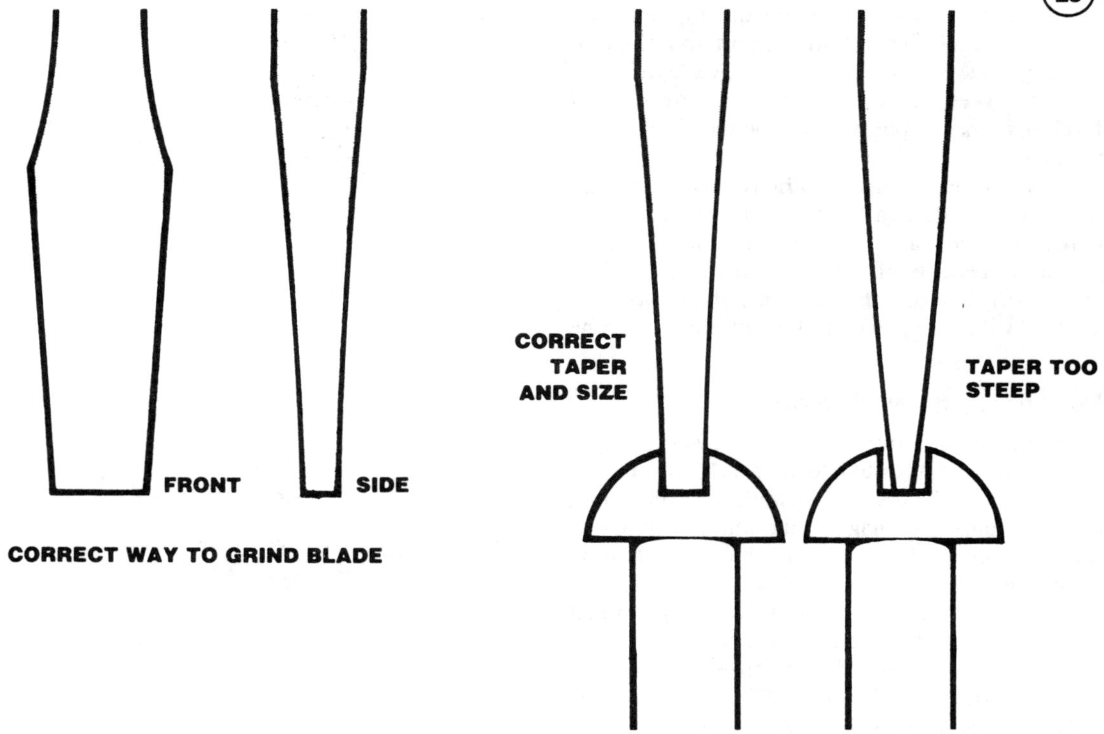

Pliers

Pliers come in a wide range of types and sizes. Pliers are useful for cutting, bending and crimping. They should never be used to cut hardened objects or to turn bolts or nuts. **Figure 24** shows several pliers useful in bike repairs.

Each type of pliers has a specialized function. Slip joint pliers are general purpose pliers and are used mainly for holding things and for bending. Vise Grips are used to hold objects very tight, like a vise, but avoid using them unless absolutely necessary. The jaws of the Vise Grips will permanently scar any objects which are held. Needlenose pliers are used to hold or bend small objects. Channel-lock pliers can be adjusted to hold various sizes of objects; the jaws remain parallel to grip around objects such as pipe or tubing. There are many more types of pliers. The ones described here are most suitable for bike repairs.

Box and Open-end Wrenches

Box and open-end wrenches are available in sets or separately in a variety of sizes. The size number stamped near the end refers to the distance between 2 parallel flats on the hex head bolt or nut.

Box wrenches are usually superior to open-end wrenches. Open-end wrenches grip the nut or bolt on only 2 flats. Unless it fits well, it may slip and round off the points on the nut or bolt. The box wrench grips all 6 flats. Both 6-point and 12-point openings on box wrenches are available. The 6-point gives superior holding power and durability; the 12-point works better within tight confines.

Combination wrenches (**Figure 25**) which are open on one side and boxed on the other are also available and are favored by professional mechanics because of their versatility; use the box end to break loose the fastener, then speed its removal with the open end. Both ends are the same size.

Adjustable (Crescent) Wrenches

An adjustable wrench (also called a crescent wrench) can be adjusted to fit nearly any nut or bolt head. See **Figure 26**. However, it can loosen and slip, causing damage to the nut and injury to your knuckles. Use an adjustable wrench only when other wrenches are not available. Adjustable wrenches are directional: the moveable jaw must never be used to transmit the loosening force.

Adjustable wrenches come in sizes ranging from 4-18 in. overall. A 6- or 8-in. wrench is recommended as an all-purpose wrench.

24

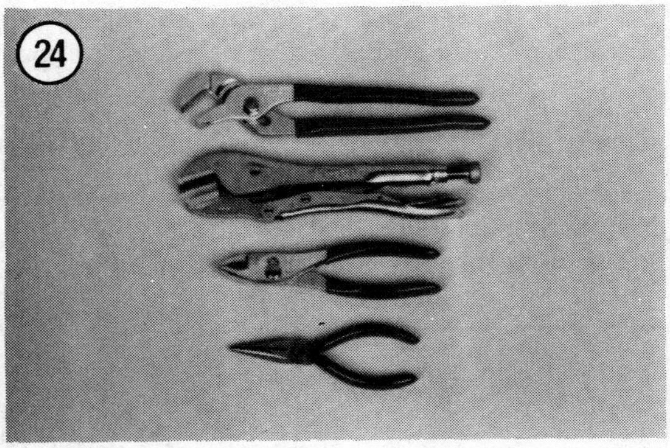

25

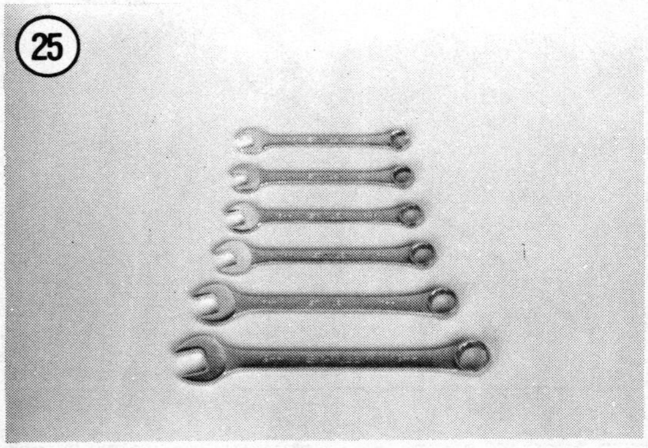

26

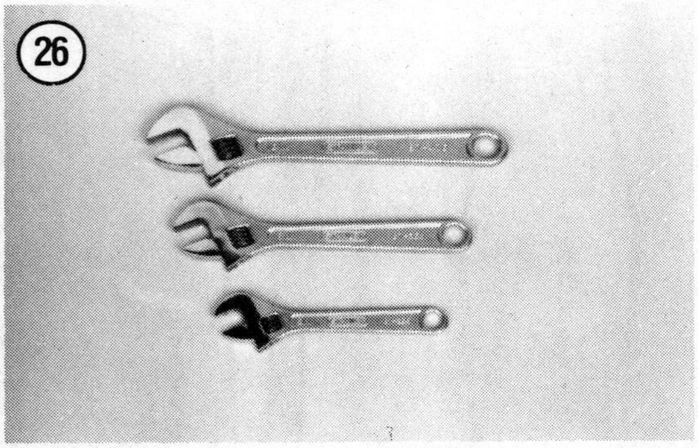

27

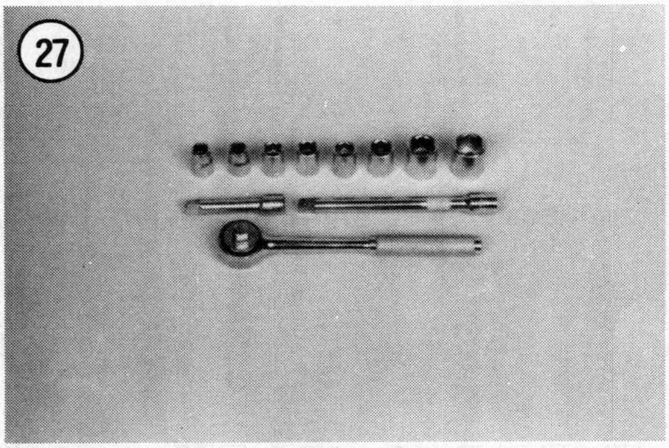

(28)

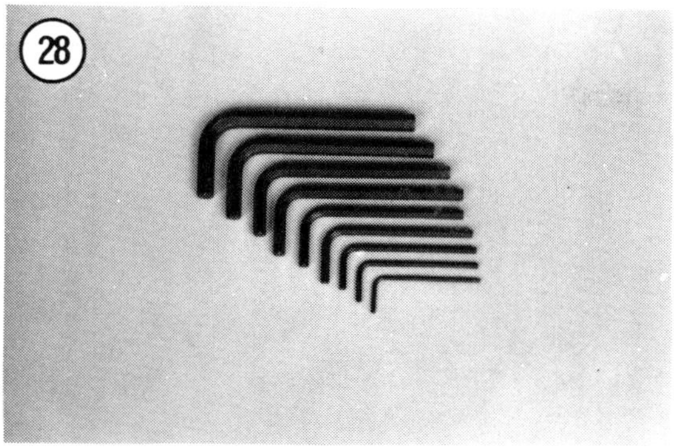

(29)

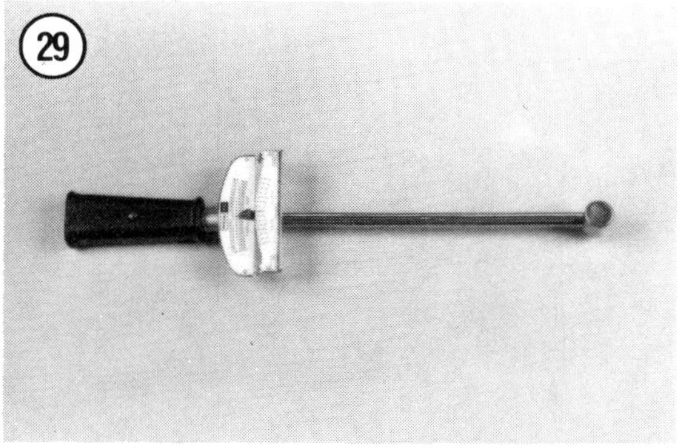

(30)

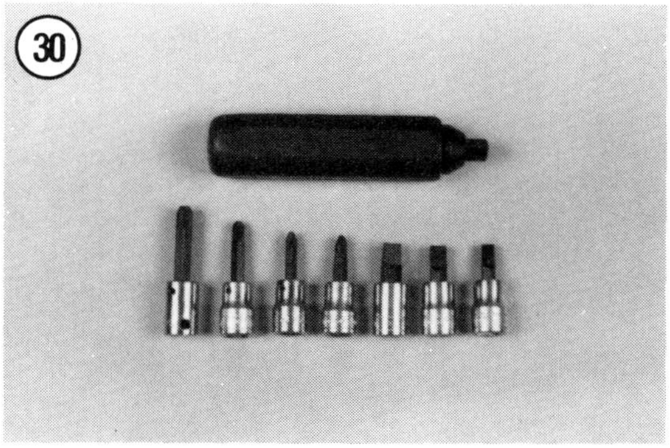

(31)

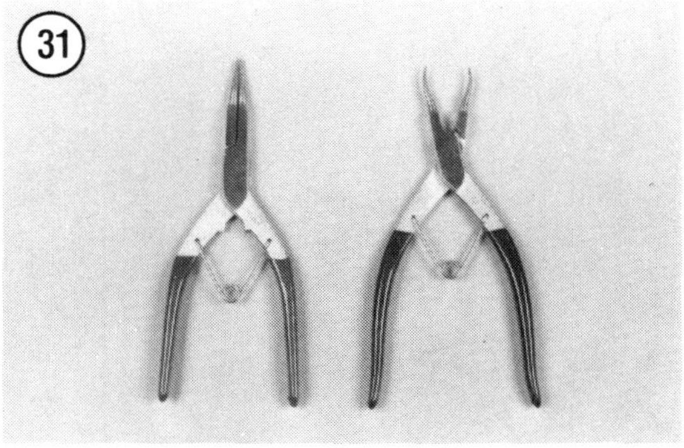

Socket Wrenches

This type is undoubtedly the fastest, safest and most convenient to use. See **Figure 27**. Sockets which attach to a ratchet handle are available with 6-point or 12-point openings and 1/4, 3/8, 1/2 and 3/4 inch drives. The drive size indicates the size of the square hole which mates with the ratchet handle.

Allen Wrenches

Allen wrenches (**Figure 28**) are available in sets or separately in a variety of sizes. These sets come in SAE and metric size, so be sure to buy a metric set. Suzuki uses a lot of Allen bolts (sometimes called socket head bolts) on the engine and on the front fairing.

Torque Wrench

A torque wrench is used with a socket or offset crowsfoot to measure how tightly a nut or bolt is installed. They come in a wide price range and with either 3/8 or 1/2 in. square drive (**Figure 29**). The drive size indicates the size of the square drive which mates with the socket. Purchase one that measures 0-207 N•m (0-150 ft.-lb.).

Impact Driver

This tool might have been designed with the bike in mind. See **Figure 30**. It makes removal of engine and clutch parts easy and eliminates damage to bolts and screw slots. It also works well on fasteners which are frozen because of rust, corrosion, etc. Impact drivers are available at most large hardware, motorcycle or auto parts stores.

Circlip Pliers

Circlip pliers (sometimes referred to as snap-ring pliers) are necessary to remove the circlips used on the transmission shaft assemblies and the suspension assemblies. They are available in internal and external types. See **Figure 31**.

Hammers

The correct hammer is necessary for bike repairs. Use only a hammer with a face (or head) of rubber or plastic or the soft-faced type that is filled with buckshot. These are sometimes necessary in engine tear-downs. *Never* use a metal-faced hammer on the actual part as severe damage will result in most cases. You can always produce the same amount of force with a soft-faced hammer.

Ignition Gauge

This tool (**Figure 32**) has both flat and wire measuring gauges and is used to measure spark plug gap. This device is available at most auto or motorcycle supply stores.

32

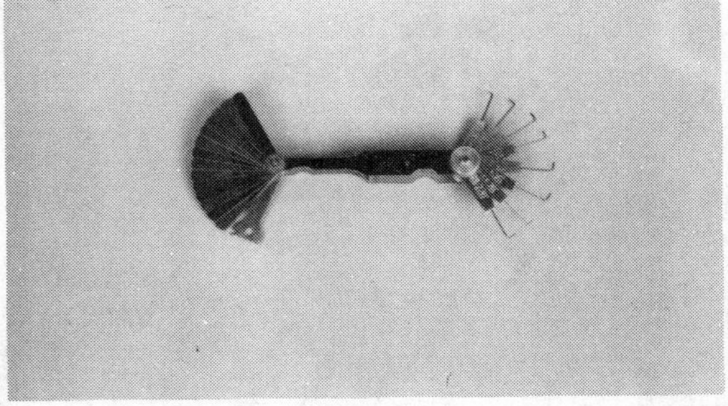

Other Special Tools

A few other special tools may be required for major service. These are described in the appropriate chapters and are available either from a Suzuki dealer or other manufacturers as indicated.

TUNE-UP AND TROUBLESHOOTING TOOLS

Multimeter or Volt-ohm Meter

This instrument (**Figure 33**) is invaluable for electrical system troubleshooting and service. A few of its functions may be duplicated by homemade test equipment, but for the serious mechanic it is a must. Its uses are described in the applicable sections of the book.

33

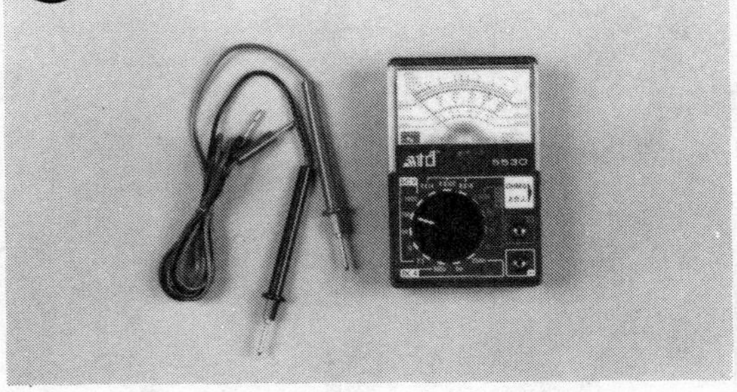

Strobe Timing Light

This instrument is necessary for checking ignition timing. By flashing a light at the precise instant the spark plug fires, the position of the timing mark can be seen. Marks on the alternator flywheel line up with the stationary mark on the crankcase while the engine is running.

Suitable lights range from inexpensive neon bulb types to powerful xenon strobe lights (**Figure 34**). Neon timing lights are difficult to see and must be used in dimly lit areas. Xenon strobe timing lights can be used outside in bright sunlight. Both types work on the bike; use according to the manufacturer's instructions.

Ignition timing is not adjustable on modern, emissions-regulated motorcycles. Because of this, the ignition timing is only checked when a problem is suspected. For such infrequent use, it may be better to rent a timing light from a rental company.

34

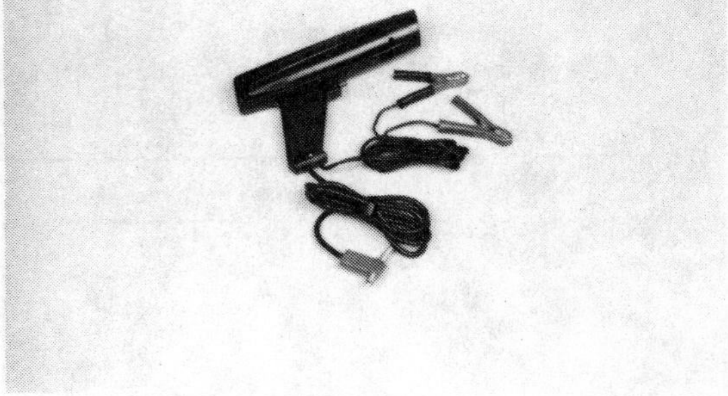

Portable Tachometer

A portable tachometer is necessary for tuning (**Figure 35**). Ignition timing and carburetor adjustments must be performed at the specified engine speed. The best instrument for this purpose is one with a low range of 0-2,000 rpm and a high range of 0-6,000. The instrument should be capable of detecting changes of 25 rpm on the low range.

35

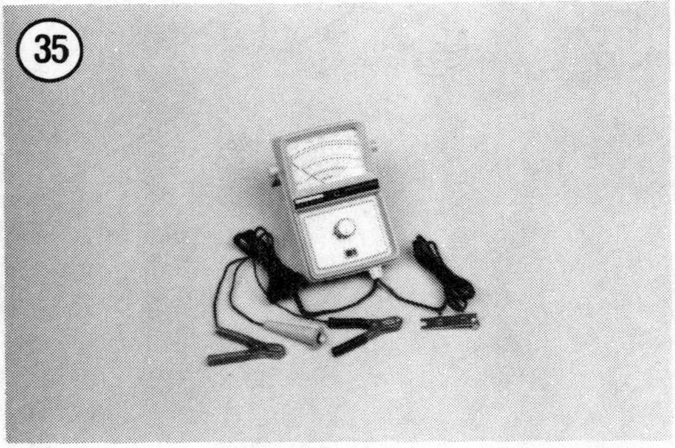

(36)

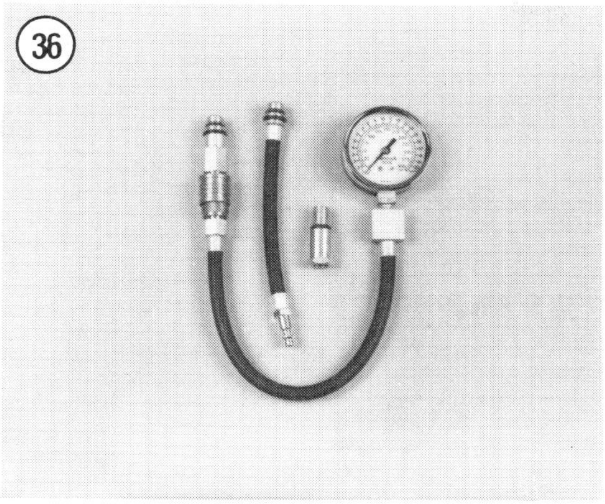

(37)

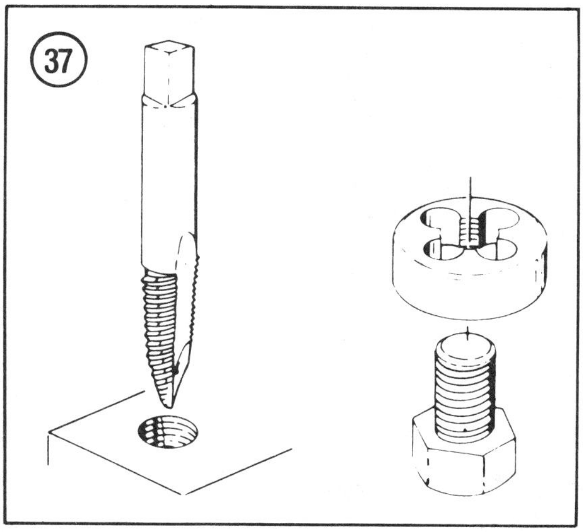

(38)

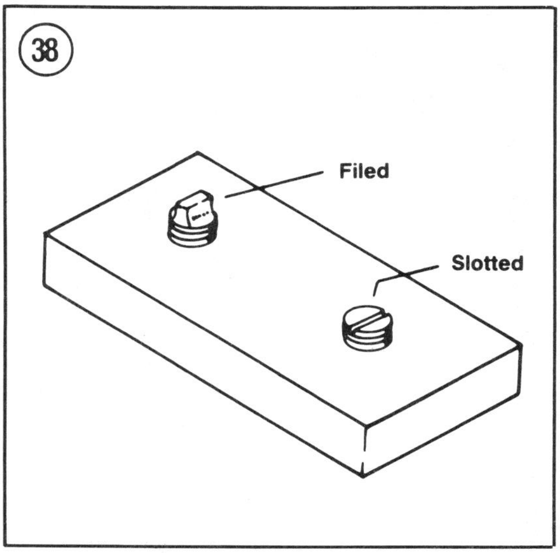

Compression Gauge

A compression gauge (**Figure 36**) mea engine compression. The results, when interpreted, can indicate general ring a condition. They are available from moto auto supply stores and mail order outlets.

MECHANIC'S TIPS

Removing Frozen Nuts and Screws

When a fastener rusts and cannot be r several methods may be used to loosen apply penetrating oil such as Liquid Wr WD-40 (available at any hardware or auto store). Apply it liberally and let it penet 10-15 minutes. Rap the fastener several tin a small hammer; do not hit it hard enough damage. Reapply the penetrating oil if nec

For frozen screws, apply penetrating described, then insert a screwdriver in the rap the top of the screwdriver with a hamm loosens the rust so the screw can be remove normal way. If the screw head is too chew use a screwdriver, grip the head with Vi and twist the screw out. For frozen scr and bolts, an impact driver with th attachment may ease removal.

Remedying Stripped Threads

Occasionally, threads are stripp carelessness or impact damage. Often can be cleaned up by running a tap threads on nuts) or die (for externa bolts) through or over the threads. S

Removing Broken Screws or Bolts

When the head breaks off a screwg methods are available for removir portion. it,

If a large portion of the remaining try gripping it with Vise Grips. t a portion is too small, file it to fit slot in it to fit a screwdriver. Screw

If the head breaks off flush, trthis out using a small chisel andctor. doesn't work, you'll need to uson of To do this, centerpunch the rescrew the screw or bolt. Drill a smascrew and tap the extractor into the ire 39. out with a wrench on the extr

REMOVING BROKEN SCREWS AND BOLTS

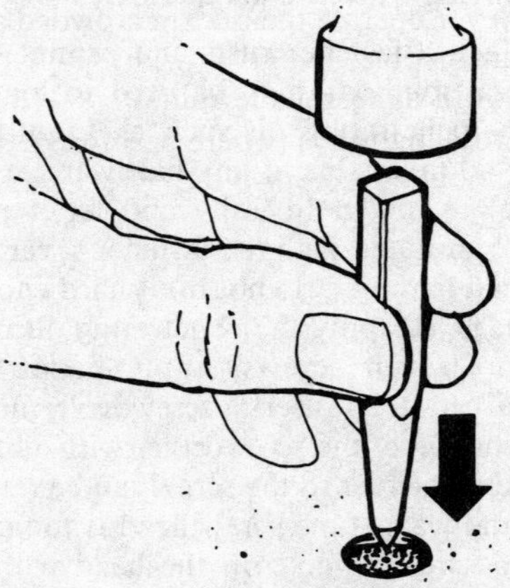

1. Center punch broken stud

2. Drill hole in stud

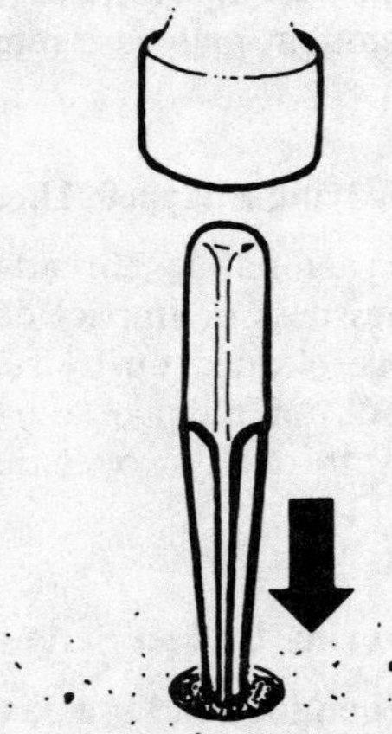

3. Tap in screw extractor

4. Remove broken stud

RIDING SAFETY

General Tips

1. Read your owner's manual and know your machine.
2. Check the throttle and brake controls before starting the engine.
3. Know how to make an emergency stop.
4. Never add fuel while anyone is smoking in the area or when the engine is running.
5. Never wear loose scarves, belts or boot laces that could catch on moving parts.
6. Always wear eye and head protection and protective clothing to protect your *entire* body. Today's riding apparel is very stylish and you will be ready for action as well as being well protected.
7. Riding in the winter months requires a good set of clothes to keep your body dry and warm, otherwise your entire trip may be miserable. If you dress properly, moisture will evaporate from your body. If you become too hot and if your clothes trap the moisture, you will become cold. Even mild temperatures can be very uncomfortable and dangerous when combined with a strong wind or traveling at high speed. See **Table 4** for wind chill factors. Always dress according to what the wind chill factor is, not the ambient temperature.
8. Never allow anyone to operate the bike without proper instruction. This is for their bodily protection and to protect your machine from damage or destruction. Many motorcycle accidents occur when an inexperienced rider takes his or her first ride on a friend's motorcycle.
9. Use the "buddy system" for long trips, just in case you have a problem or run out of gas.
10. Never attempt to repair your machine with the engine running except when necessary for certain tune-up procedures.
11. Check all of the machine components and hardware frequently, especially the wheels and the steering.

Operating Tips

1. Never operate the bike in crowded areas or steer toward people.
2. Avoid dangerous terrain.
3. Cross highways (where permitted) at a 90° angle after looking in both directions. Post traffic guards if crossing in groups.
4. Do not ride the bike on or near railroad tracks. The bike's engine and exhaust noise can drown out the sound of an approaching train.
5. Keep the headlight, turn signal lights and taillight free of dirt.
6. Always steer with both hands.
7. Be aware of the terrain and avoid operating the bike at excessive speed.
8. Do not panic if the throttle sticks. Turn the engine stop switch to the OFF position.
9. Do not tailgate. Rear end collisions can cause injury and machine damage.
10. Do not mix alcoholic beverages or drugs with riding—*ride straight*.
11. Check your fuel supply regularly. Do not travel farther than your fuel supply will allow.

Tables on the following pages.

Table 1 DECIMAL AND METRIC EQUIVALENTS

Fractions	Decimal in.	Metric mm	Fractions	Decimal in.	Metric mm
1/64	0.015625	0.39688	33/64	0.515625	13.09687
1/32	0.03125	0.79375	17/32	0.53125	13.49375
3/64	0.046875	1.19062	35/64	0.546875	13.89062
1/16	0.0625	1.58750	9/16	0.5625	14.28750
5/64	0.078125	1.98437	37/64	0.578125	14.68437
3/32	0.09375	2.38125	19/32	0.59375	15.08125
7/64	0.109375	2.77812	39/64	0.609375	15.47812
1/8	0.125	3.1750	5/8	0.625	15.87500
9/64	0.140625	3.57187	41/64	0.640625	16.27187
5/32	0.15625	3.96875	21/32	0.65625	16.66875
11/64	0.171875	4.36562	43/64	0.671875	17.06562
3/16	0.1875	4.76250	11/16	0.6875	17.46250
13/64	0.203125	5.15937	45/64	0.703125	17.85937
7/32	0.21875	5.55625	23/32	0.71875	18.25625
15/64	0.234375	5.95312	47/64	0.734375	18.65312
1/4	0.250	6.35000	3/4	0.750	19.05000
17/64	0.265625	6.74687	49/64	0.765625	19.44687
9/32	0.28125	7.14375	25/32	0.78125	19.84375
19/64	0.296875	7.54062	51/64	0.796875	20.24062
5/16	0.3125	7.93750	13/16	0.8125	20.63750
21/64	0.328125	8.33437	53/64	0.828125	21.03437
11/32	0.34375	8.73125	27/32	0.84375	21.43125
23/64	0.359375	9.12812	55/64	0.859375	21.82812
3/8	0.375	9.52500	7/8	0.875	22.22500
25/64	0.390625	9.92187	57/64	0.890625	22.62187
13/32	0.40625	10.31875	29/32	0.90625	23.01875
27/64	0.421875	10.71562	59/64	0.921875	23.41562
7/16	0.4375	11.11250	15/16	0.9375	23.81250
29/64	0.453125	11.50937	61/64	0.953125	24.20937
15/32	0.46875	11.90625	31/32	0.96875	24.60625
31/64	0.484375	12.30312	63/64	0.984375	25.00312
1/2	0.500	12.70000	1	1.00	25.40000

Table 2 STANDARD TORQUE SPECIFICATIONS

Bolt diameter (mm)	N•m	ft.-lb.
Conventional or "4" Marked bolt*		
4	1-2	0.7-1.5
5	2-4	1.5-3.0
6	4-7	3-5
8	10-16	7-11.5
10	22-35	16-25.5
12	35-55	25.5-40
14	50-80	36-58
16	80-130	58-94
18	130-190	94-137.5

(continued)

1

Table 2 STANDARD TORQUE SPECIFICATIONS (cont.)

Bolt diameter (mm)	N•m	ft.-lb.
"7" Marked bolt*		
4	1.5-3	1-2
5	3-6	2-4.5
6	8-12	6-8.5
8	18-28	13-20
10	40-60	29-43.5
12	70-100	50.5-72.5
14	110-160	79.5-115.5
16	170-250	123-181
18	200-280	144-202

* Number is marked on top of Suzuki bolt head. These are Suzuki numbers and do not appear on aftermarket bolts.

Table 3 WORKSHOP TOOLS

Tool	Size or Specifications
Screwdriver	
Common	5/16×8 in. blade
Common	3/8×12 in. blade
Phillips	Size 2 tip, 6 in. overall
Pliers	
Slip-joint pliers	6 in. overall
Vise grips	10 in. overall
Needlenose	6 in. overall
Channel lock	12 in. overall
Snap ring	—
Wrenches	
Box-end set	5-17 mm, plus 24/28 mm
Open-end set	5-17 mm, plus 24/28 mm
Crescent	6 in. and 12 in. overall
Socket set	1/2 in. drive ratchet with 5-17 mm sockets
Other special tools	
Strap wrench	—
Impact driver	1/2 in. drive with assorted bits
Torque wrench	1/2 in. drive 0-50 ft.-lb.
Ignition gauge	—

Table 4 WIND CHILL FACTOR

Estimated wind speed in MPH	Actual thermometer reading (° F)											
	50	40	30	20	10	0	−10	−20	−30	−40	−50	−60
	Equivalent temperature (° F)											
Calm	50	40	30	20	10	0	−10	−20	−30	−40	−50	−60
5	48	37	27	16	6	−5	−15	−26	−36	−47	−57	−68
10	40	28	16	4	−9	−21	−33	−46	−58	−70	−83	−95
15	36	22	9	−5	−18	−36	−45	−58	−72	−85	−99	−112
20	32	18	4	−10	−25	−39	−53	−67	−82	−96	−110	−124
25	30	16	0	−15	−29	−44	−59	−74	−88	−104	−118	−133
30	28	13	−2	−18	−33	−48	−63	−79	−94	−109	−125	−140
35	27	11	−4	−20	−35	−49	−67	−82	−98	−113	−129	−145
40	26	10	−6	−21	−37	−53	−69	−85	−100	−116	−132	−148
*	Little Danger (for properly clothed person)				Increasing Danger			Great Danger				
					Danger from freezing of exposed flesh							

* Wind speed greater than 40 mph have little additional effect.

NOTE: If you own a GSX600F Katana, first refer to Chapter 13 for specific service information.

2

CHAPTER TWO

TROUBLESHOOTING

Diagnosing mechanical problems is relatively simple if you use orderly procedures and keep a few basic principles in mind.

The troubleshooting procedures in this chapter analyze typical symptoms and show logical methods of isolating causes. These are not the only methods. There may be several ways to solve a problem, but only a systematic, methodical approach can guarantee success.

Never assume anything. Do not overlook the obvious. If you are riding along and the engine suddenly quits, check the easiest, most accessible problems first. Is there gasoline in the tank? Is the fuel shutoff valve in the ON position? Has a spark plug wire cap become loose? Check the ignition switch and key. Sometimes the weight of the key ring may turn the ignition off suddenly.

If nothing obvious turns up in a quick check, look a little further. Learning to recognize and describe symptoms will make repairs easier for you or a mechanic at the shop. Describe problems accurately and fully. Saying that "it won't run" isn't the same as saying "it quit at high speed and won't start" or that "it sat in my garage for 3 months and then wouldn't start."

Gather as many symptoms together as possible to aid in diagnosis. Note whether the engine lost power gradually or all at once. Remember that the more complicated a machine is, the easier it is to troubleshoot because symptoms point to specific problems.

After the symptoms are defined, areas which could cause the problems are tested and analyzed. Guessing at the cause of a problem may provide the solution, but it can easily lead to frustration, wasted time and a series of expensive, unnecessary parts replacements.

You do not need fancy equipment or complicated test gear to determine whether repairs can be attempted at home. A few simple checks could save a large repair bill and time lost while the bike sits in a dealer's service department. On the other hand, be realistic and don't attempt repairs beyond your abilities. Service departments tend to charge a lot for putting together a disassembled engine that may have been abused. Some dealers won't even take on such a job—so use common sense and don't get in over your head.

OPERATING REQUIREMENTS

An engine needs 3 basics to run properly: correct fuel-air mixture, compression and a spark at the correct time. If one or more are missing, the engine just won't run. The electrical system is the weakest link of the 3 basics. More problems result from electrical breakdowns than from any other source. Keep that in mind before you begin tampering with carburetor adjustments and the like.

If the bike has been sitting for any length of time and refuses to start, check and clean the spark plugs and then look to the gasoline delivery system. This includes the fuel tank, fuel shutoff valve and the fuel line to the carburetor and the vacuum line to the fuel shutoff valve. Gasoline deposits may have formed and gummed up the carburetor's jets and air passages. Gasoline tends to lose its potency after standing for long periods. Condensation may contaminate the fuel with water. Drain the old fuel and try starting with a fresh tankful.

EMERGENCY TROUBLESHOOTING

When the bike is difficult to start or won't start at all, it does not help to wear down the battery with the starter. Check for obvious problems even before getting out your tools. Go down the following list step by step. Do each one; you may be embarrassed to find your engine stop switch is stuck in the OFF position, but that is better than wearing down the battery. If it still will not start, refer to the appropriate troubleshooting procedure which follows in this chapter.

WARNING

Do not use an open flame to check in the tank. A serious explosion is certain to result.

1. Is there fuel in the tank? Open the filler cap (**Figure 1**) and rock the bike. Listen for fuel sloshing around.
2. Is the fuel shutoff valve (**Figure 2**) in the ON position and is the vacuum line to the valve from the engine still connected?
3. Make sure the engine stop switch (**Figure 3**) is not in the OFF position.
4. Are the spark plug wire caps (**Figure 4**) on tight? Push all of them on and slightly rotate them to clean the electrical connection between the plug and the connector.
5. Is the choke in the correct position? The knob (**Figure 5**) should be pulled *out* for a cold engine and pushed *in* for a warm engine.
6. Is the vent tube (**Figure 6**) from the fuel tank blocked? Clean out if necessary with compressed air.
7. Has the circuit breaker tripped (**Figure 7**)? The circuit breaker protects the electrical system when the main circuit load exceeds the rated amperage. When an overload occurs, the red button pops out on the breaker face panel and the circuit is opened. The circuit will remain open until the problem is solved and the breaker is reset. To reset, wait approximately 10 minutes for the circuit breaker to cool down, then push the red button in. If the red button pops out again, the problem still exists in the electrical system and must be corrected. Refer to Chapter Eight.

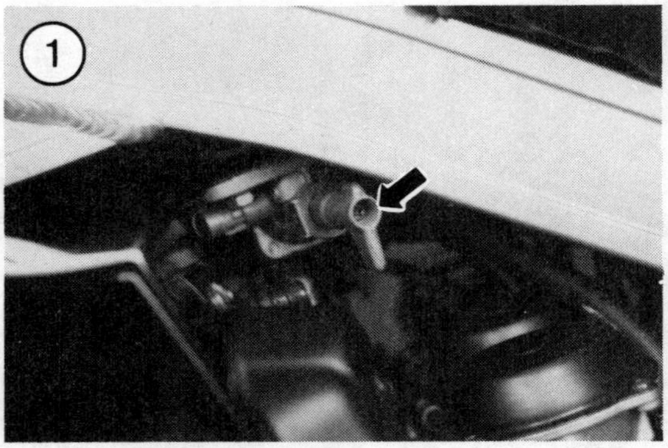

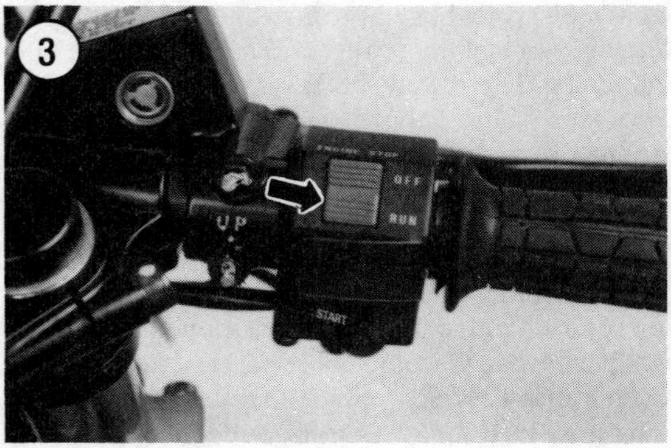

5

6

7

8

ENGINE STARTING

An engine that refuses to start or is difficult to start is very frustrating. More often than not, the problem is very minor and can be found with a simple and logical troubleshooting approach.

The following items show a beginning point from which to isolate engine starting problems.

Engine Fails to Start

Perform the following spark test to determine if the ignition system is operating properly.

1. Remove one of the spark plugs from the cylinder.
2. Connect the spark plug wire and connector to the spark plug and touch the spark plug's base to a good ground such as the engine cylinder head (**Figure 8**). Make sure the spark plug is against some a bare metal, not a painted surface. Position the spark plug so you can see the electrodes, but away from the hole in the cylinder head.
3. Crank the engine over with the starter. A fat blue spark should be evident across the plug's electrodes.

WARNING
If it is necessary to hold the high voltage lead, do so with an insulated pair of pliers. The high voltage generated by the ignition pulse generator and ignitor unit could produce serious or fatal shocks.

4. If the spark is good, check for one or more of the following possible malfunctions:
   a. Obstructed fuel line.
   b. Low compression.
   c. Leaking head gasket.
   d. Choke not operating properly.
   e. Throttle not operating properly.
5. If spark is not good, check for one or more of the following:
   a. Loose or broken ignition coil ground wire.
   b. Weak ignition coil.
   c. Weak ignition pulse generator.
   d. Weak or faulty ignitor unit.
   e. Broken or shorted high tension lead to the spark plug.
   f. Loose electrical connections.

Engine Is Difficult to Start

Check for one or more of the following possible malfunctions:

a. Fouled spark plugs.
b. Improperly adjusted choke.
c. Contaminated fuel system.
d. Improperly adjusted carburetor.
e. Weak ignition coil.
f. Weak ignition pulse generator.
g. Weak or faulty igniter unit.
h. Incorrect type ignition coil.
i. Poor compression.

Engine Will Not Crank

Check for one or more of the following possible malfunctions:

a. Discharged battery.
b. Broken starter gears.
c. Seized piston.
d. Seized crankshaft bearings.
e. Broken connecting rod(s).
f. Locked-up transmission or clutch assembly.

ENGINE PERFORMANCE

In the following checklist, it is assumed that the engine runs, but is not operating at peak performance. This will serve as a starting point from which to isolate a performance malfunction.

The possible causes for each malfunction are listed in a logical sequence and in order of probability.

Engine Will Not Start Or Is Hard To Start

a. Fuel tank empty.
b. Obstructed fuel line or fuel shutoff valve.
c. Sticking float valve in carburetor(s).
d. Carburetors incorrectly adjusted.
e. Improper choke operation.
f. Fouled or improperly gapped spark plugs.
g. Weak ignition pulse generator.
h. Weak or faulty ignitor unit.
i. Ignition timing incorrect (faulty component in system).
j. Shorted or open ignition coil.
k. Improper valve timing.
l. Clogged air filter element.
m. Contaminated fuel.

Engine Will Not Idle or Idles Erratically

a. Carburetor(s) incorrectly adjusted.
b. Fouled or improperly gapped spark plugs.
c. Leaking head gasket or vacuum leak.
d. Weak ignition pulse generator.
e. Weak or faulty ignitor unit.
f. Ignition timing incorrect (faulty component in system).
g. Improper valve timing.
h. Obstructed fuel line or fuel shutoff valve.

Engine Misses at High Speed

a. Fouled or improperly gapped spark plugs.
b. Improper ignition timing (faulty component in system).
c. Improper carburetor main jet selection.
d. Clogged jets in the carburetor(s).
e. Weak ignition coil.

NOTE: If you own a GSX600F Katana, first refer to Chapter 13 for specific service information.

CHAPTER THREE

LUBRICATION, MAINTENANCE AND TUNE-UP

A motorcycle, even in normal use, is subjected to tremendous heat, stress and vibration. When neglected, any bike becomes unreliable and actually dangerous to ride.

To gain the utmost in safety, performance and useful life from the Suzuki GSX-R, it is necessary to make periodic inspections and adjustments. Frequently, minor problems are found during these inspections that are simple and inexpensive to correct at the time. If they are not found and corrected at this time they could lead to major and more expensive problems later on.

Start out by doing simple tune-up, lubrication and maintenance. Tackle more involved jobs as you become more acquainted with the bike.

Tables 1-9 are located at the end of this chapter.

ROUTINE CHECKS

The following simple checks should be performed at each fuel stop.

Engine Oil Level

Refer to *Engine Oil Level Check* under *Periodic Lubrication* in this chapter.

General Inspection

1. Quickly inspect the engine for signs of oil or fuel leakage.
2. Check the tires for embedded stones. Pry them out with your ignition key.
3. Make sure all lights work.

WARNING

At least check the brake light. It can burn out at any time. Motorists cannot stop as quickly as you and need all the warning you can give.

Tire Pressure

Tire pressure must be checked with the tires cold. Correct tire pressure varies with the load you are carrying or if you have a passenger. See **Table 1**.

Battery

The electrolyte level must be between the upper and lower level marks on the case (**Figure 1**). For complete details see *Battery Removal, Installation and Electrolyte Level Check* in this chapter.

Check the level more frequently in hot weather; electrolyte will evaporate rapidly as heat increases.

Crankcase Breather Hose

Inspect the hose for cracks and deterioration and make sure that the hose clamps are tight.

Evaporative Emission Control System (California Models)

Inspect the hoses to make sure they are not kinked or bent and that they are securely connected to their respective parts.

Lights and Horn

With the engine running, check the following.

1. Pull the front brake lever on and check that the brake light comes on.
2. Push the rear brake pedal down and check that the brake light comes on soon after you have begun depressing the pedal.
3. If during the test, the rear brake pedal traveled too far before the brakelight came on, adjust the rear brake light switch as described in Chapter Eight.
4. Turn the ignition switch to the ON position. Press the headlight dimmer switch to both the HI and LO positions and check to see that both headlight elements are working in BOTH headlights.
5. Push the turn signal switch to the left and right positions and check that all 4 turn signals are working.
6. Push the horn button and make sure that the horn blows loudly.
7. If the horn or any of the lights failed to operate properly, refer to Chapter Eight.

PRE-CHECKS

The following checks should be performed before the first ride of the day.

1. Inspect all fuel lines and fittings for wetness.
2. Make sure the fuel tank is full of fresh gasoline.
3. Make sure the engine oil level is correct.
4. Check the operation of the front brake. Add hydraulic fluid to the front brake master cylinder if necessary.

5A. On GSX-R750R Limited Edition models, check the operation of the clutch. If necessary, adjust the clutch free-play as described under *Clutch Adjustment (GSX-R750R Limited Edition Models)* in this chapter.

5B. On all other models, check the operation of the clutch. Add hydraulic fluid to the clutch master cylinder if necessary.

6. Check the throttle and the rear brake pedal. Make sure they operate properly with no binding.
7. Inspect the front and rear suspensions; make sure they have a good solid feel with no looseness.
8. Check tire pressure. Refer to **Table 1**.
9. Check the exhaust system for damage.
10. Check the tightness of all fasteners, especially engine mounting hardware.

SERVICE INTERVALS

The services and intervals shown in **Table 2** are recommended by the factory. Strict adherence to these recommendations will ensure long service from the Suzuki. If the bike is run in an area of high humidity, the lubrication services must be done more frequently to prevent possible rust damage.

For convenience when maintaining your motorcycle, most of the services shown in these tables are described in this chapter. However, some procedures which require more than minor disassembly or adjustment are covered elsewhere in the appropriate chapter.

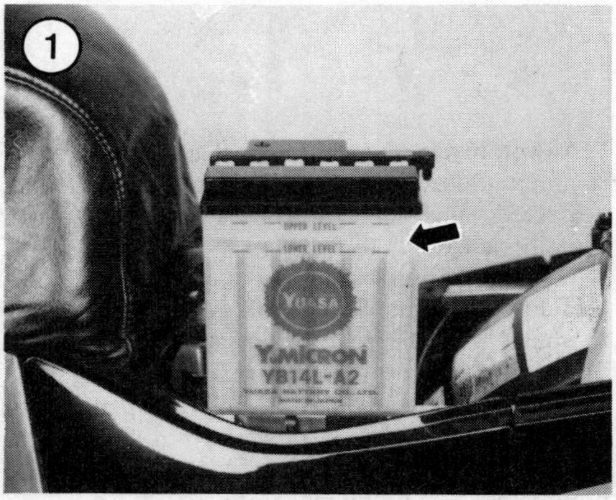

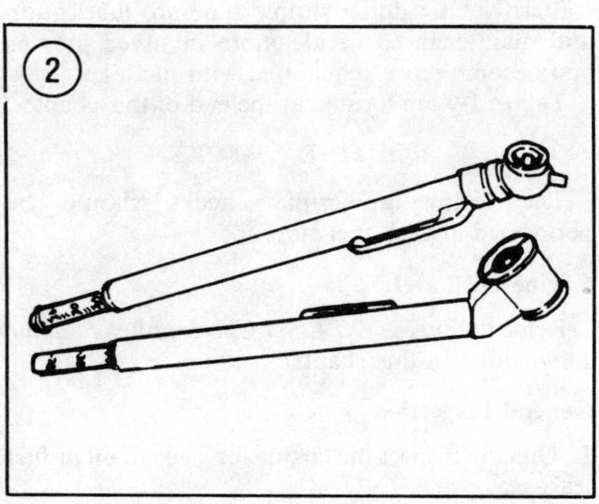

TIRES AND WHEELS

Tire Pressure

Tire pressure should be checked and adjusted to maintain the smoothness of the tire, good traction and handling and to get the maximum life out of the tire. A simple, accurate gauge (**Figure 2**) can be purchased for a few dollars and should be carried in your motorcycle tool kit. The appropriate tire pressures are shown in **Table 1**.

3

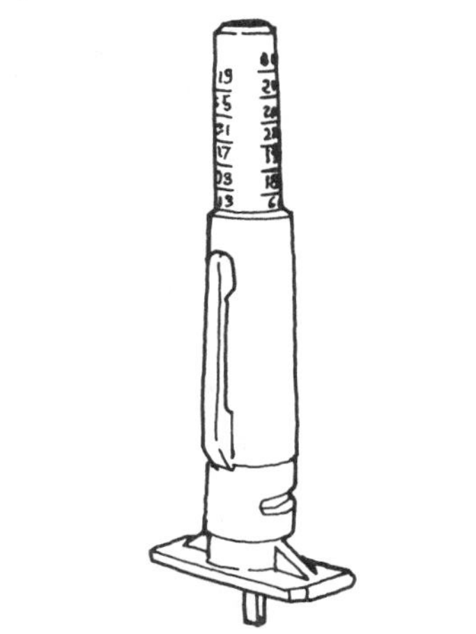

4

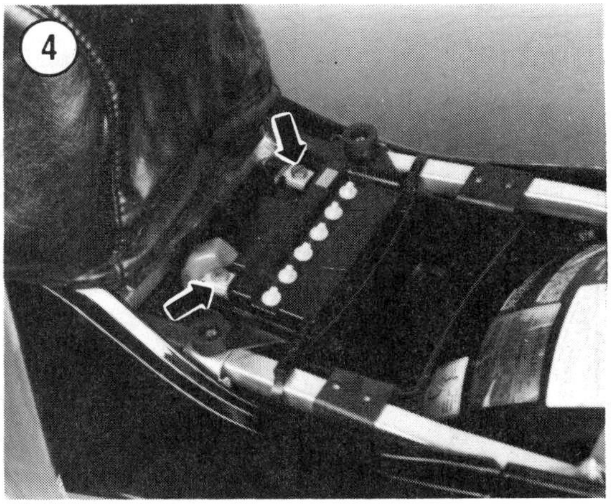

NOTE
After checking and adjusting the air pressure, make sure to install the air valve cap. The cap prevents small pebbles and dirt from collecting in the valve stem; this could allow air leakage or result in incorrect tire pressure readings.

3

Tire Inspection

The tires take a lot of punishment, so inspect them periodically for excessive wear, cuts, abrasions, etc. If you find a nail or other object in the tire, mark its location with a light crayon before removing it. This will help locate the hole for repair. Refer to Chapter Nine for tire changing and repair information.

Check local traffic regulations concerning minimum tread depth. Measure the tread depth at the center of the tire tread using a tread depth gauge (**Figure 3**) or small ruler. Suzuki recommends that original equipment tires be replaced when the tread depth has worn to the following dimension or less:

a. Front tire: 1.6 mm (0.06 in.).
b. Rear tire: 2.0 mm (0.08 in.).

Rim Inspection

Frequently inspect the wheel rims. If a rim has been damaged it might have been enough to create excessive runout: wobble in an up-and-down or side-to-side plane. Excessive runout can cause severe vibration and result in an unsafe riding condition.

BATTERY

Removal, Installation and Electrolyte Level Check

The battery is the heart of the electrical system. Check and service the battery at the interval indicated in **Table 2**. Most electrical system troubles can be attributed to neglect of this vital component.

1. Remove the seat as described in Chapter Twelve.
2. First disconnect the battery negative lead, then the positive lead, from the battery terminals (**Figure 4**).
3. Disconnect the breather tube from the battery. Leave the breather tube routed through the frame.

4. Carefully pull the battery up and out of the bike's frame.
5. The electrolyte level should be maintained between the 2 marks on the battery case (**Figure 1**).

WARNING
Protect your eyes, skin and clothing. If electrolyte gets into your eyes, flush your eyes thoroughly with clean water and get prompt medical attention.

CAUTION
Be careful not to spill battery electrolyte on plastic, painted or plated surfaces. The liquid is highly corrosive and will damage the finish. If it is spilled, wash it off immediately with soapy water and thoroughly rinse with clean water.

6. Remove the cap from the battery cells and add distilled water to correct the level. Never add electrolyte (acid) to correct the level.

NOTE
If distilled water has been added, reinstall the battery caps and gently shake the battery for several minutes to mix the existing electrolyte with the new water.

7. After the fluid level has been corrected and the battery allowed to stand for a few minutes, remove the battery caps and check the specific gravity of the electrolyte with a hydrometer (**Figure 5**). See *Battery Testing* in this chapter.
8. After the battery has been refilled, recharged or replaced, install it by reversing these removal steps.

CAUTION
*If you removed the breather tube from the frame, be sure to route it so that residue will not drain onto any part of the bike's frame as shown in **Figure 6**. The tube must be free of bends or twists as any restrictions may pressurize the battery and damage it.*

Testing

Hydrometer testing is the best way to check battery condition. Use a hydrometer with numbered graduations from 1.100 to 1.300 rather than one with just color-coded bands. To use the hydrometer, squeeze the rubber ball, insert the tip into the cell and release the pressure on the ball. Draw enough electrolyte to float the weighted float inside the hydrometer. Note the number (on the

5

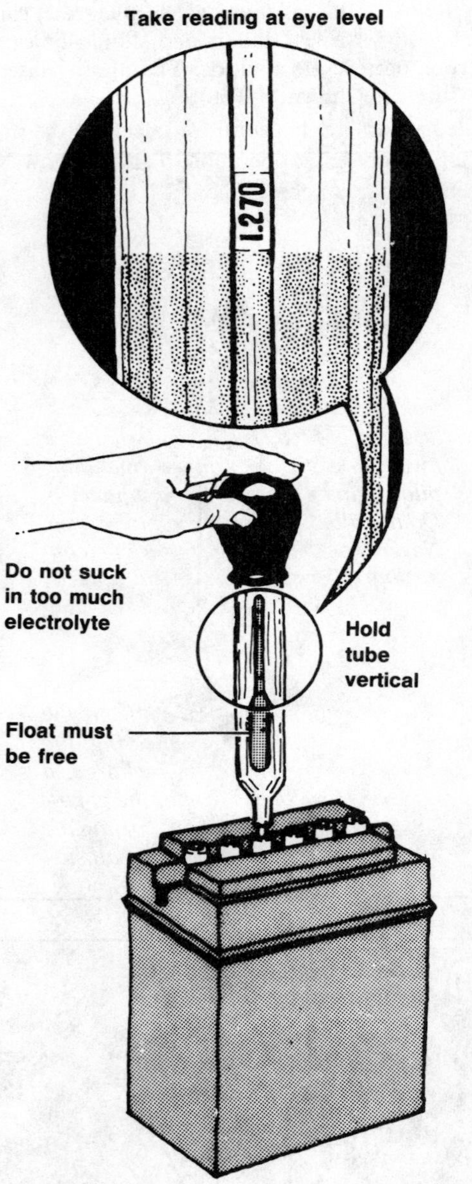

float) aligned with the surface of the electrolyte; this is the specific gravity for this cell. Squeeze the rubber ball again and return the electrolyte to the cell from which it came.

The specific gravity of the electrolyte in each battery cell is an excellent indication of that cell's condition. A fully charged cell will read from 1.260-1.280, while a cell in good condition reads from 1.230-1.250 and anything below 1.140 is discharged.

The hydrometer is useful for checking the progress of the charging operation. **Table 3** shows approximate state of charge.

Charging

WARNING
During the charging process, highly explosive hydrogen gas is released from the battery. The battery should be charged only in a well-ventilated area away from any open flames (including pilot lights on home gas appliances). Do not allow any smoking in the area. Never check the charge by arcing (connecting pliers or other metal objects) across the terminals; the resulting spark can ignite the hydrogen gas.

CAUTION
Always remove the battery from the bike's frame before connecting the battery charger. Never recharge a battery in the bike's frame; the corrosive mist that is emitted during the charging process will corrode all surrounding surfaces.

6

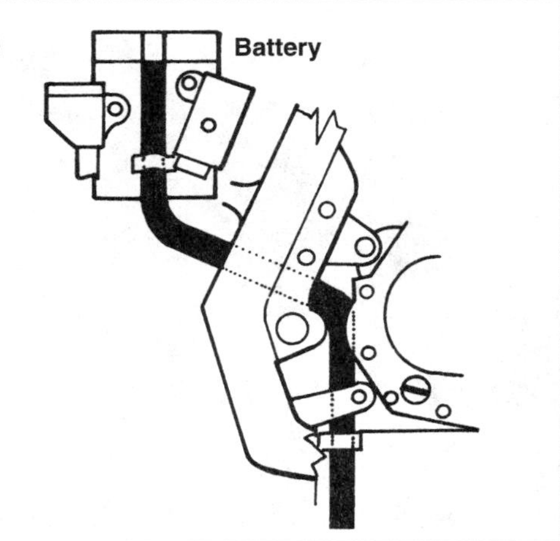

1. Connect the positive (+) charger lead to the positive (+) battery terminal and the negative (–) charger lead to the negative (–) battery terminal.
2. Remove all vent caps from the battery, set the charger to 12 volts and switch the charger ON. If the output of the charger is variable, it is best to select a low setting—1 1/2 to 2 amps.

CAUTION
The electrolyte level must be maintained at the upper level during the charging cycle; check and refill as necessary.

3. After the battery has been charged for about 8 hours, turn the charger off, disconnect the leads and check the specific gravity of each cell. It should be within the limits specified in **Table 3**. If it is, and remains stable for 1 hour, the battery is considered charged.
4. Clean the battery terminals, electrical cable connectors and surrounding case and reinstall the battery in the frame, reversing the removal steps. Coat the battery terminals with Vaseline or light grease to retard corrosion.

CAUTION
Route the breather tube so that is does not drain onto any part of the frame.The tube must be free of bends or twists as any restriction may pressurize the battery and damage it.

New Battery Installation

When replacing the old battery with a new one, be sure its electrolyte level is ok and charge it completely (specific gravity 1.260-1.280) before installing it in the bike. Failure to do so will permanently damage the new battery.

PERIODIC LUBRICATION

Oil

Oil is graded according to its viscosity, which is an indication of how thick it is. The Society of Automotive Engineers (SAE) system distinguishes oil viscosity by numbers. Thick oils have higher viscosity numbers than thin oils. For example, an SAE 5 oil is a thin oil while an SAE 90 oil is relatively thick. If an oil has been tested in cold weather it is denoted with a "W" after the number such as "SAE 5W."

Grease

A good quality grease (preferably waterproof) should be used. Water does not wash grease off parts as easily as it washes oil off. In addition, grease maintains its lubricating qualities better than oil over long periods of time. In a pinch, though, the wrong lubricant is better than none at all. But correct the situation as soon as possible.

Engine Oil Level Check

Engine oil level is checked with the oil level inspection window, located at the right-hand side of the engine on the clutch cover.

1. Place the bike on level ground.
2. Start the engine and let it idle for 2-3 minutes.
3. Shut off the engine and let the oil settle for 1-2 minutes.
4. Have an assistant hold the bike in the true vertical position. A false reading will be given if the bike is tipped either to the right or left.

NOTE

*On GSX-R750R Limited Edition models, check oil level in the **upper** window (A, **Figure** 7). The lower window (B, **Figure** 7) is used when the bike is raced. During a pit stop, when there is no time to wait for the oil to drain down, the oil level is considered okay if it is within the lower window.*

5. Look at the oil level inspection window. The oil level should be between the 2 lines. Refer to **Figure 8** for GSX-R750R Limited Edition or **Figure 9** for all other models. If the level is below the lower "F" line, add the recommended engine oil **(Figure 10)** to correct the level.

Engine Oil and Oil Filter Change

Change the engine oil and the oil filter at the recommended oil change interval indicated in **Table 2**. This assumes that the motorcycle is operated in moderate climates. In extreme climates, oil should be changed every 30 days. The time interval is more important than the mileage interval because acids formed by combustion blowby will contaminate the oil even if the motorcycle is not run for several months. If the motorcycle is operated under dusty conditions, the oil will get dirty more quickly and should be changed more frequently than recommended.

Use only a high-quality detergent motor oil with an API classification of SE or SF. The quality rating is stamped on top of the can or printed on the label

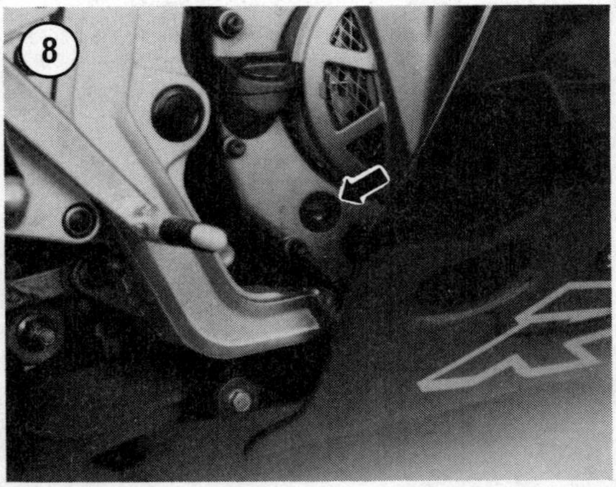

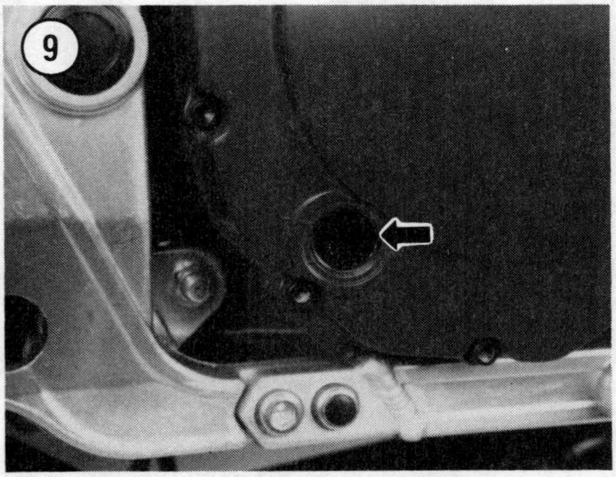

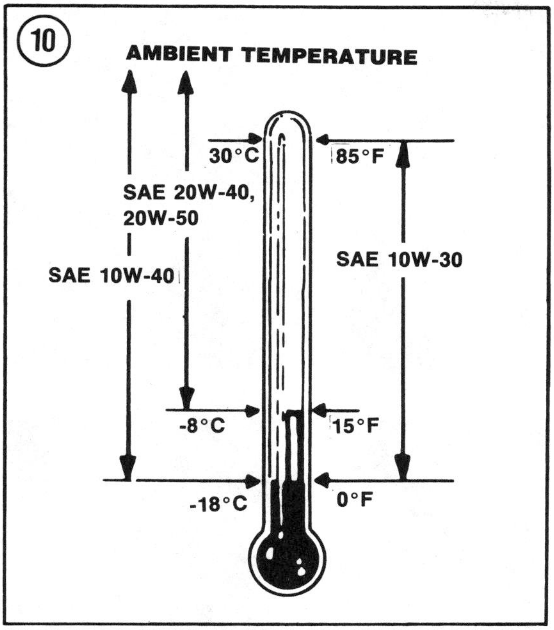

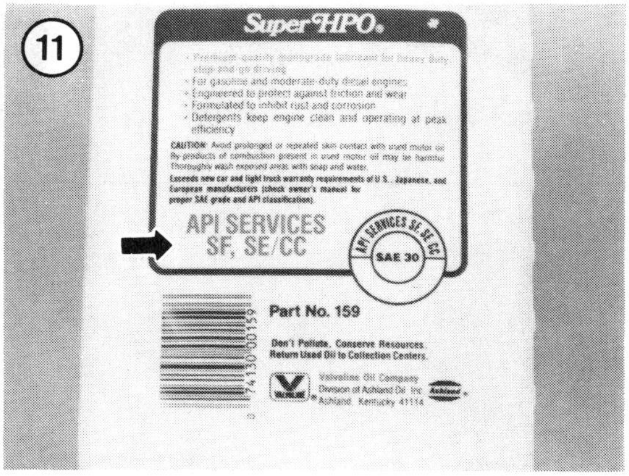

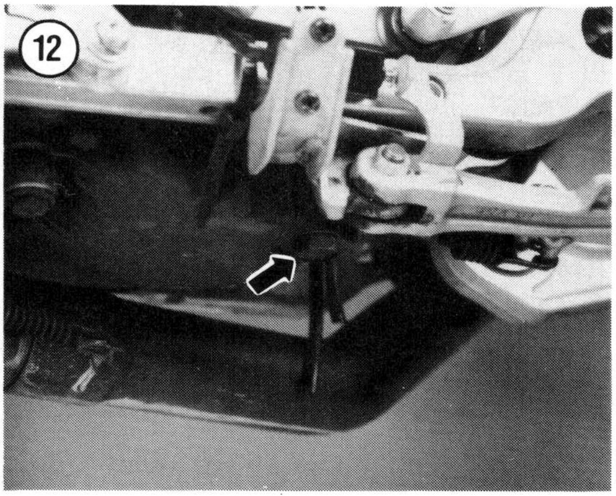

on the plastic bottle (**Figure 11**). Try to use the same brand of oil at each change. Use of oil additives is not recommended as they may cause clutch slippage (wet-clutch models). Refer to **Figure 10** for correct oil viscosity to use under anticipated ambient temperatures (not engine oil temperature).

CAUTION

On wet-clutch models, do not add any friction-reducing additives to the oil as they will cause clutch slippage. Also, do not use an engine oil with graphite added. The use of graphite oil will void any applicable Suzuki warranty. Graphite could build up on the clutch friction plates and cause clutch slippage. Until further testing is done by the oil and motorcycle industries, do not use this type of oil.

To change the engine oil and filter you will need the following:

a. Drain pan.
b. Funnel.
c. Can opener or pour spout (oil in cans).
d. 21 mm wrench (drain plug).
e. Oil filter wrench.
f. Oil (refer to **Table 4** for quantity).
g. Oil filter element.

NOTE

Never dispose of motor oil in the trash, on the ground, or down a storm drain. Many service stations accept used motor oil and waste haulers provide curbside used motor oil collection. Do not combine other fluids with motor oil to be recycled. To locate a recycler, contact the American Petroleum Institute (API) at ***www.recycleoil.org****.*

1. Start the engine and let it reach operating temperature; 10 minutes of stop-and-go riding is usually sufficient.
2. Turn the engine off and place the bike on level ground on the side stand.
3. Remove the lower section of the fairing as described under *Front Fairing Removal/Installation* in Chapter Twelve.
4. Place a drain pan under the left-hand rear portion of the crankcase and remove the drain plug (**Figure 12**). Remove the dipstick/oil filler cap; this

will speed up the flow of oil. Refer to A, **Figure 13** for GSX-R750R Limited Edition models or **Figure 14** for all other models.

5. Inspect the sealing washer on the crankcase drain plug. Replace if its condition is in doubt.
6. Install the drain plug and washer and tighten to the torque specification listed in **Table 5**.
7. Move the drain pan under the oil filter at the front of the engine.

NOTE
Because the exhaust system (especially most aftermarket systems) is so close to the oil filter there is very little working room for oil filter removal and installation. The easiest way to remove the oil filter is to use a Suzuki oil filter wrench (part No. 09915-40610) with a ratchet and socket.

8. Use the special tool and socket wrench to unscrew the oil filter (**Figure 15**) from the engine.
9. Clean off the oil filter mating surface on the crankcase with a shop rag and cleaning solvent. Remove any sludge or road dirt. Wipe it dry with a clean, lint-free cloth.
10. Apply a light coat of clean engine oil to the O-ring seal on the new oil filter (**Figure 16**).
11. Screw on the new oil filter by hand until the O-ring seal contacts the crankcase surface.
12. Make a mark on the face of the oil filter wrench with a permanent marker pen so it can be easily seen. Position this mark at the 12 o'clock position and install the wrench on the oil filter. Tighten the oil filter until this mark moves around to the 10 o'clock position, then stop. The filter is now tight enough.
13. During oil filter removal, some oil may drip onto the exhaust pipes. Before starting the engine,

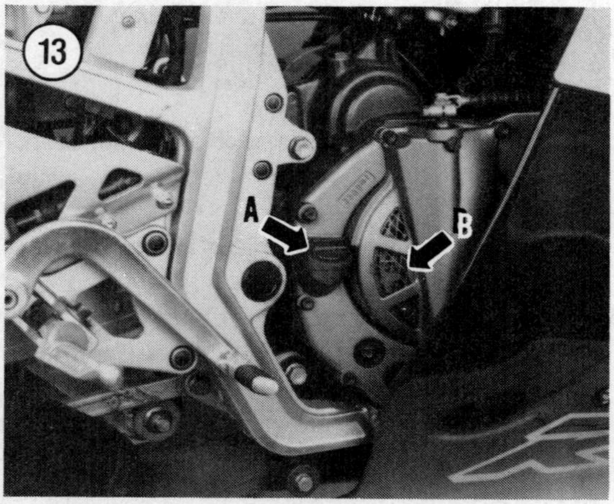

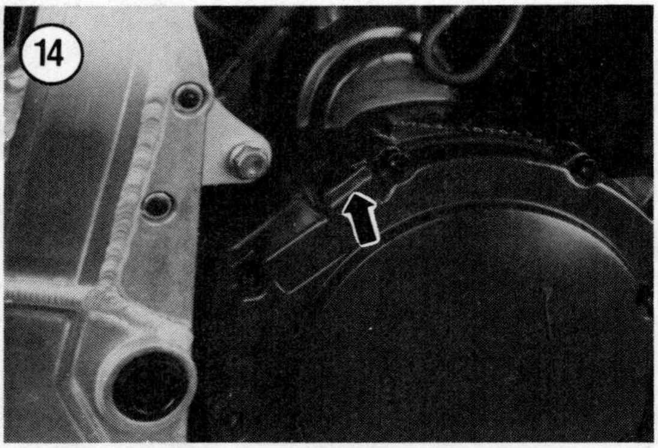

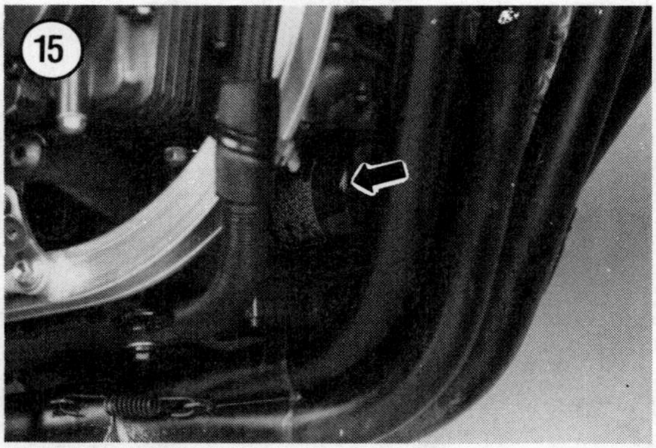

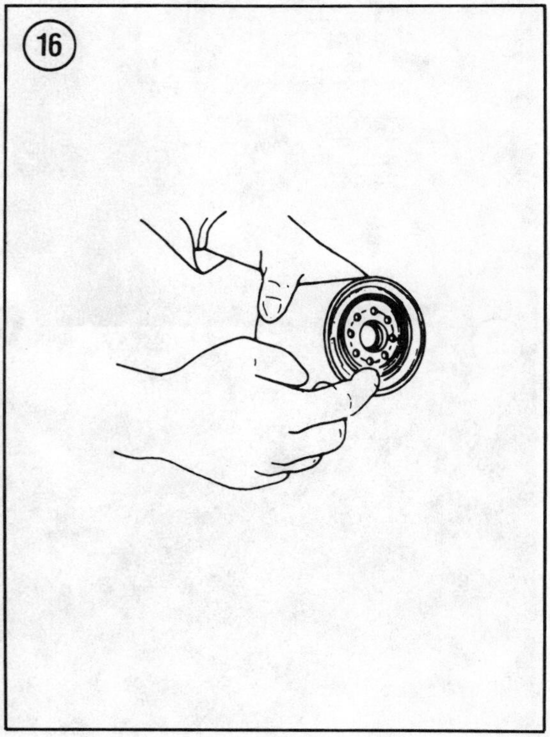

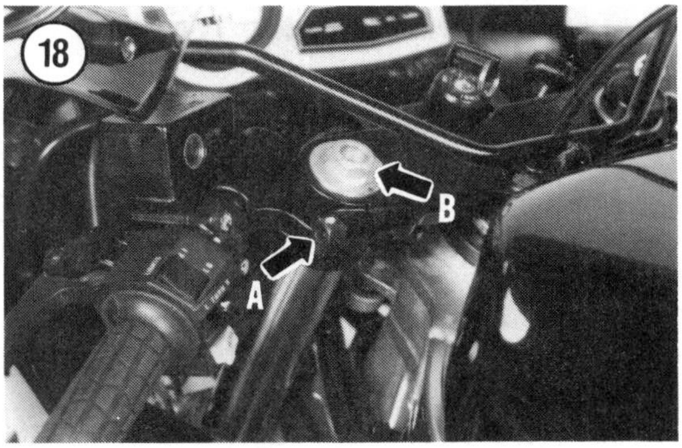

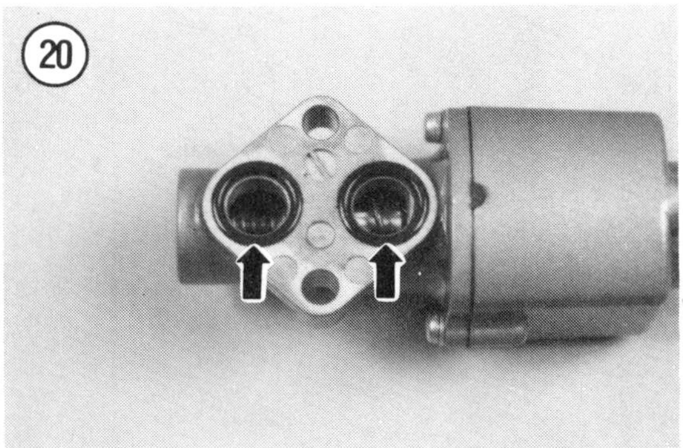

wipe off any spilled oil with a shop cloth. If necessary, spray some electrical contact cleaner on the pipes to remove the oil residue. If the oil is not cleaned off it will smoke once the exhaust pipes get hot.

CAUTION
On GSXR-750R Limited Edition dry-clutch models, be careful not to spill any oil onto the area of the clutch friction plates or clutch discs (B, ***Figure 13****). These clutch items must be free of oil at all times.*

14. Insert a funnel into the oil fill hole and fill the engine with the correct viscosity and quantity of oil. Refer to **Table 4**.
15. Install the dipstick/oil filler cap.
16. Start the engine, let it run at idle speed and check for leaks.
17. Turn the engine off and check the oil level; adjust as necessary.
18. Install the lower section of the front fairing as described under *Front Fairing Removal/ Installation* in Chapter Twelve.

Front Fork Oil Change

It is a good practice to change the fork oil at the interval listed in **Table 2** or once a year. If it becomes contaminated with dirt or water, change it immediately.

1. Remove the lower section of the fairing as described under *Front Fairing Removal/ Installation* in Chapter Twelve.
2. Place wood block(s) under the frame on each side to support the bike securely with the front wheel off the ground.
3. Remove the fork cap (**Figure 17**).
4. Loosen the upper fork bridge bolt (A, **Figure 18**).
5. Remove the upper fork cap bolt and spring seat (B, **Figure 18**).
6. Place a drip pan under the fork.

CAUTION
Cover the brake discs with shop cloths or plastic. Do not allow the fork oil to contact the discs. If any oil comes in contact with it, clean off with lacquer thinner or electrical contact cleaner. Remove all oil residue from the discs or the brake will be useless.

7. Remove the Allen bolts securing the NEAS unit (**Figure 19**) to the front fork. Remove the NEAS unit from the fork leg. Remove the O-ring seals (**Figure 20**) from the recesses in the NEAS unit. Discard the O-ring seals.

8. Repeat Steps 3-7 for the other fork assembly.
9. Allow the fork oil to drain for at least 5 minutes. Never reuse fork oil.

CAUTION
Do not allow the fork oil to come in contact with any of the brake components.

10. Place a shop cloth around the top of the fork tube and the upper fork bridge to catch remaining fork oil while the fork spring is removed. Withdraw the fork spring from each fork tube.
11. Install new O-ring seals (**Figure 20**) in the recesses in the NEAS unit and install the NEAS unit on the fork tube.
12. Apply Locktite Lock N' Seal to the Allen bolts prior to installation.
13. Install the Allen bolts securing the NEAS unit to the fork leg and tighten to the torque specification listed in **Table 5**.

NOTE
Suzuki recommends that the fork oil level be measured, if possible, to ensure a more accurate filling.

14. Remove the wood block(s) from under the engine.
15. Compress the forks completely.

NOTE
To measure the correct amount of fluid, use a plastic baby bottle. These bottles have measurements in fluid ounces (oz.) and cubic centimeters (cc) on the side.

16. Add the recommended type and quantity of fork oil as specified in **Table 6**.
17. Use an accurate ruler or the Suzuki oil level gauge (part No. 09943-74110) to achieve the oil level as specified in **Table 6** and measure to the center of the fork tube.

NOTE
*An oil level measuring device can be made as shown in **Figure 21**. Position the lower edge of the hose clamp the specified oil level distance up from the small diameter hole. Fill the fork with a few cubic centimeters more than the required amount of oil. Position the hose clamp on the top edge of the tube and draw out the excess oil. Oil is sucked out until the level reaches the small diameter hole. A precise oil level can be achieved with this simple device.*

18. Allow the oil to settle completely and recheck the oil level measurement. Adjust the oil level if necessary.

21

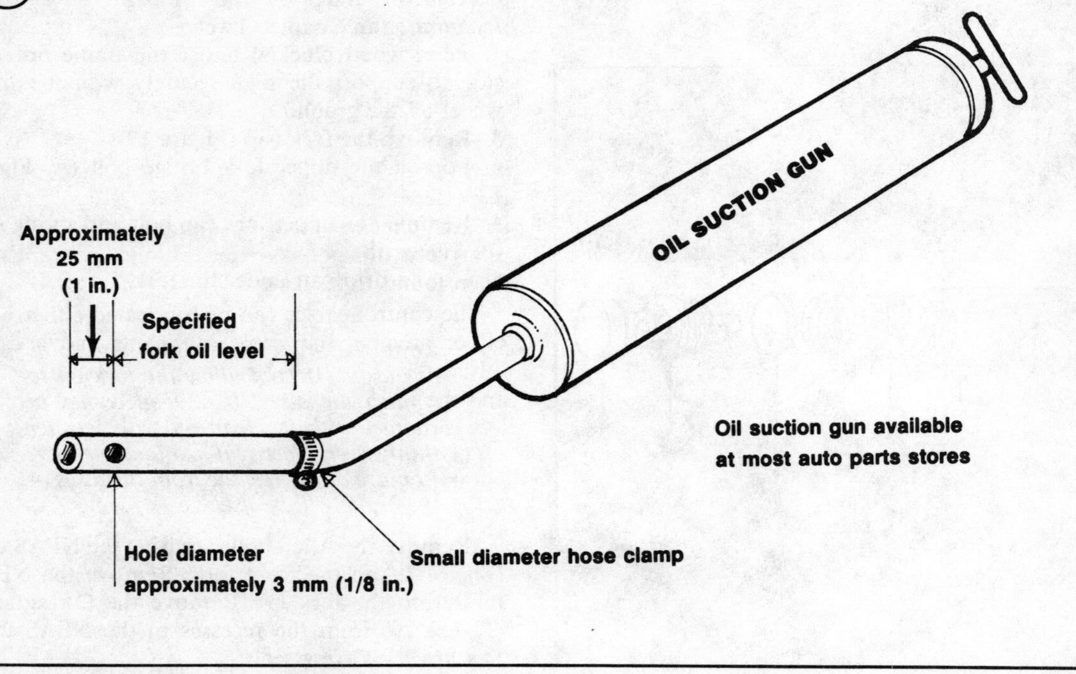

22

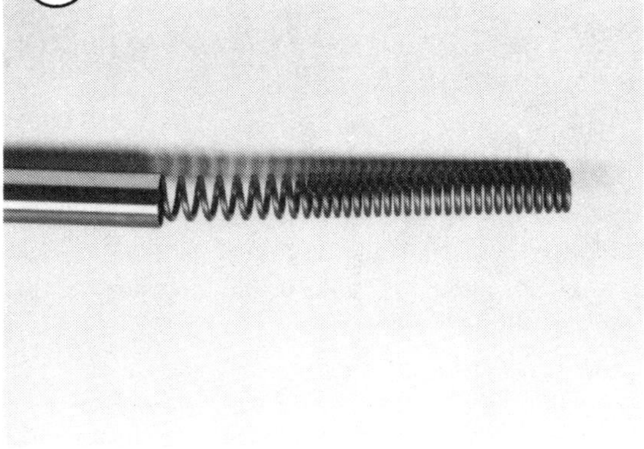

23

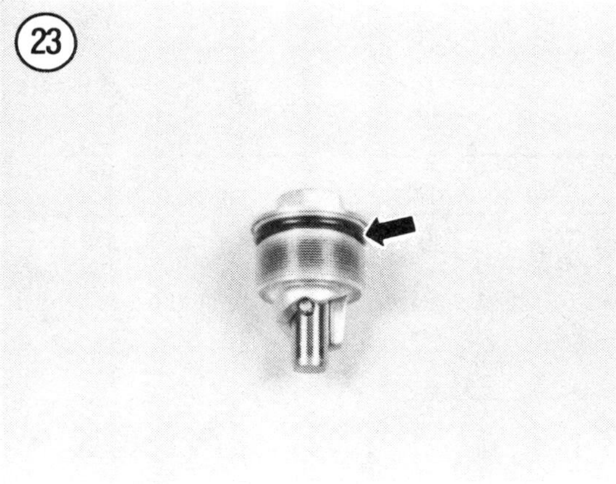

24

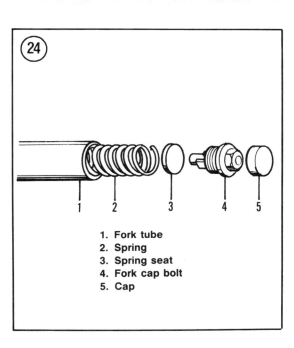

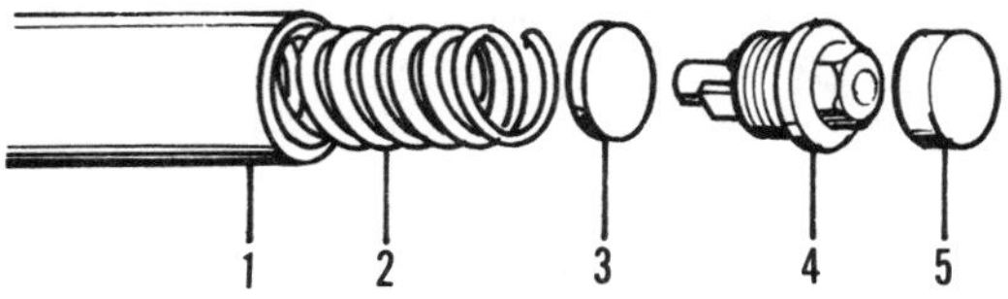

1. Fork tube
2. Spring
3. Spring seat
4. Fork cap bolt
5. Cap

19. Place wood block(s) under the frame to support the bike securely with the front wheel off the ground.
20. Install the fork spring with the tighter wound coils (**Figure 22**) going in last.
21. Inspect the O-ring seal (**Figure 23**) on the fork cap bolt; replace if necessary.
22. Install the spring seat and the fork cap bolt (**Figure 24**) while pushing down on the spring. Start the bolt slowly; don't cross-thread it. Tighten to the torque specification listed in **Table 5**.
23. Tighten the upper fork bridge bolt to the torque specification listed in **Table 5**.
24. Repeat Steps 10-23 for the other fork assembly.
25. Install the lower section of the front fairing as described under *Lower Fairing Removal/ Installation* in Chapter Twelve.
26. Road test the bike and check for leaks.

Drive Chain Lubrication

Oil the drive chain at the interval indicated in **Table 2** or sooner if it becomes dry.

1. Place wood block(s) under the engine or frame to support the bike securely with the rear wheel off the ground.
2. Oil the bottom run with a good grade of commercial chain lubricant formulated for O-ring chains. Concentrate on getting the oil down between the side plates of the chain links, into the pins, bushings and rollers.
3. Rotate the rear wheel to bring the unoiled portion of the chain within reach. Continue until all the chain is lubricated.

Control Cables

The control cables should be lubricated at the interval listed in **Table 2**. They should also be inspected at this time for fraying and the cable sheath checked for chafing. The cables are relatively inexpensive and should be replaced when found to be faulty.

The control cables can be lubricated either with oil or any popular cable lubricants and a cable lubricator. The first method requires more time and the complete lubrication of the entire cable is less certain.

On the throttle cable it is necessary to remove the screws securing the right-hand switch assembly together to gain access to the throttle cable end.

Oil method

1. Disconnect the cable from the clutch (GSX-R750R Limited Edition) and the throttle grip assembly.

3

2. Make a cone of stiff paper and tape it to the end of the cable sheath (**Figure 25**).
3. Hold the cable upright and pour a small amount of thin oil (SAE 10W-30) into the cone. Work the cable in and out of the sheath for several minutes to help the oil work its way down to the end of the cable.

NOTE
To avoid a mess, place a shop cloth at the end of the cable to catch the oil as it runs out.

4. Remove the cone, reconnect the cable and adjust the cable(s) as described in this chapter.

NOTE
While the throttle cable is removed and the switch assembly disassembled, apply a light coat of oil to the metal surfaces of the throttle grip assembly.

Lubricator method

1. Disconnect the cable from the clutch (GSX-R750R Limited Edition) and the throttle grip assembly.
2. Attach a lubricator following the manufacturer's instructions (**Figure 26**).
3. Insert the nozzle of the lubricant can in the lubricator, press the button on the can and hold down until the lubricant begins to flow out the other end of the cable.
4. Remove the lubricator, reconnect the cable(s) and adjust the cable as described in this chapter.

Miscellaneous Lubrication Points

Lubricate the clutch lever, front brake lever, side stand pivot point and the footpeg pivot points. Use SAE 10W-40 engine oil.

PERIODIC MAINTENANCE

Drive Chain Adjustment

The drive chain should be checked and adjusted at the interval listed in **Table 2** or more often if ridden in wet or dusty conditions. The correct amount of chain free play, when pushed up midway between the sprockets on the lower chain run, is listed in **Table 7**. See **Figure 27**. If the adjustment is necessary, perform the following.
1. Place the bike on the side stand for the most accurate adjustment.
2. Place the transmission in NEUTRAL.
3. Remove the cotter pin and loosen the axle nut (A, **Figure 28**).

25

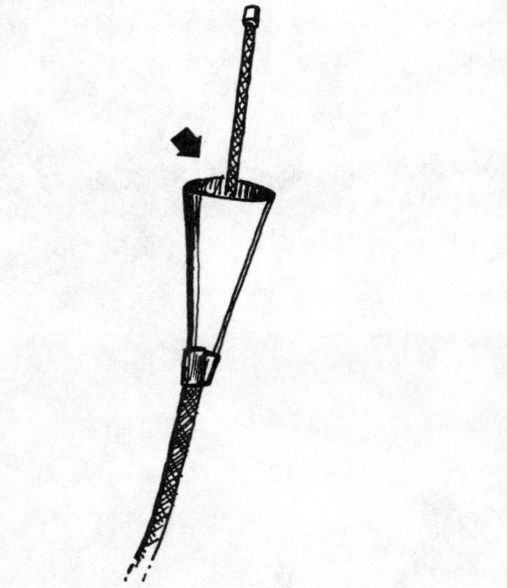

26

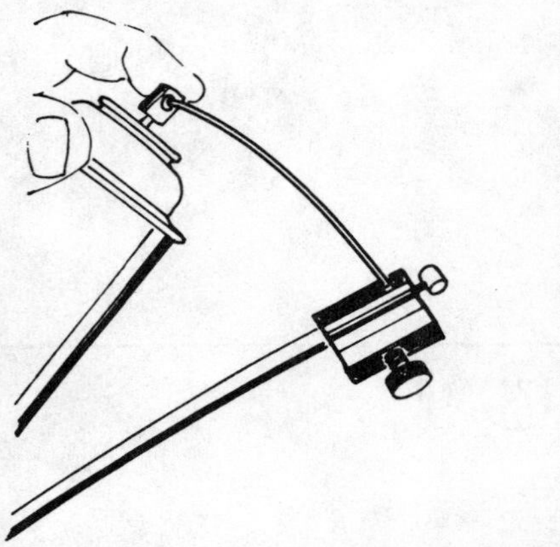

27

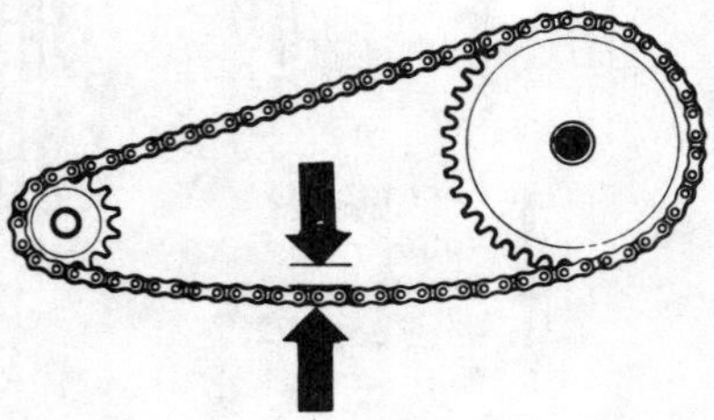

4. Turn the adjuster nuts (B, **Figure 28**) in either direction, in equal amounts, to either increase or decrease drive chain tension. After adjustment is complete, make sure the notches on the rear axle special washers (both sides) are on the same scale mark (**Figure 29**) on the swing arm on both sides.
5. Roll the bike forward to rotate the rear wheel and move the chain to another position, then recheck the free play; chains rarely wear or stretch evenly and, as a result, the free play will not remain constant over the entire length.

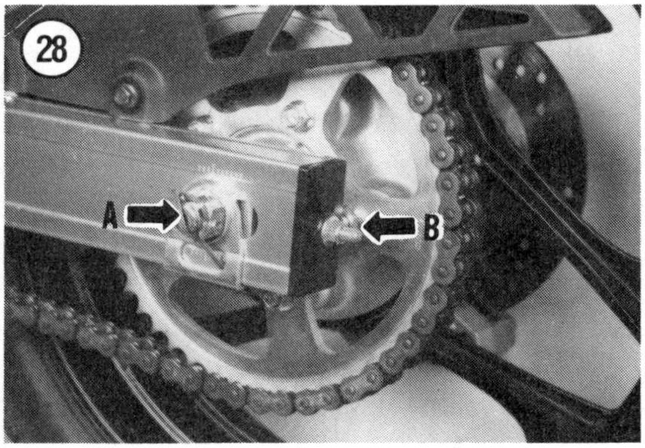

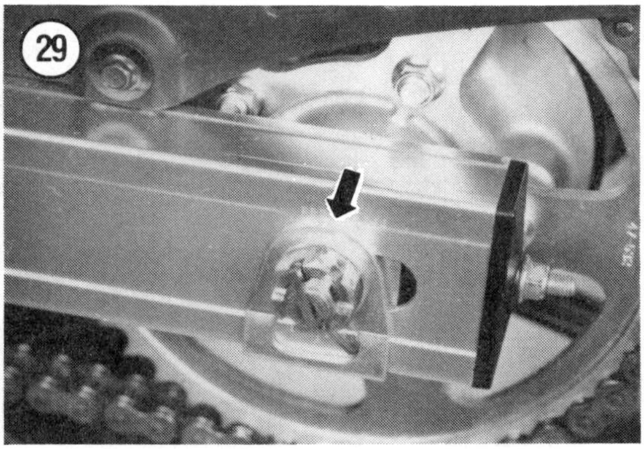

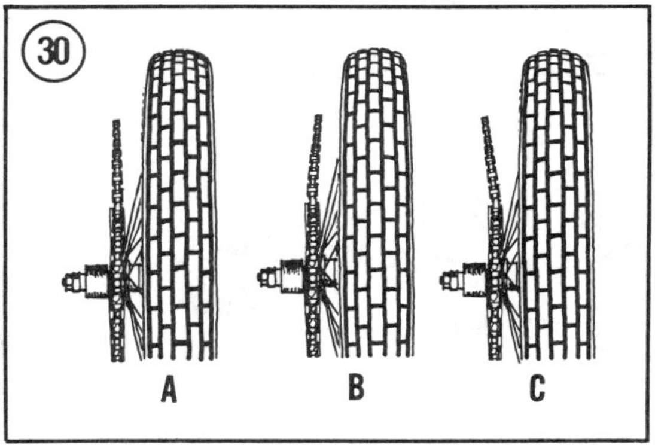

WARNING
Excessive free play can result in chain breakage which could cause a serious accident.

6. If the chain cannot be adjusted within the limits in **Table 7**, it is excessively worn and stretched and should be replaced. Always replace both sprockets when replacing the drive chain; never install a new chain over worn sprockets. The drive chain replacement numbers are listed in **Table 8**.
7. When the adjustment is correct, sight along the chain from the rear sprocket to see that it is correctly aligned. It should leave the top of the rear sprocket in a straight line (A, **Figure 30**). If it is cocked to one side or the other (B or C, **Figure 30**), the rear wheel is incorrectly aligned and must be corrected by turning the adjusters counter to one another until the chain and sprocket are correctly aligned.
8. Tighten the rear axle nut to the torque specification listed in **Table 5**.
9. Install a new cotter pin and bend both ends over completely. Always install a new cotter pin—never reuse a cotter pin.

Drive Chain Cleaning, Inspection and Lubrication

Clean and lubricate the drive chain at the interval indicated in **Table 2**, or more frequently if ridden in dusty or muddy terrain.

NOTE
All models are equipped with an O-ring type drive chain.

1. Remove the drive chain as described under *Drive Chain Removal/Installation* in Chapter Ten.
2. Immerse the drive chain in a pan of kerosene or high flash point solvent that will not destroy the rubber O-rings.
3. Allow it to soak for about 10-15 minutes. Move it around and flex it during this period so that the dirt between the links may work its way out.
4. Scrub the rollers and side plates with a soft brush and rinse away loosened grit (**Figure 31**). Rinse the chain a couple of times to make sure all dirt is washed out. Wipe the chain dry with a shop cloth; hang it up and allow it to dry thoroughly.
5. After cleaning the chain, examine it carefully for wear or damage. If any signs are visible, replace the chain.
6. Lay the chain on the workbench. Stretch the chain out and measure the distance between 21 pins with a vernier caliper (**Figure 32**). If the chain

has stretched to the service limit listed in **Table 7**, it must be replaced. The replacement drive chain numbers are listed in **Table 8**.

CAUTION
*Always check both the drive and the driven sprockets (**Figure 33**) every time the drive chain is removed. If any wear is visible on the teeth, replace the sprocket. Never install a new chain over worn sprockets or a worn chain over new sprockets.*

7. Check the inner faces of the inner plates. They should be lightly polished on both sides. If they show considerable wear on both sides, the sprockets are not aligned. Adjust alignment as described in this chapter.
8. Lubricate the drive chain with SAE 80 or 90 gear oil or a good grade of chain lubricant (formulated for O-ring chains) carefully following the manufacturer's instructions.

CAUTION
Do not use engine oil as a lubricant as it will damage the O-rings. Use a chain lubricant specifically formulated for use with this type of chain or the specified gear oil.

9. Reinstall the drive chain as described under *Drive Chain Removal/Installation* in Chapter Ten.
10. Adjust the drive chain tension as described in this chapter.

Drive Chain Slider Inspection/Replacement

A drive chain slider (**Figure 34**) is attached to the left-hand side of the swing arm near the pivot point. There are no factory-specified wear limit dimensions for the slider. If the slider is worn unevenly or if the wear groove is worn more than halfway through the material, replace the slider.

1. Remove the swing arm as described under *Swing Arm Removal/Installation* in Chapter Nine.

32

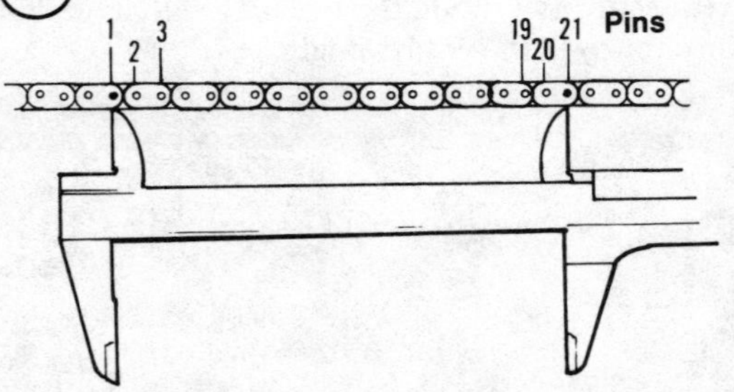

33

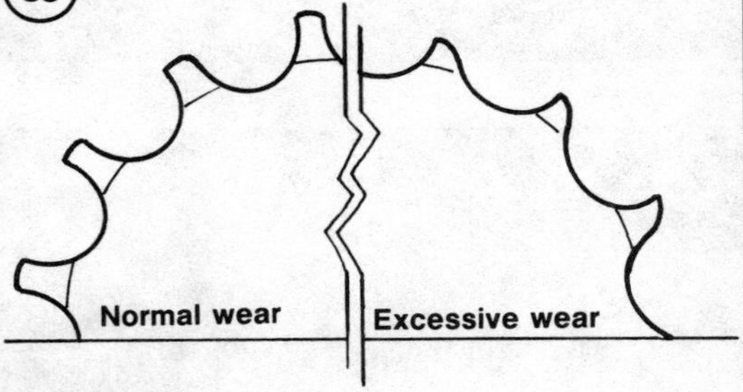

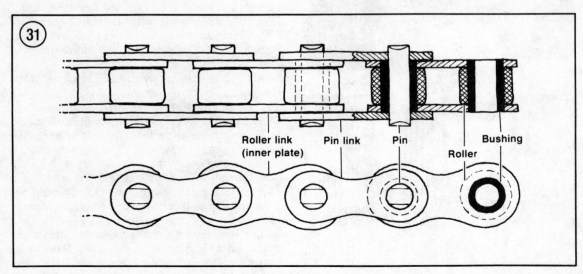

31

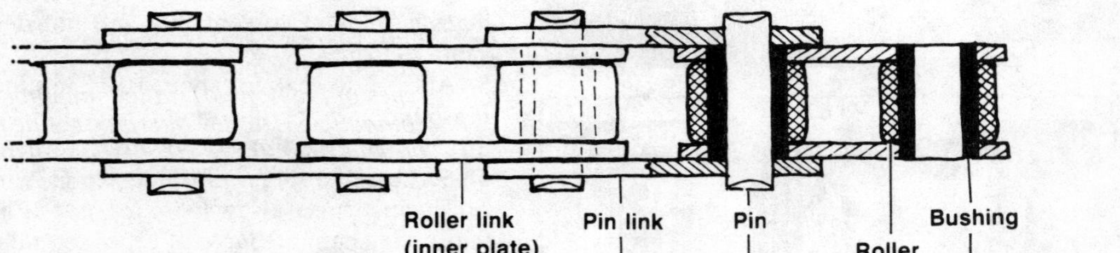

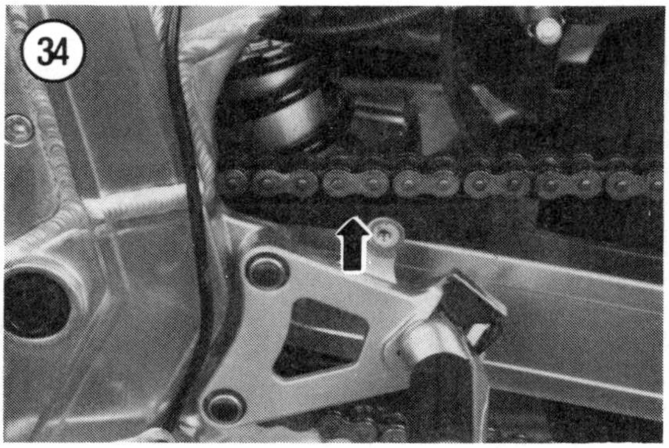
34

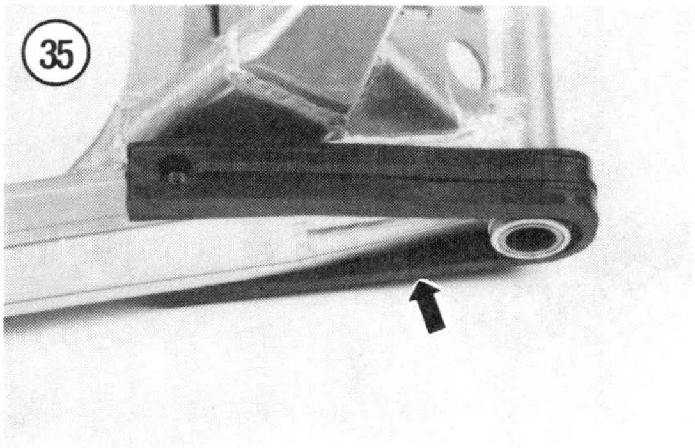
35

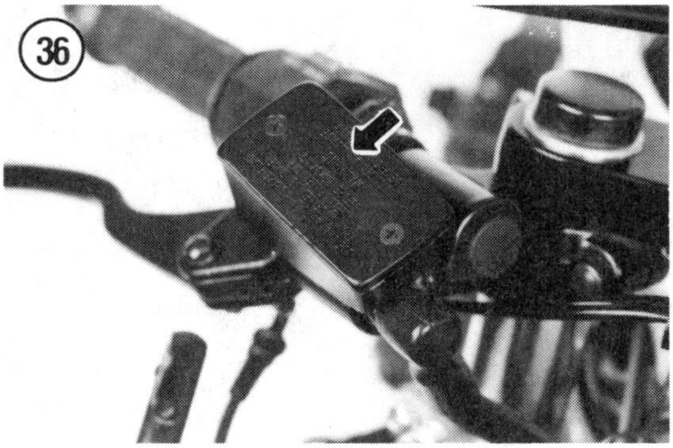
36

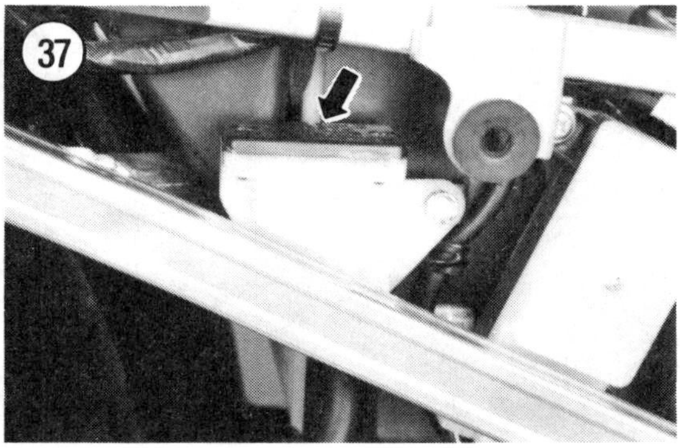
37

2. Remove the screw, washer and collar securing the slider (**Figure 35**) to the swing arm.
3. Remove the old slider and install a new slider.
4. Tighten the screws securely.
5. Install the swing arm as described under *Swing Arm Removal/Installation* in Chapter Ten.

Disc Brake Fluid Level

The fluid level should be up between the upper and lower mark within the reservoir. If the brake fluid level reaches the lower level mark, visible through the viewing port on the front master cylinder or on the side of the rear master cylinder reservoir, the fluid level must be corrected by adding fresh brake fluid.

1. Place the bike on level ground and position the handlebars so the front master cylinder reservoir is level.
2. Remove the right-hand side cover in order to check the rear master cylinder.
3. Clean any dirt from the area around the top cover before removing the cover.
4. Remove the screws securing the top cover. Remove the top cover and the diaphragm. Refer to **Figure 36** for the front master cylinder or **Figure 37** for the rear master cylinder.
5. Add brake fluid until the level is to the upper level line within the master cylinder reservoir. Refer to **Figure 38** for the front master cylinder or **Figure 39** for the rear master cylinder. Use fresh brake fluid from a sealed brake fluid container.

WARNING
Use brake fluid from a sealed container and clearly marked DOT 3 or DOT 4 only (specified for disc brakes). Others may vaporize and cause brake failure. Do not intermix different brands or types of brake fluid as they may not be compatible. Do not intermix a silicone based (DOT 5) brake fluid as it can cause brake component damage leading to brake system failure.

CAUTION
Be careful when handling brake fluid. Do not spill it on painted or plated surfaces or plastic parts as it will destroy the surface. Wash the area immediately with soapy water and thoroughly rinse it off.

6. Reinstall the diaphragm and the top cover. Tighten the screws securely.

Disc Brake Lines

Check brake lines between the master cylinders and the brake calipers. If there is any leakage, tighten the connections and bleed the brakes as described under *Bleeding the System* in Chapter Eleven. If this does not stop the leak or if a brake line is obviously damaged, cracked or chafed, replace the brake line(s) and bleed the system.

Disc Brake Pad Wear

Inspect the brake pads for excessive or uneven wear, scoring and oil or grease on the friction surface. If any of these conditions exist, replace the pads as described in Chapter Eleven. Remove the caliper dust cover (**Figure 40**). Look into the caliper assembly and check the wear lines on the brake pads. Replace both pads if the wear line on the pads reaches the brake disc. On front brakes, replace both pads in both calipers at the same time.

Disc Brake Fluid Change

Every time the reservoir cap is removed, a small amount of dirt and moisture enters the brake fluid. The same thing happens if a leak occurs or any part of the hydraulic system is loosened or disconnected. Dirt can clog the system and cause unnecessary wear. Water in the brake fluid vaporizes at high temperature, impairing the hydraulic action and reducing the brake's stopping ability.

To maintain peak performance, change the brake fluid as indicated in **Table 2**. To change brake fluid, follow the *Bleeding the System* procedure in Chapter Eleven. Continue adding new fluid to the master cylinders and bleeding out at the calipers until the fluid leaving the caliper is clean and free of contaminants.

WARNING
Use brake fluid from a sealed container and clearly marked DOT 3 or DOT 4 only (specified for disc brakes). Others may vaporize and cause brake failure. Do not intermix different brands or types of brake fluid as they may not be compatible. Do not intermix a silicone based (DOT 5) brake fluid as it can cause brake component damage leading to brake system failure.

Rear Brake Pedal Height Adjustment

The rear brake pedal height should be adjusted at the interval listed in **Table 2**. The top of the brake pedal should be positioned below the top surface of the footpeg (**Figure 41**) the following distance:

a. 750 cc models: 60 mm (2.4 in.).
b. 1100 cc models: 55 mm (2.2 in.).

1. Make sure the brake pedal is in the at-rest position.

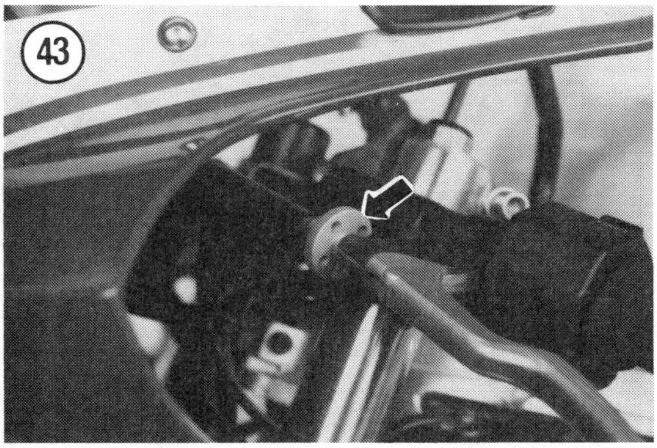

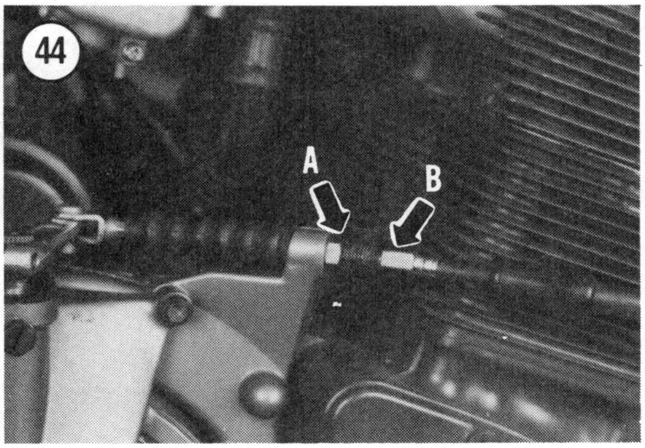

2. To change height position, loosen the locknut (A, **Figure 42**) and turn the master cylinder pushrod (B, **Figure 42**) until the correct height is achieved. Tighten the locknut (A) securely.

Clutch Adjustment (GSX-R750R Limited Edition)

This type of clutch will always have a rattling sound when the engine is running. This is due to the clutch design and the rattle cannot be "adjusted out" with this adjustment procedure.

NOTE
The GSX-R750R Limited Edition model is equipped with a dry-type clutch that ***does*** *require routine adjustment. All other models, covered in this book have a wet-type clutch with a hydraulic slave cylinder and do not require any type of adjustment.*

Adjust the clutch at the interval indicated in **Table 2**. For the clutch to fully engage and disengage, there must be 2-3 mm (0.08-0.12 in.) of free play between the lever and the lever housing.

1. Minor adjustments can be made at the upper adjuster at the hand lever. Turn the adjuster (**Figure 43**) in or out to obtain the correct amount of free play.

NOTE
If the proper amount of free play cannot be achieved at the hand lever, additional adjustment can be made at the clutch actuating lever on the right-hand crankcase cover.

2. Major adjustments are made at the clutch actuating lever as follows:
   a. At the clutch lever, turn the adjuster (**Figure 43**) in all the way toward the hand grip.
   b. Near the right-hand crankcase cover, loosen the locknut (A, **Figure 44**) and turn the adjuster (B, **Figure 44**) until the correct amount of free play can be achieved.
   c. Tighten the locknut (A).
3. If necessary, do some final adjusting at the clutch lever as described in Step 1.
4. After adjustment is complete, check that the locknut is tight at the clutch actuating lever on the crankcase cover.
5. Road test the bike to make sure the clutch fully disengages when the lever is pulled in; if it does not, the bike will creep in gear when stopped. Also make sure the clutch fully engages; if it does not, the clutch will slip, particularly when accelerating in high gear.

6. If the proper amount of adjustment cannot be achieved using this procedure, the cable has stretched to the point where it needs replacing. Refer to Chapter Five for complete procedure.

Throttle Cable Adjustment

The throttle cable should have 0.5-1.0 mm (0.02-0.04 in.) of free play. If adjustment is necessary, perform the following:

1. Remove the fuel tank as described under *Fuel Tank Removal/Installation* in Chapter Seven.
2. At the carburetor assembly end of the throttle cable, loosen the locknut and slide the adjuster in either direction until the correct amount of free play is achieved.
3. Tighten the locknut.
4. If the proper amount of adjustment cannot be achieved using this procedure, the cable has stretched to the point where it needs replacing. Refer to *Throttle Cable Replacement* in Chapter Seven.
5. Check the throttle cable from the throttle grip to the carburetor. Make sure it is not kinked or chafed. Replace as necessary.
6. Make sure the throttle grip rotates freely from a fully closed to fully open position. Check with the handlebar at center, at full right and at full left. If necessary, remove the throttle grip and apply a lithium base grease to the rotating surfaces.

WARNING

*With the engine idling, move the handlebar from side to side. If idle speed increases during this movement, the throttle cable may need adjusting or may be incorrectly routed through the frame. Correct this problem immediately. Do **not** ride the bike in this unsafe condition.*

7. Install the fuel tank as described under *Fuel Tank Removal/Installation* in Chapter Seven.

Camshaft Chain Tensioner Adjustment

There is *no* provision for cam chain tensioner adjustment on this engine. Camshaft chain tension is maintained automatically.

Air Filter Element

The air filter element should be removed and cleaned at the interval listed in **Table 2**. The air filter element should be replaced at the interval listed in **Table 2** or sooner if soiled, severely clogged or broken in any area.

The air filter removes dust and abrasive particles from the air before the air enters the carburetors and the engine. Without the air filter, very fine particles could enter into the engine and cause rapid wear of the piston rings, cylinders and bearings and might clog small passages in the carburetors. Never run the bike without the air filter element installed.

Proper air filter servicing can do more to ensure long service from your engine than almost any other single item.

Air Filter Element Removal/Cleaning/Installation

1. Place the bike on the side stand.
2. Remove the seat as described under *Seat Removal/Installation* in Chapter Twelve.
3. Remove the fuel tank as described under *Fuel Tank Removal/Installation* in Chapter Seven.

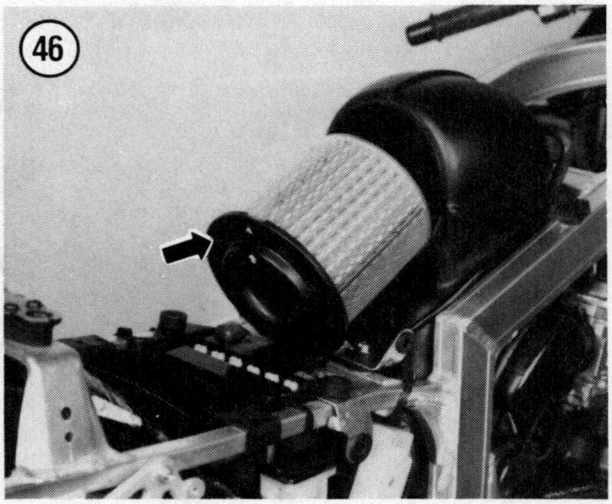

4. Remove the wing nut and washer (**Figure 45**) securing the air filter element into the air box.
5. Withdraw the element assembly from the air box (**Figure 46**).
6. Wipe out the interior of the air box with a shop rag dampened with cleaning solvent. Remove any foreign matter that may have passed through a broken element.
7. Gently tap the air filter element to loosen the dust.

CAUTION
In the next step, do not direct compressed air toward the inside surface of the element. If air pressure is directed to the inside surface it will force the dirt and dust into the pores of the element thus restricting air flow.

47

48

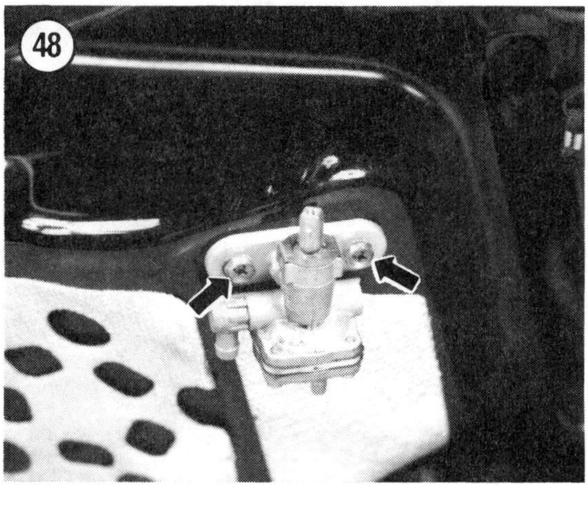

8. Apply compressed air toward the *outside surface* of the element to remove all loosened dirt and dust from the element.
9. Inspect the element; if it is torn or damaged in any area it must be replaced. Do *not* run the bike with a damaged element as it may allow dirt to enter the engine.
10. Install the new air filter element and position it with the raised arrow (**Figure 47**) facing UP.
11. Make sure the element is correctly seated into the air box so there is no air leak, then install the washer and wing nut. Tighten the wing nut securely.
12. Install the fuel tank and seat.

Fuel Shutoff Filter and Valve Removal/Installation

The fuel filter is built into the shutoff valve and removes particles which might otherwise enter into the carburetor and may cause the float needle to remain in the open position.
1. Remove the fuel tank as described under *Fuel Tank Removal/Installation* in Chapter Seven.
2. If necessary, drain the fuel from the fuel tank into a clean and sealable metal container. If the fuel is kept clean it can be reused.
3. Place an old blanket or several shop cloths on the workbench to protect the fuel tank's painted surface. Place the fuel tank on these protective items.
4. Remove the screws and washers (**Figure 48**) securing the fuel shutoff valve to the fuel tank.
5. Remove the valve from the fuel tank. Don't lose the O-ring seal between the fuel tank and the valve.
6. After removing the valve from the fuel tank, insert a corner of a lint-free cloth into the opening in the tank to prevent the entry of foreign matter or tape it closed.
7. Clean the filter with a medium soft toothbrush and blow out with compressed air. Replace the filter if it is broken in any area.
8. Install by reversing these removal steps, noting the following.
9. Be sure to install the O-ring seal between the shutoff valve and the fuel tank. Tighten the screws securely.
10. Install the fuel tank as described under *Fuel Tank Removal/Installation* in Chapter Seven.
11. Start the engine and check for fuel leaks.

Fuel Line Inspection

Inspect the fuel line from the fuel shutoff valve to the carburetor. If it is cracked or starting to deteriorate it must be replaced. Make sure the hose clamps are in place and holding securely.

WARNING

A damaged or deteriorated fuel line presents a very dangerous fire hazard to both the rider and the vehicle if fuel should spill onto a hot engine or exhaust pipe.

Crankcase Breather (U.S. Only)

Inspect the breather hose (**Figure 49**) from the cylinder head breather cover to the air filter air case. If it is cracked or starting to deteriorate it must be replaced. Make sure the hose clamps are in place and holding securely.

Evaporative Emission Control System (California Models Only)

Fuel vapor from the fuel tank is routed into a charcoal canister when the engine is stopped. When the engine is started, these vapors are drawn through the vacuum controlled valves, into the carburetors and into the engine to be burned. Make sure all vacuum hoses are correctly routed and attached. Inspect the hoses and replace any if necessary.

Refer to Chapter Seven for detailed information on the evaporative emission control system and for vacuum hose routing.

Exhaust System

Check for leakage at all fittings. Tighten all bolts and nuts. Replace any gaskets if necessary. Refer to *Exhaust System* in Chapter Seven.

Wheel Bearings

There is no factory-recommended mileage interval for cleaning and repacking the wheel bearings. They should be inspected and serviced, if necessary, every time the wheel is removed or whenever there is a likelihood of water contamination. The correct service procedures are covered in Chapter Nine and Chapter Ten.

49

50

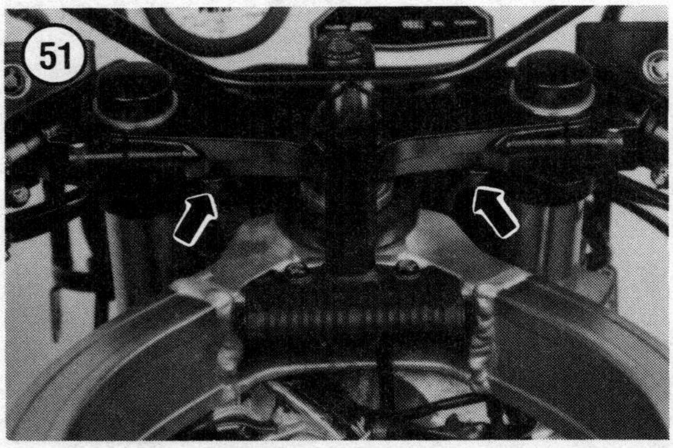
51

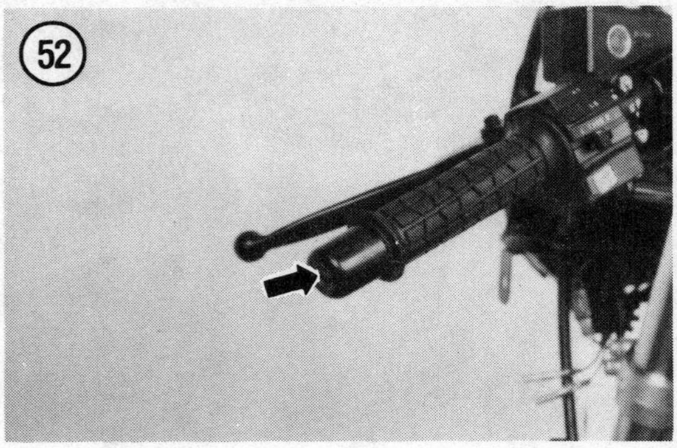
52

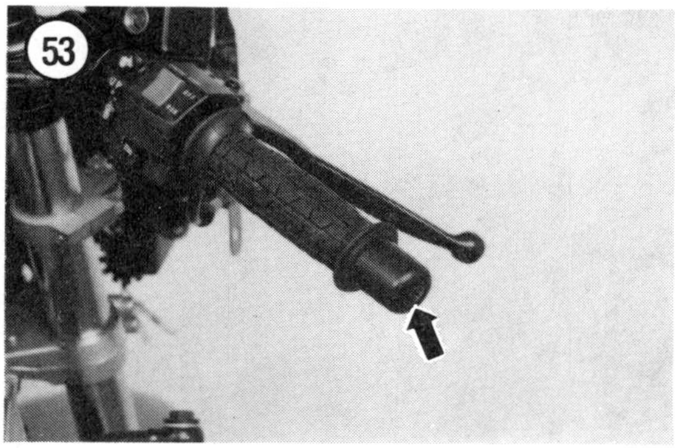

Front Suspension Check

1. Apply the front brake and pump the forks up and down as vigorously as possible. Check for smooth operation and check for any oil leaks.
2. Make sure the upper and lower fork bridge bolts are tight (**Figure 50**).
3. Make sure the bolts (**Figure 51**) securing the handlebars are tight and that the handlebars are secure.
4. Make sure the screws securing the handlebar balancer weights are tight and secure. Refer to **Figure 52** and **Figure 53**.
5. Make sure the front axle nut is tight and that the cotter pin is in place (**Figure 54**).

CAUTION
If any of the previously mentioned bolts and nuts are loose, refer to Chapter Nine for correct procedures and torque specifications.

Rear Suspension Check

1. Remove the lower fairing. Place a wood block(s) under each side of the frame to support it securely with the rear wheel off the ground.
2. Push hard on the rear wheel (sideways) to check for side play in the rear swing arm bearings. Remove the wood block(s).
3. Check the tightness of the upper (**Figure 55**) and lower (**Figure 56**) mounting bolts and nuts on the shock absorber.
4. Remove the plastic cap (**Figure 57**) and make sure the swing arm pivot bolt and nut (**Figure 58**) are tight.

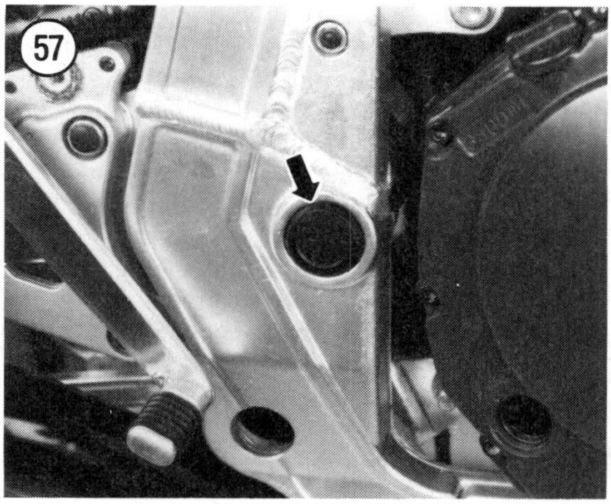

3

5. Check the tightness of the shock absorber lever assembly bolts and nuts (**Figure 59**).
6. Make sure the rear axle nut is tight and that the cotter pin is in place (**Figure 60**).
7. Check the tightness of the rear brake torque arm bolts and nuts. Make sure the cotter pins are in place.

CAUTION
If any of the previously mentioned bolts and nuts are loose, refer to Chapter Ten for correct procedures and torque specifications.

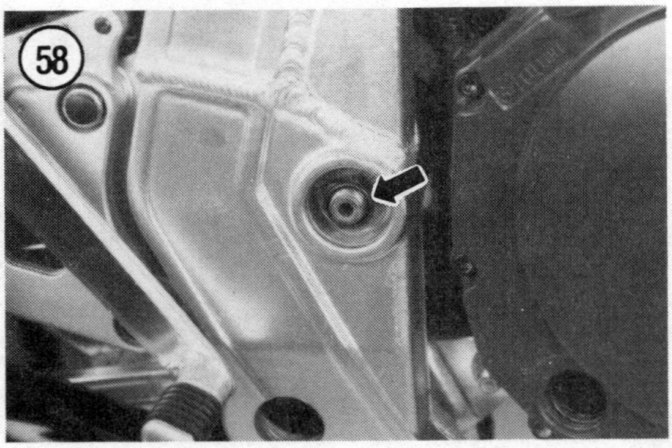

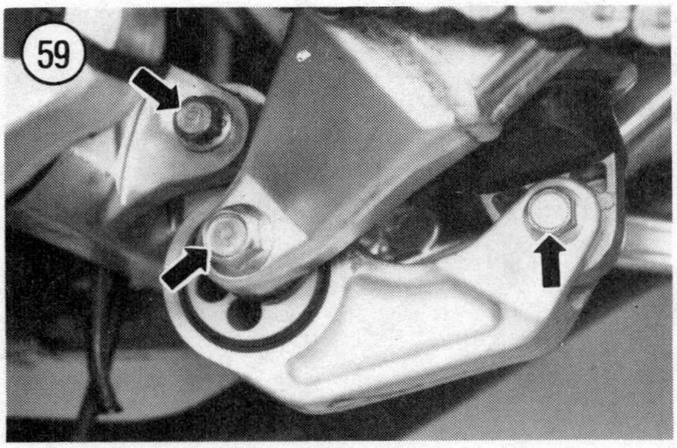

Nuts, Bolts and Other Fasteners

Constant vibration can loosen many of the fasteners on the motorcycle. Check the tightness of all fasteners, especially those on:

a. Engine mounting hardware.
b. Engine crankcase covers.
c. Handlebar and front forks.
d. Gearshift lever.
e. Brake pedal and lever.
f. Sprocket bolts and nuts.
g. Exhaust system.
h. Lighting equipment.

Steering Head Adjustment Check

Check the steering head bearings for looseness at the interval listed in **Table 2**.

Remove the lower fairing. Place a wood block(s) under each side of the frame to support it securely with the front wheel off the ground.

Hold onto the front fork tube and gently rock the fork assembly back and forth. If you feel looseness, refer to Chapter Nine.

TUNE-UP

Perform a complete tune-up at the interval listed in **Table 2** (4,000 miles or 12 months) if the bike is used for normal riding. More frequent tune-ups may be required if the bike is ridden in stop-and-go traffic. The purpose of the tune-up is to restore the performance lost due to normal wear and deterioration of parts.

The spark plugs should be routinely replaced at every other tune-up or if the electrodes show signs of erosion. In addition, this is a good time to clean the air filter element. Have the new parts on hand before you begin.

Because the different systems in an engine interact, the procedures should be done in the following order:

62

a. Tighten the cylinder head nuts.
b. Adjust valve clearances.
c. Run a compression test.
d. Set the idle speed.

Table 9 summarizes tune-up specifications.

To perform a tune-up on your Suzuki, you will need the following tools and equipment:

a. 18 mm (5/8 in.) spark plug wrench.
b. Socket wrench and assorted sockets.
c. Flat feeler gauge.
d. Compression gauge.
e. Spark plug wire feeler gauge and gapper tool.

63

64

65

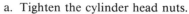

Cylinder Head and Cylinder Nuts and Bolt Tightening

The cylinder head (not the cylinder head cover) is held in place with 12 nuts. There is also 1 cylinder head-to-cylinder bolt and 1 cylinder-to-crankcase nut.

The nuts should be tightened after the first 600 miles (1,000 km) of the purchase of a new bike, after the cylinder head has been removed for service and at every tune-up.

1. Place the bike on the side stand.
2. Remove the seat as described under *Seat Removal/Installation* in Chapter Twelve.
3. Remove the fuel tank as described under *Fuel Tank Removal/Installation* in Chapter Seven.
4. Remove the front fairing as described under *Front Fairing Removal/Installation* in Chapter Twelve.
5. Disconnect the crankcase breather hose (**Figure 61**) from the cylinder head cover.
6. Disconnect all spark plug caps and wires (**Figure 62**).

NOTE
The following steps are shown with the engine removed from the frame for clarity. It is not necessary to remove the engine to tighten the cylinder head and cylinder nuts and bolt.

7. Remove the Allen bolts securing the oil hose fittings (**Figure 63**) to the cylinder head cover. Move the oil hoses away from the cylinder head cover. Discard the O-ring seals in each oil hose fitting. To prevent an oil leak, these O-rings must be replaced every time the oil hoses are disconnected from the cylinder head cover.
8. Using a crisscross pattern, loosen then remove the Allen bolts (**Figure 64**) and the hex bolts (and washers) (**Figure 65**) securing the cylinder head cover.

9. Remove the cylinder head cover (**Figure 66**) and gaskets. Don't lose the small rubber gasket that surrounds each spark plug hole in the cover.

NOTE

***Figure 67** is shown with the camshafts removed for clarity. It is not necessary to remove the camshafts to tighten the cylinder head nuts.*

10. First, using a crisscross pattern, loosen all cylinder head nuts (**Figure 67**).
11. Tighten all cylinder head nuts in a crisscross pattern starting from the center and working out. Tighten to the torque specification listed in **Table 5**.
12. Tighten the cylinder head-to-cylinder bolt (A, **Figure 68**) and the cylinder-to-crankcase nut (B, **Figure 68**) to the torque specifications listed in **Table 5**.
13. Leave off all parts that have been removed and adjust the valves as described *Valve Clearance Measurement and Adjustment* in this chapter.

Valve Clearance Measurement and Adjustment

Valve clearance measurement and adjustment must be performed with the engine cool, at room temperature (below 35° C/95° F). The correct valve clearance for all models is listed in **Table 9**. The exhaust valves are located at the front of the engine and the intake valves are located at the rear of the engine. There are 2 intake valves and 2 exhaust valves per cylinder.

For this procedure the camshaft lobes must face away from the cam follower surface of the rocker arm as shown in A or B, **Figure 69**.

1. Perform Steps 1-9 of *Cylinder Head and Cylinder Nuts and Bolt Tightening* in this chapter.

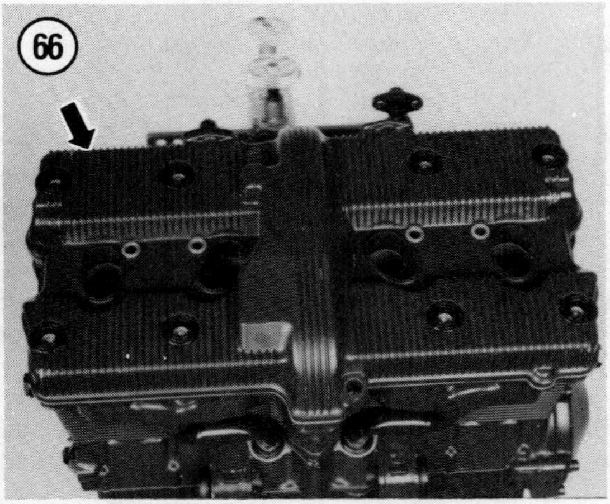

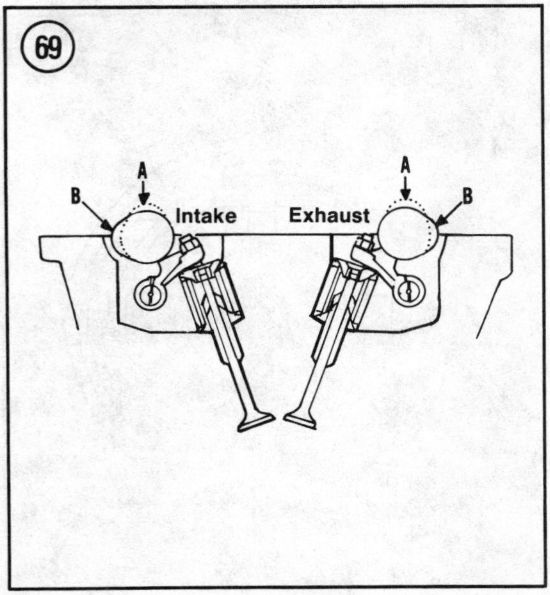

NOTE
The following steps are shown with the engine removed from the frame for clarity. It is not necessary to remove the engine to adjust the valves.

2. Remove all spark plugs. This will make it easier to rotate the engine.
3. Remove the bolts securing the signal generator cover (**Figure 70**) and remove the cover and gasket.

CAUTION
*In the next step, rotate the engine with a 19 mm wrench on the flats of the signal generator rotor (A, **Figure 71**). Do **not** use the Allen bolt (B, **Figure 71**) that secures the rotor to the crankshaft as the bolt may shear off.*

4. Use a 19 mm wrench on the signal generator rotor (A, **Figure 71**). Rotate the engine *clockwise* until the signal generator rotor "T" mark aligns with the center of the 1.4 pickup coil (**Figure 72**). Also, the notch on the right-hand end of both the intake and exhaust camshafts must point *away* from the engine (**Figure 73**). If the camshafts are not in this position, rotate the engine 360° (one full turn) until the notches are pointing *away* from the engine. Also make sure the "T" mark is still aligned correctly.

NOTE
The cylinders are numbered 1,2,3 and 4 from left to right. The left-hand side refers to a rider sitting on the seat looking forward.

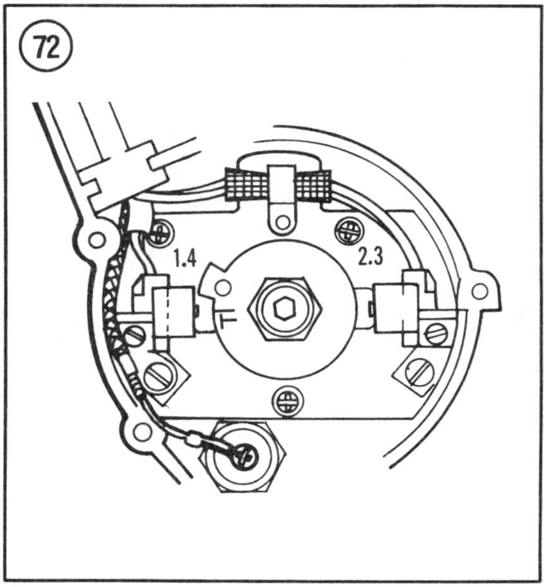

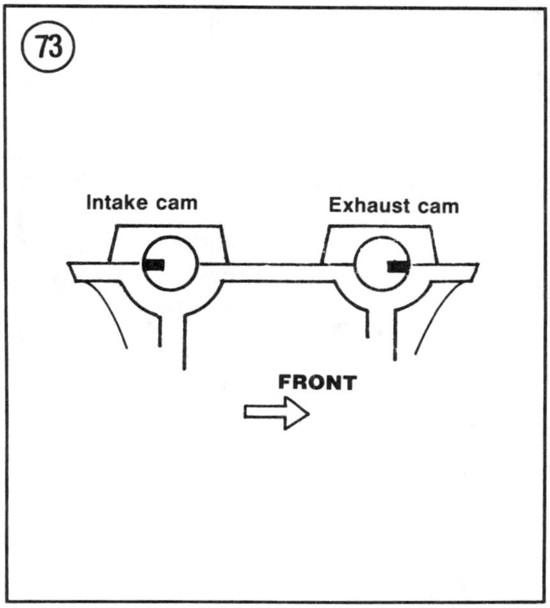

5. With the engine in this position, check the clearance of the intake and exhaust valves identified as C, **Figure 74**. The valves to be checked are as follows:
   a. Cylinder No. 1: intake and exhaust valves.
   b. Cylinder No. 2: exhaust valves.
   c. Cylinder No. 3: intake valves.
6. Check the clearance by inserting a flat feeler gauge between the adjusting screw and each valve stem (A, **Figure 75**). When the clearance is correct, there will be a slight drag on the feeler gauge when it is inserted and withdrawn.
7. To correct the clearance, perform the following:
   a. Loosen the adjuster locknut (B, **Figure 75**).
   b. Screw the adjuster in or out so there is a slight resistance felt on the feeler gauge.
   c. Hold the adjuster to prevent it from turning further and tighten the locknut securely.
   d. Then, recheck the clearance to make sure the adjuster did not turn after the correct clearance was achieved. Readjust if necessary.
   e. Repeat for the adjuster of the other valve controlled by the same rocker arm.
   f. Repeat this step for all valves indicated in C, **Figure 74**.
8. Use a 19 mm wrench on the signal generator rotor (A, **Figure 71**). From the position in Step 4; rotate the engine 360° (one full turn) *clockwise* until the signal generator rotor "T" mark again aligns with the center of the 1.4 pickup coil (**Figure 72**). Also the notch on the right-hand end of both the intake and exhaust camshafts must point *in* toward the engine (**Figure 76**).
9. With the engine in this position, check the clearance of the intake and exhaust valves as shown in D, **Figure 74**. The valves to be checked are as follows:
   a. Cylinder No. 2: intake valves.
   b. Cylinder No. 3: exhaust valves.
   c. Cylinder No. 4: intake and exhaust valves.
10. Check the clearance by inserting a flat feeler gauge between the adjusting screw and each valve stem (A, **Figure 75**). When the clearance is correct, there will be a slight drag on the feeler gauge when it is inserted and withdrawn.
11. To correct the clearance, perform the following:
   a. Loosen the adjuster locknut (B, **Figure 75**).
   b. Screw the adjuster in or out so there is a slight resistance felt on the feeler gauge.

74

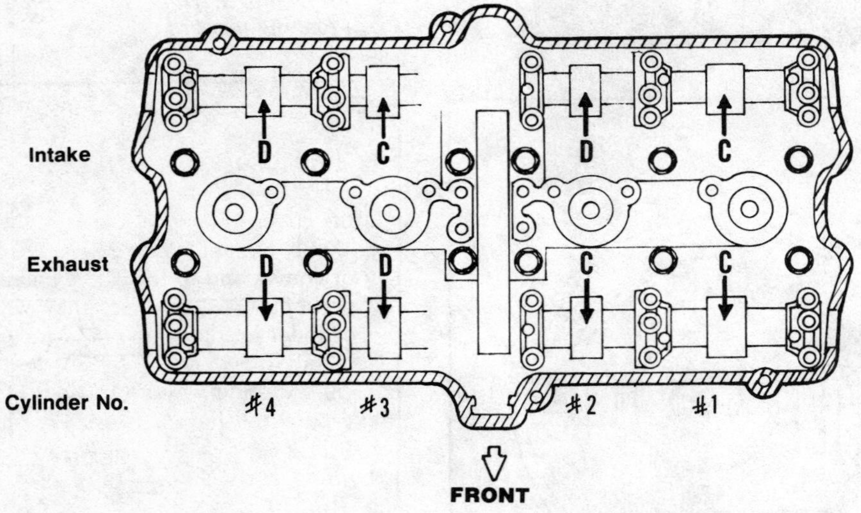

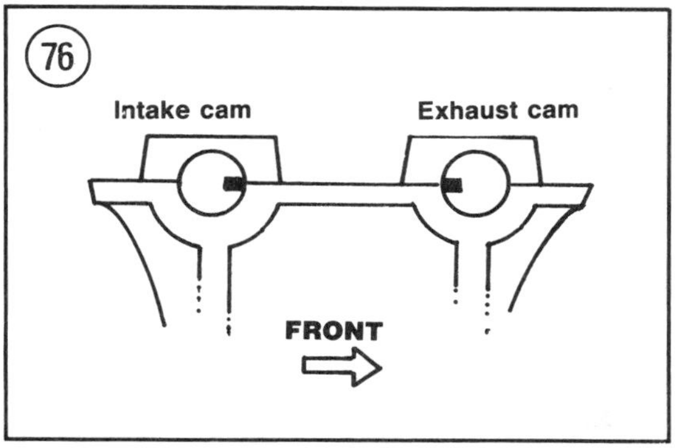

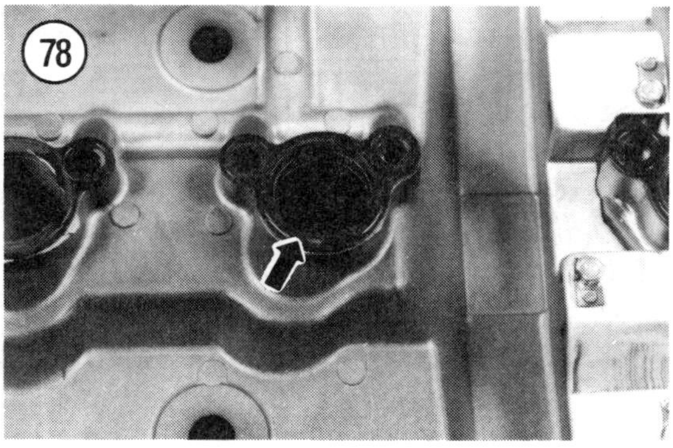

c. Hold the adjuster to prevent it from turning further and tighten the locknut securely.
d. Then, recheck the clearance to make sure the adjuster did not turn after the correct clearance was achieved. Readjust if necessary.
e. Repeat for the adjuster of the other valve controlled by the same rocker arm.
f. Repeat this step for all valves indicated in D, **Figure 74**.

12. Inspect the rubber gasket (**Figure 77**) around the perimeter of the cylinder head cover. Also inspect the rubber gasket at each spark plug hole (**Figure 78**). If they are starting to deteriorate or harden they should be replaced; replace as a set even if only one is bad.

NOTE
New gaskets must be installed onto the cylinder head cover using the following method to help prevent an oil leak.

13. If the gaskets are to be replaced, perform the following:
a. Remove the old gaskets and clean off all gasket sealer residue from the cylinder head cover.
b. Clean out the gasket groove around the perimeter of the cover and around each spark plug hole.
c. Apply Suzuki Bond No. 1207B liquid gasket, or equivalent, to the gasket grooves in the cover following the manufacturer's instructions.
d. Install all gaskets. Make sure they are correctly seated in their respective grooves in the cover.
e. Apply Suzuki Bond No. 1207B liquid gasket, or equivalent, to the camshaft end caps of the perimeter gasket where they will contact the cylinder head.

14. Install the cylinder head cover. Make sure none of the spark plug hole gaskets have fallen off. Make sure the camshaft end caps are correctly seated into the cylinder head.
15. Install the hex bolts and washers (**Figure 65**) and tighten finger-tight at this time.
16. Make sure all 8 gaskets are in place on the cylinder head cover, then install the Allen bolts (**Figure 64**).
17. Tighten the Allen bolts and hex bolts in a crisscross pattern to the torque specification listed in **Table 5**.

18. Install a *new* O-ring seal into each fitting of the oil hoses. To prevent an oil leak, these O-rings must be replaced every time the oil hoses are disconnected from the cylinder head cover.
19. Move the fittings into place on the cylinder head cover and install the Allen bolts (**Figure 63**). Tighten the Allen bolts to the torque specification listed in **Table 5**.
20. Install all spark plugs and connect all spark plug caps and wires.
21. Install the signal generator cover and gasket (**Figure 70**). Install and tighten the bolts securely.
22. Connect the crankcase breather hose onto the cylinder head cover.
23. Install the front fairing as described under *Front Fairing Removal/Installation* in Chapter Twelve.
24. Install the fuel tank as described under *Fuel Tank Removal/Installation* in Chapter Seven.
25. Install the seat as described under *Seat Removal/Installation* in Chapter Twelve.

Compression Test

Check the cylinder compression at the interval indicated in **Table 2**. Record the results and compare them to the results at the next interval. A running record will show trends in deterioration so that corrective action can be taken before complete failure.

The results, when properly interpreted, can indicate general cylinder, piston ring and valve condition. To ensure accurate readings, the valves must be adjusted before checking the compression since loose or tight valves can greatly affect the readings. The air filter element must also be clean to ensure adequate air reaches the cylinders.

1. Warm the engine to normal operating temperature, then shut it off. Make sure the choke valve is off.
2. Remove all spark plugs.
3. Connect the compression tester to one cylinder following the manufacturer's instructions.
4. With the throttle wipe open, have an assistant crank the engine over until there is no further rise in pressure.
5. Remove the tester and record the reading. When interpreting the results, actual readings are not as important as the difference between the readings. The recommended cylinder compression pressure and the maximum allowable difference between cylinders are listed in **Table 9**. Greater differences than that listed in **Table 9** indicate broken rings, leaky or sticking valves, a blown head gasket or a combination of all.

79

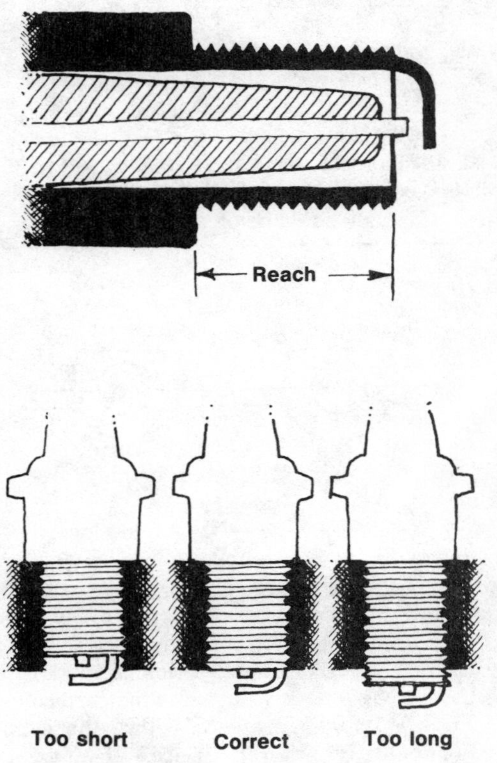

80

If the compression readings do not differ between the cylinders by more than 10%, the rings and valves are in good condition.

If a low reading (10% or more) is obtained it indicates valve or ring trouble. To determine which, pour about a teaspoon of engine oil through the spark plug hole onto the top of the piston. Turn the engine over once to distribute the oil, then take another compression test and record the reading. If the compression increases significantly, the valves are good but the rings are defective. If the compression does not increase, the valves require servicing. A valve(s) could be hanging open, but not burned, or a piece of carbon could be on a valve seat.

Spark Plug Selection

Spark plugs are available in various heat ranges, hotter or colder than plugs originally installed at the factory.

Select plugs of a heat range designed for the loads and temperature conditions under which the bike will be run. The use of overly-hot heat ranges can cause seized pistons, scored cylinder walls or damaged piston crowns.

In general, use a hot plug for low speeds, low engine loads and low temperatures. Use a cold plug for high speeds, high engine loads and high temperatures. The plug should operate hot enough to burn off unwanted deposits, but not so hot that it is damaged or causes preignition. A spark plug of the correct heat range will show a light tan color on the portion of the insulator within the cylinder after the plug has been in service.

81

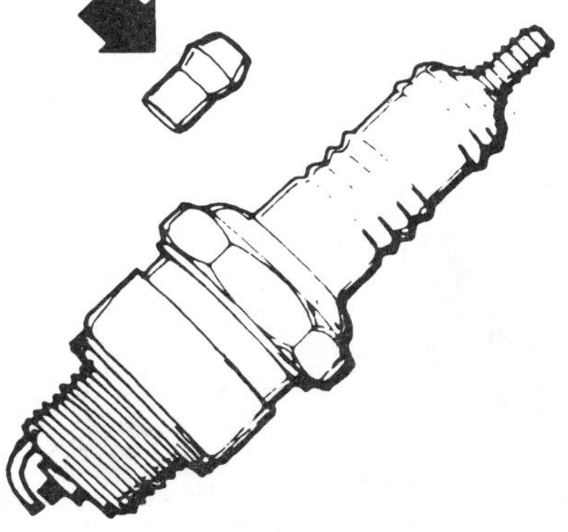

The reach (length) of a plug is also important (**Figure 79**). A longer than normal plug could interfere with the valves and pistons, causing severe damage. The recommended spark plugs are listed in **Table 9**.

Spark Plug Removal/Cleaning

1. Remove the lower and middle portions of the front fairing as described under *Front Fairing Removal/Installation* in Chapter Twelve.
2. Grasp each spark plug lead (**Figure 80**) and carefully pull it off the plug. If the boot is stuck to the plug, twist it slightly to break it loose.

CAUTION
If any dirt falls into the cylinder when the plugs are removed, it could cause serious engine damage.

3. Use compressed air and blow away any dirt that may have passed by the rubber boot on the spark plug lead and accumulated in the spark plug well.
4. Remove spark plugs with an 18 mm spark plug wrench. Keep the spark plugs in the order that they were removed. If anything turns up during the inspection step, you will know which cylinder is suspect.

NOTE
If plugs are difficult to remove, apply penetrating oil around base of plugs and let it soak in about 10-20 minutes.

5. Inspect the spark plug carefully. Look for a plug with broken center porcelain, excessively eroded electrodes and excessive carbon or oil fouling. Replace such a plug. If deposits are light, the plug may be cleaned in solvent with a wire brush or in a special spark plug sandblast cleaner. Regap the plug as explained in this chapter.

Spark Plug Gapping and Installation

A new plug should be carefully gapped to ensure a reliable, consistent spark. You must use a special spark plug gapping tool with a wire feeler gauge.

1. Remove the new plug from the box. Do *not* screw on the small piece (**Figure 81**) that is sometimes loose in the box, they are not to be used.

2. Insert a wire feeler gauge between the center and the side electrode of each plug (**Figure 82**). The correct gap is listed in **Table 9**. If the gap is correct, you will feel a slight drag as you pull the wire through. If there is no drag or the gauge won't pass through, bend the side electrode *with the gapping tool* (**Figure 83**) to set the proper gap.
3. Put a *small* drop of oil or aluminum anti-seize compound on the threads of the spark plug.
4. Screw each spark plug in by hand until it seats. Very little effort is required. If force is necessary, you have the plug cross-threaded; unscrew it and try again.
5. Tighten the spark plugs an additional 1/2 turn after the gasket has made contact with the head. If you are reinstalling old, regapped plugs and are reusing the old gasket, only tighten an additional 1/4 turn.

CAUTION
Do not overtighten. This will only squash the gasket and destroy its sealing ability.

6. Install the spark plug leads; make sure the leads are on tight and that the rubber boot is positioned correctly in the receptacle in the cylinder head cover.
7. Install the lower and middle portions of the front fairing as described under *Front Fairing Removal/Installation* in Chapter Twelve.

Reading Spark Plugs

Much information about engine and spark plug performance can be determined by careful examination of the spark plugs. This information is more valid after performing the following steps.

1. Ride the bike a short distance at full throttle in any gear.
2. Turn the engine stop switch (**Figure 84**) to the OFF position before closing the throttle and simultaneously pull in the clutch or shift to NEUTRAL; coast and brake to a stop.
3. Remove one spark plug at a time and examine it. Compare it to **Figure 85**. If the insulator is white or burned, the plug is too hot and should be replaced with a colder one. A too-cold plug will have sooty or oily deposits ranging in color from dark brown to black. Check for too-rich carburetion or evidence of oil blowby at the piston rings. If these are okay, replace with a hotter plug. If the plug has a light tan or gray colored deposit and no abnormal gap wear or electrode erosion is evident, the plug and the engine are running

82

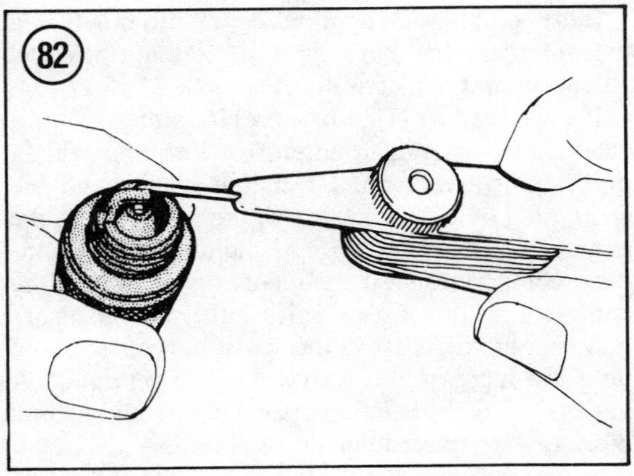

83

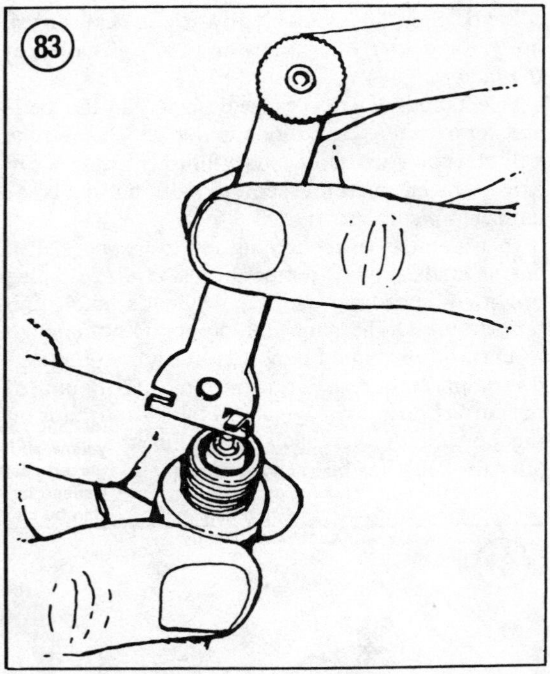

84

85

SPARK PLUG CONDITION

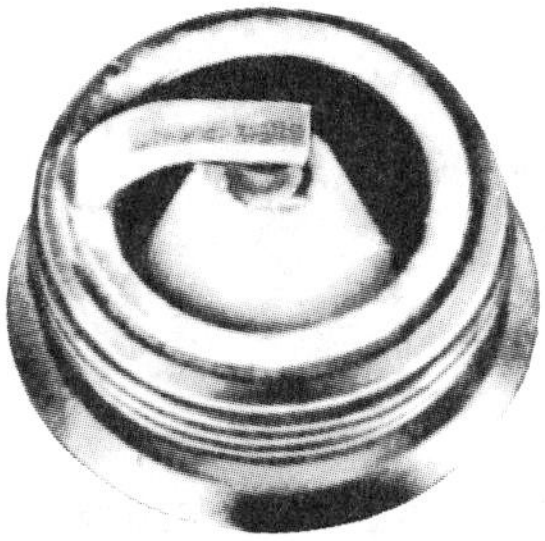

NORMAL

- Identified by light tan or gray deposits on the firing tip.
- Can be cleaned.

GAP BRIDGED

- Identified by deposit buildup closing gap between electrodes.
- Caused by oil or carbon fouling. If deposits are not excessive, the plug can be cleaned.

OIL FOULED

- Identified by wet black deposits on the insulator shell bore and electrodes.
- Caused by excessive oil entering combustion chamber through worn rings and pistons, excessive clearance between valve guides and stems, or worn or loose bearings. Can be cleaned. If engine is not repaired, use a hotter plug.

CARBON FOULED

- Identified by black, dry fluffy carbon deposits on insulator tips, exposed shell surfaces and electrodes.
- Caused by too cold a plug, weak ignition, dirty air cleaner, too rich a fuel mixture, or excessive idling. Can be cleaned.

LEAD FOULED

- Identified by dark gray, black, yellow, or tan deposits or a fused glazed coating on the insulator tip.
- Caused by highly leaded gasoline. Can be cleaned.

WORN

- Identified by severely eroded or worn electrodes.
- Caused by normal wear. Should be replaced.

FUSED SPOT DEPOSIT

- Identified by melted or spotty deposits resembling bubbles or blisters.
- Caused by sudden acceleration. Can be cleaned.

OVERHEATING

- Identified by a white or light gray insulator with small black or gray brown spots and with bluish-burnt appearance of electrodes.
- Caused by engine overheating, wrong type of fuel, loose spark plugs, too hot a plug, or incorrect ignition timing. Replace the plug.

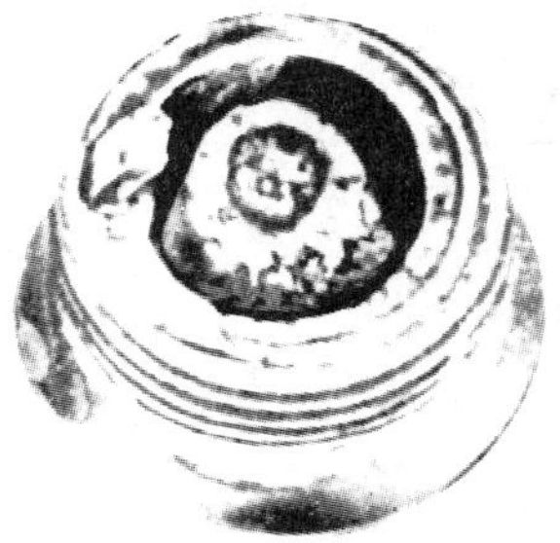

PREIGNITION

- Identified by melted electrodes and possibly blistered insulator. Metallic deposits on insulator indicate engine damage.
- Caused by wrong type of fuel, incorrect ignition timing or advance, too hot a plug, burned valves, or engine overheating. Replace the plug.

properly. If the plug exhibits a black insulator tip, a damp and oily film over the firing end and a carbon layer over the entire nose, it is oil fouled. An oil fouled plug can be cleaned, but it is better to replace it.

4. Repeat for all 4 spark plugs. Replace as a set if any are bad.

Carburetor Idle Speed Adjustment

1. Start the engine and let reach normal operating temperature. Make sure the choke knob is in the off position.
2. Connect a portable tachometer following the manufacturer's instructions.
3. Turn the idle adjust knob (**Figure 86**) in or out to adjust idle speed.
4. The correct idle speed is listed in **Table 9**.
5. Open and close the throttle a couple of times; check for variations in idle speed. Readjust if necessary.

WARNING

*With the engine running at idle speed, move the handlebar from side to side. If the idle speed increases during this movement, the throttle cable may need adjusting or it may be incorrectly routed through the frame. Correct this problem immediately. Do **not** ride the bike in this unsafe condition.*

Carburetor Idle Mixture

The idle mixture (pilot screw) is preset at the factory and *is not to be reset*. Do not adjust the pilot screw unless the carburetors have been overhauled. If so, refer to Chapter Seven for service procedures.

86

Table 1 TIRE INFLATION PRESSURE (COLD)*

Load	Tire pressure			
	Front		Rear	
	psi	kPa	psi	kPa
Solo riding	36	250	36	250
Dual riding	36	250	42	290

* Tire inflation pressure for factory equipped tires. Aftermarket tires may require different inflation pressure. The standard tire on this motorcycle is 110/80VR18-240 (250) on the front and 140/70VR18-V240 (250) on the rear. Suzuki states the use of tires other than those originally equipped may cause instability.

Table 2 MAINTENANCE SCHEDULE*

Prior to each ride	
	• Inspect tires and rims and check inflation pressure • Check steering for smooth operation with no excessive play or binding • Check brake operation and for brake fluid leakage • Check fuel supply. Make sure there is enough fuel for the intended ride • Check for fuel leakage • Check all lights for proper operation • Check engine oil level • Check for smooth throttle operation • Check gearshift lever operation • Check clutch operation and for fluid leakage (wet-type clutch models) • Inspect drive chain • Check drive chain tension, adjust if necessary • Check drive chain slider for wear
Every 600 miles (1,000 km)	
	• Inspect, clean and lubricate drive chain
Every 2,000 miles (3,000 km) or 6 months	
	• Clean the air filter element
Every 4,000 miles (6,000 km) or 12 months	
	• Tune up engine • Check battery electrolyte level • Tighten cylinder head nuts and exhaust pipe nuts • Replace the air filter element • Inspect and adjust, if necessary, the valve clearance • Check and adjust idle speed • Clean and inspect spark plugs • Run a compression test • Replace engine oil and filter • Check and adjust clutch operation and free play (dry-type clutch) • Inspect brake hoses (front and rear) for leakage • Inspect clutch hose for leakage (wet-type clutch) • Check brake fluid level in both brake master cylinders • Check hydraulic fluid level in clutch master cylinder (wet-type clutch) • Inspect fuel lines for damage or leakage • Inspect evaporation emission lines for damage or leakage (California models) • Check all brake system components • Inspect the brake pads for wear • Check and tighten the axle nuts • Lubricate control cables • Inspect and lubricate drive chain • Inspect drive and driven sprockets for wear and mounting tightness
Every 7,500 miles (12,000 km) or 24 months	
	• Major carburetor service (if necessary) • Inspect steering head bearings

(continued)

3

Table 2 MAINTENANCE SCHEDULE* (cont.)

	• Check all suspension components for wear or damage • Replace all spark plugs
Every 2 years	
	• Drain and replace hydraulic brake fluid
Every 4 years	
	• Replace all brake hoses • Replace fuel lines • Replace evaporative emission lines (California models)

* This Suzuki factory maintenance schedule should be considered as a guide to general maintenance and lubrication intervals. Harder than normal use and exposure to mud, water, sand, high humidity, etc. (or if used for racing) will naturally dictate more frequent attention to most maintenance items.

Table 3 STATE OF CHARGE

Specific Gravity	State of Charge
1.110-1.130	Discharged
1.140-1.160	Almost discharged
1.170-1.190	One-quarter charged
1.200-1.220	One-half charged
1.230-1.250	Three-quarters charged
1.260-1.280	Fully charged

Table 4 ENGINE OIL CAPACITY

	Oil change		Oil/filter change		Overhaul	
Model	Liters	U.S. qt.	Liters	U.S. qt.	Liters	U.S. qt.
GSX-R750	3.6	3.8	3.8	4.0	5.0	5.3
GSX-R750R Limited Edition	3.3	3.5	3.51	3.7	4.81	5.1
GSX-R1100	3.4	3.6	3.7	3.9	4.7	5.0

Table 5 MAINTENANCE AND TUNE-UP TORQUE SPECIFICATIONS

Item	N·m	ft.-lb.
Oil drain plug	20-25	14-18
NEAS unit mounting bolts	6.8-8.0	4.5-6.0
Fork cap bolt	15-30	11-22
Upper fork bridge bolts	85-115	61-83
Cylinder head nuts	35-40	25-29
Cylinder head bolts	7-11	5-8
Cylinder block nut	7-11	5-8
Cylinder head cover bolts (all)	13-15	9-11
Oil hose fitting Allen bolts	8-12	6-9

Table 6 FRONT FORK OIL CAPACITY* AND DIMENSION

Model	Capacity cc	Capacity oz.	Distance mm	Distance in.	Fork oil
GSX-R750	456	15.4	107	4.21	SAE 15
GSX-R750R Limited Edition	427	14.4	130	5.21	SAE 10
GSX-R1100	417	14.1	159	6.26	SAE 15

* Each fork leg.

Table 7 DRIVE CHAIN SLACK AND SERVICE LIMIT

Model	Slack	Service limit length*
750 cc models	25-30 mm (1.0-1.2 in.)	319.4 mm (12.6 in.)
1100 cc models	20-25 mm (0.8-1.0 in.)	319.4 mm (12.6 in.)

* Drive chain length between 21 link pins.

Table 8 DRIVE CHAIN REPLACEMENT NUMBERS

Model	Number	Number of links
GSX-R750	DID50VA	110
	Takasago RK 50HF0-22	110
GSX-R750 Limited Edition	Takasago RK,GB 50HF0-24	110
GSX-R1100	DID532ZL	114
	Takasago RK 532GSV	114

Table 9 TUNE-UP SPECIFICATIONS

Valve clearance	
Intake and exhaust	0.10-0.15 mm (0.004-0.006 in.)
Spark plug type	
Standard heat range	
GSX-R750, GSX-R750R Limited Edition	NGK D9EA
GSX-R1100	NGK J9A
Hotter heat range	
GSX-R750, GSX-R750R Limited Edition	NGK D8EA
Colder heat range	
GSX-R1100	NGK J10A
Spark plug gap	0.6-0.7 mm (0.02-0.03 in.)
Idle speed	1,100 ±100 rpm
Firing order	1, 2, 4, 3
Ignition timing (all models)	13° BTDC below 1,500 rpm 35° BTDC above 2,350 rpm
Cylinder compression	Standard 1,000-1,400 kPa (142-199 psi) Limit 800 kPa (114 psi)

NOTE: If you own a GSX600F Katana, first refer to Chapter 13 for specific service information.

CHAPTER FOUR

ENGINE

The Suzuki GSX-R series bikes are equipped with an air/oil-cooled, 4-stroke, 4-cylinder engine with double overhead camshafts. The cylinder head incorporates 4 valves per cylinder with each set having its own rocker arm. Each valve has its own adjuster, but two adjusters are combined onto one rocker arm to minimize valve reciprocating mass. The camshafts are chain-driven from the sprocket on the center of the crankshaft.

This chapter provides complete service and overhaul procedures including information for removal, disassembly, inspection, service and reassembly of the engine. Although the clutch and transmission are located within the engine, the clutch is covered in Chapter Five and the transmission is covered in Chapter Six to simplify this material.

Refer to **Table 1** for complete specifications for the 750 cc engine or to **Table 2** for the 1100 cc engine. **Tables 1-8** are located at the end of this chapter.

Before starting any work, re-read Chapter One of this book. You will do a better job with this information fresh in your mind.

Throughout the text there is frequent mention of the right-hand and left-hand side of the engine. This refers to the engine as it sits in the bike's frame, *not* as it sits on your workbench. "Right-" and "left-hand" refer to a rider sitting on the seat facing forward.

ENGINE PRINCIPLES

Figure 1 explains how the engine works. This will be helpful when troubleshooting or repairing the engine.

ENGINE COOLING

Cooling is provided by a unique oil system that helps dissipate the engine heat. In addition to the normal engine components that require lubrication the engine oil is routed through the cylinder head, sprayed onto the lower portion of the pistons and piston pins and directed to any portion of the engine where there is any normal heat build-up.

The oil is pumped out of the engine and into a frame-mounted oil cooler in front of the engine. Fresh air is drawn through the front fairing and through the oil cooler. The cooled oil then returns to the engine.

The cylinder head cover, cyinder head and cylinder block have shallow cooling fins which also help to dissipate the engine heat.

SERVICING ENGINE IN FRAME

The following components can be serviced while the engine is mounted in the frame (the bike's

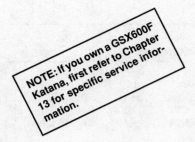

1 4-STROKE OPERATING PRINCIPLES

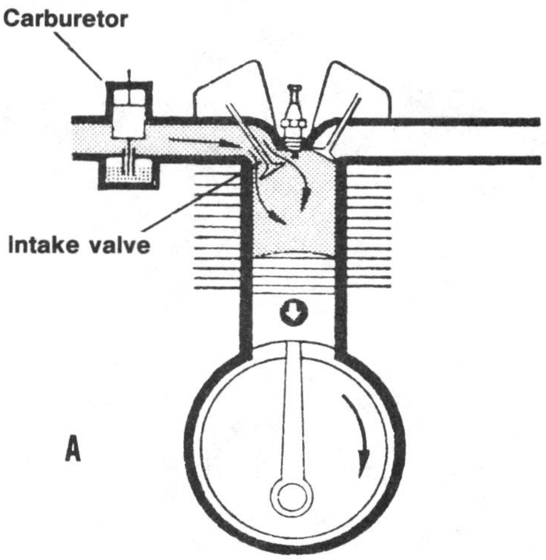

As the piston travels downward, the exhaust valve is closed and the intake valve opens, allowing the new fuel/air mixture from the carburetor to be drawn into the cylinder. When the piston reaches the bottom of its travel (BDC), the intake valve closes and remains closed for the next revolution-and-a-half of the crankshaft.

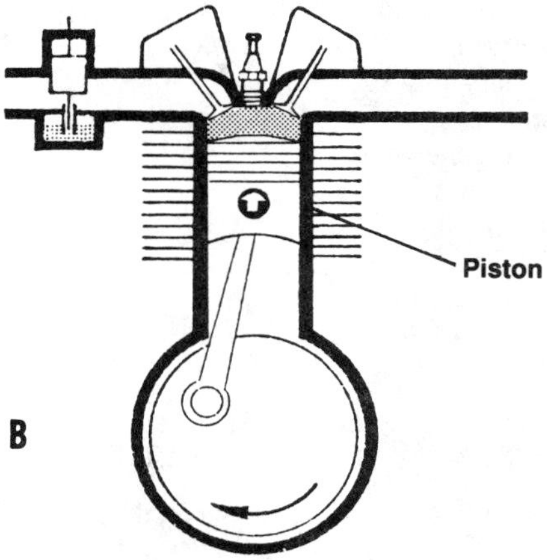

While the crankshaft continues to rotate, the piston moves upward, compressing the fuel/air mixture.

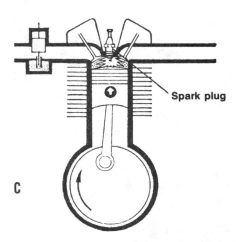

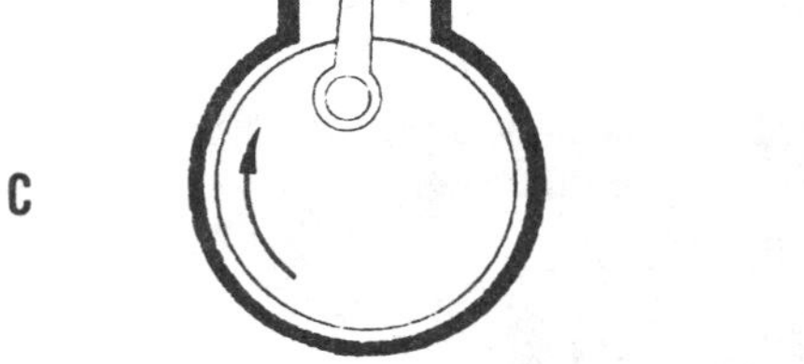

As the piston almost reaches the top of its travel, the spark plug fires, igniting the compressed fuel/air mixture. The piston continues to top dead center (TDC) and is pushed downward by the expanding gases.

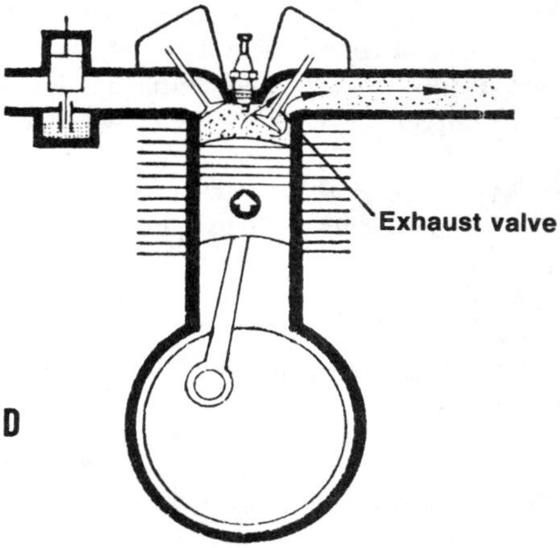

When the piston almost reaches BDC, the exhaust valve opens and remains open until the piston is near TDC. The upward travel of the piston causes the exhaust gases to be pushed out of the cylinder. After the piston has reached TDC, the exhaust valve closes and the cycle starts all over again.

frame is a great holding fixture for breaking loose stubborn bolts and nuts):

a. Carburetor assembly.
b. Exhaust system.
c. Alternator and starter.
d. Camshaft and cylinder head.
e. Cylinder block.
f. Pistons.
g. Signal generator.
h. Clutch assembly.
i. External shift mechanism.

ENGINE REMOVAL/INSTALLATION

1. Remove the seat as described under *Seat Removal/Installation* in Chapter Twelve.
2. Remove the front fairing as described under *Front Fairing Removal/Installation* in Chapter Twelve.
3. Remove the fuel tank as described under *Fuel Tank Removal/Installation* in Chapter Seven.
4. Remove the battery as described under *Battery Removal/Installation* in Chapter Three.
5. Remove the exhaust system as described under *Exhaust System Removal/Installation* in Chapter Seven.
6. Disconnect the breather hose (**Figure 2**) from the cylinder head cover.
7. Remove the carburetor assembly as described under *Carburetor Removal/Installation* in Chapter Seven.
8. Drain the engine oil and remove the oil filter as described under *Engine Oil and Filter Change* in Chapter Three. The oil filter must be removed in order for the engine to clear the frame later in this procedure.
9. Disconnect the spark plug leads and tie them up out of the way.
10. Remove the gearshift lever as follows:

a. Remove the circlip (**Figure 3**) and the washer (**Figure 4**) securing the gearshift lever to the pivot post.
b. Remove the bolt (**Figure 5**) securing the gearshift lever to the shift shaft and remove the gearshift lever assembly.

11. On GSX-R750R Limited Edition models, perform the following:

a. Loosen the adjusting barrel at the clutch hand lever and remove the cable from the lever.

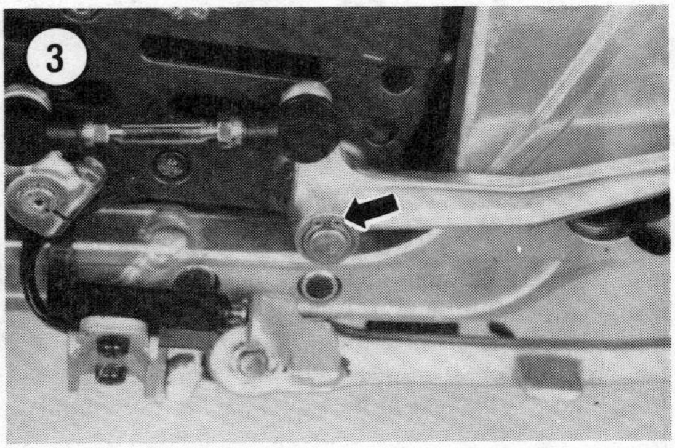

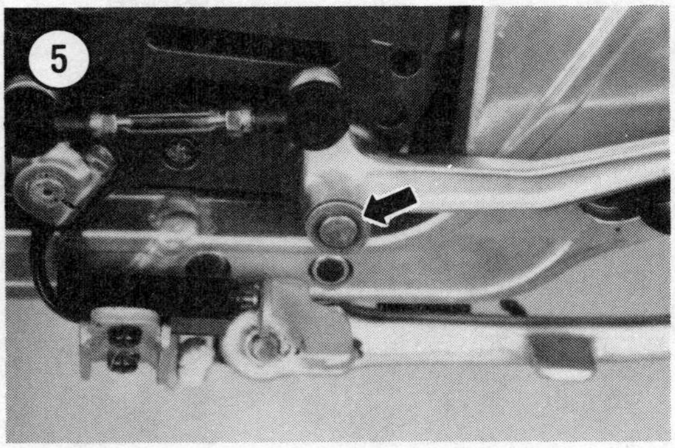

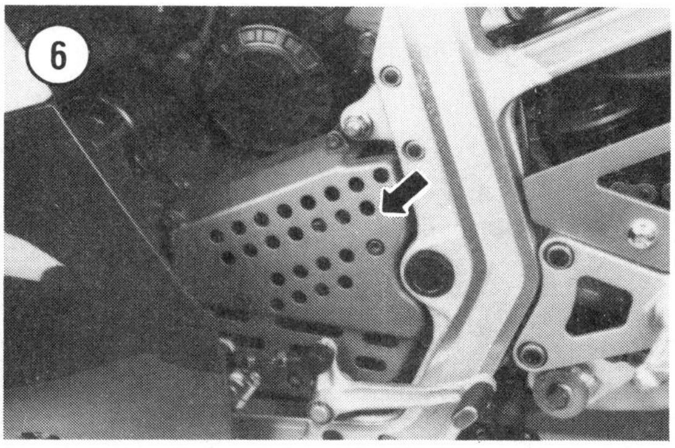

b. Disconnect the clutch cable from the clutch release arm.
c. Disconnect the clutch cable from the receptacle on the clutch outer cover.

12A. On GSX-R750R Limited Edition models, remove the bolts securing the drive sprocket cover (**Figure 6**) and remove the cover.

12B. On all other models, remove the bolts securing the drive sprocket cover (**Figure 7**) and remove the cover.

13. Have an assistant apply the rear brake. Loosen the drive sprocket bolt (A, **Figure 8**) and nut (B, **Figure 8**).

14. To provide slack in the drive chain, perform the following:
  a. Remove the cotter pin and loosen the rear axle nut (A, **Figure 9**).
  b. Loosen the drive chain adjuster nut (B, **Figure 9**) on each side of the swing arm.
  c. Push the rear wheel forward to achieve slack in the drive chain.

15. Remove the drive chain (C, **Figure 8**) from the drive sprocket.

16. Refer to **Figure 10** and disconnect the following electrical connectors:
  a. Alternator.
  b. Neutral indicator.
  c. Signal generator.
  d. Oil pressure indicator switch.
  e. Side stand indicator.

17. Place a drain pan under the front of the engine and remove the union bolts and sealing washers securing the oil cooler hoses to the crankcase oil pan. Refer to **Figure 11** for the right-hand side and **Figure 12** for the left-hand side. Move the oil hoses out of the way.

NOTE
If you are just removing the engine and are not planning to disassemble it, do not perform Step 18.

18. If the engine is going to be disassembled, remove the following parts while the engine is still in the frame. Removal procedures are in this chapter unless otherwise noted:
   a. Alternator and starter (Chapter Eight).
   b. Camshafts and cylinder head.
   c. Cylinder block.
   d. Pistons.
   e. Signal generator.
   f. Clutch assembly (Chapter Five).
   g. External shift mechanism (Chapter Six).
19. Take a final look all over the engine to make sure everything has been disconnected.
20. Place a suitable size jack, with a piece of wood to protect the crankcase, under the engine. Apply a small amount of jack pressure under the engine.

NOTE
*There are many different bolt sizes and lengths, different combinations of washers, conical washers, lockwashers and different spacer lengths. As **each set** of bolts, nuts, washers, spacers and holding plates are removed, place in a separate plastic bag or box the set. This will save a lot of time when installing the engine.*

CAUTION
Continually adjust jack height during engine removal and installation to prevent damage to the mounting bolt threads and hardware. Ideally, the jack should support the engine so its mounting bolts can be easily removed or installed.

21A. On 750 cc models, refer to **Figure 13** and remove the following:
   a. Front upper bolts, washers and holding plates (A, **Figure 14**).
   b. Front lower bolts, washers, lockwashers and holding plates (B, **Figure 14**).
   c. Rear upper bolts, washers and holding plates (C, **Figure 14**).
   d. Rear upper through-bolt, nut and spacers (D, **Figure 14**).
   e. Rear lower through-bolt, spacers, mounting bracket and nut (E, **Figure 14**).

NOTE
Don't lose the spacers between the frame and the engine. Be sure to reinstall them in the correct locations.

11

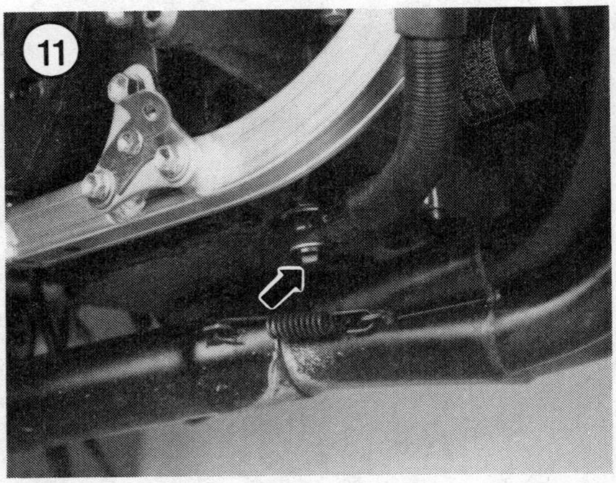

12

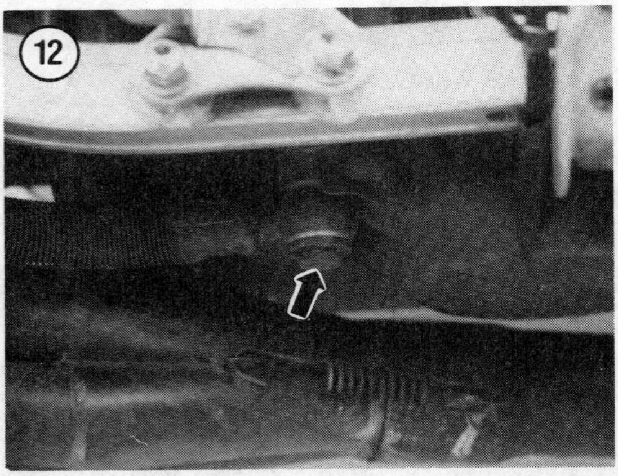

14

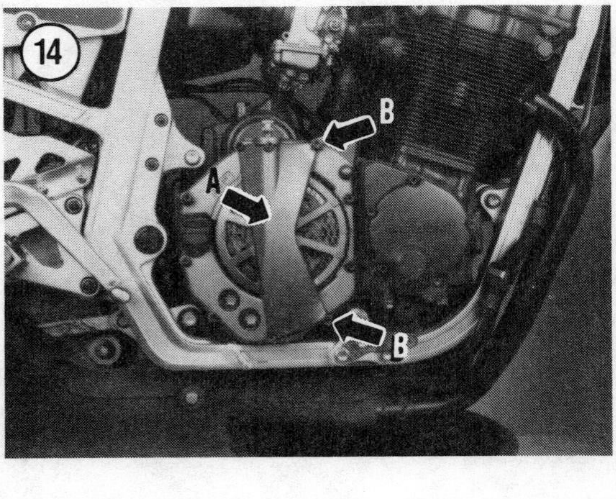

(13)

ENGINE MOUNTING HARDWARE (750 CC MODELS)

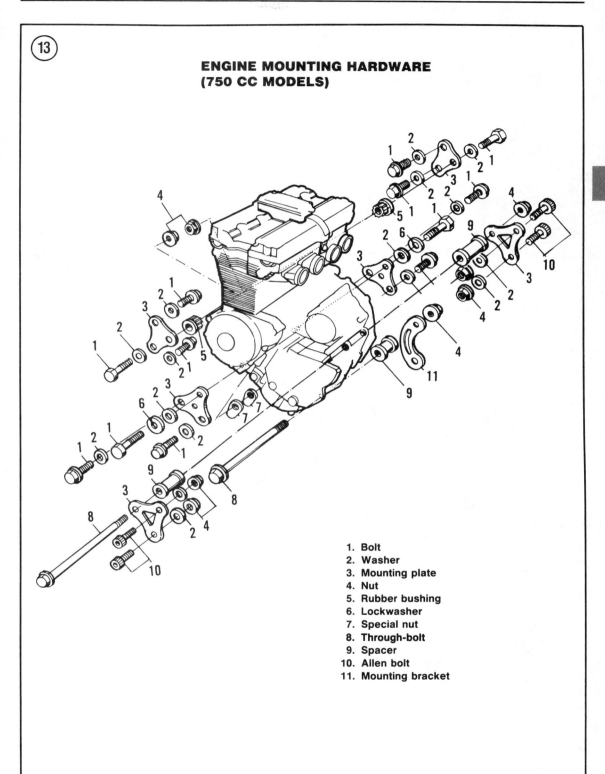

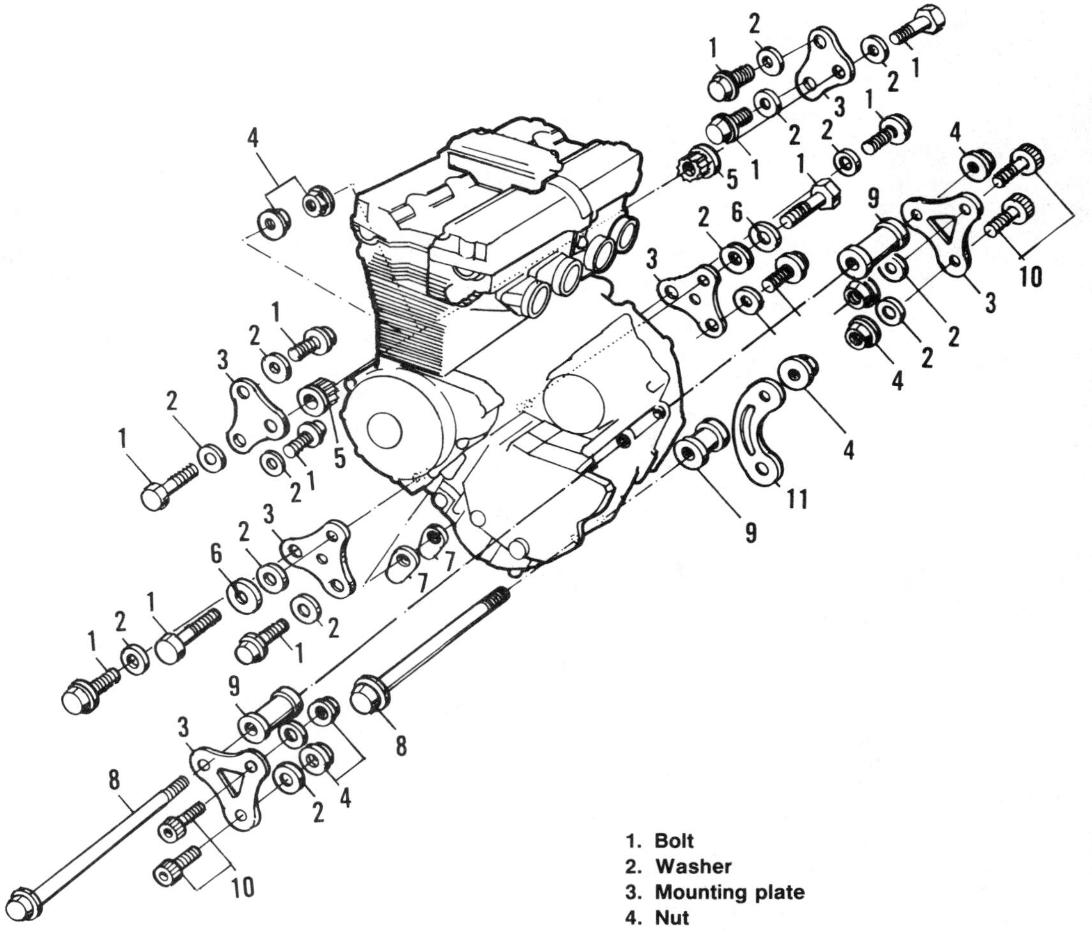

1. Bolt
2. Washer
3. Mounting plate
4. Nut
5. Rubber bushing
6. Lockwasher
7. Special nut
8. Through-bolt
9. Spacer
10. Allen bolt
11. Mounting bracket

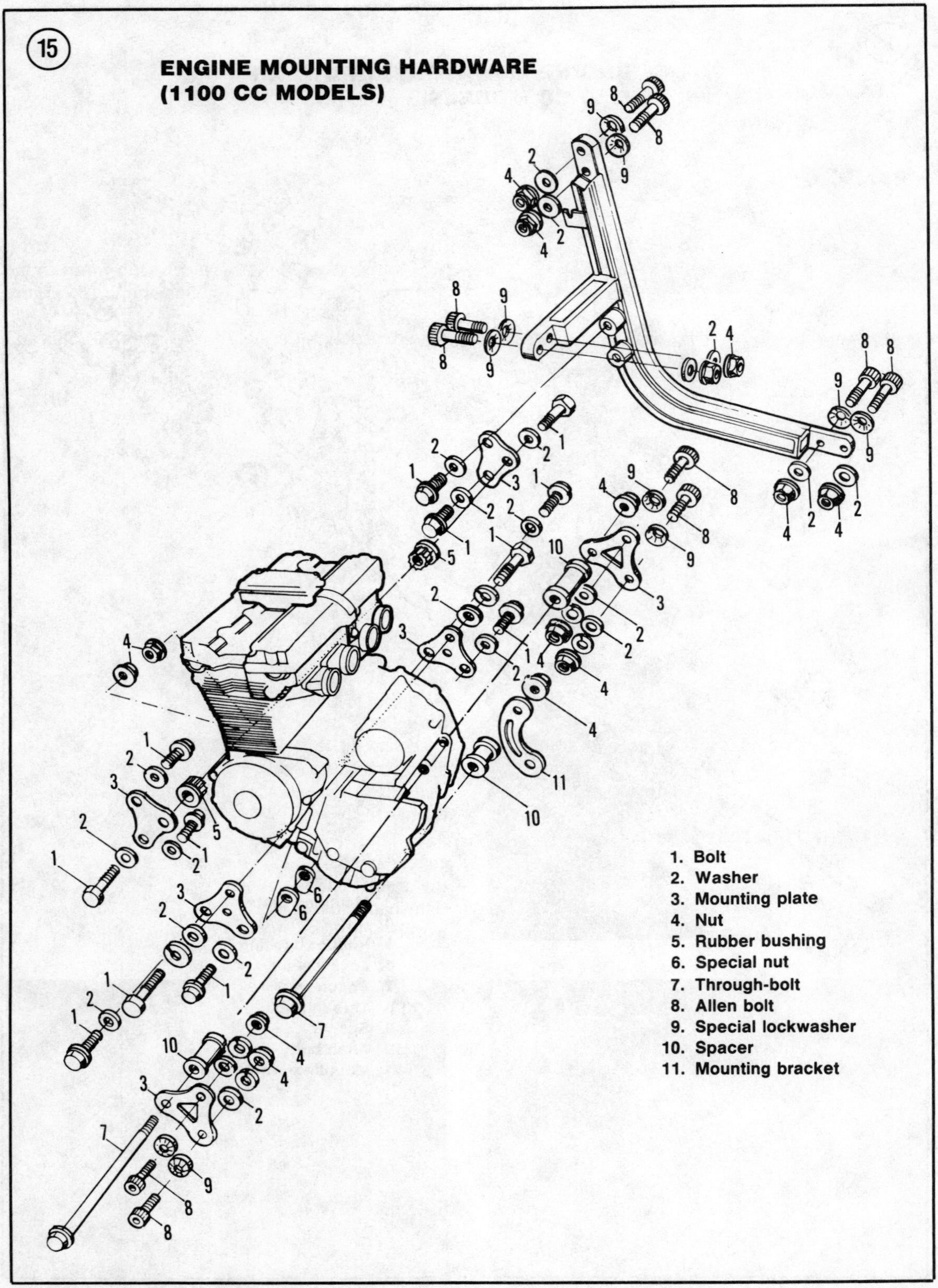
15
ENGINE MOUNTING HARDWARE
(1100 CC MODELS)
1. Bolt
2. Washer
3. Mounting plate
4. Nut
5. Rubber bushing
6. Special nut
7. Through-bolt
8. Allen bolt
9. Special lockwasher
10. Spacer
11. Mounting bracket

21B. On 1100 cc models, refer to **Figure 15** and remove the following:

a. Front upper bolts, washers and holding plates (**Figure 16**).
b. Front lower bolts, washers, lockwashers and holding plates (**Figure 17**).
c. Rear upper bolts, conical washers, washers, lockwashers and holding plates (A, **Figure 18**).
d. Rear upper through-bolt, nut and spacers (B, **Figure 18**).
e. The bolts (A, **Figure 19**), conical washers, washers and nuts securing the sub-frame to the frame and remove the sub-frame (B, **Figure 19**).
f. Rear lower through-bolt (**Figure 20**), nut and spacer.

NOTE
Don't lose the spacers between the frame and the engine. Be sure to reinstall them in the correct locations.

CAUTION
The following steps require the aid of a helper to safely remove the engine assembly from the frame. Due to the weight of the engine, it is suggested that at least one helper, preferably 2 assist you in the removal of the engine.

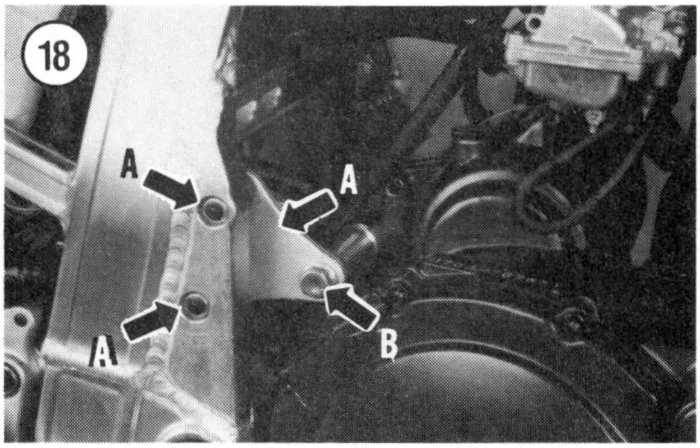

22A. On 750 cc models, gradually raise the engine assembly to clear the frame and pull the engine out through the right-hand side of the frame. It may be necessary to remove the breather cover from the cylinder head cover to provide additional clearance. Take the engine to a workbench for further disassembly.

22B. On 1100 cc models, gradually lower the engine assembly to clear the remaining portions of the frame and pull the engine out through the right-hand side of the frame. Take the engine to a workbench for further disassembly.

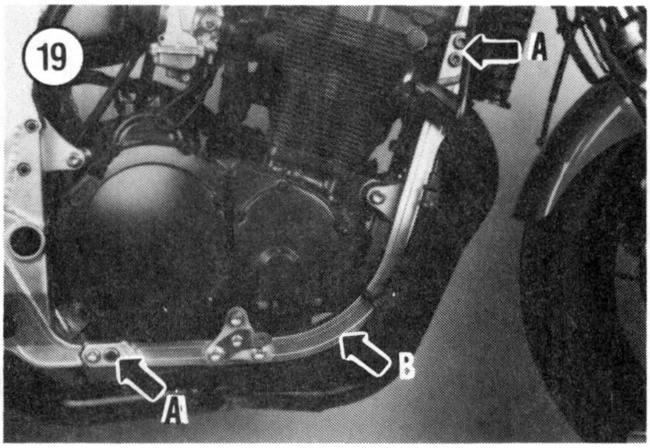

23. Install by reversing these removal steps, noting the following.
24. Tighten the mounting bolts to the torque specifications in **Table 3**.
25. Fill the engine with the recommended type and quantity of oil; refer to Chapter Three.
26. On GSX-R750R Limited Edition models, adjust the clutch as described under *Clutch Adjustment* in Chapter Three.
27. Adjust the drive chain as described under *Drive Chain Adjustment* in Chapter Three.
28. Start the engine and check for leaks.

CYLINDER HEAD COVER

Removal

1. Place the bike on the side stand.
2. Remove the seat as described under *Seat Removal/Installation* in Chapter Twelve.
3. Remove the fuel tank as described under *Fuel Tank Removal/Installation* in Chapter Seven.
4. Remove the entire front fairing as described under *Front Fairing Removal/Installation* in Chapter Twelve.
5. Disconnect the crankcase breather hose (**Figure 21**) from the cylinder head cover.
6. Disconnect all spark plug caps and wires (**Figure 22**).

NOTE
The following steps are shown with the engine removed from the frame for clarity. It is not necessary to remove the engine to remove the cylinder head cover.

7. Remove the Allen bolts securing the oil hose fittings (**Figure 23**) to the cylinder head cover. Move the oil hoses away from the cylinder head cover. Discard the O-ring seals in each oil hose fitting. To prevent an oil leak, these O-rings must be replaced every time the oil hoses are disconnected from the cylinder head cover.
8. Using a crisscross pattern, loosen then remove the Allen bolts (**Figure 24**) and the hex bolts (and washers) (**Figure 25**) securing the cylinder head cover.
9. Remove the cylinder head cover (**Figure 26**) and gaskets. Don't lose the small rubber gasket that surrounds each spark plug hole in the cover.

Installation

1. Inspect the rubber gasket (**Figure 27**) around the perimeter of the cylinder head cover. Also inspect the rubber gasket at each spark plug hole (**Figure**

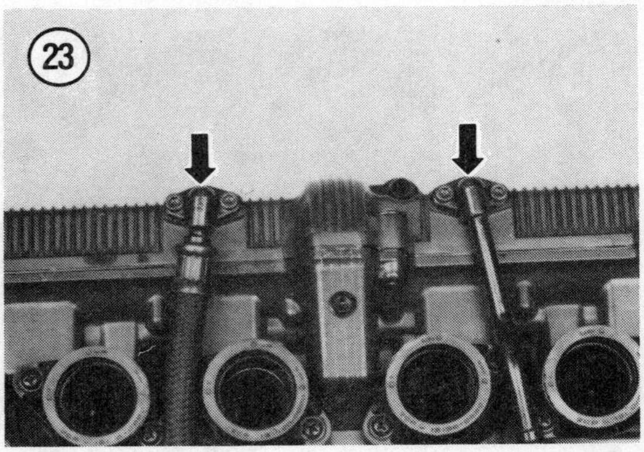

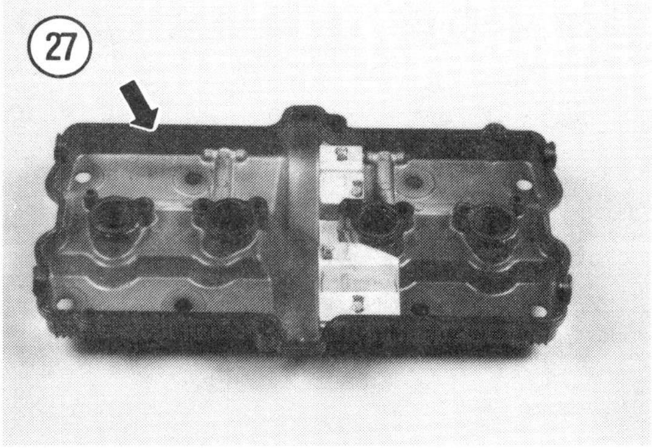

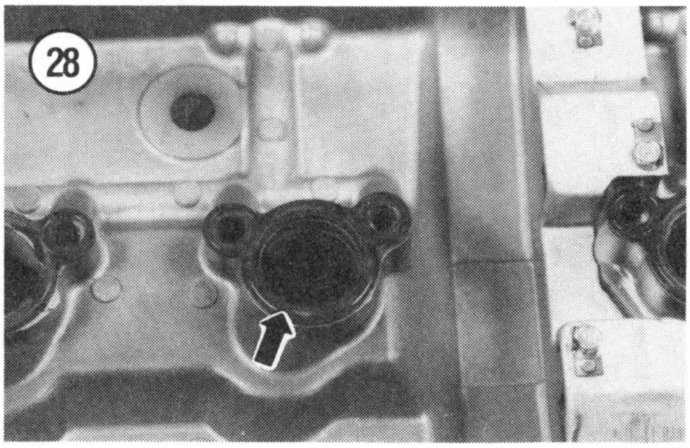

28). If they are starting to deteriorate or harden they should be replaced; replace as a set even if only one is bad.

NOTE
New gaskets must be installed onto the cylinder head cover using the following method to help prevent an oil leak.

2. If the gaskets are to be replaced, perform the following:
   a. Remove the old gaskets and clean off all gasket sealer residue from the cylinder head cover.
   b. Clean out the gasket groove around the perimeter of the cover and around each spark plug hole.
   c. Apply Suzuki Bond No. 1207B liquid gasket, or equivalent, to the gasket grooves in the cover following the manufacturer's instructions.
   d. Install all gaskets. Make sure they are correctly seated in their respective grooves in the cover.
   e. Apply Suzuki Bond No. 1207B liquid gasket, or equivalent, to the camshaft end caps of the perimeter gasket where they will contact the cylinder head.
3. Install the cylinder head cover. Make sure none of the spark plug hole gaskets have fallen off. Make sure the camshaft end caps are correctly seated into the cylinder head.
4. Install the hex bolts and washers (**Figure 25**) and tighten finger-tight at this time.
5. Make sure all 8 gaskets are in place on the cylinder head cover, then install the Allen bolts (**Figure 24**).
6. Tighten the Allen bolts and hex bolts in a crisscross pattern to the torque specification listed in **Table 3**.
7. Install a *new* O-ring seal (**Figure 29**) into each fitting of the oil hoses. To prevent an oil leak, these

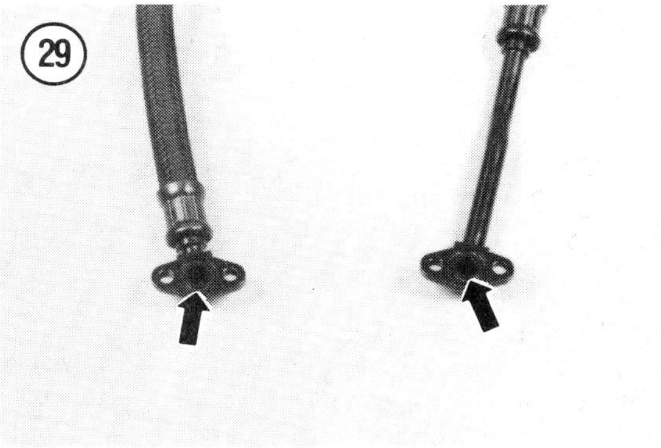

4

O-rings must be replaced every time the oil hoses are disconnected from the cylinder head cover.

8. Move the fittings into place on the cylinder head cover and install the Allen bolts (**Figure 23**). Tighten the Allen bolts to the torque specification listed in **Table 3**.

9. Install all spark plugs and connect all spark plug caps and wires.

10. Install the signal generator cover and gasket (**Figure 30**). Install and tighten the bolts securely.

11. Connect the crankcase breather hose (**Figure 21**) onto the cylinder head cover.

12. Install the front fairing as described under *Front Fairing Removal/Installation* in Chapter Twelve.

13. Install the fuel tank as described under *Fuel Tank Removal/Installation* in Chapter Seven.

14. Install the seat as described under *Seat Removal/Installation* in Chapter Twelve.

CAMSHAFTS

Removal

1. Remove the cylinder head cover as described under *Cylinder Head Cover Removal* in this chapter.

2. Remove all spark plugs. This will make it easier to rotate the engine.

3. Remove the cam chain tensioner spring holder bolt and sealing washer (**Figure 31**), then withdraw the cam chain tensioner spring (**Figure 32**) from the tensioner body.

4. Remove the bolts (**Figure 33**) securing the tensioner assembly to the cylinder block and remove the tensioner assembly and gasket.

5. Remove the bolts securing the signal generator cover (**Figure 30**) and remove the cover and gasket.

CAUTION
*In the next step, rotate the engine with a 19 mm wrench on the flats on the signal generator rotor (A, **Figure 34**). Do **not** use the Allen bolt (B, **Figure 34**) that secures the rotor to the crankshaft as the bolt may shear off.*

6. Use a 19 mm wrench on the signal generator rotor (A, **Figure 34**). Rotate the engine *clockwise* until the signal generator rotor "T" mark aligns with the center of the 1.4 pickup coil (**Figure 35**).

34

7. Remove the bolts (**Figure 36**) securing the camshaft chain idler and remove the idler, rubber cushions, plate and locating dowels.
8. Using a crisscross pattern, loosen then remove the bolts securing the camshaft bearing caps on the intake camshaft (A, **Figure 37**).
9. Using a crisscross pattern, loosen then remove the bolts securing the camshaft bearing caps on the exhaust camshaft (B, **Figure 37**).

NOTE
*Each camshaft bearing cap has its own unique mark as shown in **Figure 38**. Each bearing cap must be reinstalled in the same location.*

35

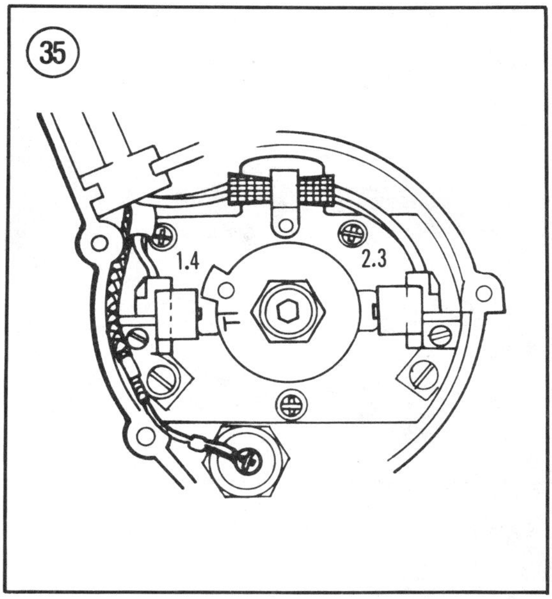

10. Remove all bearing caps from both camshafts. Don't lose the locating dowels in each cap.
11. Disengage the camshaft drive chain from the camshaft sprockets and remove both the intake and exhaust camshafts from the cylinder head.

CAUTION
If the crankshaft must be rotated when the camshafts are removed, pull up on the camshaft chain and keep it taut while rotating the crankshaft. Make certain that the drive chain is positioned correctly on the crankshaft timing sprocket. If this is not done, the drive chain may become kinked and may damage both the chain and the timing sprocket on the crankshaft.

36

37

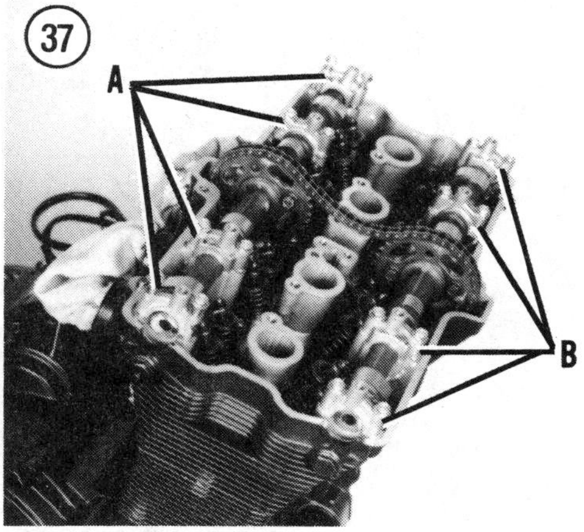

12. Tie a piece of wire to the camshaft drive chain and tie the loose end to the exterior of the engine (**Figure 39**).
13. Inspect the camshafts as described under *Camshaft Inspection* in this chapter.

Inspection

1. Measure the camshaft bearing journals (**Figure 40**) with a micrometer (A, **Figure 41**) for wear and scoring. Compare to the dimensions given in **Table 1** or **Table 2**. If worn to the service limit or less, the camshaft must be replaced.
2. Check the camshaft lobes for wear. The lobes should show no signs of scoring and the edges should be square.
3. Even though the camshaft lobe surface appears to be satisfactory, with no visible signs of wear, the camshaft lobes (**Figure 42**) must be measured with a micrometer (B, **Figure 41**). Compare to the dimensions given in **Table 1** or **Table 2**. If worn to the service limit or less, the camshaft must be replaced.
4. Place the camshaft on a set of V-blocks and check its runout with a dial indicator (**Figure 43**). Compare to the dimension given in **Table 1** or **Table 2**. If the runout is to the service limit or more, the camshaft must be replaced.
5. Inspect the camshaft bearing surfaces in the cylinder head (**Figure 44**) and camshaft bearing caps (**Figure 45**). They should not be scored or excessively worn. Replace the cylinder head and camshaft bearing caps if the bearing surfaces are worn or scored.

39

40

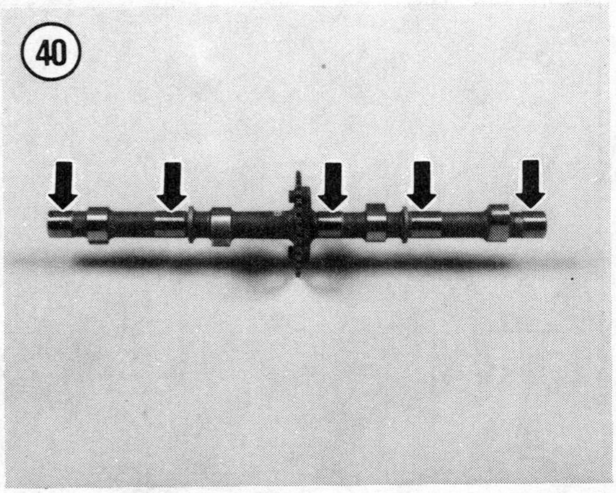

38

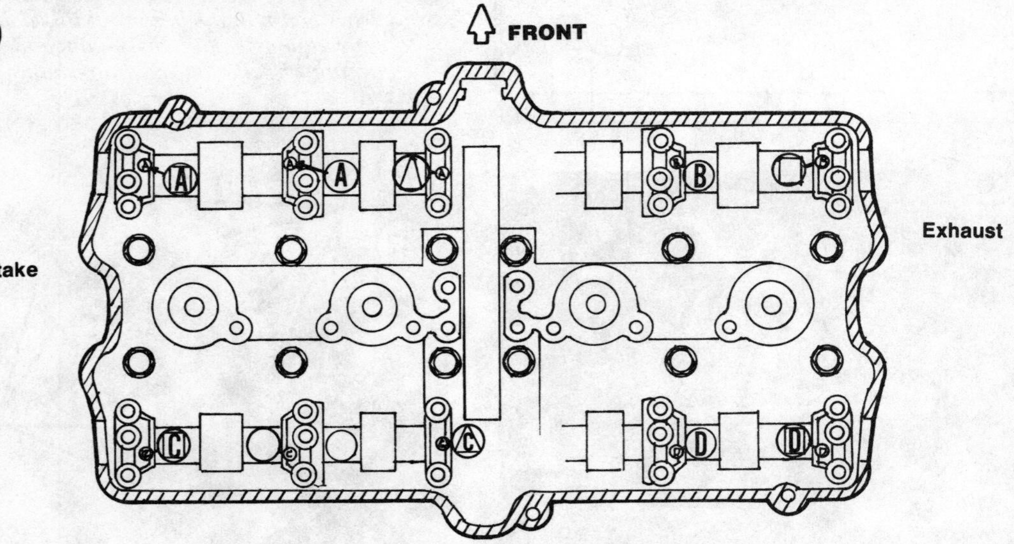

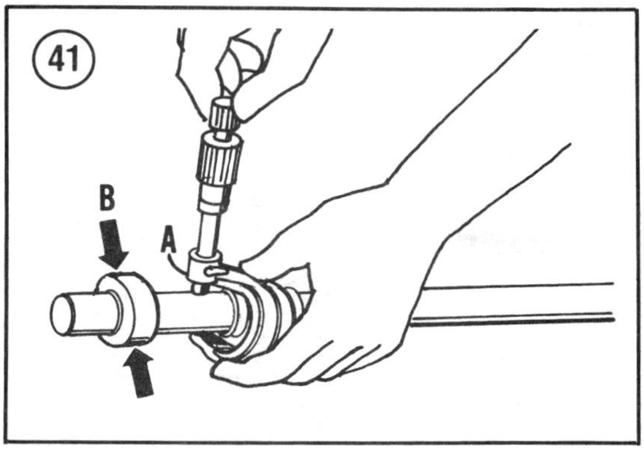

41

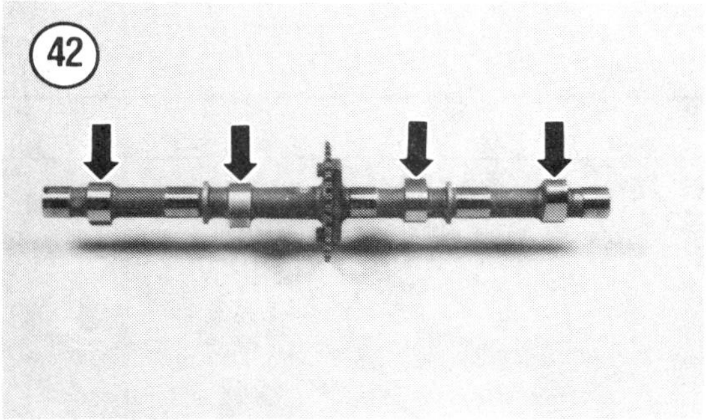

42

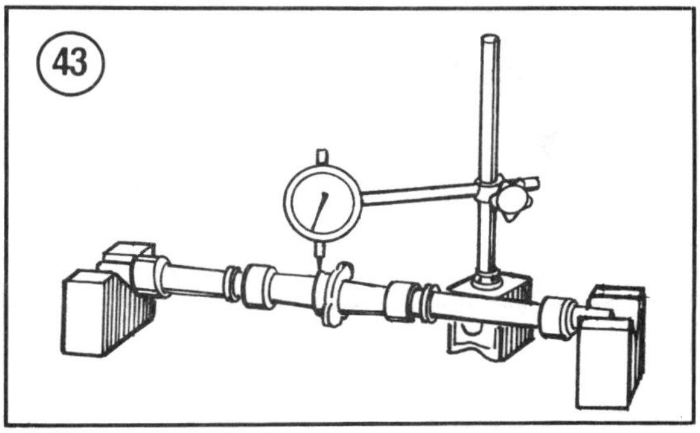

43

44

6. Inspect the camshaft sprocket teeth for wear; replace if necessary.

7. Rotate the camshaft chain idler sprocket (**Figure 46**) by hand. The sprocket should rotate smoothly with no noise or binding. If worn or damaged, replace the idler assembly.

8. Make sure the bolt holes (**Figure 47**) are not elongated or damaged. If damaged, replace the idler assembly.

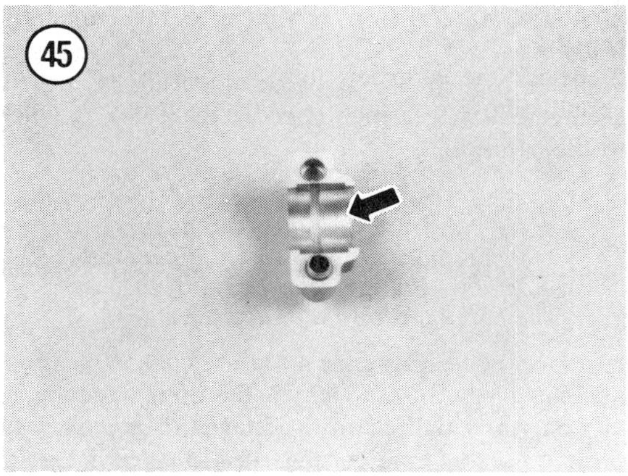

45

46

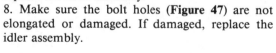

47

Camshaft Bearing Clearance Measurement

This procedure requires a Plastigage set. The camshafts must be installed into the cylinder head. Before installing the camshafts, wipe all oil residue from each camshaft bearing journal and bearing surface in the cylinder head and camshaft bearing caps.

1. Install the camshafts into the cylinder head. Do not engage the drive chain onto the sprockets.
2. Install all locating dowels into the camshaft bearing caps.
3. Place a strip of Plastigage material on top of each camshaft bearing journal (**Figure 48**), parallel to the camshaft.

NOTE
*Each camshaft bearing cap has its own unique mark as shown in **Figure 38**. Each bearing cap must be reinstalled in the same location and direction.*

4. Place the bearing caps into their correct position and install the bolts. Tighten the bolts finger-tight at first, then tighten in 2-3 stages in a crisscross pattern to the final torque specification listed in **Table 3**.

CAUTION
Do not rotate the camshafts with the Plastigage material in place.

5. Loosen the bearing cap bolts in 2-3 stages in a crisscross pattern. Carefully remove all bearing caps.
6. Measure the width of the flattened Plastigage material (**Figure 49**) at the widest point, according to the manufacturer's instructions.

CAUTION
Be sure to remove all traces of Plastigage material from the groove in each bearing cap. If any material is left in the engine it can plug an oil control orifice and cause severe engine damage.

7. Remove *all* Plastigage material from the camshafts and the bearing caps.
8. If the oil clearance is greater than specified in **Table 1** or **Table 2**, perform the following:
   a. Remove both camshafts from the cylinder head.

NOTE
*Each camshaft bearing cap has its own unique mark as shown in **Figure 38**. Each bearing cap must be reinstalled in the same location and direction.*

48

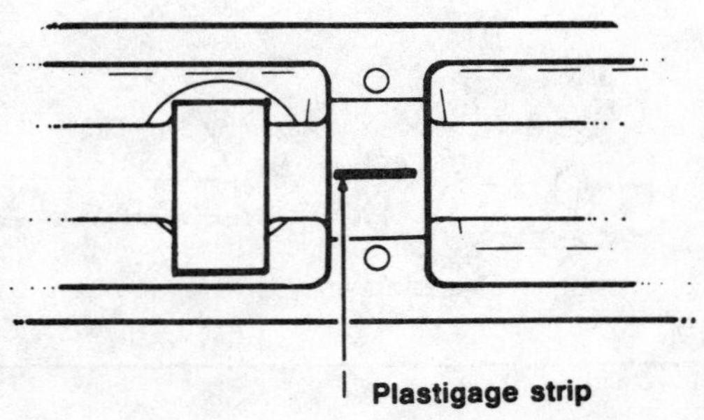

49

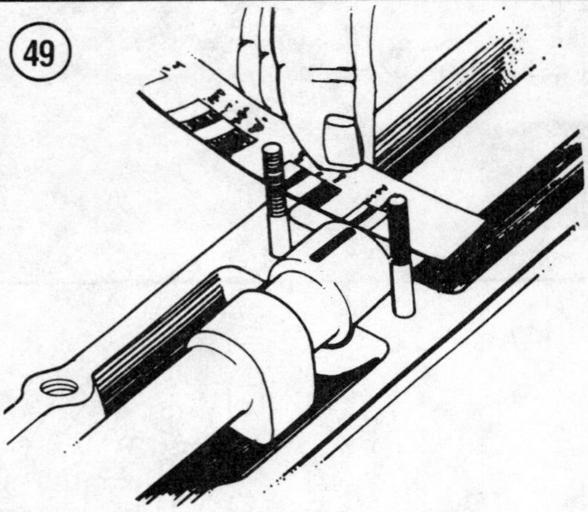

50

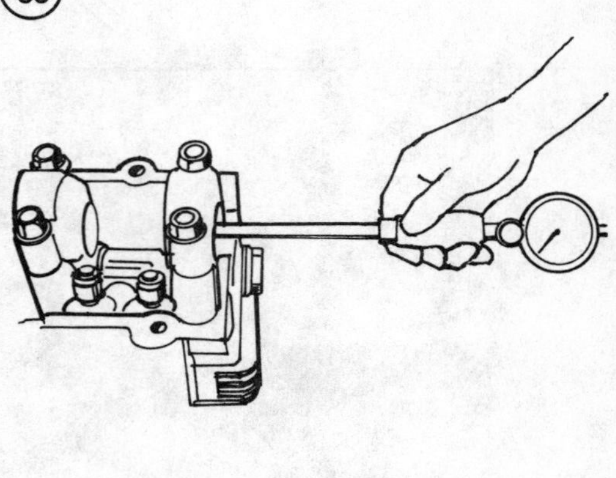

b. Place the bearing caps into their correct positions and install the bolts. Tighten the bolts to the torque specification listed in **Table 3**.
c. Use a bore gauge and measure the inside diameter of each camshaft journal holder (**Figure 50**).
d. Compare to dimensions listed in **Table 1** or **Table 2**. If any of the dimensions exceeds the wear limit in **Table 1** or **Table 2**, and the camshaft bearing journal dimensions were within specification in *Camshaft Inspection*, replace the cylinder head and camshaft bearing caps as a set.
e. Remove the bolts securing the bearing caps and remove the bearing caps and locating dowels.

51

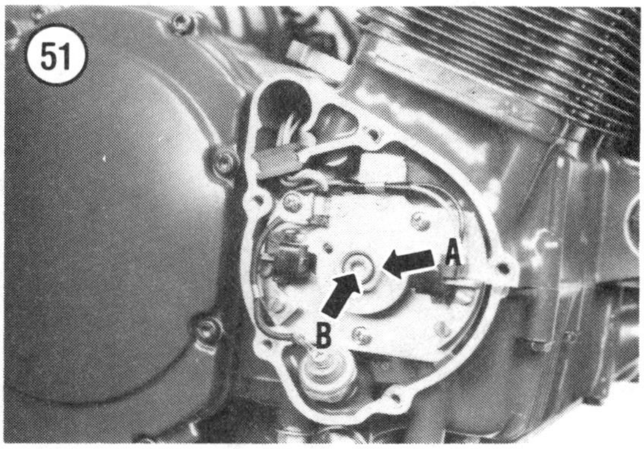

52

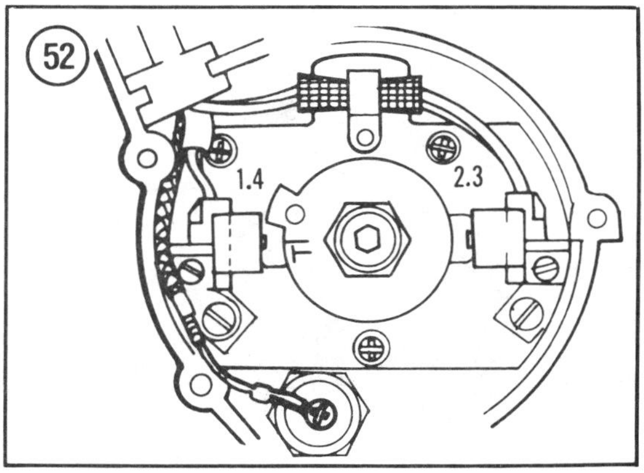

53

Installation

1. Pull up on the camshaft drive chain and make sure it properly meshed with the drive sprocket on the crankshaft.

CAUTION

*In the next step, rotate the engine with a 19 mm wrench on the flats on the signal generator rotor (A, **Figure 51**). Do **not** use the Allen bolt (B, **Figure 51**) that secures the rotor to the crankshaft as the bolt may shear off.*

2. Use a 19 mm wrench on the signal generator rotor (**Figure 51**). Rotate the engine *clockwise* until the signal generator rotor "T" mark aligns with the center of the 1.4 pickup coil (**Figure 52**).
3. Apply a light, but complete coat, of molybdenum disulfide grease to each camshaft bearing journal (**Figure 53**). Coat all bearing surfaces in the cylinder head with clean engine oil.
4. Make sure the camshaft sprocket bolts (**Figure 54**) are tight on both camshafts. If they are loose, remove the bolts and apply Loctite Lock N' Seal to the threads. Install the bolts and tighten to the torque specification listed in **Table 3**.
5. Each camshaft is marked with an IN (intake) or EX (exhaust) as shown in **Figure 55**. Also there is a notch on the right-hand end of each camshaft.
6. Position the exhaust camshaft with the notch facing toward the right-hand side of the engine. Install the camshaft through the drive chain and onto the cylinder head bearing surfaces.
7. Rotate the exhaust camshaft until the "1" arrow (A, **Figure 56**) is level with the top surface of the cylinder head.
8. Pull up on the front of the camshaft drive chain and mesh the chain (B, **Figure 56**) with the exhaust camshaft sprocket.

54

4

9. Insert a drift or wrench (**Figure 57**) through the intake camshaft side of the camshaft drive chain to keep the chain in position on the exhaust camshaft.
10. Make sure the locating dowels are in place in each bearing cap. Refer to **Figure 38** and install the exhaust camshaft bearing caps and bolts. Tighten the bolts in 2-3 stages in a crisscross pattern to the torque specification listed in **Table 3**.

CAUTION
In the next step, rotate the engine with a 19 mm wrench on the flats on the signal generator rotor (A, ***Figure 51****). Do* ***not*** *use the Allen bolt (B,* ***Figure 51****) that secures the rotor to the crankshaft as the bolt may shear off.*

11. Use a 19 mm wrench on the signal generator rotor (**Figure 51**). Rotate the engine *counterclockwise* slightly 2-3°.
12. Pull on the camshaft drive chain with your fingers (**Figure 58**).
13. Use a 19 mm wrench on the signal generator rotor (**Figure 51**). Rotate the engine back *clockwise* until the signal generator rotor "T" mark again aligns with the center of the 1.4 pickup coil (**Figure 52**).
14. Recheck to make sure the exhaust camshaft "1" arrow (A, **Figure 56**) is still level with the top surface of the cylinder head. If alignment is not correct, readjust the camshaft drive chain to the camshaft sprocket at this time.
15. Position the intake camshaft with the notch facing toward the right-hand side of the engine. Install the camshaft through the drive chain and onto the cylinder head bearing surfaces.
16. Rotate the intake camshaft until the "3" arrow (A, **Figure 59**) is pointing straight up.
17. The exhaust camshaft "2" arrow (C, **Figure 56**) should be pointing straight up. From the pin that the "2" arrow is pointing to (D, **Figure 56**) start counting back toward the intake camshaft until you reach the 21st pin on the chain.
18. Align the camshaft drive chain with the intake camshaft sprocket so the "3" arrow is pointing to the 21st pin on the drive chain (B, **Figure 59**) and mesh the chain onto the sprocket.
19. Recheck the following:
   a. Refer to Step 13 and make sure the "T" mark is still properly aligned (**Figure 52**). Readjust if necessary.

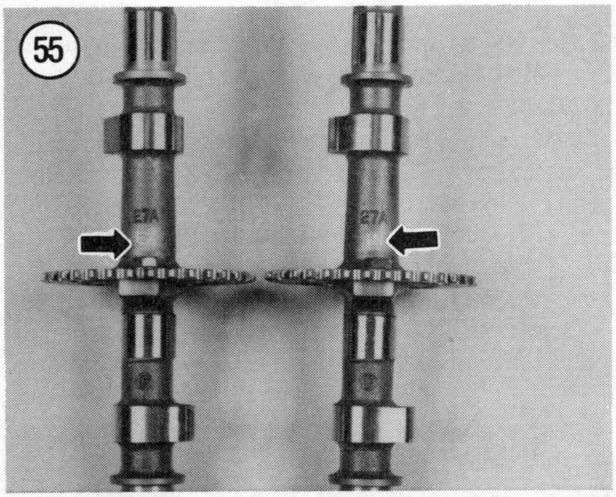

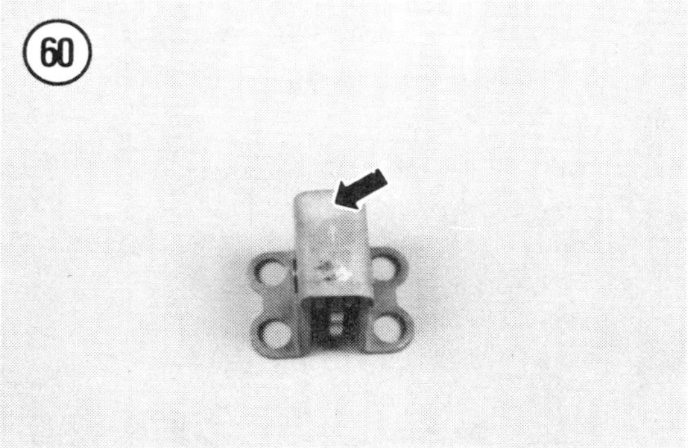

b. Make sure the exhaust camshaft "1" arrow (A, **Figure 56**) is still level with the top surface of the cylinder head.

c. Make sure the intake camshaft "3" arrow is pointing to the 21st pin on the drive chain for 750cc models or to the 22nd pin for 1100cc models (B, **Figure 59**).

d. If alignment is incorrect, reposition the camshaft chain on the sprockets and again recheck the alignment.

CAUTION

Very expensive damage could result from improper camshaft drive chain-to-camshafts alignment. Recheck your work several times to be sure alignment is correct.

20. Make sure the locating dowels are in place in each bearing cap. Refer to **Figure 38** and install the intake camshaft bearing caps and bolts. Tighten the bolts in 2-3 stages in a crisscross pattern to the torque specification listed in **Table 3**.

21. Position the cam chain idler with the arrow (**Figure 60**) facing toward the front of the engine. Refer to **Figure 61** and install the idler components onto the cylinder head as follows:

a. Metal plate, rubber cushion and locating dowels.

b. Idler assembly, rubber cushion and bolts (**Figure 62**).

c. Tighten the bolts to the torque specification listed in **Table 3**.

22. After the idler is installed, again check the alignment of all marks as shown in **Figure 63**. If any of the alignment points are incorrect, repeat this procedure until *all* are correct.

CAUTION

If there is any binding while rotating the crankshaft, ***stop****. Determine the cause before proceeding.*

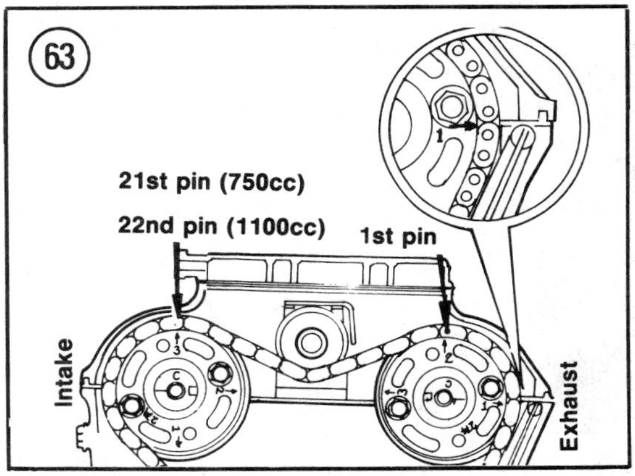

64

CAMSHAFT CHAIN TENSIONER

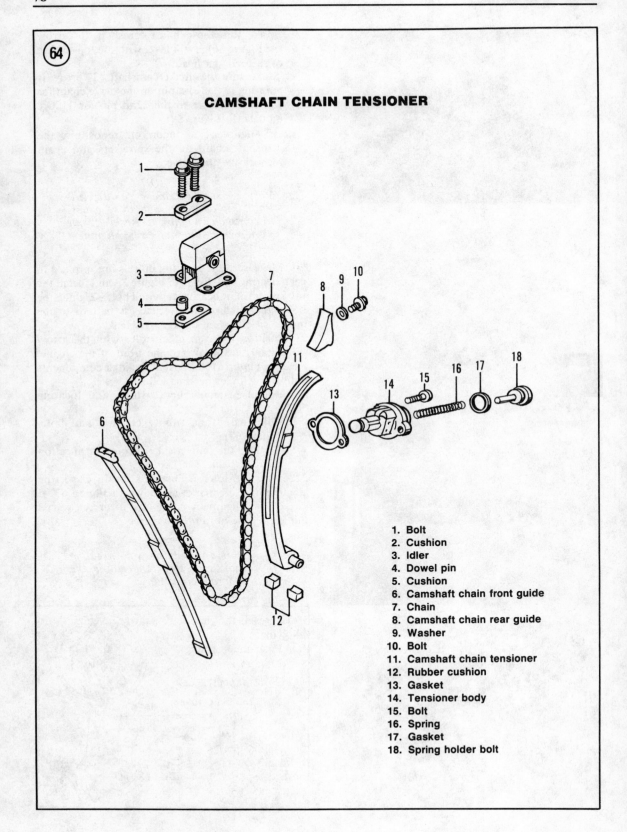

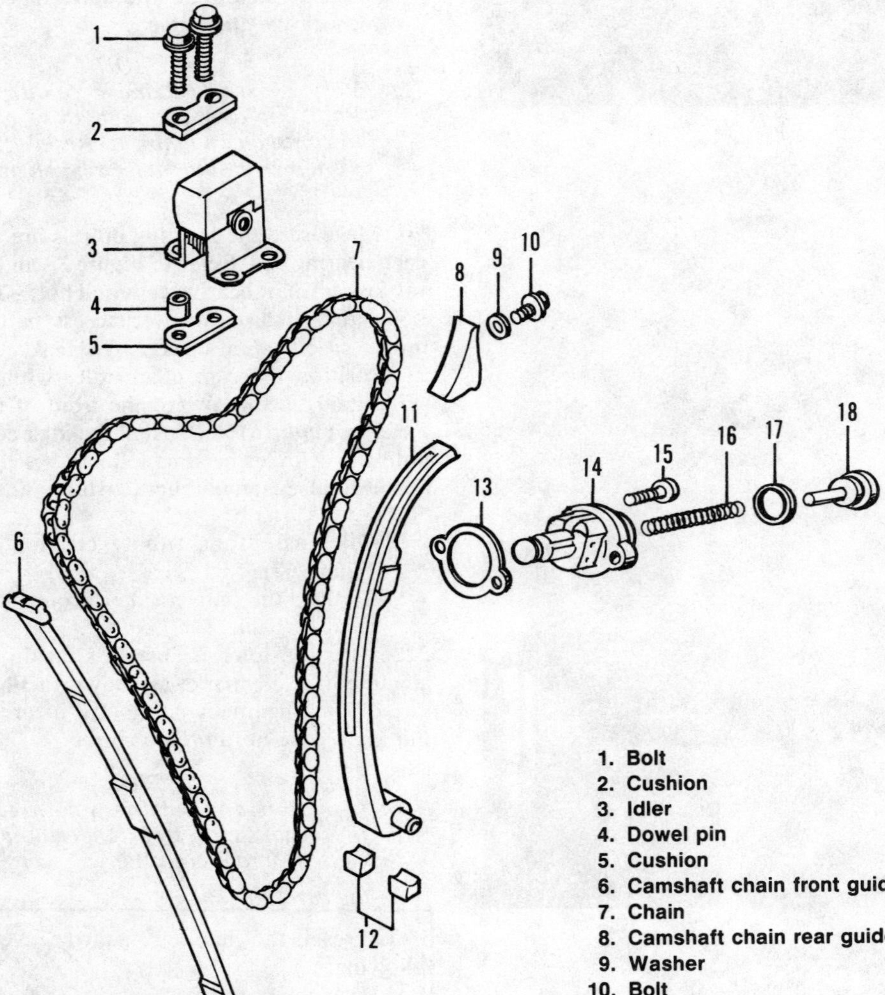

1. Bolt
2. Cushion
3. Idler
4. Dowel pin
5. Cushion
6. Camshaft chain front guide
7. Chain
8. Camshaft chain rear guide
9. Washer
10. Bolt
11. Camshaft chain tensioner
12. Rubber cushion
13. Gasket
14. Tensioner body
15. Bolt
16. Spring
17. Gasket
18. Spring holder bolt

65

66

67

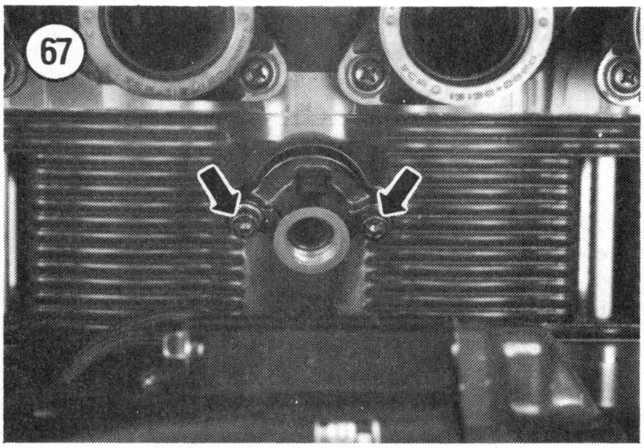

68

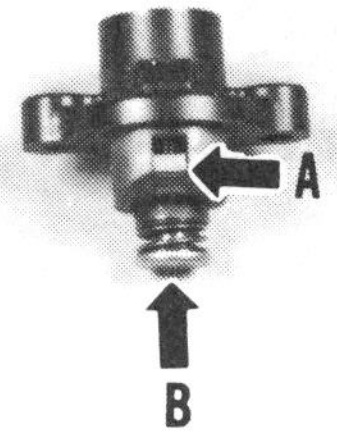

23. After installation is complete, rotate the crankshaft several times using a 19 mm wrench on the signal generator rotor (**Figure 51**).
24. Fill the oil pockets in the cylinder head with new engine oil so the cam lobes are submerged in the oil.
25. Reset the camshaft chain tensioner pushrod and install the camshaft chain tensioner assembly as described under *Camshaft Chain Tensioner Removal/Installation* in this chapter.
26. Install all spark plugs and reconnect the spark plug leads. Make sure the rubber boots are properly seated in the cylinder head cover.
27. Install the signal generator cover and gasket. Install and tighten the bolts securely.
28. Install the cylinder head cover as described under *Cylinder Head Cover Installation* in this chapter.
29. Adjust the valves as described under *Valve Clearance Measurement and Adjustment* in Chapter Three.

4

CAMSHAFT CHAIN TENSIONER

Removal/Installation

Refer to **Figure 64** for this procedure.

1. Remove the cam chain tensioner spring holder bolt and sealing washer (**Figure 65**).
2. Withdraw the cam chain tensioner spring (**Figure 66**) from the tensioner body.
3. Remove the bolts (**Figure 67**) securing the tensioner assembly to the cylinder block.
4. Remove the tensioner assembly and gasket.

CAUTION
Be sure to reset the ratchet pushrod before installing the tensioner assembly. This is necessary in order to apply the correct amount of pressure on the camshaft chain.

5. To reset the ratchet pushrod, perform the following:
   a. Push the spring ratchet pawl (A, **Figure 68**) forward and push the ratchet pushrod (B, **Figure 68**) all the way into the body.
   b. Release the ratchet pawl. The pushrod should stay within the body. If it does not, replace the tensioner assembly.
6. Install the tensioner assembly and gasket onto the cylinder block.
7. Install the mounting bolts and tighten to the torque specification listed in **Table 3**.
8. Install the spring (**Figure 66**) into the tensioner body.

9. Make sure the sealing washer (**Figure 69**) is in place on the spring holder bolt and install the bolt.
10. Tighten the bolt to the torque specification listed in **Table 3**.

Inspection

Inspect all parts of the camshaft tensioner assembly for wear or damage (**Figure 70**). Suzuki does not provide any service specifications for the tensioner assembly. If any part of the tensioner body is worn or damaged, replace the body assembly. Replacement parts are not available.

ROCKER ARM ASSEMBLIES

NOTE
This procedure is shown with the engine removed from the frame for clarity. It is not necessary to remove the engine to perform this procedure.

Removal

1. Remove the bolt (**Figure 71**) securing the rocker arm shaft into the cylinder head.
2. Unscrew the end plug (**Figure 72**) and sealing washer from the cylinder head.
3. Screw an 8 mm bolt (**Figure 73**) into the end of the rocker arm shaft.
4. Pull the rocker arm shaft out and remove the rocker arms and springs.
5. Repeat for all rocker arm shaft assemblies.

NOTE
Mark the shafts and rocker arms with an "I" (intake) or "E" (exhaust) and cylinder number (No. 1, 2, 3 or 4) as they must be reinstalled into their original position. The No. 1 cylinder is on the left-hand side of the bike; No. 2, 3 and 4 cylinders continue from left to right across the engine.

6. Wash all parts in solvent and thoroughly dry with compressed air.

69

70

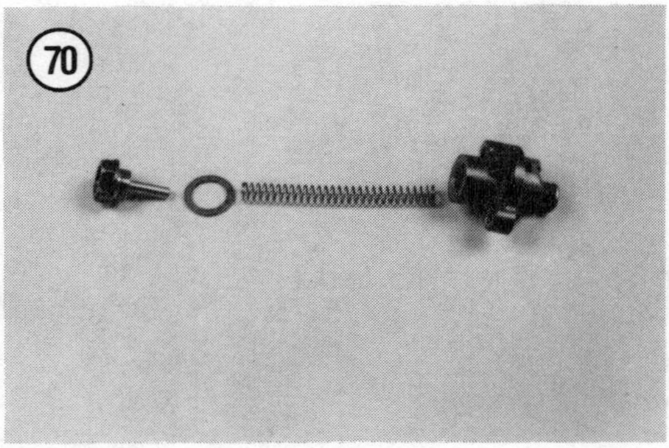

71

72

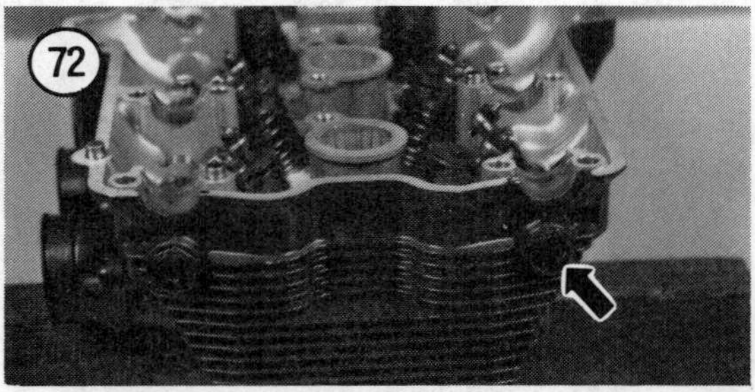

73

74

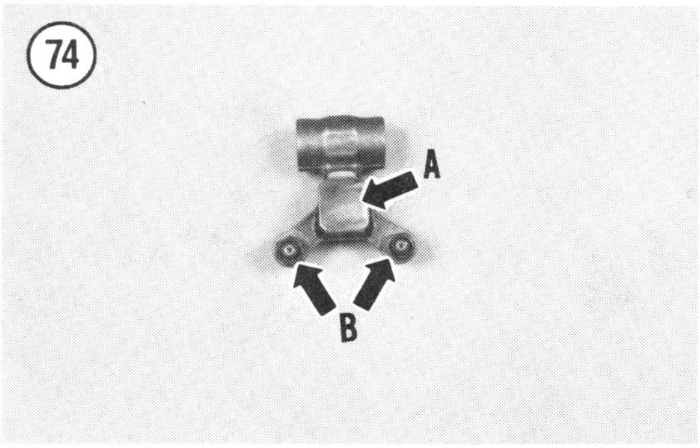

75

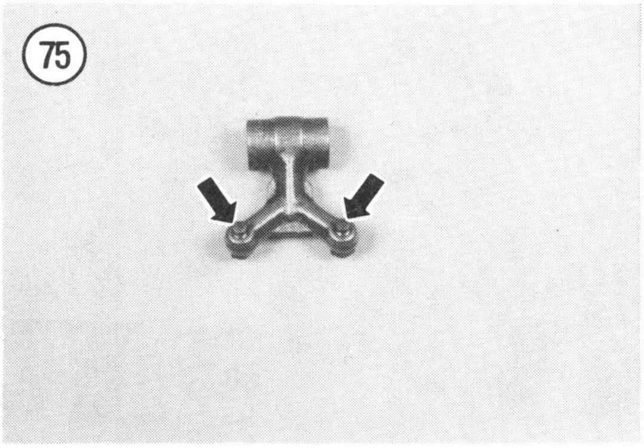

76

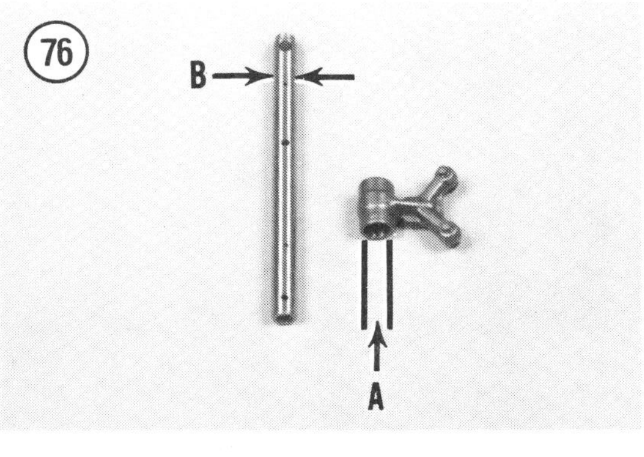

77

Inspection

1. Inspect the rocker arm pad where it rides on the cam lobe (A, **Figure 74**) and where the adjusters ride on the valve stems (B, **Figure 74**). If the pad is scratched or unevenly worn, inspect the cam lobe for scoring, chipping or flat spots. Replace the rocker arm if defective. If the adjuster top is pitted, replace it.
2. Inspect the valve adjusters (**Figure 75**) for wear or damage. Replace the adjusters if defective.
3. Measure the inside diameter of the rocker arm bore (A, **Figure 76**) with an inside micrometer and check against the dimensions in **Table 1** or **Table 2**. Replace if worn to the service limit or greater.
4. Inspect the rocker arm shaft for signs of wear or scoring. Measure the outside diameter (B, **Figure 76**) with a micrometer and check against the dimensions in **Table 1** or **Table 2**. Replace if worn to the service limit or less.
5. Make sure the oil holes in the rocker arm shaft are clean and clear. If necessary, clean out with a piece of wire and thoroughly clean with solvent. Dry with compressed air.
6. Check the rocker arm springs for breakage or distortion; replace if necessary.

Installation

1. Coat the rocker arm shaft, rocker arm bore and the shaft receptacles in the cylinder head with assembly oil or clean engine oil.
2. Refer to marks made in Step 5, *Removal,* and be sure to install the rocker arm and shafts back into their original locations.
3. Install the rocker arm (A, **Figure 77**) and the spring (B, **Figure 77**). The spring goes toward the outside surface of the engine, away from the cam chain cavity.
4. Position the rocker arm shaft so the bolt hole (**Figure 78**) is vertical.

78

5. Partially install the rocker arm shaft into the cylinder head, through the spring and then the rocker arm.
6. Rotate the rocker arm shaft so the bolt hole (A, **Figure 79**) is aligned with the bolt hole in the cylinder head (B, **Figure 79**). Pull the rocker arm shaft back enough to install the next rocker arm and spring.
7. Install the next rocker arm (A, **Figure 80**) and the spring (B, **Figure 80**). The spring goes toward the outside surface of the engine, away from the cam chain cavity.
8. Push the shaft all the way in and, if necessary, rotate it slightly to align its hole with the bolt hole in the cylinder head.
9. Install the bolt securing the rocker arm shaft and tighten to the torque specification listed in **Table 3**.
10. Inspect the sealing washer (**Figure 81**) on the end plug; replace if necessary.

NOTE
*The end plugs for intake and exhaust rocker arms are different. The ones with the threaded hole (A, **Figure 82**) must be installed on the side, at the rear of the cylinder head. These holes are used for front fairing bracket bolts.*

11. Install the end plug (B, **Figure 82**) and sealing washer and tighten to the torque specification listed in **Table 3**.

CYLINDER HEAD

NOTE
This procedure is shown with the engine removed from the frame for clarity. It is not necessary to remove the engine to perform this procedure.

Removal

CAUTION
To prevent any warpage and damage, remove the cylinder head only when the engine is at room temperature.

1. Remove the carburetors as described under *Carburetor Removal/Installation* in Chapter Seven.
2. Remove the exhaust system as described under *Exhaust System Removal/Installation* in Chapter Seven.
3. Remove the cylinder head cover as described under *Cylinder Head Cover Removal/Installation* in this chapter.
4. Remove the camshafts and rocker arm assemblies as described under *Camshafts Removal* and *Rocker Arm Assemblies Removal* in this chapter.

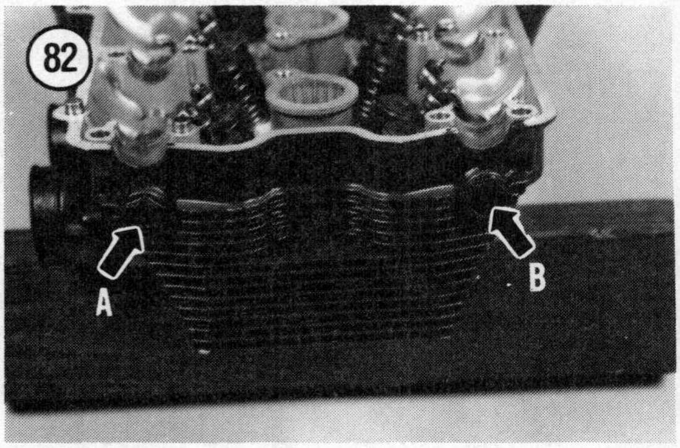

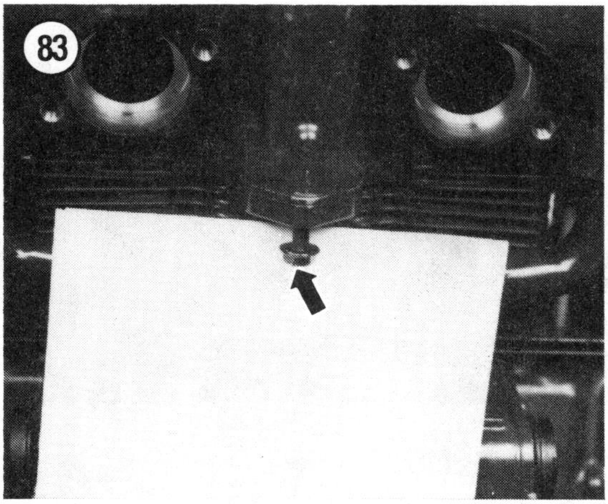

83

5. Remove the bolt **(Figure 83)** securing the cylinder head to the cylinder block.
6. Remove the cam chain's front guide.

CAUTION
The conventional nuts (not acorn) are located at the outer 4 corners of the cylinder head. These nuts must be reinstalled in the same location.

7. Loosen the cylinder head nuts **(Figure 84)** in 2-3 stages in the pattern shown in **Figure 85**. Remove the nuts and washers.
8. Loosen the cylinder head by tapping around the perimeter with a rubber or soft faced mallet. If necessary, *gently* pry the head loose with a broad-tipped screwdriver.

CAUTION
Remember the cooling fins are fragile and may be damaged if tapped or pried on too hard. Never use a metal hammer.

84

9. Lift the cylinder head straight up and off the cylinder and crankcase studs. Guide the camshaft chain through the opening in the cylinder head and retie the wire to the exterior of the engine. This will prevent the drive chain from falling down into the crankcase.
10. Remove the cylinder head gasket and discard it. Don't lose the locating dowels.
11. Place a clean shop cloth into the camshaft chain opening in the cylinder block to prevent the entry of foreign matter.

85

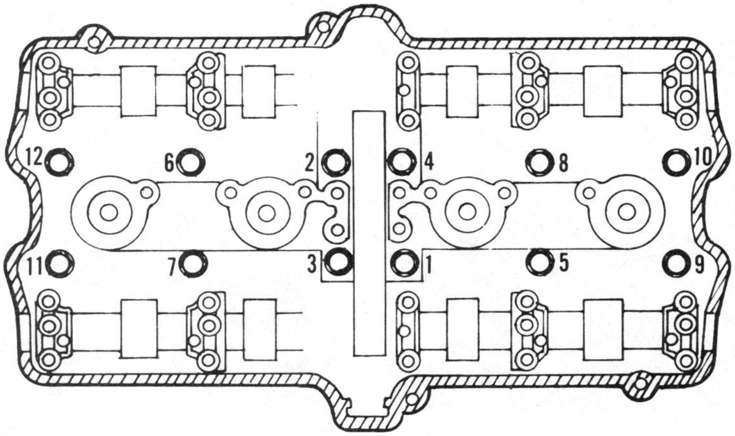

12. Remove the front external oil pipes from the crankcase and discard the O-ring seals. To help prevent an oil leak, the O-ring seals must be replaced whenever the oil pipes are removed.

Inspection

1. Remove all traces of gasket material from the cylinder head mating surfaces (**Figure 86**).
2. *Without removing the valves,* remove all carbon deposits from the combustion chambers (**Figure 87**) and valve ports with a wire brush. A blunt screwdriver may be used if care is taken not to damage the head, valves and spark plug threads.
3. After the carbon is removed from the combustion chambers and the intake and exhaust ports, clean the entire head in cleaning solvent. Blow dry with compressed air.
4. Clean away all carbon from the piston crowns. Do not remove the carbon ridge at the top of the cylinder bore.
5. Check for cracks in the combustion chamber and exhaust ports. A cracked head must be replaced.
6. After the head has been thoroughly cleaned, place a straightedge across the cylinder head/cylinder gasket surface at several points. Measure the warpage by inserting a flat feeler gauge between the straightedge and the cylinder head at each location. There should be no warpage; if a small amount is present, it can be resurfaced by a dealer or qualified machine shop. Replace the cylinder head and cylinder head cover as a set if the gasket surface is warped to or beyond the limit listed in **Table 1** or **Table 2**.

86

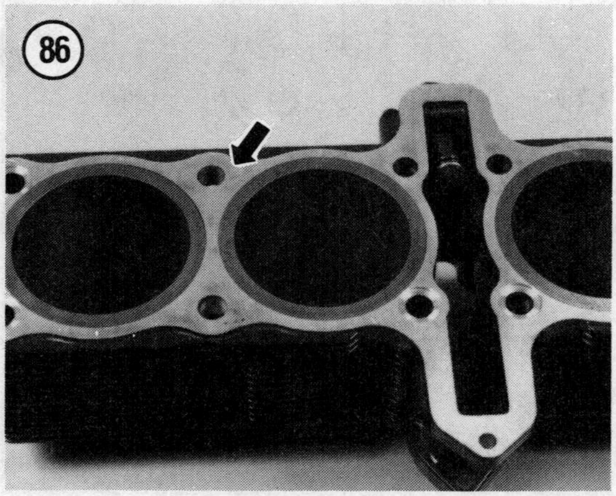

87

88

89

90

7. Check the cylinder head cover mating surface using the procedure in Step 6. There should be no warpage.

8. Check the valves and valve guides as described in this chapter.

9. Inspect the hole (**Figure 88**) in each oil pipe. Make sure it is clean. If necessary, remove the oil pipes (**Figure 89**) and clean with solvent, then thoroughly dry with compressed air. Install the oil pipe with the enlarged end (**Figure 90**) going in last.

10. Inspect the cam chain guide (**Figure 91**) for wear or damage. To replace, perform the following:

a. Remove the bolt and washer (**Figure 92**) securing the guide and remove the guide.

b. Install a new guide.

c. Apply Loctite Lock N' Seal to the bolt threads prior to installation.

d. Install the bolt and washer and tighten securely.

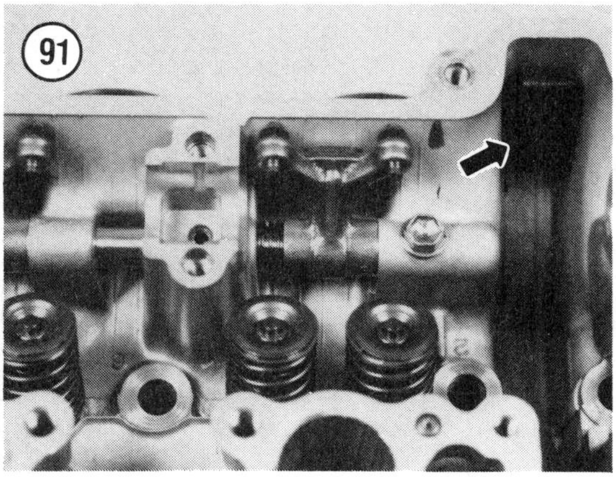

NOTE

*Each intake pipe is unique and must be reinstalled at the correct location on the cylinder head. Mark each pipe prior to removal to ensure proper installation. If installing new intake pipes, refer to **Figure 93** for correct identification numbers and cylinder locations.*

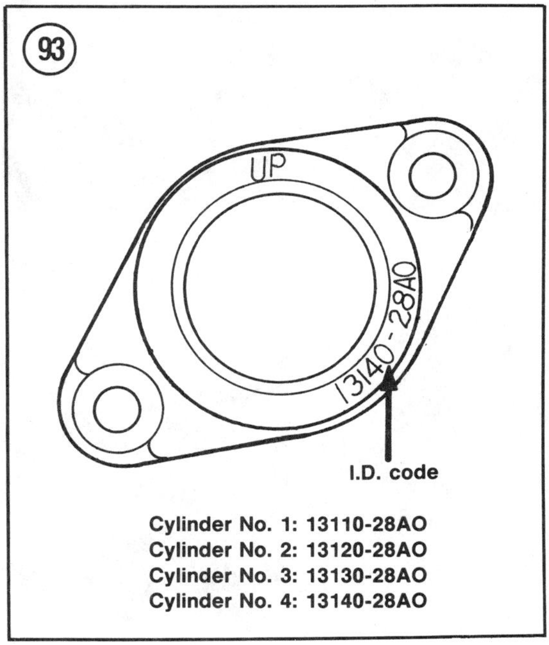

11. If necessary, remove the screws securing the intake pipes (**Figure 94**) onto the cylinder head. To prevent a vacuum leak, install a new O-ring seal between the intake pipe and the cylinder head. Install the intake pipes and tighten the screws securely.

Installation

1. Install a new O-ring seal (**Figure 95**) at each end of both front external oil pipes.
2. Install both oil pipes (**Figure 96**) into the receptacles in the crankcase.
3. If removed, install the locating dowel (**Figure 97**) at each end of the cylinder block.
4. Remove the shop rag from the camshaft chain opening in the cylinder block.
5. Install a new cylinder head gasket (**Figure 98**) with the UP mark (**Figure 99**) facing up.
6. Carefully slide the cylinder head onto the cylinder. Feed the camshaft chain through the chain cavity in the cylinder head and secure the other end of the wire again (**Figure 100**).
7. Apply oil to the threads of the crankcase threaded studs.
8. Install the cylinder head washers and nuts. Refer to **Figure 101** for the correct location of the conventional nuts and the acorn nuts.

95

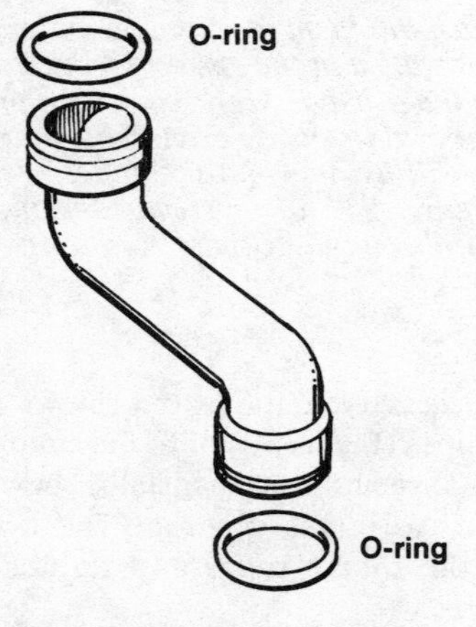

96

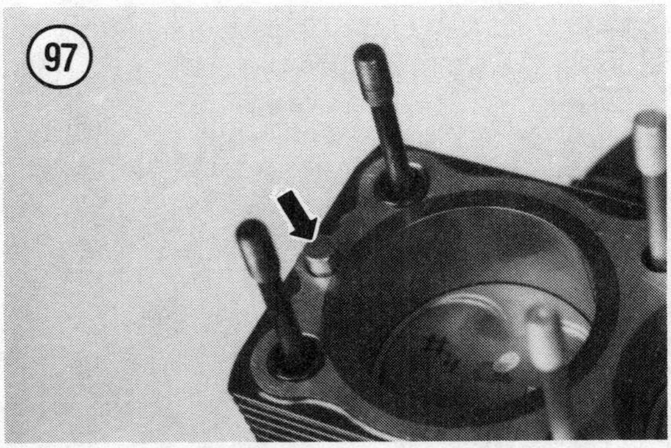

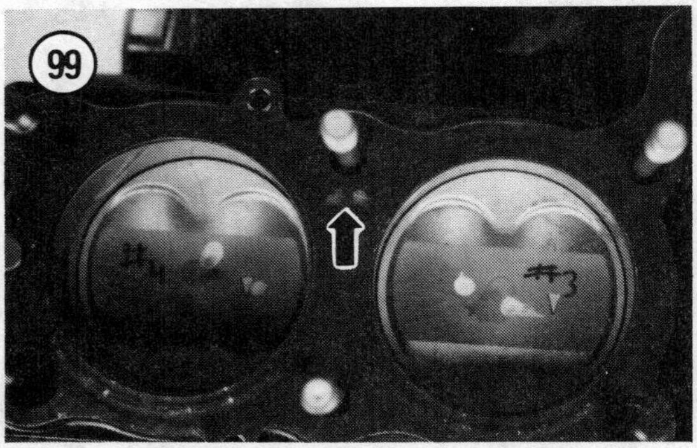

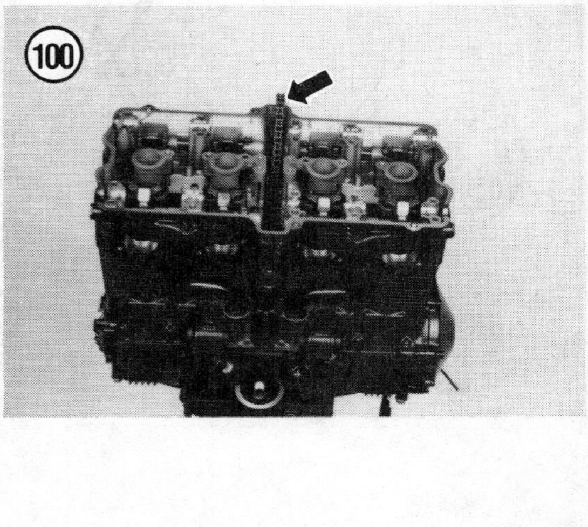

9. Tighten the nuts in the torque pattern shown in **Figure 85** to the torque specification listed in **Table 3**.
10. Install the cylinder head-to cylinder bolt (**Figure 83**) and tighten to the torque specification listed in **Table 3**.

(102)

11. Install the cam chain's front guide (**Figure 102**) and its bolt (**Figure 92**).
12. Install the rocker arm assemblies and camshafts as described under *Rocker Arm Assemblies Installation* and *Camshafts Installation* in this chapter.
13. Install the cylinder head cover as described under *Cylinder Head Cover Installation* in this chapter.
14. Install the carburetor and exhaust system as described in Chapter Seven.
15. Adjust the valves as described under *Valve Clearance Measurement and Adjustment* in Chapter Three.

VALVES AND VALVE COMPONENTS

General practice among those who do their own service is to remove the cylinder head and take it to a machine shop or dealer for inspection and service. Since the cost is low relative to the required effort and equipment, this is the best approach, even for experienced mechanics.

(101)

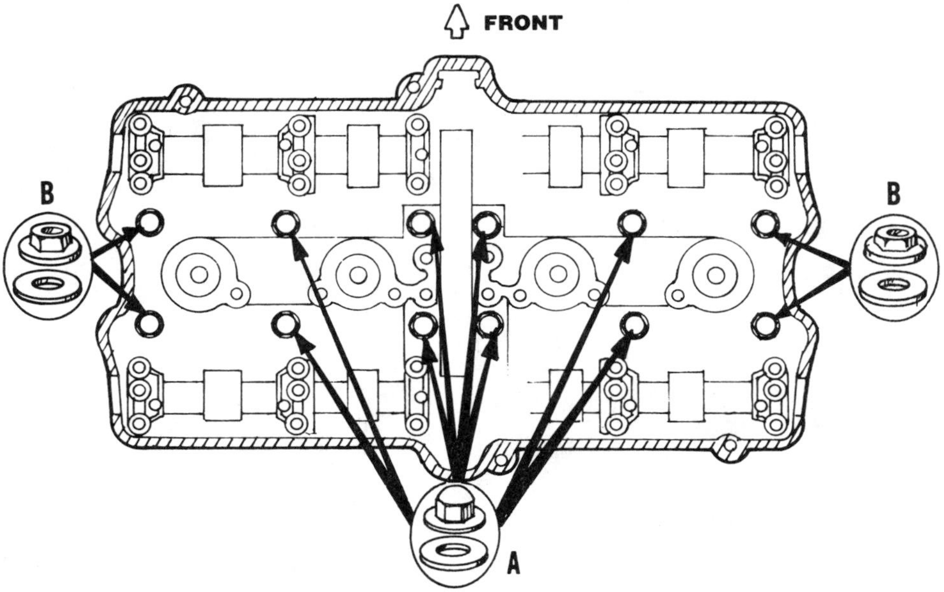

4

103

VALVE ASSEMBLY

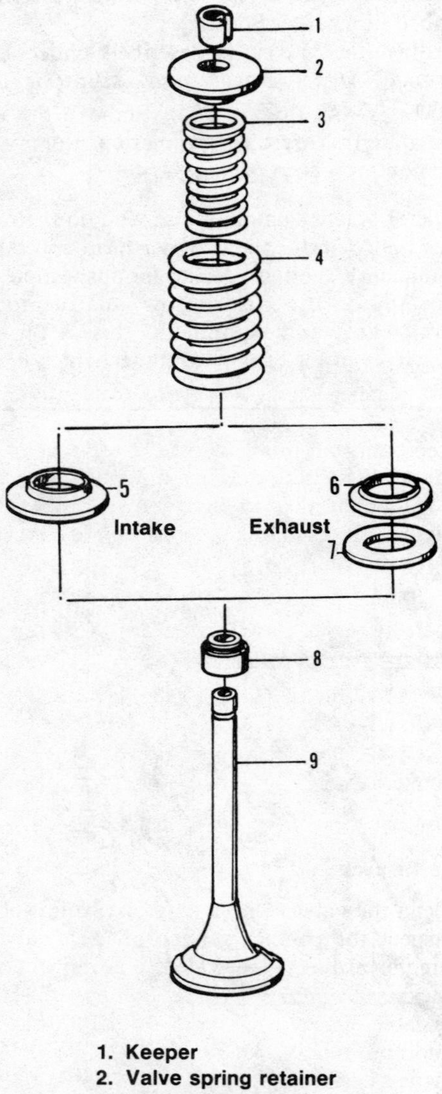

1. Keeper
2. Valve spring retainer
3. Inner spring
4. Outer spring
5. Valve seat
6. Inner valve spring seat
7. Outer valve spring seat
8. Oil seal
9. Valve

104

105

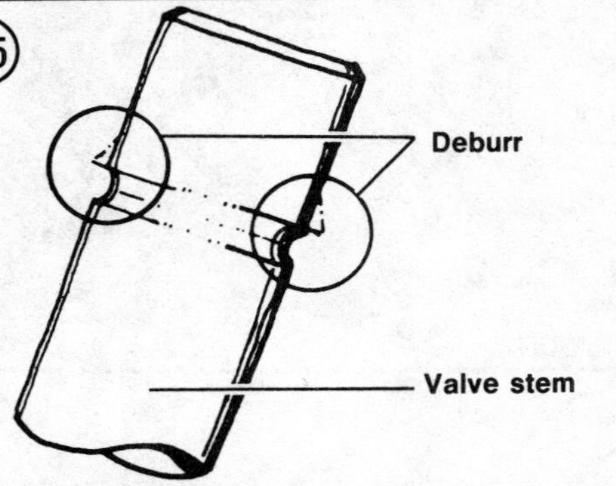

106

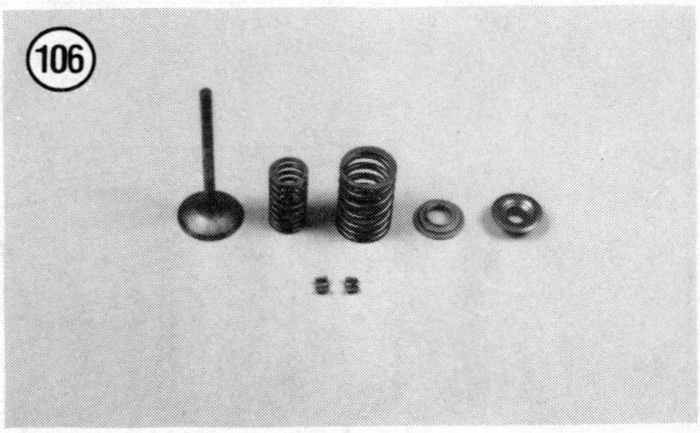

107

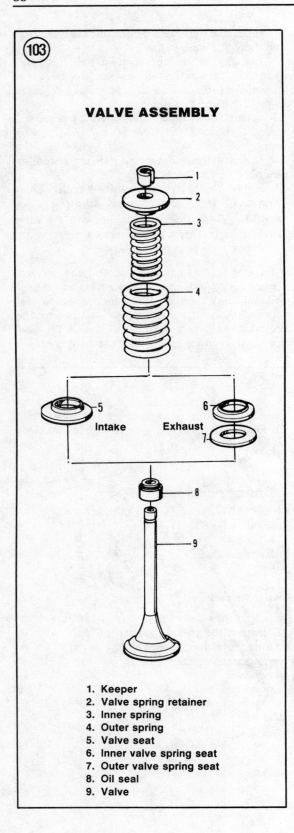

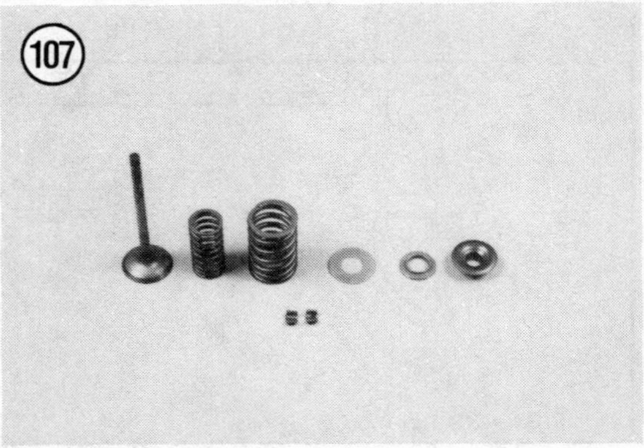

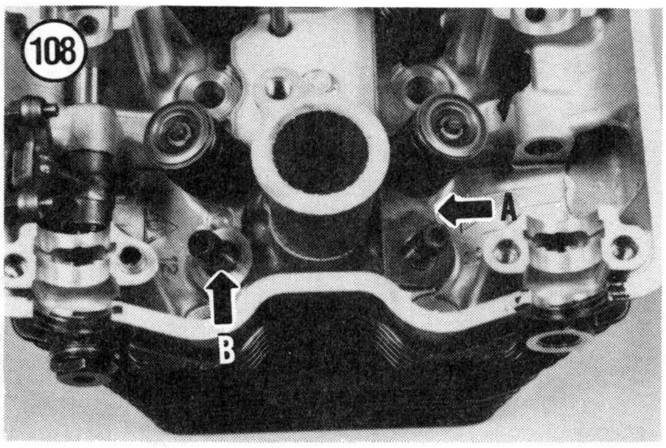

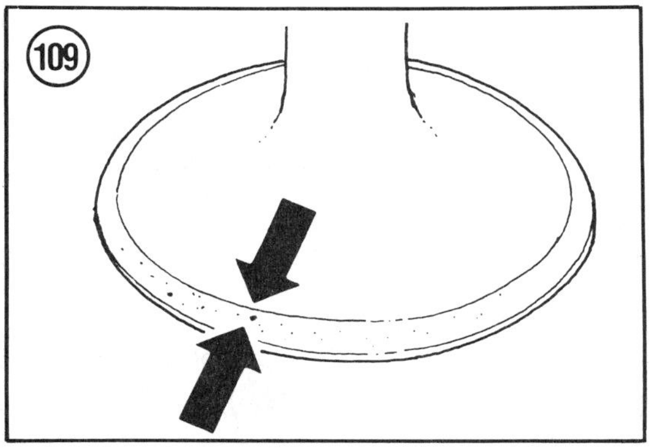

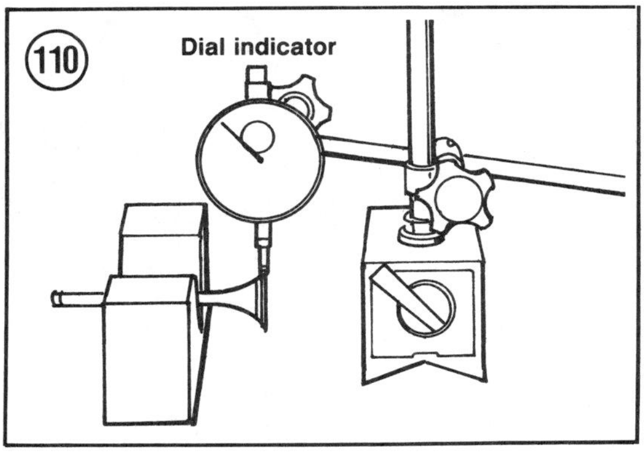

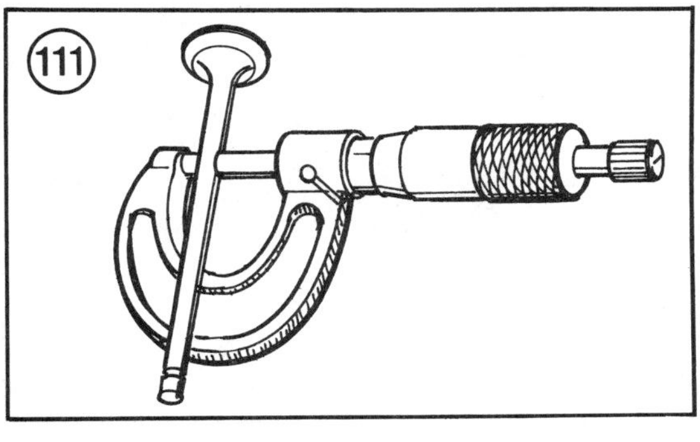

This procedure is included for those who choose to do their own valve service. Refer to **Figure 103**.

Valve Removal

1. Remove the cylinder head as described under *Cylinder Head Removal* in this chapter.

CAUTION
To avoid loss of spring tension, do not compress the springs any more than necessary to remove the keepers.

2. Compress the valve springs with a valve compressor tool (**Figure 104**). Remove the valve keepers and release the compression. Remove the valve compressor tool.
3. Remove the valve spring retainer and valve springs.
4. Before removing the valve, remove any burrs from the valve stem (**Figure 105**). Otherwise the valve guide will be damaged.
5. Remove the valve.
6. On intake valves, remove the spring seat.
7. On exhaust valves remove the inner and outer spring seats.
8. Repeat for all intake and exhaust valves.
9. Mark all parts as they are disassembled so that they will be installed in their same locations. Refer to **Figure 106** for intake valves or **Figure 107** for exhaust valves.

NOTE
It is easiest to store valve parts in several muffin tins.

10. Remove the metal plates (A, **Figure 108**) from the exhaust valve side.
11. Remove the oil seal (B, **Figure 108**) from each valve guide.

Valve Inspection

1. Clean the valves with a wire brush and solvent.
2. Inspect the contact surface of each valve for burning or pitting (**Figure 109**). Unevenness of the contact surface is an indication that the valve is not serviceable. The valve contact surface can *not* be ground and must be replaced if defective.
3. Inspect each valve head for wear and roughness and measure the vertical runout of the valve head as shown in **Figure 110**. The runout should not exceed the service limit listed in **Table 1** or **Table 2**.
4. Measure each valve stem for wear (**Figure 111**). If worn beyond specifications in **Table 1** or **Table 2**, or less the valve must be replaced.

5. Measure each valve's margin for wear (**Figure 112**). If worn to the wear limit listed in **Table 1** or **Table 2** or less, the valve must be replaced.
6. Remove all carbon and varnish from each valve guide bore with a stiff spiral wire brush.
7. Insert each valve in its guide. Hold the valve with the head off the valve seat (approximately 8 mm) and rock it sideways in 2 directions, "X" and "Y," perpendicular to each other as shown in **Figure 113**. If the valve-to-valve guide clearance measured exceeds the limit listed in **Table 1** or **Table 2**, measure the valve stem. If the valve stem is worn, replace the valve. If the valve stem is within tolerances, replace the valve guide.
8. Measure each valve spring free length with a vernier caliper (**Figure 114**). All should be within the length specified in **Table 1** or **Table 2** with no signs of bends or distortion. Replace defective springs in pairs (inner and outer).
9. Check the valve spring retainer and valve keepers. If they are in good condition they may be reused; replace as necessary.
10. Inspect the valve seats. If worn or burned, they must be reconditioned as described in this chapter.

112

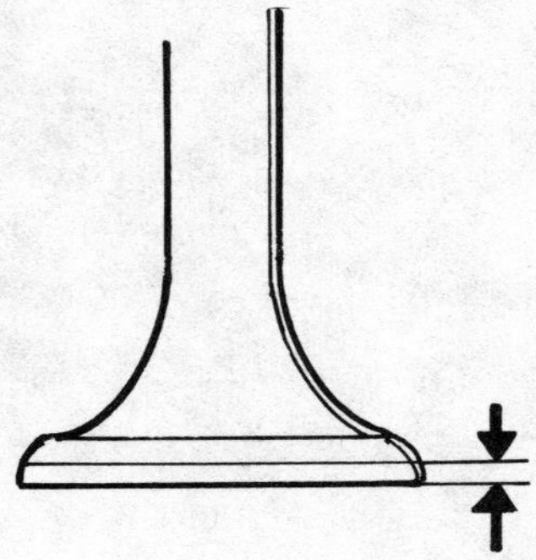

113

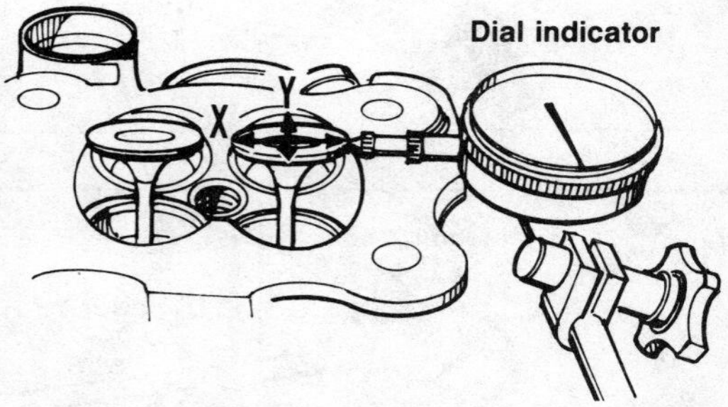

114

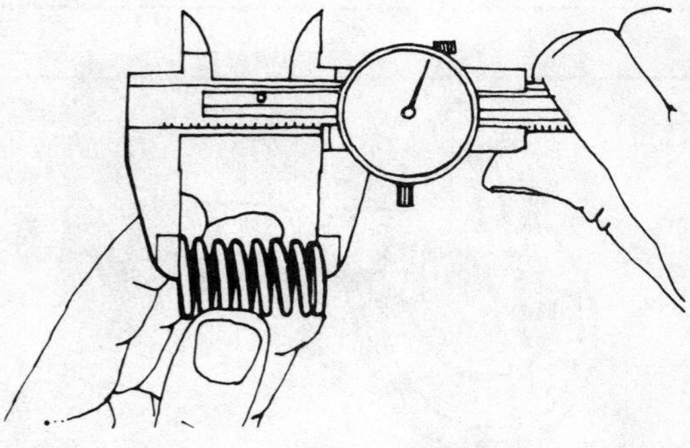

Valve Installation

1. Install the metal plates (A, **Figure 108**) on the exhaust valves side.
2. Install a new seal (B, **Figure 108**) on each valve guide.
3. On intake valves, install the valve seat.
4. On exhaust valves, install the inner and outer valve seats.
5. Coat the valve stems with molybdenum disulfide grease. To avoid damage to the valve stem seal, turn the valve slowly while inserting the valve into the cylinder head.
6. Install the valve springs with their closer wound coils (**Figure 115**) facing the cylinder head.
7. Install the valve spring retainer on top of the valve springs.

CAUTION
To avoid loss of spring tension, do not compress the springs any more than necessary to install the keepers.

8. Compress the valve springs with a compressor tool (**Figure 104**) and install the valve keepers. Make sure the keepers fit snugly into the rounded groove in the valve stem.
9. Remove the compression tool.
10. Gently tap the end of the valve stem with a plastic hammer. This will ensure that the keepers are properly seated.

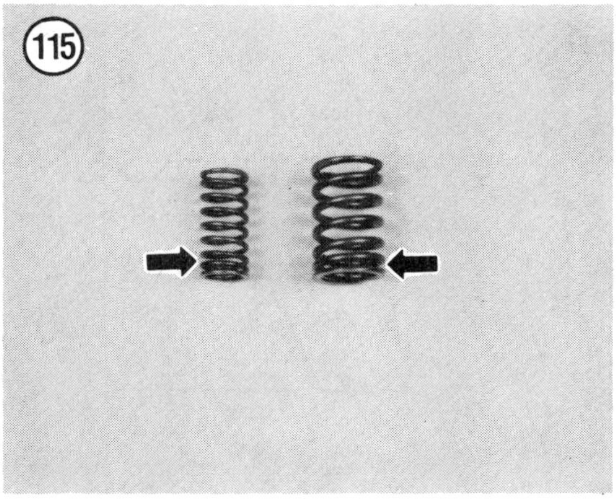

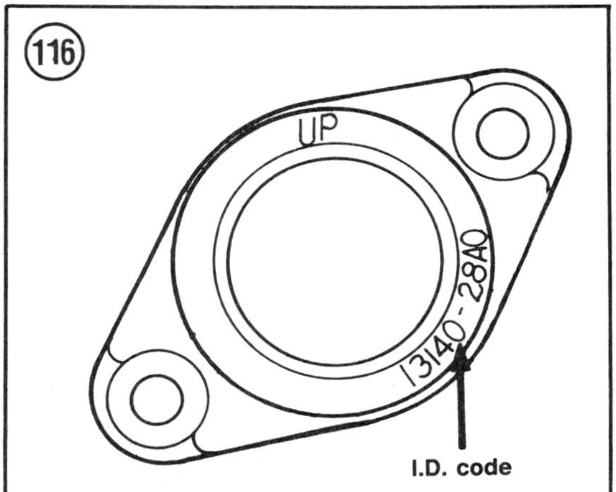

Cylinder No. 1: 13110-28AO
Cylinder No. 2: 13120-28AO
Cylinder No. 3: 13130-28AO
Cylinder No. 4: 13140-28AO

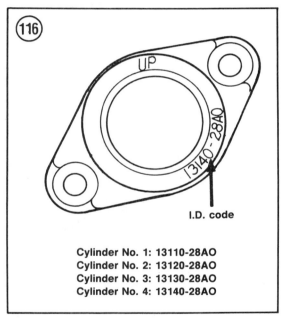

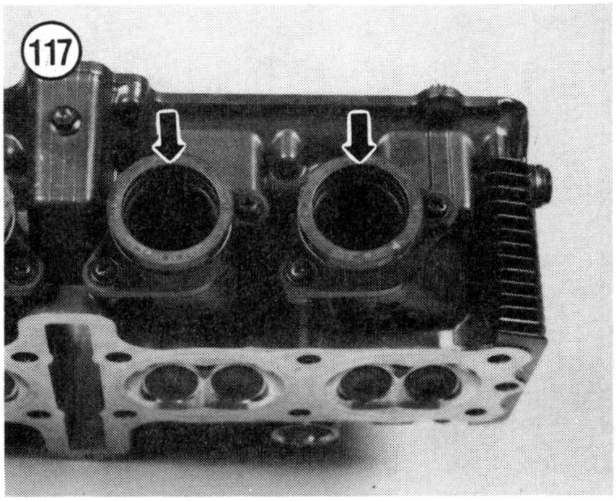

11. Repeat for all valve assemblies.
12. Install the cylinder head as described under *Cylinder Head Installation* in this chapter.

Valve Guide Replacement

Worn valve guides can create excessive valve stem-to-guide clearance or valve wobble. In such cases, the guides must be replaced. This job should be done only by a dealer, as special tools and considerable expertise are required. If the valve guide is replaced, also replace its valve.

The following procedure is provided if you choose to perform this task yourself.

CAUTION
*There **may** be a residual oil or solvent odor left in the oven after heating the cylinder head. If you use a household oven, first check with the person who uses the oven for food preparation to avoid getting into trouble.*

NOTE
*Each intake pipe is unique and must be reinstalled at the correct location on the cylinder head. Mark each pipe prior to removal to ensure proper installation. If installing new intake pipes, refer to **Figure 116** for correct identification numbers and cylinder locations as follows: 13110-28A0 for No. 1, 13120-28A0 for No. 2, 13130-28A0 for No. 3 and 13140-28A0 for No. 4.*

1. Remove the screws securing the intake pipes (**Figure 117**) onto the cylinder head. Remove all intake pipes before placing the cylinder head in the oven.
2. The valve guides are installed with a slight interference fit. Place the cylinder head in a heated oven (or on a hot plate). Heat the cylinder head to a temperature between 100-150° C (212-300° F). An easy way to check the proper temperature is to drop tiny drops of water on the cylinder head; if they sizzle and evaporate immediately, the temperature is correct.

CAUTION
Do not heat the cylinder head with a torch (propane or acetylene); never bring a flame into contact with the cylinder head or valve guide. The direct heat will destroy the case hardening of the valve guide and will likely cause warpage of the cylinder head.

3. Remove the cylinder head from the oven and hold onto it with kitchen pot holders, heavy gloves or heavy shop cloths—*it is very hot.*

4. While heating up the cylinder head, place the new valve guides in a freezer (or refrigerator) if possible. Chilling them will slightly reduce their outside diameter, while the hot cylinder head is slightly larger due to heat expansion. This will make valve guide installation much easier.
5. Turn the cylinder head upside down on wood blocks. Make sure the cylinder is properly supported on the wood blocks.
6. From the combustion chamber side of the cylinder head, drive out the old valve guide (**Figure 118**) with a hammer and valve guide remover. Use Suzuki special tool, Valve Guide Remover/ Installer, part No. 09916-44310. Remove the special tool.
7. Remove and discard the valve guide and the ring. *Never* reinstall a valve guide or ring that has been removed as it is no longer true nor within tolerances.
8. Insert the valve guide hole reamer into the valve guide hole in the cylinder head. Use Suzuki special tools, Valve Guide Hole Reamer, part No. 09916-34580 and Reamer Handle, part No. 09916-34541. Rotate the reamer *clockwise* as shown in **Figure 119**. Continue to rotate the reamer and work it down through the entire length of the valve guide hole in the cylinder head.
9. Rotate the reamer *clockwise* and withdraw the reamer from the valve guide hole in the cylinder head. Remove the reamer and handle.
10. Install a new ring onto the valve guide.

CAUTION
Failure to apply fresh engine oil to both the valve guide and the valve guide hole in the cylinder head will result in damage to the cylinder head and/or the new valve guide.

11. Apply fresh engine oil to the new valve guide and the valve guide hole in the cylinder head.

NOTE
The same Suzuki special tool is used for both removal and installation of the valve guide.

12. From the top side (valve side) of the cylinder head, drive in the new valve guide (**Figure 120**) with a hammer and valve guide remover. Drive the valve guide in until the ring completely seats in the cylinder head. Remove the special tool.
13. After installation, ream the new valve guide as follows:
   a. Use Suzuki special tools, Valve Guide Reamer, part No. 09916-34570 and Reamer Handle, part No. 09916-34541.

118

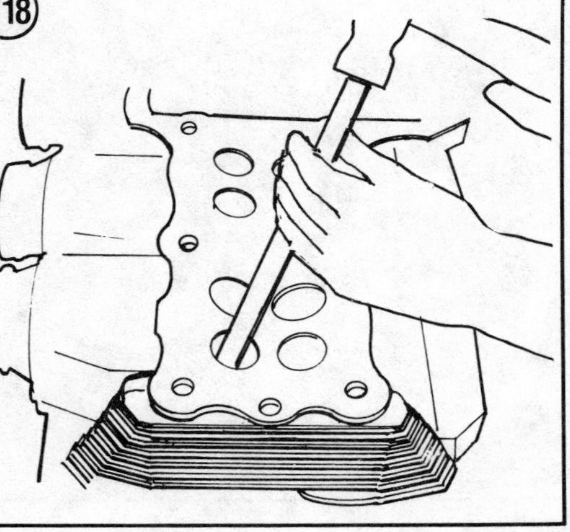

119

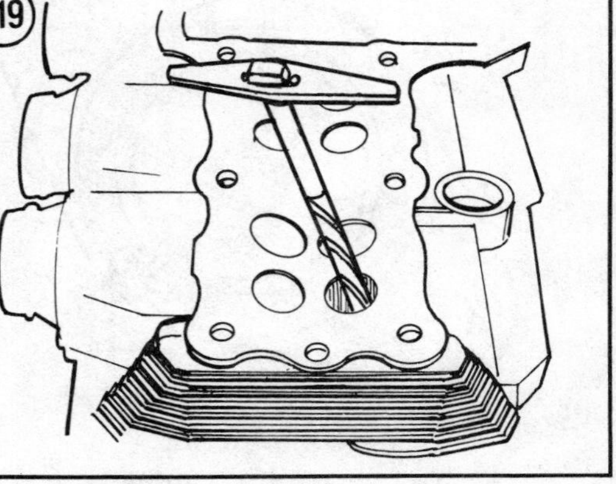

120

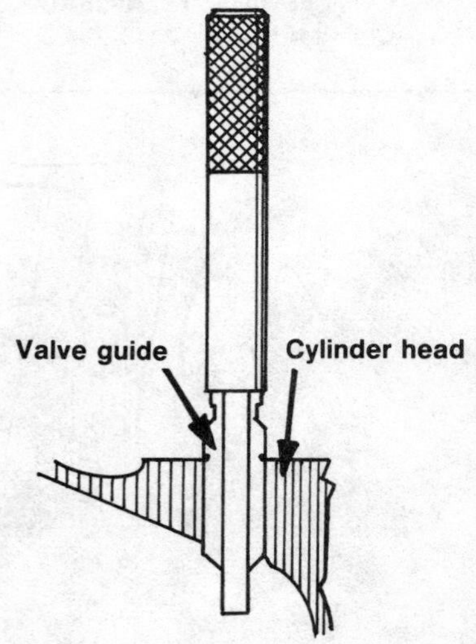

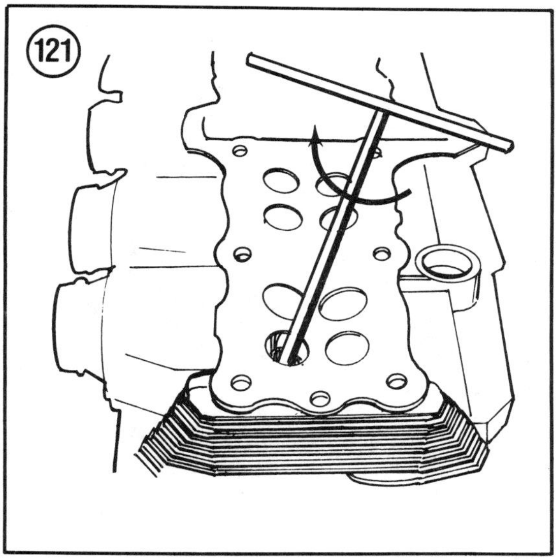

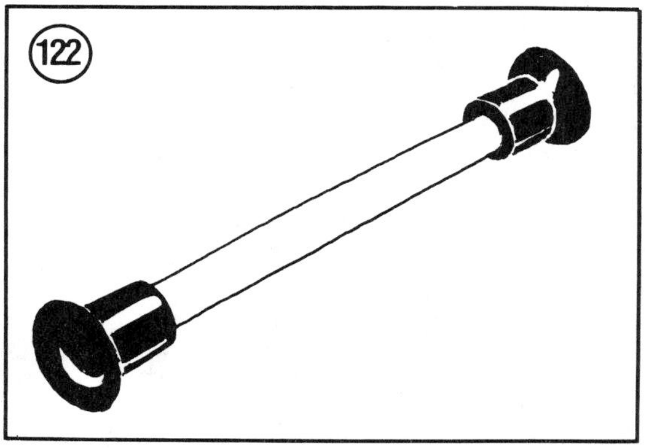

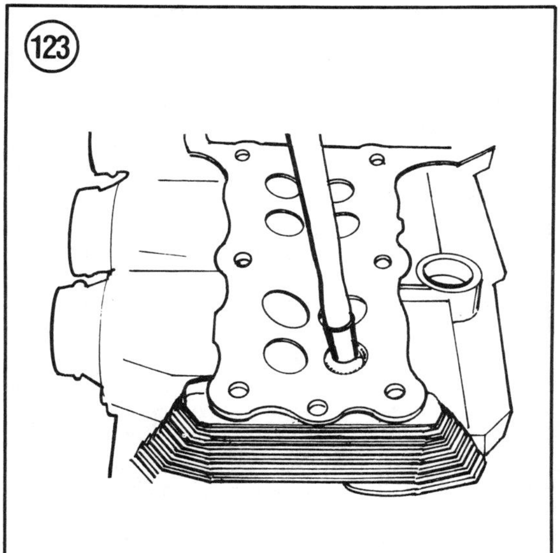

b. Apply cutting oil to both the new valve guide and the valve guide reamer.

CAUTION
***Always** rotate the valve guide reamer **clockwise**. If the reamer is rotated counterclockwise, you will dull its cutting surfaces.*

c. Rotate the reamer *clockwise* as shown in **Figure 121**. Continue to rotate the reamer and work it down through the entire length of the new valve guide. Apply additional cutting oil during this procedure.
d. Rotate the reamer *clockwise* until the reamer has traveled all the way through the new valve guide.
e. Rotate the reamer *clockwise* and withdraw the reamer from the valve guide.

14. If necessary, repeat Steps 1-13 for any other valve guides.
15. Thoroughly clean the cylinder head and valve guides with solvent to wash out all metal particles. Dry with compressed air.
16. Reface the valve seats as described in this chapter.
17. Install the intake pipes (**Figure 117**). To prevent a vacuum leak, install a new O-ring seal between the intake pipe and the cylinder head. Install the intake pipes and tighten the screws securely.

Valve Seat Inspection

1. Remove the valves as described in this chapter.
2. The most accurate method for checking the valve seat width and position is to use Prussian blue or machinist's dye, available from auto parts stores or machine shops. To check the valve seat with Prussian blue or machinist's dye, perform the following:
   a. Thoroughly clean off all carbon deposits from the valve face with solvent or detergent, then thoroughly dry.
   b. Spread a thin layer of Prussian blue or machinist's dye evenly on the valve face.
   c. Moisten the end of a suction cup valve tool (**Figure 122**) and attach it to the valve. Insert the valve into the guide.
   d. Using the suction cup tool, tap the valve up and down in the cylinder head (**Figure 123**). Do *not* rotate the valve or a false indication will result.

e. Remove the valve and examine the impression left by the Prussian blue or machinist's dye. If the impression left in the dye (on the valve or in the cylinder head) is not even and continuous and the valve seat width (**Figure 124**) is not within specified tolerance listed in **Table 1** or **Table 2**, the cylinder head valve seat must be reconditioned.

3. Closely examine the valve seat in the cylinder head. It should be smooth and even with a polished seating surface.
4. If the valve seat is okay, install the valves as described in this chapter.
5. If the valve seat is not correct, recondition the valve seat as described in this chapter.

124

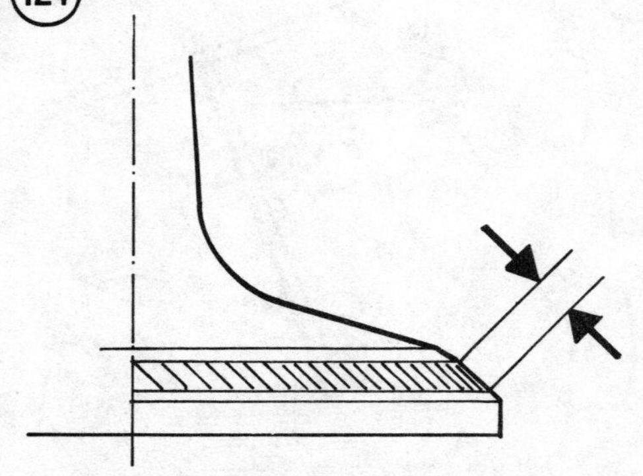

Valve Seat Reconditioning

Special valve seat cutter tools and considerable expertise are required to properly recondition the valve seats in the cylinder head. You can save considerable money by removing the cylinder head and taking just the cylinder head to a dealer or machine shop and have the valve seats ground.

The following procedure is provided if you choose to perform this task yourself.

The Suzuki valve seat cutter and T-handle are available from a Suzuki dealer or from machine shop supply outlets. Follow the manufacturer's instruction in regard to the operating the cutter. You will need the Suzuki Valve Seat Cutter (N-116), a T-handle and the Solid Pilot (N-100-5.0) or equivalent.

The valve seat for both the intake valves and exhaust valves are machined to the same angles. The valve contact surface is cut to a 45° angle and the area above the contract surface (closest to the combustion chamber) is cut to a 15° angle (**Figure 125**).

125

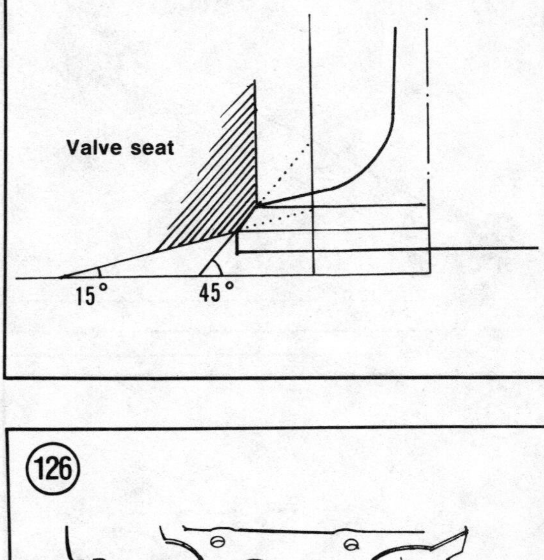

1. Carefully rotate and insert the solid pilot into the valve guide (**Figure 126**). Make sure the pilot is correctly seated.
2. Use the 45° angle side of the cutter, install the cutter and the T-handle onto the solid pilot.
3. Using the 45° cutter, descale and clean the valve seat with one or two turns (**Figure 127**).

CAUTION
Measure the valve seat contact area in the cylinder head after each cut to make sure the contact area is correct and to prevent removing too much material. If too much material is removed, the cylinder head must be replaced.

126

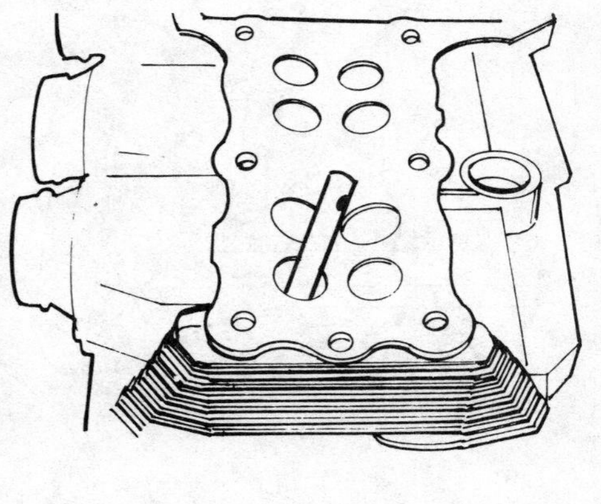

127

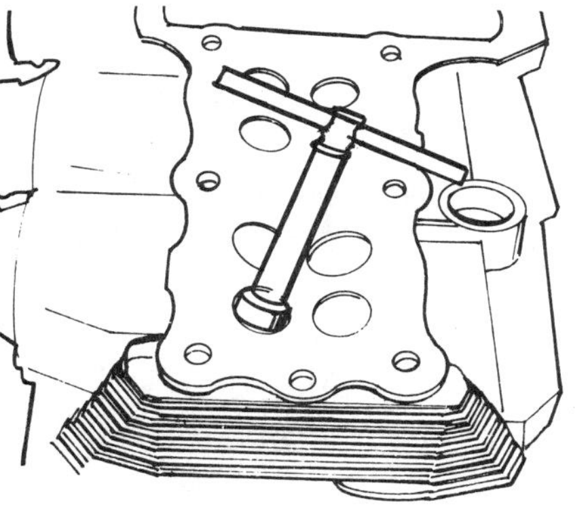

128

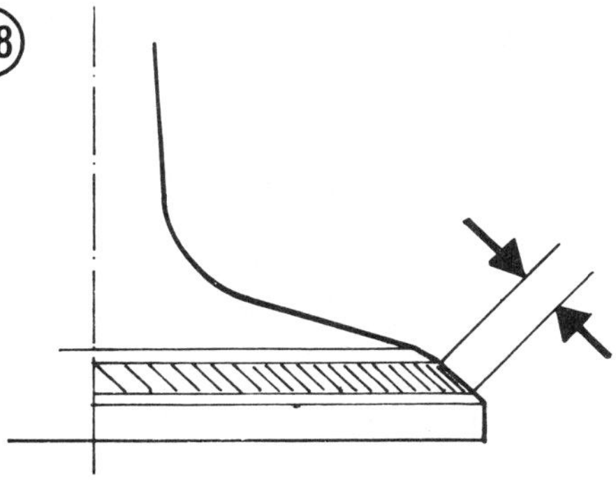

129

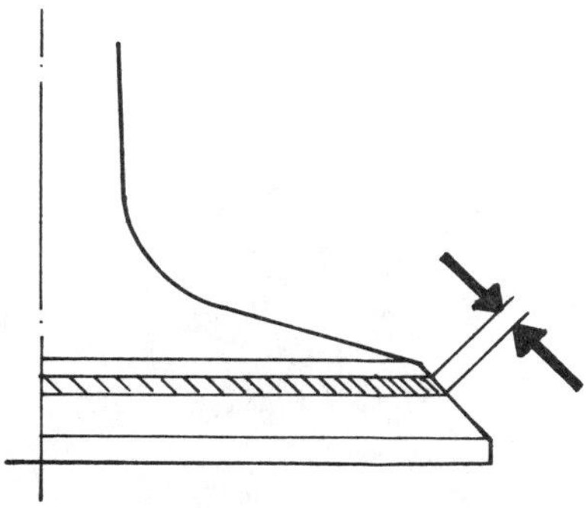

4. If the seat is still pitted or burned, turn the 45 degree cutter additional turns until the surface is clean. Refer to the previous CAUTION to avoid removing too much material from the cylinder head.
5. Remove the valve cutter, T-handle and solid pilot from the cylinder head.
6. Inspect the valve seat-to-valve face impression as follows:
   a. Spread a thin layer of Prussian Blue or machinist's dye evenly on the valve face.
   b. Moisten the end of a suction cup valve tool (**Figure 122**) and attach it to the valve. Insert the valve into the guide.
   c. Using the suction cup tool, tap the valve up and down in the cylinder head. Do *not* rotate the valve or a false indication will result.
   d. Remove the valve and examine the impression left by the Prussian Blue or machinist's dye.
   e. Measure the valve seat width as shown in **Figure 124**. Refer to **Table 1** or **Table 2** for the seat width.
7. If the contact area is too *high* on the valve, or if it is too wide, use the 15° side of the cutter and remove a portion of the top area of the valve seat material to lower and narrow the contact area (**Figure 128**).
8. If the contact area is too *low* on the valve, or too narrow, use the 45° cutter and remove a portion of the lower area of the valve seat material to raise and widen the contact area (**Figure 129**).
9. After the desired valve seat position and angle is obtained, use the 45° side of the cutter and T-handle and very lightly clean off any burrs that may have been caused by the previous cuts.

CAUTION
*Do **not** use any valve lapping compound after the final cut has been made.*

10. Check that the finish has a smooth and velvety surface; it should *not* be shiny or highly polished. The final seating will take place when the engine is first run.
11. Repeat Steps 1-10 for all remaining valve seats.
12. Thoroughly clean the cylinder head and all valve components in solvent or detergent and hot water.

4

13. If the end of the valve stem must be resurfaced, refer to the following:

a. The valve stem can be resurfaced only to the point where there is a *minimum* dimension of 2.5 mm (0.09 in.) (**Figure 130**). If the finished dimension is less than specified, the valve must be replaced.

b. After installing a valve that had its stem resurfaced, check that the tip (A, **Figure 131**) of the stem end is above the valve keeper (B, **Figure 131**). If not, the valve must be replaced.

14. If the cylinder head and valve components were cleaned in detergent and hot water, apply a light coat of engine oil to all non-aluminum metal surfaces to prevent any rust formations.

15. Install the valve assemblies as described in this chapter.

130

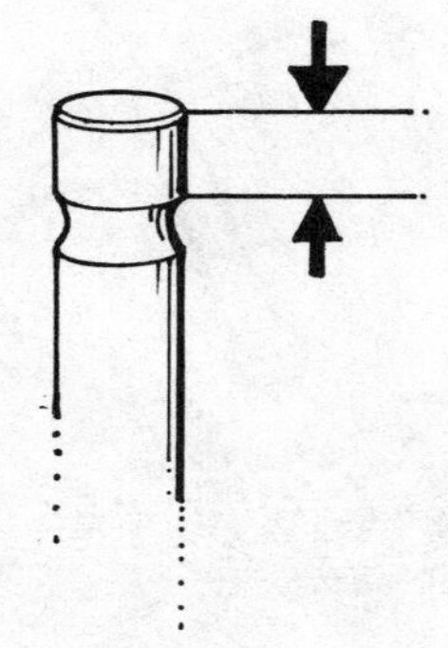

131

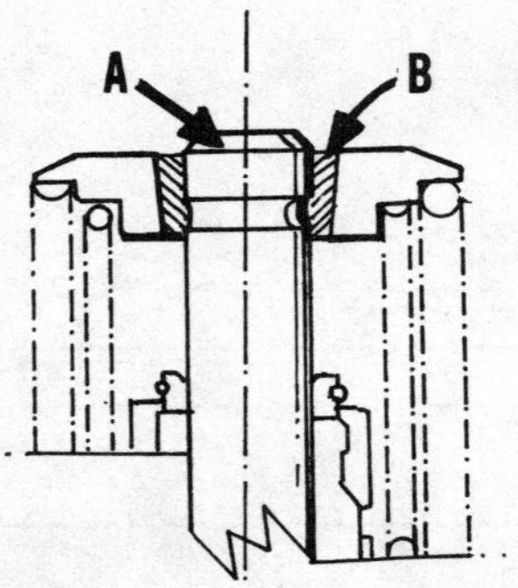

CYLINDER BLOCK

Removal

1. Remove the cylinder head as described under *Cylinder Head Removal/Installation* in this chapter.

2. Remove the bolts securing the rear external oil line (**Figure 132**) to the crankcase. Remove the oil line assembly and the O-ring seal at the base of the assembly.

3. Remove the cylinder head as described under *Cylinder Head Removal* in this chapter.

4. Remove the cylinder head gasket and the locating dowels.

5. If not already removed, remove the front oil pipes (**Figure 133**) from the crankcase. Discard the O-ring seals.

6. Remove the nut (**Figure 134**) securing the front portion of the cylinder block to the crankcase.

7. Loosen the cylinder block by tapping around the perimeter with a rubber or plastic mallet. If necessary, *gently* pry the cylinder loose with a broad-tipped screwdriver.

CAUTION

Remember, the cooling fins are fragile and may be damaged if tapped or pried on too hard. Never use a metal hammer.

8. Pull the cylinder block (**Figure 135**) straight up and off of the pistons and crankcase studs. Work the camshaft chain wire through the opening in the cylinder. Reattach the wire to the exterior of the crankcase (**Figure 136**).

132

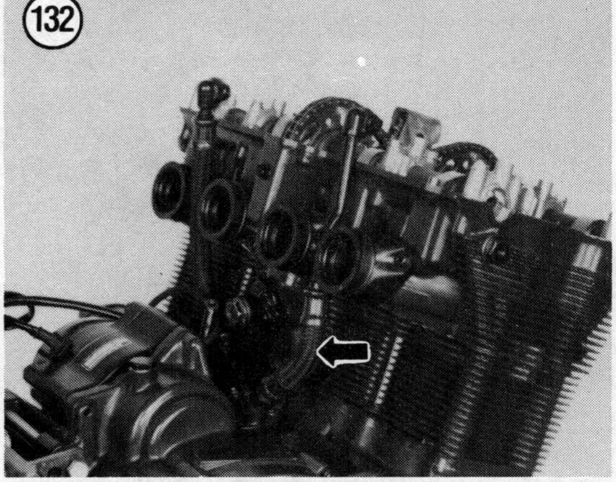

9. Remove the cylinder base gasket and discard it. Remove the locating dowels from the crankcase receptacles.
10. Stuff clean shop cloths into the crankcase openings and under the pistons to prevent the entry of foreign matter and small objects.

Inspection

The following procedure requires the use of highly specialized and expensive measuring instruments. If such equipment is not readily available, have the measurements performed by a dealer or qualified machine shop.

1. Soak with solvent any old cylinder head gasket material on the cylinder block. If necessary use a broad-tipped *dull* chisel and gently scrape off all gasket residue. Do not gouge the sealing surface as oil leaks will result.
2. Measure the cylinder bore with a cylinder bore gauge or inside micrometer at the points shown in **Figure 137**. Measure in 2 axes—in line with the piston-pin and at 90° to the pin. If the taper or out-of-round is 0.05 mm (0.002 in.) or greater in one cylinder, the cylinder block must be rebored to the next oversize and new pistons and piston rings installed. Rebore all 4 cylinders to the same size even though only one may be worn.

NOTE
The new pistons must be obtained before the cylinder are rebored so that the pistons can be measured; slight manufacturing tolerances must be taken into account to determine the actual size and working clearance.

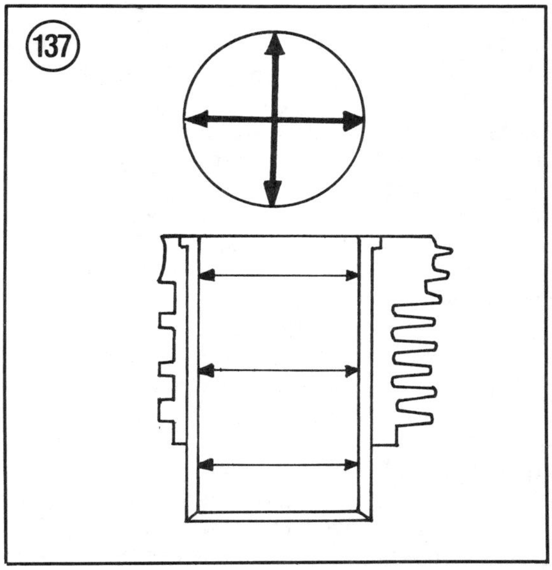

4

3. Check the cylinder walls (**Figure 138**) for deep scratches; if evident, the cylinders should be rebored.

NOTE

*The maximum wear limit on the cylinders is listed in **Table 1** or **Table 2**. If any cylinder is worn to this limit, the cylinder block must be replaced. Never rebore a cylinder(s) if the finished rebore diameter will be this dimension or greater.*

NOTE

After having the cylinder block rebored, wash it thoroughly in hot soapy water. This is the best way to clean the cylinders of all fine grit material left from the bore job. After washing the cylinder block, run a clean white cloth through each cylinder; the cloth should show no traces of dirt or other debris. If the rag is dirty, the cylinder(s) is not clean enough and must be rewashed. After the cylinder block is thoroughly clean, dry and lubricate each cylinder wall with clean engine oil to prevent the cylinder liners from rusting.

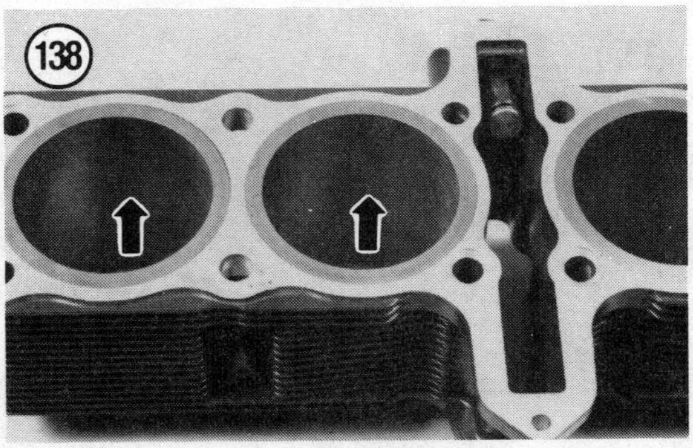
138

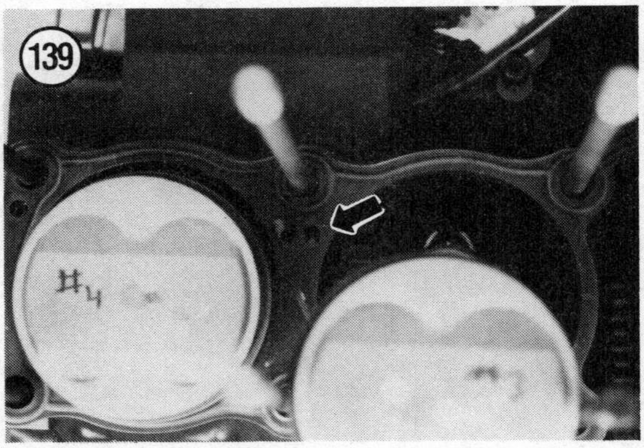
139

Installation

1. Check that the top surface of the crankcase and the bottom surface of the cylinder block are clean before installing a new base gasket.
2. Install a new cylinder base gasket with the UP mark (**Figure 139**) facing up.
3. Install the locating dowels (**Figure 140**) on the 2 front center crankcase studs.
4. Turn the crankshaft so the two inside pistons (No. 2 and No. 3) are at top dead center. Install a piston holding fixture under the 2 center pistons.
5. Make sure the end gaps of the piston rings are *not* lined up with each other—they must be staggered. Lightly oil the piston rings and the inside of the cylinder bores with clean engine oil.
6. Carefully feed the camshaft chain and wire up through the opening in the cylinder block and tie it to the engine.
7. Start the cylinder block down over the center pistons and crankcase studs (**Figure 141**). Compress each piston ring with your fingers as it enters the cylinder.
8. Slide the cylinder block down until it bottoms on the piston holding fixtures.
9. Remove the piston holding fixtures and slide the cylinder down over the outside pistons compressing the rings as they enter the cylinder.

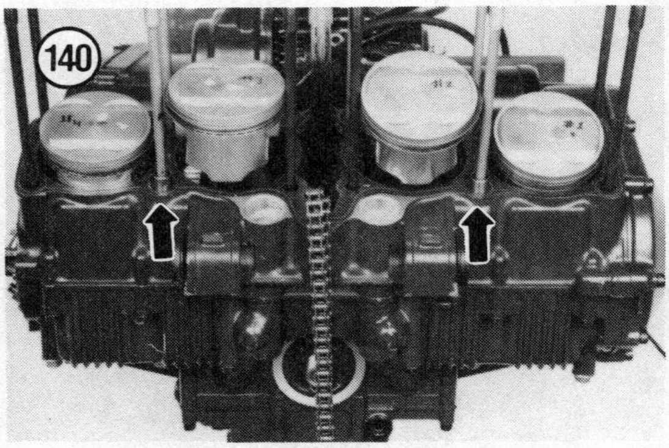
140

141

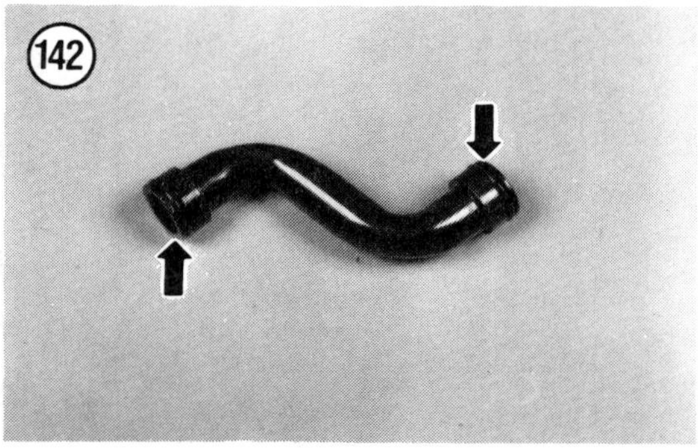

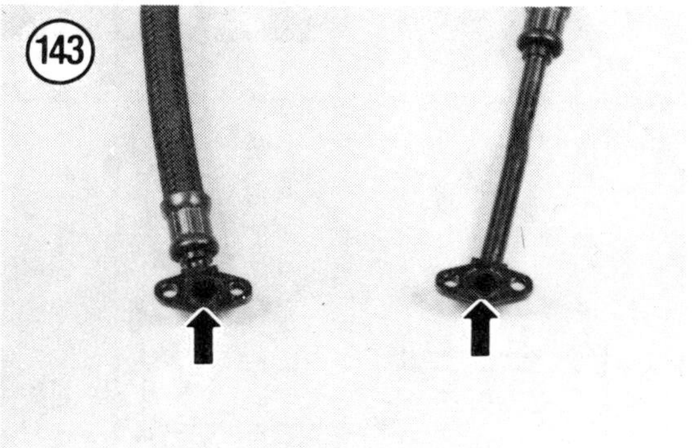

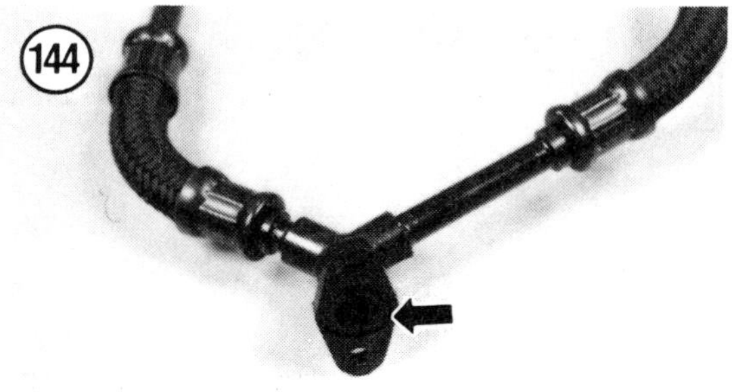

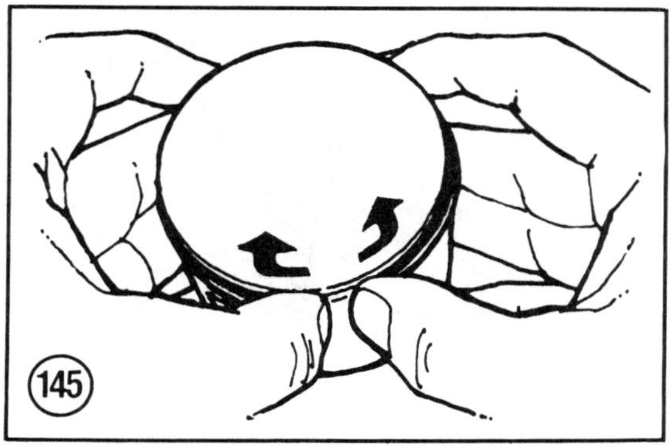

Once the outside pistons have entered the cylinder, push the cylinder block into place on the crankcase.

10. Install the nut (**Figure 134**) securing the front portion of the cylinder block to the crankcase and tighten to the torque specification listed in **Table 3**.
11. Install a new O-ring seal at each end of the front oil pipes (**Figure 142**). Install both front oil pipes into the receptacles in the crankcase.
12. Install the cylinder head as described under *Cylinder Head Installation* in this chapter.
13. Install a new O-ring seal into all 3 ends of the rear external oil line assembly. Refer to **Figure 143** and **Figure 144**.
14. Install the oil line assembly and tighten the bolts securing the rear external oil line (**Figure 132**) to the crankcase.
15. Install the cylinder head cover as described under *Cylinder Head Cover Removal/Installation* in this chapter.
16. Follow the *Break-in Procedure* in this chapter if the cylinder block was rebored or honed or new pistons or piston rings were installed.

4

PISTONS, PISTON PINS AND PISTON RINGS

The pistons are made of an aluminum alloy. The piston pins are made of steel and are full-floating in the small end of the connecting rod. The piston pin is held in place by a clip at each end.

Piston Removal

1. Remove the cylinder head and cylinder as described in this chapter.

WARNING
The edges of all piston rings are very sharp. Be careful when handling them to avoid cutting fingers.

2. Remove the top ring with a ring expander tool or by spreading the ends with your thumbs just enough to slide the ring up over the piston (**Figure 145**). Repeat for the remaining rings.
3. Before removing the piston, hold the rod tightly and try to move the piston up and down on the connecting rod. Any motion (do not confuse with the normal sliding motion) indicates wear on the piston pin, piston pin bore or connecting rod small-end bore (more likely a combination of these).

NOTE
Wrap a clean shop cloth under the piston so that the piston pin clip will not fall into the crankcase.

4. Lightly mark the top of the piston with an identification number (1 through 4), starting with the No. 1 piston on the left-hand side (**Figure 146**). The left-hand side refers to a rider sitting on the seat facing forward. These marks will make it easier to assure that the pistons will be installed into the correct cylinder bores during installation.
5. Remove the clip from each side of the piston pin bore (**Figure 147**) with a small screwdriver or scribe. Hold your thumb over one edge of the clip when removing it to prevent the clip from springing out.
6. Use a proper size wooden dowel or socket extension and push out the piston pin. Once the piston is free of the connecting rod, push the piston pin back into the piston so that they will be reassembled into the same set.

CAUTION
Be careful when removing the pin to avoid damaging the connecting rod. If it is necessary to gently tap the pin to remove it, be sure that the piston is properly supported so that lateral shock is not transmitted to the connecting rod bearing.

7. If the piston pin is difficult to remove, heat the piston and pin with a hair dryer. The pin will probably push right out. Heat the piston to only about 140° F (60° C), i.e., until it is too warm to touch, but not excessively hot. If the pin is still difficult to push out, use a homemade tool as shown in **Figure 148**.
8. If the piston is going to be left off for some time, place a piece of foam insulation tube over the end of the rod to protect it.
9. Repeat Steps 5-9 for the remaining pistons.

146
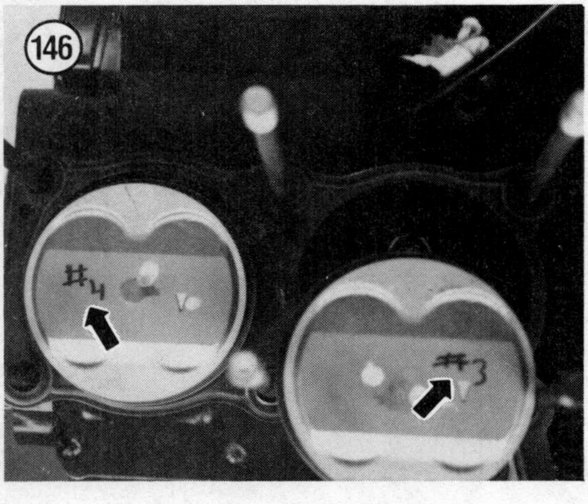

147
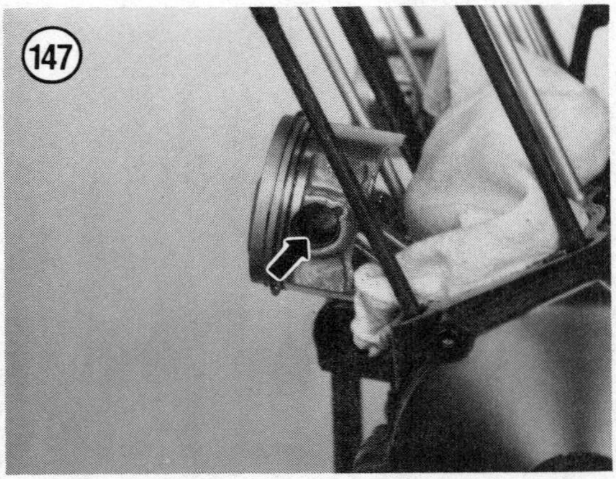

148
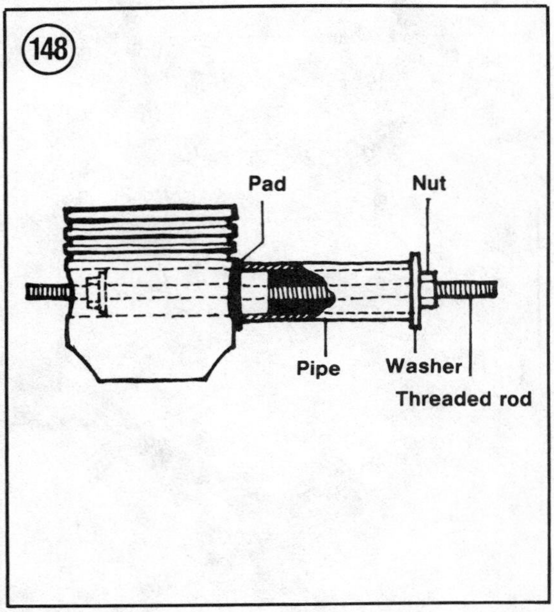

149
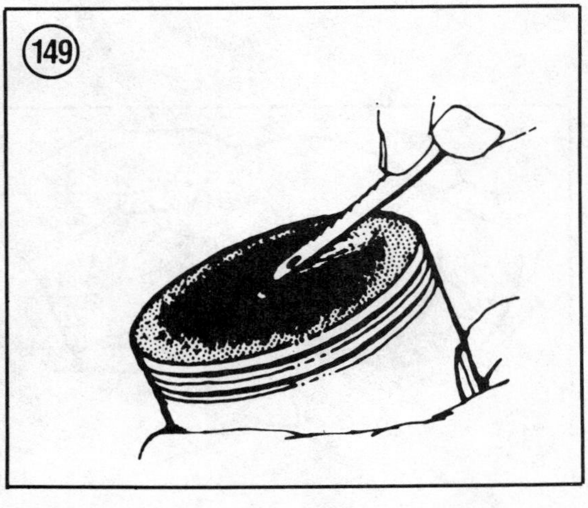

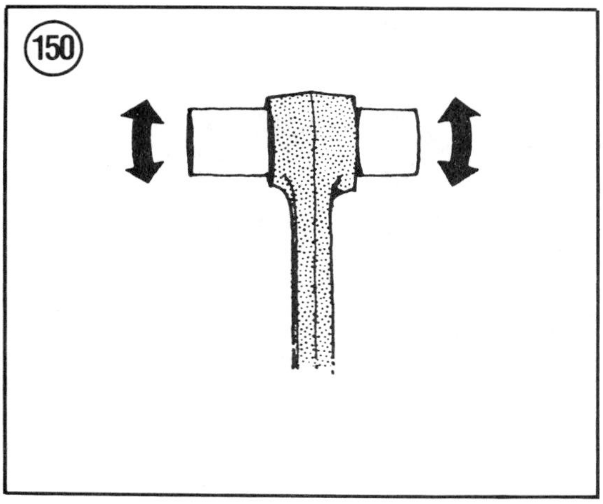

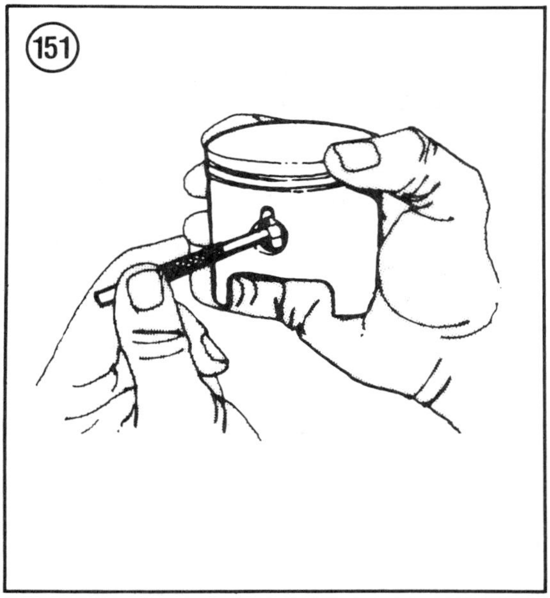

Inspection

1. Carefully clean the carbon from the piston crown with a chemical remover or with a soft scraper (**Figure 149**). Do not remove or damage the carbon ridge around the circumference of the piston above the top ring. If the pistons, rings and cylinders are found to be dimensionally correct and can be reused, removal of the carbon ring from the top of the piston or the carbon ridge from the top of the cylinder wall will promote excessive oil consumption in this cylinder.

CAUTION
Do not wire brush the piston skirts.

2. Examine each ring groove for burrs, dented edges and wide wear. Pay particular attention to the top compression ring groove as it usually wears more than the other grooves.
3. If damage or wear indicates piston replacement, select a new piston as described under *Piston Clearance* in this chapter.
4. Oil the piston pin and install it in the connecting rod. Slowly rotate the piston pin and check for radial play (**Figure 150**). If any play exists, the piston pin should be replaced, providing the rod bore is in good condition.
5. Measure the inside diameter of the piston pin bore with a snap gauge (**Figure 151**) and measure the outside diameter of the piston pin with a micrometer (**Figure 152**). Compare with dimensions given in **Table 1** or **Table 2**. Replace the piston and piston pin as a set if either or both are worn.

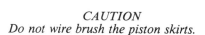

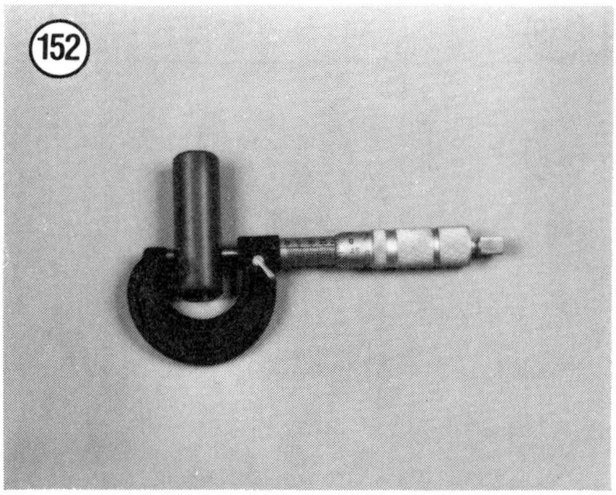

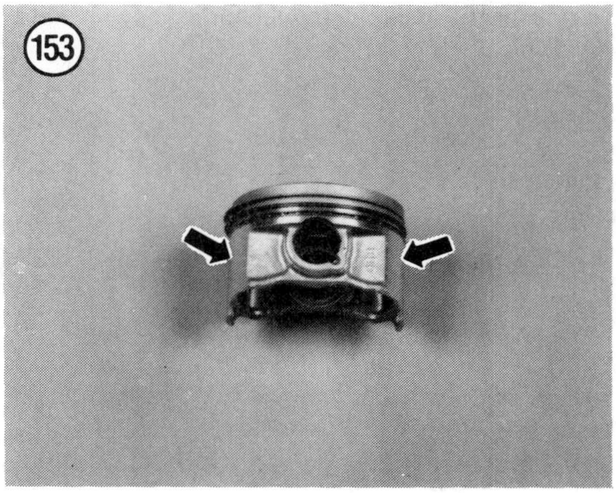

6. Check the piston skirt (**Figure 153**) for galling and abrasion which may have been caused by piston seizure. If a piston(s) shows signs of partial seizure (bits of aluminum build-up on the piston skirt), the pistons should be replaced and the cylinders bored (if necessary) to reduce the possibility of engine noise and further piston seizure.
7. Check the oil control holes in the piston pin area (**Figure 154**) for carbon or oil sludge build-up. Clean the holes with a small diameter drill bit by hand.

Piston Clearance

1. Make sure the pistons and cylinder walls are clean and dry.
2. Measure the inside diameter of the cylinder bore at a point 13 mm (1/2 in.) from the upper edge with a bore gauge.
3. Measure the outside diameter of each piston across the skirt (**Figure 155**) at right angles to the piston pin. Measure at a distance 15 mm (0.60 in.) up from the bottom of the piston skirt (**Figure 156**).
4. Piston clearance is the difference between the maximum piston diameter and the minimum cylinder diameter. Subtract the dimension of the piston from the cylinder dimension and compare to the dimension listed in **Table 1** or **Table 2**. If the clearance exceeds that specified, the cylinders should be rebored to the next oversize and a new pistons installed.
5. To establish a final overbore dimension with new pistons, add the piston skirt measurement to the specified clearance. This will determine the dimension for the cylinder overbore size. Remember, do not exceed the cylinder maximum service limit inside diameter indicated in **Table 1** or **Table 2**.

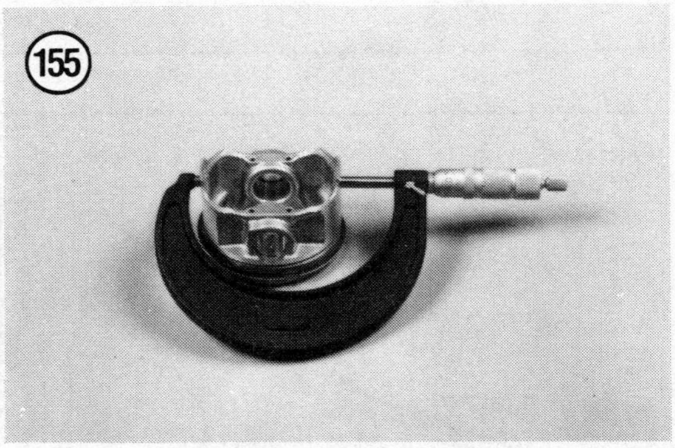

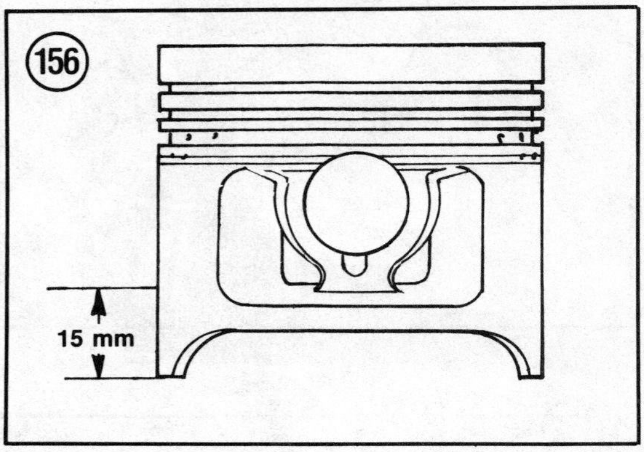

Piston Installation

1. Apply molybdenum disulfide grease to the inside surface of the connecting rod's small end.

CAUTION
New piston pin clips must be installed during assembly. Piston pin clips were not designed to be reused. A broken clip will cause severe damage to a cylinder. Install the clips with the gap away from the cutout in the piston.

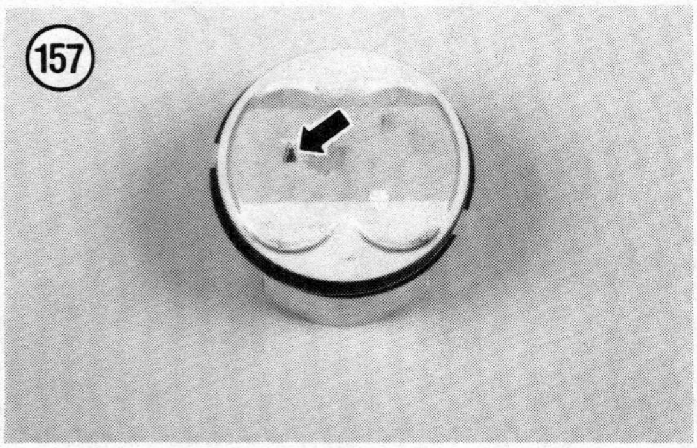

2. Install one piston pin clip in each piston on the side that faces toward the center of the engine. The ends of the clip must not align with the cutout in the piston pin bore. The arrow on top of the piston (**Figure 157**) must point toward the front of the engine.
3. Oil the piston pin with fresh engine oil and install the piston pin in the piston until its end extends slightly beyond the inside of the boss (**Figure 158**).

158

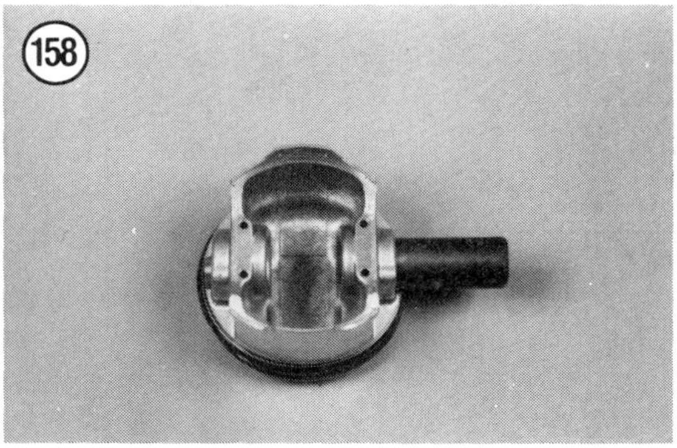

159

160

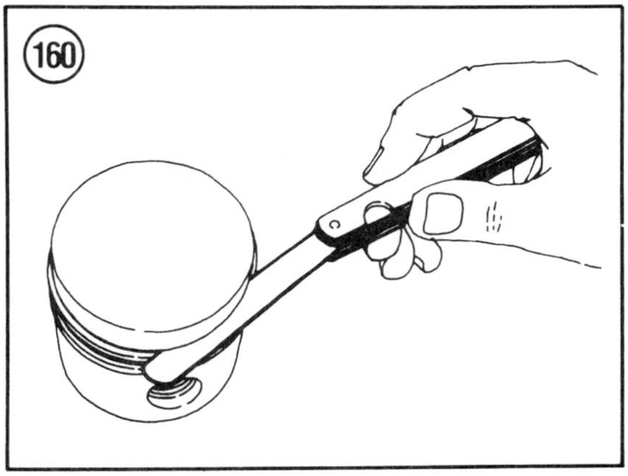

4. Place the piston over the connecting rod. If you are reusing the same pistons and connecting rods, match the pistons to the rod from which it came. If the cylinders were bored, install the pistons as marked by the machinist. Remember that the arrow on top of the piston (**Figure 157**) must point toward the front of the engine.

CAUTION
When installing the piston pin in Step 4 do not push the pin in too far, or the piston pin clip installed in Step 2 will be forced into the piston metal, destroying the clip groove and loosening the clip.

5. Line up the piston pin with the hole in the connecting rod. Push the piston pin into the connecting rod. It may be necessary to move the piston around until the piston pin enters the connecting rod. Do not use force during installation or damage may occur. Push the piston pin in until it touches the pin clip on the other side of the piston.
6. If the piston pin does not slide easily, use the homemade tool used during removal but eliminate the piece of pipe. Pull the piston pin in until it stops.
7. After the piston is installed, recheck and make sure that the arrow on top of the piston (**Figure 159**) is pointing toward the front of the engine and that you have installed the correct piston on that connecting rod.

NOTE
In the next step, install the second clip with the gap away from the cutout in the piston.

8. Install the second piston pin clip in the groove in the piston. Make sure both piston pin clips are seated in the grooves in the piston.
9. Check the installation by rocking the piston back and forth around the pin axis and from side to side along the axis. It should rotate freely back and forth but not from side to side.
10. Repeat Steps 1-9 for the remaining pistons.
11. Install the piston rings as described in this chapter.
12. Install the cylinder and cylinder head as described in this chapter.

Piston Ring Replacement

WARNING
The edges of all piston rings are very sharp. Be careful when handling them to avoid cutting fingers.

1. Measure the side clearance of each ring in its groove with a flat feeler gauge (**Figure 160**) and

compare to dimensions given in **Table 1** or **Table 2**. If the clearance is greater than specified, the rings must be replaced. If the clearance is still excessive with the new rings, the piston(s) must also be replaced.

2. Remove the old top ring by spreading the ends with your thumbs just enough to slide the ring up over the piston (**Figure 161**). Repeat for the remaining rings.
3. Carefully remove all carbon build-up from the ring grooves with a broken piston ring (**Figure 162**). Do not remove any aluminum; only carbon. Inspect the grooves carefully for burrs, nicks or broken and cracked lands. Recondition or replace the piston if necessary.
4. Roll each ring around its piston groove as shown in **Figure 163** to check for binding. Minor binding may be cleaned up with a fine-cut file.
5. Measure the thickness of each compression ring with a micrometer (**Figure 164**) and compare to dimensions given in **Table 1** or **Table 2**. If the thickness is less than specified, the ring(s) must be replaced.
6. First, measure the free end gap of each compression ring with a vernier caliper (**Figure 165**) and compare to dimensions given in **Table 1** or **Table 2**. If the end gap is greater than specified, the ring(s) must be replaced.
7. After measuring the free end gap, place each compression ring, one at a time, into the cylinder and push it in about 20 mm (3/4 in.) with the crown of the piston to ensure that the ring is square in the cylinder bore. Measure the gap with a flat feeler gauge (**Figure 166**) and compare to dimensions in **Table 1** or **Table 2**. If the gap is greater than specified, the rings should be replaced.

162

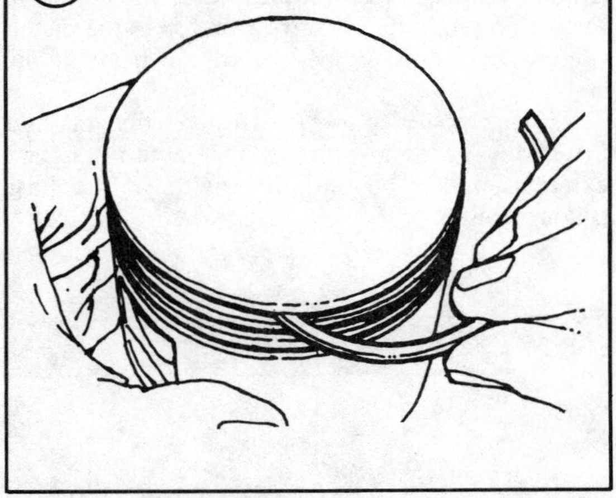

163

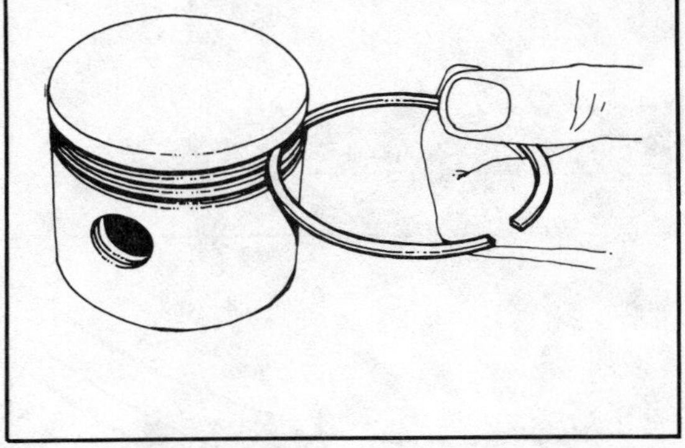

161

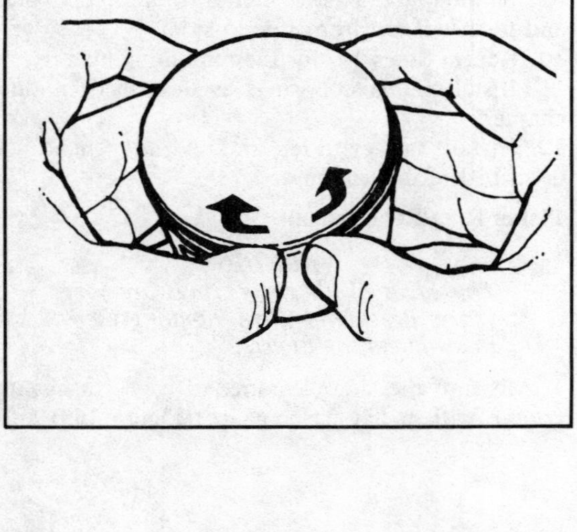

164

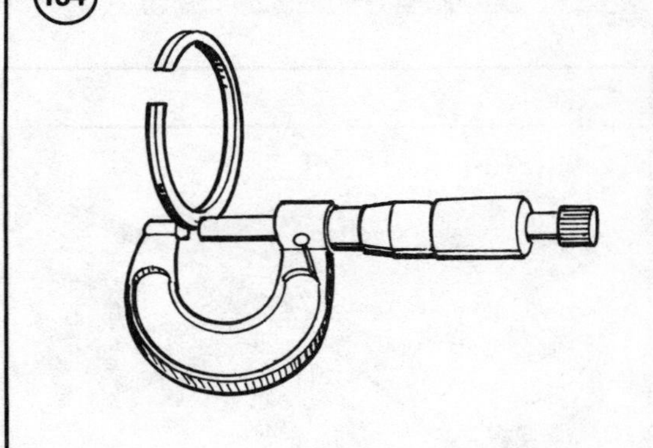

165

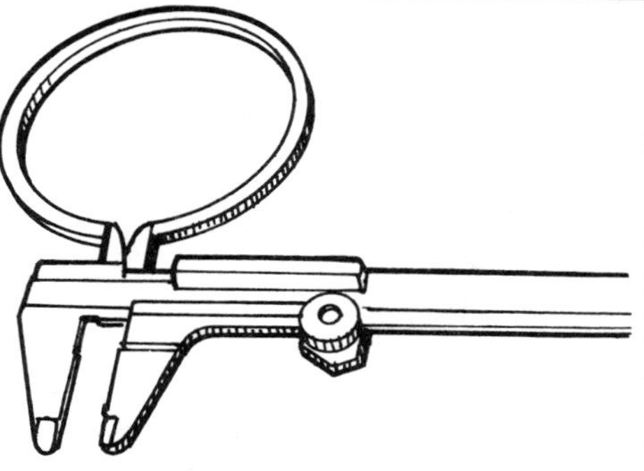

166

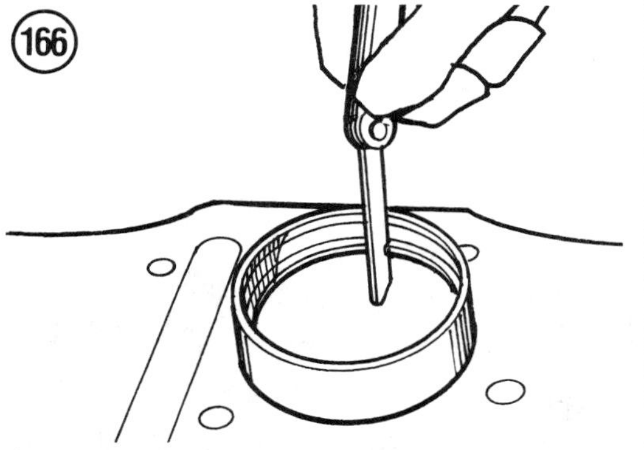

167

168

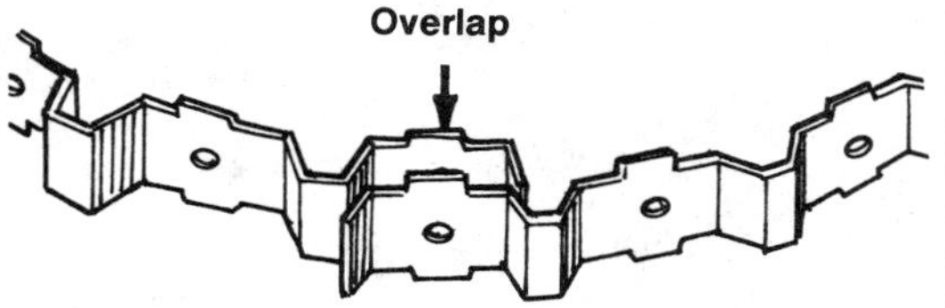

8. When installing new rings, measure their end gap as described in Step 6 and Step 7 and compare to dimensions given in **Table 1** or **Table 2**. If the end gap is greater than specified, the cylinder may be worn excessively. Check the cylinder inside diameter.

NOTE
*Install the 2nd ring with its "R" mark facing up (**Figure 167**).*

9. If new rings are installed, the cylinders must be deglazed or honed. This will help to seat the new rings. Refer honing service to a Suzuki dealer or competent machine shop. After honing, measure the end clearance of each ring (**Figure 166**) and compare to dimensions in **Table 1** or **Table 2**.

CAUTION
*If the cylinders were deglazed or honed, clean each cylinder as described under **Cylinder Block Inspection** in this chapter.*

CAUTION
*Do **not** allow the 2 ends of the oil ring spacer to overlap in the piston groove. **Figure 168** shows an **incorrect** situation.*

10. Install the oil ring spacer first (A, **Figure 169**), then both side rails (B, **Figure 169**). Suzuki factory new oil ring side rails do not have top and bottom designations and can be installed either way. If reassembling used parts, install the side rails as they were removed.

169

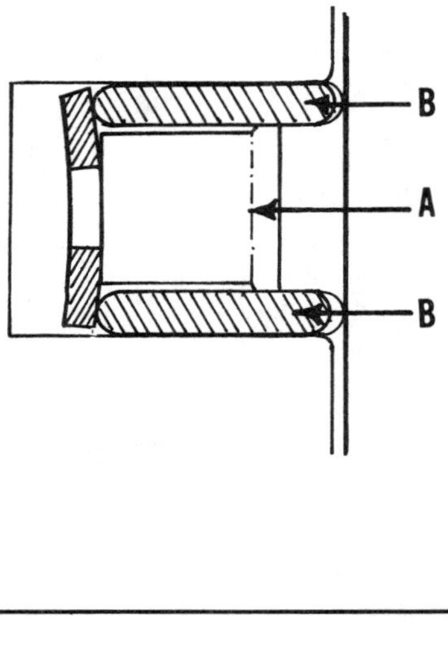

4

11. Install the second compression ring (with slight side taper), then the top by carefully spreading the ends of the ring with your thumbs and slipping ring over the top of the piston (**Figure 161**). Remember that the marks on the piston rings are toward the top of the piston and installed in the order shown in **Figure 170**.

12. Make sure the rings are seated completely in their grooves all the way around the piston and that the ends are distributed around the piston as shown in **Figure 171**. The important thing is that the ring gaps are not aligned with each other when installed to prevent compression pressures from escaping past them.

13. If installing oversized compression rings, check the ring number (A, **Figure 172**) to make sure the correct rings are being installed. The ring oversize numbers should be the same as the piston oversize numbers.

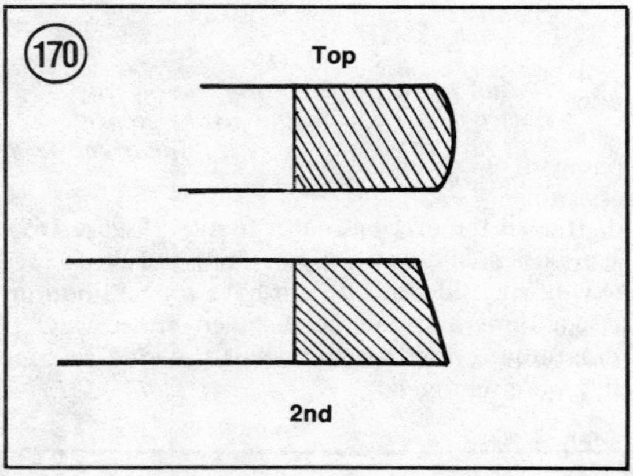

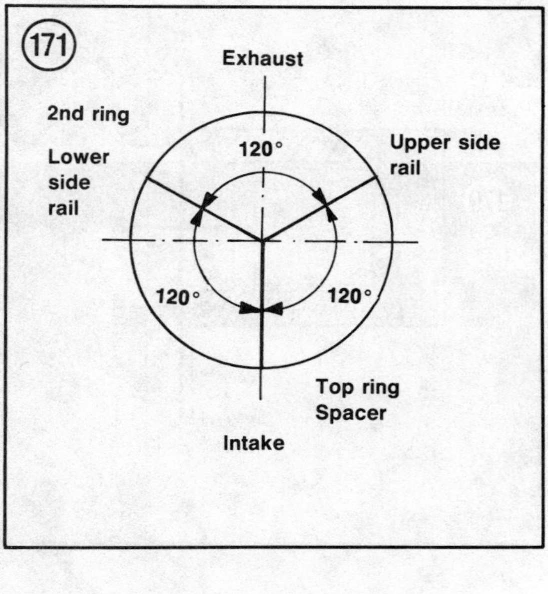

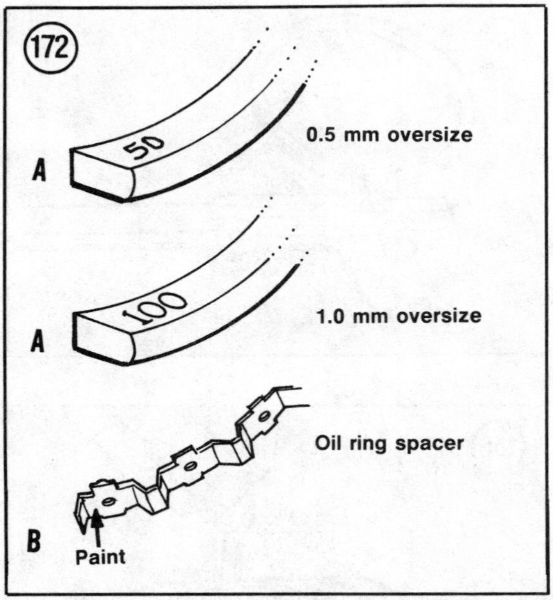

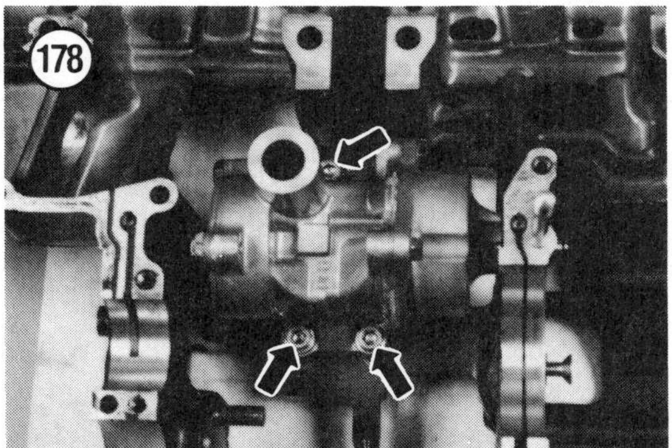

14. If installing oversized oil rings, check the paint color spot (B, **Figure 172**) to make sure the correct oil rings are being installed. The paint color spots are as follows:
   a. Blue: standard size.
   b. Red: 0.5 mm oversize.
   c. Yellow: 1.0 mm oversize.
15. Follow the *Break-in Procedure* in this chapter if new pistons or new piston rings have been installed.

4

OIL PUMP

Removal/Installation

1. Remove the engine and separate the crankcase as described under *Crankcase Disassembly* in this chapter.
2. Remove the circlip (**Figure 173**) and outer thrust washer (**Figure 174**) securing the oil pump drive sprocket to the oil pump.
3. Remove the oil pump drive sprocket (**Figure 175**) from the oil pump.
4. Remove the drive pin (**Figure 176**) and the inner thrust washer (**Figure 177**).
5. Remove the bolts (**Figure 178**) securing the oil pump to the crankcase and remove the oil pump assembly.
6. Remove the O-ring (A, **Figure 179**) and the locating dowels (B, **Figure 179**). Discard the O-ring.
7. Inspect the oil pump as described under *Oil Pump Inspection* in this chapter.

CAUTION

To prevent loss of oil pressure and to prevent an oil leak, always install a new O-ring between the crankcase and the oil pump.

8. Install the locating dowels (B, **Figure 179**) and a new O-ring (A, **Figure 179**).
9. Install the oil pump onto the crankcase.

10. Apply Loctite Lock N' Seal to the mounting bolts prior to installation. Install the bolts and tighten to the torque specification listed in **Table 3**.
11. Install the inner thrust washer (**Figure 177**) and the drive pin (**Figure 176**).
12. Align the notch in the oil pump drive sprocket with the drive pin (**Figure 180**) and install the oil pump drive sprocket (**Figure 175**) onto the oil pump.
13. Install the outer thrust washer (**Figure 174**) and the circlip (**Figure 173**) securing the oil pump drive sprocket to the oil pump.
14. Assemble the crankcase as described under *Crankcase Assembly* in this chapter.

Inspection

Replacement parts are *not* available for the oil pump. If the oil pump is not operating properly, the entire oil pump assembly must be replaced.

CAUTION
Do not try to disassemble the oil pump, as replacement parts and lockwashers are not available.

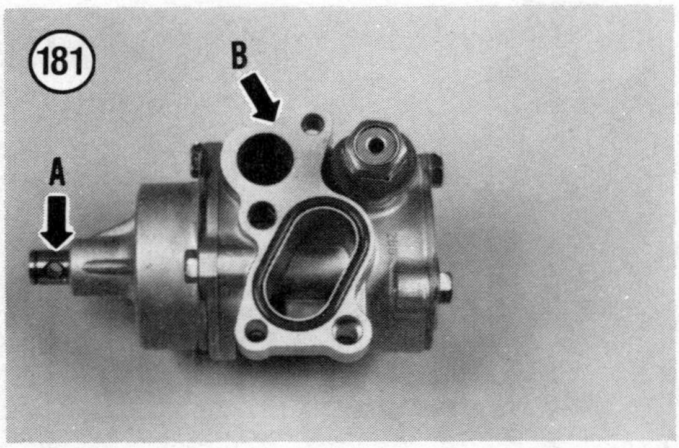

1. Rotate the drive shaft (A, **Figure 181**). If there is any binding or sign of wear; replace the oil pump assembly.
2. Make sure the locking tabs on the lockwashers are in place and bent up against one side of the bolts securing the oil pump together. Refer to **Figure 182** and **Figure 183**.
3. Inspect the oil pump body (B, **Figure 181**) for cracks or damage.
4. Make sure the integral relief valve (**Figure 184**) is secured tightly to the oil pump body.
5. Inspect the teeth on the oil pump drive sprocket. Replace the sprocket if the teeth are damaged or any are missing.

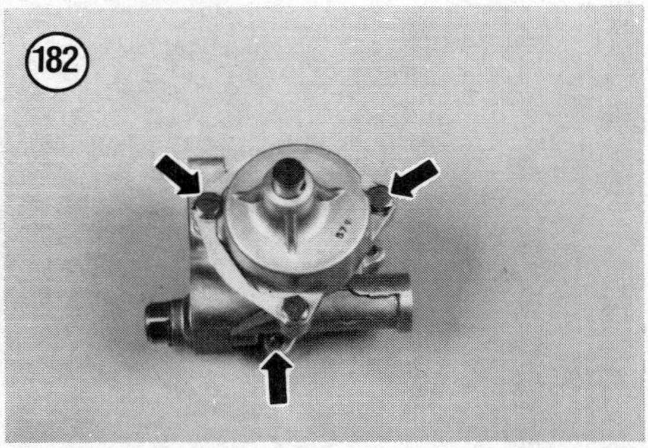

OIL COOLER

Removal/Installation

Refer to **Figure 185** for this procedure.
1. Drain the engine oil as described under *Engine Oil and Filter Change* in Chapter Three.
2. Remove the front fairing as described under *Front Fairing Removal/Installation* in Chapter Twelve.
3. Move the oil drain pan used in Step 1 under each oil line fitting, as additional oil will drain out when the union bolts are removed from the oil pan.
4. Remove the union bolts and sealing washers securing the lower portion of the oil lines to the oil pan. Refer to **Figure 186** for the right-hand side and **Figure 187** for the left-hand side.

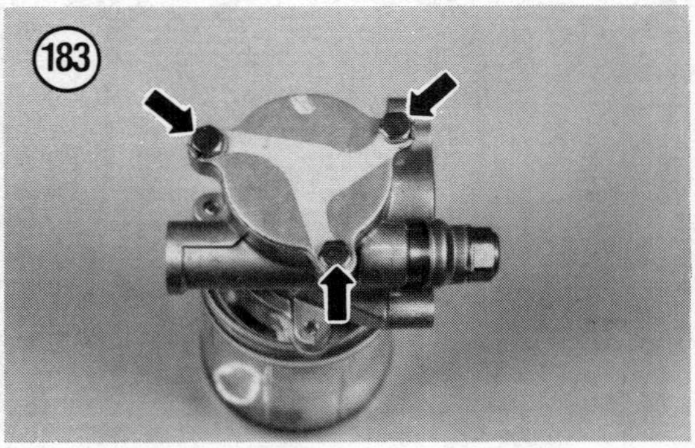

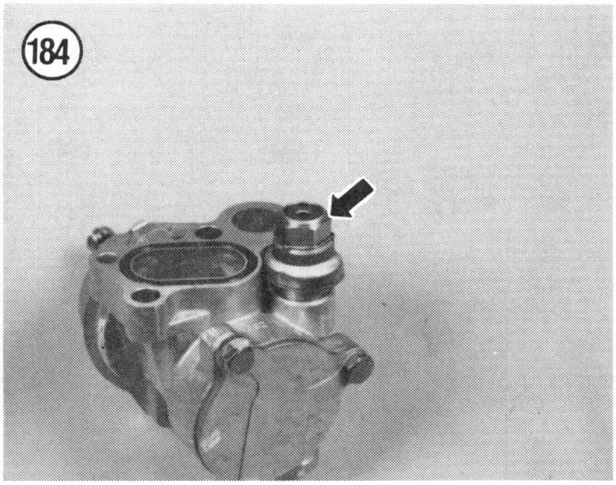

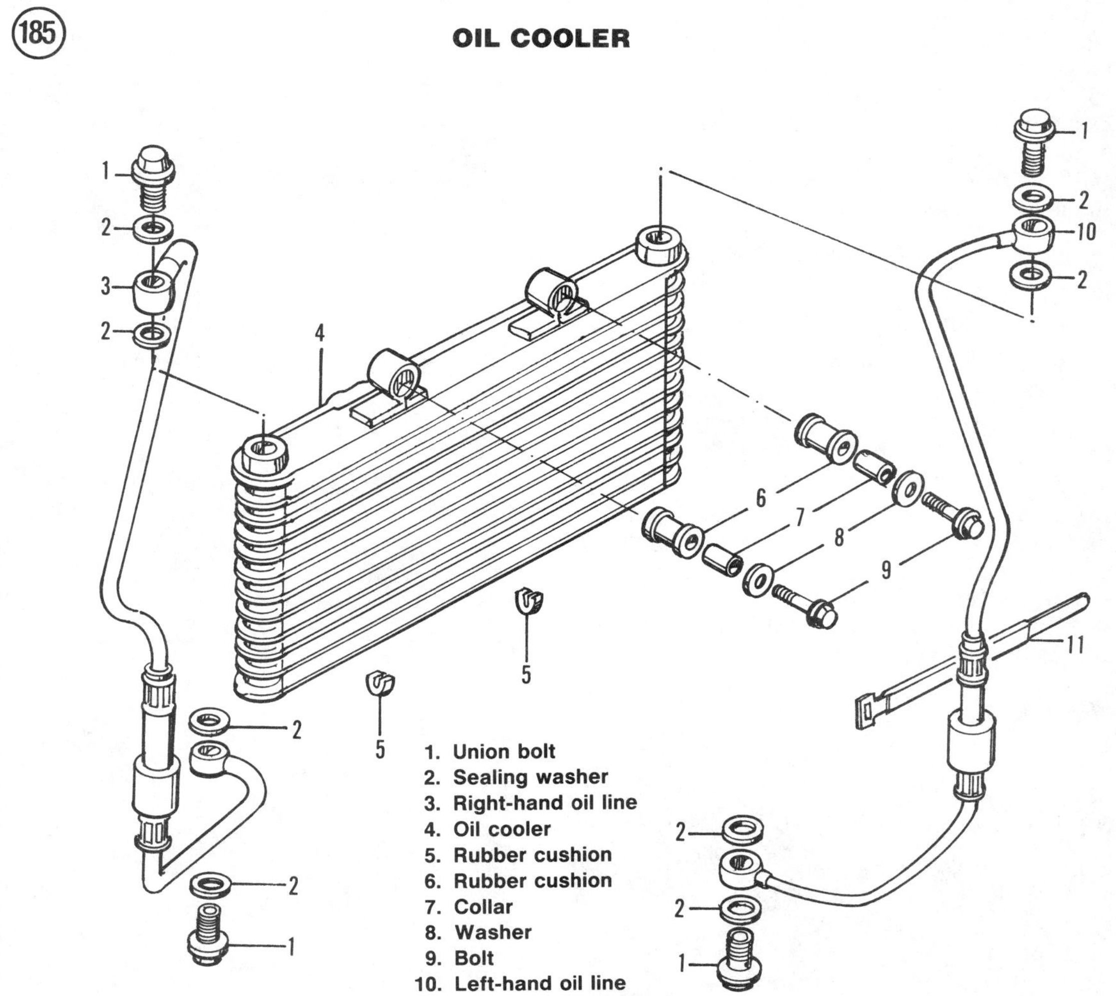

1. Union bolt
2. Sealing washer
3. Right-hand oil line
4. Oil cooler
5. Rubber cushion
6. Rubber cushion
7. Collar
8. Washer
9. Bolt
10. Left-hand oil line
11. Tie wrap

5. Loosen the bolt, washer and collar (**Figure 188**) on each side securing the oil cooler to the frame.
6. Remove the plastic tie wraps securing the oil lines to the frame on each side.
7. Remove the union bolts and sealing washers (**Figure 189**) securing the upper portion of the oil lines to the oil cooler.
8. Remove both oil lines from the frame.
9. Remove the bolt, washer and collar (**Figure 188**) on each side securing the oil cooler to the frame.
10. Pull the oil cooler up to release the lower locating tabs from the frame receptacles.
11. Install by reversing these removal steps, noting the following.
12. Clean off all road dirt and oil residue from the oil line mating surfaces on the oil pan.
13. Be sure to place a new sealing washer on each side of the oil line fittings.
14. Install the union bolts and tighten to the torque specification listed in **Table 3**.
15. Tighten the oil cooler mounting bolts securely. Don't forget to install the spacer along with the washer and bolt.
16. Refill the engine with the recommended type and quantity oil as described in Chapter Three.

OIL PAN AND OIL PRESSURE REGULATOR

Removal/Installation

NOTE
This procedure is shown with the engine removed from the frame for clarity. The oil pan can be removed with the engine installed in the frame.

1. Remove the union bolts and sealing washers securing the lower portion of the oil lines to the oil pan. Refer to **Figure 186** for the right-hand side and **Figure 187** for the left-hand side.
2. Remove the bolts securing the oil pan (**Figure 190**) to the lower crankcase.

188

189

190

187

191

192

193

194

195

3. Remove the oil pan and gasket. Discard the gasket as a new one must be installed.
4. Remove the shim (**Figure 191**) and O-ring seal (**Figure 192**) from the crankcase.
5. Install a new pan gasket (**Figure 193**).
6. Apply a light coat of cold grease to the O-ring seal (**Figure 192**) and install it in the receptacle in the crankcase.
7. Apply a light coat of cold grease to the shim and install it on top of the O-ring seal (**Figure 191**).
8. Install the oil pan and bolts. Be sure to install the copper washer under the one pan bolt (W, **Figure 190**). Tighten the bolts to the torque specification listed in **Table 3**.
9. Clean off all road dirt and oil residue from the oil line mating surfaces on the oil pan.
10. Be sure to place a new sealing washer on each side of the oil line fittings.
11. Install the union bolts and tighten to the torque specification listed in **Table 3**.

Inspection and Cleaning

1. Unscrew the oil gallery plug bolts and gaskets from the oil pan. Refer to **Figure 194** and **Figure 195**.
2. Unscrew the oil pressure regulator and washer (**Figure 196**) from the oil pan.
3. Unscrew the oil gallery plug bolt, gasket, spring and plunger from the oil pan.
4. Wash the oil pan in solvent. Clean out all of the oil galleries located behind the plug bolts.
5. Thoroughly dry with compressed air. Be sure to remove all solvent residue and any oil sludge loosened by the solvent. Any pieces of sludge left in any oil gallery may clog the gallery and any oil control orifices in the lubrication system.
6. Install the oil gallery plug bolt and gaskets into the oil pan. Tighten the plug bolts securely.

196

7. Install the plunger, spring gasket and the oil gallery plug bolt into the oil pan. Tighten the plug bolt securely.
8. Install the oil pressure regulator and washer (**Figure 196**) into the oil pan. Tighten the regulator to the torque specification listed in **Table 3**.

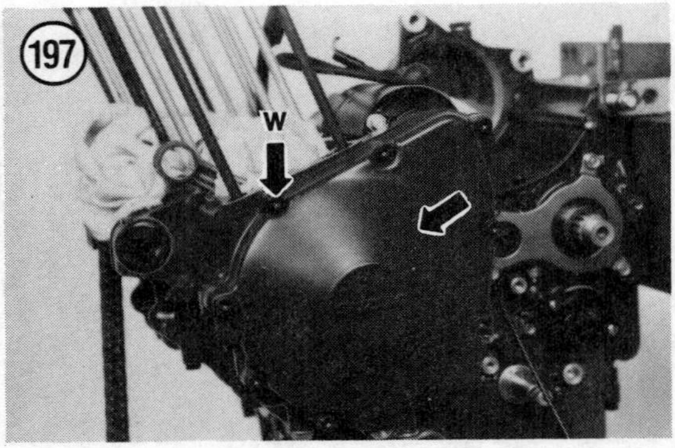

STARTER CLUTCH AND GEARS

Removal

The starter gears can be removed with the complete engine in the frame. This procedure is shown with the partially disassembled engine removed for clarity.

1. Remove the lower and the middle left-hand section of the front fairing as described under *Front Fairing Removal/Installation* in Chapter Twelve.
2. Drain the engine oil as described under *Engine Oil and Filter Change* in Chapter Three.
3. Move the oil drain pan used in Step 1 under the starter clutch cover as additional oil will drain out when the cover is removed.
4. Remove the bolts securing the starter clutch cover (**Figure 197**) and remove the cover and gasket. One of the bolts has a copper washer under it; don't lose it.
5. Remove the locating dowel (**Figure 198**).
6. Remove the starter idle gear and shaft assembly (**Figure 199**) from the crankcase.

7A. If the engine is installed in the frame, shift the transmission into gear. This is to prevent the gear from rotating while loosening the mounting bolt.

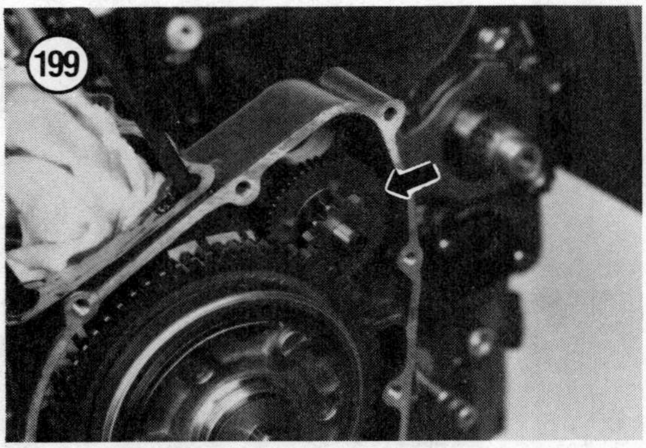

NOTE
The Grabbit special tool (part No. 969103) is available from Joe Bolger Products, Inc. Summer Street, Barre MA. 01005.

7B. If the engine is removed, attach the Grabbit special tool to the starter clutch gear. Do not overtighten the tool as it may damage the gear. This is to prevent the gear from rotating while loosening the mounting bolt.

8. Loosen, but do not remove, the bolt (A, **Figure 200**) securing the starter clutch to the end of the crankshaft. The bolt must be left in place in order to be used with the special tool in the next step.

201

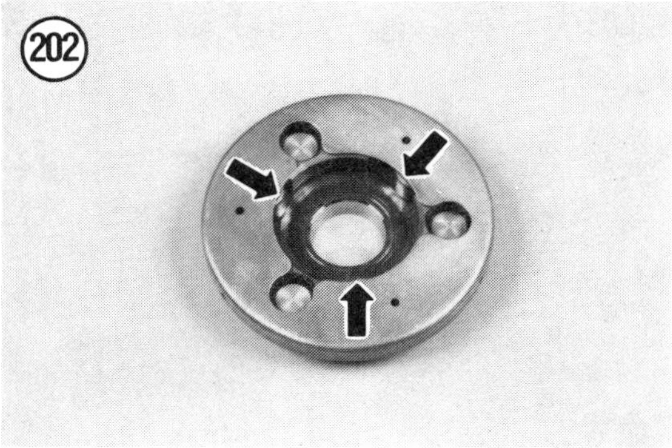
202

203

204

9. Install the Suzuki special tool (Rotor Remover, part No. 09930-33720) to the starter clutch and remove the starter clutch from the taper on the end of the crankshaft.
10. Remove the special tool, unscrew the bolt and remove the starter clutch assembly.

Installation

1. Clean the tapered end of the crankshaft and the mating surface of the starter clutch with electrical contact cleaner to remove all traces of oil. Both surfaces must be dry and free of any oil residue.
2. Install the starter clutch onto the crankshaft.
3. Apply Loctite Lock N' Seal to the mounting bolt prior to installation.
4. Use the same tool set-up used for removal to hold the starter clutch stationary while tightening the bolt.
5. Install and tighten the bolt (A, **Figure 200**) to the torque specification listed in **Table 3**.
6. Install the starter idle gear and shaft assembly.
7. Apply a light coat of Three-Bond No. 1207 gasket sealer, or equivalent, to the crankcase surfaces at the point where the upper and lower crankcase halves meet (B, **Figure 200**). This is to prevent an oil leak.
8. Install the locating dowel (**Figure 198**).
9. Install a new gasket and the starter clutch cover (**Figure 197**). Install the bolts. Install a copper washer under the one bolt (W, **Figure 197**). Tighten the bolts securely in a crisscross pattern.
10. Refill the engine with the recommended type and quantity of engine oil as described in Chapter Three.
11. Install the middle left-hand section and the lower section of the front fairing as described under *Front Fairing Removal/Installation* in Chapter Twelve.

Disassembly/Inspection/Assembly

1. Rotate the starter clutch (A, **Figure 201**) *clockwise* and remove it from the starter driven gear (B, **Figure 201**).
2. Check the rollers (**Figure 202**) in the starter clutch for uneven or excessive wear. Replace as a set if any are bad. If damaged, remove the rollers, springs and plungers (**Figure 203**).
3. Inspect the starter driven gear (**Figure 204**) for chipped or missing teeth. Look for uneven or excessive wear on the gear faces. If damaged, both the starter driven gear and starter clutch must be replaced as a set.

4

4. Inspect the starter idle gear (**Figure 205**) for chipped or missing teeth. Look for uneven or excessive wear on the gear faces. Replace if necessary.
5. Inspect the roller riding surface (**Figure 206**) of the starter driven gear for wear or abrasion. If damaged, both the starter driven gear and starter clutch must be replaced as a set.

NOTE
Do not apply any grease to the rollers in the following step to hold them in place. If grease is applied it will interfere with their movement during the normal engine starting sequence.

6. To install the rollers in the starter clutch, perform the following:
   a. Install the spring into the plunger (**Figure 207**).
   b. Install the assembled spring and plunger into the receptacle in the starter clutch (**Figure 208**).
   c. Push the plunger into the receptacle and hold it in place with a small tool similar to a dental tool (**Figure 209**).
   d. Hold the plunger and spring in place and install the roller (**Figure 210**). Push the roller in until it bottoms out and stays in place.
   e. Repeat for the other 2 sets of rollers.

205

206

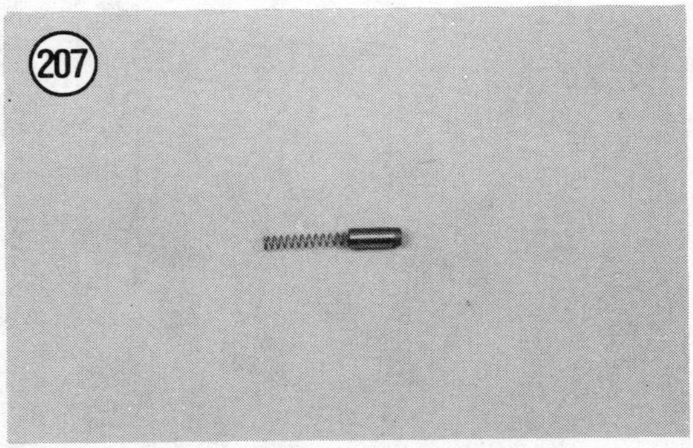
207

208

209

210

211

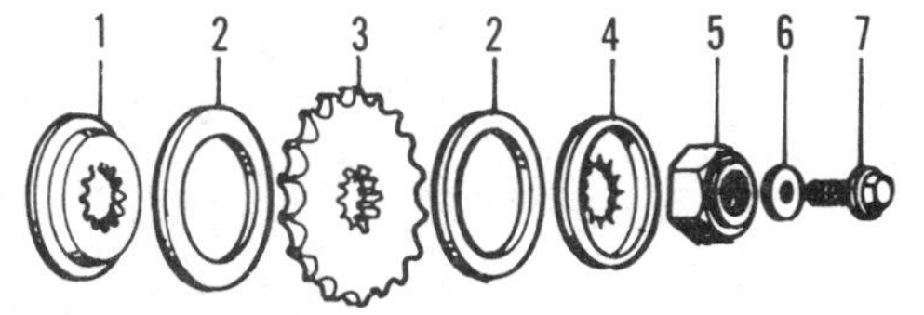

DRIVE SPROCKET

1. Inner damper holder
2. Damper
3. Drive sprocket
4. Damper holder
5. Nut
6. Washer
7. Bolt

212

213

214

7. Rotate the starter clutch (A, **Figure 201**) *counterclockwise* and install it onto the starter driven gear (B, **Figure 201**).

CRANKCASE

Service to the lower end requires that the crankcase assembly be removed from the motorcycle frame.

Disassembly

1. While the engine is still in the frame, remove the cylinder head, cylinder block, pistons, electric starter, alternator, signal generator and clutch assembly as described in this and other related chapters.
2. Remove the engine as described under *Engine Removal/Installation* in this chapter.
3. If the drive sprocket is still installed, refer to **Figure 211** and perform the following:
   a. Remove the bolt and washer (**Figure 212**) and the nut (**Figure 213**) securing the drive sprocket.
   b. Remove the outer damper holder and damper (**Figure 214**).
   c. Remove the drive sprocket (**Figure 215**).
   d. Remove the inner damper (**Figure 216**) and inner damper holder (**Figure 217**).

215

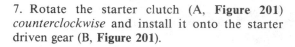

216

4

4. Straighten the locking tabs and remove the bolts (**Figure 218**) securing the oil seal retainer. Remove the oil seal retainer.
5. Remove the screws securing the neutral switch (**Figure 219**) and remove the neutral switch.
6. Remove the neutral switch O-ring (**Figure 220**) from the crankcase receptacle.
7. Remove the neutral switch contact and spring (**Figure 221**).
8. Remove the screws (**Figure 222**) securing the countershaft bearing retainer and remove the bearing retainer.
9. Remove the upper crankcase plug bolt and washer (**Figure 223**).
10. Remove the upper crankcase half bolts. Refer to **Figure 224** and **Figure 225** for bolt locations. Refer to **Figure 226** for the nut location.
11. Place the engine on a workbench upside down on a couple of 2×4 in. wood blocks. This is to protect the protruding connecting rod ends and the crankcase studs.
12. Remove the bolts securing the oil pan (**Figure 227**) to the lower crankcase. Don't lose the copper washer under the one pan bolt (W, **Figure 227**).
13. Remove the oil pan and gasket. Discard the gasket as a new one must be installed.
14. Remove the bolts (A, **Figure 228**) securing the oil sump filter assembly. Remove the assembly (B, **Figure 228**) and the gasket (**Figure 229**).

223

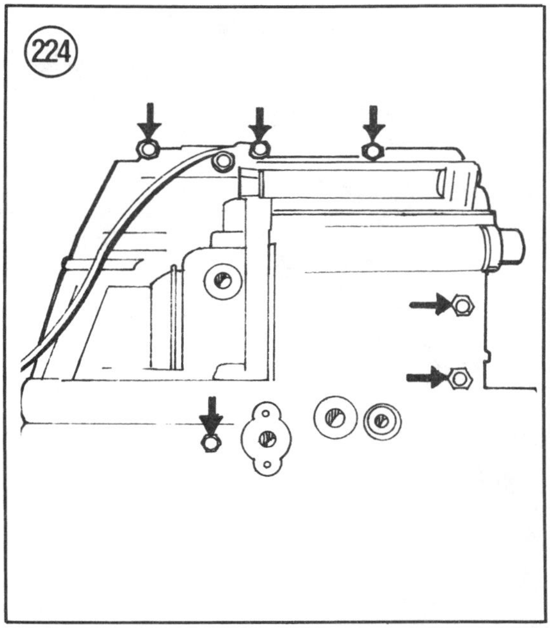
224

225

226

227
W

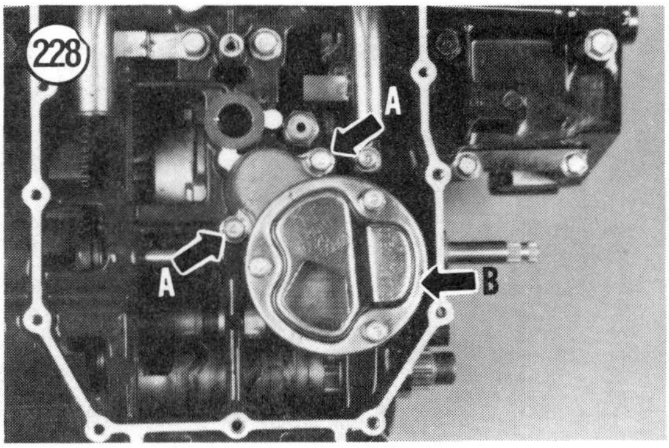
228
A
A
B

229

15. Remove the shim (**Figure 230**) and the O-ring (**Figure 231**).
16. Remove the bolts (**Figure 232**) securing the oil pipes and remove the oil pipes (**Figure 233**).
17. Remove the lower crankcase bolts (**Figure 234**). Don't forget the single bolt (**Figure 235**) at the rear corner.
18. Remove the main oil gallery plug bolt and O-ring (**Figure 236**). Discard the O-ring seal as it cannot be reused.

NOTE
*A torque sequence number is cast into the lower crankcase next to each main bearing bolt (**Figure 237**).*

19. Loosen each main bearing bolt in the descending order of the numbers (highest to lowest) cast into the lower crankcase (**Figure 238**). Remove the bolts.
20. Double check that you have removed all of the upper and lower crankcase bolts.
21. Tap the lower crankcase (**Figure 239**) with a plastic mallet and separate the 2 halves.

CAUTION
*If it is necessary to pry the halves apart, do it very **carefully** so that you do not mar the gasket surfaces. If you do, the cases will leak oil and must be replaced.*

230

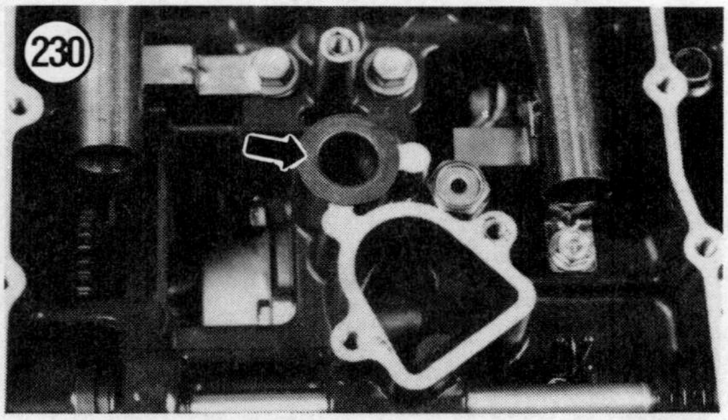

231

232

233

234

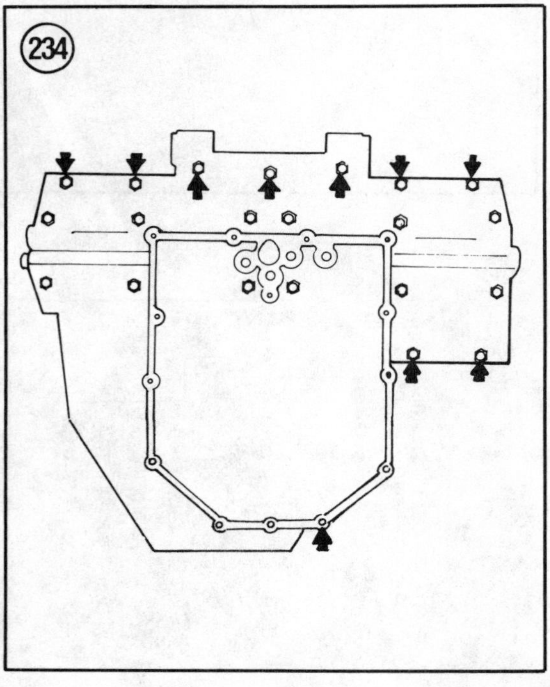

235

236

237

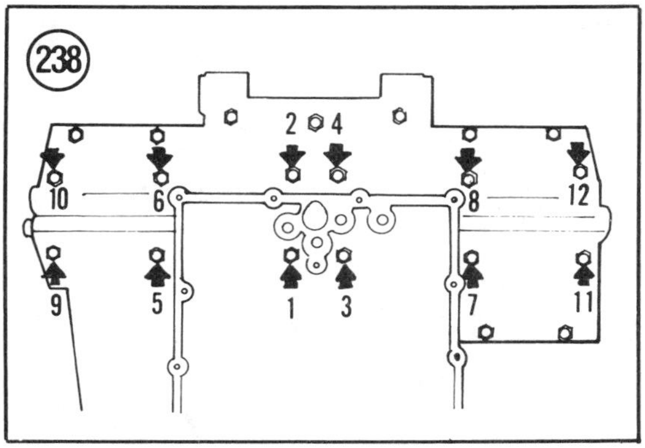

238

22. Lift the lower crankcase off the upper crankcase. Turn the lower crankcase over immediately and be careful that the crankshaft main bearing inserts do not fall out. If any do, reinstall them immediately into their original position if possible.

23. Remove both transmission assemblies (**Figure 240**) from the upper crankcase half.

24. Remove the C-rings (A, **Figure 241**) and the transmission bearing locating dowels (B, **Figure 241**).

239

240

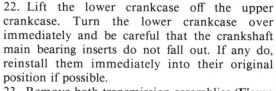

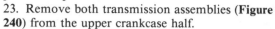

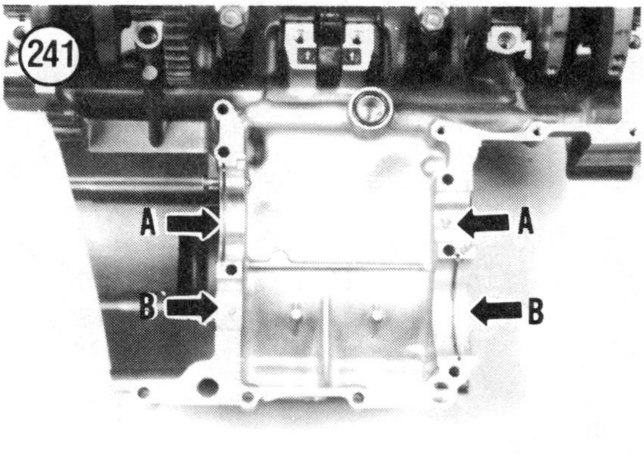

241

25. Lift the crankshaft/connecting rod assembly (**Figure 242**) out of the upper crankcase.
26. On 1100 cc models, remove the crankshaft side thrust bearings (**Figure 243**) from the upper crankcase half.
27. Remove the oil gallery O-rings (**Figure 244**).
28. Remove the camshaft drive chain guide dampers (A, **Figure 245**) and the chain guide (B, **Figure 245**).
29. Remove the oil pump as described under *Oil Pump Removal/Installation* in this chapter.
30. Remove the internal shift mechanism as described under *Internal Gearshift Mechanism Removal/Installation* in Chapter Six.
31. Remove the crankshaft main bearing inserts as described in this chapter.

Inspection

1. Thoroughly clean the inside and outside of both crankcase halves with cleaning solvent. Dry with compressed air. Make sure there is no solvent residue left in the cases as it will contaminate the new engine oil.

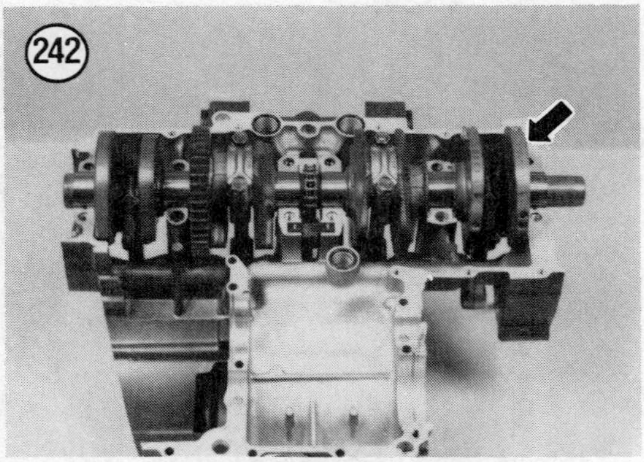
242

243

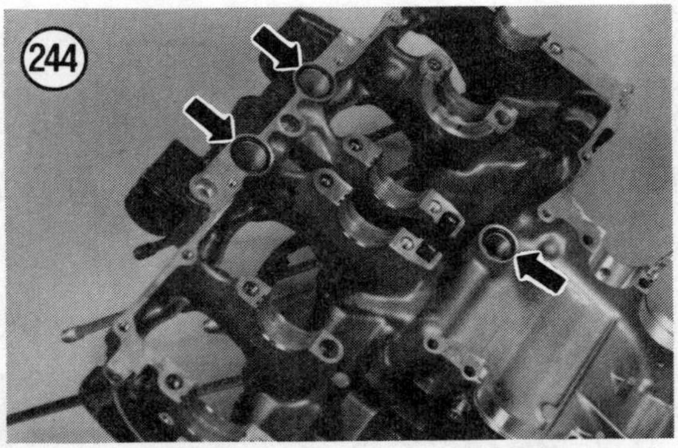
244

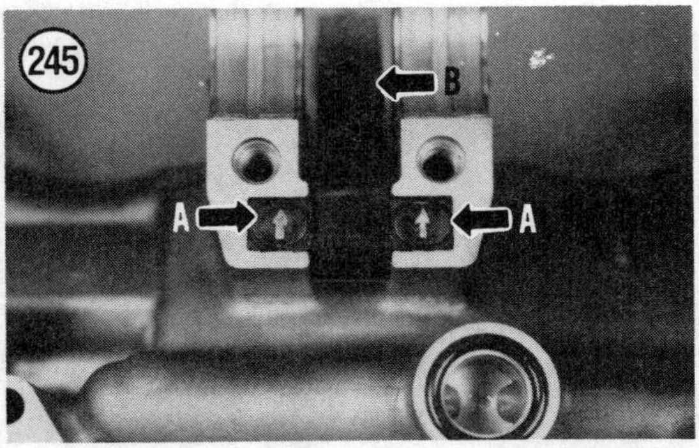

245

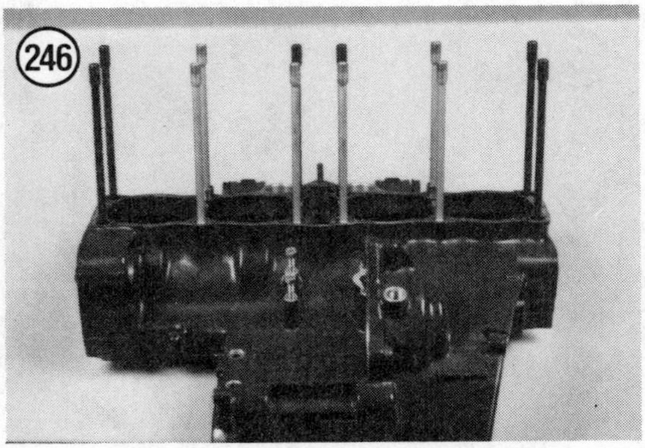
246

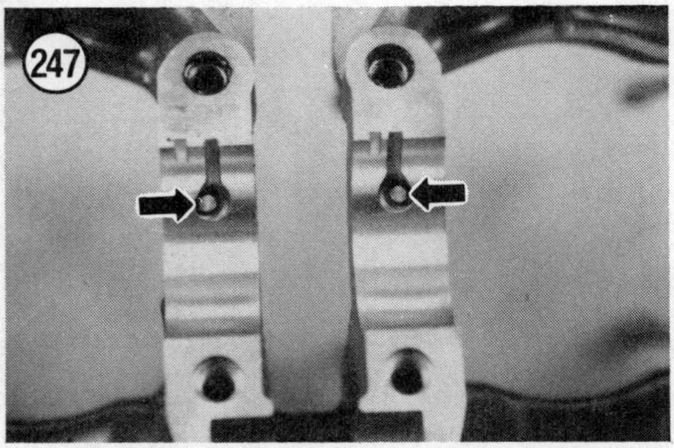
247

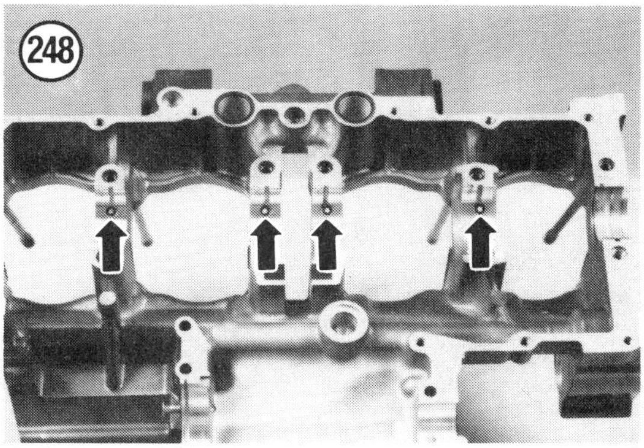

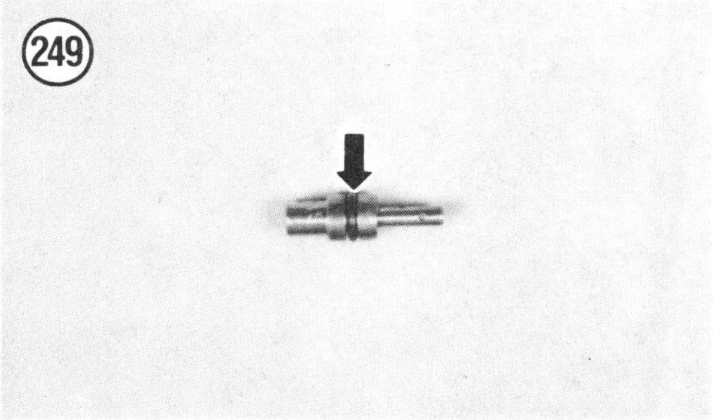

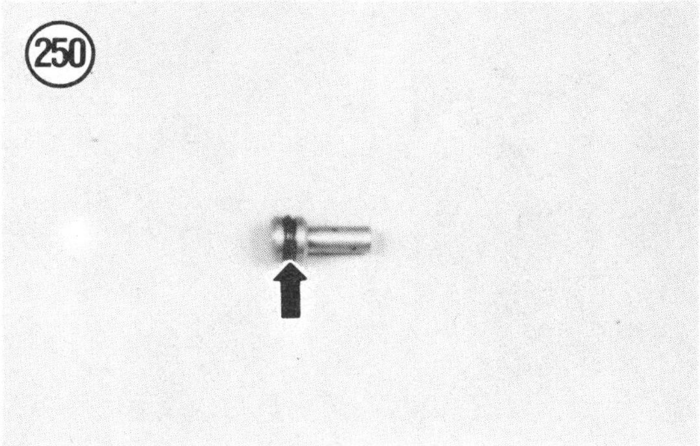

2. Remove all old gasket sealing material from both case half mating surfaces.
3. Carefully inspect the cases for cracks and fractures. Also check the areas around the stiffening ribs, bearing bosses and threaded holes. If damage is found, have it repaired by a shop specializing in the repair of precision aluminum castings or replace the crankcase halves as a set.
4. Make sure the crankcase studs are tight (**Figure 246**). Suzuki does not provide a torque specification for the studs.
5. Remove the oil control nozzles (**Figure 247**) from the upper crankcase half (**Figure 248**).
6. On 750 cc models, remove the oil plungers from the lower crankcase half.
7. Inspect the oil control nozzles (**Figure 249**), their O-rings and the oil plungers (**Figure 250**) and their O-rings for wear or deterioration. The O-rings cannot be replaced separately.
8. Make sure the oil jets are clean in the lower crankcase half. Refer to **Figure 251** and **Figure 252**.
9. Make sure the oil jets are clean at each end of the upper crankcase half (**Figure 253**).

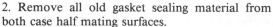

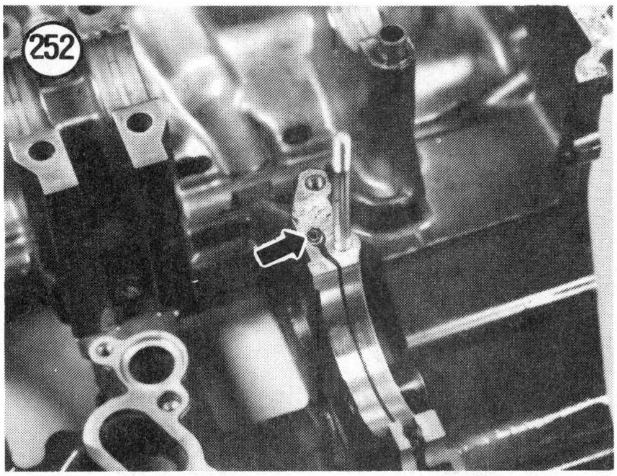

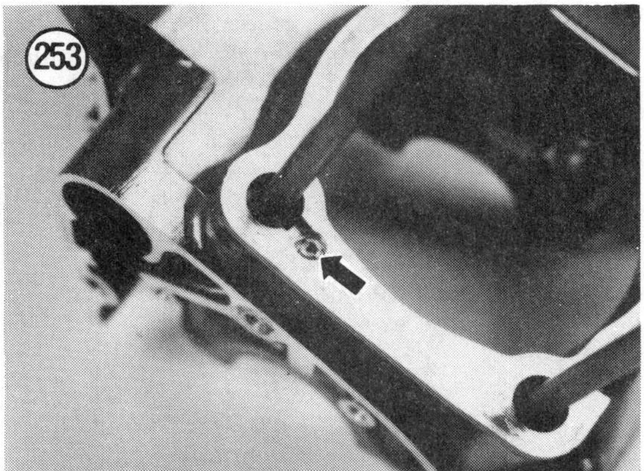

Crankcase Bearings Removal/Installation

1. Turn the shift drum bearings by hand and check for damaged races, balls or needles. Refer to **Figure 254** and **Figure 255**. Replace the bearing(s) if it has excessive side play. If the bearings are okay, oil the races or needles with fresh engine oil. If necessary, replace the bearings as follows.

NOTE

If bearing replacement is required, purchase the new bearing(s) and place them in a freezer for approximately 2 hours before installation. Chilling the bearings will slightly reduce their overall diameter while the hot crankcase is slightly larger due to heat expansion. This will make bearing installation much easier.

2. Remove the circlip securing the ball bearing into the inner surface of the crankcase.

WARNING

Prior to heating the crankcase half as described in Step 3, first wash the crankcase thoroughly in soap and water to remove all traces of gasoline or solvent.

CAUTION

Even though the crankcase has been washed, there ***may*** *be a residual oil or solvent odor left in the oven after heating the crankcase. If you use a household oven, first check with the person who uses the oven for food preparation to avoid getting into trouble.*

3. The bearings are installed with a slight interference fit. The crankcase half must be heated in an oven to a temperature of about 100° C (212° F). An easy way to check the proper temperature is to drop tiny drops of water on the case; if they sizzle and evaporate immediately, the temperature is correct.

CAUTION

Do not heat the cases with a torch (propane or acetylene); never bring a flame into contact with the bearing or case. The direct heat will destroy the case hardening of the bearing and will likely cause warpage of the case.

WARNING

Wear insulated gloves (insulated kitchen mitts) when handling heated parts.

4. Remove the case from the oven and place on wood blocks. Hold onto the crankcase with kitchen mitts or heavy gloves—it is *hot*.

5. Carefully tap the bearing(s) out of the crankcase with a block of wood, socket or piece of pipe the same size as the bearing inner or outer race.

CAUTION

If the bearings are difficult to remove or install, don't take a chance on expensive crankcase damage. Have the work performed by a dealer or competent machine shop.

254

255

256

6. Reheat the crankcase half in the oven.
7. Remove the case from the oven and place on wood blocks. Hold onto the crankcase with kitchen mitts or heavy gloves—it is *hot*.
8. While the crankcase is still hot, press each new bearing(s) into place in the crankcase by hand until it seats completely. Do not hammer it in. If the bearing will not seat, remove it and cool it again. Reheat the crankcase and install the bearing again.
9. Install the circlip retaining the ball bearing. Make sure the circlip is seated correctly in the groove.

Assembly

NOTE
If reusing the old bearing inserts, make sure that they are installed in the same location as noted during ***Removal***.

257

258

1. Install the crankshaft main bearing inserts into the crankcase halves as described in this chapter.
2. Install the internal shift mechanism as described under *Internal Gearshift Mechanism Removal/Installation* in Chapter Six.
3. Install the oil pump as described under *Oil Pump Removal/Installation* in this chapter.
4. Install the camshaft drive chain guide (B, **Figure 245**).
5. On models so marked, position the chain guide dampers (A, **Figure 245**) with the arrow facing toward the front of the engine.
6. Install new oil gallery O-rings (**Figure 244**).
7. On 1100 cc models, install the crankshaft side thrust bearings (**Figure 243**) into the upper crankcase half with the grooved side facing away from the bearing saddle (**Figure 256**).

NOTE
Prior to installation, coat all bearing surfaces with assembly oil or fresh engine oil.

8. Install the crankshaft/connecting rod assembly (**Figure 242**) into the upper crankcase.
9. Install the C-rings (A, **Figure 241**) and the transmission bearing locating pins (B, **Figure 241**).
10. Install both transmission assemblies (**Figure 240**) into the upper crankcase half.
11. Make sure the crankshaft main bearing inserts are in place in the lower crankcase half.
12. Shift the transmission into NEUTRAL. The shift forks should be located in the upper crankcase in the approximate positions shown in **Figure 257**.
13. If removed, install the locating dowels (**Figure 258**) into the lower crankcase half.
14. Make sure case half sealing surfaces are perfectly clean and dry. Clean off with electrical contact cleaner and wipe off with a lint-free cloth.

NOTE
Use Three Bond No. 1207, or equivalent. When selecting an equivalent, avoid thick and hard setting materials.

15. Apply a light coat of gasket sealer, or equivalent, to the sealing surfaces of the lower crankcase half. Cover only flat surfaces, *not curved bearing surfaces*. Make the coating as thin as possible, but still covers completely.

4

16. Position the lower crankcase onto the upper crankcase. Set the front portion down first and lower the rear while making sure the shift forks engage properly with their respective transmission gears and that the guide pins are still engaged in the shift drum grooves (**Figure 259**). Join both halves and tap them together lightly with a plastic mallet—do not use a metal hammer as it will damage the case.

CAUTION

Crankcase halves should fit together without force. If the crankcase halves do not fit together completely, do not attempt to pull them together with the crankcase bolts. Separate the crankcase halves and investigate the cause of the interference. If the transmission shafts were disassembled, recheck to make sure that a gear is not installed backwards. Do not risk damage by trying to force the cases together.

17. Before installing the bolts, slowly spin the transmission shafts and shift the transmission through all gears using the shift drum. Make sure the shift forks are operating properly and that you

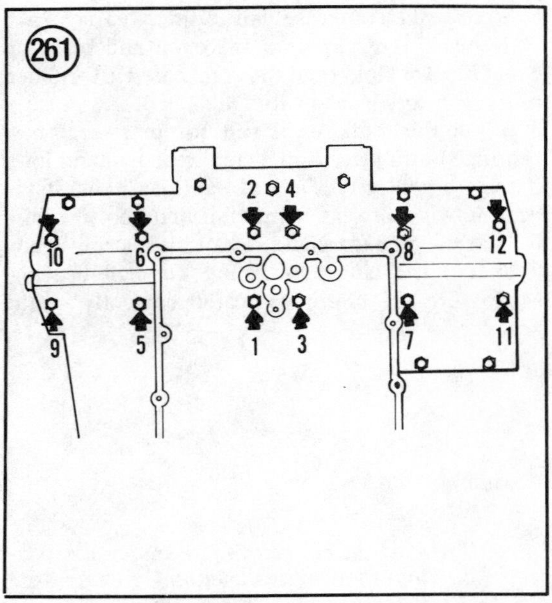

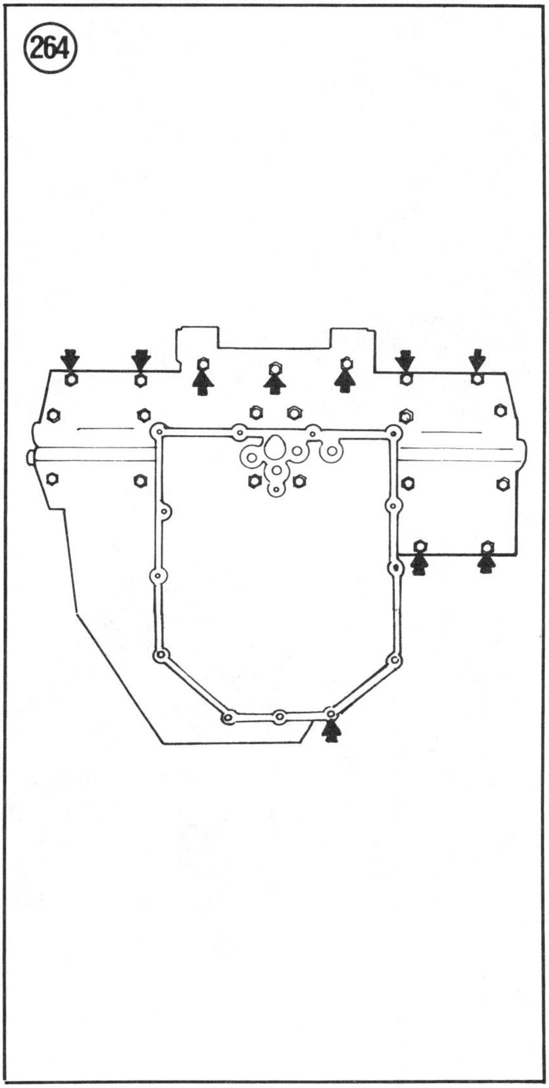

can shift through all gears. This is the time to find that something may be installed incorrectly—not after the engine is installed in the frame.

18. Install the oil pipes (**Figure 260**) and bolts. Tighten the bolts securely.

19. Apply a light coat of oil to the bolts prior to installation. Install the main bearing bolts. Place a copper washer under the No. 9 and No. 11 bolts (**Figure 261**).

NOTE
*A torque sequence number is cast into the lower crankcase next to each main bearing bolt (**Figure 262**).*

20. Tighten the main bearing bolt in the ascending order (lowest to highest) of the numbers cast into the lower crankcase (**Figure 261**). Tighten first to the initial torque specification listed in **Table 3** and then to the final torque specification listed in **Table 3**.

21. Install the main oil gallery plug bolt and new O-ring (**Figure 263**). Tighten to the torque specification listed in **Table 3**.

22. Apply a light coat of oil to the bolts prior to installation. Install the lower crankcase bolts (**Figure 264**). Don't forget the single bolt (**Figure 265**) at the rear corner. Tighten first to the initial torque specification listed in **Table 3** and then to the final torque specification listed in **Table 3**.

23. Install the O-ring (**Figure 266**) and the shim (**Figure 267**).

24. Install a new oil sump filter assembly gasket (**Figure 268**).

CAUTION
*Be sure to install the oil sump filter assembly with the FRONT arrow (**Figure 269**) facing toward the front of the engine.*

25. Install the oil sump filter assembly and bolts (**Figure 270**). Tighten the bolts securely.
26. Install the oil pan and bolts. Be sure to install the copper washer under the one pan bolt (W, **Figure 271**). Tighten the bolts to the torque specification listed in **Table 3**.
27. Place the engine on workbench upside down on a couple of 2×4 in. wood blocks. This is to protect the protruding connecting rod ends and the crankcase studs.
28. Apply a light coat of oil to the bolts prior to installation. Install the upper crankcase half bolts. Refer to **Figure 272** and **Figure 273** for bolt locations. Refer to **Figure 274** for the nut location. Tighten the bolts first to the initial torque specification listed in **Table 3** and then to the final torque specification listed in **Table 3**.

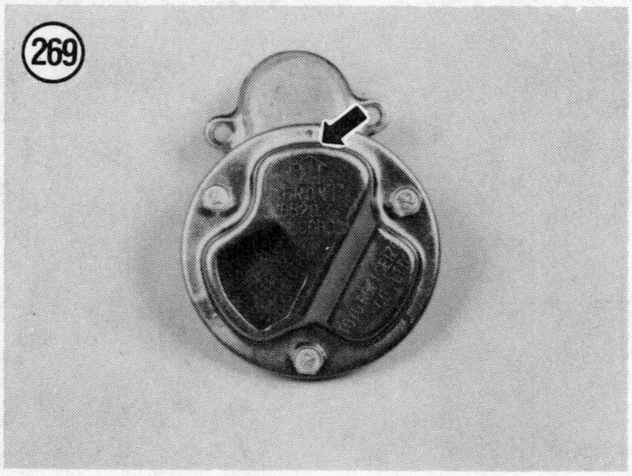

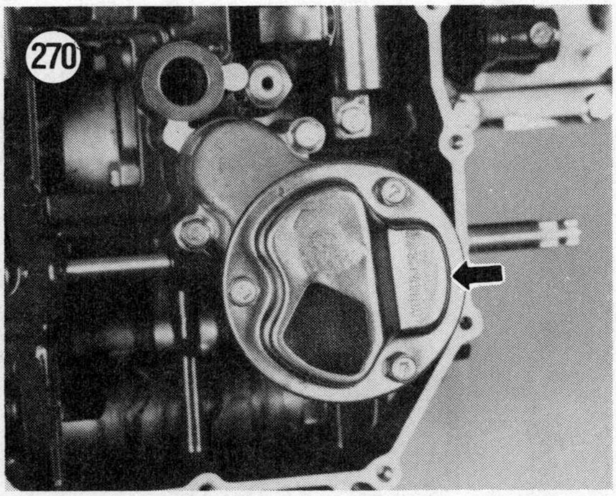

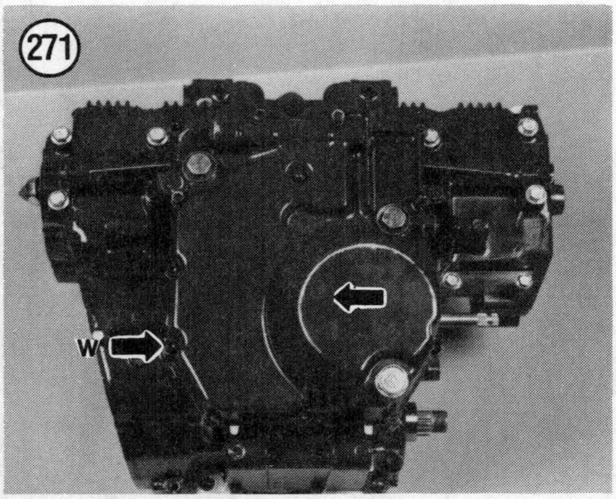

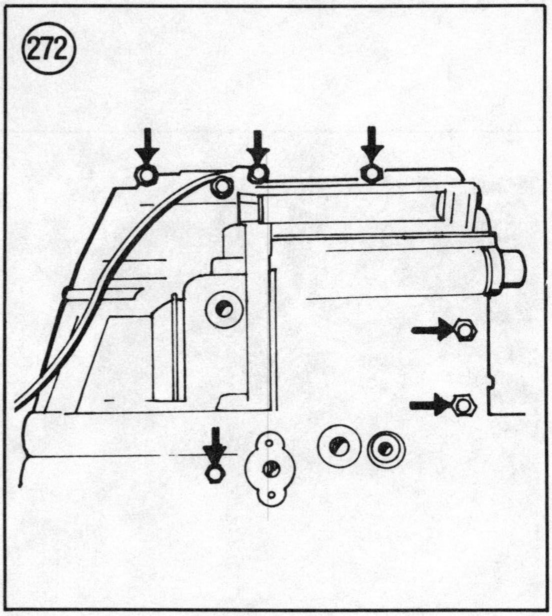

273

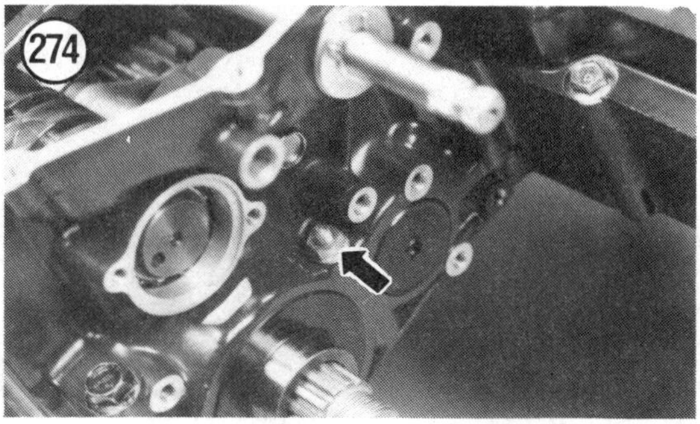

274

275

276

29. Install the upper crankcase plug bolt and washer (**Figure 275**) and tighten securely.
30. Apply a light coat of Loctite Lock N' Seal to the screw threads prior to installation. Install the countershaft bearing retainer and screws (**Figure 276**) and tighten securely.
31. Install the neutral switch contact and spring.
32. Install the neutral switch O-ring seal into the groove in the crankcase.
33. Install the neutral switch and screws. Tighten the screws securely.
34. Install the oil seal retainer and bolts (**Figure 277**). Tighten the bolts securely. Bend up the locking tab against the one of the flats of the bolts.
35. If the drive sprocket is going to be installed at this time, refer to **Figure 278** and perform the following:

277

278

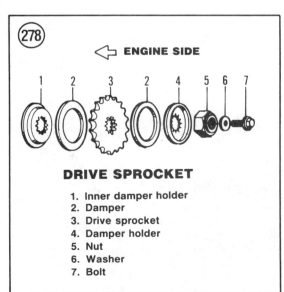

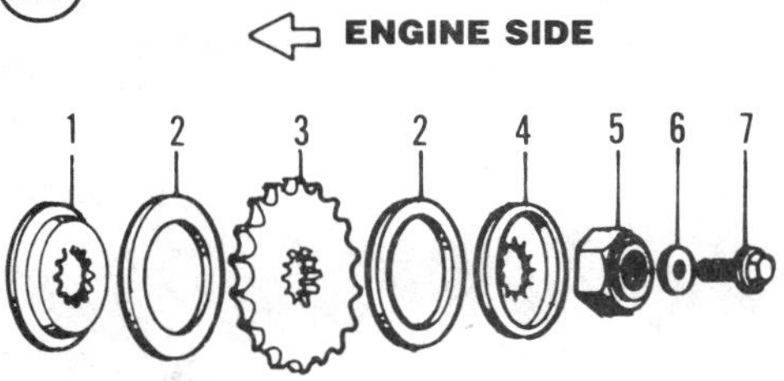

DRIVE SPROCKET

1. Inner damper holder
2. Damper
3. Drive sprocket
4. Damper holder
5. Nut
6. Washer
7. Bolt

a. Install the inner damper holder (**Figure 279**) and inner damper (**Figure 280**).
b. Install the drive sprocket (**Figure 281**).
c. Install the damper and the outer damper holder (**Figure 282**).
d. Insall the nut (**Figure 283**) securing the drive sprocket. Tighten the nut to the torque specification listed in **Table 3**.

NOTE
It will be necessary to hold the sprocket with a suitable holder, such as the "Grabbit",available from Joe Bolger Products, Inc., Barre, MA 01005, before the sprocket nut can be torqued.

e. Install the bolt and washer (**Figure 284**) and tighten securely.

36. Install the engine as described under *Engine Removal/Installation* in this chapter.
37. Install all exterior components removed as described in this and other related chapters.

CRANKSHAFT

Removal/Installation

1. Disassembly the crankcase as described under *Crankcase Disassembly* in this chapter.
2. Remove the crankshaft/connecting rod assembly and camshaft chain (**Figure 285**) from the upper crankcase half. Remove the connecting rods as described in this chapter.

NOTE
In Step 3, the No. 1-6 marks go from left to right across the engine. The left-hand side of the engine refers to the engine as it sits in the bike frame—not as it sits on your bench upside down.

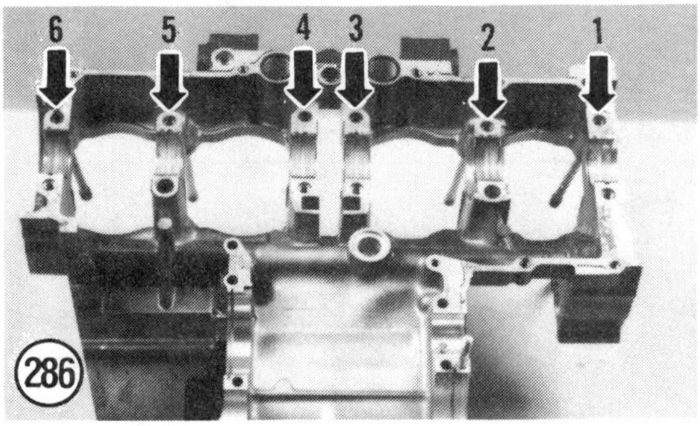

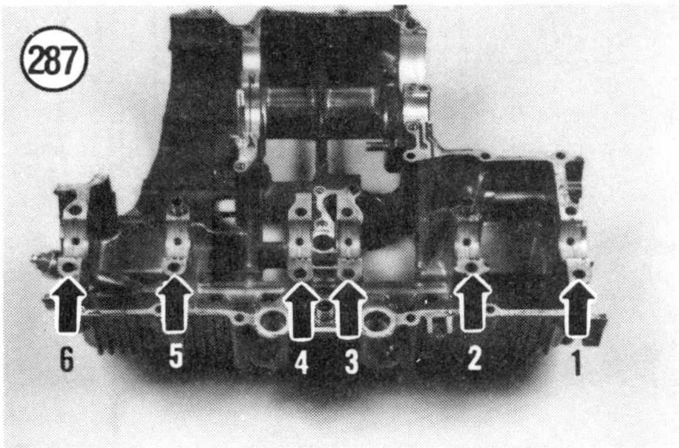

3. If the bearing inserts are going to be removed for cleaning, perform the following;
   a. Remove the main bearing inserts from the upper (**Figure 286**) and lower (**Figure 287**) crankcase half.
   b. Mark the backside of the inserts with a 1, 2, 3, 4, 5 or 6 and "U" (upper) or "L" (lower). Remember that the inserts with an oil hole are for the lower crankcase (**Figure 288**).

CAUTION
If the old bearings are reused, be sure that they are installed in their original locations.

4. Inspect the crankshaft and main bearings as described in this chapter.
5. Reinstall the connecting rods as described in this chapter.
6. Install the crankshaft/connecting rod assembly and camshaft chain (**Figure 285**) into the upper crankcase half.
7. Assemble the crankcase as described under *Crankcase Assembly* in this chapter.

Inspection

1. Clean crankshaft thoroughly with solvent. Clean oil holes with rifle cleaning brushes; flush thoroughly and dry with compressed air.

288

1. **Grooved bearing (upper crankcase half)**
2. **Grooved bearing with oil hole (lower crankcase half)**

2. Carefully inspect each main bearing journal (**Figure 289**) for scratches, ridges, scoring, nicks, etc. Very small nicks and scratches may be removed with crocus cloth. More serious damage will require crankshaft replacement.
3. Inspect the camshaft chain sprocket teeth (**Figure 290**). If damaged, the crankshaft must be replaced.
4. Inspect the primary drive gear teeth (**Figure 291**). If damaged, the crankshaft must be replaced.
5. If the surface finish on all journals is satisfactory, measure the journals with a micrometer (**Figure 292**) and check out-of-roundness, taper, and wear on the journals. Check against measurements given in **Table 1** or **Table 2** for journal runout.

Crankshaft Main Bearing Clearance Measurement

1. Check each main bearing insert for evidence of wear, abrasion and scoring. If the bearings are good, they may be reused. If any insert is questionable, replace the entire set.
2. Clean the bearing surfaces of the crankshaft and the main bearing inserts.
3. Place the upper crankcase on a workbench upside down on a couple of 2×4 in. wood blocks. This is to protect the protruding connecting rod ends and the crankcase studs.
4. Install the existing main bearing inserts in the upper (**Figure 286**) and the lower (**Figure 287**) case halves in their original positions. Remember that the inserts with a hole go into the lower crankcase (**Figure 288**).
5. Install the crankshaft into the upper crankcase (**Figure 285**).

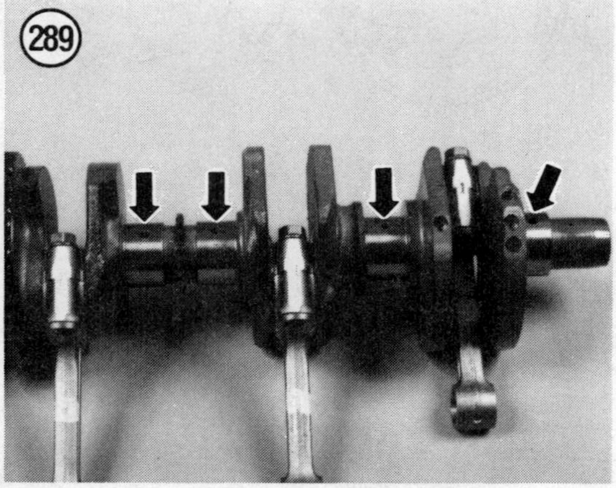

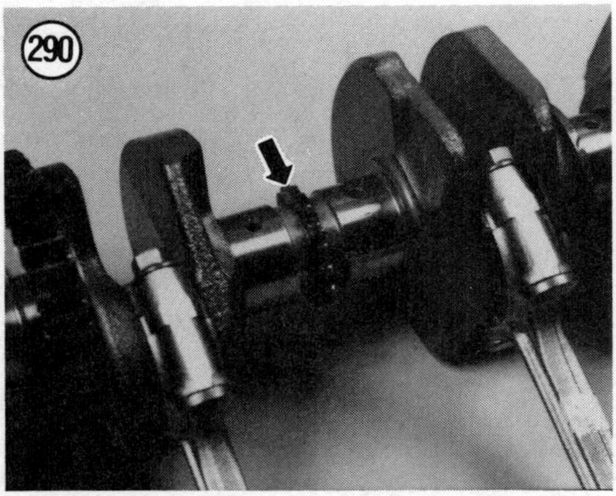

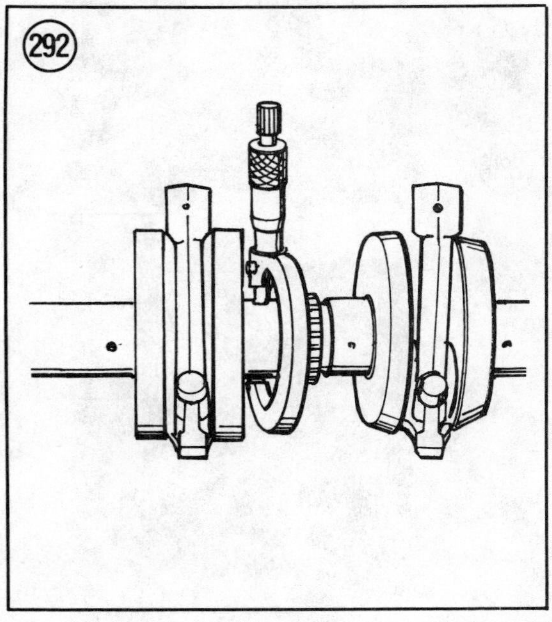

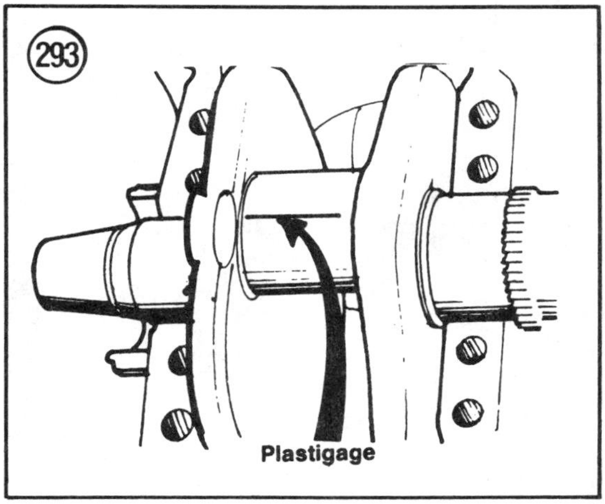

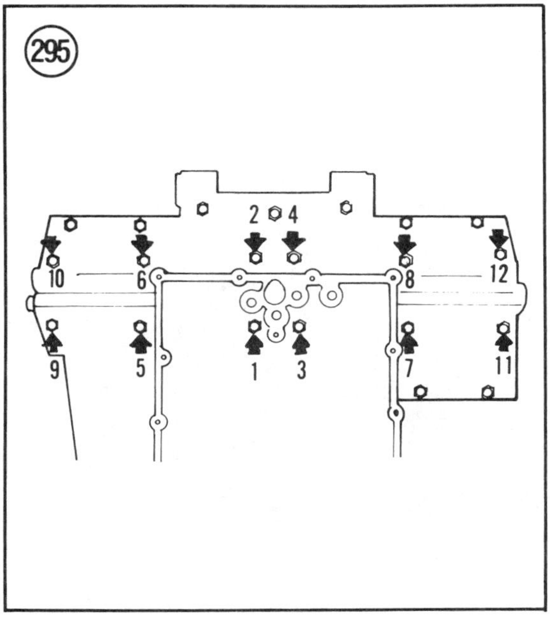

6. Place a piece of Plastigage over each main bearing journal parallel to the crankshaft (**Figure 293**). Do not place the Plastigage material over an oil hole in the crankshaft.

CAUTION
Do not rotate the crankshaft while the Plastigage is in place.

7. Position the lower crankcase onto the upper crankcase. Set the front portion down first and lower the rear. If the transmission shafts are still installed, make sure the shift forks engage properly with their respective transmission gears and that the guide pins are still engaged in the shift drum grooves (**Figure 294**). Join both halves and tap them together lightly with a plastic mallet—do not use a metal hammer, as it will damage the case.

CAUTION
Crankcase halves should fit together without force. If the crankcase halves do not fit together completely, do not attempt to pull them together with the crankcase bolts. Separate the crankcase halves and investigate the cause of the interference. If the transmission shafts were disassembled, recheck to make sure that a gear is not installed backwards. Do not risk damage by trying to force the cases together.

8. Apply a light coat of oil to the bolts prior to installation. Install the main bearing bolts. Place a copper washer under the No. 9 and No. 11 bolts (**Figure 295**).

NOTE
*A torque sequence number is cast into the lower crankcase next to each main bearing bolt (**Figure 296**).*

4

9. Tighten the main bearing bolt in the ascending order (lowest to highest) of the numbers cast into the lower crankcase (**Figure 295**). Tighten first to the initial torque specification listed in **Table 3** and then to the final torque specification listed in **Table 3**.
10. Loosen each main bearing bolt in the descending order (highest to lowest) of the numbers cast into the lower crankcase (**Figure 295**). Remove the bolts.
11. Carefully remove the lower crankcase half.
12. Measure the width of the flattened Plastigage according to manufacturer's instructions. Measure at both ends of Plastigage strip (**Figure 297**). A difference of 0.025 mm (0.001 in.) or more indicates a tapered journal. Confirm with a micrometer. Bearing clearance for new bearings are listed in **Table 1** or **Table 2**.
13. Remove the Plastigage strips from the main bearing journals.
14. If the bearing clearance is greater than specified, select new bearings as described in this chapter.

Crankshaft Main Bearing Selection

1. The crankshaft main bearing journals are marked with an "A," "B" or "C" (A, **Figure 298**). The stamped letters relate to the journals as shown in **Figure 299**.
2. The crankcase journal I.D. code letters ("A" or "B") are stamped on the rear surface of the upper crankcase (**Figure 300**). The stamped letters are in the same order as the journals and are located in the crankcase.
3. Select new bearings by cross-referencing the main journal letters (A, **Figure 298**) in the vertical column of **Table 4** with the crankcase I.D. letters (**Figure 300**). Where the columns intersect, the new bearing insert color is indicated. **Table 4** gives the bearing color and **Table 5** gives bearing color, part number and thickness. Always replace all 12 bearing inserts as a complete set.
4. After new bearing inserts have been installed, recheck the clearance by repeating the *Crankshaft Main Bearing Clearance Measurement* procedure in this chapter. If the clearance is still out of specifications, either the crankcases or the crankshaft are worn beyond the service limit and requires replacement.

Crankshaft Side Thrust Clearance Inspection (1100 cc Models)

NOTE
The 750 cc engine is not equipped with side thrust bearings.

1. Disassemble the crankcase as described under *Crankcase Disassembly* in this chapter.
2. With the crankshaft and both right- and left-hand thrust bearings in place (**Figure 301**), perform the following.

297

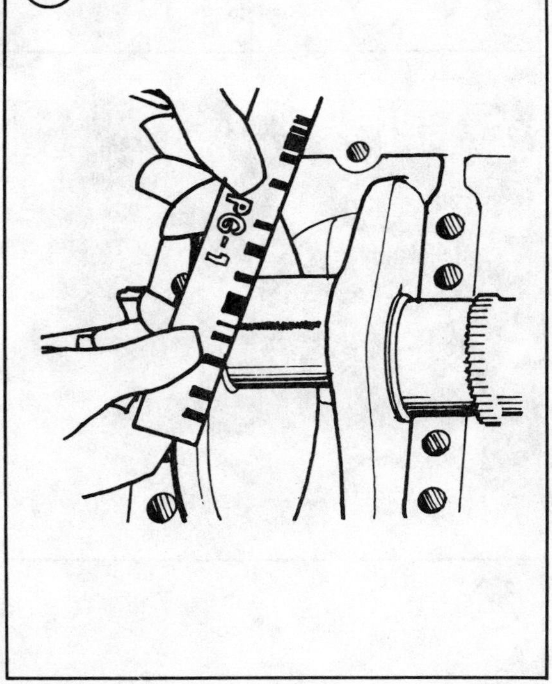

298

299

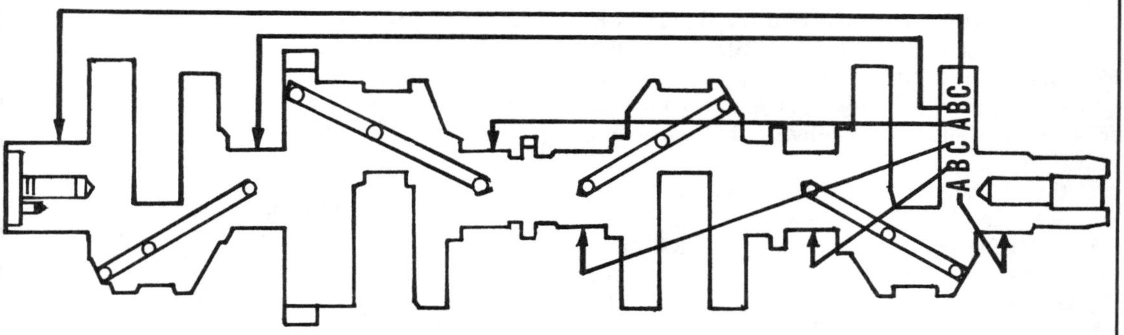

4

3. Push on the right-hand end of the crankshaft until there is no clearance between the crankshaft and the right-hand thrust bearing (**Figure 302**).
4. Install a flat feeler gauge between the left-hand thrust bearing and the machined surface of the crankshaft. Refer to **Figure 303** and **Figure 304**. Compare to dimensions listed in **Table 2**. If the clearance is greater than specified, perform the following.
5. Remove the right-hand thrust bearing and measure its thickness with a micrometer. Compare to dimension listed in **Table 2**. If the thickness is within specifications, proceed to Step 6. If the thickness is less than specified, replace the right-hand thrust bearing with a new one and repeat Step 3 and Step 4. Install the right-hand thrust bearing.
6. If the clearance is still greater than specified, remove the left-hand thrust bearing.
7. Install a flat feeler gauge between the left-hand surface of the crankcase and the machined surface of the crankshaft (**Figure 305**). Compare the dimension to those listed in **Table 6**. **Table 6** gives the left-hand thrust bearing color (**Figure 306**), part number and thickness.

303

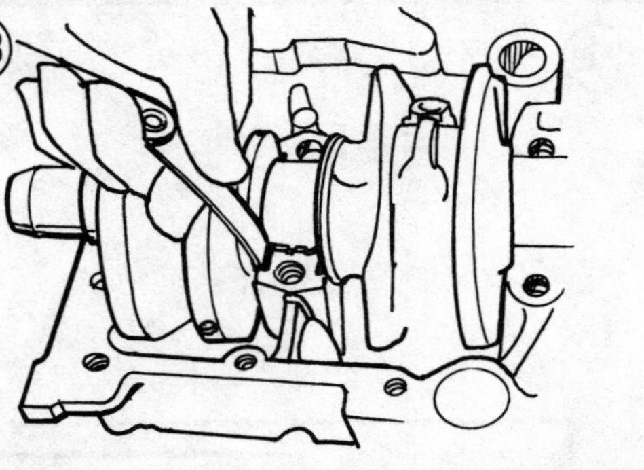

304

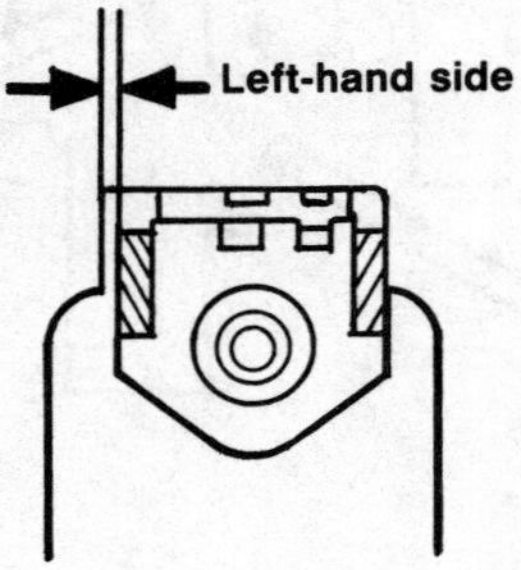

302

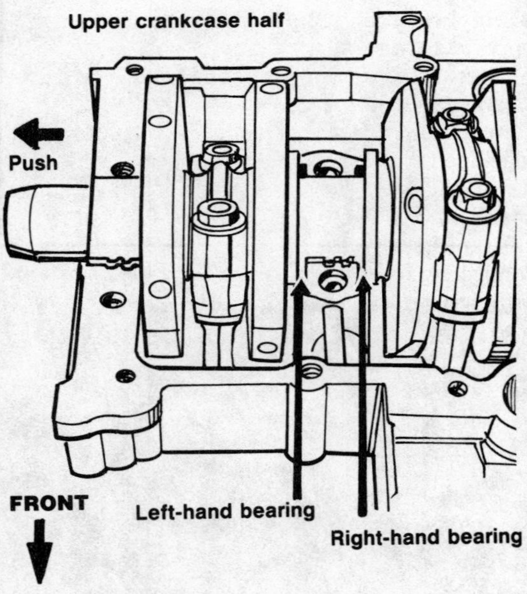

305

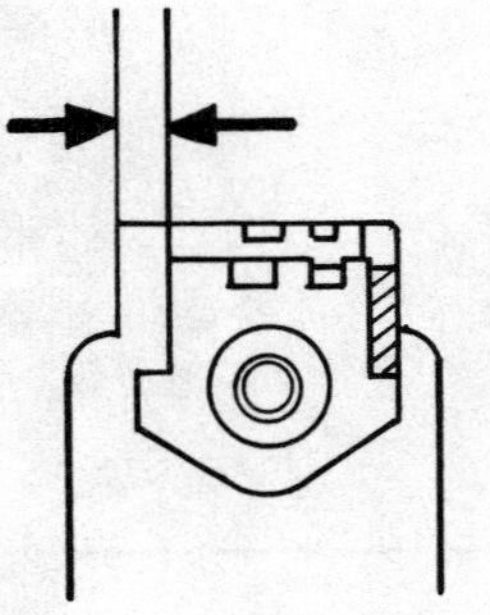

306

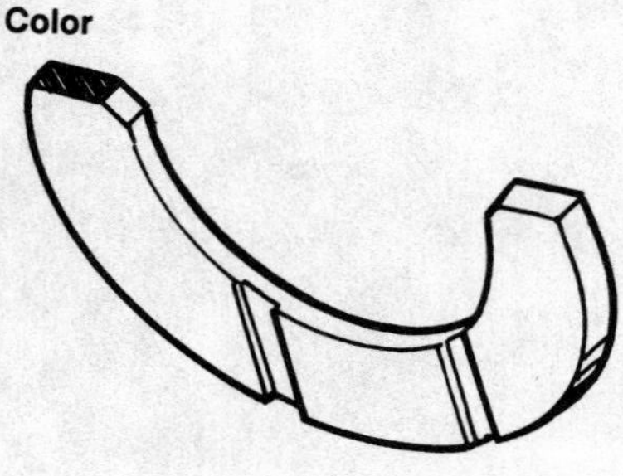

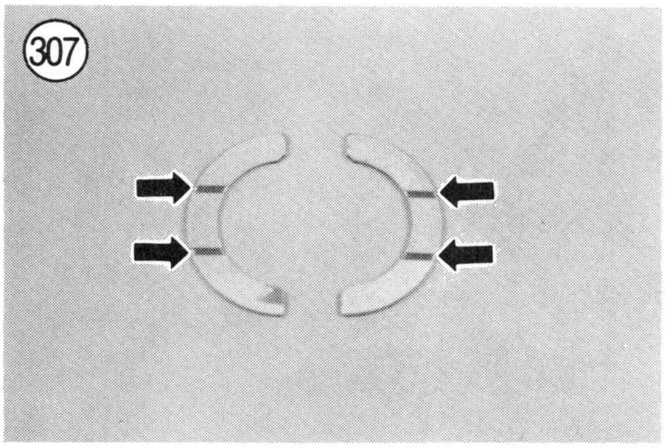

8. Refer to **Table 6** and choose the correct thrust bearing thickness. Install the new left-hand thrust bearing, then repeat Step 3 and Step 4.

9. If the clearance cannot brought into specification with the different thrust bearings, replace the crankshaft.

CAUTION

*Install both the right- and left-hand thrust bearings with their oil grooves (**Figure 307**) facing toward the crankshaft and away from the crankcase bearing saddle.*

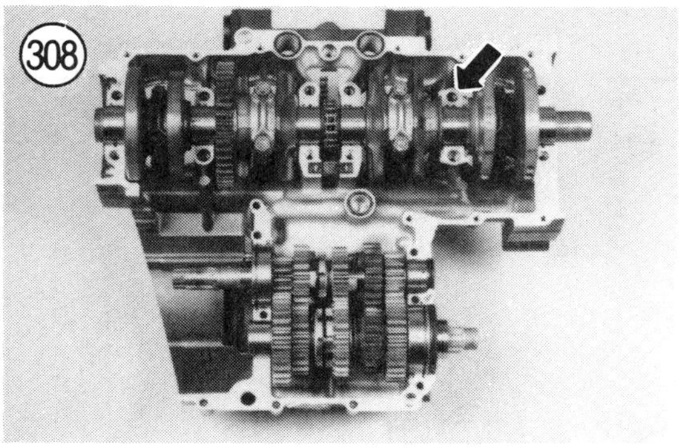

10. After the clearance has been correctly adjusted, remove both thrust bearings and apply a coat of molybdenum disulfide grease to each side of both bearings. Install both bearings into the crankcase with their oil grooves facing toward the crankshaft and away from the crankcase bearing saddle.

CONNECTING RODS

Removal/Installation

1. Disassemble the crankcase as described under *Crankcase Disassembly* in this chapter.

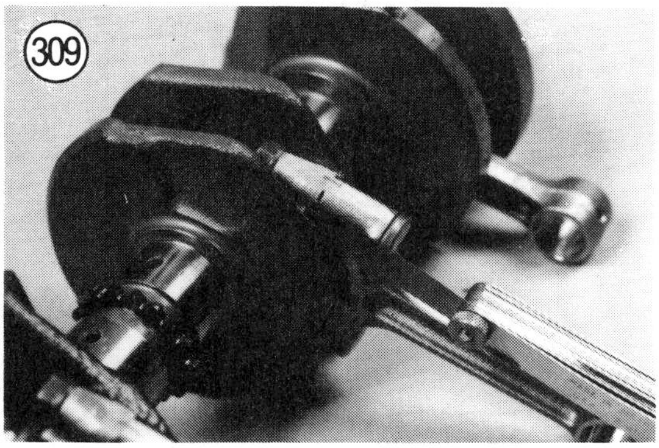

2. Remove the crankshaft/connecting rod assembly and camshaft chain (**Figure 308**) from the upper crankcase half.

3. Measure the connecting rod big end side clearance. Insert a flat feeler gauge between a connecting rod big end and either crankshaft machined web (**Figure 309**). Record the clearance for each connecting rod and compare to the specifications listed in **Table 1** or **Table 2**. If the clearance is greater than specified, inspect the connecting rod width and the crankshaft pin width as described in this chapter.

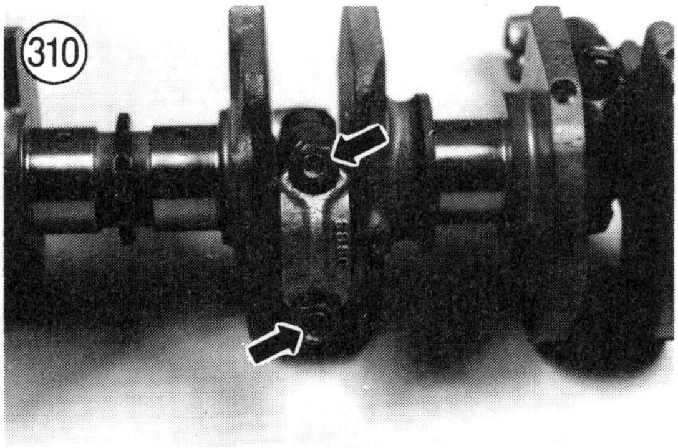

NOTE

Before disassembling the connecting rods, mark the rods and caps with a "1", "2", "3" and "4" starting from the left-hand side. The No. 1 cylinder is on the left-hand side. The No. 1-4 marks relate to the left- and right-hand side of the engine as it sits in the bike frame—not as it sits on your bench.

4. Remove the connecting rod cap nuts (**Figure 310**) and separate the rods from the crankshaft.

Keep each cap with its original rod with the weight mark on the end of the cap matching the mark on the rod (**Figure 311**).

NOTE
Keep each bearing insert in its original place in the crankcase, rod or rod cap. If you are going to assemble the engine with the original inserts, they must be installed exactly as removed in order to prevent rapid wear.

5. Inspect the connecting rods and bearings as described in this chapter.
6. If new bearing inserts are going to be installed, check the bearing clearance as described in this chapter.
7. Apply a light, even coat of molybdenum disulfide grease to the connecting rod bearing journals and to the connecting rod bearing inserts.
8. Install the connecting rod onto the crankshaft, being careful not to damage the bearing surface of the crankshaft with the rod's threaded studs.
9. Match the weight mark on the end of the cap with the mark on the rod (**Figure 311**) and install the cap.
10. Apply a light coat of oil to the connecting rod threaded studs and install the cap nuts (**Figure 310**). Tighten the cap nuts in 2-3 stages to the final torque listed in **Table 3**.
11. After the connecting rods are installed and the cap nuts tightened to the correct torque, rotate the connecting rod several times and check that the bearings are not too tight. Make sure there is no binding.

Connecting Rod Inspection

CAUTION
Never try to remove the connecting rod bolts from the connecting rod. If loosened and retightened, the bearing cap will never fit properly.

1. Check each connecting rod for obvious damage such as cracks and burns.
2. Check the piston pin bore for wear or scoring.
3. Take the connecting rods to a machine shop and check for twisting or bending.
4. Examine the bearing inserts for wear, scoring, or burning. They are reusable if in good condition. Make a note of the bearing color identification on the side of the insert if the bearing is to be discarded.
5. If the connecting rod big end clearance is greater than specified as measured in Step 3, *Connecting Rod Removal/Installation* in this chapter, perform the following:

311
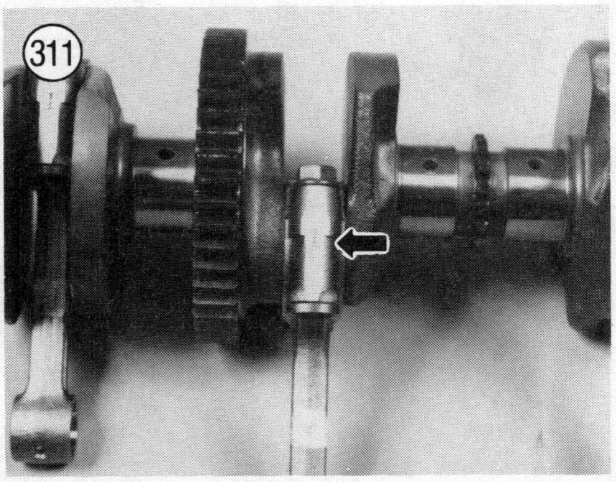

312
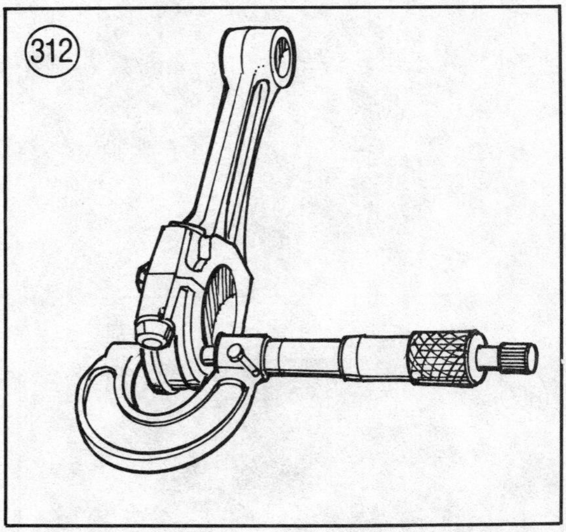

313
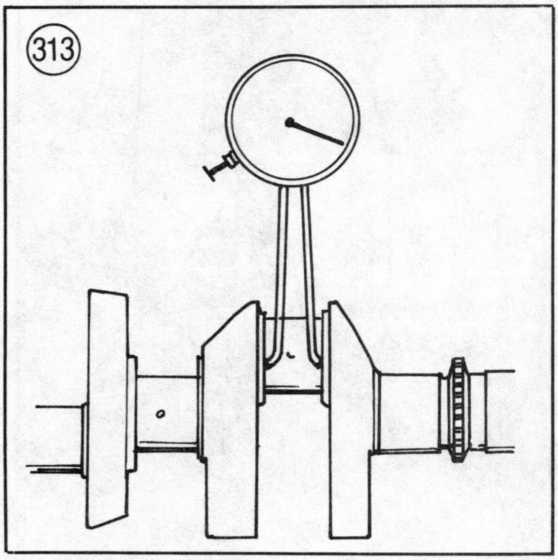

314

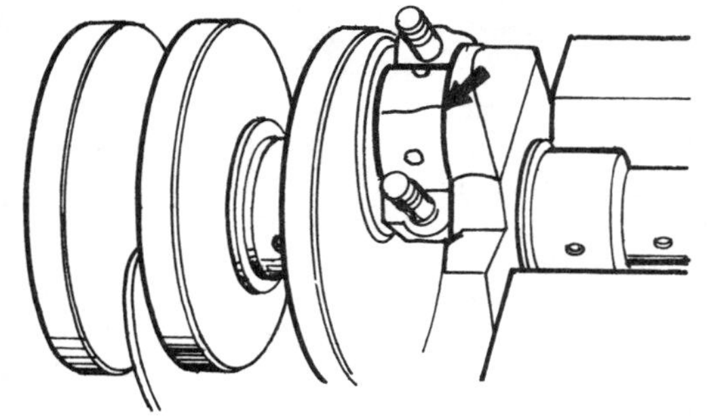

315

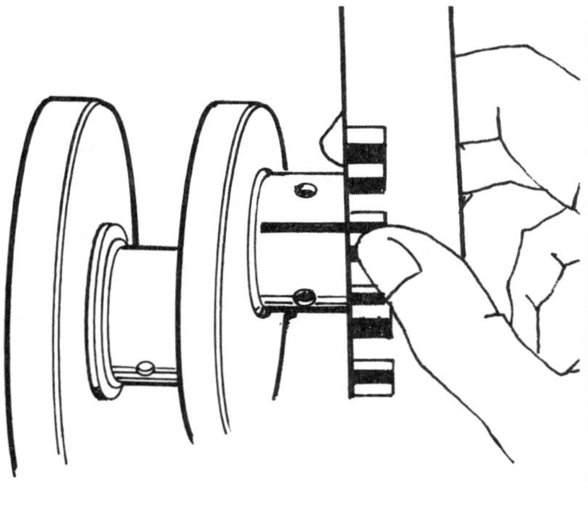

a. Measure the width of the connecting rod big end with a micrometer (**Figure 312**) and compare to dimensions listed in **Table 1** or **Table 2**. If the width is less than specified, replace the connecting rod assembly.

b. Measure the crankpin width with a dial caliper (**Figure 313**) and compare to dimensions listed in **Table 1** or **Table 2**. If the width is greater than specified, replace the crankshaft.

Connecting Rod Bearing Clearance Measurement

1. Check each rod bearing insert for evidence of wear, abrasion, and scoring. If the bearings are good, they may be reused. If any insert is questionable, replace as a set.
2. Clean the bearing surfaces of the crankshaft and the connecting rod bearing inserts.
3. Install the rod bearing inserts in the connecting rod and bearing cap. Make sure they are locked in place correctly.
4. Install the connecting rod onto the crankshaft, being careful not to damage the bearing surface of the crankshaft with the rod's threaded studs.
5. Place a piece of Plastigage over the rod bearing journal parallel to the crankshaft (**Figure 314**). Do not place the Plastigage material over an oil hole in the crankshaft.

CAUTION
Do not rotate the crankshaft while the Plastigage is in place.

6. Match the weight mark on the end of the cap with the mark on the rod (**Figure 311**) and install the cap.
7. Apply a light coat of oil to the connecting rod threaded studs and install the cap nuts (**Figure 310**). Tighten the cap nuts in 2-3 stages to the final torque listed in **Table 3**.
8. Loosen the cap nuts and carefully remove the cap from the connecting rod.
9. Measure the width of the flattened Plastigage according to manufacturer's instructions. Measure at both ends of Plastigage strip (**Figure 315**). A difference of 0.025 mm (0.001 in.) or more indicates a tapered journal. Confirm with a micrometer. Bearing clearance for new connecting rod bearings is listed in **Table 1** or **Table 2**.
10. Remove the Plastigage strips from the main bearing journals.
11. If the bearing clearance is greater than specified, select new bearings as described in this chapter.

Connecting Rod Bearing Selection

1. The crankshaft connecting rod bearing journals are marked with a "1," "2" or "3" (B, **Figure 298**). The stamped letters relate to the crankshaft journals as shown in **Figure 316**.
2. The connecting rod bearing I.D. code number ("1" or "2") is marked on the side of each connecting rod and cap **(Figure 311)**.
3. Select new bearings by cross-referencing the rod bearing journal numbers (B, **Figure 298**) in the vertical column of **Table 7** with the connecting rod I.D. numbers (**Figure 311**). Where the columns intersect, the new bearing insert color is indicated. **Table 7** gives the bearing color and **Table 8** gives bearing color, part number and thickness. Always replace all 8 bearing inserts as a set.
4. After new bearing inserts have been installed, recheck the clearance by repeating the *Connecting Rod Bearing Clearance Measurement* procedure in this chapter. If the clearance is still out of specifications, either the connecting rod or the crankshaft is worn beyond the service limit and requires replacement.

BREAK-IN

Following cylinder servicing (boring, honing, new rings, etc.) and major lower end work, the engine should be broken in just as though it were new. The performance and service life of the engine depend greatly on a careful and sensible break-in.

For the first 800 km (500 miles), no more than one-third throttle should be used and speed should be varied as much as possible within the one-third throttle limit. Prolonged, steady running at one speed, no matter how moderate, is to be avoided, as is hard acceleration.

Following the 800 km (500-mile) service, increasingly more throttle can be used but full throttle should not be used until the motorcycle has covered at least 1,600 km (1,000 miles) and then it should be limited to short bursts until 2,410 km (1,500 miles) have been logged.

During this period, oil consumption will be higher than normal. It is therefore important to frequently check and correct the oil level. At no time, during break-in or later, should the oil level be allowed to drop below the bottom line on the dipstick; if the oil level is low, the oil will become overheated, resulting in insufficient lubrication and increased wear.

800 KM (500-MILE) SERVICE

It is essential that oil and filter be changed after the first 800 km (500 miles). In addition, it is a good idea to change the oil and filter at the completion of break-in (about 2,410 km/1,500 miles) to ensure that all of the particles produced during break-in are removed from the lubrication system. The small added expense may be considered a smart investment that will pay off in increased engine life.

316

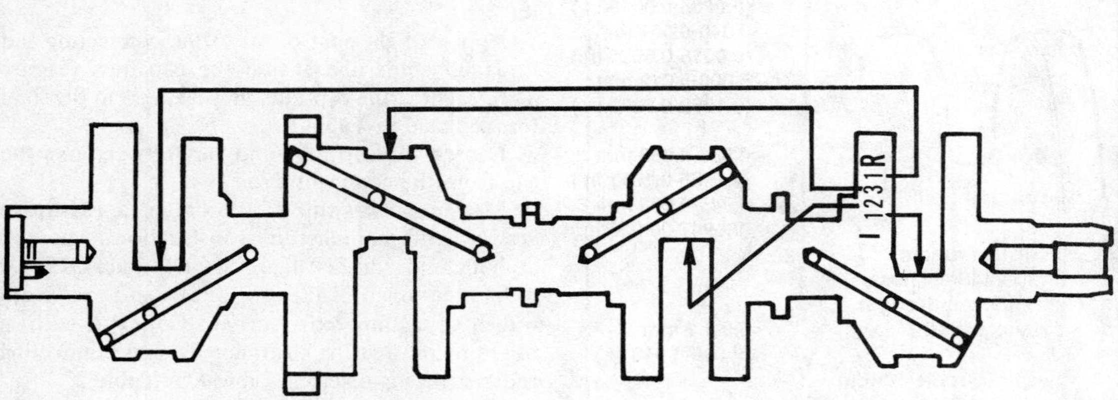

Table 1 ENGINE SPECIFICATIONS (750 CC MODELS)

	Specification	Wear limit
General		
Type and number of cylinders	Inline 4-cylinder, DOHC, oil cooled	
Bore × strole	70.0 × 48.7 mm (2.76 × 1.92 in.)	
Displacement	749 cc (45.7 cu. in.)	
Compression pressure	1,000-1,400 kPa (142-199 psi)	
Camshaft		
Cam lobe height		
Intake	33.594-33.634 mm* 33.563-33.603 mm** (1.3226-1.3242 in.) (1.3224-1.3240 in.)	33.300 mm* 33.270 mm** (1.3110 in.) (1.3108 in.)
Exhaust	32.882-32.992 mm* 33.146-33.186 mm** (1.2946-1.2989 in.) (1.3067-1.3075 in.)	32.590 mm* 32.850 mm** (1.2831 in.) (1.2942 in.)
Journal O.D.		
Intake and exhaust	21.959-21.980 mm (0.8645-0.8654 in.)	–
Journal oil clearance		
Intake and exhaust	0.032-0.066 mm (0.0013-0.0026 in.)	0.150 mm (0.0059 in.)
Journal holder I.D.		
Intake and exhaust	22.012-22.025 mm (0.8666-0.8671 in.)	–
Runout	–	0.10 mm (0.004 in.)
Drive chain (20 pitch length)	–	158.0 mm (6.22 in.)
Rocker assembly		
Rocker arm bore I.D.	12.000-12.018 mm (0.4724-0.4731 in.)	–
rocker arm shaft O.D.	11.973-11.984 mm (0.4711-0.4718 in.)	–
Cylinder head distortion	–	0.20 mm (0.008 in.)
Valves		
Diameter		
Intake	26 mm (1.0 in.)	–
Exhaust	24 mm (0.9 in.)	–
Valve lift		
Intake	8.3 mm (0.326 in.)* 8.2 mm (0.323 in.)**	–
Exhaust	7.0 mm (0.275 in.)* 7.5 mm (0.295 in.)**	–
Valve stem-to-guide clearance		
Intake	0.020-0.047 mm (0.0008-0.0019 in.)	0.35 mm (0.014 in.)
Exhaust	0.040-0.067 mm (0.0016-0.0026 in.)	0.35 mm (0.014 in.)
Valve guide I.D.	5.000-5.012 mm (0.1969-0.1973 in.)	–
Valve stem O.D.		
Intake	4.965-4.980 mm (0.1955-0.1961 in.)	–
Exhaust	4.945-4.960 mm (0.1947-0.1953 in.)	–
Valve stem runout	–	0.05 mm (0.002 in.)
Valve head thickness	–	0.5 mm (0.02 in.)
Valve stem end length	–	2.5 mm (0.10 in.)
Valve seat width	0.9-1.1 mm (0.035-0.043 in.)	–
Valve head radial runout	–	0.03 mm (0.001 in.)
Valve spring free length		
Inner	–	35.0 mm (1.38 in.)
Outer	–	38.4 mm (1.51 in.)

(continued)

Table 1 ENGINE SPECIFICATIONS (750 CC MODELS) (continued)

	Specification	Wear limit
Cylinders		
Bore	70.000-70.015 mm (2.7559-2.7565 in.)	70.080 mm (2.7590 in.)
Cylinder/piston clearance	0.050-0.060 mm (0.0020-0.0024 in.)	0.120 mm (0.0047 in.)
Out-of-round	–	0.05 mm (0.002 in.)
Pistons		
Outer diameter	69.945-69.960 mm (2.7537-2.7543 in.)	69.880 mm (2.7512 in.)
Clearance in bore	0.050-0.060 mm (0.0020-0.0024 in.)	0.120 mm (0.0047 in.)
Piston pin bore	18.002-18.008 mm (0.7087-0.7090 in.)	18.030 mm (0.7098 in.)
Piston pin outer diameter	17.996-18.000 mm (0.7085-0.7086 in.)	17.980 mm (0.7079 in.)
Piston ring groove width		
Top	0.81-0.83 mm (0.032-0.033 in.)	–
Second	1.01-1.03 mm (0.039-0.040 in.)	–
Oil	2.01-2.03 mm (0.079-0.080 in.)	–
Piston rings		
Number per piston		
Compression	2	–
Oil control	1	–
Ring end gap		
Top and second	0.1-0.3 mm (0.004-0.012 in.)	0.7 mm (0.03 in.)
Ring end gap (free)		
Top	Approx. 9.1 mm (0.36 in.)	7.3 mm (0.29 in.)
Second	Approx 7.5 mm (0.30 in.)	6.0 mm (0.24 in.)
Ring side clearance		
Top	–	0.180 mm (0.007 in.)
Second	–	0.150 mm (0.006 in.)
Ring thickness		
Top	0.77-0.79 mm (0.030-0.031 in.)	–
Second	0.97-0.99 mm (0.038-0.039 in.)	–
Connecting rods		
Piston pin hole I.D.	18.010-18.018 mm (0.7091-0.7094 in.)	18.040 mm (0.7102 in.)
Big end side clearance	0.10-0.20 mm (0.004-0.008 in.)	0.30 mm (0.01 in.)
Big end width	20.95-21.00 mm (0.825-0.827 in.)	–
Big end oil clearance	0.032-0.056 mm (0.0013-0.0022 in.)	0.080 mm (0.0031 in.)
Crankshaft		
Crankpin width	21.10-21.15 mm (0.831-0.833 in.)	–
Crankpin journal O.D.		
Code A	31.992-32.000 mm (1.2595-1.2598 in.)	–

(continued)

Table 1 ENGINE SPECIFICATIONS (750 CC MODELS) (continued)

	Specification	Wear limit
Code B	31.984-31.992 mm (1.2592-1.2595 in.)	–
Code C	31.976-31.984 mm (1.2589-1.2592 in.)	–
Crankpin O.D.	33.976-34.000 mm (1.3376-1.3386 in.)	–
Crankpin journal oil clearance	0.020-0.044 mm (0.0008-0.0017 in.)	0.080 mm (0.0031 in.)
Crankpin journal O.D.	31.976-32.000 mm (1.2589-1.2598 in.)	–
Thrust clearance	0.04-0.18 mm (0.002-0.007 in.)	0.25 mm (0.010 in.)
Journal holder width	23.88-23.96 mm (0.940-0.943 in.)	–
Journal width	24.00-24.05 mm (0.945-0.947 in.)	–
Runout	–	0.05 mm (0.002 in.)
Crankcase crankshaft bearing insert I.D.		
Code A	35.000-35.008 mm (1.3780-1.3783 in.)	–
Code B	35.008-35.016 mm (1.3783-1.3786 in.)	–

*U.S. models
**UK models

Table 2 ENGINE SPECIFICATIONS (1100 CC MODELS)

	Specification	Wear limit
General		
Type and number of cylinders	Inline 4-cylinder, DOHC, oil cooled	
Bore × stroke	76.0 × 58.0 mm (2.90 × 1.30 in.)	
Displacement	1,052 cc (64.2 cu. in.)	
Compression pressure	1,000-1,400 kPa (142-199 psi)	
Camshaft		
Cam lobe height		
Intake	33.878-33.918 mm (1.3338-1.3354 in.)	33.580 mm (1.3220 in.)
Exhaust	33.533-33.573 mm (1.3202-1.3218 in.)	33.240 mm (1.3087 in.)
Journal O.D.		
Intake and exhaust	21.959-21.980 mm (0.8645-0.8654 in.)	–
Journal oil clearance		
Intake and exhaust	0.032-0.066 mm (0.0013-0.0026 in.)	0.150 mm (0.0059 in.)
Journal holder I.D.		
Intake and exhaust	22.012-22.025 mm (0.8666-0.8671 in.)	–
Runout	–	0.10 mm (0.004 in.)
Drive chain (20 pitch length)	–	158.0 mm (6.22 in.)

(continued)

Table 2 ENGINE SPECIFICATIONS (1100 CC MODELS) (cont.)

	Specification	Wear limit
Rocker assembly		
Rocker arm bore I.D.	12.000-12.018 mm (0.4724-0.4731 in.)	—
Rocker arm shaft O.D.	11.973-11.984 mm (0.4711-0.4718 in.)	—
Cylinder head distortion	—	0.20 mm (0.008 in.)
Valves		
Diameter		
Intake	28.5 mm (1.12 in.)	—
Exhaust	25 mm (1.0 in.)	—
Valve lift		
Intake	8.8 mm (0.35 in.)	—
Exhaust	8.2 mm (0.32 in.)	—
Valve stem-to-guide clearance		
Intake	0.020-0.047 mm (0.0008-0.0019 in.)	0.35 mm (0.014 in.)
Exhaust	0.040-0.067 mm (0.0016-0.0026 in.)	0.35 mm (0.014 in.)
Valve guide I.D.	5.000-5.012 mm (0.1969-0.1973 in.)	—
Valve stem O.D.		
Intake	4.965-4.980 mm (0.1955-0.1961 in.)	—
Exhaust	4.945-4.960 mm (0.1947-0.1953 in.)	—
Valve stem runout	—	0.05 mm (0.002 in.)
Valve head thickness	—	0.05 mm (0.002 in.)
Valve stem end length	—	2.5 mm (0.10 in.)
Valve seat width	0.9-1.1 mm (0.035-0.043 in.)	—
Valve head radial runout	—	0.03 mm (0.001 in.)
Valve spring free length		
Inner	—	35.0 mm (1.38 in.)
Outer	—	38.4 mm (1.51 in.)
Cylinders		
Bore	76.000-76.015 mm (2.9921-2.9927 in.)	76.065 mm (2.9947 in.)
Cylinder/piston clearance	0.065-0.075 mm (0.0022-0.0026 in.	0.120 mm (0.0047 in.)
Out-of-round	—	0.05 mm (0.002 in.)
Pistons		
Outer diameter	75.930-75.945 mm (2.9894-2.9899 in.)	75.880 mm (2.9874 in.)
Clearance in bore	0.065-0.075 mm (0.0022-0.0026 in.	0.120 mm (0.0047 in.)
Piston pin bore	20.002-20.008 mm (0.7875-0.7877 in.)	20.030 mm (0.7886 in.)
Piston pin outer diameter	19.996-20.000 mm (0.7872-0.7874 in.)	19.980 mm (0.7866 in.)
Piston ring groove width		
Top	1.01-1.03 mm (0.039-0.040 in.)	—
Second	1.01-1.03 mm (0.039-0.040 in.)	—
Oil	2.01-2.03 mm (0.079-0.080 in.)	—

(continued)

Table 2 ENGINE SPECIFICATIONS (1100 CC MODELS) (cont.)

	Specification	Wear limit
Piston rings		
Number per piston		
Compression	2	—
Oil control	1	—
Ring end gap		
Top and second	0.2-0.35 mm (0.008-0.014 in.)	0.7 mm (0.03 in.)
Ring end gap (free)		
Top	Approx 9.7 mm (0.38 in.)	7.8 mm (0.31 in.)
Second	Approx 8.2 mm (0.32 in.)	6.6 mm (0.26 in.)
Ring side clearance		
Top	—	0.180 mm (0.007 in.)
Second	—	0.150 mm (0.006 in.)
Ring thickness		
Top	0.97-0.99 mm (0.038-0.039 in.)	—
Second	0.97-0.99 mm (0.038-0.039 in.)	—
Connecting rods		
Piston pin hole I.D.	20.010-20.018 mm (0.7878-0.7881 in.)	20.040 mm (0.7890 in.)
Big end side clearance	0.10-0.2 mm (0.004-0.008 in.)	0.30 mm (0.01 in.)
Big end width	20.95-21.00 mm (0.825-0.827 in.)	—
Big end oil clearance	0.032-0.056 mm (0.0013-0.0022 in.)	0.080 mm (0.0031 in.)
Crankshaft		
Crankpin width	21.10-21.15 mm (0.831-0.833 in.)	—
Crankpin O.D.	37.976-38.000 mm (1.4951-1.4961 in.)	—
Crankpin journal oil clearance	0.020-0.044 mm (0.0008-0.0017 in.)	0.080 mm (0.0031 in.)
Crankpin journal O.D.		
Code A	35.992-36.000 mm (1.4170-1.4173 in.)	—
Code B	35.984-35.992 mm (1.4167-1.4170 in.)	—
Code C	35.976-36.000 mm (1.4164-1.4167 in.)	—
Thrust clearance	0.04-0.16 mm (0.002-0.006 in.)	—
Thrust bearing thickness		
Left-hand side	2.33-2.51 mm (0.092-0.099 in.)	—
Right-hand side	2.39-2.45 mm (0.094-0.096 in.)	—
Runout	—	0.05 mm (0.002 in.)
Crankcase crankshaft bearing insert I.D.		
Code A	39.000-39.008 mm 1.5354-1.5357 in.)	—
Code B	39.008-39.016 mm 1.5357-1.5361 in.)	—

Table 3 ENGINE TORQUE SPECIFICATIONS

Item	N•m	ft.-lb.
Engine mounting bolts and nuts		
Through-bolts	70-88	51-64
Bolts (55 mm long)	50-60	36-44
All other bolts	25-38	18-28
Cylinder head cover bolts	13-15	9-11
Oil hose fitting Allen bolts	8-12	6-9
Camshaft sprocket bolts	24-26	17-19
Camshaft bearing cap bolts	8-12	6-9
Camshaft chain idler bolts	9-11	7-8
Camshaft chain tensioner spring bolt	30-45	21-33
Camshaft chain tensioner mounting bolts	6-8	4.5-6
Rocker arm shaft bolt	8-12	6-8
Rocker arm shaft end plug	25-30	18-22
Cylinder base nut	7-11	5-8
Cylinder head nuts	35-40	25-29
Cylinder head bolt	7-11	5-8
Oil pump mounting bolts	8-12	6-8
Oil cooler oil line union bolts	25-30	18-22
Oil pan bolts	12-16	8-12
Oil pressure regulator	25-30	18-22
Starter clutch bolt	110-130	80-94
Crankcase bolts		
Initial torque		
6 mm	6	4.5
8 mm	13	10
Final torque		
6 mm	13	10
8 mm	24	18
Main oil gallery plug bolt	35-45	26-33
Connecting rod cap nuts	33-37	24-27
Drive sprocket		
Nut	100-130	73-94
Bolt	9-12	6-9
Oil strainer bolt	10-14	7-10

Table 4 CRANKSHAFT MAIN BEARING INSERT SELECTION

Crankshaft O.D.	Code	A	B	C
Crankcase I.D.	A	Green	Black	Brown
	B	Black	Brown	Yellow

Table 5 CRANKSHAFT INSERT COLOR, PART NO., THICKNESS

Color @ Part No.	Specification
Green 12229-06B00-0A0	1.486-1.490 mm (0.0585-0.0587 in.)
Black 12229-06B00-0B0	1.490-1.494 mm (0.0587-0.0588 in.)
Brown 12229-06B00-0C0	1.494-1.498 mm (0.0588-0.0590 in.)
Yellow 12229-06B00-0D0	1.498-1.502 mm (0.0590-0.0591 in.)

Table 6 THRUST BEARING SELECTION (1100 CC MODELS)

Clearance before inserting left side thrust bearing	Color and part No.	Thrust bearing thickness
2.43-2.49 mm (0.096-0.098 in.)	Black 12228-06B00-0C0	2.33-2.39 mm (0.092-0.094 in.)
2.49-2.55 mm (0.098-0.100 in.)	Green 12228-06B00-0B0	2.39-2.45 mm (0.094-0.096 in.)
2.55-2.62 mm (0.100-0.103 in.)	Red 12228-06B00-0A0	2.45-2.51 mm (0.096-0.099 in.)

Table 7 CONNECTING ROD BEARING INSERT SELECTION

Crankpin O.D.	Code	1	2	3
Connecting rod	1	Green	Black	Brown
I.D.	2	Black	Brown	Yellow

Table 8 CONNECTING ROD INSERT COLOR, PART NO., THICKNESS

Color @ Part No.	Specification
Green 12164-27A00-0A0	1.480-1.484 mm (0.0583-0.0584 in.)
Black 12164-27A00-0B0	1.484-1.488 mm (0.0584-0.0586 in.)
Brown 12164-27A00-0C0	1.488-1.492 mm (0.0586-0.0587 in.)
Yellow 12164-27A00-0D0	1.492-1.496 mm (0.0587-0.0589 in.)

NOTE: If you own a GSX600F Katana, first refer to Chapter 13 for specific service information.

CHAPTER FIVE

CLUTCH

This chapter provides complete service procedures for the clutch and clutch release mechanism.

The clutch on the GSX R750R Limited Edition is a dry multi-plate type. It is mounted on the right-hand end of the transmission mainshaft. The inner clutch hub is splined to the mainshaft and the outer housing can rotate freely on the mainshaft. The outer housing is geared to the crankshaft.

The clutch on all other models is a wet multi-plate type which operates immersed in the engine oil. It is mounted on the right-hand end of the transmission mainshaft. The inner clutch hub is splined to the mainshaft and the outer housing can rotate freely on the mainshaft. The outer housing is geared to the crankshaft.

On GSX-R750R Limited Edition models, the clutch release mechanism is mounted within the clutch outer cover and is operated by a clutch cable and hand lever mounted on the left-hand handlebar. This type of clutch *does* require routine adjustment as the cable stretches with use. Refer to Chapter Three.

On all other models, the clutch release mechanism is hydraulic and requires no adjustment. The mechanism consists of a clutch master cylinder on the left-hand handlebar, a slave cylinder on the left-hand side of the engine and a pushrod that rides within the channel in the transmission mainshaft.

Specifications for the GSX-R750R Limited Edition (dry clutch) are listed in **Table 1**. Specifications for all other models (wet clutch) are listed in **Table 2**. **Tables 1-3** are located at the end of this chapter.

CLUTCH—DRY TYPE (GSX-R750R LIMITED EDITION)

Removal/Disassembly

The clutch can be removed with the engine in the frame. Refer to **Figure 1** for this procedure.

1. Remove the lower section and the right-hand middle section of the front fairing as described under *Front Fairing Removal/Installation* in Chapter Twelve.
2. Drain the engine oil as described under *Engine Oil and Filter Change* in Chapter Three.
3. Slacken the clutch cable at the hand lever (**Figure 2**).
4. Disconnect the clutch cable from the clutch release arm (A, **Figure 3**).

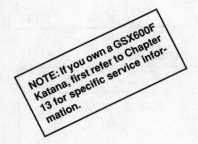

1

CLUTCH—DRY TYPE
(GSX-R750R LIMITED EDITION)

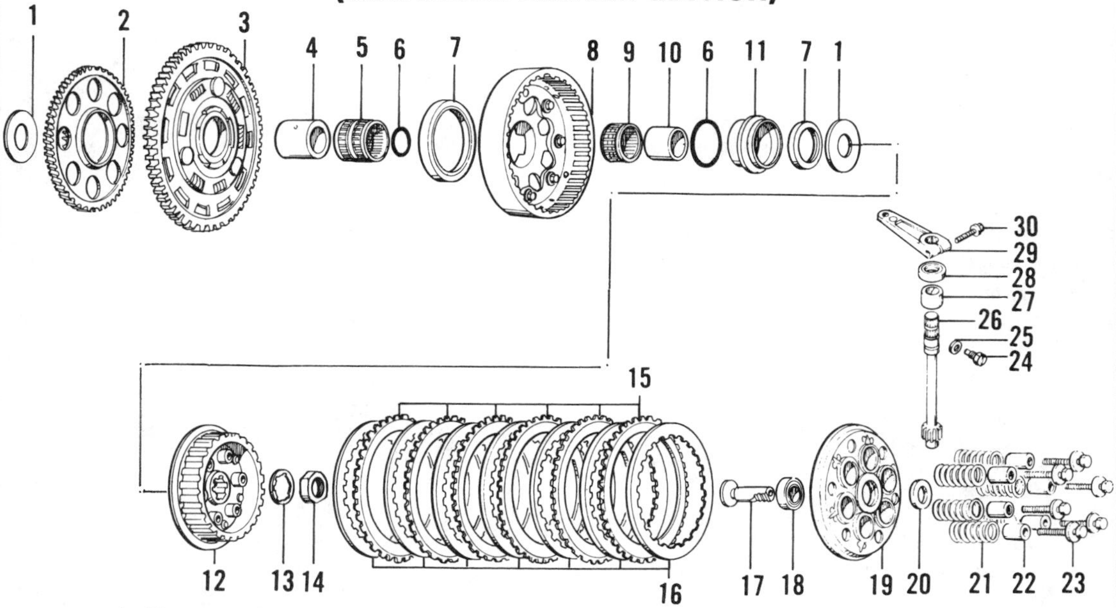

1. Thrust washer
2. Alternator/oil pump drive gear
3. Primary driven gear
4. Inner spacer
5. Inner needle bearing
6. O-ring
7. Oil seal
8. Clutch outer housing
9. Outer needle bearing
10. Outer spacer
11. Clutch outer housing collar
12. Clutch hub
13. Lockwasher
14. Clutch nut
15. Drive plate
16. Driven plate
17. Clutch release rack
18. Bearing
19. Pressure plate
20. Oil seal
21. Clutch spring
22. Spacer
23. Clutch bolt
24. Bolt
25. Washer
26. Clutch release rack
27. Bushing
28. Oil seal
29. Clutch release arm
30. Bolt

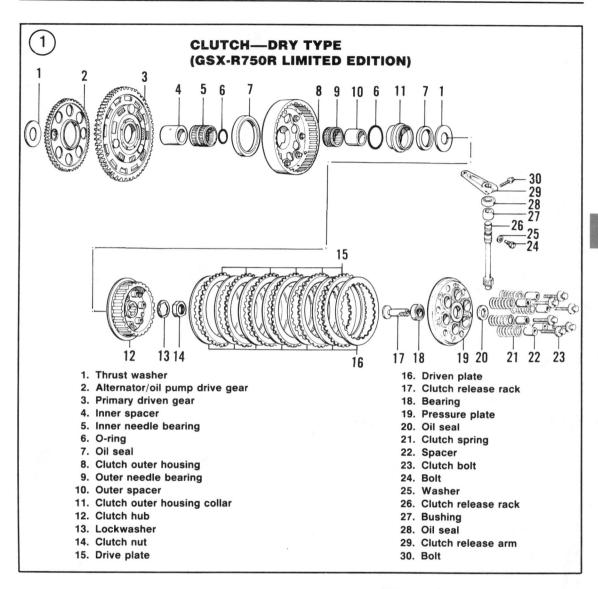

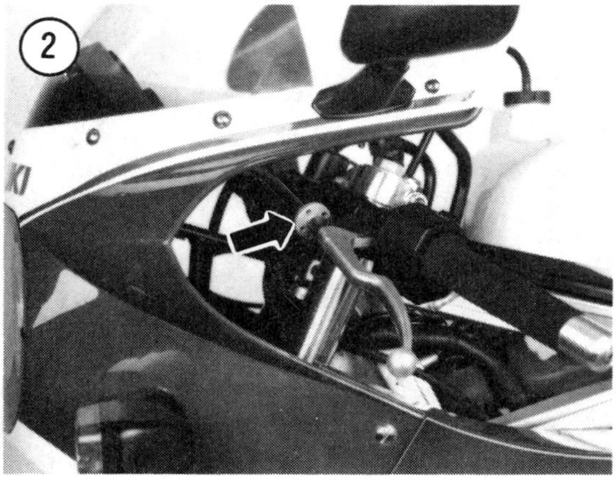

5. Disconnect the clutch cable from the receptacle on the clutch outer cover (B, **Figure 3**).
6. Remove the bolts securing the clutch outer cover (**Figure 4**) and remove the clutch outer cover.
7. Using a crisscross pattern remove the clutch bolts (**Figure 5**) securing the clutch pressure plate.
8. Remove the clutch bolts and springs.
9. Remove the pressure plate (A, **Figure 6**) and release rack (B, **Figure 6**).
10. Remove all of the drive and driven plates (**Figure 7**) from the clutch hub and clutch outer housing.
11. Straighten the locking tab on the lockwasher (**Figure 8**).

NOTE

The following special tool is manufactured for American Honda (not Suzuki) and is very versatile. It can be adjusted to work on almost all types of Japanese motorcycle clutch assemblies—not just Honda. If you work on different motorcycles this is a very handy tool to have in your tool box.

10

11

12

13

12A. To loosen the clutch nut with a special tool, perform the following:

a. Hold onto the clutch center to prevent it from turning. Use Honda special tool (Clutch Center Holder—part No. 07923-4280000) (**Figure 9**) or equivalent.

b. Loosen the clutch nut. Remove the nut and lockwasher.

12B. To remove the clutch nut without special tool, perform the following:

a. Hold onto the clutch center to prevent it from turning.

b. Use an impact driver and loosen the clutch nut. Remove the nut and lockwasher.

13. Slide the clutch hub (**Figure 10**) off the transmission mainshaft.

14. Remove the thrust washer (**Figure 11**).

15. Slide the clutch outer housing (**Figure 12**) off the transmission mainshaft.

16. Remove the bolts securing the clutch inner cover (A, **Figure 13**). Don't lose the copper washers under the 2 bolts (W, **Figure 13**) at the rear.

17. Remove the clutch inner cover and gasket. Don't lose the locating dowels.

18. Slide off the outer needle bearing (single row) (**Figure 14**).

19. Slide off the outer spacer (**Figure 15**).

14

15

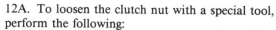

20. Remove the O-ring (**Figure 16**) from the transmission mainshaft.
21. Slide off the inner needle bearing (double row) (**Figure 17**).
22. Slide off the inner spacer (A, **Figure 18**).
23. Remove the primary driven gear assembly and alternator/oil pump drive gear (B, **Figure 18**).
24. Remove the thrust washer (**Figure 19**).
25. Inspect all components as described in this chapter.

Inspection

Refer to **Table 1** for clutch specifications.

CAUTION
*Do **not** wash the clutch drive or clutch driven plates in a petroleum-based solvent. This type of solvent will leave an oil residue and will render the plates useless. These plates are to be **free** of any oil or grease residue. If any engine oil has leaked past the oil seal in the clutch mechanism, replace the clutch drive and driven plates as a set. The plates cannot be completely cleaned after becoming oil-contaminated—not even with carbon tetrachloride.*

1. Clean all clutch parts (except the drive and driven plates) in petroleum-based solvent such as kerosene and thoroughly dry with compressed air.
2. Measure the free length of each clutch spring as shown in **Figure 20**. Compare to the specifications listed in **Table 1**. Replace the springs as a set if any have sagged to the service limit or less.
3. Measure the thickness of each clutch drive plate at several places around the plate as shown in **Figure 21**. Compare to the specifications listed in **Table 1**. Replace any plate that is worn to the service limit or less.

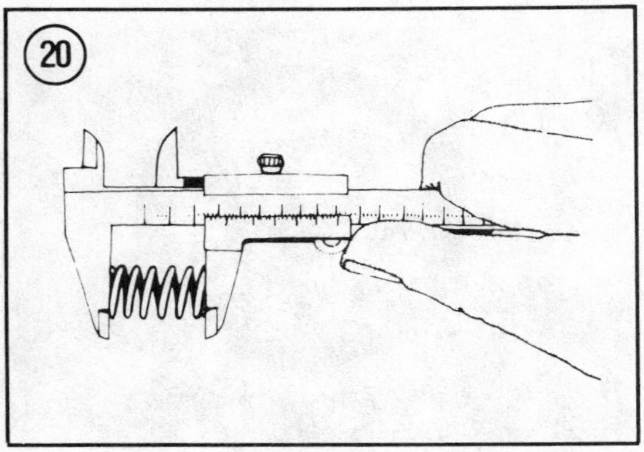

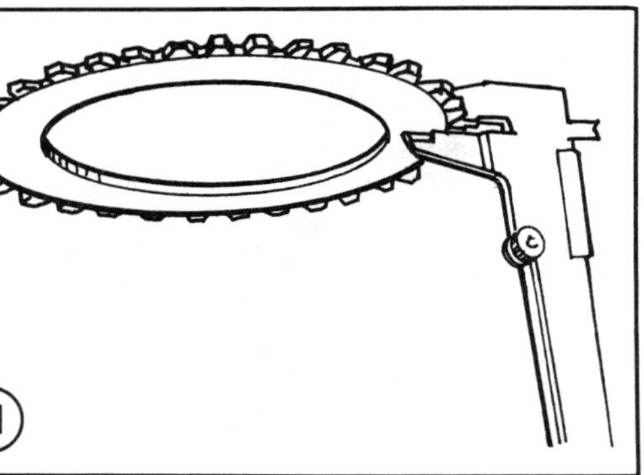

21

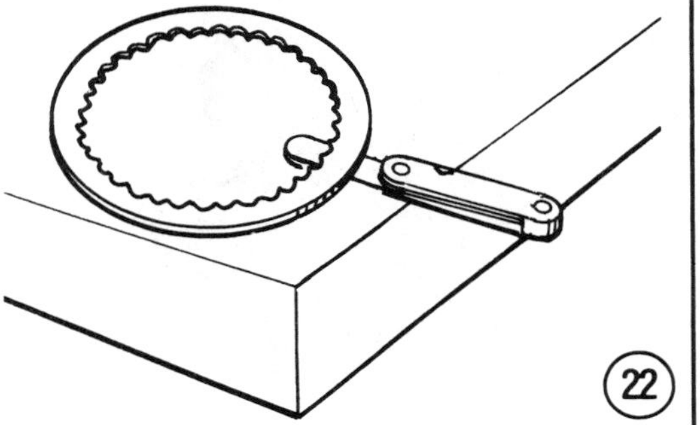

22

4. Check the clutch driven plates for warpage on a surface plate such as a piece of plate glass (**Figure 22**). Compare to the specifications listed in **Table 1**. Replace any plate that is warped to the service limit or more.

5. Check the clutch drive plates (**Figure 23**) and clutch driven plates (**Figure 24**) for wear, scratches or surface damage. Replace any plate that is damaged or worn.

NOTE

If any of the clutch drive plates, clutch driven plates or clutch springs require replacement, you should consider replacing all of them as a set to retain maximum clutch performance.

6. Inspect the grooves in the clutch outer housing (**Figure 25**) for nicks or galling where they come in contact with the clutch drive plate tabs. If any severe damage is evident, the housing must be replaced.

7. Inspect the locating tabs (**Figure 26**) on the backside of the clutch outer housing for nicks or damage where they come in contact with the locating grooves in the primary driven gear assembly. If any severe damage is evident, the housing must be replaced.

23

25

24

26

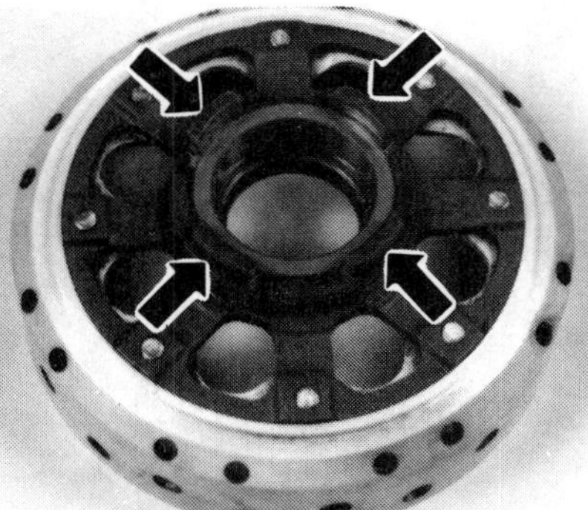

8. Inspect the grooves in the clutch hub (**Figure 27**) for nicks or galling where they come in contact with the clutch driven plate tabs. If any severe damage is evident, the hub must be replaced.
9. Inspect the inner splines in the clutch hub (**Figure 28**) for damage. If any severe damage is evident, the clutch hub must be replaced.
10. Inspect the bearing (**Figure 29**) in the clutch pressure plate. It must rotate smoothly with no signs of wear or damage. Replace if necessary.
11. Inspect the gear teeth on the primary driven gear assembly (A, **Figure 30**) and the alternator/oil pump drive gears (A, **Figure 31**) for damage. Remove any small nicks with an oilstone. If damage is severe, the gear assembly must be replaced. Also check the teeth on the drive gear of the crankshaft; if damaged the driven gear may also need replacing.
12. Inspect the splines on the primary driven gear assembly (B, **Figure 30**) and the alternator/oil pump drive gears (B, **Figure 31**) for damage. Remove any small nicks with an oilstone. If damage is severe, the gear assembly must be replaced.

27

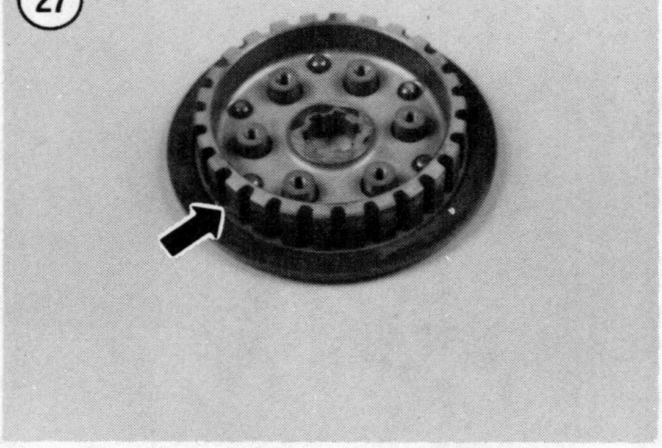

28

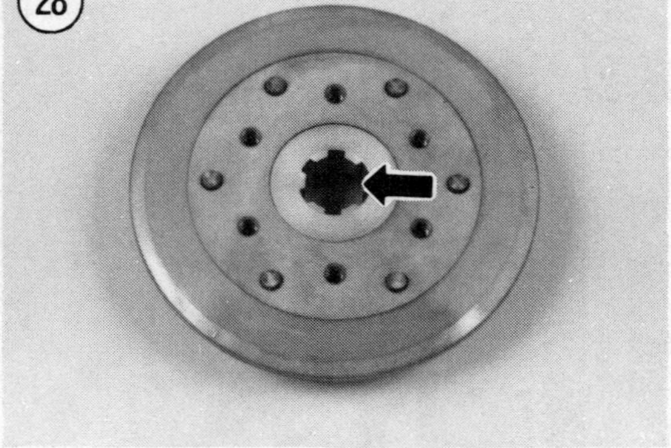

29

30

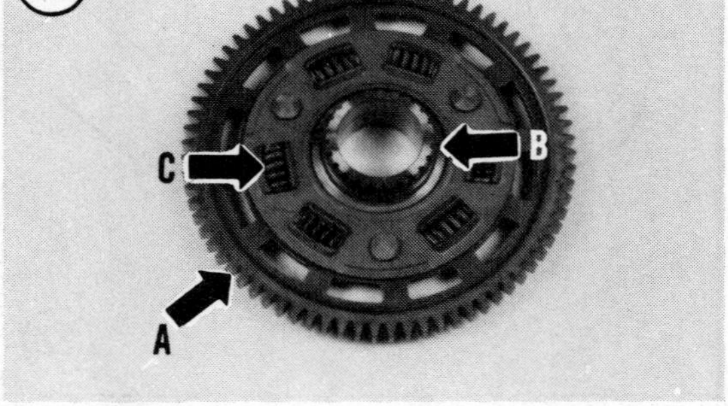

31

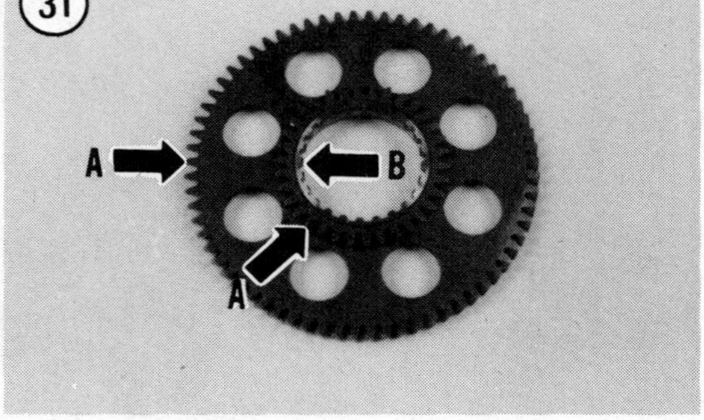

32

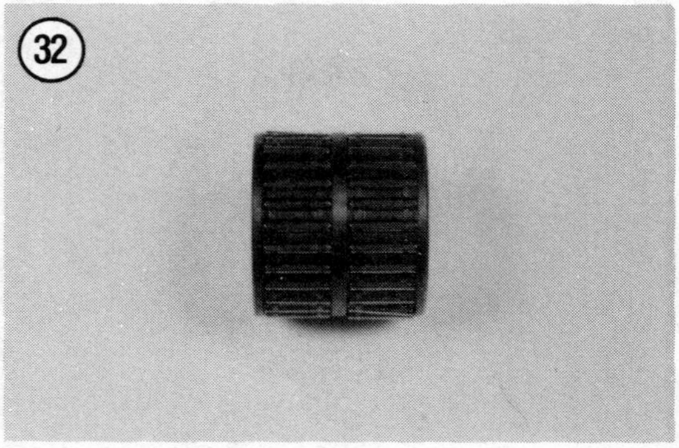

33

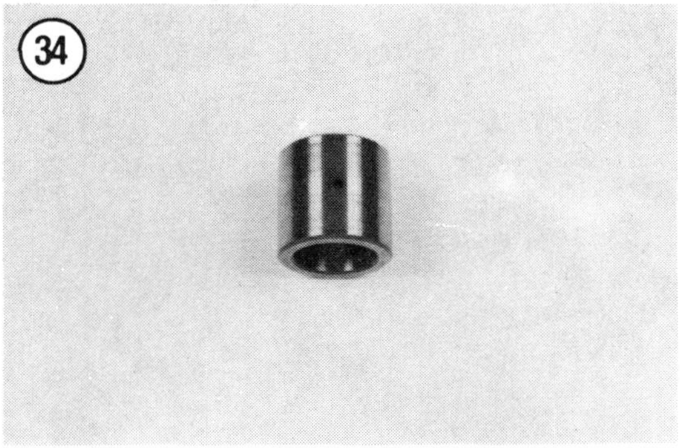

34

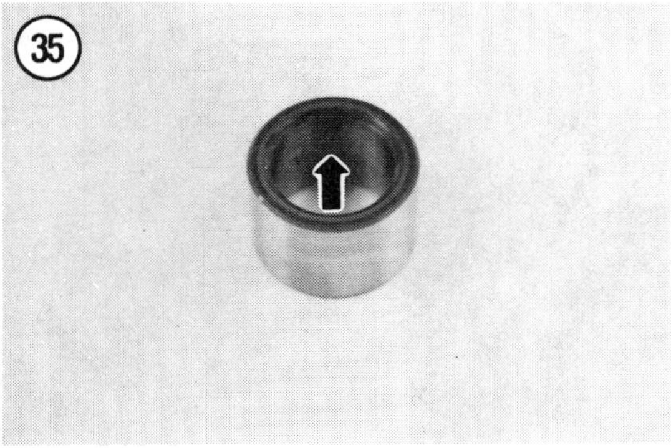

35

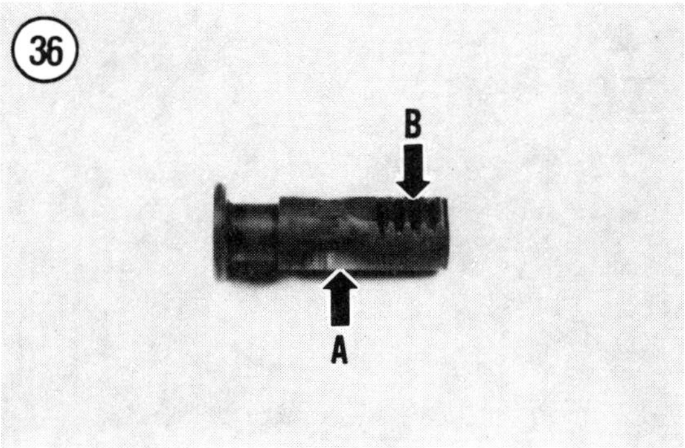

36

13. Inspect the damper springs (C, **Figure 30**). If they are sagging or broken, the primary driven gear assembly must be replaced.

14. Check the inner needle bearing (**Figure 32**) and the outer needle bearing (**Figure 33**). Make sure they rotate smoothly with no signs of wear or damage. Replace if necessary.

15. Check the inner and outer surfaces of both the inner spacer (**Figure 34**) and the outer spacer (**Figure 35**) for signs of wear or damage. Replace if necessary.

16. Check the clutch release rack outer surface (A, **Figure 36**) and the rack teeth (B, **Figure 36**) for signs of wear or damage. Replace if necessary.

17. Check the clutch inner cover oil seal (**Figure 37**) for wear or damage. Replace if necessary.

18. Install a new O-ring (**Figure 38**) on the clutch outer housing collar.

19. Check the movement of the clutch release shaft in the clutch outer cover. If the arm binds, it must be replaced. To remove the shaft perform the following:

   a. Remove the screw and washer securing the clutch release shaft to the clutch outer cover.

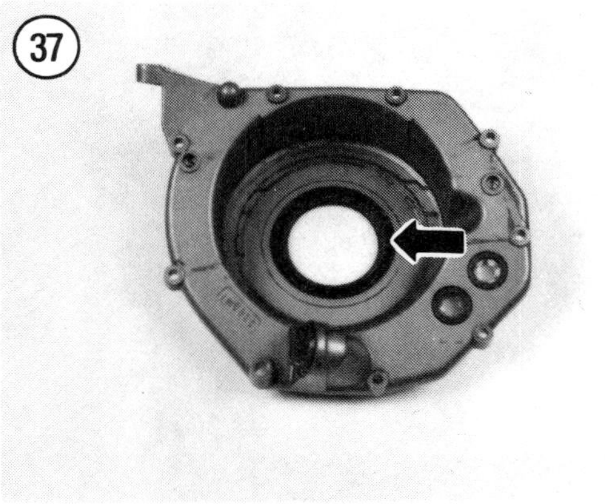

37

38

b. Withdraw the clutch release shaft (A, **Figure 39**) from the clutch outer cover.
c. Inspect the O-ring (B, **Figure 39**) on the clutch outer cover; replace if necessary.
d. Apply multipurpose grease to the clutch release shaft and install it into the clutch outer cover. Secure the shaft with the screw and washer. Tighten the screw securely.

Assembly/Installation

1. Position the thrust washer with the beveled side (**Figure 40**) going on first and install the thrust washer (**Figure 41**).
2. Slide on the inner spacer (A, **Figure 42**).
3. Install the primary driven gear assembly and alternator/oil pump drive gear (B, **Figure 42**).
4. Slide on the inner needle bearing (double row) (**Figure 43**).
5. Install a new O-ring (**Figure 44**) onto the transmission mainshaft and push it all the way up against the inner spacer.
6. Slide on the outer spacer (**Figure 45**).

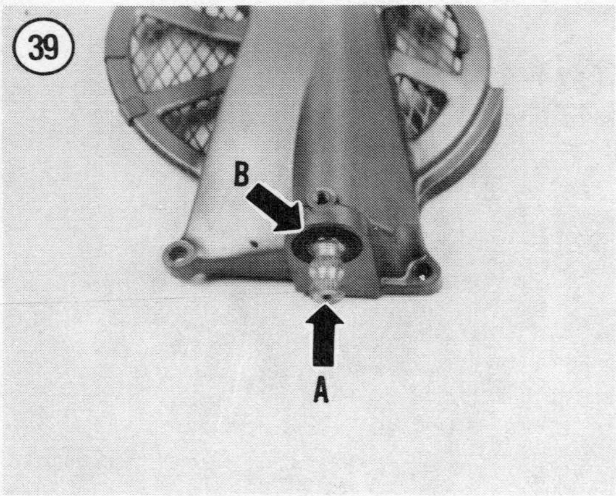

7. Slide on the outer needle bearing (single row) (**Figure 46**).
8. If removed, make sure the locating dowels are installed either on the crankcase or on the clutch inner cover.
9. Install a new clutch inner cover gasket.
10. Install the clutch inner cover (A, **Figure 47**) and bolts. Be sure to install the copper washers under the 2 bolts (W, **Figure 47**) at the rear. Tighten the bolts securely.
11. Apply a light coat of grease to the oil seal lips (B, **Figure 47**).
12. Apply a light coat of grease to the oil seal lips (**Figure 48**) in the clutch outer housing.
13. Slide the clutch outer housing (**Figure 49**) onto the transmission mainshaft. Slowly rotate the clutch outer housing and align the tabs on the backside of the clutch outer housing with the locating recesses in the primary driven gear assembly. Push the clutch outer housing on all the way and make sure the 2 parts are indexed to each other correctly. If they are not indexed correctly, the clutch will not operate and the clutch nut will not go on completely.
14. Install the thrust washer (**Figure 50**).

5

15. Slide the clutch hub (**Figure 51**) onto the transmission mainshaft.
16. Install a new lockwasher and clutch nut (**Figure 52**).
17A. To tighten the clutch nut with a special tool, perform the following:
   a. Hold onto the clutch center to prevent it from turning. Use Honda special tool (Clutch Center Holder—part No. 07923-4280000) (**Figure 53**) or equivalent.
   b. Tighten the clutch nut to the torque specification listed in **Table 3**.
17B. To tighten the clutch nut without the special tool, perform the following:
   a. Shift the transmission into gear.
   b. Have an assistant hold the rear brake on.
   c. Tighten the nut to the torque specification listed in **Table 3**.
18. Bend down a locking tab of a new lockwasher onto one of the flats on the clutch nut (**Figure 54**).
19. Install a driven plate onto the clutch hub (**Figure 55**).
20. Install a drive plate (**Figure 56**).
21. Continue to install a driven plate and then a drive plate, alternating them until all are installed. The last item installed is a driven plate (**Figure 57**).

51

52

53

54

55

56

22. Install the pressure plate (A, **Figure 58**) and release rack (B, **Figure 58**).
23. Install the clutch bolts and springs (**Figure 59**).
24. Using a crisscross pattern tighten the clutch bolts to the torque specification listed in **Table 3**.
25. Position the clutch release rack with the teeth facing toward the rear (**Figure 60**). This is necessary for proper engagement with the teeth on the clutch release shaft in the clutch outer cover.
26. Apply a very light coat of grease to the oil seal (**Figure 61**) in the clutch outer cover.

CAUTION
In the following step, the clutch release shaft gears and the teeth on the clutch release rack must mesh properly. If they don't, the clutch outer cover will not go on correctly nor will the clutch operate correctly.

27. Install the clutch outer cover (A, **Figure 62**). If necessary, slightly rotate the clutch release shaft to ensure proper engagement with the clutch release rack. Install the flanged mounting bolts (B, **Figure 62**) at the front of the cover. Tighten the bolts securely.

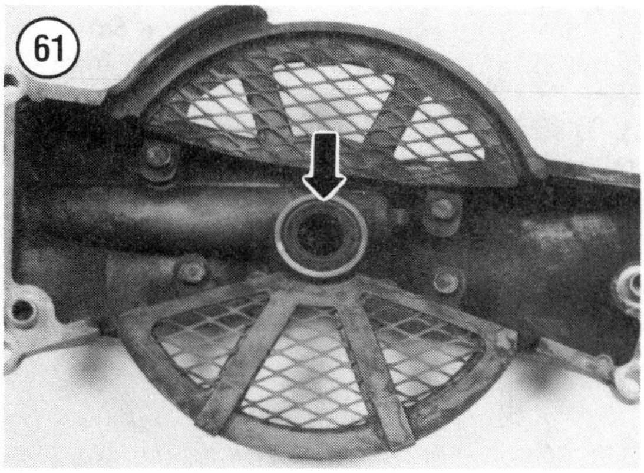

28. Connect the clutch cable into the receptacle on the clutch outer cover (A, **Figure 63**).
29. Connect the clutch cable onto the clutch release arm (B, **Figure 63**).
30. Refill the engine oil with the recommended type and quantity as described under *Engine Oil and Filter Change* in Chapter Three.
31. Install the right-hand middle and lower sections of the front fairing as described under *Front Fairing Removal/Installation* in Chapter Twelve.
32. Adjust the clutch as described under *Clutch Adjustment (GSX-R750R Limited Edition)* in Chapter Three.

Clutch Cable Replacement

In time, the clutch cable will stretch to the point where it is no longer useful and will have to be replaced.

1. Remove the lower section and the right-hand middle section of the front fairing as described under *Front Fairing Removal/Installation* in Chapter Twelve.
2. Loosen the adjusting barrel (**Figure 64**) at the clutch hand lever and remove the cable from the lever.
3. Disconnect the clutch cable from the clutch release arm (B, **Figure 63**).
4. Disconnect the clutch cable from the receptacle on the clutch outer cover (A, **Figure 63**).

NOTE
Before removing the cable, make a drawing of the cable routing through the frame. It is very easy to forget how it was, once it has been removed. Replace the cable exactly as it was, avoiding any sharp turns.

5. Pull the clutch cable out from behind the steering head area and out of the retaining loop and clips on the frame.
6. Remove the cable and replace it with a new cable.
7. Install by reversing these removal steps, noting the following.
8. Adjust the clutch as described in Chapter Three.

CLUTCH—WET-TYPE (GSX-R750, GSX-R1100)

Removal/Disassembly

The clutch assembly can be removed with the engine in the frame. This procedure is shown with the engine removed and partially disassembled for clarity.

Refer to **Figure 65** for GSX-R750 models or **Figure 66** for GSX-R1100 models for this procedure. The clutch assemblies used in these 2 models are basically the same. Where differences occur they are identified.

1. Remove the lower section and the right-hand middle section of the front fairing as described under *Front Fairing Removal/Installation* in Chapter Twelve.
2. Drain the engine oil as described under *Engine Oil and Filter Change* in Chapter Three.
3. Shift the transmission into gear.

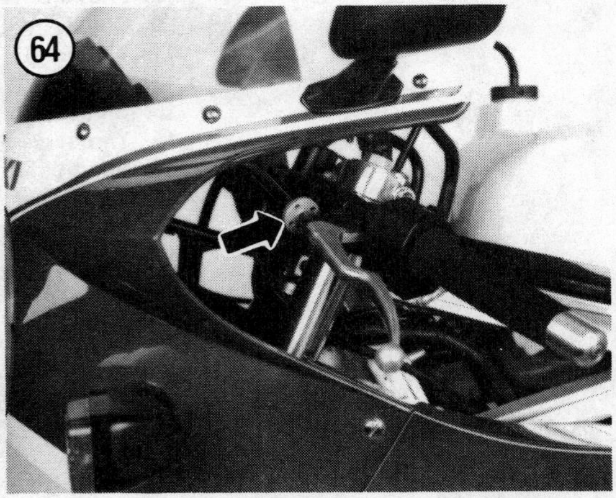

65

CLUTCH—WET-TYPE (GSX-R750)

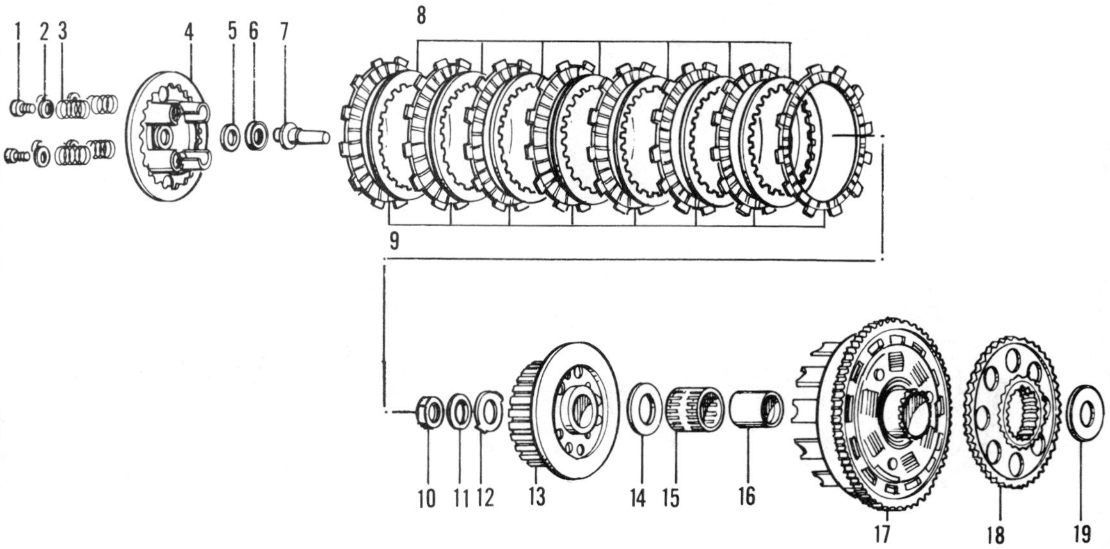

1. Clutch bolt
2. Washer
3. Clutch spring
4. Pressure plate
5. Thrust washer
6. Bearing
7. Clutch push piece
8. Clutch plate
9. Friction disc
10. Clutch nut
11. Washer
12. Lockwasher
13. Clutch hub
14. Thrust washer
15. Needle bearing
16. Spacer
17. Clutch outer housing
18. Alternator/oil pump driven gear
19. Thrust washer

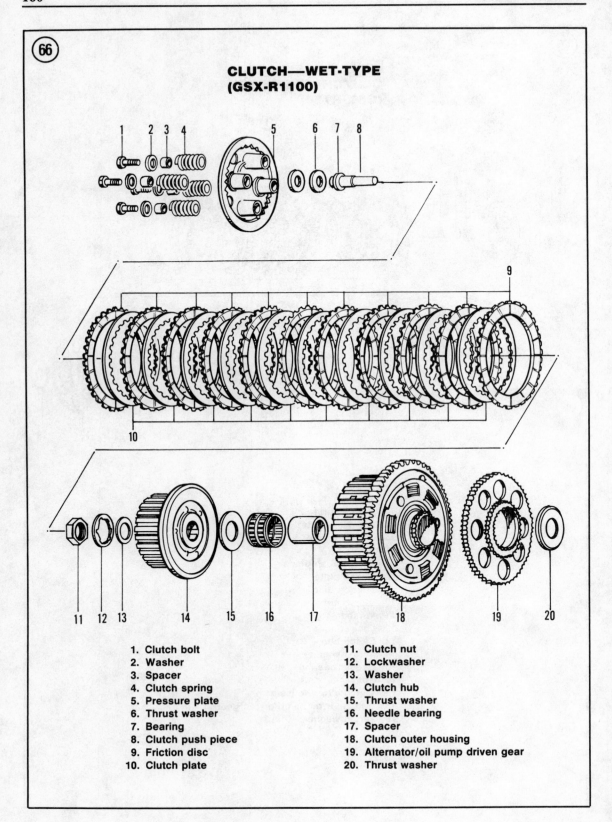

(66)

CLUTCH—WET-TYPE (GSX-R1100)

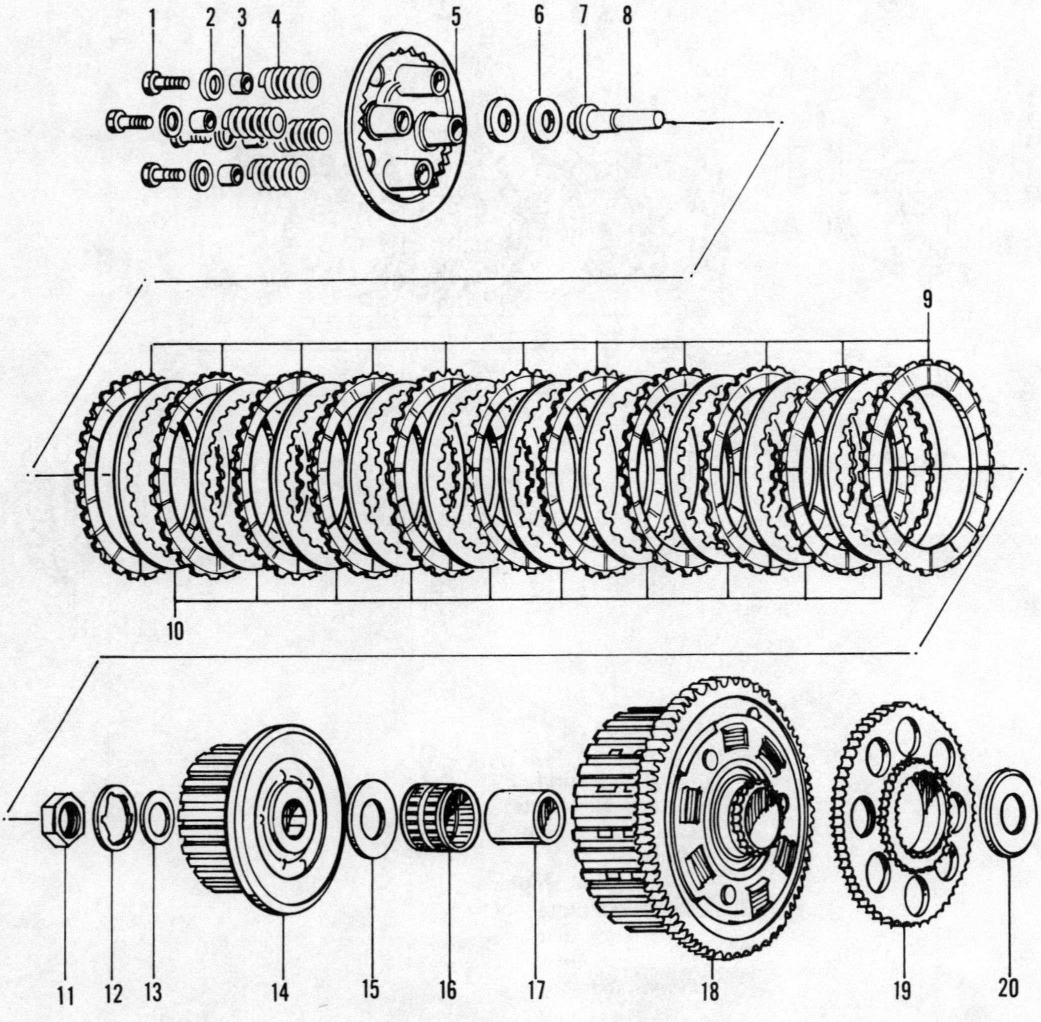

1. Clutch bolt
2. Washer
3. Spacer
4. Clutch spring
5. Pressure plate
6. Thrust washer
7. Bearing
8. Clutch push piece
9. Friction disc
10. Clutch plate
11. Clutch nut
12. Lockwasher
13. Washer
14. Clutch hub
15. Thrust washer
16. Needle bearing
17. Spacer
18. Clutch outer housing
19. Alternator/oil pump driven gear
20. Thrust washer

4. Remove the bolts (**Figure 67**) securing the clutch cover. Remove the clutch cover and gasket. Don't lose the locating dowels.
5. With the transmission in gear; have an assistant hold the rear brake on.
6. Using a crisscross pattern, loosen the clutch bolts (**Figure 68**).

7A. On 750 cc models, remove the bolts and washers.
7B. On 1100 cc models, remove the bolts, washers and spacers (**Figure 69**).
8. Remove the clutch springs (**Figure 70**) and the pressure plate (**Figure 71**).
9. Remove the thrust washer, bearing and clutch push piece.
10. Remove the friction discs and clutch plates.
11. Remove the clutch pushrod from the transmission shaft.
12. Straighten the locking tab on the lockwasher.

NOTE
The "Grabbit" (part No. 969103) is available from Joe Bolger Products Inc., Summer Street, Barre, MA 01005.

CAUTION
Do not clamp the "Grabbit" on too tight as it may damage the grooves in the clutch hub.

5

13. To keep the clutch hub from turning in the next step, attach a special tool such as the "Grabbit" (A, **Figure 72**) to it.
14. Loosen and then remove the clutch locknut (B, **Figure 72**).
15. Remove the special tool from the clutch center.
16A. On 750 cc models, remove the plain washer and the lockwasher. Discard the lockwasher as a new one must be installed.
16B. On 1100 cc models, remove the lockwasher and plain washer. Discard the lockwasher as a new one must be installed.
17. Remove the clutch hub (**Figure 73**).
18. Remove the thrust washer (**Figure 74**).
19. Slide the clutch outer housing forward enough to pull the needle bearing and spacer out until you can grab hold of these two parts.
20. Hold onto the clutch outer housing and slide off the clutch outer housing needle bearing and spacer.
21. Remove the clutch outer housing and alternator drive gear.
22. Slide off the thrust washer.
23. Inspect all components as described in this chapter.

Inspection

Refer to **Table 2** for clutch specifications.
1. Separate the alternator drive gear (**Figure 75**) from the backside of the clutch outer housing.
2. Clean all clutch parts in petroleum-based solvent such as kerosene and thoroughly dry with compressed air.
3. Measure the free length of each clutch spring as shown in **Figure 76**. Compare to the specifications listed in **Table 2**. Replace any springs that have sagged to the service limit or less.

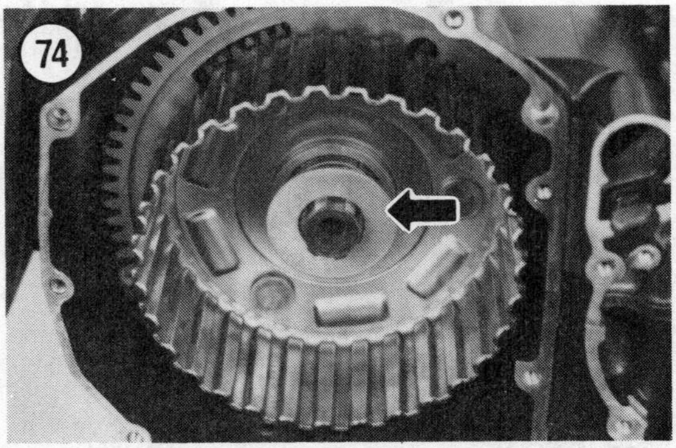

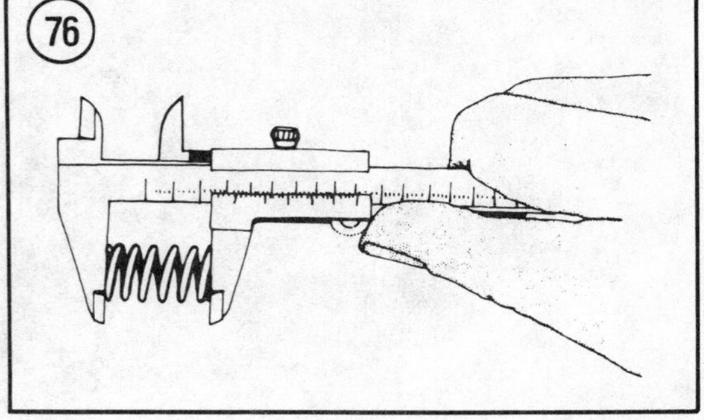

77

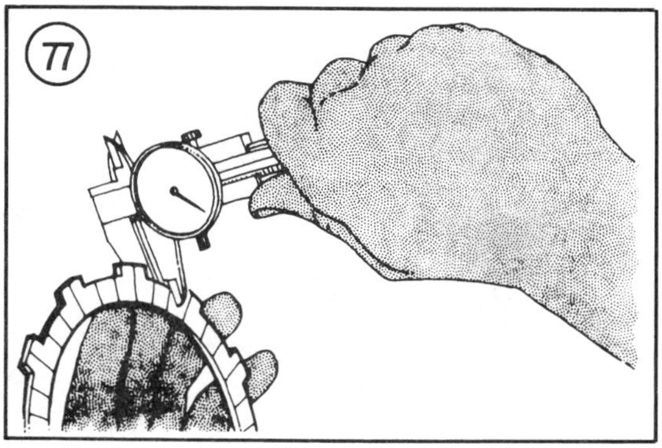

78

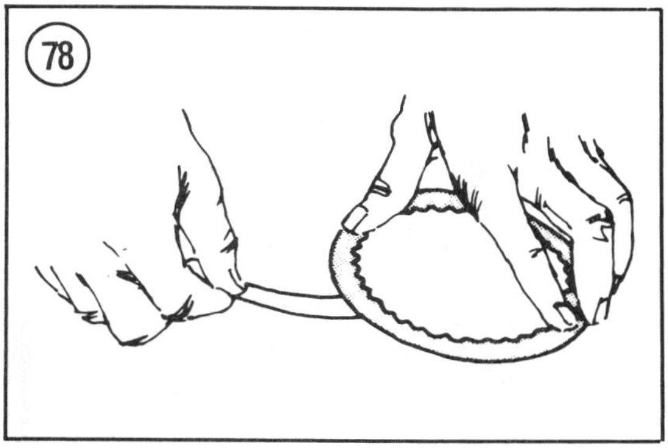

79

80

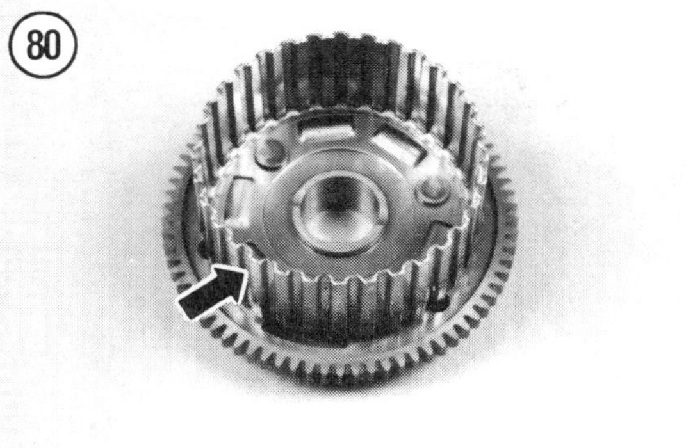

4. Measure the thickness of each friction disc at several places around the disc as shown in **Figure 77**. Compare to the specifications listed in **Table 2**. Replace any disc that is worn to the service limit or less.
5. Check the clutch plates for warpage on a surface plate such as a piece of plate glass (**Figure 78**). Compare to the specifications listed in **Table 2**. Replace any plate that is discolored or warped to the service limit.

NOTE
If any of the friction discs, clutch plates or clutch springs require replacement, you should consider replacing all of them as a set to retain maximum clutch performance.

6A. On 750 cc models, inspect the slots (**Figure 79**) in the clutch outer housing for cracks, nicks or galling where they come in contact with the friction disc tabs. If any severe damage is evident, the housing must be replaced.
6B. On 1100 cc models, inspect the grooves in the clutch outer housing (**Figure 80**) for cracks, nicks or galling where they come in contact with the friction disc tabs. If any severe damage is evident, the housing must be replaced.
7. Inspect the gear teeth on the clutch outer housing for damage. Refer to A, **Figure 81** for 750 cc models or A, **Figure 82** for 1100 cc models. Remove any small nicks with an oilstone. If damage is severe, the clutch outer housing must be replaced. Also check the teeth on the drive gear of the crankshaft; if damaged the driven gear may also need replacing.
8. Inspect the damper springs. Refer to B, **Figure 81** for 750 cc models or B, **Figure 82** for 1100 cc models. If they are sagged or broken, the housing must be replaced.

81

9. Inspect the outer splines of the clutch outer housing (**Figure 83**) and the inner splines of the alternator drive gear (**Figure 84**) for damage. Remove any small nicks with an oilstone. If damage is severe, the clutch outer housing and/or the alternator drive gear must be replaced.

10. Inspect the gear teeth (**Figure 85**) on the alternator drive gear for damage. Remove any small nicks with an oilstone. If damage is severe, the alternator drive gear must be replaced.

11. Inspect the grooves and studs in the clutch hub. Refer to **Figure 86** for 750 cc models or **Figure 87** for 1100 cc models. If either shows signs of wear or galling, the clutch hub should be replaced.

12. Inspect the inner splines (**Figure 88**) in the clutch hub for damage. Remove any small nicks with an oilstone. If damage is severe, the clutch hub must be replaced.

13. Inspect the grooves and spring towers in the clutch pressure plate (**Figure 89**). If either shows signs of wear or galling, the clutch pressure plate should be replaced.

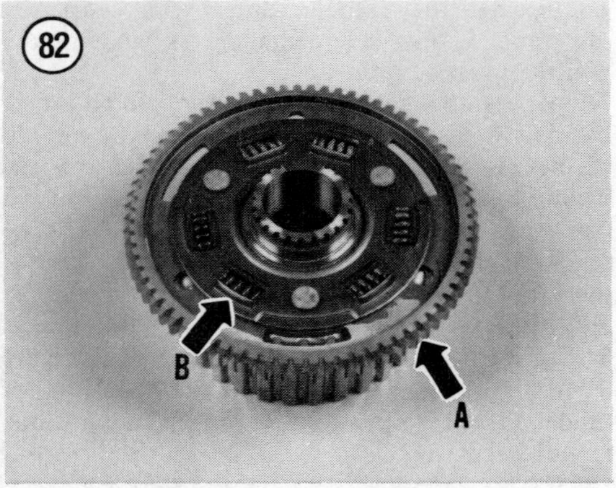

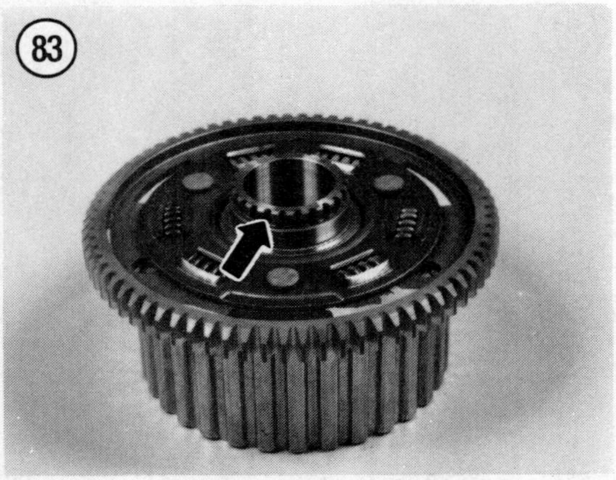

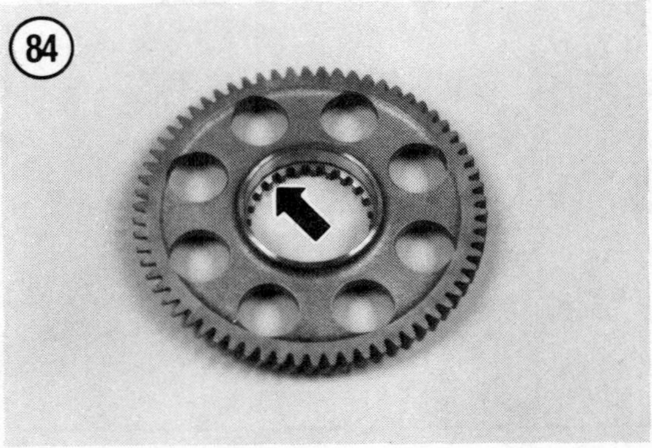

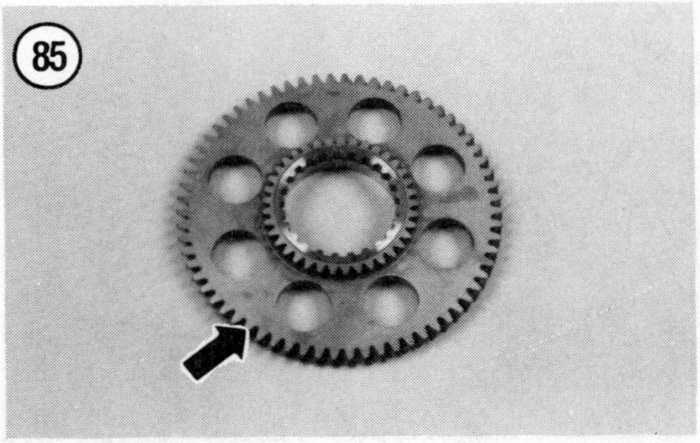

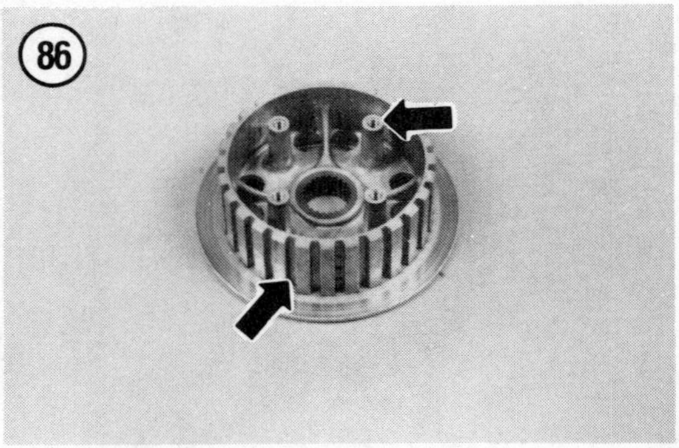

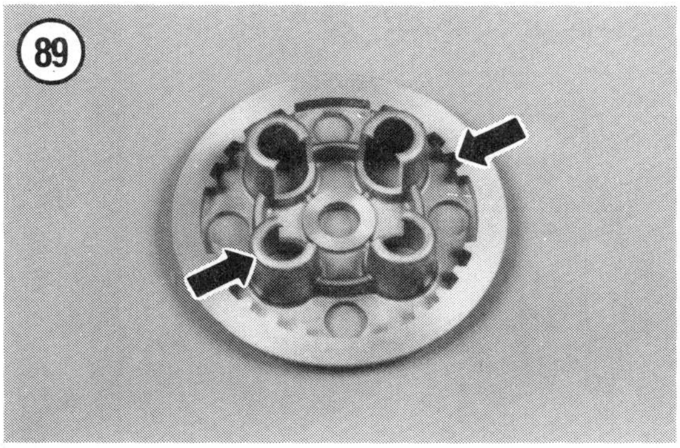

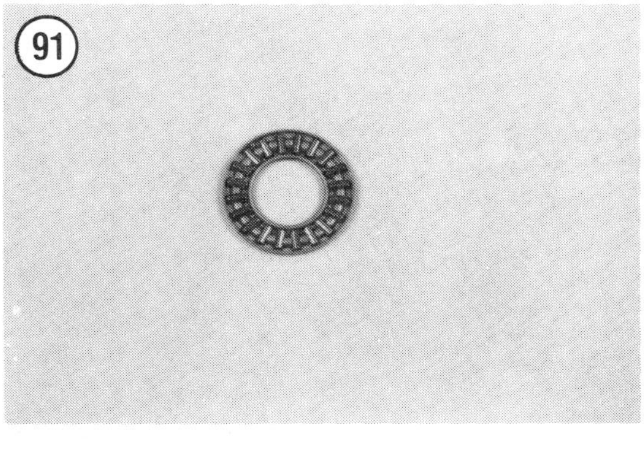

14. Check the needle bearing (**Figure 90**). Make sure it rotates smoothly with no signs of wear or damage. Replace if necessary.
15. Check the clutch push piece bearing (**Figure 91**). Make sure it rotates smoothly with no signs of wear or damage. Replace if necessary.
16. Check the inner and outer surfaces of the spacer (**Figure 92**) for signs of wear or damage. Replace if necessary.
17. Inspect the clutch right-hand pushrod (A, **Figure 93**) and left-hand pushrod (B, **Figure 93**) for bending. Roll it on a surface plate or piece of plate glass. Suzuki does not provide service information for this component, but if the rod(s) is bent or deformed in any way it must be replaced. Otherwise it may hang up in the transmission shaft, causing erratic clutch operation.
18. Check the clutch push piece (C, **Figure 93**) for wear or damage. Replace if necessary.

5

Assembly/Installation

Refer to **Figure 94** for GSX-R750 models or **Figure 95** for GSX-R1100 models for this procedure.

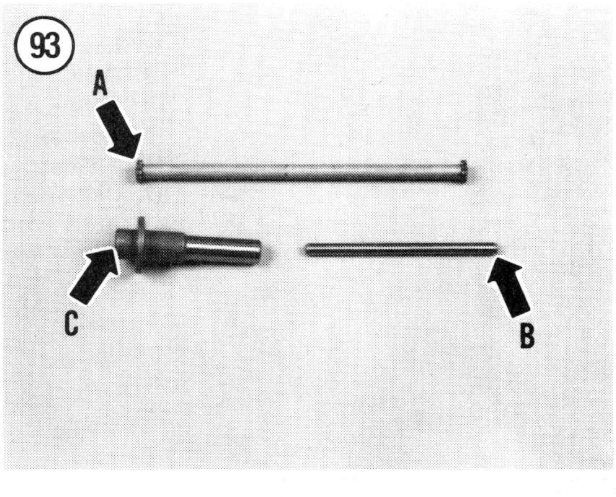

94

CLUTCH—WET-TYPE (GSX-R750)

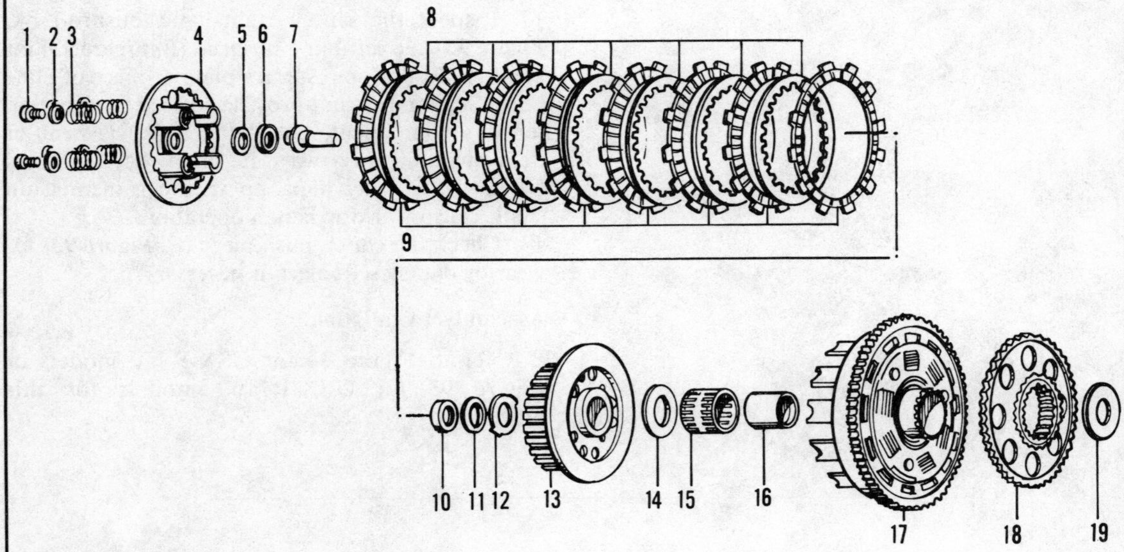

1. Clutch bolt
2. Washer
3. Clutch spring
4. Pressure plate
5. Thrust washer
6. Bearing
7. Clutch push piece
8. Clutch plate
9. Friction disc
10. Clutch nut
11. Washer
12. Lockwasher
13. Clutch hub
14. Thrust washer
15. Needle bearing
16. Spacer
17. Clutch outer housing
18. Alternator/oil pump driven gear
19. Thrust washer

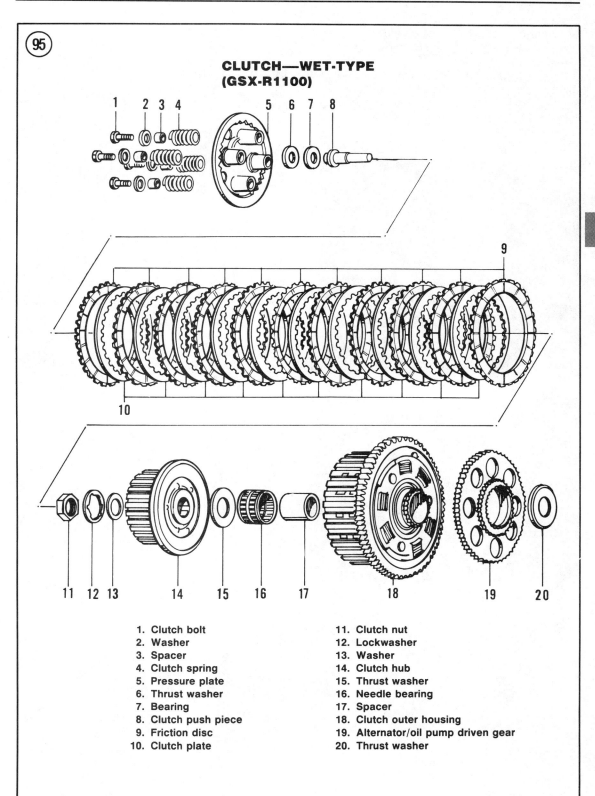

95

CLUTCH—WET-TYPE (GSX-R1100)

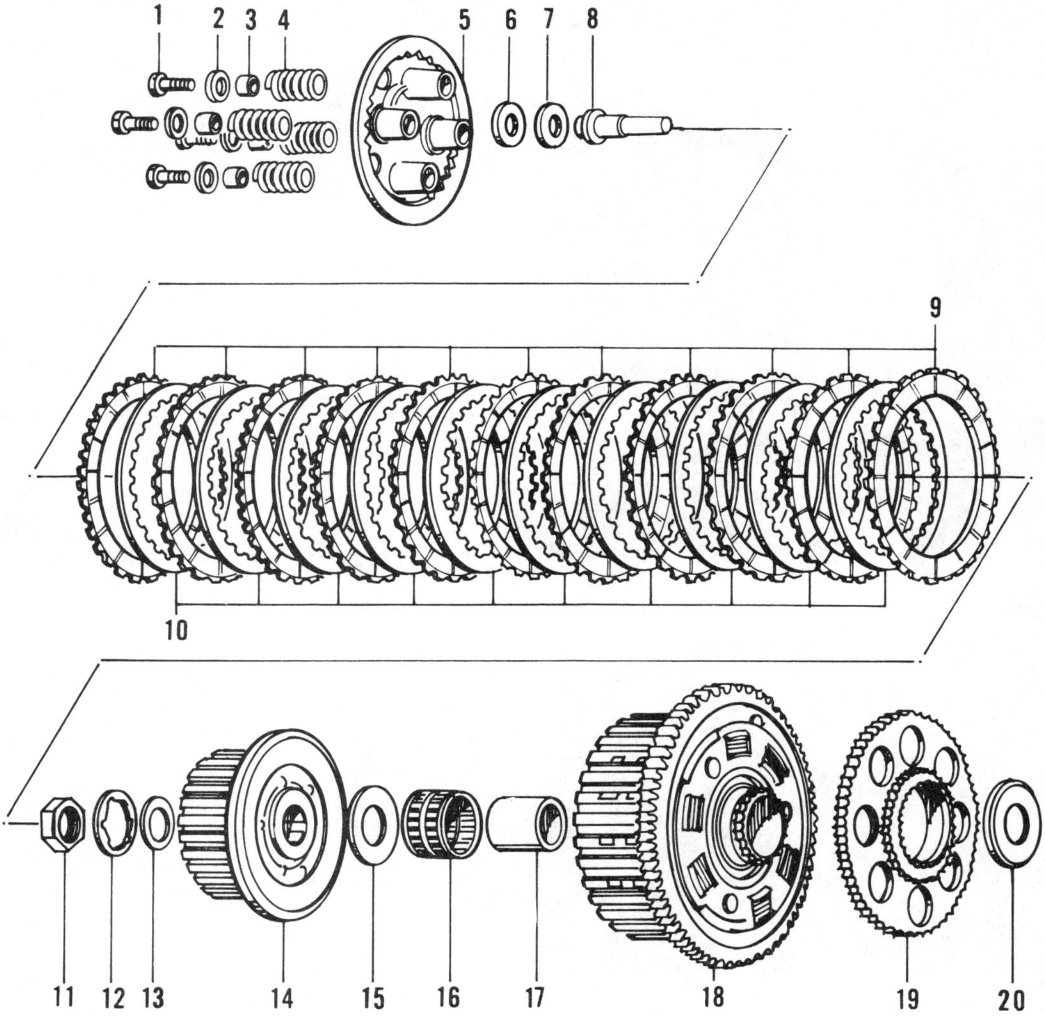

1. Clutch bolt
2. Washer
3. Spacer
4. Clutch spring
5. Pressure plate
6. Thrust washer
7. Bearing
8. Clutch push piece
9. Friction disc
10. Clutch plate
11. Clutch nut
12. Lockwasher
13. Washer
14. Clutch hub
15. Thrust washer
16. Needle bearing
17. Spacer
18. Clutch outer housing
19. Alternator/oil pump driven gear
20. Thrust washer

1. Position the thrust washer with the beveled side (**Figure 96**) going on first and install the thrust washer (**Figure 97**).
2. Install the alternator drive gear (**Figure 98**) into the backside of the clutch outer housing.
3. Install the clutch outer housing and alternator drive gear assembly onto the transmission shaft (**Figure 99**).

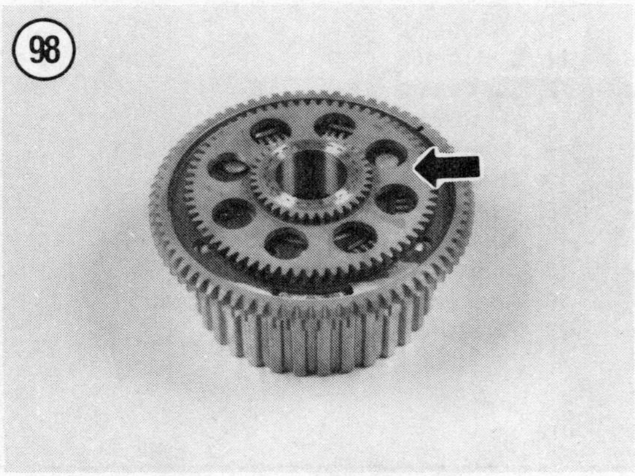

4. Hold onto the clutch outer housing and slide on the clutch outer housing needle bearing (**Figure 100**) and the spacer (**Figure 101**).
5. Push the clutch outer housing toward the rear until it stops. Make sure it is engaged properly with the driven gear on the countershaft.
6. Install the thrust washer (**Figure 102**).
7. Install the clutch hub (**Figure 103**).
8A. On 750 cc models, install a new lockwasher and the plain washer.
8B. On 1100 cc models, install the plain washer (**Figure 104**) and a new lockwasher (**Figure 105**).
9. Use the same special tool (A, **Figure 106**) setup used in Step 13 of *Removal/Disassembly* to hold the clutch hub for the following step.
10. Install then tighten the clutch locknut (B, **Figure 106**). Tighten to the torque specification listed in **Table 3**.
11. Remove the special tool from the clutch hub.
12. Bend up one of the tabs of the lockwasher against one side of the clutch nut.
13. Install the clutch right-hand pushrod (**Figure 107**) into the transmission shaft.
14. Install the clutch push piece (**Figure 108**), the bearing (**Figure 109**) and the thrust washer (A, **Figure 110**).

103

104

105

106

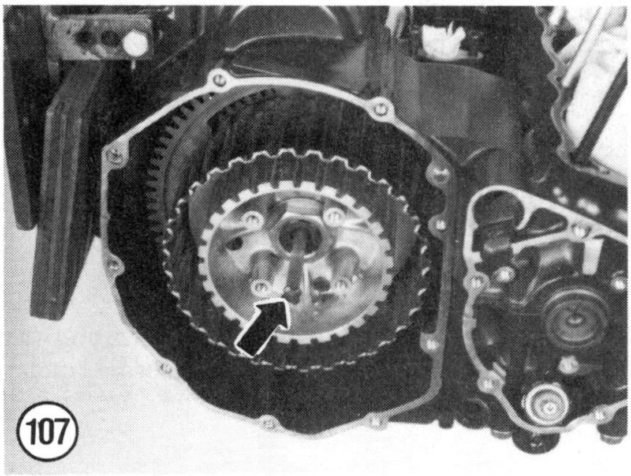
107

108

NOTE
If new friction discs and clutch plates are being installed, apply new engine oil to all surfaces to avoid having the clutch lock up when used for the first time.

15. Install a friction disc (B, **Figure 110**) then a clutch plate (**Figure 111**) onto the clutch hub.
16. Continue to install the friction discs and clutch plates, alternating them until all are installed. The last item installed is a friction disc (**Figure 112**).
17. Install the clutch pressure plate (**Figure 113**).
18A. On 750 cc models, install the washers and bolts.
18B. On 1100 cc models, install the spacers (**Figure 114**), the washers and bolts (**Figure 115**).
19. Make sure the transmission is still in gear and have an assistant hold the rear brake on.
20. Using a crisscross pattern, tighten the clutch bolts (**Figure 115**) to the torque specification listed in **Table 3**.
21. Apply a light coat of Three-Bond No. 1207 gasket sealer, or equivalent, to the crankcase surfaces at the point where the upper and lower crankcase halves meet (A, **Figure 116**). This is to prevent an oil leak.
22. Make sure the locating dowels (B, **Figure 116**) are in place.
23. Install a new clutch cover gasket.
24. Install the clutch cover and the bolts (**Figure 117**). Tighten the bolts securely.
25. Refill the engine oil as described under *Engine Oil and Filter Change* in Chapter Three.
26. Install the right-hand middle section and the lower section of the front fairing as described under *Front Fairing Removal/Installation* in Chapter Twelve.

CLUTCH HYDRAULIC SYSTEM (WET-TYPE CLUTCH)

The clutch is actuated by hydraulic fluid pressure and is controlled by the hand lever on the clutch master cylinder. As clutch components wear, the piston within the clutch slave cylinder moves out and automatically adjusts for wear. There is no routine adjustment necessary nor possible.

When working on the clutch hydraulic system, it is necessary that the work area and all tools be

109

110

111

112

113

114

115

116

absolutely clean. Any tiny particles or foreign matter and grit in the clutch slave cylinder or the master cylinder can damage the components. Also, sharp tools must not be used inside the slave cylinder or on the piston. If there is any doubt about your ability to correctly and safely carry out major service on the clutch hydraulic components, take the job to a dealer or other qualified specialist.

WARNING
Throughout the text, reference is made to hydraulic fluid. Hydraulic fluid is the same as DOT 3 or DOT 4 brake fluid. Use only DOT 3 or DOT 4 brake fluid; ***do not use other types of fluids*** *as they are not compatible. Do not intermix silicone based (DOT 5) brake fluid as it can cause clutch component damage leading to clutch system failure.*

Master Cylinder Removal/Installation

1. Remove the front fairing as described under *Front Fairing Removal/Installation* in Chapter Twelve.

CAUTION
Cover the fuel tank, front fender and instrument cluster with a heavy cloth or plastic tarp to protect them from accidental hydraulic fluid spills. Wash hydraulic fluid off any painted or plated surfaces or plastic parts immediately, as it will destroy the finish. Use soapy water and rinse completely.

2. Disconnect the starter interlock switch electrical connector from the main wiring harness.
3. Pull back the rubber boot on the union bolt on the master cylinder.
4. Place a shop cloth under the union bolt to catch any spilled hydraulic fluid that will leak out.

117

5. Unscrew the union bolt (**Figure 118**) securing the clutch hose to the master cylinder. Don't lose the sealing washer on each side of the hose fitting. Tie the loose end of the hose up to the handlebar and cover the end to prevent the entry of moisture and foreign matter.
6. Remove the clamping bolts, washers (A, **Figure 119**) and the clamp securing the master cylinder to the handlebar and remove the master cylinder.
7. Install by reversing these removal steps, noting the following.
8. Install the clamp with the UP arrow (B, **Figure 119**) facing up. Align the face of the clamp with the punch mark on the handlebar. Tighten the upper bolt first, then the lower to the torque specification listed in **Table 3**.
9. Place a new sealing washer on each side of the brake hose fitting and install the union bolt.
10. Tighten the union bolt to the torque specification listed in **Table 3**.
11. Bleed the clutch as described under *Bleeding the System* in this chapter.

Master Cylinder Disassembly

Refer to **Figure 120** for this procedure.
1. Remove the master cylinder as described in this chapter.

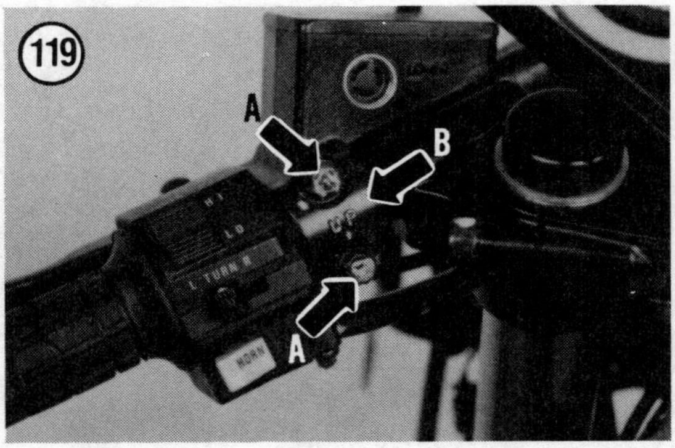

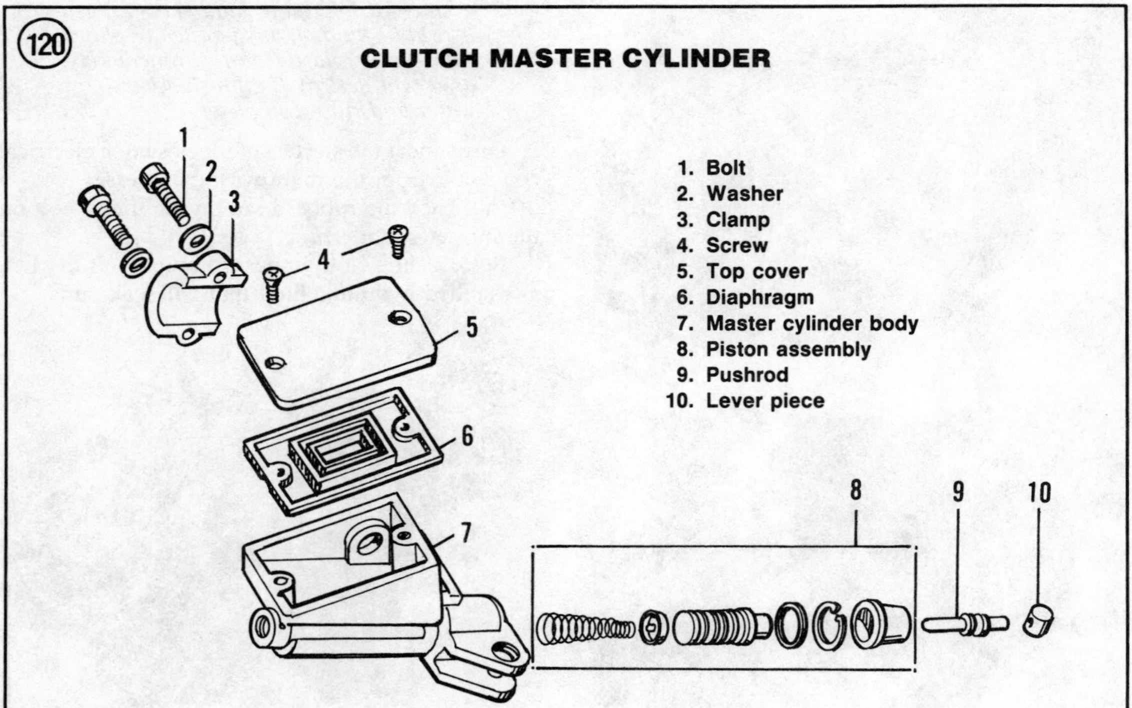

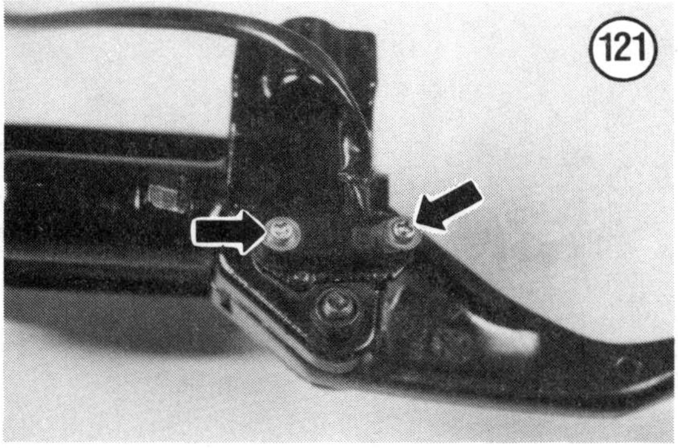

121

122

2. Remove the screws, washers and lockwashers (**Figure 121**) securing the starter interlock switch to the master cylinder and remove the switch assembly.
3. Remove the screws securing the top cover and remove the top cover and the diaphragm.
4. Pour out any residual hydraulic fluid and discard it. *Never* re-use hydraulic fluid.
5. Remove the bolt and nut (**Figure 122**) securing the hand lever and remove the lever.
6. Remove the rubber boot (**Figure 123**) from the area where the hand lever actuates the piston assembly.
7. Using circlip pliers, remove the internal circlip (**Figure 124**) from the body. On models so equipped, remove the washer behind the circlip.
8. Remove the piston assembly and the spring (**Figure 125**).

Master Cylinder Inspection

1. Clean all parts in denatured alcohol or fresh hydraulic fluid.
2. Inspect the body cylinder bore (**Figure 126**) surface for signs of wear and damage. If less than perfect, replace the master cylinder assembly. The body cannot be replaced separately.

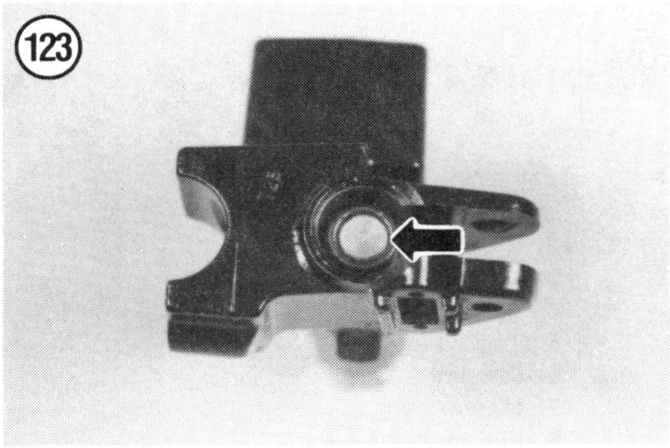

123

124

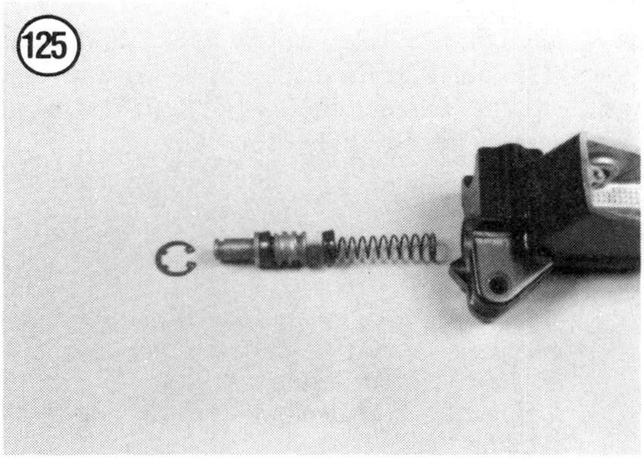

125

126

3. Remove the secondary cup (**Figure 127**) from the piston.
4. Inspect the piston contact surfaces (A, **Figure 128**) for signs of wear and damage. If less than perfect, replace the piston assembly.
5. Check the end of the piston (B, **Figure 128**) for wear caused by the hand lever. If worn, replace the piston assembly.
6. Replace the piston assembly if either the primary or secondary cup requires replacement.
7. Inspect the pivot hole (**Figure 129**) in the hand lever. If worn or elongated, it must be replaced.
8. Make sure the passages (**Figure 130**) in the bottom of the master cylinder body are clear.
9. Check the top cover (**Figure 131**) and diaphragm (**Figure 132**) for damage and deterioration and replace as necessary.
10. Inspect the threads in the bore for the union bolt. If worn or damaged, clean out with a thread tap or replace the master cylinder assembly.
11. Check the hand lever pivot lugs (**Figure 133**) on the master cylinder body for cracks. If damaged, replace the master cylinder assembly.

127
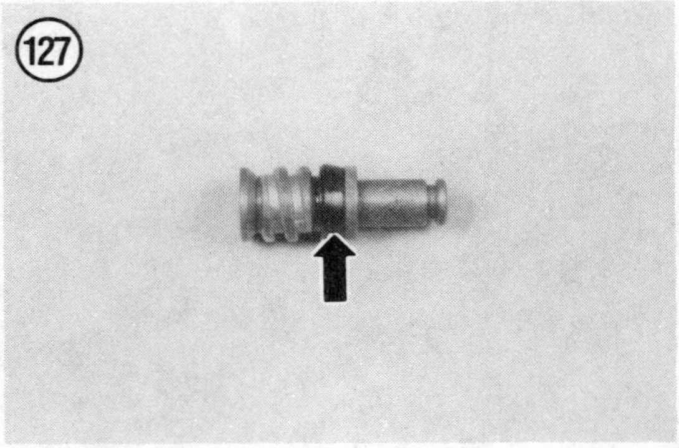

128
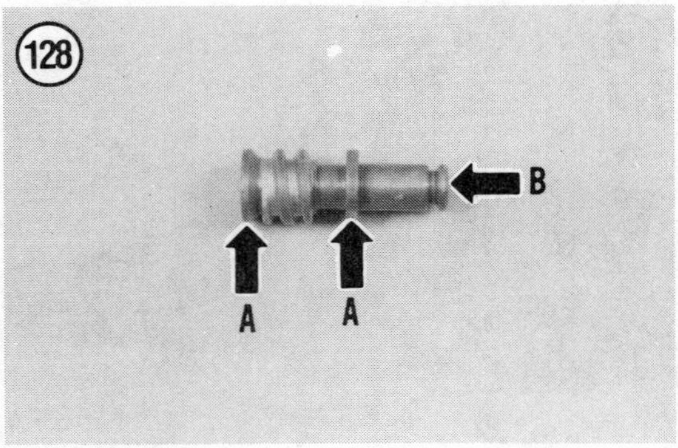

Master Cylinder Assembly

1. Soak the new cups in fresh hydraulic fluid for at least 15 minutes to make them pliable. Coat the inside of the cylinder bore with fresh hydraulic fluid prior to the assembly of parts.

CAUTION
When installing the piston assembly, do not allow the cups to turn inside out as they will be damaged and allow hydraulic fluid leakage within the cylinder bore.

2. Install the spring and piston assembly into the cylinder together. Install the spring with the tapered end (**Figure 134**) facing toward the primary cup on the piston.
3. On models so equipped, install the washer.
4. Install the circlip (**Figure 124**) and slide in the rubber boot (**Figure 123**).
5. Install the diaphragm and top cover. Do not tighten the cover screws at this time as hydraulic fluid will have to be added later when the system is bled.

129
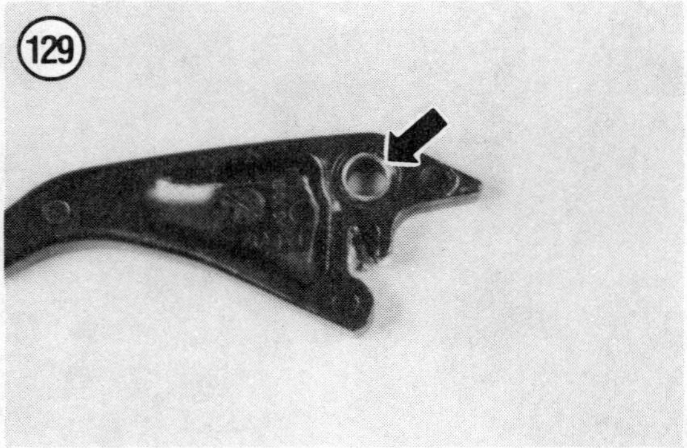

130
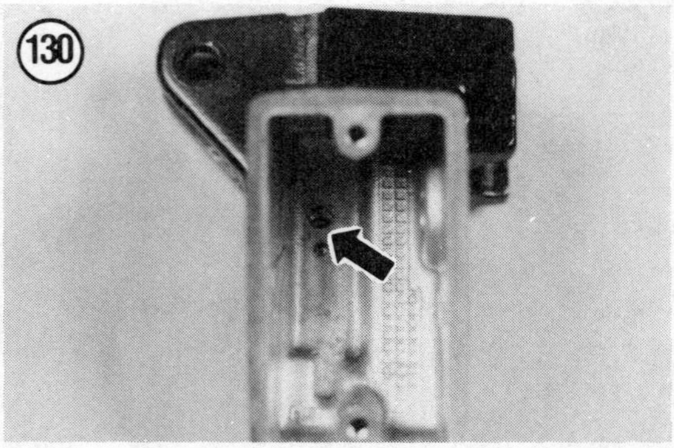

(131)

(132)

(133)

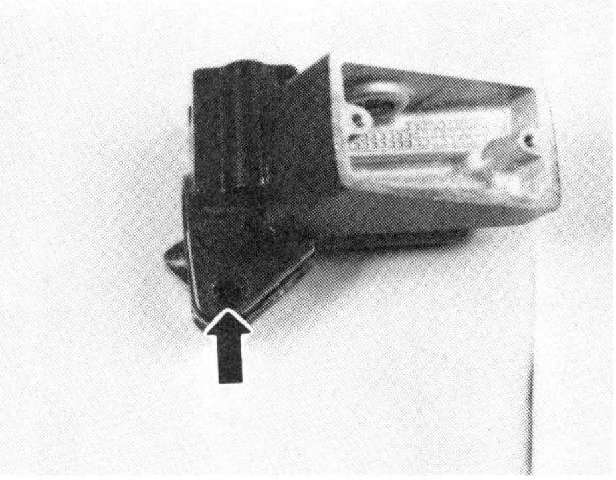

(134)

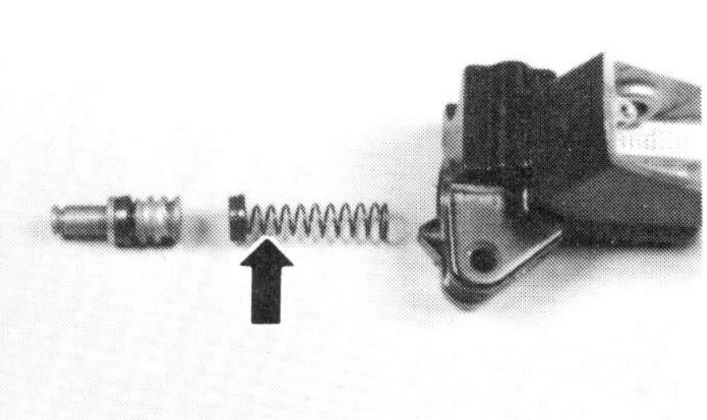

6. Install the starter interlock switch, washers, lockwashers and screws to the master cylinder. Tighten the screws securely.
7. Install the master cylinder as described in this chapter.

Clutch Hose Replacement

There is no factory-recommended replacement interval but it is a good idea to replace the clutch hose every four years or when it shows signs of cracking or damage.

Refer to **Figure 135** for this procedure.

1. Remove the front fairing as described under *Front Fairing Removal/Installation* in Chapter Twelve.

CAUTION
Cover the fuel tank, front fender and instrument cluster with a heavy cloth or plastic tarp to protect them from accidental hydraulic fluid spills. Wash hydraulic fluid off any painted or plated surfaces or plastic parts immediately, as it will destroy the finish. Use soapy water and rinse completely.

2. Clean the top of the master cylinder of all dirt and foreign matter.
3. Loosen the screws (**Figure 136**) securing the master cylinder top cover. Pull up and loosen the cover and the diaphragm. This will allow air to enter the reservoir and allow the hydraulic fluid to drain out more quickly in the next steps.
4. Place a container under the clutch hose at the slave cylinder.
5. Remove the union bolt and sealing washers (**Figure 137**) securing the clutch hose to the slave cylinder.
6. Remove the clutch hose and let the hydraulic fluid drain out into the container. Dispose of this hydraulic fluid—never re-use hydraulic fluid. To prevent the entry of moisture and dirt, tape over the threaded bore in the slave cylinder.

WARNING
Dispose of this hydraulic fluid—never re-use hydraulic fluid. Contaminated hydraulic fluid can cause clutch problems.

135

CLUTCH HYDRAULIC HOSE

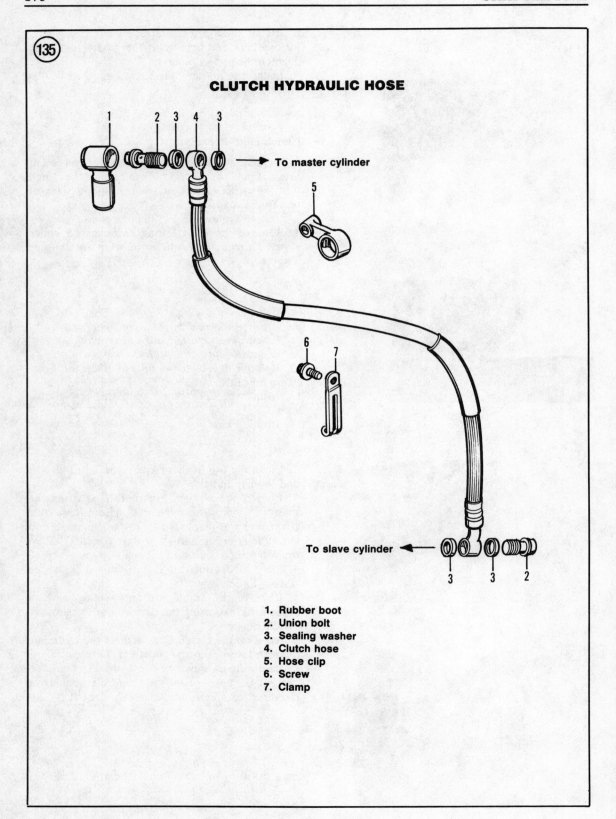

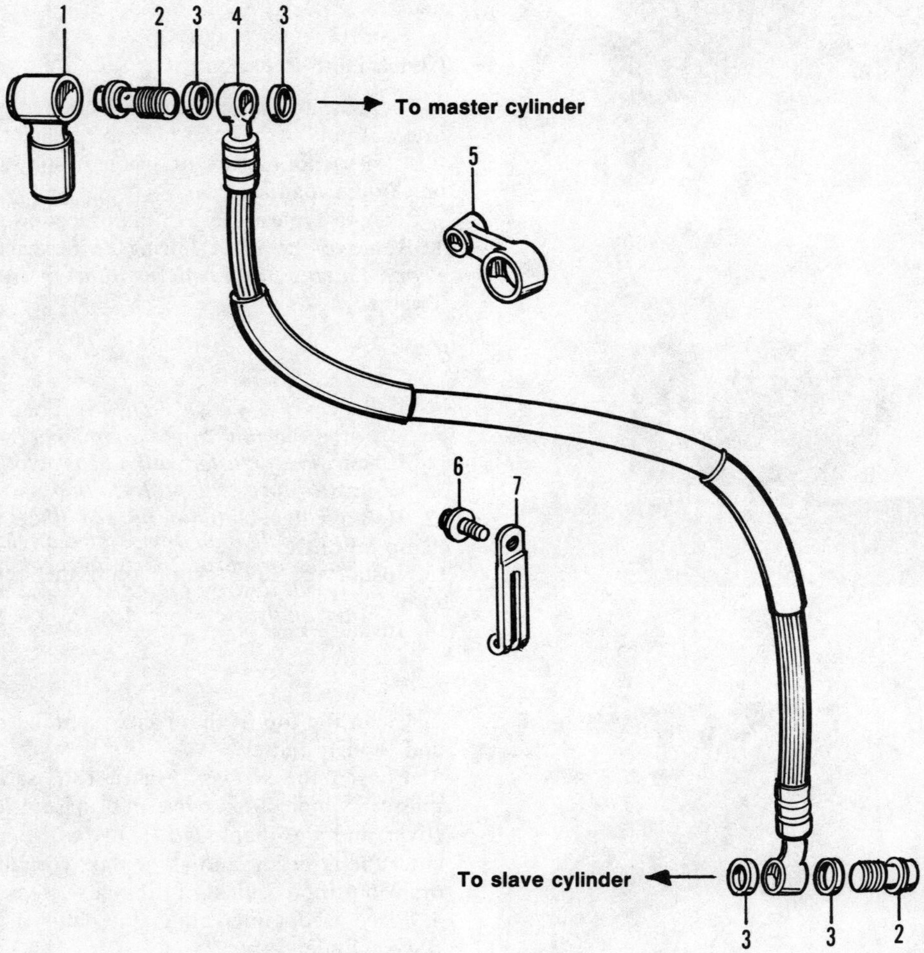

1. Rubber boot
2. Union bolt
3. Sealing washer
4. Clutch hose
5. Hose clip
6. Screw
7. Clamp

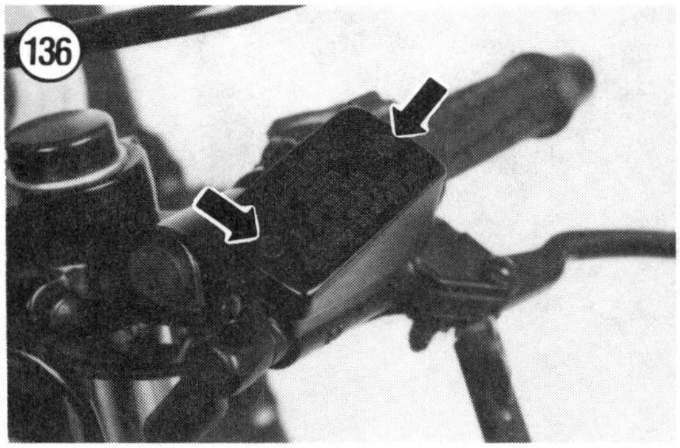

7. Pull back the rubber boot from the union bolt on the clutch master cylinder.
8. Place a shop cloth under the union bolt to catch any spilled hydraulic fluid that will leak out.
9. Unscrew the union bolt (**Figure 138**) securing the clutch hose to the master cylinder. Don't lose the sealing washer on each side of the hose fitting.
10. Remove the screw securing the hose clamp (A, **Figure 139**) to the frame. The hose clamp will stay with the hose.

NOTE
Before removing the clutch hose make a drawing of the hose routing through the frame. It is very easy to forget how it was, once it has been removed. Replace the hose exactly as it was, avoiding any sharp turns.

11. Pull the clutch hose (B, **Figure 139**) out from the front fork area and from between the carburetors. Unhook any additional retaining clips on the frame.
12. Remove the clutch hose and slide the hose clamp off of the old hose.
13. Install the hose clamp onto the new clutch hose.
14. Install a new hose, sealing washers and union bolts in the reverse order of removal. Be sure to install new sealing washers and in the correct positions.
15. Tighten the fittings and union bolts to the torque specifications listed in **Table 3**.
16. Bleed the clutch system as described under *Bleeding the System* in this chapter.
17. Test ride the bike slowly at first to make sure the clutch is operating correctly.

Slave Cylinder Removal

1. Remove the lower section and the left-hand middle section of the front fairing as described under *Front Fairing Removal/Installation* in Chapter Twelve.

CAUTION
Cover the fuel tank, front fender and instrument cluster with a heavy cloth or plastic tarp to protect them from accidental hydraulic fluid spills. Wash hydraulic fluid off any painted or plated surfaces or plastic parts immediately, as it will destroy the finish. Use soapy water and rinse completely.

2. Remove the gearshift lever as follows:
   a. Remove the circlip (**Figure 140**) and the washer (**Figure 141**) securing the gearshift lever to the pivot post.
   b. Remove the bolt (**Figure 142**) securing the gearshift lever to the shift shaft and remove the gearshift lever assembly.

3. Clean the top of the master cylinder of all dirt and foreign matter.
4. Loosen the screws (**Figure 136**) securing the master cylinder top cover. Pull up and loosen the cover and the diaphragm. This will allow air to enter the reservoir and allow the hydraulic fluid to drain out more quickly in the next steps.
5. Place a container under the clutch hose at the slave cylinder.
6. Remove the union bolt and sealing washers (A, **Figure 143**) securing the clutch hose to the slave cylinder.
7. Remove the clutch hose and let the hydraulic fluid drain out into the container. Dispose of this hydraulic fluid—never re-use hydraulic fluid. To prevent the entry of moisture and dirt, tape over the threaded bore in the slave cylinder.

WARNING

Dispose of this hydraulic fluid—never re-use hydraulic fluid. Contaminated hydraulic fluid can cause clutch problems.

8. Remove the bolts securing the drive sprocket cover (B, **Figure 143**) and remove the cover.
9. Unscrew the bleed valve (A, **Figure 144**) from the slave cylinder.
10. Remove the bolts (B, **Figure 144**) securing the slave cylinder to the drive sprocket cover.
11. Remove the screws (A, **Figure 145**) securing the piston retainer (B, **Figure 145**) to the backside of the drive sprocket cover.
12. Remove the slave cylinder assembly from the sprocket cover.

Slave Cylinder Disassembly/ Inspection/Assembly

Refer to **Figure 146** for this procedure.

1. Place a shop cloth or piece of soft wood at the end of the slave cylinder against the piston.
2. Place the slave cylinder assembly on the workbench with the piston facing down.

WARNING

*In the next step, the piston may shoot out of the slave cylinder body like a bullet. Keep your fingers out of the way. Wear shop gloves and apply air pressure gradually. Do **not** use high*

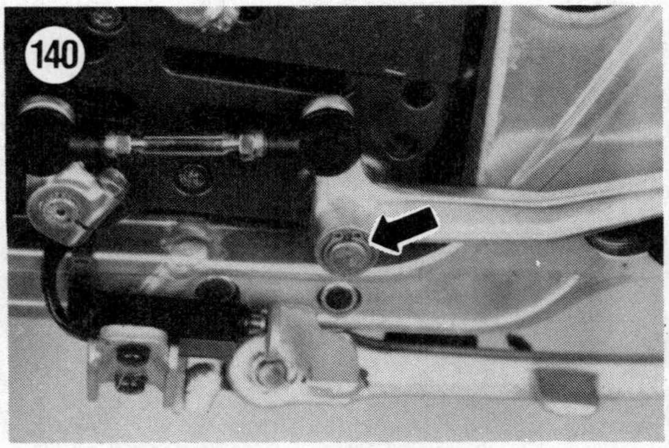

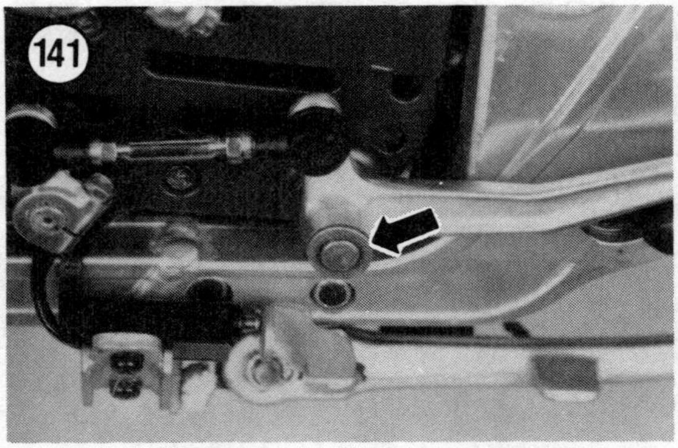

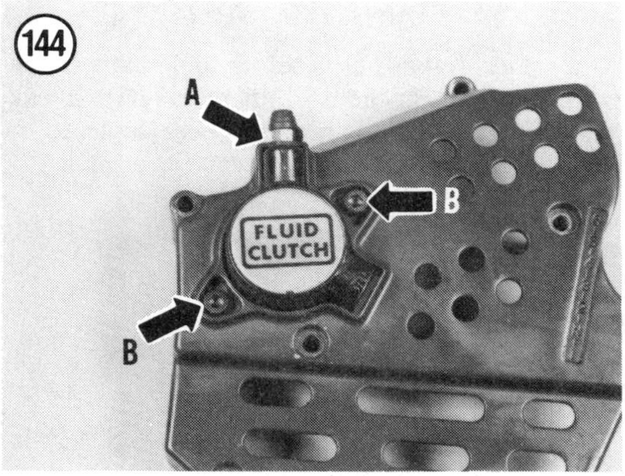

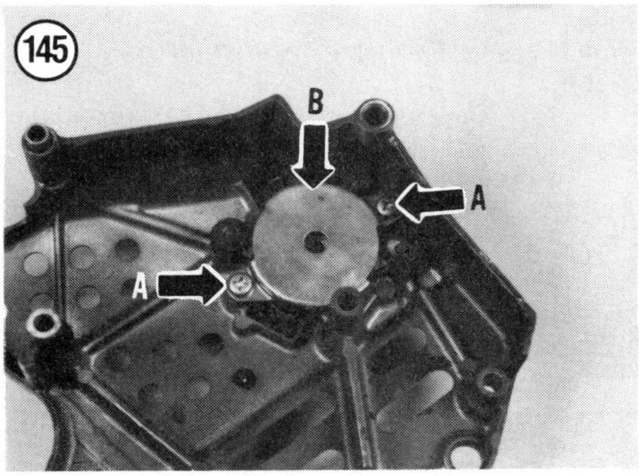

pressure air or place the air hose nozzle directly against the hydraulic line fitting inlet in the slave cylinder body. Hold the air nozzle away from the inlet allowing some of the air to escape.

3. Place your finger over the bleed valve fitting inlet to seal off the cylinder.
4. Apply the air pressure in short spurts to the hydraulic line fitting inlet and force the piston out. Use a service station air hose if you don't have an air compressor.
5. Remove the piston, seal and spring.

CAUTION
In the following step, do not use a sharp tool to remove the piston seal from the piston. Do not damage the piston surface.

6. Use a piece of plastic or wood and carefully remove the piston seal from the piston. Discard the piston seal as it must be replaced.
7. Inspect the slave cylinder body for damage. If damaged, replace the slave cylinder as an assembly. The body cannot be replaced separately.
8. Inspect the piston for scratches, scoring or other damage. If damaged, replace the slave cylinder as an assembly. The piston cannot be replaced separately.
9. Inspect the spring for damage or sagging. Replace if necessary. Suzuki does not provide service information for spring free length.

146

CLUTCH SLAVE CYLINDER

1. Right-hand pushrod
2. Left-hand pushrod
3. Oil seal
4. Screw
5. Piston retainer
6. Piston
7. Piston seal
8. Spring
9. Slave cylinder body
10. Bleed valve
11. Cap
12. Locating dowel
13. Allen bolt

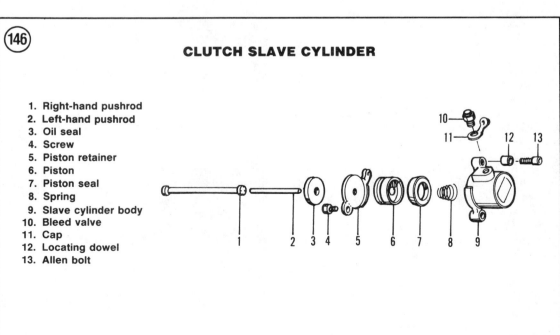

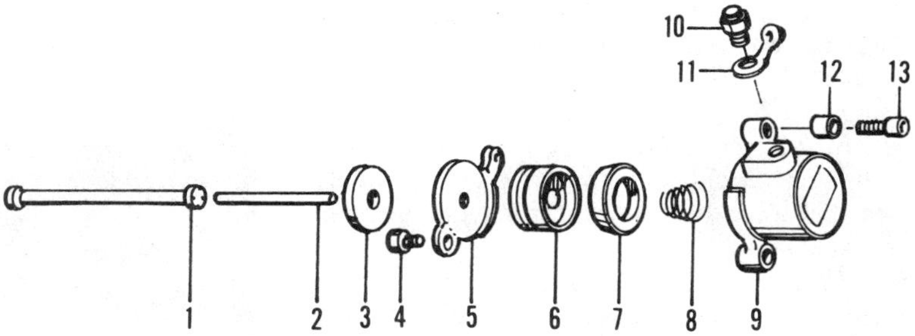

10. If serviceable, clean the slave cylinder with rubbing alcohol and rinse with clean hydraulic fluid.

NOTE
Never reuse the old piston seal. Very minor damage or age deterioration can make the seal useless.

11. Coat the new piston seal with fresh hydraulic fluid.
12. Carefully install the new piston seal in the groove in piston. Make sure the seal is properly seated in the groove.
13. Coat the piston and cylinder wall with fresh hydraulic fluid.
14. Position the spring with the tapered end toward the piston and install the spring into the backside of the piston.
15. Carefully install the piston into the slave cylinder. Push the piston in until it bottoms out.

Slave Cylinder Installation

1. Install the slave cylinder assembly into the sprocket cover.
2. Install the piston retainer (B, **Figure 145**) and screws (A, **Figure 145**) securing the piston retainer to the backside of the drive sprocket cover. Tighten the screws securely.
3. Install the bolts (B, **Figure 144**) securing the slave cylinder to the drive sprocket cover. Tighten the bolts securely.
4. Install the bleed valve (A, **Figure 144**) into the slave cylinder. Tighten the bleed valve securely.
5. Make sure the locating dowels are in place.
6. Install the drive sprocket cover (B, **Figure 143**) and bolts. Tighten the bolts securely.
7. Install a sealing washer on each side of the hose fitting. Install the union bolt (A, **Figure 143**) securing the clutch hose to the slave cylinder. Tighten the union bolt to the torque specification listed in **Table 3**.
8. Install the gearshift lever as follows:
   a. Install the gearshift lever onto the shift shaft and install the bolt. Tighten the bolt securely.
   b. Install the gearshift lever onto the pivot post. Install the washer and the circlip.
9. Install the left-hand middle portion and lower portion of the front fairing as described under *Front Fairing Removal/Installation* in Chapter Twelve.

BLEEDING THE SYSTEM

This procedure is not necessary unless the clutch feels spongy (air in the line), there has been a leak in the system, a component has been replaced or the clutch hydraulic fluid has been replaced.

Brake Bleeder Process

This procedure uses a brake bleeder that is available from motorcycle or automotive supply stores or from mail order outlets.

1. Remove the front fairing as described under *Front Fairing Removal/Installation* in Chapter Twelve.
2. Remove the dust cap (**Figure 147**) from the bleed valve on the slave cylinder assembly.

147

148

3. Connect the brake bleeder to the bleed valve on the slave cylinder assembly (**Figure 148**).

CAUTION
Cover the front fender and front wheel with a heavy cloth or plastic tarp to protect it from the accidental spilling of hydraulic fluid. Wash any hydraulic fluid off of any plastic, painted or plated surface immediately; as it will destroy the finish. Use soapy water and rinse completely.

4. Clean the top cover of the clutch master cylinder of all dirt and foreign matter.
5. Remove the screws (**Figure 149**) securing the top cover and remove the top cover and diaphragm.
6. Fill the reservoir almost to the top lip; insert the diaphragm and the top cover loosely. Leave the top cover in place during this procedure to prevent the entry of dirt.

WARNING
Use hydraulic brake fluid from a sealed container marked DOT 3 or DOT 4 only. Other types may vaporize and cause clutch failure. Do not intermix different brands or types as they may not be compatible. Do not intermix a silicone based (DOT 5) brake fluid as it can cause clutch component damage leading to clutch system failure.

7. Open the bleed valve on the slave cylinder about one-half turn and pump the brake bleeder.

NOTE
If air is entering the brake bleeder hose from around the bleed valve, apply several layers of Teflon tape to the bleed valve. This should make a good seal between the bleed valve and the brake bleeder hose.

8. As the fluid enters the system and exits into the brake bleeder the level will drop in the reservoir. Maintain the level at about 3/8 inch from the top of the reservoir to prevent air from being drawn into the system.
9. Continue to pump the lever on the brake bleeder until the fluid emerging from the hose is completely free of bubbles. At this point, tighten the bleed valve.

NOTE
Do not allow the reservoir to empty during the bleeding operation or more air will enter the system. If this occurs, the entire procedure must be repeated.

10. When the hydraulic fluid is free of bubbles, tighten the bleed valve, remove the brake bleeder tube and install the bleed valve dust cap.
11. If necessary, add fluid to correct the level in the reservoir. It should be to the upper level line.
12. Install the diaphragm and the reservoir top cover. Tighten the screws securely.
13. Test the feel of the clutch lever. It should be firm and should offer the same resistance each time it's operated. If it feels spongy, it is likely that there is still air in the system and it must be bled again. When all air has been bled from the system and the fluid level is correct in the reservoir, double-check for leaks and tighten all fittings and connections.
14. Install the front fairing as described under *Front Fairing Removal/Installation* in Chapter Twelve.
15. Test ride the bike slowly at first to make sure that the clutch is operating properly.

Without a Brake Bleeder

1. Remove the front fairing as described under *Front Fairing Removal/Installation* in Chapter Twelve.
2. Remove the dust cap (**Figure 147**) from the bleed valve on the slave cylinder assembly.

5

3. Connect the bleed hose to the bleed valve on the caliper assembly (**Figure 150**).
4. Place the other end of the tube into a clean container. Fill the container with enough fresh hydraulic fluid to keep the end submerged. The tube should be long enough to prevent air from being drawn into the slave cylinder during bleeding.

CAUTION
Cover the front fender and front wheel with a heavy cloth or plastic tarp to protect it from the accidental spilling of hydraulic fluid. Wash any hydraulic fluid off of any plastic, painted or plated surface immediately, as it will destroy the finish. Use soapy water and rinse completely.

5. Clean the top of the clutch master cylinder of all dirt and foreign matter.
6. Remove the screws (**Figure 149**) securing the reservoir top cover and remove the reservoir top cover and diaphragm.
7. Fill the reservoir almost to the cover lip; insert the diaphragm and the top cover loosely. Leave the top cover in place during this procedure to prevent the entry of dirt.
8. If the clutch master cylinder was drained, it must be bled first as follows:
   a. Remove the hose joint bolt and hose from the master cylinder.
   b. While holding your thumb over the hole in the master cylinder, pump the clutch lever several times then hold the lever depressed.
   c. Reduce your thumb pressure over the hole. Some brake fluid and air bubbles will ooze out. Reapply thumb pressure. Repeat this procedure until only brake fluid comes out and you have some feel at the lever.
   d. Refill the master cylinder, if necessary.
   e. Reconnect the hose joint bolt and hole. Pump the lever several times then hold the lever depressed.
   f. Loosen the joint bolt 1/4 turn. Some fluid and air bubbles will ooze out. Tighten the bolt and repeat this procedure until only brake fluid comes out.
   g. Refill the master cylinder, if necessary.

WARNING
Use hydraulic brake fluid from a sealed container marked DOT 3 or DOT 4 only. Other types may vaporize and cause clutch failure. Do not intermix different brands or types as they may not be compatible. Do not intermix a silicone based (DOT 5) brake fluid as it can cause clutch component damage leading to clutch system failure.

9. Slowly apply the clutch lever several times as follows:
   a. Pull the lever in. Hold the lever in the applied position.
   b. Open the bleed valve about one-half turn. Allow the lever to travel to its limit.
   c. When this limit is reached, tighten the bleed screw.

10. As the fluid enters the system, the level will drop in the reservoir. Maintain the level at about 3/8 inch from the cover of the reservoir to prevent air from being drawn into the system.
11. Continue to pump the lever and fill the reservoir until the fluid emerging from the hose is completely free of bubbles.

NOTE
Do not allow the reservoir to empty during the bleeding operation or more air will enter the system. If this occurs, the entire procedure must be repeated.

12. Hold the clutch lever in, tighten the bleed valve, remove the bleed tube and install the bleed valve dust cap.
13. If necessary, add fluid to correct the level in the reservoir. It should be to the upper level line.

150

14. Install the diaphragm and reservoir top cover. Tighten the screws securely.
15. Test the feel of the clutch lever. It should be firm and should offer the same resistance each time it's operated. If it feels spongy, it is likely that there is still air in the system and it must be bled again. When all air has been bled from the system and the fluid level is correct in the reservoir, double-check for leaks and tighten all fittings and connections.
16. Install the front fairing as described under *Front Fairing Removal/Installation* in Chapter Twelve.
17. Test ride the bike slowly at first to make sure that the clutch is operating properly.

Table 1 CLUTCH SPECIFICATIONS (GSX-R750R LIMITED EDITION)

Item	Standard	Wear limit
Drive plate thickness	1.4-1.6 mm (0.05-0.06 in.)	1.1 mm (0.04 in.)
Driven plate distortion	—	0.10 mm (0.004 in.)
Clutch spring free length	—	33.3 mm (1.31 in.)

Table 2 CLUTCH SPECIFICATIONS (GSX-R750, GSX-R1100)

Item	Standard	Wear limit
Friction disc thickness	2.92-3.08 mm (0.115-0.121 in.)	2.62 mm (0.103 in.)
Friction disc claw width	15.8-16.0 mm (0.622-0.630 in.)	15.0 mm (0.591 in.)
Clutch plate warpage	—	0.10 mm (0.004 in.)
Clutch spring free length	—	34.0 mm (1.34 in.)

Table 3 CLUTCH TORQUE SPECIFICATIONS

Item	N•m	ft.-lb.
Clutch nut	50-70	36-51
Clutch spring bolts	11-13	8-10
Master cylinder mounting bolts	5-8	3-6
Clutch hose union bolts	20-25	14-18

5

CHAPTER SIX

TRANSMISSION AND GEARSHIFT MECHANISMS

This chapter provides complete service procedures for the transmission and the external and the internal shift mechanism.

EXTERNAL GEARSHIFT MECHANISM

The external gearshift mechanism is located on the same side of the crankcase as the clutch assembly. To remove the internal shift mechanism (shift drum and shift forks), it is necessary to remove the engine and split the crankcase. This procedure is covered in Chapter Four.

The gearshift lever is subject to a lot of abuse. If the bike has been in a hard spill, the gearshift lever may have been hit and the gearshift shaft bent. It is very hard to straighten the shaft without subjecting the crankcase halves to abnormal stress where the shaft enters the crankcase. If the shaft is bent enough to prevent it from being withdrawn from the crankcase, there is little recourse but to cut the shaft off with a hacksaw very close to the crankcase. It is much cheaper in the long run to replace the shaft than risk damaging a very expensive crankcase assembly.

Removal

This procedure is shown with the crankcase separated for clarity. It is not necessary to separate the crankcase for this procedure.

1. Remove the clutch assembly as described under *Clutch Removal/Installation* in Chapter Five for your specific model.
2. Remove the clip (**Figure 1**) and the washer (**Figure 2**) from the gearshift shaft.
3. On the other side of the crankcase, withdraw the gearshift shaft (**Figure 3**) from the crankcase. See information regarding a bent gearshift shaft in the introductory paragraph of this procedure.
4. Remove the screws securing the pawl retainer (**Figure 4**) and remove the pawl retainer.
5. Remove the screws securing the cam guide (**Figure 5**) and remove the cam guide.

6. Remove the cam gear assembly (**Figure 6**) from the end of the shift drum. Don't lose the pawls, springs and pins in the assembly. Store the cam gear assembly in a spray paint can top to keep all components together.

Inspection

1. Inspect the return spring (**Figure 7**) on the gearshift shaft assembly. If broken or weak it must be replaced.
2. Inspect the gearshift shaft assembly (**Figure 8**) for bending, wear or other damage; replace if necessary.

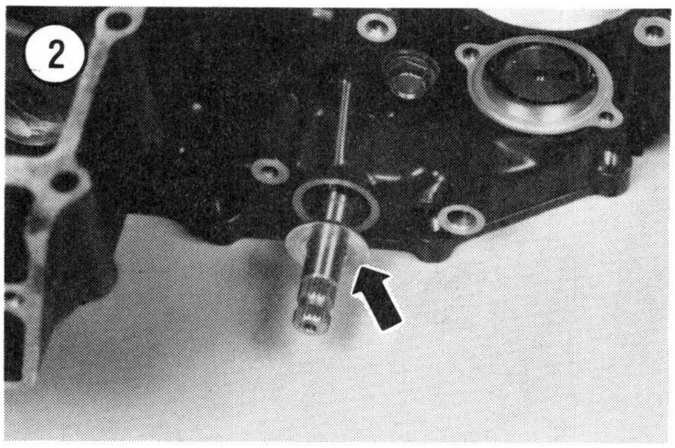

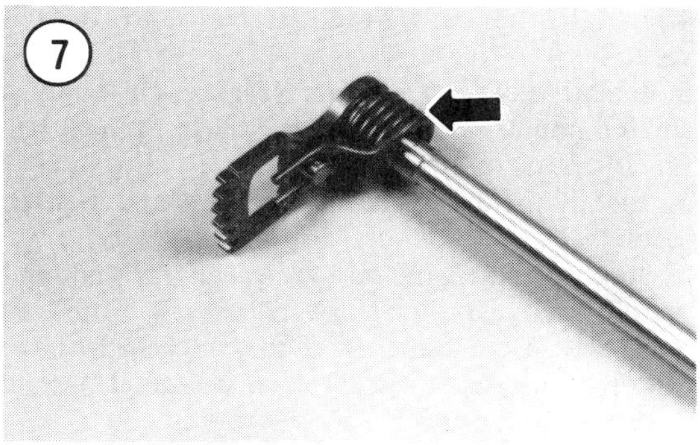

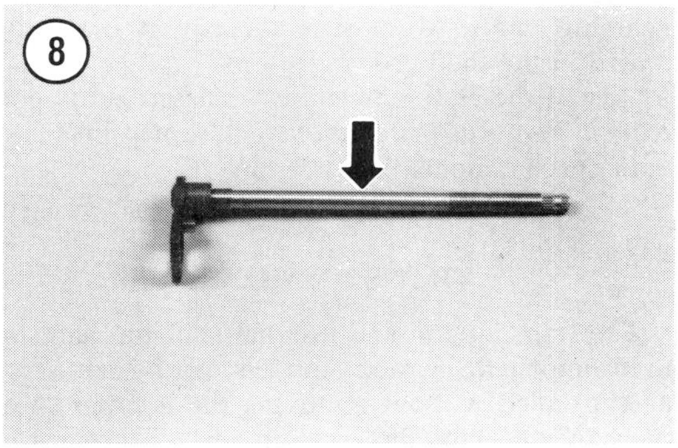

3. Inspect the gear teeth (**Figure 9**) on the gearshift shaft assembly. If broken or weak it must be replaced.
4. Disassemble the cam gear assembly (**Figure 10**) and inspect the pawls, springs and pins for wear or damage.
5. Assemble the cam gear assembly as follows:
   a. Install the springs into the cam gear body.
   b. Position the pawl pins with the rounded end facing out and install them onto the springs.
   c. Install the pawls onto the pins and into the cam gear body.
   d. The pin grooves in the pawls are offset. When the pawls are installed correctly the wider shoulder (W, **Figure 11**) must face toward the outside.
   e. Hold the pawls in place and place the assembly into the spray paint can top.

Installation

1. Remove the cam gear assembly from the spray paint can top and keep all components together.
2. Compress the spring-loaded shift pawls with your fingers. Install the cam gear assembly into the receptacle of the shift drum as shown in **Figure 6**.
3. Install the cam guide (**Figure 5**). Apply a small amount of Loctite Lock N' Seal to the screw threads prior to installation.
4. Install the cam guide screws and tighten securely.
5. Install the pawl retainer (**Figure 4**). Apply a small amount of Loctite Lock N' Seal to the screw threads prior to installation.
6. Install the pawl retainer screws and tighten securely.
7. Apply clean engine oil to the gearshift shaft and install the gearshift shaft (**Figure 3**) into the crankcase. Align the center of the cam gear with the center of the gearshift shaft gear (**Figure 12**), then push the shaft assembly all the way in.
8. On the other side of the crankcase, install the washer (**Figure 2**) and the clip (**Figure 1**) onto the gearshift shaft. Make sure the clip is correctly seated in the shaft groove.
9. Install the clutch assembly as described under *Clutch Removal/Installation* in Chapter Five for your specific model.

TRANSMISSIONS

The transmission and internal shift mechanism used among the various models can be removed and installed without removing the internal shift mechanism. Once the crankcase is split, removal

9

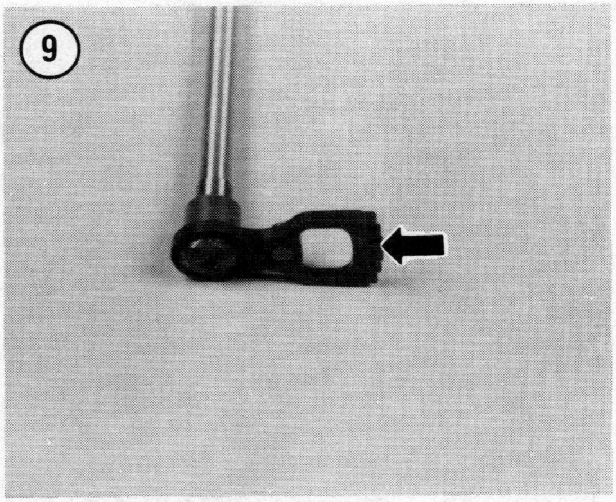

10

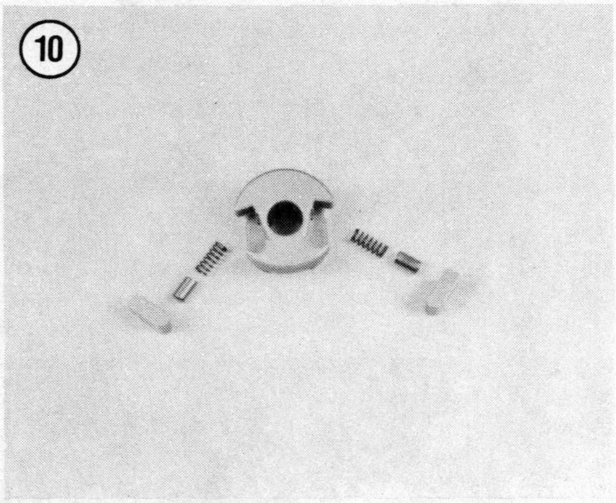

11

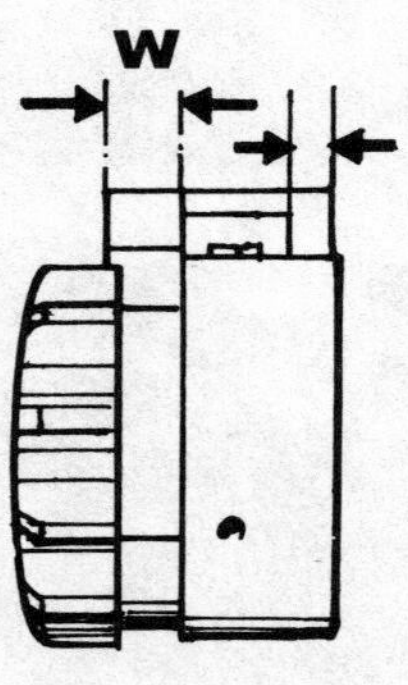

and installation of the transmission assemblies is a simple task of pulling the shaft assemblies up and out of the lower crankcase.

There are 2 different transmissions used among the various models. The 750 cc engine use a 6-speed gear unit while the 1100 cc engine uses a 5-speed unit. Be sure to use the correct procedure for your specific model.

Refer to **Table 1** for 750 cc models or **Table 2** for 1100 cc models at the end of the chapter for transmission and gearshift mechanism specifications.

To gain access to the transmission and internal shift mechanism it is necessary to remove the engine and split the crankcase as described in Chapter Four.

Preliminary Inspection (All Models)

After the transmission shaft assemblies have been removed from the crankcase, clean and inspect the assemblies prior to disassembling them. Place the assembled shaft into a large can or plastic bucket and thoroughly clean with a petroleum-based solvent such as kerosene and a stiff brush. Dry with compressed air or let it sit on rags to drip dry. Repeat for the other shaft assembly.

1. After they have been cleaned, visually inspect the components of the assemblies for excessive wear. Any burrs, pitting or roughness on the teeth of a gear will cause wear on the mating gear.

NOTE
Defective gears should be replaced. It's a good idea to replace the mating gear on the other shaft even though it may not show as much wear or damage.

2. Carefully check the engagement dogs (**Figure 13**). If any are chipped, worn, rounded or missing, the affected gear must be replaced.
3. Rotate the transmission bearings on the transmission shafts by hand. Check for roughness, noise and radial play. Any bearing that is suspect should be replaced as described in this chapter.
4. If the transmission shafts are satisfactory and are not going to be disassembled, apply assembly oil or engine oil to all components and reinstall them in the crankcase as described in this chapter.

NOTE
If disassembling a used, well run-in (high mileage) transmission for the first time by yourself, pay particular attention to any additional shims that may have been added by a previous owner. These may have been added to take up the tolerance of worn components and must be reinstalled in the same position. If new parts are going to be installed these shims may be eliminated. This is something you will have to determine upon reassembly.

6-SPEED TRANSMISSION (750 CC ENGINES)

Removal/Installation

1. Remove the engine and split the crankcase as described under *Crankcase Disassembly* in Chapter Four.

12

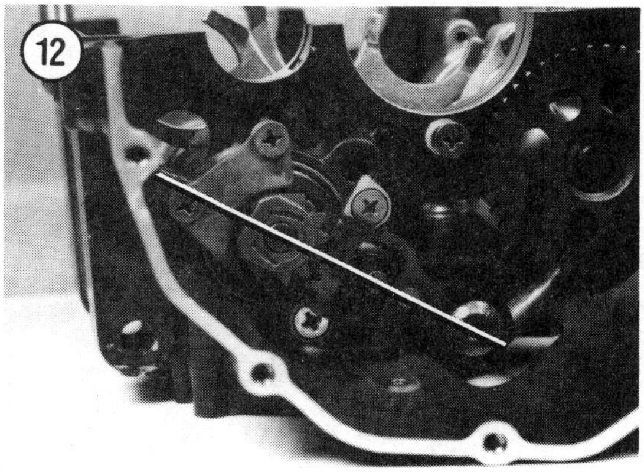

13

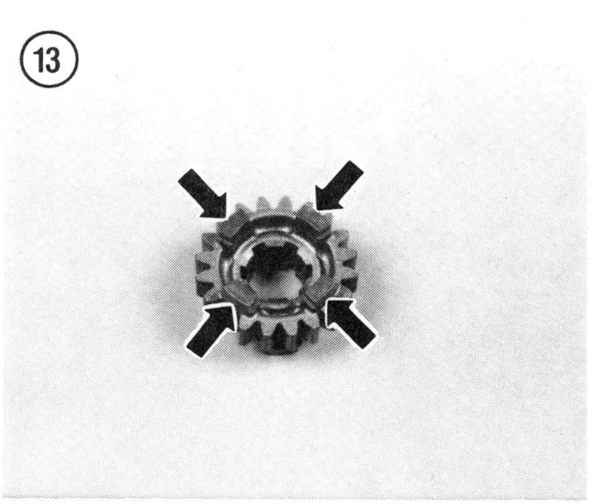

2. Remove the mainshaft assembly (**Figure 14**) and countershaft assembly (A, **Figure 15**).
3. Inspect the transmission shaft assemblies as described under *Preliminary Inspection* in this chapter.

NOTE
Prior to installation, coat all bearing surfaces with assembly oil.

4. Install the 2 bearing set rings (A, **Figure 16**) and bearing locating dowels (B, **Figure 16**) into the upper crankcase.
5. Install the countershaft assembly (A, **Figure 15**) and check the following:
   a. On models so equipped, make sure the end cap (**Figure 17**) is in place on the end of the countershaft.
   b. Make sure the bearings are properly indexed into the set ring (B, **Figure 15**) and locating dowel.
6. Install the mainshaft assembly (**Figure 14**) and check the following:
   a. Make sure the end cap (A, **Figure 18**) is in place on the end of the countershaft.
   b. Make sure the bearings are properly indexed into the set ring (B, **Figure 18**) and locating dowel.
7. After both transmission assemblies are installed, perform the following:
   a. Hold onto the mainshaft and rotate the countershaft. The countershaft should rotate freely. If it does not, shift the gear that is engaged so that both shafts are in NEUTRAL.
   b. Rotate both shaft assemblies by hand. Make sure there is no binding. This is the time to find that something may be installed incorrectly—not after the crankcase is completely assembled.
8. Reassemble the crankcase as described under *Crankcase Assembly* and install the engine as described in Chapter Four.

Mainshaft Disassembly/Inspection

Refer to **Figure 19** for this procedure.

NOTE
*A helpful "tool" that should be used for transmission disassembly is a large egg flat (the type that restaurants get their eggs in) as shown in **Figure 20**. As you remove a part from the shaft, set it in one of the depressions in the same position from which it was removed. This is an easy way to remember the correct relationship of all parts.*

18

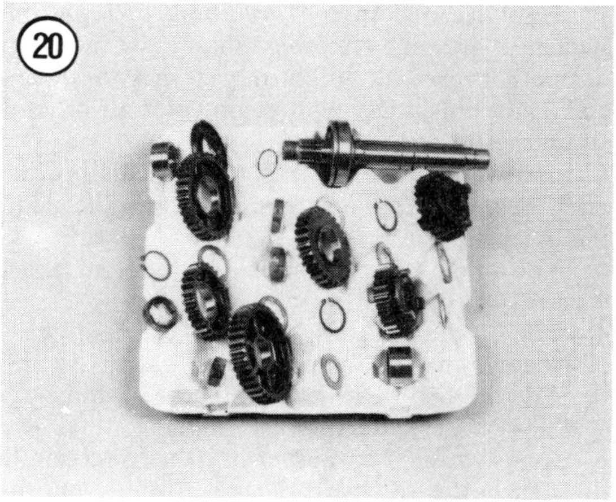

20

19

6-SPEED TRANSMISSION (750 CC ENGINES)

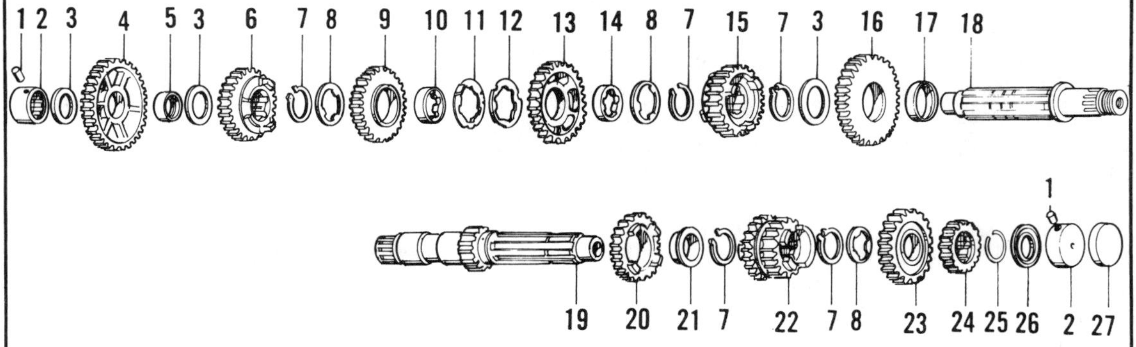

1. Locating pin
2. Needle bearing assembly
3. Thrust washer
4. Mainshaft 1st gear
5. Mainshaft 1st gear bushing
6. Mainshaft 5th gear
7. Circlip
8. Splined washer
9. Mainshaft 4th gear
10. Mainshaft 4th gear bushing
11. Splined lockwasher
12. Splined washer
13. Mainshaft 3rd gear
14. Mainshaft 3rd gear bushing
15. Mainshaft 6th gear
16. Mainshaft 2nd gear
17. Mainshaft 2nd gear bushing
18. Mainshaft
19. Countershaft/1st gear
20. Countershaft 5th gear
21. Countershaft 5th gear bushing
22. Countershaft 3rd/4th combination gear
23. Countershaft 6th gear
24. Countershaft 2nd gear
25. Snap ring
26. Oil seal
27. Cap (models so equipped)

1. If not cleaned in the *Preliminary Inspection* sequence, place the assembled shaft into a large can or plastic bucket and thoroughly clean with solvent and a stiff brush. Dry with compressed air or let it sit on rags to dry.
2. Remove the outer bearing race, needle bearing and thrust washer. Don't lose the locating dowel in the outer bearing race.
3. Slide off the 1st gear, 1st gear bushing and thrust washer.
4. Slide off the 5th gear.
5. Remove the circlip and splined washer.
6. Slide off the 4th gear and 4th gear bushing.
7. Slide off the splined lockwasher.
8. Rotate the splined washer in either direction to disengage the tangs from the grooves on the transmission shaft. Slide off the splined washer.
9. Slide off the 3rd gear and 3rd gear bushing.
10. Slide off the splined washer.
11. Remove the circlip.
12. Slide off the 6th gear.
13. Remove the circlip and the thrust washer.
14. Slide off the 2nd gear and 2nd gear bushing.
15. From the other end of the shaft, remove the oil seal, the spacer and the O-ring. Discard the O-ring; it must be replaced.
16. If necessary, remove the ball bearing (A, **Figure 21**) from the shaft.
17. Check each gear for excessive wear, burrs, pitting, or chipped or missing teeth (A, **Figure 22**). Make sure the lugs (B, **Figure 22**) on the gears are in good condition.
18. Check each gear bushing (**Figure 23**) for excessive wear, pitting or damage.
19. Inspect the shift fork-to-gear clearance as described under *Internal Gearshift Mechanism* in this chapter.

NOTE
Defective gears should be replaced. It is a good idea to replace the mating gear on the countershaft even though it may not show as much wear or damage.

20. Make sure that all gears and bushings slide smoothly on the mainshaft splines.

NOTE
All circlips should be replaced every time the transmission is disassembled to ensure proper gear alignment. Do not expand a circlip more than necessary to slide it over the shaft.

21

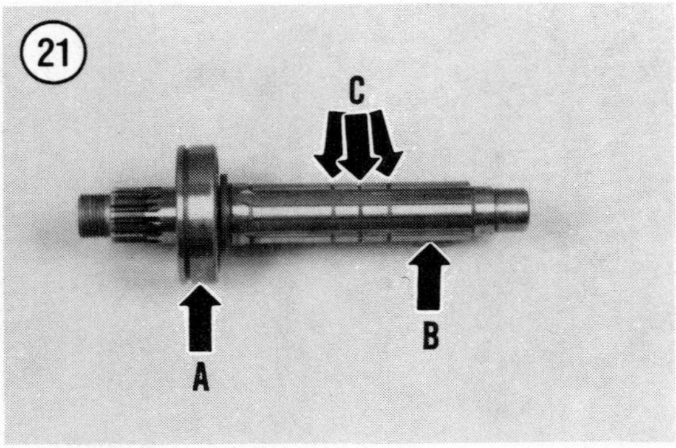

22

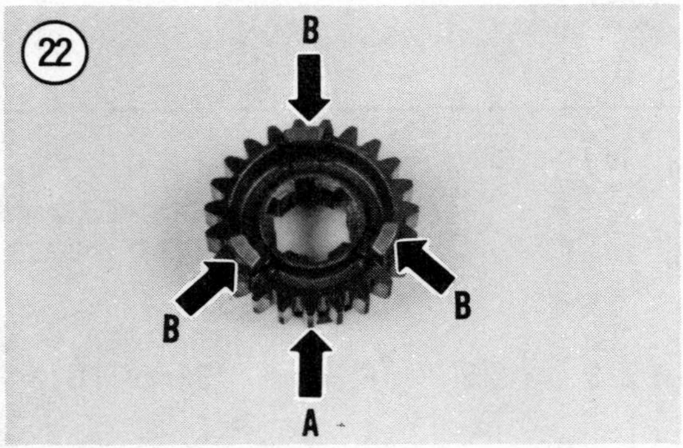

23

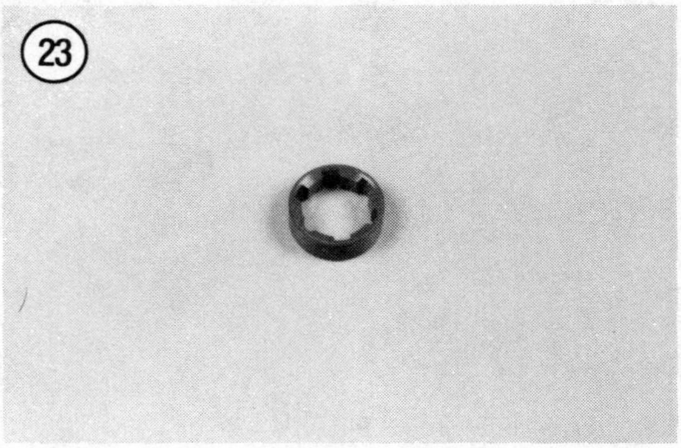

24

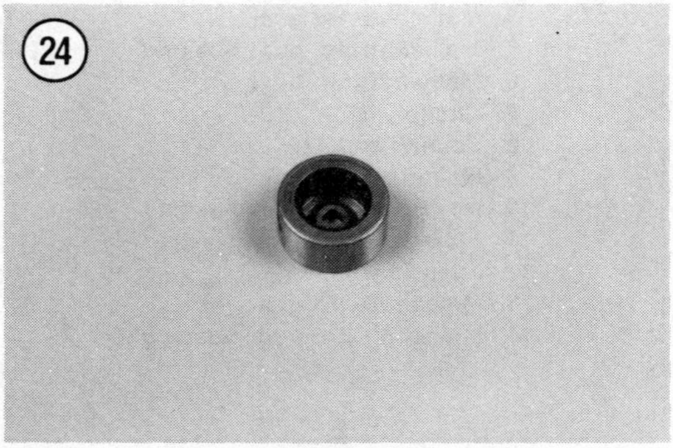

(25)

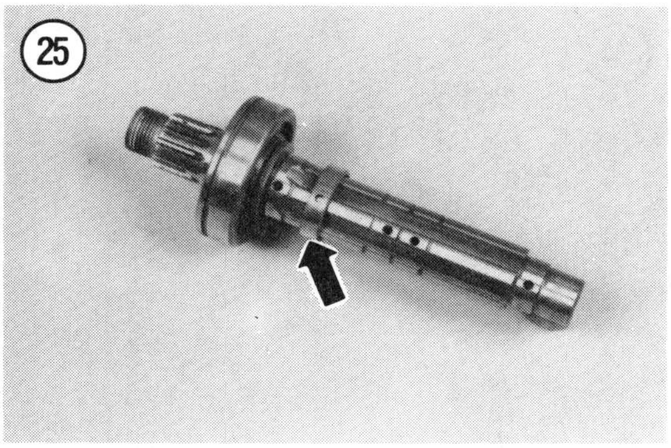

(26)

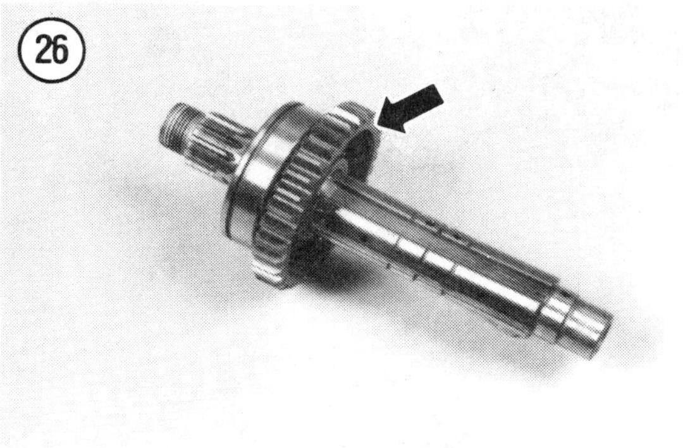

(27)

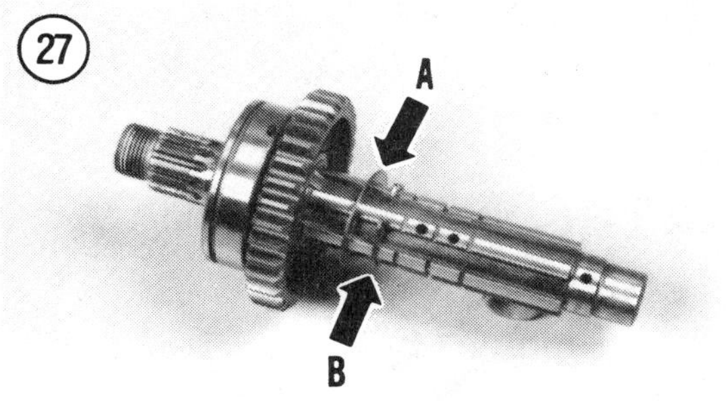

(28)

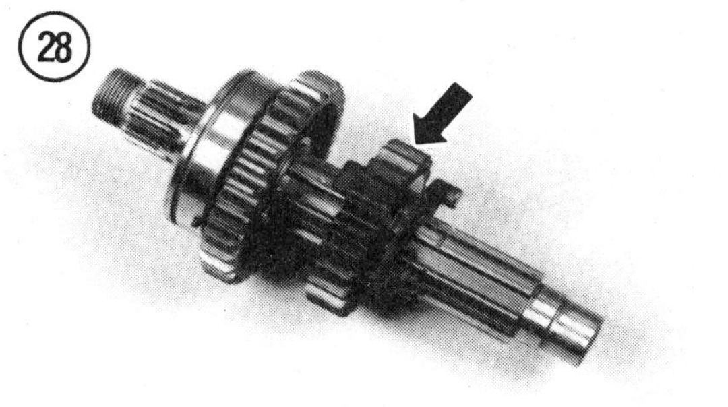

21. Inspect the splines (B, **Figure 21**) and circlip grooves (C, **Figure 21**) of the mainshaft. If any are damaged, the shaft must be replaced.
22. Check the needle bearing (**Figure 24**). Make sure the needles rotate smoothly with no signs of wear or damage. Replace as necessary.

Mainshaft Assembly

1. Apply a light coat of clean engine oil to all sliding surfaces prior to installing any parts.
2. Slide on the 2nd gear bushing (**Figure 25**) and the 2nd gear (**Figure 26**).
3. Slide on the thrust washer (A, **Figure 27**) and install the circlip (B, **Figure 27**).
4. Slide on the 6th gear (**Figure 28**).
5. Install the circlip (A, **Figure 29**) and slide on the splined washer (B, **Figure 29**).
6. Align the oil hole in the 3rd gear bushing with the transmission shaft oil hole and slide on the bushing (**Figure 30**). This alignment is necessary for proper gear lubrication.

6

(29)

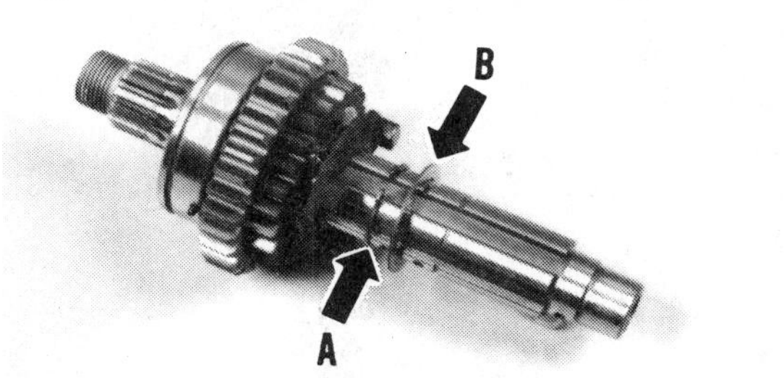

(30)

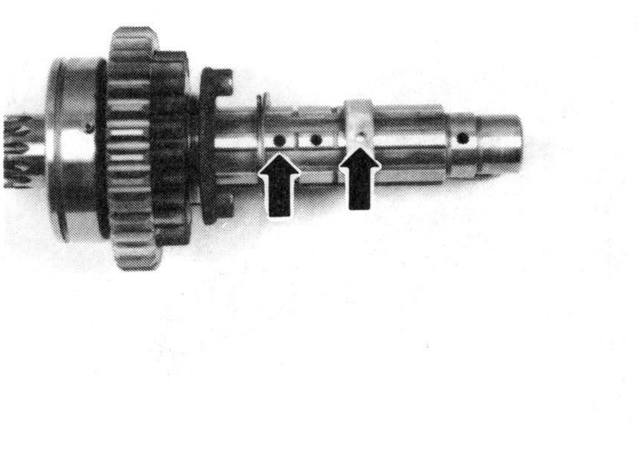

7. Slide on the 3rd gear (**Figure 31**).
8. Slide on the splined washer. Rotate the splined washer in either direction to engage the tangs into the grooves on the transmission shaft (**Figure 32**).
9. Slide on the splined lockwasher (**Figure 33**). Push it on until the tangs go into the open areas of the splined washer and lock the washer into place (**Figure 34**).
10. Align the oil hole in the 4th gear bushing with the transmission shaft oil hole and slide on the bushing (**Figure 35**). This alignment is necessary for proper gear lubrication.
11. Slide on the 4th gear (**Figure 36**).
12. Slide on the thrust washer (A, **Figure 37**) and install the circlip (B, **Figure 37**).
13. Slide on the 5th gear (**Figure 38**) and the thrust washer (**Figure 39**).

31

32

33

34

35

36

37

38

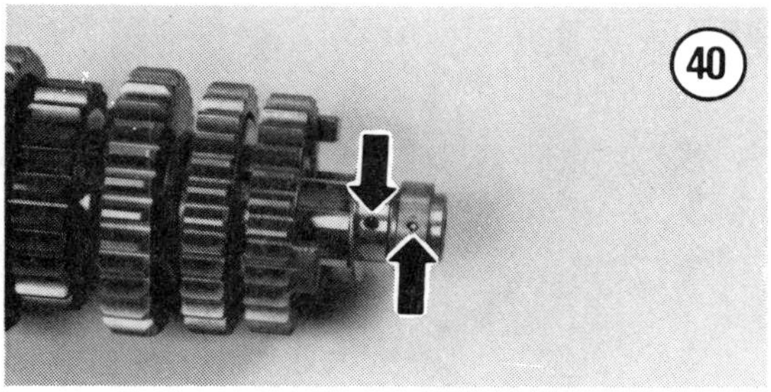

14. Align the oil hole in the 1st gear bushing with the transmission shaft oil hole and slide on the bushing (**Figure 40**). This alignment is necessary for proper gear lubrication.

15. Slide on the 1st gear (**Figure 41**).

16. Install the thrust washer (**Figure 42**) and the needle bearing (**Figure 43**).

17. Onto the other end of the shaft, install the following:
   a. Install a new O-ring (**Figure 44**) and the spacer (**Figure 45**).
   b. Apply a light coat of multipurpose grease to the lips of the oil seal prior to installation. Install the oil seal (**Figure 46**).

18. Make sure each gear engages properly to the adjoining gear where applicable.

6

Countershaft Disassembly/Inspection

Refer to **Figure 19** for this procedure.

NOTE

Use the same large egg flat (used on the mainshaft disassembly) during the countershaft disassembly ***(Figure 47)****. This is an easy way to remember the correct relationship of all parts.*

1. If not cleaned in the *Preliminary Inspection* sequence, place the assembled shaft into a large can or plastic bucket and thoroughly clean with solvent and a stiff brush. Dry with compressed air or let it sit on rags to dry.
2. On models so equipped, remove the oil seal.
3. Remove the outer bearing race and needle bearing assembly.
4. Slide off the oil seal.
5. Release the circlip (7, **Figure 19**) from the countershaft groove. Move it down the shaft toward the 3rd/4th combination gear.
6. Slide the 6th and 2nd gear down toward the 3rd/4th combination gear.
7. Secure the countershaft vertically in a vise with soft jaws.
8. Use a scribe and pry one end of the snap ring out of the groove (25, **Figure 19**) then secure this end with needlenose pliers. Hold onto the circlip with the needlenose pliers, work around the shaft with the scribe, pry the circlip out of the groove and remove it. This circlip must be replaced as it will be severely distorted during removal.
9. Slide off the 2nd gear.
10. Slide off the 6th gear.
11. Slide off the splined washer and remove the circlip.
12. Slide off the 3rd/4th combination gear.
13. Remove the circlip.
14. Slide off the 5th gear and the 5th gear bushing.
15. Remove ball bearing (A, **Figure 48**) if necessary.
16. Check each gear for excessive wear, burrs, pitting or chipped or missing teeth (A, **Figure 49**). Make sure lugs (B, **Figure 49**) on gears are in good condition.

47

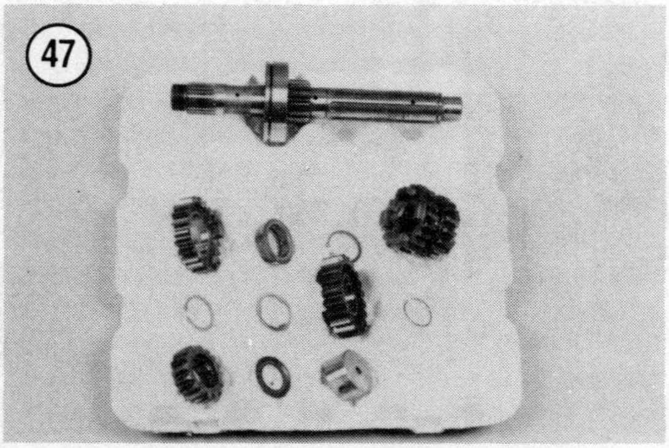

48

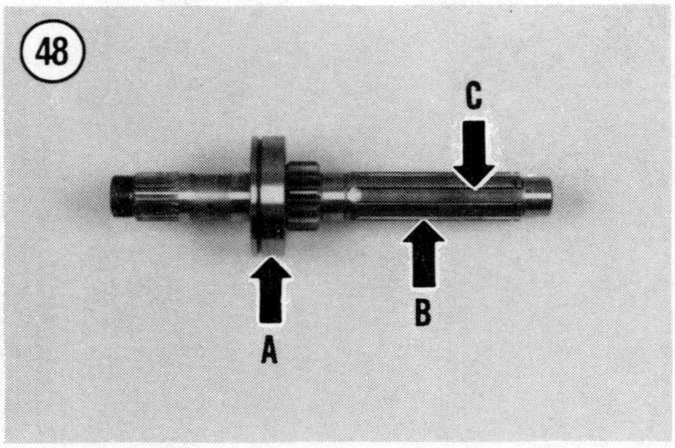

49

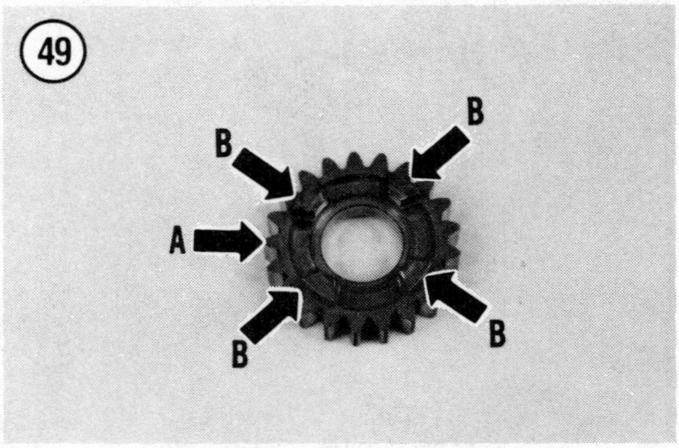

50

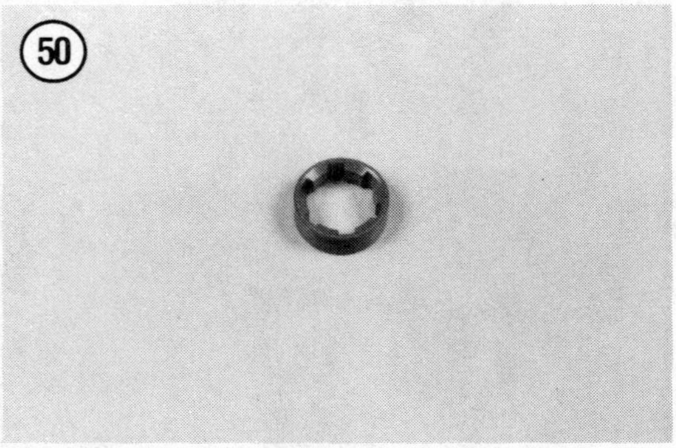

51

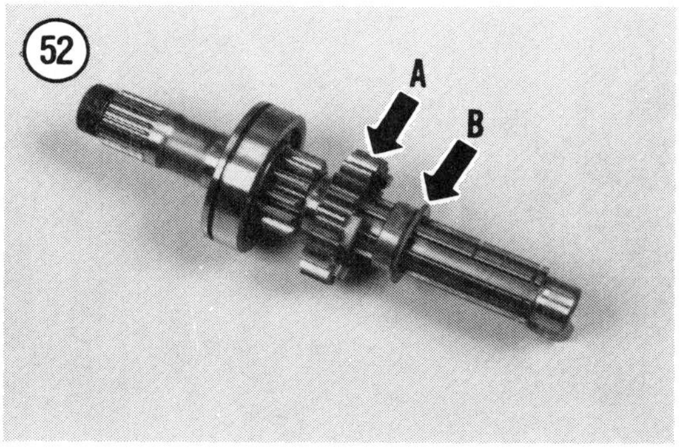

52

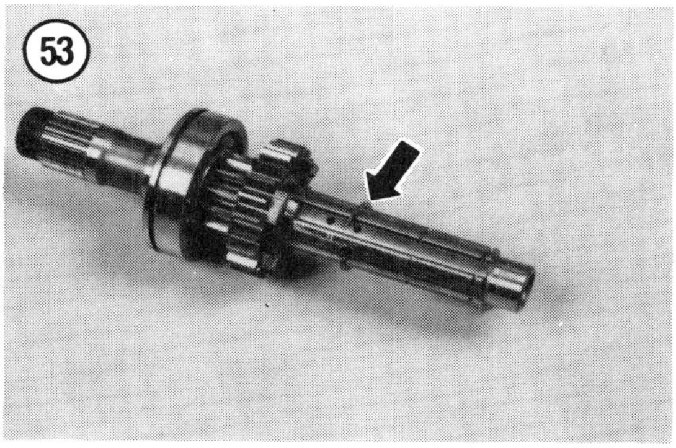
53

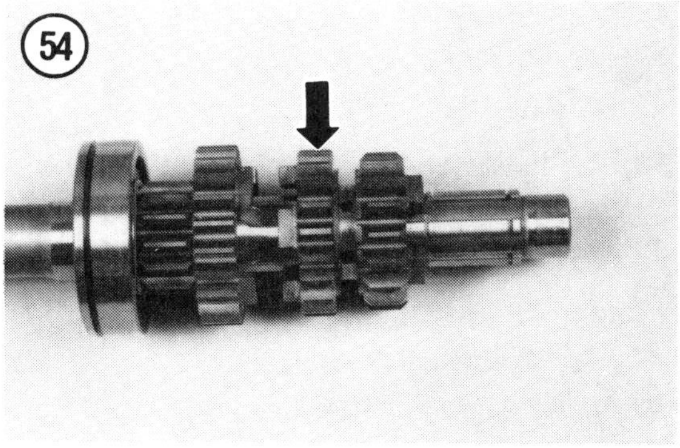
54

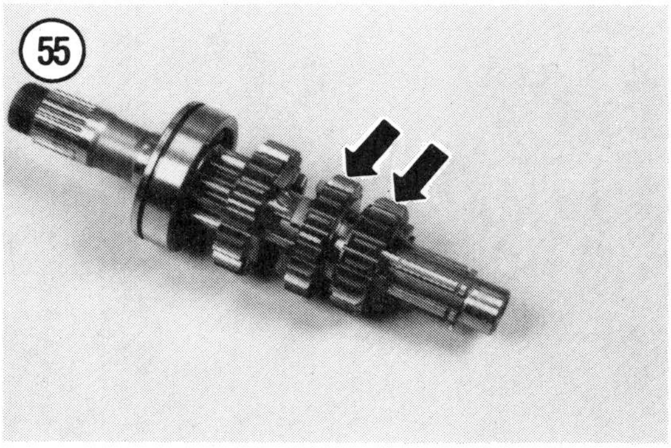
55

17. Check each gear bushing (**Figure 50**) for excessive wear, pitting or damage.
18. Inspect the shift fork-to-gear clearance as, described under *Internal Gearshift Mechanism* in this chapter.

NOTE
Defective gears should be replaced. It is a good idea to replace the mating gear on the mainshaft even though it may not show as much wear or damage.

NOTE
The 1st gear is part of the countershaft. If the gear is defective, the countershaft must be replaced.

19. Make sure that all gears slide smoothly on the countershaft splines.

NOTE
It is recommended that all circlips be replaced every time the transmission is disassembled to ensure proper gear alignment. Do not expand a circlip more than necessary to slide it over the shaft.

20. Inspect the splines (B, **Figure 48**) and circlip grooves (C, **Figure 48**) of the countershaft. If any are damaged, the shaft must be replaced.
21. Check the needle bearing (**Figure 51**). Make sure the needles rotate smoothly with no signs of wear or damage. Replace as necessary.

Countershaft Assembly

1. Apply a light coat of clean engine oil to all sliding surfaces prior to installing any parts.
2. Position the 5th gear with the flush side going on first. Slide on the 5th gear (A, **Figure 52**).
3. Position the 5th gear bushing with the flange side going on last. Slide on the 5th gear bushing (B, **Figure 52**) and push it all the way into the 5th gear.
4. Install the circlip (**Figure 53**).
5. Position the 3rd/4th combination gear with the larger diameter 4th gear going on first (**Figure 54**) and slide the combination gear on (**Figure 55**).
6. Install the circlip (A, **Figure 56**), *but not in its correct groove* (B, **Figure 56**). Slide the

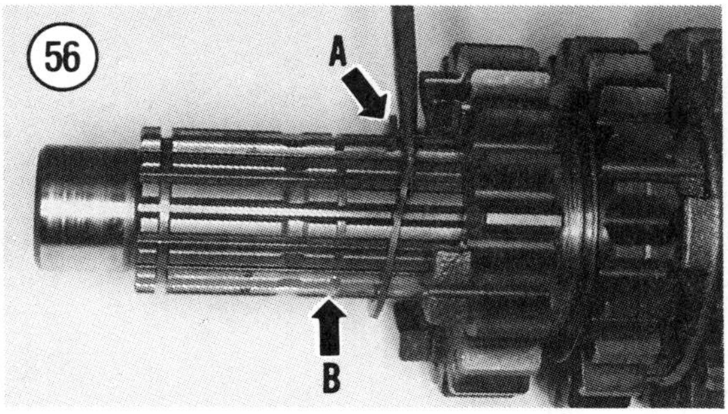

56

circlip down toward the 3rd/4th combination gear.

7. Slide on the splined washer (**Figure 57**).
8. Position the 6th gear with the flush side going on last and slide on the 6th gear (**Figure 58**).
9. Position the 2nd gear with the shoulder side going on first (**Figure 59**). Slide on the 2nd gear (**Figure 60**).
10. Install the snap ring (**Figure 61**). Make sure it is correctly seated in the countershaft groove.
11. Push the 2nd and 6th gears toward the end of the countershaft.
12. Move the circlip (B, **Figure 56**), installed in Step 6, into its correct groove in the countershaft. Make sure it is correctly seated in the countershaft groove.
13. Position the thrust washer with the convex side going on first and install the thrust washer (**Figure 62**).
14. Install the needle bearing (**Figure 63**).
15. On models so equipped, install the oil seal.
16. Make sure each gear engages properly to the adjoining gear where applicable.

5-SPEED TRANSMISSION (1100 CC ENGINES)

Removal/Installation

1. Remove the engine and split the crankcase as described under *Crankcase Disassembly* in Chapter Four.
2. Remove the mainshaft assembly (**Figure 64**) and countershaft assembly (A, **Figure 65**).
3. Inspect the transmission shaft assemblies as described under *Preliminary Inspection* in this chapter.

57

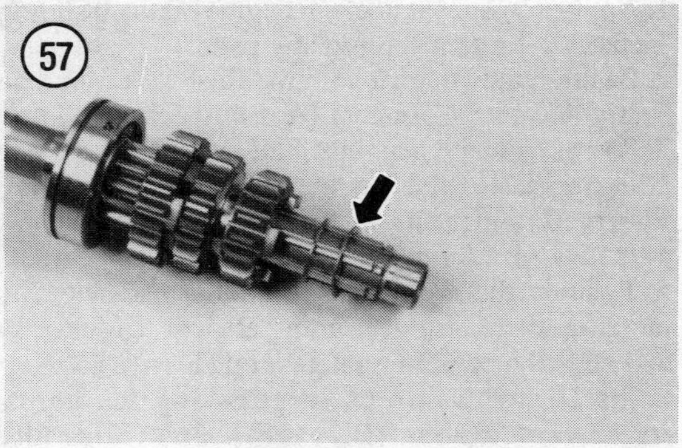

58

59

60

61

62

NOTE
Prior to installation, coat all bearing surfaces with assembly oil.

4. Install the 2 bearing set rings (A, **Figure 66**) and bearing locating dowels (B, **Figure 66**) into the upper crankcase.
5. Install the countershaft assembly (A, **Figure 65**) and check the following:
   a. Make sure the end cap (**Figure 67**) is in place on the end of the countershaft.
   b. Make sure the bearings are properly indexed into the set ring (B, **Figure 65**) and locating dowels.
6. Install the mainshaft assembly (**Figure 64**) and check the following:
   a. Make sure the end cap (A, **Figure 68**) is in place on the end of the countershaft.
   b. Make sure the bearings are properly indexed into the set ring (B, **Figure 68**) and locating dowels.
7. After both transmission assemblies are installed, perform the following:
   a. Hold onto the mainshaft and rotate the countershaft. The countershaft should rotate freely. If it does not, shift the gear that is engaged so that both shafts are in NEUTRAL.

(69)

5-SPEED TRANSMISSION (1100 CC ENGINES)

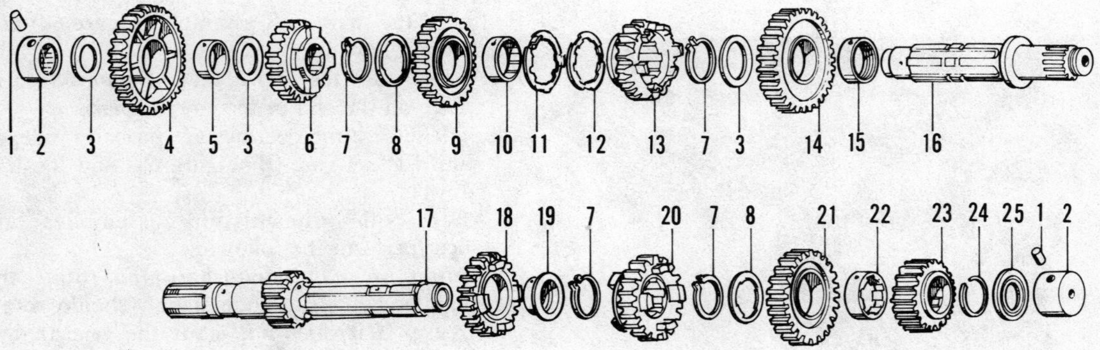

1. Locating pin
2. Needle bearing assembly
3. Thrust washer
4. Mainshaft 1st gear
5. Mainshaft 1st gear bushing
6. Mainshaft 4th gear
7. Circlip
8. Splined washer
9. Mainshaft 3rd gear
10. Mainshaft 3rd gear bushing
11. Splined lockwasher
12. Splined washer
13. Mainshaft 5th gear
14. Mainshaft 2nd gear
15. Mainshaft 2nd gear bushing
16. Mainshaft
17. Countershaft/1st gear
18. Countershaft 4th gear
19. Countershaft 4th gear bushing
20. Countershaft 3rd gear
21. Countershaft 5th gear
22. Countershaft 5th gear bushing
23. Countershaft 2nd gear bushing
24. Snap ring
25. Oil seal

70

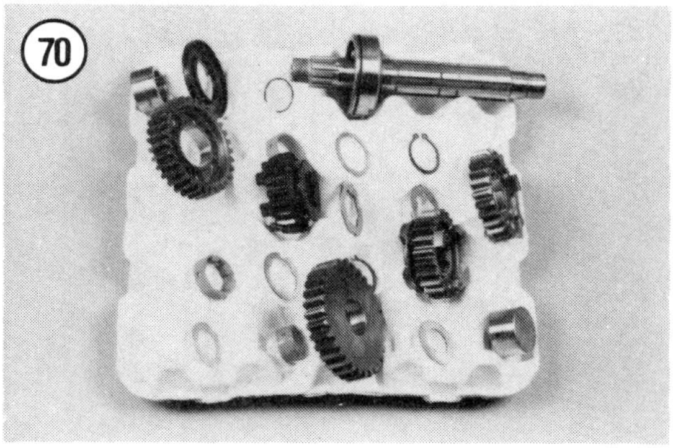

71

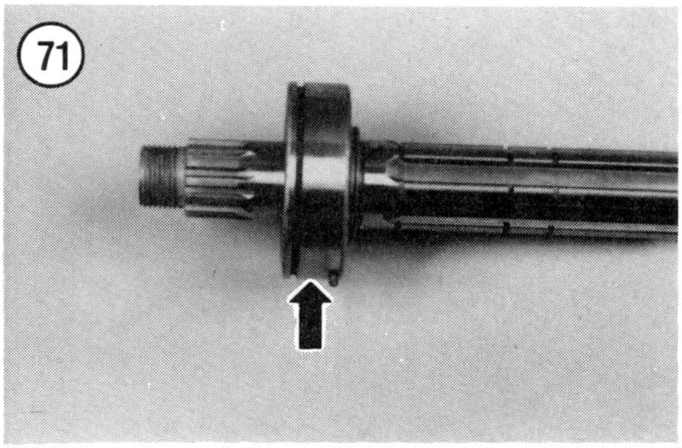

72

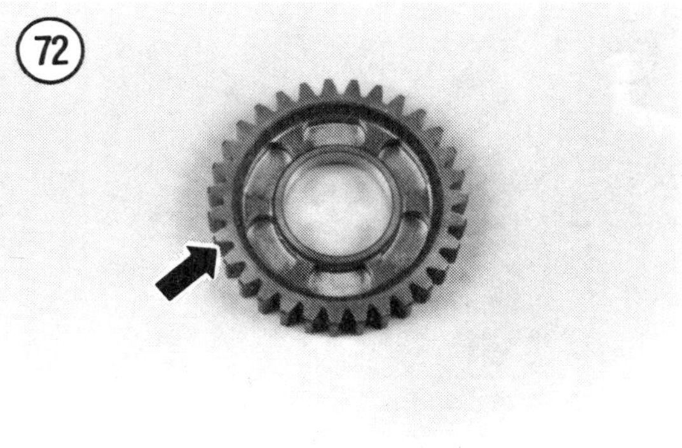

73

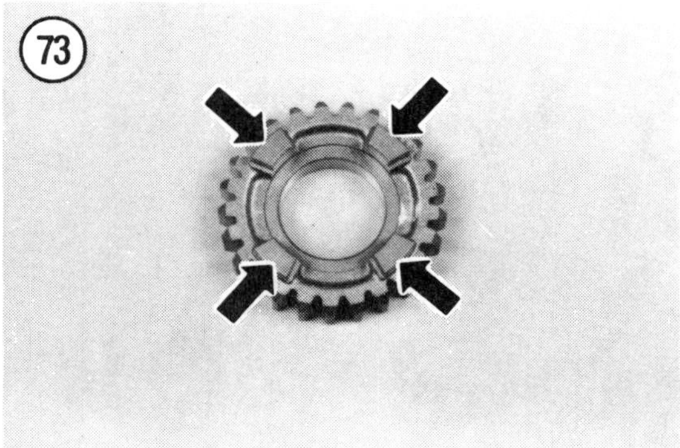

b. Rotate both shaft assemblies by hand. Make sure there is no binding. This is the time to find that something may be installed incorrectly—not after the crankcase is completely assembled.

8. Reassemble the crankcase as described under *Crankcase Assembly* and install the engine as described in Chapter Four.

Mainshaft Disassembly/Inspection

Refer to **Figure 69** for this procedure.

NOTE

*A helpful "tool" that should be used for transmission disassembly is a large egg flat (the type that restaurants get their eggs in) as shown in **Figure 70**. As you remove a part from the shaft, set it in one of the depressions in the same position from which it was removed. This is an easy way to remember the correct relationship of all parts.*

1. If not cleaned in the *Preliminary Inspection* sequence, place the assembled shaft into a large can or plastic bucket and thoroughly clean with solvent and a stiff brush. Dry with compressed air or let it sit on rags to dry.
2. Remove the outer bearing race, needle bearing and thrust washer. Don't lose the locating dowel in the outer bearing race.
3. Slide off the 1st gear, 1st gear bushing and thrust washer.
4. Slide off the 4th gear.
5. Remove the circlip and splined washer.
6. Slide off the 3rd gear and 3rd gear bushing.
7. Slide off the splined lockwasher.
8. Rotate the splined washer in either direction to disengage the tangs from the grooves on the transmission shaft. Slide off the splined washer.
9. Slide off the 5th gear.
10. Remove the circlip and the thrust washer.
11. Slide off the 2nd gear and 2nd gear bushing.
12. Onto the other end of the shaft, remove the oil seal, needle bearing and O-ring seal. Discard the O-ring as a new one must be installed.
13. If necessary, remove the ball bearing (**Figure 71**) from the shaft.
14. Check each gear for excessive wear, burrs, pitting, or chipped or missing teeth (**Figure 72**). Make sure the lugs (**Figure 73**) on the gears are in good condition.

6

15. Check each gear bushing (**Figure 74**) for excessive wear, pitting or damage.
16. Inspect the shift fork-to-gear clearance as described under *Internal Gearshift Mechanism* in this chapter.

NOTE
Defective gears should be replaced. It is a good idea to replace the mating gear on the countershaft even though it may not show as much wear or damage.

17. Make sure that all gears and bushings slide smoothly on the mainshaft splines.

NOTE
All circlips should be replaced every time the transmission is disassembled to ensure proper gear alignment. Do not expand a circlip more than necessary to slide it over the shaft.

18. Inspect the splines and circlip grooves of the mainshaft (**Figure 75**). If any are damaged, the shaft must be replaced.
19. Check the needle bearing (**Figure 76**). Make sure the needles rotate smoothly with no signs of wear or damage. Replace as necessary.

74

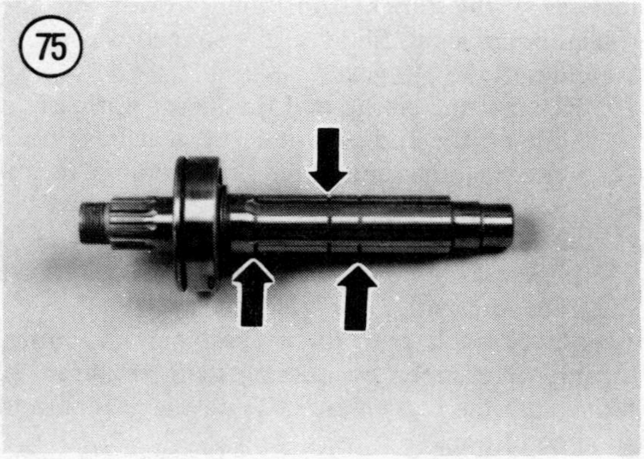
75

76

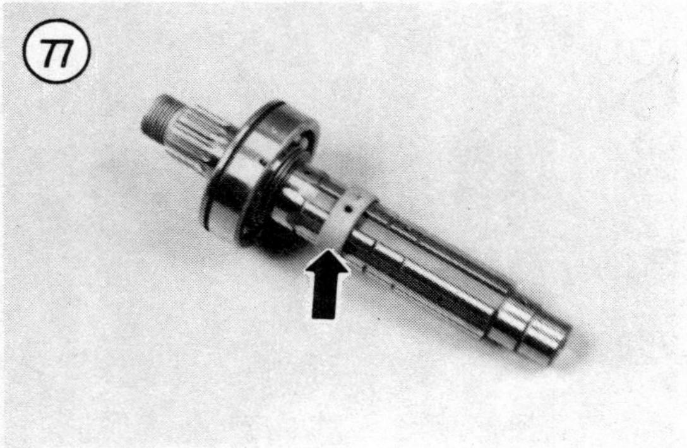
77

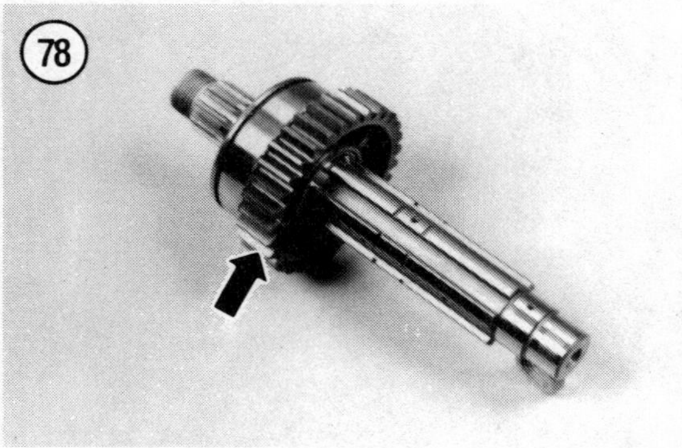
78

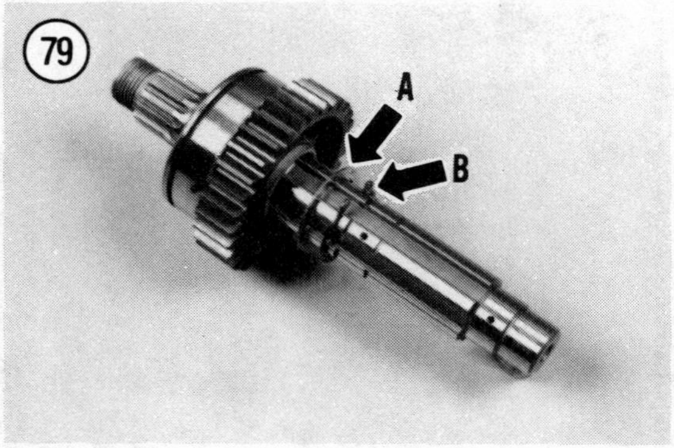

79

Mainshaft Assembly

1. Apply a light coat of clean engine oil to all sliding surfaces prior to installing any parts.
2. Slide on the 2nd gear bushing (**Figure 77**) and the 2nd gear (**Figure 78**).
3. Slide on the thrust washer (A, **Figure 79**) and install the circlip (B, **Figure 79**).
4. Slide on the 5th gear (**Figure 80**).
5. Slide on the splined washer. Rotate the splined washer in ether direction to engage the tangs into the grooves on the transmission shaft (A, **Figure 81**).
6. Slide on the splined lockwasher (B, **Figure 81**). Push it on until the tangs go into the open areas of the splined washer and lock the washer into place (**Figure 82**).
7. Align the oil hole in the 3rd gear bushing with the transmission shaft oil hole and slide on the bushing (**Figure 83**). This alignment is necessary for proper gear lubrication.
8. Slide on the 3rd gear (**Figure 84**).
9. Slide on the thrust washer (A, **Figure 85**) and install the circlip (B, **Figure 85**).

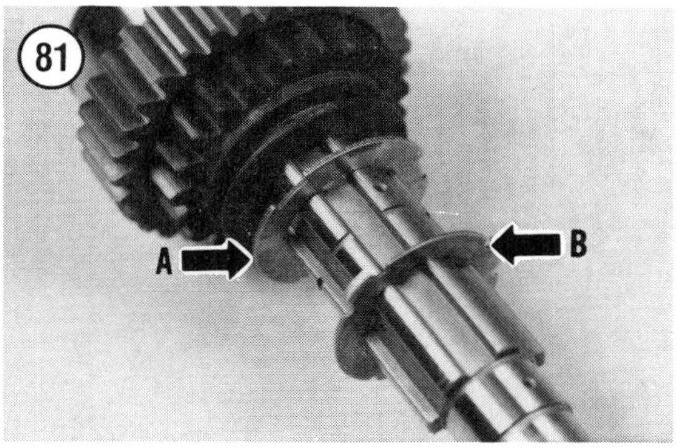

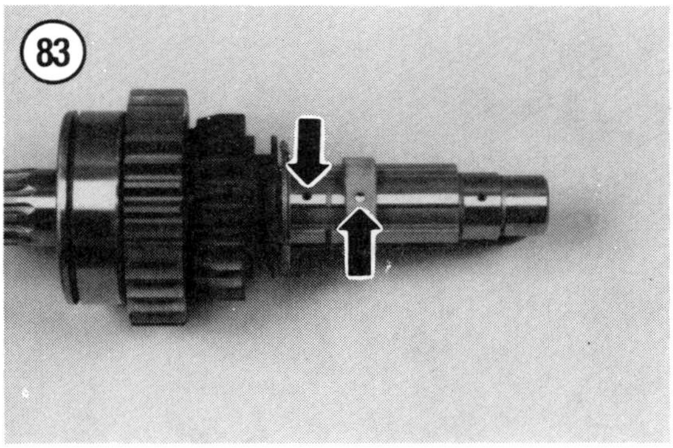

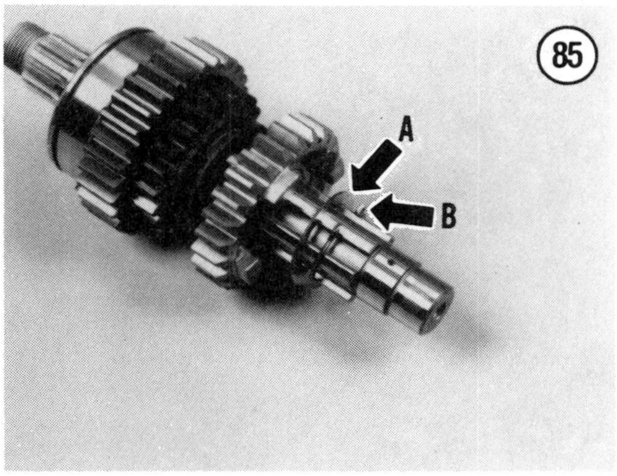

10. Slide on the 4th gear (**Figure 86**) and the thrust washer (**Figure 87**).
11. Align the oil hole in 1st gear bushing with the transmission oil hole, then slide on the 1st gear bushing (**Figure 88**) and the 1st gear (**Figure 89**).
12. Install the thrust washer (**Figure 90**) and the needle bearing (**Figure 91**).
13. Onto the other end of the shaft, install the following:

a. Install a new O-ring (**Figure 92**) and the needle bearing (**Figure 93**).
b. Apply a light coat of multipurpose grease to the lips of the oil seal prior to installation. Install the oil seal (**Figure 94**).

14. Refer to **Figure 95** for correct placement of all gears. Make sure all circlips are seated correctly in the mainshaft grooves.
15. Make sure each gear engages properly to the adjoining gear where applicable.

86

87

88

89

90

91

92

93

94

95

Countershaft Disassembly/Inspection

Refer to **Figure 69** for this procedure.

NOTE

*Use the same large egg flat (used on the mainshaft disassembly) during the countershaft disassembly (**Figure 96**). This is an easy way to remember the correct relationship of all parts.*

1. If not cleaned in the *Preliminary Inspection* sequence, place the assembled shaft into a large can or plastic bucket and thoroughly clean with solvent and a stiff brush. Dry with compressed air or let it sit on rags to dry.
2. Remove the needle bearing assembly.
3. Slide off the oil seal.
4. Release the circlip (7, **Figure 69**) from the countershaft groove. Move it down the shaft toward the third gear.
5. Slide the 5th and 2nd gear down toward the third gear.
6. Secure the countershaft vertically in a vise with soft jaws.
7. Use a scribe and pry one end of the snap ring out of the groove (24, **Figure 69**) then secure this end with needlenose pliers. Hold onto the circlip with the needlenose pliers, work around the shaft with the scribe, pry the circlip out of the groove and remove it. This circlip *must be replaced* as it will be severely distorted during removal.

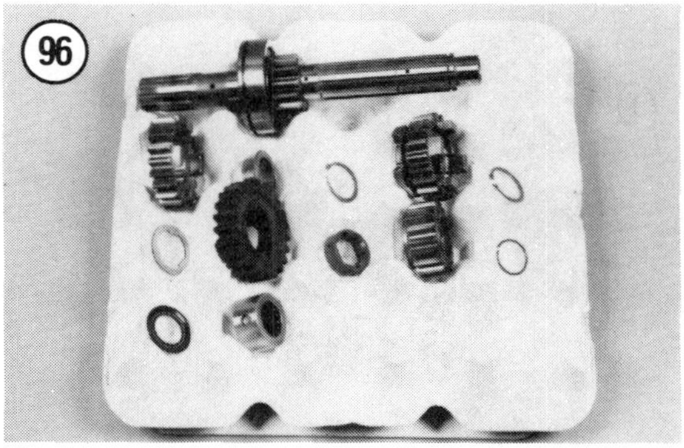
96

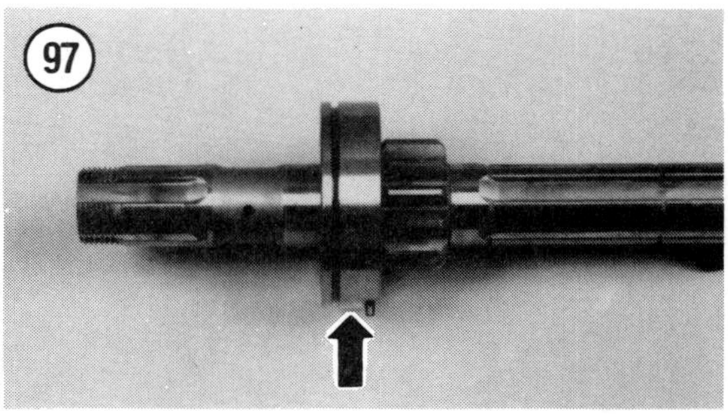
97

6

8. Slide off the 2nd gear.
9. Slide off the 5th gear and 5th gear bushing.
10. Slide off the splined washer and remove the circlip.
11. Slide off the 3rd gear.
12. Slide off the 4th gear and 4th gear bushing.
13. Remove the ball bearing (**Figure 97**) if necessary.
14. Check each gear for excessive wear, burrs, pitting or chipped or missing teeth. Make sure the lugs (**Figure 98**) on the gears are in good condition.
15. Check each gear bushing (**Figure 99**) for excessive wear, pitting or damage.
16. Inspect the shift fork-to-gear clearance as described under *Internal Gearshift Mechanism* in this chapter.

NOTE

Defective gears should be replaced. It is a good idea to replace the mating gear on the mainshaft even though it may not show as much wear or damage.

NOTE

The 1st gear is part of the countershaft. If the gear is defective, the countershaft must be replaced.

17. Make sure that all gears and bushings slide smoothly on the countershaft splines.

NOTE

It is recommended that all circlips be replaced every time the transmission is disassembled to ensure proper gear

98

99

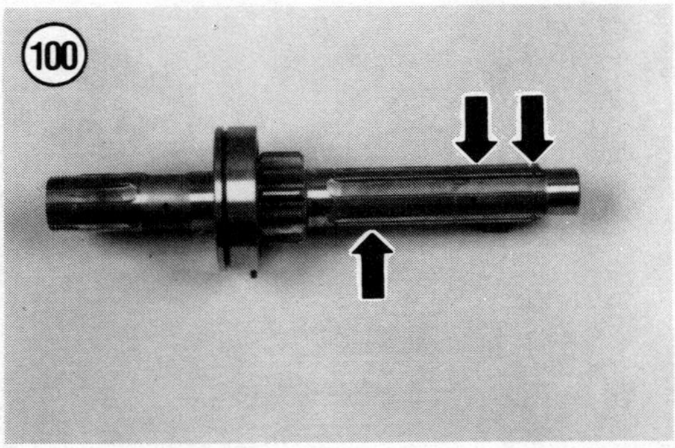
100

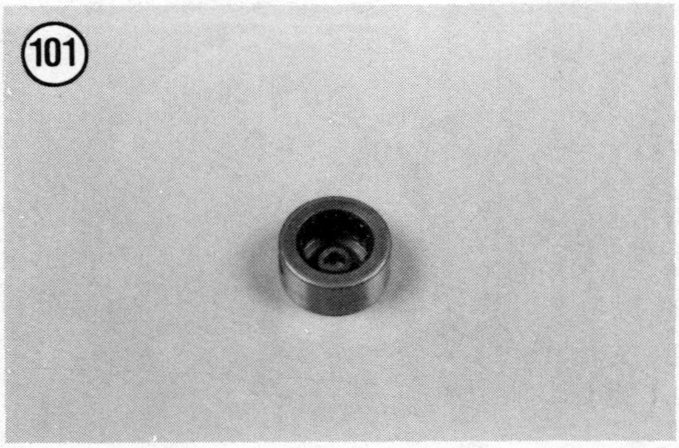
101

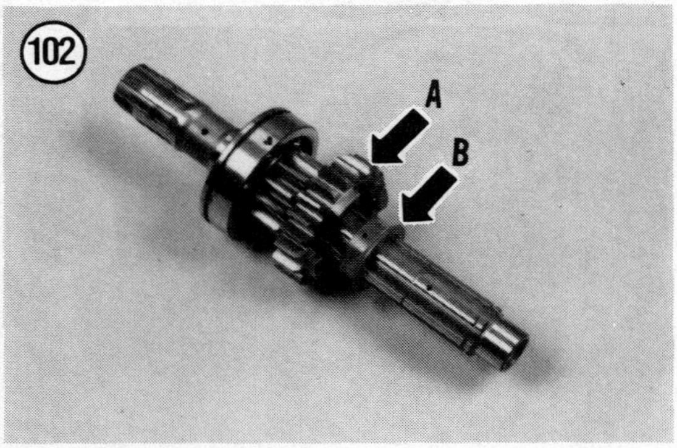

102

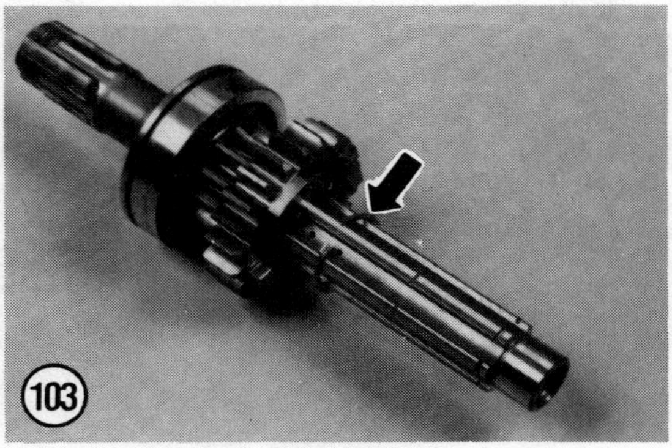
103

104

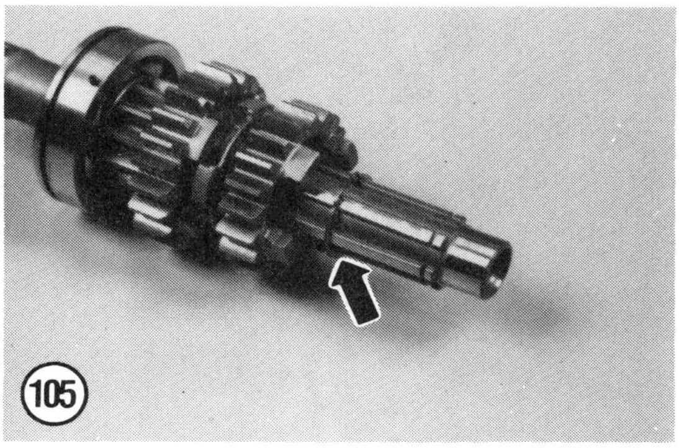
105

106

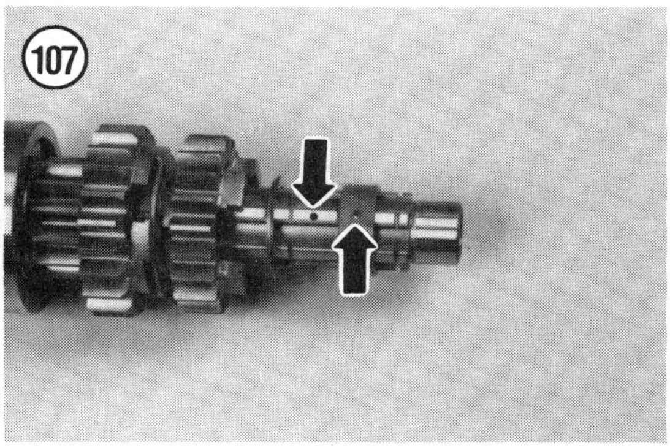
107

alignment. Do not expand a circlip more than necessary to slide it over the shaft.

18. Inspect the splines and circlip grooves of the countershaft (**Figure 100**). If any are damaged, the shaft must be replaced.
19. Check the needle bearing (**Figure 101**). Make sure the needles rotate smoothly with no signs of wear or damage. Replace as necessary.

Countershaft Assembly

1. Apply a light coat of clean engine oil to all sliding surfaces before installing any parts.
2. Position the 4th gear with the flush side going on first. Slide on the 4th gear (A, **Figure 102**).
3. Position the 4th gear bushing with the flange side going on last. Slide on the 4th gear bushing (B, **Figure 102**) and push it all the way into the 4th gear.
4. Install the circlip (**Figure 103**).
5. Slide on the 3rd gear (**Figure 104**).
6. Install the circlip (**Figure 105**) *but not in its correct groove*. Slide the circlip down toward 3rd gear.
7. Slide on the splined washer (**Figure 106**).
8. Align the oil hole in the 5th gear bushing with the transmission shaft oil hole and slide on the bushing (**Figure 107**). This alignment is necessary for proper gear lubrication.
9. Slide on the 5th gear (**Figure 108**).
10. Position the 2nd gear with the shoulder side going on first (**Figure 109**). Slide on the 2nd gear (**Figure 110**).

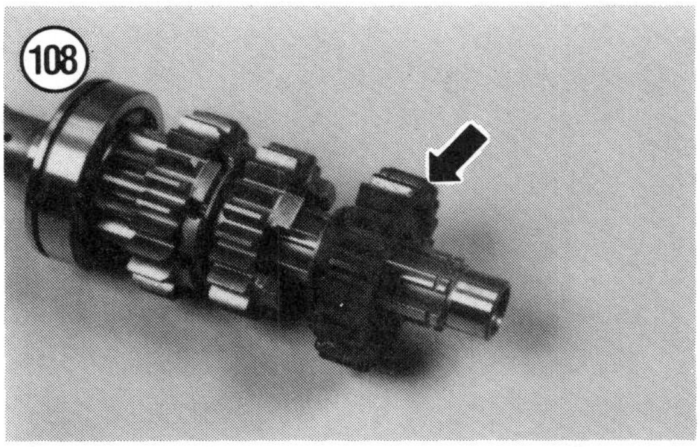
108

109

11. Install a *new* snap ring (**Figure 111**). Make sure it is correctly seated in the countershaft groove.
12. Push the 2nd and 5th gears toward the end of the countershaft. Recheck the 5th gear bushing alignment.
13. Move the circlip (**Figure 105**), installed in Step 6, into its correct groove in the countershaft. Make sure it is correctly seated in the countershaft groove.
14. Position the oil seal with the convex side going on first (**Figure 112**) and install the oil seal (**Figure 113**).
15. Install the needle bearing (**Figure 114**).
16. Refer to **Figure 115** for correct placement of all gears. Make sure all circlips are seated correctly in the countershaft grooves.
17. Make sure each gear engages properly to the adjoining gear where applicable.

INTERNAL GEARSHIFT MECHANISM

The internal gearshift mechanism is the same for both the 5-speed and 6-speed transmission. Refer to **Figure 116** for this procedure.

Removal/Disassembly

1. Remove the engine and split the crankcase as described under *Crankcase Disassembly* in Chapter Four.
2. Remove the external gearshift mechanism as described under *External Gearshift Mechanism Removal* in this chapter.

110

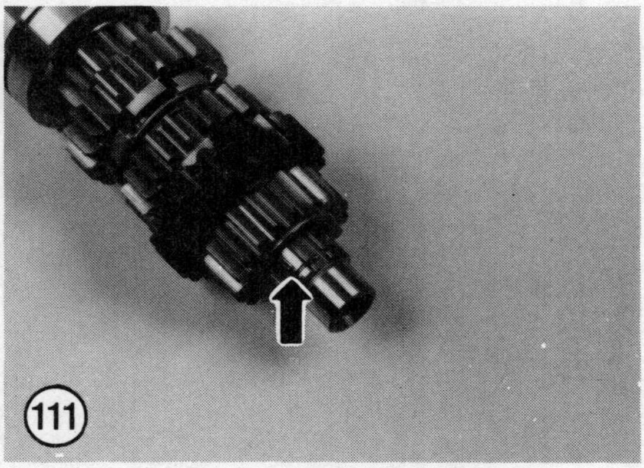
111

112

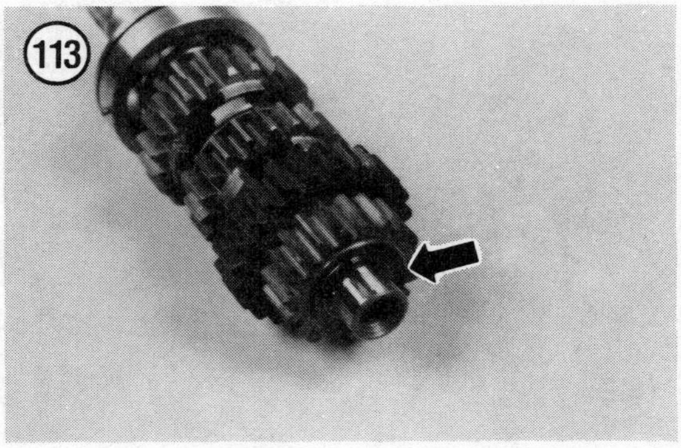
113

114

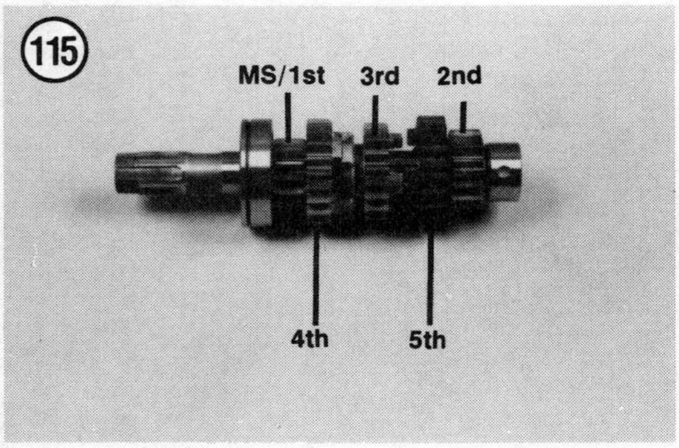

115

116

GEARSHIFT MECHANISM

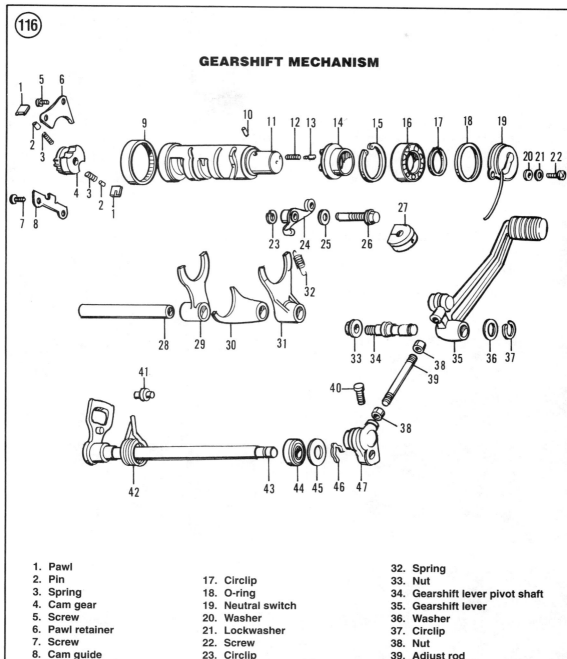

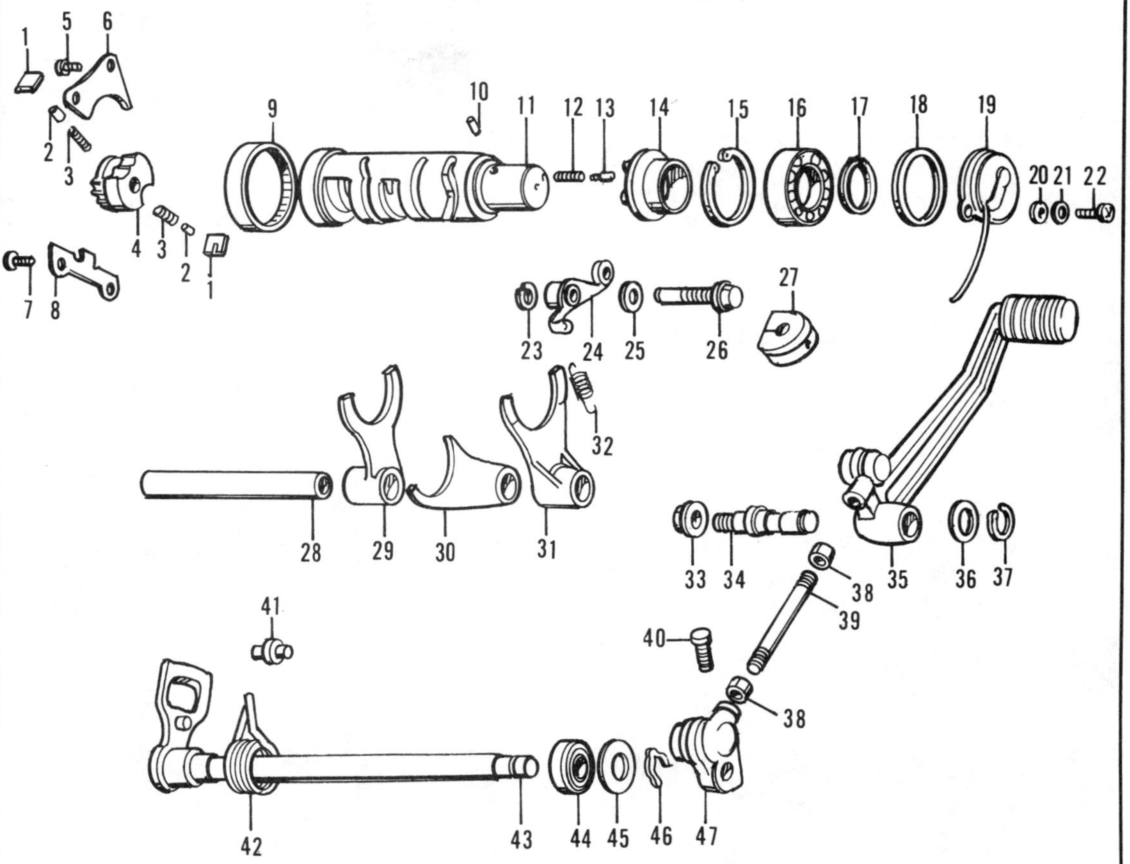

1. Pawl
2. Pin
3. Spring
4. Cam gear
5. Screw
6. Pawl retainer
7. Screw
8. Cam guide
9. Needle bearing
10. Locating pin
11. Shift drum
12. Spring
13. Contact plunger
14. Stopper plate
15. Circlip
16. Ball bearing
17. Circlip
18. O-ring
19. Neutral switch
20. Washer
21. Lockwasher
22. Screw
23. Circlip
24. Shift drum stopper
25. Washer
26. Bolt
27. Grommet
28. Shift fork shaft
29. Shift fork No. 1
30. Shift fork No. 2
31. Shift fork No. 3
32. Spring
33. Nut
34. Gearshift lever pivot shaft
35. Gearshift lever
36. Washer
37. Circlip
38. Nut
39. Adjust rod
40. Bolt
41. Spring stopper pin
42. Return spring
43. Gearshift shaft
44. Oil seal
45. Washer
46. Clip
47. Joint

3. Remove the transmission assemblies as described under *Transmission Removal/ Installation* for your specific model in this chapter.
4. Remove the screws securing the neutral switch (**Figure 117**) and remove the neutral switch assembly.
5. Remove the O-ring (**Figure 118**) from the receptacle in the crankcase.
6. Remove the switch contact plunger and spring (**Figure 119**) from the end of the gearshift drum.
7. Hold onto the shift forks and withdraw the shift fork shaft . Remove the shift fork shaft and all shift forks.
8. Turn the crankcase over.
9. Unhook the spring (**Figure 120**) from the lug on the crankcase.
10. Remove the circlip (**Figure 121**) securing the shift drum into the crankcase.
11. Carefully withdraw the shift drum (**Figure 122**) from the crankcase.
12. Remove the circlip (**Figure 123**) securing the shift drum stopper to the threaded stud.

117

118

119

120

121

122

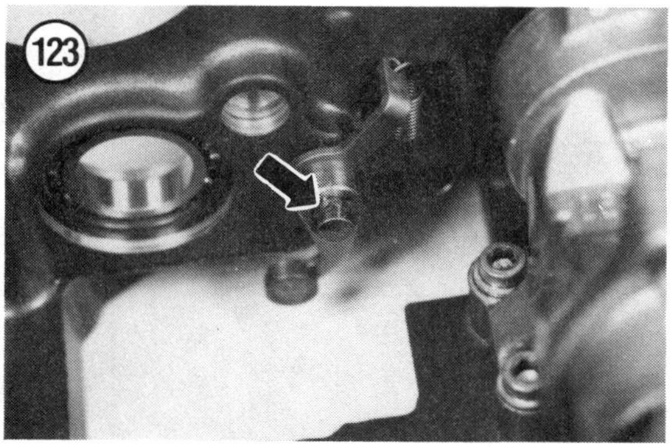
123

124

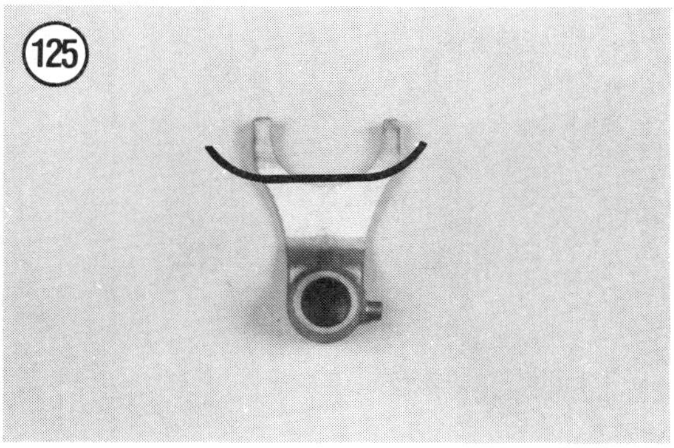
125

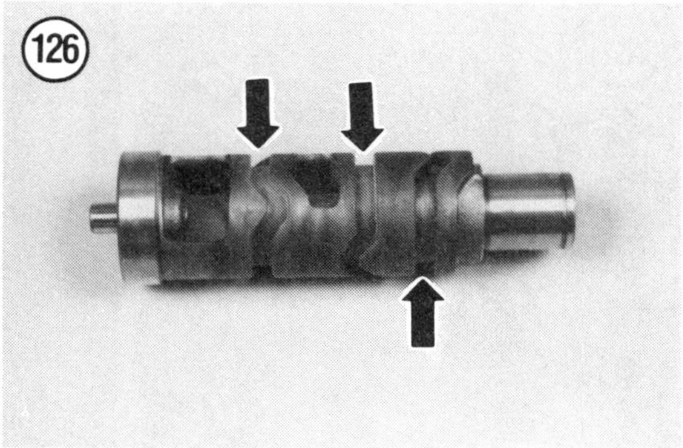
126

13. Remove the shift drum stopper (**Figure 124**) and spring from the threaded stud.
14. Thoroughly clean all parts in solvent and dry with compressed air.

Inspection

1. Inspect each shift fork for signs of wear or cracking. Check for bending and make sure each fork slides smoothly on the shaft. Replace any worn or damaged forks.
2. Check for any arc-shaped (**Figure 125**) wear or burned marks on the shift forks. This indicates that the shift fork has been forced against the gear. If the fork fingers have become excessively worn, the fork must be replaced.
3. Check the grooves in the shift drum (**Figure 126**) for wear or roughness. If any of the groove profiles have excessive wear or damage, replace the shift drum.
4. Inspect the cam gear receptacle (**Figure 127**) in the end of the shift drum for wear or damage. Replace the shift drum if necessary.
5. Check the shift drum stopper plate (**Figure 128**) for wear; replace as necessary.

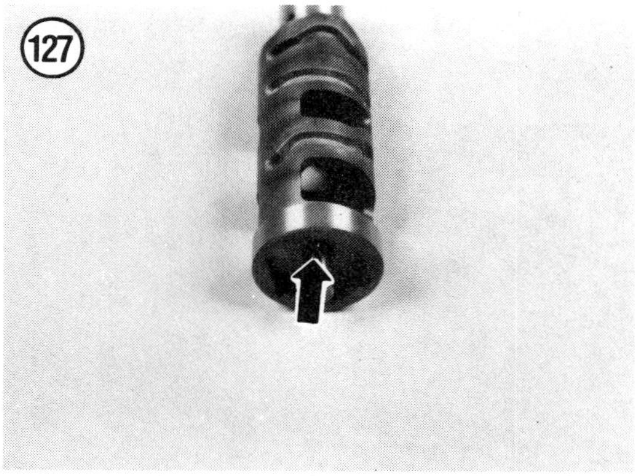
127

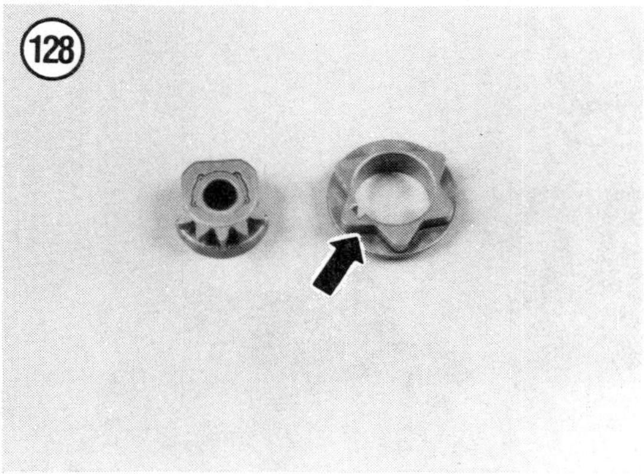
128

6. Check the neutral switch contact plunger and spring (**Figure 129**) for wear or damage. If the spring has sagged, replace it.
7. Make sure the locating pin (**Figure 130**) is a tight fit in the shift drum. If the pin is loose, replace it.
8. Check the shift drum bearings. Refer to **Figure 131** and **Figure 132**. Make sure they operate smoothly with no signs of wear or damage. If damaged, replace as described under *Crankcase Bearings Removal/Installation* in Chapter Four.
9. Check the cam pin followers (**Figure 133**) on each shift fork that rides in the shift drum for wear or damage. Replace the shift fork(s) as necessary.
10. Roll the shift fork shaft on a flat surface such as a piece of plate glass and check for any bends. If the shaft is bent, it must be replaced.
11. Inspect the roller (**Figure 134**) on the end of the shift drum stopper. If worn or damaged, replace the shift drum stopper.

CAUTION
Marginally worn shift forks should be replaced. Worn forks can cause the transmission to slip out of gear, leading to more serious and expensive damage.

12. Inspect the shift fork-to-gear clearance as follows:

131

132

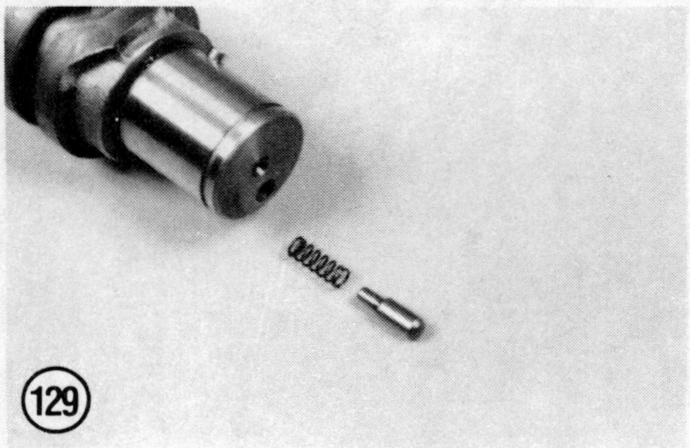
129

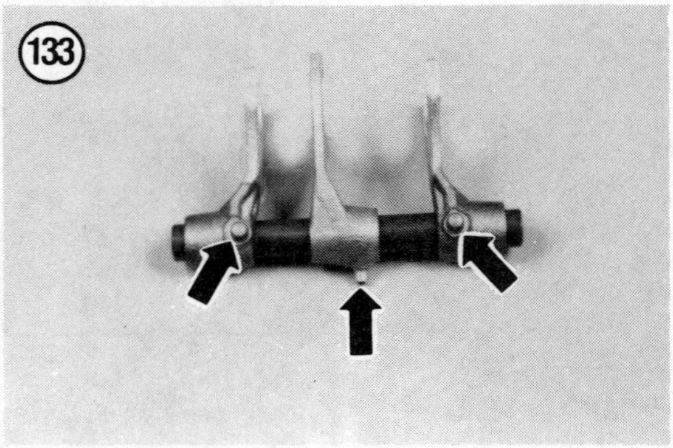
133

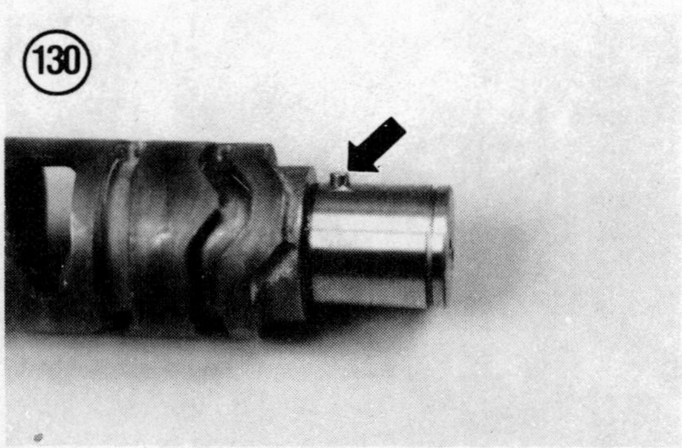
130

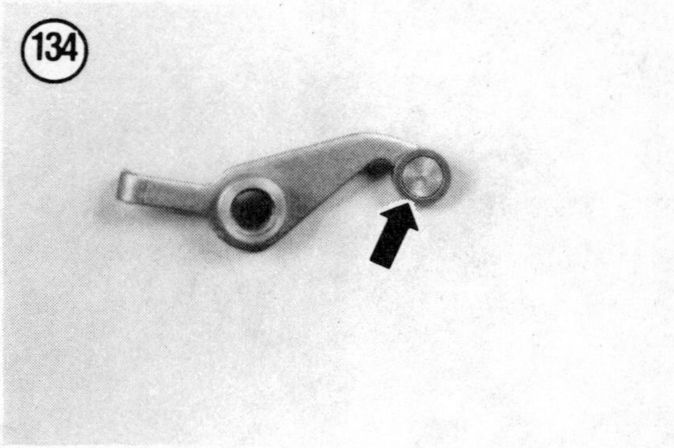
134

135

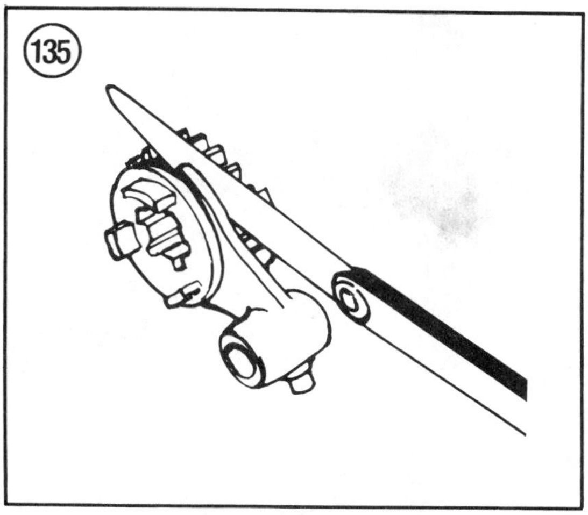

136

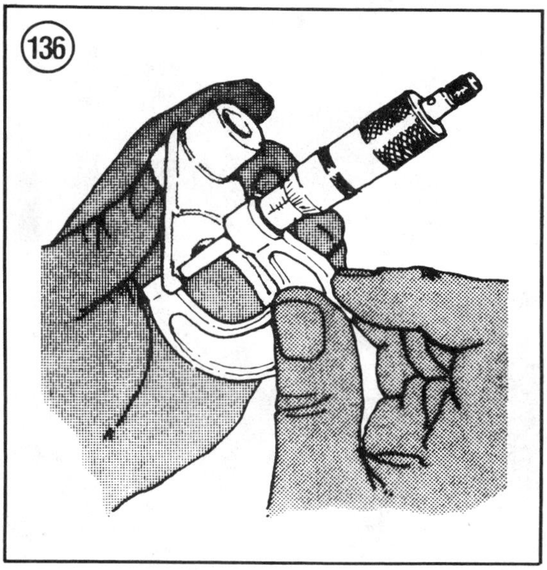

137

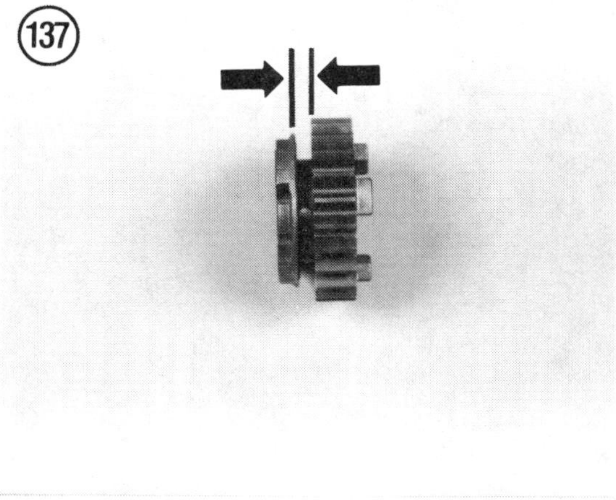

a. Install each shift fork into its respective gear. Use a flat feeler gauge and measure the clearance between the fork and the gear as shown in **Figure 135**. Compare to the specifications listed in **Table 1** or **Table 2**.

b. If the clearance is greater than specified in **Table 1** or **Table 2**, measure the width of the gearshift fork fingers with a micrometer (**Figure 136**). Replace the shift fork(s) if worn to the service limit listed in **Table 1** or **Table 2** or less.

c. If the shift fork finger width is within tolerance, measure the shift fork groove width (**Figure 137**) in the gears. Compare to the specifications listed in **Table 1** or **Table 2**. Replace the gear(s) if the groove is worn to the service limit or more.

Assembly/Installation

1. Apply a light coat of oil to the shift fork shafts and the inside bores of the shift forks prior to installation.
2. Install the shift drum stopper (**Figure 138**) and spring onto the threaded stud.
3. Install the circlip (**Figure 139**) securing the shift drum stopper to the threaded stud.

138

139

4. Make sure the locating pin (A, **Figure 140**) is in place in the shift drum.
5. Position the stopper plate with the flange side going on last and install the stopper plate (B, **Figure 140**). Push the stopper plate on until it bottoms (**Figure 141**).
6. Carefully install the gearshift drum (**Figure 142**) into the crankcase. Push it in until it stops.

NOTE
After installing the shift drum, make sure it rotates smoothly with no binding.

7. Install the circlip (**Figure 143**) securing the shift drum into the crankcase. Make sure the circlip is correctly seated in the shift drum groove.
8. Hook the shift drum stopper spring (**Figure 144**) onto the lug on the crankcase. Rotate the shift drum to the NEUTRAL position and make sure the shift drum stopper roller is correctly seated in the neutral detent of the stopper plate (**Figure 145**).

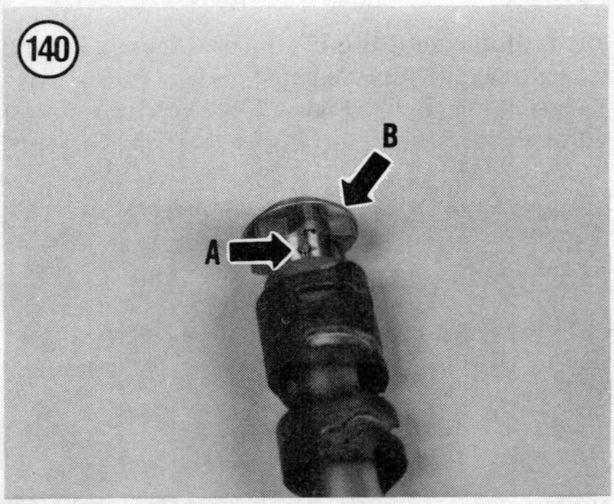

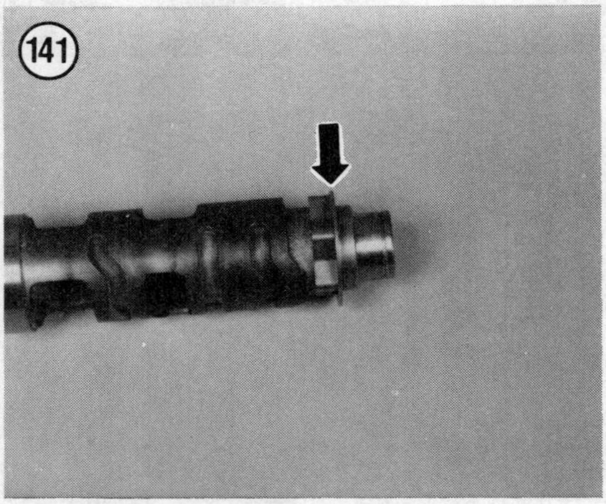

146

147

148

149

9. Partially install the shift fork shaft (A, **Figure 146**) into the crankcase.

NOTE
Make sure the shift fork guide pins are correctly meshed with the grooves in the shift drum.

10. Hold the No. 1 shift fork (B, **Figure 146**) in position and push the shift fork shaft through it. Make sure the shift fork guide pin is indexed into its respective groove in the shift drum.
11. Hold the No. 2 shift fork (**Figure 147**) in position and push the shift fork shaft through it. Make sure the shift fork guide pin is indexed into its respective groove in the shift drum.
12. Hold the No. 3 shift fork (**Figure 148**) in position and push the shift fork shaft through it. Make sure the shift fork guide pin is indexed into its respective groove in the shift drum.
13. Push the shift fork shaft all the way through all shift forks until it bottoms out in the crankcase.
14. Make sure the shift fork guide pins are correctly meshed with the grooves in the shift drum (**Figure 149**).
15. The shift fork shaft can slide out at this point. To prevent this from happening, install part of the external shift mechanism:
   a. Remove the cam gear assembly from the spray paint can top and keep all components together.
   b. Compress the spring-loaded shift pawls with your fingers. Install the cam gear assembly into the receptacle of the shift drum as shown in **Figure 150**.

150

6

c. Install the cam guide (**Figure 151**). Apply a small amount of Loctite Lock N' Seal to the screw threads prior to installation.

d. Install the cam guide screws and tighten securely.

16. Install the neutral switch contact spring and plunger (**Figure 152**) into the end of the gearshift drum.

17. Install a new O-ring (**Figure 153**) into the receptacle in the crankcase.

18. Install the neutral switch (**Figure 154**) and screws. Tighten the screws securely.

19. Install the transmission assemblies as described under *Transmission Removal/ Installation* for your specific model in this chapter.

20. Perform Steps 7-9 of *External Gearshift Mechanism Installation* in this chapter.

21. Assemble the crankcase as described under *Crankcase Assembly* in Chapter Four.

22. Install the engine as described under *Engine Removal/Installation* in Chapter Four.

151

152

153

154

Table 1 TRANSMISSION AND GEARSHIFT SPECIFICATIONS (750 CC)

Item	Specifications	Wear limit
Shift fork-to-groove in gear clearance	0.1-0.3 mm 0.004-0.012 in.)	0.50 mm (0.02 in.)
Shift fork groove width in gear		
Shift fork No. 1, and No. 3	4.8-4.9 mm (0.189-0.193 in.)	—
Shift fork No. 2	5.0-5.1 mm (0.197-0.201 in.)	—
Shift fork finger thickness		
Shift fork No. 1, and No. 3	4.6-4.7 mm (0.181-0.185 in.)	—
Shift fork No. 2	4.8-4.9 mm (0.189-0.193 in.)	—
Transmission gear ratios		
1st gear	2.769	
2nd gear	2.062	
3rd gear	1.647	
4th gear	1.400	
5th gear	1.227	
6th gear	1.095	

6

Table 2 TRANSMISSION AND GEARSHIFT SPECIFICATIONS (1100 CC)

Item	Specifications	Wear limit
Shift fork-to-groove in gear clearance	0.1-0.3 mm 0.004-0.012 in.)	0.50 mm (0.02 in.)
Shift fork groove width in gear	5.0-5.1 mm (0.197-0.201 in.)	—
Shift fork finger thickness	4.8-4.9 mm (0.189-0.193 in.)	—
Transmission gear ratios		
1st gear	2.385	
2nd gear	1.632	
3rd gear	1.250	
4th gear	1.045	
5th gear	0.913	

NOTE: If you own a GSX600F Katana, first refer to Chapter 13 for specific service information.

CHAPTER SEVEN

FUEL, EMISSION CONTROL AND EXHAUST SYSTEMS

The fuel system consists of the fuel tank, the shutoff valve, 4 carburetors and an air filter. The exhaust system consists of a 4-into-1 exhaust pipe and a muffler assembly.

The emission controls consist of a crankcase emission system and on California models an evaporative emission control system.

This chapter includes service procedures for all parts of the fuel system and exhaust system. Air filter service is covered in Chapter Three.

Carburetor specifications are covered in **Table 1** at the end of this chapter.

CARBURETOR OPERATION

For proper operation a gasoline engine must be supplied with fuel and air mixed in proper proportions by weight. A mixture in which there is an excess of fuel is said to be rich. A lean mixture is one which contains insufficient fuel. A properly adjusted carburetor supplies the proper mixture to the engine under all operating conditions.

Each carburetor consists of several major systems. A float and float valve mechanism maintain a constant fuel level in the float bowls. The pilot jet system supplies fuel at low speeds. The main jet fuel system supplies fuel at medium and high speeds. A starter (choke) system supplies the very rich mixture needed to start a cold engine.

CARBURETOR SERVICE

Major carburetor service (removal and cleaning) should be performed at the intervals indicated in **Table 2** in Chapter Three or when poor engine performance, hesitation and little or no response to mixture adjustment is observed. Alterations in jet size, throttle slide cutaway, and changes in jet needle position, etc., should be attempted only if you're experienced in this type of "tuning" work; a bad guess could result in costly engine damage or, at least, poor performance. If, after servicing the carburetor and making the adjustments described in this chapter, the bike does not perform correctly (and assuming that other factors affecting performance are correct, such as ignition component condition, etc.), the bike should be checked by a dealer or a qualified performance tuning specialist.

CARBURETOR ASSEMBLY

Removal/Installation

Remove all 4 carburetors as an assembled unit.

1. Remove the seat as described under *Seat Removal/Installation* in Chapter Twelve.
2. Remove the lower section and both right and left-hand middle sections of the front fairing as

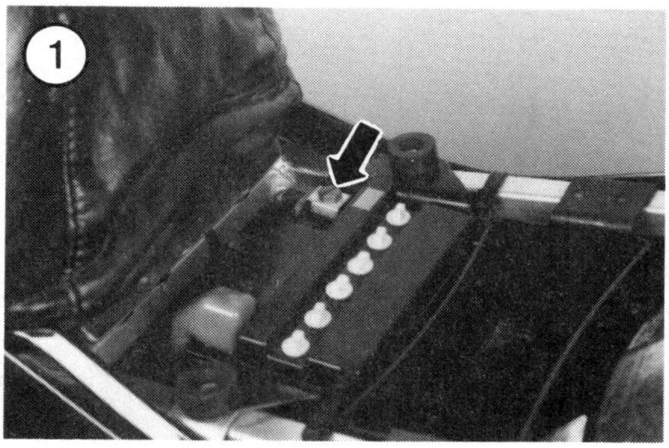

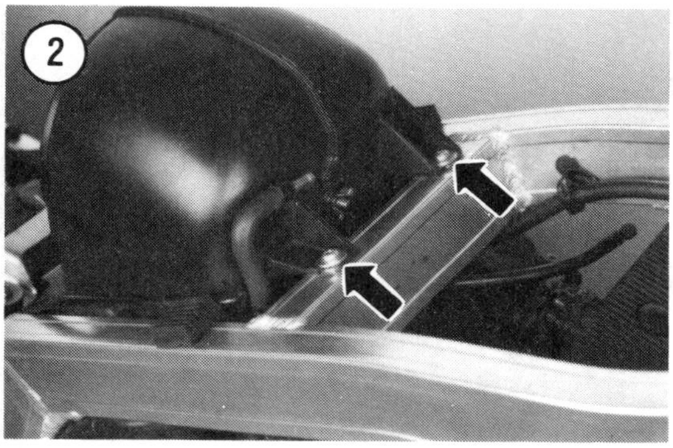

described under *Front Fairing Removal/ Installation* in Chapter Twelve.

3. Remove the fuel tank as described under *Fuel Tank Removal/Installation* in this chapter.
4. Disconnect the battery negative lead (**Figure 1**).
5. Remove the bolts securing the air filter case at the front (**Figure 2**) and at the rear (**Figure 3**).
6. Disconnect the crankcase breather hose (**Figure 4**) from the cylinder head cover.
7. Loosen the screw on the clamping bands (**Figure 5**) on each end of all 4 carburetors.
8. Pull the air filter air case toward the rear (**Figure 6**) and disengage it from all 4 carburetors.
9. Pull the carburetor assembly toward the rear to free the assembly from the intake tubes on the cylinder head.
10. Pull the carburetor assembly slightly toward the right-hand side.
11. Loosen the throttle cable locknut at the carburetor assembly.
12. Disconnect the throttle cable from the throttle wheel.

NOTE
Before disconnecting, mark each carburetor tube with the carburetor number (1 through 4), starting with the

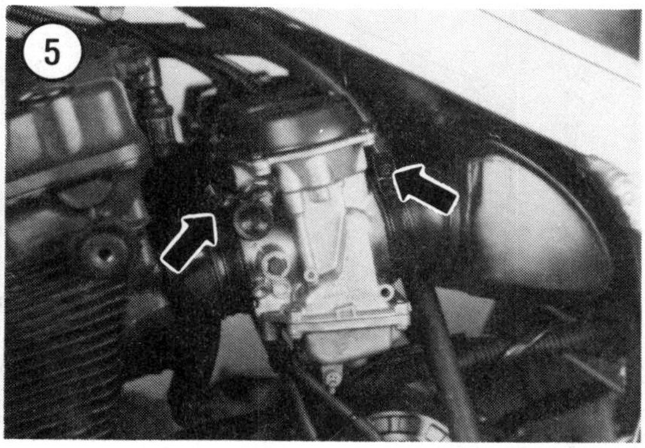

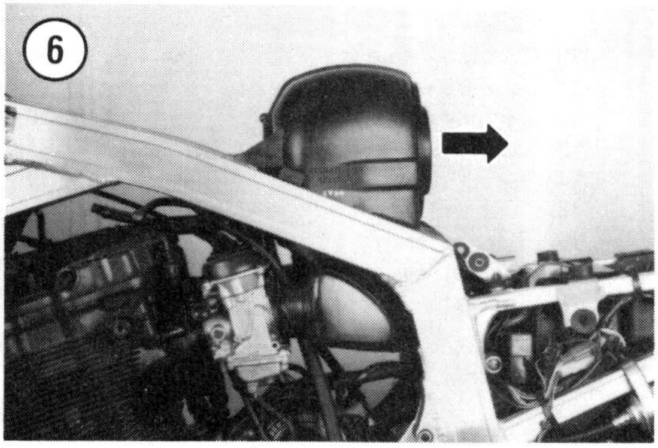

(7)

CARBURETOR ASSEMBLY

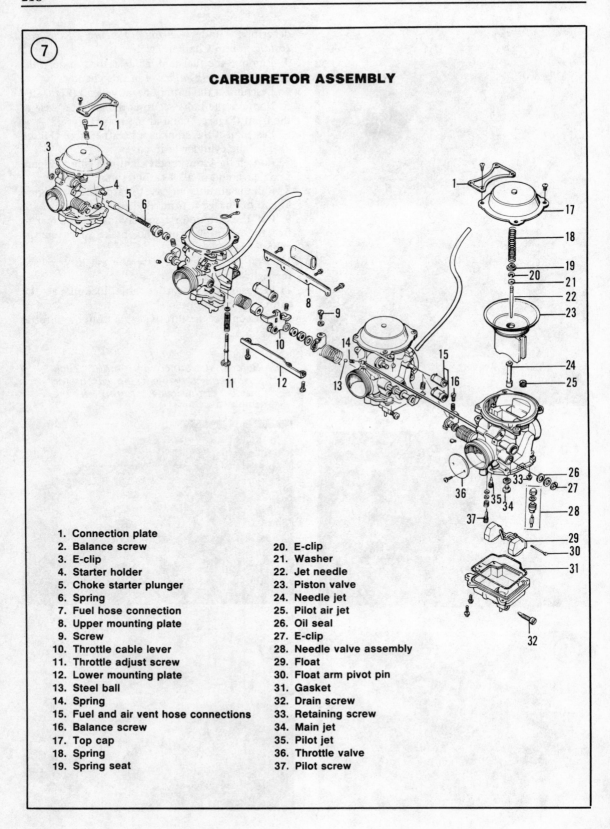

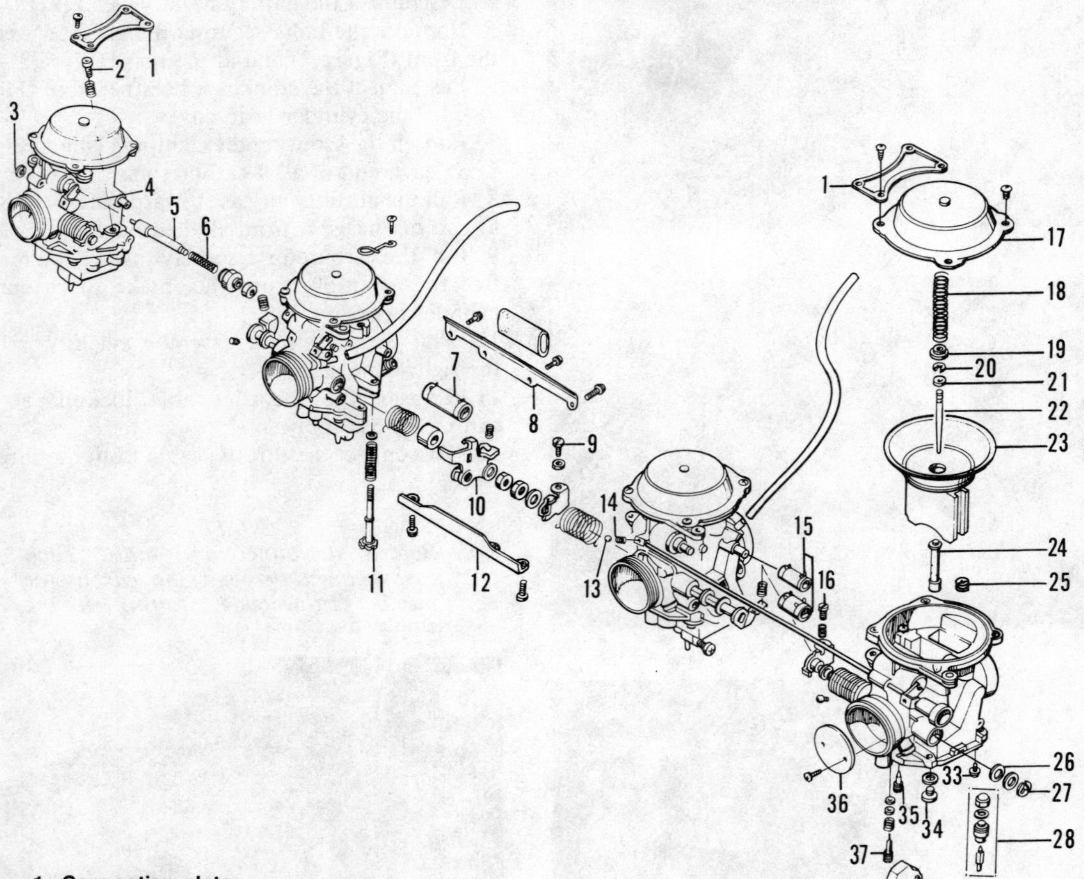

1. Connection plate
2. Balance screw
3. E-clip
4. Starter holder
5. Choke starter plunger
6. Spring
7. Fuel hose connection
8. Upper mounting plate
9. Screw
10. Throttle cable lever
11. Throttle adjust screw
12. Lower mounting plate
13. Steel ball
14. Spring
15. Fuel and air vent hose connections
16. Balance screw
17. Top cap
18. Spring
19. Spring seat
20. E-clip
21. Washer
22. Jet needle
23. Piston valve
24. Needle jet
25. Pilot air jet
26. Oil seal
27. E-clip
28. Needle valve assembly
29. Float
30. Float arm pivot pin
31. Gasket
32. Drain screw
33. Retaining screw
34. Main jet
35. Pilot jet
36. Throttle valve
37. Pilot screw

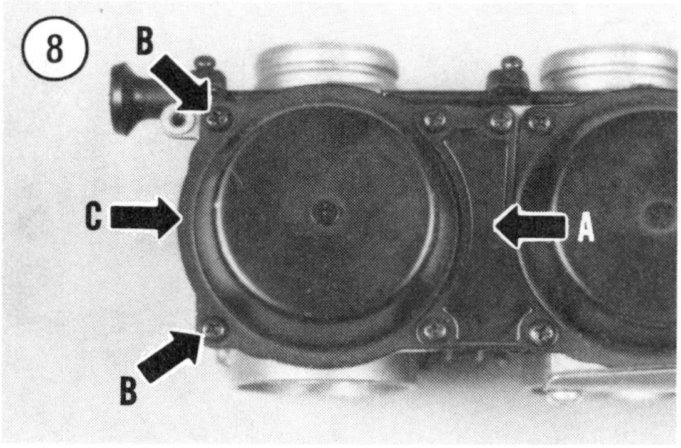

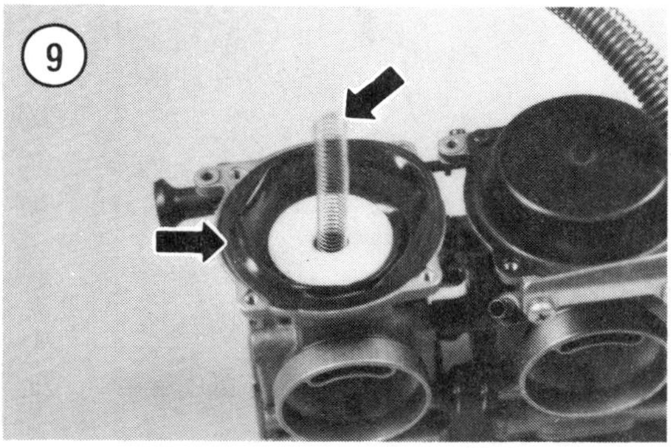

No. 1 carburetor on the left-hand side. Use masking tape and a felt-tipped pen. The left-hand side refers to a rider sitting on the seat facing forward. This identification will make it easier to assure that the tubes are connected to the correct carburetor during installation.

13. On California models, disconnect the evaporative emission tube from each carburetor.
14. Carefully remove the carburetor assembly from the engine and frame and take it a workbench for disassembly and cleaning.
15. Install by reversing these removal steps, noting the following.
16. Make sure the carburetors are fully seated forward in the rubber holders in the cylinder head. You should feel a solid "bottoming out" when they are correctly seated.
17. Make sure the screws on the clamping bands are tight to avoid a vacuum loss and possible valve damage due to a lean fuel mixture.
18. Adjust the throttle cable as described under *Throttle Cable Adjustment* in Chapter Three.

CARBURETOR

Disassembly/Assembly

Refer to **Figure 7** for this procedure. It is recommended that one carburetor be disassembled at a time. This will prevent a mixup of parts.

1. Remove the screws securing the connector plate (A, **Figure 8**) and remove the connector plate.
2. Remove the remaining screws (B, **Figure 8**) securing the top cover and remove the cover (C, **Figure 8**) and gasket.
3. Remove the piston valve and spring (**Figure 9**) from the carburetor.
4. Unscrew the pilot air jet (**Figure 10**).
5. Remove the screws (**Figure 11**) securing the float bowl and remove the float bowl.
6. Remove the float pivot pin (A, **Figure 12**).

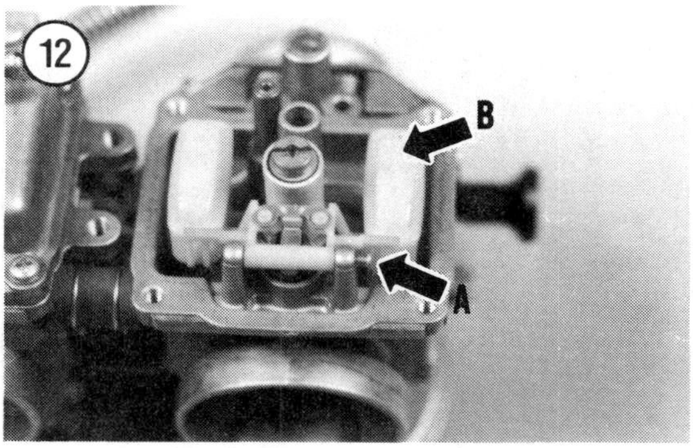

7

7. Remove the float (B, **Figure 12**).
8. Remove the float valve (**Figure 13**).
9. Remove the screw (**Figure 14**) securing the float valve housing and remove the housing (**Figure 15**).
10. Unscrew the main jet (**Figure 16**) and remove the main jet washer (**Figure 17**).
11. Unscrew the pilot jet (**Figure 18**).

NOTE
*Do not remove the pilot screw (**Figure 19**), spring and washers.*

12. Turn the carburetor over and gently tap the side of the body. Catch the needle jet (**Figure 20**) as it falls out into your hand. If the needle jet does not fall out, use a plastic or fiber tool and gently push the needle jet out. Do not use any metal tools for this purpose.
13. Remove the seal (**Figure 21**) from the float bowl.

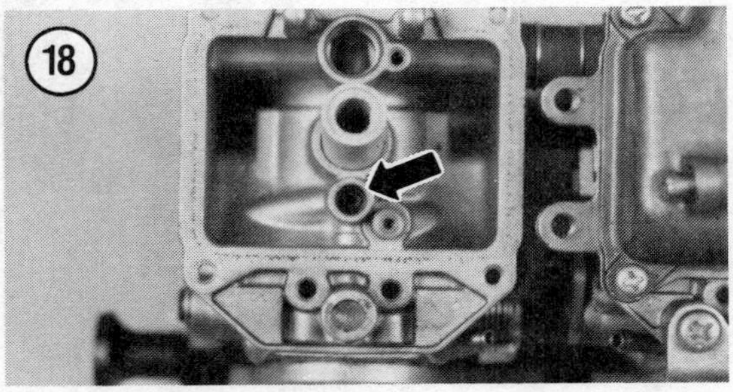

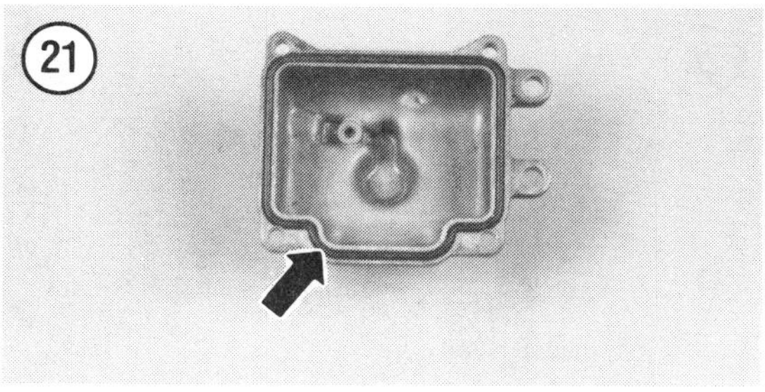
21

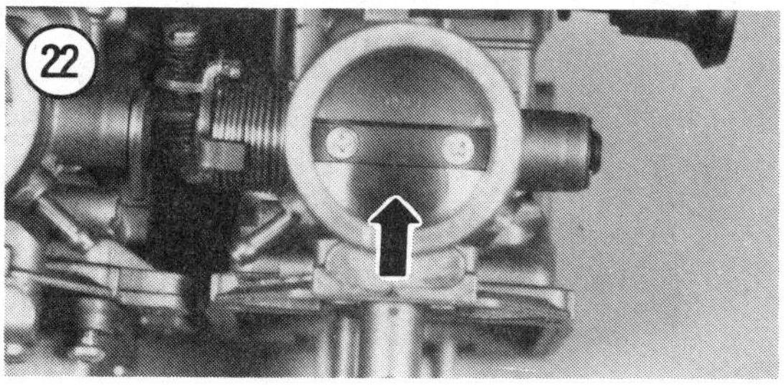
22

23

NOTE
*Further disassembly is neither necessary nor recommended. If throttle shafts or butterflies (**Figure 22**) are damaged, take the carburetor body to a dealer for replacement.*

14. Clean and inspect all parts as described under *Cleaning and Inspection* in this chapter.
15. Assembly is the reverse of these disassembly steps, noting the following.
16. Install the pilot jet with the threaded portion going in last as shown in **Figure 23**.

CAUTION
In the next step, make sure that the flat portion on the needle jet is correctly aligned with the protrusion in the main jet stanchion. If alignment is not correct, you will be unable to screw the main jet into the needle jet.

17. Install the needle jet so the flat portion (**Figure 24**) aligns with the protrusion (**Figure 25**) in the main jet stanchion of the carburetor body. Carefully push the needle jet all the way in until it bottoms out (**Figure 26**).
18. Check the float height and adjust if necessary as described in this chapter.
19. Make sure the vacuum diaphragm sealing lip is positioned correctly in the groove in the carburetor body (**Figure 27**). Using your finger, push up on the piston valve just enough so there is no crease in the diaphragm lip. Install the carburetor top cap and screws.

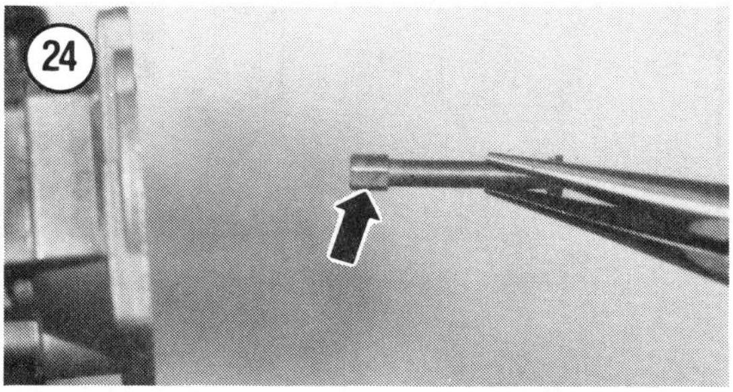
24

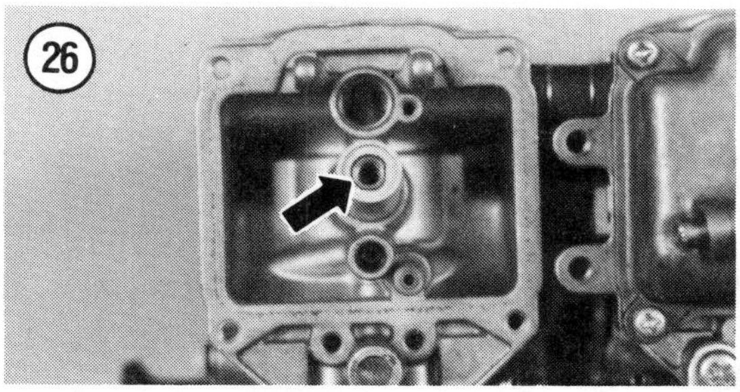
26

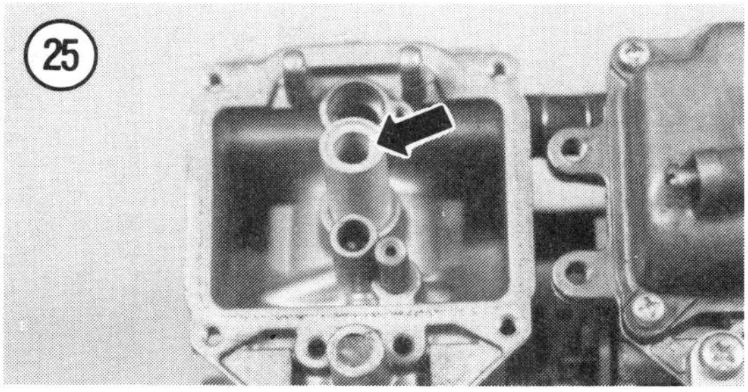
25

27

20. Install a new float bowl rubber seal (A, **Figure 28**) and make sure it is correctly seated in the float bowl groove.

Cleaning and Inspection

1. Clean all parts, except rubber or plastic parts, with spray carburetor cleaner. It is possible to clean the parts in a special carburetor cleaning solution. But such solutions can clog air and fuel passages with sediment and will also remove any paint or corrosion protective coating from the carburetors. Use this method only in extreme cases. This solution is available at most automotive or motorcycle supply stores in a small, resealable tank with a dip basket for just a few dollars. If it is tightly sealed when not in use, the solution will last for several cleanings. Follow the manufacturer's instructions for correct soak time (usually about 1/2 hour).
2. Remove all parts from the cleaner and blow dry with compressed air. Blow out the jets and needle jet holder with compressed air.

CAUTION
*If compressed air is not available, allow the parts to air dry or use a clean lint-free cloth. Do **not** use a paper towel to dry carburetor parts, as small paper particles may plug openings in the carburetor body or jets. Blow through all air and fuel passages with spray contact cleaner to ensure that they are clear and unobstructed.*

CAUTION
***Do not** use a piece of wire to clean jets as this will enlarge the jet orifices which may upset the fuel/air mixture.*

3. Remove the drain screw (**Figure 29**) from the float bowl.
4. Be sure to clean out the drain tube in the float bowl from both ends (B, **Figure 28**).

28
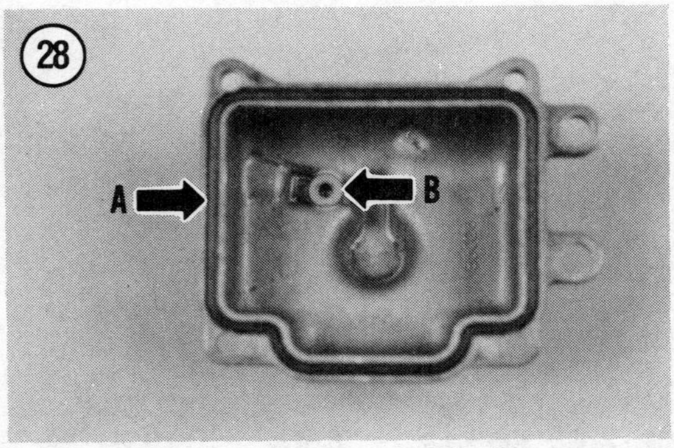

29

30
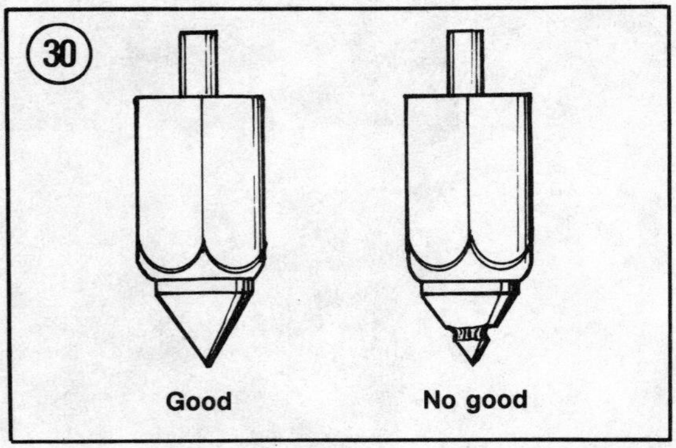

31
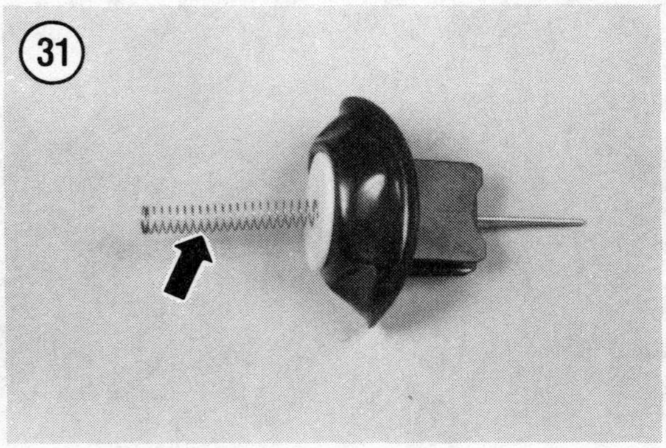

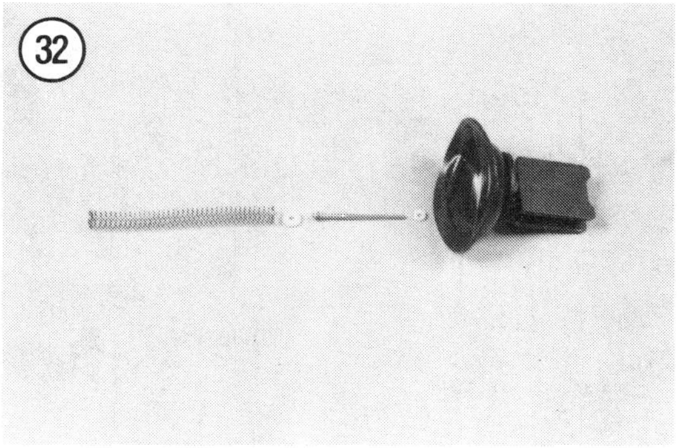

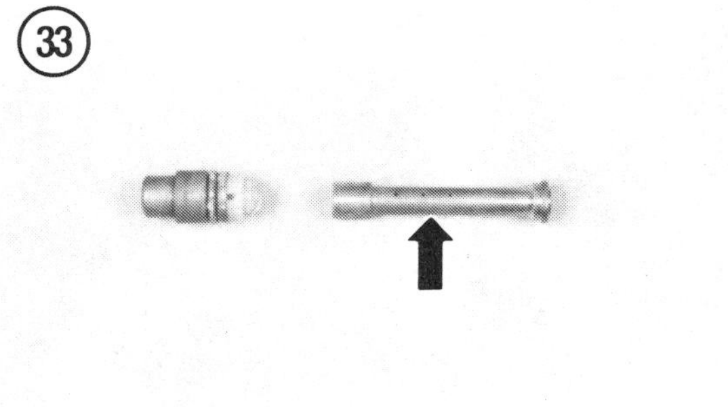

5. Inspect the end of the float valve (**Figure 30**) for wear or damage. Also check the inside of the valve seat. If either part is damaged, replace as a set. A damaged valve or a particle of dirt or grit in the valve seat assembly will cause the carburetor to flood and overflow fuel.
6. Inspect all O-rings. O-rings tend to become hardened after prolonged use and heat and therefore lose their ability to seal properly.
7. Remove the spring (**Figure 31**) from the piston valve.
8. Disassemble the piston valve (**Figure 32**) and examine all parts for wear or damage. Make sure the diaphragm is not torn or cracked. Replace any damaged or worn parts. Reassemble the piston valve.
9. Make sure the air bleed holes in the side of the needle jet (**Figure 33**) are clear. Clean out if they are plugged in any way. Replace the needle jet if you cannot unplug the holes.
10. Make sure all openings in the carburetor body are clear. Refer to **Figure 34** and **Figure 35**. Clean out if they are plugged in any way.

7

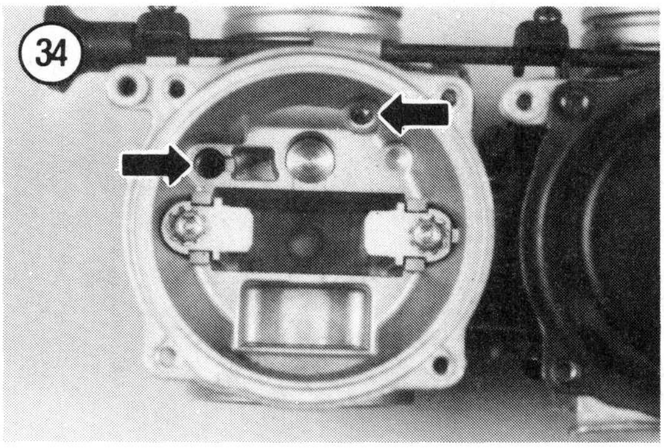

CARBURETOR SEPARATION

1. Remove the carburetor assembly as described under *Carburetor Removal/Installation* in this chapter.
2. Remove the E-clip (A, **Figure 36**) at the end of the starter shaft.

NOTE
*The Phillips head screws in the next step had a locking agent applied prior to assembly. The screws are small and will be damaged when removed. Discard the screws and replace with new ones. Do **not** try to re-use these*

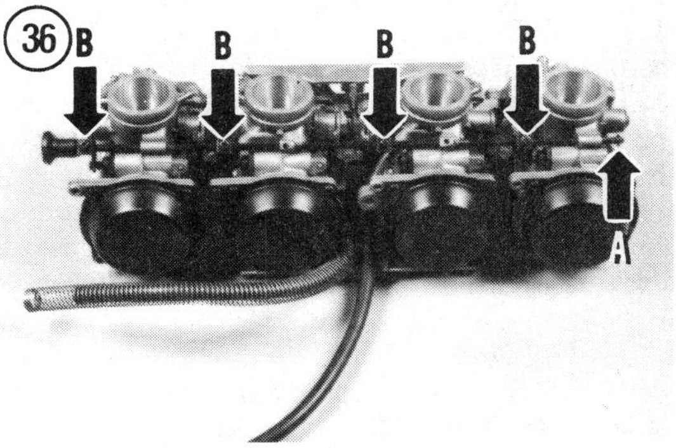

screws as they will not tighten properly, leading to choke problems.

3. Loosen the Phillips screws (B, **Figure 36**) at each carburetor.
4. Slide out the starter shaft. Retrieve the spring and steel ball in the No. 2 and No. 3 carburetor body at the screw location (**Figure 37**) when the shaft is withdrawn.
5. Remove the screws securing the upper mounting plate (**Figure 38**) and the lower mounting plate (**Figure 39**).
6. Slide the hose clamps in toward the center of the center fuel hose (**Figure 40**). Disconnect the fuel hose from one of the carburetors and separate the No. 1 and No. 2 carburetor from the No. 3 and No. 4 carburetors. Split the 4 carburetors into 2 pairs of carburetors then separate the pairs as follows:
7. Remove the screws (**Figure 41**) securing the 2 carburetor float bowls together.
8. Remove the screws (**Figure 42**) securing the connection plate that secures the 2 carburetor bodies together.
9. Slide the hose clamps in toward the center of the fuel and air vent hoses. Disconnect the fuel hose and the air vent hose from one of the carburetors.
10. Carefully pull the 2 carburetor bodies apart. Do not damage the air vent hose or the fuel hose joining the 2 carburetors.
11. Assemble the carburetors by reversing these disassembly steps, noting the following.
12. Place one of the carburetors onto its adjacent carburetor, carefully aligning the air vent hose and the fuel hose.
13. Push the 2 carburetor bodies together until they are completely seated.
14. Make sure the throttle valve control levers are positioned correctly (**Figure 43**).
15. Install the upper and lower mounting plates. Apply Loctite Lock N' Seal to the screw threads prior to installation. Tighten the screws securely.
16. Apply a light coat of grease to the starter shaft.
17. Partially insert the starter shaft into the carburetor assembly from the left-hand side.
18. Slide the starter shaft in and install the steel ball and spring on the No. 2 and No. 3 carburetor bodies at the screw location (**Figure 37**).
19. Push the starter shaft all the way in and make sure that the detent marks on the shaft aligns with each hole. Install the E-clip (A, **Figure 36**) on the right-hand end of the shaft.
20. Apply Loctite Lock N' Seal to the *new* Phillips screw threads prior to installation. Install the screws (B, **Figure 36**) and tighten securely.

37

38

39

40

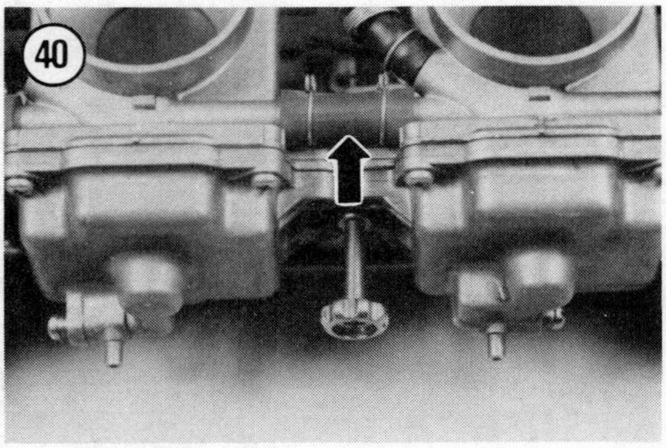

CARBURETOR ADJUSTMENTS

Fuel Level

The fuel level in the carburetor float bowls is critical to proper performance. The fuel flow rate from the bowl up to the carburetor bore depends not only on the vacuum in the throttle bore and the size of the jets, but also on the fuel level. Suzuki gives a specification of actual fuel level, measured from the top edge of the float bowl with assembly installed on the engine. Refer to **Table 1**.

The measurement is more useful than a simple float height measurement because the actual fuel level can vary from bike to bike even when their floats are set at the same height. Fuel level inspection requires a special fuel level gauge (Suzuki part No. 09913-14511).

1. Start the engine and let it reach normal operating temperature. 10-15 minutes of stop-and-go riding is usually sufficient.
2. Turn the engine off.
3. Place the bike in a vertical position.
4. Attach a small drain hose with metal container to the float bowl drain fitting. Loosen the drain screw. After all fuel has drained, remove the float bowl drain screw (**Figure 44**) and install the fuel level gauge.
5. Start the engine and let it idle at 1,000-1,200 rpm.
6. Align the middle line of the fuel level gauge with the mating surface of the float bowl-to-carburetor body at the middle of the carburetor body as shown in **Figure 45**.

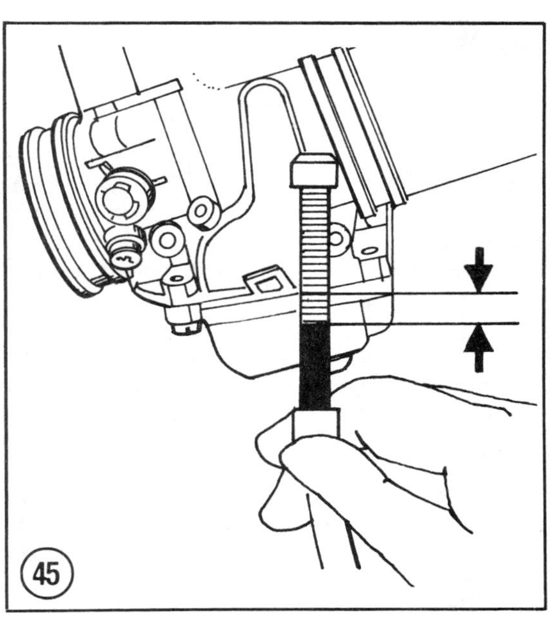

7

7. The fuel level should be within the specified range listed in **Table 1**.
8. Record the fuel level in each carburetor.
9. If the fuel level is not correct, remove the carburetors and adjust the float as described in this chapter.
10. Reinstall the carburetor assembly and recheck the fuel level in each carburetor.

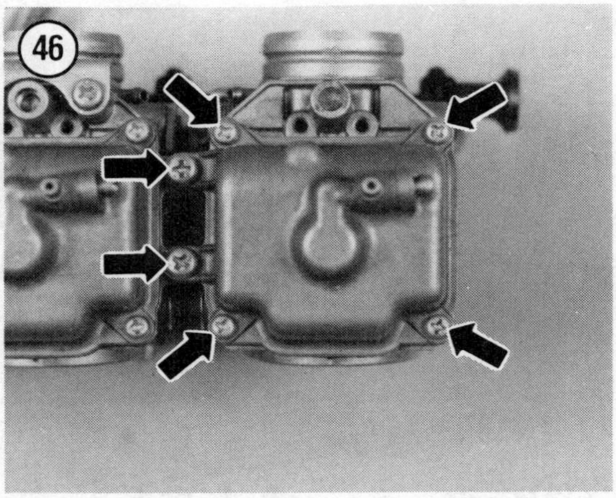
46

Float Adjustment

The carburetor assembly has to be removed and partially disassembled for this adjustment.

1. Remove the carburetor assembly as described under *Carburetor Removal/Installation* in this chapter.
2. Remove the screws (**Figure 46**) securing the float bowls and remove them.
3. Hold the carburetor assembly with the carburetor inclined approximately 15° from vertical so that the float arm is just touching the float needle—not pushing it down. Use a float level gauge, vernier caliper or small ruler and measure the distance from the carburetor body to the bottom surface of the float body (**Figure 47**). The correct height is listed in **Table 1**.
4. Adjust by carefully bending the tang (**Figure 48**) on the float arm. If the float level is too high, the result will be a rich fuel/air mixture. If it is too low, the mixture will be too lean.

NOTE
The floats on all carburetors must be adjusted at the same height to maintain the same fuel/air mixture.

5. Reassemble and install the carburetors.

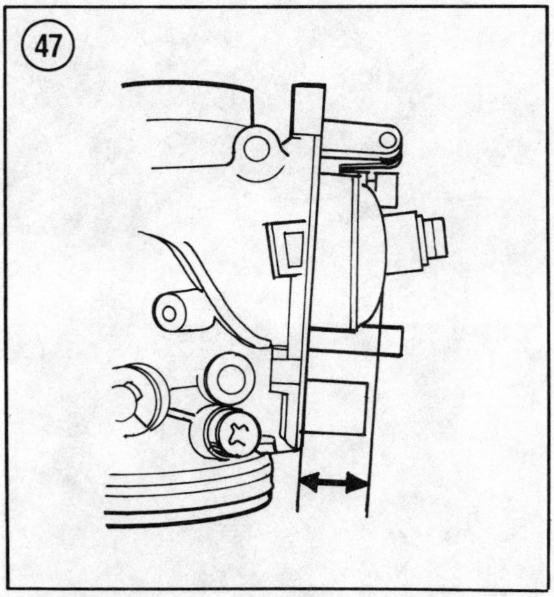
47

Rejetting The Carburetors

Do not try to solve a poor running engine problem by rejetting the carburetors if all of the following conditions hold true:

a. The engine has held a good tune in the past with the standard jetting.
b. The engine has not been modified.
c. The motorcycle is being operated in the same geographical region under the same general climatic conditions as in the past.
d. The motorcycle was and is being ridden at average highway speeds.

If those conditions all hold true, the chances are that the problem is due to a malfunction in the carburetor. More than likely, another component not needs to be adjusted or repaired. Changing carburetor jet size probably won't solve the

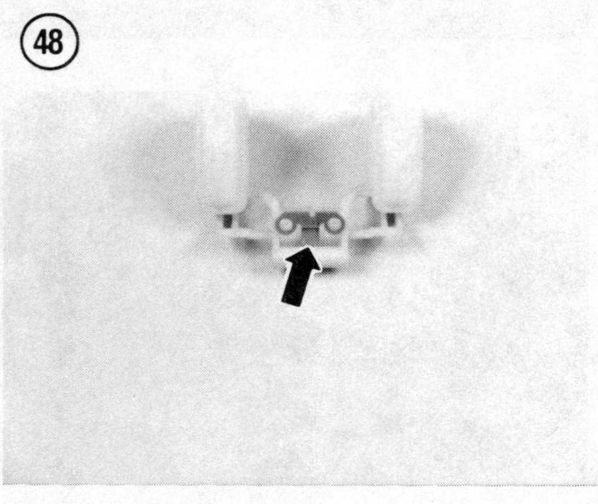
48

49

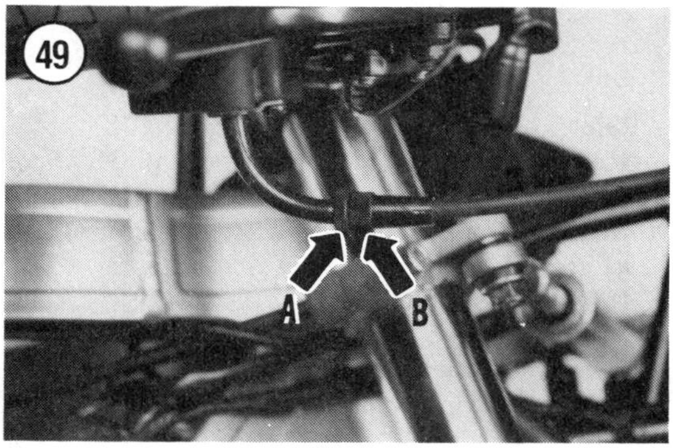

50

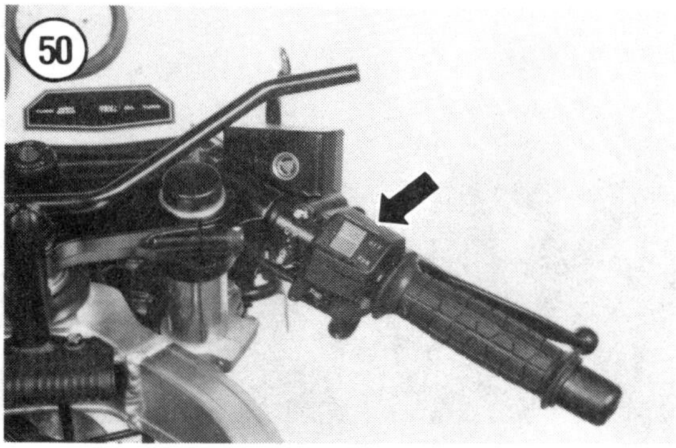

51

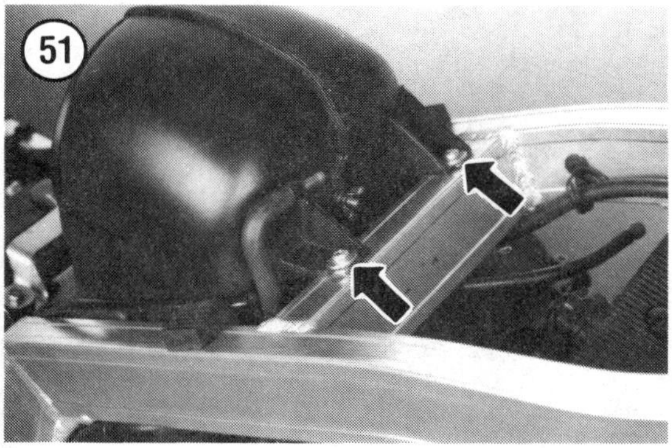

52

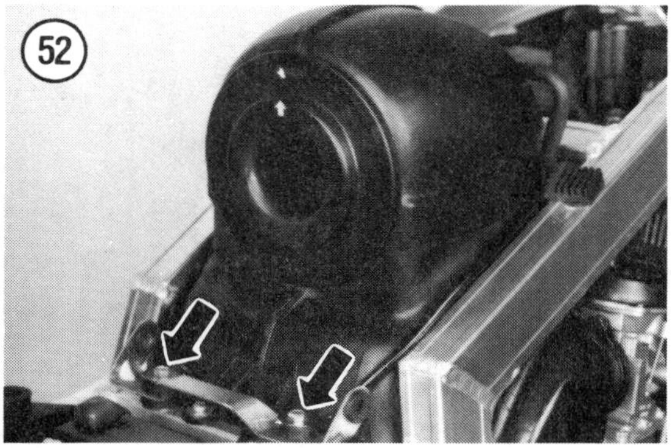

problem. Rejetting the carburetors may be necessary if any of the following conditions hold true:

a. A non-standard type of air filter element is being used.
b. A non-standard exhaust system is installed on the motorcycle.
c. Any of the top end components in the engine (pistons, camshafts, valves, compression ratio, etc.) have been modified.
d. The motorcycle is in use at considerably higher or lower altitudes or in a considerably hotter or colder climate than in the past.
e. The motorcycle is being operated at considerably higher speeds than before and changing to colder spark plugs does not solve the problem.
f. Someone has previously changed the carburetor jetting.
g. The motorcycle has never held a satisfactory engine tune.

If it is necessary to rejet the carburetors, check with a dealer or motorcycle performance tuner for recommendations as to the size of jets to install for your specific situation.

If you do change the jets, do so only one size at a time. After rejetting, test ride the bike and perform a spark plug test; refer to *Reading Spark Plugs* in Chapter Three.

THROTTLE CABLE REPLACEMENT

1. Remove the seat as described under *Seat Removal/Installation* in Chapter Twelve.
2. Remove the front fairing as described under *Front Fairing Removal/Installation* in Chapter Twelve.
3. Remove the fuel tank as described under *Fuel Tank Removal/Installation* in this chapter.
4. Loosen the throttle cable locknut (A, **Figure 49**) at the carburetor assembly. Turn the adjuster (B, **Figure 49**) to achieve the maximum amount of slack in the throttle cable.
5. Remove the screws securing the right-hand switch assembly (**Figure 50**), then disengage the throttle cable from the throttle grip.
6. Remove the bolts securing the air filter case at the front (**Figure 51**) and at the rear (**Figure 52**).
7. Disconnect the crankcase breather hose (**Figure 53**) from the cylinder head cover.
8. Loosen the screw on the clamping bands (**Figure 54**) on each end of all 4 carburetors.
9. Pull the air filter air case toward the rear (**Figure 55**) and disengage it from all 4 carburetors.

10. Pull the carburetor assembly toward the rear and free the assembly from the intake tubes on the cylinder head.
11. Pull the carburetor assembly slightly toward the right-hand side.
12. Loosen the throttle cable locknut at the carburetor assembly.
13. Disconnect the throttle cable from the throttle wheel.

NOTE
The piece of string attached in the next step will be used to pull the new throttle cable back through the frame so it will be routed in exactly the same position as the old one was.

14. Tie a piece of heavy string or cord (approximately 7 ft./2 m long) to the carburetor end of both throttle cables. Wrap this end with masking or duct tape. Do not use an excessive amount of tape as it must be pulled through the frame during removal. Tie the other end of the string to the frame or air box.
15. At the throttle grip end of the cable, carefully pull the cable (and attached string) out through the frame. Make sure the attached string follows the same path as the cable through the frame.
16. Remove the tape and untie the string from the old cable.
17. Lubricate the new cable as described under *Control Cable* in Chapter Three.
18. Tie the string to the new throttle cable and wrap it with tape.
19. Carefully pull the string back through the frame, routing the new cable through the same path as the old cable.
20. Remove the tape and untie the string from the cable and the frame.
21. Attach the throttle cable to the throttle wheel.
22. Install the right-hand switch housing and tighten the screws securely.
23. Operate the throttle grip and make sure the carburetor throttle linkage is operating correctly, with no binding. If operation is incorrect or there is binding, carefully check that the cables are attached correctly and there are no tight bends in the cable.
24. Install the carburetor assembly, fuel tank, front fairing and seat.
25. Adjust the throttle cable as described under *Throttle Cable Adjustment* Chapter Three.
26. Test ride the bike slowly at first and make sure the throttle is operating correctly.

AIR FILTER AIR CASE

Removal/Installation

Refer to **Figure 56** for this procedure.
1. Remove the seat as described under *Seat Removal/Installation* in Chapter Twelve.
2. Remove the fuel tank as described under *Fuel Tank Removal/Installation* in this chapter.
3. Remove the bolts securing the air filter case at the front (**Figure 51**) and at the rear (**Figure 52**).
4. Disconnect the crankcase breather hose (**Figure 53**) from the cylinder head cover.

53

54

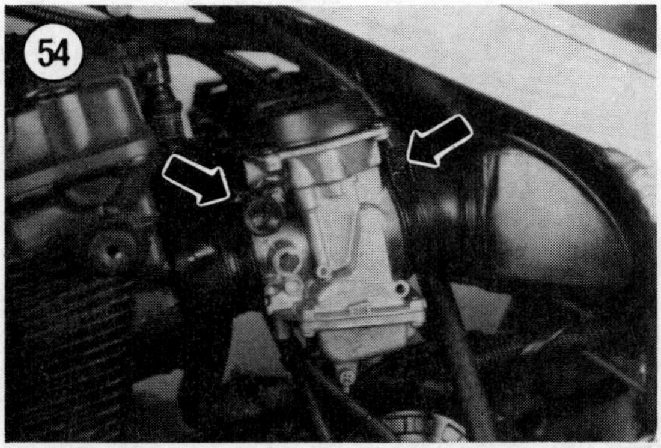

55

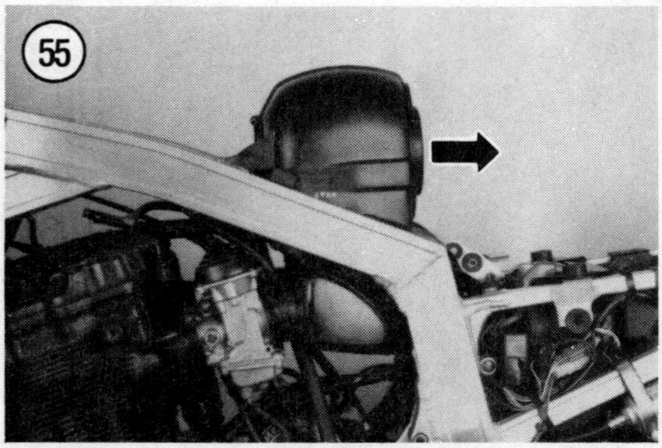

56

AIR FILTER AIR CASE

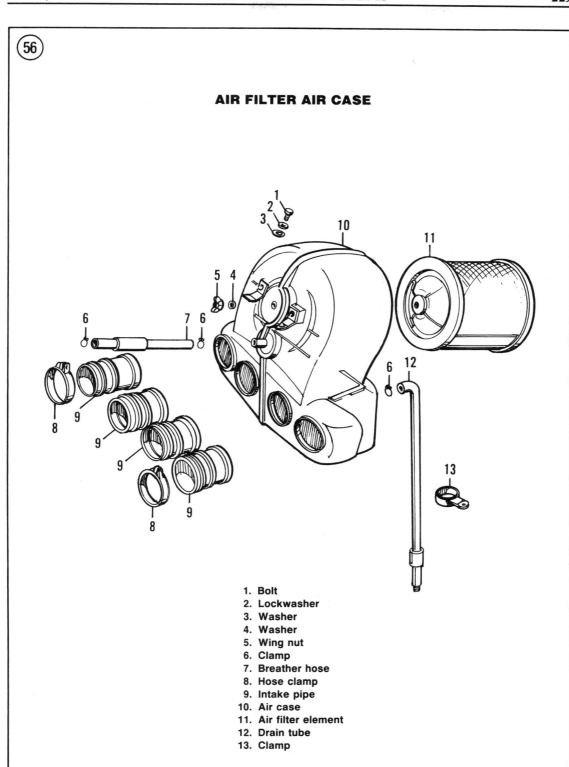

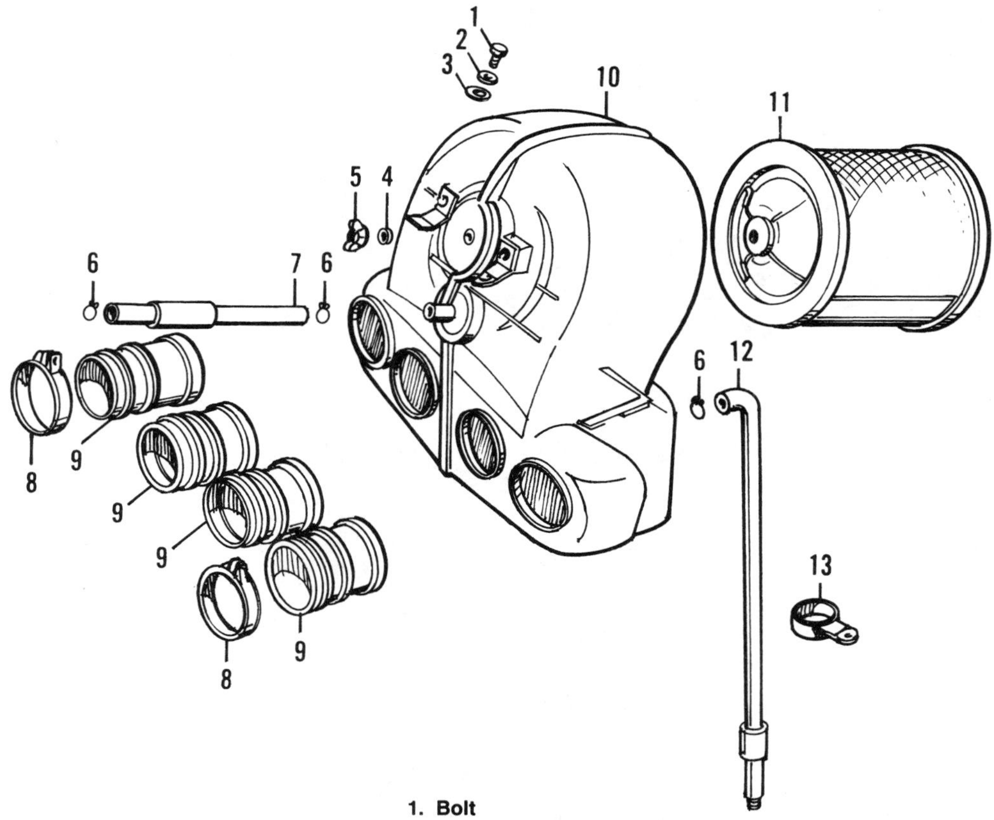

1. Bolt
2. Lockwasher
3. Washer
4. Washer
5. Wing nut
6. Clamp
7. Breather hose
8. Hose clamp
9. Intake pipe
10. Air case
11. Air filter element
12. Drain tube
13. Clamp

(58)

FUEL TANK

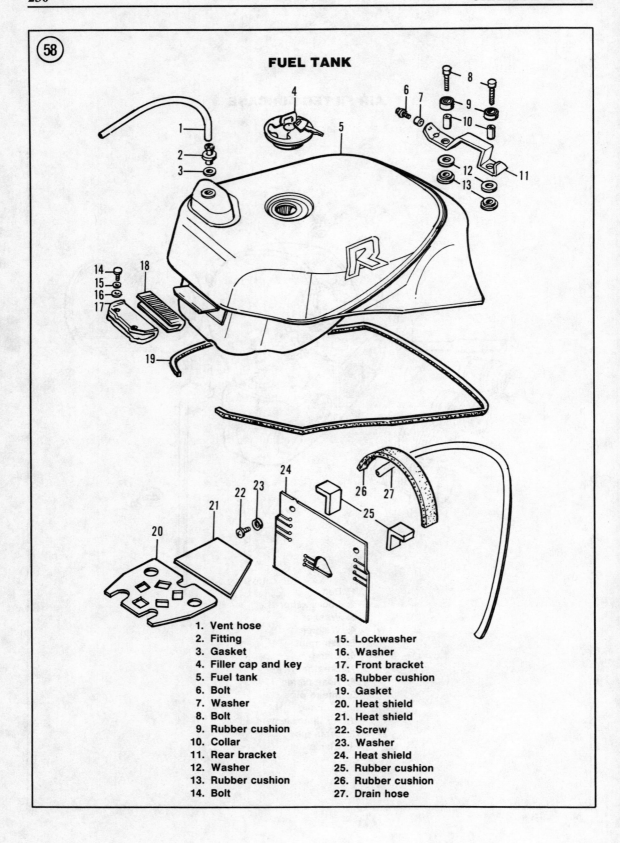

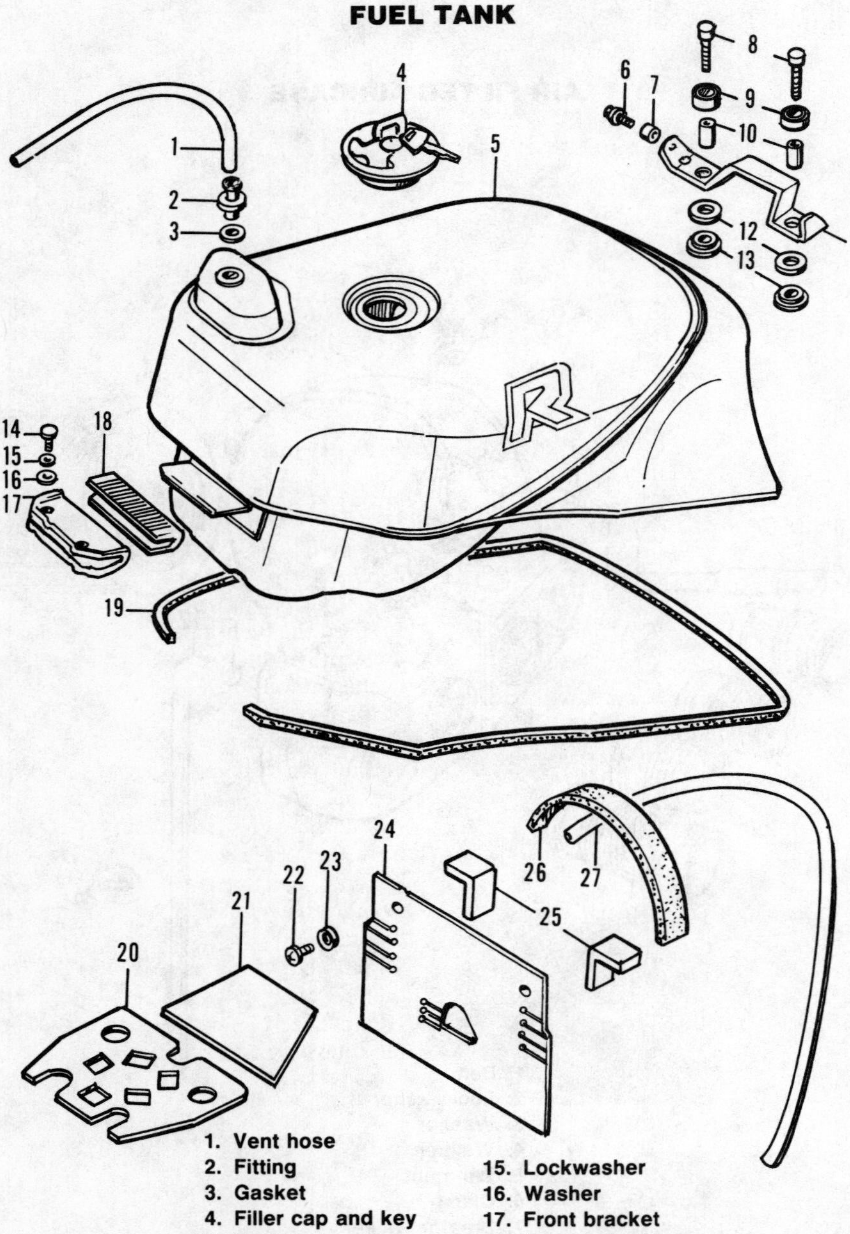

1. Vent hose
2. Fitting
3. Gasket
4. Filler cap and key
5. Fuel tank
6. Bolt
7. Washer
8. Bolt
9. Rubber cushion
10. Collar
11. Rear bracket
12. Washer
13. Rubber cushion
14. Bolt
15. Lockwasher
16. Washer
17. Front bracket
18. Rubber cushion
19. Gasket
20. Heat shield
21. Heat shield
22. Screw
23. Washer
24. Heat shield
25. Rubber cushion
26. Rubber cushion
27. Drain hose

57

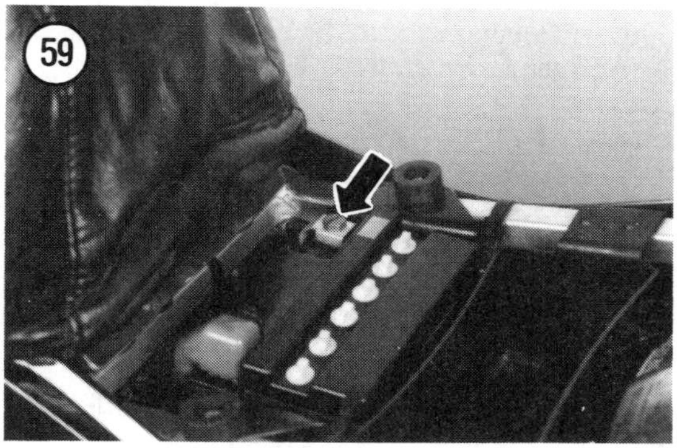
59

60

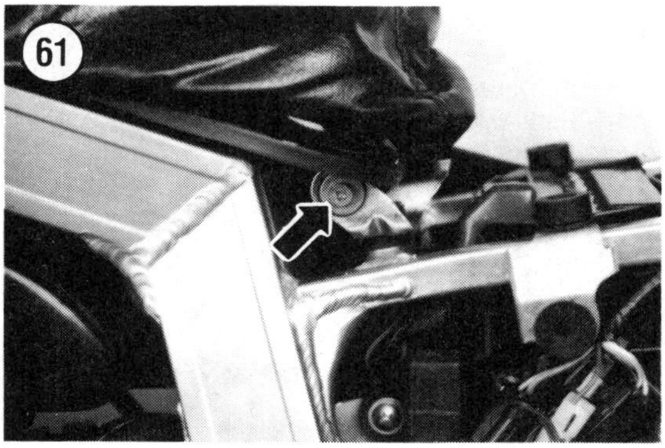
61

5. Loosen the screw on the rear clamping bands (**Figure 57**) on all 4 carburetors.
6. Pull the air filter air case toward the rear (**Figure 55**) and disengage it from all 4 carburetors.
7. Remove the air filter air case from the frame.
8. Install by reversing these removal steps, noting the following.
9. Make sure the air box rubber holders are fully seated against the carburetor inlets. You should feel a solid "bottoming out" when they are correctly seated.
10. Make sure the screws on the clamping bands are tight to avoid a vacuum loss which could lead to possible engine damage due to a lean fuel mixture.

FUEL TANK

Removal/Installation

Refer to **Figure 58** for this procedure.
1. Remove the seat as described under *Seat Removal/Installation* in Chapter Twelve.
2. Disconnect the battery negative lead (**Figure 59**).
3. Turn the fuel shutoff valve to the OFF position.
4. Remove the screw securing the lever (**Figure 60**) to the shutoff valve. Remove the lever.
5. Remove the bolt and washer (**Figure 61**) on each side securing the rear of the fuel tank.
6. Pull the fuel tank partially up and disconnect the fuel line to the carburetor assembly.
7. Pull the fuel filler cap vent tube (**Figure 62**) from the steering head receptacle or fuel filler cap.
8. On California models, disconnect the evaporative emission system vent line from the fuel tank.
9. Lift up and pull the tank to the rear and remove the fuel tank.
10. Install by reversing these removal steps, noting the following.

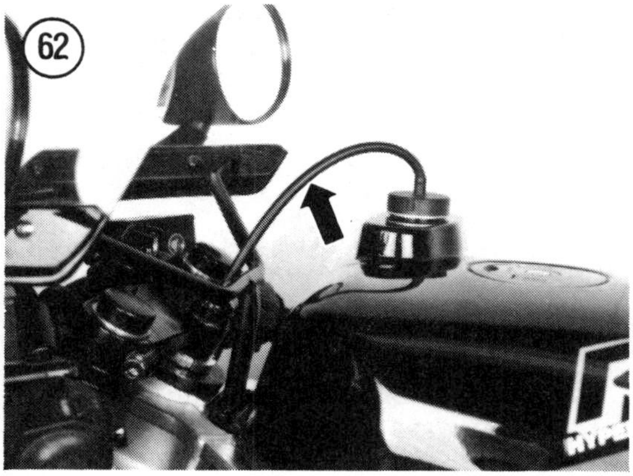
62

11. Inspect the rubber cushion (**Figure 63**) where the front of the fuel tank attaches to the frame. Replace the cushion if it is damaged or starting to deteriorate.
12. Turn the fuel shutoff valve ON and check for fuel leaks.

FUEL FILTER

The GSX-R models are equipped with a small fuel filter screen in the fuel shutoff valve. Considering the dirt and residue that is often found in today's gasoline, it is good idea to install an inline fuel filter to help keep the carburetor clean. A good quality inline fuel filter (A.C. part No. GF453 or equivalent) is available at most auto and motorcycle supply stores. Just cut the fuel line from the fuel tank to the carburetor and install the filter. Cut out a section of the fuel line the length of the filter so the fuel line does not kink and restrict fuel flow. Insert the fuel filter and make sure the fuel line is secured to the filter at each end.

GASOLINE/ALCOHOL BLEND TEST

Gasoline blended with alcohol is available in many areas. Most states and most fuel suppliers require labeling of gasoline pumps that dispense gasoline containing a certain percentage of alcohol (methyl or wood). If in doubt, ask the service station operator if their fuel contains any alcohol. A gasoline/alcohol blend, even if it contains co-solvents and corrosion inhibitors for methanol, may be damaging to the fuel system. It may also cause poor performance, hot engine restart or hot-engine running problems.

If you are not sure if the fuel you purchased contains alcohol, run this simple and effective test. A blended fuel doesn't look any different from straight gasoline so it must be tested.

WARNING

Gasoline is very volatile and presents an extreme fire hazard. Be sure to work in a well-ventilated area away from any open flames (including pilot lights on household appliances). Do not allow anyone to smoke in the area and have a fire extinguisher rated for gasoline fires handy.

During this test keep the following facts in mind:

a. Alcohol and gasoline mix together.
b. Alcohol mixes *easier* with water.
c. Gasoline and water do *not* mix.

NOTE

If cosolvents have been used in the gasoline, this test may not work with water. Repeat this test using automotive antifreeze instead of water.

Use an 8 oz. transparent baby bottle with a sealable cap.

1. Set the baby bottle on a level surface and add water up to the 1.5 oz mark. Mark this lire on the bottle with a fine-line permanent marking pen. This will be the reference line used later in this test.
2. Add the suspect fuel into the baby bottle up to the 8 oz. mark.
3. Install the sealable cap and shake the bottle vigorously for about 10 seconds.
4. Set the baby bottle upright on the level surface used in Step 1 and wait for a few minutes for the mixture to settle down.
5. If there is *no* alcohol in the fuel the gasoline/water separation line will be exactly on the 1.5 oz reference line made in Step 1.
6. If there *is* alcohol in the fuel the gasoline/water separation line will be *above* the 1.5 oz. reference line made in Step 1. The alcohol has separated from the gasoline and mixed in with the water (remember it is easier for the alcohol to mix with water than gasoline).

WARNING

After the test, discard the baby bottle or place it out of reach of small children. There will always be a gasoline and alcohol residue in it and should ***not*** *be used to drink out of.*

63

CRANKCASE BREATHER SYSTEM (U.S. ONLY)

To comply with air pollution standards, all models are equipped with a closed crankcase breather system. The system routes the engine's oil vapors into the air filter air box where they are burned in the engine.

Inspection/Cleaning

Make sure the hose clamps at each end of the hose (**Figure 53**) are tight. Check the hose for deterioration and replace as necessary.

Remove the drain plug on the end of the air box drain hose and drain out all residue. This cleaning procedure should be done more frequently if a considerable amount of riding is done at full throttle or in the rain.

EVAPORATIVE EMISSION CONTROL SYSTEM (CALIFORNIA MODELS ONLY)

Fuel vapor from the fuel tank is routed into a charcoal canister when the engine is not running. When the engine is starting these vapors are drawn through a purge control valve and into the carburetors. Refer to **Figure 64** for 750 cc models or **Figure 65** for 1100 cc models.

Make sure all hose clamps are tight. Check all hoses for deterioration and replace as necessary.

When removing the hoses from any component in the system, mark the hose and the fitting with a piece of masking tape and identify where the hose goes. There are so many vacuum hoses on these models that reconnecting the hoses can be very confusing. The charcoal canister is located just forward of the rear wheel. Refer to **Figure 66** and **Figure 67** for canister hose routing.

Vacuum Control Valves and Charcoal Canister Removal/Installation

NOTE
Removal of the some of the sections of the front fairing is not necessary but it does allow additional work space.

1. Remove the lower section and both right and left-hand middle sections of the front fairing as described under *Front Fairing Removal/Installation* in Chapter Twelve.

NOTE
Prior to removing the hoses from the vacuum control valves and the charcoal canister, mark the hose and the fitting with a piece of masking tape and identify where the hose goes.

2. Disconnect the hoses going to the charcoal canister and to each vacuum control valve.
3. Remove the bolt, lockwasher and washer on each side securing the charcoal canister and the vacuum control valves assembly to the frame and remove the canister assembly. Don't lose the spacer located within the rubber grommet on each side of the bracket.
4. Install by reversing these removal steps.
5. Be sure to install the hoses to their correct fittings on the charcoal canister and the vacuum control valves.
6. Make sure the hoses are not kinked, twisted or in contact with any sharp surfaces.

EXHAUST SYSTEM

The exhaust system is a vital performance component and frequently, because of its design, it is a vulnerable piece of equipment. Check the exhaust system for deep dents and fractures and repair or replace them immediately. Check the muffler frame mounting flanges for fractures and loose bolts. Check the cylinder head mounting flanges for tightness. A loose exhaust pipe connection can rob the engine of power.

The exhaust system consists of a 4-into-1 exhaust pipe/muffler assembly.

Removal/Installation

Refer to **Figure 68** for this procedure.

1. Remove the lower section and both right and left-hand middle sections of the front fairing as described under *Front Fairing Removal/Installation* in Chapter Twelve.

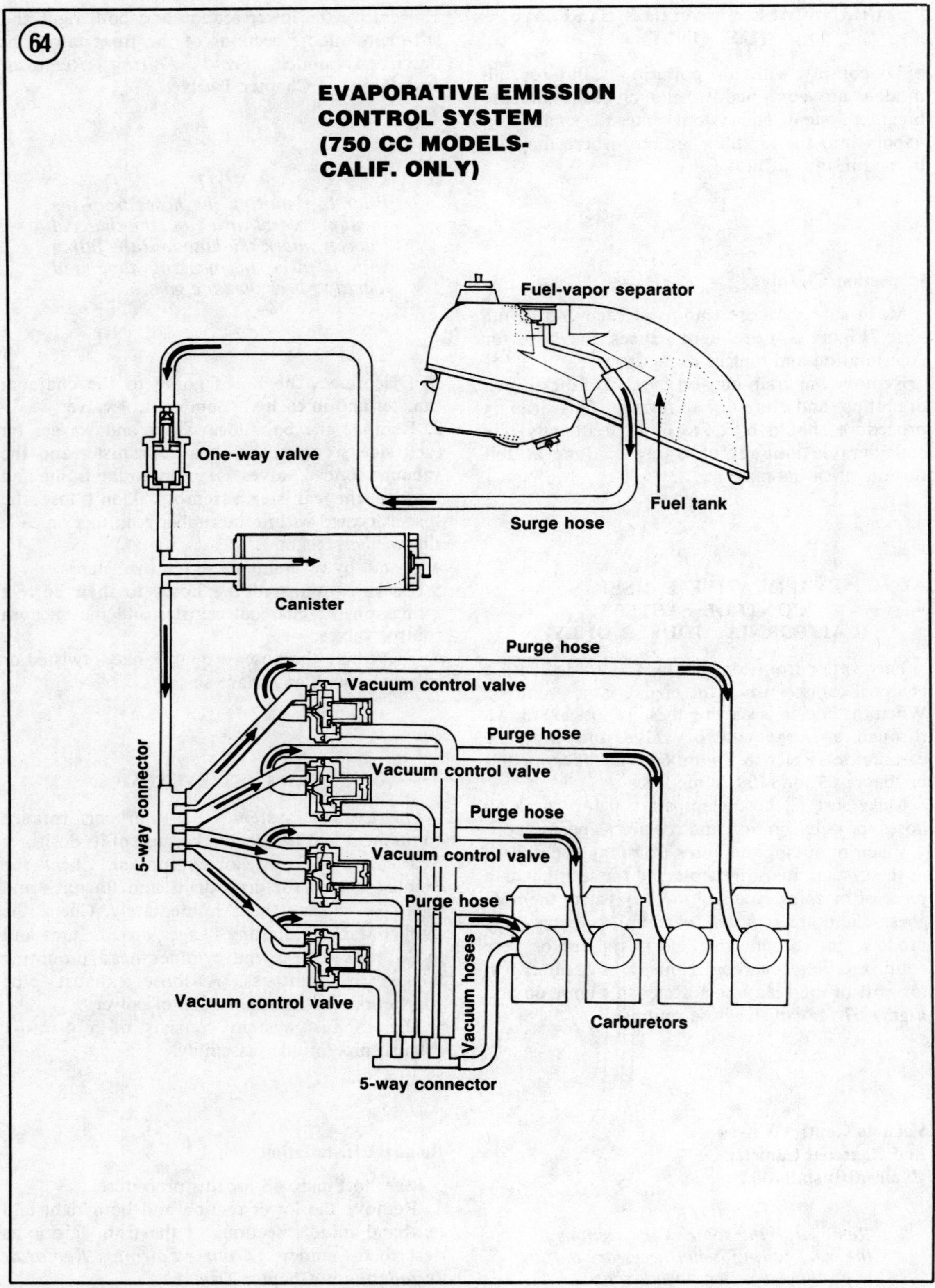
64
EVAPORATIVE EMISSION
CONTROL SYSTEM
(750 CC MODELS-
CALIF. ONLY)
Fuel-vapor separator
One-way valve
Fuel tank
Surge hose
Canister
Purge hose
Vacuum control valve
Purge hose
Vacuum control valve
Purge hose
5-way connector
Vacuum control valve
Purge hose
Vacuum hoses
Vacuum control valve
Carburetors
5-way connector

(65)

EVAPORATIVE EMISSION CONTROL SYSTEM (1100 CC MODELS- -CALIF. ONLY)

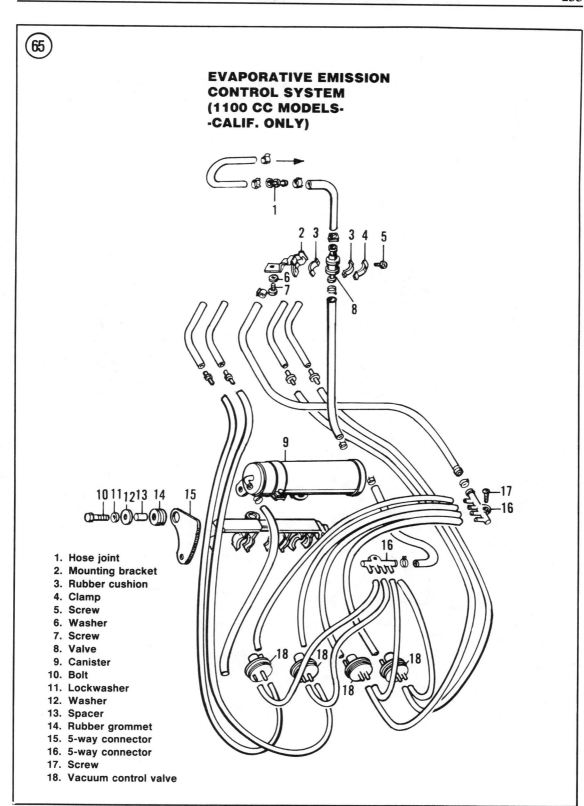

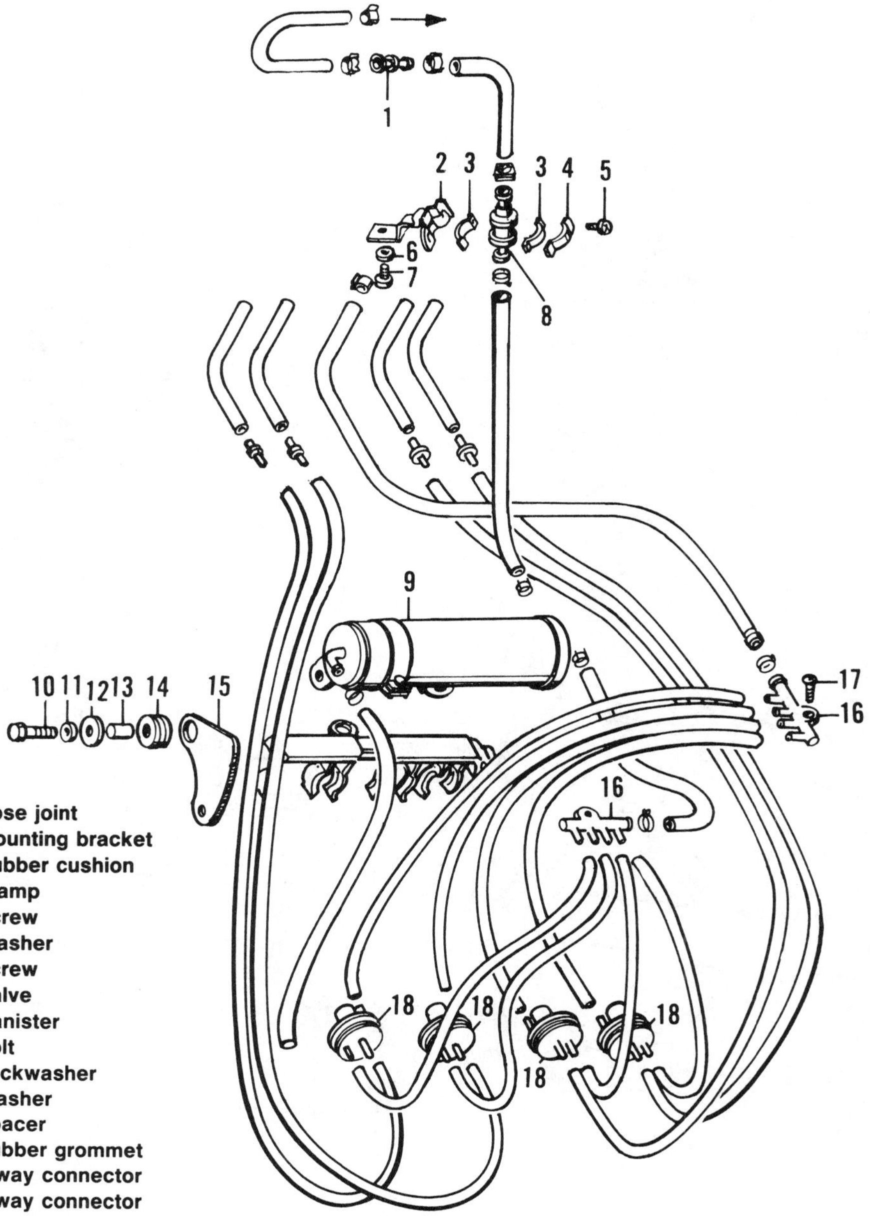

1. Hose joint
2. Mounting bracket
3. Rubber cushion
4. Clamp
5. Screw
6. Washer
7. Screw
8. Valve
9. Canister
10. Bolt
11. Lockwasher
12. Washer
13. Spacer
14. Rubber grommet
15. 5-way connector
16. 5-way connector
17. Screw
18. Vacuum control valve

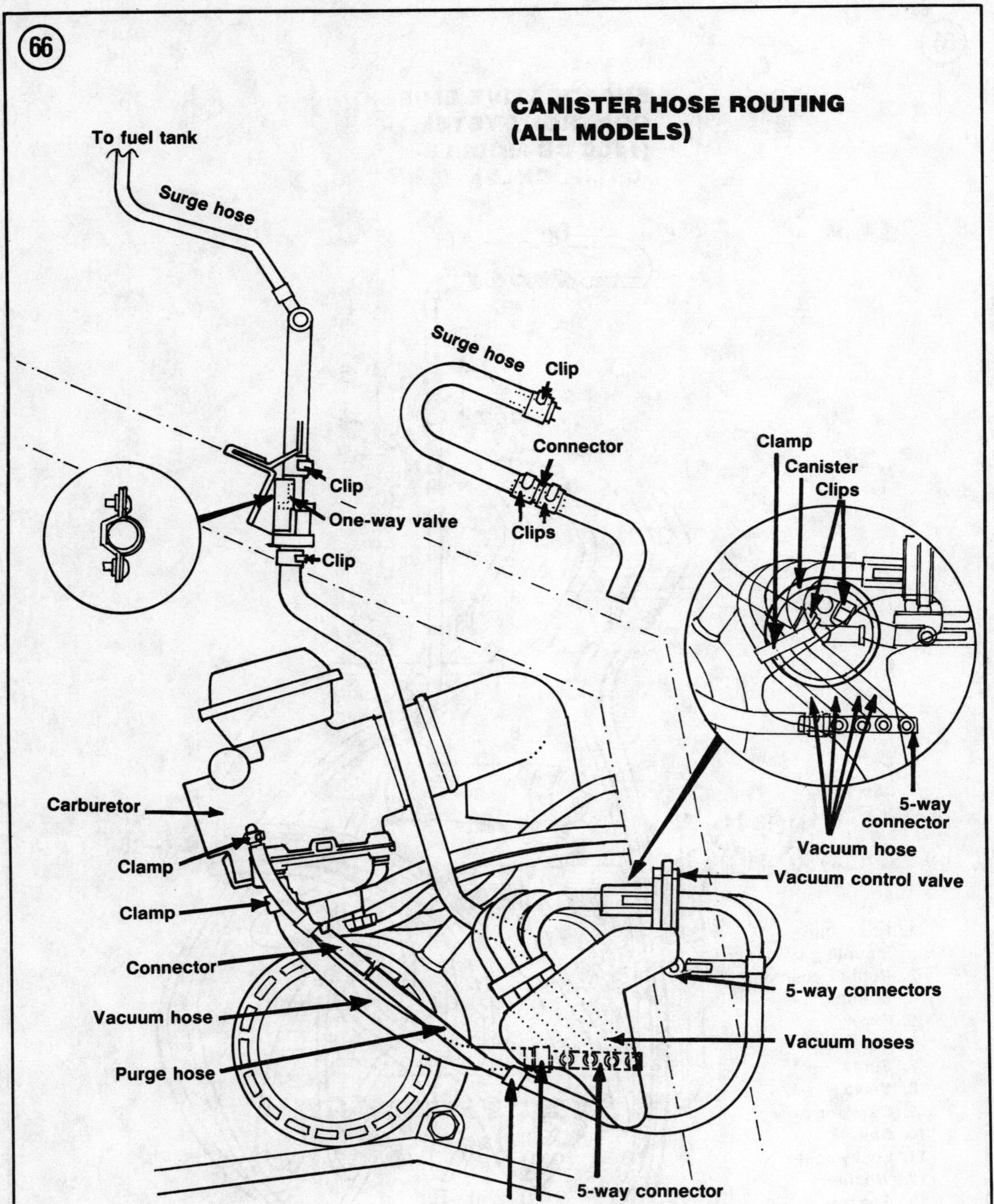
66
CANISTER HOSE ROUTING
(ALL MODELS)
To fuel tank
Surge hose
Surge hose
Clip
Connector
Clip
One-way valve
Clips
Clip
Clamp
Canister
Clips
5-way
connector
Vacuum hose
Vacuum control valve
Carburetor
Clamp
Clamp
Connector
Vacuum hose
Purge hose
5-way connectors
Vacuum hoses
5-way connector
Clips

67

CANISTER HOSE ROUTING (ALL MODELS)

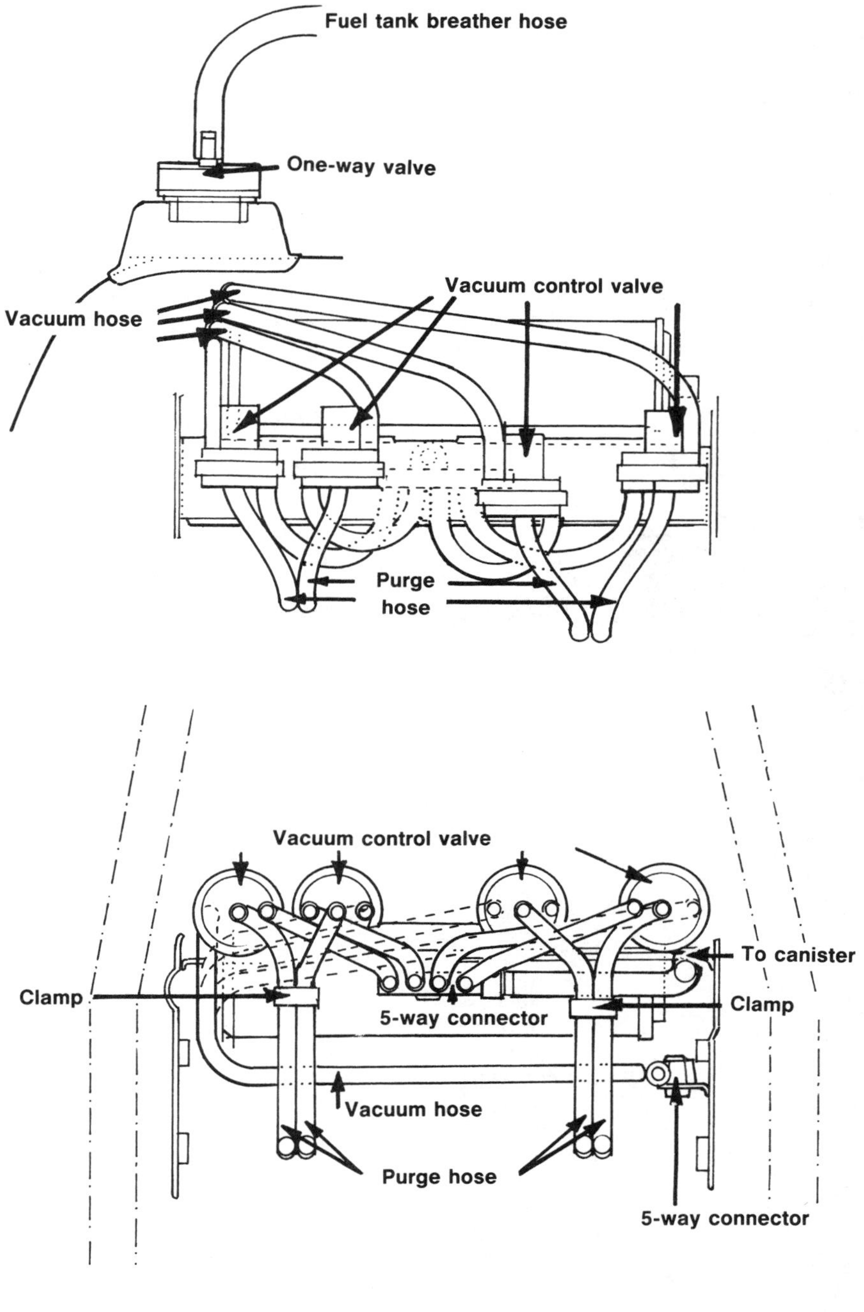

68

EXHAUST SYSTEM

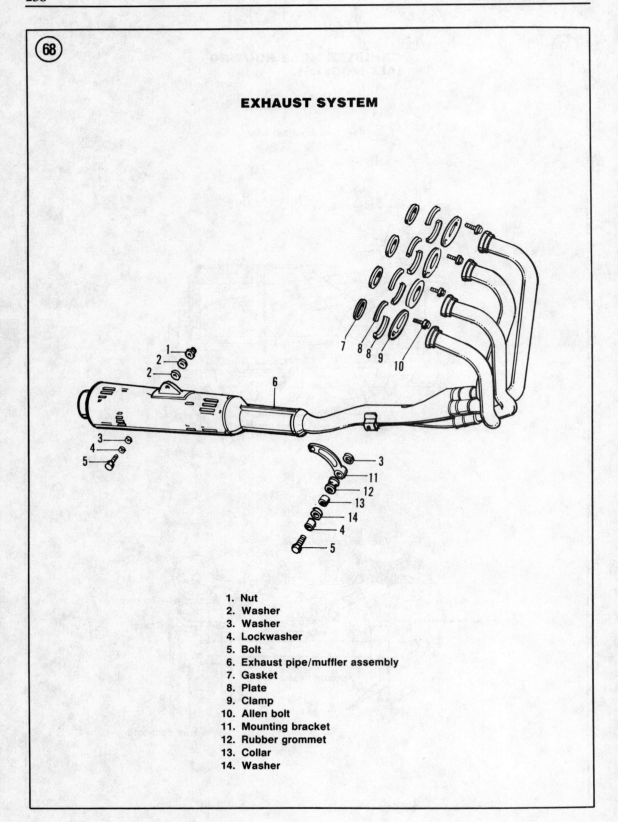

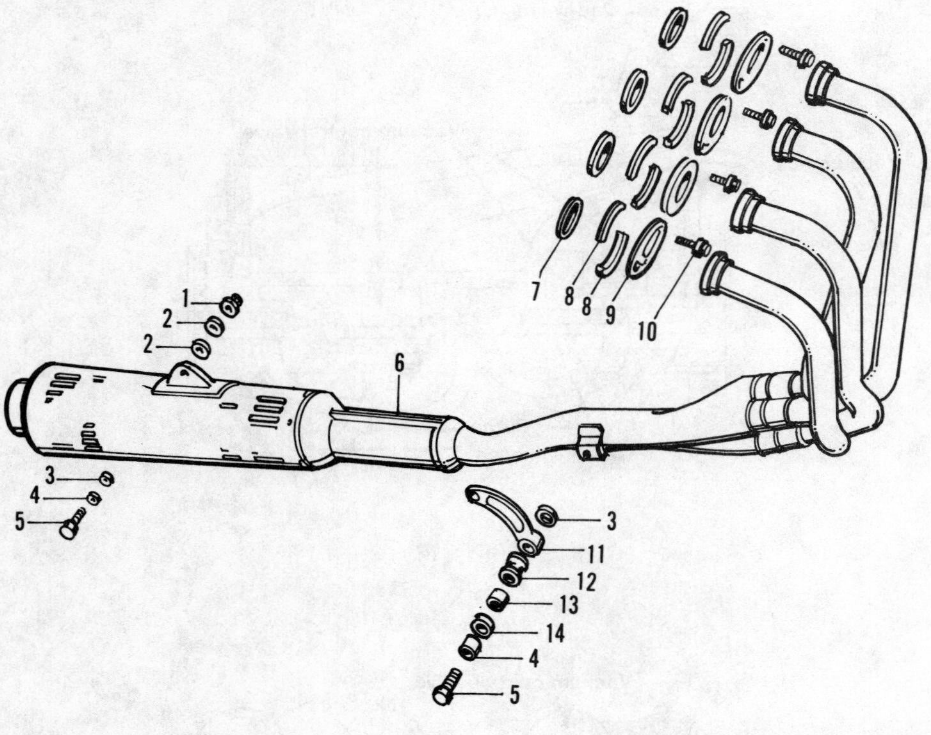

1. Nut
2. Washer
3. Washer
4. Lockwasher
5. Bolt
6. Exhaust pipe/muffler assembly
7. Gasket
8. Plate
9. Clamp
10. Allen bolt
11. Mounting bracket
12. Rubber grommet
13. Collar
14. Washer

2. Remove the Allen bolts (**Figure 69**) securing each exhaust pipe clamp to the cylinder head.

NOTE
Don't lose the 2 plates at each exhaust port when the exhaust pipe is removed from the cylinder head.

69

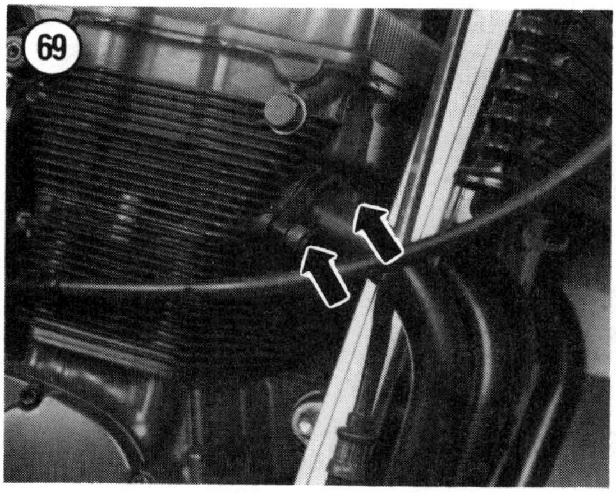

70

3. Remove the bolt, lockwasher and washer securing the rear portion of the exhaust system to the frame.
4. Remove the bolt, lockwasher and washer (**Figure 70**) securing the center portion of the exhaust system to the frame.
5. Move the exhaust system forward and withdraw the system out from the frame.
6. Inspect the gaskets at all joints; replace as necessary.
7. Be sure to install a new gasket in each exhaust port in the cylinder head.
8. Install the exhaust system onto the frame and engine.
9. Install one cylinder head Allen bolt (at each exhaust port) only finger-tight until the rest of the bolts and washers are installed.
10. Install the exhaust system mounting bolts, lockwasher and washers; do not tighten at this time. Make sure the head pipes inlet is correctly seated in the exhaust ports.
11. Remove the cylinder head Allen bolts. Install the plates (2 plates per exhaust port) and slide the exhaust clamp into position. Make sure the plates are correctly seated into the cylinder head exhaust port.

NOTE
Tightening the cylinder head Allen bolts first will minimize exhaust leaks at the cylinder head. Tighten the bolts securely.

12. Tighten the rest of the exhaust system bolts securely.
13. After installation is complete, start the engine and make sure there are no exhaust leaks.
14. Install the lower section and both right and left-hand middle sections of the front fairing as described under *Front Fairing Removal/Installation* in Chapter Twelve.

7

Table 1 is on the next page.

Table 1 CARBURETOR SPECIFICATIONS

750 cc Models			
Item	**1986 (U.S.)**	**1987 (U.S.)**	**1986-1987 (UK)**
Carburetor type	Mikuni BST31SS	Mikuni BST34SS	Mikuni VM29SS
Model No.			
49-state	28A00	27B30	27A01 (1986)
California	28A10	27B40	27B20 (1987)
Venturi diameter	31 mm (1.20 in.)	34 mm (1.34 in.)	29 mm (1.143 in.)
Fuel level	1.0-2.0 mm (0.04-0.08 in.)	1.0-2.0 mm (0.04-0.08 in.)	1.5-2.5 mm (0.059-0.098 in.)
Float leven	13.6-15.6 mm (0.53-0.61 in.)	13.6-15.6 mm (0.53-0.61 in.)	13.2-15.2 mm (0.520-0.598 in.)
Needle clip position	fixed	fixed	third
Jet needle	4C71	4C09-1	6DP2
Needle jet	P-8	O-6	P-5
Main jet No.	117.5	112.5	97.5
Main air jet No.	1.7 mm (0.067 in.)	1.8 mm (0.07 in.)	0.5 mm (0.02 in.)
Pilot jet No.	32.5	35	32.5
Pilot outlet	0.7 mm (0.03 in.)	0.7 mm (0.03 in.)	0.7 mm (0.03 in.)
Starter jet No.	40	45	42.5
Pilot screw	pre-set	pre-set	pre-set
Pilot air jet No.	160	145	1.6 mm (0.06 in.)

1100 cc Models		
Item	**1986-1987 (U.S.)**	**1986-1987 (UK)**
Carburetor type	Mikuni BST34SS	Mikuni BST34SS
Model No.		
49-state	06B10	06B00
California	06B20	
Venturi diameter	34 m (1.34 in.)	34 mm (1.34 in.)
Fuel level	1.0-2.0 mm (0.04-0.08 in.)	1.0-2.0 mm (0.04-0.08 in.)
Float level	13.6-15.6 mm (0.53-0.61 in.)	13.6-15.6 mm (0.53-0.61 in.)
Needle clip position	fixed	third
Jet needle	5D29	4D13
Needle jet	P-2	O-9
Main jet No.	130	130
Main air jet No.	0.6 mm (0.024 in.)	0.6 mm (0.024 in.)
Pilot jet No.	32.5	42.5
Pilot outlet	0.8 mm (0.031 in.)	0.7 mm (0.03 in.)
Starter jet No.	42.5	42.5
Pilot screw	pre-set	2 turns out
Pilot air jet No.	135	150

NOTE: If you own a GSX600F Katana, first refer to Chapter13 for specific service information.

CHAPTER EIGHT

ELECTRICAL SYSTEM

This chapter contains operating principles, service and test procedures for all electrical and ignition components. Information regarding the battery and spark plug are covered in Chapter Three.

The electrical system includes the following systems:

a. Charging system.
b. Ignition system.
c. Lighting system.

Table 1 and **Table 2** are at the end of this chapter.

CHARGING SYSTEM

The charging system consists of the battery, alternator and a solid-state voltage regulator/rectifier (**Figure 1**).

Alternating current generated by the alternator is rectified to direct current. The voltage regulator maintains the voltage to the electrical load (lights, ignition, etc.) at a constant voltage regardless of variations in engine speed and load.

Charging System Test

Whenever charging system trouble is suspected, make sure the battery is fully charged and in good condition before going any further. Clean and test the battery as described in Chapter Three. Make sure all electrical connectors are tight and free of corrosion.

1. Start the engine and let it reach normal operating temperature; shut off the engine.
2. Remove the seat as described under *Seat Removal/Installation* in Chapter Twelve.
3. Start the engine and let it idle.
4. Connect a 0-15 DC voltmeter to the battery negative (-) and positive (+) terminals (**Figure 2**).
5. Increase engine speed to 5,000 rpm. The voltage reading should be above 13.5 V. If the voltage is less than specified, inspect the alternator as described in this chapter. The voltage regulator and rectifier are integral parts of the alternator.
6. If the charging voltage is too high; the voltage regulator/rectifier is probably at fault.
7. After the test is completed, disconnect the voltmeter and shut off the engine.

ALTERNATOR

The voltage regulator and rectifier are built into the alternator. These 2 components can be removed and replaced separately.

Removal/Installation

1. Remove the lower section and both right and left-hand middle sections of the front fairing as described under *Front Fairing Removal/ Installation* in Chapter Twelve.
2. Remove the left-hand side cover (**Figure 3**).
3. Remove the gearshift lever as follows:

1

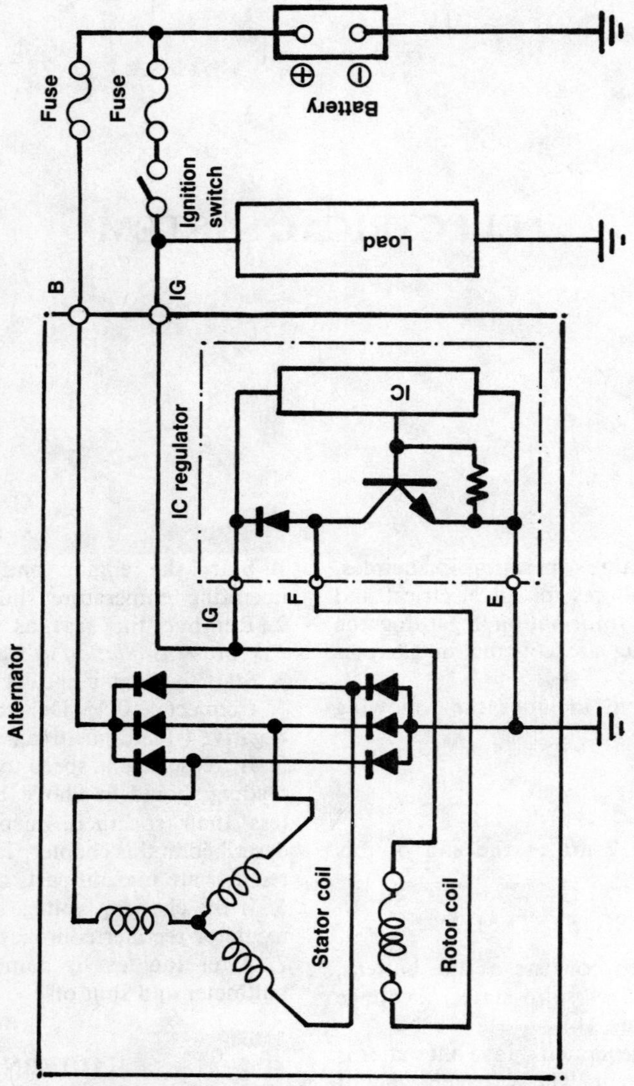

CHARGING SYSTEM

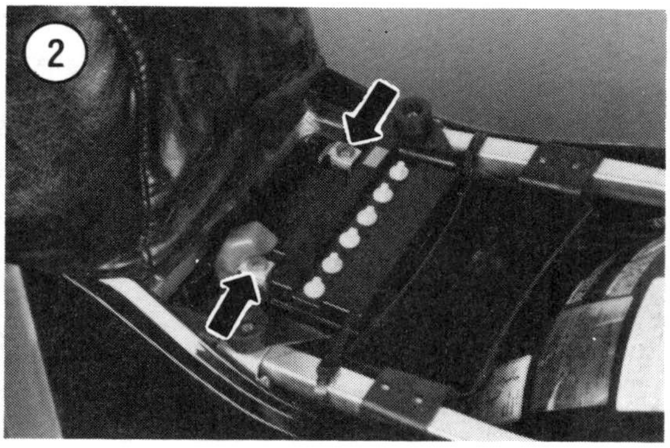
2

a. Remove the circlip (**Figure 4**) and the washer (**Figure 5**) securing the gearshift lever to the pivot post.
b. Remove the bolt (**Figure 6**) securing the gearshift lever to the shift shaft and remove the gearshift lever assembly.

4A. On GSX-R750R Limited Edition models, remove the bolts securing the drive sprocket cover (**Figure 7**) and remove the cover.

4B. On all other models, remove the bolts securing the drive sprocket cover (**Figure 8**) and move the cover out of the way.

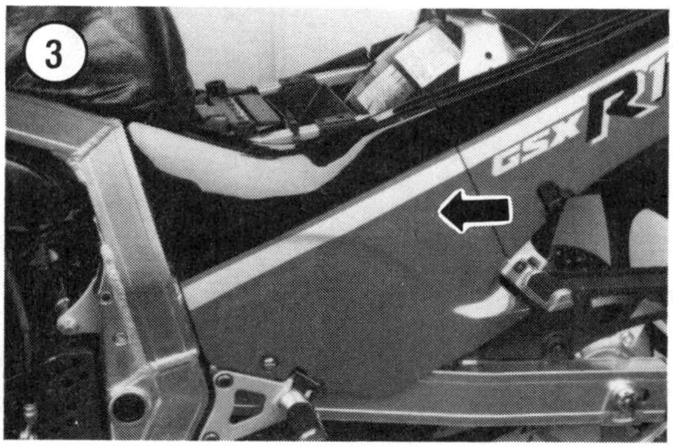
3

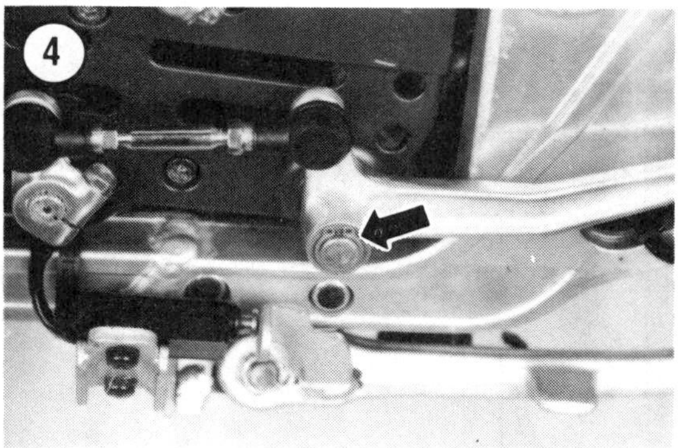
4

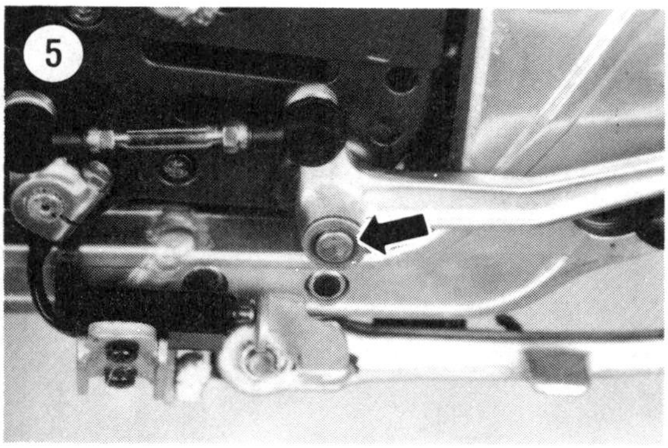
5

6

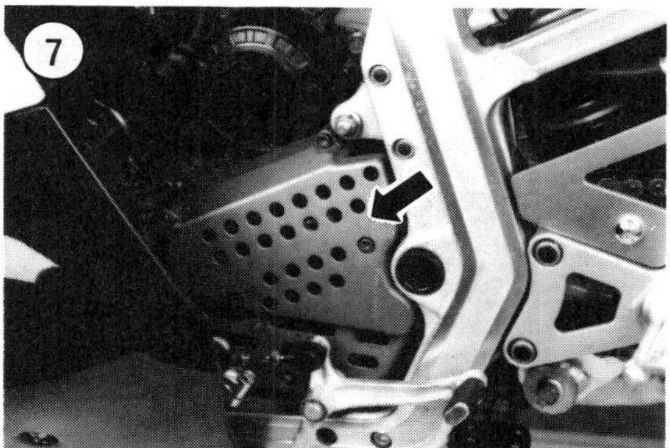
7

8

5. Disconnect the battery negative lead (**Figure 9**).
6. Unhook the tie-wrap (**Figure 10**) securing the electrical connectors and electrical wires to the frame.
7. Disconnect the alternator 2-pin electrical connector (**Figure 11**) containing 1 red wire and 1 orange wire.
8. Remove the bolts securing the alternator (A, **Figure 12**) to the crankcase. Carefully pull the alternator and electrical wires (B, **Figure 12**) from the crankcase.
9. Install by reversing these removal steps, noting the following.
10. Inspect the O-ring seal (**Figure 13**) on the alternator housing. Replace the seal if it is starting to harden or deteriorate.
11. Inspect the gear teeth (**Figure 14**) for wear or damage. Check for chipped or missing teeth. If damaged, replace the gear.
12. Tighten the bolts securing the alternator assembly securely.
13. Make sure the electrical connector is free of corrosion and is tight.

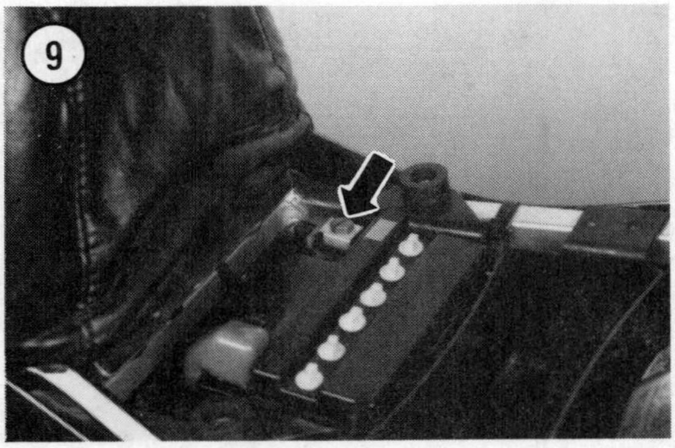

Testing

The alternator has to be partially disassembled to perform these tests. If you feel unqualified to perform these tests, have them performed by a Suzuki dealer or qualified electrical shop.

To test the voltage regulator portion of the alternator, a special piece of test equipment is required. Have the voltage regulator tested by a Suzuki dealer.

1. Remove the screws securing the end cover (**Figure 15**) and remove the end cover.

CAUTION

In the following step, do not apply excessive heat from the soldering gun, to the electrical terminals when unsoldering the wires. Excess heat can destroy the components within the rectifier. Place the soldering gun on the terminal just long enough to melt the solder and remove the wire. Remove the soldering gun ***immediately***.

2. Use a soldering gun and unsolder the stator coil electrical wires (A, **Figure 16**) and battery lead wire connector (B, **Figure 16**) from the rectifier portion of the alternator.
3. Remove the screws (C, **Figure 16**) securing the brush holder, IC regulator and rectifier and remove these items and the electrical wires as an assembly.

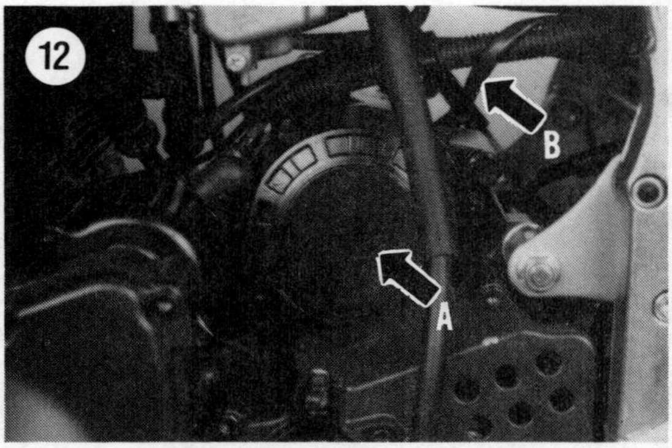

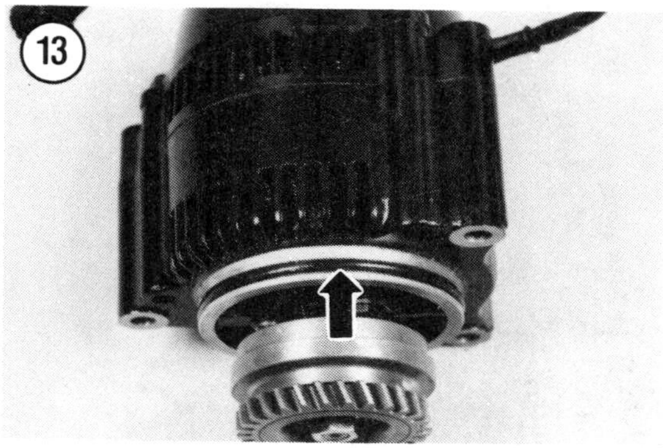

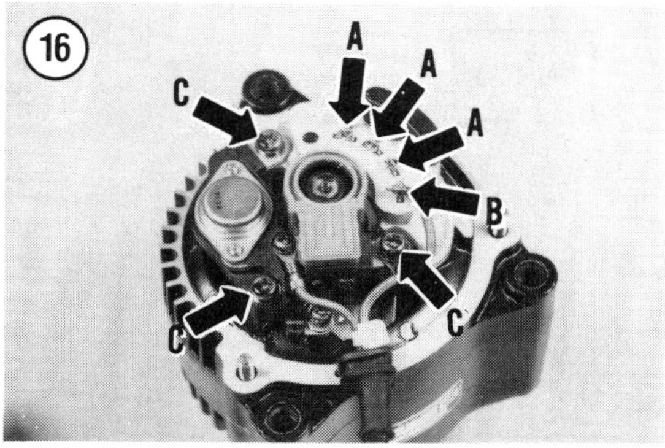

4. To test the stator portion, perform the following:
   a. Use an ohmmeter set at R×10 and check for continuity between each stator wire.
   b. There should be continuity (low resistance). If there is no continuity (infinite resistance) the stator assembly is faulty and must be replaced. This procedure must be performed by a Suzuki dealer, as special tools and a press are required to disassemble the alternator assembly.
5. To test the rotor portion, perform the following:
   a. Use an ohmmeter set at R×10 and check for continuity between the 2 slip rings on the end of the rotor assembly.
   b. There should be continuity (low resistance). If there is no continuity (infinite resistance) the rotor assembly is faulty and must be replaced. This procedure must be performed by a Suzuki dealer as special tools and a press are required to disassemble the alternator assembly.
6. To test the rectifier, perform the following:
   a. Use an ohmmeter set at R×10 and check for continuity between each terminal and ground. Refer to **Figure 17**.
   b. Connect one test lead to the "B" terminal and the other test lead to ground and then to each of the "P" terminals.
   c. Reverse the test leads and repeat step 6b. The results should be just the opposite. If in Step 6b the readings showed continuity (low resistance) then in Step 6c they should all show no continuity (infinite resistance) or vice-versa.
   d. If the rectifier fails *any* part of this test, it is faulty and must be replaced.

8

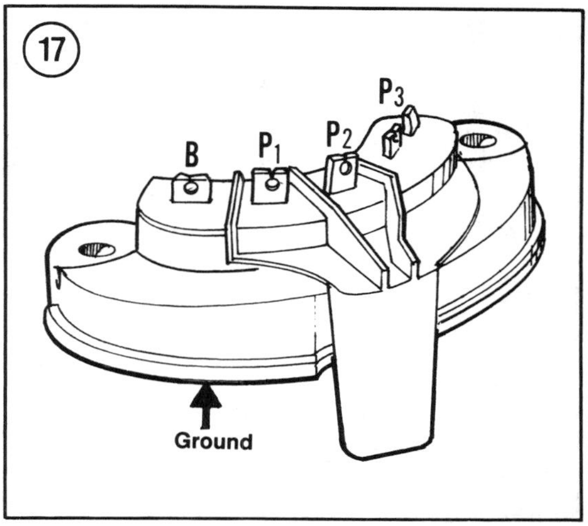

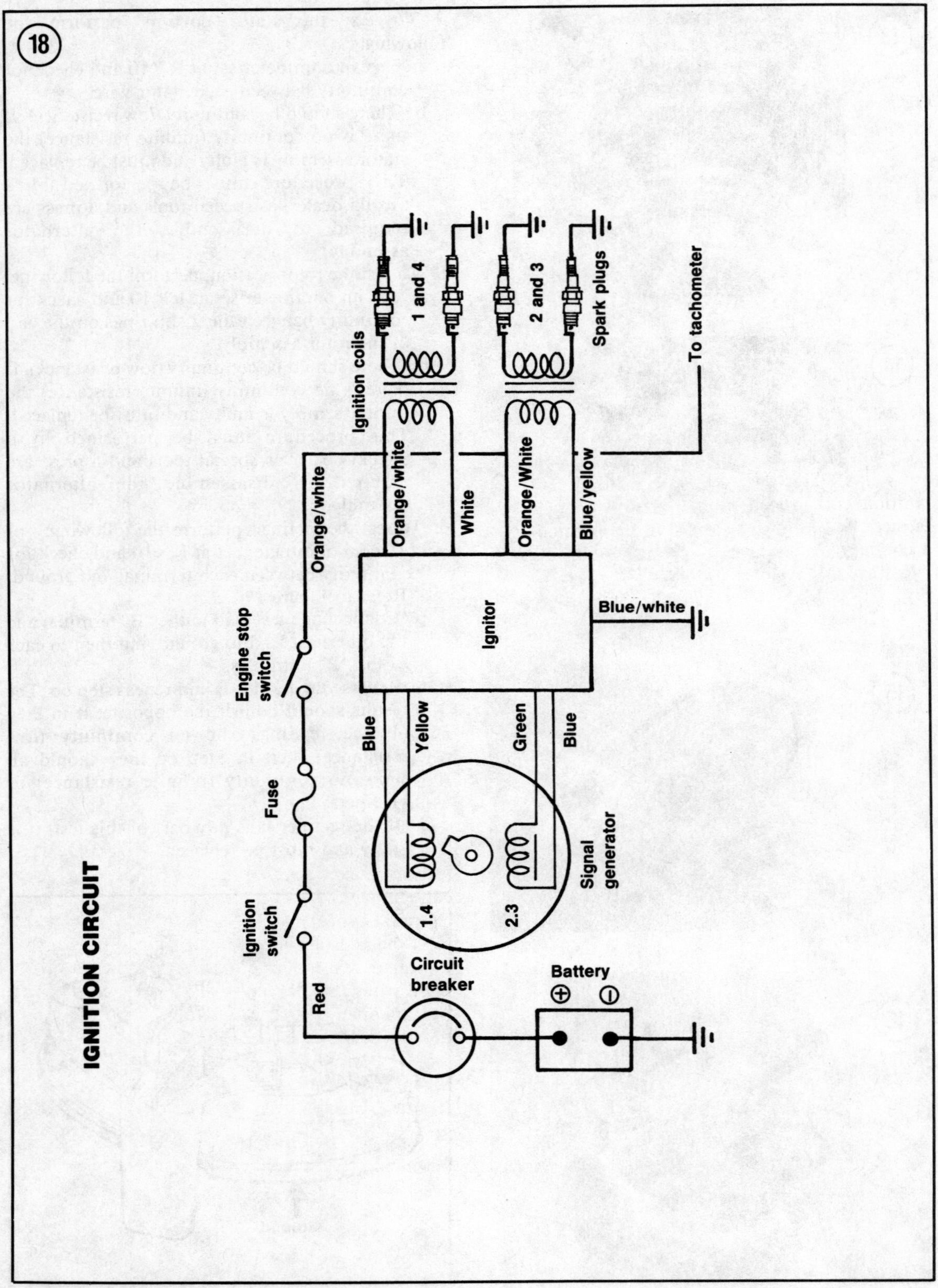
18
IGNITION CIRCUIT
Ignition coils
1 and 4
2 and 3
Spark plugs
To tachometer
Orange/white
Orange/white
White
Orange/White
Blue/yellow
Ignitor
Blue/white
Engine stop switch
Fuse
Ignition switch
Red
Blue
Yellow
Green
Blue
1.4
2.3
Signal generator
Circuit breaker
Battery
⊕
⊖

7. Reassemble the alternator by reversing these steps, noting the following.
8. Use a solder gun and solder the stator coil electrical wires (A, **Figure 16**) and battery lead wire connector (B, **Figure 16**) onto the rectifier portion of the alternator.
9. Make sure all electrical connectors are free of corrosion and are tight.

TRANSISTORIZED IGNITION

All models are equipped with a transistorized ignition system, a solid-state system that uses no breaker points. The ignition circuit is shown **Figure 18**.

The signal generator is mounted on the right-hand end of the crankshaft. As the signal generator rotor is turned by the crankshaft its signal it sent to the ignitor unit. This signal turns the ignitor unit transistor alternately on and off. As the transistor is turned on and off, the current passing through the primary windings of the ignition coil is also turned on and off. Thus it induces the secondary current in the ignition coils secondary windings and produces the current necessary to fire the spark plugs.

There is a cut-off circuit built into the ignition system to prevent over-revving the engine. If the engine reaches 11,500 rpm, the circuit cuts off the ignition primary current to all spark plugs.

Transistorized Ignition System Precautions

Certain measures must be taken to protect the ignition system. Instantaneous damage to the semiconductors in the system will occur if the following precautions are not observed.
1. Never disconnect any of the electrical connections while the engine is running.
2. Keep all connections between the various units clean and tight. Be sure that the wiring connectors are pushed together firmly to help keep out moisture.
3. Do not substitute another type of ignition coil.

Troubleshooting

Problems with the transistorized ignition system fall into one of the following categories. See **Table 1**.

a. Weak spark.
b. No spark.

Signal Generator Testing

1. Remove the seat as described under *Seat Removal/Installation* in Chapter Twelve.
2. Remove the left-hand side cover (**Figure 3**).
3. Disconnect both 2-pin electrical connectors from the signal generator (**Figure 19**). One connector contains 1 green wire and 1 black wire while the other connector contains 1 blue wire and 1 yellow wire.
4. Use an ohmmeter set at R×100 and check the resistance between both wires in each electrical connector. The specified resistance for both electrical connectors is 130-180 ohms.
5. If the resistance shown is greater or there is no indicated resistance (infinite resistance) between the 2 wires in *either* terminal, the signal generator has an open or short and must be replaced as described in this chapter.

Signal Generator Removal/Installation

1. Remove the lower section and both right and left-hand middle sections of the front fairing as described under *Front Fairing Removal/Installation* in Chapter Twelve.
2. Remove the left-hand side cover (**Figure 3**).
3. Remove the bolts securing the signal generator cover (**Figure 20**). Remove the cover and gasket.

8

NOTE
In the following steps, the engine is shown removed from the frame and partially disassembled for clarity. It is not necessary to remove the engine nor disassemble it for this procedure.

4. Disconnect the oil pressure sending switch wire (A, **Figure 21**).
5. Hold onto the signal generator rotor with a wrench and loosen the Allen bolt (B, **Figure 21**) securing the rotor and remove the rotor.
6. Remove the screws securing the signal generator stator plate (C, **Figure 21**) to the crankcase.
7. Carefully remove the rubber grommet (D, **Figure 21**) from the crankcase. Pull the electrical wires through the opening in the crankcase (E, **Figure 21**) and remove the stator plate assembly.
8. Install by reversing these removal steps, noting the following.
9. Apply a light coat of gasket sealer to the area in the crankcase where the rubber grommet fits.
10. Align the notch in the back of the rotor with the pin on the end of the crankshaft and install the rotor and Allen bolt.
11. Hold onto the signal generator rotor with a wrench and tighten the Allen bolt (B, **Figure 21**) securing the rotor. Tighten the Allen bolt to 25-35 N•m (18-25 ft.-lb.).
12. Install a new gasket and install the cover. Tighten the screws securely.
13. Make sure all electrical connectors are free of corrosion and are tight.

Ignition Coil

Testing

The ignition coil is a form of transformer which develops the high voltage required to jump the spark plug gap. The only maintenance required is that of keeping the electrical connections clean and tight and occasionally checking to see that the coils are mounted securely.

If the condition of the coil(s) is doubtful, there are several checks which may be made.

NOTE
The spark plug must ground out against a piece of bare metal on the engine or frame. If necessary, carefully scrape away some of the engine paint.

First as a quick check of coil condition, disconnect the high voltage lead from the spark plug. Remove one of the spark plugs from the cylinder head. Connect a new or known good spark plug to the high voltage lead and place the spark plug base on a good ground like the engine cylinder head (**Figure 22**). Position the spark plug so you can see the electrodes, but away from the spark plug hole.

WARNING
If it is necessary to hold the high voltage lead, do so with an insulated pair of pliers. The high voltage generated by the signal generator could produce serious or fatal shocks.

Turn the engine over with the starter. If a fat blue spark occurs the coil is in good condition; if not, proceed as follows. Make sure that you are using a known good spark plug for this test. If the spark plug used is defective the test results will be incorrect.

Reinstall the spark plug in the cylinder head and connect the high voltage lead.

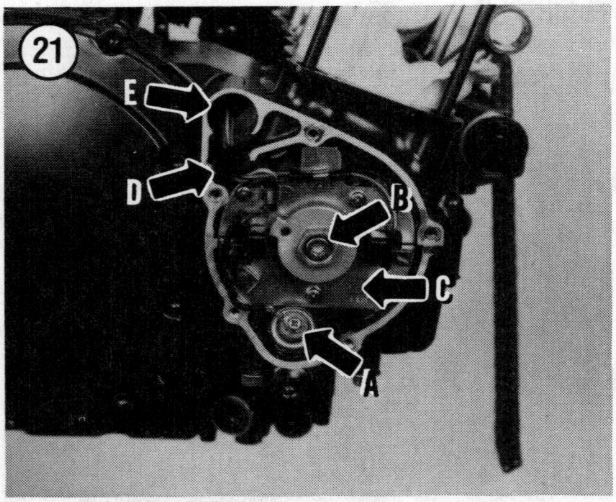

NOTE
In order to get accurate resistance measurements the coil must be at least at room temperature (minimum temperature is 20° C/68° F). If necessary, start the engine and let it warm up to normal operating temperature which will warm the coils. If the engine won't run and the coil temperature is below 68° F, warm the coils with a hair dryer.

1. Disconnect all ignition coil wires (including the spark plug leads from the spark plugs) before testing.
2. Use an ohmmeter set at R×1 and measure the primary coil resistance between the positive (+) and the negative (-) terminals on the top of the ignition coil. The specified resistance value is 3-5 ohms.
3. Use an ohmmeter set at R×1,000 measure the secondary coil resistance between the 2 spark plug leads (with the spark plug caps attached). The specified resistance value is 25,000-45,000 ohms.

23

24

4. If the coil resistance does not meet either of these specifications, the coil must be replaced. If the coil exhibits visible damage, it should be replaced.
5. Reconnect all ignition coil wires to the ignition coil.
6. Repeat this procedure for the other ignition coil.

Ignition Coil Removal/Installation

1. Remove the lower section and both right and left-hand middle sections of the front fairing as described under *Front Fairing Removal/ Installation* in Chapter Twelve.
2. Remove the seat as described under *Seat Removal/Installation* in Chapter Twelve.
3. Disconnect the battery negative lead (**Figure 9**).
4. Remove the fuel tank as described under *Fuel Tank Removal/Installation* in Chapter Seven.

NOTE
On the original equipment ignition coil and high voltage leads, the spark plug cylinder number is marked on each lead. If these marks are no longer legible or are missing, mark each lead with its cylinder number. The No. 1 cylinder is on the left-hand side and working across from left to right are the No. 2, No. 3 and No. 4 cylinders. These marks will ease installation and will ensure that the correct leads go to the correct cylinders.

5. Disconnect the high voltage lead (**Figure 23**) from each spark plug.
6. Remove the screws securing the ignition coil (**Figure 24**) to the frame.
7. Carefully pull the ignition coil away from the frame and disconnect the primary electrical wires from the coil.
8. If necessary, repeat Steps 5-7 for the other ignition coil.
9. Install by reversing these removal steps, noting the following.
10. Make sure all electrical connections are free of corrosion and are tight.

Ignitor Unit Testing

Complete testing of the ignitor unit requires 2 special Suzuki tools and should be done by a Suzuki dealer as these tools are expensive. If the signal generator and the ignition coils are working correctly, then this simple test will check if the ignitor unit is working.

The dealer will either test the ignitor unit with the special tools or perform a "remove and replace" test to see if the ignitor unit is faulty. This type of test is expensive if performed by yourself. Remember, if you purchase a new ignitor unit and it does *not* solve your particular ignition system problem, you cannot return the ignitor unit for refund. Most motorcycle dealers will *not* accept returns on any electrical component since they could be damaged internally even though they look okay externally.

Make sure all connections between the various components are clean and tight. Be sure that the wiring connectors are pushed together firmly to help keep out moisture.

1. Remove the lower section and both right and left-hand middle sections of the front fairing as described under *Front Fairing Removal/Installation* in Chapter Twelve.
2. Remove both side covers (**Figure 25**).
3. Test the signal generator and both ignition coils as described in this chapter prior to performing this test. If any one of these units is faulty, this test will not provide any usable test results.
4. Test the ignitor's unit ability to produce a spark. Perform the following:
   a. Disconnect the high voltage lead from one of the spark plugs. Remove the spark plug from the cylinder head.

NOTE
The spark plug must ground out against a piece of bare metal on the engine or frame. If necessary, carefully scrap away some of the engine paint.

   b. Connect a new or known good spark plug to the high voltage lead and place the spark plug base on a good ground like the engine cylinder head cover (**Figure 22**). Position the spark plug so you can see the electrodes, but away from the spark plug hole.

WARNING
If it is necessary to hold the high voltage lead, do so with an insulated pair of pliers. The high voltage generated by the ignitor unit could produce serious or fatal shocks.

   c. Turn the engine over with the starter and check for a spark. If there is a fat blue spark, the ignitor unit is working properly.

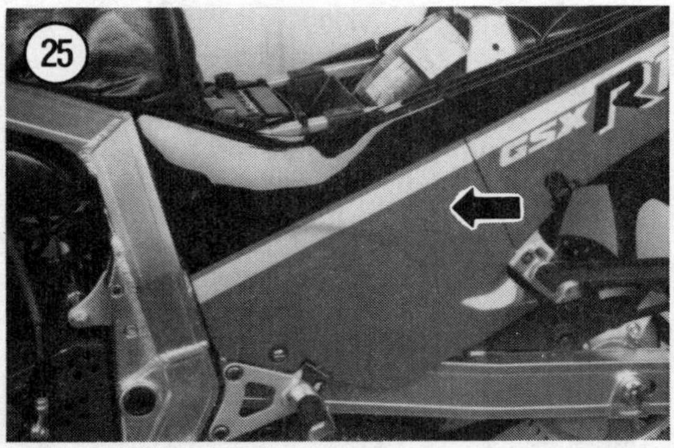

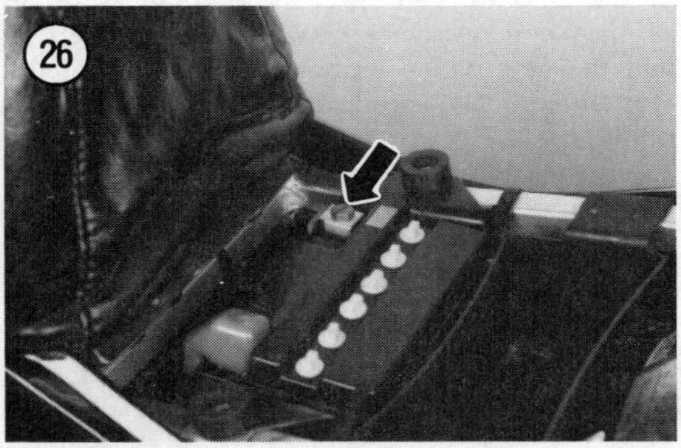

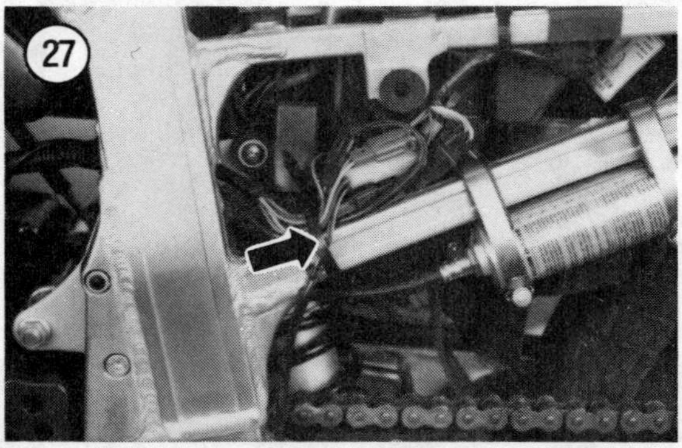

d. If a weak spark or no spark is obtained and the signal generator and ignition coils are okay, have the ignitor unit tested by a Suzuki dealer.
e. Reinstall the spark plug and connect the high voltage lead onto the spark plug.

5. If all of the ignition components are okay, then check the following:
a. Check for an open or short in the wire harness between each component in the system.
b. Again, make sure all connections between the various components are clean and tight. Be sure that the wiring connectors are pushed together firmly to help keep out moisture.

Ignitor Unit Replacement

1. Remove the lower section and both right and left-hand middle sections of the front fairing as described under *Front Fairing Removal/ Installation* in Chapter Twelve.
2. Remove the left-hand side cover (**Figure 25**).
3. Disconnect the battery negative lead (**Figure 26**).
4. Unhook the tie-wrap (**Figure 27**) securing the electrical connectors and electrical wires to the frame. Move the electrical connectors and wires out of the way.
5. Remove the screws (**Figure 28**) securing the ignitor unit. Carefully pull the ignitor unit from the frame.
6. Disconnect both of the ignitor unit's 4-pin electrical connectors.
7. Remove the ignitor unit.
8. Install a new ignitor unit onto the frame. Attach both electrical wires to it. Make sure both electrical connectors are free of corrosion and are tight.
9. Install and tighten the screws securely.
10. Install all parts removed.

ELECTRIC STARTER

The starter system includes a starter switch, starter interlock switch, starter solenoid, battery and starter motor as shown in **Figure 29**.

29

STARTER SYSTEM

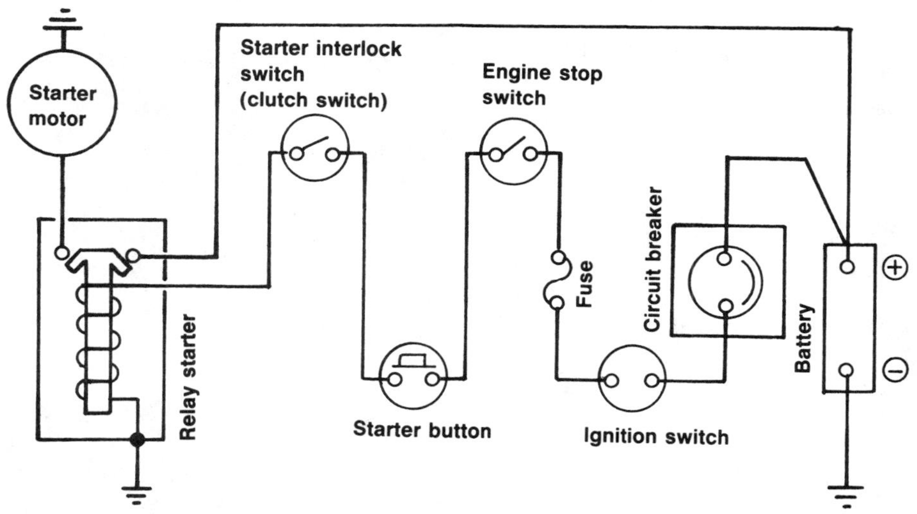

8

Removal/Installation

1. Remove the lower section and the left-hand middle section of the front fairing as described under *Front Fairing Removal/Installation* in Chapter Twelve.
2. Remove the seat as described under *Seat Removal/Installation* in Chapter Twelve.
3. Disconnect the battery negative lead (**Figure 26**).
4. Slide back the rubber boot on the electrical cable connector.
5. Disconnect the starter electrical cable (A, **Figure 30**) from the starter.
6. Remove the bolts securing the starter (B, **Figure 30**) to the crankcase.
7. Lift up and withdraw the starter from the top of the crankcase.
8. Install by reversing these removal steps.

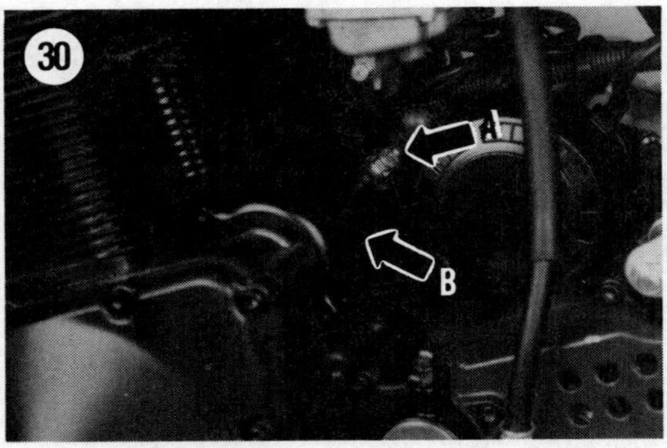

Preliminary Inspection

The overhaul of a starter motor is best left to an expert. This procedure shows how to detect a defective starter.

Inspect the O-ring seal (A, **Figure 31**). O-ring seals tend to harden after prolonged use and heat and therefore lose their ability to seal properly. Replace as necessary.

Inspect the gear (B, **Figure 31**) for chipped or missing teeth. If damaged, the starter assembly must be replaced.

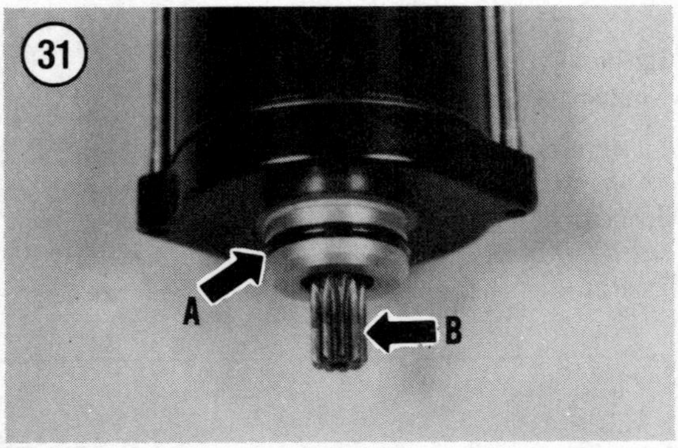

Disassembly

Refer to **Figure 32** for this procedure.

1. Remove the case screws and washers (**Figure 33**), then separate the front and rear covers from the case.

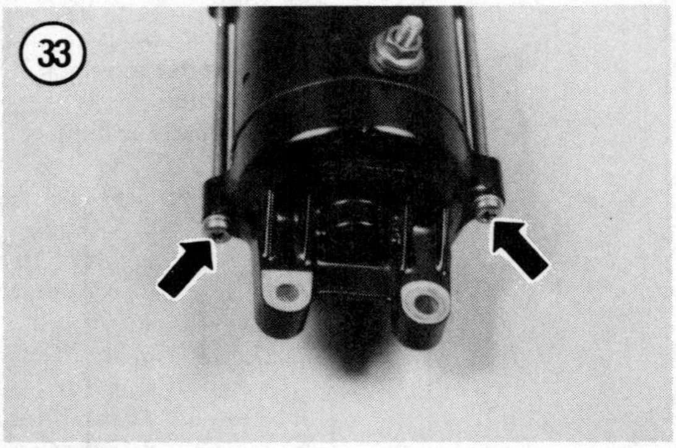

NOTE
Write down the number of shims used on the shaft next to the commutator and next to the rear cover. Be sure to install the same number when reassembling the starter.

2. Remove the special washer and shims (**Figure 34**) from the front cover end of the shaft.

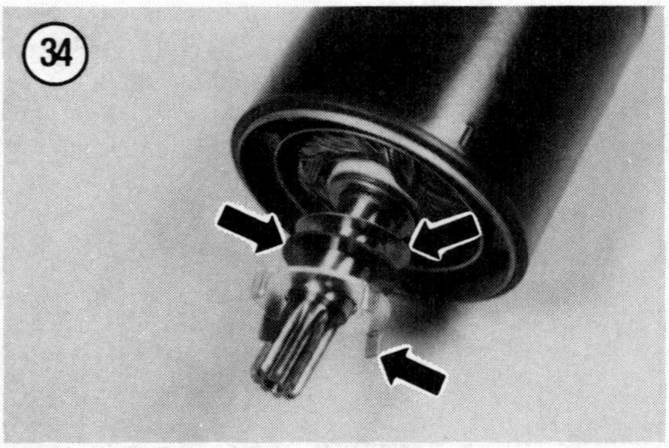

(32)

STARTER MOTOR

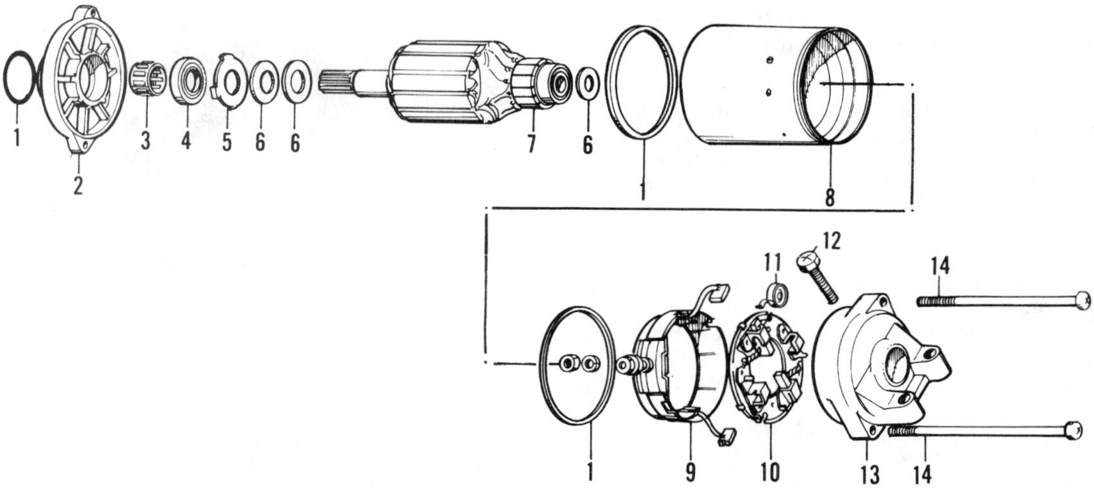

1. O-ring
2. Front cover
3. Needle bearing
4. Oil seal
5. Special washer
6. Shim
7. Armature
8. Starter motor case assembly
9. Brush terminal set
10. Brush holder assembly
11. Brush spring
12. Bolt
13. Rear cover
14. Case screws

3. Remove the washers (**Figure 35**) from the armature end of the shaft.
4. Withdraw the armature coil assembly (**Figure 36**) from the front end of the case.
5. Remove the brush holder assembly (**Figure 37**) from the end of the case.

NOTE

Before removing the nuts and washers, write down their description and order. They must be reinstalled in the same order to insulate this set of brushes from the case.

6. Remove the nuts, washers and O-ring (A, **Figure 38**) securing the brush terminal set. Remove the brush terminal set (B, **Figure 38**).

CAUTION

Do not immerse the wire windings in the case or the armature coil in solvent as the insulation may be damaged. Wipe the windings with a cloth lightly moistened with solvent and thoroughly dry.

7. Clean all grease, dirt and carbon from all components.
8. Inspect the starter motor as described in this chapter.

35

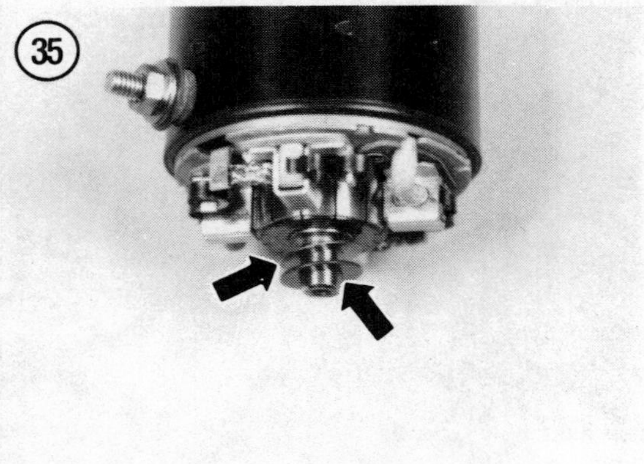

36

37

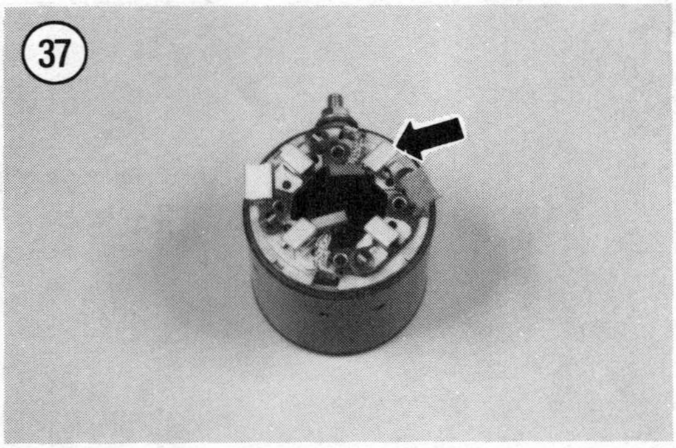

38

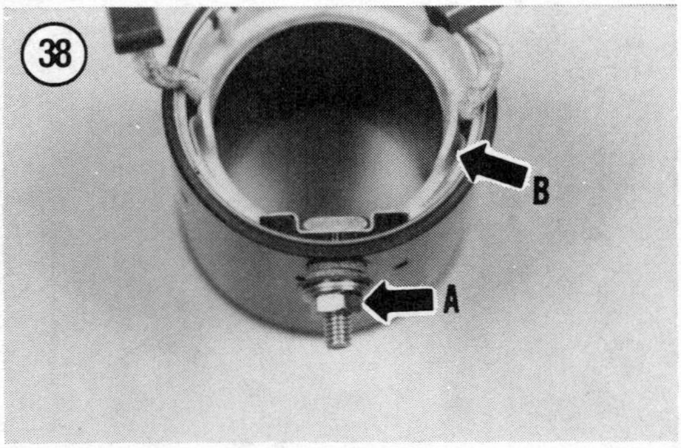

39

40

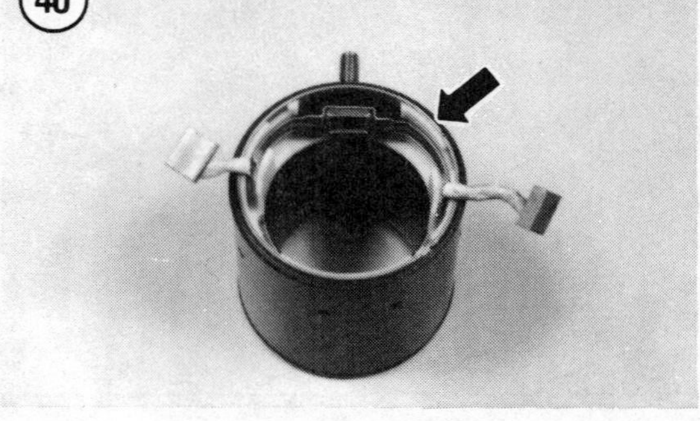

41

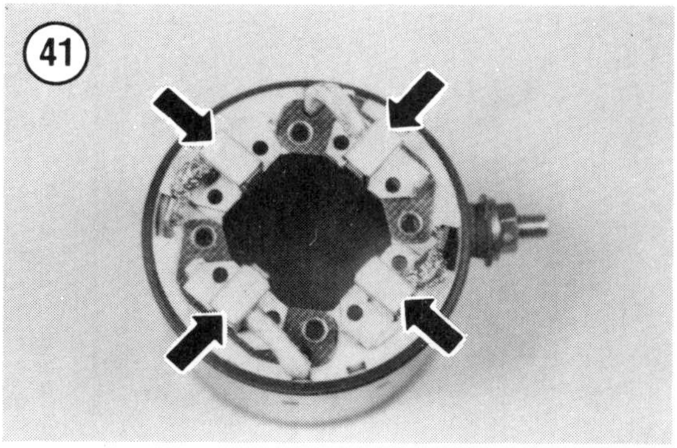

42

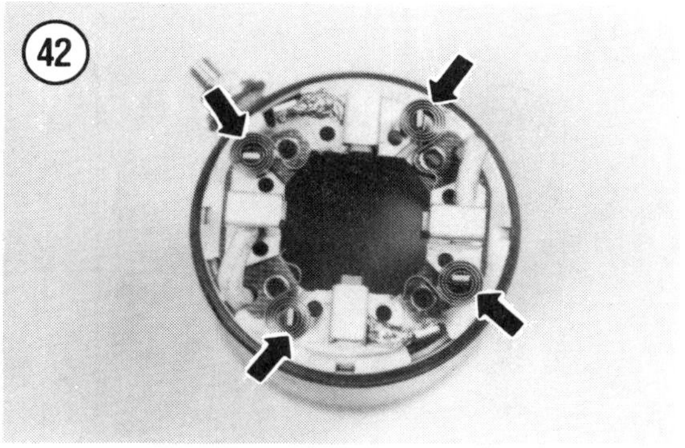

43

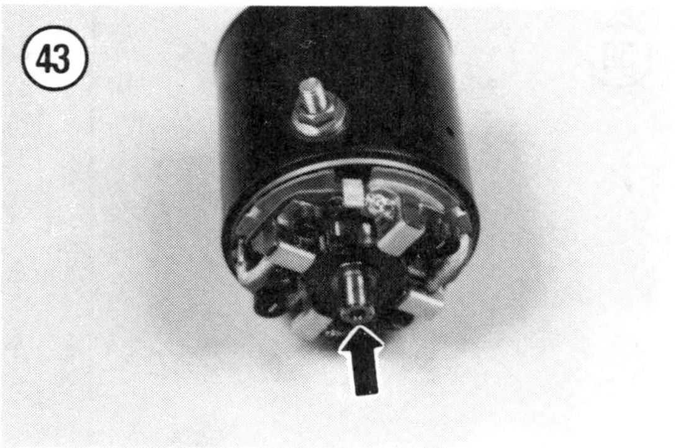

44

Assembly

1. Install the brush holder assembly (**Figure 39**).

NOTE
In the next step, reinstall all parts in the same order as noted during removal. This is essential in order to insulate this set of brushes from the case.

2. Install the O-ring, washers and nuts (A, **Figure 38**) securing the brush terminal set to the case.
3. Install the brush holder assembly (**Figure 37**) onto the end of the case. Align the holder locating tab with the case notch (**Figure 40**).
4. Install the brushes into their receptacles (**Figure 41**).
5. Install the brush springs (**Figure 42**) but do not place them against the brushes at this time.
6. Insert the armature coil assembly (**Figure 43**) into the front end of the case. Do not damage the brushes during this step.
7. Bring the end of the spring up and onto the backside of the brush. Refer to **Figure 44** and **Figure 45** for correct spring-to-brush installation. Repeat for all remaining brushes.
8. Install the washers (**Figure 35**) onto the armature end of the shaft.
9. Align the raised tab on the brush holder with the locating notch (**Figure 46**) in the rear cover and install the rear cover.

45

46

10. Align the raised marks (**Figure 47**) on the rear cover with the case.
11. Install the shims and special washer (**Figure 34**) onto the front cover end of the shaft.
12. Install the front cover (A, **Figure 48**), then the case screws and washers (B, **Figure 48**). Tighten the screws securely.

Inspection

1. Measure the length of each brush (**Figure 49**) with a vernier caliper. If the length is 6.0 mm (0.20 in.) or less for any one of the brushes, the brush holder assembly and brush terminal set must be replaced. The brushes cannot be replaced individually.
2. Inspect the commutator (**Figure 50**). The mica in a good commutator is below the surface of the copper bars. On a worn commutator the mica and copper bars may be worn to the same level (**Figure 51**). If necessary, have the commutator serviced by a dealer or electrical repair shop.
3. Inspect the commutator copper bars for discoloration. If a pair of bars are discolored, the armature may be grounded.
4. Use an ohmmeter and perform the following:
   a. Check for continuity between the commutator bars (**Figure 52**); there should be continuity (indicated resistance) between pairs of bars.
   b. Check for continuity between the commutator bars and the shaft (**Figure 53**); there should be *no* continuity (infinite resistance).
   c. If the unit fails either of these tests, the starter assembly must be replaced. The armature is not available separately.
5. Use an ohmmeter and perform the following:
   a. Check for continuity between the starter cable terminal and the starter case; there should be continuity (indicated resistance).

47

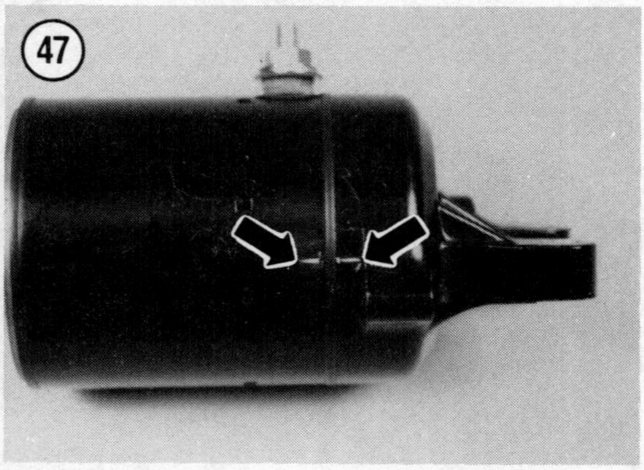

48

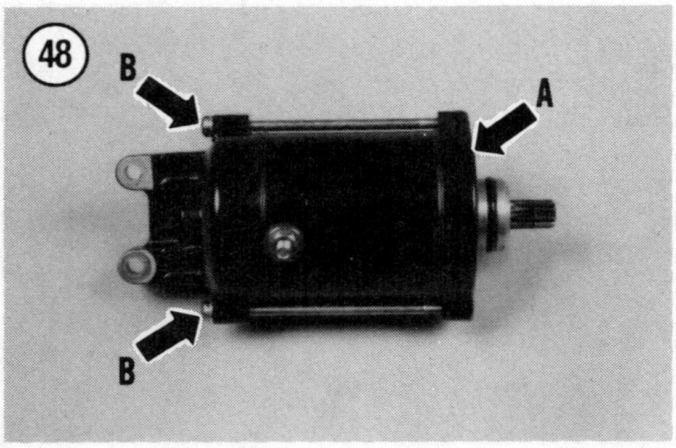

49

50

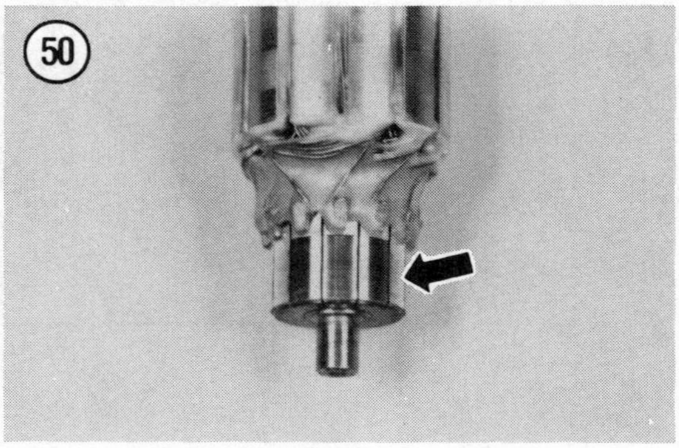

51

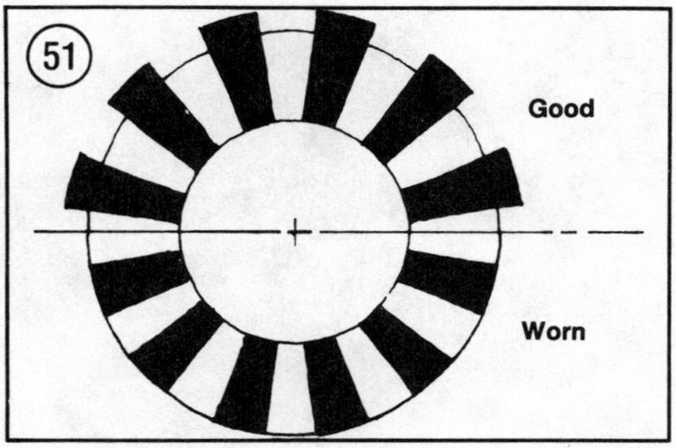

52

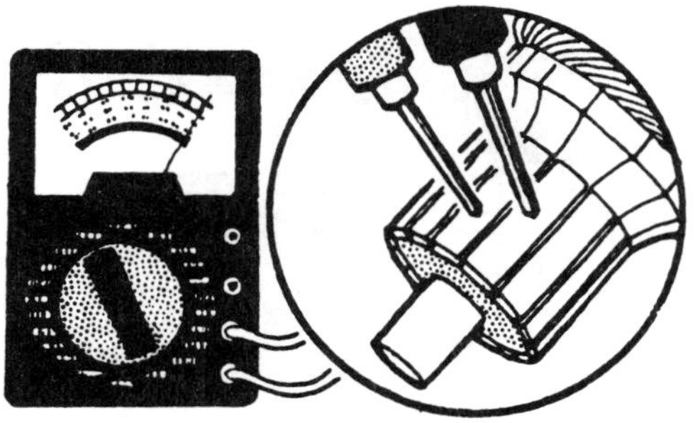

53

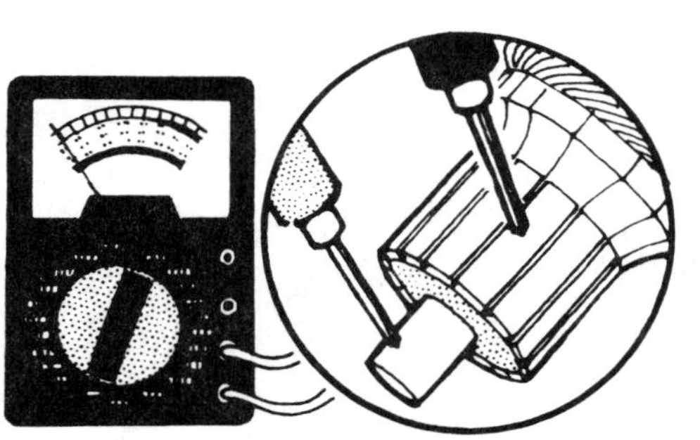

54

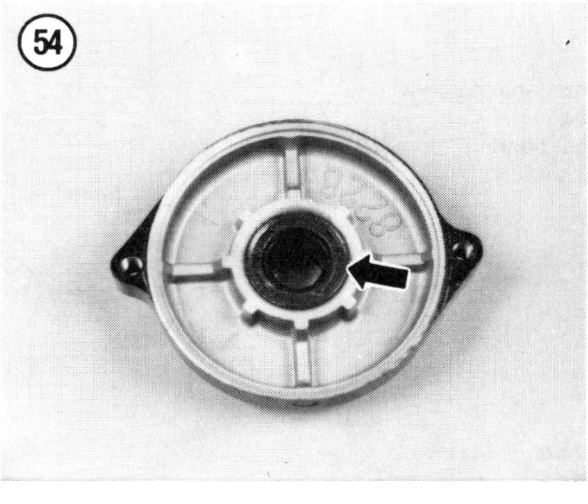

b. Check for continuity between the starter cable terminal and the brush wire terminal; there should be *no* continuity (infinite resistance).

c. If the unit fails either of these tests, the starter assembly must be replaced. The case/field coil is not available separately.

6. Inspect the oil seal and bushing **(Figure 54)** in the front cover for wear or damage. If either is damaged, replace the starter assembly as these parts are not available separately.

7. Inspect the bushing **(Figure 55)** in the rear cover for wear or damage. If it is damaged, replace the starter assembly as this part is not available separately.

STARTER SOLENOID

Testing

1. Remove the seat as described under *Seat Removal/Installation* in Chapter Twelve.
2. Remove the battery as described under *Battery Removal, Installation and Electrolyte Level Check* in Chapter Three.
3. Reconnect the battery to the battery terminals with jumper cables. Make sure the electrical contacts are good otherwise the results of this test will be inaccurate.
4. Disconnect the electrical wire going from the starter solenoid to the starter. Leave the other electrical wire connected to the solenoid.
5. Shift the transmission into NEUTRAL.
6. Turn the ignition switch on.
7. Pull in on the clutch lever until it bottoms out.
8. Press the START button.
9. Have an assistant connect an ohmmeter between the positive and negative terminals on top of the solenoid and check for continuity. If there is continuity (low resistance), the solenoid is okay. If there is no continuity (infinite resistance), the solenoid is faulty; proceed to Step 10.

55

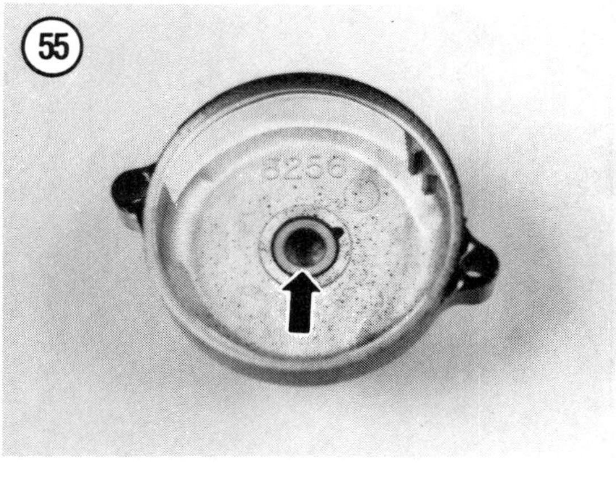

8

10. Disconnect the 2 small electrical wires from the top of the solenoid. Connect an ohmmeter to these small terminals (**Figure 56**) and check the resistance. The specified resistance is 3-5 ohms. If the resistance is not within specified range, the solenoid is faulty and must be replaced.
11. If the solenoid checks out okay, install all electrical wires to the solenoid, and tighten the nuts on the large terminals. Make sure the electrical connectors are on tight and that the rubber boot is properly installed to keep out moisture.
12. Install the battery as described under *Battery Removal, Installation and Electrolyte Level Check* in Chapter Three.
13. Install the seat as described under *Seat Removal/Installation* in Chapter Twelve.

56

57

HEADLIGHT ASSEMBLY

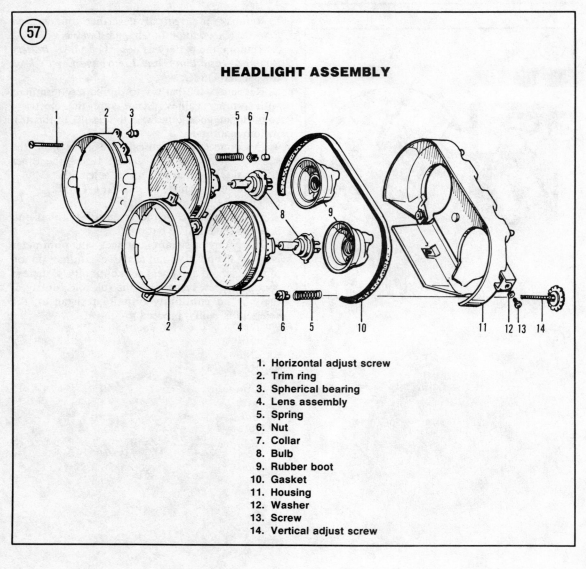

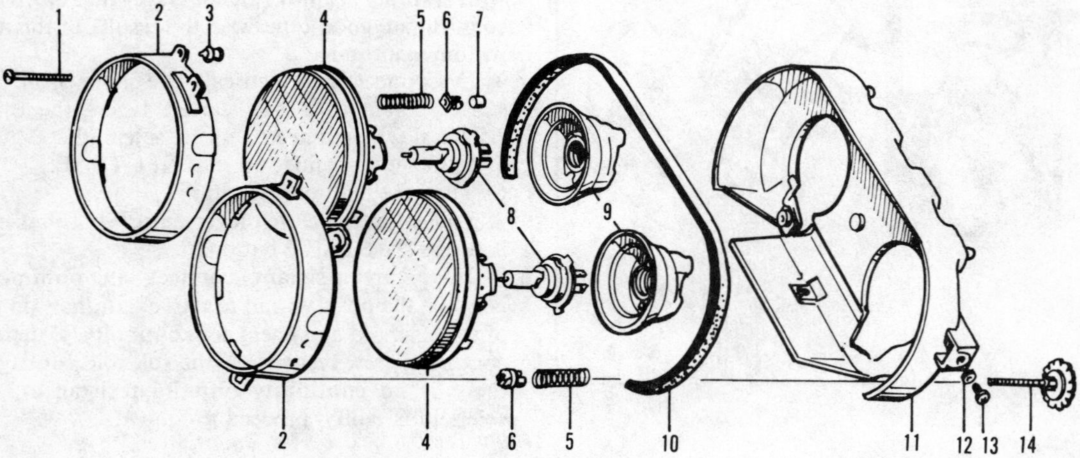

1. Horizontal adjust screw
2. Trim ring
3. Spherical bearing
4. Lens assembly
5. Spring
6. Nut
7. Collar
8. Bulb
9. Rubber boot
10. Gasket
11. Housing
12. Washer
13. Screw
14. Vertical adjust screw

Removal/Installation

1. Remove the seat as described under *Seat Removal/Installation* in Chapter Twelve.
2. Remove the battery as described under *Battery Removal, Installation and Electrolyte Level Check* in Chapter Three.

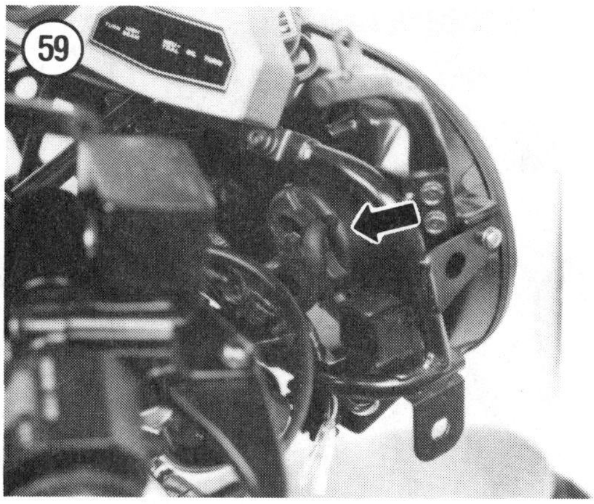

3. Slide off the rubber protective boots and disconnect the large electrical wires from the top terminals of the solenoid.
4. Disconnect the 2 small electrical wires from the top of the solenoid.
5. Remove the screws securing the solenoid to the frame and remove the solenoid.
6. Replace by reversing these removal steps, noting the following.
7. Install all electrical wires to the solenoid, and tighten the nuts on the large terminals securely. Make sure the electrical connectors are on tight and that the rubber boot is properly installed to keep out moisture.

LIGHTING SYSTEM

The lighting system consists of a headlight, taillight/brakelight, directional lights, indicator lights and a speedometer illumination light. **Table 2** lists replacement bulbs for these components.

Always use the correct wattage bulb as indicated in this section. The use of a larger wattage bulb will give a dim light and a smaller wattage bulb will burn out prematurely.

8

Headlight Replacement

Refer to **Figure 57** for this procedure.

NOTE
This procedure is shown with the front fairing removed for clarity. It is not necessary to remove the front fairing to replace either headlight bulb.

1. Disconnect the electrical connector (**Figure 58**) from the backside of the bulb.
2. Remove the rubber cover (**Figure 59**) from the back of the headlight bulb.

CAUTION
Carefully read all instructions shipped with the replacement quartz bulb. Do not touch the bulb glass with your fingers because any traces of skin oil on the quartz halogen bulb will create hot spots which will drastically reduce bulb life. Clean any traces of oil from the bulb with a cloth moistened in alcohol or lacquer thinner.

3. Unhook the clip (**Figure 60**) and remove the light bulb. Replace with a new bulb.
4. Install by reversing the removal steps.

Headlight Lens and Housing Removal/Installation

1. Remove the front fairing as described under *Front Fairing Removal/Installation* in Chapter Twelve.
2. Remove the headlight bulb as described in this chapter.
3. To remove the headlight lens, perform the following:
   a. Completely unscrew the vertical adjust screw (**Figure 61**) and spring.
   b. Completely unscrew the horizontal adjust screw (**Figure 62**) and spring.
   c. Remove the headlight lens and trim ring assembly from the headlight housing.
4. Remove the screw and washer on each side securing the headlight housing to the front fairing mounting bracket and remove the housing assembly.
5. Install by reversing these removal steps.
6. Adjust the headlight as described in this chapter.

Headlight Adjustment

NOTE
This procedure is shown with the front fairing removed for clarity. It is not necessary to remove the front fairing to adjust the headlight.

Adjust the headlight horizontally and vertically according to Department of Motor Vehicles regulations in your area.

To adjust the headlight horizontally, turn the screw (**Figure 62**). Turn the screw either clockwise or counterclockwise until the aim is correct.

For vertical adjustment, turn the knob (**Figure 61**). Turn the knob either clockwise or counterclockwise until the aim is correct.

Taillight/Brake Light Replacement (GSX-R750R Limited Edition)

Refer to **Figure 63** for this procedure.

1. Remove the screws securing the lens and remove the lens and gasket.
2. Wash out the inside and outside of the lens with a mild detergent and wipe dry.
3. Inspect the lens gasket and replace it if damaged or deteriorated.
4. Replace the bulb and install the lens; do not overtighten the screws as the lens may crack.

Taillight/Brake Light Replacement (All Models Except GSX-R750R Limited Edition)

1. Remove the seat as described under *Seat Removal/Installation* in Chapter Twelve.
2. Disconnect the electrical connector (**Figure 64**) going to the taillight/brake light bulb socket.

61

62

64

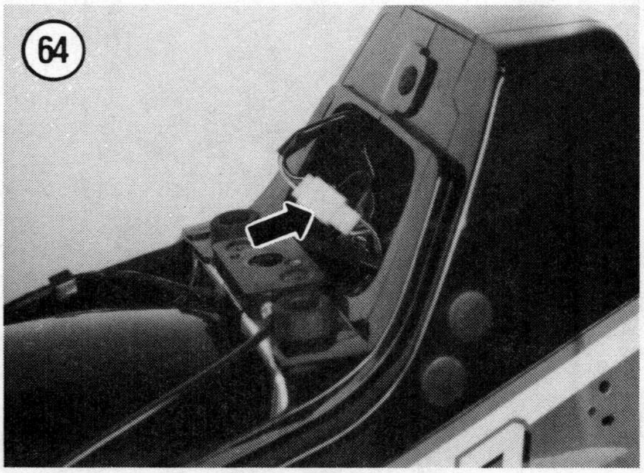

(63)

TAILLIGHT/BRAKELIGHT/ LICENSE PLATE LIGHT (GSX-R750R LIMITED EDITION)

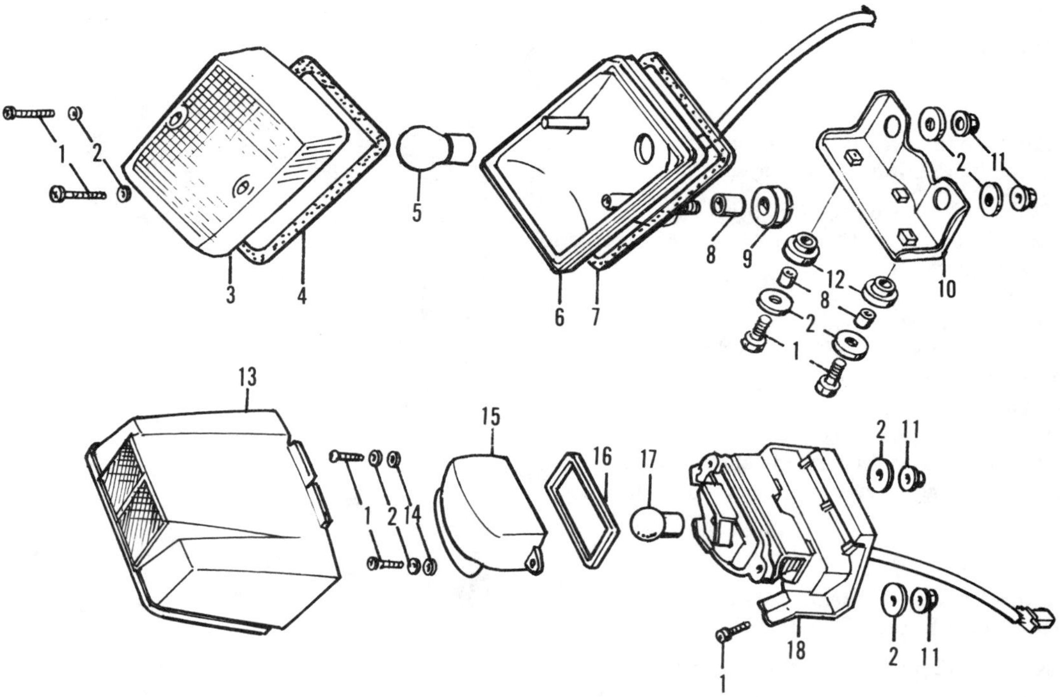

1. Screw
2. Washer
3. Taillight/brake light lens
4. Gasket
5. Bulb
6. Housing
7. Gasket
8. Collar
9. Rubber grommet
10. Mounting bracket
11. Nut
12. Rubber cushion
13. License plate light cover
14. Washer
15. License plate lens
16. Gasket
17. Bulb
18. Housing

NOTE
***Figure 65** is shown with the rear fender panel removed from the frame for clarity. It is not necessary to remove the rear fender panel to remove the bulb/socket assembly.*

3. Reach into the rear fender panel, turn and remove the bulb/socket assembly (**Figure 65**) from the backside of the taillight/brake light lens assembly.
4. Replace the bulb and install the bulb/socket assembly. Make sure it is tightened securely to prevent the entry of moisture.

65

License Plate Light Replacement (GSX-R750R Limited Edition)

Refer to **Figure 63** for this procedure.

1. Remove the screws securing the cover and remove the cover.
2. Remove the screws securing the lens and remove the lens and gasket.
3. Wash out the inside and outside of the lens with a mild detergent and wipe dry.
4. Inspect the lens gasket and replace it if it is damaged or deteriorated.
5. Replace the bulb and install the lens; do not overtighten the screws as the lens may crack.

67

License Plate Light Replacement (All Models Except GSX-R750R Limited Edition)

Refer to **Figure 66** for this procedure.

1. Remove the screws securing the cover (**Figure 67**) and remove the cover.
2. Remove the screws securing the lens and remove the lens and gasket.
3. Wash out the inside and outside of the lens with a mild detergent and wipe dry.
4. Inspect the lens gasket and replace it if damaged or deteriorated.
5. Replace the bulb and install the lens; do not overtighten the screws as the lens may crack.

68

Directional Signal Light Replacement

1. Remove the screws securing the lens and remove the lens. Refer to **Figure 68** or **Figure 69**.
2. Wash out the inside and outside of the lens with a mild detergent and wipe dry.
3. Replace the bulb and install the lens; do not overtighten the screws as the lens may crack.

69

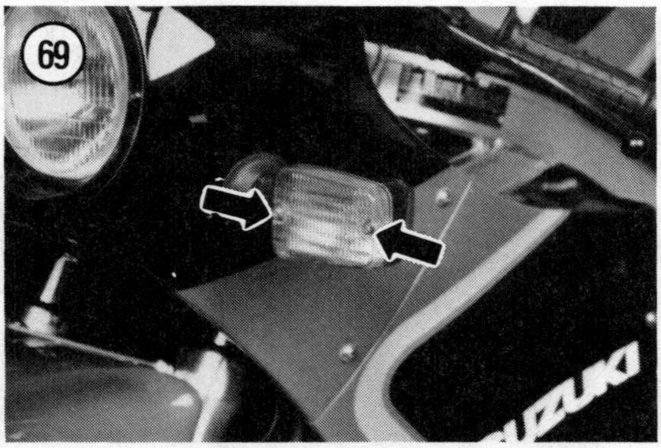

66

TAILLIGHT/BRAKELIGHT/ LICENSE PLATE LIGHT (ALL MODELS EXCEPT GSX-R750R LIMITED EDITION)

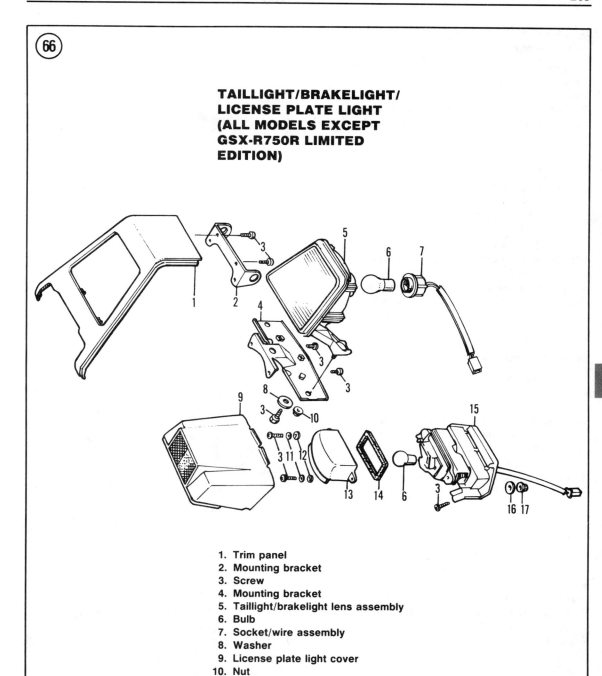

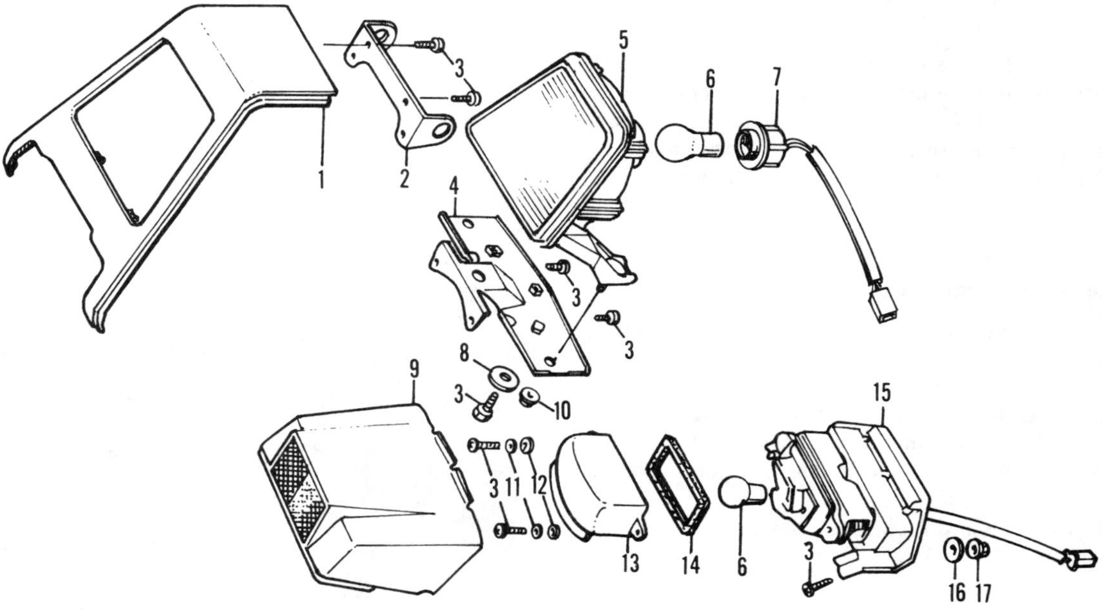

1. Trim panel
2. Mounting bracket
3. Screw
4. Mounting bracket
5. Taillight/brakelight lens assembly
6. Bulb
7. Socket/wire assembly
8. Washer
9. License plate light cover
10. Nut
11. Lockwasher
12. Washer
13. License plate light lens
14. Gasket
15. Housing
16. Washer
17. Nut

8

Speedometer and Tachometer Illumination Light Replacement

1. Remove the front fairing as described under *Front Fairing Removal/Installation* in Chapter Twelve.
2. Carefully pull the defective lamp holder/electrical wire assembly **(Figure 70)** from the backside of the housing.
3. Remove and replace the defective bulb.

NOTE
If a new bulb will not work, check the wire connections for loose or broken wires. Also check the bulb socket for corrosion. Replace as necessary.

4. Push the lamp socket/electrical wire assembly back into the housing. Make sure it is completely seated to prevent the entry of water and moisture.
5. Install the front fairing as described under *Front Fairing Removal/Installation* in Chapter Twelve.

Indicator Light Replacement

1. Remove the instrument cluster assembly as described under *Instrument Cluster Removal/Installation* in this chapter.
2. Carefully pull the lamp holder/electrical wire assembly down and out of the backside of the indicator panel on the backside of the instrument cluster.
3. Remove and replace the defective bulb.

NOTE
If a new bulb will not work, check the wire connections for loose or broken wires. Also check the bulb socket for corrosion. Replace as necessary.

4. Push the lamp socket/electrical wire assembly back into the panel. Make sure it is completely seated to prevent the entry of water and moisture.
5. Install the instrument cluster assembly as described under *Instrument Cluster Removal/Installation* in this chapter.

SWITCHES

Ignition Switch Continuity Test

The ignition switch cannot be separated. If either the electrical or mechanical portion of the switch becomes defective, the entire switch assembly must be replaced.

1. Remove the front fairing as described under *Front Fairing Removal/Installation* in Chapter Twelve.
2. In front of the instrument cluster, locate the ignition switch 4-pin electrical connector containing 4 wires (1 red, 1 orange, 1 gray and 1 brown). Disconnect this electrical connector **(Figure 71)**.
3. Use an ohmmeter and check for continuity. Connect the test leads to the ignition switch side of the electrical connector as follows:
   a. Turn the ignition switch on: there should be continuity (low resistance) between the red and orange wires and between the gray and brown wires.
   b. Turn the ignition switch off: there should be *no* continuity (infinite resistance) between any of these wires.
   c. Turn the ignition switch to the "P" position: there should be continuity (low resistance) between the red and brown wires.

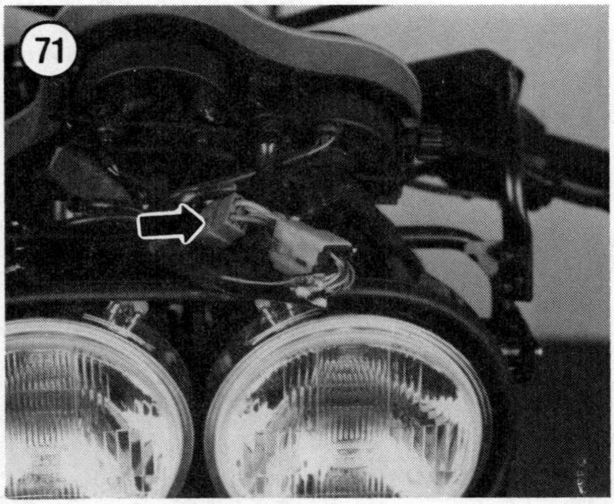

4. If the ignition switch fails any one of these tests, the switch must be replaced as described in this chapter.
5. Reconnect the 4-pin electrical connector. Make sure the electrical connector is free of corrosion and is tight.
6. Install the front fairing as described under *Front Fairing Removal/Installation* in Chapter Twelve.

Ignition Switch Removal/Installation

1. Remove the front fairing as described under *Front Fairing Removal/Installation* in Chapter Twelve.
2. In front of the instrument cluster, locate the ignition switch 4-pin electrical connector containing 4 wires (1 red, 1 orange, 1 gray and 1 brown). Disconnect this electrical connector (**Figure 71**).
3. Remove the mounting screws and washers securing the ignition switch (**Figure 72**) to the upper fork bridge.

4. Remove the switch assembly from the upper fork bridge.
5. Install the new ignition switch onto the upper fork bridge and tighten the screws securely.
6. Reconnect the 4-pin electrical connector. Make sure the electrical connector is free of corrosion and is tight.
7. Install the front fairing as described under *Front Fairing Removal/Installation* in Chapter Twelve.

Right-hand Combination Switch (Engine Start and Stop Switch) Testing

The right-hand combination switch assembly contains both the engine start and engine stop switch. If either switch is faulty, the entire switch assembly must be replaced.
1. Remove the seat as described under *Seat Removal/Installation* in Chapter Twelve.
2. Remove the fuel tank as described under *Fuel Tank Removal/Installation* in Chapter Seven.
3. Unhook the tie wrap and locate the engine start and stop switch 6-pin electrical connector containing 5 wires (1 orange/black, 1 orange/white, 1 gray, 1 orange/blue and 1 orange/red). Disconnect this electrical connector (**Figure 73**).
4. Unhook the single electrical connector on the yellow/green wire. This wire goes from the start switch to the starter interlock switch at the clutch lever.
5. Use an ohmmeter and check for continuity. Connect the test leads to the right-hand combination switch side of the electrical connector as follows:
   a. Turn the engine stop switch to the RUN position: there should be continuity (low resistance) between the orange and the orange/white wires.
   b. Turn the engine stop switch to the OFF position: there should be *no* continuity (infinite resistance) between the orange, orange/white or yellow/green wires.
   c. Press the START switch: there should be continuity (low resistance) between the orange/white and the yellow/green wires.
6. If the right-hand combination switch fails any one of these tests, the switch must be replaced as described in this chapter.
7. Reconnect the 6-pin electrical connector containing 5 wires and the single electrical connector on the yellow/green wire.

8. Make sure the electrical connectors are free of corrosion and are tight. Install the tie wrap to hold the electrical wires to the front of the frame. The wires must be retained in this manner to allow room of the fuel tank.
9. Install the fuel tank as described under *Fuel Tank Removal/Installation* in Chapter Seven.
10. Install the seat as described under *Seat Removal/Installation* in Chapter Twelve.

Right-hand Combination Switch (Engine Start and Stop Switch) Removal/Installation

The right-hand combination switch assembly contains both the engine start and engine stop switch. If either switch is faulty the entire switch assembly must be replaced.

1. Remove the seat as described under *Seat Removal/Installation* in Chapter Twelve.
2. Remove the fuel tank as described under *Fuel Tank Removal/Installation* in Chapter Seven.
3. Unhook the tie wrap and locate the engine start and stop switch 6-pin electrical connector containing 5 wires (1 orange/black, 1 orange/white, 1 gray, 1 orange/blue and 1 orange/red). Disconnect this electrical connector (**Figure 73**).
4. Unhook the single electrical connector on the yellow/green wire. This wire goes from the start switch to the starter interlock switch at the clutch lever.
5. Unhook the single electrical connector on the yellow/white wire. This wire goes from the 6-pin electrical connector to the headlight dimmer switch.
6. Remove the electrical wire harness from any clips on the frame and carefully pull the harness out from the frame.
7. Remove the screws securing the right-hand combination switch together and remove the switch assembly (**Figure 74**).
8. Install a new switch and tighten the screws securely. Do not overtighten the screws or the plastic switch housing may crack.
9. Reconnect the 6-pin electrical connector containing 5 wires and the 2 single electrical connectors.
10. Make sure the electrical connectors are free of corrosion and are tight. Install the tie wrap to hold the electrical wires to the front of the frame. The wires must be retained in this manner to allow room of the fuel tank.
11. Install the fuel tank as described under *Fuel Tank Removal/Installation* in Chapter Seven.
12. Install the seat as described under *Seat Removal/Installation* in Chapter Twelve.

Left-hand Combination Switch (Headlight Dimmer Switch, Turn Signal Switch and Horn Switch) Testing

The left-hand combination switch assembly contains the headlight dimmer switch, turn signal switch and the horn switch.

If any of the switches are faulty,the entire switch assembly must be replaced.

1. Remove the seat as described under *Seat Removal/Installation* in Chapter Twelve.
2. Remove the fuel tank as described under *Fuel Tank Removal/Installatton* in Chapter Seven.
3. Unhook the tie wrap and locate the engine start and stop switch 8-pin electrical connector containing 8 wires (1 white, 1 yellow, 1 black, 1 black/white, 1 black, 1 light blue, 1 light green and 1 orange/red). Disconnect this electrical connector (**Figure 73**).

NOTE
In the following tests, connect the test leads to the left-hand combination switch side of the electrical connector.

4. To test the headlight dimmer switch, perform the following:
   a. Use an ohmmeter and check for continuity.
   b. Turn the headlight dimmer switch to the HI position: there should be continuity (low resistance) between the yellow and the yellow/white wires.
   c. Turn the headlight dimmer switch to the LO position: there should be continuity (low resistance) between the black and the light blue wires.
5. To test the turn signal switch, perform the following:
   a. Use an ohmmeter and check for continuity.
   b. Turn the turn signal switch to the "R" position: there should be continuity (low resistance) between the light blue and the light green wires.

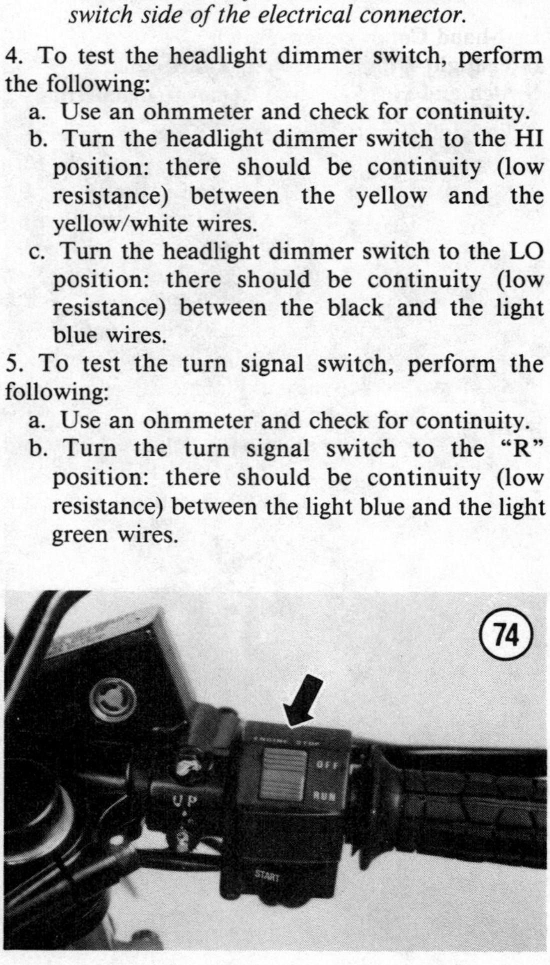

c. Turn the turn signal switch to the "L" position: there should be continuity (low resistance) between the black and the light blue wires.

6. To test the horn switch, perform the following:
   a. Use an ohmmeter and check for continuity.
   b. Press the HORN button: there should be continuity (low resistance) between the green and the black/white wires.

7. If the left-hand combination switch fails any one of these tests, the switch must be replaced as described in this chapter.

8. Reconnect the 8-pin electrical connector.

9. Make sure the electrical connector is free of corrosion and is tight. Install the tie wrap to hold the electrical wires to the front of the frame. The wires must be retained in this manner to allow room for the fuel tank.

10. Install the fuel tank as described under *Fuel Tank Removal/Installation* in Chapter Seven.

11. Install the seat as described under *Seat Removal/Installation* in Chapter Twelve.

Left-hand Combination Switch (Headlight Dimmer Switch, Turn Signal Switch and Horn Switch) Removal/Installation

The left-hand combination switch assembly contains both the headlight dimmer switch, turn signal switch and horn switch. If any of the switches are faulty the entire switch assembly must be replaced.

1. Remove the seat as described under *Seat Removal/Installation* in Chapter Twelve.

2. Remove the fuel tank as described under *Fuel Tank Removal/Installation* in Chapter Seven.

3. Unhook the tie wrap and locate the engine start and stop switch 8-pin electrical connector containing 8 wires (1 white, 1 yellow, 1 black, 1 black/white, 1 black, 1 light blue, 1 light green and 1 orange/red). Disconnect this electrical connector (**Figure 73**).

4. Remove the screws securing the right-hand combination switch together and remove the switch assembly (**Figure 75**).

5. Remove the electrical wire harness from any clips on the frame and carefully pull the harness out from the frame.

6. Install a new switch and tighten the screws securely. Do not overtighten the screws or the plastic switch housing may crack.

7. Reconnect the 8-pin electrical connector.

8. Make sure the electrical connector is free of corrosion and is tight. Install the tie wrap to hold the electrical wires to the front of the frame. The wires must be retained in this manner to allow room for the fuel tank.

9. Install the fuel tank as described under *Fuel Tank Removal/Installation* in Chapter Seven.

10. Install the seat as described under *Seat Removal/Installation* in Chapter Twelve.

Starter Interlock Switch (Clutch Lever) Testing

1. Remove the seat as described under *Seat Removal/Installation* in Chapter Twelve.

2. Remove the fuel tank as described under *Fuel Tank Removal/Installation* in Chapter Seven.

3. Unhook the tie wrap and locate the starter interlock switch's 2 individual yellow/green wires. Disconnect these 2 individual electrical connectors (**Figure 73**).

4. Use an ohmmeter and check for continuity. Connect the test leads to the starter interlock switch side of the electrical connectors as follows:
   a. Squeeze the clutch lever to the fully applied position: there should be continuity (low resistance) between the 2 yellow/green wires.
   b. Release the clutch lever: there should be no continuity (infinite resistance) between the 2 yellow/green wires.

5. If the starter interlock switch fails any one of these tests, the switch must be replaced as described in this chapter.

6. Reconnect the 2 individual electrical connectors.

7. Make sure the electrical connectors are free of corrosion and are tight. Install the tie wrap to hold the electrical wires to the front of the frame. The wires must be retained in this manner to allow room for the fuel tank.

8. Install the fuel tank as described under *Fuel Tank Removal/Installation* in Chapter Seven.

9. Install the seat as described under *Seat Removal/Installation* in Chapter Twelve.

Starter Interlock Switch (Clutch Lever) Removal/Installation

1. Remove the seat as described under *Seat Removal/Installation* in Chapter Twelve.
2. Remove the fuel tank as described under *Fuel Tank Removal/Installation* in Chapter Seven.
3. Unhook the tie wrap and locate the starter interlock switch's 2 individual yellow/green wires. Disconnect these 2 individual electrical connectors (**Figure 73**).
4. Remove the screws securing the starter interlock switch to the clutch lever housing and remove the switch assembly (**Figure 76**).
5. Remove the electrical wire harness from any clips on the frame and carefully pull the harness out from the frame.
6. Install a new switch and tighten the screws securely.
7. Reconnect the 2 individual electrical connectors.
8. Make sure the electrical connectors are free of corrosion and are tight. Install the tie wrap to hold the electrical wires to the front of the frame. The wires must be retained in this manner to allow room for the fuel tank.
9. Install the fuel tank as described under *Fuel Tank Removal/Installation* in Chapter Seven.
10. Install the seat as described under *Seat Removal/Installation* in Chapter Twelve.

Front Brake Light Switch Testing

1. Remove the seat as described under *Seat Removal/Installation* in Chapter Twelve.
2. Remove the fuel tank as described under *Fuel Tank Removal/Installation* in Chapter Seven.
3. Unhook the tie wrap and locate the front brake light switch individual orange/green and white/black wires. Disconnect these 2 individual electrical connectors (**Figure 73**).
4. Use an ohmmeter and check for continuity. Connect the test leads to the front brake light switch side of the electrical connectors as follows:
   a. Squeeze the front brake lever to the fully applied position: there should be continuity (low resistance) between the orange/green and the white/black wires.
   b. Release the clutch lever: there should be no continuity (infinite resistance) between the orange/green and white/black wires.
5. If the front brake lever switch fails any one of these tests, the switch must be replaced as described in this chapter.
6. Reconnect the 2 individual electrical connectors.
7. Make sure the electrical connectors are free of corrosion and are tight. Install the tie wrap to hold the electrical wires to the front of the frame. The wires must be retained in this manner to allow room for the fuel tank.
8. Install the fuel tank as described under *Fuel Tank Removal/Installation* in Chapter Seven.
9. Install the seat as described under *Seat Removal/Installation* in Chapter Twelve.

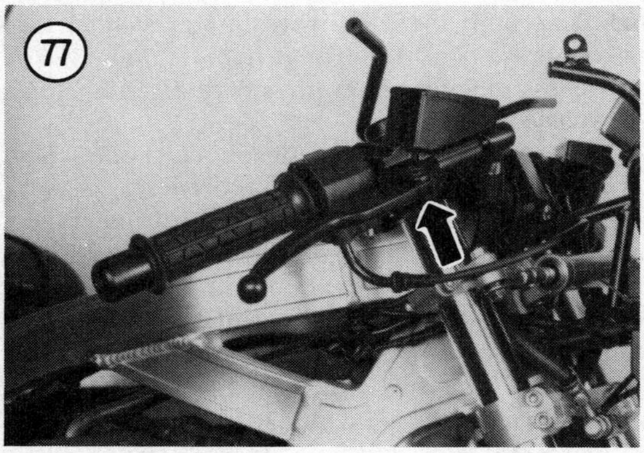

Front Brake Light Switch Removal/Installation

1. Remove the seat as described under *Seat Removal/Installation* in Chapter Twelve.
2. Remove the fuel tank as described under *Fuel Tank Removal/Installation* in Chapter Seven.
3. Unhook the tie wrap and locate the front brake light switch individual orange/green and white/black wires. Disconnect these 2 individual electrical connectors (**Figure 73**).
4. Remove the screws securing the front brake light switch to the front brake lever housing and remove the switch assembly (**Figure 77**).
5. Remove the electrical wire harness from any clips on the frame and carefully pull the harness out from the frame.
6. Install a new switch and tighten the screws securely.
7. Reconnect the 2 individual electrical connectors.
8. Make sure the electrical connectors are free of corrosion and are tight. Install the tie wrap to hold the electrical wires to the front of the frame. The wires must be retained in this manner to allow room of the fuel tank.

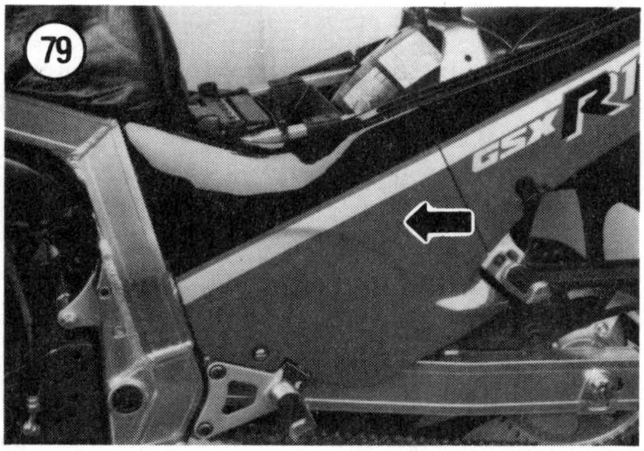

9. Install the fuel tank as described under *Fuel Tank Removal/Installation* in Chapter Seven.
10. Install the seat as described under *Seat Removal/Installation* in Chapter Twelve.

Rear Brake Light Switch Testing

The rear brake light switch is mounted on the backside of the rear master cylinder (**Figure 78**).

1. Disconnect the electrical connector wires going to the rear brake pedal switch.
2. Have an assistant apply the rear brake. Use an ohmmeter set at R×1 and connect the 2 leads of the ohmmeter to the electrical terminals on top of the rear brake light switch.
3. If the switch is good, there will be continuity (very low resistance).
4. If the switch fails to pass this test, the switch is faulty and must be replaced.
5. To remove the switch, refer to *Rear Master Cylinder Removal/Installation* in Chapter Eleven.
6. Install a new switch and adjust as described in this chapter.
7. Connect the electrical connector wires to the rear brake pedal switch.

Rear Brake Light Switch Adjustment

1. Turn the ignition switch to the ON position.
2. Depress the brake pedal. The brake light should come on just as the brake begins to work.
3. To make the brake light come on earlier, hold the brake light switch body and turn the adjusting nut *clockwise* as viewed from the top. Turn the adjusting nut *counterclockwise* to delay the light from coming on.

NOTE

Some riders prefer the brake light to come on a little early. This way, they can tap the pedal without braking to warn drivers who are following too closely.

Neutral Indicator Light Switch Testing

1. Remove the left-hand side cover (**Figure 79**).
2. Shift the transmission into NEUTRAL.
3. Unhook the tie-wrap (**Figure 80**) securing the electrical connectors and electrical wires to the frame.
4. Disconnect the neutral indicator light switch individual blue wire connector.

5. Use an ohmmeter and check for continuity. Connect one of the test leads to the blue wire on the neutral indicator switch side of the electrical connector (male side). Connect the other test lead to ground.
6. There should be continuity (low resistance) between the orange/green and the white/black wires.
7. If the switch is good, there will be continuity (very low resistance).
8. If the switch fails to pass this test, the switch is faulty and must be replaced.
9. Remove the switch as described in this chapter.
10. Reconnect the individual electrical connector.
11. Make sure the electrical connector is free of corrosion and is tight. Install the tie wrap to hold the electrical wires to the frame.
12. Install the left-hand side cover.

Neutral Switch Removal/Installation

1. Remove the lower section and both right and left-hand middle sections of the front fairing as described under *Front Fairing Removal/Installation* in Chapter Twelve.
2. Remove the left-hand side cover (**Figure 79**).
3. Remove the gearshift lever as follows:
   a. Remove the circlip (**Figure 81**) and the washer (**Figure 82**) securing the gearshift lever to the pivot post.
   b. Remove the bolt (**Figure 83**) securing the gearshift lever to the shift shaft and remove the gearshift lever assembly.

4A. On GSX-R750R Limited Edition models, remove the bolts securing the drive sprocket cover (**Figure 84**) and remove the cover.
4B. On all other models, remove the bolts securing the drive sprocket cover (**Figure 85**) and move the cover out of the way.
5. Remove the screws (A, **Figure 86**) securing the neutral switch and remove the neutral switch assembly.

NOTE
Step 6 and Step 7 are shown with the engine removed from the frame and partially disassembled for clarity. It is not necessary to remove the engine from the frame for this procedure.

6. Remove the O-ring (**Figure 87**) from the receptacle in the crankcase.
7. Don't lose the switch contact plunger and spring (**Figure 88**) from the end of the gearshift drum.

81
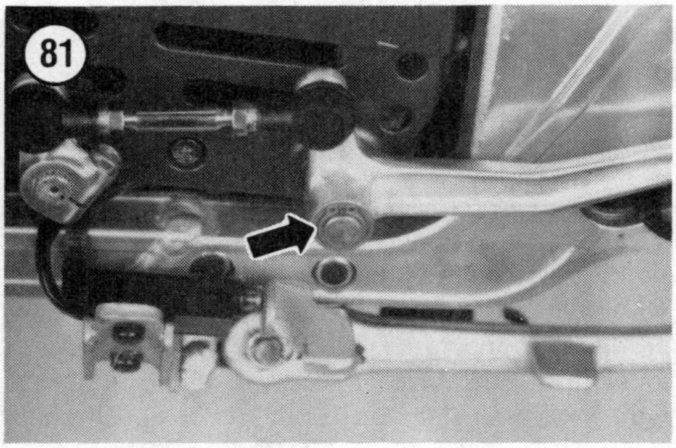

82
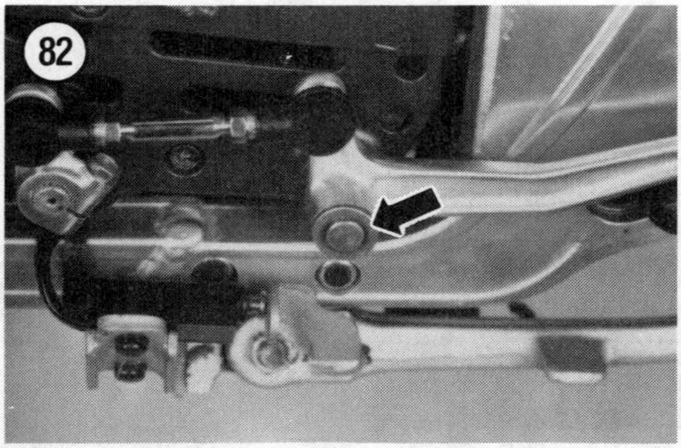

83
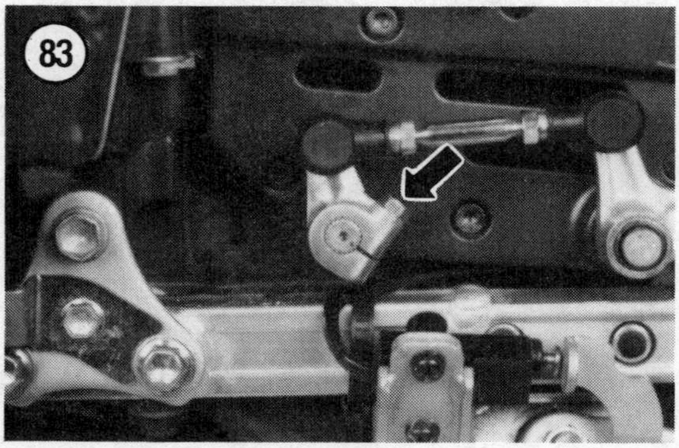

84
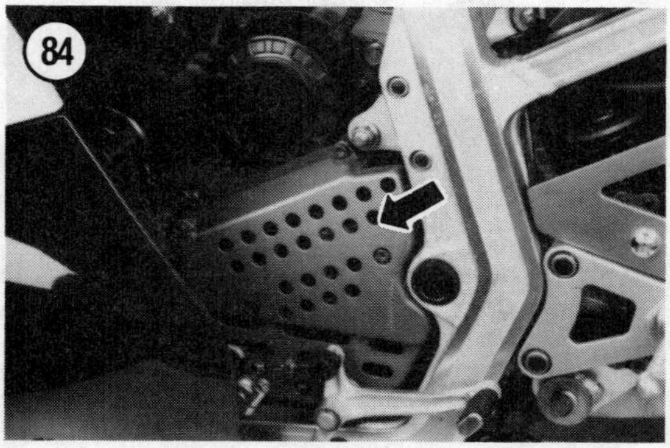

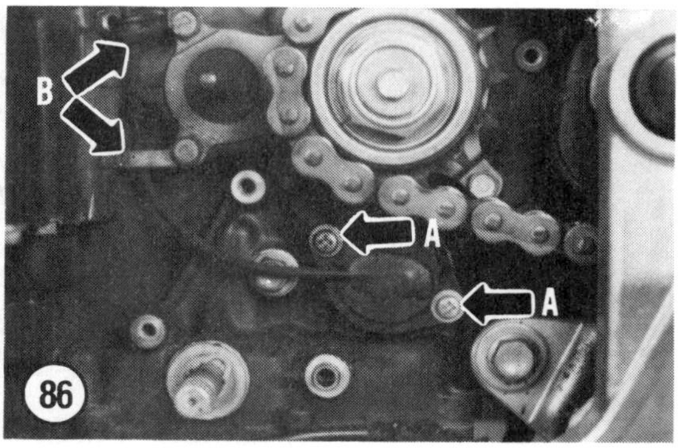

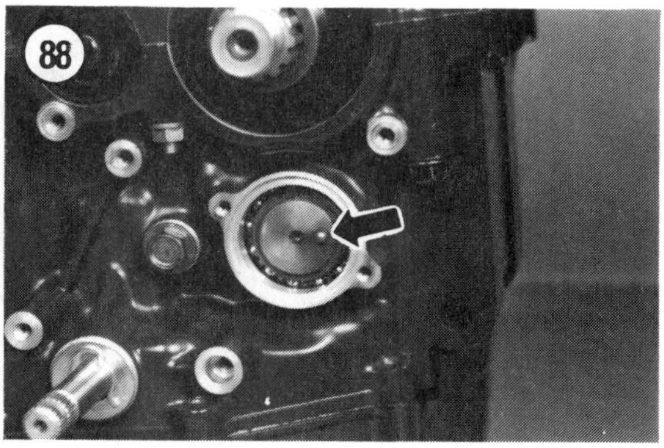

8. Carefully remove the electrical wire from the retaining loops (B, **Figure 86**) on the crankcase and pull the wire out from under the starter motor.
9. Install by reversing these removal steps, noting the following.
10. Install a new O-ring seal into the receptacle in the crankcase.
11. Make sure the electrical connector is free of corrosion and is tight. Install the tie wrap to hold the electrical wires to the frame.
12. Attach the tie wrap (**Figure 80**) securing the electrical wires to the frame.

Sidestand Check Switch Testing

1. Remove the left-hand side cover (**Figure 79**).
2. Unhook the tie wrap (**Figure 80**) securing the electrical connectors and electrical wires to the frame.
3. Disconnect the sidestand check switch 2-pin electrical connector containing 2 wires (1 green/white wire and 1 black/white wire).
4. Use an ohmmeter and check for continuity. Connect the test leads to the sidestand check switch side of the electrical connectors as follows:
   a. Place the sidestand in the down position: there should be continuity (low resistance) between the green/white and the black/white wires.
   b. Have an assistant hold the bike in the upright position, raise the sidestand and check for continuity: there should be no continuity (infinite resistance) between the green/white and black/white wires.
5. If the sidestand check switch fails either one of these tests, the switch must be replaced as described in this chapter.
6. Remove the switch as described in this chapter.
7. Reconnect the 2-pin electrical connector.
8. Reconnect the individual electrical connector.
9. Make sure the electrical connector is free of corrosion and is tight. Install the tie wrap to hold the electrical wires to the frame.
10. Install the left-hand side cover.

Sidestand Check Switch Removal/Installation

1. Remove the left-hand side cover (**Figure 79**).
2. Unhook the tie wrap (**Figure 80**) securing the electrical connectors and electrical wires to the frame.
3. Disconnect the sidestand check switch 2-pin electrical connector containing 2 wires (1 green/white wire and 1 black/white wire).

4. Unhook the tie wraps (**Figure 89**) securing the electrical wire harness to the frame.
5. Have an assistant hold the bike in the upright position.
6. Remove the screws (A, **Figure 90**) securing the sidestand check switch (B, **Figure 90**) to the frame and remove the switch.
7. Install a new sidestand check switch and tighten the screws securely.
8. Route the electrical wire harness through the frame and install the tie wraps securing the harness to the frame.
9. Reconnect the 2-pin electrical connector.
10. Make sure the electrical connector is free of corrosion and is tight. Install the tie wrap to hold the electrical wires to the frame.
11. Install the left-hand side cover.

Oil Pressure Switch Testing

NOTE
Prior to starting this test procedure, make sure the oil level is correct in the engine as described under ***Engine Oil Level Check*** *in Chapter Three. If the oil level is low it may give a false reading for the test.*

1. Start the engine and let it reach normal operating temperature. Usually 10-15 minutes of stop-and-go riding is sufficient. Shut off the engine.
2. Remove the left-hand side cover (**Figure 79**).
3. Unhook the tie-wrap (**Figure 80**) securing the electrical connectors and electrical wires to the frame.
4. Disconnect the oil pressure switch individual green/yellow wire connector.
5. Start the engine and let it idle.
6. Use an ohmmeter and check for continuity. Connect one of the test leads to the green/yellow wire on the oil pressure switch side of the electrical connector (male side). Connect the other test lead to ground.
7. There should be continuity (low resistance) between the green/yellow wire and ground.
8. Shut off the engine.
9. Use an ohmmeter and check for continuity. Connect the one of the test leads to the green/yellow wire on the oil pressure switch side of the electrical connector (male side). Connect the other test lead to ground.
10. There should be no continuity (infinite resistance) between the green/yellow wire and ground.
11. If the sidestand check switch fails either one of these tests, the switch must be replaced as described in this chapter.

12. Reconnect the individual electrical connector.
13. Make sure the electrical connector is free of corrosion and is tight. Install the tie wrap to hold the electrical wires to the frame.
14. Install the left-hand side cover.

Oil Pressure Switch Removal/Installation

1. Remove the lower section and both right and left-hand middle sections of the front fairing as described under *Front Fairing Removal/ Installation* in Chapter Twelve.
2. Remove the left-hand side cover (**Figure 79**).
3. Remove the bolts securing the signal generator cover (**Figure 91**). Remove the cover and gasket.

NOTE
In the following steps, the engine is shown removed from the frame and partially disassembled for clarity. It is not necessary to remove the engine nor disassemble it for this procedure.

4. Disconnect the oil pressure sending switch wire.
5. Unscrew the oil pressure switch (**Figure 92**) from the crankcase.
6. Apply a light coat of gasket sealer to the switch threads prior to installation. Install the switch and tighten securely.
7. Connect the oil pressure sending switch wire and tighten the screw securely.
8. Install a new gasket and install the signal generator cover. Tighten the screws securely.
9. Make sure all electrical connectors are free of corrosion and are tight.
10. Install the left-hand side cover (**Figure 79**).
11. Install both right and left-hand middle sections and the lower section of the front fairing as described under *Front Fairing Removal/ Installation* in Chapter Twelve.

93

94

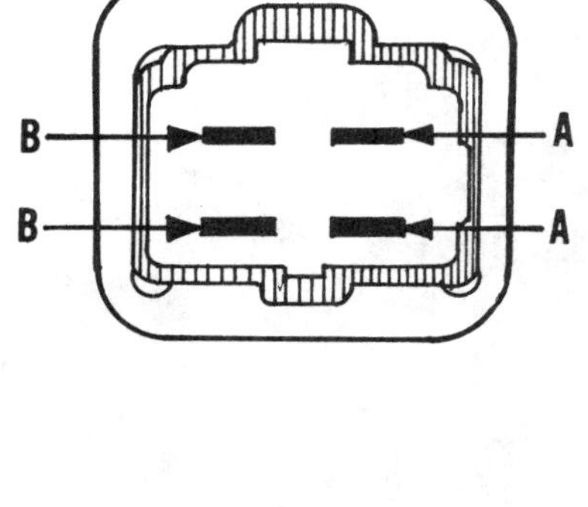

RELAYS (1100 CC MODELS)

Headlight Relay Removal/Installation and Testing

1. Remove the seat as described under *seat Removal/Installation* in Chapter Twelve.
2. Remove the fuel tank as described under *Fuel Tank Removal/Installation* in Chapter Seven.
3. Disconnect the electrical connector (A, **Figure 93**) from each headlight relay.
4. Unhook each headlight relay (B, **Figure 93**) from its rubber mount on the frame and remove both relays.
5. Connect a 12-volt battery to terminals A, **Figure 94** on the relay.
6. With the battery connected to terminals A, use an ohmmeter and check for continuity. Connect the test leads to terminals B, **Figure 94** of the relay: there should be continuity (low resistance) between terminals B, **Figure 94**.
7. If there is no continuity (infinite resistance) the relay is defective and must be replaced.
8. If the existing relay(s) checks out okay, reinstall the old relay. If the relay(s) is defective, install a new relay(s).
9. Reconnect the electrical connector to each relay.
10. Make sure the electrical connectors are free of corrosion and are tight.
11. Install the fuel tank as described under *Fuel Tank Removal/Installation* in Chapter Seven.
12. Install the seat as described under *Seat Removal/Installation* in Chapter Twelve.

8

NEAS Relay
Removal/Installation and Testing

NOTE
This procedure is shown with the front fairing removed for clarity. It is not necessary to remove the front fairing for this procedure.

1. Disconnect the electrical connector from the NEAS relay (**Figure 95**).
2. Unhook the NEAS relay from its rubber mount on the front fairing mounting bracket.
3. Connect a 12-volt battery to terminals A, **Figure 94** on the relay.
4. Use an ohmmeter and check for continuity. Connect the test leads to terminals B, **Figure 94** of the relay: there should be continuity (low resistance) between terminals B, **Figure 94**.
5. If there is no continuity (infinite resistance) the relay is defective and must be replaced.
6. If the existing relay checks out okay, reinstall the old relay. If the relay is defective, install a new relay.
7. Reconnect the electrical connector to the relay.
8. Make sure the electrical connectors are free of corrosion and are tight.

NEAS Solenoid

1. Disconnect the electrical connector (**Figure 96**) from the NEAS relay. There is an electrical connector for each NEAS solenoid on each fork leg.
2. Use an ohmmeter and check for continuity. Connect the test leads to the NEAS solenoid side of the electrical connector.
3. There should be continuity. The specified resistance is 5.4-8 ohms.
4. If the solenoid fails this test, the NEAS solenoid must be replaced as described under *Front Fork Oil Change* in Chapter Three.
5. Remove any tie wraps securing the NEAS solenoid electrical wire to the front fork and steering stem area. Carefully pull the electrical wire from the frame.
6. If the existing relay checks out okay, reinstall the old relay. If the relay is defective, install a new relay.
7. Reconnect the electrical connector to the relay.
8. Make sure the electrical connectors are free of corrosion and are tight.
9. If the NEAS solenoid was replaced, refill the front fork oil as described under *Front Fork Oil Change* in Chapter Three.

ELECTRICAL COMPONENTS

This section contains information on all electrical components except switches and relays.

Instrument Cluster
Removal/Installation

Refer to **Figure 97** for this procedure.

1. Remove the seat as described under *Seat Removal/Installation* in Chapter Twelve.
2. Remove the front fairing as described under *Front Fairing Removal/Installation* in Chapter Twelve.
3. Disconnect the battery negative lead (**Figure 98**).

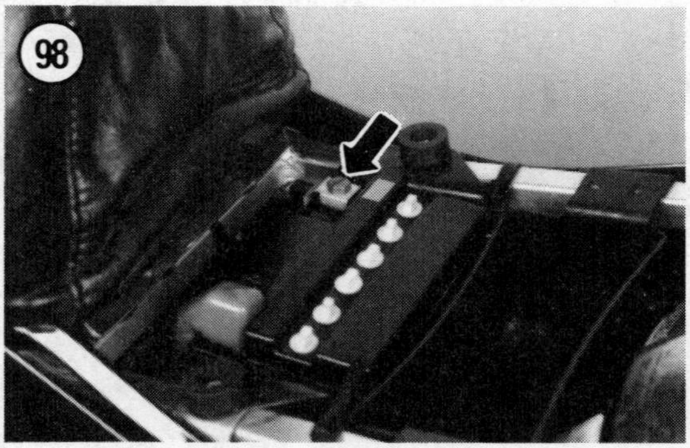

(97)

INSTRUMENT CLUSTER

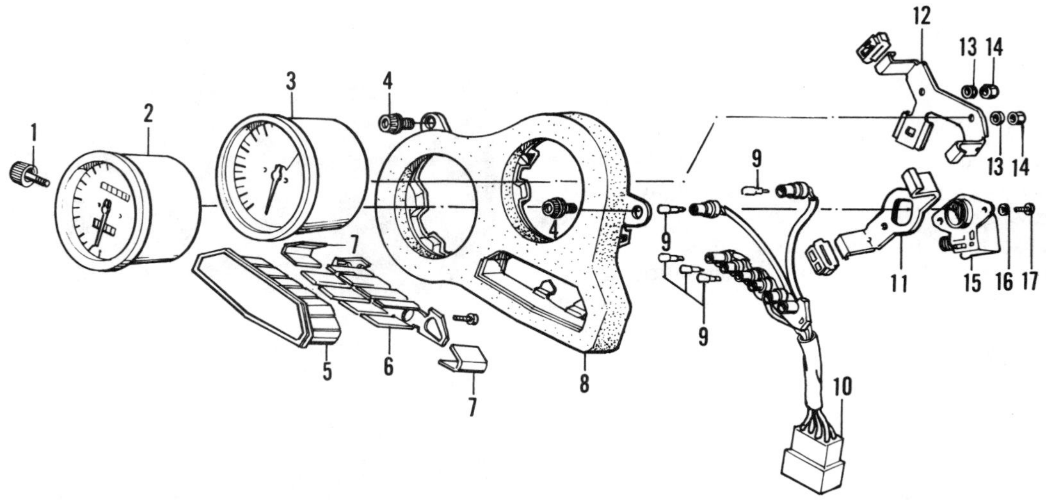

1. Odometer reset knob
2. Speedometer
3. Tachometer
4. Allen bolt
5. Indicator light panel
6. Mounting plate
7. End cap
8. Face panel
9. Indicator bulb
10. Wire harness
11. Speedometer mounting plate
12. Tachometer mounting plate
13. Washer
14. Nut
15. Speedometer gear box
16. Washer
17. Screw

4. Unscrew the speedometer drive cable (A, **Figure 99**) from the back of the speedometer.
5. In back of the instrument cluster, disconnect the instrument cluster electrical connector (B, **Figure 99**).
6. Remove the screws (**Figure 100**) securing the front of the instrument cluster to the mounting bracket.
7. Remove the screw (C, **Figure 99**) securing the rear of the instrument cluster to the mounting bracket.
8. Remove the instrument cluster assembly.
9. Install by reversing these removal steps, noting the following.
10. Make sure the electrical connector is free of corrosion and is tight.

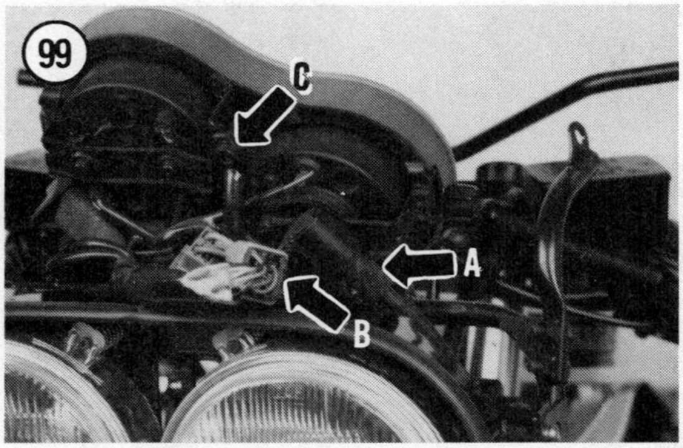

Horn Testing

1. Remove the front fairing as described under *Front Fairing Removal/Installation* in Chapter Twelve.
2. Disconnect horn wires from harness.
3. Connect a 12-volt battery to the horn.
4. If the horn is good it will sound. If not, replace it.

Horn Removal/Installation

1. Remove the front fairing as described under *Front Fairing Removal/Installation* in Chapter Twelve.
2. Disconnect the electrical connectors (A, **Figure 101**) from the horn.
3. Remove the screw and washers securing the horn (B, **Figure 101**) to the bracket. Remove the horn.
4. Install by reversing these removal steps, noting the following.
5. Make sure the electrical connector is free of corrosion and is tight.

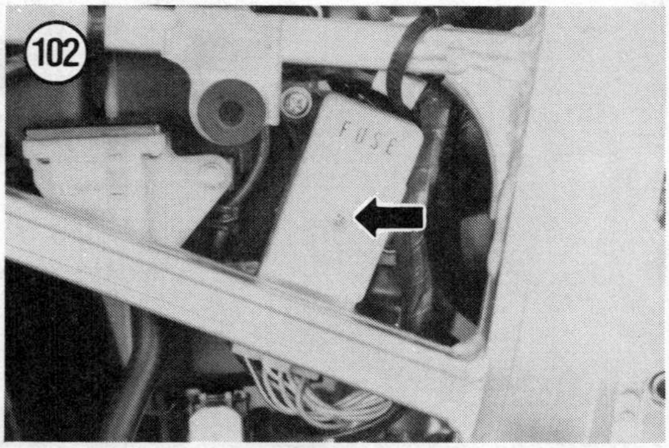

FUSES

The fuse panel is located under the right-hand side panel. Whenever the fuse blows, find out the reason for the failure before replacing the fuse.

103

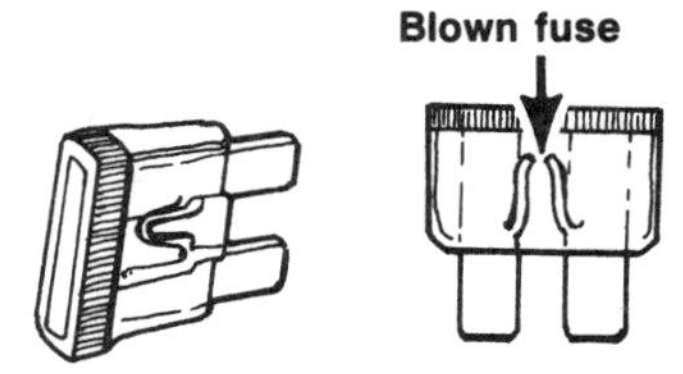

104

105

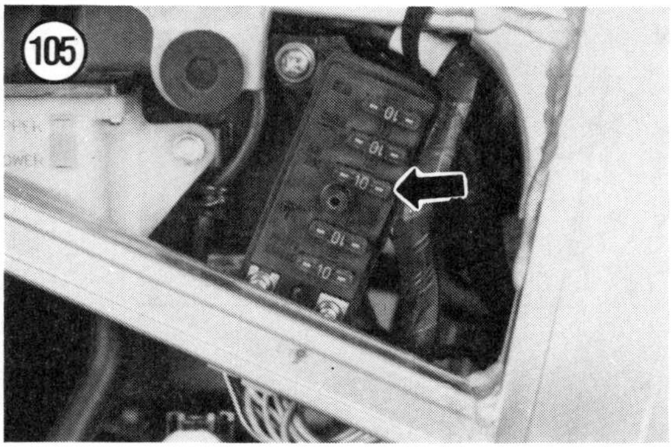

106

Usually, the trouble is a short circuit in the wiring. This may be caused by worn-through insulation or a disconnected wire shorted to ground.

CAUTION
Never substitute metal foil or wire for a fuse. Never use a higher amperage fuse than specified. An overload could result in a fire and complete loss of the bike.

CAUTION
When replacing a fuse, make sure the ignition switch is in the OFF position. This will lessen the chance of a short circuit.

Fuse Replacement

1. Remove the right-hand side cover.
2. Remove the screw (**Figure 102**) securing the fuse panel cover and remove the cover.

NOTE
*These fuses (**Figure 103**) are not the typical glass tube with metal ends. Carry extra fuses in your tool box.*

3. Remove the fuse and install a new one. Inside the cover there is 1 spare fuse (**Figure 104**).
4. Install the cover and screw. Tighten the screw securely but do not overtighten as the cover may crack.
5. Install the right-hand side cover.

8

Fuse Panel Removal/Installation

1. Remove the seat as described under *Seat Removal/Installation* in Chapter Twelve.
2. Disconnect the battery negative lead (**Figure 98**).
3. Remove the right-hand side cover.
4. Remove the screw (**Figure 102**) securing the fuse panel cover and remove the cover.
5. Remove the screws and washers securing the fuse panel (**Figure 105**) to the frame.
6. Partially pull the fuse panel up and out of the frame.
7. Disconnect the electrical connector from the base of the fuse panel and remove the fuse panel.
8. Install by reversing these removal steps, noting the following.
9. Make sure the electrical connector is free of corrosion and is tight.

CIRCUIT BREAKER

The wiring harness is protected by a circuit breaker that is located just below and behind the fuse panel (**Figure 106**). The circuit breaker protects the electrical system when the main circuit load exceeds the rated amperage. When an overload occurs, the red button pops out on the breaker face panel and the circuit is opened. The circuit will remain open until the problem is solved and the breaker is reset.

To reset, wait approximately 10 minutes for the circuit breaker to cool down, then push the red button in. If the red button pops out again, the problem still exists in the electrical system and must be corrected.

WIRING DIAGRAMS

Wiring diagrams for all models are located at the end of this book.

Table 1 IGNITION TROUBLESHOOTING

Symptoms	Probable cause
Weak spark	Poor connections in circuit (clean and retighten all connections)
	High voltage leak (replace defective wire)
	Defective ignition coil (replace coil)
No spark	Broken wire (replace wire)
	Faulty engine stop switch (replace switch)
	Defective ignition coil (replace coil)
	Defective signal generator (replace signal generator assembly)
	Defective ignitor unit (replace ignitor unit)

Table 2 REPLACEMENT BULBS

Item	Voltage/wattage U.S.	UK
Headlight	12V 55/60W	12V 60/55W
Parking light	–	12V 4W
Taillight/brake light	12V 8/23W	12V 5/21W
License plate light	12V 8W	12V 5W
Turn signal light	12V 23W	12V 21W
Illumination light (speedometer, tachometer, sidestand check light)	12V 3W	12V 3W
Indicator light (turn signal, light beam, oil pressure)	12V 1.7W	12V 1.7W
Indicator light (neutral)	12V 3W	12V 3W

NOTE: If you own a GSX600F Katana, first refer to Chapter 13 for specific service information.

CHAPTER NINE

FRONT SUSPENSION AND STEERING

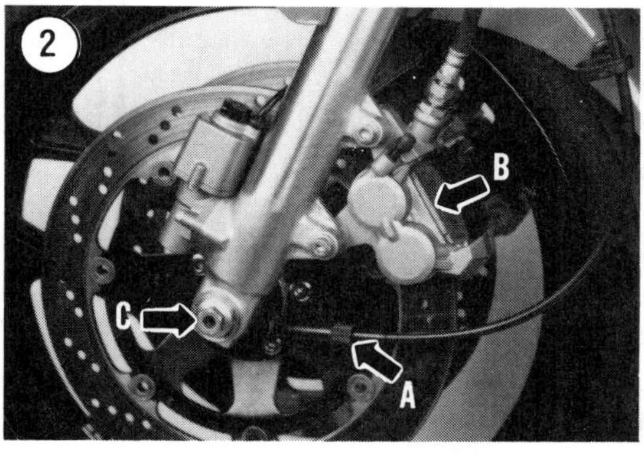

This chapter describes procedures for the repair and maintenance ofr the front wheel, front forks and steering components.

Front suspension torque specifications are covered in **Table 1**. **Table 1** and **Table 2** are at the end of this chapter.

FRONT WHEEL

Removal

1. Remove the lower portion of the front fairing as described under *Front Fairing Removal/Installation* in Chapter Twelve.
2. Remove the cotter pin (A, **Figure 1**) and loosen the front axle pinch bolt and nut (B, **Figure 1**) on the right-hand side.
3. Place wood block(s) under each side of the frame to support the bike securely with the front wheel off the ground.
4. Remove the speedometer cable (A, **Figure 2**) from the speedometer gear box.
5. Remove either the right- or left-hand front caliper assembly (B, **Figure 2**) as described under *Front Brake Caliper Removal/Installation* in Chapter Eleven. It is only necessary to remove one of the caliper assemblies.
6. Remove the front axle nut (C, **Figure 1**).
7. Withdraw the front axle (C, **Figure 2**) from the left-hand side.

8. Pull the wheel down and forward and remove it. This allows the brake disc to slide out of the remaining caliper assembly.
9. Remove the wheel. Don't lose the spacers (**Figure 3**) on the right-hand side.

CAUTION
Do not set the wheel down on the disc surface as it may get scratched or bent. Set the sidewalls on 2 wooden blocks.

NOTE
Insert a piece of vinyl tubing or wood in each caliper in place of the brake disc. That way if the brake lever is inadvertently squeezed, the piston will not be forced out of the cylinder. If this does happen, the caliper may have to be disassembled to reseat the piston and the system will have to be bled.

Installation

1. Make sure the axle bearing surfaces of the fork sliders and axle are free from burrs and nicks.
2. Remove the vinyl tubing or pieces of wood from the brake calipers.
3. Position the wheel into place; carefully insert the brake disc between the brake pads in the caliper assembly.
4. Make sure the wheel spacers (**Figure 3**) are in place on the right-hand side.

NOTE
Make sure the speedometer gear box seats completely. If the speedometer components do not mesh properly, the hub components of the wheel will be too wide for installation.

5. Apply a light coat of grease to the front axle. Insert the front axle from the left-hand side through the speedometer gear box and the wheel hub.
6. Install the front axle nut but do not tighten at this time.
7. Slowly rotate the wheel and install the speedometer cable into the speedometer housing. Position the speedometer housing and cable so that the cable does not have a sharp bend in it.
8. Tighten the front axle nut to the torque specification listed in **Table 1**.
9. Install the front caliper assembly (B, **Figure 2**) that was removed as described under *Front Brake Caliper Removal/Installation* in Chapter Eleven.
10. Remove the wood block(s) from under each side of the frame.
11. With the front brake applied, push down hard on the handlebars and pump the forks several times to seat the front axle.
12. Tighten the front axle pinch bolt and nut to the torque specification listed in **Table 1**.
13. Install a new cotter pin (A, **Figure 1**) and bend the ends over completely. Never re-use an old cotter pin as the ends may break off and the pin may fall out.
14. After the wheel is completely installed, rotate it several times to make sure that it rotates freely. Apply the front brake as many times as necessary to make sure all brake pads are against both brake discs correctly.

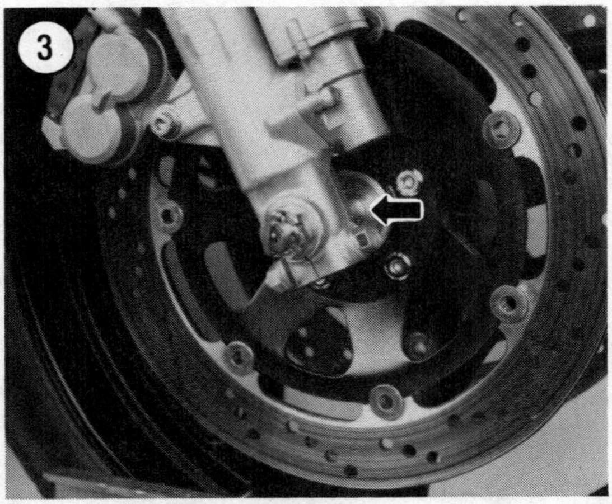

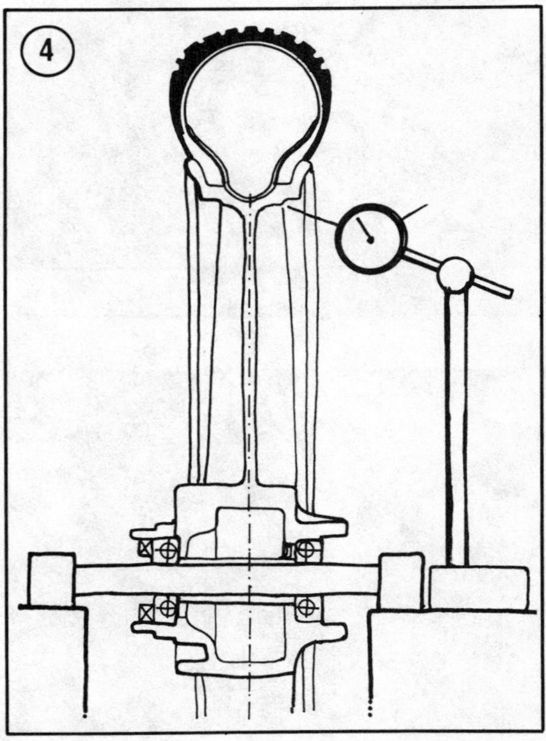

5

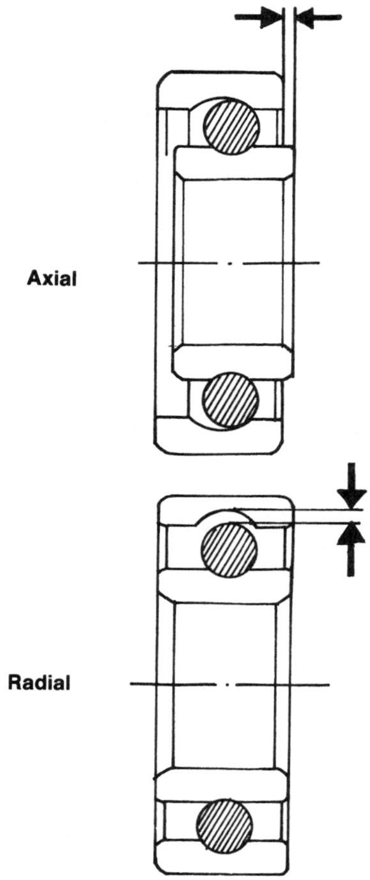

6

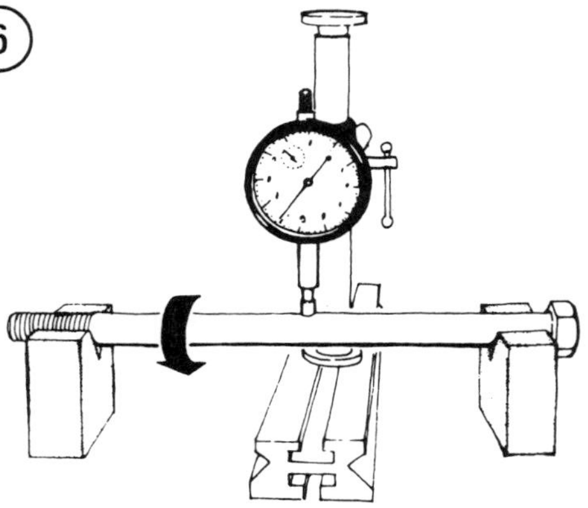

WHEEL INSPECTION

Measure the axial runout (end play) and radial runout (side play) of the wheel with a dial indicator as shown in **Figure 4**. The maximum axial and radial runout is 2.0 mm (0.08 in.). If the runout exceeds this dimension, check the wheel bearing condition.

Check the front axle runout as described under *Front Hub* in this chapter.

FRONT HUB

Inspection

Inspect each wheel bearing prior to removing it from the wheel hub.

CAUTION
Do not remove the wheel bearings for inspection purposes as they will be damaged during the removal process. Remove wheel bearings only if they are to be replaced.

1. Perform Steps 1-3 of *Disassembly* in this chapter.
2. Turn each bearing by hand. Make sure bearings turn smoothly.
3. Inspect the play of the inner race (**Figure 5**) or each wheel bearing. Check for excessive axial play (end play) and radial play (side play). Replace the bearing if it has an excess amount of free play.
4. On non-sealed bearings, check the balls for evidence of wear, pitting or excessive heat (bluish tint). Replace the bearings if necessary; always replace as a complete set. When replacing the bearings, be sure to take your old bearings along to ensure a perfect matchup.

NOTE
Fully sealed bearings are available from many bearing specialty shops. Fully sealed bearings provide better protection from dirt and moisture that may get into the hub.

5. Check the axle for wear and straightness. Use V-blocks and a dial indicator as shown in **Figure 6**. If the runout is 0.2 mm (0.01 in.) or greater, the axle should be replaced.

Disassembly

Refer to **Figure 7** for this procedure.

1. Remove the front wheel as described under *Front Wheel Removal* this chapter.
2. Remove the speedometer gear box from the hub.

7

FRONT WHEEL/HUB

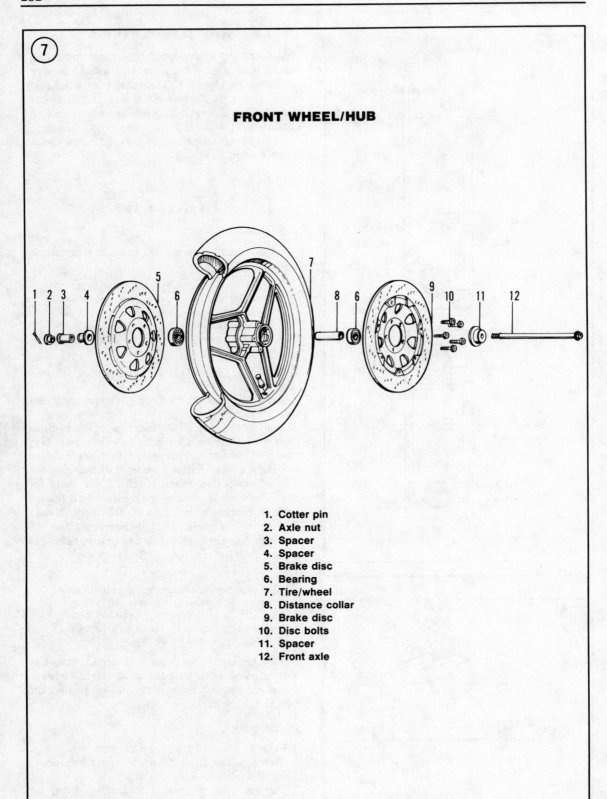

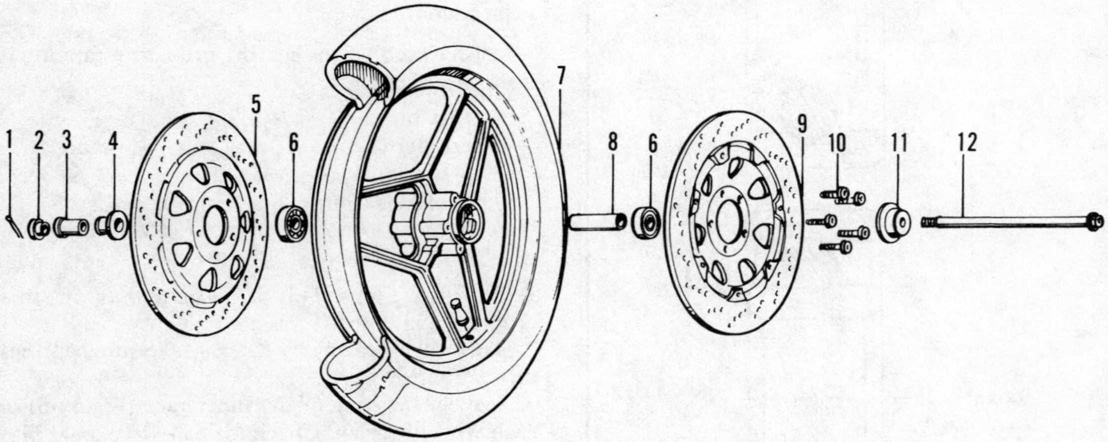

1. Cotter pin
2. Axle nut
3. Spacer
4. Spacer
5. Brake disc
6. Bearing
7. Tire/wheel
8. Distance collar
9. Brake disc
10. Disc bolts
11. Spacer
12. Front axle

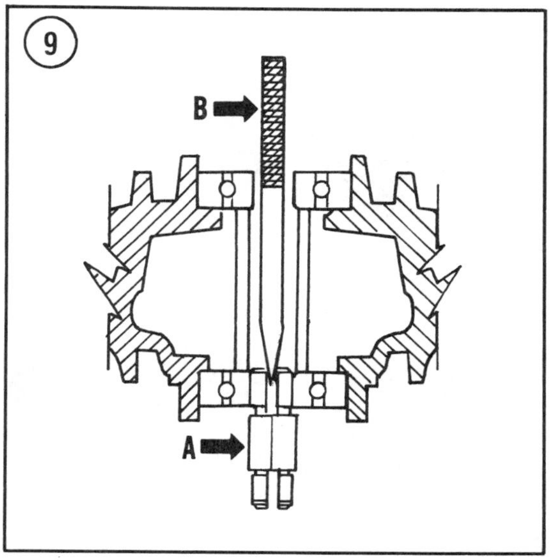

3. Remove the bolts (**Figure 8**) securing the brake disc and remove the disc. Remove the brake disc from each side.

4. Before proceeding further, inspect the wheel bearings as described in this chapter. If they must be replaced, proceed as follows.

5A. A special Suzuki tool (Suzuki part No. 09941-50110) can be used to remove the wheel bearings as follows:

a. Insert the adaptor (A, **Figure 9**) into one of the wheel bearings from the outer surface of the wheel.
b. Turn the wheel over and insert the wedge bar (B, **Figure 9**) into the backside of the adaptor. Tap the wedge bar and force it into the slit in the adaptor (**Figure 10**). This will wedge the adaptor against the inner bearing race.
c. Tap on the end of the wedge bar with a hammer (**Figure 11**) and drive the bearing out of the hub. Remove the bearing and the distance collar.
d. Repeat for the bearing on the other side.

5B. If the special tools are not used, perform the following:

a. To remove the right- and left-hand bearings and distance collar, insert a soft aluminum or brass drift into one side of the hub.
b. Push the distance collar over to one side and place the drift on the inner race of the lower bearing.
c. Tap the bearing out of the hub with a hammer, working around the perimeter of the inner race.
d. Repeat for the bearing on the other side.

6. Clean the inside and the outside of the hub with solvent. Dry with compressed air.

9

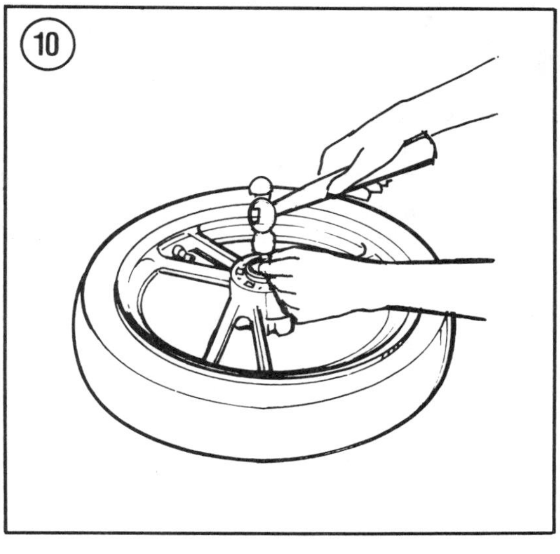

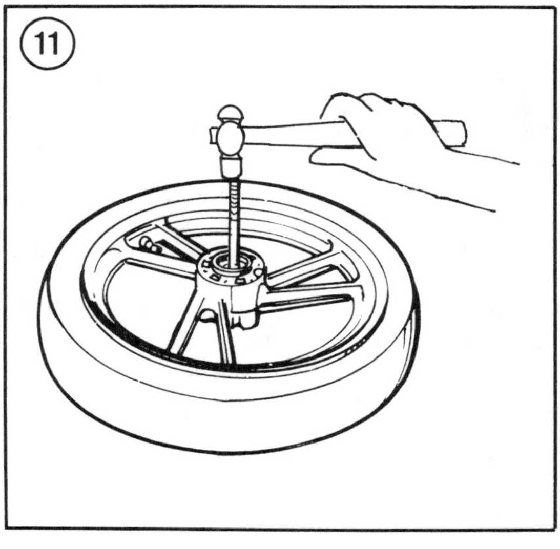

Assembly

1. On non-sealed bearings, pack the bearings with a good quality bearing grease. Work the grease in between the balls thoroughly; turn the bearing by hand a couple of times to make sure the grease is distributed evenly inside the bearing.
2. Blow any dirt or foreign matter out of the hub prior to installing the bearings.

CAUTION
Install non-sealed bearings with the single sealed side facing outward. Tap the bearings squarely into place and tap on the outer race only. Do not tap on the inner race or the bearing might be damaged. Be sure that the bearings are completely seated.

3A. A special Suzuki tool (Suzuki part No. 09924-84510) can be used to install the wheel bearings as follows:

a. Install the left-hand bearing into the hub first.
b. Set the bearing with the sealed side facing out and install the bearing installer as shown in **Figure 12.**
c. Tighten the bearing installer (**Figure 13**) and pull the bearing into the hub until it is completely seated (**Figure 14**). Remove the bearing installer.
d. Turn the wheel over (right-hand side up) on the workbench and install the distance collar.
e. Set the bearing with the sealed side facing out and install the bearing installer as shown in **Figure 15.**
f. Tighten the bearing installer (**Figure 13**) and pull the bearing into the hub until it is completely seated (**Figure 16**).
g. Remove the bearing installer.

3B. If special tools are not used, perform the following:

a. Tap the left-hand bearing squarely into place, tapping only on the outer race. The sealed side of the bearing must face out. Use a socket (**Figure 17**) that matches the outer race diameter. Do not tap on the inner race or the bearing will be damaged. Be sure that the bearing is completely seated.
b. Turn the wheel over (right-hand side up) on the workbench and install the distance collar.
c. Use the same tool set-up and drive in the right-hand bearing. The sealed side of the bearing must face out.

12

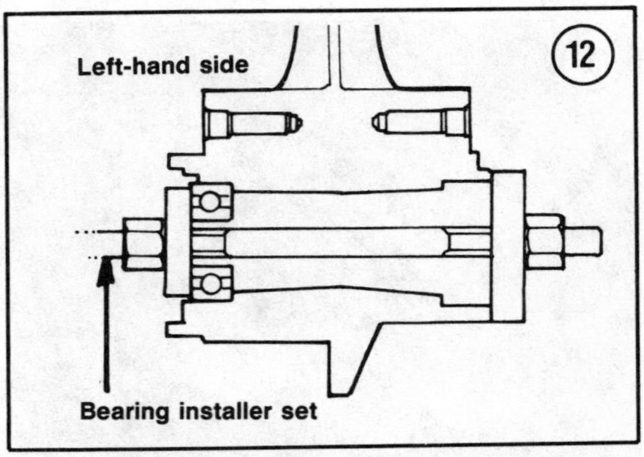

13

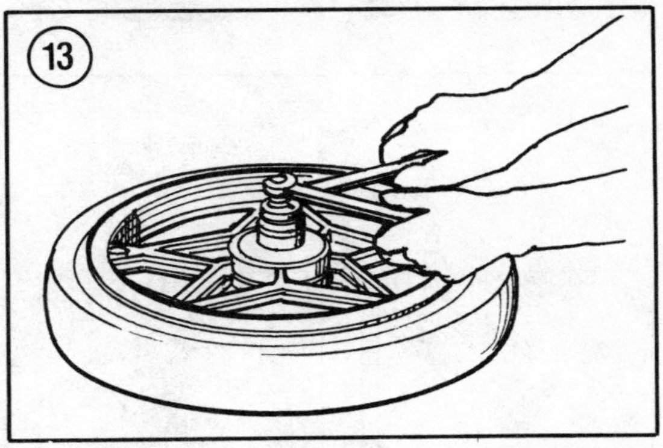

14

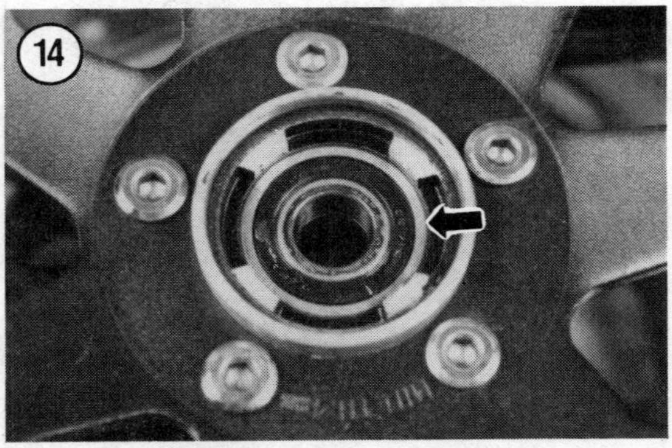

15

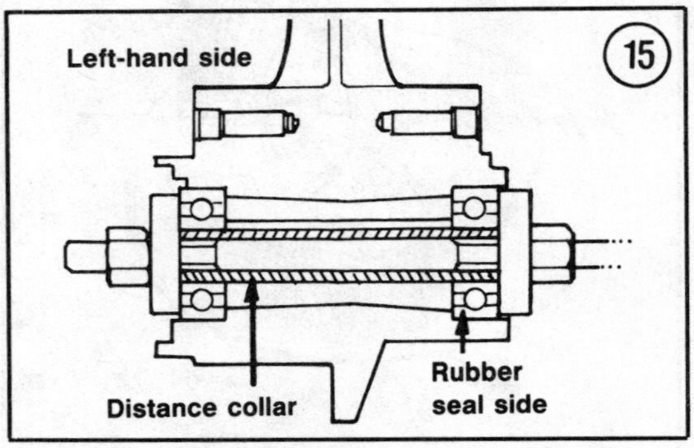

16

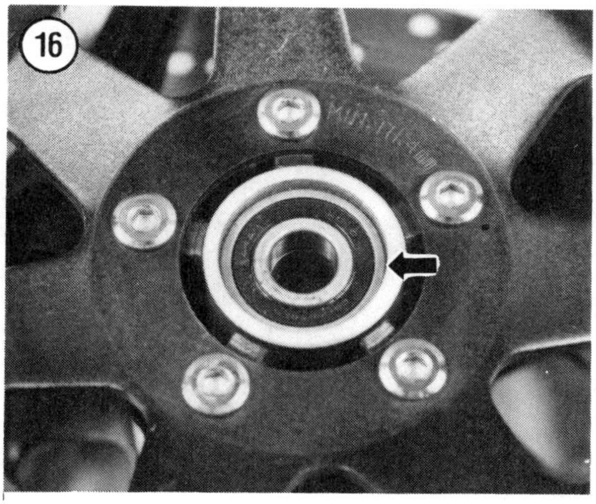

17

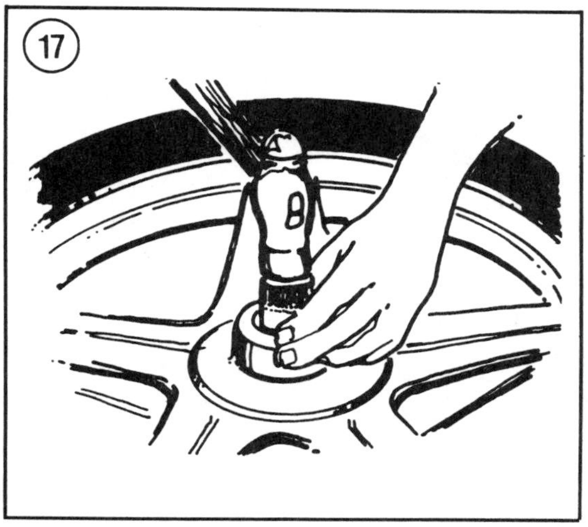

18

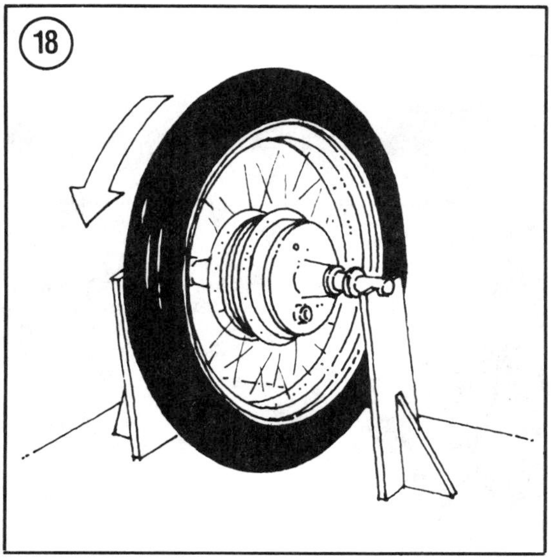

4. Apply Loctite Lock N' Seal to the brake disc bolts prior to installation.
5. Install the brake disc and bolts (**Figure 8**). Tighten to the torque specifications listed in **Table 1**.
6. Align the tangs of the speedometer drive gear with the notches in the front hub and install the speedometer gearbox.

NOTE
Make sure the speedometer gear box seats completely. If the speedometer components do not mesh properly, the wheel will be too wide for installation.

7. Install the front wheel as described in this chapter.

WHEELS

Wheel Balance

An unbalanced wheel is unsafe. Depending on the degree of unbalance and the speed of the motorcycle, the rider may experience anything from a mild vibration to a violent shimmy which may even result in loss of control.

The weights are attached to the rim. Weight kits are available from motorcycle dealers. These kits contain test weights and strips of adhesive-backed weights that can be cut to the desired length and attached directly to the rim.

Before you attempt to balance the wheel, check to be sure that the wheel bearings are in good condition and properly lubricated and that the brakes do not drag. The wheel must rotate freely.

NOTE
When balancing the wheels, do so with the brake discs (front and rear wheel) attached and with the driven sprocket assembly attached to the rear wheel. These components rotate with the wheels and they affect the balance.

1. Remove the wheel as described in this chapter or Chapter Ten.
2. Mount the wheel on a fixture such as the one shown in **Figure 18** so it can rotate freely.
3. Give the wheel a spin and let it coast to a stop. Mark the tire at the lowest point (6 o'clock).
4. Spin the wheel several more times. If the wheel keeps coming to rest at the same point, it is out of balance.
5. Tape a test weight to the upper side (12 o'clock) of the wheel.

6. Experiment with different weights until the wheel, when spun, comes to a rest at a different position each time.
7. Remove the test weight and install the correct size weight.

Wheel Alignment

Refer to **Figure 19** for this procedure.

1. Measure the tires at their widest point.
2. Subtract the small dimension from the larger dimension.
3. Make an alignment tool out of 3/4 in. plywood approximately 7 feet long, with an offset equal to one-half of the dimension obtained in Step 2. Refer to (D).
4. If the wheels are not aligned as in (A) and (C), the rear wheel must be shifted to correct the alignment.
5. Remove the cotter pin and loosen the rear axle nut (A, **Figure 20**).
6. Loosen the drive chain adjuster locknut (B, **Figure 20**) on either side and move the rear wheel until the wheels align.
7. Adjust the drive chain as described under *Drive Chain Adjustment* in Chapter Three.

WARNING
After the wheel alignment has been changed, ride the bike carefully at first since you may have altered its handling characteristics.

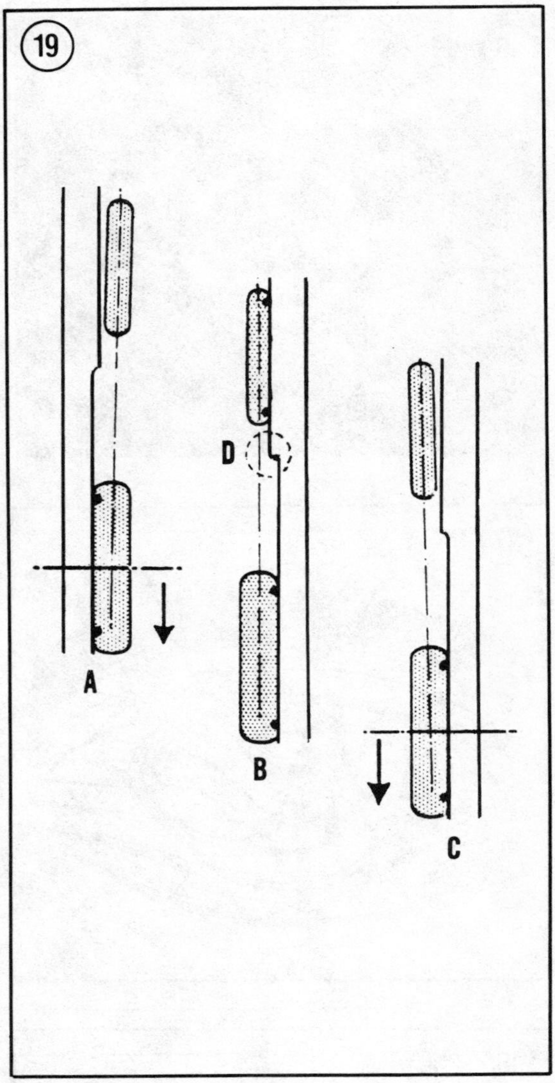

TIRE CHANGING

Removal

1. Mark the valve stem location on the tire, so the tire can be installed in the same position for easier balancing.
2. Remove the valve core to deflate the tire.

NOTE
*Removal of tubeless tires from their rims can be very difficult because of the exceptionally tight bead/rim seal. Breaking the bead seal may require a special tool (**Figure 21**). If you are unable to break the seal loose, take the wheel to a motorcycle dealer and have them break it loose.*

CAUTION
The inner rim and tire bead area are sealing surfaces on the tubeless tire. Do not scratch the inside of the rim or damage the tire bead.

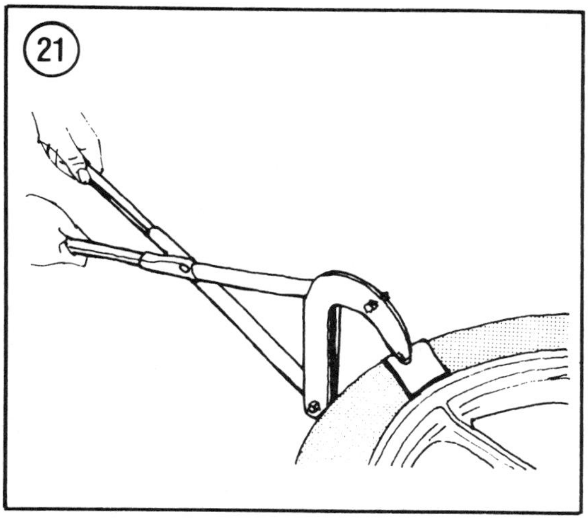

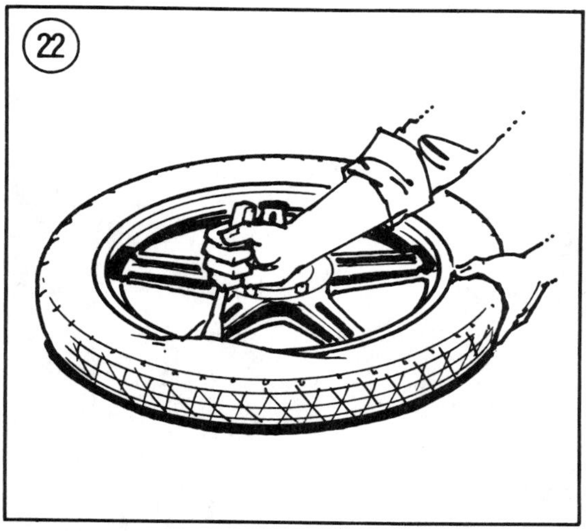

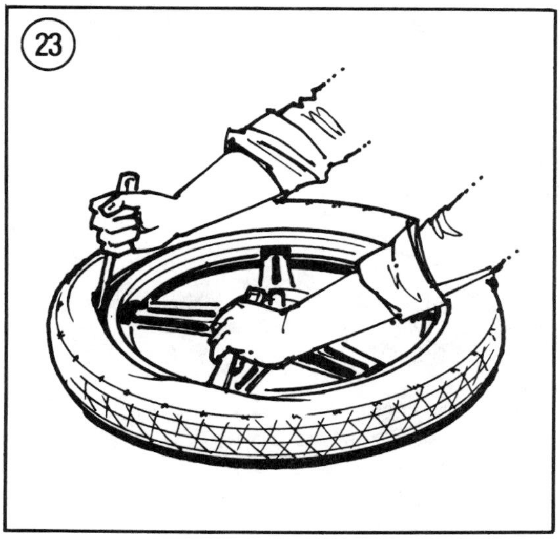

3. Press the entire bead on both sides of the tire into the center of the rim.
4. Lubricate the beads with soapy water.

CAUTION
Use rim protectors or insert scraps of thick leather between the tire irons and the rim to protect the rim from damage.

5. Insert the tire iron under the bead next to the valve (**Figure 22**). Force the bead on the opposite side of the tire into the center of the rim and pry the bead over the rim with the tire iron.
6. Insert a second tire iron next to the first to hold the bead over the rim. Then work around the tire with the first tire iron, prying the bead over the rim (**Figure 23**).
7. Turn the tire over. Insert the tire iron between the second bead and the side of the rim that the first bead was pried over (**Figure 24**). Force the bead on the opposite side from the tire iron into the center of the rim. Pry the second bead off the rim, working around as with the first.
8. Inspect the valve stem seal. Because rubber deteriorates with age, it is advisable to replace the valve stem when replacing the tire.
9. Remove the old valve stem and discard it. Inspect the valve stem hole in the rim. Remove any dirt or corrosion from the hole and wipe dry with a clean cloth.

9

Tire and Rim Inspection

1. Wipe off the inner surfaces of the wheel rim. Clean off any rubber residue or any oxidation.

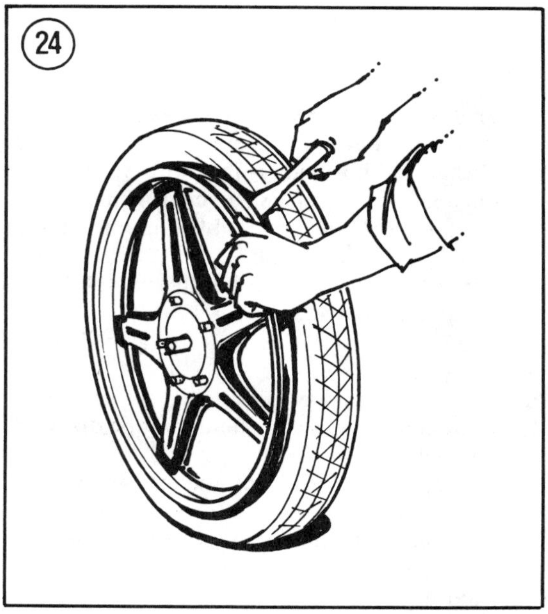

2. If a can of pressurized tire sealant was used for a temporary fix of a flat, thoroughly clean off all sealant residue. Any remaining residue will present a problem when reinstalling the tire and achieving a good seal of the tire bead against the rim.

WARNING
Since the GSX-R is a high-performance bike, carefully consider whether a tire should be patched or replaced. If there is any doubt about the quality of the existing tire, ***replace it with a new one****. Don't take a chance on a tire failure during a "canyon run".*

3. If a tire is going to be patched, thoroughly inspect the tire. If any one of the following is observed, do not repair the tire; *replace it with a new one*:

a. A puncture or split whose total length or diameter exceeds 6 mm (0.24 in.).
b. A scratch or split on the side wall.
c. Any type of ply separation.
d. Tread separation or excessive abnormal wear pattern.
e. Tread depth of less than 1.6 mm (0.06 in.) in the front tire or less than 2.0 mm (0.08 in.) in the rear tire on original equipment tires. Aftermarket tires' tread depth minimum may vary.
f. Scratches on either sealing bead.
g. Any cut in the cord.
h. Flat spots in the tread from skidding.
i. Any abnormality in the inner liner.

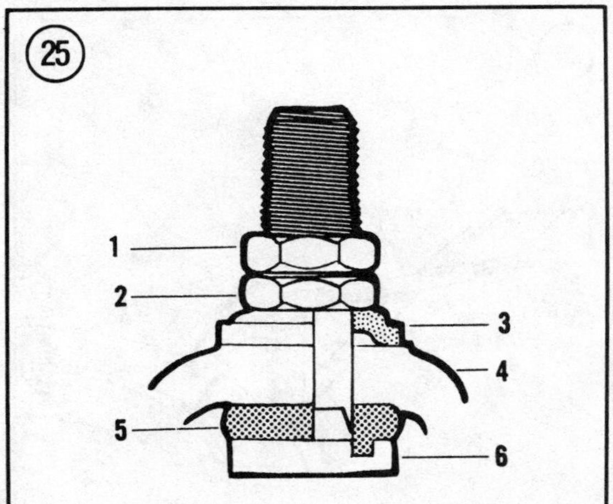

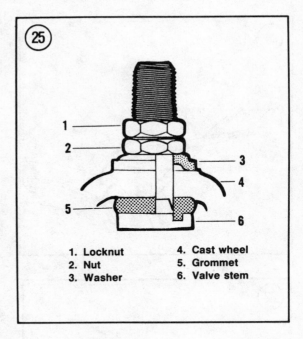

1. Locknut
2. Nut
3. Washer
4. Cast wheel
5. Grommet
6. Valve stem

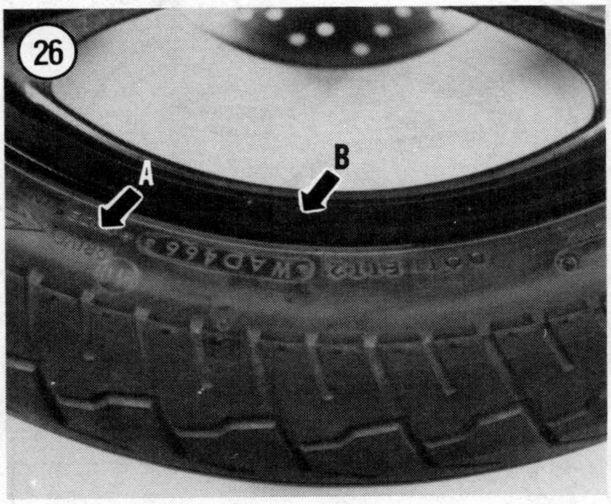

Installation

1. Install a new valve stem (**Figure 25**) as follows:
   a. Insert the new valve stem into the rim.
   b. Install the nut and tighten with your fingers only. Do not use pliers and overtighten the nut as it may distort the rubber grommet that could cause an air leak.
   c. Hold onto the nut and install and tighten the locknut securely.
2. Carefully inspect the tire for any damage, especially inside.
3. A new tire may have balancing rubbers inside. These are not patches and should not be disturbed or removed.
4. Lubricate both beads of the tire with soapy water.
5. When installing the tire onto the rim make sure the direction arrow (A, **Figure 26**) faces the direction of wheel rotation.

28

29

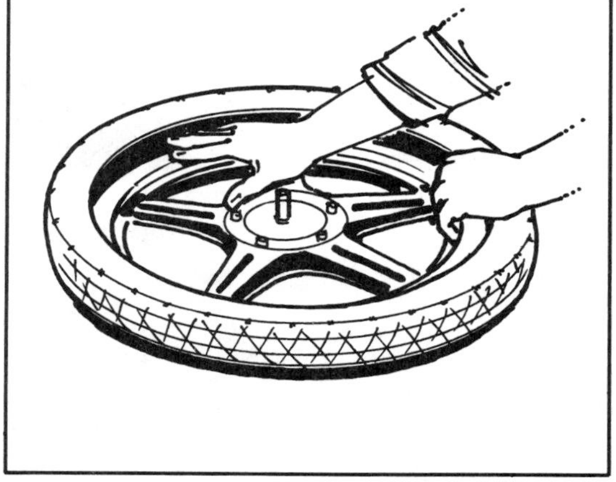

30

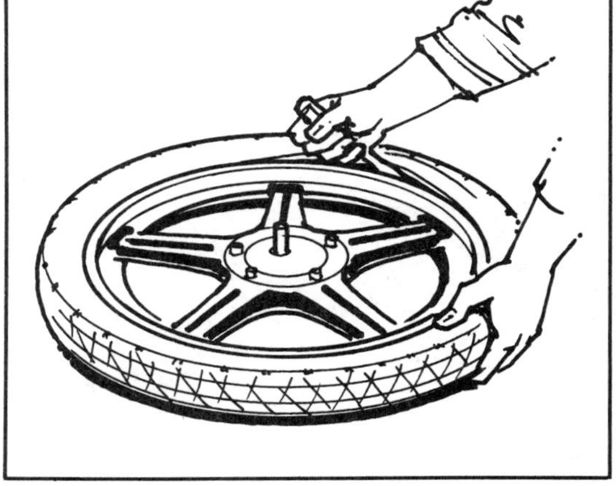

6. If remounting the old tire, align the mark made in Step 1, *Removal* with the valve stem. If a new tire is being installed, align the colored spot near the bead (indicating a lighter point on the tire) with the valve stem.
7. Place the backside of the tire into the center of the rim. The lower bead should go into the center of the rim and the upper bead outside. Work around the tire in both directions (**Figure 27**). Use a tire iron for the last few inches of bead (**Figure 28**).
8. Press the upper bead into the rim opposite the valve stem (**Figure 29**). Pry the bead into the rim on both sides of the initial point with a tire iron, working around the rim to the valve (**Figure 30**).
9. Check the bead on both sides of the tire for even fit around the rim.
10. Bounce the wheel several times, rotating it each time. This will force the tire beads against the rim flanges. After the tire beads are in contact with the rim evenly, inflate the tire to seat the beads.

WARNING
In the next step never exceed 56 psi (4.0 kg/cm²) inflation pressure as the tire could burst, causing severe injury. Never stand directly over a tire while inflating it.

11. Place an inflatable band around the circumference of the tire. Slowly inflate the band until the tire beads are pressed against the rim. Inflate the tire enough to seat it, deflate the band and remove it.
12. After inflating the tire, check to see that the beads are fully seated and that the tire rim lines (B, **Figure 26**) are the same distance from the rim all the way around the tire. If the beads won't seat, deflate the tire and relubricate the rim and beads with soapy water.
13. Reinflate the tire to the required pressure. Install the valve stem cap.
14. Balance the wheel as described in this chapter.

WARNING
If you have repaired a tire, do not ride the bike any faster than 30 mph (50 km/h) for the first 24 hours. It takes at least 24 hours for a patch to cure. Also ***never*** *ride the bike faster than 80 mph (130 km/h) with a repaired tire.*

9

TIRE REPAIRS

Patching a tubeless tire on the road is very difficult. If both beads are still against the rim, a can of pressurized tire sealant may inflate the tire and seal the hole, although this is only a temporary fix. The beads must be against the rim for this method to work.

Suzuki (and the tire industry) recommends that the tubeless tire be patched from the inside. Use a combination plug/patch applied from inside the tire (**Figure 31**). Do not patch the tire with an external type plug. If you find an external patch on the tire, it is recommended that it be patch-reinforced from the inside.

Due to the variations of material supplied with different tubeless tire repair kits, follow the instructions and recommendations supplied with the repair kit.

HANDLEBAR

Removal/Installation

1. Remove the front fairing as described under *Front Fairing Removal/Installation* in Chapter Twelve.
2. Remove the front wheel (A, **Figure 32**) as described under *Front Wheel Removal/Installation* in this chapter.
3. Remove the screws securing the front fender to the front fork stabilizer. Remove the spacers (**Figure 33**) from the front fender and remove the front fender (B, **Figure 32**).
4. Remove the screws securing the front fork stabilizer to the front forks and remove the front fork stabilizer (C, **Figure 32**).
5. Disconnect the brake light switch electrical connector from the brake lever.
6. Remove the screws securing the right-hand handlebar switch assembly (A, **Figure 34**) together and remove the right-hand switch assembly from the handlebar.

CAUTION
Cover the frame and fuel tank with a heavy cloth or plastic tarp to protect it from accidental spilling of brake fluid. Wash any spilled brake fluid off any painted or plated surface immediately, as it will destroy the finish. Use soapy water and rinse thoroughly.

7. Remove the screw securing the right-hand balance set (B, **Figure 34**) and remove all parts from the end of the handlebar.
8. Disconnect the throttle cable from the throttle assembly. Slide the throttle assembly (C, **Figure 34**) off the end of the handlebar. Carefully lay the

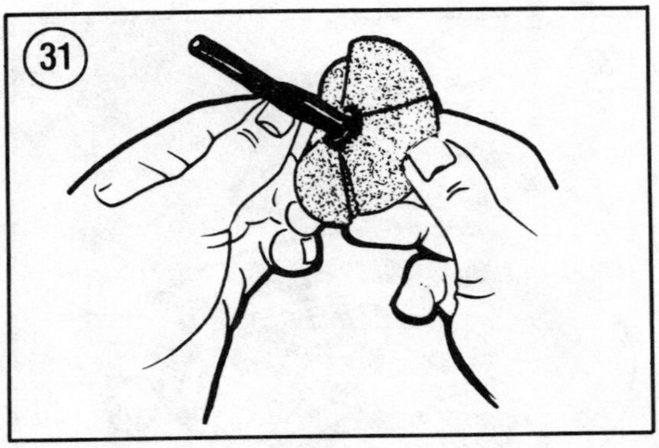

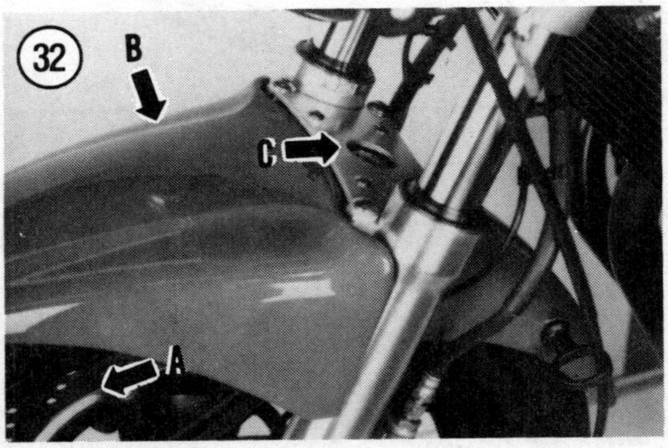

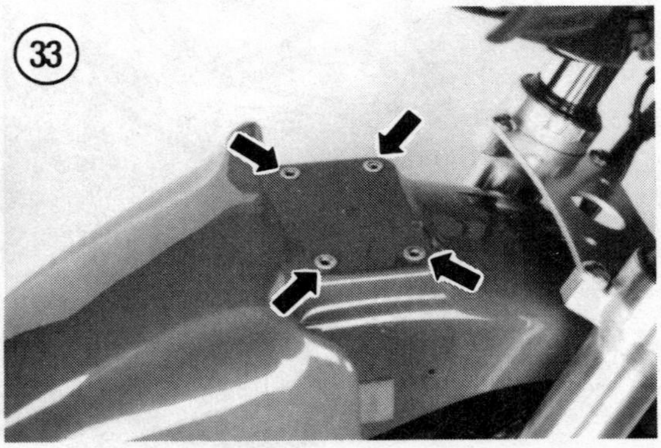

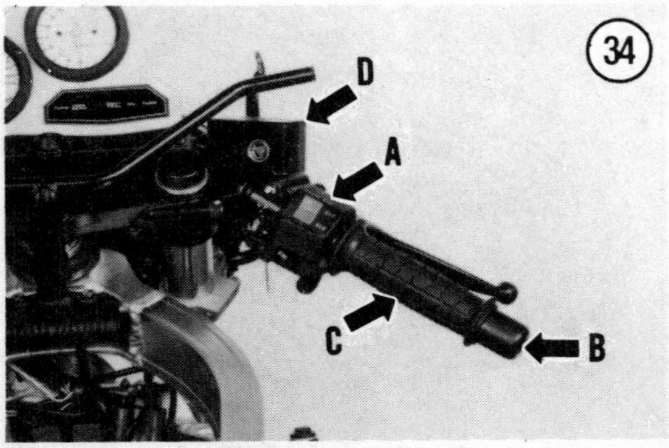

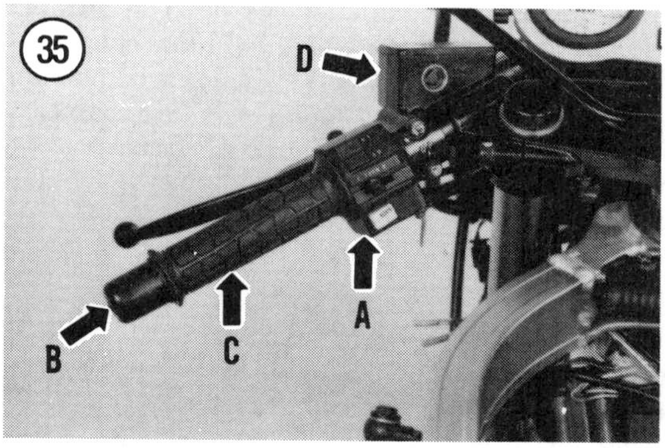

35

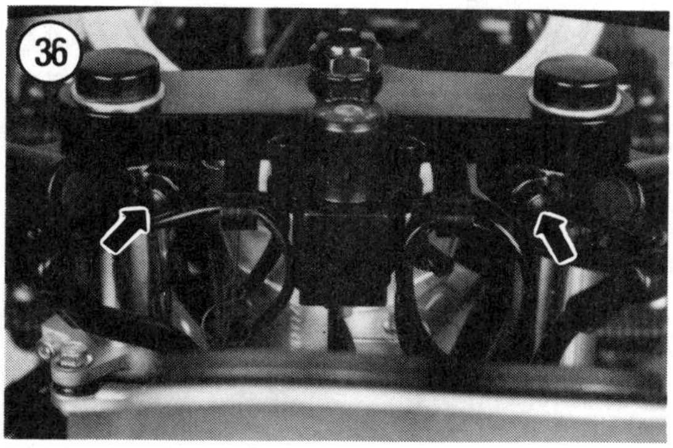
36

37

38

throttle cable over the fender or back over the frame. Be careful that the cable does not get crimped or damaged.

9. Remove the bolts securing the brake master cylinder (D, **Figure 34**). Tie the master cylinder up to the front fairing mounting bracket and keep the reservoir in the upright position. This is to minimize loss of brake fluid and to keep air from entering into the brake system. It is not necessary to remove the hydraulic brake line.

10. Disconnect the starter interlock switch electrical connector from the clutch lever.

11. Remove the screws securing the left-hand handlebar switch assembly (A, **Figure 35**) together and remove the left-hand switch assembly from the handlebar.

12. Remove the screw securing the left-hand balance set (B, **Figure 35**) and remove all parts from the end of the handlebar.

13. Slide the left-hand handgrip (C, **Figure 35**) off the end of the handlebar.

14. On models so equipped, remove the bolts securing the clutch master cylinder (D, **Figure 35**). Tie the master cylinder up to the front fairing mounting bracket and keep the reservoir in the upright position. This is to minimize loss of hydraulic fluid and to keep air from entering into the clutch system. It is not necessary to remove the hydraulic brake line.

15. Remove the cap and loosen the Allen bolt (**Figure 36**) clamping each handlebar to the fork tube.

16. Remove the mounting bolt (**Figure 37**) securing each handlebar to the upper fork bridge.

17. Remove the handlebar from each fork tube.

18. To remove the handlebar holder, perform the following:

   a. Loosen the upper and lower fork bridge bolts (**Figure 38**).
   b. Lower the fork tube and remove the handlebar holder from the fork tube.

19. Install by reversing these removal steps, noting the following.

39

20. If the handlebar holder was removed, perform the following:
   a. Install the handlebar holder onto the fork tube.
   b. Install the fork tubes so that the top of the fork tube aligns with the top surface of the upper fork bridge (**Figure 39**).
   c. Tighten the bolts to the torque specification listed in **Table 1**.
21. Apply a light coat of multipurpose grease to the throttle grip area on the handlebar prior to installing the throttle grip assembly.
22. Tighten all mounting bolts and clamping bolts to the torque specification listed in **Table 1**.
23. Install the brake master cylinder onto the handlebar. Install the clamp with the UP arrow (**Figure 40**) facing up and align the clamp mating surface with the punch mark on the handlebar. Tighten the upper bolt first and then the lower bolt.

WARNING
After installation is completed, make sure the brake lever does not come in contact with the throttle grip assembly when it is pulled on fully. If it does, the brake fluid may be low in the reservoir; refill as necessary. Refer to ***Front Disc Brakes*** *in Chapter Eleven.*

24. On models so equipped, install the clutch master cylinder onto the handlebar. Install the clamp with the UP arrow (**Figure 41**) facing up and align the clamp mating surface with the punch mark on the handlebar. Tighten the upper bolt first and then the lower bolt.

WARNING
After installation is completed, make sure the clutch lever does not come in contact with the handgrip when it is pulled on fully. If it does, the hydraulic fluid may be low in the reservoir; refill as necessary. Refer to ***Clutch Hydraulic System*** *in Chapter Five.*

25. Adjust the throttle operation as described in Chapter Three.

STEERING HEAD AND STEM

Disassembly

Refer to **Figure 42** for this procedure.

1. Remove the front wheel as described under *Front Wheel Removal* in this chapter.
2. Remove the front fairing as described under *Front Fairing Removal/Installation* in Chapter Twelve.
3. Remove the handlebars as described under *Handlebar Removal/Installation* in this chapter.
4. Remove the front forks as described under *Front Fork Removal/Installation* in this chapter.
5. Remove the bolts (**Figure 43**) securing the ignition switch and move the ignition switch out of the way.

40

41

43

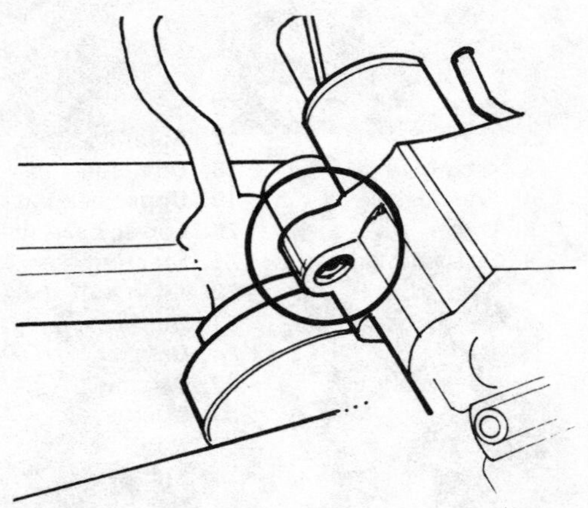

(42)

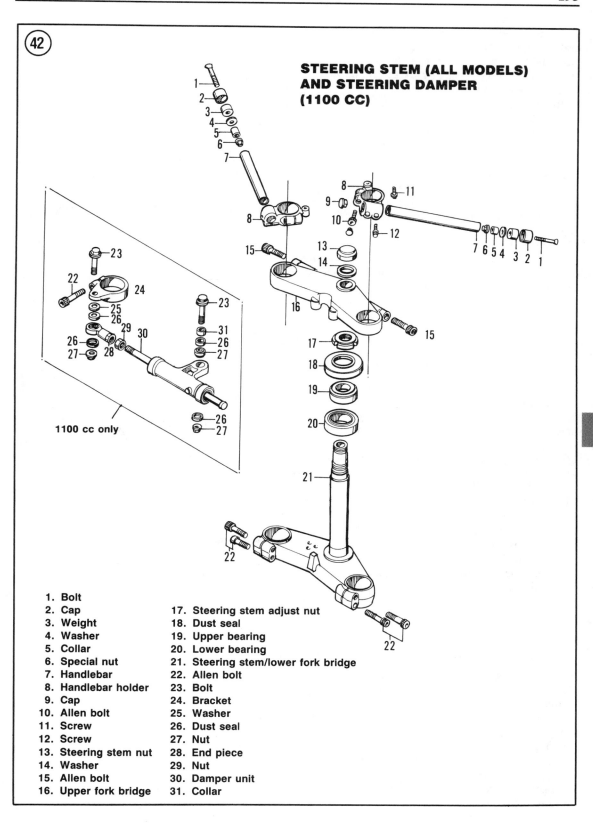

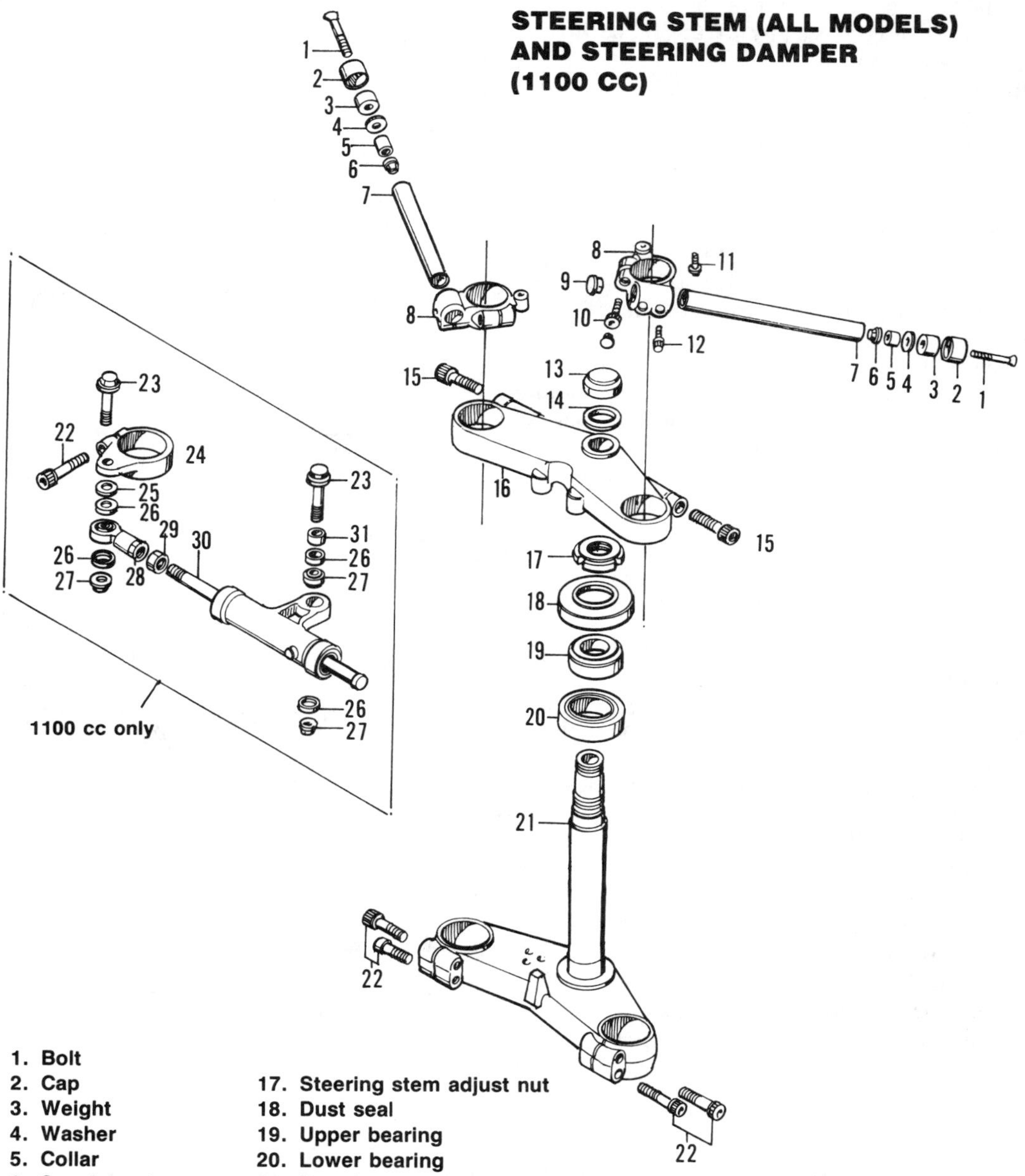

1. Bolt
2. Cap
3. Weight
4. Washer
5. Collar
6. Special nut
7. Handlebar
8. Handlebar holder
9. Cap
10. Allen bolt
11. Screw
12. Screw
13. Steering stem nut
14. Washer
15. Allen bolt
16. Upper fork bridge
17. Steering stem adjust nut
18. Dust seal
19. Upper bearing
20. Lower bearing
21. Steering stem/lower fork bridge
22. Allen bolt
23. Bolt
24. Bracket
25. Washer
26. Dust seal
27. Nut
28. End piece
29. Nut
30. Damper unit
31. Collar

6. Remove the bolt (**Figure 44**) securing the front brake hydraulic hose 3-way joint. Move the 3-way joint and hose assembly out of the way. It is not necessary to disconnect any of the brake hoses from the 3-way joint.
7. Remove the steering stem nut and washer (A, **Figure 45**).
8. Remove the upper fork bridge (B, **Figure 45**).
9. Loosen the steering stem adjust nut. To loosen the adjust nut, use a large drift and hammer or use the easily improvised tool shown in **Figure 46**.
10. Hold onto the lower end of the steering stem assembly and remove the steering stem adjust nut.
11. Remove the dust seal from the top of the headset.
12. Lower the steering stem assembly down and out of the steering head. Don't worry about catching any loose steel balls as the steering stem is equipped with caged roller bearings.
13. Remove the upper bearing from the top of the headset area of the frame.

44

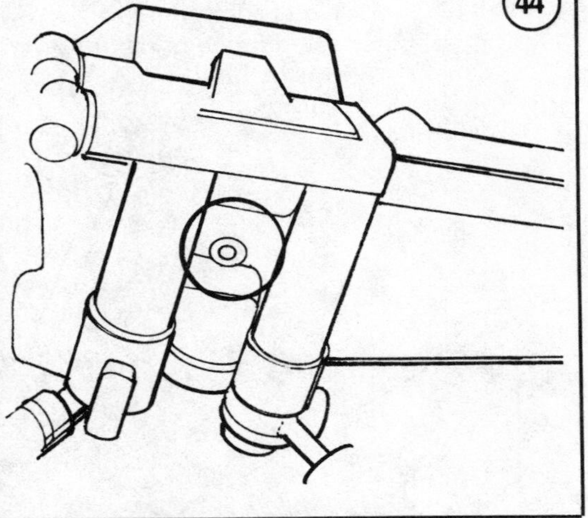

45

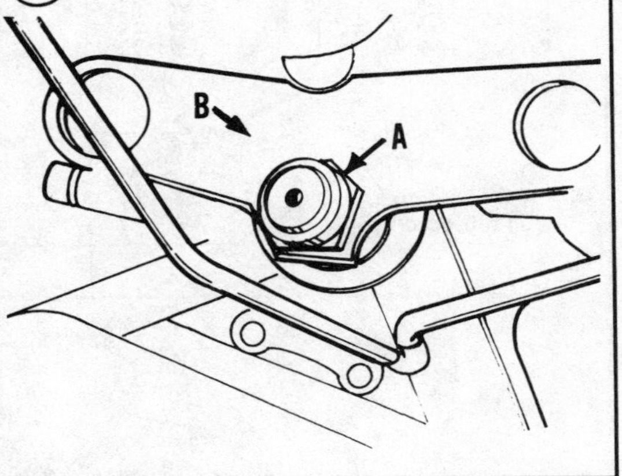

Inspection

1. Clean the bearing races in the steering head and the bearings with solvent.
2. Check the welds around the steering head for cracks and fractures. If any are found, have them repaired by a competent frame shop or welding service that is knowledgeable in the welding of aluminum.
3. Check the rollers for pitting, scratches or discoloration indicating wear or corrosion. Replace them in sets if any are bad.
4. Check the races for pitting, galling and corrosion. If any of these conditions exist, replace the races as described in this chapter.
5. Check the steering stem for cracks, damage or wear. If damaged in any way replace the steering stem.

46

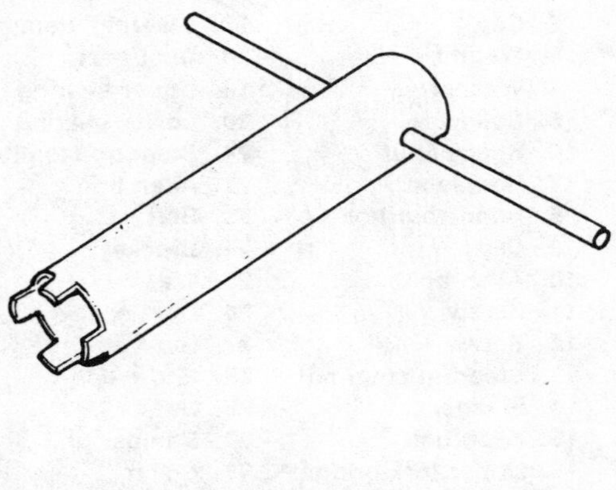

Steering Stem Assembly

Refer to **Figure 42** for this procedure.

1. Make sure the steering head outer races are properly seated.
2. Apply an even complete coat of wheel bearing grease to the steering head outer races and to both bearings.
3. Install the upper bearing into the steering head (**Figure 47**).
4. Install the steering stem into the head tube and hold it firmly in place.

5. Install the dust seal onto the top of the headset.
6. Install the steering stem adjust nut and tighten it to the initial torque specification listed in **Table 1**.
7. Turn the steering stem from lock-to-lock 5-6 times to seat the bearings.
8. Loosen the steering stem nut 1/4 to 1/2 turn.

47

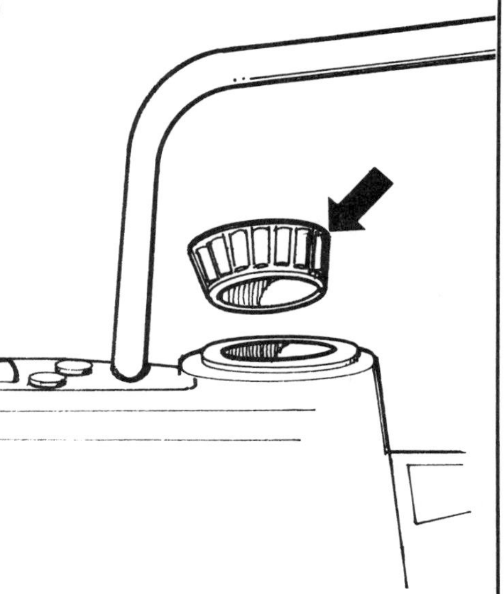

48

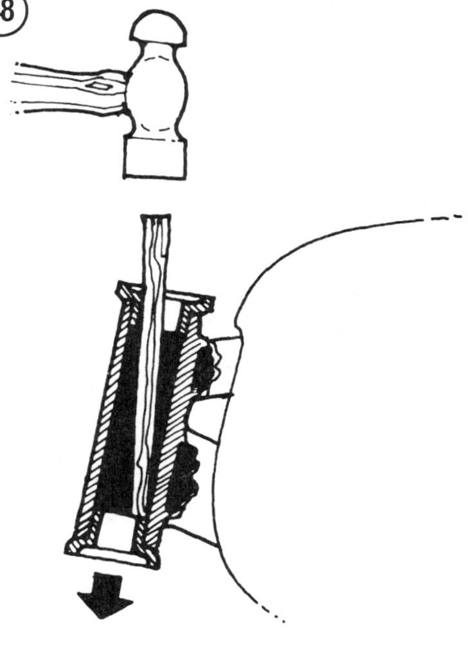

9. Retighten the steering stem adjust nut to the final torque specification listed in **Table 1**.

NOTE
If during Step 6 and Step 9 the adjust nut will not tighten, remove the nut and inspect both the nut and the steering stem threads for dirt and/or burrs. Clean both parts with a tap and die if necessary, then repeat Steps 6-9.

10. Install the upper fork bridge, washer and steering stem nut only finger-tight at this time.

NOTE
Steps 10-13 must be performed in this order to assure proper upper and lower fork bridge to fork alignment.

11. Temporarily slide the fork tubes into position so the top surface of the fork tube aligns with the top surface of the upper fork bridge.
12. Tighten the *lower* fork bridge bolts to the torque specification listed in **Table 1**.
13. Tighten the steering stem nut to the torque specification listed in **Table 1**.
14. Loosen the lower fork bridge bolt and slide the front fork tubes down and out.
15. Move the 3-way joint and hose assembly into position and install the mounting bolt (**Figure 44**). Tighten the bolt securely.
16. Move the ignition switch into position and install the mounting bolts (**Figure 43**). Tighten the bolts securely.
17. Install the front forks as described under *Front Fork Removal/Installation* in this chapter.
18. Install the handlebars as described under *Handlebar Removal/Installation* in this chapter.
19. Install the front fairing as described under *Front Fairing Removal/Installation* in Chapter Twelve.
20. Install the front wheel as described under *Front Wheel Installation* in this chapter.

STEERING HEAD BEARING RACES

The headset and steering stem bearing races are pressed into place. Because they are easily bent, do not remove them unless they are worn and require replacement.

Headset Bearing Race Removal/Installation

To remove the headset race, insert a soft punch into the head tube (**Figure 48**) and carefully tap the race out from the inside. After it is started, tap around the race so that neither the race nor the head tube is damaged.

To install the headset race, tap it in slowly with a block of wood, a suitable size socket or piece of pipe (**Figure 49**). Make sure that the race is squarely seated in the headset race bore before tapping it into place. Tap the race in until it is flush with the steering head surface (**Figure 50**).

49

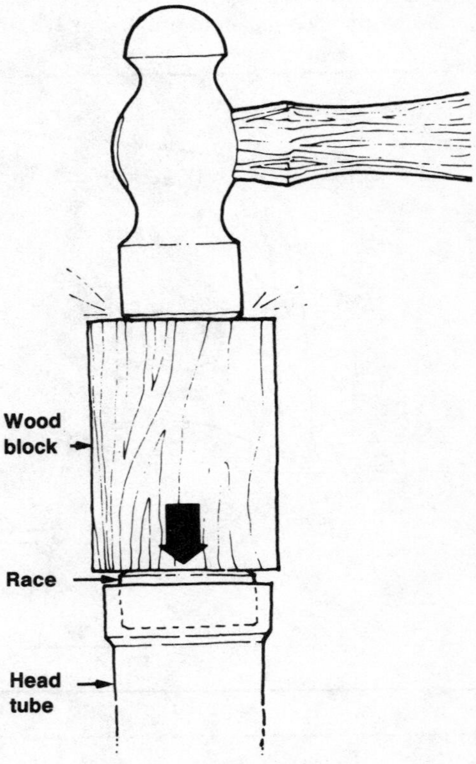

Steering Stem Bearing Removal/Installation

1. Screw the steering stem nut onto the steering stem (A, **Figure 51**).
2. Install the Suzuki special tool (bearing remover part No. 09941-84510) onto the steering stem assembly (B, **Figure 51**).
3. Tighten the upper bolt (C, **Figure 51**) and withdraw the lower bearing from the steering stem.
4. Unscrew the steering stem nut.
5. Remove the special tool and the lower bearing from the steering stem.
6. Install the lower bearing on the steering stem and slide it down onto the top of the shoulder at the base of the steering stem.
7. Install a flat washer on top of the lower bearing.
8. Install the Suzuki special tool (steering stem bearing installer, part No. 09941-74910) on top of the washer and lower bearing.
9. Using a hammer, carefully tap on the bearing installer (**Figure 52**) and drive the lower bearing into place.
10. Remove the bearing installer and the washer.
11. Make sure it is seated squarely and is all the way down (**Figure 53**).

50

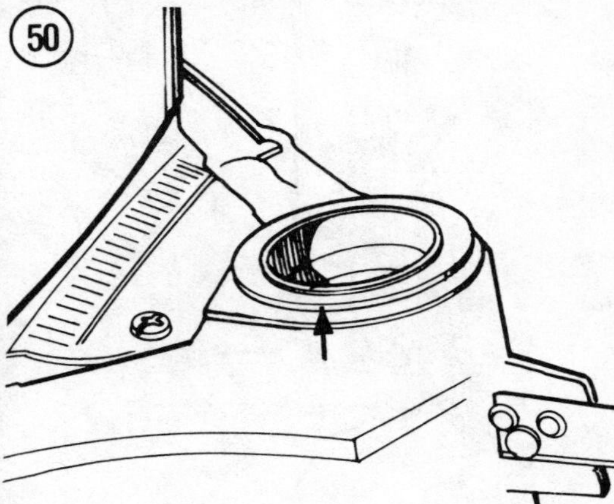

STEERING DAMPER (GSX-R1100)

Removal

Refer to **Figure 42** for this procedure.

1. Remove the front fairing as described under *Front Fairing Removal/Installation* in Chapter Twelve.
2. Remove the outer bolt and nut (**Figure 54**) securing the end of the steering damper to the bracket on the right-hand fork tube.
3. Remove the inner bolt and nut (**Figure 55**) securing the damper unit to the steering head portion of the frame.
4. Remove the steering damper assembly from the frame.

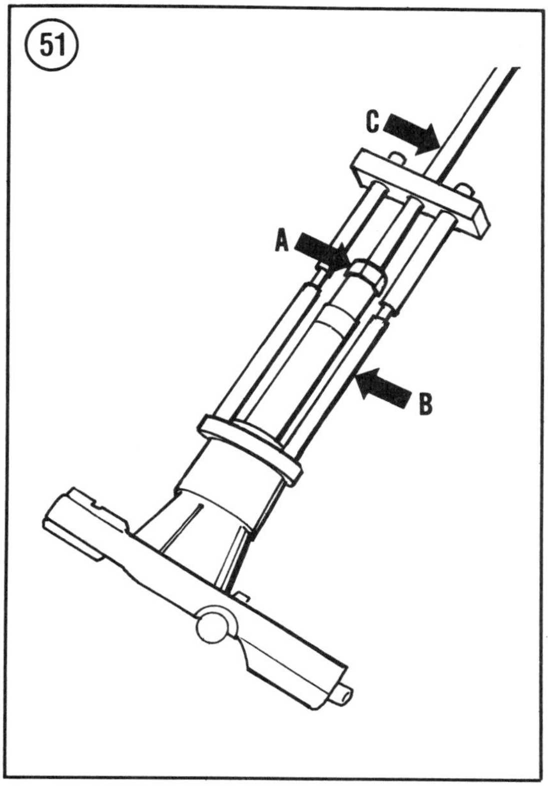
51
C
A
B

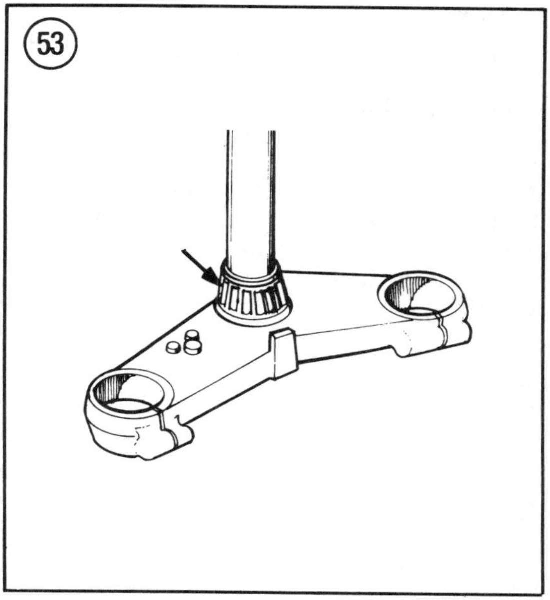
53

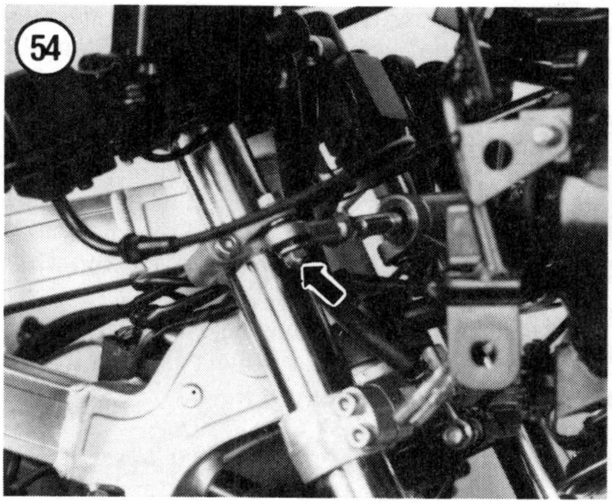
54

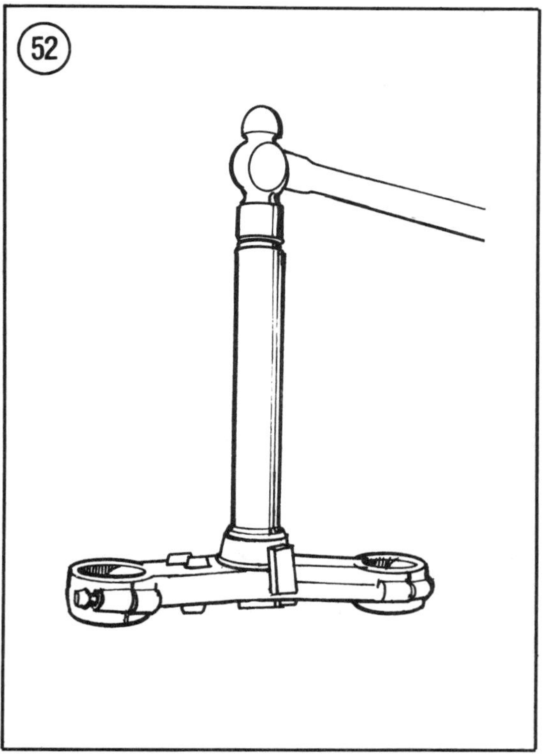
52

55

Inspection

1. Inspect the steering damper unit (A, **Figure 56**) for oil leakage. If there is leakage, replace the damper unit as it cannot be serviced.
2. Inspect all rubber parts for wear and deterioration. Replace as necessary. **Figure 57** shows the dust seals on the inner bolt and nut.
3. Stroke the damper rod (B, **Figure 56**) back and forth in the damper unit. Check for smooth movement. If the movement is rough or erratic, replace the damper unit assembly.

56

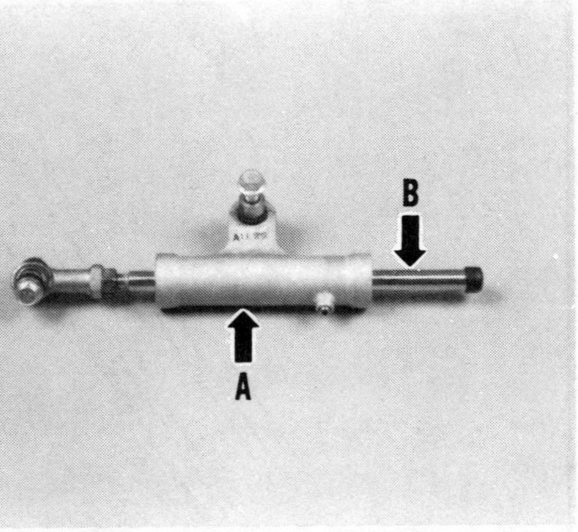

Installation

1. Apply a light coat of grease to the dust seals and bearings.
2. Refer to **Figure 58** and install the steering damper onto the frame and mounting bracket on the right-hand fork tube. Do not tighten the mounting bolts and nuts at this time.
3. Turn the front wheel to the full left lock position. Measure the distance between the nut and the end of the damper unit (**Figure 59**). The specified distance is 8 mm (0.3 in.). If the distance is incorrect, perform the following:
   a. Loosen the clamping bolt (**Figure 60**) on the fork leg bracket.
   b. Rotate the bracket on the fork leg until the specified dimension is achieved. Don't tighten the clamping bolt at this time. Proceed to Step 4.
4. Measure the distance between the lower surface of the bracket and the top surface of the lower fork bridge (**Figure 61**). The specified distance is 80-84 mm (3.1-3.3 in.). If the distance is incorrect, perform the following:
   a. Move the bracket up or down to achieve the correct distance.
   b. Again check the distance dimension in Step 3b. When both dimensions are correct, tighten the clamping bolt to the torque specification listed in **Table 1**.
5. Tighten the mounting bolts and nuts to the torque specification listed in **Table 1**.
6. Move the handlebars back and forth from full right lock to full left lock. Check for smooth operation. Make sure that there are no electrical wires in the way of the damper unit.
7. Install the front fairing as described under *Front Fairing Removal/Installation* in Chapter Twelve.

57

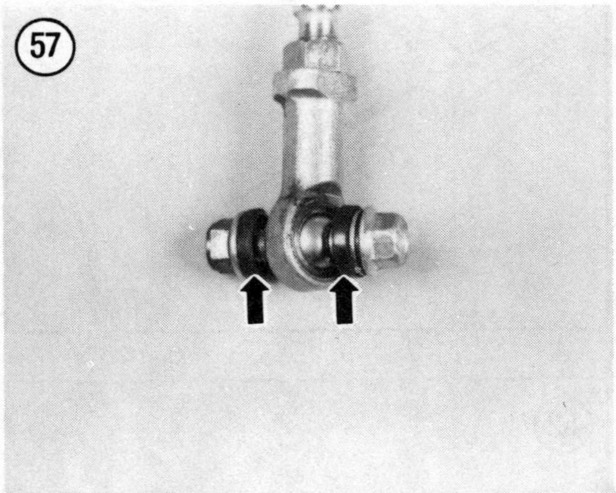

58

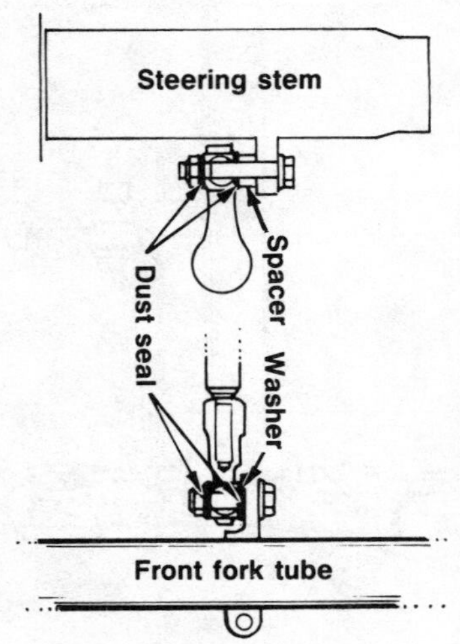

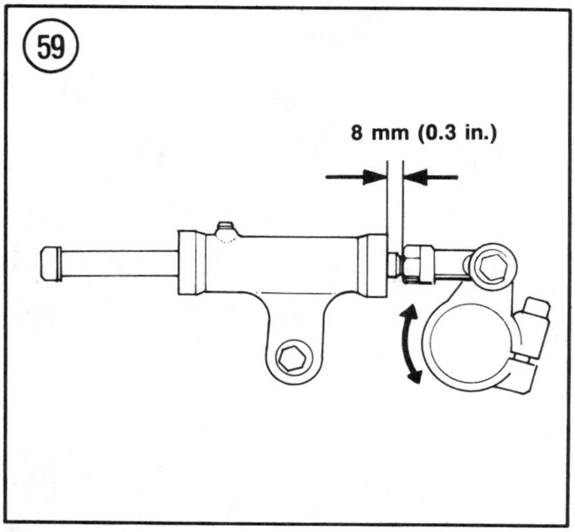

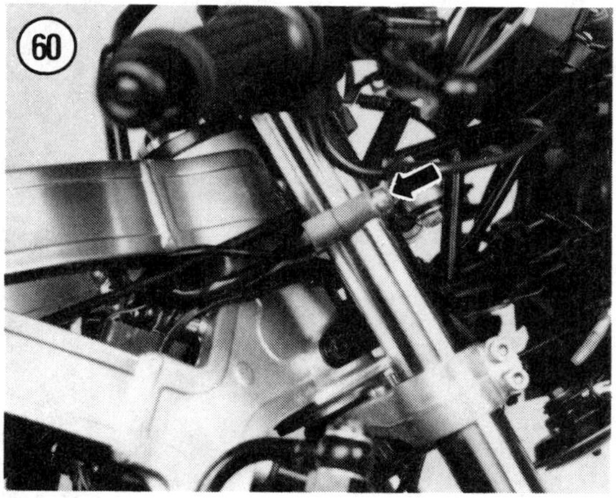

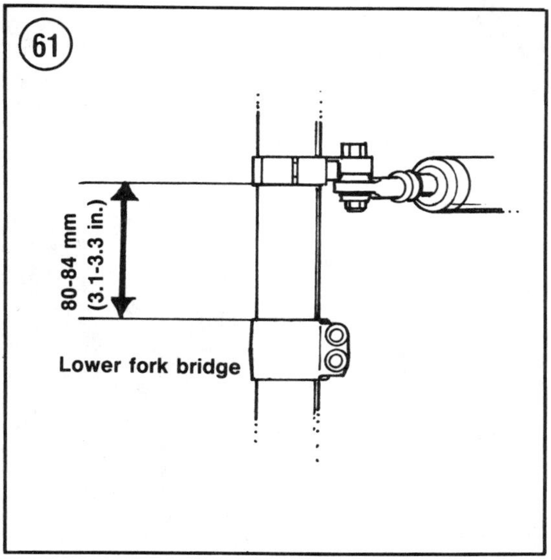

FRONT FORKS

The front suspension on all models uses spring controlled, hydraulically damped, telescopic forks.

Front Fork Adjustment

The front fork is adjustable for both spring pre-load and anti-dive action.

Spring pre-load adjustment

The spring pre-load can be adjusted to 4 different settings. Position 1 (completely counterclockwise) is the softest setting and position 4 (completely clockwise) is the stiffest setting. The bike is delivered from the factory on the No. 2 setting.

WARNING

Both fork springs must be adjusted to the ***same setting****. If the springs are set on different settings, it will greatly disturb the handling stability which may lead to an accident. Make sure each adjuster is set correctly onto one of the setting detents and not in between any 2 of them (****Figure 62****).*

NOTE

Figure 62 *is shown with the fork cap bolt removed to show where the detents are located within the fork cap bolt. Do not remove the fork cap bolt for this procedure.*

1. Remove the lower section of the front fairing as described under *Front Fairing Removal/ Installation* in Chapter Twelve.
2. Place wood blocks under the frame on each side to support the bike securely with the front wheel off the ground. There should be no weight on the forks during the adjustment procedure.

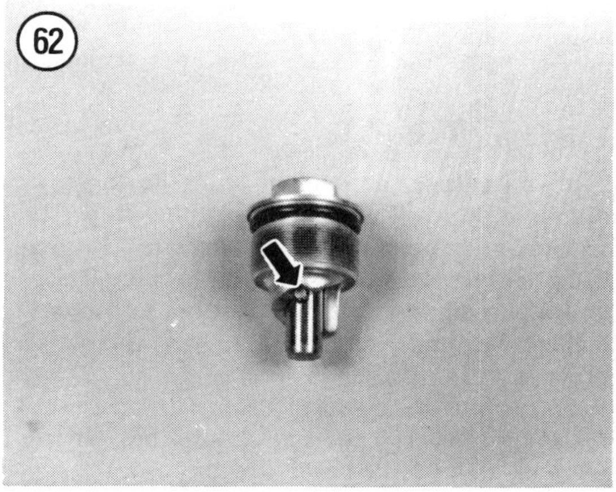

9

3. Remove the cap (**Figure 63**) from the fork cap bolt.
4. Insert a flat-bladed screwdriver into the slot in the adjuster (**Figure 64**) in the fork cap bolt.

WARNING
*Make sure each adjuster is set correctly onto one of the setting detents and not in between any 2 of them (**Figure 62**).*

5. Using the screwdriver, turn the adjuster *clockwise* to increase pre-load or *counterclockwise* to decrease pre-load.
6. Repeat for the other fork assembly.
7. Install the cap (**Figure 63**) onto the fork cap bolt.
8. Remove the wood blocks from under the frame on each side.
9. Install the lower section of the front fairing as described under *Front Fairing Removal/ Installation* in Chapter Twelve.

Anti-dive or compression damping adjustment

The front fork anti-dive and compression damping can be adjusted to 3 different settings. Position 1 provides the least amount of anti-dive or compression damping while position 3 provides the greatest amount of anti-dive or compression damping. The bike is delivered from the factory with the adjuster on the No. 1 setting.

The adjuster knob is located on top of the NEAS unit (**Figure 65**) on the front fork slider.

The anti-dive adjustment varies the following:

a. The amount of anti-dive when the front brake is applied.
b. The amount of compression damping force when the front brake is not applied.

Rotate the adjuster to the desired setting (align the number to the arrow). Make sure that the adjuster is located into one of the detents and not in between any 2 settings.

Front Fork Service

If you suspect a problem with the forks, first drain the fork oil and refill with the proper type and quantity; refer to *Front Fork Oil Change* in Chapter Three. If you still have trouble, such as poor damping, a tendency to bottom or top out or leakage around the seals, follow the service procedures in this section.

To simplify fork service and to prevent the mixing of parts, the legs should be removed, serviced and installed individually.

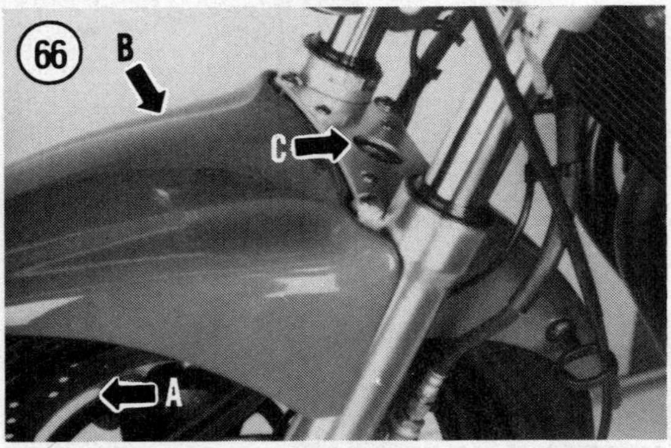

Removal/Installation

1. Remove the front fairing as described under *Front Fairing Removal/Installation* in Chapter Twelve.
2. Remove the front wheel (A, **Figure 66**) as described under *Front Wheel Removal/Installation* in this chapter.
3. Remove the screws securing the front fender to the front fork stabilizer. Remove the spacers (**Figure 67**) from the front fender and remove the front fender (B, **Figure 66**).

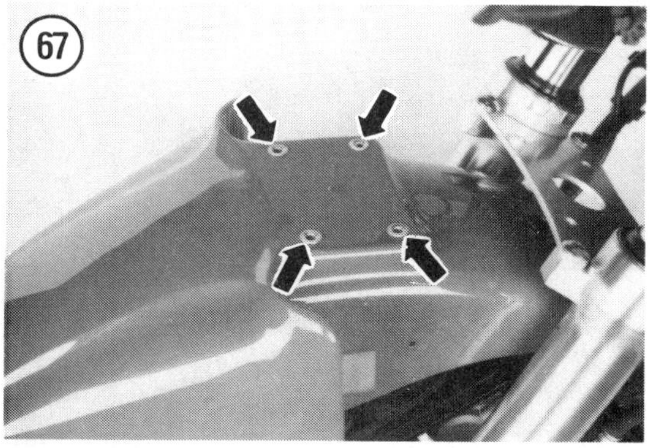
67

68

69

4. Remove the screws securing the front fork stabilizer to the front forks and remove the front stabilizer (C, **Figure 66**).
5. Remove the remaining front caliper assembly as described under *Front Brake Caliper Removal/Installation* in Chapter Eleven.
6. Remove the handlebars as described under *Handlebar Removal* in this chapter.

NOTE
The Allen bolt at the base of the slider has been secured with Loctite and is often very difficult to remove because the damper rod will turn inside the slider. It sometimes can be removed with an air impact driver. If you are unable to remove it, take the fork tubes to a dealer and have the bolts removed.

7. If the fork assembly is going to be disassembled, use an Allen wrench to slightly loosen the Allen bolt at the base of the slider. If the bolt is loosened too much, fork oil may start to drain out of the slider.
8. On 1100 cc models, loosen the steering damper bracket clamping bolt (**Figure 60**) on the right-hand fork tube.
9. Remove the cap (**Figure 63**) from the fork cap bolt.

NOTE
Do not try to loosen the fork cap bolt at this time as there is insufficient room for a wrench.

10. Loosen the upper and lower fork bridge bolts (**Figure 68**).

CAUTION
On 1100 cc models, the right-hand fork leg also goes through the steering damper bracket as well as the upper and lower fork bridges. Remember this while sliding the fork tube in and out of the fork bridges.

11. Slide the fork tube out of the upper fork bridge and retighten the lower fork bridge bolts. It may be necessary to slightly rotate the fork tube while pulling it down and out.
12. Loosen the fork cap bolt (**Figure 69**).
13. Loosen the lower fork bridge bolts and slide the fork tube from the lower fork bridge. It may be necessary to slightly rotate the fork tube while pulling it down and out.
14. Install by reversing these removal steps, noting the following.

15. Install the fork tubes so that the top of the fork tube aligns with the top surface of the upper fork bridge (**Figure 70**).
16. Tighten the upper and lower fork bridge bolts to the torque specifications listed in **Table 1**.

70

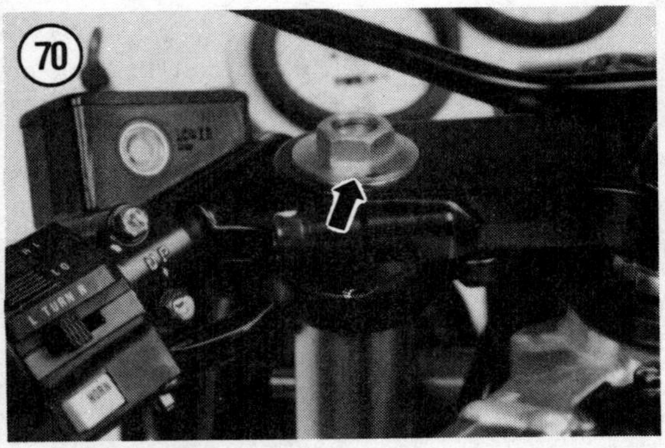

Disassembly

Refer to **Figure 71** during the disassembly and assembly procedures.

1. Clamp the axle boss of the slider in a vise with soft jaws.
2. If not loosened during the fork removal sequence, loosen the Allen bolt on the bottom of the slider.

NOTE
If you have the special Suzuki tools used for fork disassembly, loosen the Allen bolt in Step 10.

NOTE
This bolt has been secured with Loctite and is often very difficult to remove because the damper rod will turn inside the slider. It sometimes can be removed with an air impact driver. If you are unable to remove it, take the fork tubes to a dealer and have the bolts removed.

3. Remove the Allen bolt and gasket from the slider.
4. Hold the fork tube in a vise with soft jaws and loosen the fork cap bolt (if it was not loosened during the fork removal sequence).

WARNING
Be careful when removing the fork cap bolt as the spring is under pressure. Protect your eyes accordingly.

5. Remove the fork cap bolt from the fork tube.
6. Remove the spring seat and the fork spring.
7. Remove the fork from the vise, pour the fork oil out and discard it. Pump the fork several times by hand to expel most of the remaining oil.
8. Remove the dust seal (**Figure 72**) from the slider.
9. Remove the circlip and washer (**Figure 73**) from the slider.
10. If the Allen bolt was not loosened before, use special Suzuki tools and perform the following:
   a. Install the attachment "G" (part No. 09940-34592) onto the "T" handle (part No. 09940-34520) as shown in **Figure 74**.
   b. Insert this special tool setup into the fork tube and index it into the top of the damper rod to hold the damper rod in place.

72

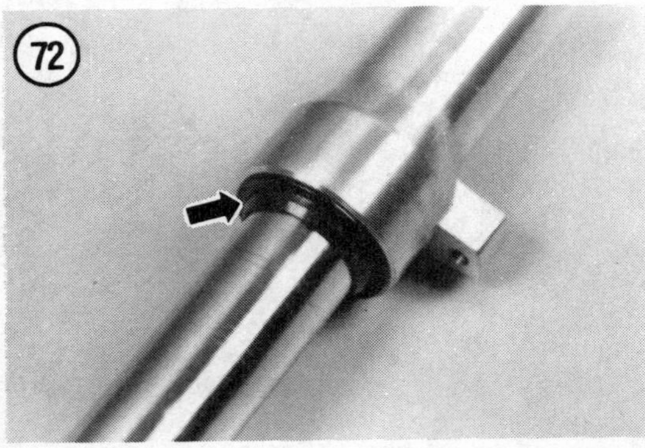

73

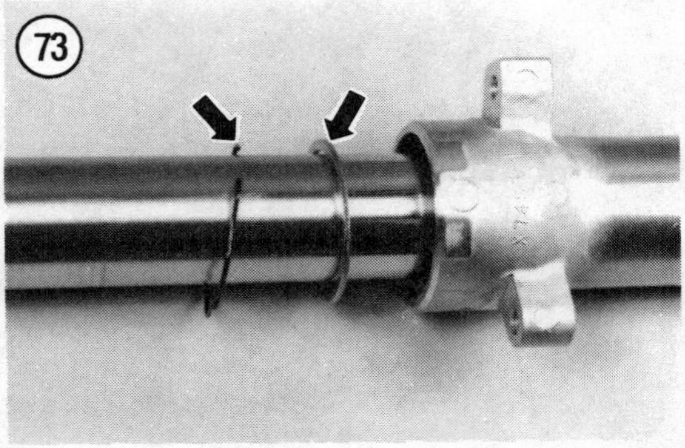

74

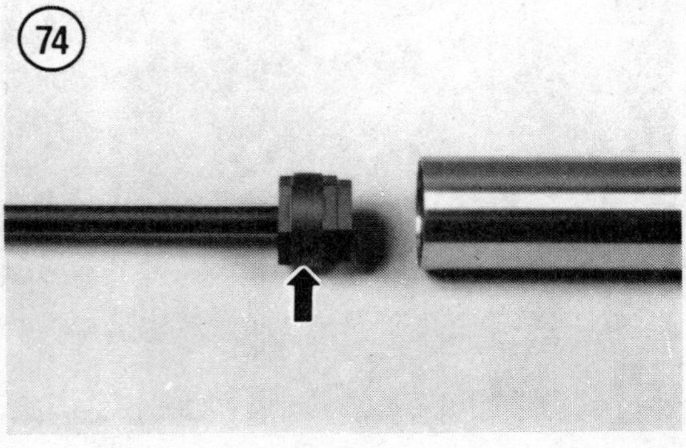

(71)

FRONT FORK ASSEMBLY

1. Cap
2. Fork cap bolt
3. O-ring
4. Spring seat
5. Fork spring
6. Piston ring
7. Damper rod
8. Rebound spring
9. Fork tube
10. Dust seal
11. Circlip
12. Washer
13. Oil seal
14. Washer
15. Slider bushing
16. Wave washer
17. Washer
18. Oil lock piece
19. Fork slider
20. Allen bolt
21. NEAS unit
22. Pinch bolt
23. Washer
24. Lockwasher
25. Nut
26. Gasket
27. Allen bolt
28. Fork tube bushing

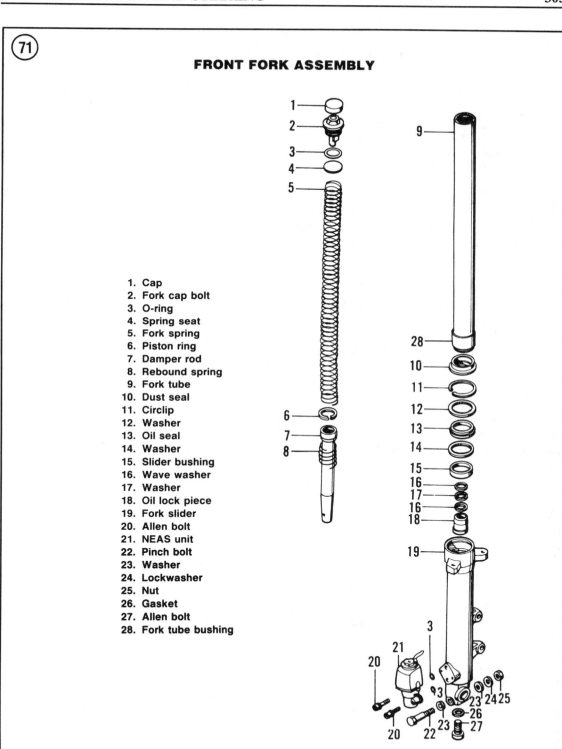

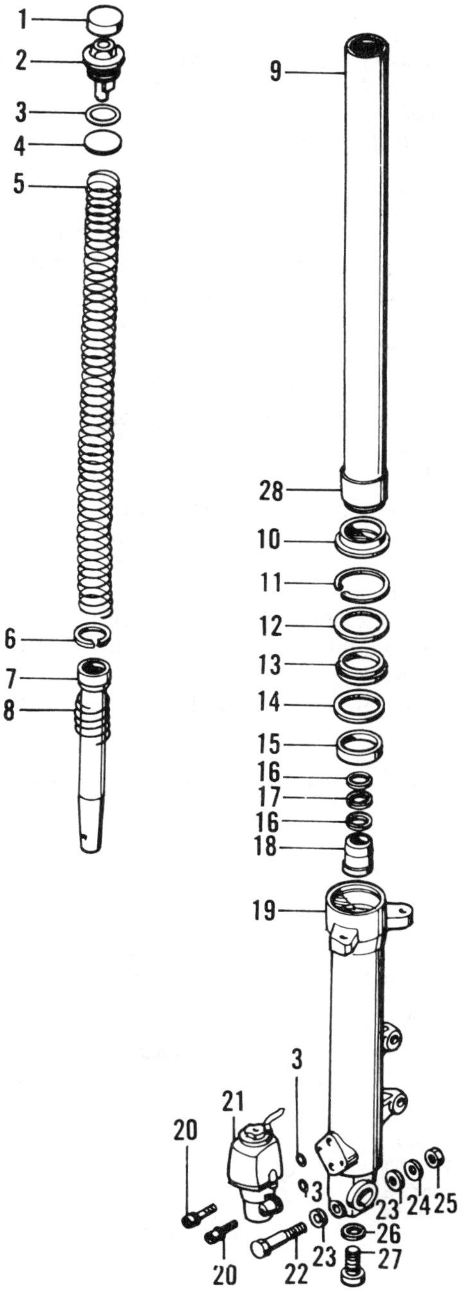

c. Using an Allen wrench, loosen then remove the Allen bolt and washer from the base of the slider.

NOTE
On this type of fork, a pressed in bushing keeps the slider and fork tube from separatin. To remove the fork tube from the slider, you'll need to use these parts as a slide hammer.

11. Hold the slider in one hand and the fork tube in the other hand.
12. Pull hard on the fork tube using quick in-and-out strokes (**Figure 75**). Doing so will withdraw the bushing, washer and oil seal from the slider.
13. Separate the fork tube from the slider.

NOTE
Do not remove the fork tube bushing unless it is going to be replaced. Inspect it as described in this chapter.

14. Remove the oil lock piece, wave washers and washer.
15. Remove the damper rod and rebound spring from the fork tube.
16. Remove the screws (**Figure 76**) securing the NEAS unit to the fork slider. Remove the NEAS unit and the O-rings.
17. Inspect the components as described in this chapter.

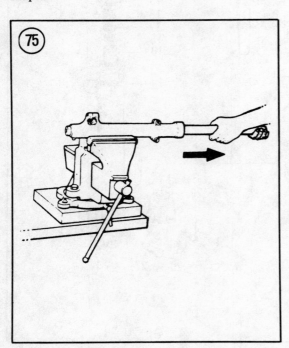

75

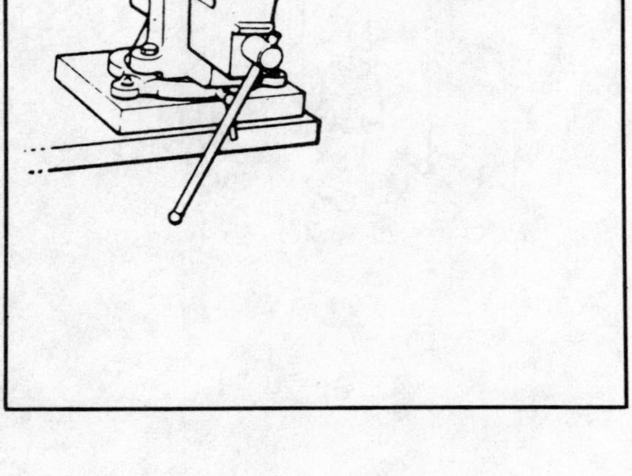

76

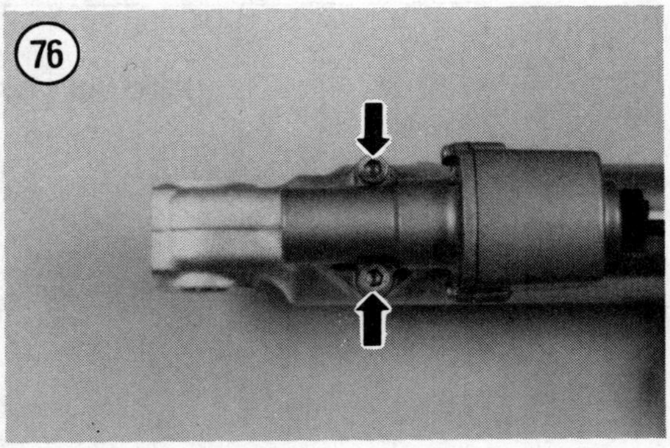

77

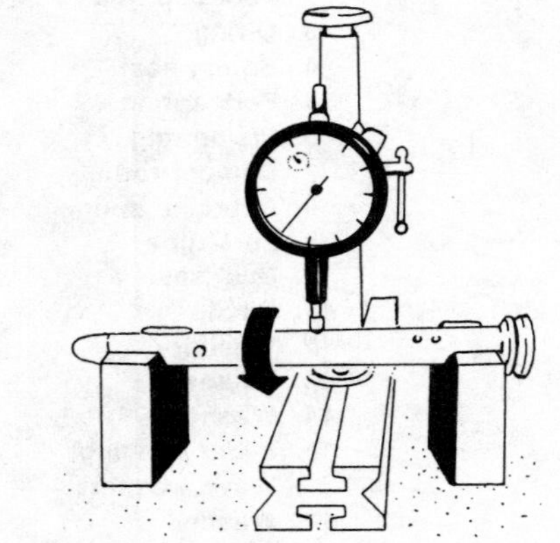

78

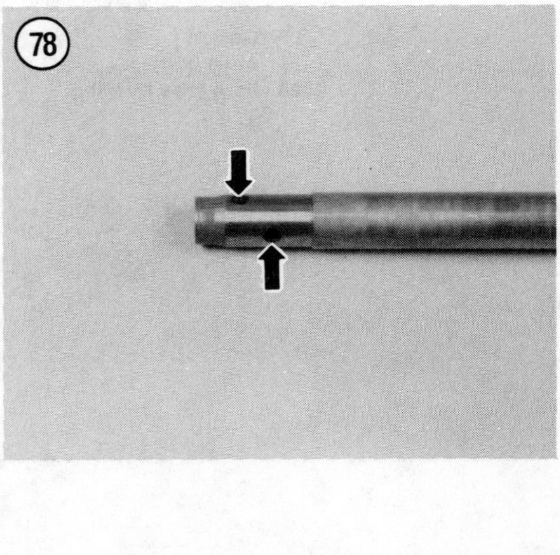

79

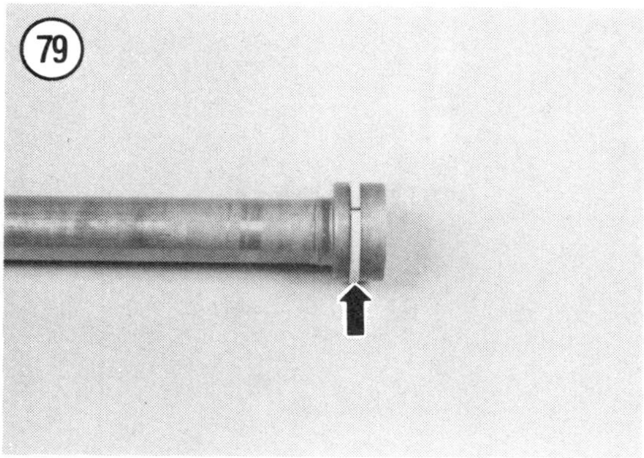

80

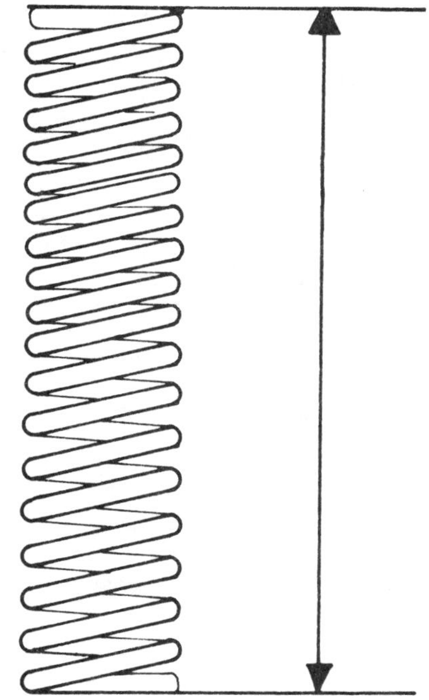

81

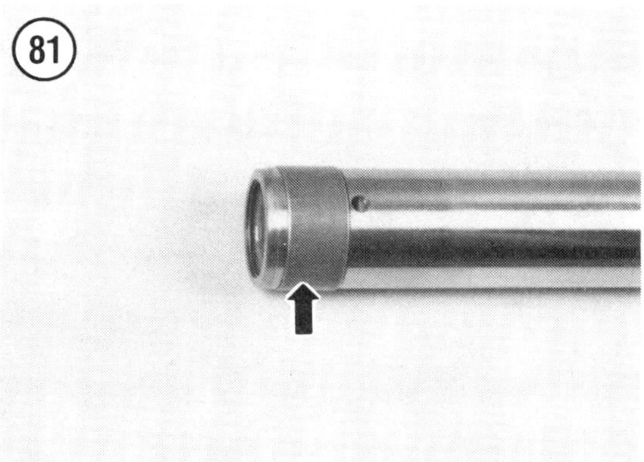

Inspection

1. Thoroughly clean all parts in solvent and dry them. Check the fork tube for signs of wear or scratches.
2. Check the damper rod for straightness. **Figure 77** shows one method. The damper rod should be replaced if the runout is 0.2 mm (0.008 in.) or greater.
3. Make sure the oil holes (**Figure 78**) in the damper rod are clear. Clean out if necessary.
4. Inspect the damper rod and piston ring (**Figure 79**) for wear or damage. Replace as necessary.
5. Check the upper fork tube for straightness. If bent or severely scratched, it should be replaced.
6. Check the lower slider for dents or exterior damage that may cause the upper fork tube to hang up during riding. Replace if necessary.
7. Measure the free length of the fork spring (not rebound spring) as shown in **Figure 80**. If the spring has sagged to the service limit dimensions listed in **Table 2**, the spring must be replaced.
8. Inspect the fork tube bushing (**Figure 81**). If either is scratched or scored they must be replaced. If the Teflon coating is worn off so that the copper base material is showing on approximately 3/4 of the total surface, the bushing must be replaced. Also check for distortion on the check points of the washer; replace as necessary. Refer to **Figure 82**.

9

82

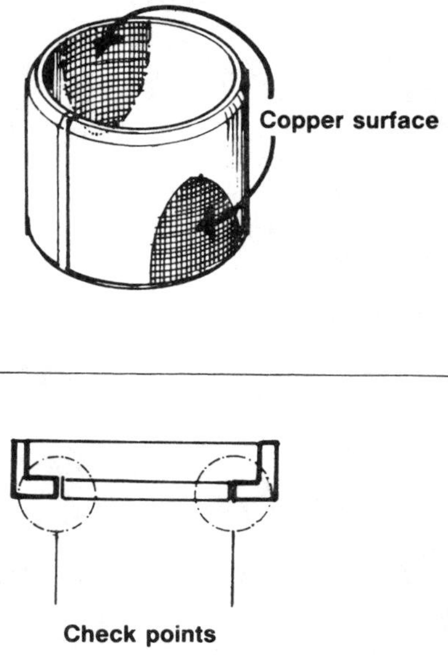

9. Inspect the gasket on the allen bolt (**Figure 83**); replace if damaged.
10. Inspect the NEAS unit (**Figure 84**) for fork oil leakage. If any leakage is found, replace the NEAS unit, as the unit cannot be serviced.
11. Any parts that are worn or damaged should be replaced.
Simply cleaning and reinstalling unserviceable components will not improve performance of the front suspension.

Assembly

1. Coat all parts with fresh DEXRON automatic transmission fluid or SAE 15W fork oil prior to installation.
2. Install new O-rings (**Figure 85**) into the NEAS unit.
3. Install the NEAS unit onto the fork leg.
4. Apply Loctite Lock N' Seal to the NEAS screw threads prior to installation and install the NEAS unit mounting screws (**Figure 76**). Tighten the screws to the torque specification listed in **Table 1**.

83

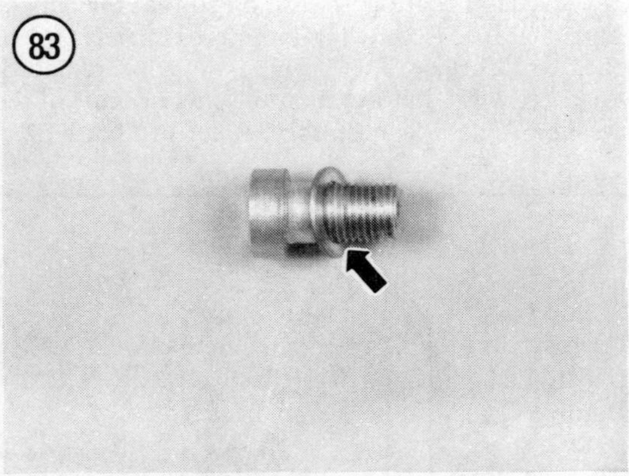

84

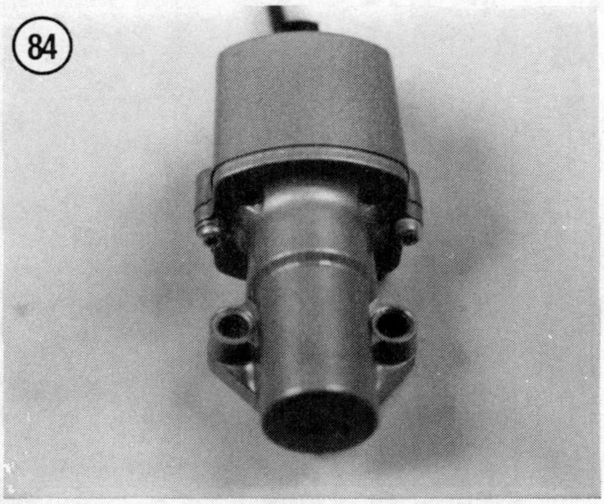

85

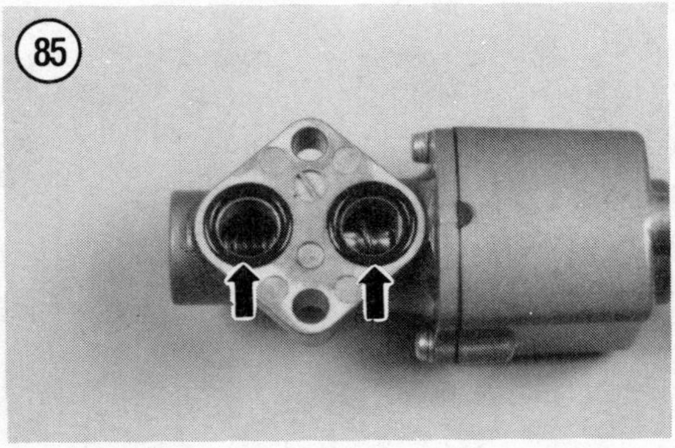

86

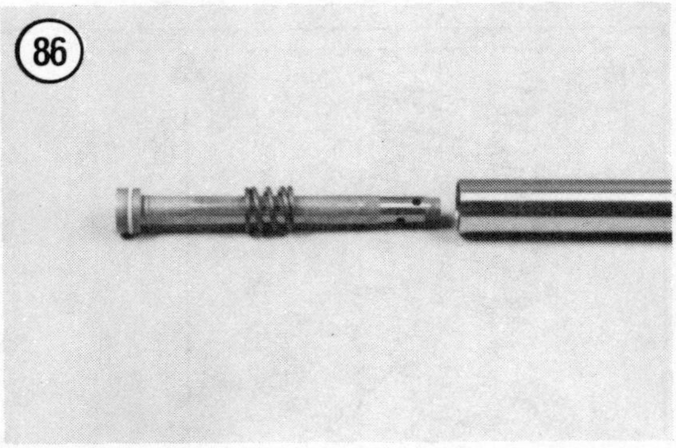

87

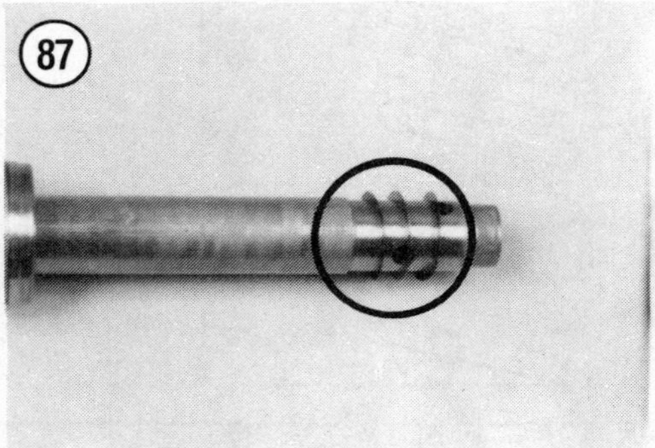

88

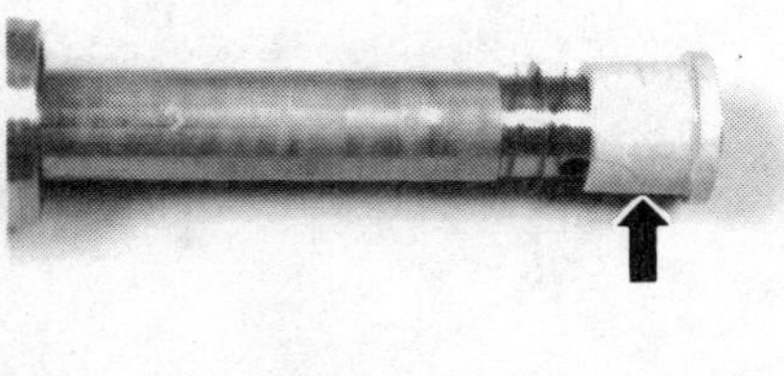

89

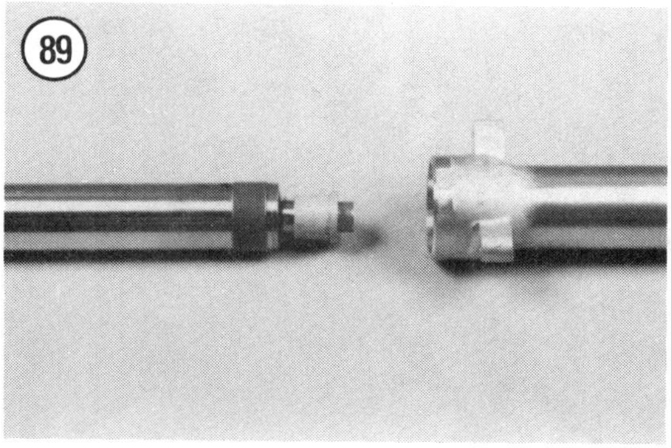

90

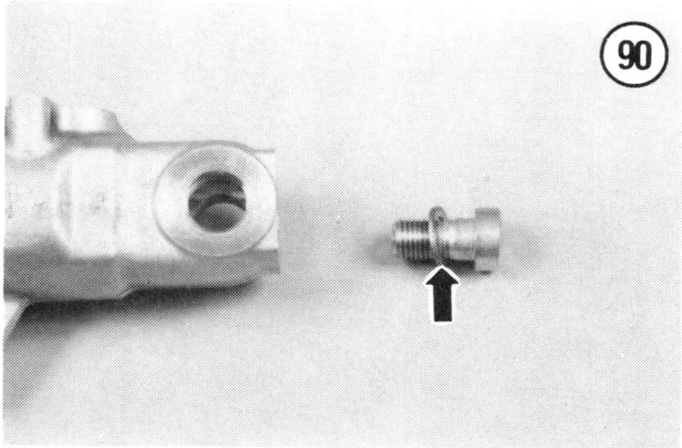

91

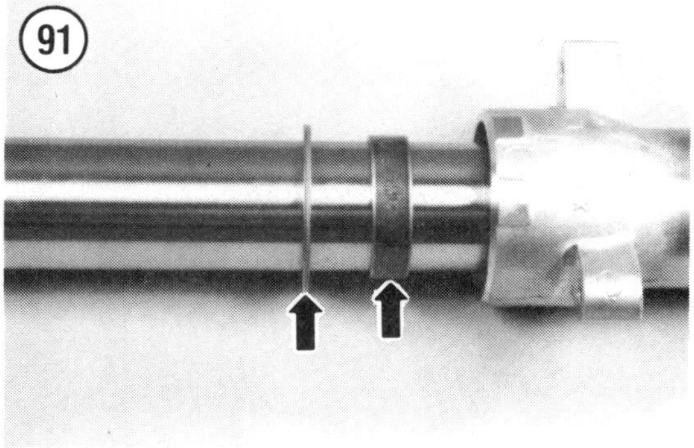

92

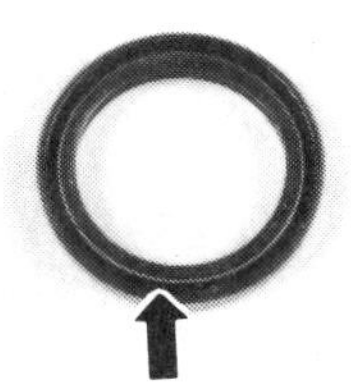

5. Install the rebound spring onto the damper rod and insert this assembly into the fork tube (**Figure 86**).
6. Temporarily install the fork spring, spring seat and fork cap bolt to hold the damper rod in place. Tighten the fork cap bolt securely.
7. Install a wave washer, washer, then another wave washer onto the damper rod (**Figure 87**).
8. Install the oil lock piece onto the damper rod (**Figure 88**).
9. Install the fork tube assembly into the slider (**Figure 89**).
10. Make sure the gasket (**Figure 90**) is on the Allen bolt.
11. Apply Loctite Lock N' Seal to the threads of the Allen bolt prior to installation. Install it in the fork slider and tighten to the torque specification listed in **Table 1**.
12. Slide the fork slider bushing and the lower washer (**Figure 91**) down the fork tube and rest it on top of the fork slider.
13. Install the new oil seal as follows:
   a. Coat the new seal with ATF (automatic transmission fluid).
   b. Position the seal with the open groove facing downward (**Figure 92**) and slide the oil seal (**Figure 93**) and upper washer down onto the fork tube.
   c. Drive the seal, washers and bushing into the slider with Suzuki special tool Front Fork Oil Seal Installer (part No. 09940-50112).
   d. Drive the oil seal in until the circlip groove in the slider can be seen above the top surface of the upper washer.
14. Position the circlip with the sharp side facing up and install the circlip. Make sure the circlip (**Figure 94**) is completely seated in the groove in the fork slider.

93

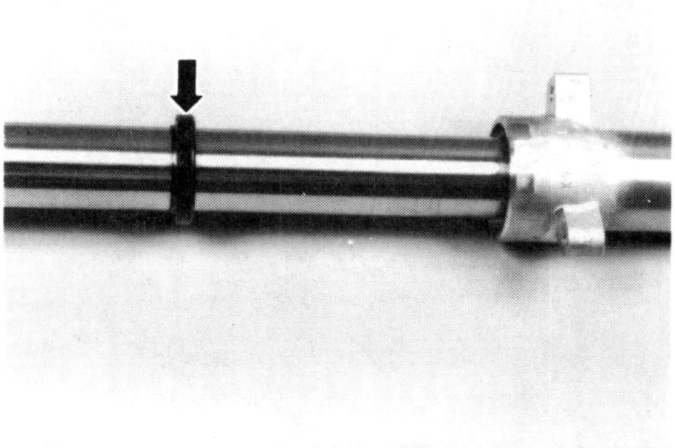

15. Install the dust seal (**Figure 95**) into the slider.
16. Remove the fork cap bolt, the spring seat and the fork spring.
17. Fill the fork tube with the correct quantity of DEXRON automatic transmission fluid or SAE 10W or 15W fork oil. Refer to **Table 2** for specified type, quantity and oil level.
18. Check the fork oil level in each fork assembly as follows:
  a. Hold the fork tube vertical and *completely* compress the fork tube into the slider.
  b. Use an accurate ruler or the Suzuki Oil Level Gauge (part No. 09943-74111) and measure the distance from the top surface of the fork tube. Adjust the oil level as necessary.

NOTE
An oil level measuring device can be made as shown in ***Figure 96****. Position the lower edge of the hose clamp the specified oil level distance up from the end of the tube. Fill the fork with a few cc's more than the required amount of oil. Position the hose clamp on the top edge of the fork tube and draw out the excess oil. Oil is sucked out until the level reaches the end of the tube. A precise oil level can be achieved with this simple device.*

19. Install the fork spring with the tighter wound coils (**Figure 97**) going in last.
20. Inspect the O-ring seal (**Figure 98**) on the fork cap bolt; replace if necessary.
21. Install the spring seat and the fork cap bolt (**Figure 99**) while pushing down on the spring. Start the bolt slowly, don't cross-thread it.
22. Place the fork tube in a vise with soft jaws and tighten the top fork cap bolt to the torque specifications listed in **Table 1**.
23. Repeat for the other fork assembly.
24. Install the fork assemblies as described in this chapter.

95
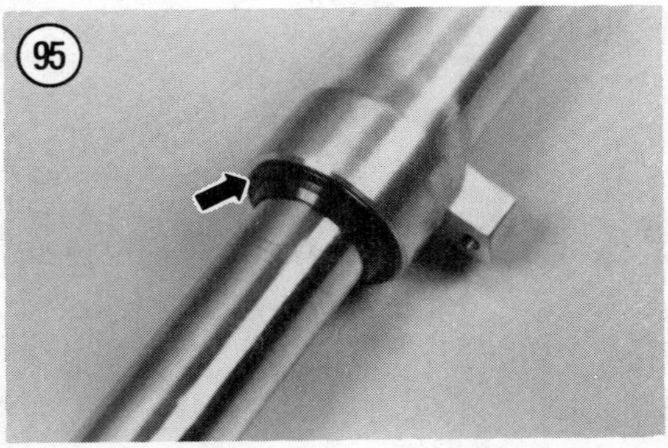

97
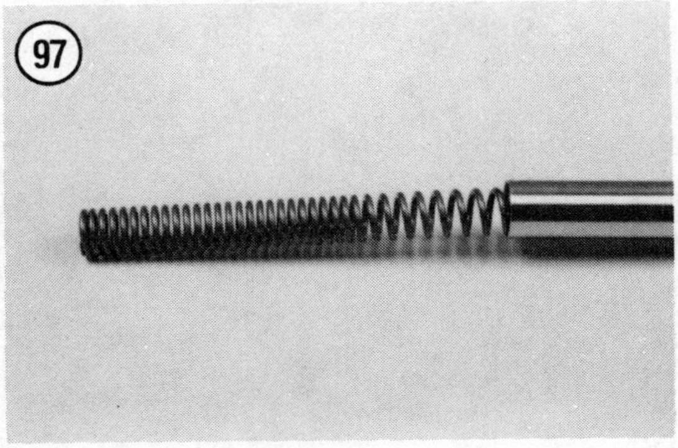

98
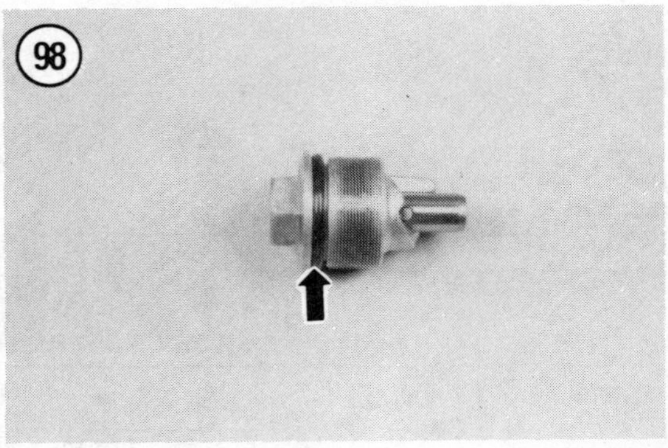

94

99
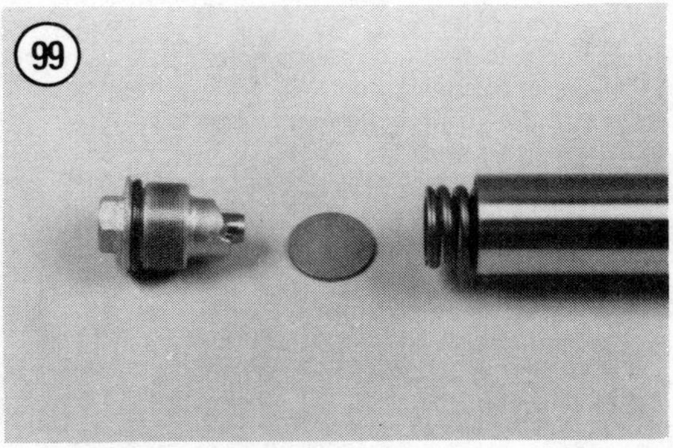

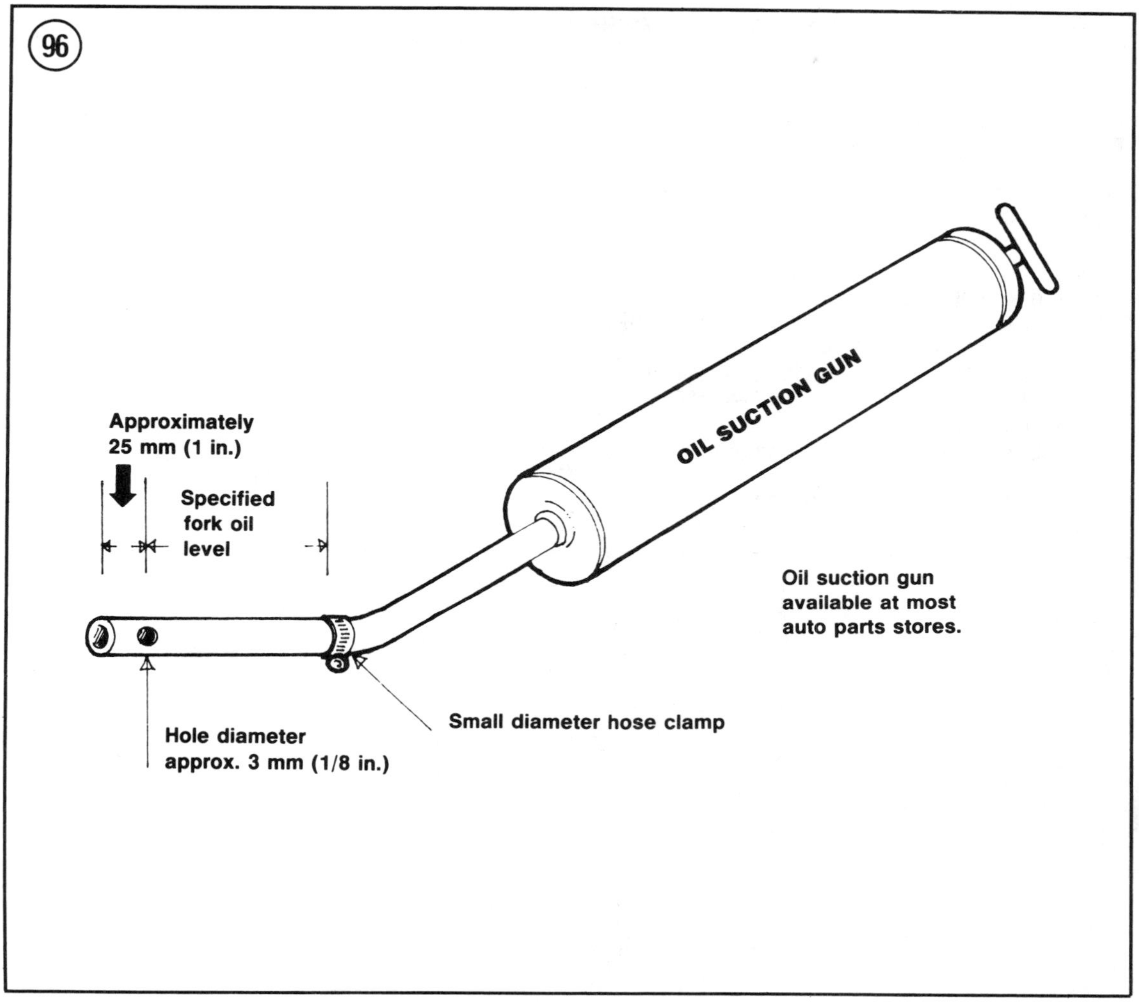

Table 1 FRONT SUSPENSION TORQUE SPECIFICATIONS

Item	N•m	ft.-lb.
Front axle nut	36-52	26-38
Front axle pinch bolt and nut	15-25	11-18
Brake disc bolts	15-25	11-18
Handlebar-to-fork tube clamp bolt	15-25	11-18
Handlebar mounting bolt	6-10	4-7
Fork bridge clamp bolts (upper and lower)	20-30	14-22
Steering stem nut		
Initial torque	40-50	29-36
Final torque	30-40	21-29
Steering damper mounting bolts and nuts	15-20	11-15
Steering damper bracket clamp bolt	20-25	15-18
NEAS unit mounting screws	6-8	4-6
Front damper Allen bolt	54-70	40-51

Table 2 FRONT SUSPENSION SPECIFICATIONS

Item	Standard	Wear limit	Fork oil
Front fork spring free length			
GSX-R750		377 mm (14.8 in.)	
GSX-R750R Limited Edition		382 mm (15.0 in.)	
GSX-R1100			
1986		459 mm (18.1 in.)	
1987		463 mm (18.2 in.)	
Front fork oil capacity			
GSX-R750	456 cc (15.4 U.S. oz.)		SAE 15
GSX-R750R			
Limited Edition	427 cc (14.4 U.S. oz.)		SAE 10
GSX-R1100	417 cc (14.1 U.S. oz.)		SAE 15
Front fork oil level dimension			
GSX-R750	107 mm (4.2 in.)		
GSX-R750R			
Limited Edition	130 mm (5.12 in.)		
GSX-R1100	159 mm (6.26 in.)		

NOTE: If you own a GSX600F Katana, first refer to Chapter 13 for specific service information.

CHAPTER TEN

REAR SUSPENSION

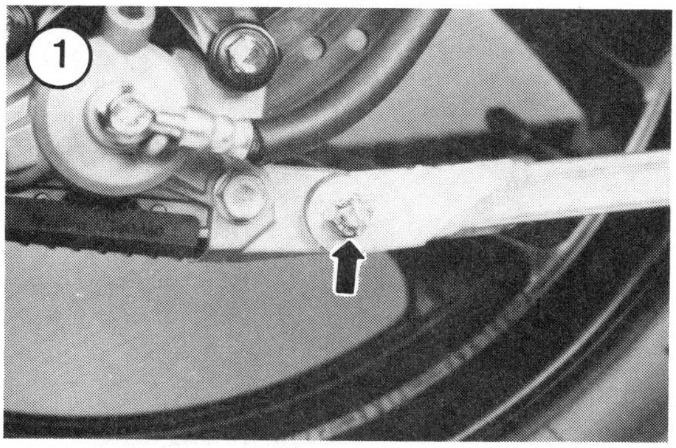

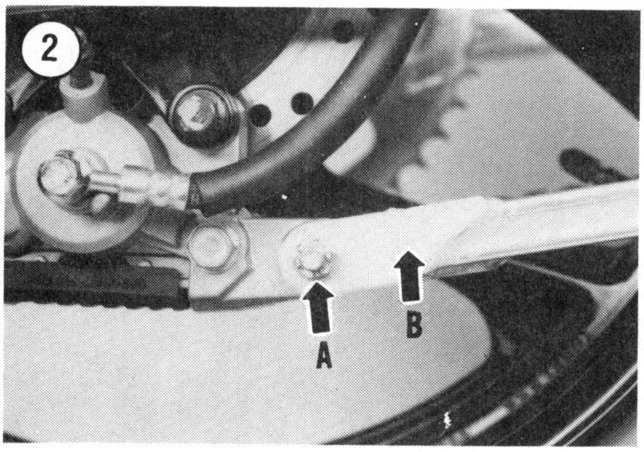

This chapter includes repair and replacement procedures for the rear wheel and rear suspension components. Tire changing and wheel balancing are covered in Chapter Nine.

Refer to **Table 1** for rear suspension torque specifications and **Table 2** for shock absorber settings. **Table 1** and **Table 2** are located at the end of this chapter.

10

REAR WHEEL

Removal/Installation

1. Remove the lower portion of the front fairing as described under *Front Fairing Removal/ Installation* in Chapter Twelve.
2. Place wood block(s) under each side of the frame to support the bike securely with the rear wheel off the ground.
3. Remove the cotter pin (**Figure 1**) on the rear caliper torque link. Discard the cotter pin.
4. Remove the bolt, washer and nut (A, **Figure 2**) and let the torque link (B, **Figure 2**) pivot down to the ground.
5. Remove the bolts (**Figure 3**) securing the rear brake caliper to the caliper bracket.
6. Carefully pull the caliper off of the rear disc and tie it up the frame or swing arm with a Bungee cord.

NOTE
Insert a piece of vinyl tubing or wood in the caliper in place of the brake disc. That way if the brake lever is inadvertently squeezed, the piston will not be forced out of the cylinder. If this does happen, the caliper may have to be disassembled to reseat the piston and the system will have to be bled.

7. Loosen the drive chain adjuster nut (**Figure 4**) on each side of the swing arm so the wheel can be moved forward for maximum chain slack.
8. Remove the cotter pin (**Figure 5**) on the rear axle nut. Discard the cotter pin.
9. Remove the rear axle nut (**Figure 6**), washer (**Figure 7**) and special washer (**Figure 8**).
10. Move the wheel forward (A, **Figure 9**), then rotate the rear wheel and derail the drive chain (B, **Figure 9**) from the driven sprocket.
11. Withdraw the rear axle (A, **Figure 10**) and special washer (B, **Figure 10**) from the right-hand side. Remove the caliper bracket from the right-hand side of the wheel.
12. Slide the wheel to the rear and remove it. Don't lose the spacer on each side of the wheel hub.

CAUTION
Do not set the wheel down on the disc surface as it may get scratched or bent. Set the sidewalls on 2 wood blocks.

13. Inspect the rear hub and caliper bracket as described in this chapter.
14. Install by reversing these removal steps, noting the following.
15. Refer to **Figure 11** for the components relating to the rear axle.
16. Position the right-hand spacer with the shoulder (**Figure 12**) side facing in toward the bearing. This shoulder must be against the bearing

3

4

5

6

7

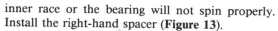

inner race or the bearing will not spin properly. Install the right-hand spacer (**Figure 13**).

17. Install the left-hand spacer (**Figure 14**) into the hub.

18. Adjust the drive chain as described in Chapter Three.

19. Tighten the rear axle nut to the torque specification listed in **Table 1**.

20. After the wheel is completely installed, rotate it several times to make sure that it rotates freely. Apply the rear brake as many times as necessary to make sure the brake pads are against the brake disc correctly.

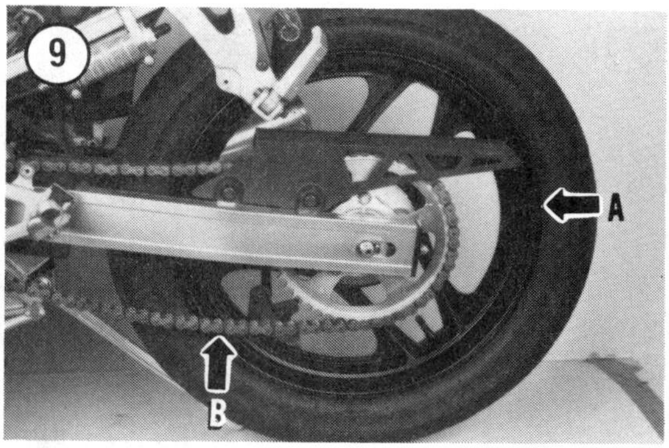

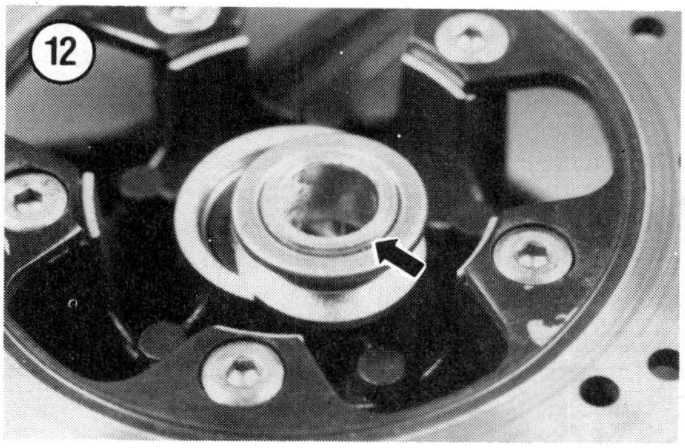

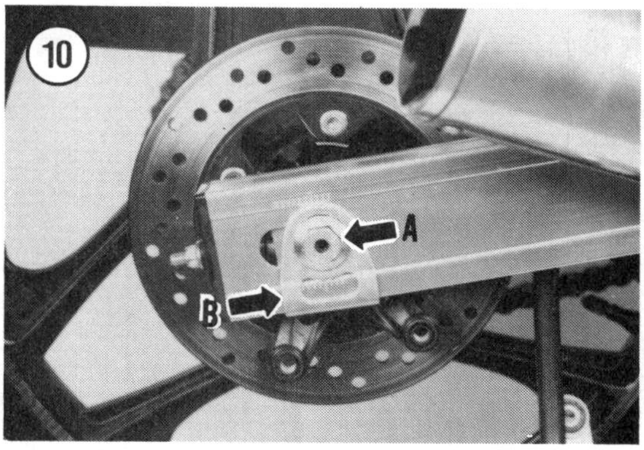

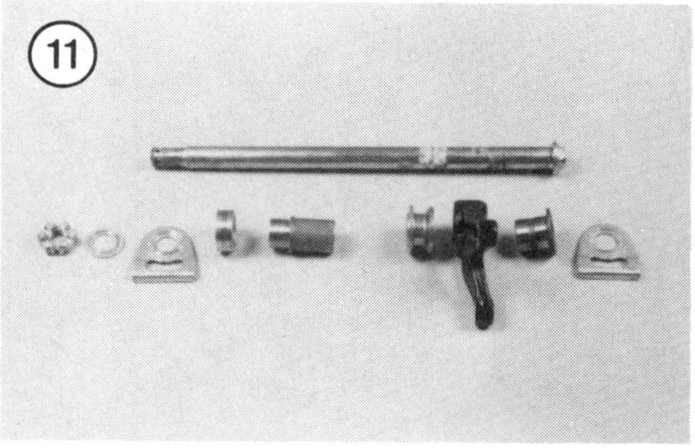

Inspection

Measure the axial and radial runout of the wheel with a dial indicator as shown in **Figure 15**. The maximum axial runout (end play) and radial runout (side play) is 2.0 mm (0.08 in.).

Check axle runout as described in this chapter.

CALIPER BRACKET

Inspection

1. Remove the spacer (**Figure 16**) from the caliper bracket.
2. Remove the oil seal (**Figure 17**) from each side of the caliper bracket.
3. Check the caliper bracket (**Figure 18**) for wear, cracks or damage. If any damage is found, replace the bracket.
4. Inspect the inner (**Figure 19**) and the outer (**Figure 20**) surfaces of the spacer for wear or scratches. Replace if necessary.
5. Inspect the inner bronze bushing surface (**Figure 21**) of the caliper bracket for wear or scratches. Replace the caliper bracket if the surfaces is worn or damaged.
6. Inspect the oil seals for wear or deterioration. Replace if necessary. Install an oil seal into each side of the caliper bracket.
7. Install the spacer into the caliper bracket with the flange side (**Figure 22**) toward the outside. Push the spacer in until it seats completely.

15

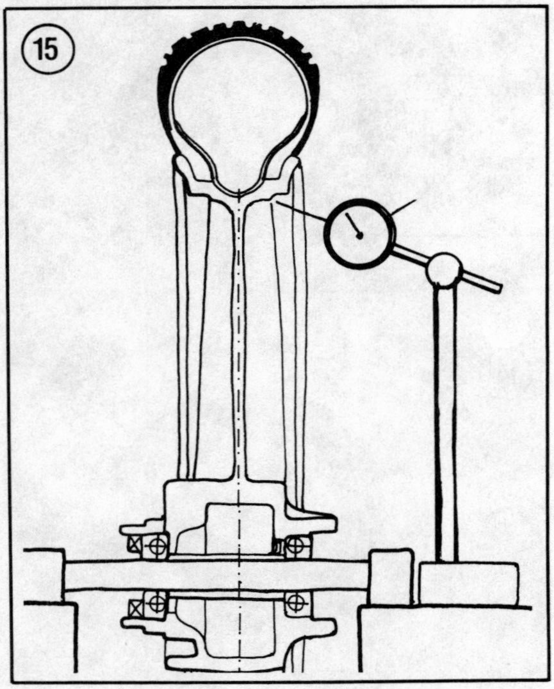

16

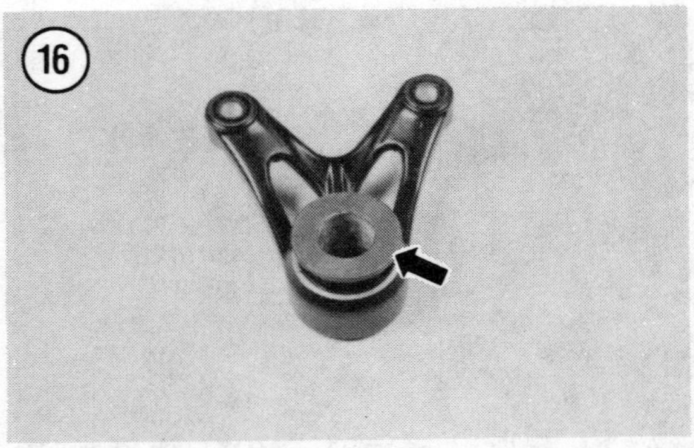

17

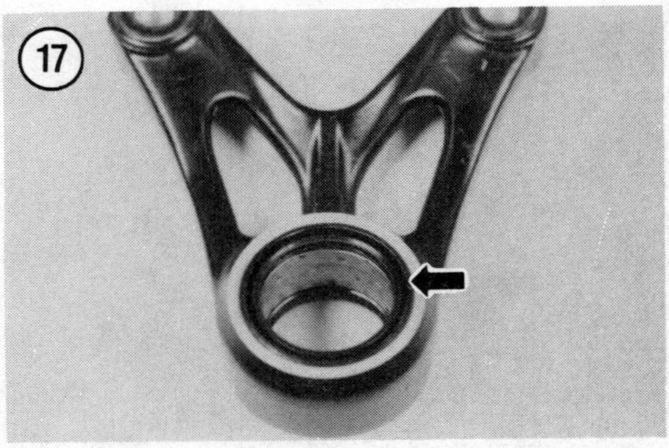

18

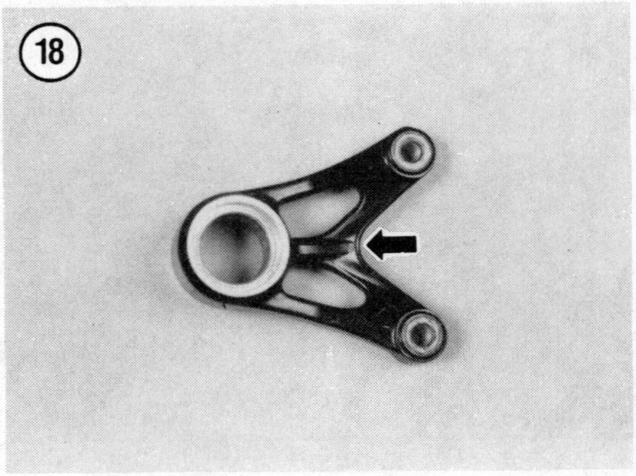

19

REAR HUB

Inspection

Inspect each wheel bearing prior to removing it from the wheel hub.

CAUTION
Do not remove the wheel bearings for inspection purposes as they will be damaged during the removal process. Remove wheel bearings only if they are to be replaced.

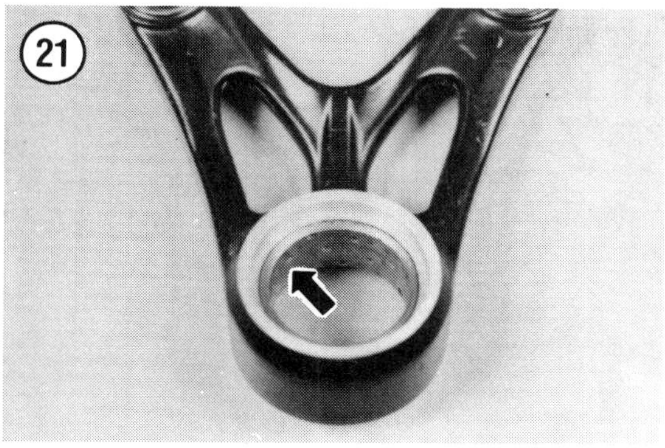

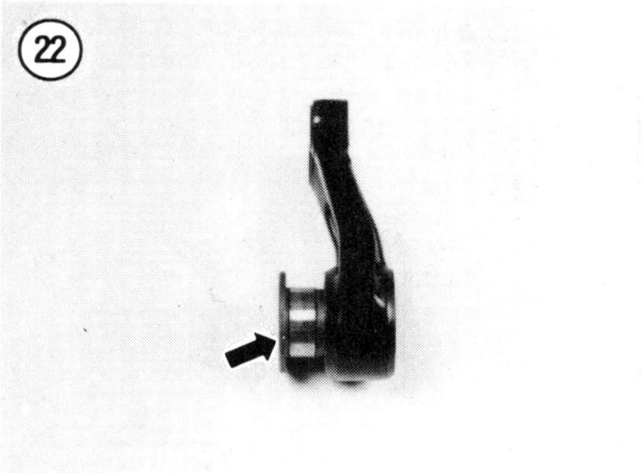

1. Perform Steps 1-7 of *Disassembly* in this chapter.
2. Turn each bearing by hand. Make sure the bearings turn smoothly.
3. On non-sealed bearings, check the balls for evidence of wear, pitting or excessive heat (bluish tint). Replace the bearings if necessary; always replace as a complete set. When replacing the bearings, be sure to take your old bearings along to ensure a perfect matchup.

NOTE
Fully sealed bearings are available from many bearing specialty shops. Fully sealed bearings provide better protection from dirt and moisture that may get into the hub.

4. Check the axle for wear and straightness. Use V-blocks and a dial indicator as shown in **Figure 23**. If the runout is 0.2 mm (0.01 in.) or greater, the axle should be replaced.
5. Inspect the raised webs (**Figure 24**) where the rubber dampers fit. Check for cracks or wear. If any damage is visible, replace the wheel.

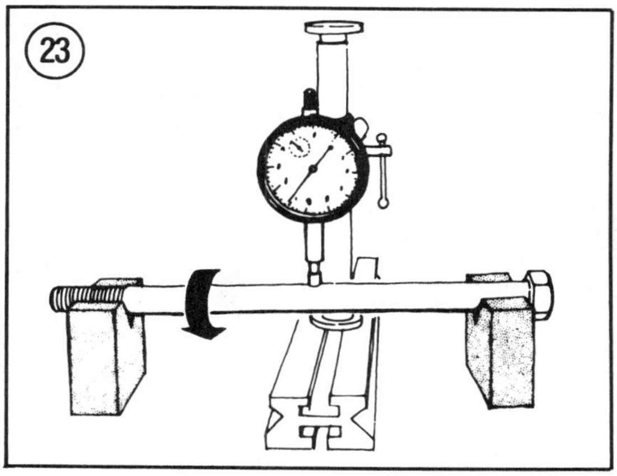

Disassembly

Refer to **Figure 25** for this procedure.

1. Remove the rear wheel as described in this chapter.
2. Remove the spacer (**Figure 26**) from the right-hand side.
3. Turn the wheel over and remove the spacer (**Figure 27**) from the left-hand side.
4. If the driven sprocket is going to be replaced, loosen the nuts (**Figure 28**) at this time. The wheel makes a great holding fixture.
5. Remove the driven sprocket and drum assembly (**Figure 29**) from the rear wheel hub.

26

25

REAR WHEEL/HUB/DRIVEN SPROCKET

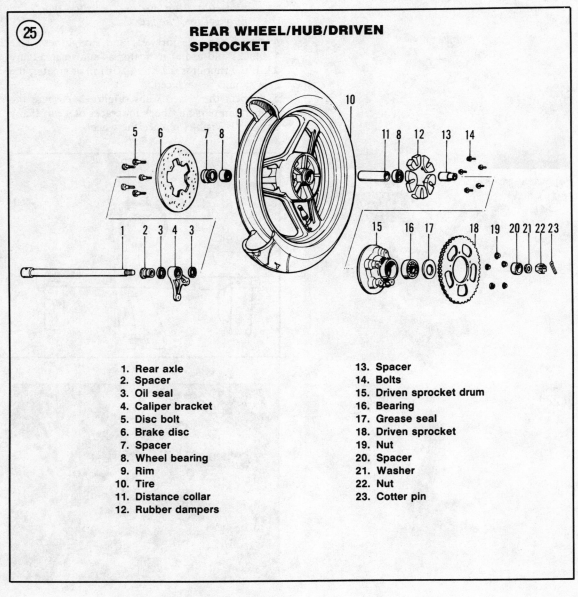

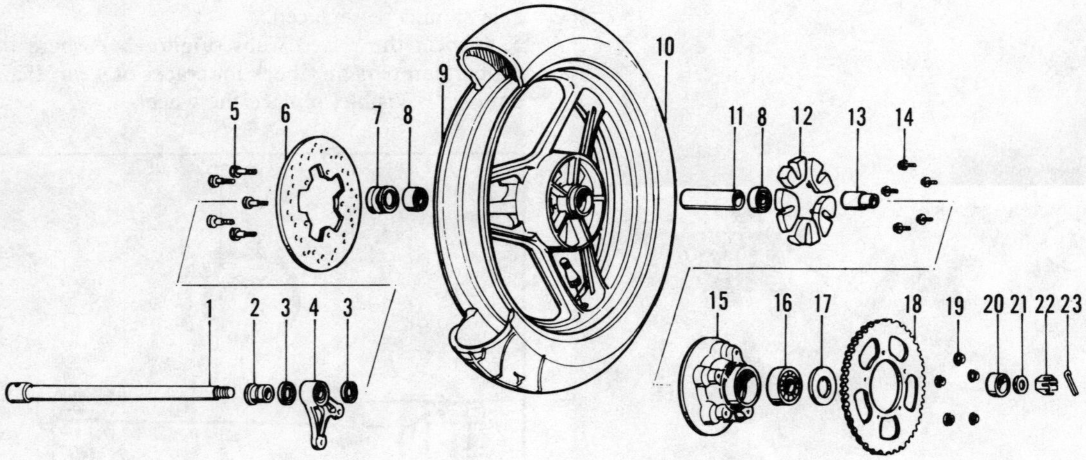

1. Rear axle
2. Spacer
3. Oil seal
4. Caliper bracket
5. Disc bolt
6. Brake disc
7. Spacer
8. Wheel bearing
9. Rim
10. Tire
11. Distance collar
12. Rubber dampers
13. Spacer
14. Bolts
15. Driven sprocket drum
16. Bearing
17. Grease seal
18. Driven sprocket
19. Nut
20. Spacer
21. Washer
22. Nut
23. Cotter pin

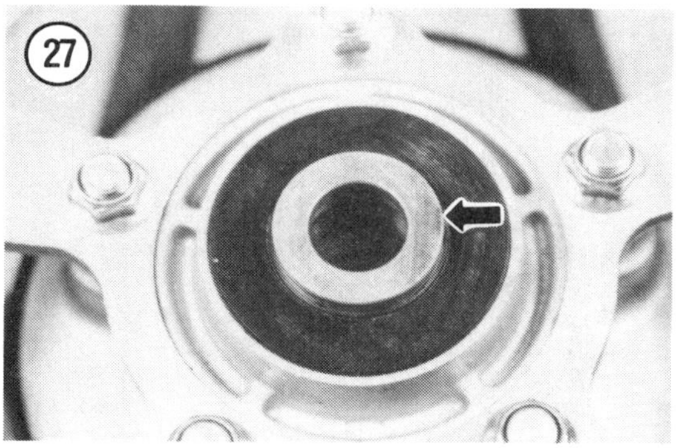

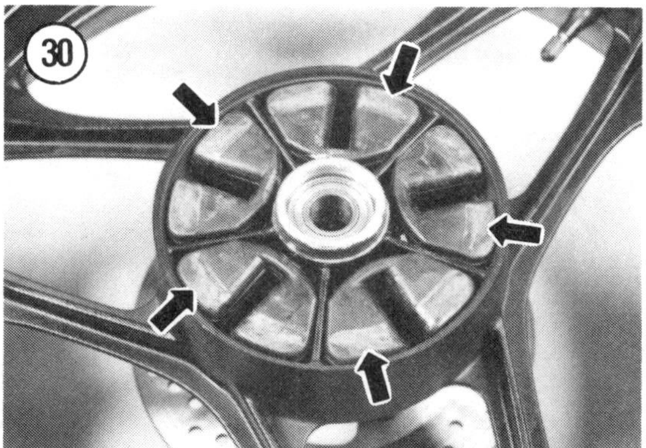

6. Remove the rubber dampers (**Figure 30**) from the rear hub.
7. Remove the bolts (**Figure 31**) securing the brake disc and remove disc.
8. Before proceeding further, inspect the wheel bearings as described in this chapter. If they must be replaced, proceed as follows.
9A. A special Suzuki tool (Suzuki part No. 09941-50110) can be used to remove the wheel bearings as follows:
  a. Insert the adaptor (A, **Figure 32**) into one of the wheel bearings from the outer surface of the wheel.
  b. Turn the wheel over and insert the wedge bar (B, **Figure 32**) into the backside of the adaptor. Tap the wedge bar and force it into the slit in

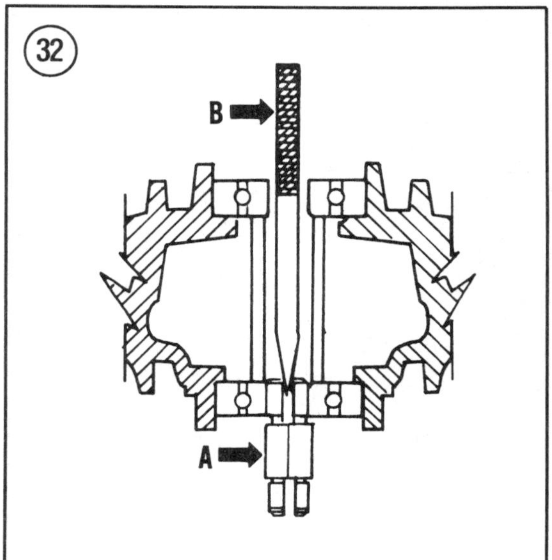

the adaptor (**Figure 33**). This will wedge the adaptor against the inner bearing race.

c. Tap on the end of the wedge bar with a hammer (**Figure 34**) and drive the bearing out of the hub. Remove the bearing and the distance collar.

d. Repeat for the bearing on the other side.

9B. If the special tools are not used, perform the following:

a. To remove the right- and left-hand bearings and distance collar, insert a soft aluminum or brass drift into one side of the hub.

b. Push the distance collar over to one side and place the drift on the inner race of the lower bearing.

c. Tap the bearing out of the hub with a hammer, working around the perimeter of the inner race.

d. Repeat for the other bearing.

10. Clean the inside and the outside of the hub with solvent. Dry with compressed air.

Assembly

1. On non-sealed bearings, pack the bearings with a good quality bearing grease. Work the grease in between the balls thoroughly; turn the bearing by hand a couple of times to make sure the grease is distributed evenly inside the bearing.

2. Blow any dirt or foreign matter out of the hub prior to installing the bearings.

CAUTION

Install non-sealed bearings with the sealed side facing outward. Tap the bearings squarely into place and tap on the outer race only. Do not tap on the inner race or the bearing will be damaged. Be sure that the bearings are completely seated.

34

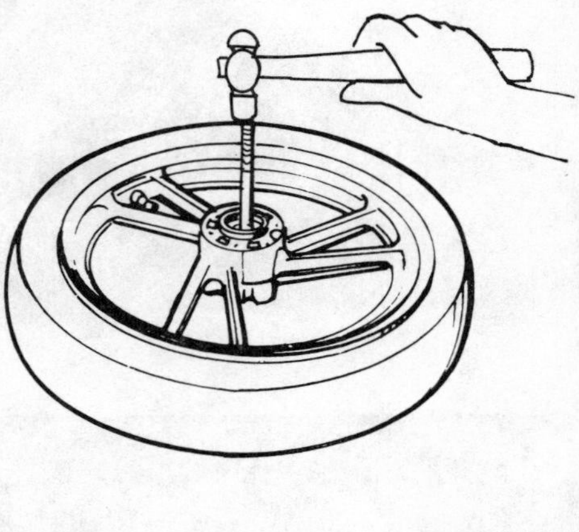

35

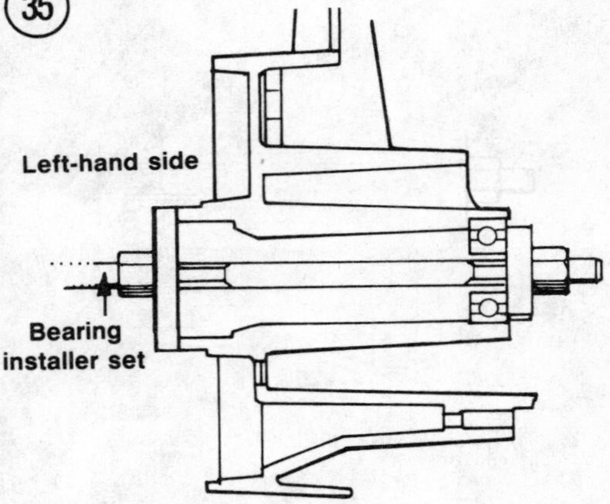

33

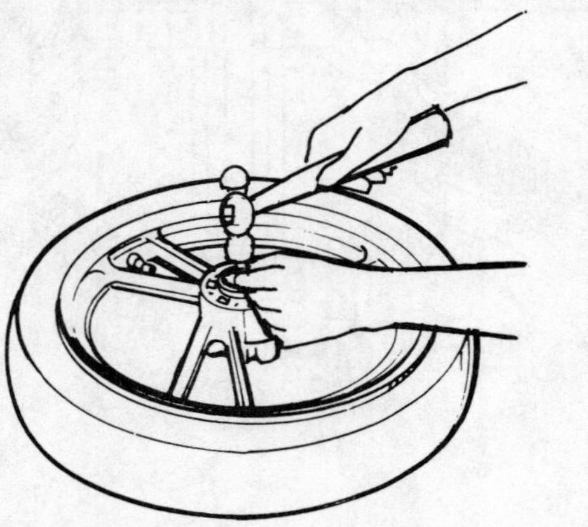

36

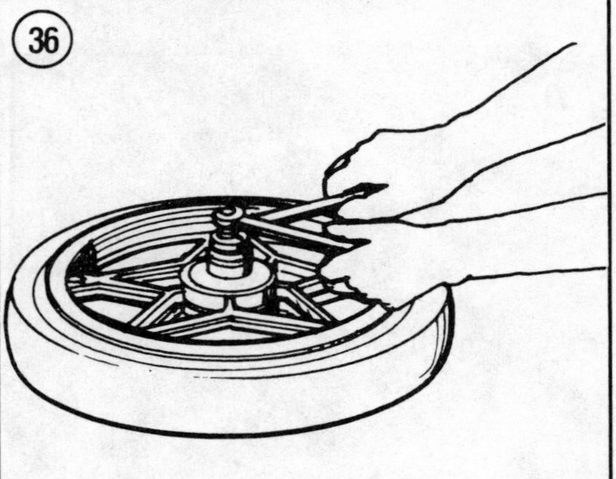

37

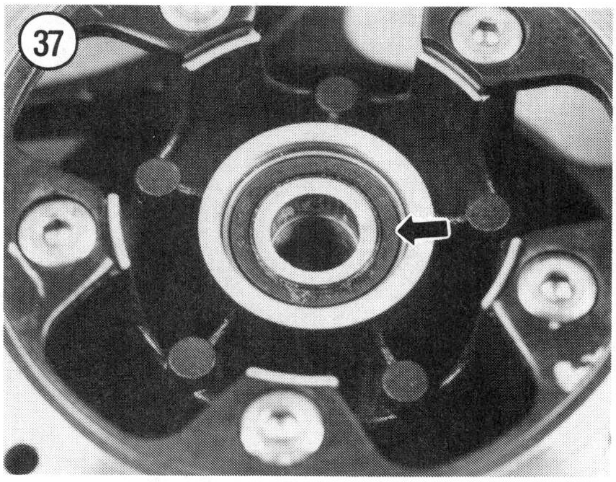

38

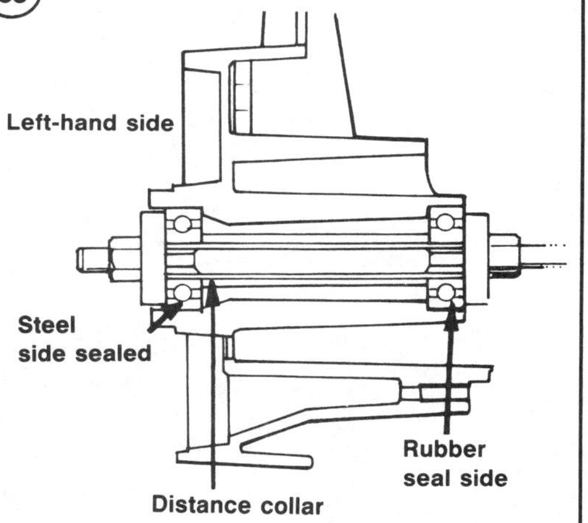

39

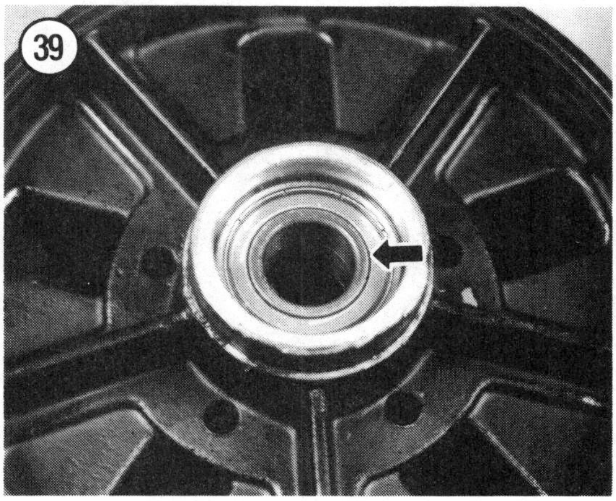

3A. A special Suzuki tool (Suzuki part No. 09924-84510) can be used to install the wheel bearings as follows:

a. Install the left-hand bearing into the hub first.
b. Set the bearing with the sealed side facing out and install the bearing installer as shown in **Figure 35**.
c. Tighten the bearing installer (**Figure 36**) and pull the bearing into the hub until it is completely seated (**Figure 37**). Remove the bearing installer.
d. Turn the wheel over (right-hand side up) on the workbench and install the distance collar.
e. Set the bearing with the sealed side facing out and install the bearing installer as shown in **Figure 38**.
f. Tighten the bearing installer (**Figure 36**) and pull the bearing into the hub until it is completely seated (**Figure 39**).
g. Remove the bearing installer.

3B. If special tools are not used, perform the following:

a. Tap the left-hand bearing squarely into place and tap on the outer race only. Use a socket (**Figure 40**) that matches the outer race diameter. Do not tap on the inner race or the bearing will be damaged. Be sure that the bearing is completely seated.
b. Turn the wheel over (right-hand side up) on the workbench and install the distance collar.
c. Use the same tool and drive in the right-hand bearing.

4. Apply Loctite Lock N' Seal to the brake disc bolts prior to installation.

5. Install the brake disc and bolts (**Figure 31**). Tighten to the torque specifications listed in **Table 1**.

6. Install the rubber dampers (**Figure 30**) into the rear hub.

40

7. Install the driven sprocket and drum assembly (**Figure 29**) into the rear wheel hub.
8. If the driven sprocket was replaced, tighten the nuts (**Figure 28**) at this time. Tighten to the torque specification listed in **Table 1**.
9. Install the left-hand spacer (**Figure 41**) into the hub.
10. Turn the wheel over and position the right-hand spacer with the shoulder (**Figure 42**) side facing in toward the bearing. This shoulder must be against the bearing inner race or the bearing will not spin properly. Install the right-hand spacer (**Figure 43**).
11. Install the rear wheel as described in this chapter.

DRIVEN SPROCKET AND DRUM

Disassembly/Assembly

Refer to **Figure 44** for this procedure.
1. Remove the rear wheel as described in this chapter.
2. Loosen the nuts (**Figure 45**) with the driven sprocket and drum installed in the rear hub of the wheel. The wheel makes a great holding fixture.
3. Remove the driven sprocket and drum assembly (**Figure 46**) straight up and out of the rear hub.

NOTE
If the driven sprocket and drum assembly is difficult to remove, tap on the backside of the sprocket (from the opposite side of the wheel through the wheel spokes) with the wooden handle of a hammer. Tap evenly around the perimeter of the sprocket until the assembly is free.

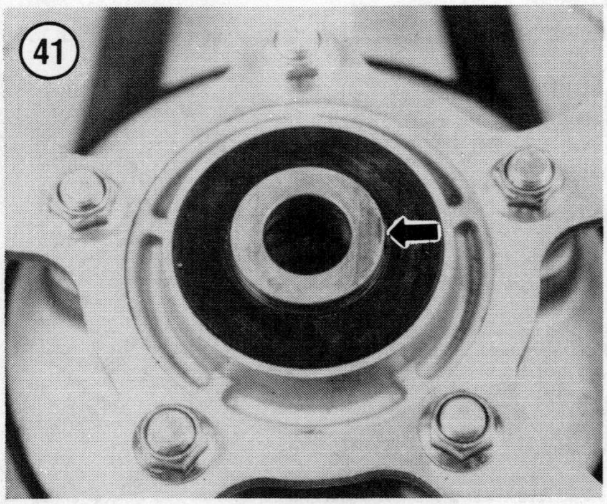
41

42

43

45

46

(44)

REAR WHEEL/HUB/DRIVEN SPROCKET

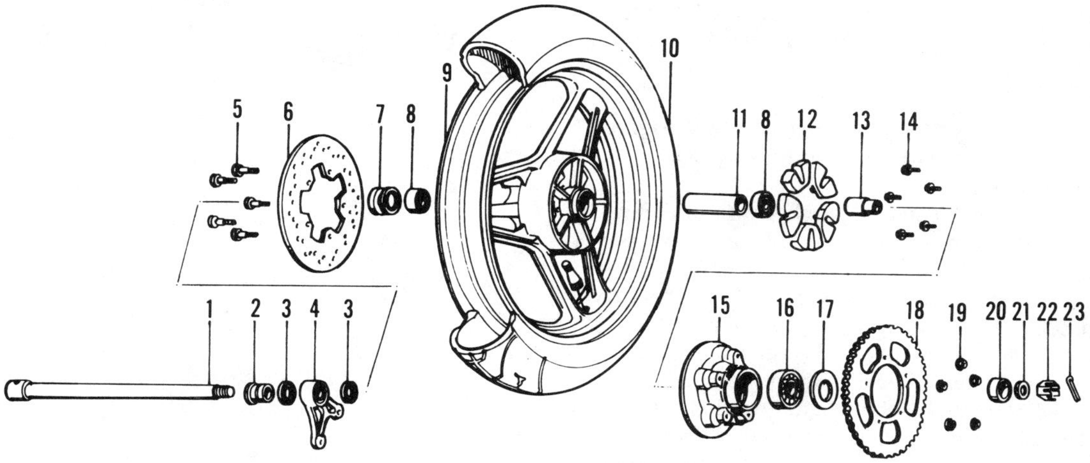

1. Rear axle
2. Spacer
3. Oil seal
4. Caliper bracket
5. Disc bolt
6. Brake disc
7. Spacer
8. Wheel bearing
9. Rim
10. Tire
11. Distance collar
12. Rubber dampers
13. Spacer
14. Bolts
15. Driven sprocket drum
16. Bearing
17. Grease seal
18. Driven sprocket
19. Nut
20. Spacer
21. Washer
22. Nut
23. Cotter pin

4. Remove the rubber dampers (**Figure 47**) from the rear hub.
5. Remove the spacer (**Figure 48**) from the driven sprocket and drum assembly.
6. Remove the driven sprocket nuts (**Figure 49**) and separate the driven sprocket from the drum (**Figure 50**).
7. Install by reversing these removal steps, noting the following.
8. If the driven sprocket was removed, tighten the nuts to the torque specification listed in **Table 1**.

Inspection

1. Visually inspect the rubber dampers (**Figure 51**) for signs of damage or deterioration. Replace as a complete set.
2. Inspect the driven sprocket drum (**Figure 50**) assembly for cracks or damage; replace if necessary.
3. Inspect the teeth (**Figure 52**) of the driven sprocket. If the teeth are visibly worn (**Figure 53**), remove nuts and replace the sprocket.
4. If the driven sprocket requires replacement, also inspect the drive chain and the drive sprocket. They also may be worn and need replacing.
5. Inspect the bearing, turn each bearing by hand. Make sure it turns smoothly. Replace if necessary.
6. On non-sealed bearings, check the balls for evidence of wear, pitting or excessive heat (bluish tint). Replace the bearings if necessary; always replace as a complete set. When replacing the bearings, be sure to take your old bearings along to ensure a perfect matchup.

NOTE
Fully sealed bearings are available from many bearing specialty shops. Fully sealed bearings provide better protection from dirt and moisture that may get into the hub.

47

48

49

50

51

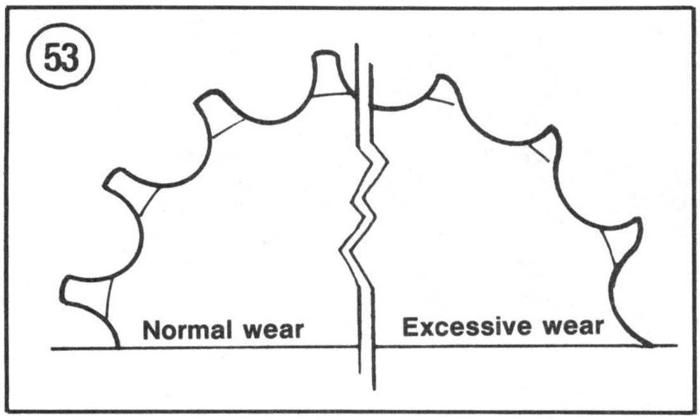

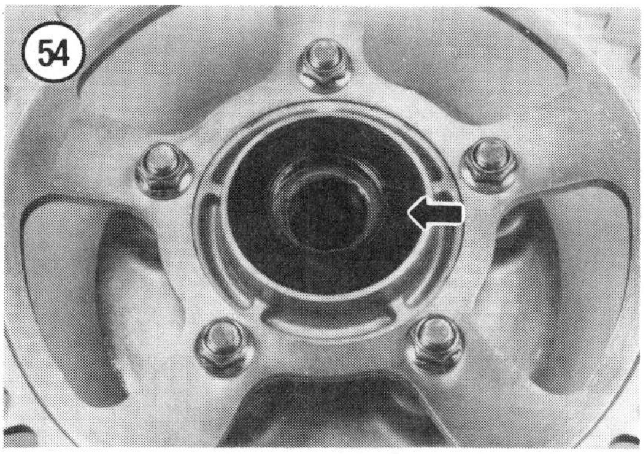

Bearing Replacement

1. Remove the grease seal (**Figure 54**) from the drum.
2. To remove the bearing, insert a soft aluminum or brass drift into one side of the drum.
3. Place the drift on the inner race of the bearing (**Figure 55**).
4. Tap the bearing out of the drum with a hammer, working around the perimeter of the inner race.
5. On a non-sealed bearing, pack the bearing with a good quality bearing grease. Work the grease in between the balls thoroughly; turn the bearing by hand a couple of times to make sure the grease is distributed evenly inside the bearing.
6. Blow any dirt or foreign matter out of the drum prior to installing the bearing.
7. Tap the bearing squarely into place and tap on the outer race only. Use a socket (**Figure 56**) that matches the outer race diameter. Do not tap on the inner race or the bearing will be damaged. Be sure that the bearing is completely seated.
8. Turn the drum over and install the grease seal.

DRIVE CHAIN

Removal/Installation

WARNING
The original equipment Suzuki drive chain is manufactured as an endless loop with no master link. Do ***not*** *cut it with a chain cutter as this will result in future chain failure and possible loss of control under riding conditions.*

NOTE
If an aftermarket drive chain has been installed, it may be equipped with a master link. Follow the chain manufacturer's instructions for removal.

1. Remove the gearshift lever as follows:
   a. Remove the circlip (**Figure 57**) and the washer (**Figure 58**) securing the gearshift lever to the pivot post.
   b. Remove the bolt (**Figure 59**) securing the gearshift lever to the shift shaft and remove the gearshift lever assembly.

2A. On GSX-R750R Limited Edition models, remove the bolts securing the drive sprocket cover (**Figure 60**) and remove the cover.

2B. On all other models, remove the bolts securing the drive sprocket cover (**Figure 61**) and remove the cover.

3. Have an assistant apply the rear brake. Loosen the drive sprocket bolt (A, **Figure 62**) and nut (B, **Figure 62**).

4. To provide slack in the drive chain, perform the following:
   a. Remove the cotter pin and loosen the rear axle nut (A, **Figure 63**).
   b. Loosen the drive chain adjuster nut (B, **Figure 63**) on each side of the swing arm.
   c. Push the rear wheel forward to achieve slack in the drive chain.

5. Remove the drive chain (C, **Figure 62**) from the drive sprocket.

6. Remove the swing arm as described under *Swing Arm Removal* in this chapter.

7. Inspect the drive chain as described under *Drive Chain Cleaning, Inspection, Lubrication* in Chapter Three.

8. Install the drive chain by reversing these removal steps, noting the following.

9. Feed the drive chain through the swing arm and the frame. Install the swing arm as described under *Swing Arm Installation* in this chapter.

10. Tighten the sprocket nut and bolt to the torque specification in **Table 1**.

11. Adjust the drive chain as described under *Drive Chain Adjustment* in Chapter Three.

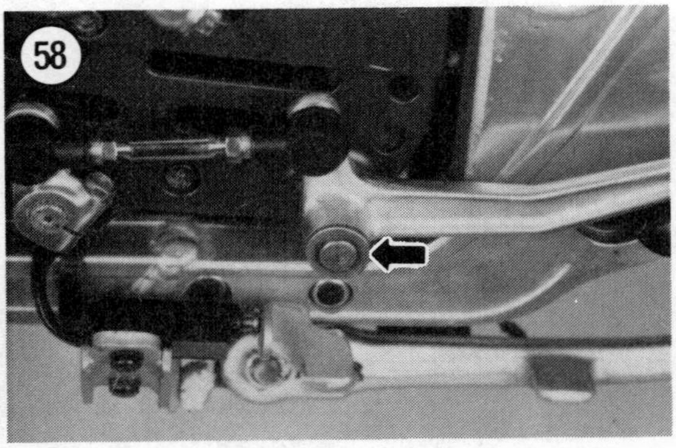

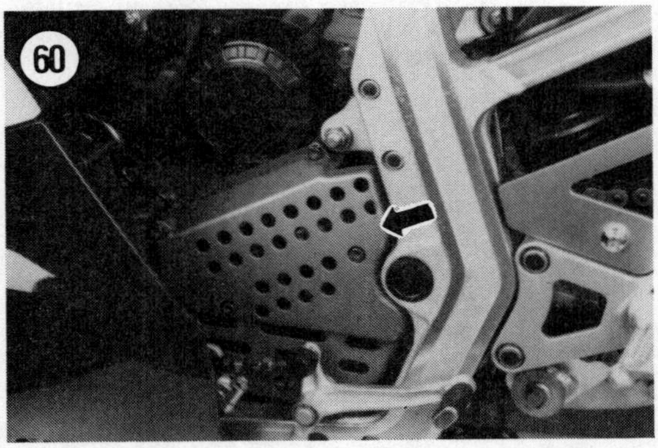

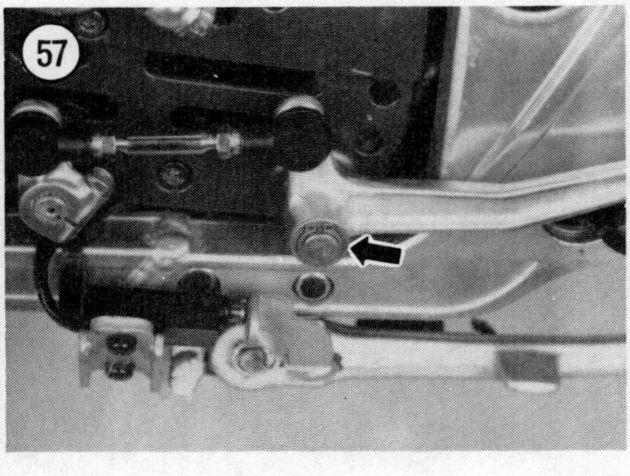

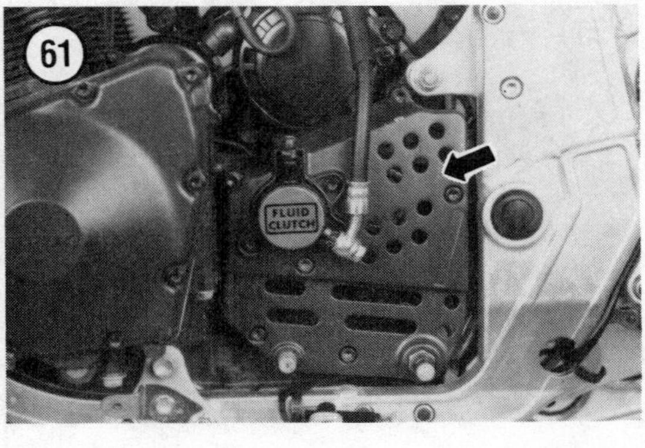

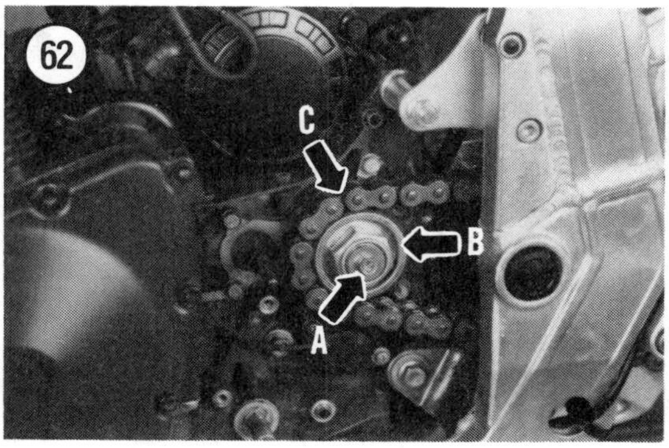

SWING ARM

In time, the needle bearings will wear and will have to be replaced. The condition of the bearings can greatly affect handling performance and if worn parts are not replaced they can produce erratic and dangerous handling. Common symptoms are wheel hop, pulling to one side during acceleration and pulling to the other side during braking.

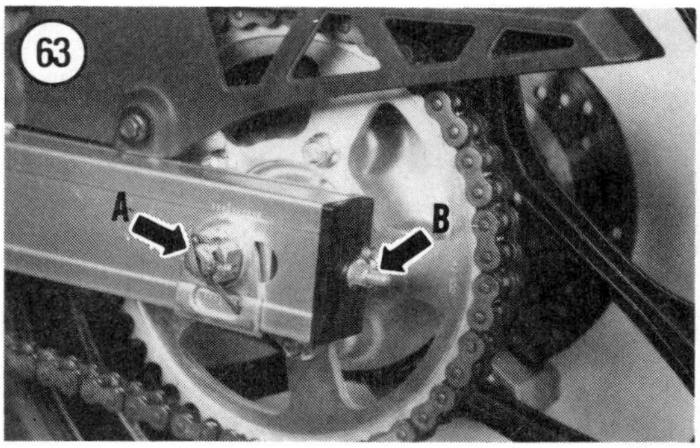

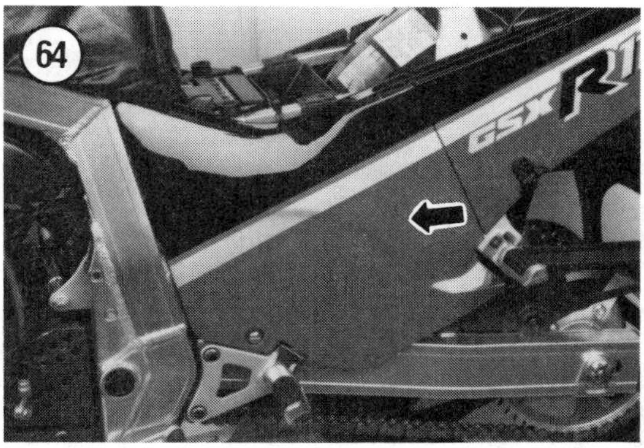

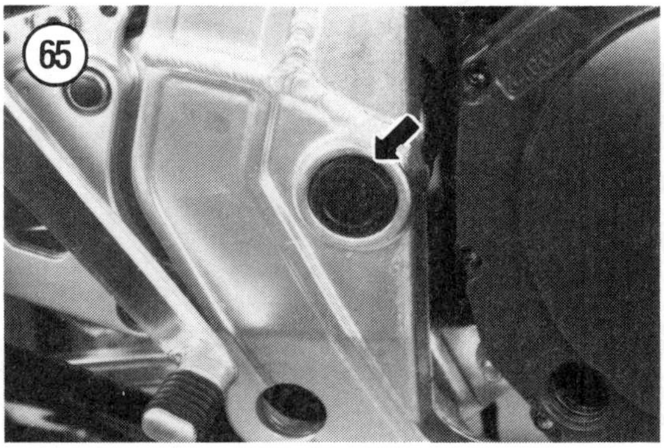

Removal

1. Remove the lower portion of the front fairing as described under *Front Fairing Removal/ Installation* in Chapter Twelve.
2. Remove the seat as described under *Seat Removal/Installation* in Chapter Twelve.
3. Place wood block(s) under each side of the frame to support the bike securely with the rear wheel off the ground.
4. Remove both side covers (**Figure 64**).
5. Remove the cap (**Figure 65**) from each side of the frame covering the pivot bolt and nut.
6. Remove the shock absorber as described under *Shock Absorber Removal* in this chapter.
7. Remove the shock absorber lever as described under *Shock Absorber Removal* in this chapter.
8. Remove the rear brake caliper and disconnect the brake hose from the caliper. Refer to *Rear Caliper Removal/Installation* in Chapter Eleven.
9. Remove the rear wheel as described under *Rear Wheel Removal/Installation* in this chapter.
10. Remove the screws and washer securing the drive chain cover and remove the cover (**Figure 66**).

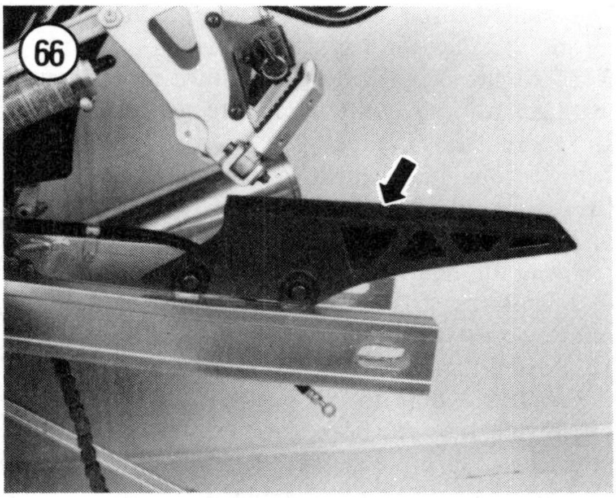

11. Grasp the rear end of the swing arm (**Figure 67**) and try to move it from side to side in a horizontal arc. There should be no noticeable side play. If play is evident and the pivot bolt is tightened correctly, the needle bearings should be replaced.
12. Remove the bolt securing the rear brake hose clamp and remove the clamp (A, **Figure 68**). Pull the brake hose through the other hose clamp (B, **Figure 68**) on the swing arm. Tie the brake hose up to the frame.
13. Remove the self-locking nut (**Figure 69**) and withdraw the pivot bolt from the left-hand side.
14. Pull back on the swing arm, free it from the drive chain and remove the swing arm from the frame.
15. Inspect the swing arm as described in this chapter.

NOTE
Don't lose the dust seal and washer on each side of the pivot points; they will usually fall off when the swing arm is removed.

Installation

1. Position the drive chain over the left-hand side of the swing arm.
2. Make sure the washer and dust seal (**Figure 70**) are correctly installed at each side of the swing arm.
3. Position the swing arm into the mounting area of the frame. Align the holes in the swing arm with the holes in the frame. To help align the holes, insert a drift in from the right-hand side.
4. Apply a light coat of molybdenum disulfide grease to the pivot bolt and install the pivot bolt from the left-hand.
5. Install the self-locking nut and tighten to the torque specification listed in **Table 1**.
6. Move the swing arm up and down several times to make sure all components are properly seated and there is no binding.
7. Insert the brake hose through the hose clamp (B, **Figure 68**) on the swing arm.
8. Install the clamp and bolt (A, **Figure 68**) securing the rear brake hose to the swing arm.
9. Install the drive chain cover and tighten the screws securely.
10. Install the rear wheel as described under *Rear Wheel Installation* in this chapter.
11. Install the rear brake caliper and connect the brake hose onto the caliper. Refer to *Rear Caliper Removal/Installation* in Chapter Eleven.

67

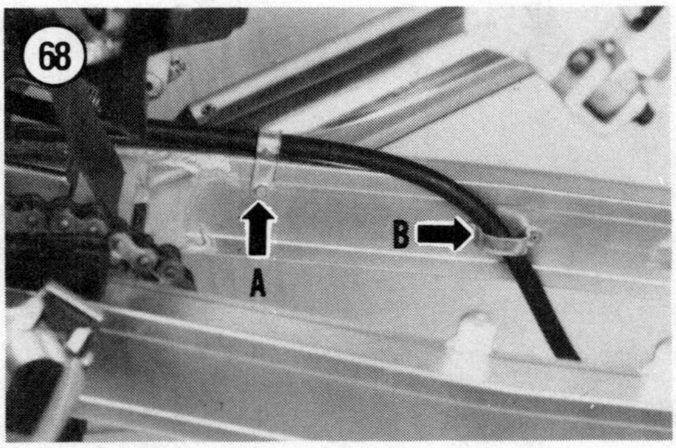

68

69

70

12. Install the shock absorber lever as described under *Shock Absorber Lever Installation* in this chapter.
13. Install the shock absorber as described under *Shock Absorber Installation* in this chapter.
14. Install the cap on each side of the frame covering the pivot bolt and nut.
15. Install both side covers.
16. Install the seat as described under *Seat Removal/Installation* in Chapter Twelve.
17. Install the lower portion of the front fairing as described under *Front Fairing Removal/Installation* in Chapter Twelve.

Disassembly/Inspection/Assembly

Refer to the following illustrations for this procedure:

a. **Figure 71**: 750 cc models.
b. **Figure 72**: 1100 cc models.

(71)

SWING ARM (750 CC MODELS)

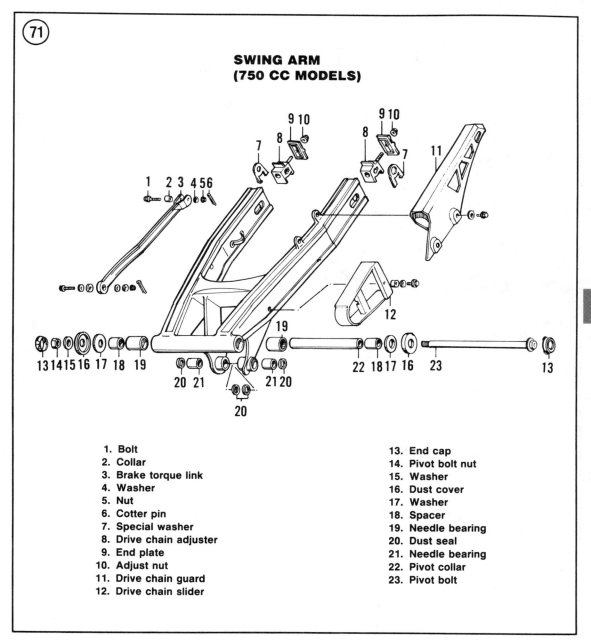

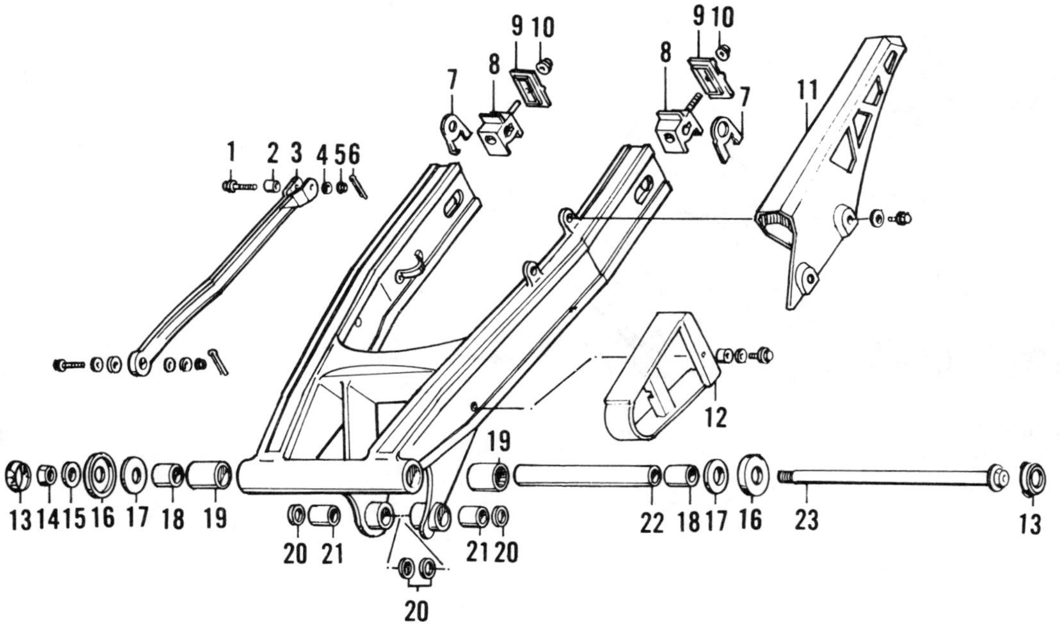

1. Bolt
2. Collar
3. Brake torque link
4. Washer
5. Nut
6. Cotter pin
7. Special washer
8. Drive chain adjuster
9. End plate
10. Adjust nut
11. Drive chain guard
12. Drive chain slider
13. End cap
14. Pivot bolt nut
15. Washer
16. Dust cover
17. Washer
18. Spacer
19. Needle bearing
20. Dust seal
21. Needle bearing
22. Pivot collar
23. Pivot bolt

(72)

SWING ARM
(1100 CC MODELS)

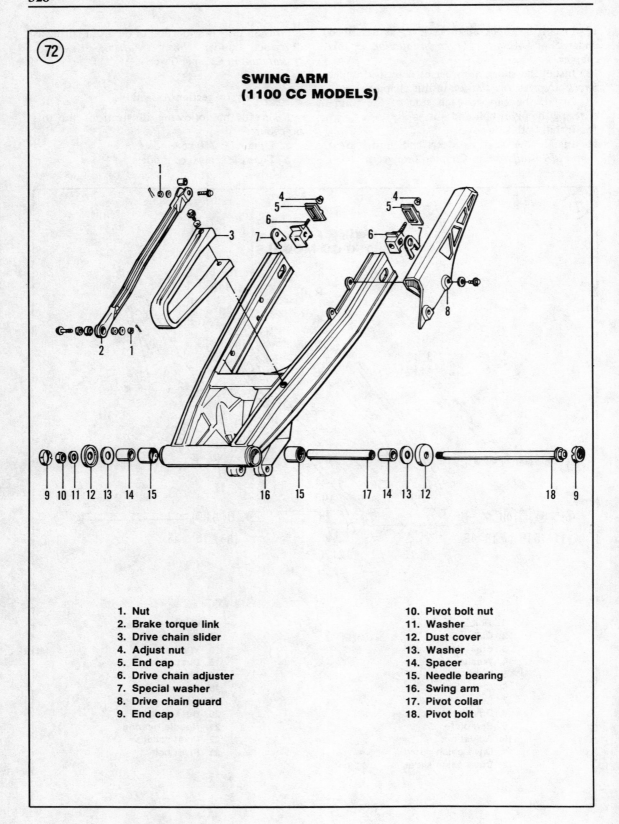

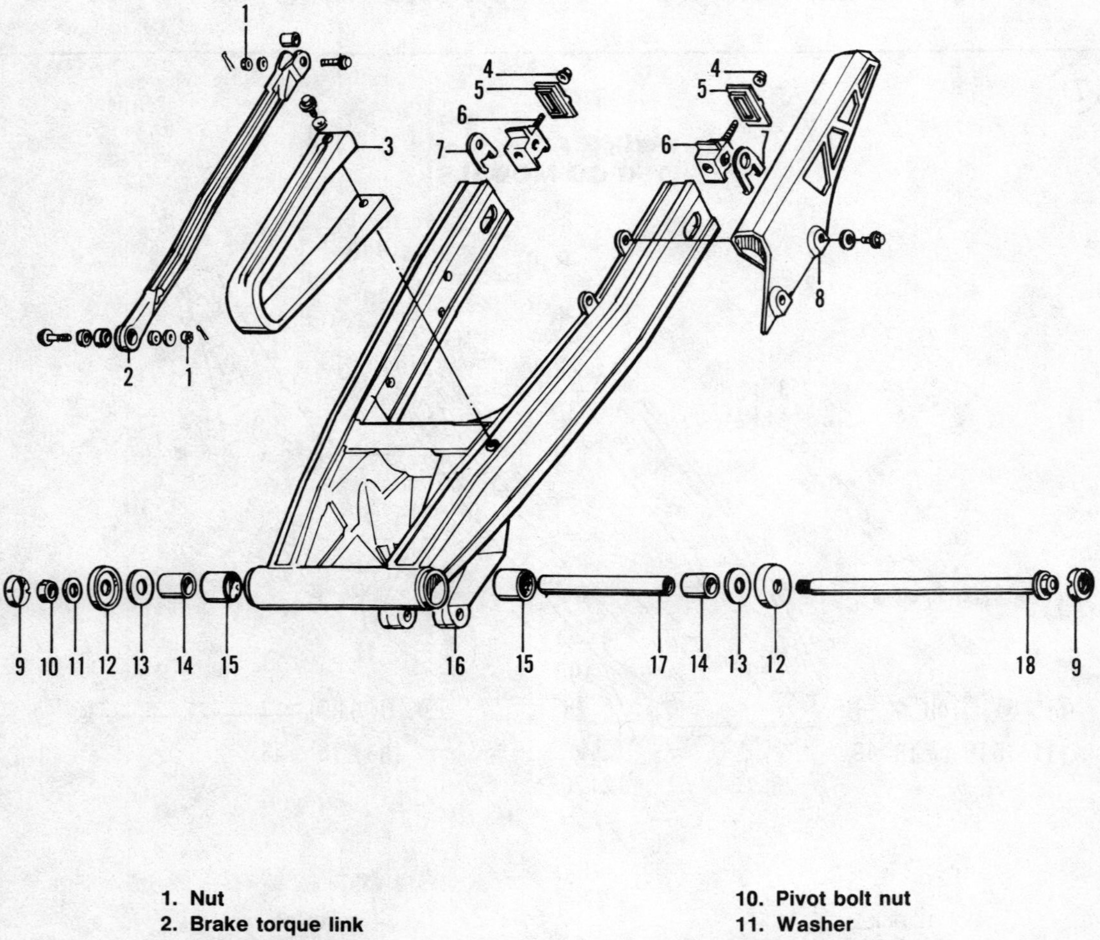

1. Nut
2. Brake torque link
3. Drive chain slider
4. Adjust nut
5. End cap
6. Drive chain adjuster
7. Special washer
8. Drive chain guard
9. End cap
10. Pivot bolt nut
11. Washer
12. Dust cover
13. Washer
14. Spacer
15. Needle bearing
16. Swing arm
17. Pivot collar
18. Pivot bolt

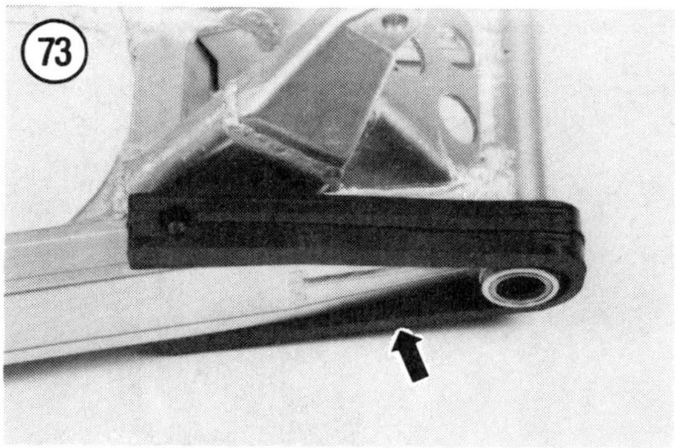

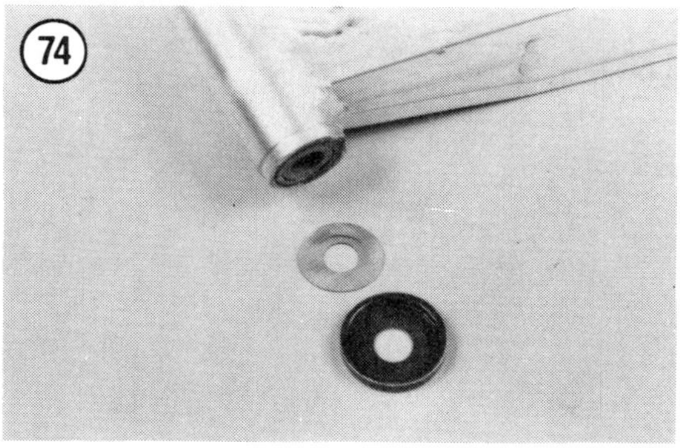

1. Remove the swing arm as described under *Swing Arm Removal* in this chapter.
2. Remove the screws securing the drive chain slider (**Figure 73**) and remove the guard.
3. Remove both dust seals and washers (**Figure 74**) if they have not already fallen off during the removal sequence.
4. Withdraw the spacer (**Figure 75**) and pivot collar (**Figure 76**).

NOTE
Some 750 cc model may have a shim on one side of the shock absorber lever where it attaches to the swing arm. It was installed at the factory to adjust the clearance. Don't lose this shim as it must be reinstalled to maintain the proper clearance between the 2 parts.

5. Remove the bolt (**Figure 77**) and nut securing the shock absorber lever and remove the lever assembly.
6. Remove the drive chain adjuster assemblies from the rear of the swing arm.
7. Clean all parts (**Figure 78**) in solvent and thoroughly dry.

NOTE
There are no factory specifications for the outside diameter of the spacers or pivot collar.

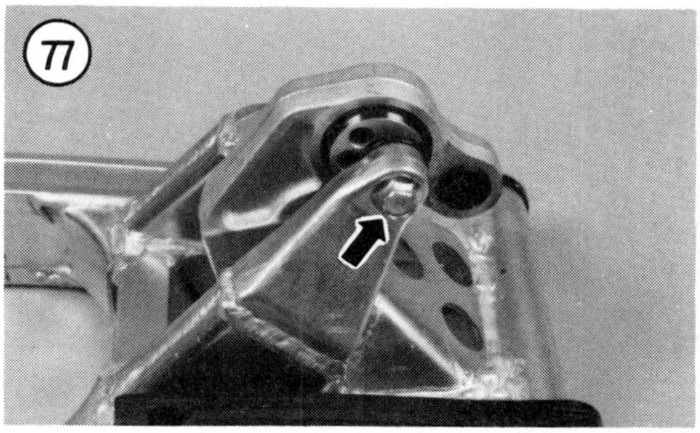

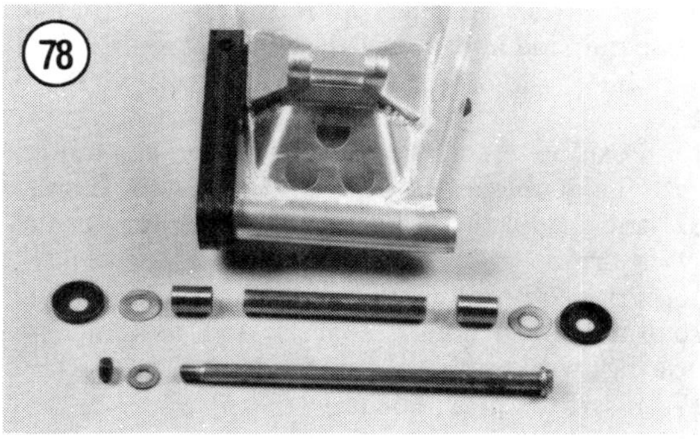

8. Inspect the spacers and the pivot collar for abnormal wear, scratches or score marks. Replace if necessary.

NOTE

If the spacers and the pivot collar are replaced, the needle bearing at each end must also be replaced at the same time.

9. Inspect the needle bearings as follows:
   a. Wipe off any excess grease from the needle bearing at each end of the swing arm.
   b. Turn each bearing (**Figure 79**) with your fingers; make sure they rotate smoothly. The needle bearings wear very slowly and wear is very difficult to measure.
   c. Check the rollers for evidence of wear, pitting or color change (bluish tint) indicating heat from lack of lubrication.

NOTE

Always replace both needle bearings even though only one may be worn.

10. Inspect the shock absorber lever mounting bracket pivot holes (**Figure 80**). If the holes are elongated or worn, replace the swing arm.
11. Check the welded sections (**Figure 81**) on the swing arm for cracks or fractures.
12. Inspect the drive chain adjuster assemblies (**Figure 82**) for wear or damage; replace if necessary.

NOTE

If so equipped on 750 cc models, install the shim between the shock absorber lever and the swing arm. This shim must be reinstalled to maintain the proper clearance between the 2 parts.

13. Prior to installing the shock absorber lever mounting bolt, coat it with molybdenum disulfide grease.
14. Position the shock absorber lever as shown in **Figure 77**. Install the mounting bolt from the left-hand side and install the nut. tighten the bolt and nut to the torque specification listed in **Table 1**.
15. Position the drive chain adjuster assemblies with the double leg side toward the bottom (**Figure 82**) and install the assemblies into the rear of the swing arm.
16. Prior to installing the pivot collar and spacers, coat the pivot collar, spacers and both needle bearings with molybdenum disulfide grease.
17. Insert the pivot collar.
18. Insert the spacer into each end.

79

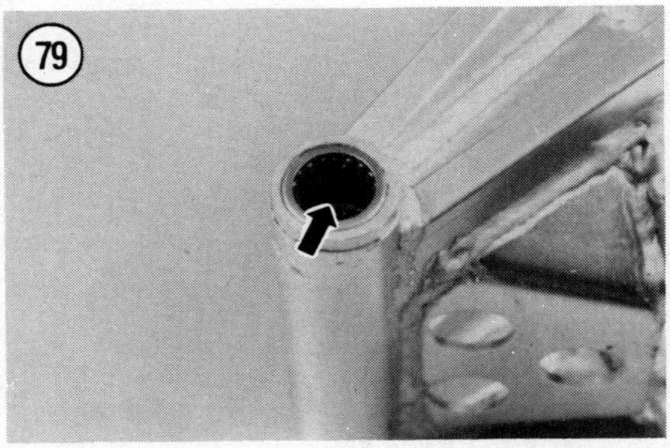

80

81

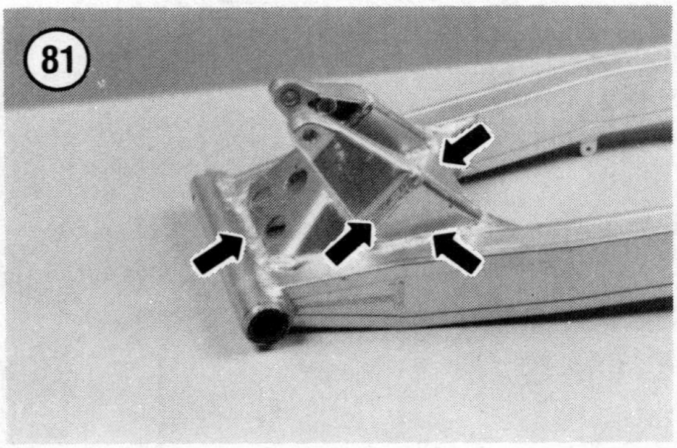

82

19. Coat the inside of both dust caps and the washers with molybdenum disulfide grease and install them onto the ends of the swing arm.
20. Install the drive chain slider and tighten the screws securely.
21. Install the swing arm as described under *Swing Arm Installation* in this chapter.

Pivot Point
Needle Bearing Replacement

The swing arm is equipped with a needle bearing at each end. The bearing is pressed in place and has to be removed with force. The bearing will be distorted during removal, so don't remove it unless absolutely necessary.

The bearings must be removed and installed with special tools that are available from a Suzuki dealer.

1. Remove the swing arm as described under *Swing Arm Removal* in this chapter.
2. Remove both dust seals and washers (**Figure 74**) if they have not already fallen off during the removal sequence.
3. Withdraw the spacer (**Figure 75**) and pivot collar (**Figure 76**).
4. Either the right- or left-hand bearing can be removed first.

83

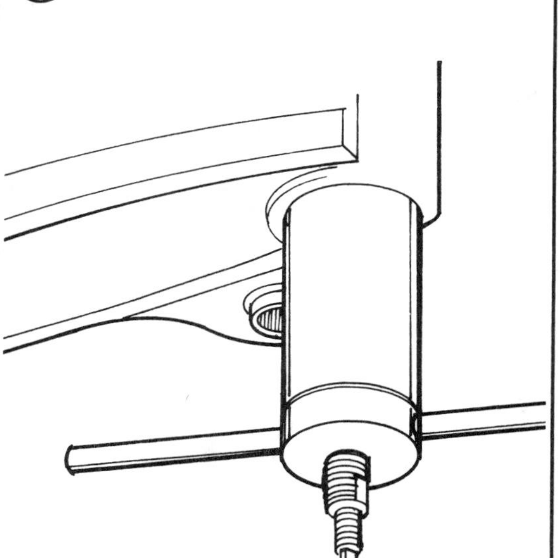

5. Install the swing arm in a vise with soft jaws.

NOTE
The special tool grabs the inner surface of the bearing and then withdraws it from the swing arm.

6. Install the bearing remover (Suzuki Swingarm Bearing Remover, part No, 09941-44510) through the hole in the bearing and expand the tool behind the bearing.
7. Turn the handle on the bearing remover and withdraw the needle bearing from the swing arm (**Figure 83**).
8. Remove the bearing and the special tool.
9. Turn the swing arm over in the vise and repeat Steps 6-8 for the other bearing.
10. Thoroughly clean out the inside of the swing arm with solvent and dry with compressed air.
11. Apply a light coat of molybdenum disulfide grease to all parts prior to installation.

NOTE
Either the right- or left-hand bearing race can be installed first.

12. Apply a light coat of molybdenum disulfide grease to all parts prior to installation.

CAUTION
Never reinstall a needle bearing that has been removed. During removal it becomes slightly distorted and is no longer true. If reinstalled, it will damage the pivot collar, create binding and possibly cause an unsafe riding condition.

13. Position the new needle bearing with its marks facing up toward the outside.
14. Install the bearing installer (Suzuki Steering Outer Race Installer, part No, 09941-34513) through the hole in the bearing and through the swing arm.
15. Turn the nut on the installer and press the new needle bearing into the swing arm.
16. Remove the installer from the swing arm.
17. Turn the swing arm over in the vise and repeat Steps 13-16 for the other bearing.
18. Prior to installing the pivot collar and spacers, coat both needle bearings, the pivot collar and spacers with molybdenum disulfide grease.
19. Insert the pivot collar (**Figure 76**).
20. Insert the spacer (**Figure 75**) into each end.
21. Coat the inside of both dust caps and the washers with molybdenum disulfide grease and install them onto the ends of the swing arm.

10

22. Install the drive chain slider and tighten the screws securely.
23. Install the swing arm as described under *Swing Arm Installation* in this chapter.

Shock Absorber Lever Pivot Needle Bearing Replacement (750 cc Models)

The swing arm is equipped with needle bearings where the shock absorber lever attaches to it. The bearings are pressed in place and have to be removed with force. The bearings will be distorted during removal, so don't remove them unless you are planning to replace the bearings.

The bearings must be removed and installed with special tools that are available from a Suzuki dealer.

1. Remove the swing arm as described under *Swing Arm Removal* in this chapter.
2. Remove both dust seals and spacers (**Figure 84**) from each pivot point.
3. Either bearing can be removed first.
4. Install the swing arm in a vise with soft jaws.

NOTE
These special tools grab the inner surface of the bearing and then withdraw it from the swing arm with the use of a tool similar to a body shop slide hammer.

5. Install the bearing remover (Suzuki Bearing Puller, part No, 09923-73210) through the hole in the bearing and expand the tool behind the bearing (A, **Figure 85**).
6. Attach the slide hammer (Suzuki Sliding Shaft, part No. 09930-30102) to the bearing remover (B, **Figure 85**).
7. Slide the weight on the hammer back and forth several times until the bearing and bearing collar are withdrawn from the swing arm.
8. Remove the bearing and the special tools.
9. Turn the swing arm over in the vise and repeat Steps 5-7 for the other bearing.
10. Thoroughly clean out the inside of the bearing area of the swing arm with solvent and dry with compressed air.

NOTE
Either bearing race can be installed first.

11. Apply a light coat of molybdenum disulfide grease to all parts prior to installation.

CAUTION
Never reinstall a needle bearing that has been removed. During removal it becomes slightly distorted and is no longer true. If reinstalled, it will damage the pivot collar, create binding and possibly cause an unsafe riding condition.

12. Support the shock absorber lever pivot point so the dust seal sealing surface will not be damaged.
13. Correctly position the needle bearing onto the pivot point.
14. Tap the needle bearing squarely into place and tap on the outer race only. Use a socket that matches the outer diameter.
15. Tap the bearing into until it is centered in the pivot area. There should be an equal gap on each side. This gap is necessary for the dust seals on each side.

84

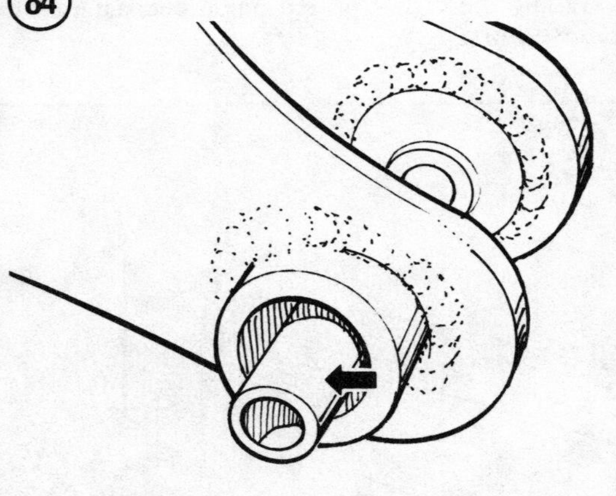

85

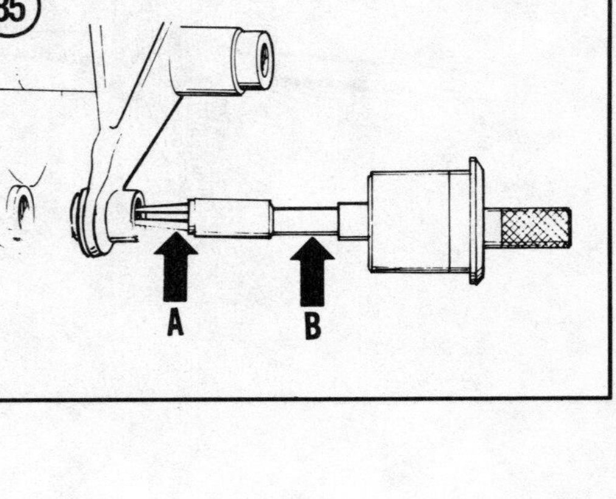

16. Turn the swing arm over in the vise and repeat Steps 10-14 for the other bearing.
17. Prior to installing the spacers, coat the spacers and both needle bearings with molybdenum disulfide grease.
18. Insert the spacer into each pivot point.
19. Coat the inside of both dust seals with molybdenum disulfide grease and install them onto each end of both pivot points.
20. Install the swing arm as described under *Swing Arm Installation* in this chapter.

FULL FLOATER REAR SUSPENSION SYSTEM

The single shock absorber and linkage of the Full Floater rear suspension system is attached to the swing arm just aft of the swing arm pivot point and to the lower rear portion of the frame and the shock absorber. All of these items are located forward of the rear wheel.

The shock absorber lever works together with the matched spring rate and damping rates of the shock absorber to achieve a "progressive rising rate" rear suspension. This system provides the rider with the best of two worlds—greater rider comfort at low speeds with greater resistance to bottoming at high speeds.

86

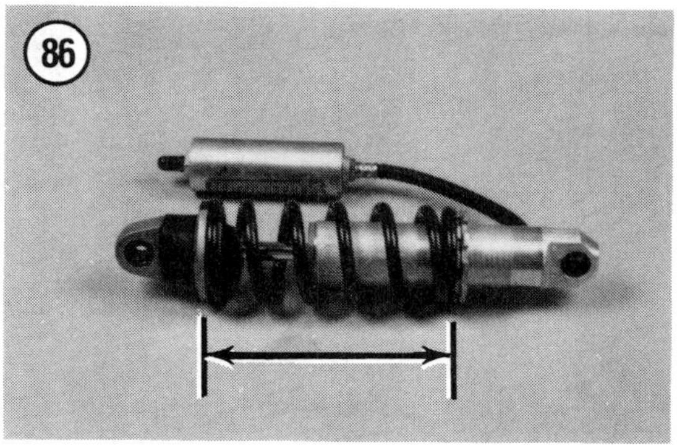

87

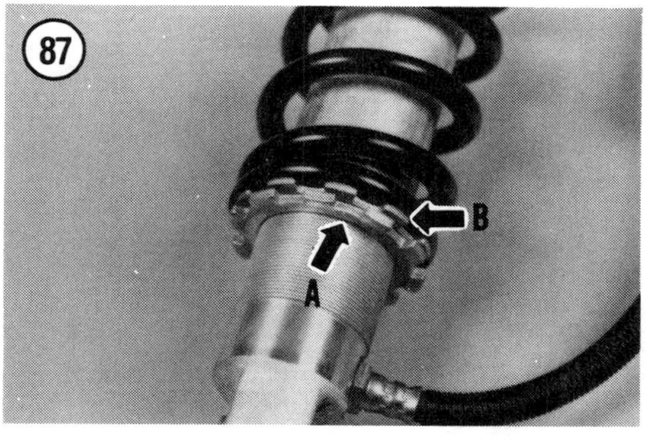

SHOCK ABSORBER

The single shock absorber on the GSX-R750R Limited Edition and the GSX-R1100 models has a remote oil/nitrogen reservoir. The remote reservoir helps prevent the oil from frothing. The GSX-R750 model is not equipped with a remote reservoir.

The shock is adjustable for both rate and damping action.

Spring Preload Adjustment

There must be preload on the spring at all times. Never ride the bike without spring preload as possible loss of control will result.

The spring length (preload) must be maintained within the dimensions listed in **Table 2**. Suzuki recommends that the spring preload and the damping adjustment be set in relation to each other as shown in **Table 2**. When both adjustments are set in relation to each other the rider will get the best possible ride.

Special Suzuki tools are required for the lockring and the adjuster. These are as follows:

a. GSX-R750R Limited Edition and GSX-R1100: Universal Clamp Wrench, part NO. 09910-60611.
b. GSX-R750: Spring Retainer Wrench, part No. 09940-71411 and Spring Lockring Wrench, part No. 09940-71420.

1. Remove the shock absorber from the frame as described under *Shock Absorber Removal* in this chapter.
2. Measure the existing spring length (**Figure 86**).
3. To adjust, use the special tools and loosen the lockring (A, **Figure 87**). Turn the adjuster (B, **Figure 87**) in the desired direction. Tightening the adjuster *increases* spring preload and loosening it *decreases* preload.

NOTE
*Remember, the spring length (preload) must be maintained within the dimensions listed in **Table 2**.*

CAUTION
*Refer to the minimum spring preload dimension listed in **Table 2**. **Never** adjust the spring beyond the minimum dimension.*

4. After the desired spring length is achieved, tighten the lockring securely.
5. Install the shock absorber into the frame as described under *Shock Absorber Removal/Installation* in this chapter.

Damping Adjustment

Damping can be adjusted to 4 different settings (I, II, III and IIII). Position I is the softest setting and position IIII is the stiffest setting. The adjuster knob is located at the base of the shock absorber on the GSX-R1100 (**Figure 88**). On the GSX-R750R Limited Edition and the GSX-R750, the adjuster is located at the top of the shock absorber (**Figure 89**).

Pull back the rubber boot (**Figure 90**) and rotate the adjuster to the desired setting. Make sure that the adjuster is located into one of the detents and not in between any 2 settings.

Suzuki recommends that the damping adjustment and spring preload setting be set in relation to each other as shown in **Table 2**. When both adjustments are set in relation to each other the rider will get the best possible ride.

Removal

NOTE
This procedure is shown on a GSX-R1100 model. Where differences occur in the procedure they are identified.

NOTE
This procedure is shown with the rear wheel removed for clarity. It is not necessary to remove the rear wheel for this procedure.

1. Remove the lower portion of the front fairing as described under *Front Fairing Removal/ Installation* in Chapter Twelve.
2. Remove both side covers.
3. Place wood block(s) under each side of the frame to support the bike securely with the rear wheel off the ground just a little.
4. On GSX-R750R Limited Edition and GSX-R1100 models, perform the following.
   a. Loosen the clamping screws (**Figure 91**) on the remote reservoir.
   b. Slide the clamps off of the remote reservoir and remove the rubber dampers.
   c. Let the remote reservoir rest on the frame or swing arm (**Figure 92**).
5. Remove the nut from the lower mounting bolt (**Figure 93**) securing the shock absorber to the shock absorber lever.
6. Have a helper pull up on the rear wheel to take the strain off of the mounting bolt. Withdraw the bolt from the left-hand side. Let the swing arm and rear wheel rest on the ground.

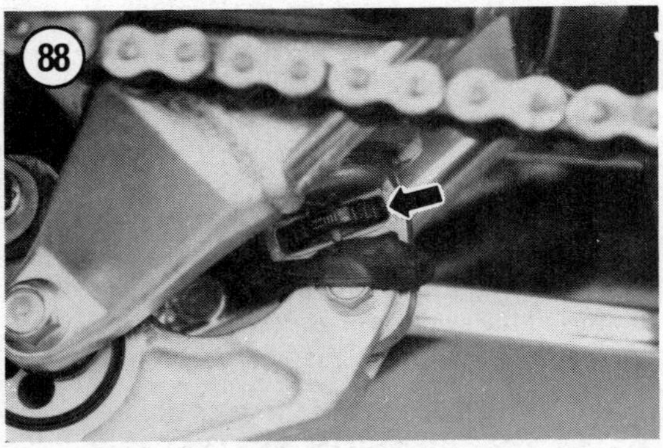

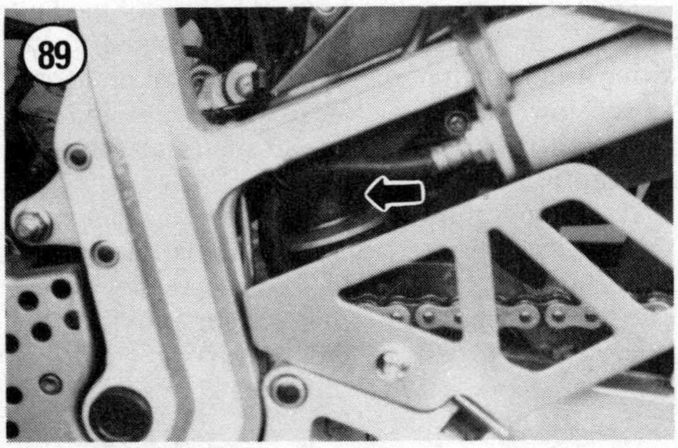

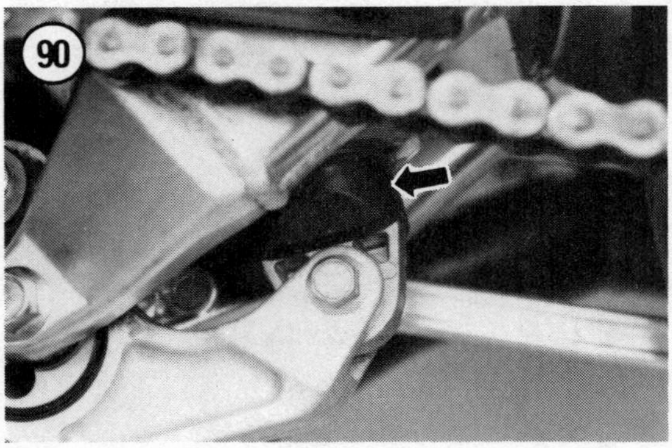

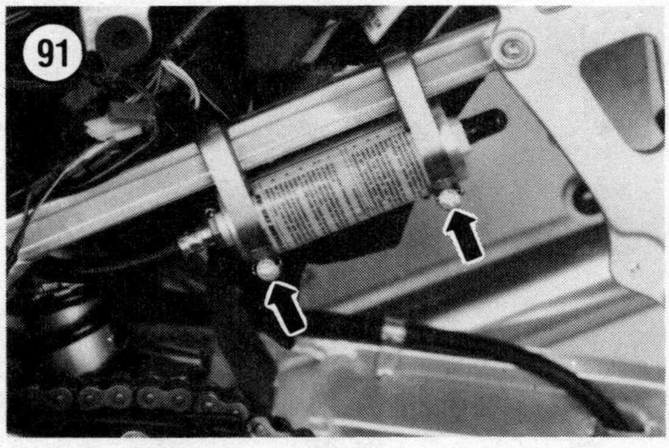

7. Remove the nut from the upper mounting bolt (**Figure 94**) securing the shock absorber to the frame. Withdraw the bolt from the left-hand side.
8. On models so equipped, note the location of the remote reservoir hose in relation to the shock absorber and the frame. The shock absorber must be reinstalled in the same direction so the remote reservoir will be on the correct side of the frame.
9. Carefully remove the shock absorber out from the frame.

92

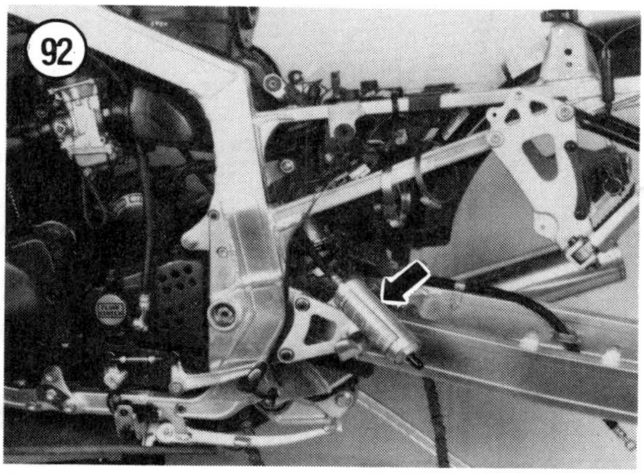

93

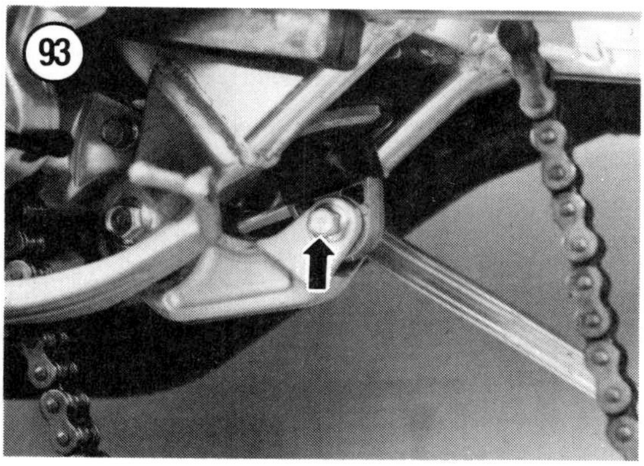

94

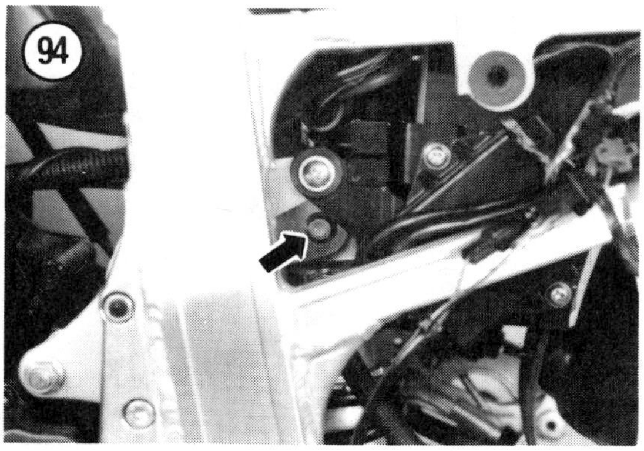

Installation

WARNING
*All bolts and nuts used on the Full Floater suspension are specifically designed for that purpose. Do **not** use a replacement bolt or nut of lesser quality or substitute design, as this may affect the performance of the system or result in failure of the part which will lead to loss of control of the bike. Torque values listed in **Table 1** must be used during installation to assure proper retention of these parts.*

1. Apply a light coat of molybdenum disulfide grease to the upper mounting bracket on the frame and to the bearing surfaces of the shock absorber lever.
2. On models so equipped, position the shock absorber assembly in the frame with the remote reservoir hose on the correct side as noted in Step 8 of *Removal.*

NOTE
Position the shock absorber into the frame with the damper adjuster marks toward the left-hand side.

3. Position the shock absorber onto the frame mounting area and install the upper mounting bolt (**Figure 94**) from the left-hand side. Install the nut but do not tighten at this time.

NOTE
The next step requires the aid of a helper to raise the rear wheel and swing arm. On models so equipped, make sure the remote reservoir hose does not get damaged.

4. Slowly raise the rear wheel and move the lower portion of the shock absorber into alignment with the mounting flange on the shock absorber lever.
5. Install the shock absorber lower mounting bolt (**Figure 93**) from the left-hand side. Install the nut.
6. Tighten the upper and lower mounting bolts and nuts to the torque specification listed in **Table 1**.

NOTE
*Since the hose routing on the GSX-R750R Limited Edition models is quite complex, refer to **Figure 95** for correct remote reservoir hose routing and position.*

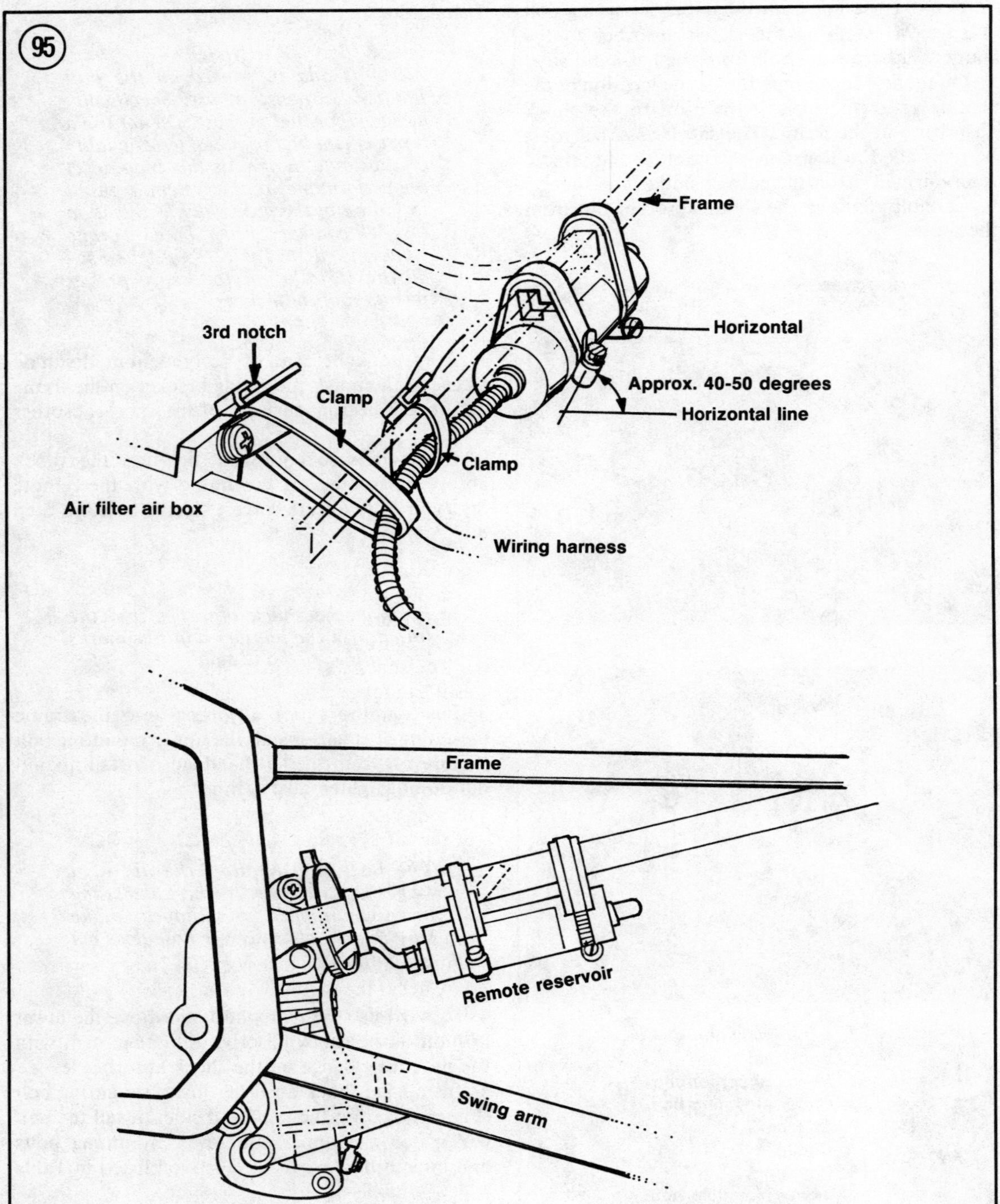
95
Frame
Horizontal
3rd notch
Clamp
Approx. 40-50 degrees
Horizontal line
Clamp
Air filter air box
Wiring harness
Frame
Remote reservoir
Swing arm

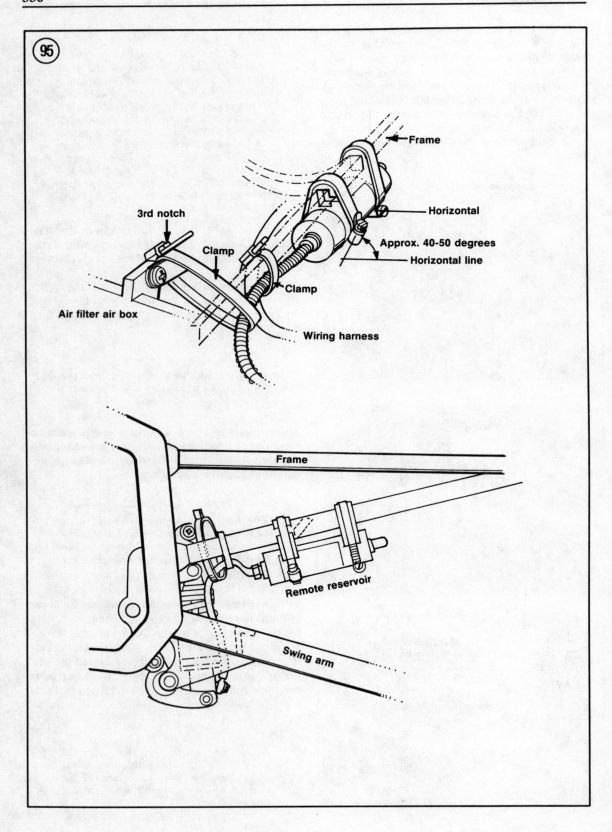

(96)

REAR SHOCK ABSORBER (GSX-R750)

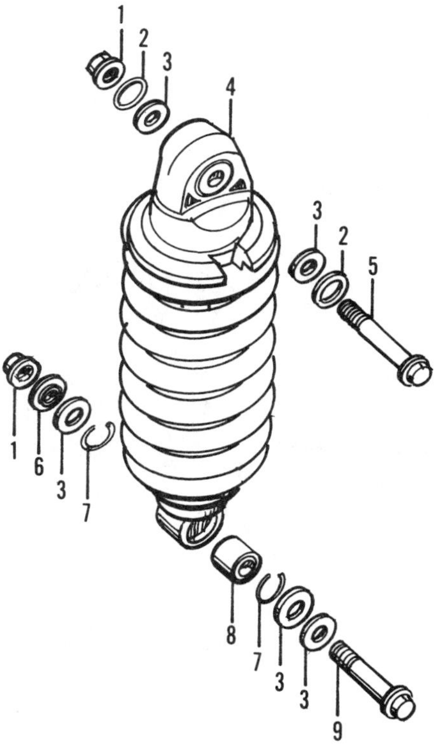

1. Nut
2. Rubber washer
3. Dust seal
4. Shock absorber unit
5. Upper mounting bolt
6. Spacer
7. Circlip
8. Bearing
9. Lower mounting bolt

7. On models equipped with a remote reservoir, perform the following:
   a. Position the remote reservoir onto the frame.
   b. Install the rubber dampers into the clamps and tighten the screws securely.
   c. Make sure the remote reservoir hose is correctly routed through the frame and is not kinked or touching any moving part of the bike.
8. Remove the wood block(s) from under the frame. Push down on the rear of the bike and make sure the rear suspension is operating properly. Make sure the remote reservoir hose is not rubbing on the shock absorber. Relocate if necessary.
9. Install both side covers.
10. Install the lower portion of the front fairing as described under *Front Fairing Removal/ Installation* in Chapter Twelve.

Inspection

Refer to the following illustrations for this procedure:

a. **Figure 96**: GSX-R750.
b. **Figure 97**: GSX-R750R Limited Edition.
c. **Figure 98**: GSX-R1100.

The shock absorber should not be disassembled as it cannot be serviced. There are *no* replacement parts available except those mentioned in this procedure. Under no circumstances should you attempt to disconnect the reservoir hose (models so equipped) or disassemble the shock absorber unit or reservoir due to the high internal pressure of the nitrogen.

1. Make sure the spring adjuster locknut (A, **Figure 99**) and adjuster (B, **Figure 99**) are tight.
2. On models so equipped, check the remote reservoir hose (A, **Figure 100**) for deterioration or damage. If damaged, replace the shock absorber.
3. Check the damper unit (B, **Figure 100**) for dents, oil leakage or other damage. Make sure the damper rod is straight.

WARNING
The shock absorber damper unit and remote reservoir (models so equipped) contain high-pressure nitrogen gas. Do not tamper with or attempt to open the damper unit or disconnect the reservoir hose from either unit. Do not place it near an open flame or other extreme heat. Do not dispose of the damper assembly yourself. Take it to a dealer where it can be deactivated and disposed of properly. Never attempt to remove the valve core from the base of the reservoir.

97

REAR SHOCK ABSORBER (GSX-R750R LIMITED EDITION)

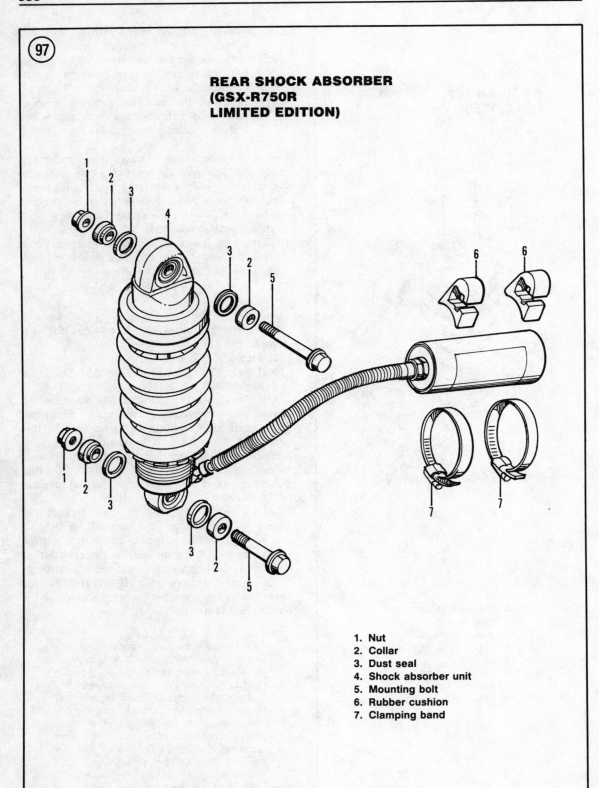

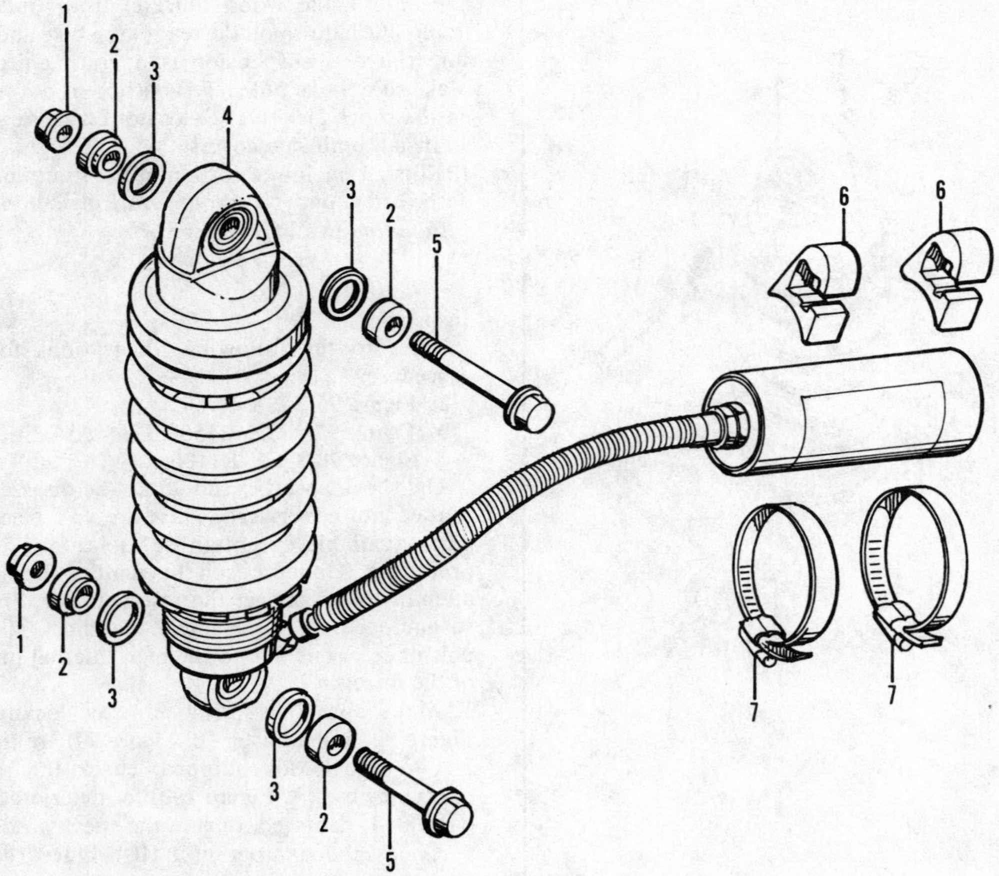

1. Nut
2. Collar
3. Dust seal
4. Shock absorber unit
5. Mounting bolt
6. Rubber cushion
7. Clamping band

(98)

REAR SHOCK ABSORBER (GSX-R1100)

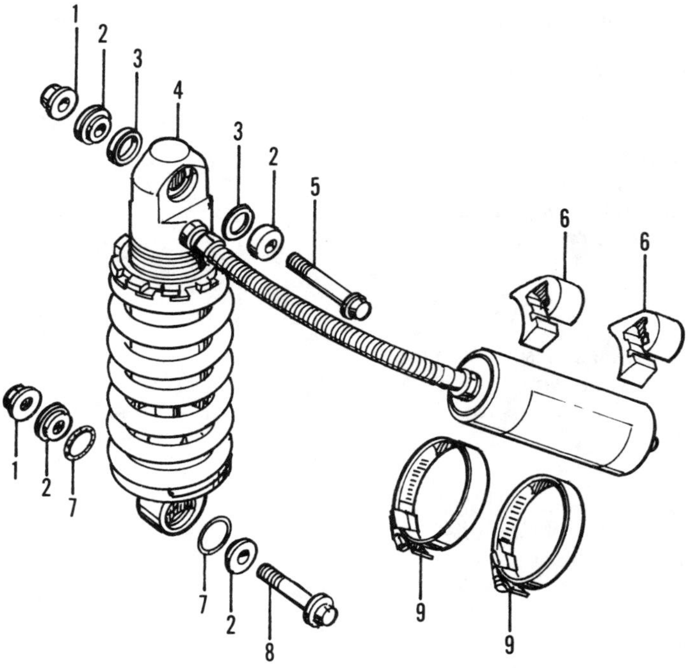

1. Nut
2. Collar
3. Dust seal
4. Shock absorber unit
5. Upper mounting bolt
6. Rubber cushion
7. Dust seal
8. Lower mounting bolt
9. Clamping band

4. Inspect the mounting spacers and dust seals at each end of the shock absorber. Refer to **Figure 101** and **Figure 102**. Replace any that are worn or starting to deteriorate.

SHOCK ABSORBER LEVER

Removal

Refer to the following illustrations for this procedure:

a. **Figure 103**: GSX-R750 and GSX-R750R Limited Edition.
b. **Figure 104**: GSX-R1100.

NOTE
This procedure is shown on a GSX-R1100 model. Where differences occur in the procedure they are identified.

1. Remove the swing arm as described under *Swing Arm Removal* in this chapter.

NOTE
Some 750cc models may have a shim on one side of the shock absorber lever where it attaches to the swing arm. It was installed at the factory to adjust the clearance. Don't lose this shim as it must be reinstalled to maintain the proper clearance between the 2 parts.

2. Remove the bolt (**Figure 105**) and nut securing the shock absorber lever and remove the lever assembly.
3. Remove the dust seal and washer (A, **Figure 106**) and the spacer and dust seal (B, **Figure 106**) from the pivot points.
4. Remove the pivot collar (**Figure 107**) from the pivot spacer.
5. Remove the pivot spacer (**Figure 108**) from the lever assembly.
6. Inspect all components as described in this chapter.

Inspection

1. Clean all parts in solvent and thoroughly dry with compressed air.

99

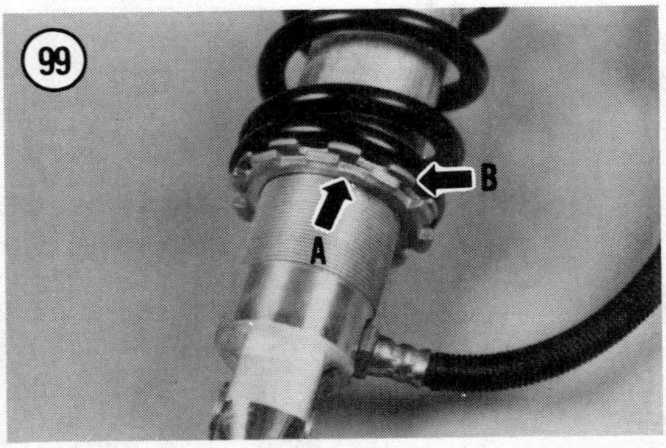

100

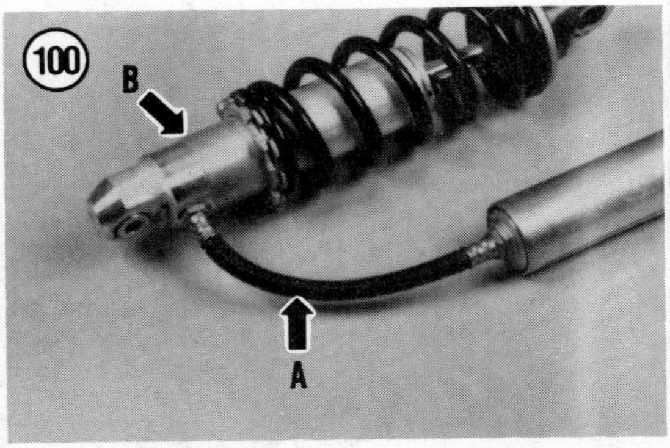

101

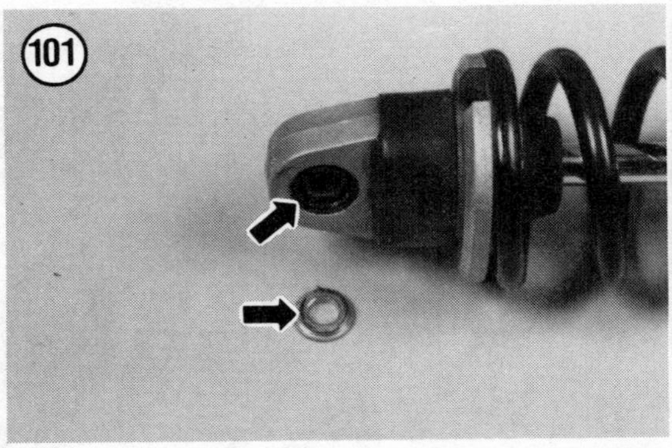

102

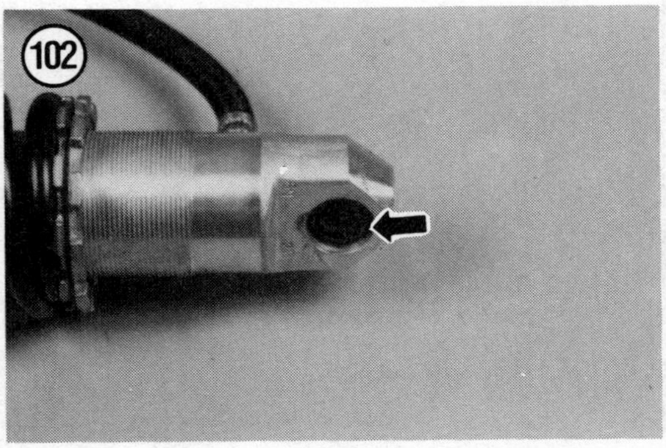

(103)

SHOCK LEVER (GSX-R750, GSX-R750R LIMITED EDITION)

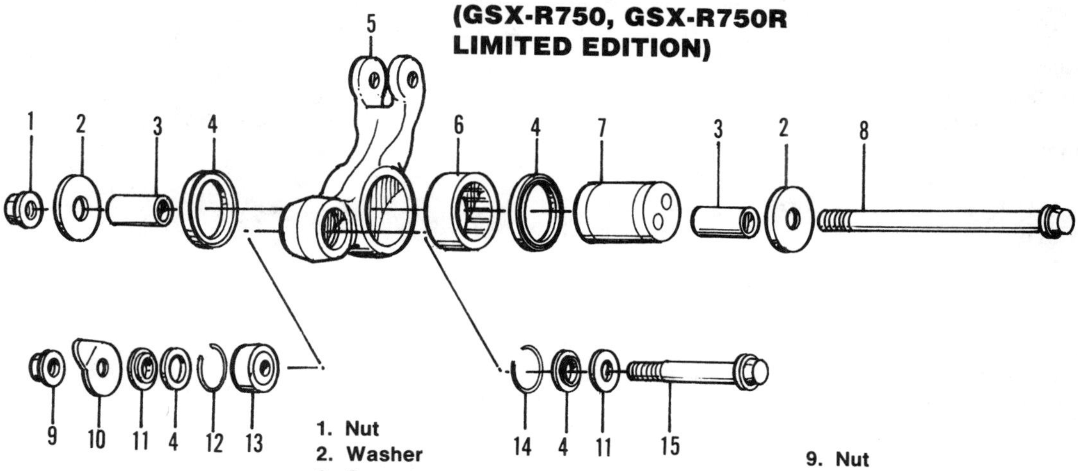

1. Nut
2. Washer
3. Spacer
4. Dust seal
5. Shock lever
6. Needle bearing
7. Pivot spacer
8. Shock lever-to-swing arm mounting bolt
9. Nut
10. Shim
11. Spacer
12. Circlip
13. Bearing
14. Circlip
15. Shock lever-to-frame mounting bolt

(104)

SHOCK LEVER (GSX-R1100)

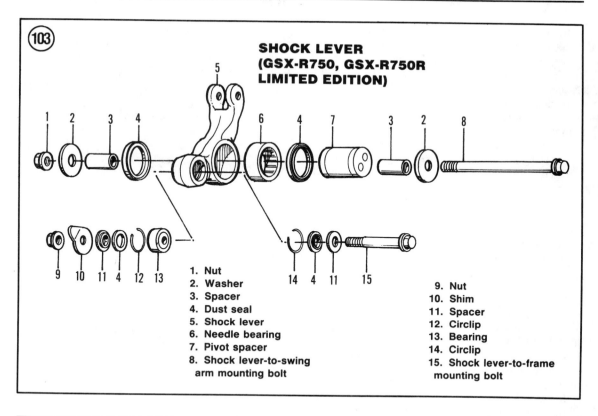

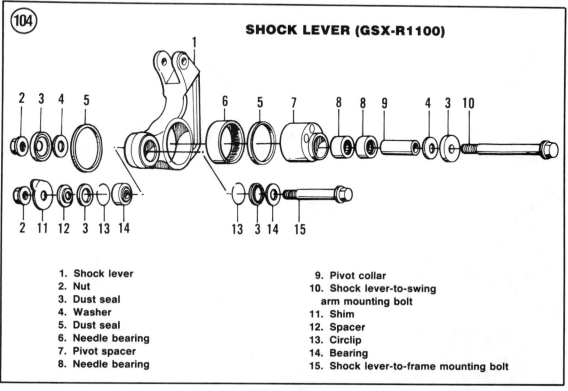

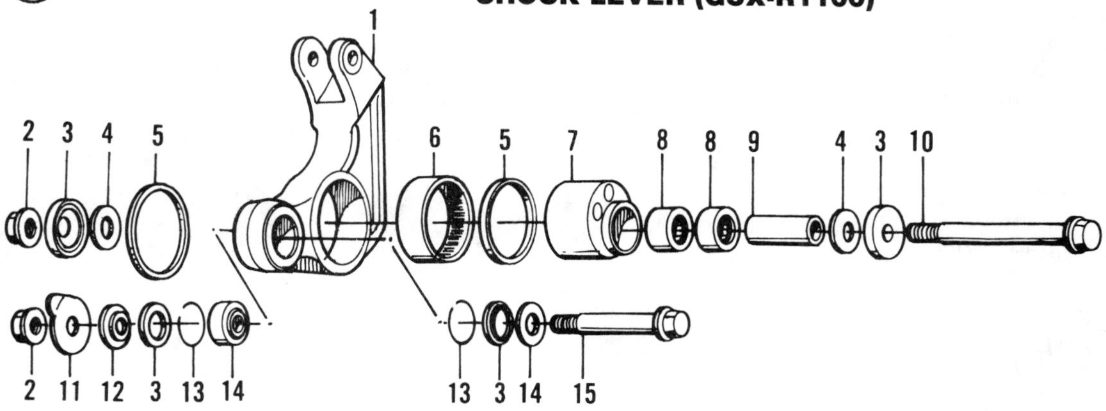

1. Shock lever
2. Nut
3. Dust seal
4. Washer
5. Dust seal
6. Needle bearing
7. Pivot spacer
8. Needle bearing
9. Pivot collar
10. Shock lever-to-swing arm mounting bolt
11. Shim
12. Spacer
13. Circlip
14. Bearing
15. Shock lever-to-frame mounting bolt

2. Inspect the lever assembly (A, **Figure 109**) for cracks or damage; replace as necessary.
3. Inspect the pivot point (B, **Figure 109**) where the lever attaches to the frame. If worn or elongated, the lever assembly must be replaced.
4. Inspect the lever needle bearing (A, **Figure 110**) and the pivot spacer needle bearing (**Figure 111**) as follows:
   a. Wipe off any excess grease from the needle bearing at each end of the swing arm.
   b. Turn the bearing with your fingers; make sure it rotates smoothly. The needle bearing wears very slowly and wear is very difficult to measure.
   c. Check the rollers for evidence of wear, pitting or color change (bluish tint) indicating heat from lack of lubrication.
   d. Replace if necessary as described in this chapter.
5. Inspect the spherical bearing (B, **Figure 110**) for wear. Turn the bearing with your fingers; make sure it rotates smoothly. Replace if necessary as described in this chapter.
6. Inspect the pivot spacer (**Figure 112**) for scratches, abrasion or abnormal wear; replace as necessary.
7. Inspect the dust seals (**Figure 113**). Replace all of them as a set if any are worn or starting to deteriorate. If the dust seals are in poor condition they will allow dirt to enter into the pivot areas and cause the bearings to wear.
8. Coat all surfaces of the pivot receptacles, the bearings and the inside of the dust seals with molybdenum disulfide grease.

NOTE
Make sure the dust seal lips seat correctly. If not, they will allow dirt and moisture into the bearing areas and cause wear.

105

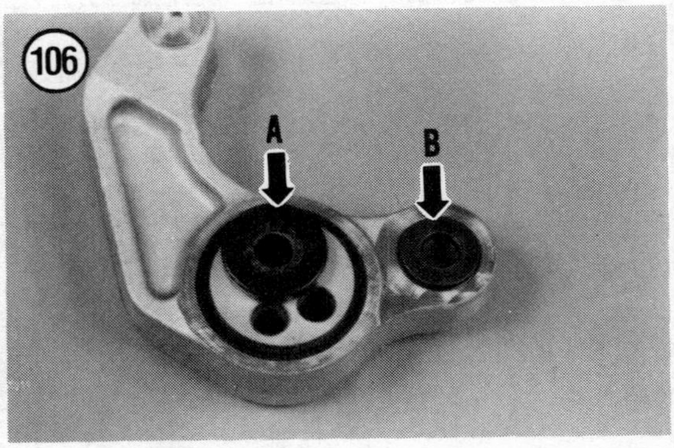

106

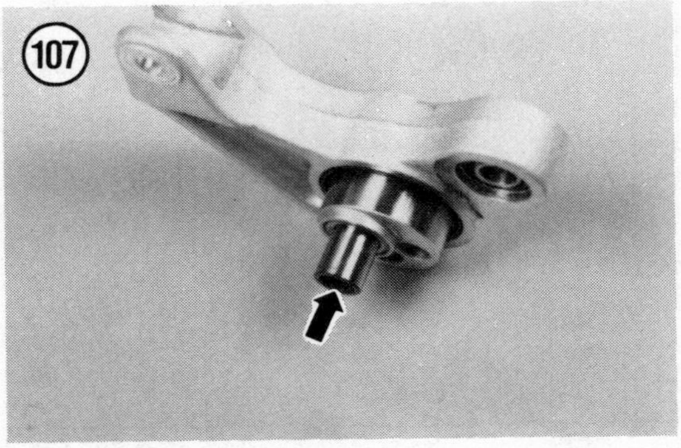

107

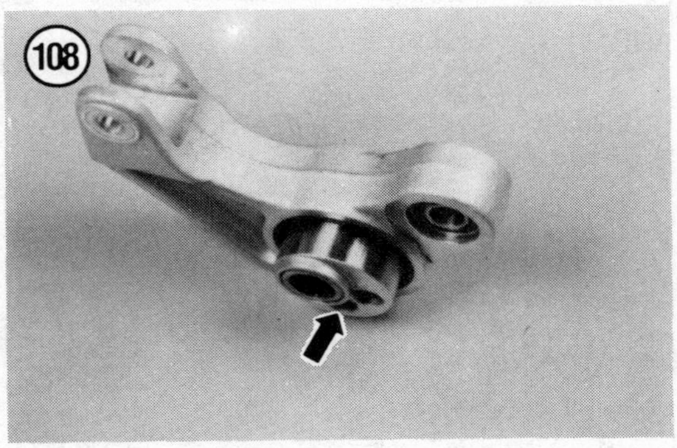

108

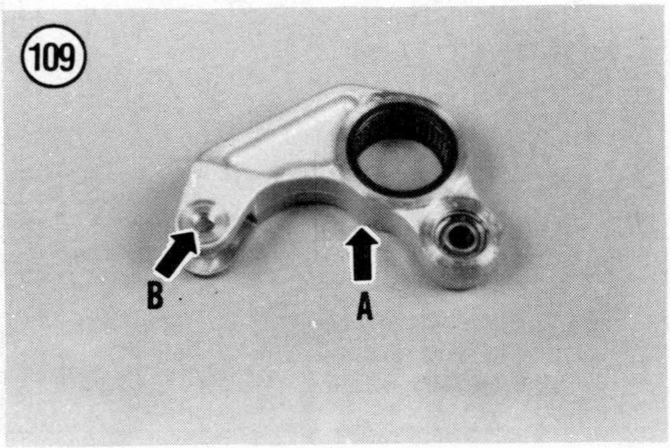

109

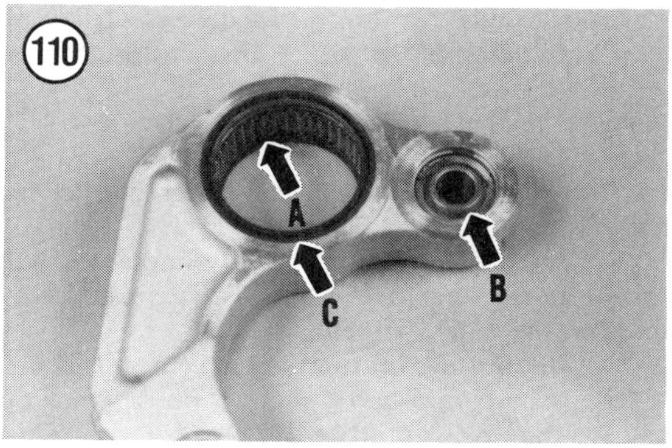

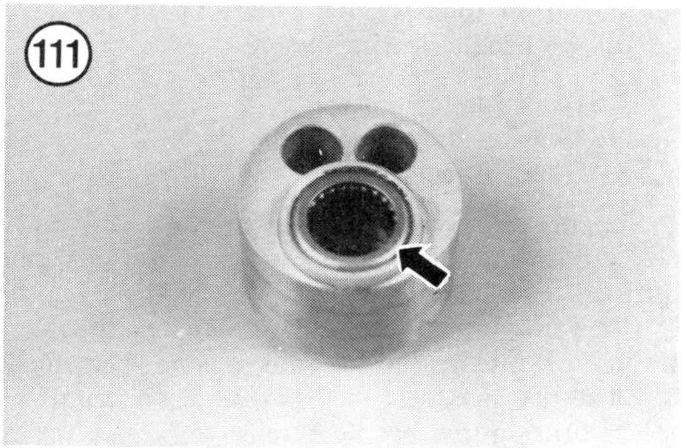

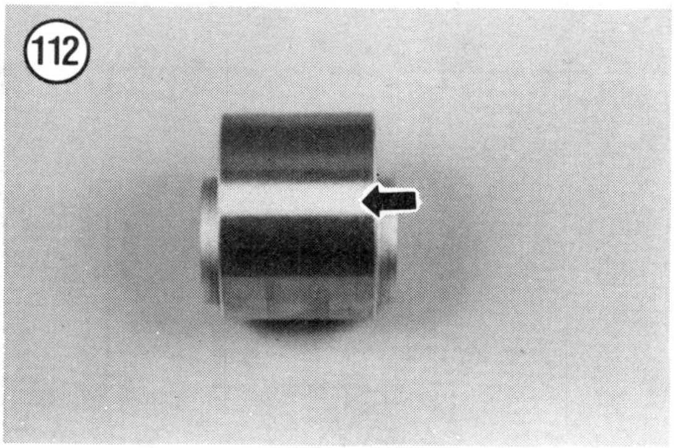

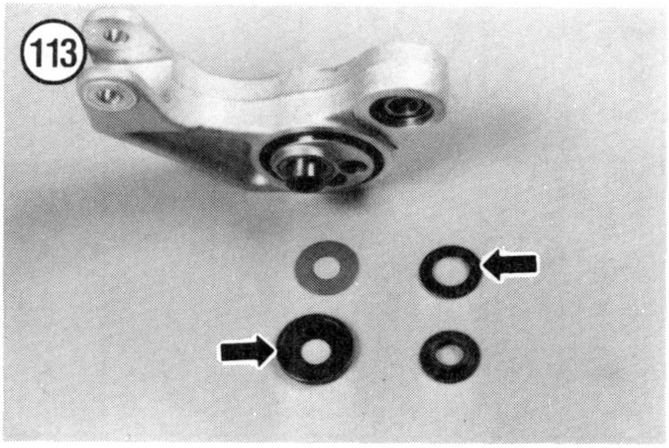

Installation

1. Install the pivot spacer (**Figure 108**) into the lever assembly.
2. Install the pivot collar (**Figure 107**) into the pivot spacer.
3. Install the washer and dust seal (A, **Figure 106**) and the dust seal and spacer (B, **Figure 106**) into the pivot points.

NOTE
If so equipped on 750 cc models, install the shim between the shock absorber lever and the swing arm. This shim must be reinstalled to maintain the proper clearance between the 2 parts.

4. Before installing the shock absorber lever mounting bolt, coat it with molybdenum disulfide grease.
5. Position the shock absorber lever as shown in **Figure 105**. Install the mounting bolt from the left-hand side and install the nut. Tighten the bolt and nut to the torque specification listed in **Table 1**.
6. Install the swing arm as described under *Swing Arm Installation* in this chapter.
7. On GSX-R750 models, after the swing arm is installed, refer to **Figure 114** as a final check for the correct position of the shock absorber lever and the shock absorber.

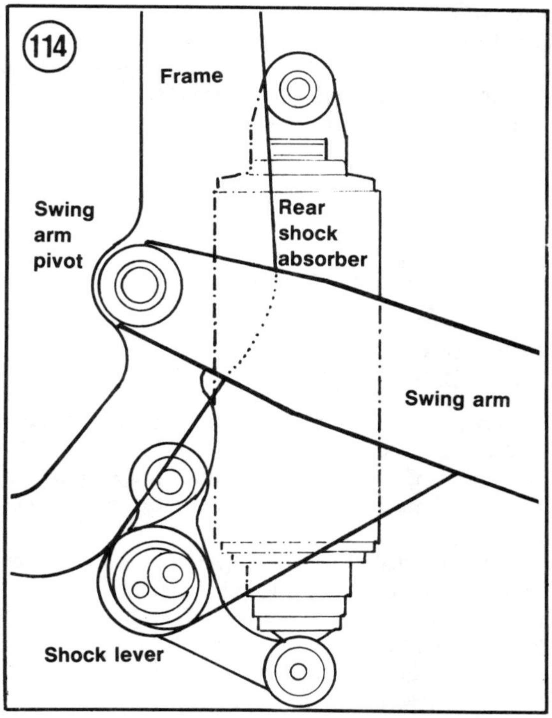

10

SHOCK ABSORBER LEVER BEARING REPLACEMENT

Spherical Bearing Replacement

1. Remove the washer and dust seal (B, **Figure 106**) from each side of the spherical bearing.
2. Remove the circlip from each side of the spherical bearing.
3. Support the lever assembly on 2 blocks of wood. Be careful that the dust seal surfaces do not get damaged.
4. Use a suitable size socket that matches the outer diameter and drive out the spherical bearing. Discard the bearing—never reinstall a bearing that has been removed.
5. Thoroughly clean the lever assembly in solvent and blow dry with compressed air.
6. Apply a light coat of oil to the inner surface of the lever assembly prior to installation of the new spherical bearing.
7. Support the lever assembly so the dust seal sealing surface will not be damaged.
8. Correctly position the spherical bearing onto the lever assembly.
9. Tap the spherical bearing squarely into place, tapping on the outer race only. Use a socket that matches the outer diameter.
10. Tap the bearing into until it is centered in the lever assembly. There should be an equal gap on each side. This gap is necessary for the circlips on each side.
11. Install a circlip on each side. Make sure the circlip is properly seated in the lever groove.
12. Install the dust seal and washer (B, **Figure 106**) onto each side of the spherical bearing.

Pivot Spacer Outer Needle Bearing Replacement

1. Remove the dust seal (C, **Figure 110**) from each side of the needle bearing.
2. Support the lever assembly on 2 blocks of wood. Be careful that the dust seal surfaces do not get damaged.
3. Use a suitable size socket that matches the outer diameter and drive out the needle bearing. Discard the needle bearing—never reinstall a needle bearing that has been removed.
4. Thoroughly clean the lever assembly in solvent and blow dry with compressed air.
5. Apply a light coat of oil to the inner surface of the lever assembly prior to installation of the needle bearing.
6. Support the lever assembly so the dust seal sealing surface will not be damaged.
7. Correctly position the needle bearing onto the lever assembly.
8. Tap the needle bearing squarely into place and tap on the outer race only. Use a socket that matches the outer diameter.
9. Tap the bearing into until it is centered in the lever assembly. There should be a gap of approximately 4 mm (0.15 in.) on each side. This gap is necessary for the dust seal on each side.
10. Install the dust seal (C, **Figure 110**) onto each side of the needle bearing.

Pivot Spacer Inner Needle Bearing Replacement (GSX-R1100 Models)

1. Support the pivot spacer on 2 blocks of wood. Be careful that the pivot surfaces do not get damaged.
2. Use a suitable size socket that matches the outer diameter and drive out the needle bearings. Discard the needle bearings—never reinstall a needle bearing that has been removed.
3. Thoroughly clean the pivot spacer in solvent and blow dry with compressed air.

115

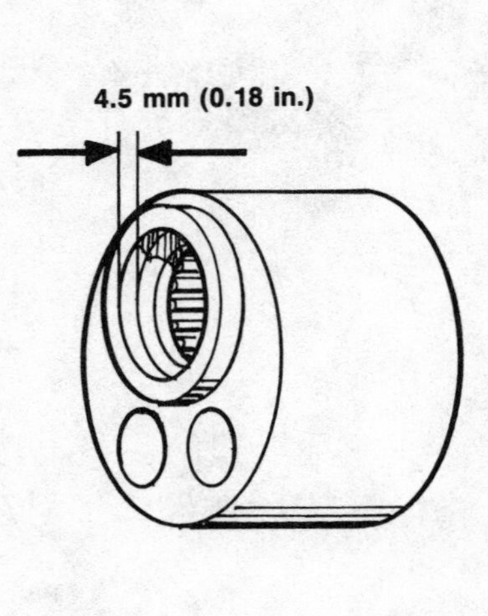

4. Apply a light coat of oil to the inner surface of the pivot spacer prior to installation of the needle bearings.
5. Support the pivot spacer on 2 blocks of wood. Be careful that the pivot surfaces do not get damaged.

NOTE
Install the bearings so that the markings face toward the outside.

6. Correctly position one of the needle bearings onto the pivot spacer.
7. Tap the needle bearing squarely into place and tap on the outer race only. Use a socket that matches the outer diameter.
8. Tap the bearing in until it is 4.5 mm (0.8 in.) past the outer surface of the pivot spacer (**Figure 115**).
9. Turn the pivot spacer over and repeat Steps 5-8 for the other bearing.

Table 1 REAR SUSPENSION TORQUE SPECIFICATIONS

Item	N•m	ft.-lb.
Rear axle nut	85-115	61-83
Rear caliper mounting bolt	15-25	14-18
Brake disc bolts	15-25	11-18
Driven sprocket nuts	48-72	35-52
Drive sprocket nut	80-100	58-72
Swing arm pivot bolt and nut		
750 cc	50-80	36-58
1100 cc	55-85	40-62
Shock absorber		
Mounting bolts and nuts	40-60	29-43
Shock lever bolt and nut	70-100	50-72
Drive sprocket		
Nut	100-130	73-94
Bolt	9-12	6-94

Table 2 REAR SHOCK ABSORBER DAMPING FORCE AND SPRING PRE-LOAD DIMENSION

Ride type	Damping force setting	Spring preload dimension	Number of rider(s)
GSX-R750*			
Standard	3	175 mm (6.89 in.)	Solo riding
Softer	2	180 mm (7.09 in.)	Solo riding
Stiffer	4	170 mm (6.69 in.)	Solo riding
Dual riding	4	170 mm (6.69 in.)	Dual riding
GSX-R750R Limited Edition**			
Standard	2	162 mm (6.40 in.)	Solo riding
Softer	1	167 mm (6.60 in.)	Solo riding
Stiffer	3	157 mm (6.20 in.)	Solo riding
GSX-R1100***			
Standard	4	190 mm (7.48 in.)	Solo riding
Softer	3	191.5 mm (7.54 in.)	Solo riding
Stiffer	4	188.5 mm (7.54 in.)	Solo riding
Dual riding	4	187 mm (7.36 in.)	Dual riding

* On GSX-R750 models, do NOT set the spring length to less than 165 mm (6.50 in.).

** On GSX-R750R Limited Edition models, do NOT set the spring length to less than 152 mm (5.98 in.) nor more than 172 mm (6.77 in.).

*** On GSX-R1100 models, do NOT set the spring length to less than 185 mm (7.28 in.) nor more than 195 mm (7.68 in.).

NOTE: If you own a GSX600F Katana, first refer to Chapter 13 for specific service information.

CHAPTER ELEVEN

BRAKES

The brake system on all models consists of a dual disc on the front wheel and a single disc on the rear. This chapter describes repair and replacement procedures for all brake components.

Table 1 contains the brake system torque specifications and **Table 2** contains brake system specifications. **Table 1** and **Table 2** are located at the end of this chapter.

DISC BRAKES

The disc brakes are actuated by hydraulic fluid and are controlled by a hand lever (front brakes) or brake pedal (rear brakes) that is attached to the front or rear master cylinder. As the brake pads wear, they automatically adjust for wear.

When working on hydraulic brake systems, it is necessary that the work area and all tools be absolutely clean. Any tiny particles of foreign matter and grit in the caliper assembly or the master cylinder can damage the components. Also, sharp tools must not be used inside the calipers or on the piston. If there is any doubt about your ability to correctly and safely carry out major service on the brake components, take the job to a Suzuki dealer or brake specialist.

When adding brake fluid, use only a brake fluid clearly marked DOT 3 or DOT 4 from a sealed container. Other types may vaporize and cause brake failure. Always use the same brand name; do not intermix as many brands are not compatible. Brake fluid will draw moisture which greatly reduces its ability to perform correctly, so it is a good idea to purchase brake fluid in small containers.

WARNING

Do not intermix silicone based (DOT 5) brake fluid as it can cause brake component damage leading to brake system failure.

Whenever *any* component has been removed from the brake system the system is considered "opened" and must be bled to remove air bubbles. Also if the brake feels "spongy," this usually means there are air bubbles in the system and it must be bled. For safe operation, refer to *Bleeding the System* in this chapter.

CAUTION

Disc brake components rarely require disassembly, so do not disassemble them unless necessary. Do not use solvents of any kind on the brake system's internal components. Solvents will cause the seals to swell and distort and require replacement. When disassembling and cleaning brake components (except brake pads) use new brake fluid.

FRONT BRAKE PAD REPLACEMENT

There is no recommended mileage interval for changing the friction pads in the disc brakes. Pad wear depends greatly on riding habits and conditions. The pads should be checked for wear every 6 months and replaced when the wear indicator reaches the edge of the brake disc. To maintain an even brake pressure on the disc, always replace both pads in the caliper at the same time. Also replace the pads in both calipers at the same time.

Disconnecting the hydraulic brake hose from the brake caliper is not necessary for brake pad replacement. Disconnect the hose only if the caliper assembly is going to be removed.

CAUTION
Check the pads more frequently when the wear line approaches the disc. On some pads the wear line is very close to the metal backing plate. If pad wear happens to be uneven for some reason the backing plate may come in contact with the disc and cause damage.

Refer to **Figure 1** for this procedure.

This procedure is shown with the caliper assembly removed from the disc and fork slider for clarity. The pads can be replaced without removing the caliper assembly.

1. Remove the dust cover from the brake caliper.
2. Remove the clips securing the pad pins.
3. Withdraw both pad pins and remove the pad springs.
4. Withdraw both brake pads and shims (models so equipped) from the caliper assembly.
5. Clean the pad recess and the end of the pistons with a soft brush. Do not use solvent, a wire brush or any hard tool which would damage the cylinders or pistons.
6. Carefully remove any rust or corrosion from the disc.
7. Lightly coat the end of the pistons and the backs of the new pads (*not* the friction material) with disc brake lubricant.

NOTE
When purchasing new pads, check with your dealer to make sure the friction compound of the new pad is compatible

(1)

FRONT BRAKE CALIPER ASSEMBLY

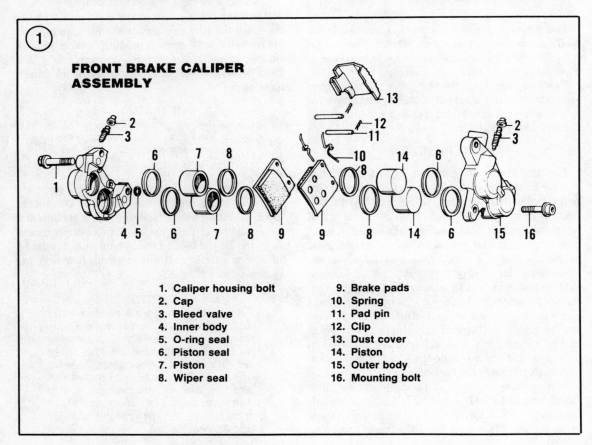

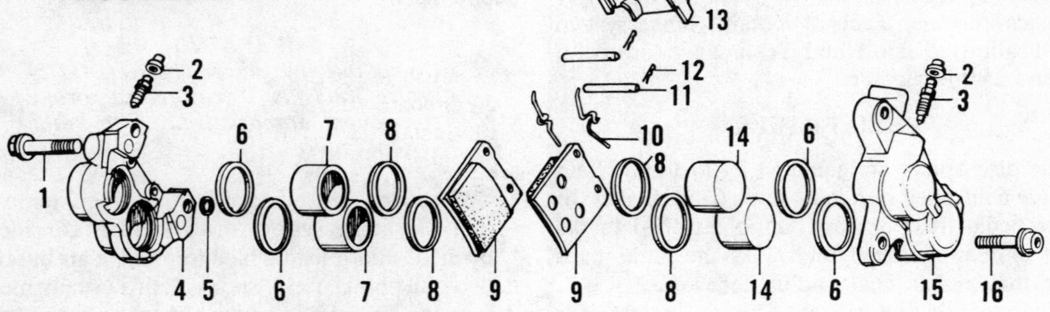

1. Caliper housing bolt
2. Cap
3. Bleed valve
4. Inner body
5. O-ring seal
6. Piston seal
7. Piston
8. Wiper seal
9. Brake pads
10. Spring
11. Pad pin
12. Clip
13. Dust cover
14. Piston
15. Outer body
16. Mounting bolt

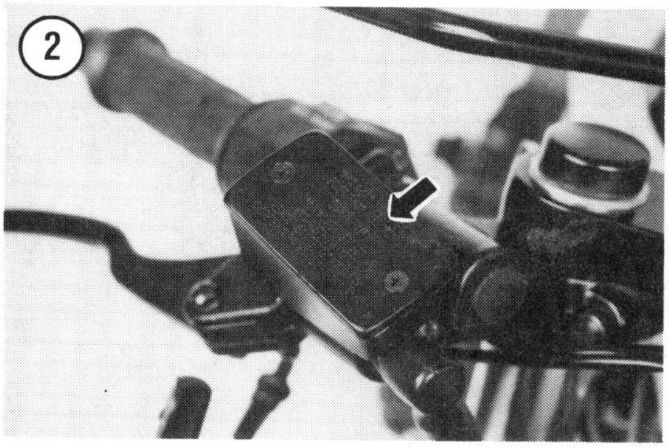
2

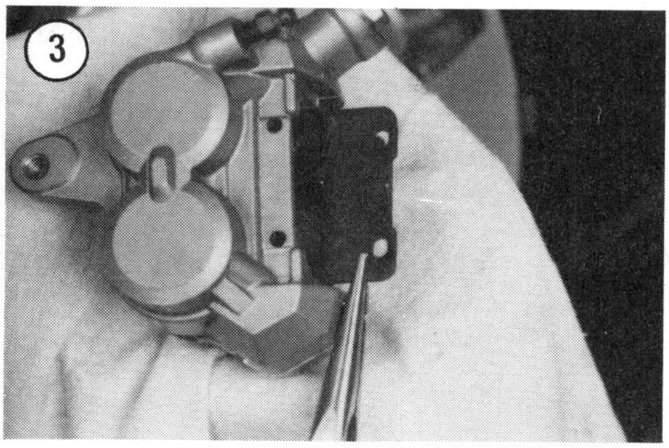
3

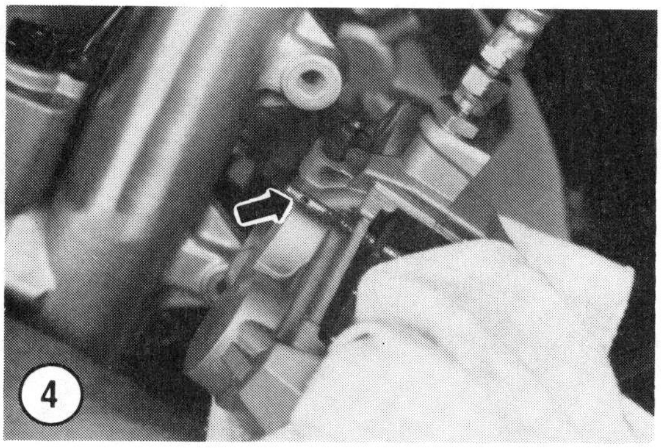
4

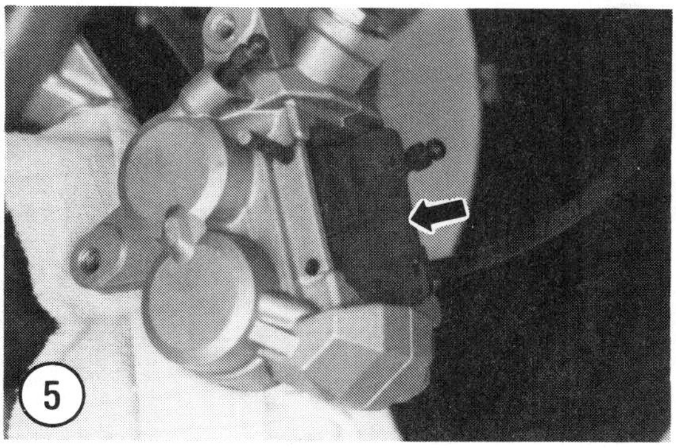
5

with the disc material. Remove any roughness from the backs of the new pads with a fine-cut file; blow them clean with compressed air.

8. When new pads are installed in the caliper, the master cylinder brake fluid level will rise as the caliper pistons are repositioned. Perform the following:
   a. Clean the top of the master cylinder of all dirt and foreign matter.
   b. Remove the screws securing the cover (**Figure 2**). Remove the cover and the diaphragm from the master cylinder and slowly push the caliper pistons into the caliper. Constantly check the reservoir to make sure brake fluid does not overflow. Remove fluid, if necessary, before it overflows.
   c. The pistons should move freely. If they don't and there is evidence of them sticking in the cylinder, the caliper should be removed and serviced as described in this chapter.
9. Push the caliper pistons in all the way to allow room for the new pads.
10. Install the outboard pad (**Figure 3**) into the caliper.
11. Partially install one of the pad pins (**Figure 4**) through one of the holes in the outboard pad.
12. Install the inboard pad into the caliper (**Figure 5**).
13. Push the pad pin through one of the holes in the inboard pad. Push the pad pin until it stops.
14. Install the clip (**Figure 6**) into the hole in the pad pin. Push the clip in until it seats completely on the pad pin.

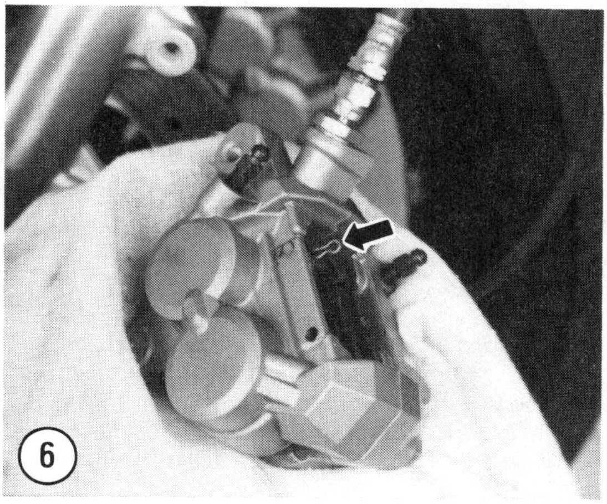
6

15. Hook one of the springs under one of the pad pins and index it onto the top of the brake pad (**Figure 7**).
16. Partially install the other pad pin (A, **Figure 8**) and hook the spring under the pad pin (B, **Figure 8**).
17. Hook the other spring under one of the pad pins and index it onto the top of the brake pad (**Figure 9**).
18. Push the pad pin farther in, hook the spring under the pad pin and push the pad pin until it stops.
19. Install the remaining clip (**Figure 10**) into the hole in the pad pin. Push the clip in until it seats completely on the pad pin.
20. Install the dust cap. Make sure it snaps into place, otherwise it will fly off when you hit the first bump in the road.
21. Repeat Steps 1-20 for the other caliper assembly.
22. Remove the lower portion of the front fairing as described under *Front Fairing Removal/Installation* in Chapter Twelve.
23. Place wood block(s) under each side of the frame to support the bike securely with the front wheel off the ground. Spin the front wheel and activate the front brake lever as many times as it takes to correctly locate both sets of pads.

WARNING
Use brake fluid clearly marked DOT 3 or DOT 4 from a sealed container. Other types may vaporize and cause brake failure. Always use the same brand name; do not intermix as many brands are not compatible. Do not intermix silicone based (DOT 5) brake fluid as it can cause brake component damage leading to brake system failure.

24. Refill the master cylinder reservoir, if necessary, to maintain the correct fluid level as seen through the viewing port on the side. Install the diaphragm and cover. Tighten the screws securely.

WARNING
*Do not ride the motorcycle until you are sure the brakes are operating correctly with full hydraulic advantage. If necessary, bleed the brake as described under **Bleeding the System** in this chapter.*

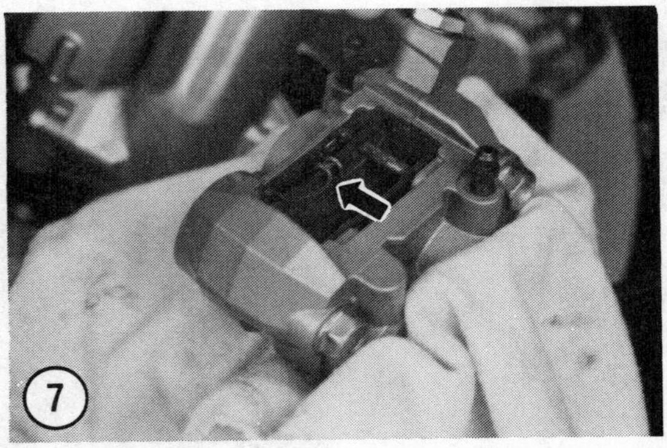
7

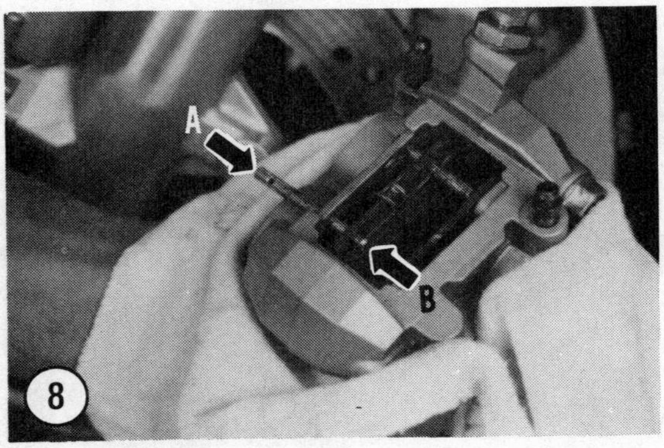

8

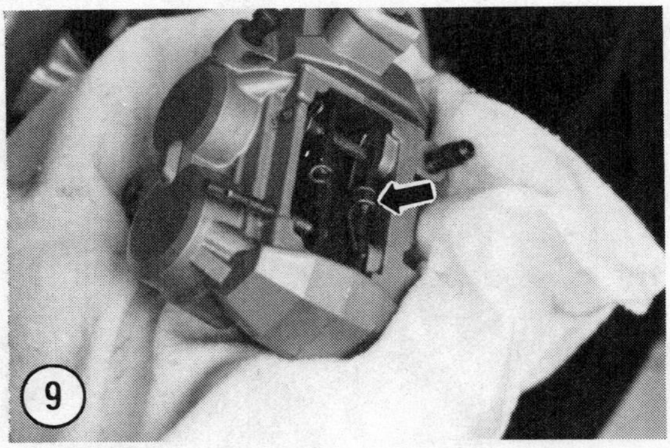
9

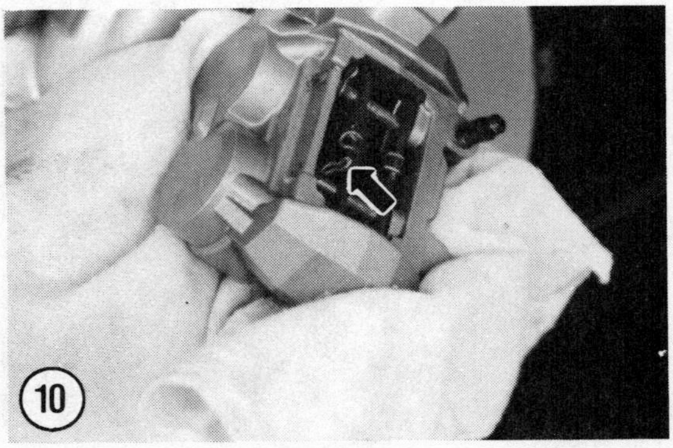
10

25. Bed in the pads gradually for the first 10 days of riding by using only light pressure as much as possible. Immediate hard application will glaze the new friction pads and greatly reduce the effectiveness of the brake.

FRONT MASTER CYLINDER

Removal/Installation

1. Remove the front fairing as described under *Front Fairing Removal/Installation* in Chapter Twelve.

CAUTION
Cover the fuel tank, front fender and instrument cluster with a heavy cloth or plastic tarp to protect them from accidental brake fluid spills. Wash brake fluid off any painted or plated surfaces or plastic parts immediately, as it will destroy the finish. Use soapy water and rinse completely.

11

12

13

2. Disconnect the brake light switch electrical connector from the main wiring harness.
3. Pull back the rubber boot (**Figure 11**) on the master cylinder union bolt.
4. Place a shop cloth under the union bolt to catch any spilled brake fluid that will leak out.
5. Unscrew the union bolt securing the upper brake hose to the master cylinder. Don't lose the sealing washer on each side of the hose fitting. Tie the loose end of the hose up to the handlebar and cover the end to prevent the entry of moisture and foreign matter.
6. Remove the clamping bolts (**Figure 12**) and clamp securing the master cylinder to the handlebar and remove the master cylinder.
7. Install by reversing these removal steps, noting the following.
8. Install the clamp with the UP arrow (**Figure 13**) facing up. Align the face of the clamp with the punch mark on the handlebar. Tighten the upper bolt first, then the lower to the torque specification listed in **Table 1**.
9. Place a new sealing washer on each side of the brake hose fitting and install the union bolt.
10. Tighten the union bolt to the torque specification listed in **Table 1**.
11. Bleed the front brakes as described under *Bleeding the System* in this chapter.

Disassembly

Refer to **Figure 14** for this procedure.

1. Remove the master cylinder as described in this chapter.
2. Remove the screws, washers and lockwashers (**Figure 15**) securing the brakelight switch to the master cylinder and remove the switch assembly.
3. Remove the screws securing the top cover and remove the top cover and the diaphragm.
4. Pour out any residual hydraulic fluid and discard it. *Never* re-use hydraulic fluid.

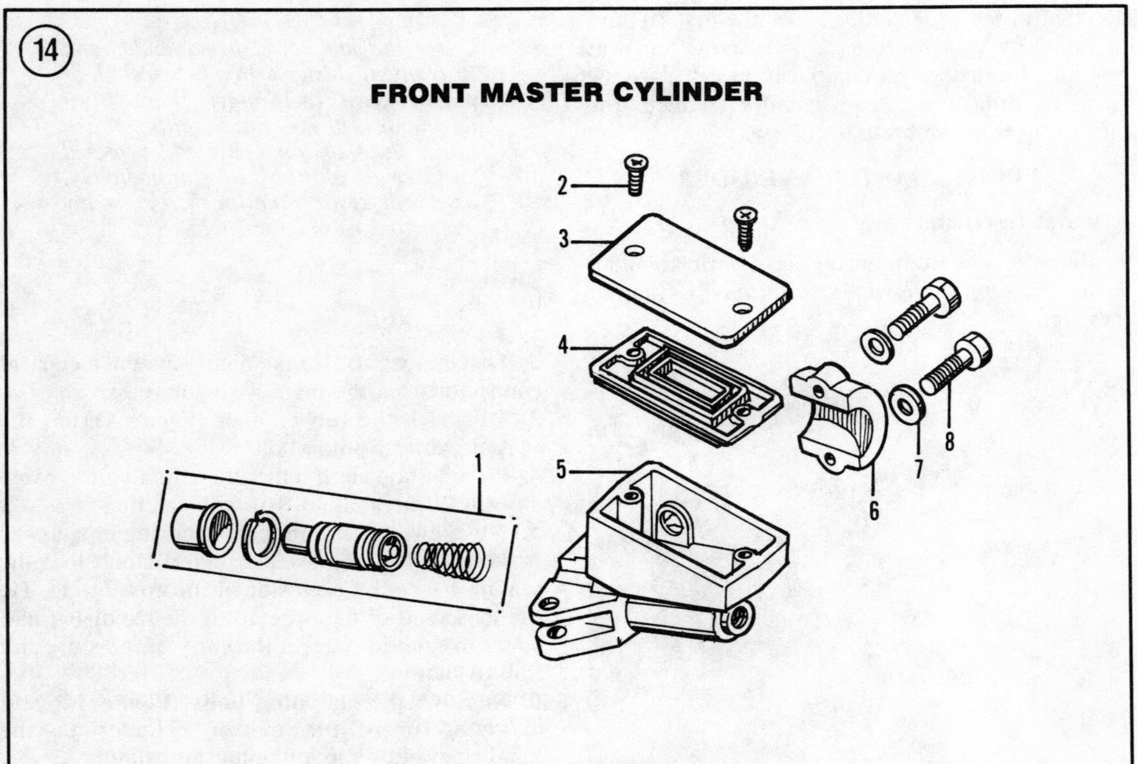

1. Piston assembly
2. Screw
3. Top cover
4. Diaphragm
5. Master cylinder body
6. Clamp
7. Washer
8. Bolt

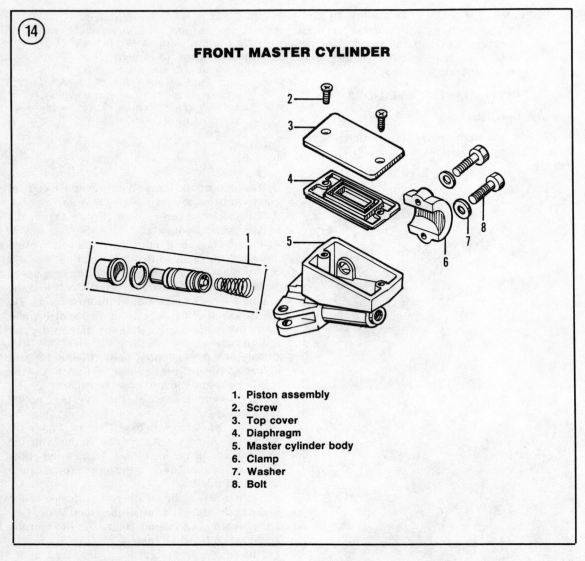

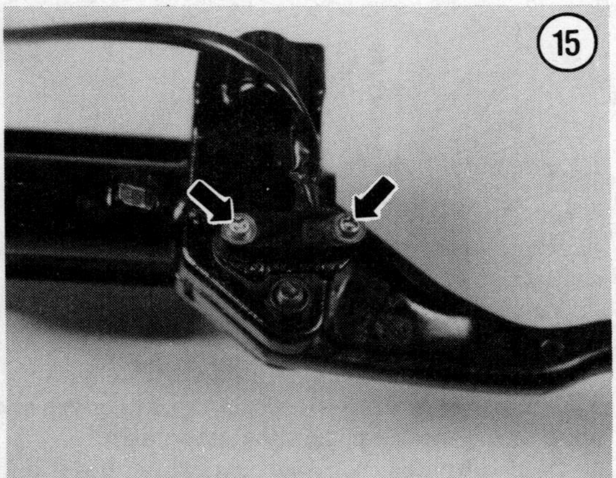

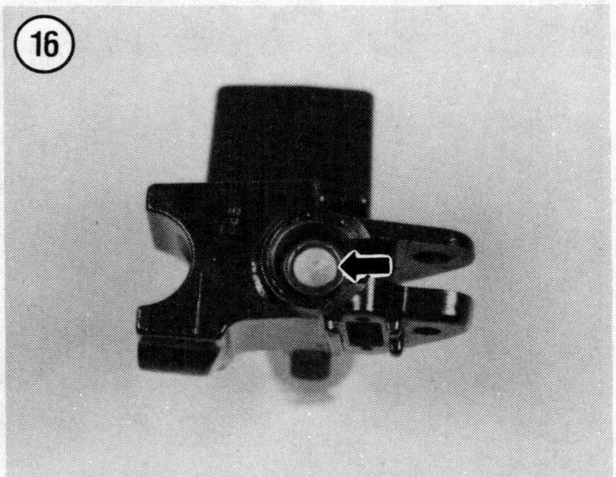

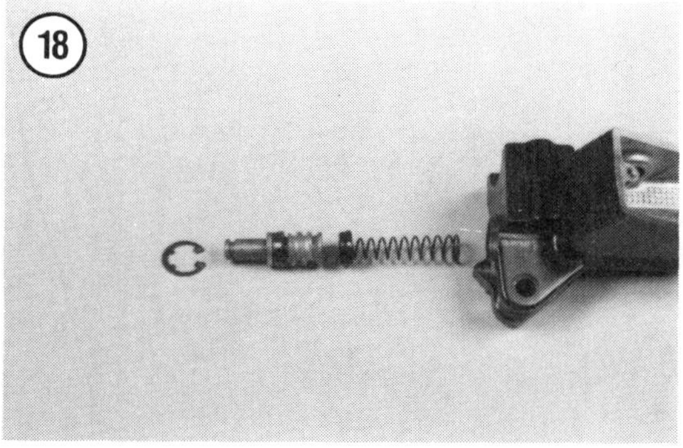

5. Remove the rubber boot (**Figure 16**) from the area where the hand lever actuates the piston assembly.
6. Using circlip pliers, remove the internal circlip (**Figure 17**) from the body.
7. Remove the piston assembly and the spring (**Figure 18**).

Inspection

1. Clean all parts in denatured alcohol or fresh hydraulic fluid.
2. Inspect the bore (**Figure 19**) for signs of wear and damage. If less than perfect, replace the master cylinder assembly. The body cannot be replaced separately.
3. Remove the secondary cup (**Figure 20**) from the piston.
4. Inspect the piston contact surfaces (A, **Figure 21**) for signs of wear and damage. If less than perfect, replace the piston assembly.
5. Check the end of the piston (B, **Figure 21**) for wear caused by the hand lever. If worn, replace the piston assembly.
6. Replace the piston assembly if either the primary or secondary cup requires replacement.
7. Inspect the pivot hole (**Figure 22**) in the hand lever. If worn or elongated it must be replaced.

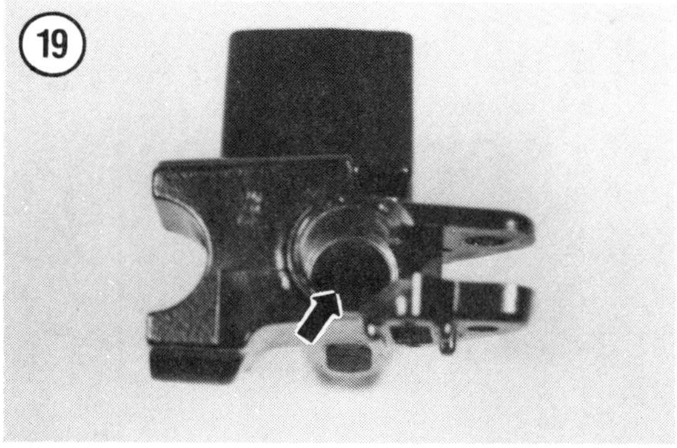

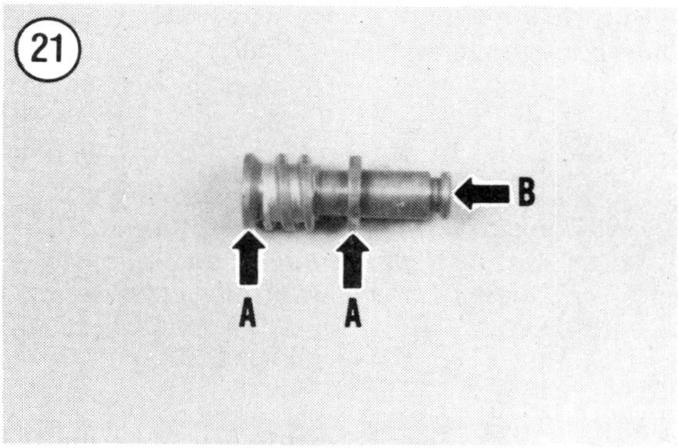

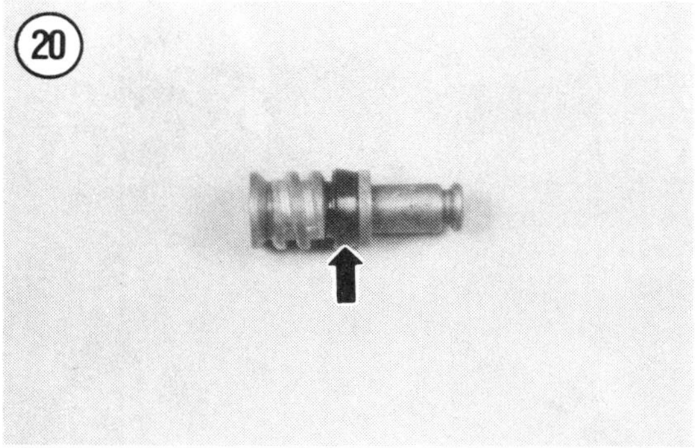

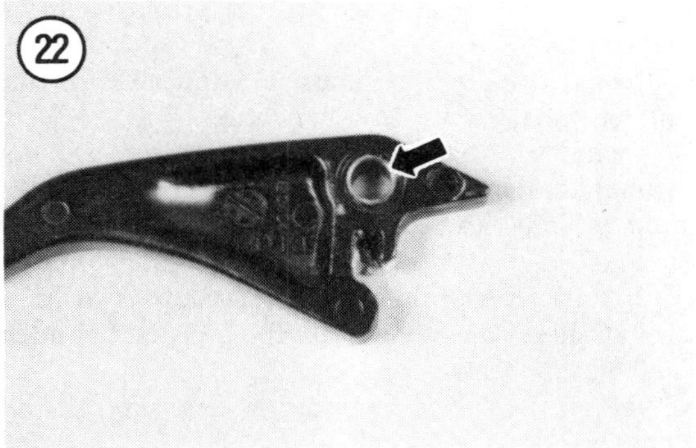

11

8. Make sure the passages (**Figure 23**) in the bottom of the master cylinder body are clear.

NOTE
There are two passages. The large hole feeds the system and rarely becomes plugged. The small hole is the return orifice and can become plugged if the brake fluid becomes dirty. If the return orifice becomes plugged, the brakes can be applied, but will not release.

23

9. Check the top cover (**Figure 24**) and diaphragm (**Figure 25**) for damage and deterioration and replace as necessary.
10. Inspect the threads in the bore for the union bolt. If worn or damaged, clean out with a thread tap or replace the master cylinder assembly.
11. Check the hand lever pivot lugs (**Figure 26**) on the master cylinder body for cracks. If damaged, replace the master cylinder assembly.

24

Assembly

1. Soak the new cups in fresh brake fluid for at least 15 minutes to make them pliable. Coat the inside of the cylinder bore with fresh hydraulic fluid prior to the assembly of parts.

CAUTION
When installing the piston assembly, do not allow the cups to turn inside out as they will be damaged and allow brake fluid leakage within the cylinder bore.

25

2. Install the spring and piston assembly into the cylinder together. Install the spring with its small end (**Figure 27**) facing toward the primary cup on the piston.
3. Install the circlip (**Figure 17**) and slide on the rubber boot (**Figure 16**).
4. Install the diaphragm and top cover. Do not tighten the cover screws at this time as hydraulic fluid will have to be added later when the system is bled.
5. Install the brake light switch, washers, lockwashers and screws to the master cylinder. Tighten the screws securely.
6. Install the master cylinder as described in this chapter.

26

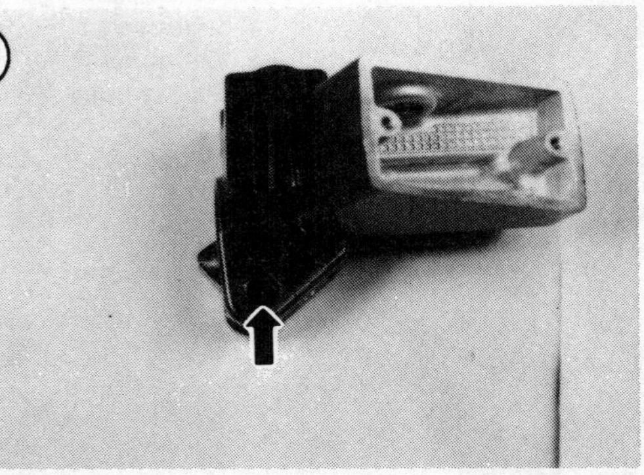

(27)

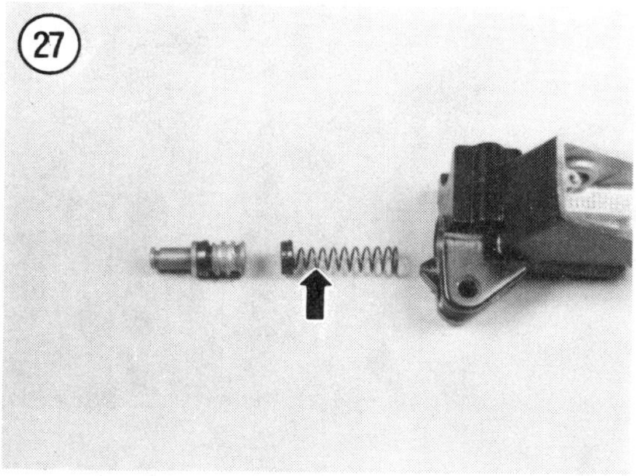

FRONT CALIPER

Removal/Installation

Refer to **Figure 28** for this procedure.

It is not necessary to remove the front wheel in order to remove the caliper assembly.

CAUTION

Do not spill any brake fluid on the front fork or front wheel. Wash off any spilled brake fluid immediately, as it will destroy the finish. Use soapy water and rinse completely.

1. Clean the top of the master cylinder of all dirt and foreign matter.

(28)

FRONT BRAKE CALIPER ASSEMBLY

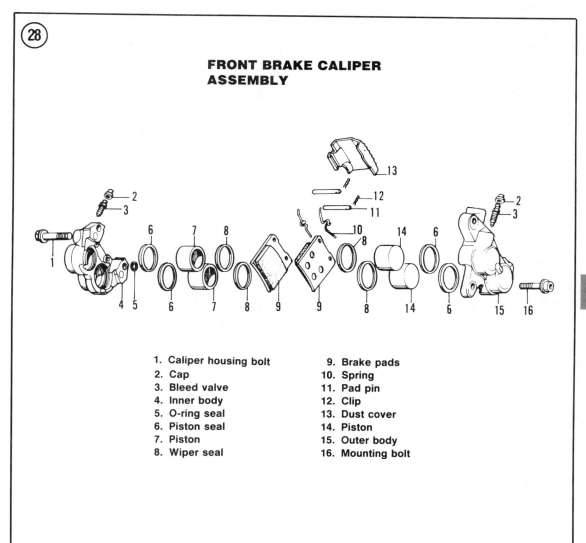

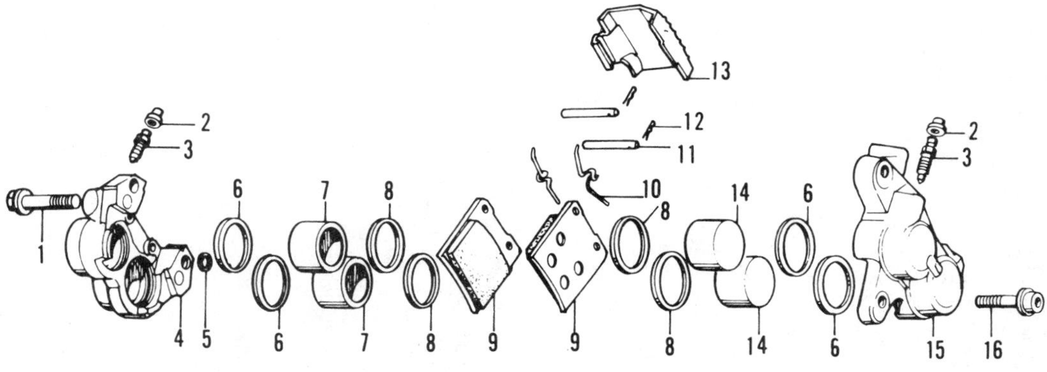

1. Caliper housing bolt
2. Cap
3. Bleed valve
4. Inner body
5. O-ring seal
6. Piston seal
7. Piston
8. Wiper seal
9. Brake pads
10. Spring
11. Pad pin
12. Clip
13. Dust cover
14. Piston
15. Outer body
16. Mounting bolt

2. Loosen the screws (**Figure 29**) securing the master cylinder cover. Pull up and loosen the cover and the diaphragm. This will allow air to enter the reservoir and allow the brake fluid to drain out more quickly in the next step.
3. Place a container under the brake line at the caliper.
4. Hold onto the locknut (A, **Figure 30**) with an open end wrench. Loosen the nut adapter (B, **Figure 30**) securing the brake hose to the caliper assembly.
5. Remove the brake hose (A, **Figure 31**) and let the brake fluid drain out into the container. Dispose of this brake fluid—never reuse brake fluid. To prevent the entry of moisture and dirt, cap the end of the brake hose and tie the loose end up to the forks.
6. Loosen the bolts (B, **Figure 31**) securing the brake caliper assembly to the front fork. Push in on the caliper while loosening the bolts to push the pistons back into the caliper bores.
7. Remove the bolts securing the brake caliper assembly to the front fork (B, **Figure 31**).
8. Remove the caliper assembly from the brake disc.
9. Install by reversing these removal steps, noting the following.
10. Carefully install the caliper assembly onto the disc, being careful not to damage the leading edge of the brake pads.
11. Install the bolts securing the brake caliper assembly to the front fork and tighten to the torque specifications listed in **Table 1**.
12. Screw the brake hose into the caliper.
13. Hold onto the locknut (A, **Figure 30**) with an open end wrench. Tighten the nut adaptor (B, **Figure 30**) securing the brake hose to the caliper assembly. Tighten the nut adapter to the torque specification listed in **Table 1**, then tighten the locknut.
14. If necessary, repeat Steps 3-13 for the other caliper assembly.
15. Remove the master cylinder top cover and diaphragm.

WARNING
Use brake fluid clearly marked DOT 3 or DOT 4 from a sealed container. Other types may vaporize and cause brake failure. Always use the same brand name; do not intermix as many brands are not compatible. Do not intermix silicone-based (DOT 5) brake fluid as it can cause brake component damage leading to brake system failure.

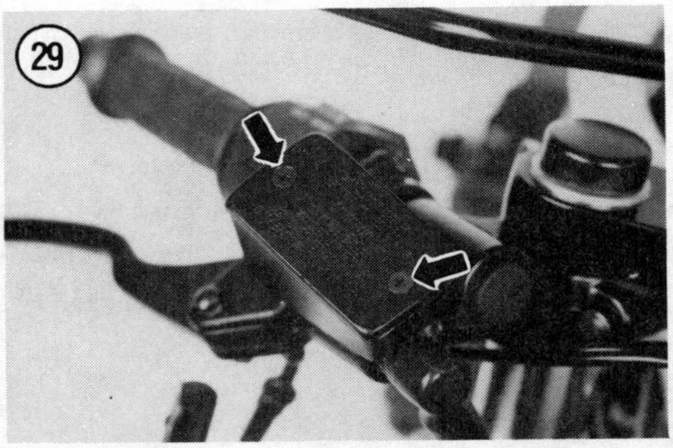

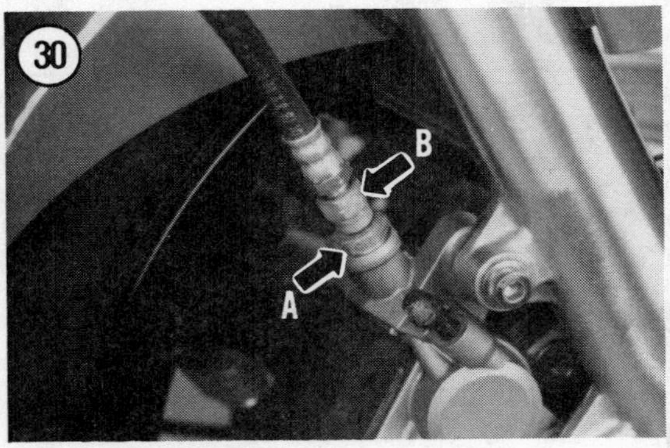

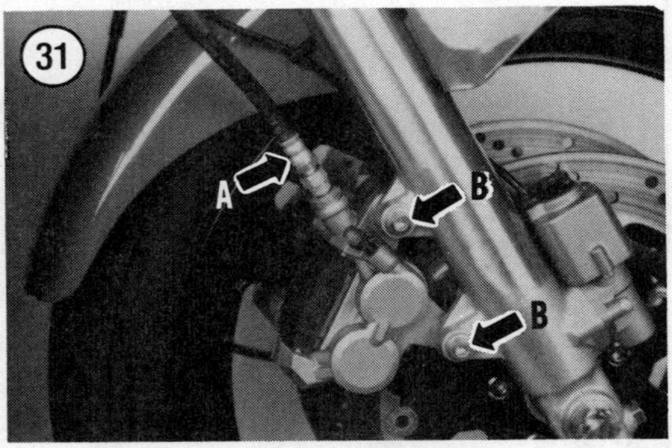

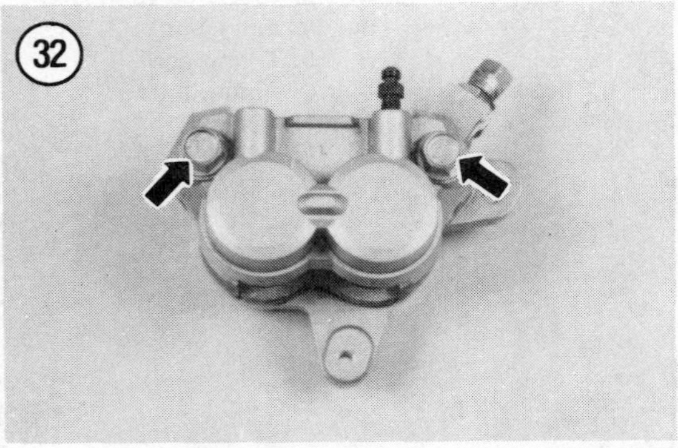

16. Push the bike forward enough to turn the front wheel several revolutions. As you do this, operate the front brake lever as many times as it takes to correctly locate the front brake pads.
17. Refill the master cylinder reservoir. Install the diaphragm and cover. Do not tighten the screws at this time.

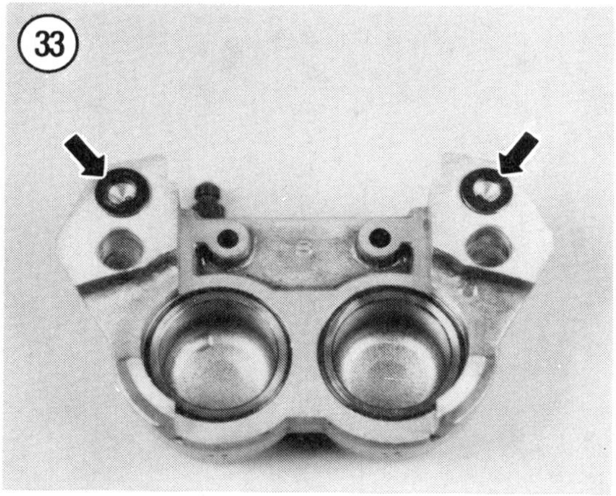

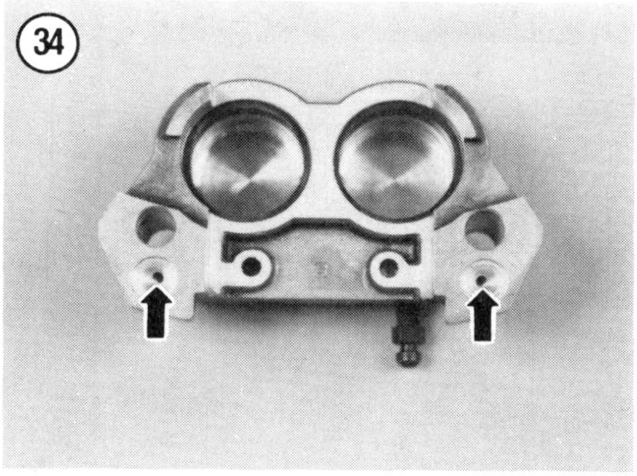

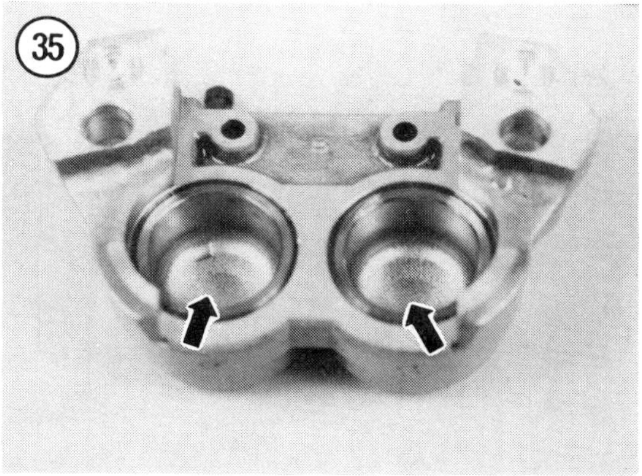

18. Bleed the brake as described under *Bleeding the System* in this chapter.

WARNING
Do not ride the motorcycle until you are sure that the brakes are operating properly.

Caliper Rebuilding

Refer to **Figure 28** for this procedure.
1. Remove the caliper and brake pads as described in this chapter.
2. Remove the caliper housing bolts **(Figure 32)** securing the caliper inner body to the caliper outer body.
3. Separate the 2 caliper bodies.
4. Remove the O-rings (**Figure 33**) from the caliper inner body.
Discard these O-rings as they must be replaced every time the caliper is disassembled.
5. Place a shop cloth or piece of soft wood over the ends of the pistons of the outer caliper body.
6. Perform this step above and close to a workbench top. Hold the caliper body with the pistons facing away from you.

WARNING
*In the next step, the pistons may shoot out of the caliper body like bullets. Keep your fingers out of the way. Wear shop gloves and apply air pressure gradually. Do **not** use high pressure air or place the air hose nozzle directly against the hydraulic line fitting inlet in the caliper body. Hold the air nozzle away from the inlet allowing some of the air to escape.*

7. Apply the air pressure in short spurts to the hydraulic fluid passageways **(Figure 34)** and force both pistons out (**Figure 35**). Use a service station air hose if you don't have an air compressor.

CAUTION
In the following step, do not use a sharp tool to remove the dust and piston seals from the caliper cylinders. Do not damage the cylinder surface.

11

8. Use a piece of plastic or wood and carefully push the wiper seal and the piston seal (**Figure 36**) in toward the caliper cylinder and out of their grooves. Remove the wiper and piston seals from both cylinders and discard all seals.
9. Inspect the seal grooves in caliper body (**Figure 37**) for damage. If damaged or corroded, replace the caliper assembly.
10. Inspect the caliper body (**Figure 38**) for damage; replace the caliper body if necessary.
11. Inspect the hydraulic fluid passageways (**Figure 39**) at each end of the caliper body. Make sure it is clean and open. Apply compressed air to the opening and make sure it is clear. Clean out if necessary with fresh brake fluid.
12. Inspect the cylinder walls (**Figure 40**) and the pistons (**Figure 41**) for scratches, scoring or other damage. Replace the pistons or the caliper assembly, if they are rusty or corroded.
13. Inspect the caliper mounting bolt holes (**Figure 42**) on the outer body. If worn or damaged, replace the caliper assembly.
14. Remove the bleed screw (**Figure 43**). Make sure it is clean and open. Apply compressed air to the opening and make sure it is clear. Clean out if necessary with fresh brake fluid.
15. If serviceable, clean the caliper body with rubbing alcohol and rinse with clean brake fluid.

NOTE
Never reuse the old wiper seals or piston seals. Very minor damage or age deterioration can make the seals useless.

16. Coat the new wiper seals and piston seals with fresh DOT 3 or DOT 4 brake fluid.
17. Carefully install the new wiper seals and piston seals in the grooves in each caliper cylinder. Make sure the seals are properly seated in their respective grooves (**Figure 36**).
18. Coat the pistons and caliper cylinders with fresh DOT 3 or DOT 4 brake fluid.
19. Position the pistons with the open ends facing out toward the brake pads and install the pistons into the caliper (**Figure 44**). Push the pistons in until they bottom out (**Figure 35**).
20. Repeat Steps 5-19 for the inner caliper body.
21. Install new O-rings (**Figure 33**) onto the caliper inner body.

36

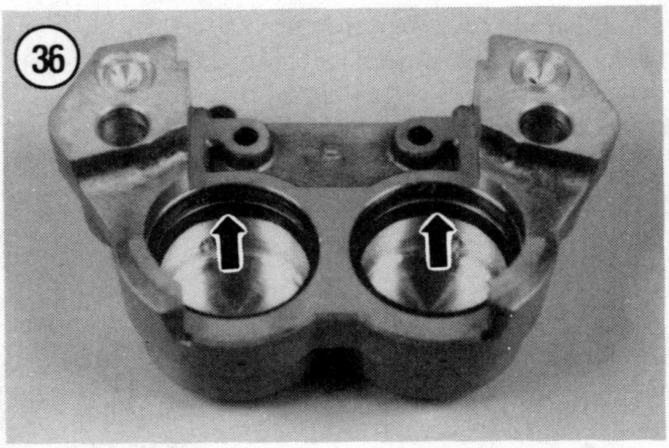

37

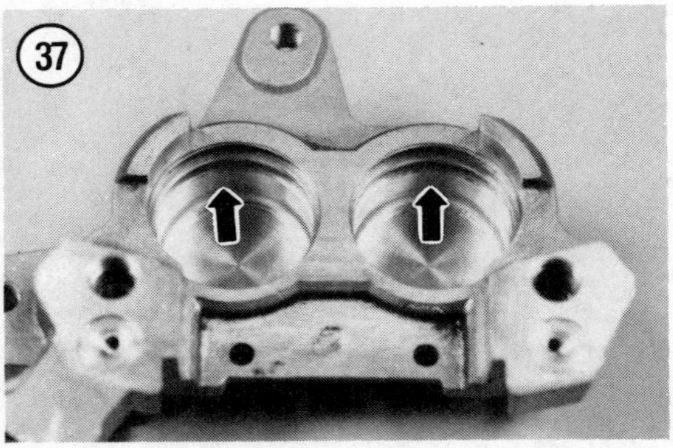

38

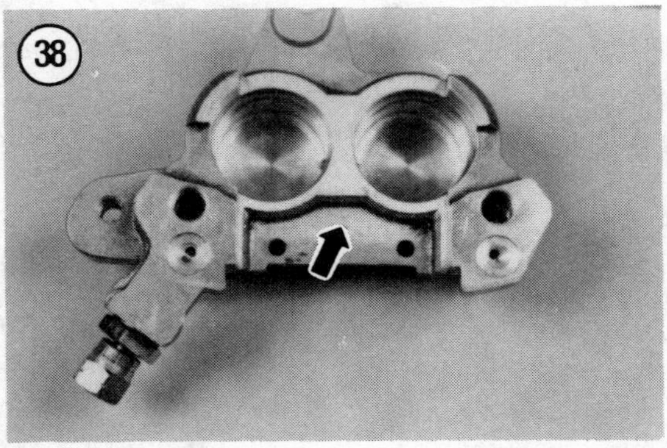

39

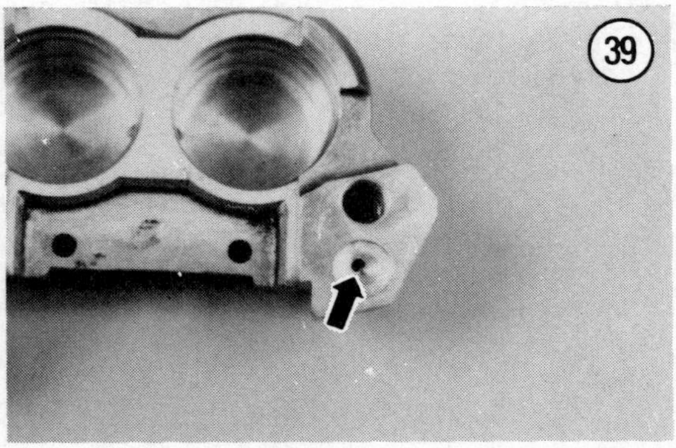

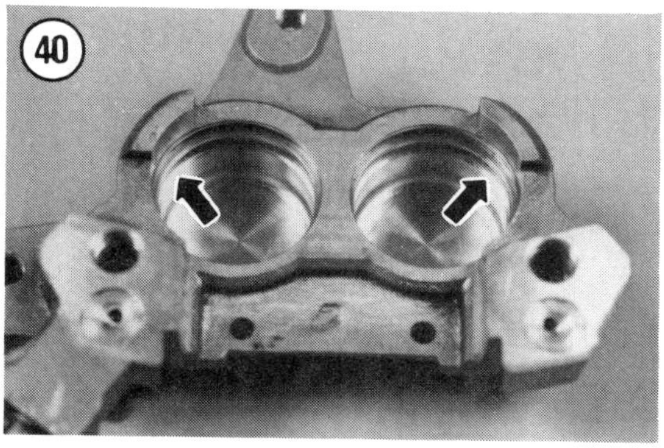
40

41

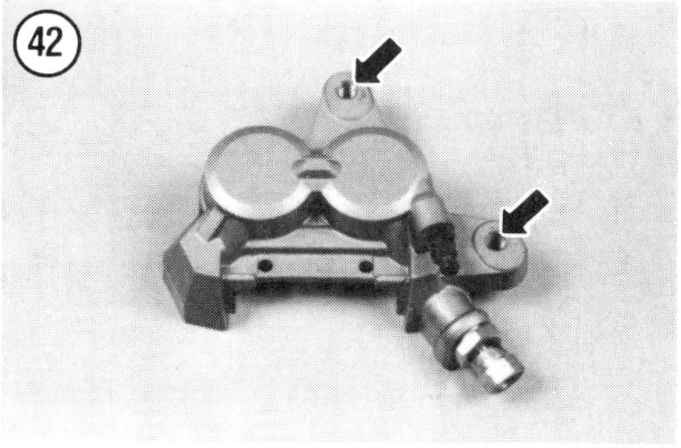
42

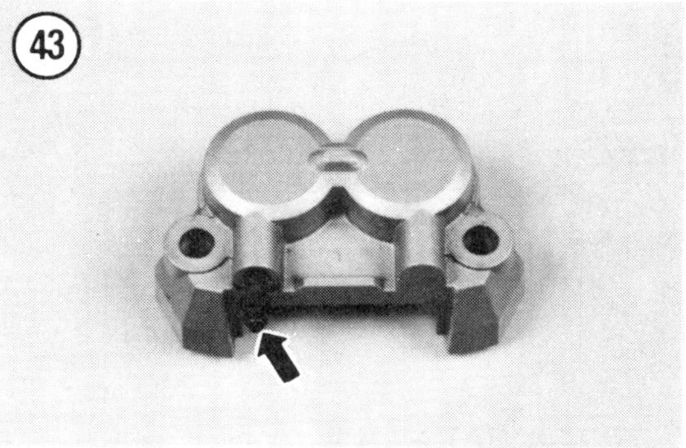
43

22. Assemble the 2 caliper bodies and install the caliper housing bolts (**Figure 32**). Tighten the bolts to the torque specification listed in **Table 1**.
23. Install the caliper and brake pads as described in this chapter.

FRONT BRAKE HOSE REPLACEMENT

Suzuki recommends replacing all brake hoses every four years or when they show signs of cracking or damage.

Refer to **Figure 45** for this procedure.

1. Remove the front fairing as described under *Front Fairing Removal/Installation* in Chapter Twelve.

CAUTION
Cover the fuel tank, front fender and instrument cluster with a heavy cloth or plastic tarp to protect them from accidental brake fluid spills. Wash brake fluid off any painted or plated surfaces or plastic parts immediately, as it will destroy the finish. Use soapy water and rinse completely.

2. Clean the top of the master cylinder of all dirt and foreign matter.
3. Loosen the screws securing the master cylinder cover (**Figure 46**). Pull up and loosen the cover and the diaphragm. This will allow air to enter the reservoir and allow the brake fluid to drain out more quickly in the next step.

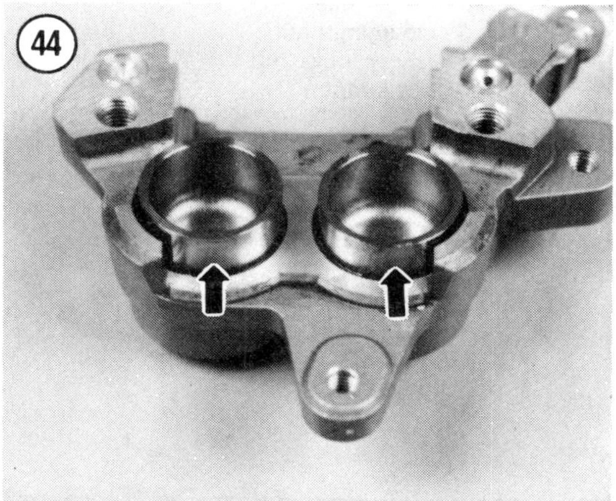
44

(45)

FRONT BRAKE HOSES

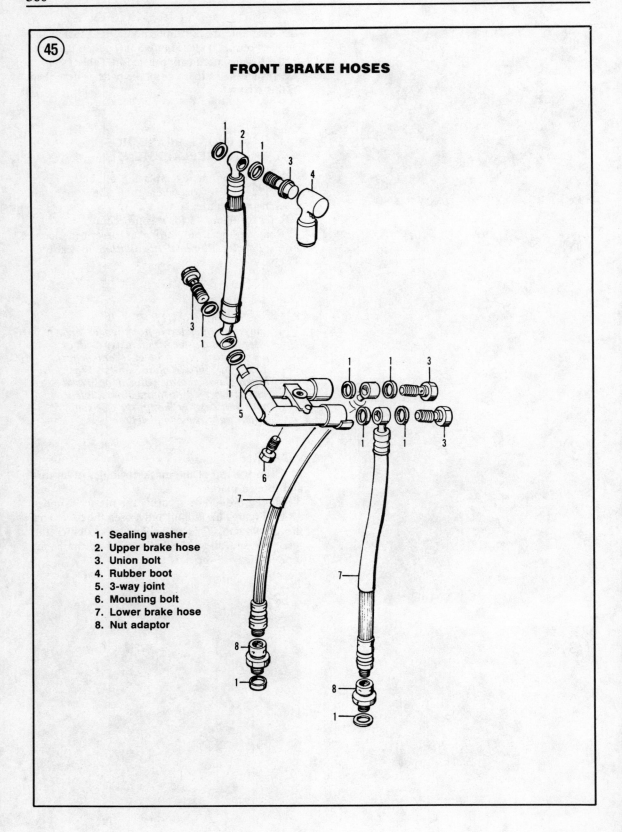

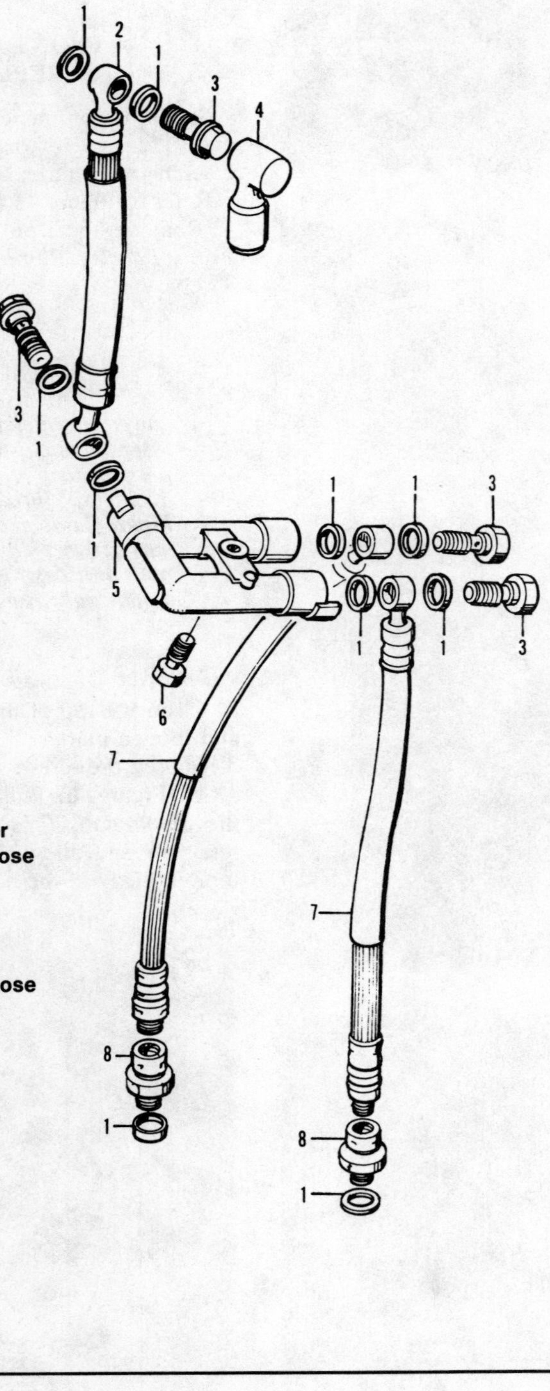

1. Sealing washer
2. Upper brake hose
3. Union bolt
4. Rubber boot
5. 3-way joint
6. Mounting bolt
7. Lower brake hose
8. Nut adaptor

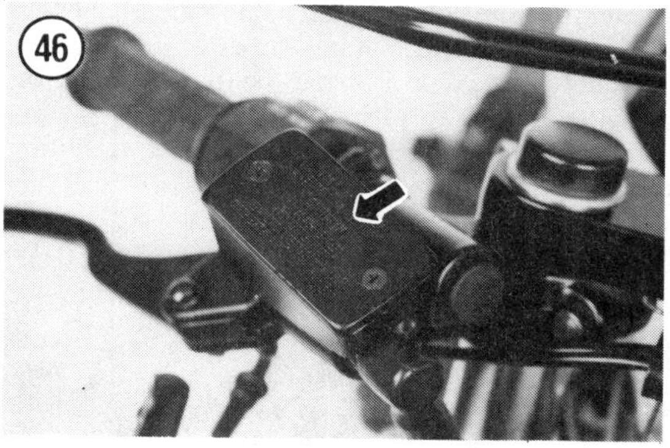

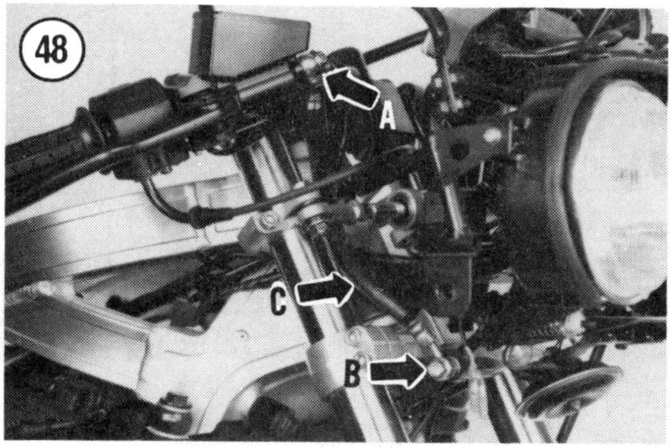

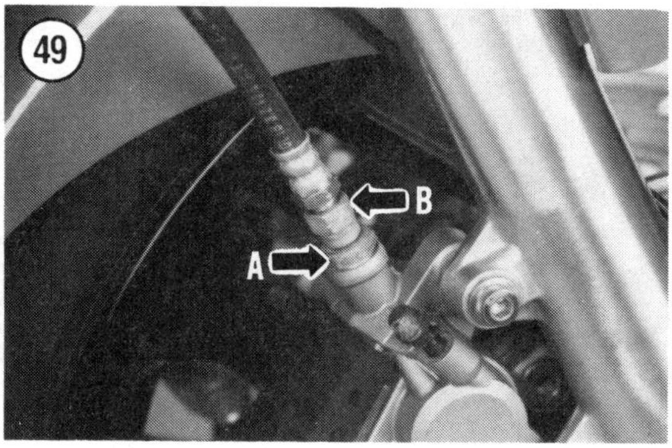

4. Pull back the rubber boot (**Figure 47**) on the union bolt.
5. Place a shop cloth under the union bolt (A, **Figure 48**) to catch any spilled brake fluid that will leak out.
6. Unscrew the union bolt securing the upper brake hose to the master cylinder. Don't lose the sealing washer on each side of the hose fitting.
7. Unscrew the union bolt (B, **Figure 48**) securing the upper brake hose to the 3-way joint. Don't lose the sealing washer on each side of the hose fitting.
8. Remove the upper brake hose (C, **Figure 48**) from the frame.
9. Hold onto the locknut (A, **Figure 49**) with an open end wrench. Loosen the nut adapter (B, **Figure 49**) securing the brake hose to the caliper assembly.
10. Place a container under the caliper. Remove the brake hose (**Figure 50**) and let the brake fluid drain out into the container. Dispose of this brake fluid—never reuse brake fluid.
11. Repeat Step 9 and Step 10 for the other lower brake hose.

NOTE
***Figure 51** is shown with the left-hand fork assembly removed for clarity. It is not necessary to remove the fork assembly to remove the brake hoses.*

12. Unscrew the union bolt (A, **Figure 51**) securing each lower brake hose to the 3-way joint. Don't lose the sealing washer on each side of the hose fitting.
13. Unhook the lower brake hoses (B, **Figure 51**) from the cable clips and remove both hoses.
14. If necessary, remove the mounting bolt securing the 3-way joint (C, **Figure 51**) to the frame and remove the 3-way joint.

11

15. Install new hoses, sealing washers and union bolts in the reverse order of removal. Be sure to install new sealing washers in their correct positions.
16. Tighten the fittings and union bolts to the torque specifications listed in **Table 1**.
17. Refill the master cylinder reservoir, if necessary, to maintain the correct fluid level as seen through the viewing port on the side (**Figure 52**). Install the diaphragm and cover. Do not tighten the screws at this time.

WARNING
Use brake fluid clearly marked DOT 3 or DOT 4 from a sealed container. Other types may vaporize and cause brake failure. Always use the same brand name; do not intermix as many brands are not compatible. Do not intermix silicone-based (DOT 5) brake fluid as it can cause brake component damage leading to brake system failure.

WARNING
Do not ride the motorcycle until you are sure that the brakes are operating properly.

18. Bleed the brake as described under *Bleeding the System* in this chapter.

FRONT BRAKE DISC

Removal/Installation

1. Remove the front wheel as described under *Front Wheel Removal* in Chapter Nine.

NOTE
Place a piece of wood or vinyl tube in the caliper in place of the disc. This way, if the brake lever is inadvertently squeezed the pistons will not be forced out of the cylinders. If this does happen, the caliper might have to be disassembled to reseat the pistons and the system will have to be bled.

CAUTION
Do not set the wheel down on the disc surface, as it may get scratched or bent. Set the wheel on 2 blocks of wood.

2. Remove the bolts (**Figure 53**) securing the brake disc to the hub and remove the disc.
3. If necessary, repeat Step 2 for the brake disc on the other side.
4. Install by reversing these removal steps, noting the following.

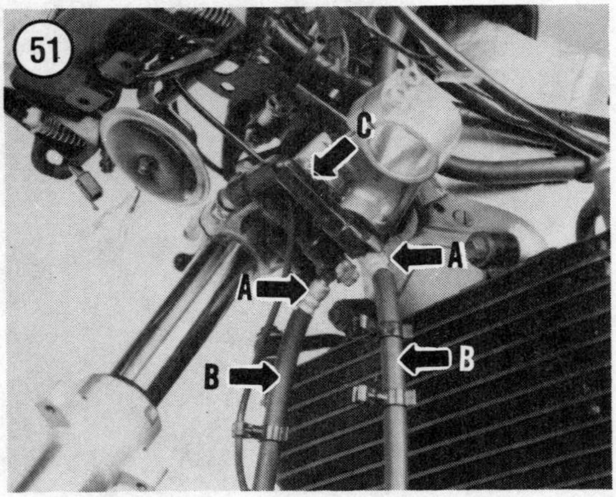

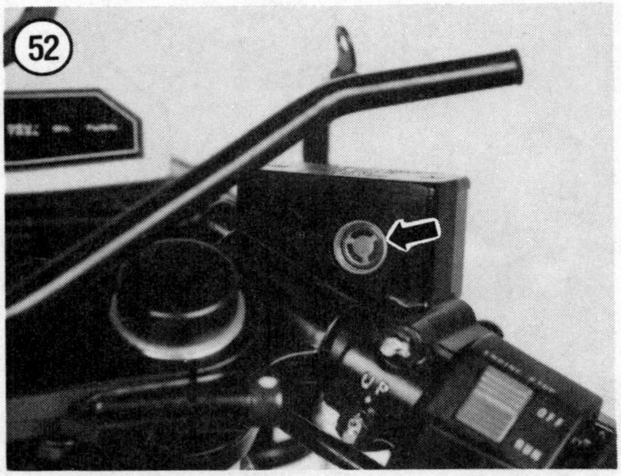

54

55

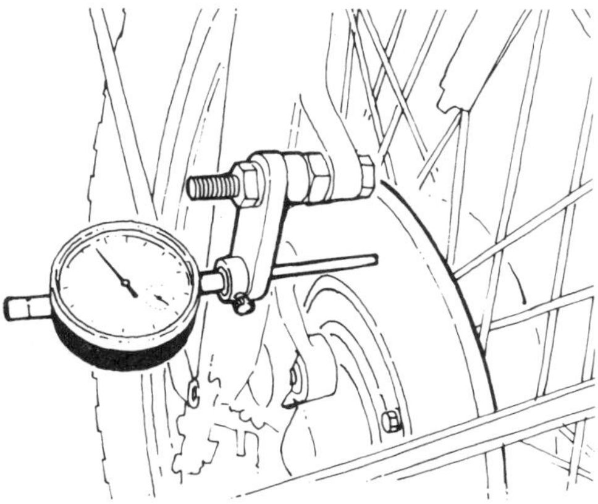

5. Apply Loctite Lock N' Seal to the disc mounting bolt threads prior to installation. Tighten the disc mounting bolts to the torque specifications listed in **Table 1**.

Inspection

It is not necessary to remove the disc(s) from the wheel to inspect it. Small marks on the disc are not important, but radial scratches deep enough to snag a fingernail reduce braking effectiveness and increase brake pad wear. If these grooves are found, the disc should be replaced. Refinishing the disc surface on a brake grinder is not recommended.

1. Measure the thickness of the disc at several locations around the disc with a micrometer (**Figure 54**) or vernier caliper. The disc must be replaced if the thickness in any area is less than that specified in **Table 2**.
2. Make sure the disc mounting bolts are tight prior to running this check. Check the disc runout with a dial indicator as shown in **Figure 55**.
3. Slowly rotate the wheel and watch the dial indicator. If the runout exceeds that listed in **Table 2** the disc must be replaced.
4. Clean the disc of any rust or corrosion and wipe clean with brake cleaner. Never use an oil-based solvent that may leave an oil residue on the disc.

REAR BRAKE PAD REPLACEMENT

There is no recommended mileage interval for changing the friction pads in the disc brake. Pad wear depends greatly on riding habits and conditions. The pads should be checked for wear every 6 months and replaced when the wear indicator reaches the edge of the brake disc. To maintain an even brake pressure on the disc, always replace both pads in the caliper at the same time.

Disconnecting the hydraulic brake hose from the brake caliper is not necessary for brake pad replacement. Disconnect the hose only if the caliper assembly is going to be removed.

CAUTION

Check the pads more frequently when the wear line approaches the disc. On some pads the wear line is very close to the metal backing plate. If pad wear happens to be uneven for some reason, the backing plate may come in contact with the disc and cause damage.

56

REAR BRAKE CALIPER

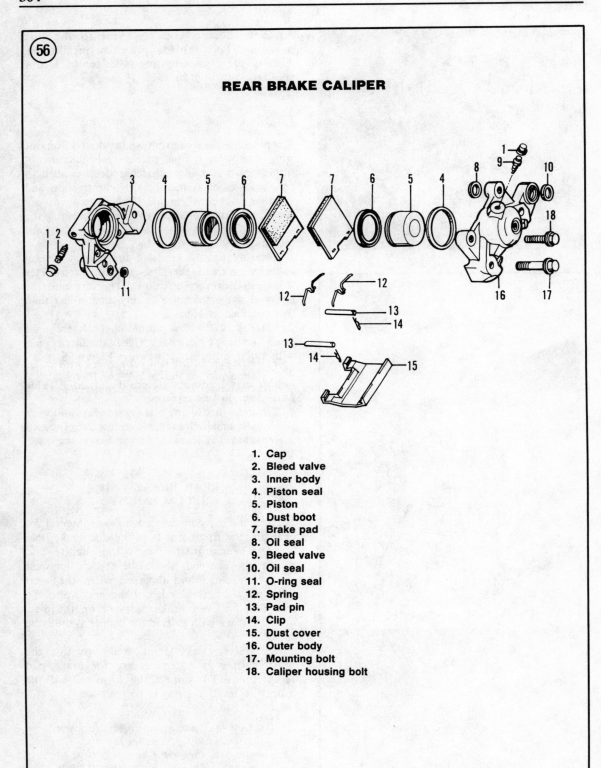

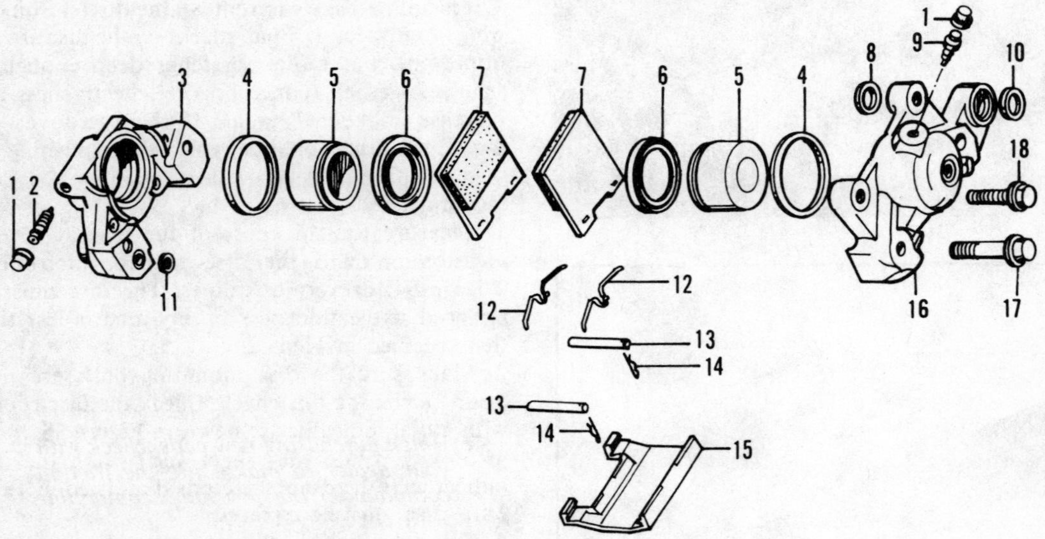

1. Cap
2. Bleed valve
3. Inner body
4. Piston seal
5. Piston
6. Dust boot
7. Brake pad
8. Oil seal
9. Bleed valve
10. Oil seal
11. O-ring seal
12. Spring
13. Pad pin
14. Clip
15. Dust cover
16. Outer body
17. Mounting bolt
18. Caliper housing bolt

(57)

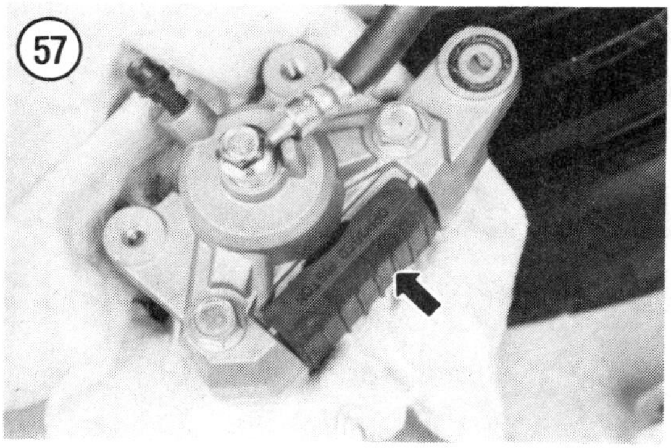

(58)

(59)

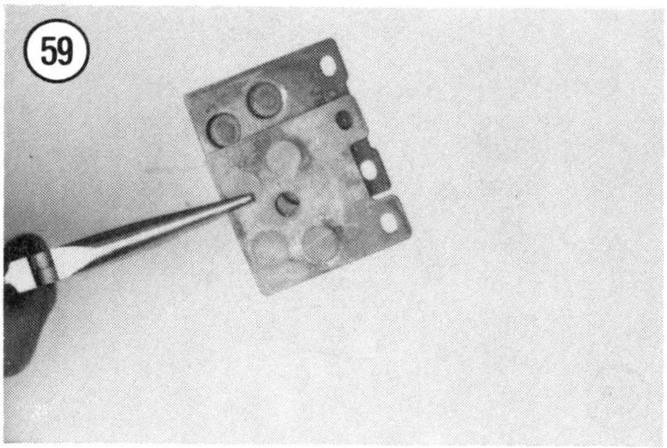

(60)

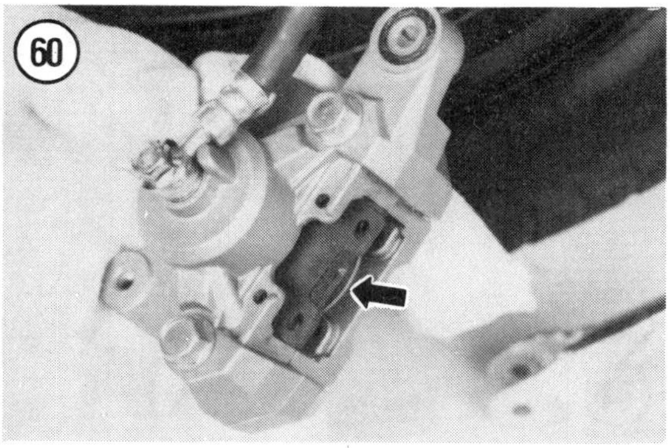

Refer to **Figure 56** for this procedure.

This procedure is shown with the caliper assembly removed from the disc for clarity. The pads can be replaced without removing the caliper assembly.

1. Remove the dust cover (**Figure 57**) from the brake caliper.
2. Remove the clips securing the pad pins.
3. Withdraw both pad pins and remove the pad springs.
4. Withdraw both brake pads and on models so equipped, the shims from the caliper assembly.
5. Clean the pad recess and the end of the pistons with a soft brush. Do not use solvent, a wire brush or any hard tool which would damage the cylinders or pistons.
6. Using brake cleaner, carefully remove any rust or corrosion from the disc.
7. Lightly coat the ends of the pistons and the backs of the new pads (*not* the friction material) with disc brake lubricant.

NOTE

When purchasing new pads, check with your dealer to make sure the friction compound of the new pad is compatible with the disc material. Remove any roughness from the backs of the new pads with a fine-cut file; blow them clean with compressed air.

8. When new pads are installed in the caliper the master cylinder brake fluid level will rise since the caliper pistons must be pushed into their bores to make room for the additional brake pad thickness. Perform the following:
   a. Remove the right-hand side cover.
   b. Clean the top of the master cylinder of all dirt and foreign matter.
   c. Remove the screws securing the cover (**Figure 58**). Remove the cover and the diaphragm from the master cylinder and slowly push the caliper pistons into the caliper. Constantly check the reservoir to make sure brake fluid does not overflow. Remove fluid, if necessary, prior to it overflowing.
   d. The pistons should move freely. If they don't and there is evidence of them sticking in the cylinder, the caliper should be removed and serviced as described in this chapter.
9. Push the caliper pistons in all the way to allow room for the new pads.
10. Install the shim (models so equipped) and the outboard pad (**Figure 59**) into the caliper (**Figure 60**).

11

11. Partially install one of the pad pins (**Figure 61**) through one of the holes in the outboard pad.
12. Install the shim (models so equipped) and the inboard pad into the caliper (**Figure 62**).
13. Push the pad pin (**Figure 63**) through one of the holes in the inboard pad. Push the pad pin until it stops.
14. Install the clip (**Figure 64**) into the hole in the pad pin. Push the clip in until it seats completely on the pad pin.
15. Hook one of the springs under one of the pad pins and index it onto the top of the brake pad (**Figure 65**).
16. Partially install the other pad pin (A, **Figure 66**) and hook the spring under the pad pin (B, **Figure 66**).
17. Hook the other spring under one of the pad pins and index it onto the top of the brake pad (**Figure 67**).
18. Push the pad pin farther in, hook the spring under the pad pin and push the pad pin until it stops (**Figure 68**).
19. Install the remaining clip (**Figure 69**) into the hole in the pad pin. Push the clip in until it seats completely on the pad pin.
20. Install the dust cap. Make sure it snaps into place, otherwise it will fly off when you hit the first bump in the road.
21. Shift the transmission into NEUTRAL.
22. Remove the lower section of the front fairing as described under *Front Fairing Removal/Installation* in Chapter Twelve.
23. Place wood block(s) under each side of the frame to support the bike securely with the rear wheel off the ground. Spin the rear wheel and activate the brake lever as many times as it takes to correctly locate both pads.

WARNING
Use brake fluid clearly marked DOT 3 or DOT 4 from a sealed container. Other types may vaporize and cause brake failure. Always use the same brand name; do not intermix as many brands are not compatible. Do not intermix silicone based (DOT 5) brake fluid as it can cause brake component damage leading to brake system failure.

24. Refill the master cylinder reservoir, if necessary, to maintain the fluid to the upper level (**Figure 70**) as seen through the transparent side of the master cylinder. Install the diaphragm and cover. Tighten the screws securely.

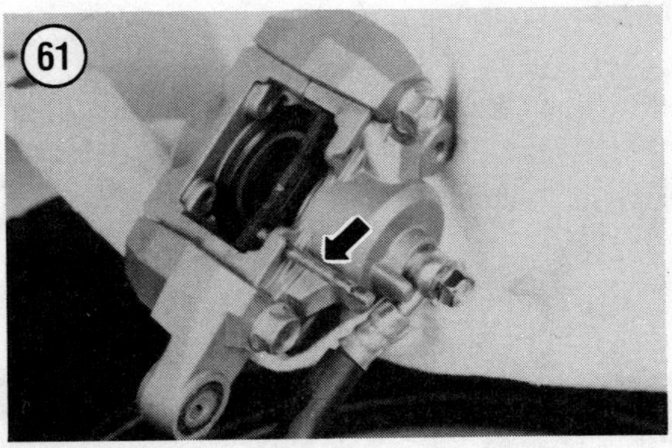

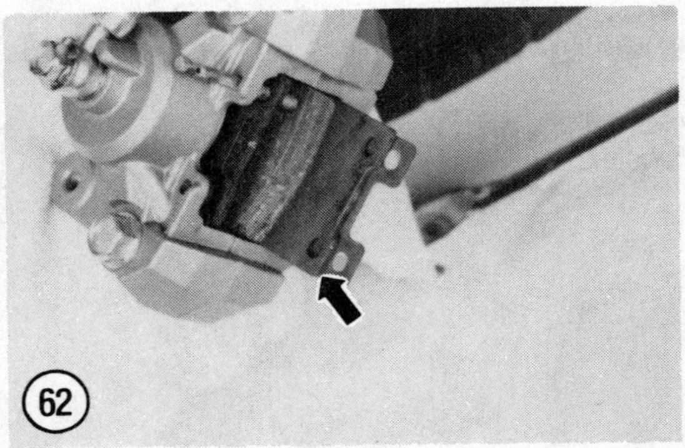

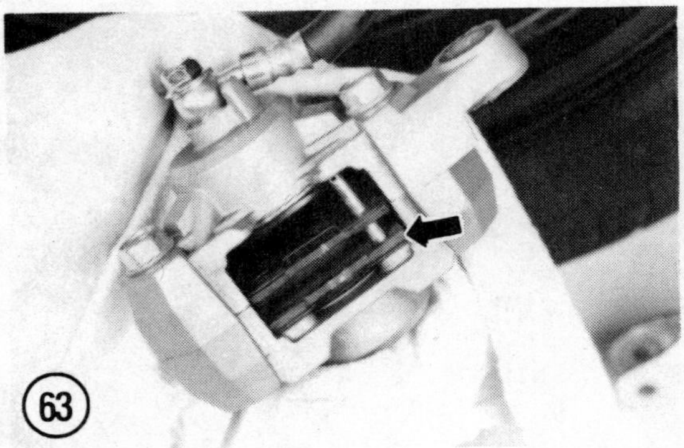

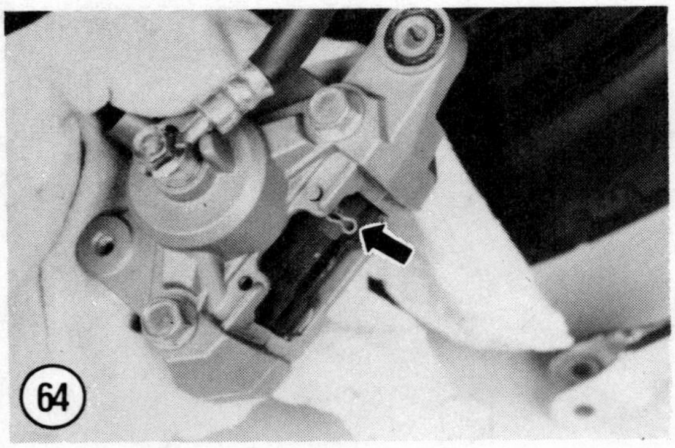

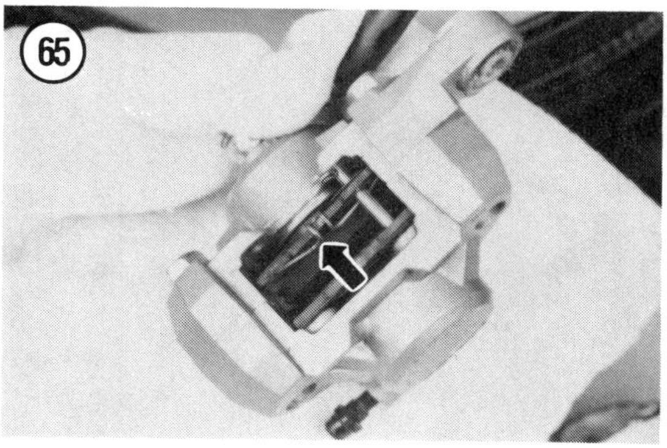

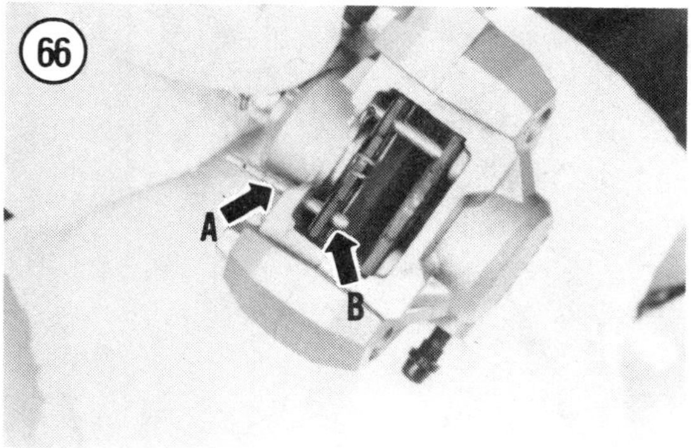

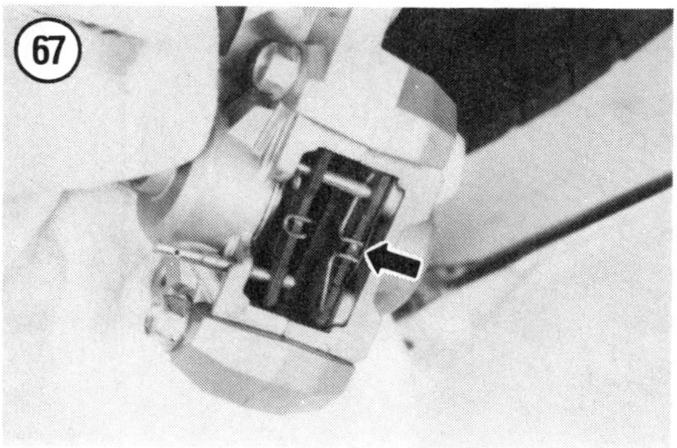

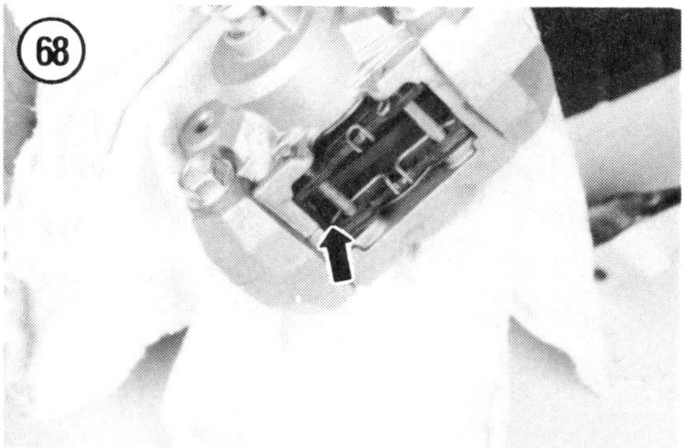

WARNING
Do not ride the motorcycle until you are sure the brakes are operating correctly with full hydraulic advantage. If necessary, bleed the brake as described under ***Bleeding the System*** *in this chapter.*

25. Bed in the pads gradually for the first 200 miles of riding by using only light pressure as much as possible. Immediate hard application will glaze the new friction pads and greatly reduce the effectiveness of the brake.

REAR MASTER CYLINDER

Removal/Installation

CAUTION
Cover the swing arm and rear wheel with a heavy cloth or plastic tarp to protect them from accidental brake fluid spills. Wash brake fluid off any painted or plated surfaces or plastic parts immediately, as it will destroy the finish. Use soapy water and rinse completely.

1. Remove the right-hand side cover.

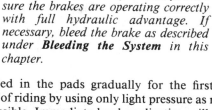

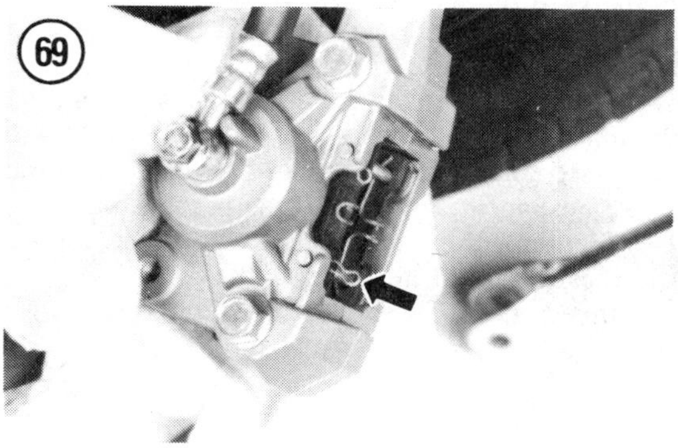

11

2. Place a container under the brake hose at the rear caliper.
3. Unscrew the union bolt (**Figure 71**) securing the brake hose to the rear caliper. Don't lose the sealing washer on each side of the hose fitting.
4. Remove the brake hose and let the brake fluid drain out into the container. Apply the rear brake pedal several times to pump the brake fluid out of the master cylinder reservoir, master cylinder and brake hose. Dispose of this brake fluid—never reuse brake fluid. To prevent the entry of moisture and dirt, cap the end of the brake hose and tie the loose end up to the frame.
5. Remove the cotter pin and washer and withdraw the pivot pin (A, **Figure 72**) from the brake pedal assembly.
6. Remove the bolt securing the master cylinder reservoir (A, **Figure 73**) to the frame.
7. Place a shop cloth under the brake hose and the master cylinder union bolt to catch any remaining brake fluid that will leak out.
8. Unscrew the union bolt (B, **Figure 72**) securing the brake hose to the backside of the master cylinder. Don't lose the sealing washer on each side of the hose fitting. Cover the end of the hose fitting to prevent the entry of moisture and foreign matter.
9. Remove the bolts securing the master cylinder to the right-hand footpeg assembly (B, **Figure 73**).
10. Remove the reservoir, reservoir hose and master cylinder assembly from the frame.
11. Install by reversing these removal steps, noting the following.
12. Place a new sealing washer on each side of the brake hose fitting and install the union bolt.
13. Tighten the union bolt to the torque specification listed in **Table 1**.
14. Bleed the rear brake as described under *Bleeding the System* in this chapter.

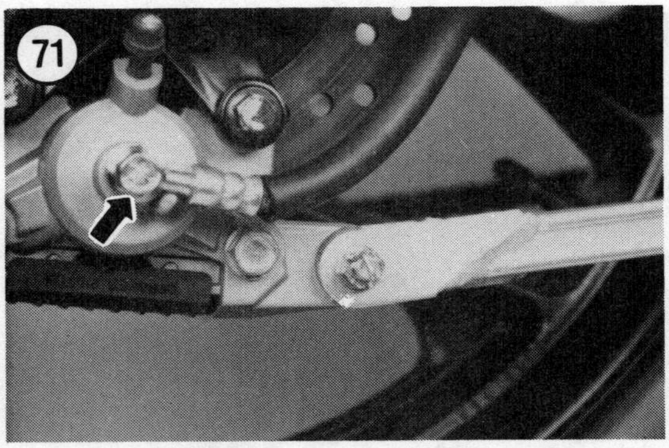

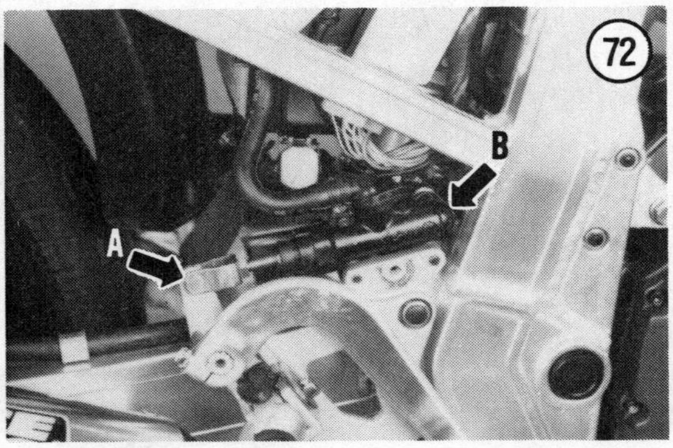

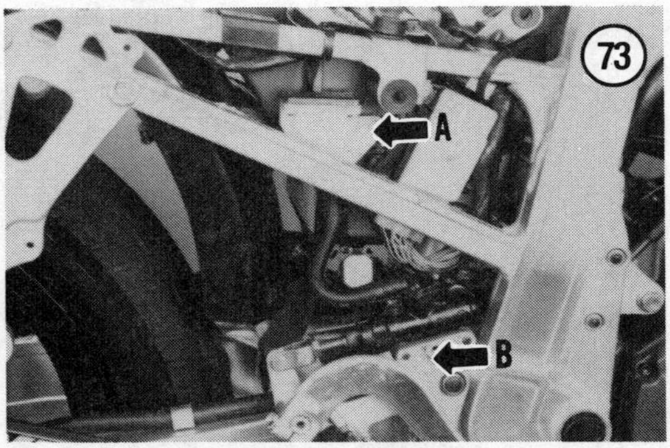

Disassembly

Refer to **Figure 74** for this procedure.
1. Remove the master cylinder as described in this chapter.
2. Remove the screw (**Figure 75**) securing the reservoir hose connector to the master cylinder body. Remove the connector and the O-ring seal (**Figure 76**). Discard the O-ring as it must be replaced.
3. Slide the dust cover (**Figure 77**) down the master cylinder rod.

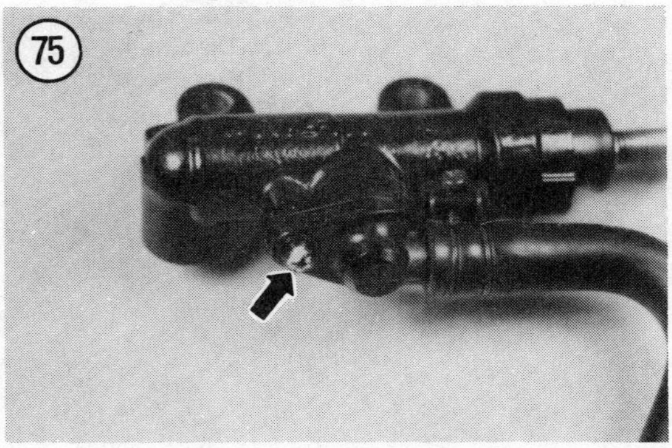

(74)

REAR MASTER CYLINDER

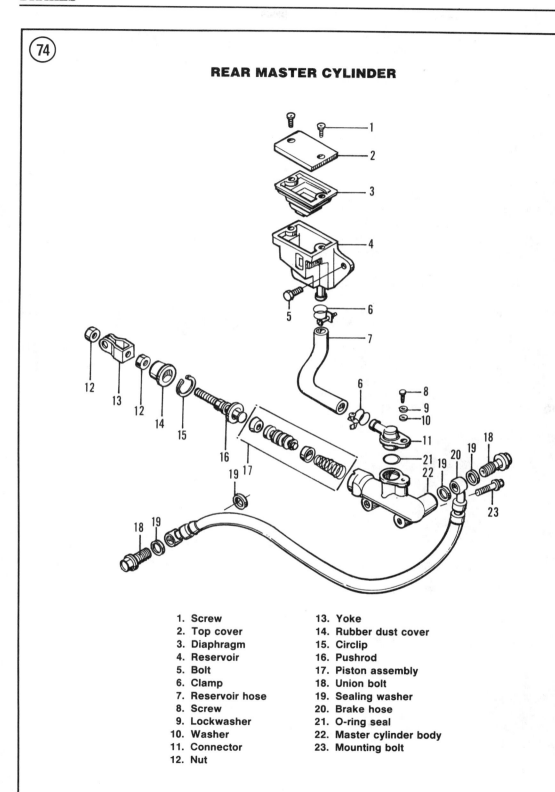

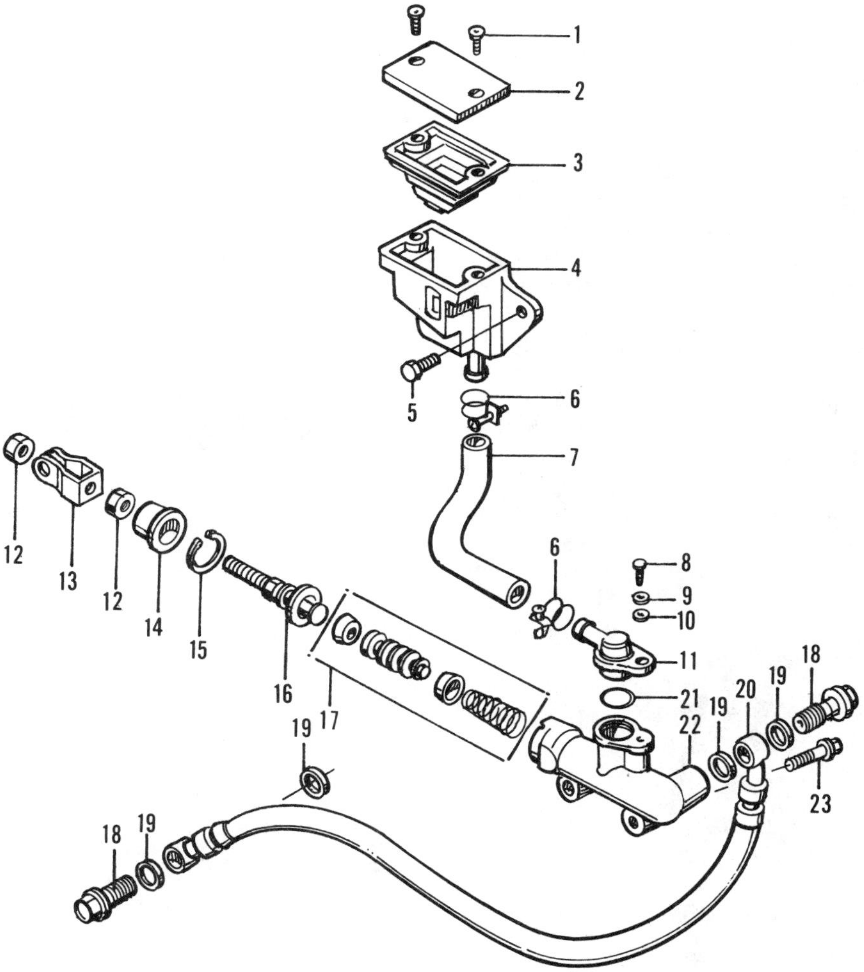

1. Screw
2. Top cover
3. Diaphragm
4. Reservoir
5. Bolt
6. Clamp
7. Reservoir hose
8. Screw
9. Lockwasher
10. Washer
11. Connector
12. Nut
13. Yoke
14. Rubber dust cover
15. Circlip
16. Pushrod
17. Piston assembly
18. Union bolt
19. Sealing washer
20. Brake hose
21. O-ring seal
22. Master cylinder body
23. Mounting bolt

4. Using circlip pliers, remove the internal circlip (A, **Figure 78**) securing the rod in the master cylinder body.
5. Withdraw the rod assembly (B, **Figure 78**) from the master cylinder body.
6. Remove the piston assembly and the spring (**Figure 79**).
7. Pour out any residual brake fluid and discard it. *Never* re-use hydraulic fluid.

Inspection

1. Clean all parts in denatured alcohol or fresh hydraulic fluid.
2. Inspect the bore (**Figure 80**) for signs of wear and damage. If less than perfect, replace the master cylinder assembly. The body cannot be replaced separately.
3. Remove the piston cups (**Figure 81**) from the piston.
4. Inspect the piston contact surfaces (A, **Figure 82**) for signs of wear and damage. If less than perfect, replace the piston assembly.
5. Check the end of the piston (B, **Figure 82**) for wear caused by the rod. If worn, replace the piston assembly.
6. Replace the piston assembly if either the primary or secondary cup requires replacement.

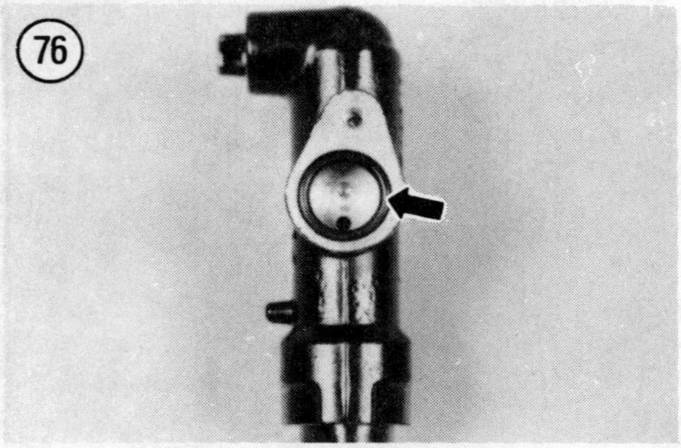

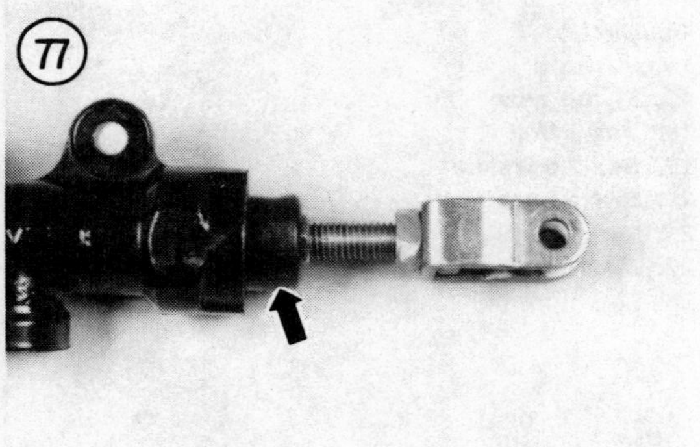

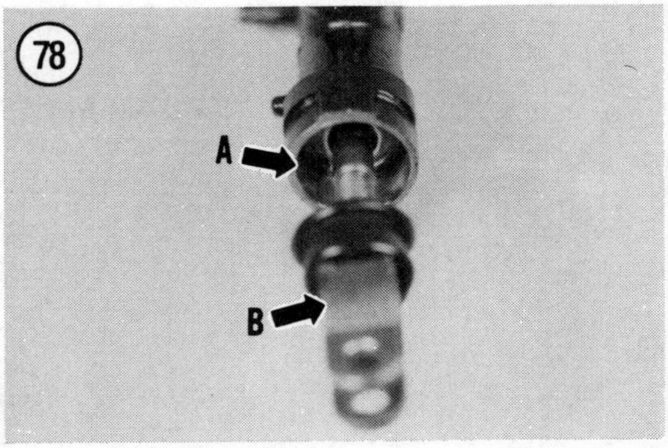

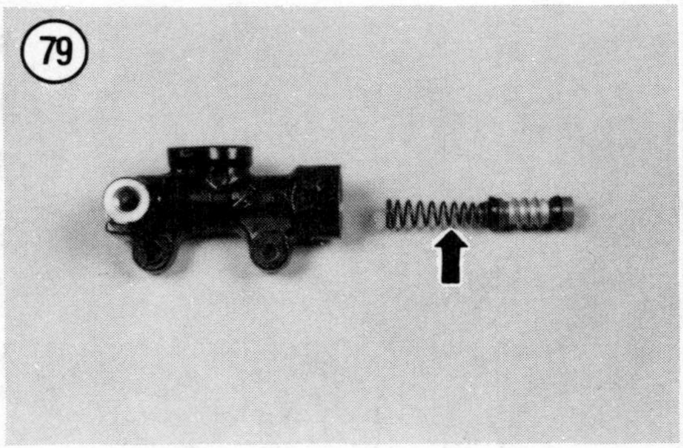

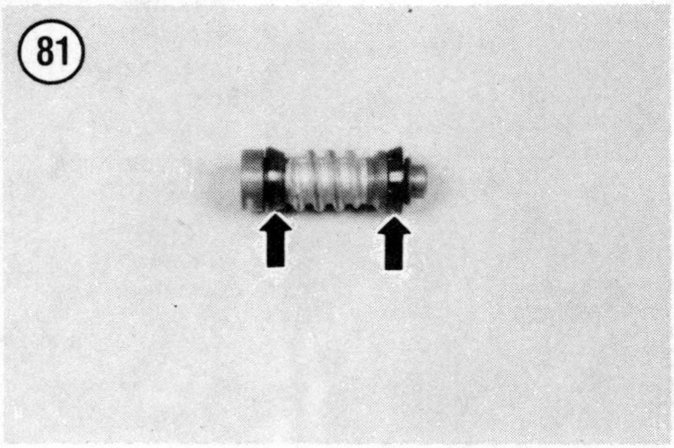

82

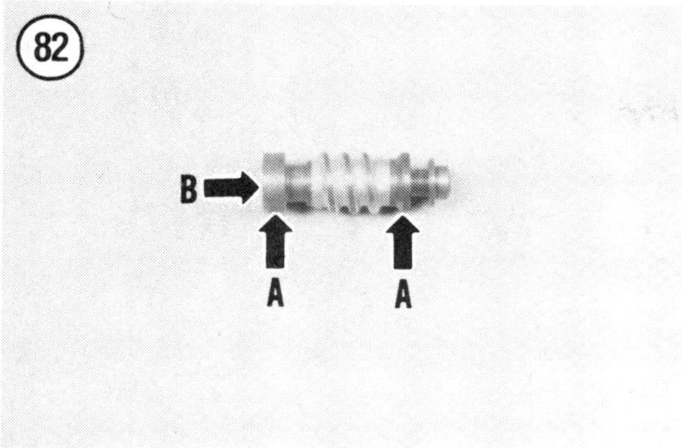

83

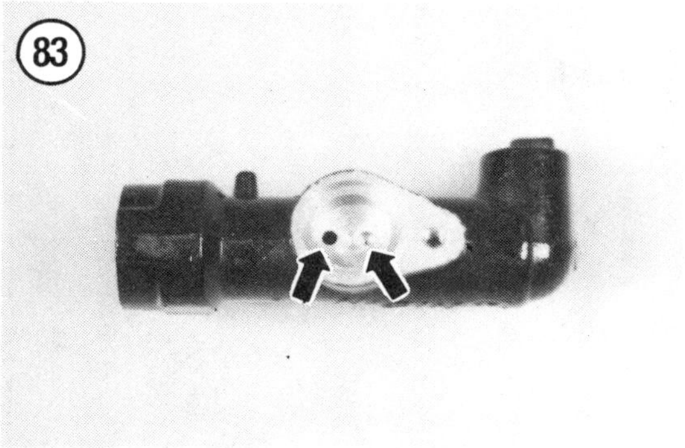

84

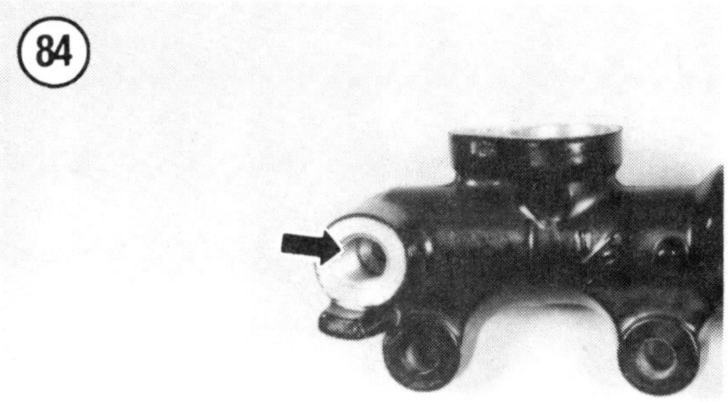

85

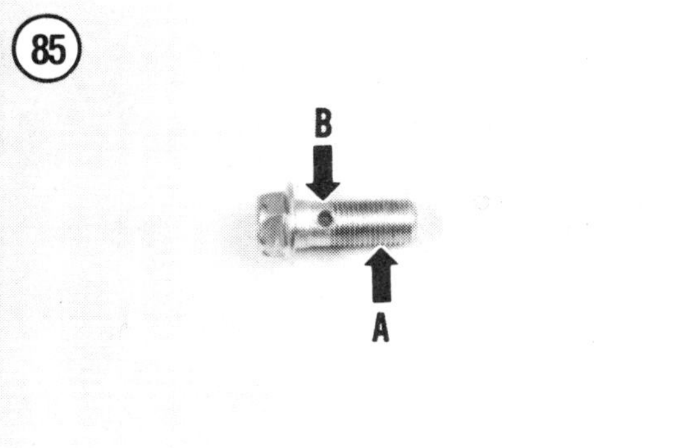

7. Make sure the passages (**Figure 83**) in the master cylinder body are clear. Clean out if necessary with fresh brake fluid and compressed air.

NOTE
There are two passages. The large hole feeds the system and rarely becomes plugged. The small hole is the return orifice and can become plugged if the brake fluid becomes dirty. If the return orifice becomes plugged, the brakes can be applied but will not release.

8. Check the reservoir top cover and diaphragm for damage and deterioration and replace as necessary.
9. Inspect the threads in the bore (**Figure 84**) for the union bolt. If worn or damaged, clean out with a thread tap or replace the master cylinder assembly.
10. Inspect the union bolt threads (A, **Figure 85**) for wear or damage. Clean out with a thread die or replace the union bolt.
11. Inspect the brake fluid hole in the union bolt (B, **Figure 85**). Make sure it is clean. Clean out or replace if necessary.
12. Inspect the rod assembly (**Figure 86**) for wear or damage. Make sure the dust boot is in good condition; replace if necessary.
13. Inspect the reservoir hose (**Figure 87**) for wear or deterioration. Replace as necessary.

86

87

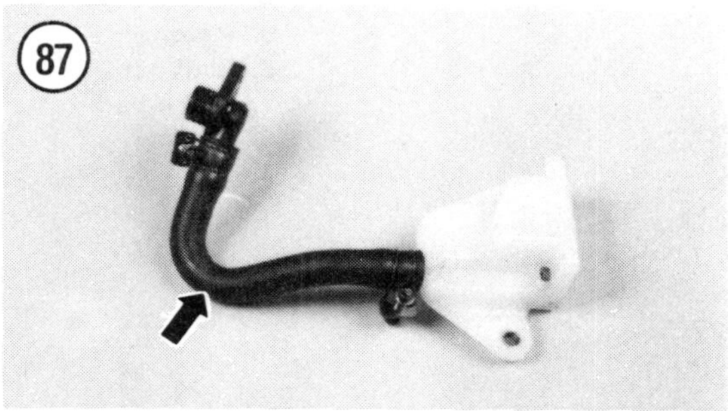

11

Assembly

1. Soak the new cups in fresh brake fluid for at least 15 minutes to make them pliable. Coat the inside of the cylinder bore with fresh hydraulic fluid prior to the assembly of parts.

CAUTION

When installing the piston assembly, do not allow the cups to turn inside out as they will be damaged and allow brake fluid leakage within the cylinder bore.

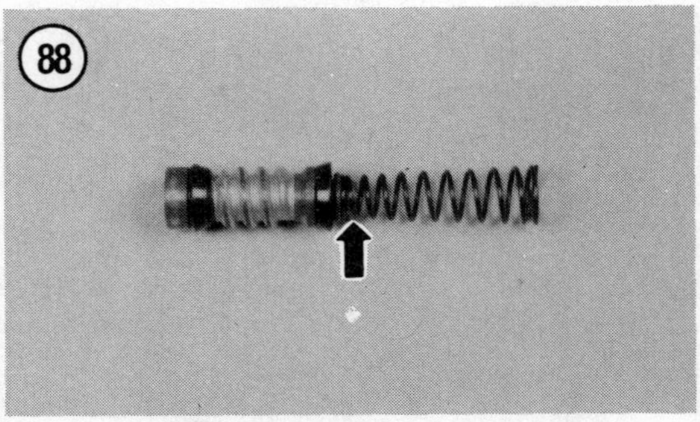

89

REAR BRAKE CALIPER

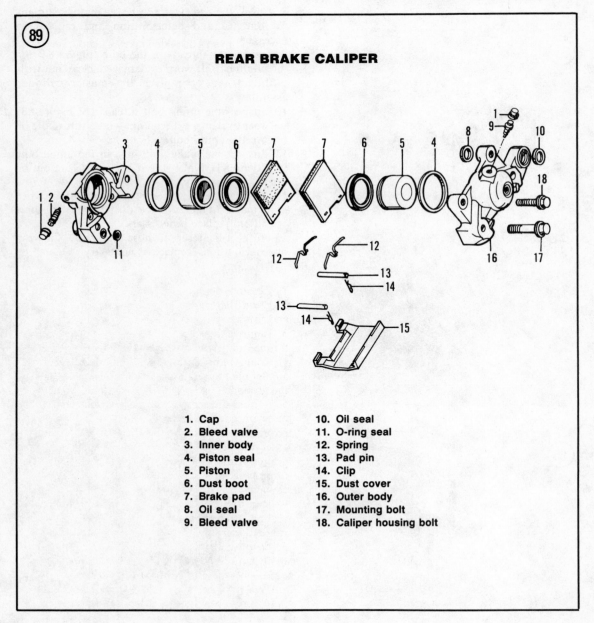

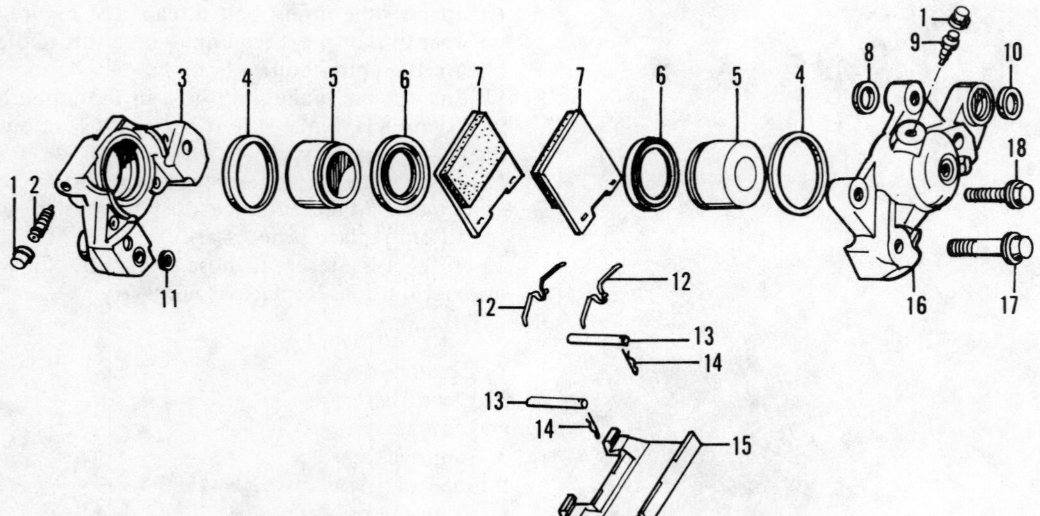

1. Cap
2. Bleed valve
3. Inner body
4. Piston seal
5. Piston
6. Dust boot
7. Brake pad
8. Oil seal
9. Bleed valve
10. Oil seal
11. O-ring seal
12. Spring
13. Pad pin
14. Clip
15. Dust cover
16. Outer body
17. Mounting bolt
18. Caliper housing bolt

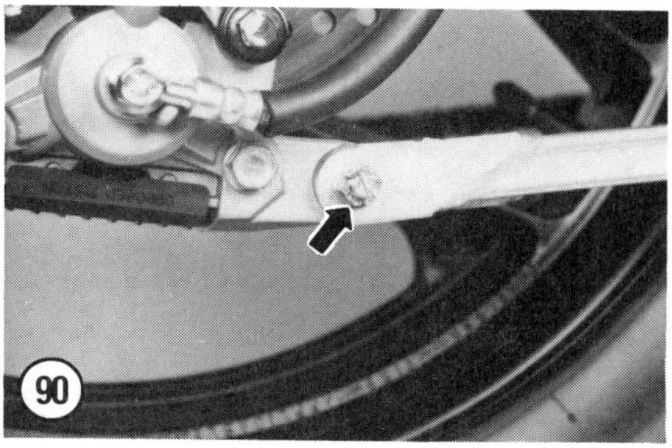

90

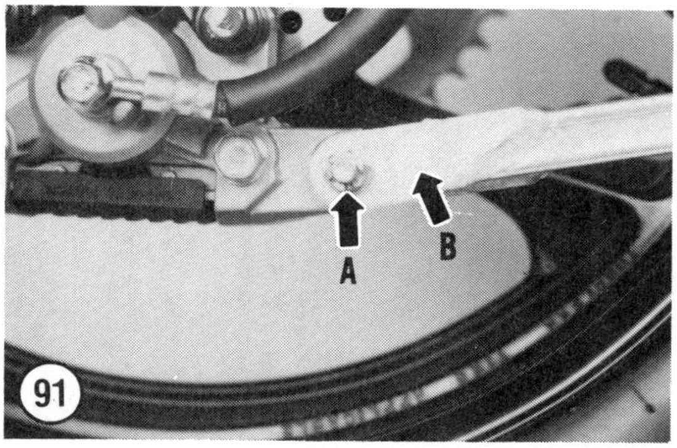

91

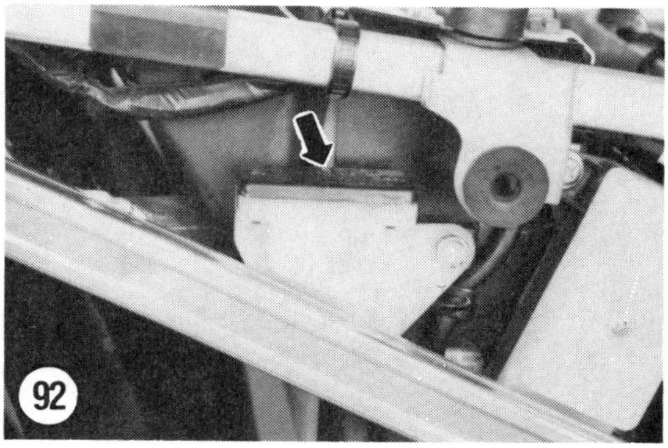

92

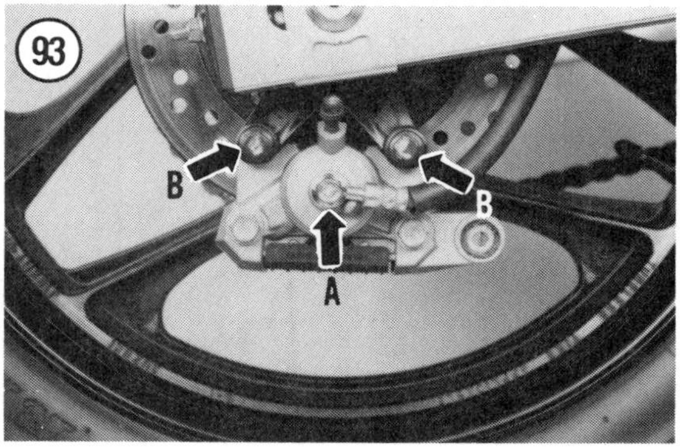

93

2. Install the spring and piston assembly into the cylinder together. Install the spring with its small end (**Figure 88**) facing toward the primary cup on the piston.
3. Install the rod assembly (B, **Figure 78**) and install the circlip (A, **Figure 78**). Make sure the circlip is correctly seated in the groove.
4. Slide the dust cover (**Figure 77**) into place.
5. Install a new O-ring (**Figure 76**) into the receptacle in the master cylinder body.
6. Install the reservoir hose connector to the master cylinder body. Tighten the screw securely (**Figure 75**).
7. Install the diaphragm and top cover. Do not tighten the cover screws at this time as hydraulic fluid will have to be added later when the system is bled.
8. Install the master cylinder as described in this chapter.

REAR CALIPER

Removal/Installation

Refer to **Figure 89** for this procedure.

CAUTION
Do not spill any brake fluid on the rear wheel. Wash off any spilled brake fluid immediately, as it will destroy the finish. Use soapy water and rinse completely.

1. Remove the right-hand side cover.
2. Clean the top of the master cylinder of all dirt and foreign matter.
3. Remove the cotter pin (**Figure 90**) on the caliper torque link. Discard the cotter pin.
4. Remove the bolt, washer and nut (A, **Figure 91**) and let the torque link (B, **Figure 91**) pivot down to the ground.
5. Loosen the screws securing the master cylinder reservoir cover (**Figure 92**). Pull up and loosen the cover and the diaphragm. This will allow air to enter the reservoir and allow the brake fluid to drain out more quickly in the next step.
6. Place a container under the brake hose at the caliper.
7. Remove the union bolt (A, **Figure 93**) and sealing washers securing the brake hose to the caliper assembly.
8. Remove the brake hose and let the brake fluid drain out into the container. Dispose of this brake fluid—never reuse brake fluid. To prevent the entry of moisture and dirt, cap the end of the brake hose and tie the loose end up to the frame.

9. Loosen the bolts (B, **Figure 93**) securing the brake caliper assembly to the caliper bracket. Push in on the caliper while loosening the bolts to push the pistons back into the caliper bores.
10. Remove the bolts securing the brake caliper assembly to the caliper bracket.
11. Remove the caliper assembly from the brake disc.
12. Install by reversing these removal steps, noting the following.
13. Carefully install the caliper assembly onto the disc being careful not to damage the leading edge of the brake pads.
14. Install the bolts securing the brake caliper assembly to the caliper bracket and tighten to the torque specifications listed in **Table 1**.
15. Install the brake hose, with a new sealing washer on each side of the fitting, onto the caliper. Install the union bolt and tighten to the torque specification listed in **Table 1**.
16. Remove the master cylinder reservoir top cover and diaphragm.

WARNING

Use brake fluid clearly marked DOT 3 or DOT 4 from a sealed container. Other types may vaporize and cause brake failure. Always use the same brand name; do not intermix as many brands are not compatible. Do not intermix silicone-based (DOT 5) brake fluid as it can cause brake component damage leading to brake system failure.

17. Shift the transmission into NEUTRAL.
18. Push the bike forward enough to turn the rear wheel several revolutions. As you do this, operate the rear brake lever as many times as it takes to correctly locate the rear brake pads.
19. Refill the master cylinder reservoir. Install the diaphragm and cover. Do not tighten the screws at this time.
20. Bleed the brake as described under *Bleeding the System* in this chapter.

WARNING

Do not ride the motorcycle until you are sure that the brake is operating properly.

Caliper Rebuilding

Refer to **Figure 89** for this procedure.

1. Remove the caliper and brake pads as described in this chapter.
2. Remove the caliper housing bolts (**Figure 94**) securing the caliper inner body to the caliper outer body.

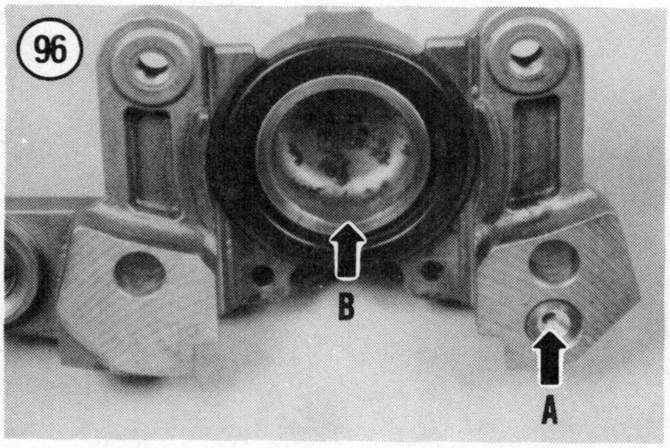

98

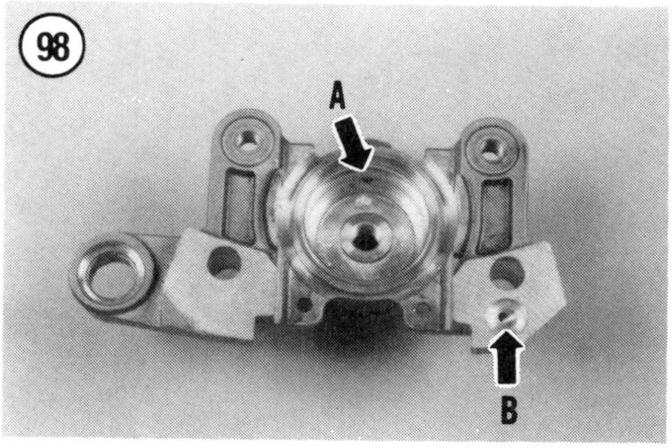

99

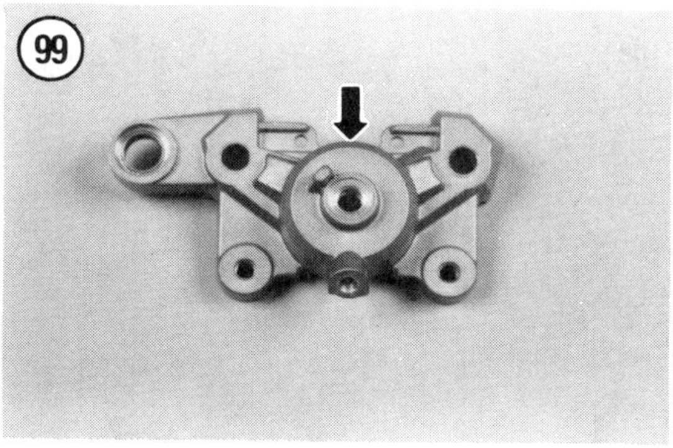

100

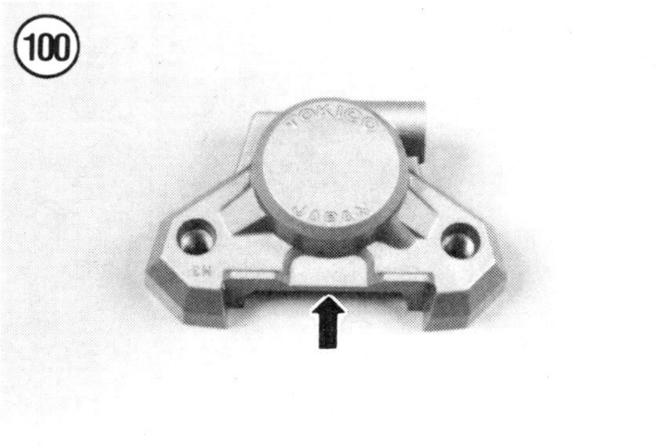

101

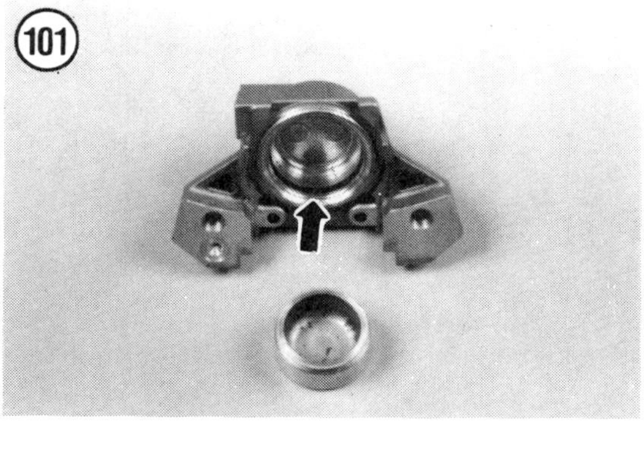

3. Separate the 2 caliper bodies.
4. Remove the O-ring (**Figure 95**) from the caliper inner body. Discard the O-ring as it must be replaced every time the caliper is disassembled.
5. Place a shop cloth or piece of soft wood over the end of the piston.
6. Perform this step over and close down to a workbench top. Hold the caliper body with the piston facing away from you.

WARNING
*In the next step, the piston may shoot out of the caliper body like a bullet. Keep your fingers out of the way. Wear shop gloves and apply air pressure gradually. Do **not** use high pressure air or place the air hose nozzle directly against the hydraulic line fitting inlet in the caliper body. Hold the air nozzle away from the inlet allowing some of the air to escape.*

7. Apply the air pressure in short spurts to the hydraulic fluid passageway (A, **Figure 96**) and force out the piston (B, **Figure 96**) and dust boot assembly. Use a service station air hose if you don't have an air compressor.

CAUTION
In the following step, do not use a sharp tool to remove the piston seal from the caliper cylinder. Do not damage the cylinder surface.

8. Use a piece of plastic or wood and carefully push the piston seal (**Figure 97**) in toward the caliper cylinder and out of its groove. Remove the piston seal from the cylinder and discard the seal.
9. Inspect the seal groove in caliper body (A, **Figure 98**) for damage. If damaged or corroded, replace the caliper assembly.
10. Inspect the caliper body for damage. Replace the caliper body if necessary. Refer to **Figure 99** and **Figure 100**.
11. Inspect the hydraulic fluid passageways (B, **Figure 98**) in each caliper body. Make sure it is clean and open. Apply compressed air to the opening and make sure it is clear. Clean out if necessary with fresh brake fluid.
12. Inspect the cylinder wall (**Figure 101**) and the piston (**Figure 102**) in each caliper body for scratches, scoring or other damage. Replace the pistons or the caliper assembly, if either is rusty or corroded.

13. Inspect the dust seal groove in the piston (**Figure 103**) in each piston for wear or corrosion. If rusty or corroded, replace the piston.
14. Inspect the caliper housing bolt holes (**Figure 104**) on the inner body. If worn or damaged, replace the caliper assembly.
15. Remove the bleed screws. Make sure they are clean and open (**Figure 105**). Apply compressed air to the opening and make sure they are clear. Clean out if necessary with fresh brake fluid.
16. Remove the spacer (**Figure 106**) from the torque link pivot point.
17. Inspect the grease seal (A, **Figure 107**) on each side of the torque link pivot point bronze bushing. If damaged or starting to deteriorate, replace as set.
18. Inspect the bronze bushing (B, **Figure 107**) in the torque link pivot point. If worn or damaged, replace the caliper assembly.
19. If serviceable, clean the caliper body with rubbing alcohol and rinse with clean brake fluid.

NOTE
Never reuse the old wiper seals or piston seals. Very minor damage or age deterioration can make the seals useless.

20. Coat the new piston seals with fresh DOT 3 or DOT 4 brake fluid.
21. Carefully install the new piston seal in the groove in the caliper cylinder. Make sure the seal is properly seated in the groove (**Figure 97**).
22. Coat the piston and caliper cylinder with fresh DOT 3 or DOT 4 brake fluid.
23. Position the piston with the open end facing out toward the brake pads and install the piston into the caliper cylinder (**Figure 108**).

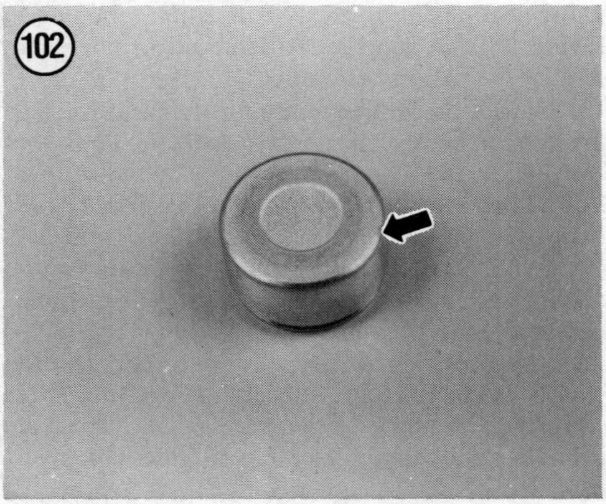

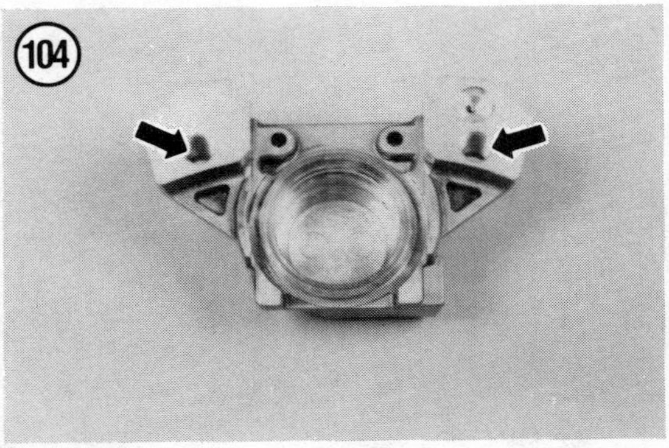

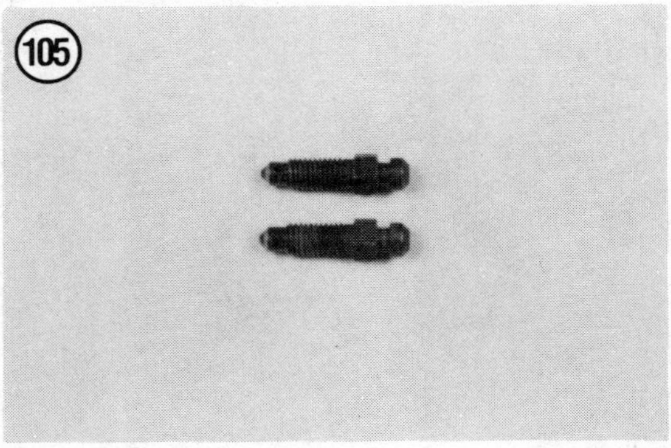

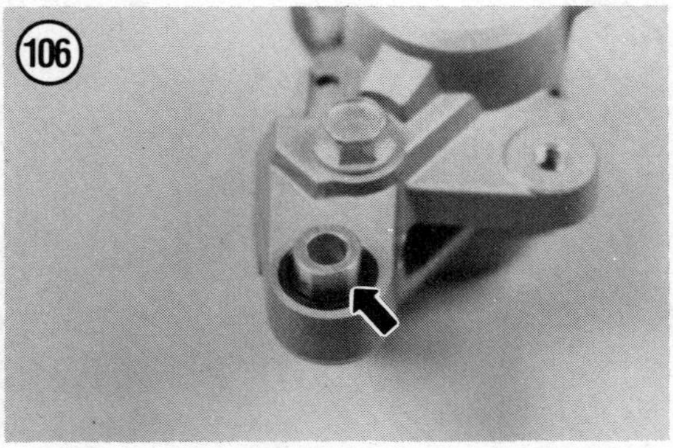

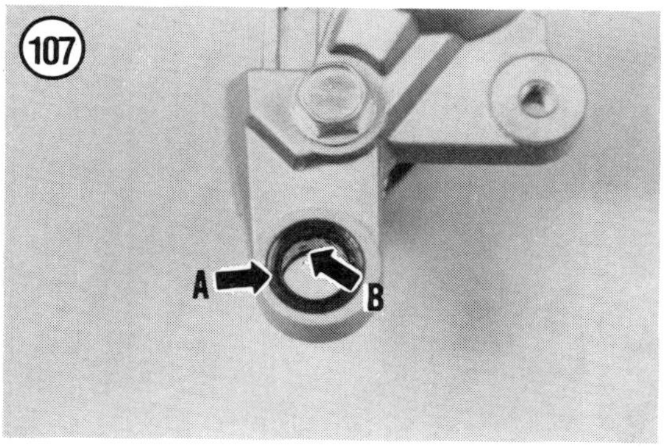

24. Install the dust seal (**Figure 109**) into the piston groove. Make sure the seal is correctly seated in the piston groove all the way around.
25. Push the piston in until it bottoms out (**Figure 110**).
26. Repeat Steps 5-25 for the other caliper body.
27. Install a new O-ring (**Figure 95**) onto the caliper outer body.
28. Assemble the 2 caliper bodies and install the caliper housing bolts (**Figure 94**). Tighten the bolts to the torque specification listed in **Table 1**.
29. Install the bleed valve (**Figure 111**) into each caliper body. Tighten the valves to the torque specification listed in **Table 1**.
30. Install the caliper and brake pads as described in this chapter.

REAR BRAKE HOSE REPLACEMENT

Suzuki recommends replacing the brake hose every four years or when it shows signs of cracking or damage.

Refer to **Figure 112** for this procedure.

1. Remove the right-hand side cover.

CAUTION

Cover the swing arm and the rear wheel with a heavy cloth or plastic tarp to protect them from accidental brake fluid spills. Wash brake fluid off any painted or plated surfaces or plastic parts immediately, as it will destroy the finish. Use soapy water and rinse completely.

2. Place a container under the brake hose at the rear caliper.

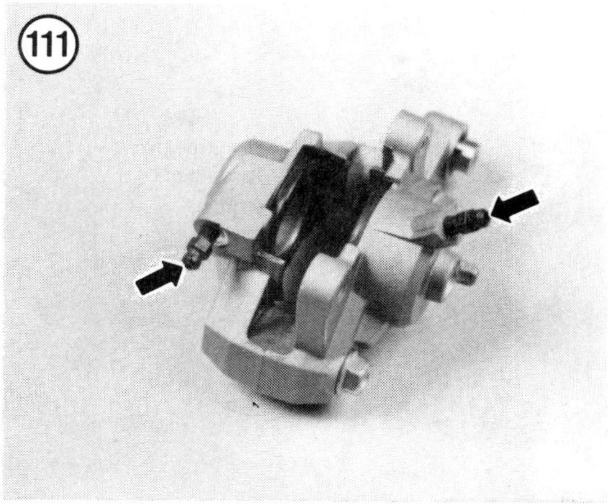

(112)

REAR MASTER CYLINDER

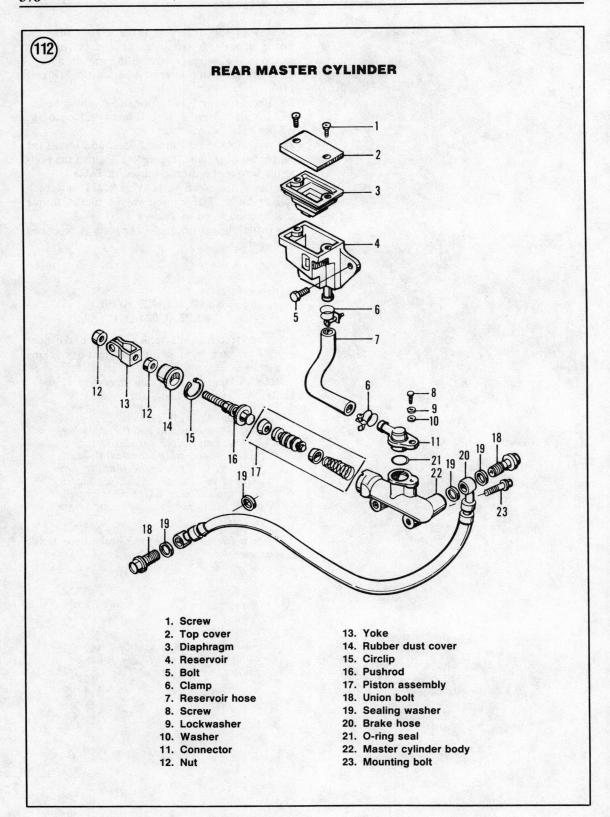

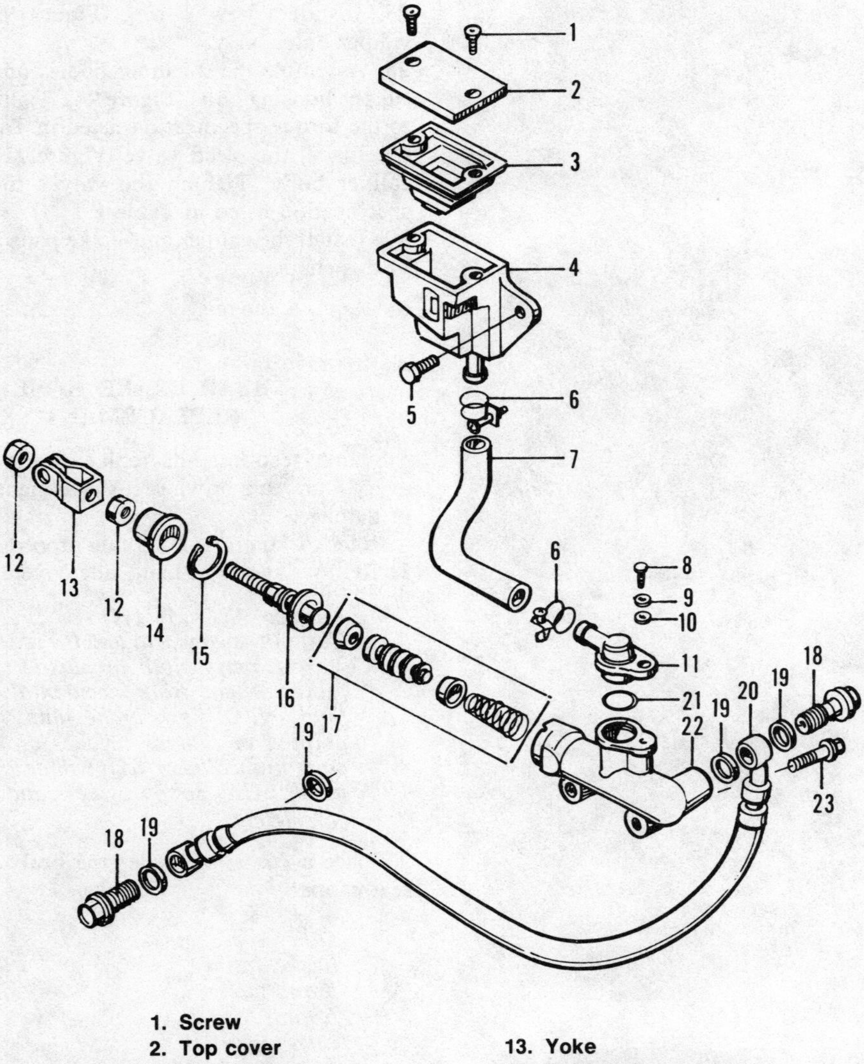

1. Screw
2. Top cover
3. Diaphragm
4. Reservoir
5. Bolt
6. Clamp
7. Reservoir hose
8. Screw
9. Lockwasher
10. Washer
11. Connector
12. Nut
13. Yoke
14. Rubber dust cover
15. Circlip
16. Pushrod
17. Piston assembly
18. Union bolt
19. Sealing washer
20. Brake hose
21. O-ring seal
22. Master cylinder body
23. Mounting bolt

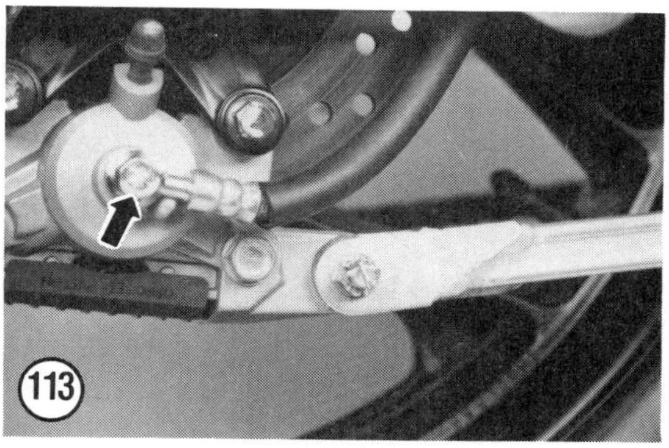

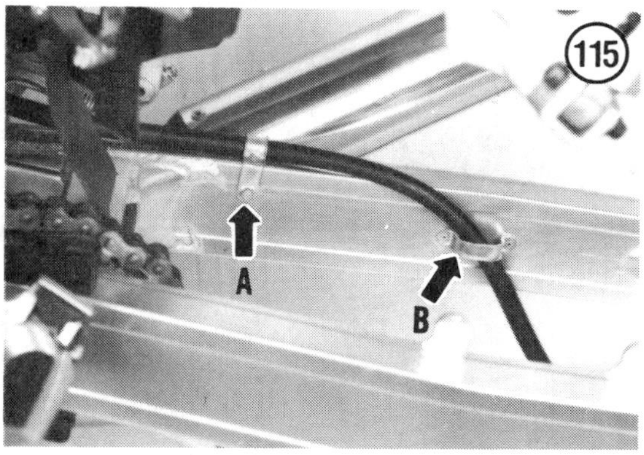

3. Unscrew the union bolt (**Figure 113**) securing the brake hose to the rear caliper. Don't lose the sealing washer on each side of the hose fitting.
4. Remove the brake hose and let the brake fluid drain out into the container. Apply the rear brake pedal several times to pump the brake fluid out of the master cylinder reservoir, master cylinder and brake hose. Dispose of this brake fluid—never reuse brake fluid.
5. Place a shop cloth under the brake hose and the master cylinder union bolt to catch any remaining brake fluid that will leak out.
6. Unscrew the union bolt (**Figure 114**) securing the brake hose to the backside of the master cylinder. Don't lose the sealing washer on each side of the hose fitting.
7. Remove the rear wheel as described under *Rear Wheel Removal* in Chapter Nine.
8. Remove the bolt securing the rear brake hose clamp and remove the clamp (A, **Figure 115**). Pull the brake hose through the other hose clamp (B, **Figure 115**) on the swing arm.
9. Remove the brake hose from the swing arm.
10. Install the new hose, sealing washers and the union bolts in the reverse order of removal. Be sure to install new sealing washers and in their correct positions.
11. Tighten the union bolts to the torque specification listed in **Table 1**.
12. Refill the master cylinder reservoir, if necessary, to maintain the fluid to the upper level (**Figure 116**) as seen through the transparent side of the master cylinder. Install the diaphragm and cover and loosely install the screws.

WARNING
Use brake fluid clearly marked DOT 3 or DOT 4 from a sealed container. Other types may vaporize and cause brake failure. Always use the same brand name; do not intermix as many brands are not compatible. Do not intermix silicone-based (DOT 5) brake fluid as it can cause brake component damage leading to brake system failure.

WARNING
Do not ride the motorcycle until you are sure that the brake is operating properly.

13. Bleed the brake as described under *Bleeding the System* in this chapter.

REAR BRAKE DISC

Removal/Installation

1. Remove the rear wheel as described under *Rear Wheel Removal/Installation* in Chapter Ten.

NOTE
Place a piece of wood or vinyl tube in the caliper in place of the disc. This way, if the brake pedal is inadvertently pressed the pistons will not be forced out of the cylinders. If this does happen, the caliper might have to be disassembled to reseat the pistons and the system will have to be bled.

CAUTION
Do not set the wheel down on the disc surface, as it may get scratched or bent. Set the wheel on 2 blocks of wood.

2. Remove the bolts (**Figure 117**) securing the brake disc to the hub and remove the disc.
3. Install by reversing these removal steps, noting the following.
4. Apply Loctite Lock N' Seal to the disc mounting bolt threads prior to installation. Tighten the disc mounting bolts to the torque specifications listed in **Table 1**.

Inspection

It is not necessary to remove the disc(s) from the wheel to inspect it. Small marks on the disc are not important, but radial scratches deep enough to snag a fingernail reduce braking effectiveness and increase brake pad wear. If these grooves are found, the disc should be replaced.

NOTE
Refinishing the disc surface on a brake cylinder is not recommended.

1. Measure the thickness of the disc at several locations around the disc with a micrometer (**Figure 118**) or vernier caliper. The disc must be replaced if the thickness in any area is less than that specified in **Table 2**.
2. Make sure the disc mounting bolts are tight before running this check. Check the disc runout with a dial indicator as shown in **Figure 119**.
3. Slowly rotate the wheel and watch the dial indicator. If the runout exceeds that listed in **Table 2**, the disc must be replaced.
4. Clean the disc of any rust or corrosion and wipe clean with lacquer thinner. Never use an oil-based solvent that may leave an oil residue on the disc.

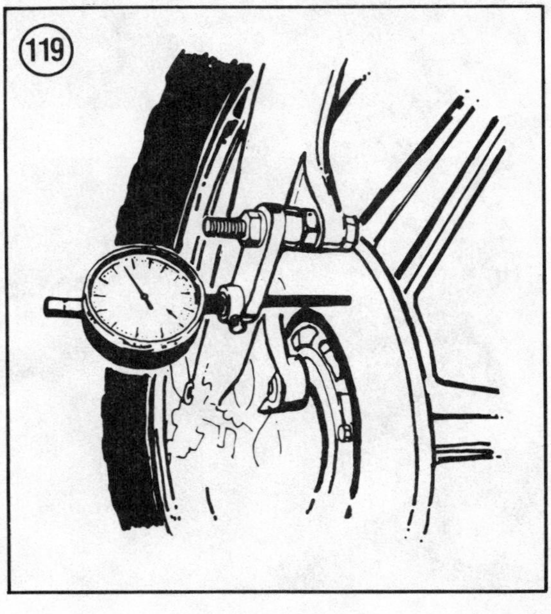

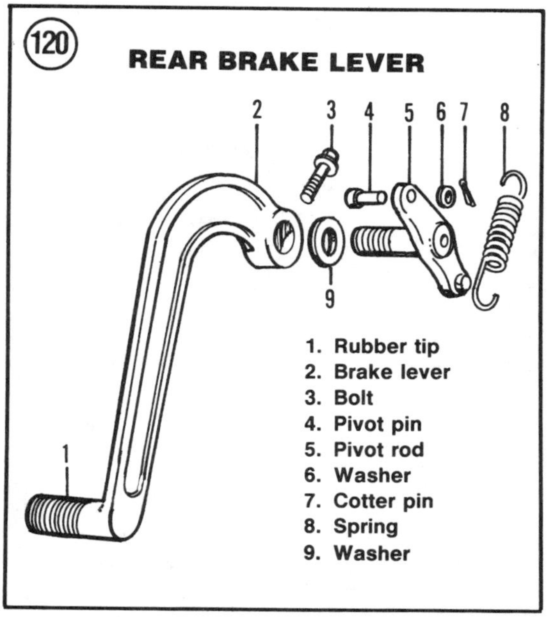

REAR BRAKE PEDAL

Removal/Installation

Refer to **Figure 120** for this procedure.

1. Remove the bolt (A, **Figure 121**) clamping the brake pedal to the pivot rod.
2. Slide off the brake pedal (B, **Figure 121**) and the washer.
3. Remove the cotter pin and washer and withdraw the pivot pin (C, **Figure 121**) securing the master cylinder pushrod assembly to the brake pedal assembly.
4. Remove the bolts (D, **Figure 121**) securing the right-hand footpeg and master cylinder assembly to the frame.
5. Carefully pull the top of the footpeg assembly down to gain access to the backside of the assembly.
6. Disconnect the brake pedal and rear brake light switch return springs from the pivot rod.
7. Remove the pivot rod from the footpeg assembly.
8. Install by reversing these removal steps.

BLEEDING THE SYSTEM

This procedure is not necessary unless the brakes feel spongy, there has been a leak in the system, a component has been replaced or the brake fluid has been replaced. This procedure is shown on the front brakes. Bleeding the rear brake is identical.

Because both the front and rear caliper assemblies have piston(s) in each caliper half there are 2 bleed valves per caliper (total of 4 for the front wheel). Start with one of the bleed valves and then switch to the other bleed valve on the same caliper. Bleed both calipers on the front wheel. It doesn't make any difference which caliper is bled first as they are both the same distance from the front master cylinder.

Brake Bleeder Process

This procedure uses a brake bleeder, that is available from motorcycle or automotive supply stores or from mail order outlets.

1. Remove the dust caps from the bleed valves on the caliper assembly. Refer to **Figure 122** for the front calipers and **Figure 123** for the rear (inner caliper body bleed valve is not visible).

2. Connect the brake bleeder to one of the bleed valves on the caliper assembly (**Figure 124**).

CAUTION
Cover the front wheel and rear wheel with a heavy cloth or plastic tarp to protect it from the accidental spilling of brake fluid. Wash any brake fluid off of any plastic, painted or plated surface immediately; as it will destroy the finish. Use soapy water and rinse completely.

3. Clean the top of the master cylinder of all dirt and foreign matter.
4. Remove the screws securing the reservoir cover and remove the reservoir cover and diaphragm. Refer to **Figure 125** for the front brakes and **Figure 126** for the rear brake.
5. Fill the reservoir almost to the top lip; insert the diaphragm and the cover loosely. Leave the cover in place during this procedure to prevent the entry of dirt.

WARNING
Use brake fluid from a sealed container marked DOT 3 or DOT 4 only (specified for disc brakes). Other types may vaporize and cause brake failure. Do not intermix different brands or types as they may not be compatible. Do not intermix a silicone based (DOT 5) brake fluid as it can cause brake component damage leading to brake system failure.

6. Open the bleed valve about one-half turn and pump the brake bleeder.

NOTE
If air is entering the brake bleeder hose from around the bleed valve, apply several layers of Teflon tape to the bleed valve. This should make a good seal between the bleed valve and the brake bleeder hose.

7. As the fluid enters the system and exits into the brake bleeder the level will drop in the reservoir. Maintain the level at about 3/8 inch from the top of the reservoir to prevent air from being drawn into the system.
8. Continue to pump the lever on the brake bleeder until the fluid emerging from the hose is completely free of bubbles. At this point, tighten the bleed valve.

NOTE
Do not allow the reservoir to empty during the bleeding operation or more air will enter the system. If this occurs, the entire procedure must be repeated.

9. When the brake fluid is free of bubbles, tighten the bleed valve, remove the brake bleeder tube and install the bleed valve dust cap.
10. If necessary, add fluid to correct the level in the reservoir. It should be to the upper level line. Refer to **Figure 127** for front brakes and **Figure 128** for the rear brake.

127

128

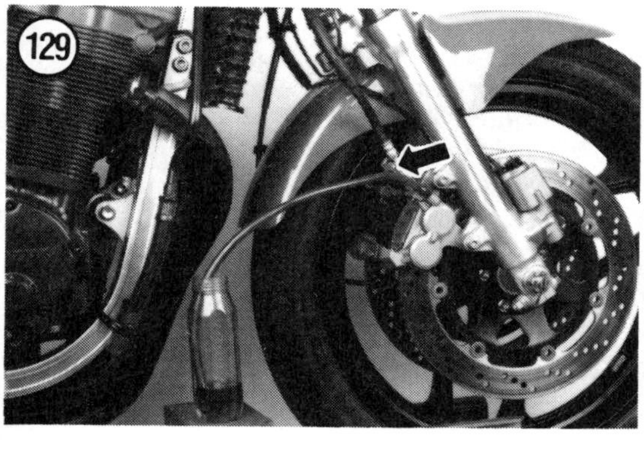

129

11. Repeat Step 2 and Steps 6-9 for the other bleed valve on the same caliper.
12. On the front wheel, repeat this procedure for the other caliper.
13. Install the diaphragm and the reservoir cover. Tighten the screws securely.
14. Test the feel of the brake lever or pedal. It should be firm and should offer the same resistance each time it's operated. If it feels spongy, it is likely that there is still air in the system and it must be bled again. When all air has been bled from the system and the fluid level is correct in the reservoir, double-check for leaks and tighten all fittings and connections.

WARNING
Before riding the bike, make certain that the brake is operating correctly by operating the lever several times.

15. Test ride the bike slowly at first to make sure that the brakes are operating properly.

Without a Brake Bleeder

1. Remove the dust caps from the bleed valves on the caliper assembly. Refer to **Figure 122** for the front calipers and **Figure 123** for the rear (inner caliper body bleed valve is not visible).
2. Connect the bleed hose to one of the bleed valves on the caliper assembly (**Figure 129**).
3. Place the other end of the tube into a clean container. Fill the container with enough fresh brake fluid to keep the end submerged to prevent air from being drawn into the caliper during bleeding.

CAUTION
Cover the front fender and front wheel with a heavy cloth or plastic tarp to protect it from the accidental spilling of brake fluid. Wash any brake fluid off of any plastic, painted or plated surface immediately, as it will destroy the finish. Use soapy water and rinse completely.

4. Clean the top of the master cylinder of all dirt and foreign matter.
5. Remove the screws securing the reservoir cover and remove the reservoir cover and diaphragm. Refer to **Figure 125** for the front brakes and **Figure 126** for the rear brake.

6. Fill the reservoir almost to the cover lip; insert the diaphragm and the cover loosely. Leave the cover in place during this procedure to prevent the entry of dirt.

WARNING
Use brake fluid from a sealed container marked DOT 3 or DOT 4 only (specified for disc brakes). Other types may vaporize and cause brake failure. Do not intermix different brands or types as they may not be compatible. Do not intermix a silicone based (DOT 5) brake fluid as it can cause brake component damage leading to brake system failure.

NOTE
During this procedure, all the hose junctions in the brake system will be bled of air. It is very important to check the fluid level in the master cylinder often. If the reservoir runs dry, you'll introduce more air into the system which will require starting over.

7. If the master cylinder was drained, it must be bled first. Remove the union bolt and hose from the master cylinder. Slowly apply the brake lever, or brake pedal, several times while holding your thumb securely over the opening in the master cylinder.
   a. With the lever or pedal held depressed, slightly release your thumb pressure. Some fluid and air bubbles will escape.
   b. Apply thumb pressure and pump the lever or pedal once more.
   c. Repeat this procedure until you can feel resistance at the lever or pedal.
   d. Refill the master cylinder.
8. Reinstall the hose and union bolt. Tighten the union bolt and pump the lever or pedal again.
   a. Loosen the union bolt 1/4 turn. Some fluid and air bubbles will escape.
   b. Tighten the union bolt and repeat this procedure until no air bubbles escape.
   c. Refill the master cylinder.
9. If working on the front brakes, each union bolt at the 3-way joint must be bled using the same procedure detailed in Step 8.
   a. Bleed the union bolts in this order: first, hose end from master cylinder; second, hose to brake closest to master cylinder hose; third, hose to brake farthest to master cylinder hose.
   b. Refill the master cylinder.
10. Slowly apply the brake lever, or brake pedal, several times. Hold the lever in the applied position or the pedal in the depressed position.
   a. Open the caliper bleed valve about one-half turn. Allow the lever or pedal to travel to its limit.
   b. When this limit is reached, tighten the bleed screw.
11. As the fluid enters the system, the level will drop in the reservoir. Maintain the level at about 3/8 inch from the cover of the reservoir to prevent air from being drawn into the system.
12. Continue to pump the lever and fill the reservoir until the fluid emerging from the hose is completely free of bubbles.

NOTE
Do not allow the reservoir to empty during the bleeding operation or more air will enter the system. If this occurs, the entire procedure must be repeated.

13. Hold the lever in, tighten the bleed valve, remove the bleed tube and install the bleed valve dust cap.
14. If necessary, add fluid to correct the level in the reservoir. It should be to the upper level line. Refer to **Figure 127** for front brakes and **Figure 128** for the rear brake.
15. Repeat Steps 2-3 and Steps 10-12 for the other bleed valve on the same caliper.
16. On the front wheel, repeat this procedure for the other caliper.
17. Install the diaphragm and reservoir cover. Tighten the screws securely.
18. Test the feel of the brake lever. It should be firm and should offer the same resistance each time it's operated. If it feels spongy, it is likely that there is still air in the system and it must be bled again. When all air has been bled from the system and the fluid level is correct in the reservoir, double-check for leaks and tighten all fittings and connections.

WARNING
Before riding the bike, make certain that the brakes are operating correctly by operating the lever or pedal several times.

19. Test ride the bike slowly at first to make sure that the brakes are operating properly.

Table 1 BRAKE TORQUE SPECIFICATIONS

Item	N•m	ft.-lb.
Front master cylinder		
Clamping bolts	5-8	3-6
Union bolt	20-25	14-18
Front caliper		
Mounting bolts	15-25	11-18
Union bolt	20-25	14-18
Bleed valve	6-9	4-7
Housing bolts	30-36	21-26
Brake hose nut adaptor	20-25	14-18
Rear caliper		
Mounting bolts	15-25	11-18
Bleed valve	6-9	4-7
Union bolt	20-25	14-18
Housing bolts	30-36	21-26
Brake disc mounting bolt	15-25	11-18

Table 2 BRAKE SPECIFICATIONS

Item	Specification	Wear limit
Front master cylinder		
Cylinder bore I.D.	15.870-15.913 mm (0.6253-0.6265 in.)	—
Piston O.D.	15.827-15.854 mm (0.6231-0.6242 in.)	—
Front caliper		
Cylinder bore I.D.	32.030-32.106 mm (1.2610-1.2640 in.)	—
Piston O.D.	31.995-32.000 mm (1.2596-1.2598 in.)	—
Front disc		
Thickness	4.3-4.7 mm (0.169-0.185 in.)	4.0 mm (0.15 in.)
Runout	—	0.30 mm (0.012 in.)
Rear master cylinder		
Cylinder bore I.D	12.700-12.743 mm (0.5000-0.5017 in.)	—
Piston O.D.	12.657-12.684 mm (0.4983-0.4994 in.)	—
Rear caliper		
Cylinder bore I.D.	38.180-38.256 mm (1.5031-1.5061 in.)	—
Piston O.D.	38.098-38.148 mm (1.5000-1.5019 in.)	—
Rear disc		
Thickness	5.8-6.2 mm (0.228-0.244 in.)	5.5 mm (0.22 in.)
Runout	—	0.30 mm (0.012 in.)

NOTE: If you own a GSX600F Katana, first refer to Chapter 13 for specific service information.

CHAPTER TWELVE

BODY AND FRAME

This chapter contains removal and installation procedures for all body panels and frame components.

SEAT

Removal/Installation (GSX-R750, GSX-R1100)

Refer to **Figure 1** for this procedure.

1. Insert the ignition key into the seat/helmet lock (**Figure 2**) on the left-hand side of the rear fender cover.
2. Turn the ignition key *clockwise* until the seat lock is released.
3. Pull up on the rear of the seat and move the seat toward the rear.
4. Remove the seat assembly (**Figure 3**).
5. Install by reversing these removal steps, noting the following.
6. Make sure the locating tab on the front of the seat is correctly hooked onto the metal seat bracket on the frame.

WARNING
After the seat is installed, pull up on it firmly to make sure it is securely locked in place. If the seat is not correctly locked in place it may slide to one side or the other when riding the bike. This could lead to the loss of control and a possible accident.

7. Push the seat firmly down until the seat latch "snaps" into the locked position.

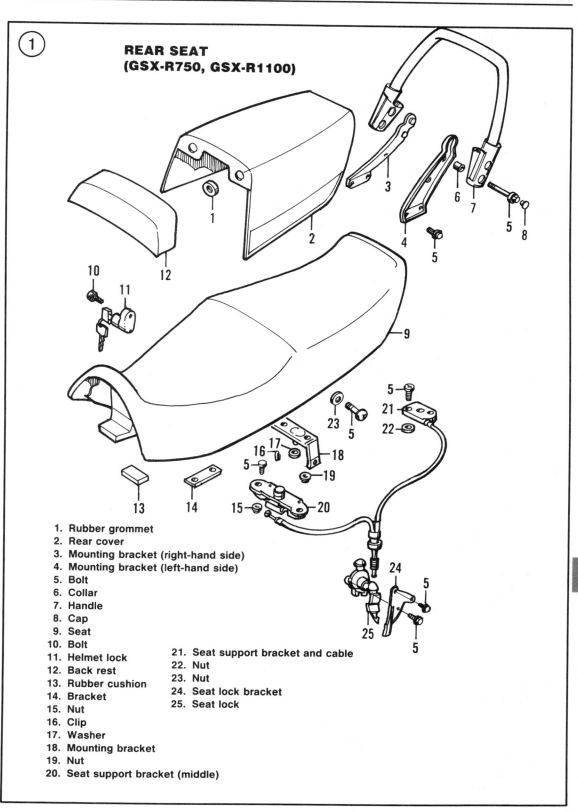

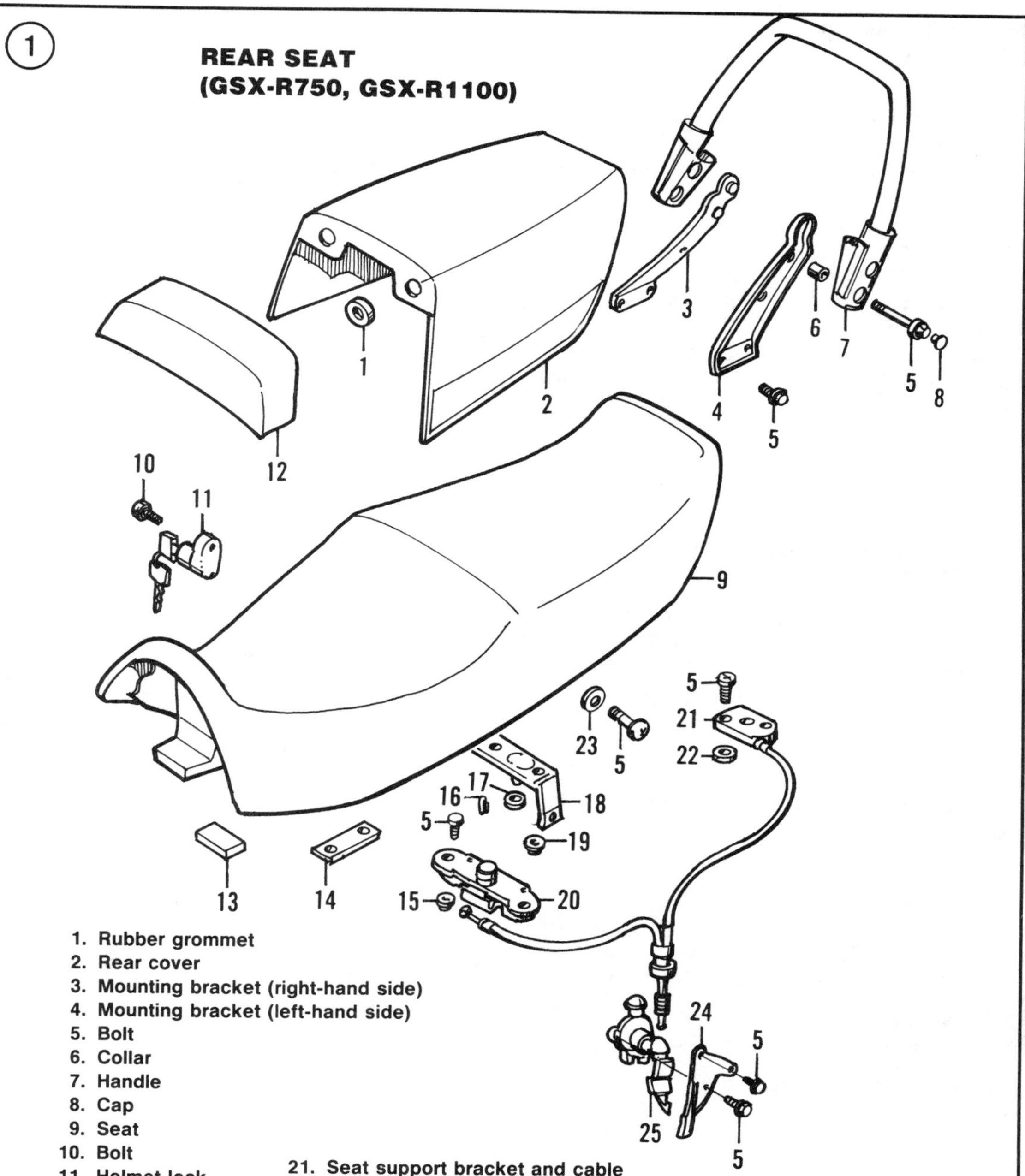

1. Rubber grommet
2. Rear cover
3. Mounting bracket (right-hand side)
4. Mounting bracket (left-hand side)
5. Bolt
6. Collar
7. Handle
8. Cap
9. Seat
10. Bolt
11. Helmet lock
12. Back rest
13. Rubber cushion
14. Bracket
15. Nut
16. Clip
17. Washer
18. Mounting bracket
19. Nut
20. Seat support bracket (middle)
21. Seat support bracket and cable
22. Nut
23. Nut
24. Seat lock bracket
25. Seat lock

Removal/Installation (GSX-R750R Limited Edition)

Refer to **Figure 4** for this procedure.

1. Insert the ignition key into the seat/helmet lock on the left-hand side of the rear fender cover.
2. Turn the ignition key *clockwise* until the seat lock is released.
3. Pull up on the rear of the seat and move the seat toward the rear.
4. Remove the seat.
5. Install by reversing these removal steps, noting the following.
6. Make sure the locating tab on the front of the seat is correctly hooked onto the metal seat bracket on the frame.

WARNING

After the seat is installed, pull up on it firmly to make sure it is securely locked in place. If the seat is not correctly locked in place it may slide to one side or the other when riding the bike. This could lead to the loss of control and a possible accident.

7. Push the seat firmly down until the seat latch "snaps" into the locked position.

FRONT FAIRING AND MOUNTING BRACKET

Front Fairing Removal/Installation

Refer to **Figure 5** for this procedure.

CAUTION

*Removal of the lower section requires the aid of a helper or some means to hold onto the lower section of the fairing. Once the fasteners on one side are removed, you then have to remove the fasteners on the other side. After the fasteners on the first side are removed, do **not** allow the first side to "hang down" by itself or part of the fairing or its fasteners will be damaged.*

(4)

REAR SEAT (GSX-R750R LIMITED EDITION)

1. Seat
2. Screw
3. Mounting bracket
4. Plate
5. Nut
6. Collar
7. Seat support bracket and cable
8. Rubber stopper
9. Seat lock and bracket
10. Cap

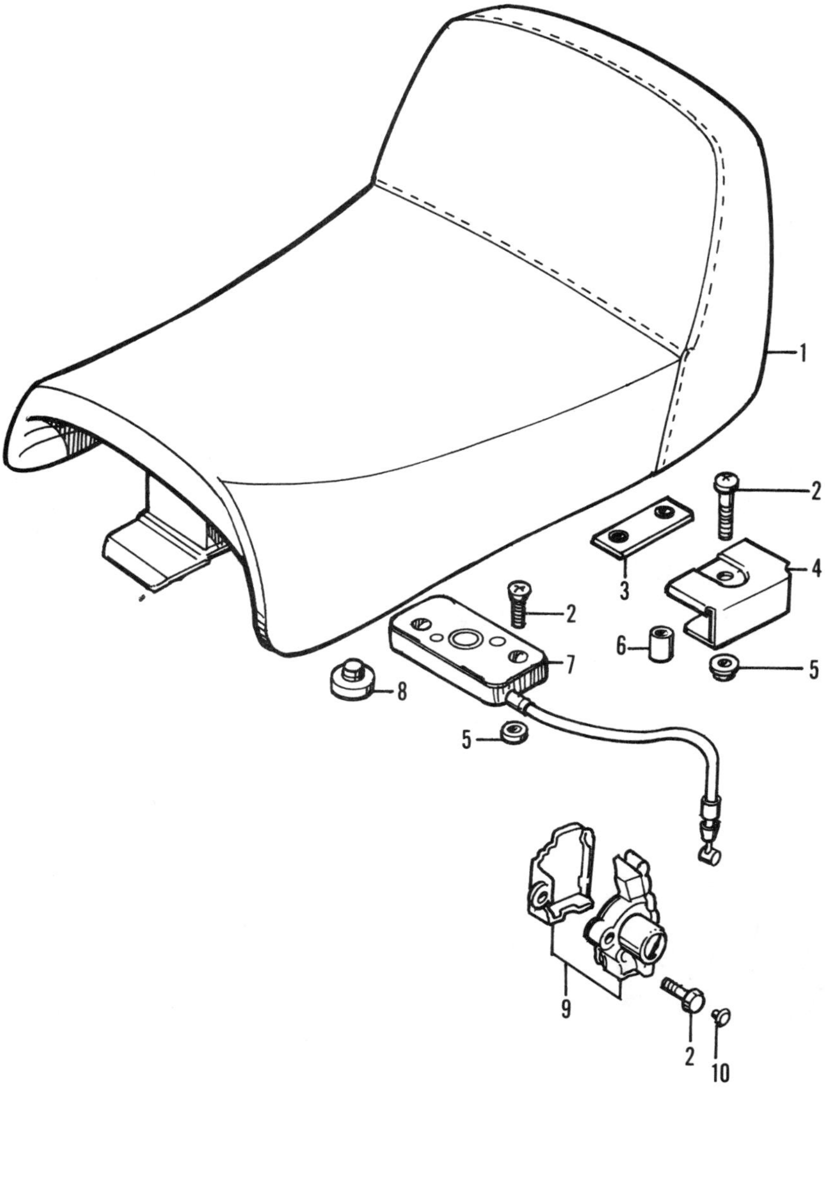
1
2
3
4
2
6
5
7
8
5
9
2
10

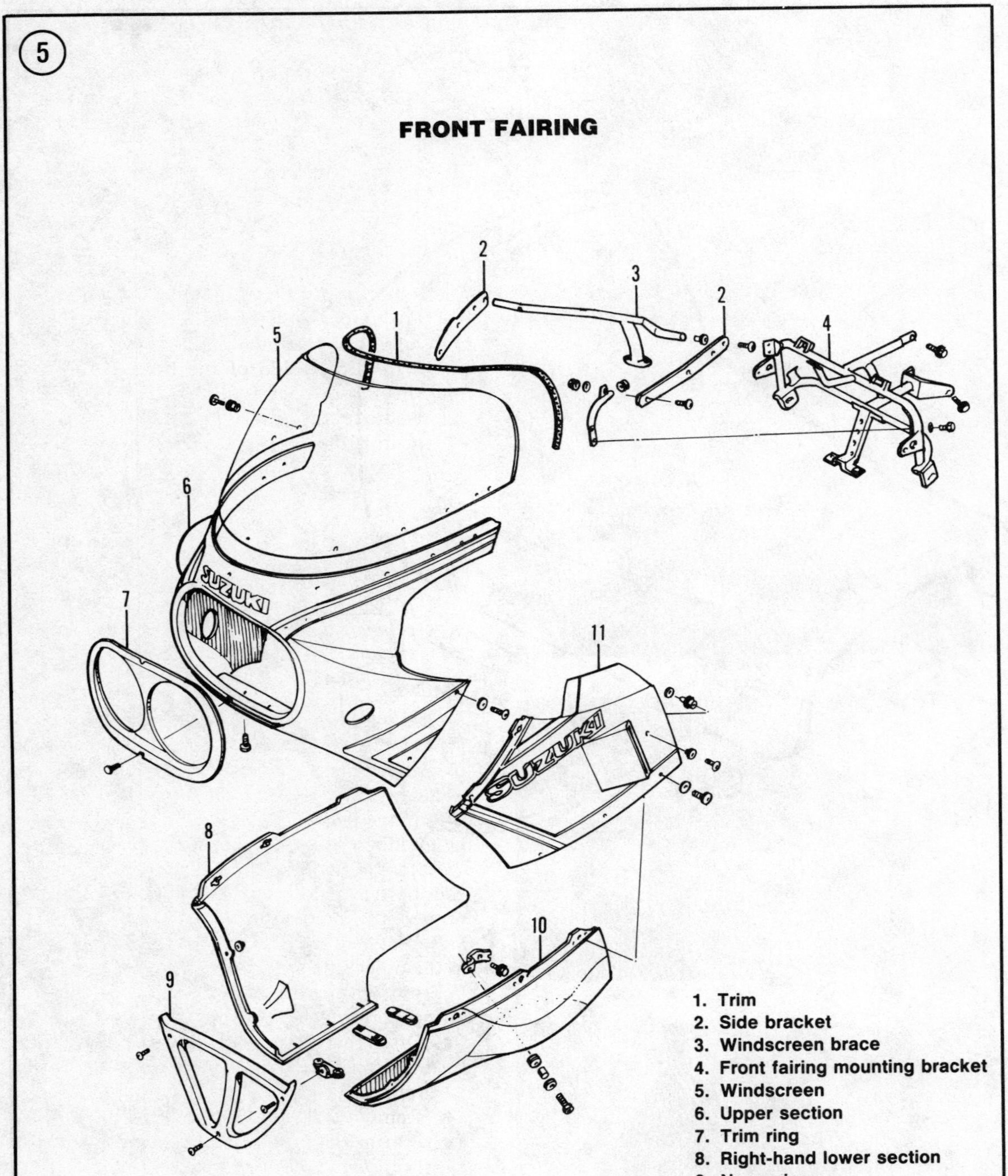

1. Trim
2. Side bracket
3. Windscreen brace
4. Front fairing mounting bracket
5. Windscreen
6. Upper section
7. Trim ring
8. Right-hand lower section
9. Nose piece
10. Left-hand lower section
11. Middle section

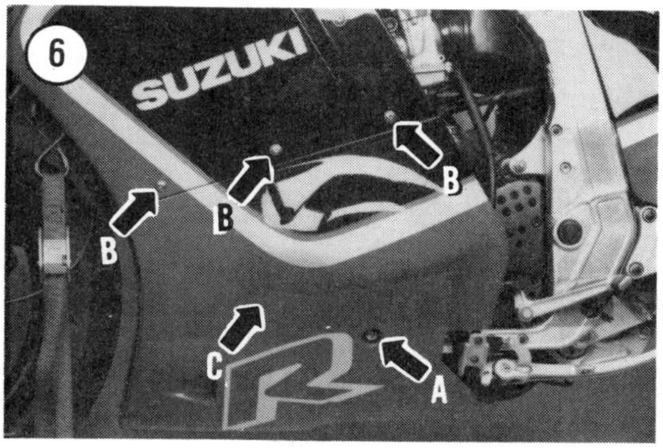

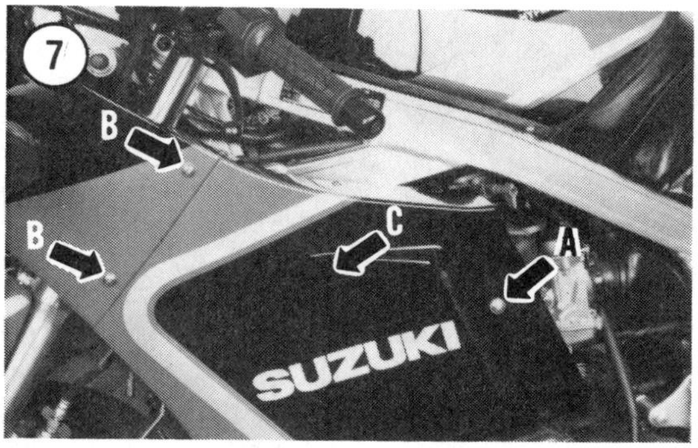

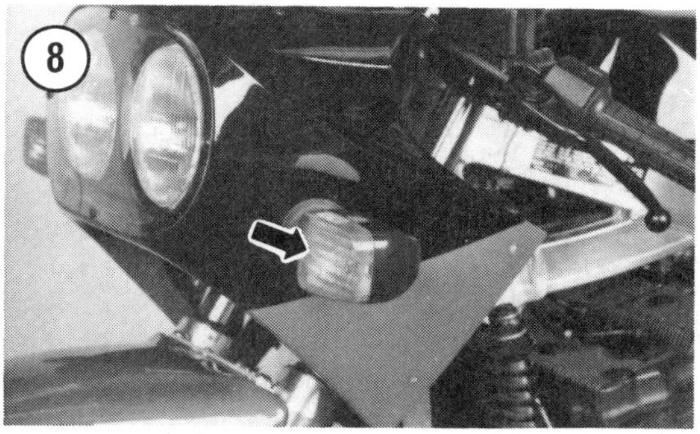

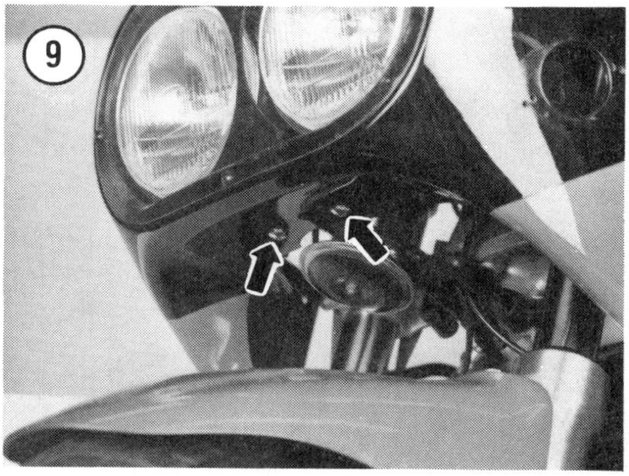

1. Place a blanket or towels on the ground under the front fairing lower section. This is to protect the fairing finish during removal of the lower section.
2. On one side of the bike, perform the following:
   a. Remove the lower fastener (A, **Figure 6**) securing the lower section to the frame.
   b. Remove the upper fasteners (B, **Figure 6**) securing the lower section to the middle section.
3. Either have an assistant hold onto the side where the fasteners were removed or place wood block(s) or a box under the lower section (C, **Figure 6**) to hold it in position.
4. On the other side of the bike, perform the following:
   a. Remove the lower fastener (A, **Figure 6**) securing the lower section to the frame.
   b. Remove the upper fasteners (B, **Figure 6**) securing the lower section to the middle section.

WARNING
If the engine has been run recently, protect yourself accordingly as the exhaust system may still be HOT.

5. Ease the lower section down and rest it on the blanket. Slightly rotate the lower section sideways (to either side) out from under the frame and exhaust system. Remove the lower section.
6. Remove the rear fastener (A, **Figure 7**) securing the middle section to the cylinder head.
7. Remove the front fasteners (B, **Figure 7**) securing the middle section to the upper section. Remove the middle section (C, **Figure 7**).
8. Repeat Step 6 and Step 7 for the middle section on the other side.
9. From within the upper section of the front fairing, perform the following:
   a. Disconnect the black and the black/white individual electrical connectors going to each front turn signal assembly.
   b. Remove the nut, washer and inner spacer securing the turn signal assembly (**Figure 8**) to the upper section. Remove the turn signal assembly and outer spacer. The rubber grommet will either stay in the fairing or come out with the turn signal assembly.
10. Repeat Step 9b for the other turn signal assembly and remove that assembly.
11. Remove both screws (**Figure 9**), under the headlights, securing the upper section to the mounting bracket.

NOTE
The following step is easier with the aid of a helper. It can be accomplished by one person but it is a little tricky.

12. Remove the screws (**Figure 10**) securing one side of the upper section to the windscreen brace and front fairing mounting bracket.
13. Have an assistant hold onto that side of the upper section and remove the screw securing the other side of the upper section to the windscreen brace.
14. Carefully pull the upper section (**Figure 11**) forward and disengage it from the headlight housing area. The headlight assembly will stay with the front fairing mounting bracket.
15. Install by reversing these removal steps, noting the following.
16. Tighten all screws securely. Do not overtighten as the plastic panels may fracture.

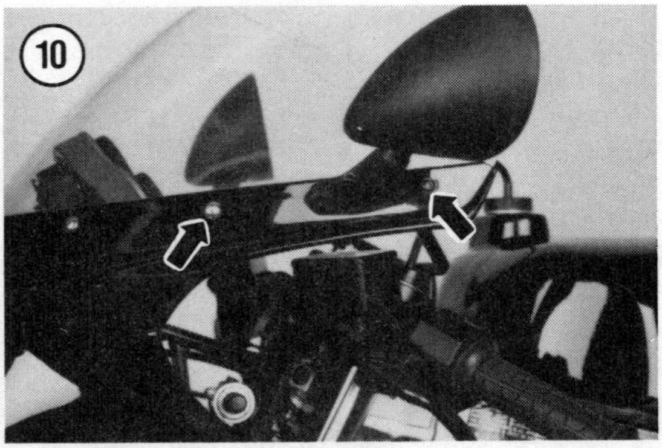

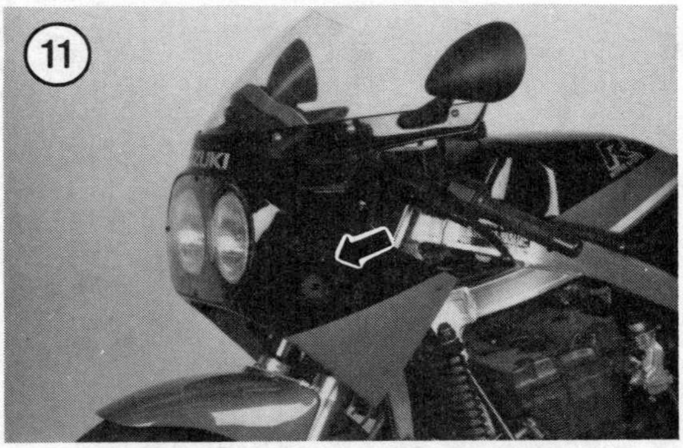

Front Fairing Mounting Bracket Removal/Installation

Refer to **Figure 5** for this procedure. This procedure is shown with the headlight assembly and the instrument cluster still attached to the mounting bracket. If so desired, both of these assemblies can be removed from the mounting bracket, prior to bracket removal, as described in Chapter Eight.

1. Remove the front fairing as described in this chapter.
2. Disconnect the speedometer cable (A, **Figure 12**) from the base of the speedometer housing.
3. On GSX-R1100 models, disconnect the 2-pin electrical connectors (**Figure 13**) going to each NEAS relay.
4. Disconnect all electrical connectors (B, **Figure 12**) going to the instrument cluster.
5. Remove the lower bolt (**Figure 14**) on each side securing the lower section of the mounting bracket to the steering head portion of the frame.
6. Remove the upper bolt (**Figure 15**) securing the upper section of the mounting bracket to the steering head portion of the frame.
7. Carefully pull the front fairing bracket assembly forward and make sure all electrical connectors are disconnected. Remove the bracket assembly.

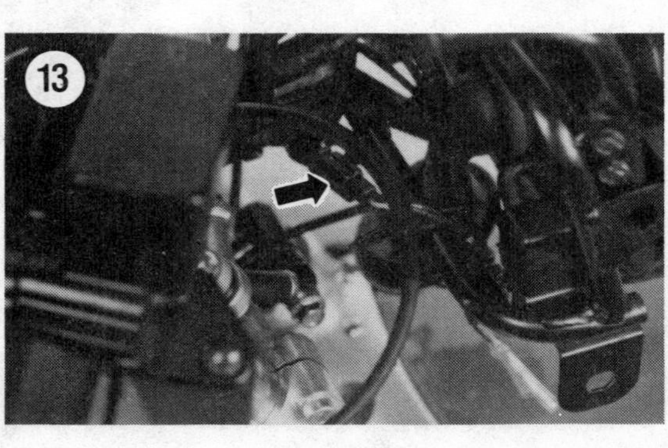

8. Remove the bolts securing the windscreen brace (**Figure 16**) to the frame and remove the windscreen brace.
9. Install by reversing these removal steps, noting the following.
10. Make sure all electrical connectors are free of corrosion and are tight.
11. Tighten all mounting bolts securely.

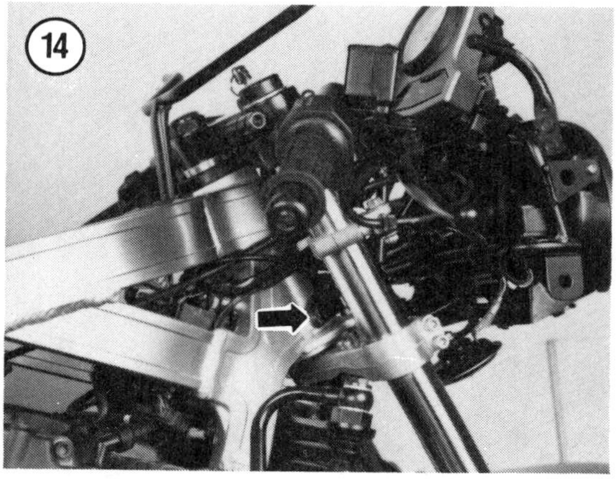

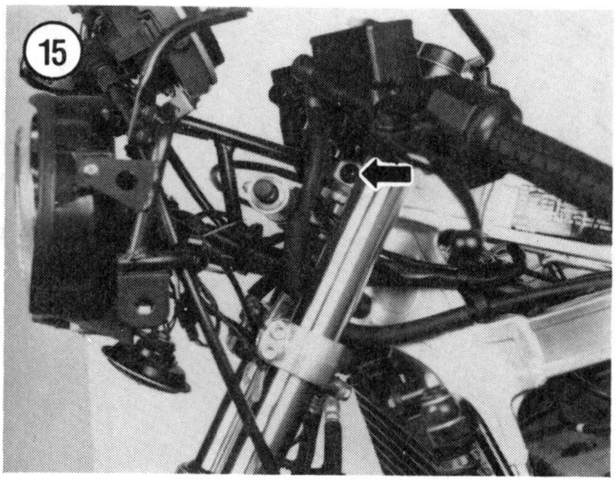

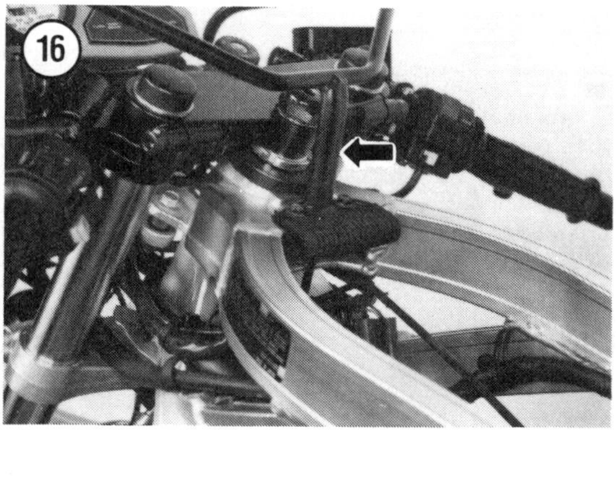

REAR FENDER COVER

Removal/Installation (GSX-R750, GSX-R1100)

Refer to **Figure 17** for this procedure.
1. Remove the seat as described in this chapter.
2. Disconnect the electrical connector (**Figure 18**) going to the taillight/brakelight assembly.
3. Remove the screws, outer washers and inner washers (A, **Figure 19**) securing the rear fender cover on one side of the frame.
4. Remove the screws, outer washers and inner washers securing the rear fender cover to the other side of the frame.
5. Remove the screws, washers and spacers (B, **Figure 19**) securing the rear portion of the rear fender cover to the frame.
6. Pull the rear fender cover (C, **Figure 19**) straight up and off the frame.
7. Install by reversing these removal steps, noting the following.
8. Make sure the rubber grommets are in place in the mounting holes in the rear fender cover. These grommets help prevent the plastic from fracturing at the attachment points.
9. Tighten all screws securely. Do not overtighten as the plastic fender may fracture.

Removal/Installation (GSX-R750R Limited Edition)

Refer to **Figure 20** for this procedure.
1. Remove the seat (A, **Figure 21**) as described in this chapter.
2. Disconnect the electrical connector going to the taillight/brakelight assembly.
3. Remove the screw, washers and spacer (B, **Figure 21**) securing the rear fender cover on one side of the frame.
4. Remove the screws, washers and spacer securing the rear fender cover to the other side of the frame.
5. Remove the screws securing the rear portion of the rear fender cover to the frame.
6. Pull the rear fender cover (C, **Figure 21**) straight up and off the frame.
7. Install by reversing these removal steps, noting the following.
8. Make sure the rubber grommets are in place in the mounting holes in the rear fender cover. These grommets help prevent the plastic from fracturing at the attachment points.
9. Tighten all screws securely. Do not overtighten as the plastic fender may fracture.

17

REAR FENDER COVER (GSX-R750, GSX-R1100)

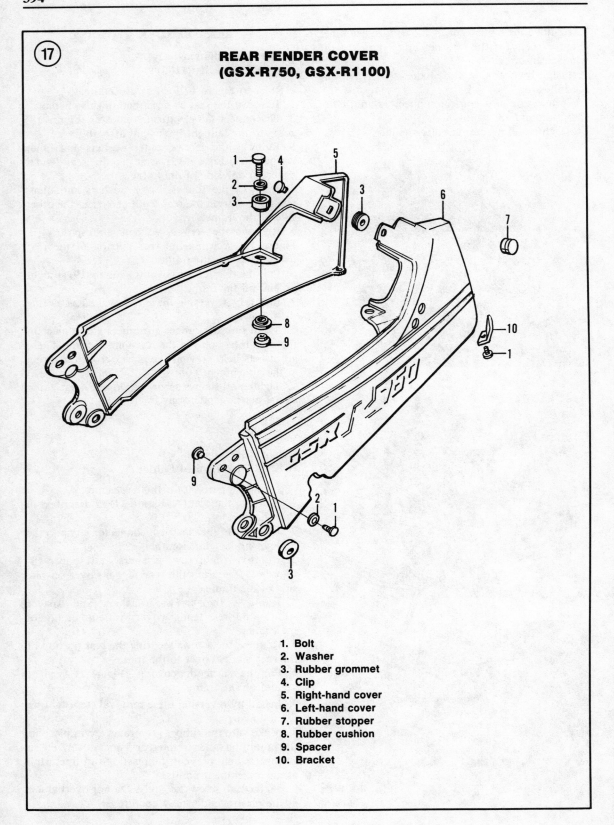

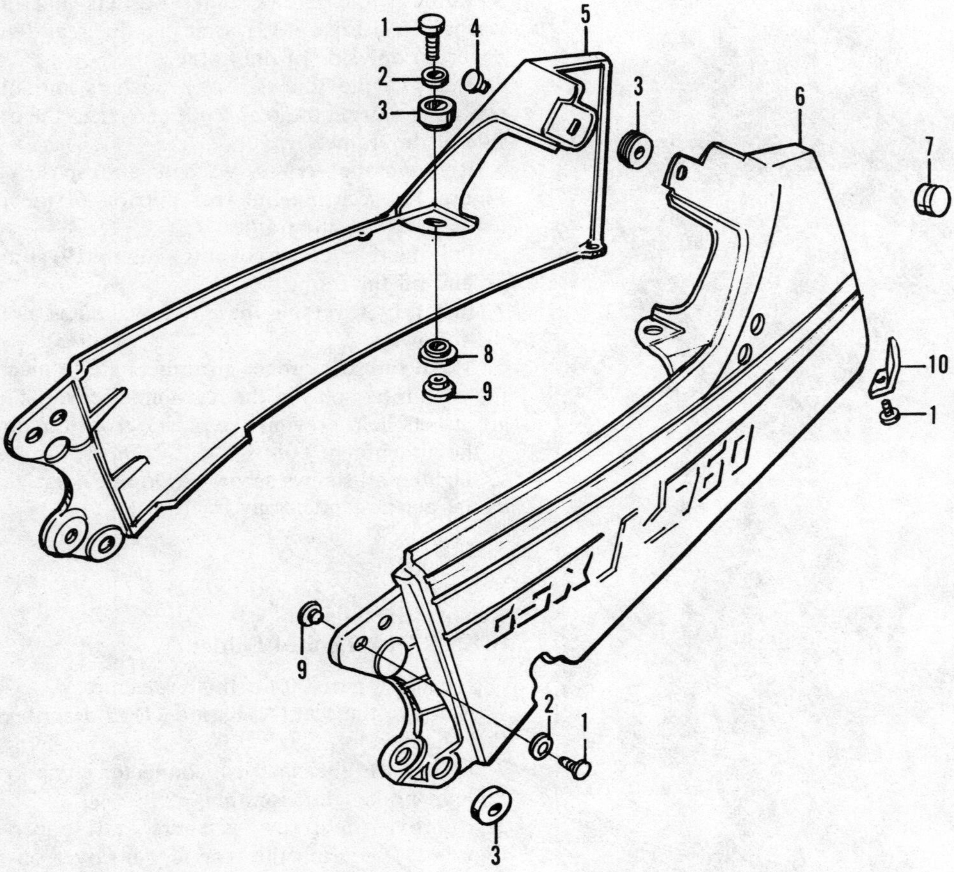

1. Bolt
2. Washer
3. Rubber grommet
4. Clip
5. Right-hand cover
6. Left-hand cover
7. Rubber stopper
8. Rubber cushion
9. Spacer
10. Bracket

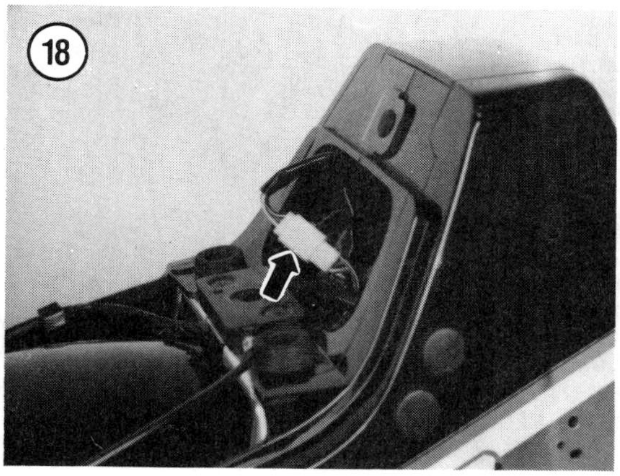

20

REAR FENDER COVER
(GSX-R750R LIMITED EDITION)

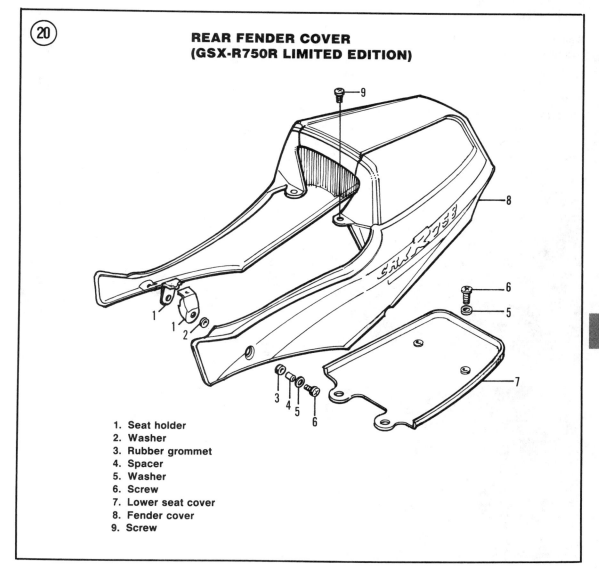

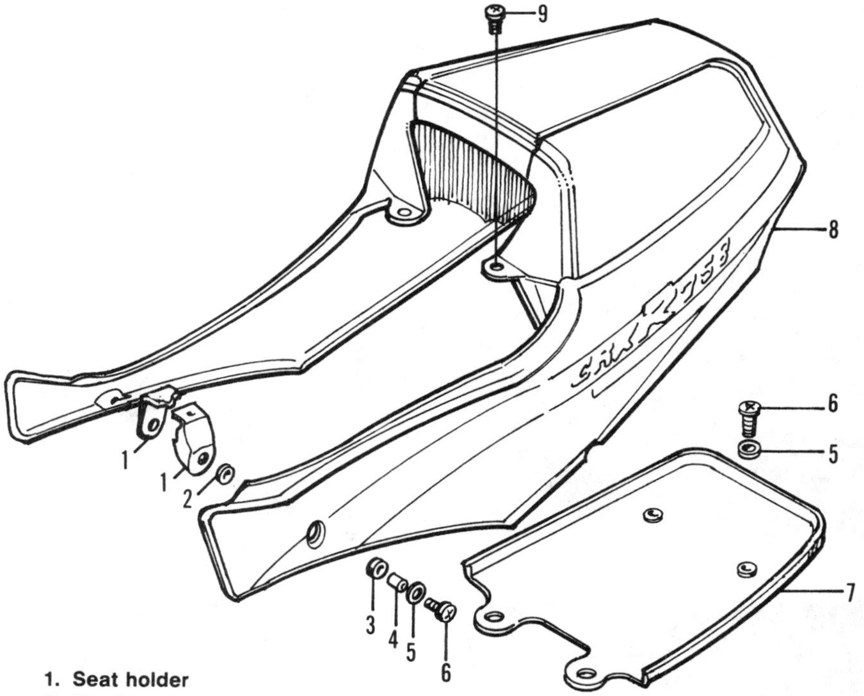

1. Seat holder
2. Washer
3. Rubber grommet
4. Spacer
5. Washer
6. Screw
7. Lower seat cover
8. Fender cover
9. Screw

FOOTPEGS

Front Footpeg Removal/Installation

1. Remove the E-clip from the end of the Allen bolt.
2. Remove the Allen bolt and washer (**Figure 22**) and nut securing the footpeg to the footpeg bracket.
3. Remove the footpeg from the mounting bracket and remove the spring and steel ball detent.
4. To remove the footpeg bracket, remove the bolts (**Figure 23**) securing the bracket to the frame and remove the assembly.
5. Install by reversing these removal steps, noting the following.
6. Tighten the bolt(s) securely and install the E-clip in the bolt groove.

Rear Footpeg Removal/Installation

1. Remove the Allen bolt (**Figure 24**) and nut securing the footpeg to the footpeg bracket.
2. Remove the footpeg from the mounting bracket and remove the spring and steel ball detent.
3. To remove the footpeg bracket, remove the bolts (**Figure 25**) securing the bracket to the frame and remove the assembly.

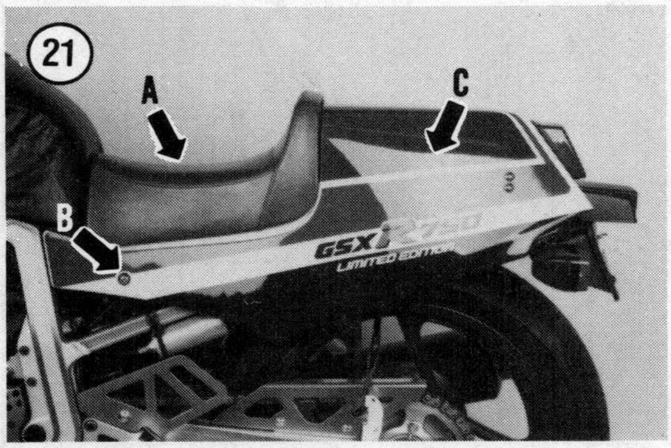

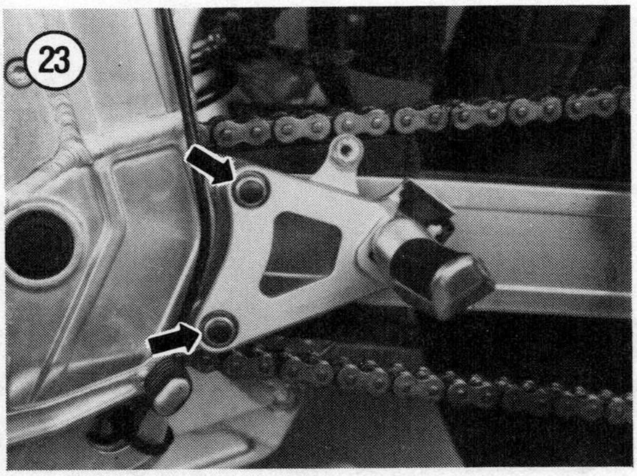

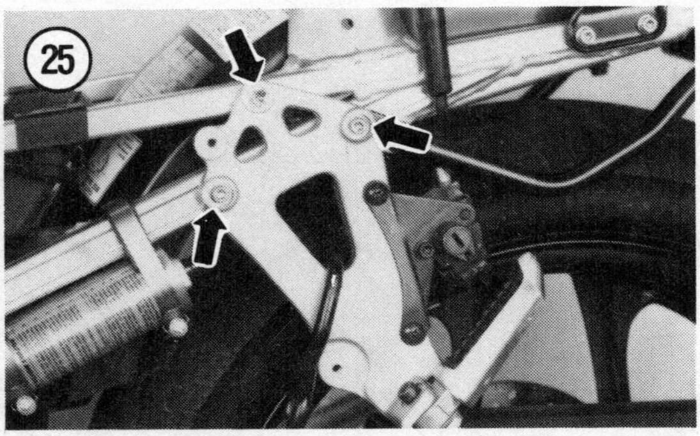

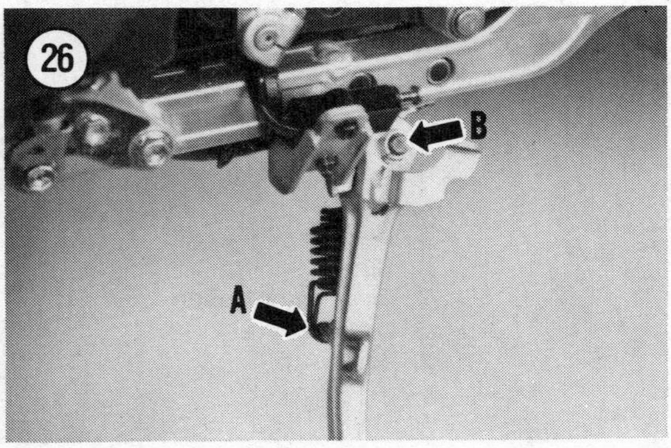

4. Install by reversing these removal steps, noting the following.
5. Tighten the bolt(s) securely.

SIDESTAND

1. Use Vise Grips and disconnect the return springs (A, **Figure 26**) from the pin on the sidestand.
2. Remove the bolt and nut (B, **Figure 26**) securing the sidestand to the frame mounting bracket.
3. Remove the sidestand from the frame.
4. Install by reversing these removal steps, noting the following.
5. Apply a light coat of multipurpose grease to the pivot points on the frame mounting area and the sidestand prior to installation.
6. Tighten the bolt and nut securely.

CHAPTER THIRTEEN

KATANA 600

This chapter contains all procedures and specifications unique to the Katana 600. If a specific procedure is not included, refer to the GSX-R750 procedure in prior chapters.

The headings in this chapter correspond to those in the other chapters of this book.

CHAPTER TWO

TROUBLESHOOTING

EMERGENCY TROUBLESHOOTING

When the bike is difficult to start or won't start at all, it does not help to wear down the battery with the starter. Check for obvious problems even before getting out your tools. Go down the following list step by step. Do each one; you may be embarrassed to find your engine stop switch is stuck in the OFF position, but that is better than wearing down the battery. If it still will not start, refer to the appropriate troubleshooting procedure which follows in this chapter.

WARNING
Do not use an open flame to check in the tank. A serious explosion is certain to result.

1. Is there fuel in the tank? Open the filler cap and rock the bike. Listen for fuel sloshing around.
2. Is the fuel shutoff valve (**Figure 1**) in the ON position and is the vacuum line to the valve from the engine still connected?
3. Make sure the engine stop switch (**Figure 2**) is not in the OFF position.

NOTE
In order to check the spark plug wire caps, it is necessary to remove the fuel tank as described in this chapter.

4. Are the spark plug wire caps on tight? Push all of them on and slightly rotate them to clean the electrical connection between the plug and the connector.
5. Is the choke in the correct position? On 1988 models, the knob (**Figure 3**) should be pulled *out* for a cold engine and pushed *in* for a warm engine. On 1989-on models, the lever should be pulled *down* for a cold engine and pushed *up* (**Figure 4**) for a warm engine.

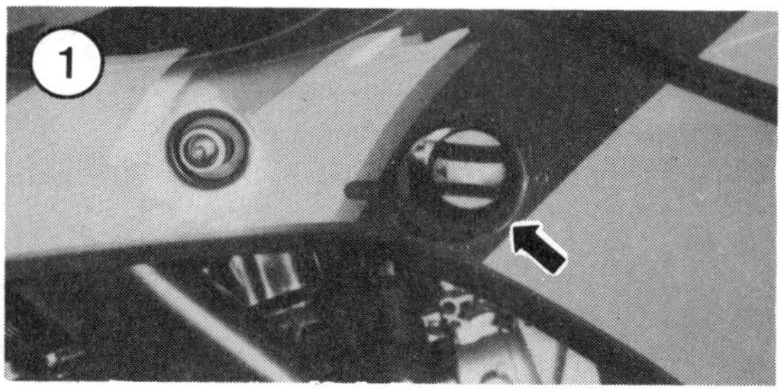

13

6. Has the circuit breaker tripped (**Figure 5**)? The circuit breaker protects the electrical system when the main circuit load exceeds the rated amperage. When an overload occurs, the red button pops out on the breaker face panel and the circuit is open. The circuit will remain open until the problem is solved and the breaker is reset. To reset, wait approximately 10 minutes for the circuit breaker to cool down, then push the red button in. If the red button pops out again, the problem still exists in the electrical system and must be corrected. Refer to Chapter Eight.

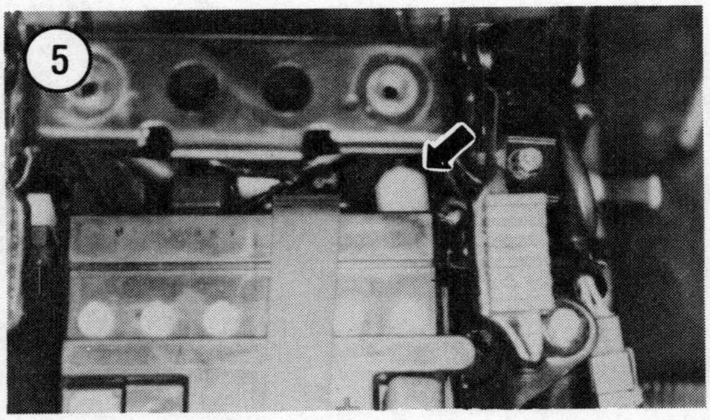

CHAPTER THREE

LUBRICATION, MAINTENANCE AND TUNE-UP

TIRES AND WHEELS

Tire Pressure

Tire pressure should be checked and adjusted to maintain the smoothness of the tire, good traction and handling and to get the maximum life out of the tire. A simple, accurate gauge (**Figure 6**) can be purchased for a few dollars and should be carried in your motorcycle tool kit. The recommended tire pressures are shown in **Table 1**.

NOTE

*After checking and adjusting the air pressure, make sure to install the air valve cap (**Figure 7**). The cap prevents small pebbles and dirt from collecting in the valve stem; this could allow air leakage or result in incorrect tire pressure readings.*

BATTERY

Removal, Installation and Electrolyte Level Check

Battery removal, installation and electrolyte level check is the same as on the GSX-R750 except for the routing of the breather tube. If the breather tube was removed, be sure to route it so that residue will not drain onto any part of the frame as shown in **Figure 8**.

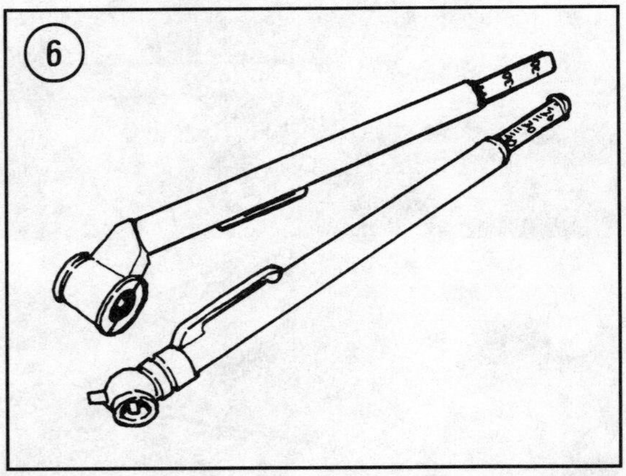

PERIODIC LUBRICATION

Engine Oil Level Check

Engine oil level is checked with the oil level inspection window, located at the right-hand side of the engine on the clutch cover.

1. Place the bike on level ground and secure in a vertical position.
2. Start the engine and let it idle for 2-3 minutes.
3. Shut off the engine and let the oil settle for 1-2 minutes.
4. Hold the bike in the true vertical position. A false reading will be given if the bike is tipped either to the right or left.

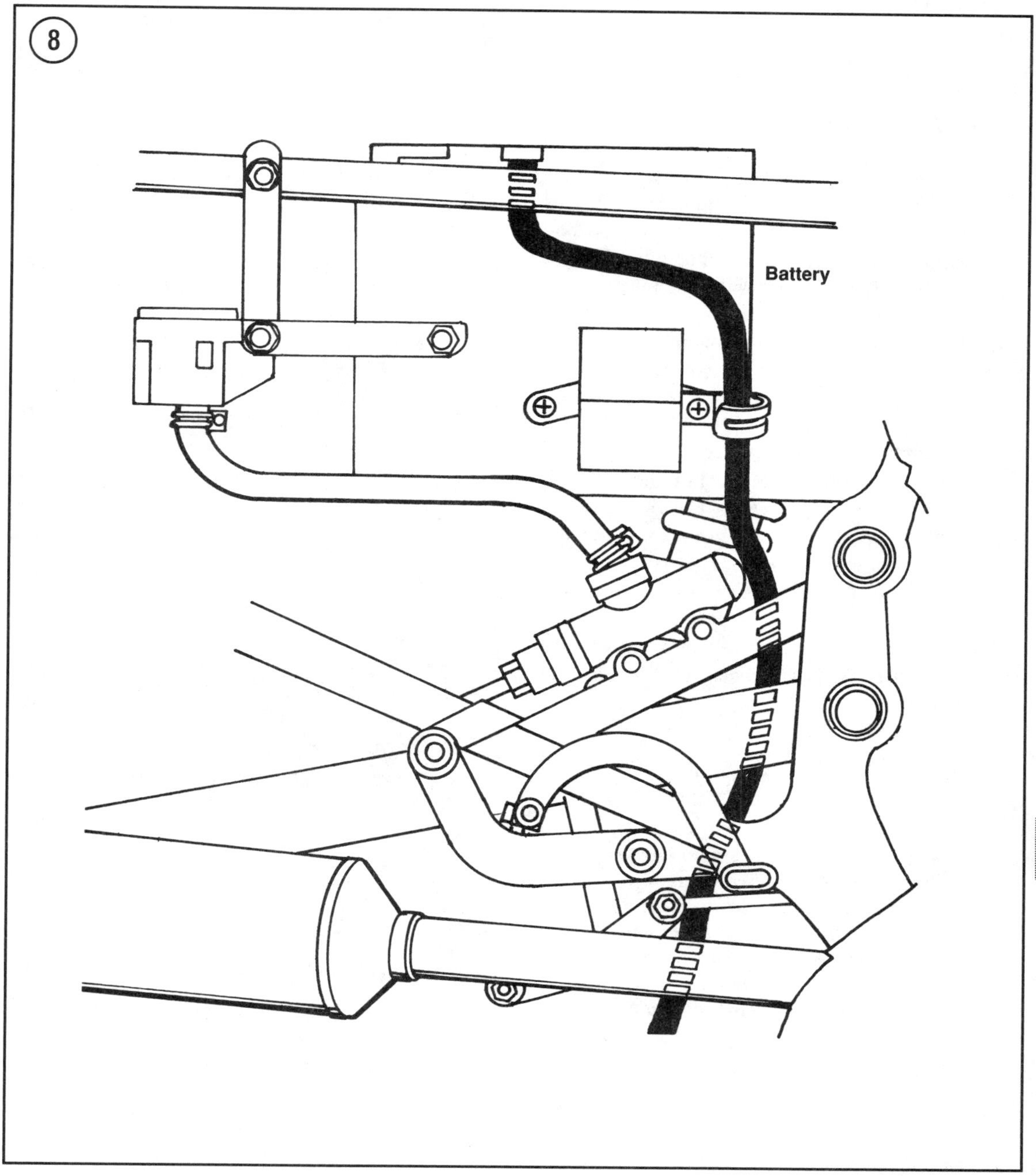

5. Look at the oil level inspection window. The oil level should be between the 2 lines (**Figure 9**). If the level is at or below the lower "L" line, perform the following:

a. Remove the screw and remove the oil filler cover (**Figure 10**).
b. Remove the dipstick/oil filler cap (**Figure 11**) and add the recommended type and weight engine oil to correct the level.
c. Reinstall the oil filler cap and the cover. Tighten the screw securely.

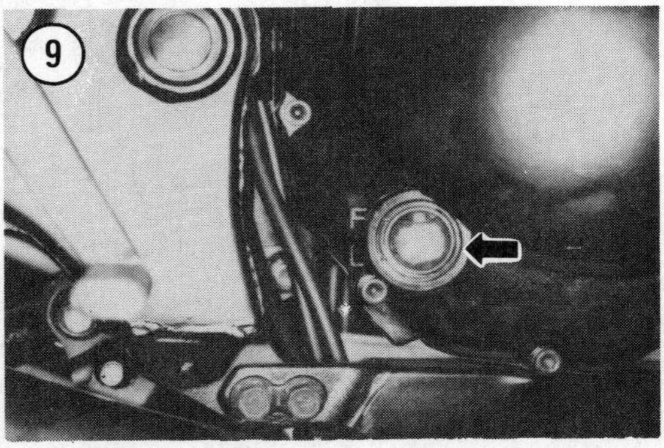
9

Engine Oil and Filter Change

Change the engine oil and the oil filter at the recommended oil change interval indicated in **Table 2**. This assumes that the motorcycle is operated in moderate climates. In extreme climates, oil should be changed every 30 days. The time interval is more important than the mileage interval because acids formed by combustion blowby will contaminate the oil even if the motorcycle is not run for several months. If the motorcycle is operated under dusty conditions, the oil will get dirty more quickly and should be changed more frequently than recommended.

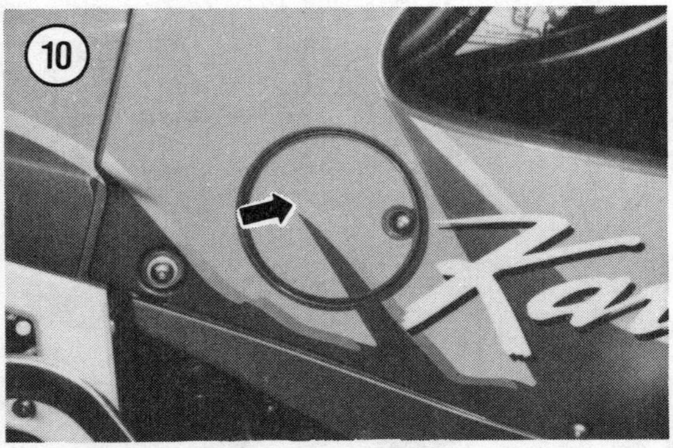
10

Use only a high-quality detergent motor oil with an API classification of SE or SF. The classification is stamped on top of the can or printed on the label on the plastic bottle (**Figure 12**). Try to use the same brand of oil at each change. Use of oil additives is not recommended as it may cause clutch slippage.

11

Refer to **Figure 13** for correct oil viscosity to use under anticipated ambient temperatures (not engine oil temperature).

CAUTION

Do not add any friction-reducing additives to the oil as they will cause clutch slippage. Also do not use an engine oil with graphite added. The use of graphite oil will void any applicable Suzuki warranty. It is not established at this time if graphite will build up on the clutch friction plates and cause clutch problems. Until further testing is done by the oil and motorcycle industries, do not use this type of oil.

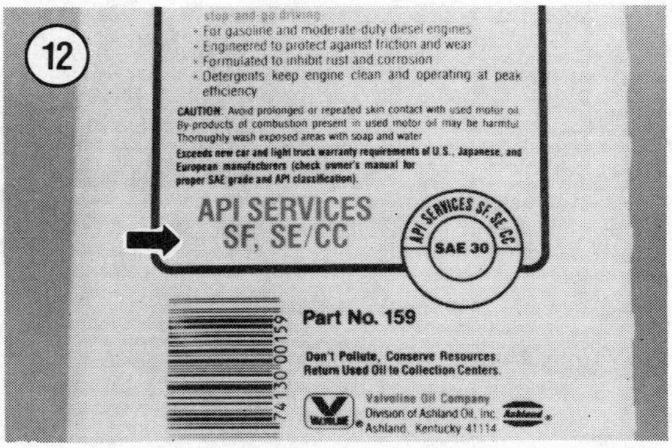

12

To change the engine oil and filter you will need the following:

a. Drain pan.

b. Funnel.
c. Can opener or pour spout (oil in cans).
d. 21 mm wrench (drain plug).

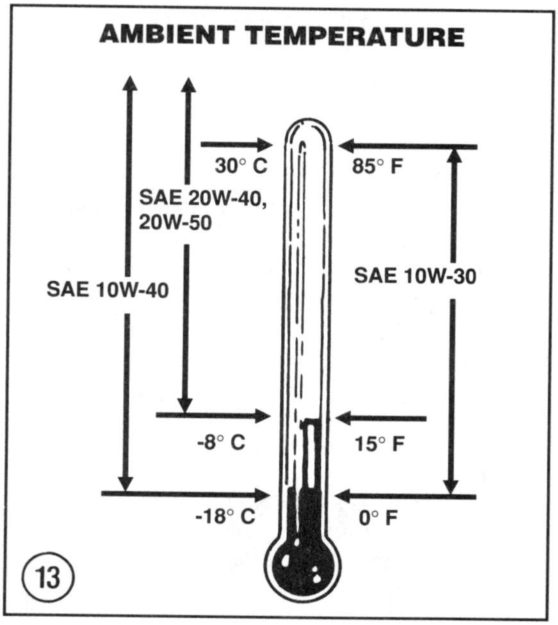

13

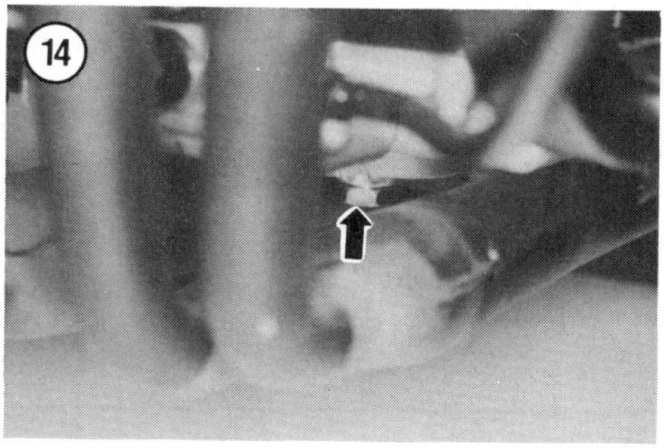

14

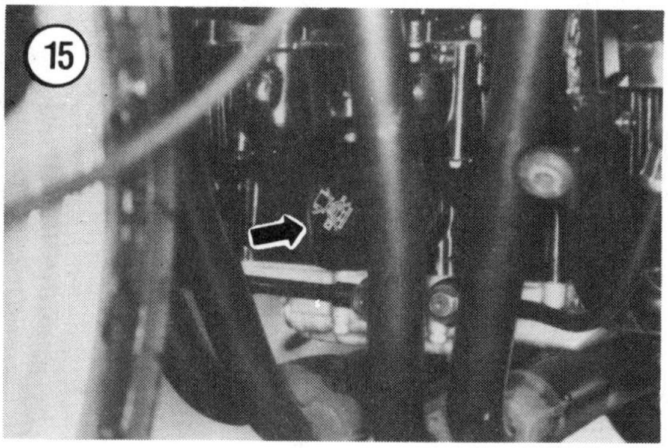

15

e. Oil filter wrench.
f. Oil (refer to **Table 3** for quantity).
g. Oil filter element.

NOTE
Never dispose of motor oil in the trash, on the ground, or down a storm drain. Many service stations accept used motor oil and waste haulers provide curbside used motor oil collection. Do not combine other fluids with motor oil to be recycled. To locate a recycler, contact the American Petroleum Institute (API) at ***www.recycleoil.org****.*

1. Start the engine and let it reach operating temperature; 15-20 minutes of stop-and-go riding is usually sufficient.
2. Turn the engine off and place the bike on level ground on the sidestand.
3. Remove the screw and remove the oil filler cover (**Figure 10**).
4. Remove the lower section of the fairing as described under *Front Fairing Removal/Installation* in this chapter.

WARNING
The exhaust system is hot; protect yourself accordingly while removing the drain plug.

5. Place a drain pan under the crankcase and remove the drain plug (**Figure 14**).
6. Remove the dipstick/oil filler cap (**Figure 11**): this will speed up the flow of oil.
7. Inspect the sealing washer on the crankcase drain plug. Replace if its condition is in doubt.
8. Install the drain plug and washer and tighten to specification shown in **Table 4.**
9. Move the drain pan under the oil filter at the front of the engine.

13

NOTE
Because the exhaust system (especially most after-market systems) is so close to the oilfiller there is very little working room for oil filter removal and installation. The easiest way to remove the oil filter is to use a Suzuki oil filter wrench (part No. 09915-40611) and a socket wrench.

10. Use the special tool and socket wrench and unscrew the oil filter (**Figure 15**) from the engine.

11. Clean off the oil filter mating surface on the crankcase with a shop rag and cleaning solvent. Remove any sludge or road dirt. Wipe it dry with a clean, lint-free cloth.

12. Apply a light coat of clean engine oil to the O-ring seal on the new oil filter (**Figure 16**).

13. Screw on the new oil filter by hand until the O-ring seal contacts the crankcase mating surface.

14. Make a mark on the face of the oil filter with a permanent marker pen so it can be easily seen. Position this mark at the 12 o'clock position and install the wrench on the oil filter. Tighten the oil filter 2 complete turns, then stop. The filter is now tight enough.

15. During oil filter removal, some oil may drip onto the exhaust pipes. Prior to starting the engine, wipe off any spilled oil with a shop cloth. If necessary, spray some electrical contact cleaner on the pipes to remove the oil residue. If the oil is not cleaned off, it will smoke once the exhaust pipes get hot.

16. Insert a long-necked funnel into the oil fill hole and fill the engine with the correct viscosity and quantity of oil. Refer to **Figure 13** and **Table 3**.

17. Install the dipstick/oil filler cap.

18. Install the oil filler cover and tighten the screw securely.

19. Start the engine, let it run at idle speed and check for leaks.

20. Turn the engine off and check for correct oil level; adjust as necessary to bring the oil level up to the "F" mark (**Figure 9**).

21. Install the lower section of the front fairing as described in this chapter.

Front Fork Oil Change (1988 Models)

It is a good practice to change the fork oil at the interval listed in **Table 2** or once a year. If it becomes contaminated with dirt or water, change it immediately.

These models are not equipped with a drain screw and it is necessary to remove both fork tubes as described under *Front Fork (1988 Models) Removal/Installation* in this chapter.

Add the recommended type and quantity of fork oil as specified in **Table 5**.

Front Fork Oil Change (1989-on)

It is a good practice to change the fork oil at the interval listed in **Table 2** or once a year. If it becomes contaminated with dirt or water, change it immediately.

1. Place the bike on the sidestand on level ground.
2. Remove the lower portion of the front fairing as described under *Front Fairing Removal/Installation* in this chapter.
3. Place wood block(s) under the crankcase between the exhaust pipes to position the bike securely with the front wheel off the ground.
4. Remove the upper fork cap bolt and rod (**Figure 17**) from the fork leg.
5. Remove the spacer and spring seat.
6. Place a drip pan under the fork slider.

CAUTION

Cover the brake discs with shop cloths or plastic. Do not allow the fork oil to contact the discs. If any oil comes in contact with them, clean off with lac-

16

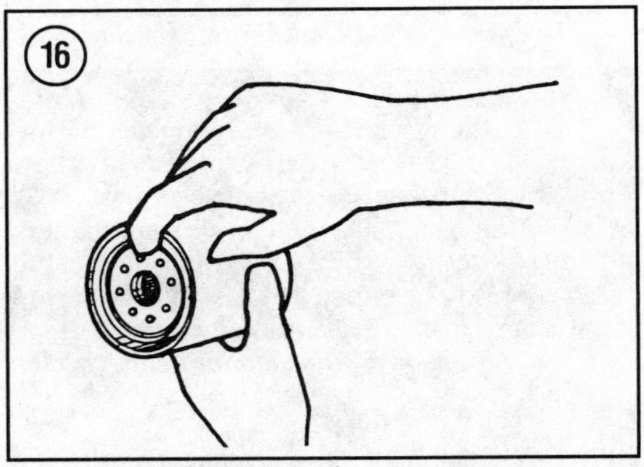

17

quer thinner or electrical contact cleaner. Remove all oil residue from the discs or the brake will be useless.

7. Remove the drain screw and sealing washer (**Figure 18**) from the slider.
8. Repeat Steps 4-7 for the other fork assembly.
9. Allow the fork oil to drain for at least 5 minutes. Never reuse fork oil.

CAUTION
Do not allow the fork oil to come in contact with any of the brake components.

10. Place a shop cloth around the top of the fork tube and the upper fork bridge to catch remaining fork oil while the fork spring is removed. Withdraw the fork spring from each fork tube.
11. Inspect the sealing washer for damage, replace if necessary.
12. Install the sealing washer and drain bolt on each fork slider. Tighten the bolts to the torque specification listed in **Table 4**.

NOTE
Suzuki recommends that the fork oil level be measured, if possible, to ensure a more accurate filling.

13. Remove the wood block(s) from under the engine and place the front wheel on the ground. Allow the front forks to compress completely.
14. Raise the rear of the motorcycle until the fork tubes are perfectly vertical. If it is inconvenient to raise the rear of the motorcycle, it will necessary to remove both fork tubes as described under *Front Fork (1989-on) Removal/Installation* in this chapter.

NOTE
To measure the correct amount of fluid, use a plastic baby bottle. These bottles have measurements in fluid ounces (oz.) and cubic centimeters (cc) on the side.

18

15. Add SAE 10W fork oil to achieve the recommended quantity of fork oil as specified in **Table 5**.
16. Use an accurate ruler or the Suzuki oil level gauge (part No. 09943-74111) to achieve the oil level as specified in **Table 5**.

NOTE
*An oil level measuring device can be made as shown in **Figure 19**. Position the lower edge of the hose clamp the specified oil level distance up from the small diameter hole. Fill the fork with a few cc's more than the required amount of oil. Position the hose clamp on the top edge of the fork tube and draw out the excess oil. Oil is sucked out until the level reaches the small diameter hole. A precise oil level can be achieved with this simple device.*

17. Allow the oil to settle completely and recheck the oil level measurement. Adjust the oil level if necessary.
18. Repeat Steps 15-17 for the other fork leg.
19. Reposition the wood block(s) under the crankcase between the exhaust pipes to position the bike securely with the front wheel off the ground.
20. Inspect the O-ring seal (**Figure 20**) on the fork cap bolt; replace if necessary.
21. Install the fork spring, spring seat and spacer into both forks.
22. Install the fork cap bolt and rod and align the flat in the end of the rod with the receptacle in the top of the damper rod. This alignment is necessary for proper fork adjustment procedures.
23. Start the fork cap bolt slowly while pushing down on the spring. Start the bolt slowly and don't cross-thread it. Tighten it securely.
24. Repeat Steps 19-23 for the other fork assembly.
25. Reinstall the lower portion of the front fairing.
26. Road test the bike and check for leaks.

Control Cables

The clutch control cable should be lubricated at the interval listed in **Table 2**. Follow the procedure relating to the GSX-R750R Limited Edition in Chapter Three.

Disc Brake Fluid Level

The fluid level should be up between the upper and lower mark within the reservoir. If the brake fluid level reaches the lower level mark, visible through the viewing port on the front master cylinder or on the side of the rear master cylinder reservoir through the opening in the right-hand side cover (**Figure 21**), the fluid level must be corrected by adding fresh brake fluid.

1. Place the bike on level ground and position the handlebars so the front master cylinder reservoir is level.
2. Remove the right-hand side cover in order to add fluid to the rear master cylinder.
3. Clean any dirt from the area around the top cover prior to removing the cover.
4. Remove the screws securing the top cover. Remove the top cover and the diaphragm. Refer to A, **Figure 22** for the front master cylinder or A, **Figure 23** for the rear master cylinder.
5. Add brake fluid until the level is to the upper level line within the master cylinder reservoir. Refer to B, **Figure 22** for the front master cylinder or B, **Figure 23** for the rear master cylinder. Use fresh brake fluid from a sealed brake fluid container.

WARNING

Use brake fluid from a sealed container and clearly marked DOT 4 only (speci-

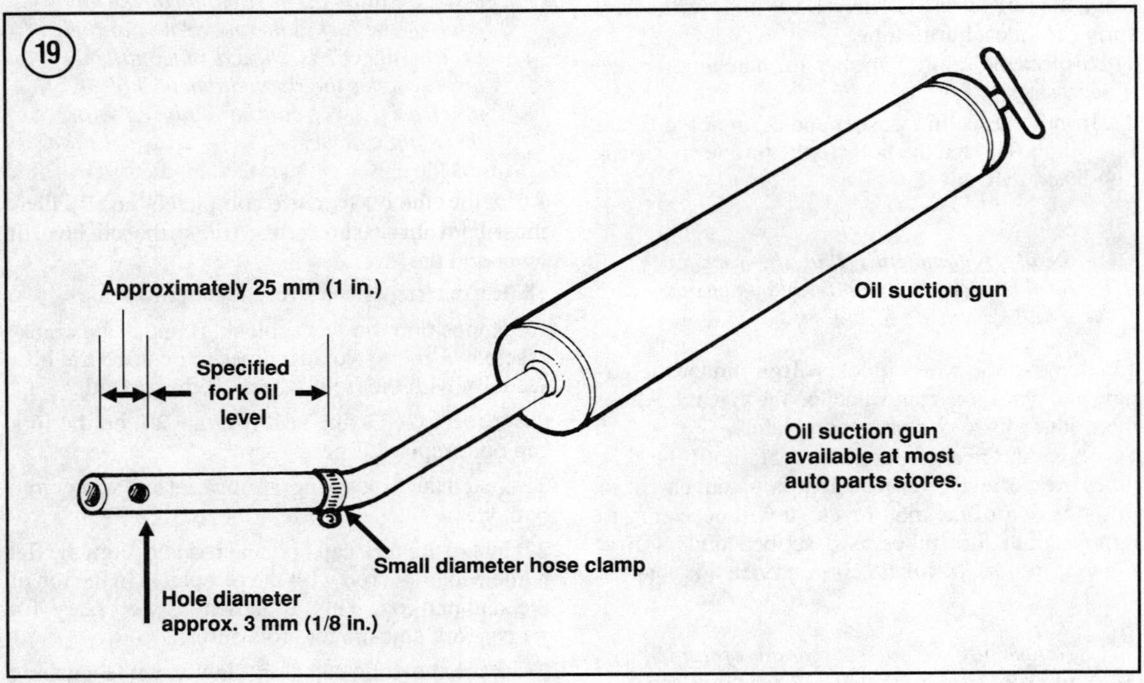

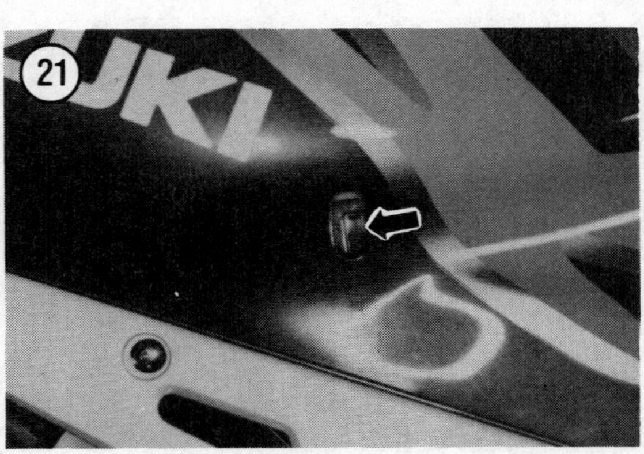

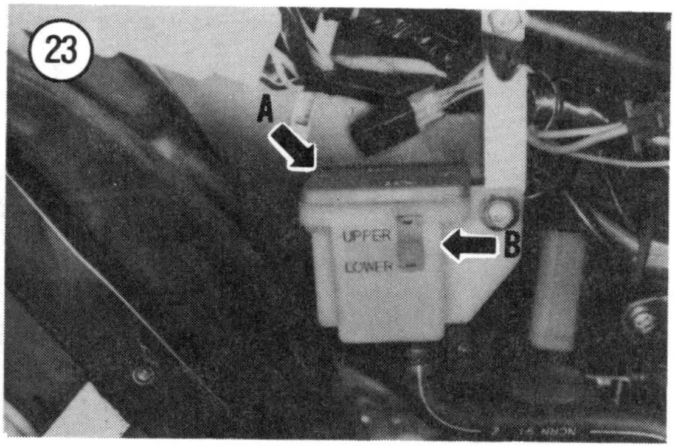

fied for disc brakes). Others may vaporize and cause brake failure. Do not intermix different brands or types of brake fluid as they may not be compatible. Do not intermix a silicone based (DOT 5) brake fluid as it can cause brake component damage leading to brake system failure.

CAUTION

Be careful when handling brake fluid. Do not spill it on painted or plated surfaces or plastic parts as it will destroy the surface. Wash the area immediately with soapy water and thoroughly rinse it off.

6. Reinstall the diaphragm and the top cover. Tighten the screws securely.
7. Install the right-hand side cover.

Clutch Adjustment

Adjust the clutch at the interval indicated in **Table 2**. For the clutch to engage and disengage fully, there must be 4 mm (0.16 in.) of free play between the lever and the lever housing.

1. At the clutch hand lever, loosen the locknut (A, **Figure 24**) and turn the upper adjuster (B, **Figure 24**) in all the way toward the hand grip.
2. Remove the left-hand lower section of the front fairing as described under *Front Fairing Removal/Installation* in this chapter.
3. At the lower adjuster on the drive sprocket cover, slide the rubber boot (A, **Figure 25**) up and off the adjuster.
4. Loosen the locknut (B, **Figure 25**) and if necessary turn the lower adjuster (C, **Figure 25**) to allow some play in the clutch hand lever.
5. Remove the clutch release cover (**Figure 26**) on the drive sprocket cover.

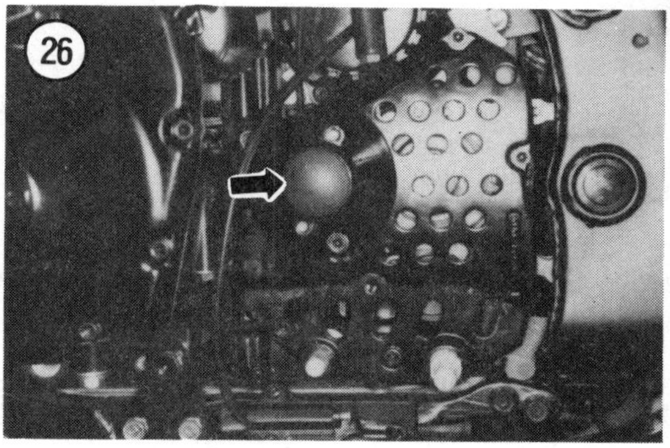

13

6. Loosen the locknut and back out the adjusting screw (**Figure 27**) 2 or 3 full rotations.

7. Slowly turn the adjusting screw in until high resistance is felt, stop at this point.

8. From the position in Step 7, turn the adjusting screw out 1/4 to 1/2 of a turn.

9. Hold the adjusting screw in this position and tighten the locknut. Do not allow the adjusting screw to move while tightening the locknut.

10. At the lower adjuster, turn the adjuster (C, **Figure 25**) to allow 4 mm (0.16 in.) of free play in the clutch hand lever. Tighten the lower locknut (B, **Figure 25**).

11. Install the clutch release cover and make sure it seats completely.

12. Install the left-hand lower section of the front fairing as described in this chapter.

13. Road test the bike to make sure the clutch fully disengages when the lever is pulled in; if it does not, the bike will creep in gear when stopped. Also make sure the clutch fully engages; if it does not, the clutch will slip, particularly when accelerating in high gear.

14. If the proper amount of adjustment cannot be achieved using this procedure, the cable has stretched to the point where it needs replacing. Refer to this chapter for the complete procedure.

Air Filter Element Removal/Cleaning/Installation

The air filter element should be removed and cleaned at the interval listed in **Table 2**. The air filter element should be replaced at the interval listed in **Table 2** or sooner if soiled, severely clogged or broken in any area.

1. Place the bike on the sidestand.

2. Remove the seat as described under *Seat Removal/Installation* in this chapter.

3. Remove the fuel tank as described under *Fuel Tank Removal/Installation* in this chapter.

4. Remove the screws securing the fuel tank bracket and remove the bracket (**Figure 28**).

5. Remove the screws securing the air filter element (A, **Figure 29**) in the air box. On models so equipped, disconnect the vacuum hoses (B, **Figure 29**) from the element.

6. Withdraw the element assembly from the air box.

7. Wipe out the interior of the air box (**Figure 30**) with a shop rag dampened with cleaning solvent. Remove any foreign matter that may have passed through a broken element.

8. Gently tap the air filter element to loosen the dust.

CAUTION

In the next step, do not direct compressed air toward the inside surface of the element. If air pressure is directed to the inside surface it will force the dirt and dust into the pores of the element thus restricting air flow.

9. Apply compressed air toward the *outside surface* of the element to remove all loosened dirt and dust from the element.

10. Inspect the element; if it is torn or damaged in any area it must be replaced. Do *not* run the bike with

27

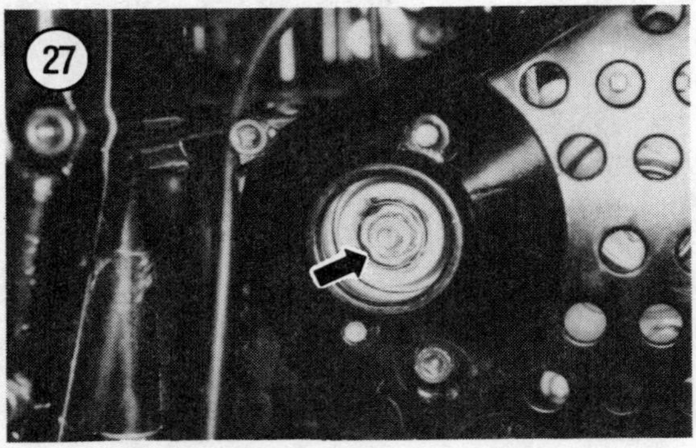

28

29

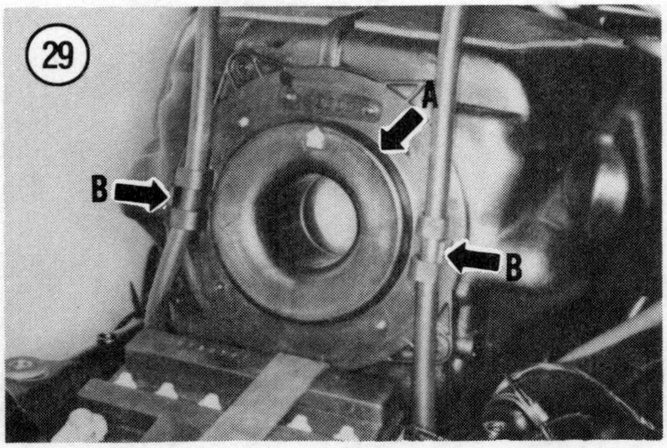

a damaged element as it may allow dirt to enter the engine.

11. Install the new air filter element and position it with the raised arrow (**Figure 31**) facing UP.

12. Make sure the element is correctly seated into the air box so there is no air leak, then install the screws and tighten securely.

13. On models so equipped, reconnect the vacuum hoses (B, **Figure 29**) onto the element.

14. Install the fuel tank bracket, fuel tank, side covers and the seat.

30

31

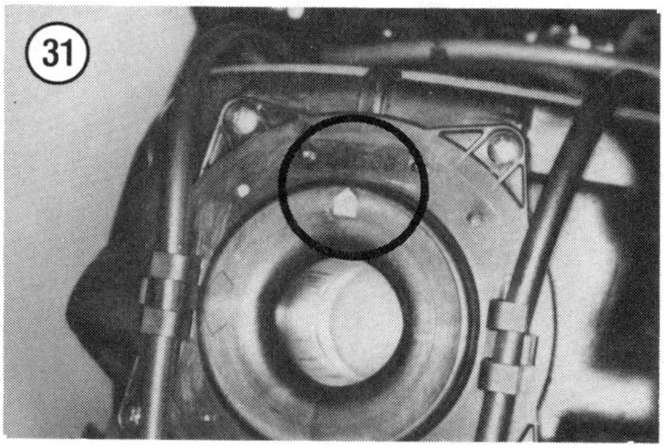

32

Fuel Shutoff Filter and Valve Removal/Installation

The fuel filter is built into the shutoff valve and removes particles which might otherwise enter into the carburetor and may cause the float needle to remain in the open position.

1. Remove the fuel tank as described under *Fuel Tank Removal/Installation* in this chapter.

2. If necessary, drain the fuel from the fuel tank into a clean and sealable metal container. If the fuel is kept clean, it can be reused.

3. Place an old blanket or several shop cloths on the workbench to protect the fuel tank's painted surface. Place the fuel tank on its side on these protective items.

4. Remove the screws and washers (**Figure 32**) securing the fuel shutoff valve to the fuel tank.

5. Remove the valve from the fuel tank. Don't lose the O-ring seal between the fuel tank and the valve.

6. After removing the valve from the fuel tank, insert a corner of a lint-free cloth into the opening in the tank to prevent the entry of foreign matter.

7. Clean the filter with a medium-soft toothbrush and blow out with compressed air. Replace the filter if it is broken in any area.

8. Install by reversing these removal steps while noting the following:

   a. Be sure to install the O-ring seal between the shutoff valve and the fuel tank. Tighten the screws securely.

   b. Install the fuel tank as described in this chapter.

   c. Start the engine and check for fuel leaks.

Evaporative Emission Control System (California Models Only)

Fuel vapor from the fuel tank is routed into a charcoal canister when the engine is stopped. When the engine is started, these vapors are drawn, through the vacuum controlled valves, into the carburetors and into the engine to be burned. Make sure all vacuum hoses are correctly routed and attached. Inspect the hoses and replace any if necessary.

Refer to *Evaporative Emission Control System (California Models Only)* later in this chapter for detailed information on the evaporative emission control system and for vacuum hose routing.

Air Suction System (California Models Only)

The air suction system consists of a vacuum switch, 2 air suction valves (reed valves) and air and vacuum hoses. This system does not pressurize air, but uses the momentary pressure differentials generated by the exhaust gas pulses to introduce fresh air into the exhaust ports. Make sure all air and vacuum hoses are correctly routed and attached. Inspect the hoses and replace any if necessary.

Refer to *Air Suction System (California Models Only)* later in this chapter for detailed information on the evaporative emission control system and for vacuum hose routing.

Front Suspension Check

1. Apply the front brake and pump the forks up and down as vigorously as possible. Check for smooth operation and check for any oil leaks.
2. Make sure the upper (**Figure 33**) and lower (**Figure 34**) fork bridge bolts are tight.
3. Remove the trim cap (**Figure 35**). Make sure the bolt securing each handlebar is tight and that the handlebars are secure.
4. Make sure the screws securing the handlebar balancer weights are tight and secure.
5. Make sure the front axle nut is tight and that the cotter pin is in place (**Figure 36**).

CAUTION

If any of the previously mentioned bolts and nuts are loose, refer to the Chapter Nine section of this chapter for correct procedures and torque specifications.

Rear Suspension Check

1. Place the bike on the sidestand.
2. Remove the lower portion of the front fairing as described under *Front Fairing Removal/Installation* in this chapter.
3. Place wood block(s) under the crankcase between the exhaust pipes to support the bike securely with the rear wheel off the ground.
4. Have an assistant hold onto the bike and then push hard on the rear wheel (sideways) to check for side play in the rear swing arm bearings.
5. Check the tightness of the shock absorber upper (**Figure 37**) and lower (**Figure 38**) mounting bolts and nuts.

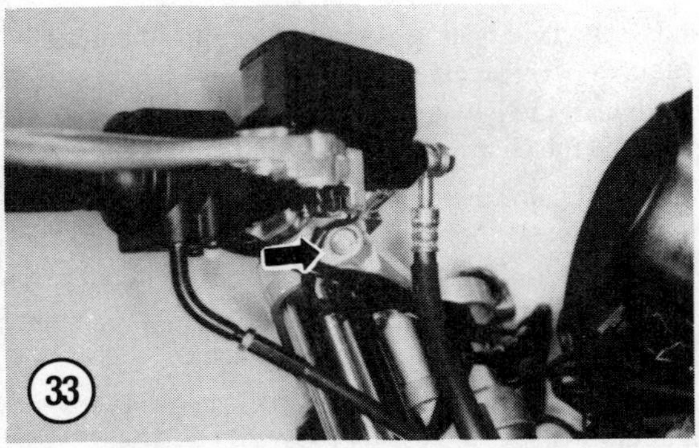
33

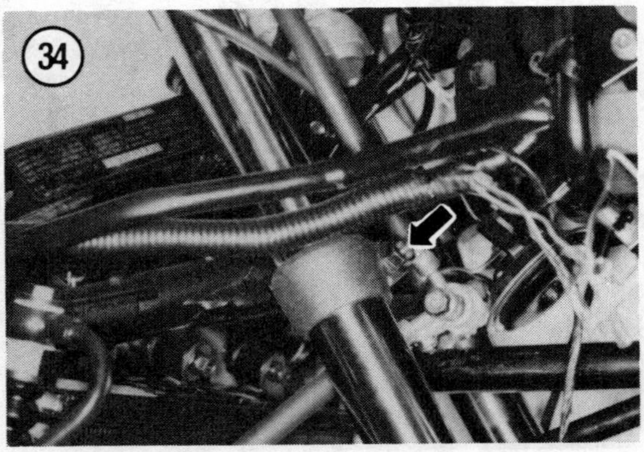
34

35

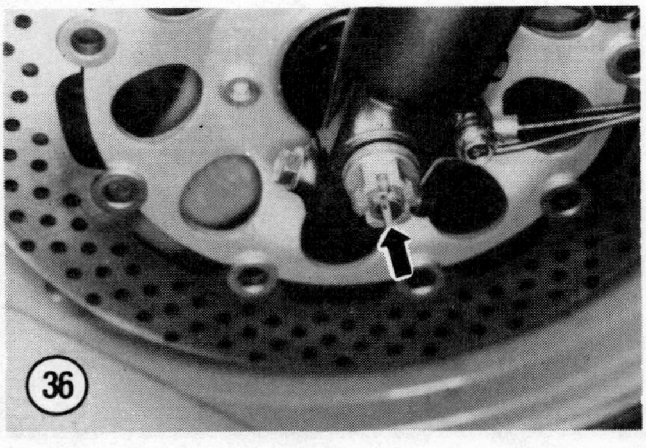
36

37

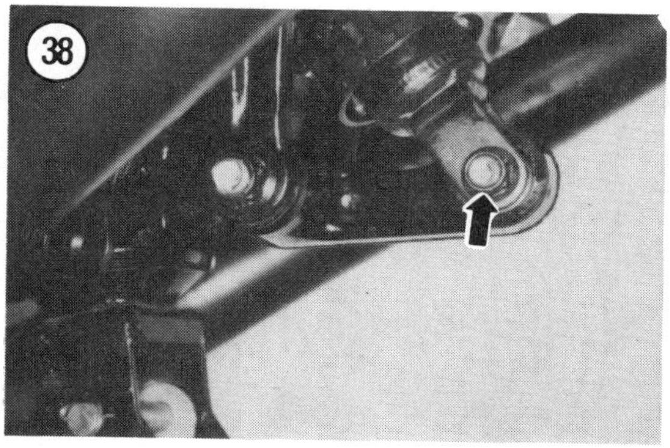

38

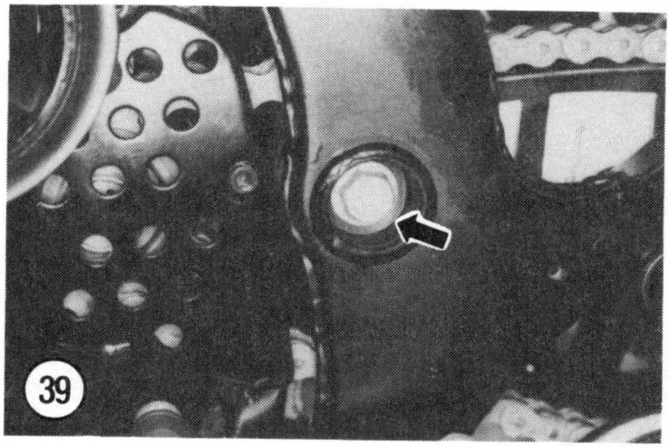

39

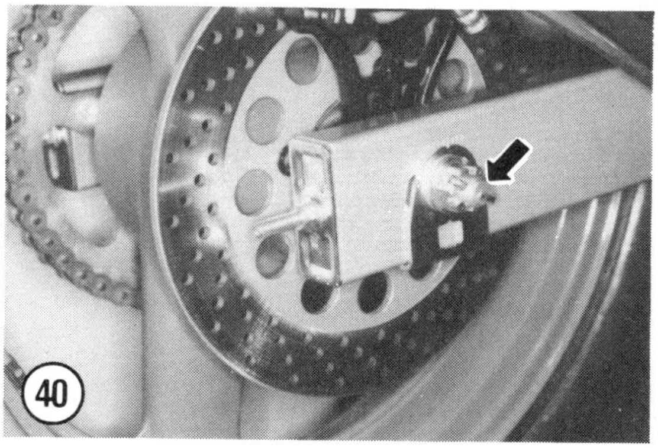

40

6. Remove the plastic cap and make sure the swing arm pivot bolt (**Figure 39**) and nut are tight.
7. Check the tightness of the shock absorber lever assembly bolts and nuts.
8. Make sure the rear axle nut is tight and that the cotter pin is in place (**Figure 40**).
9. Check the tightness of the rear brake torque arm bolts and nuts. Make sure the cotter pins are in place.
10. Reinstall the lower portion of the front fairing.

CAUTION
If any of the previously mentioned bolts and nuts are loose, refer to the Chapter Ten section of this chapter for correct procedures and torque specifications.

TUNE-UP

Valve Clearance Measurement and Adjustment (1988-1991)

Refer to the valve adjustment procedure in Chapter Three of the main body.

Valve Clearance Measurement (1992-on)

Valve clearance measurement and adjustment must be performed with the engine cool, at room temperature (below 35° C/95° F). The correct valve clearance for all models is listed in **Table 6**. The exhaust valves are located at the front of the engine and the intake valves are located at the rear of the engine. There are 2 intake valves and 2 exhaust valves per cylinder.

For this procedure, the camshaft lobes must face away from the cam follower surface of the rocker arm as shown in **Figure 41**.

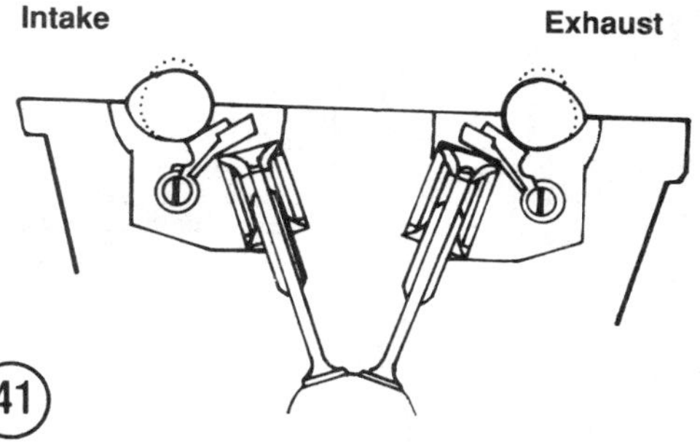

41

13

1. Remove the cylinder head cover as described under *Cylinder Head Cover Removal/Installation* in this chapter.
2. Remove all spark plugs. This will make it easier to rotate the engine.
3. Remove the bolts securing the signal generator cover (**Figure 42**) and remove the cover and gasket.

CAUTION
In the next step, rotate the engine with a 17 mm wrench on the flats on the signal generator rotor (A, ***Figure 43****). Do* ***not*** *use the Allen bolt (B,* ***Figure 43****) that secures the rotor to the crankshaft, as the bolt may shear off.*

4. Use a 17 mm wrench on the signal generator rotor (A, **Figure 43**). Rotate the engine *clockwise*, as viewed from the right-hand side of the bike, until the signal generator rotor "T" mark aligns with the cen-

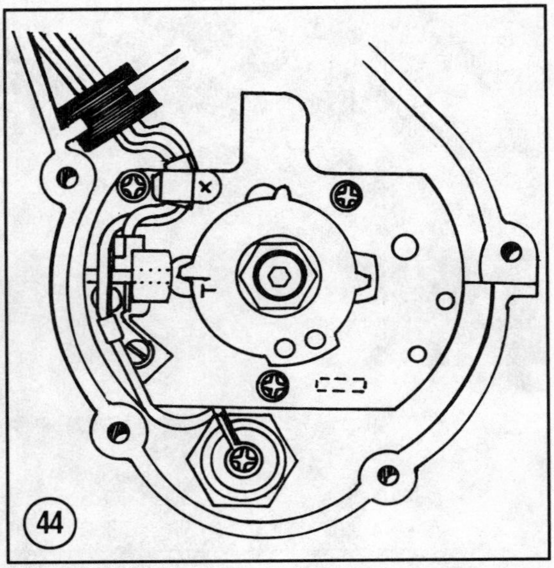

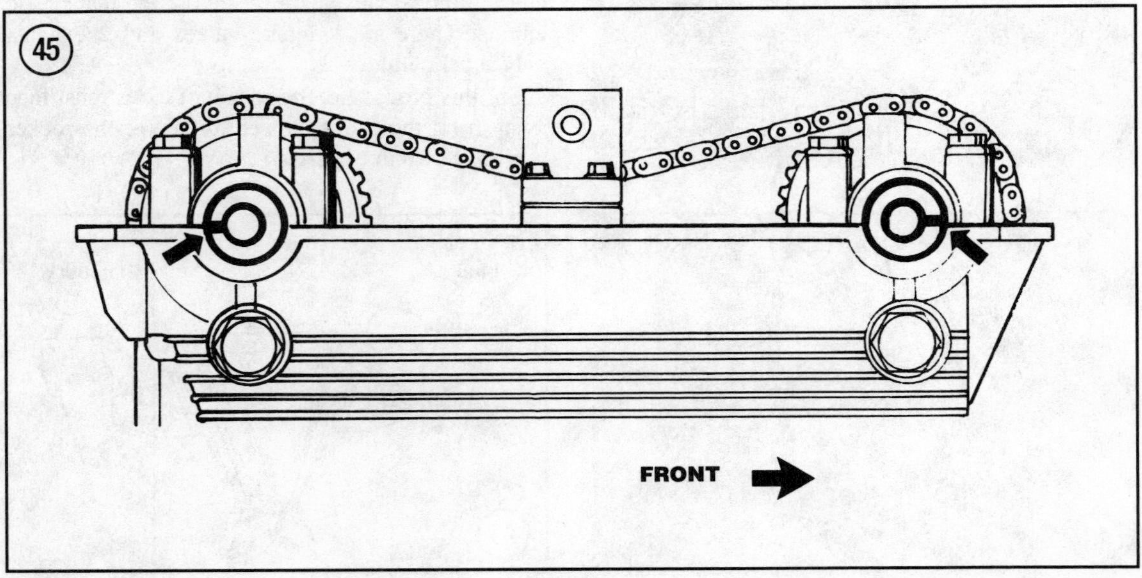

ter of the pickup coil (**Figure 44**). Also, the notch on the right-hand end of both the intake and exhaust camshafts must point *away* from the engine (**Figure 45**). If the camshafts are not in this position; rotate the engine 360° (one full turn) until the notches are pointing *away* from the engine. Also make sure the "T" mark is still aligned correctly.

NOTE
The cylinders are numbered 1, 2, 3 and 4 from left-to-right. The left-hand side refers to a rider sitting on the seat looking forward.

5. With the engine in this position, check the clearance of the intake and exhaust valves indicated in C, **Figure 46**. The valves to be checked are as follows:

47

a. Cylinder No. 1: intake and exhaust valves.

b. Cylinder No. 2: exhaust valves.

c. Cylinder No. 3: intake valves.

6. Check the clearance by inserting a flat feeler gauge between the shim and the rocker arm (**Figure 47**). When the clearance is correct, there will be a slight drag on the feeler gauge when it is inserted and withdrawn. Write the clearance on a piece of paper and identify it as to cylinder number and intake or exhaust valves. This clearance dimension will be used during the adjustment procedure, if adjustment is necessary.

7. To correct the valve clearance, the shim on top of the spring retainer must be replaced with a shim of a different thickness. The shims are available from a Suzuki dealer in 0.05 mm increments that range from 2.30 to 3.50 mm in thickness.

8. If any of the valves in this group require adjustment, do so at this time with the engine in this position. Refer to *Valve Clearance Adjustment (1992-on)* in the following procedure.

9. Use a 17 mm wrench on the signal generator rotor (A, **Figure 43**). From the position in Step 4; rotate the engine 360° (one full turn) *clockwise* until the signal generator rotor "T" mark again aligns with the center of the pickup coil (**Figure 44**). Also the notch on the right-hand end of both the intake and exhaust camshafts must point *in* toward the engine (**Figure 48**).

46

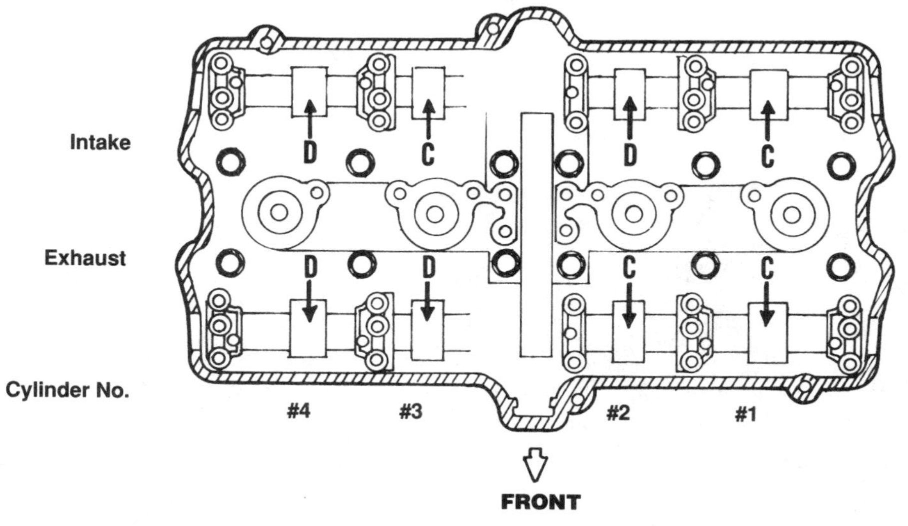

13

10. With the engine in this position, check the clearance of the intake and exhaust valves indicated in D, **Figure 46**. The valves to be checked are as follows:
   a. Cylinder No. 2: intake valves.
   b. Cylinder No. 3: exhaust valves.
   c. Cylinder No. 4: intake and exhaust valves.

11. Check the clearance by inserting a flat feeler gauge between the shim and the rocker arm (**Figure 47**). When the clearance is correct, there will be a slight drag on the feeler gauge when it is inserted and withdrawn. Write the clearance on a piece of paper and identify it as to cylinder number and intake or exhaust valves. This clearance dimension will be used during the adjustment procedure, if adjustment is necessary.

12. If any of the valves in this group require adjustment, do so at this time with the engine in this position. Refer to *Valve Clearance Adjustment (1992-on)* in the following procedure.

Valve Clearance Adjustment (1992-on)

For calculations, use the mid-point of the specified clearance. For example, if the intake valve clearance is 0.10-0.20 mm, then the mid-point would be 0.15 mm. If the exhaust valve clearance is 0.15-0.25 mm, then the mid-point would be 0.20 mm.

NOTE

If working on a well run-in engine (high mileage), measure the thickness of the old shim with a micrometer to make sure of the exact thickness of the shim. If the shim is worn to less than the indicated thickness marked on it, it will throw off calculations for a new shim. Also meas-

48

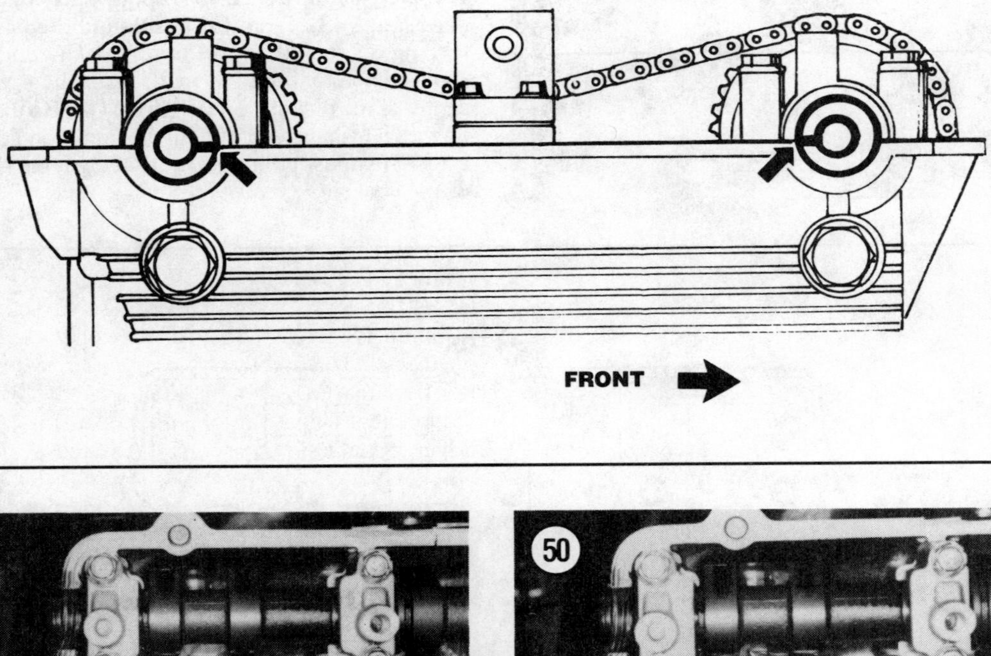

49

50

51

ure the new shim to make sure it is marked correctly.

1. Use a suitable tool and carefully slide the rocker arm (**Figure 49**) off the tappet shim and rest it on the spring retainer (**Figure 50**).
2. Use a magnetic tool and remove the shim from the spring retainer (**Figure 51**).
3. Check the number printed on the shim (**Figure 52**). If the number is no longer legible, measure it with a micrometer (**Figure 53**).

NOTE
*The following numbers are for **example only**. Use the numbers written down during the **Valve Clearance Measurement** procedure.*

Examples:	**Intake**	**Exhaust**
Actual measured clearance	0.52 mm	0.39 mm
Subtract specified clearance	0.20 mm	0.20 mm
Equals excess clearance	0.32 mm	0.19 mm
Existing shim number	220	245
Add excess clearance	+32	+19
	252	264
Equals new shim number (round off to the nearest shim number)	250	265

4. Apply clean engine oil to both sides of the new shim and to the receptacle in the spring retainer (**Figure 54**). Install the shim with the printed number facing down toward the spring retainer. Make sure the shim is correctly positioned within the spring retainer—it cannot be cocked or the spring retainer will be damaged. After the shim is installed (**Figure 55**), rotate it with a pair of tweezers or small screwdriver to make sure it is correctly seated.

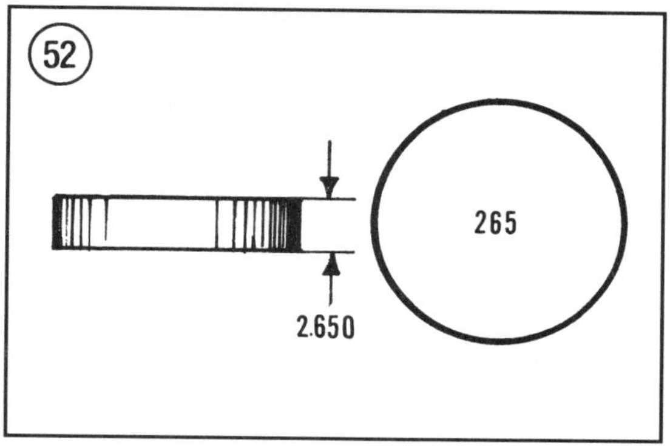

52

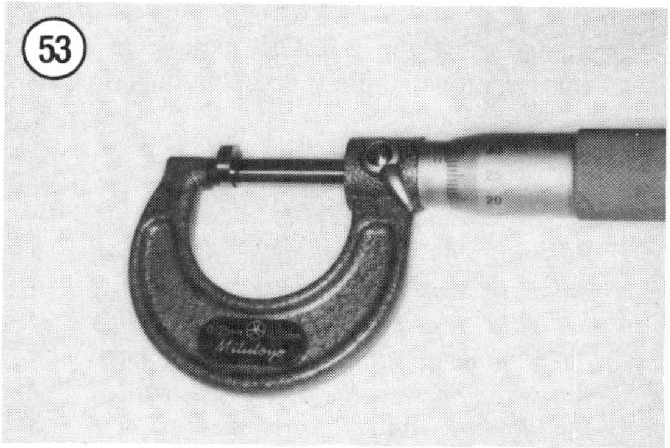
53

54

55

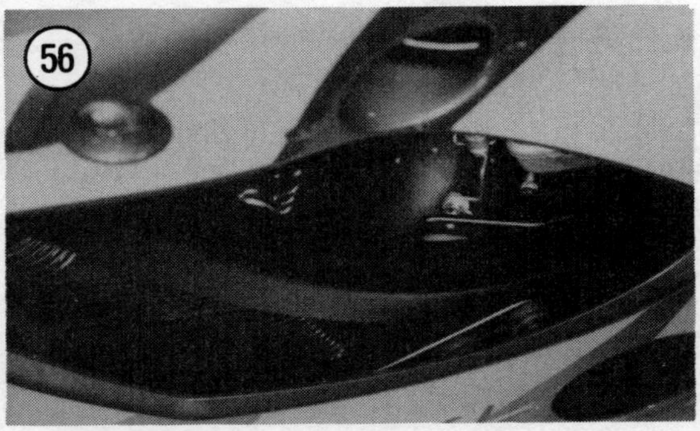

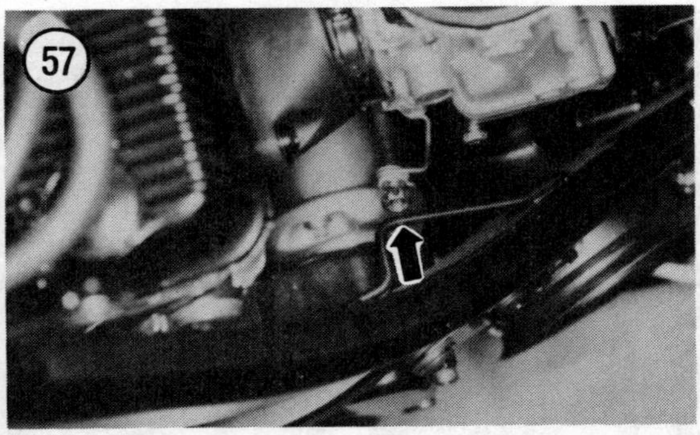

5. Use a suitable tool to slide the rocker arm back onto the tappet shim.
6. Repeat this procedure for all valve assemblies that are out of specification.
7. After all valve clearances have been adjusted, use a 17 mm wrench on the signal generator rotor (A, **Figure 43**) and rotate the engine *clockwise* several complete revolutions to seat the shims and to squeeze out any excess oil between the shim and the spring retainer.
8. Reinspect all valve clearances as described in the preceding procedure. If any of the clearances are still not within specification, repeat this procedure until all clearances are correct.
9. Install the cylinder head cover as described in this chapter.
10. Install the signal generator cover and gasket (**Figure 42**). Install and tighten the bolts securely.
11. Connect the crankcase breather hose onto the cylinder head cover.
12. Install the front fairing as described in this chapter.
13. Install the fuel tank as described in this chapter.
14. Install the seat as described in this chapter.

Carburetor Idle Speed Adjustment

Before making this adjustment, the air filter element must be clean and the engine must have adequate compression. See *Compression Test* in Chapter Three of the main body. Otherwise this procedure cannot be done properly.

1. Start the engine and let reach normal operating temperature. Make sure the choke knob (1988) or lever (1989-on) is in the open position (for warm engine).

2. Connect a portable tachometer following the manufacturer's instructions.

3. Through the opening in the left-hand fairing (**Figure 56**), turn the idle adjust knob (**Figure 57**) in or out to adjust idle speed.

4. The correct idle speed is listed in **Table 6**.

5. Open and close the throttle a couple of times; check for variations in idle speed. Readjust if necessary.

WARNING
*With the engine running at idle speed, move the handlebar from side to side. If the idle speed increases during this movement, the throttle cable may need adjusting or it may be incorrectly routed through the frame. Correct this problem immediately. Do **not** ride the bike in this unsafe condition.*

Table 1 TIRE INFLATION PRESSURE (COLD)*

Load	Tire Pressure Front psi	Front kPa	Rear psi	Rear kPa
Solo riding	33	225	36	250
Dual riding	33	225	36	250

*Tire inflation pressure for factory equipped tires. Aftermarket tires may require different inflation pressure.

Table 2 MAINTENANCE SCHEDULE*

Prior to each ride	Inspect tires and rims and check inflation pressure Check steering for smooth operation with no excessive play or restrictions Check brake operation and for fluid leakage Check fuel supply. Make sure there is enough fuel for the intended ride Check for fuel leakage Check all lights for proper operation Check engine oil level Check for smooth throttle operation Check gearshift lever operation Check clutch operation Inspect drive chain Check drive chain tension, adjust if necessary Check drive chain slider for wear
Every 600 miles (1,000 km)	Inspect, clean and lubricate drive chain
Every 2,000 miles (3,000 km) or 12 months	Clean and inspect the air filter element
Every 4,000 miles (6,000 km) or 12 months	Tighten cylinder head nuts and exhaust pipe nuts Replace the air filter element Inspect and adjust if necessary the valve clearance Check and adjust idle speed Clean and inspect spark plugs Replace engine oil and filter Check and adjust clutch operation and free play Inspect brake hoses (front and rear) for leakage Check electrolyte level in battery, add water if necessary Check brake fluid level in both brake master cylinders Inspect fuel lines for damage or leakage Inspect evaporation emission lines for damage or leakage (California models) Inspect air suction system lines for damage or leakage (California models) Check all brake system components Inspect the brake pads for wear Check and tighten the axle nuts Lubricate control cables Inspect and lubricate drive chain Inspect drive and driven sprockets for wear and mounting tightness
Every 7,500 miles (12,000 km) or 24 months	Inspect steering head bearings Check all suspension components for wear or damage Replace all spark plugs
Every 2 years	Drain and replace hydraulic brake fluid
Every 4 years	Replace all brake hoses Replace fuel lines Replace evaporative emission lines (California models)

* This Suzuki factory maintenance schedule should be considered a guide to general maintenance and lubrication intervals. Harder than normal use and exposure to mud, water, sand, high humidity, etc. will naturally dictate more frequent attention to most maintenance items.

Table 3 ENGINE OIL CAPACITY

Oil change			Oil and filter change			Overhaul		
Liters	U.S. qt.	Imp. qt.	Liters	U.S. qt.	Imp. qt.	Liters	U.S. qt.	Imp. qt.
3.6	3.8	3.2	3.8	4.0	3.3	5.0	5.3	4.4

Table 4 MAINTENANCE AND TUNE-UP TORQUE SPECIFICATIONS

Item	N·m	ft.-lb.
Oil drain plug	20-25	14-18
Fork drain bolts (1989-on models)	6-9	4.5-6.5
Cylinder head nuts	35-40	25-29
Cylinder head bolts	8-12	6-9
Cylinder block nut	7-11	5-8
Cylinder head cover bolts (all)	13-15	9-11
Oil hose fitting Allen bolts	8-12	6-9

Table 5 FRONT FORK OIL CAPACITY* AND DIMENSION

	Capacity			Distance	
Year	cc	U.S. oz.	Imp. oz.	mm	in.
1988	460	15.5	16.2	134	5.28
1989-on	478	16.1	16.9	100	3.93

* Each fork leg.

Table 6 TUNE-UP SPECIFICATIONS

Valve clearance	
1988-1991	
Intake and exhaust	0.10-0.15 mm (0.004-0.006 in.)
1992-on	
Intake	0.10-0.20 mm (0.004-0.008 in.)
Exhaust	0.15-0.25 mm (0.006-0.010 in.)
Spark plug type	
Standard heat range	NGK DR8ES
Plug gap	0.6-0.7 mm (0.024-0.028 in.)
Idle speed	1,300 ±100 rpm
Firing order	1, 2, 4, 3
Ignition timing	
1990-on California models	7° BTDC below 1,500 rpm
All other models	13° BTDC below 1,500 rpm

CHAPTER FOUR

ENGINE

ENGINE REMOVAL/INSTALLATION

1. Remove the seat as described under *Seat Removal/Installation* in this chapter.

2. Remove the front fairing as described under *Front Fairing Removal/Installation* in this chapter.

3. Remove the fuel tank as described under *Fuel Tank Removal/Installation* in this chapter.

4. Remove the battery as described under *Battery Removal/Installation* in Chapter Three of the main body.

5. Remove the exhaust system (A, **Figure 58**) as described under *Exhaust System Removal/Installation* in this chapter.

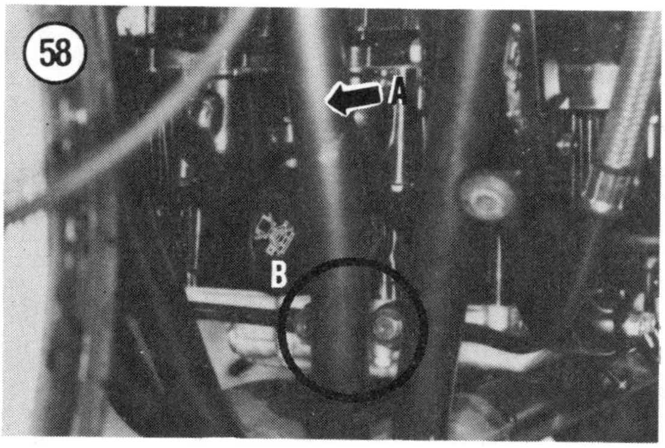

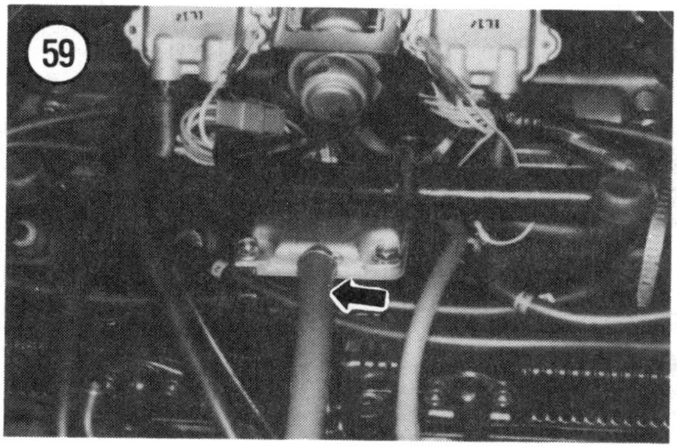

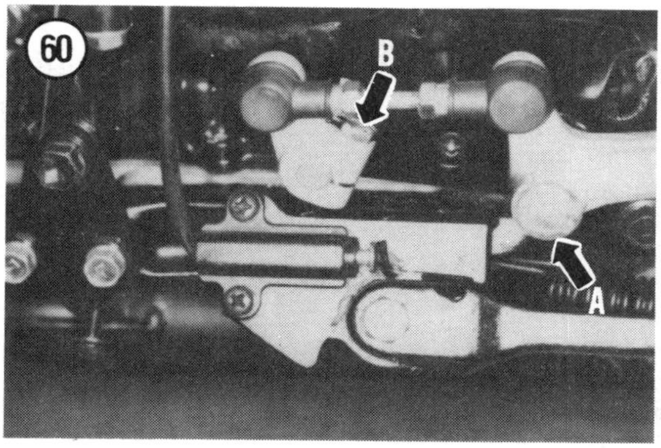

6. On California models, disconnect all hose fittings relating to the *Air Suction System* from the cylinder head.

7. Disconnect the breather hose (**Figure 59**) from the cylinder head cover.

8. Remove the carburetor assembly as described under *Carburetor Removal/Installation* in this chapter.

9. Drain the engine oil and remove the oil filter as described under *Engine Oil and Filter Change* in this chapter. The oil filter must be removed in order for the engine to clear the frame later on in this procedure.

10. Disconnect the spark plug leads and tie them up out of the way.

11. Remove the gearshift lever as follows:

a. Remove the circlip and the washer (A, **Figure 60**) securing the gearshift lever to the pivot post.

b. Remove the bolt (B, **Figure 60**) securing the gearshift lever to the shift shaft and remove the gearshift lever assembly.

12. On California models, remove the cooling fan as described in this chapter.

13. Remove the bolts securing the drive sprocket cover (**Figure 61**) and remove the cover.

14. Loosen the adjusting barrel at the clutch hand lever and remove the cable from the lever.

15. Disconnect the clutch cable from the clutch release arm within the drive sprocket cover.

16. Have an assistant apply the rear brake. Loosen the drive sprocket bolt (A, **Figure 62**) and nut (B, **Figure 62**).

17. To provide slack in the drive chain, perform the following:

a. Remove the cotter pin and loosen the rear axle nut (A, **Figure 63**).

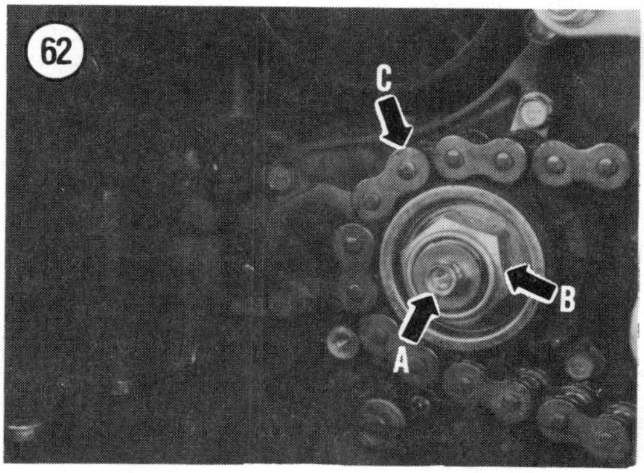

b. Loosen the drive chain adjuster nut (B, **Figure 63**) on each side of the swing arm.
c. Push the rear wheel forward to achieve slack in the drive chain.

18. Remove the drive chain (C, **Figure 62**) from the drive sprocket.
19. Refer to **Figure 64** and disconnect the following electrical connectors:
a. Alternator.
b. Neutral indicator.
c. Signal generator.
d. Oil pressure indicator switch.
e. Sidestand indicator.
20. Place a drain pan under the front of the engine and remove the union bolts and sealing washers securing the oil cooler hoses (B, **Figure 58**) to the crankcase oil pan.
21. Remove the ties (**Figure 65**) securing the oil cooler lines to the frame.
22. Remove the bolts (**Figure 66**) securing the oil cooler and remove the oil cooler and hoses from the frame.

NOTE
If you are just removing the engine and are not planning to disassemble it, do not perform Step 23.

23. If the engine is going to be disassembled, remove the following parts while the engine is still in the frame. Remove the following as described in this chapter unless otherwise noted:
a. Alternator and starter (Chapter Seven).
b. Camshafts and cylinder head (Chapter Four).
c. Cylinder block (Chapter Four).
d. Pistons (Chapter Four).
e. Signal generator.
f. Clutch assembly (Chapter Five).
g. External shift mechanism (Chapter Six).
24. Take a final look all over the engine to make sure everything has been disconnected.
25. Place a suitable size jack, with a piece of wood to protect the crankcase, under the engine. Apply a small amount of jack pressure up on the engine.

NOTE
There are many different bolt sizes and lengths, different combinations of washers and lockwashers. It is suggested that when ***each set*** *of bolts, nuts, washers and holding plates is removed that you place it in a separate plastic bag or box to keep them separated. This will save a lot of time when installing the engine.*

63
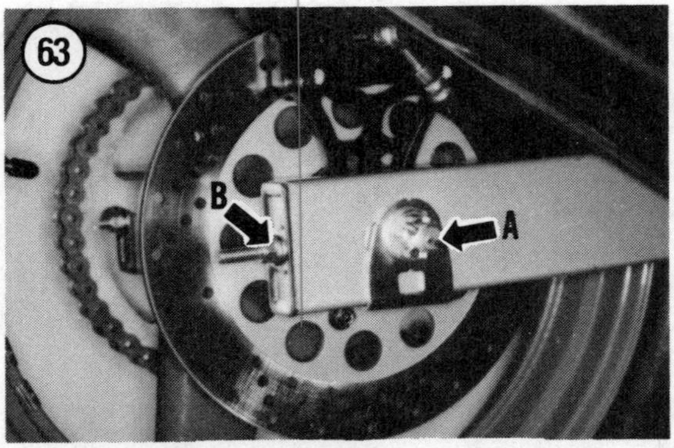

64
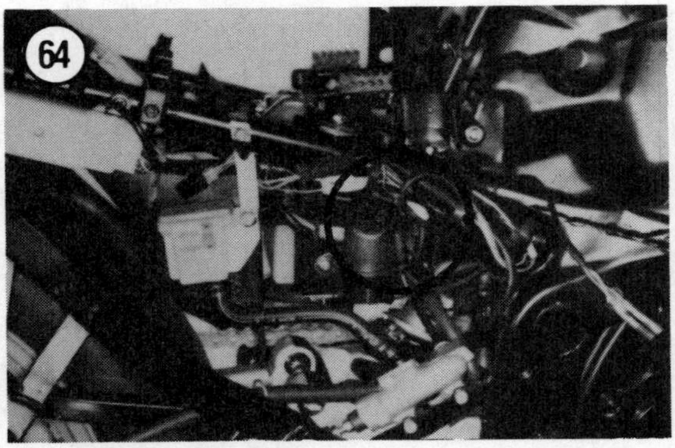

65

66
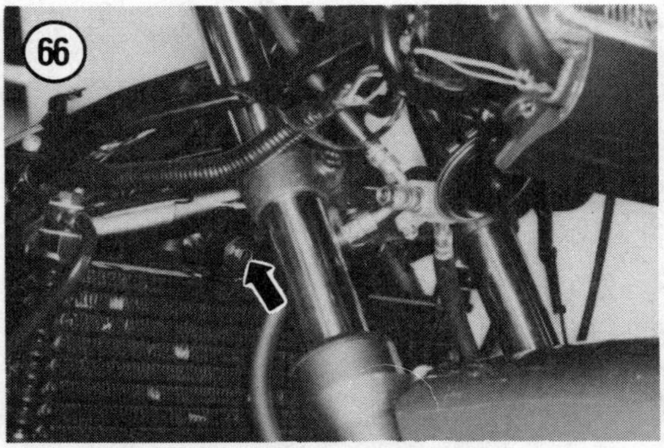

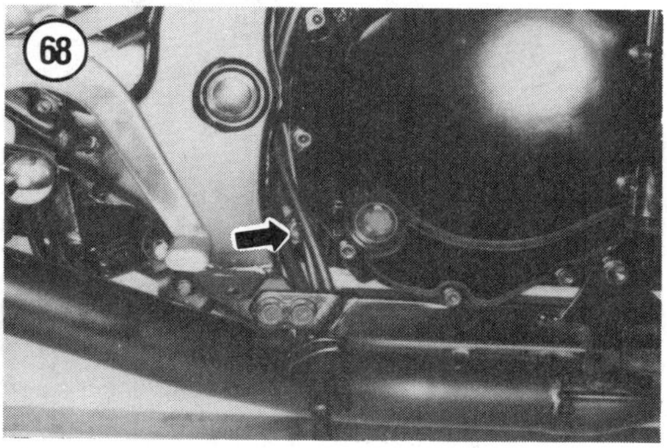

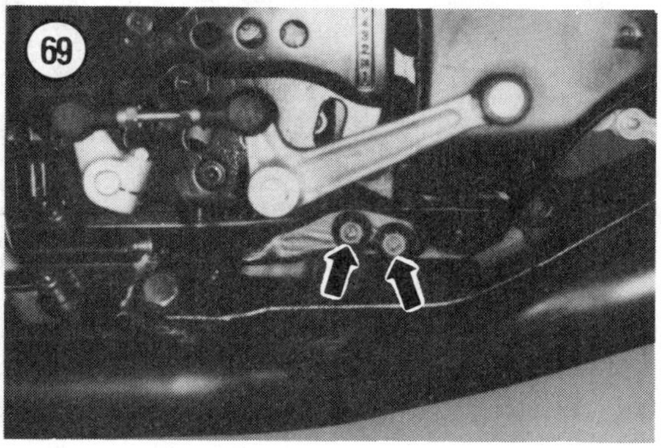

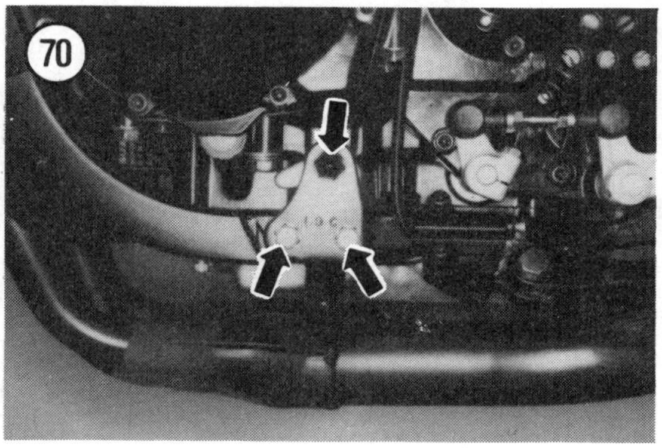

The nuts are the self-locking type and cannot be reused. New nuts must be reinstalled during engine installation.

NOTE

The following illustrations show bolt location only and the components have not been removed from the engine. Remove the previously mentioned components prior to removing the engine mounting hardware.

CAUTION

Continually adjust jack pressure during engine removal and installation to prevent damage to the mounting bolt threads and hardware.

26. Remove the rear upper through bolt, nut and right-hand spacer (**Figure 67**).
27. Remove the rear lower through bolt and nut (**Figure 68**).

NOTE

The sub-frame remains attached to the engine for removal. After the engine is removed, then the sub-frame can be removed from the engine if necessary.

28. If the sub-frame is going to be removed from the engine, loosen the sub-frame-to-engine mounting bolts and nuts prior to removing the engine from the frame:
    a. Loosen the rear bolts and self-locking nuts (**Figure 69**).
    b. Loosen the front bolts (**Figure 70**).
    c. Loosen the front upper bolts and self-locking nuts (**Figure 71**) on each side.
29. Remove the sub-frame front upper bolts and lockwashers (**Figure 72**).

13

30. Remove the sub-frame rear bolts and self-locking nuts (**Figure 73**). Discard the self-locking nuts as they cannot be reused.

CAUTION
The following steps require the aid of a helper to remove the engine and sub-frame assembly from the frame safely. Due to the weight of the engine, it is suggested that at least one helper, preferably 2, assist you in the removal of the engine.

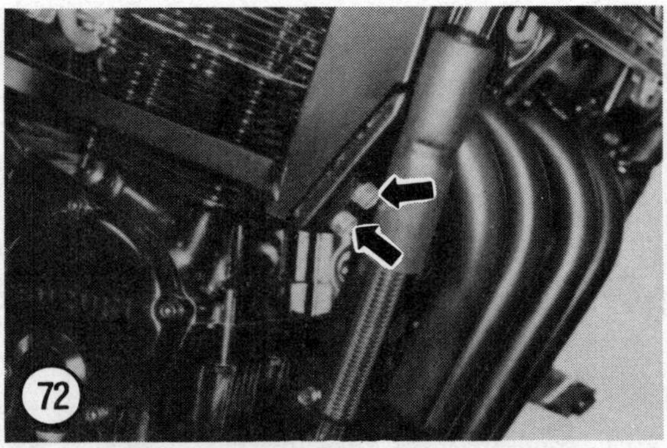
72

31. Gradually lower the engine assembly to clear the remaining portions of the frame and pull the engine out through either side. Take the engine to a workbench for further disassembly.
32. If necessary, remove the bolts and nuts securing the sub-frame to the engine.
33. Install by reversing these removal steps while noting the following:

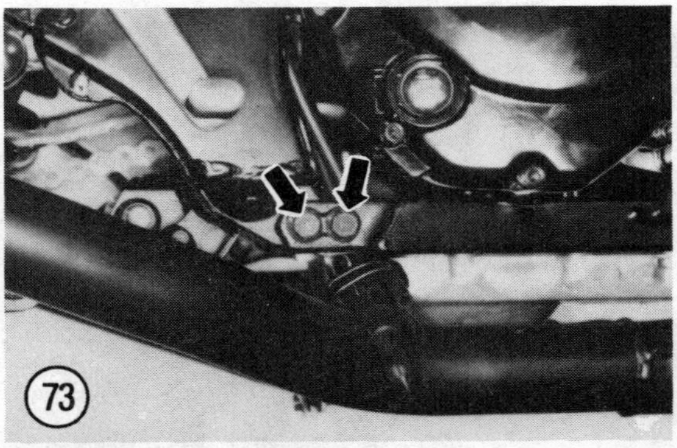
73

CAUTION
Be sure to install new self-locking nuts on all of the engine mounting bolts. Never reuse a self-locking nut that has been removed, since it has lost its locking ability and will loosen and fall off.

a. Tighten the mounting bolts to the torque specifications in **Table 7**.
b. Fill the engine with the recommended type and quantity of oil; refer to Chapter Three in the main body.
c. Adjust the clutch as described under *Clutch Adjustment* in this chapter.
d. Adjust the drive chain as described under *Drive Chain Adjustment* in Chapter Three of the main body.
e. Start the engine and check for leaks.

74

CYLINDER HEAD COVER

Removal

1. Remove the seat as described under *Seat Removal/Installation* in this chapter.
2. Remove the front fairing as described under *Front Fairing Removal/Installation* in this chapter.
3. Remove the fuel tank as described under *Fuel Tank Removal/Installation* in this chapter.
4. Place a shop cloth on the front fender.
5. Remove the tie wrap (**Figure 65**) securing the oil cooler line to the frame.

75

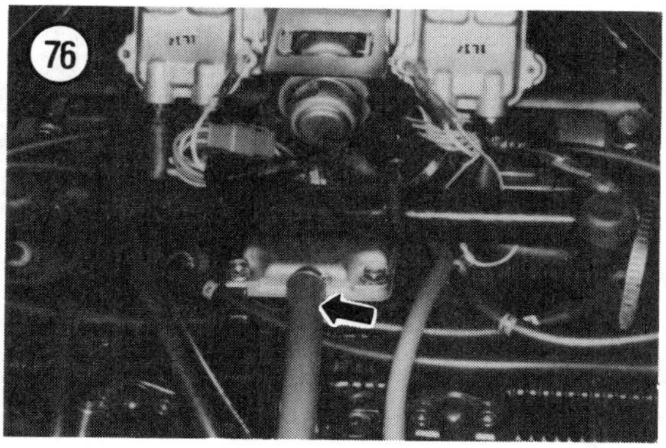
76

77

78

79

NOTE
*In **Figure 66**, only 1 bolt is visible, be sure to remove both bolts securing the oil cooler.*

6. Remove the bolts (**Figure 66**) securing the oil cooler. Lift the oil cooler out of its lower mounting tabs and rest the cooler on the front fender (**Figure 74**).

7. Remove the bolts (**Figure 75**) securing the frame upper cross member and remove it.

8. Disconnect the crankcase vent hose (**Figure 76**) from the cylinder head.

9. On California models, remove the Air Suction Valve Assembly (A, **Figure 77**) as described in this chapter.

10. Remove the bolts securing the ignition coils (B, **Figure 77**) and move them out of the way. The primary electrical wires can remain attached.

11. Remove the bolts (**Figure 78**) securing the air suction hose brackets. Move the hose and brackets forward and out of the way.

12. On 1989-on models, disconnect the choke cable from the carburetor assembly and move it out of the way.

13. Disconnect the throttle cable from the throttle control. Pull the throttle cable out from behind the steering head and from over the top of the cylinder head.

14. Disconnect all spark plug wires and caps. Move the wires out of the way.

15. Remove the Allen bolts (**Figure 79**) securing the oil hoses to the cylinder head cover. Don't lose the O-ring seal in each hose fitting. Move the hoses out of the way.

16. Remove the 4 inner union bolts (A, **Figure 80**) and outer Allen bolts (B, **Figure 80**) securing the cylinder head cover.

17. Pull the cylinder head cover straight up and slightly toward the back. Carefully work the cylin-

80

der head cover under the clutch cable and then out through the right-hand side of the frame.

Installation

1. Inspect the rubber gasket (A, **Figure 81**) around the perimeter of the cylinder head cover. Also inspect the rubber gasket (B, **Figure 81**) at each spark plug hole. If they are starting to deteriorate or harden, they should be replaced; replace as a set even if only one is bad.

NOTE

New gaskets must be installed onto the cylinder head cover using the following method to help prevent an oil leak.

2. If the gaskets are to be replaced, perform the following:
   a. Remove the old gaskets and clean off all gasket sealer residue from the cylinder head cover.
   b. Clean out the gasket groove around the perimeter of the cover and around each spark plug hole.
   c. Apply Suzuki Bond No.1207B liquid gasket, or equivalent, to the gasket grooves in the cover following the manufacturer's instructions.
   d. Install all gaskets. Make sure they are correctly seated in their respective grooves in the cover.
   e. Apply Suzuki Bond No.1207B liquid gasket, or equivalent, to the camshaft end caps of the perimeter gasket where they will contact the cylinder head.
3. Install the cylinder head cover. Make sure none of the spark plug hole gaskets have fallen off. Make

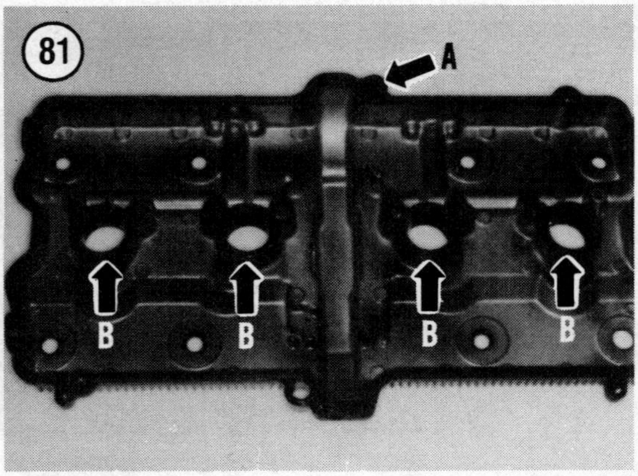

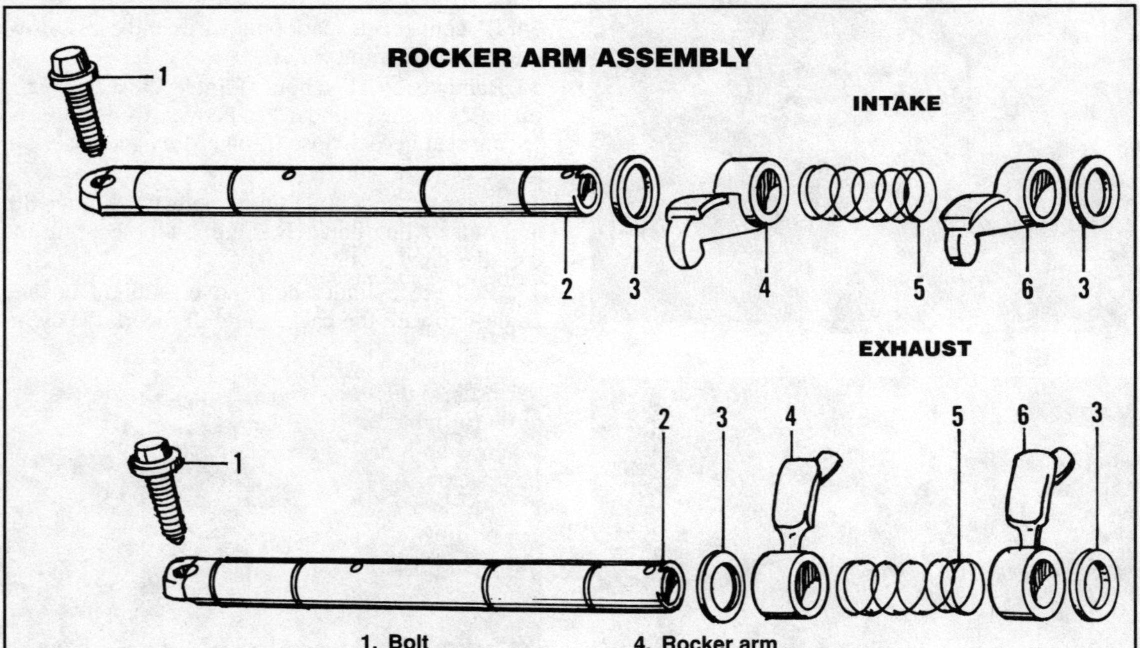

1. Bolt
2. Rocker arm shaft
3. Washer
4. Rocker arm
5. Spring
6. Rocker arm

sure the camshaft end caps are correctly seated in the cylinder head.

4. Install the 4 union bolts and washers (A, **Figure 80**) and tighten finger-tight at this time.

5. Make sure all 8 gaskets are in place on the cylinder head cover, then install the Allen bolts (B, **Figure 80**).

6. Tighten the Allen bolts and hex bolts in a crisscross pattern to the torque specification listed in **Table 7**.

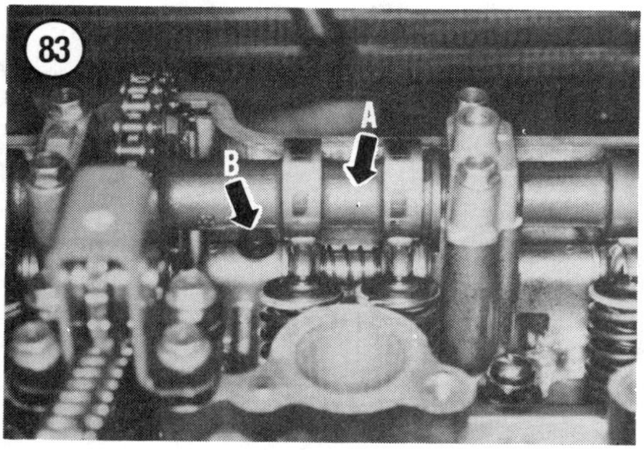

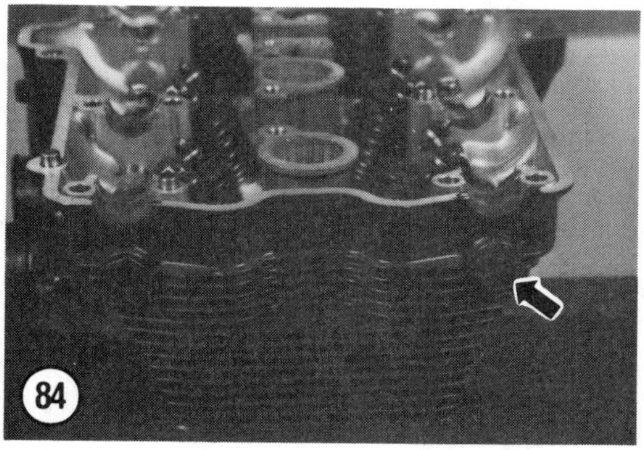

7. Install a *new* O-ring seal into each fitting of the oil hoses. To prevent an oil leak, these O-rings must be replaced every time the oil hoses are disconnected from the cylinder head cover.

8. Move the fittings into place on the cylinder head cover and install the Allen bolts (**Figure 79**). Tighten the Allen bolts to the torque specification listed in **Table 7**.

9. Install all spark plugs and connect all spark plug caps and wires.

10. Adjust the throttle and choke cables as described in Chapter Three.

11. Complete the installation by reversing Steps 1-13 of the *Removal* procedure.

CAMSHAFTS

Inspection

The removal and installation of the camshafts are identical to other models. The inspection procedure is identical also, except that the number of cam lobes is double. Each cam lobe now operates an individual valve assembly instead of one cam lobe operating a single rocker arm that operates two valves. Camshaft specifications are listed in **Table 8**.

ROCKER ARM ASSEMBLIES

Refer to **Figure 82** for this procedure.

Removal

1. Remove the cylinder head as described under *Cylinder Head* in Chapter Four of the main body.
2. Remove both camshafts (A, **Figure 83**) as described under *Camshafts* in Chapter Four of the main body.
3. Remove the bolt (B, **Figure 83**) securing the rocker arm shaft in the cylinder head.
4. Unscrew the end plug (**Figure 84**) and sealing washer from the cylinder head.
5. Screw an 8 mm bolt (**Figure 85**) into the end of the rocker arm shaft.
6. Pull the rocker arm shaft out and remove the rocker arms, washers and springs.
7. Repeat for all rocker arm shaft assemblies.

NOTE

Mark the shafts and rocker arms with an "I" (intake) or "E" (exhaust) and cylinder number (No. 1, 2, 3 or 4) as they must be reinstalled into their original positions. The No. 1 cylinder is on the left-hand side of the bike; No. 2, 3 and 4 cylinders continue from left-to-right across the engine.

8. Wash all parts in solvent and thoroughly dry with compressed air.

Inspection

1. Inspect the rocker arm pad where it rides on the cam lobe (**Figure 86**) and where it rides on the shim (**Figure 87**). If the pad is scratched or unevenly worn, inspect the cam lobe for scoring, chipping or flat spots. Replace the rocker arm if defective.

2. Measure the inside diameter of the rocker arm bore (A, **Figure 88**) with an inside micrometer and check against the dimensions in **Table 8**. Replace if worn to the service limit or greater.

3. Inspect the rocker arm shaft for signs of wear or scoring. Measure the outside diameter (B, **Figure 88**) with a micrometer and check against the dimensions in **Table 8**. Replace if worn to the service limit or less.

4. Make sure the oil holes in the rocker arm shaft are clean and clear. If necessary, clean out with a piece of wire and thoroughly clean with solvent. Dry with compressed air.

5. Check the springs for breakage or distortion; replace if necessary.

86

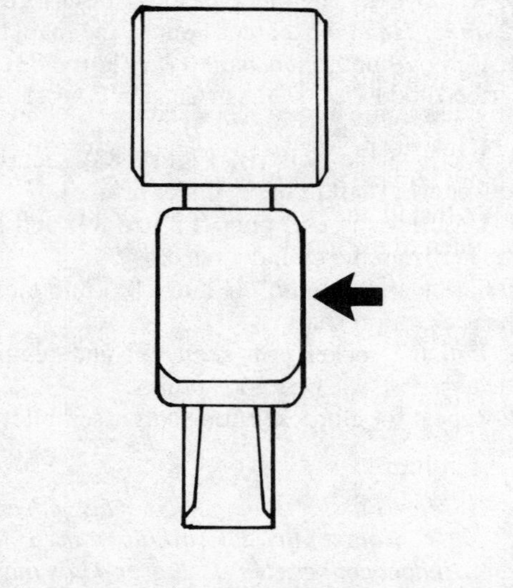

87

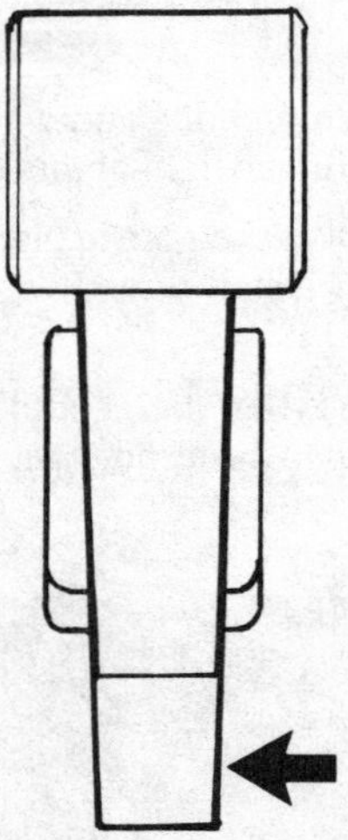

88

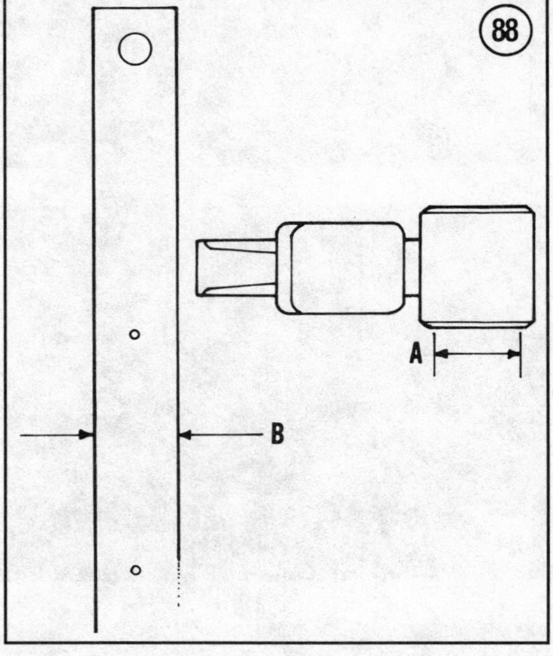

89

(90) VALVE ASSEMBLY

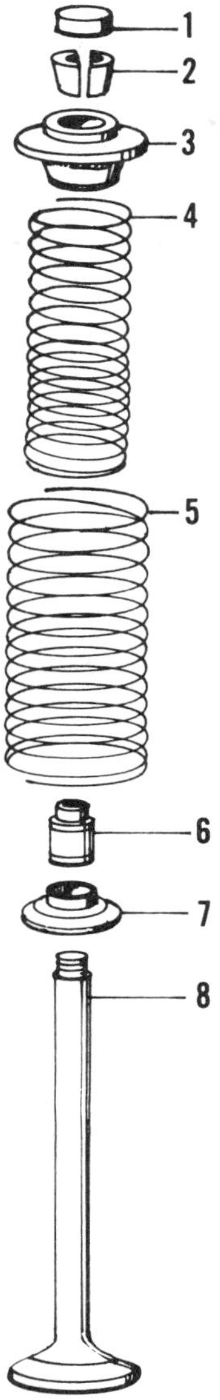

1. Shim
2. Keeper
3. Valve spring retainer
4. Inner spring
5. Outer spring
6. Oil seal
7. Valve seat
8. Valve

Installation

1. Coat the rocker arm shaft, rocker arm bore and the shaft receptacles in the cylinder head with assembly oil or clean engine oil.
2. Refer to marks made in Step 7, *Removal*, and be sure to install the rocker arms and shafts back into their original locations.
3. Install the rocker arms, spring and the washers in the outer cylinders section of the cylinder head. The spring goes between the 2 rocker arms and the washers are placed between the rocker arms and the cylinder head surfaces.
4. Position the rocker arm shaft so the bolt hole is vertical.
5. Partially install the rocker arm shaft into the cylinder head and through the first set of rocker arms. Push it through the washer, rocker arm, spring, rocker arm and washer.
6. After passing through the first set of rocker arms and through the cylinder head boss, recheck the alignment of the rocker arm shaft bolt hole with the bolt hole in the cylinder head. After alignment is correct, pull the rocker arm shaft back enough to install the next set of rocker arms.
7. Install the second set of rocker arms, spring and the washers in the inner cylinders section of the cylinder head. The spring goes between the 2 rocker arms and the washers are placed between the rocker arms and the cylinder head surfaces.
8. Push the rocker arm shaft through the second set of rocker arms. Push it through the washer, rocker arm, spring, rocker arm and washer. Push it in until it bottoms out.
9. After the shaft is installed, if necessary, rotate it to align the bolt hole with the bolt hole in the cylinder head.
10. Install the bolt securing the rocker arm shaft and tighten to the torque specification listed in **Table 7**.
11. Inspect the sealing washer (**Figure 89**) on the end plug; replace if necessary.
12. Install the end plug and sealing washer and tighten to the torque specification listed in **Table 7**.

VALVES AND VALVE COMPONENTS

The valve assembly is the same as on GSX-R750 models except for the addition of the valve adjustment shim on top of the valve spring retainer (**Figure 90**).

Prior to removing the valves, remove the shims and keep them in order so they can be reinstalled in the same location. Even if the valves have been serviced, the original shims should be used for a starting point for valve clearance adjustment.

Valve Seat Reconditioning

The valve seat reconditioning is same as on GSX-R750 models except for the valve seat cutter part numbers. The part numbers for the GSX600F are as follows:

a. 45° valve cutter: part No. N-122.

b. 15° intake valve cutter: part No. N-121.

c. 15° exhaust valve cutter: part No. N-120.

Table 7 ENGINE TORQUE SPECIFICATIONS

Item	N•m	ft.-lb.
Engine mounting bolts and nuts		
Upper and lower through bolts	70-88	51-64
Sub-frame bolts		
Front and upper front	50-60	36-44
Rear bolts	25-38	18-28
Cylinder head cover bolts	13-15	9-11
Oil hose fitting Allen bolts	8-12	6-9
Camshaft sprocket bolts	24-26	17-19
Camshaft bearing cap bolts	8-12	6-9
Camshaft chain idler bolts	8-12	6-9
Camshaft chain tensioner spring bolt	30-40	21-29
Camshaft chain tensioner mounting bolts	6-8	4.5-6
Rocker arm shaft bolt	8-10	6-7
Rocker arm shaft end plug	25-30	18-22
Cylinder head nuts	35-40	25-29
Cylinder head bolt	8-12	6-9
Oil pump mounting bolts	8-12	6-9
Oil cooler oil line union bolts	25-30	18-22
Oil pan bolts	12-16	9-12
Oil pressure regulator	25-30	18-22
Starter clutch bolt	140-160	101-115
Crankcase bolts		
Initial torque		
6 mm	6	4.5
8 mm	13	10
Final torque		
6 mm	9-13	6.5-9.5
8 mm	20-24	14-17.5
Main oil gallery plug bolt	35-45	26-33
Connecting rod cap nuts	33-37	23.5-27
Drive sprocket		
Nut	100-130	73-94
Bolt	8-12	6-9
Oil strainer bolt	10-14	7-10

Table 8 ENGINE SPECIFICATIONS

	Specification	Wear Limit
General		
Type and number of cylinders	In line 4 cylinder, DOHC, air cooled	
Bore × stroke	62.6 × 48.7 mm (2.47 × 1.92 in.)	
Displacement	599 cc (36.6 cu. in.)	
Compression pressure	1,200-1,700 kPa (171-242 psi)	
	(continued)	

Table 8 ENGINE SPECIFICATIONS (KATANA 600) (continued)

	Specification	Wear Limit
Camshaft		
Cam lobe height		
U.S. models		
Intake	33.617-33.657 mm (1.3235-1.3251 in.)	33.320 mm (1.3118 in.)
Exhaust	32.882-32.992 mm (1.2946-1.2989 in.)	32.590 mm (1.2831 in.)
UK models (1989-on)		
Intake	33.563-33.583 mm (1.3214-1.3222 in.)	33.270 mm (1.3098 in.)
Exhaust	33.146-33.186 mm (1.3050-1.3065 in.)	32.850 mm (1.2933 in.)
Journal O.D.		
Intake and exhaust	21.959-21.980 mm (0.8645-0.8654 in.)	–
Journal oil clearance		
Intake and exhaust	0.032-0.066 mm (0.0013-0.0026 in.)	0.150 mm (0.0059 in.)
Journal holder I.D.		
Intake and exhaust	22.012-22.025 mm (0.8666-0.8671 in.)	–
Runout	–	0.10 mm (0.004 in.)
Drive chain (20 pitch length)	–	158.0 mm (6.22 in.)
Rocker assembly		
Rocker arm bore I.D.	12.000-12.018 mm (0.4724-0.4731 in.)	–
Rocker arm shaft O.D.	11.973-11.984 mm (0.4711-0.4718 in.)	–
Cylinder head distortion	–	0.20 mm (0.008 in.)
Valves		
Diameter		
Intake	23 mm (0.9 in.)	–
Exhaust	20 mm (0.8 in.)	–
Valve lift		
Intake	8.2 mm (0.32 in.)	–
Exhaust		
U.S. models	7.0 mm (0.28 in.)	–
UK models	8.0 mm (0.31 in.)	–
Valve stem-to-guide clearance		
Intake	0.020-0.047 mm (0.0008-0.0019 in.)	0.35 mm (0.014 in.)
Exhaust	0.040-0.067 mm (0.0016-0.0026 in.)	0.35 mm (0.014 in.)
Valve guide I.D.	5.000-5.012 mm (0.1969-0.1973 in.)	–
Valve stem O.D.		
Intake	4.965-4.980 mm (0.1955-0.1961 in.)	–
Exhaust	4.945-4.960 mm (0.1947-0.1953 in.)	–
Valve stem runout	–	0.05 mm (0.002 in.)
Valve head thickness	–	0.05 mm (0.002 in.)
Valve stem end length	–	2.5 mm (0.10 in.)
Valve seat width	0.9-1.1 mm (0.035-0.043 in.)	–
Valve head radial runout	–	0.03 mm (0.001 in.)
Valve spring free length		
Inner	–	35.0 mm (1.38 in.)
Outer	–	38.4 mm (1.51 in.)

(continued)

13

Table 8 ENGINE SPECIFICATIONS (KATANA 600) (continued)

	Specification	Wear Limit
Cylinders		
Bore	62.600-62.615 mm (2.4646-2.4652 in.)	62.690 mm (2.4681 in.)
Cylinder/piston clearance	0.040-0.050 mm (0.0015-0.0019 in.)	0.120 mm (0.0047 in.)
Out-of-round	–	0.20 mm (0.008 in.)
Pistons		
Outer diameter	62.570-63.555 mm (2.4633-2.4628 in.)	62.480 mm (2.4598 in.)
Clearance in bore	0.040-0.050 mm (0.0016-0.0020 in.)	0.120 mm (0.0047 in.)
Piston pin bore	18.002-18.008 mm (0.7087-0.7090 in.)	18.030 mm (0.7098 in.)
Piston pin outer diameter	17.996-18.000 mm (0.7085-0.7086 in.)	17.980 mm (0.7079 in.)
Piston ring groove width		
Top	0.81-0.83 mm (0.032-0.033 in.)	–
Second	1.01-1.03 mm (0.039-0.040 in.)	–
Oil	2.01-2.03 mm (0.079-0.080 in.)	–
Piston rings		
Number per piston		
Compression	2	–
Oil control	1	–
Ring end gap		
Top and second	0.1-0.3 mm (0.004-0.012 in.)	0.7 mm (0.03 in.)
Ring end gap (free)		
Top	Approx 8.6 mm (0.34 in.)	6.9 mm (0.27 in.)
Second	Approx 6.7 mm (0.26 in.)	5.4 mm (0.21 in.)
Ring side clearance		
Top	–	0.180 mm (0.007 in.)
Second	–	0.150 mm (0.006 in.)
Ring thickness		
Top	0.77-0.79 mm (0.030-0.031 in.)	–
Second	0.97-0.99 mm (0.038-0.039 in.)	–
Connecting rods		
Piston pin hole I.D.	18.010-18.018 mm (0.7091-0.7094 in.)	18.040 mm (0.7102 in.)
Big end side clearance	0.10-0.20 mm (0.004-0.008 in.)	0.30 mm (0.01 in.)
Big end width	20.95-21.00 mm (0.825-0.827 in.)	–
Big end oil clearance	0.032-0.056 mm (0.0013-0.0022 in.)	0.080 mm (0.0031 in.)
Crankshaft		
Crankpin width	21.10-21.15 mm (0.831-0.833 in.)	–
Crankpin journal O.D.		
Code A	31.992-32.000 mm (1.2595-1.2598 in.)	–
Code B	31.984-31.992 mm (1.2592-1.2595 in.)	–

(continued)

Table 8 ENGINE SPECIFICATIONS (KATANA 600) (continued)

	Specification	Wear Limit
Crankshaft (continued)		
Crankpin journal O.D. (continued)		
Code C	31.976-31.984 mm (1.2589-1.2592 in.)	–
Crankpin O.D.	33.976-34.000 mm (1.3376-1.3386 in.)	–
Crankpin journal oil clearance	0.020-0.044 mm (0.0008-0.0017 in.)	0.080 mm (0.0031 in.)
Thrust clearance	0.04-0.18 mm (0.002-0.007 in.)	0.25 mm (0.010 in.)
Journal holder	24.00-24.05 mm (0.945-0.947 in.)	–
Runout	–	0.05 mm (0.002 in.)
Crankcase crankshaft bearing insert I.D.		
Code A	35.000-35.008 mm (1.3780-1.3783 in.)	–
Code B	35.008-35.016 mm (1.3783-1.3786 in.)	–

CHAPTER FIVE

CLUTCH

CLUTCH (1988-1991)

The clutch assembly on these models is the same as GSX-R750 Wet Type models that are covered in Chapter Five of the main body.

Tighten the clutch locknut to 60-80 N•m (43.5-58 ft.-lb.).

CLUTCH (1992-ON)

The clutch can be removed with the engine in the frame. Refer to **Figure 91** for this procedure.

Removal/Disassembly

The clutch in 1992-on models is basically the same as on prior models with the following exceptions.

1. To keep the clutch hub from turning in the next step, attach a special tool such as the "Grabbit" (A, **Figure 92**) to it.
2. Loosen and then remove the clutch locknut (B, **Figure 92**).
3. Remove the special tool from the clutch center.
4. Remove the outer plain washer, lockwasher and inner plain washer. Discard the lockwasher, as a new one must be installed.

Inspection

Inspection of the clutch components is the same as on prior years with the exception of the specifications that are listed in **Table 9**.

Assembly/Installation

The clutch in 1992-on models is basically the same as on prior models with the following exceptions.

1. After the clutch hub is installed (**Figure 93**), install the inner plain washer (**Figure 94**), a new lockwasher (**Figure 95**) and the outer plain washer.
2. Use the same special tool (A, **Figure 96**) set used during *Removal/Disassembly* to hold the clutch hub for the following step.

3. Install then tighten the clutch locknut (B, **Figure 96**). Tighten the nut to 60-80 N•m (43.5-58 ft.-lb.).

NOTE
If new friction discs and clutch plates are being installed, apply new engine oil to all surfaces to avoid having the clutch lock up when used for the first time.

4. Onto the clutch hub, install first a clutch plate, then friction disc No. 2 (**Figure 97**), and then a clutch plate.

91

CLUTCH (KATANA 600 1992-ON)

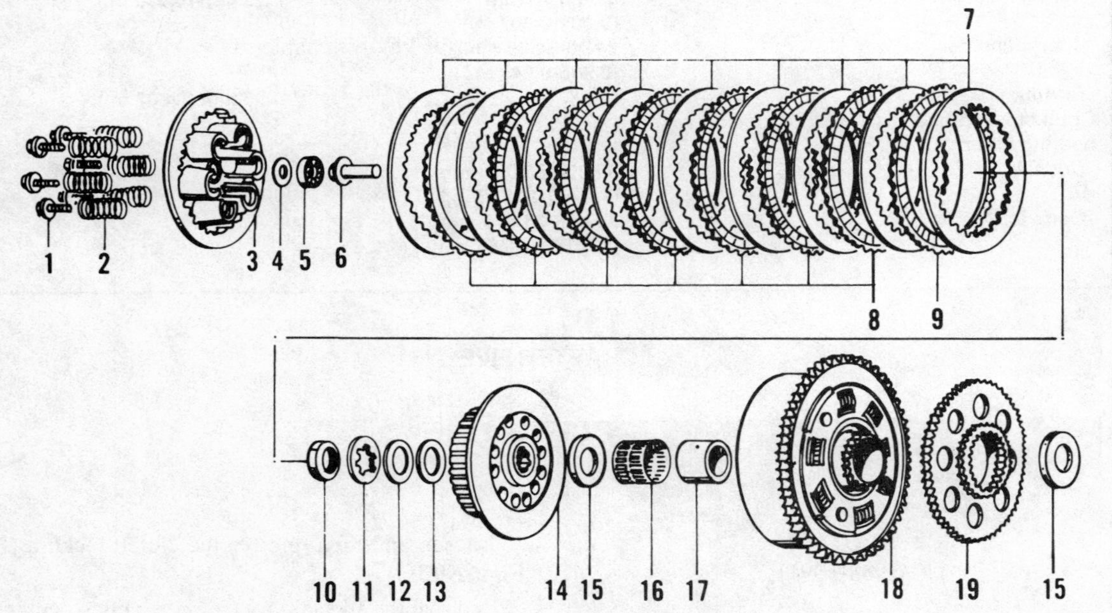

1. Clutch bolt
2. Clutch spring
3. Pressure plate
4. Thrust washer
5. Bearing
6. Clutch push piece
7. Clutch plate
8. Friction disc–No. 1 (quantity 7)
9. Friction disc–No. 2 (quantity 1)
10. Clutch nut
11. Washer
12. Wave washer
13. Washer
14. Clutch hub
15. Thrust washer
16. Needle bearing
17. Spacer
18. Clutch outer housing
19. Alternator/oil pump driven gear

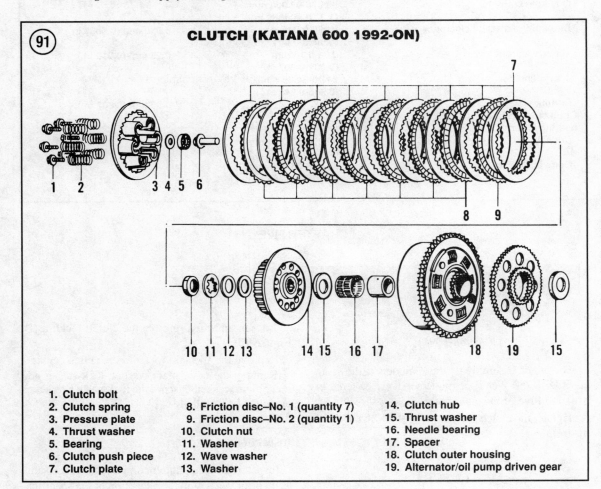

5. Continue to install the friction discs and clutch plates, alternating them until all are installed. The last item installed is a clutch plate.

Clutch Release Mechanism Removal/Installation

Refer to **Figure 98** for this procedure.

1. On California models, remove the cooling fan as described in this chapter.

2. Remove the gearshift lever as follows:

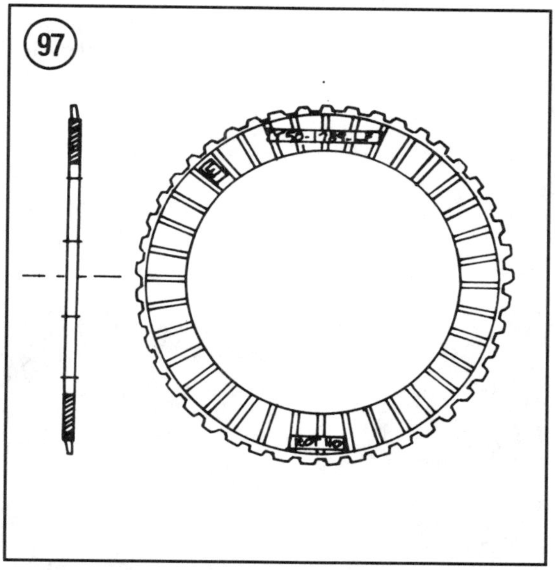

98

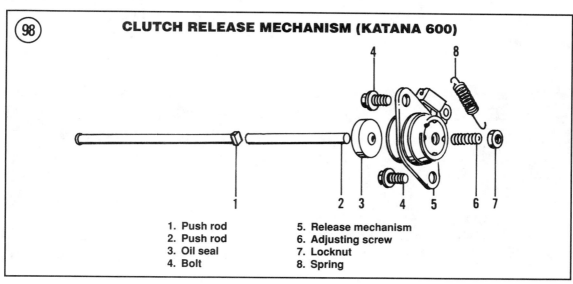

CLUTCH RELEASE MECHANISM (KATANA 600)

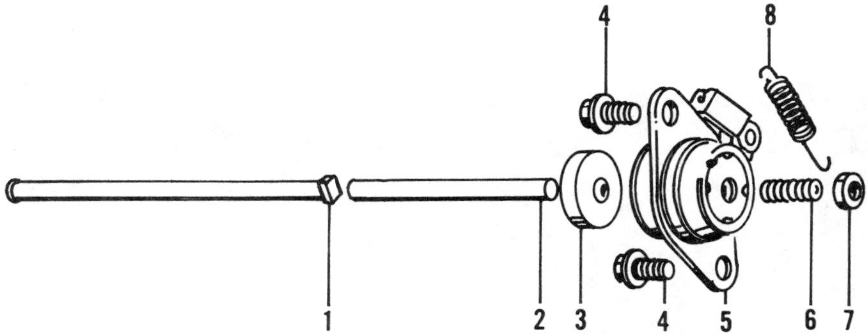

1. Push rod
2. Push rod
3. Oil seal
4. Bolt
5. Release mechanism
6. Adjusting screw
7. Locknut
8. Spring

13

a. Remove the circlip and the washer (A, **Figure 99**) securing the gearshift lever to the pivot post.
b. Remove the bolt (B, **Figure 99**) securing the gearshift lever to the shift shaft and remove the gearshift lever assembly.

3. Remove the bolts securing the drive sprocket cover (**Figure 100**) and remove the cover.
4. Loosen the locknut (A, **Figure 101**) and adjusting barrel (B, **Figure 101**) at the clutch hand lever and remove the cable from the lever.
5. Disconnect the clutch cable (**Figure 102**) from the clutch release arm within the drive sprocket cover.
6. If necessary, withdraw the clutch pushrod from the transmission shaft.
7. Install by reversing these removal steps, adjust the clutch as described under *Clutch Adjustment* in this chapter.

Clutch Cable Replacement

In time, the clutch cable will stretch to the point where it is no longer useful and will have to be replaced.

1. Remove the front fairing as described under *Front Fairing Removal/Installation* in this chapter.

2. Perform Steps 1-5 of *Clutch Release Mechanism Removal/Installation* in this chapter.

NOTE
Prior to removing the cable, make a drawing of the cable routing through the frame. It is very easy to forget how it was, once it has been removed. Replace the cable exactly as it was, avoiding any sharp turns.

3. Pull the clutch cable out from behind the steering head area and out of the retaining loop and clips on the frame.

4. Remove the cable and replace it with a new cable.

5. Install by reversing these removal steps while noting the following:

a. Lubricate the new cable prior to installation.

b. Adjust the clutch as described in this chapter.

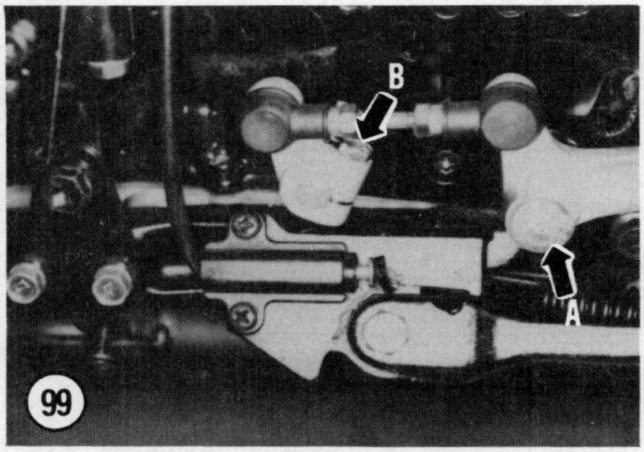

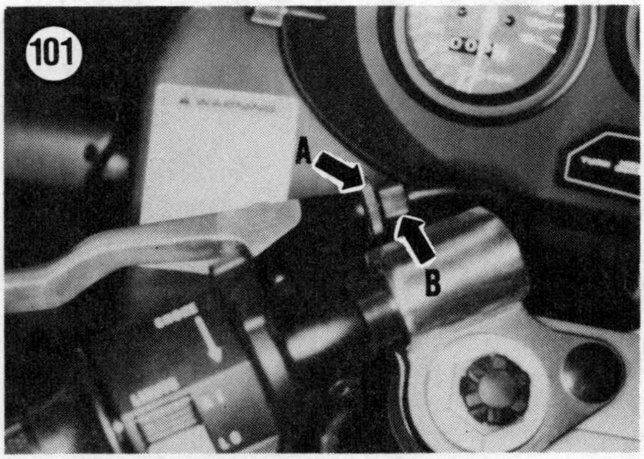

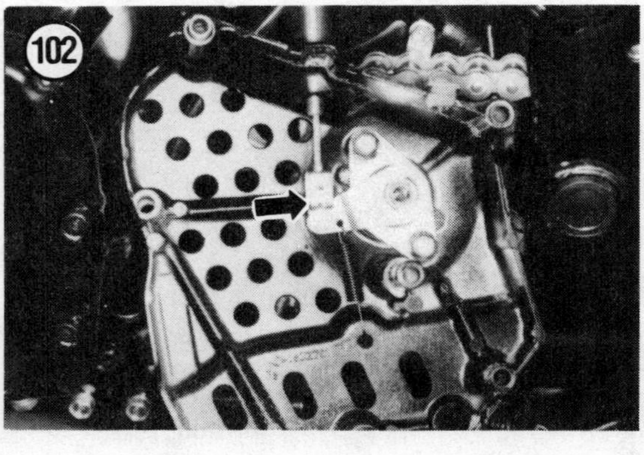

Table 9 CLUTCH SPECIFICATIONS

Item	Standard	Wear limit
Friction disc thickness	2.65-2.95 mm (0.104-0.116 in.)	2.35 mm (0.103 in.)
Friction disc claw width	15.8-16.0 mm (0.622-0.630 in.)	15.0 mm (0.591 in.)
Clutch plate warpage	–	0.10 mm (0.004 in.)
Clutch spring free length	–	33.0 mm (1.30 in.)

CHAPTER SEVEN

FUEL, EMISSION CONTROL AND EXHAUST SYSTEMS

CARBURETOR ASSEMBLY

Removal/Installation

Remove all 4 carburetors as an assembled unit.

1. Remove the seat as described under *Seat Removal/Installation* in this chapter.
2. Remove the front fairing as described under *Front Fairing Removal/Installation* in this chapter.

3. Remove the fuel tank.
4. Disconnect the battery negative lead (**Figure 103**).
5. Remove the bolt (**Figure 104**) securing the air filter case on each side.
6. Disconnect the crankcase breather hose from the cylinder head cover or air filter case.
7. Loosen the screw on the clamping bands (**Figure 105**) on each end of all 4 carburetors. Slide the clamping bands away from the carburetors.
8. Pull the air filter case toward the rear, disengage it from all 4 carburetors and remove the case.
9. Pull the carburetor assembly toward the rear and free the assembly from the intake tubes.
10. Loosen the throttle cable locknut at the carburetor assembly.
11. Disconnect the throttle cable from the throttle wheel.
12. Mark each tube with the carburetor number (1 thru 4), starting with the No. 1 carburetor on the left-hand side.
13. On California models, disconnect the evaporative emission tube from each carburetor.

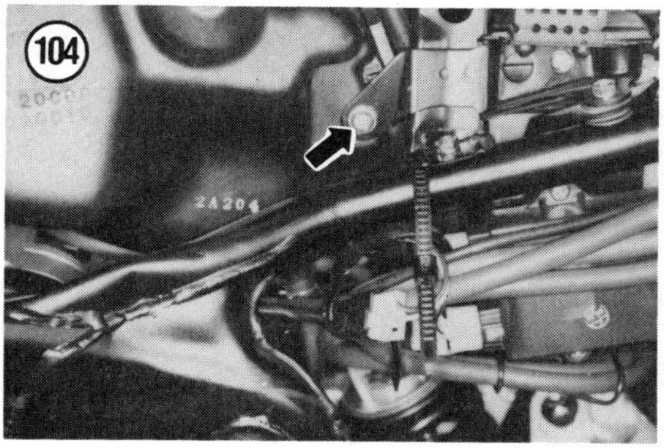

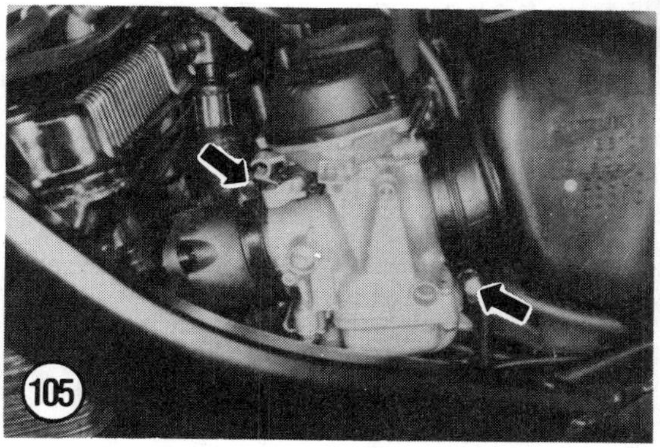

106

CARBURETOR

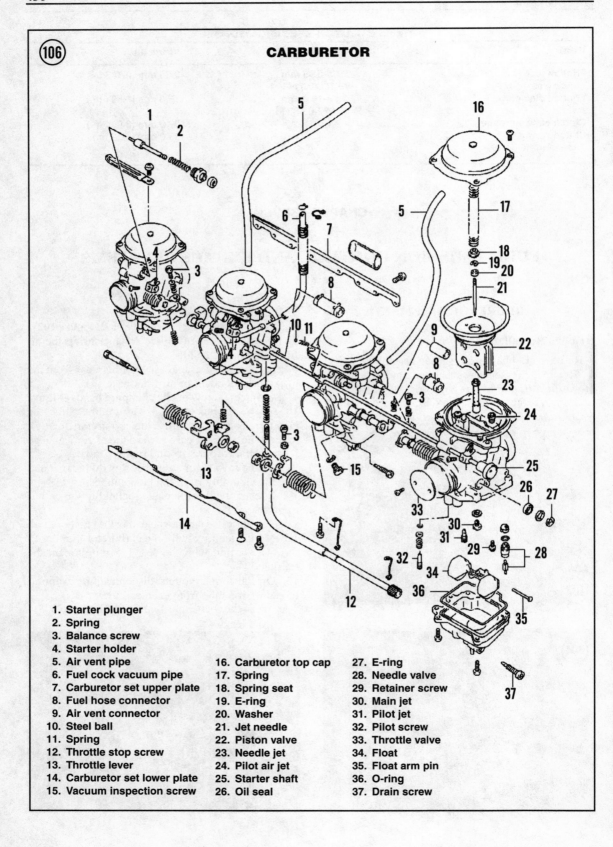

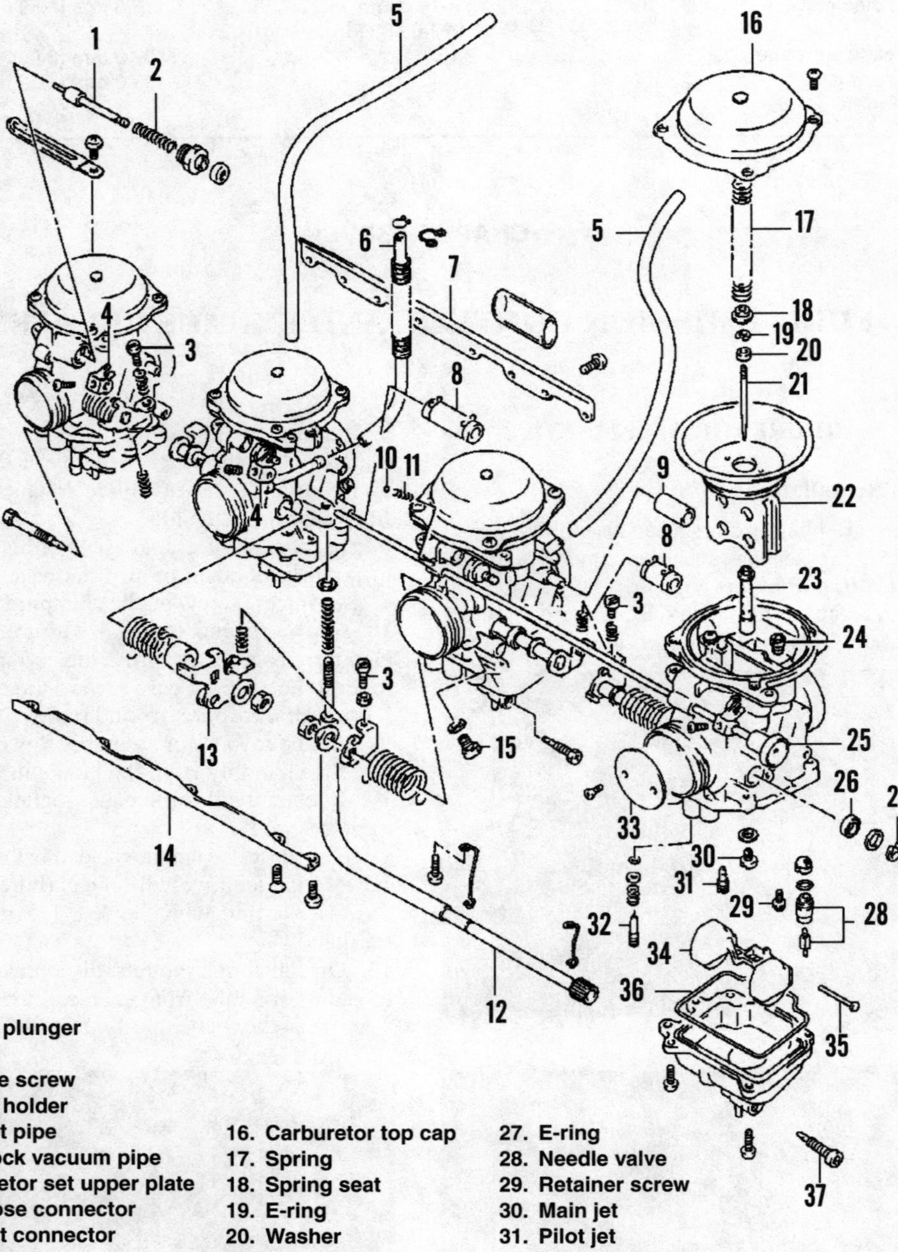

1. Starter plunger
2. Spring
3. Balance screw
4. Starter holder
5. Air vent pipe
6. Fuel cock vacuum pipe
7. Carburetor set upper plate
8. Fuel hose connector
9. Air vent connector
10. Steel ball
11. Spring
12. Throttle stop screw
13. Throttle lever
14. Carburetor set lower plate
15. Vacuum inspection screw
16. Carburetor top cap
17. Spring
18. Spring seat
19. E-ring
20. Washer
21. Jet needle
22. Piston valve
23. Needle jet
24. Pilot air jet
25. Starter shaft
26. Oil seal
27. E-ring
28. Needle valve
29. Retainer screw
30. Main jet
31. Pilot jet
32. Pilot screw
33. Throttle valve
34. Float
35. Float arm pin
36. O-ring
37. Drain screw

14. Carefully remove the carburetor assembly from the engine.
15. If overhaul is required, refer to **Figure 106** and **Table 10** in this chapter for carburetor specifications. Refer to the text in Chapter Six for typical overall instructions.
16. Install by reversing these removal steps while noting the following:
    a. Make sure the carburetors are fully seated forward in the rubber holders in the cylinder head. You should feel a solid "bottoming out" when they are correctly seated.
    b. Make sure the screws on the clamping bands are tight to avoid a vacuum loss and possible valve damage due to a lean fuel mixture.
    c. Adjust the throttle cable as described under *Throttle Cable Adjustment* in Chapter Three of the main body.

107

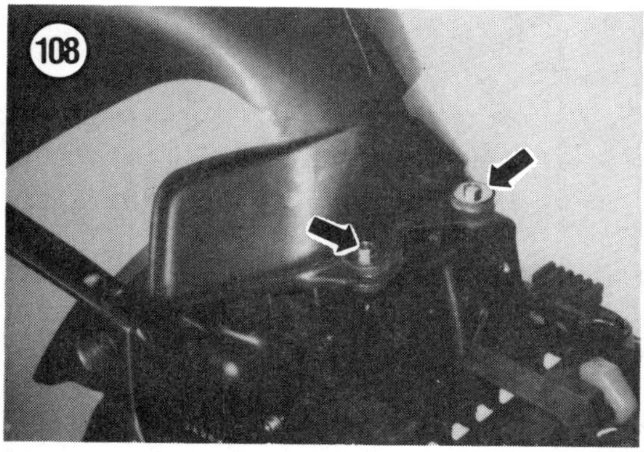
108

109

FUEL TANK

Removal/Installation

1. Remove the seat as described under *Seat Removal/Installation* in this chapter.
2. Remove the front fairing as described under *Front Fairing Removal/Installation* in this chapter.
3. Disconnect the battery negative lead (**Figure 103**).
4. Turn the fuel shutoff valve (**Figure 107**) to the OFF position.
5. Remove the bolts and washers (**Figure 108**) securing the rear of the fuel tank.
6. Pull the fuel tank partially up and disconnect the fuel line to the carburetor assembly.
7. On California models, label and disconnect the evaporation emission control hoses.
8. Disconnect the electrical connector for the fuel level gauge.
9. Lift up and pull the tank to the rear and remove the fuel tank.
10. Install by reversing these removal steps while noting the following:
    a. Inspect the rubber cushion (**Figure 109**) where the front of the fuel tank attaches to the frame. Replace the cushion if it is damaged or starting to deteriorate.
    b. Turn the fuel shutoff valve ON and check for fuel leaks.

EVAPORATIVE EMISSION CONTROL SYSTEM (CALIFORNIA MODELS ONLY)

Fuel vapor from the fuel tank is routed into a charcoal canister. This vapor is stored when the engine is not running. When the engine is running, these vapors are drawn through a purge control valve and into the carburetors. Refer to **Figure 110** for 1988-1989 models or **Figure 111** for 1990-on models.

Make sure all hose clamps are tight. Check all hoses for deterioration and replace as necessary.

(110)

EVAPORATIVE EMISSION CONTROL SYSTEM (1988-1989 KATANA 600–CALIFORNIA MODELS ONLY)

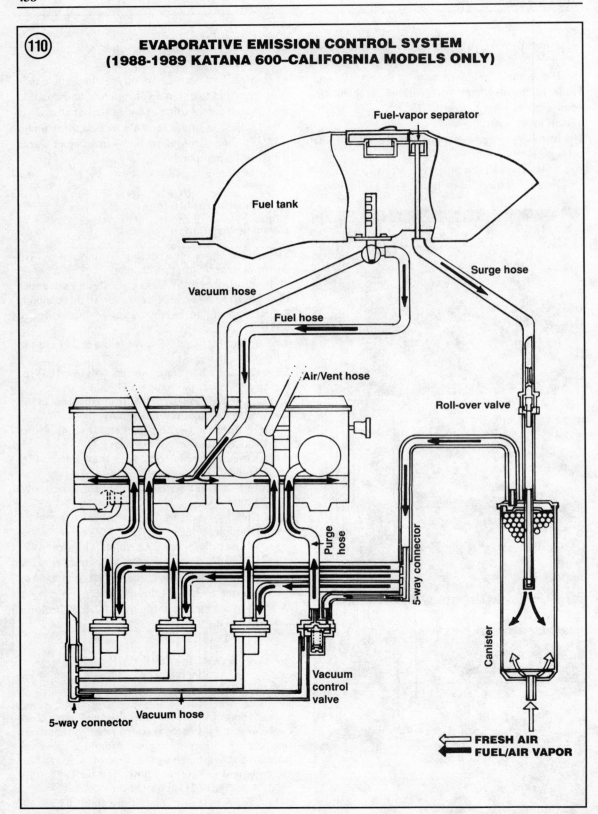

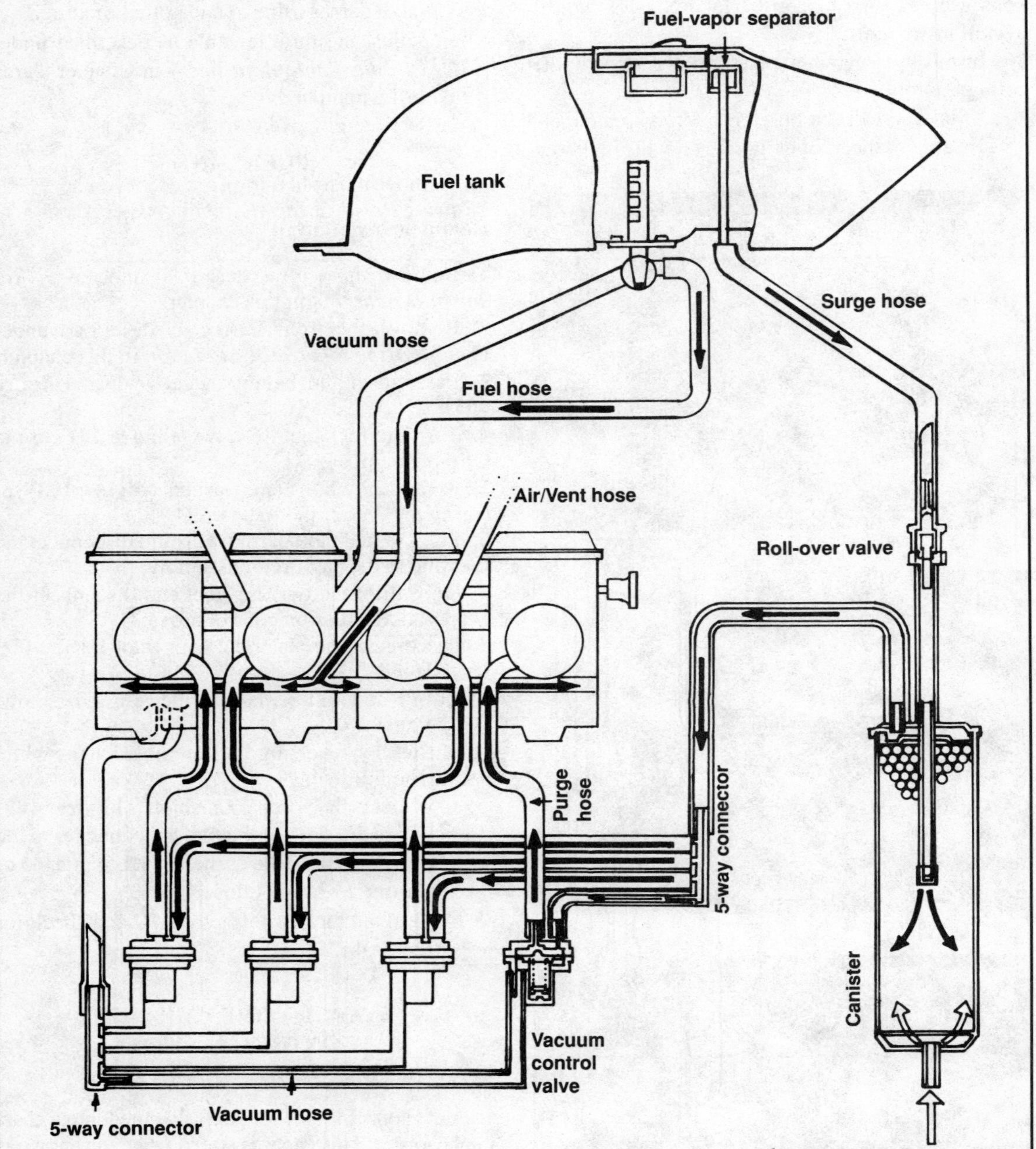

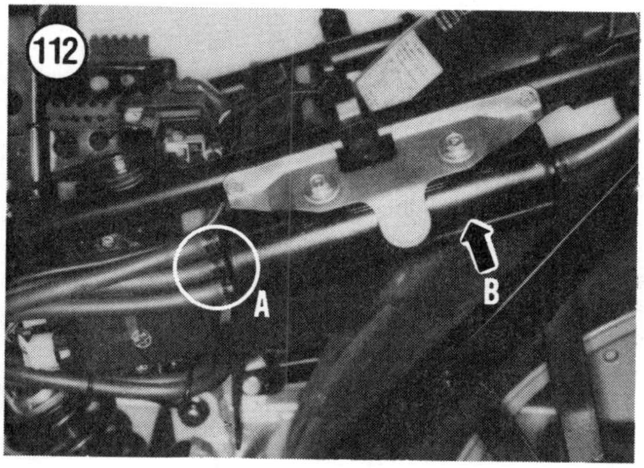

When removing the hoses from any component in the system, mark the hose and the fitting with a piece of masking tape and identify where the hose goes. There are so many vacuum hoses on these models that reconnecting the hoses can be very confusing.

The charcoal canister is located on the left-hand side of the frame under the side cover.

Vacuum Control Valves and Charcoal Canister Removal/Installation

1. Remove the front fairing as described under *Front Fairing Removal/Installation* in this chapter.

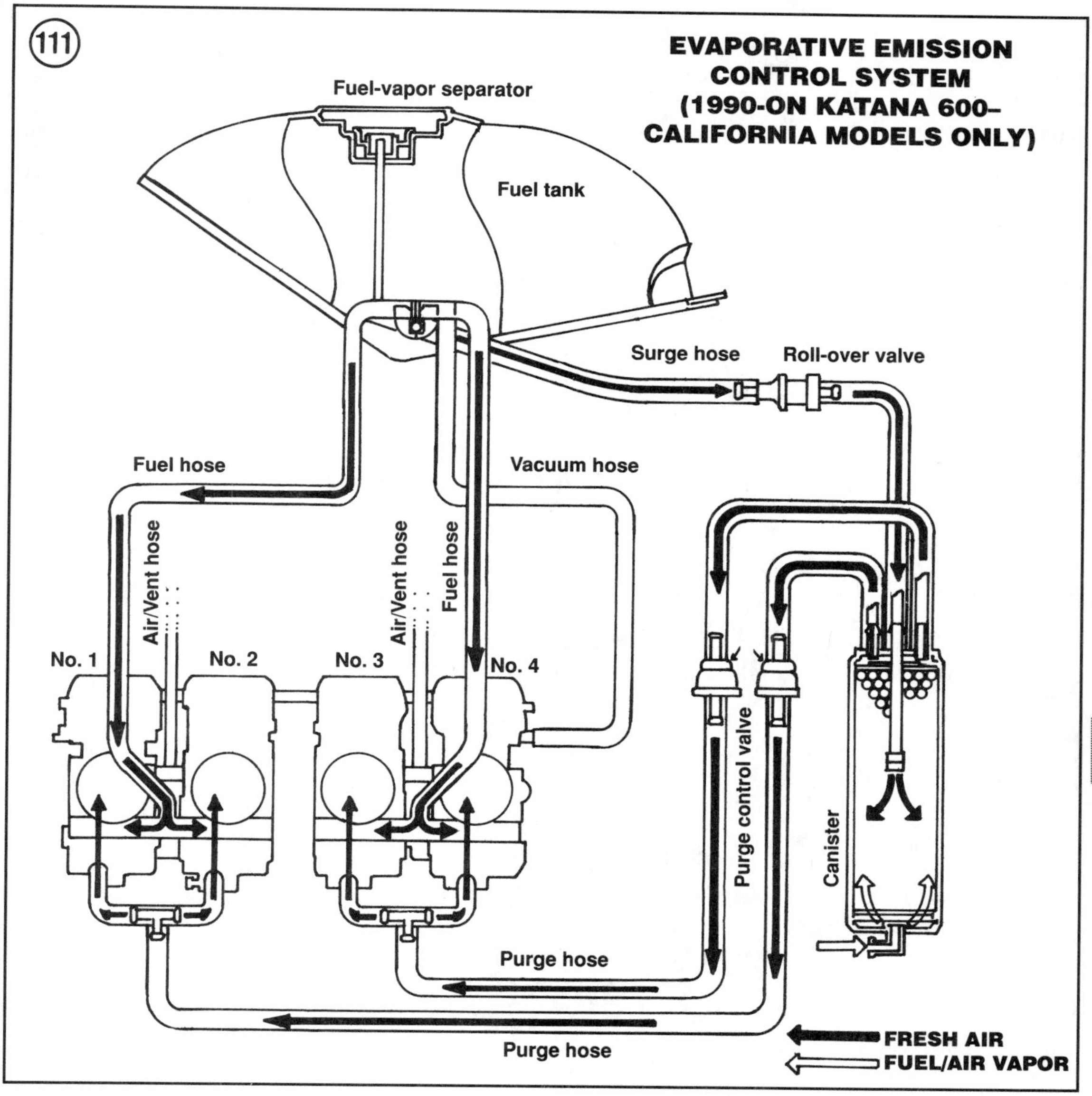

CANISTER HOSE ROUTING (ALL MODELS)

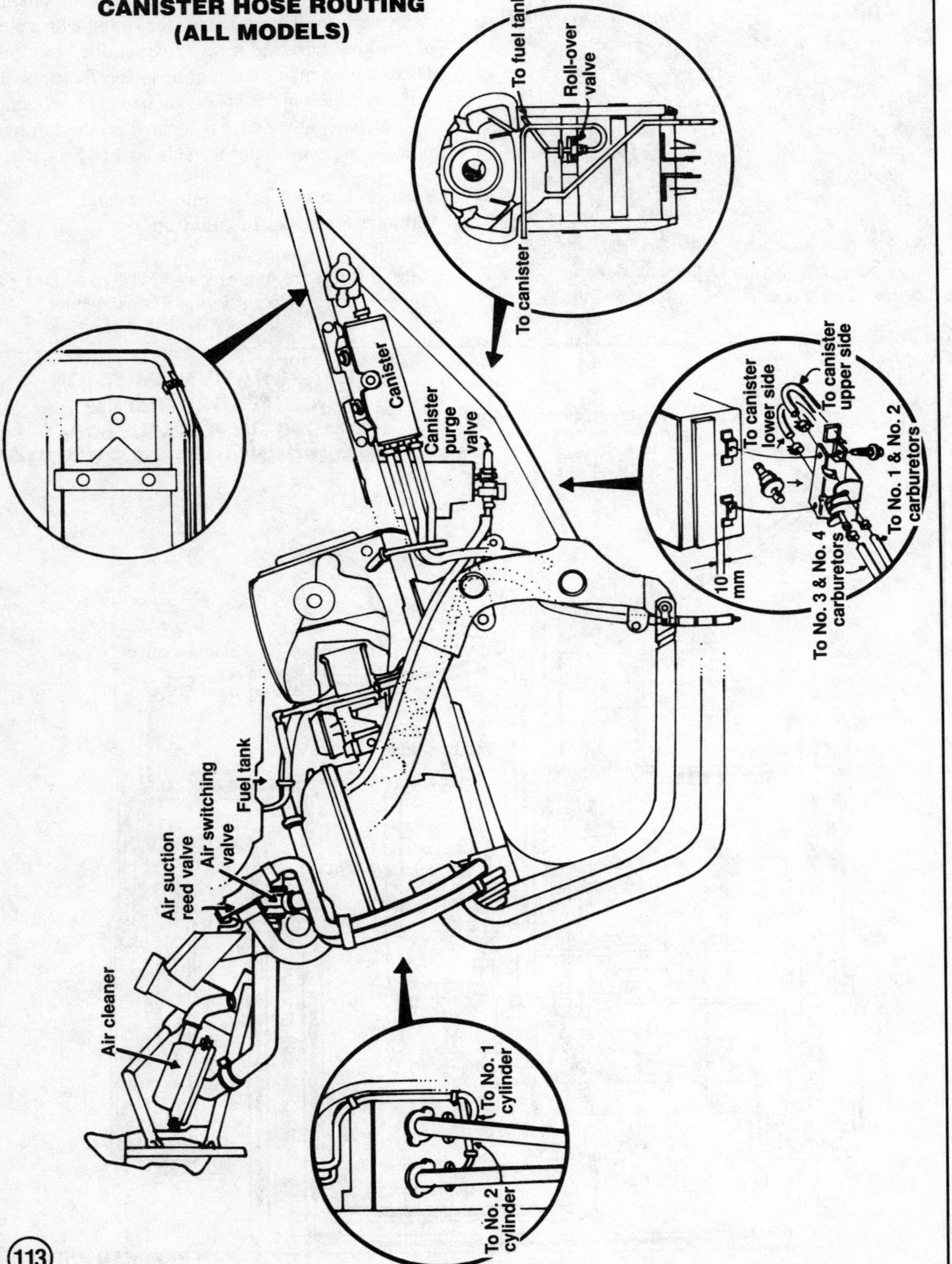

113

2. Remove the left-hand side cover as described under *Side Cover Removal/Installation* in this chapter.

NOTE
Prior to removing the hoses from the vacuum control valves and the charcoal canister, mark the hose and the fitting with a piece of masking tape and identify where the hose goes.

3. Disconnect the hoses (A, **Figure 112**) going to the charcoal canister and to each vacuum control valve.

4. Remove the bolts, lockwashers and washers securing the charcoal canister (B, **Figure 112**) to the frame bracket and remove the canister assembly. Don't lose the spacer located within the rubber grommets on the frame bracket.

5. Remove the bolts and lockwashers securing the vacuum control valves assembly and remove the valve and hose assembly.

6. Install by reversing these removal steps while noting the following:

a. Be sure to install the hoses to their correct fittings on the charcoal canister and the vacuum control valves and that they are routed correctly through the frame (**Figure 113**).
b. Make sure the hoses are not kinked, twisted or in contact with any sharp surfaces.

AIR SUCTION SYSTEM (CALIFORNIA MODELS ONLY)

The air suction system consists of a vacuum switch, 2 air suction valves (reed valves) and air and vacuum hoses (**Figure 114**). This system does not

114

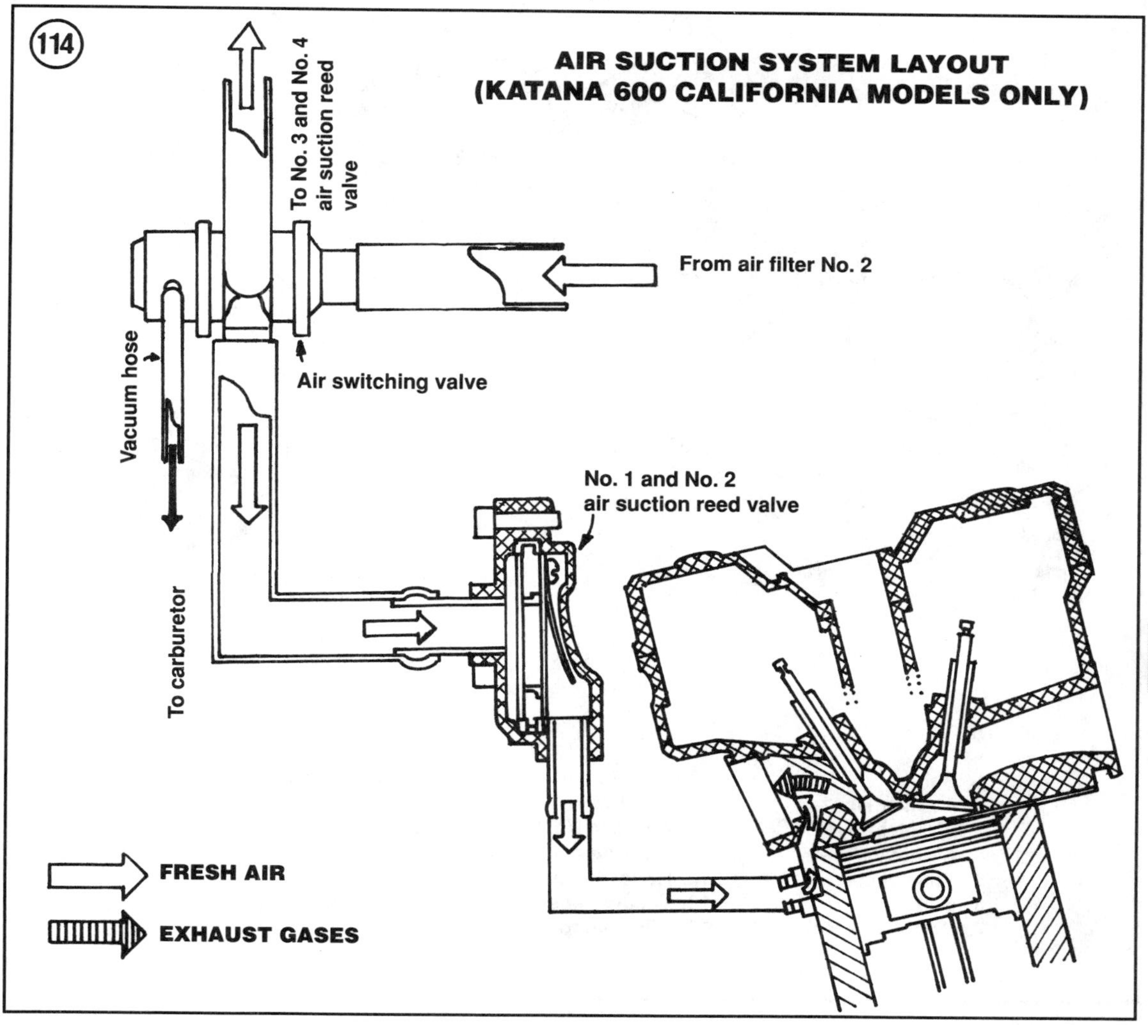

13

pressurize air, but uses the momentary pressure differentials generated by the exhaust gas pulses to introduce fresh air into the exhaust ports. Make sure all air and vacuum hoses are correctly routed and attached. Inspect the hoses and replace any if necessary.

115

AIR SUCTION SYSTEM (KATANA 600 CALIFORNIA MODELS ONLY)

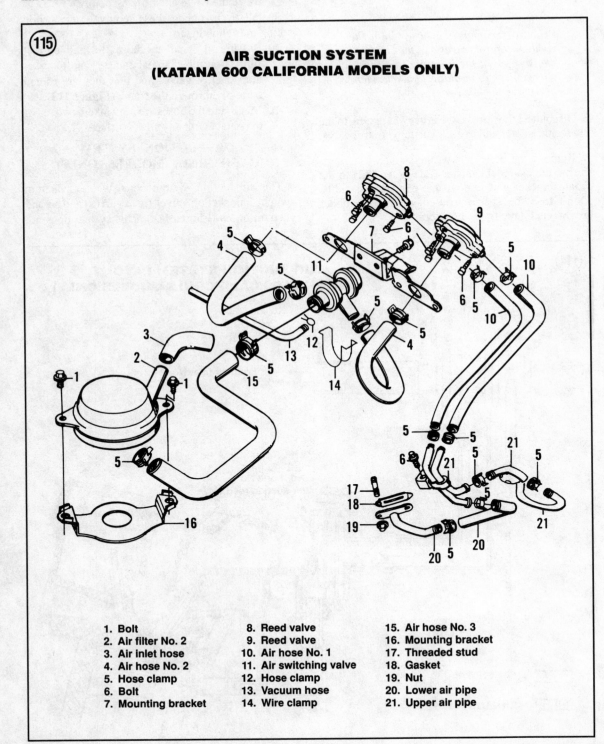

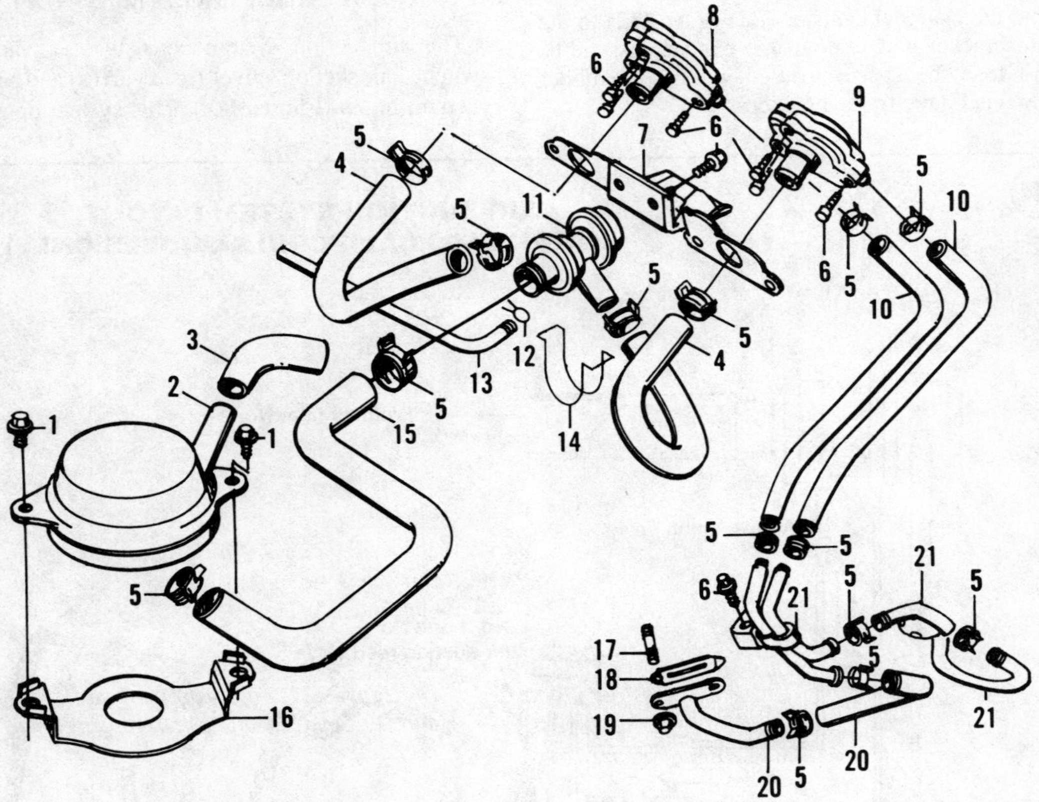

1. Bolt
2. Air filter No. 2
3. Air inlet hose
4. Air hose No. 2
5. Hose clamp
6. Bolt
7. Mounting bracket
8. Reed valve
9. Reed valve
10. Air hose No. 1
11. Air switching valve
12. Hose clamp
13. Vacuum hose
14. Wire clamp
15. Air hose No. 3
16. Mounting bracket
17. Threaded stud
18. Gasket
19. Nut
20. Lower air pipe
21. Upper air pipe

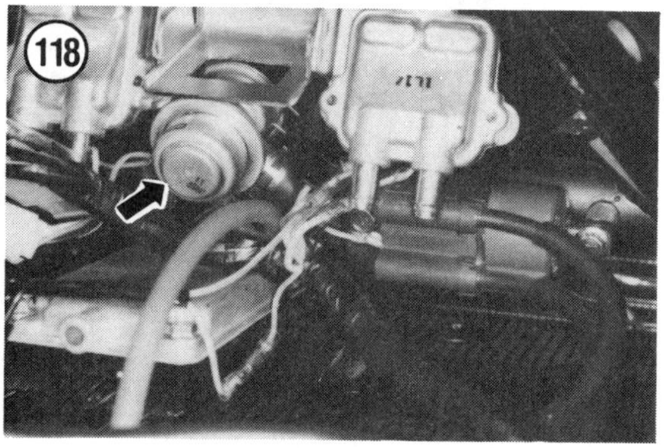

Removal/Installation

Refer to **Figure 115** for this procedure.

1. Remove the front fairing as described under *Front Fairing Removal/Installation* in this chapter.
2. Remove fuel tank as described under *Fuel Tank Removal/Installation* in this chapter.
3. Remove the exhaust system as described in this chapter.
4. Remove the bolts securing the frame upper crossmember (**Figure 116**) and remove the crossmember.
5. Remove the bolts securing the reed valve mounting bracket (A, **Figure 117**).
6. Release the clamping band securing air hose No. 1 to each reed valve (B, **Figure 117**). Pull both hoses off the fittings on each reed valve.
7. Unhook the wire clamp securing the air switching valve (**Figure 118**) to the mounting bracket and let the valve drop down.
8. Release the clamping band securing the air hose No. 3 (A, **Figure 119**) to the backside of the air switch valve. Pull the hose off the fitting on the valve.
9. Release the clamping band securing each air hose No. 2 (B, **Figure 119**) to the backside of each reed valve. Pull the hose off the fittings on each reed valve.
10. Remove the reed valve and bracket assembly from the frame.
11. Disconnect the vacuum line from the air switch valve and remove the air switch valve and air hose No. 2 assembly from the frame.
12. Place a shop cloth on the front fender.
13. Remove the tie wrap (**Figure 120**) securing the oil cooler line to the frame.

NOTE
*In **Figure 121**, only 1 bolt is visible, be sure to remove both bolts securing the oil cooler.*

14. Remove the bolts (**Figure 121**) securing the oil cooler. Lift the oil cooler out of its lower mounting tabs and rest the cooler on the front fender (**Figure 122**).
15. Remove the bolt securing the upper air pipe assembly (**Figure 123**) to the frame on each side.
16. Remove the bolts securing the lower air pipe assemblies to the cylinder head.
17. Remove the air hose No. 1, the upper air pipe assembly and the lower air pipe assembly from the engine and frame.
18. If necessary, remove the bolts securing the air filter No. 2 assembly (**Figure 124**) to the mounting bracket and remove it.
19. Install by reversing these removal steps. Be sure to install each hose to the correct fitting.

EXHAUST SYSTEM

The exhaust system is a vital performance component and frequently, because of its design, it is a vulnerable piece of equipment. Check the exhaust system for deep dents and fractures and repair or replace them immediately. Check the muffler frame mounting flanges for fractures and loose bolts. Check the cylinder head mounting flanges for tightness. A loose exhaust pipe connection can rob the engine of power.

The exhaust system consists of 2 exhaust pipe/muffler assemblies joined with a cross over tube under the crankcase.

Removal/Installation

Refer to **Figure 125** for this procedure.

1. Remove the front fairing as described under *Front Fairing Removal/Installation* in this chapter.
2. Remove the Allen bolts securing each exhaust pipe clamp (**Figure 126**) to the cylinder head.
3. Loosen the clamp bolt securing the cross over tube under the crankcase.
4. On one side of the bike, remove the bolt, washer and nut (**Figure 127**) securing the rear portion of the exhaust system to the frame.
5. Separate the exhaust system at the cross over pipe.
6. Move that side of the exhaust system forward and remove the system from the frame.
7. On the other side of the bike, remove the bolt, washer and nut securing the rear portion of the exhaust system to the frame.
8. Move that side of the exhaust system forward and remove the system from the frame.

121

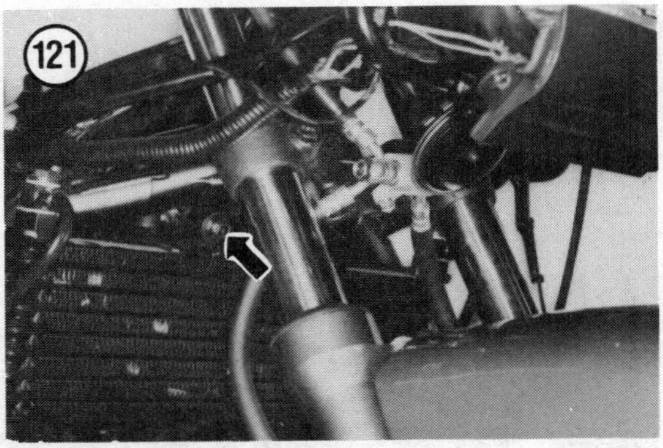

122

123

124

125

EXHAUST SYSTEM (KATANA 600)

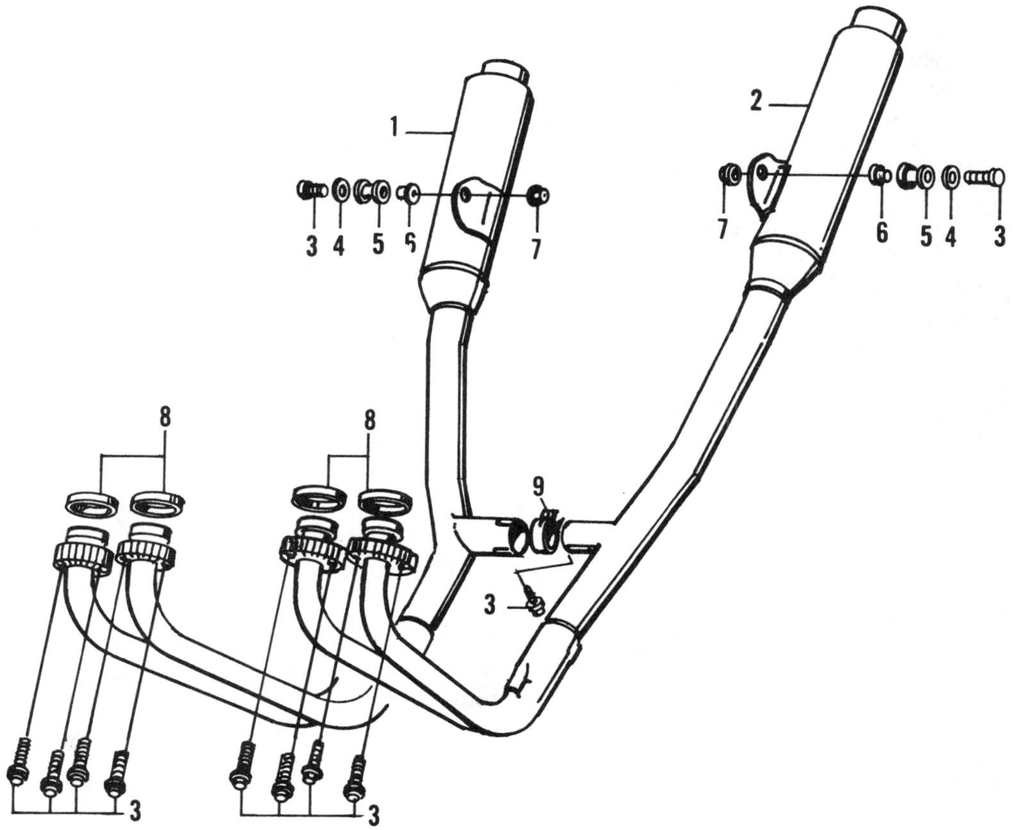

1. Exhaust pipe/muffler assembly (right-hand side)
2. Exhaust pipe/muffler assembly (left-hand side)
3. Bolt
4. Washer
5. Rubber cushion
6. Spacer
7. Nut
8. Gasket
9. Clamp

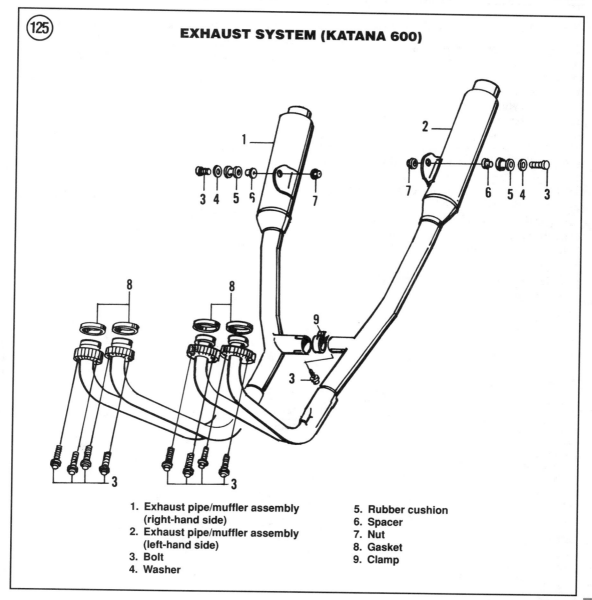

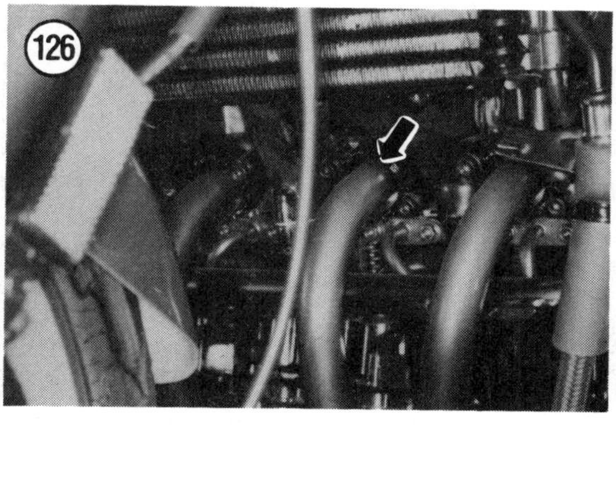

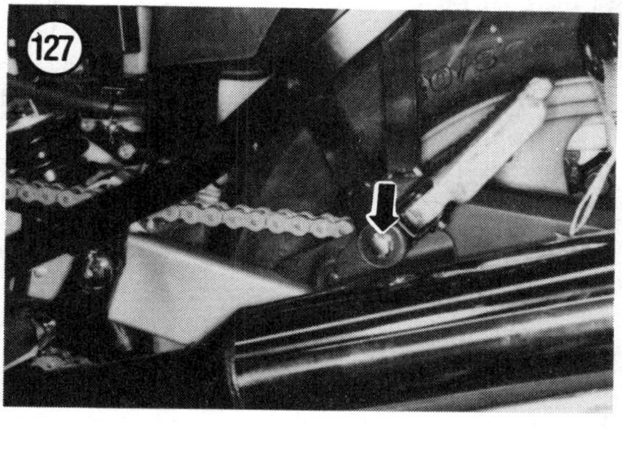

9. Don't lose the spacer located within the rubber cushion in the mounting bracket on the muffler.
10. Inspect the gaskets at all joints; replace as necessary.
11. Be sure to install a new gasket in each exhaust port in the cylinder head.
12. Install one side of the exhaust system onto the frame and engine.
13. Install one cylinder head Allen bolt (at each exhaust port) only finger-tight until the rest of the bolts and washers are installed.
14. Install the other side of the exhaust system onto the frame and engine.
15. Install one cylinder head Allen bolt (at each exhaust port) only finger-tight until the rest of the bolts and washers are installed.
16. Connect both exhaust systems at the cross over pipe. Do not tighten the clamp bolt at this time.
17. Install the exhaust system mounting bolts, washers and nuts; do not tighten at this time. Make sure the inlets for the head pipes are correctly seated in the exhaust ports.

NOTE

Tightening the cylinder head Allen bolts first will minimize exhaust leaks at the cylinder head. Tighten the bolts securely.

18. Tighten the rest of the exhaust system bolts securely, including the cross over pipe clamp bolt.
19. After installation is complete, start the engine and make sure there are no exhaust leaks.
20. Install the front fairing as described in this chapter.

Table 10 CARBURETOR SPECIFICATIONS (KATANA 600)

	U.S. Models	
Item	**1988-1989**	**1990-on**
Carburetor type	Mikuni BST31SS	Mikuni BST31SS
Model No.		
49-state	19C10	44C20
California	19C20	44C20
Venturi diameter	31 mm (1.2 in.)	31 mm (1.2 in.)
Fuel level	1.0-2.0 mm (0.04-0.08 in.)	1.0-2.0 mm (0.04-0.08 in.)
Float height	13.6-15.6 mm (0.53-0.61 in.)	13.6-15.6 mm (0.53-0.61 in.)
Needle clip position	fixed	fixed
Jet needle	4CZ-4-1	4CZ-5-1
Main jet No.		
All 4 carburetors	–	112.5
No. 1 and No. 4	137.5	–
No. 2 and No. 3	135	–
Main air jet No.		
49-state	32.5	37.5
California	0.5 mm	5F105
Pilot jet No.		
49-state	32.5	37.5
California	32.5	32.5
Pilot outlet	0.7 mm	0.9 mm
Starter jet No.	45	35
Pilot screw	pre-set	pre-set
Pilot air jet No.		
49-state	150	155
California	155	145

(continued)

Table 10 CARBURETOR SPECIFICATIONS (KATANA 600) (continued)

Non U.S. Models			
Item	**1988**		
Carburetor type	Mikuni BST31SS	Mikuni BST31SS	Mikuni GST31SS
Model No.	19C00, 19C40	19C30	19C50
Venturi diameter	31 mm (1.2 in.)	31 mm (1.2 in.)	31 mm (1.2 in.)
Fuel level	1.5 ± 0.5 mm (0.06 ± 0.02 in.)	1.5 ± 0.5 mm (0.06 ± 0.02 in.)	1.5 ± 0.5 mm (0.06 ± 0.02 in.)
Float level	14.6 ± 1.0 mm (0.57 ± 0.04 in.)	14.6 ± 1.0 mm (0.57 ± 0.04 in.)	14.6 ± 1.0 mm (0.57 ± 0.04 in.)
Jet needle	4CZ-3-3rd	4CZ-3-3rd	4CZ-3-3rd
Needle jet	P-9	P-8	P-9
Main jet No.			
No. 1 and No. 4	137.5	137.5	137.5
No. 2 and No. 3	135	135	135
Main air jet No.	1.0 mm	1.0 mm	1.0 mm
Pilot jet No.	40	32.5	32.5
Pilot outlet	0.7 mm	0.7 mm	0.7 mm
Starter jet No.	45	45	45
Pilot screw	1 7/8 turns back	Pre-set	1 7/8 turns back
Pilot air jet No.	160	150	130
Throttle valve	130	130	130
Item	**1989**		
Carburetor type	Mikuni BST31SS	Mikuni BST31SS	Mikuni BST31SS
Model No.	43C00, 43C40 43C60, 43C70	43C30	43C50
Venturi diameter	31 mm (1.2 in.)	31 mm (1.2 in.)	31 mm (1.2 in.)
Fuel level	1.5 ± 0.5 mm (0.06 ± 0.02 in.)	1.5 ± 0.5 mm (0.06 ± 0.02 in.)	1.5 ± 0.5 mm (0.06 ± 0.02 in.)
Float level	14.6 ± 1.0 mm (0.57 ± 0.04 in.)	14.6 ± 1.0 mm (0.57 ± 0.04 in.)	14.6 ± 1.0 mm (0.57 ± 0.04 in.)
Jet needle	4CZ-3-3rd	4CZ-3-3rd	4CZ-3-3rd
Needle jet	P-9	Q-0	P-9
Main jet No.			
No. 1 and No. 4	137.5	137.5	137.5
No. 2 and No. 3	135	135	135
Main air jet No.	1.0 mm	1.0 mm	1.0 mm
Pilot jet No.	40	30	32.5
Pilot outlet	0.7 mm	0.7 mm	0.7 mm
Starter jet No.	45	45	45
Pilot screw	Pre-set	Pre-set	Pre-set
Pilot air jet No.	160	145	130
Throttle valve	130	130	130
Item	**1990-on**		
Carburetor type	Mikuni BST33SS	Mikuni BST33SS	Mikuni BST33SS
Model No.	44C00, 44C40	44C10	44C20
Venturi diameter	33 mm (1.3 in.)	33 mm (1.3 in.)	33 mm (1.3 in.)
Fuel level	Not available	Not available	Not available
Float level	14.6 ± 1.0 mm (0.57 ± 0.04 in.)	14.6 ± 1.0 mm (0.57 ± 0.04 in.)	14.6 ± 1.0 mm (0.57 ± 0.04 in.)
Jet needle	5FZ102-3	5F104	5F105
Needle jet	P-3	P-2	P-2
Main jet No.	110	112.5	112.5
Main air jet	0.5 mm	0.5 mm	0.5 mm

(continued)

Table 10 CARBURETOR SPECIFICATIONS (KATANA 600) (continued)

	Non U.S. Models (continued)		
Item	1990-on (continued)		
Pilot jet No.	32.5	32.5	32.5
Pilot outlet	0.9 mm	0.9 mm	0.9 mm
Starter jet No.	35	35	35
Pilot screw	1 1/2 turns back*	Pre-set	Pre-set
Pilot air jet	1.3 mm	1.55 mm	1.45 mm
Throttle valve	120	120	115

*1 1/4 turns back on 1991-on models.

CHAPTER EIGHT

ELECTRICAL SYSTEM

TRANSISTORIZED IGNITION

All models are equipped with a transistorized ignition system that is a solid state system. The ignition circuit is shown in **Figure 128**.

Signal Generator Testing

1. Remove the seat as described under *Seat Removal/Installation* in this chapter.
2. Remove the right-hand side cover.

128

IGNITION CIRCUIT (KATANA 600)

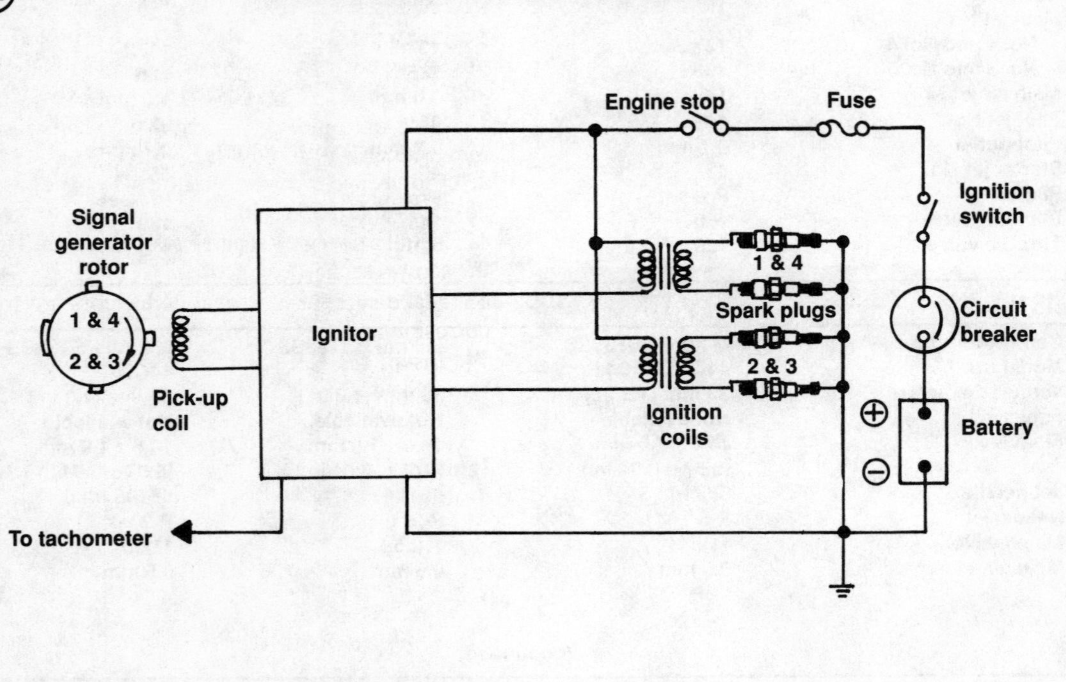

3. Disconnect the 2-pin electrical connector from the signal generator (**Figure 129**). The connector contains 1 black/blue wire and 1 yellow wire.

4. Use an ohmmeter set at R × 100 and check the resistance between the 2 wires in the electrical connector. The specified resistance is 135-200 ohms.

129
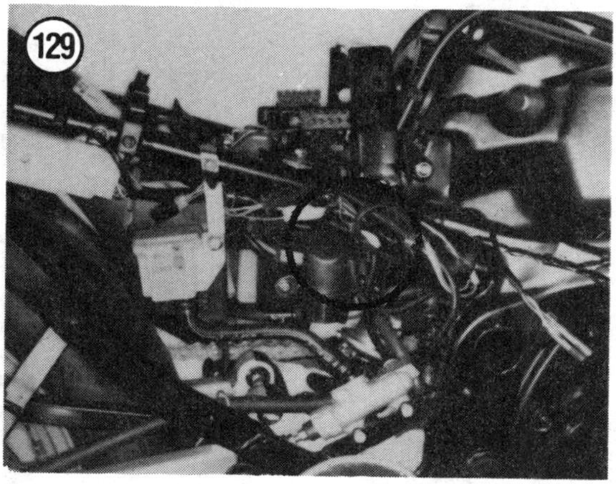

130

131
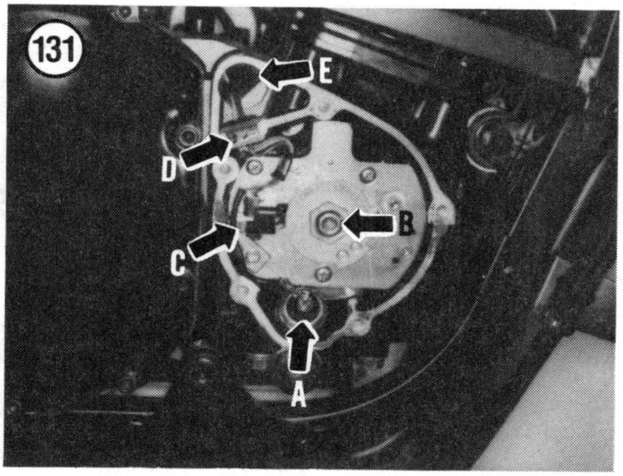

5. If the resistance shown is greater, or there is no indicated resistance (infinite resistance) between the 2 wires in the connector, the signal generator has an open or short and must be replaced as described in this chapter.

Signal Generator Removal/Installation

1. Remove the front fairing as described under *Front Fairing Removal/Installation* in this chapter.
2. Remove the right-hand side cover.
3. Disconnect the 2-pin electrical connector from the signal generator (**Figure 129**). The connector contains 1 black/blue wire and 1 yellow wire.
4. Remove the bolts securing the signal generator cover (**Figure 130**). Remove the cover and gasket.
5. Disconnect the oil pressure sending switch wire (A, **Figure 131**).
6. Hold onto the signal generator rotor with a 17 mm wrench and loosen the Allen bolt (B, **Figure 131**) securing the rotor and remove the rotor.
7. Remove the screws securing the signal generator stator plate (C, **Figure 131**) to the crankcase.
8. Carefully remove the rubber grommet (D, **Figure 131**) from the crankcase. Pull the electrical wires through the opening in the crankcase (E, **Figure 131**) and remove the stator plate assembly.
9. Apply a light coat of gasket sealer to the area in the crankcase where the rubber grommet fits into.
10. Align the notch in the back of the rotor with the pin on the end of the crankshaft and install the rotor and Allen bolt.
11. Hold onto the signal generator rotor with a 17 mm wrench and tighten the Allen bolt (B, **Figure 131**) to secure the rotor. Tighten the Allen bolt to 25-35 N•m (18-25 ft.-lb.).
12. Install a new gasket and install the cover. Tighten the screws securely.
13. Make sure all electrical connectors are free of corrosion and are tight.
14. Install the left-hand side cover and the front fairing as described in this chapter.

Ignition Coil Testing

NOTE

In order to get accurate resistance measurements, the coil must be warm (minimum temperature is 20° C/68° F). If necessary, start the engine and let it warm up to normal operating temperature.

1. Remove the fuel tank as described under *Fuel Tank Removal/Installation* in this chapter.
2. Disconnect all ignition coil wires (including the spark plug leads from the spark plugs) before testing.
3. Use an ohmmeter set at R × 1 and measure the primary coil resistance between the positive (+) and the negative (–) terminals on the top of the ignition coil. The specified resistance value is 2-4 ohms.
4. Use an ohmmeter set at R × 1,000 and measure the secondary coil resistance between the 2 spark plug leads (with the spark plug caps attached). The specified resistance value is 12,000-18,000 ohms.
5. If the coil resistance does not meet either of these specifications, the coil must be replaced. If the coil exhibits visible damage, it should be replaced.
6. Reconnect all ignition coil wires to the ignition coil.
7. Repeat this procedure for the other ignition coil.

Ignition Coil Removal/Installation

1. Remove the fuel tank as described under *Fuel Tank Removal/Installation* in this chapter.

NOTE
On the original equipment ignition coil and high voltage leads, the spark plug cylinder number is marked on each lead. If these marks are no longer legible or are missing, mark each lead as to which cylinder it is attached to. The No. 1 cylinder is on the left-hand side and working across from left-to-right are the No. 2, No. 3 and No. 4 cylinders. These marks will make it easier during installation and it will make sure that the correct leads go to the correct cylinders.

2. On California models, perform the following:
   a. Remove the bolts securing the frame upper crossmember (**Figure 132**) and remove the crossmember.
   b. Remove the bolts securing the reed valve mounting bracket (A, **Figure 133**).
   c. Release the clamping band securing air hose No. 1 to each reed valve (B, **Figure 133**). Pull both hoses off the fittings on each reed valve.
   d. Move the reed valve assembly (A, **Figure 134**) up and out of the way.

3. Disconnect the high voltage lead from each spark plug.
4. Remove the bolts securing the ignition coil (B, **Figure 134**) to the frame.
5. Carefully pull the ignition coil away from the frame and disconnect the primary electrical wires from the coil.
6. If necessary, repeat Steps 3-5 for the other ignition coil.
7. Install by reversing these removal steps. Make sure all electrical connections are free of corrosion and are tight.

Ignitor Unit Replacement

1. Remove the left-hand side cover as described in this chapter.
2. Disconnect the battery negative lead (**Figure 135**).
3. Remove the screws securing the ignitor unit (A, **Figure 136**).
4. Disconnect both of the ignitor unit's electrical connectors (B, **Figure 136**).

136

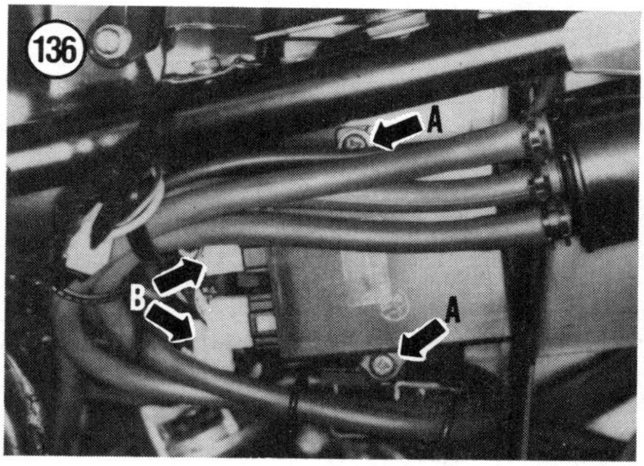

137

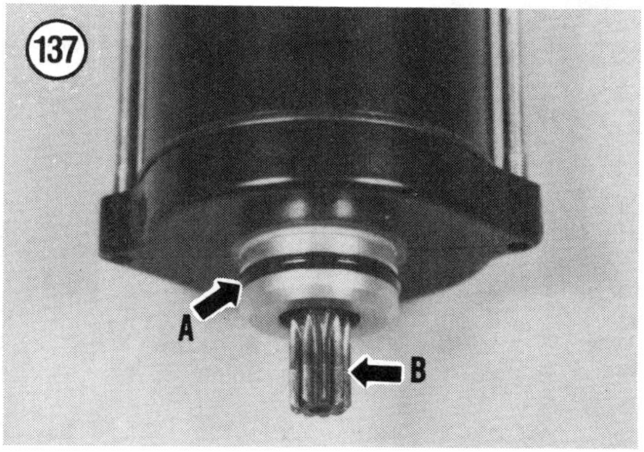

5. Carefully pull the ignitor unit from the frame.
6. Remove the ignitor unit.
7. Install a new ignitor unit onto the frame. Attach both electrical wires to it. Make sure both electrical connectors are free of corrosion and are tight.
8. Install and tighten the screws securely.
9. Connect the battery negative lead.
10. Install all parts removed.

ELECTRIC STARTER

Removal/Installation

1. Remove the front fairing as described under *Front Fairing Removal/Installation* in this chapter.
2. Disconnect the battery negative lead (**Figure 135**).
3. Remove the drive sprocket cover.
4. Slide back the rubber boot on the electrical cable connector.
5. Disconnect the starter electrical cable from the starter.
6. Remove the bolts securing the starter to the crankcase.
7. Lift up and withdraw the starter from the top of the crankcase.
8. Install by reversing these removal steps.

Preliminary Inspection

The overhaul of a starter motor is best left to an expert. This procedure shows how to detect a defective starter.

Inspect the O-ring seal (A, **Figure 137**). O-ring seals tend to harden after prolonged use and heat and therefore lose their ability to seal properly. Replace as necessary.

Inspect the gear (B, **Figure 137**) for chipped or missing teeth. If damaged, the starter assembly must be replaced.

Disassembly

Refer to **Figure 138** for this procedure.

1. Remove the case screws and washers, then separate the front and rear covers from the case.

NOTE

Write down the number of shims used on the shaft next to the commutator and next to the rear cover. Be sure to install the same number when reassembling the starter.

2. Remove the special washer and shims from the front cover end of the shaft.

3. Remove the washers from the armature end of the shaft.

4. Withdraw the armature coil assembly from the case assembly.

NOTE
Before removing the nuts and washers, write down their description and order. They must be reinstalled in the same order to insulate this set of brushes from the case.

5. Remove the nuts, washers and O-ring securing the brush holder set in the rear cover and remove the brush terminal set.

CAUTION
Do not immerse the wire windings in the case or the armature coil in solvent as the insulation may be damaged. Wipe the windings with a cloth lightly moistened with solvent and thoroughly dry.

6. Clean all grease, dirt and carbon from all components.

Assembly

1. Install the brush holder assembly in the rear cover. Align the holder locating tab with the notch in the rear cover.

NOTE
In the next step, reinstall all parts in the same order as noted during removal. This is essential in order to insulate this set of brushes from the case.

(138) **STARTER MOTOR (KATANA 600)**

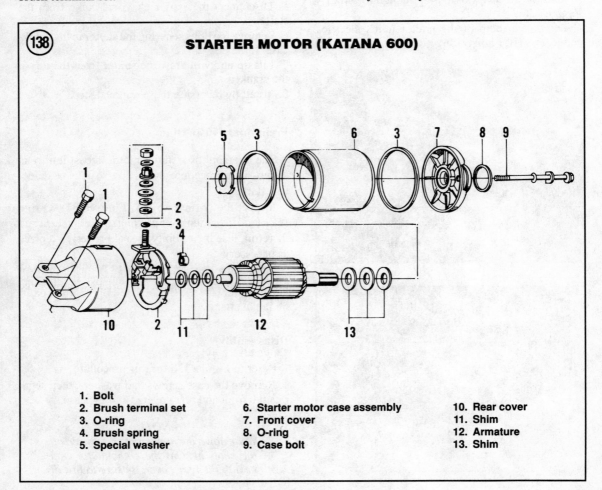

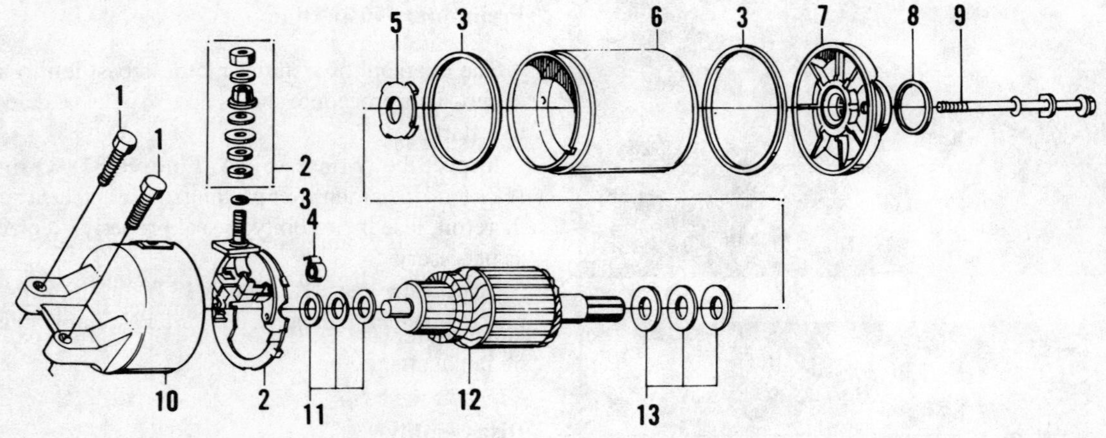

1. Bolt
2. Brush terminal set
3. O-ring
4. Brush spring
5. Special washer
6. Starter motor case assembly
7. Front cover
8. O-ring
9. Case bolt
10. Rear cover
11. Shim
12. Armature
13. Shim

2. Install the O-ring, washers and nuts securing the brush terminal set to the case.

3. Install the washers onto the armature end of the shaft.

4. Insert the armature coil assembly into the rear cover. Do not damage the brushes during this step.

5. Install the case assembly onto the armature coil assembly and rear cover.

6. Install the shims and the special washer onto the front cover end of the shaft.

7. Install the front cover.

8. Align the raised marks on the case with those on the front and rear cover.

9. Apply blue Loctite (No. 242) onto the case screw threads and install the screws and washers. Tighten the screws securely.

139

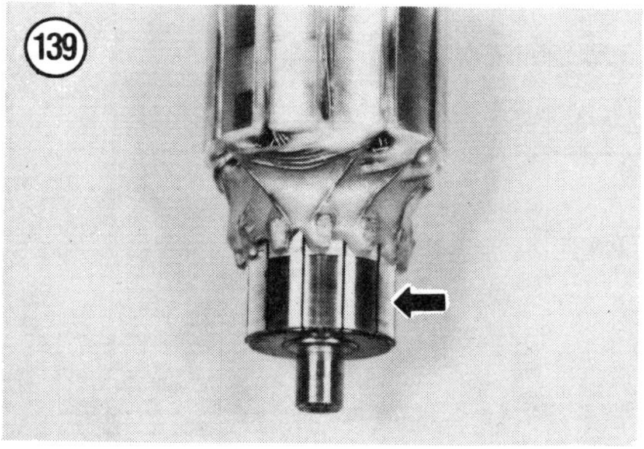

140

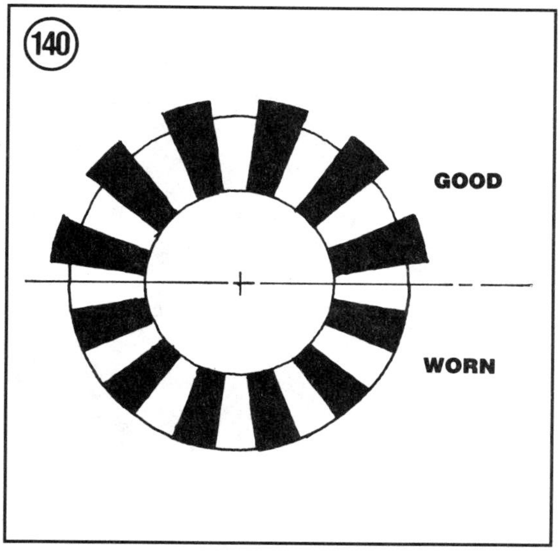

Inspection

1. Measure the length of each brush with a vernier caliper. If the length is 6.0 mm (0.20 in.) or less for any one of the brushes, the brush holder assembly and brush terminal set must be replaced. The brushes cannot be replaced individually.

2. Inspect the commutator (**Figure 139**). The mica in a good commutator is below the surface of the copper bars. On a worn commutator the mica and copper bars may be worn to the same level (**Figure 140**). If necessary, have the commutator serviced by a dealer or electrical repair shop.

3. Inspect the commutator copper bars for discoloration. If a pair of bars is discolored, grounded armature coils are indicated.

4. Use an ohmmeter and perform the following:
   a. Check for continuity between the commutator bars (**Figure 141**); there should be continuity (indicated resistance) between pairs of bars.
   b. Check for continuity between the commutator bars and the shaft (**Figure 142**); there should be *no* continuity (infinite resistance).
   c. If the unit fails either of these tests, the starter assembly must be replaced. The armature cannot be replaced individually.

5. Use an ohmmeter and perform the following:
   a. Check for continuity between the starter cable terminal and the starter case; there should be continuity (indicated resistance).
   b. Check for continuity between the starter cable terminal and the brush wire terminal; there should be *no* continuity (infinite resistance).
   c. If the unit fails either of these tests, the starter assembly must be replaced. The case/field coil assembly cannot be replaced individually.

6. Inspect the oil seal and bushing (**Figure 143**) in the front cover for wear or damage. If either is damaged, replace the starter assembly as these parts are not available separately.

7. Inspect the bushing (**Figure 144**) in the rear cover for wear or damage. If it is damaged, replace the starter assembly as this part is not available separately.

13

LIGHTING SYSTEM

Headlight Bulb Replacement

Refer to **Figure 145** for this procedure.

NOTE
This procedure is shown with the front fairing removed for clarity. It is not necessary to remove the front fairing to replace either headlight bulb.

1. Disconnect the electrical connector (A, **Figure 146**) from the backside of the bulb.
2. Remove the rubber cover (B, **Figure 146**) from the back of the headlight bulb.

CAUTION
Carefully read all instructions shipped with the replacement quartz bulb. Do not touch the bulb glass with your fingers because any traces of skin oil on the quartz halogen bulb will drastically reduce bulb life. Clean any traces of oil from the bulb with a cloth moistened in alcohol or lacquer thinner.

3. Unhook the clip (**Figure 147**) and remove the light bulb (**Figure 148**). Replace with a new bulb.
4. Install by reversing these removal steps. Install the rubber cover with the up arrow facing up.

Headlight Lens and Housing Assembly Removal/Installation

1. Remove the front fairing as described under *Front Fairing Removal/Installation* in this chapter.
2. Remove the headlight bulb as described in this chapter.
3. Remove the bolts, lockwashers and washers (**Figure 149**) on each side securing the headlight housing to the front fairing mounting bracket and remove the lens and housing assembly.
4. Install by reversing these removal steps.

141

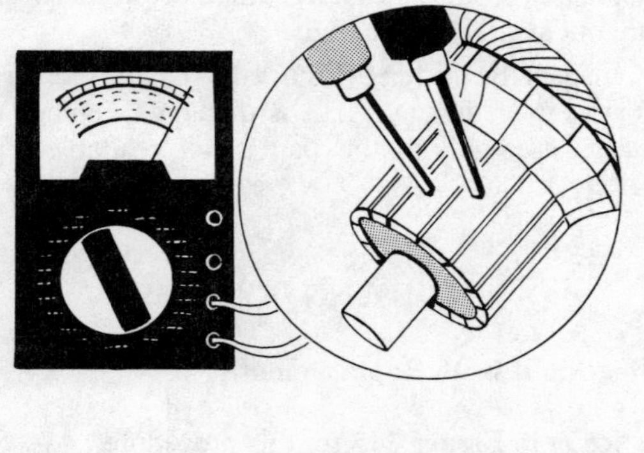

5. Adjust the headlight as described in this chapter.

Headlight Adjustment

Adjust the headlight horizontally and vertically according to Department of Motor Vehicle regulations in your area.

142

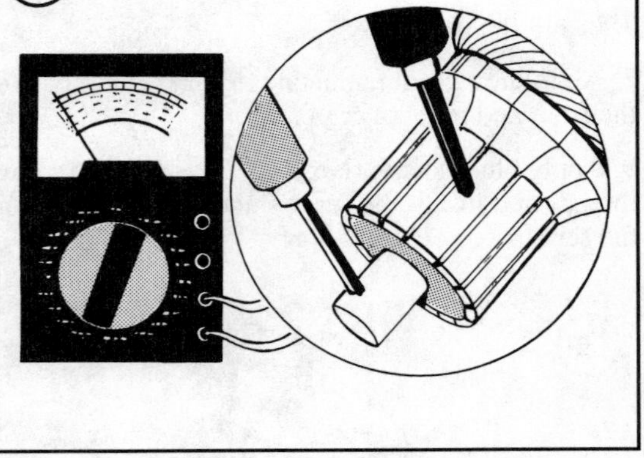

143

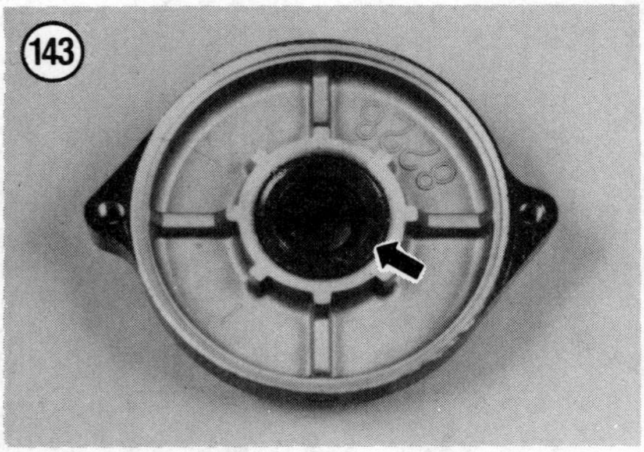

144

To adjust the headlight horizontally, turn the adjuster in the upper right-hand corner of the housing assembly. Turn the adjuster either clockwise or counterclockwise until the aim is correct.

For vertical adjustment, turn the adjuster in the lower left-hand corner of the housing assembly either clockwise or counterclockwise until the aim is correct.

Taillight/Brakelight Replacement

Refer to **Figure 150** for this procedure.

1. Remove the screws (**Figure 151**) securing the lens and remove the lens and gasket.
2. Push in on the bulb, turn it counterclockwise and remove it.

(145)

HEADLIGHT ASSEMBLY (KATANA 600)

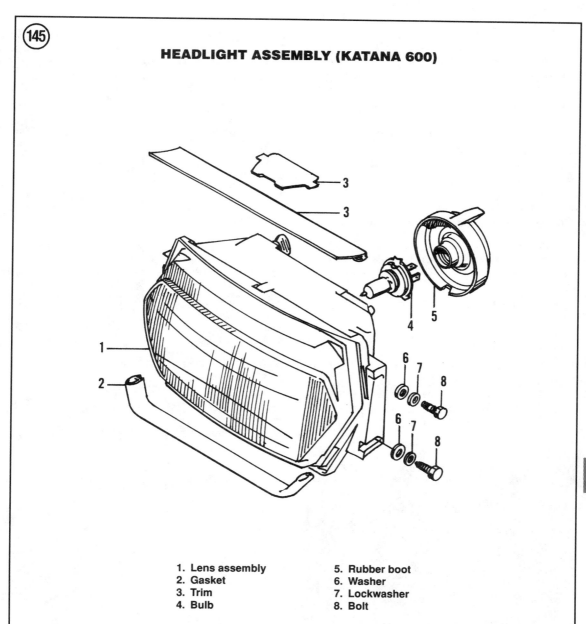

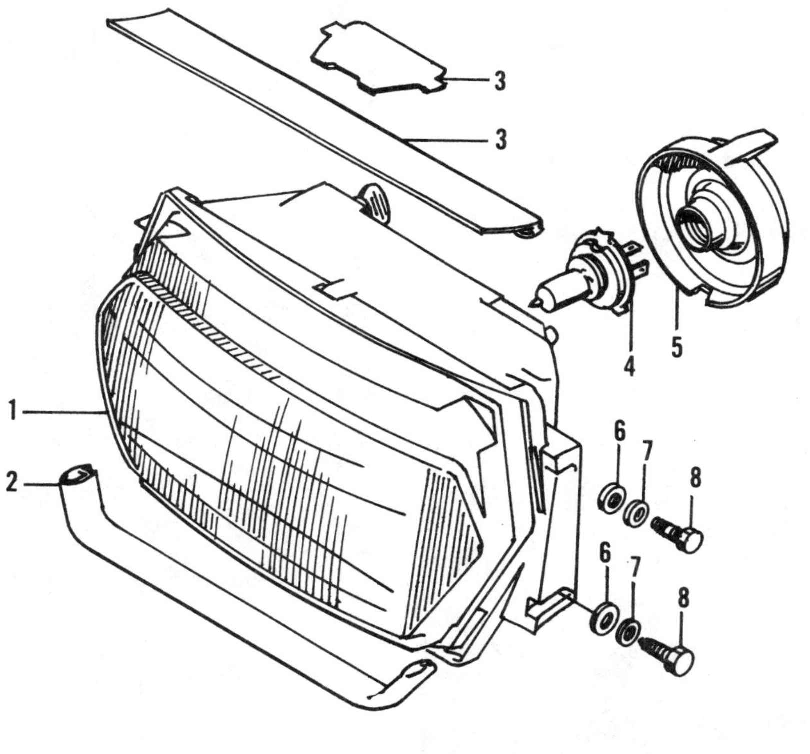

1. Lens assembly
2. Gasket
3. Trim
4. Bulb
5. Rubber boot
6. Washer
7. Lockwasher
8. Bolt

13

3. Wash out the inside and outside of the lens with a mild detergent and wipe dry.
4. Inspect the lens gasket and replace it if damaged or deteriorated.
5. Replace the bulb and install the lens; do not overtighten the screws as the lens may crack.

License Plate Light Replacement

Refer to **Figure 152** for this procedure.

1. Working under the rear fender, remove the screws securing the cover and remove the cover.
2. Remove the screws securing the lens and remove the lens and gasket.
3. Push in on the bulb, turn it counterclockwise and remove it.
4. Wash out the inside and outside of the lens with a mild detergent and wipe dry.
5. Inspect the lens gasket and replace it if damaged or deteriorated.
6. Replace the bulb and install the lens; do not overtighten the screws as the lens may crack.
7. Install the cover and tighten the screws securely.

ELECTRICAL COMPONENTS

Instrument Cluster and Indicator Light Panel Removal/Installation

Refer to **Figure 153** for this procedure.

1. Remove the seat as described under *Seat Removal/Installation* in this chapter.
2. Remove the front fairing as described under *Front Fairing Removal/Installation* in this chapter.
3. Disconnect the battery negative lead (**Figure 154**).

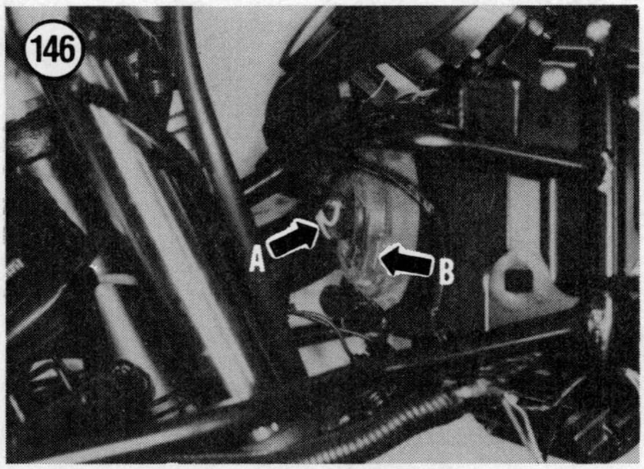

4. Remove the headlight lens and housing assembly (A, **Figure 155**) as described in this chapter.
5. To remove the speedometer, unscrew the speedometer drive cable (A, **Figure 156**) from the back of the meter.
6. At the back of each individual meter, disconnect each electrical connector(s) (B, **Figure 155**) from the meter.

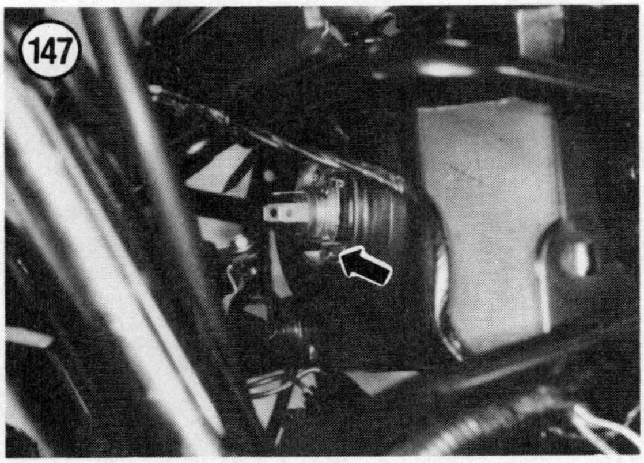

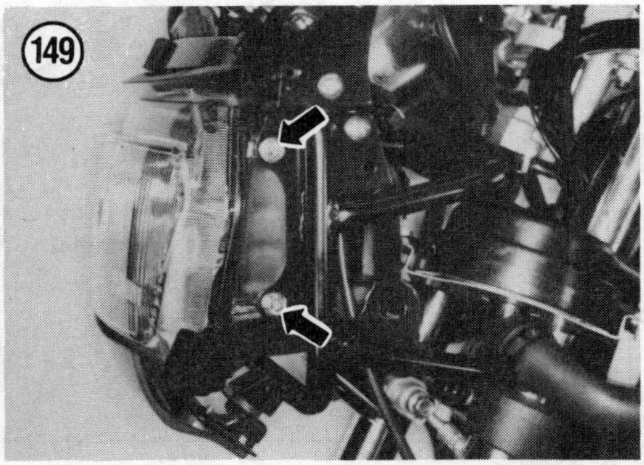

7. Remove the nuts (B, **Figure 156**) securing the meter to the mounting bracket and remove that meter (A, **Figure 157**).

8. Repeat Step 6 and Step 7 for any other meters to be removed.

151

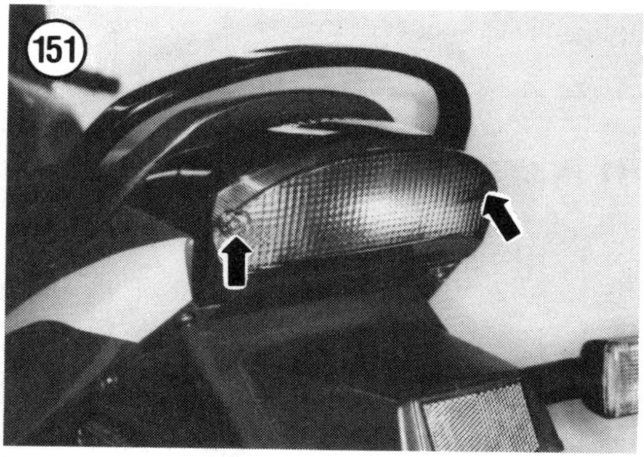

9. To remove the indicator light panel, perform the following:

a. Carefully pull the electrical socket/bulb assembly out from the backside of the bracket.
b. Remove the screws securing the bracket, plate and end caps and remove them.
c. Remove the indicator light panel and gasket (B, **Figure 157**).

10. Install by reversing these removal steps, make sure all electrical connectors are free of corrosion and are tight.

Cooling Fan (1990-on California Models)

Refer to **Figure 158** for this procedure.

150

TAILLIGHT/BRAKELIGHT (KATANA 600)

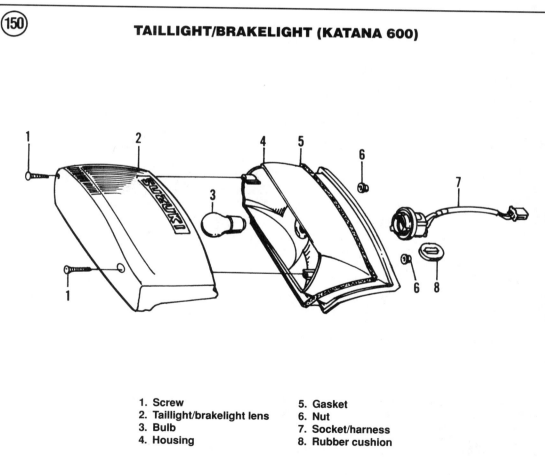

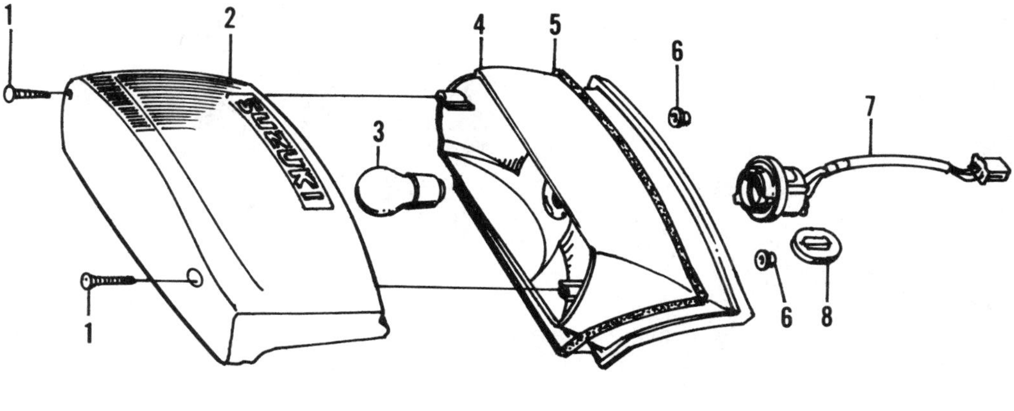

1. Screw
2. Taillight/brakelight lens
3. Bulb
4. Housing
5. Gasket
6. Nut
7. Socket/harness
8. Rubber cushion

1. Remove the front fairing as described under *Front Fairing Removal/Installation* in this chapter.

2. Disconnect the battery negative lead (**Figure 154**).

3. Remove the screws and washers (**Figure 159**) securing the cooling fan to the frame and partially remove the fan from the frame. Don't lose the collar in the rubber cushion in the mounting holes.

4. Disconnect the 2-pin electrical connector to the cooling fan and remove the fan assembly.

5. Install by reversing these removal steps, make sure the electrical connector is free of corrosion and is tight.

(152)

LICENSE PLATE LIGHT (KATANA 600)

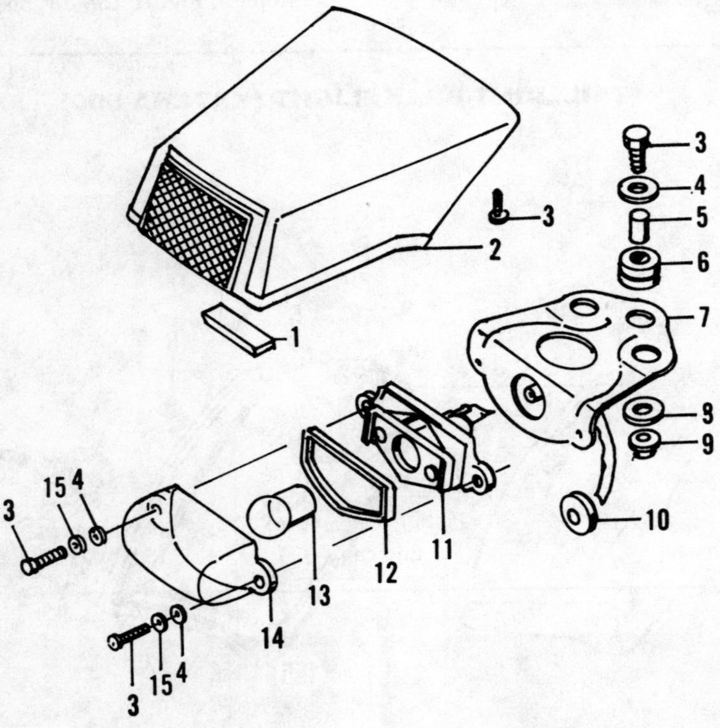

1. Rubber cushion
2. License plate light cover
3. Screw
4. Washer
5. Collar
6. Rubber cushion
7. Mounting bracket
8. Washer
9. Nut
10. Rubber grommet
11. Housing
12. Gasket
13. Bulb
14. Lens
15. Lockwasher

153

INSTRUMENT CLUSTER (KATANA 600)

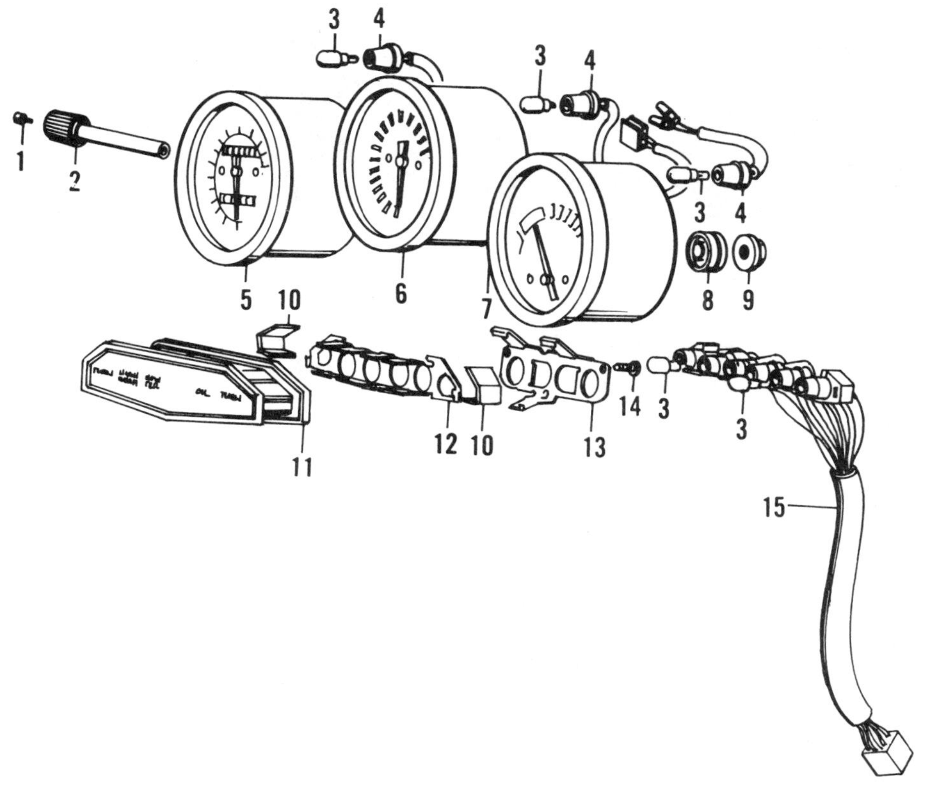

1. Screw
2. Odometer reset knob
3. Indicator bulb
4. Bulb/harness
5. Speedometer
6. Tachometer
7. Fuel gauge
8. Rubber cushion
9. Nut
10. End cap
11. Indicator light panel lens
12. Plate
13. Bracket
14. Screw
15. Bulb/harness assembly

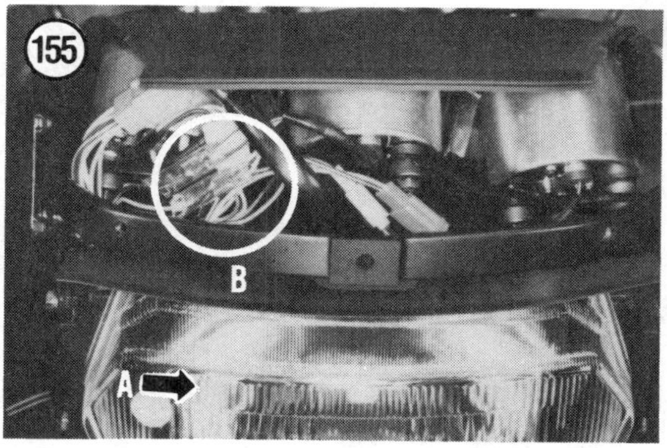

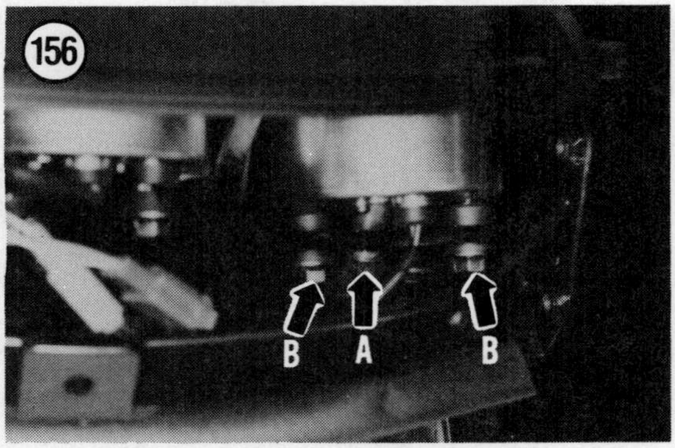

158

COOLING FAN
(1990-ON KATANA 600–CALIFORNIA MODELS ONLY)

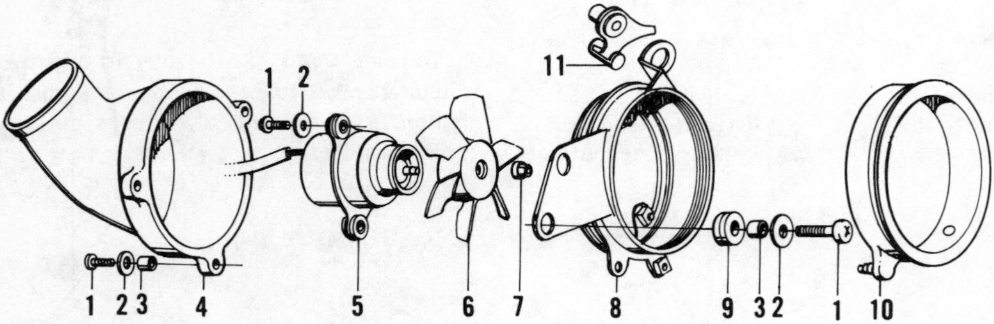

1. Bolt
2. Washer
3. Collar
4. Inner duct
5. Motor
6. Fan
7. Nut
8. Shroud
9. Rubber cushion
10. Outer duct
11. Bracket

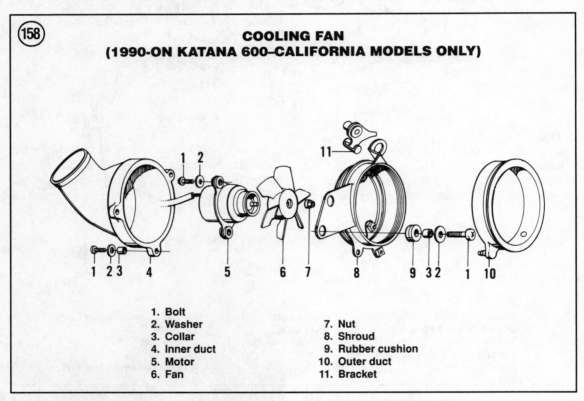

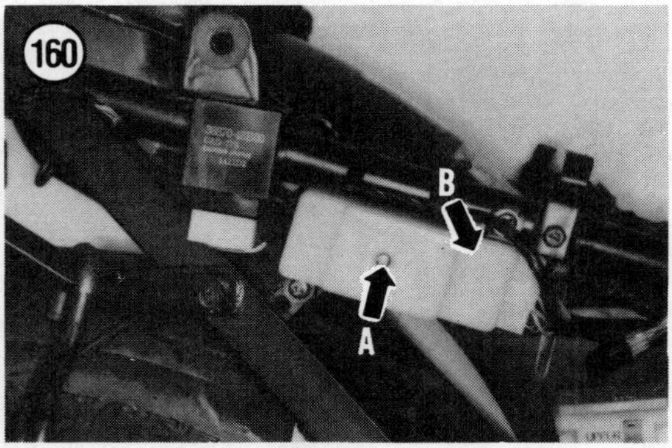

FUSES

Fuse Replacement

1. Remove the right-hand side cover.
2. Remove the screw (A, **Figure 160**) and washer securing the fuse panel cover and remove the cover (B, **Figure 160**).

NOTE
*These fuses (**Figure 161**) are not the typical glass tube with metal ends. Carry extra fuses in your tool box.*

3. Remove the fuse and install a new one.
4. There is a spare fuse (**Figure 162**) in the cover.
5. Install the cover and tighten the screw securely.
6. Install the right-hand side cover.

Fuse Panel Removal/Installation

1. Remove the seat as described under *Seat Removal/Installation* in this chapter.
2. Disconnect the battery negative lead (**Figure 154**).
3. Remove the right-hand side cover.
4. Remove the screw (A, **Figure 160**) and washer securing the fuse panel cover and remove the cover (B, **Figure 160**).
5. Release the tie-wrap securing the electrical harness to the frame.
6. Remove the screws and washers (A, **Figure 163**) securing the fuse panel to the frame.
7. Disconnect the electrical connector (B, **Figure 163**) from the end of the fuse panel and remove the fuse panel (C, **Figure 163**).
8. Install by reversing these removal steps, make sure the electrical connector is free of corrosion and is tight.

CIRCUIT BREAKER

The wiring harness is protected by a circuit breaker that is located between the battery and the right-hand side of the frame (**Figure 164**). The circuit breaker protects the electrical system when the main circuit load exceeds the rated amperage. When an overload occurs, the red button pops out on the breaker face panel and the circuit is open. The circuit will remain open until the problem is solved and the breaker is reset.

To reset, wait approximately 10 minutes for the circuit breaker to cool down, then push the red button in. If the red button pops out again, the problem still exists in the electrical system and must be corrected.

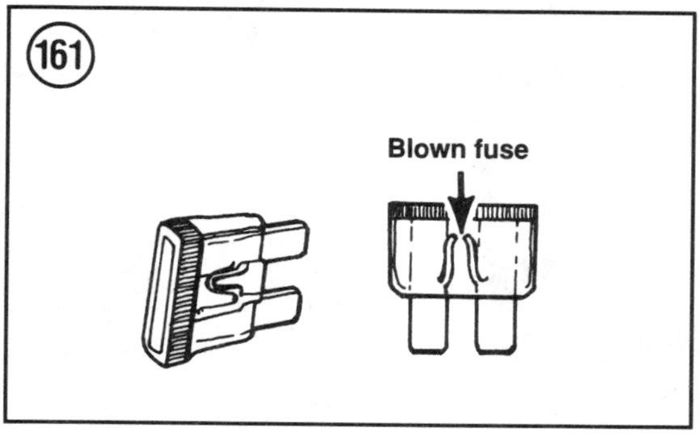

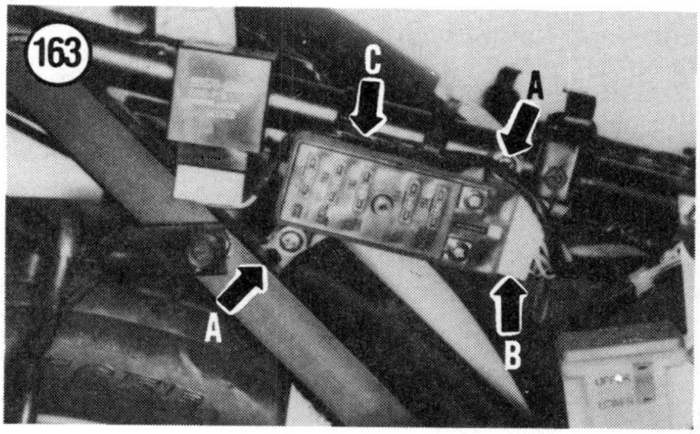

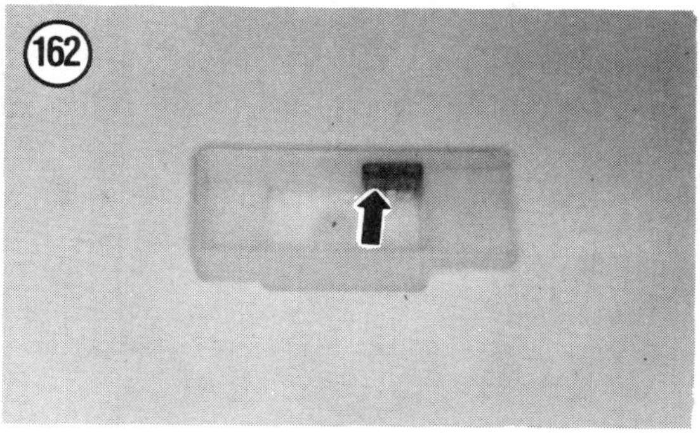

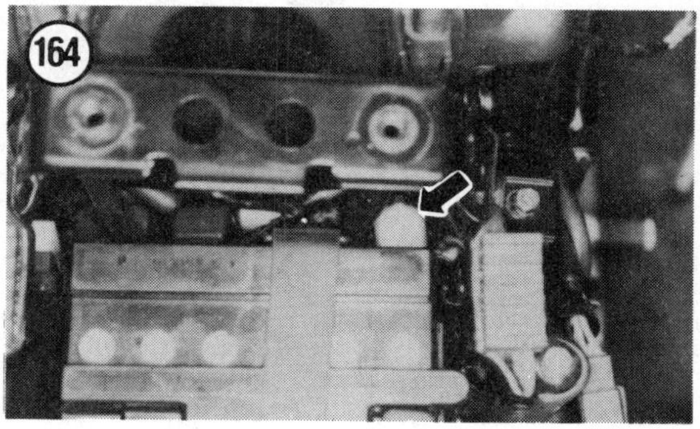

CHAPTER NINE

FRONT SUSPENSION AND STEERING

FRONT WHEEL

Removal

1. Remove the lower portion of the front fairing as described under *Front Fairing Removal/Installation* in this chapter.
2. Remove the cotter pin and loosen the front axle nut (A, **Figure 165**).
3. Loosen the front axle pinch bolt and nut (B, **Figure 165**) on the left-hand side.
4. Remove both right- and left-hand front caliper assemblies (A, **Figure 166**) as described under *Front Brake Caliper Removal/Installation* in Chapter Eleven of the main body.
5. Remove the speedometer cable (**Figure 167**) from the speedometer gear box.
6. Place wood block(s) under the crankcase between the exhaust pipes to support the bike securely with the front wheel off the ground.
7. Withdraw the front axle (B, **Figure 166**) from the forks and front wheel.
8. Pull the wheel down and forward and remove it.
9. Remove the wheel. Don't lose the spacers on each side.

CAUTION
Do not set the wheel down on the disc surface as it may get scratched or warped. Set the sidewalls on 2 wood blocks.

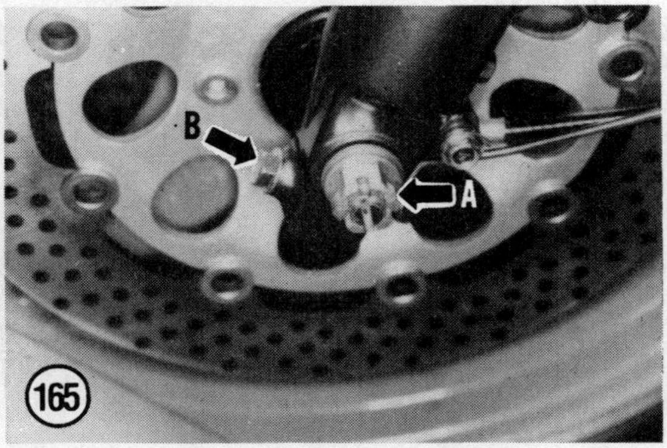

NOTE
Insert a piece of vinyl tubing or wood in each caliper in place of the brake disc. That way if the brake lever is inadvertently squeezed, the piston will not be forced out of the cylinder. If this does happen, the caliper may have to be disassembled to reseat the piston and the system will have to be bled. By using the wood, bleeding the brake is not necessary when installing the wheel.

Installation

1. Make sure the axle bearing surfaces of the fork sliders and axle are free from burrs and nicks.
2. Remove the vinyl tubing or pieces of wood from the brake calipers.

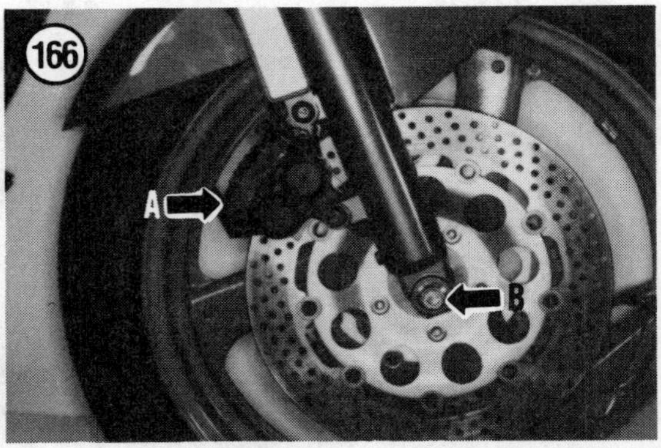

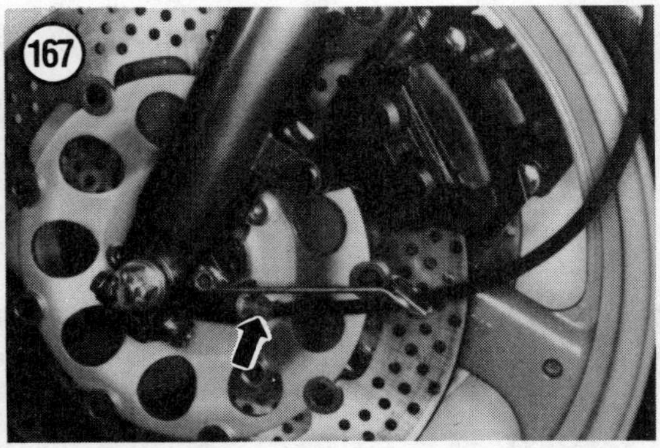

3. Make sure the wheel spacers are in place on the both sides.

NOTE
Make sure the speedometer gear box seats completely. If the speedometer components do not mesh properly, the hub components of the wheel will be too wide for installation.

4. Apply a light coat of grease to the front axle. Insert the front axle from the left-hand side through the speedometer gear box and the wheel hub.

5. Install the front axle nut but do not tighten at this time.

6. Slowly rotate the wheel and install the speedometer cable into the speedometer housing. Position the speedometer housing and cable so that the cable does not have a sharp bend in it.

7. Tighten the front axle nut to 36-52 N•m (26-37.5 ft.-lb.).

8. Install both front caliper assemblies as described in Chapter Eleven of the main body.

9. Remove the wood block(s) from under the crankcase.

10. With the front brake applied, push down hard on the handlebars and pump the forks several times to seat the front axle.

11. Tighten the front axle pinch bolt and nut to 15-25 N•m (11-18 ft.-lb.).

12. Install a new cotter pin in the front axle nut and bend the ends over completely. Never re-use an old cotter pin as the ends may break off and the pin may fall out.

13. After the wheel is completely installed, rotate it several times to make sure that it rotates freely. Apply the front brake as many times as necessary to make sure all brake pads are against both brake discs correctly.

168

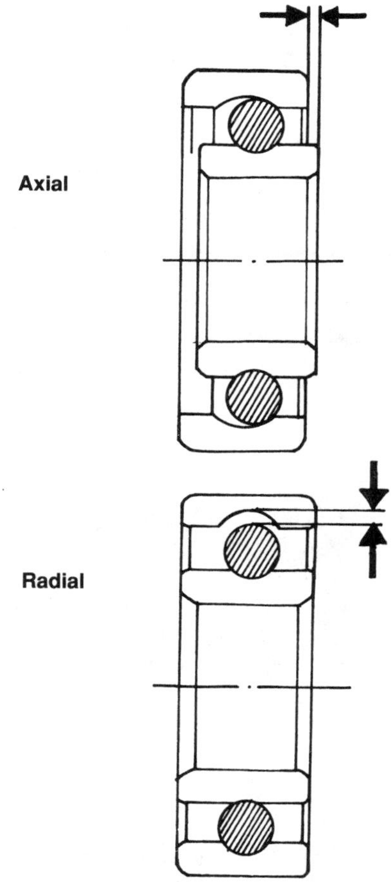

FRONT HUB

Inspection

Inspect each wheel bearing prior to removing it from the wheel hub.

CAUTION
Do not remove the wheel bearings for inspection purposes as they will be damaged during the removal process. Remove wheel bearings only if they are to be replaced.

1. Perform Steps 1-3 of *Disassembly* in Chapter Nine of the main body.
2. Turn each bearing by hand. Make sure bearings turn smoothly.
3. Inspect the play of the inner race (**Figure 168**) of each wheel bearing. Check for excessive axial (side play) and radial (end play) play. Replace the bearing if it has an excess amount of free play.
4. On non-sealed bearings, check the balls for evidence of wear, pitting or excessive heat (bluish tint). Replace the bearings if necessary; always replace as a complete set. When replacing the bearings, be sure to take your old bearings along to ensure a perfect matchup.

NOTE
Fully sealed bearings are available from many bearing specialty shops.

13

Fully sealed bearings provide better protection from dirt and moisture that may get into the hub.

5. Check the axle for wear and straightness. Use V-blocks and a dial indicator as shown in **Figure 169**. If the runout is 0.2 mm (0.01 in.) or greater, the axle should be replaced.

Disassembly and Assembly

Refer to **Figure 170** for this procedure.

The disassembly and assembly of the front hub are identical to the GSX-R750. Refer to the following illustrations that depict the components of the GSX600F Katana model:

a. Brake disc bolts: **Figure 171**.
b. Left-hand bearing: A, **Figure 172**.
c. Right-hand bearing: **Figure 173**.
d. Speedometer drive dog: B, **Figure 172**.

HANDLEBAR

Removal/Installation

1. Remove the front fairing as described under *Front Fairing Removal/Installation* in this chapter.

NOTE

If the handlebars are just being removed for front fork removal, proceed to Step 12. It is not necessary to remove all of the components from the handlebars unless they are going to be replaced.

2. Disconnect the brake light switch electrical connector from the brake lever.

169

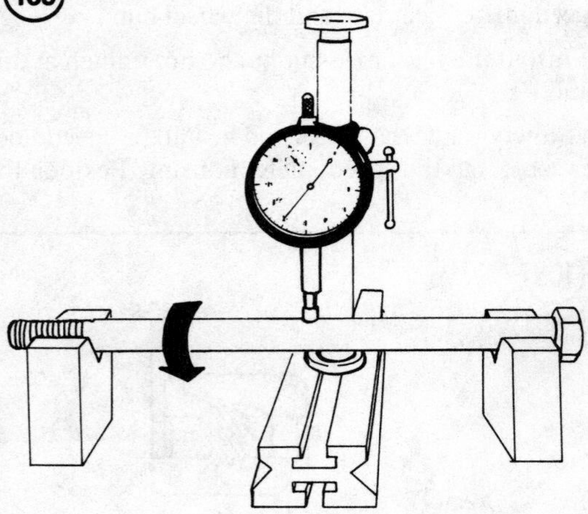

170

FRONT WHEEL/HUB (KATANA 600)

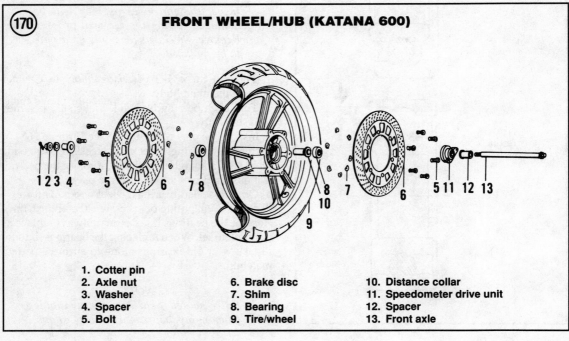

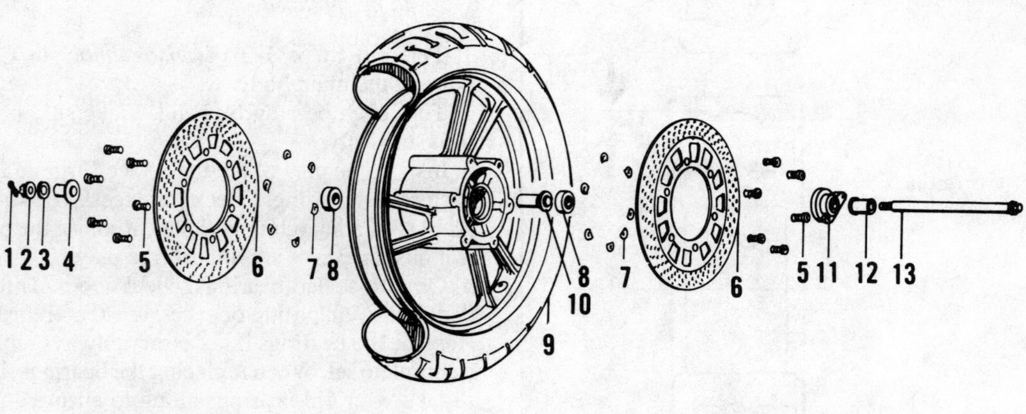

1. Cotter pin
2. Axle nut
3. Washer
4. Spacer
5. Bolt
6. Brake disc
7. Shim
8. Bearing
9. Tire/wheel
10. Distance collar
11. Speedometer drive unit
12. Spacer
13. Front axle

3. Remove the screws securing the right-hand handlebar switch assembly (A, **Figure 174**) together and remove the right-hand switch assembly from the handlebar.

CAUTION
Cover the frame and fuel tank with a heavy cloth or plastic tarp to protect them from accidental spilling of brake fluid. Wash any spilled brake fluid off any painted or plated surface immediately, as it will destroy the finish. Use soapy water and rinse thoroughly.

4. Remove the screw securing the right-hand balance set and remove all parts from the end of the handlebar.

5. Disconnect the throttle cable from the throttle assembly. Slide the throttle assembly (B, **Figure 174**) off the end of the handlebar. Carefully lay the throttle cable over the fender or back over the frame. Be careful that the cable does not get crimped or damaged.

6. Remove the bolts securing the brake master cylinder (C, **Figure 174**). Tie the master cylinder up to the front fairing and keep the reservoir in the upright position. This is to minimize loss of brake fluid and to keep air from entering into the brake system. It is not necessary to remove the hydraulic brake line.

7. Disconnect the starter interlock switch electrical connector from the clutch lever.

8. Remove the screws securing the left-hand handlebar switch assembly (A, **Figure 175**) together and remove the left-hand switch assembly from the handlebar.

9. Remove the screw securing the left-hand balance set and remove all parts from the end of the handlebar.

10. On 1989-on models, disconnect the choke cable and lever (B, **Figure 175**) on the handlebar.

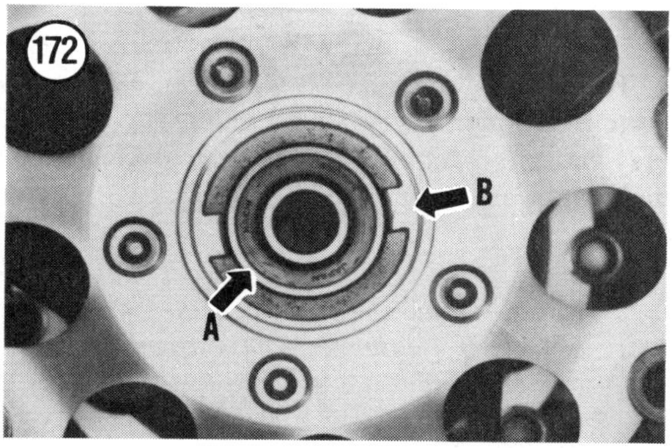

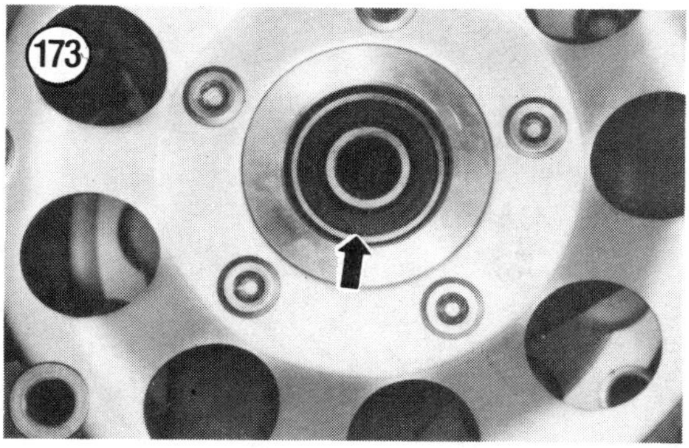

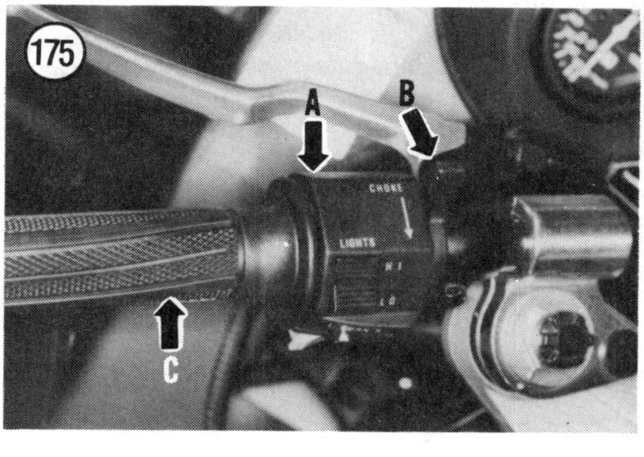

11. Slide the left-hand handgrip (C, **Figure 175**) off the end of the handlebar.
12. On 1988 models, remove the trim cap from the top of each fork tube.
13. Loosen then remove the handlebar Allen bolt nut under the upper fork bridge on each side.
14. Remove the trim cap (D, **Figure 174**) and loosen the Allen bolt securing each handlebar to the upper fork bridge.

NOTE
If the master cylinder was not removed, tie the right-hand handlebar and master cylinder up to the front fairing and keep the reservoir in the upright position. This is to minimize loss of hydraulic fluid and to keep air from entering into the clutch system. It is not necessary to remove the hydraulic brake line.

15. Remove the Allen bolts and washers securing each handlebar to the upper fork bridge and remove each handlebar from each fork tube. Reinstall the bolt, washer and nut back onto each handlebar to avoid the loss of parts.
16. Install by reversing these removal steps while noting the following:
   a. Tighten the Allen bolt first to the correct torque, then tighten the Allen bolt nut to the torque specification listed in **Table 11**.
   b. Install the brake master cylinder onto the handlebar. Install the clamp with the UP arrow (**Figure 176**) facing up and align the clamp mating surface with the punch mark on the handlebar. Tighten the upper bolt first and then the lower bolt.

WARNING
*After installation is completed, make sure the brake lever does not come in contact with the throttle grip assembly when it is pulled on fully. If it does, the brake fluid may be low in the reservoir; refill as necessary. Refer to **Front Disc Brakes** in Chapter Eleven of the main body.*

WARNING
After installation is completed, make sure the clutch lever does not come in contact with the handgrip when it is pulled on fully. If it does, it must be adjusted as described in this chapter.

   c. Adjust the throttle operation as described in Chapter Three of the main body.

FRONT FORKS

The front suspension on all models uses spring controlled, hydraulically damped telescopic forks. Refer to **Table 12** for damping force adjustments.

Front Fork Damping Force Adjustment (1989-on)

The damping force can be adjusted to 3 different settings. Position 1 is the softest setting and position 3 is the stiffest setting. The bike is delivered from the factory on the No. 2 setting.

WARNING
*Both forks must be adjusted to the **same setting**. If the damping force is set on different settings, it will greatly disturb the handling stability which may lead to an accident.*

176

177

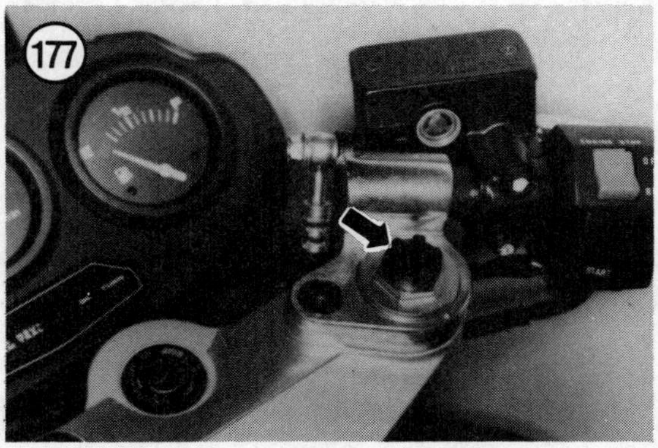

1. Turn the damping force adjuster (**Figure 177**) in the fork cap bolt to the desired setting.

WARNING
Make sure each adjuster is set correctly onto one of the setting detents and not in between any 2 of them.

2. Turn the adjuster to the desired damping.
3. Repeat for the other fork assembly.

Front Fork Service

Before suspecting major trouble, drain the front fork oil and refill with the proper type and quantity; refer to *Front Fork Oil Change* in Chapter Three. If you still have trouble, such as poor damping, a tendency to bottom or top out, or leakage around the rubber seals, follow the service procedures in this section.

To simplify fork service and to prevent the mixing of parts, the legs should be removed, serviced and installed individually.

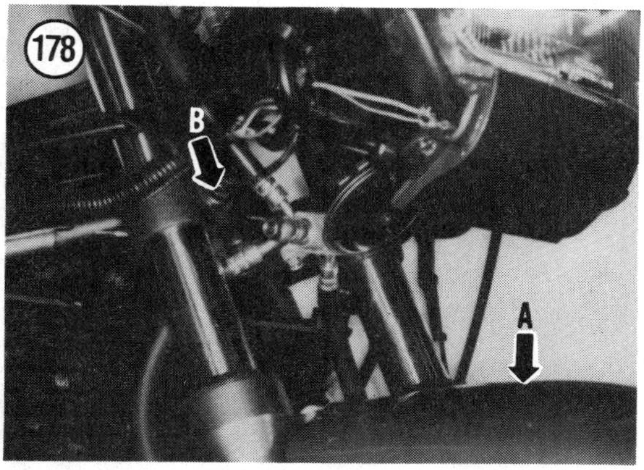

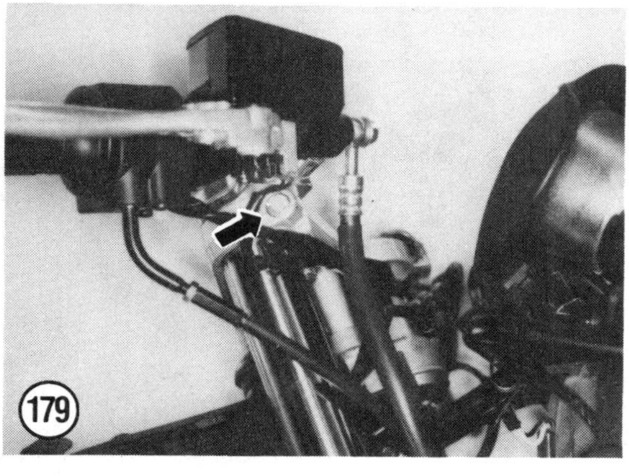

Removal/Installation

1. Remove the front wheel as described under *Front Wheel Removal/Installation* in this chapter.
2. Remove the front fender (A, **Figure 178**) and fender brace as described under *Front Fender Removal/Installation* in this chapter.

NOTE
It is not necessary to remove the front fairing but it does allow easier access to the upper and lower fork bridge clamp bolts. This procedure is shown with the fairing removed for clarity.

3. If necessary, remove the front fairing as described under *Front Fairing Removal/Installation* in this chapter.
4. Remove the handlebars as described under *Handlebar Removal* in this chapter.

NOTE
The Allen bolt at the base of the slider has been secured with Loctite and is often very difficult to remove because the damper rod will turn inside the slider. It sometimes can be removed with an air impact driver. If you are unable to remove it, take the fork tubes to a dealer and have the bolts removed.

5. If the fork assembly is going to be disassembled, using the correct size of Allen wrench, slightly loosen the Allen bolt at the base of the slider. If the bolt is loosened too much, fork oil may start to drain out of the slider.
6. Loosen the upper (**Figure 179**) and lower (B, **Figure 178**) fork bridge bolts.
7. Slide the fork tube from the upper and lower fork bridge. It may be necessary to rotate the fork tube slightly while pulling it down and out.
8. Install by reversing these removal steps while noting the following:
   a. Install the fork tubes so that the top of the fork tube aligns with the top surface of the handlebar holder (**Figure 180**).
   b. On 1989-on models, align the index mark on the fork cap bolt with the index mark on the handlebar holder (**Figure 181**).
   c. Tighten the upper and lower fork bridge bolts to the torque specifications listed in **Table 11**.

13

Disassembly (1988)

Refer to **Figure 182** during the disassembly and assembly procedures.

1. Clamp the slider in a vise with soft jaws.
2. If not loosened during the fork removal sequence, loosen the Allen bolt on the bottom of the slider.

NOTE
This bolt has been secured with Loctite and is often very difficult to remove because the damper rod will turn inside the slider. It sometimes can be removed with an air impact driver. If you are unable to remove it, take the fork tubes to a dealer and have the bolts removed.

3. Remove the Allen bolt and gasket from the slider.
4. Hold the upper fork tube in a vise with soft jaws and perform the following:
   a. Place a large Phillips screwdriver or drift in the recess in the top cap.
   b. Push down on the top cap until the stopper ring is accessible.
   c. Hold the top cap in this position and use a pick or small screwdriver and remove the stopper ring from the recess in the fork tube.

WARNING
Be careful when removing the fork top cap as the spring is under pressure. Protect your eyes accordingly.

   d. Slowly release the top cap and remove it from the fork tube.
5. Remove the spacer, spring seat and the fork spring.
6. Remove the fork from the vise, pour the fork oil out and discard it. Pump the fork several times by hand to expel most of the remaining oil.
7. Remove the dust seal from the slider.
8. Remove the stopper ring and washer from the slider.

NOTE
On this type of fork, force is needed to remove the fork tube from the slider.

9. Install the fork tube in a vise with soft jaws.
10. There is an interference fit between the bushing in the fork slider and the bushing on the fork tube. In order to remove the fork tube from the slider, pull hard on the fork tube using quick in-and-out strokes (**Figure 183**). Doing so will withdraw the bushing washer and oil seal from the slider.

NOTE
It may be necessary to heat the area on the slider around the oil seal slightly prior to removal. Use a rag soaked in hot water; do not apply a flame directly to the fork slider.

11. Withdraw the fork tube from the slider.

NOTE
Do not remove the fork tube bushing unless it is going to be replaced. Inspect it as described in this chapter.

12. Remove the oil lock piece from the damper rod.
13. Remove the damper rod and rebound spring from the slider.
14. Inspect the components as described under *Inspection (All Models)* in this chapter.

Assembly (1988)

1. Coat all parts with fresh SAE 10W fork oil prior to installation.
2. Install the rebound spring onto the damper rod and insert this assembly into the fork tube (**Figure 184**).

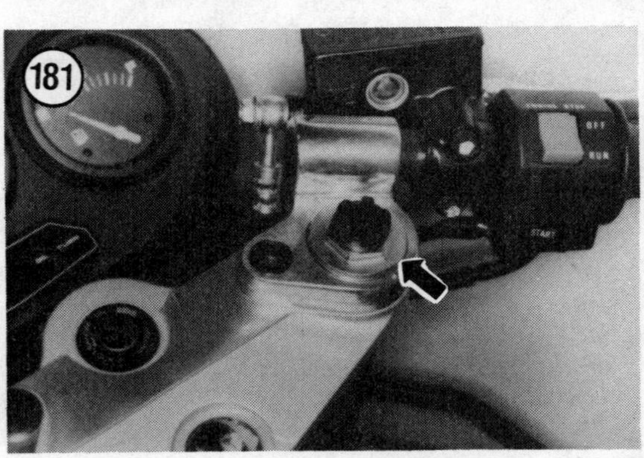

182

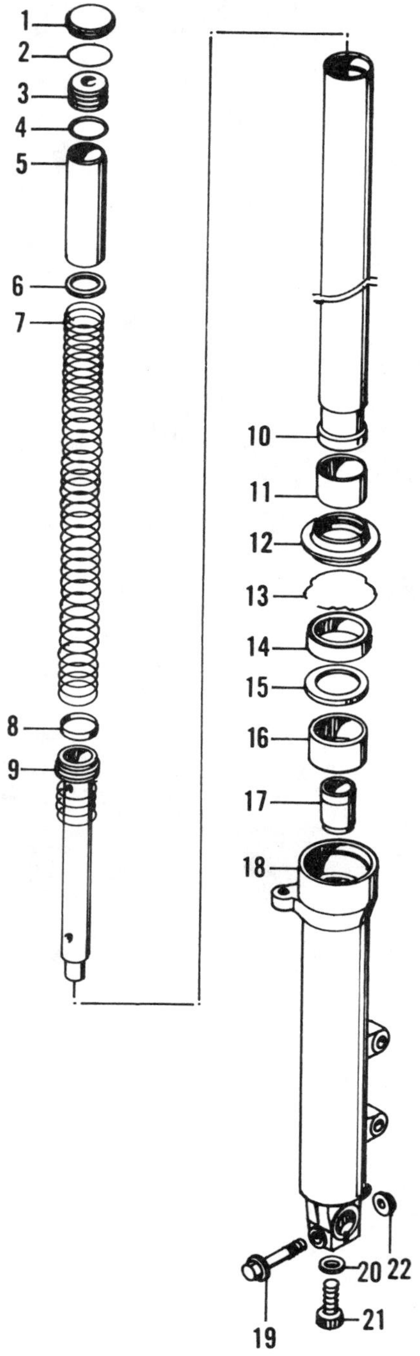

FRONT FORK ASSEMBLY (1988 KATANA 600)

1. Cap
2. Stopper ring
3. Top cap
4. O-ring
5. Spacer
6. Spring seat
7. Fork spring
8. Piston ring
9. Damper rod
10. Fork tube
11. Fork tube bushing
12. Dust seal
13. Stopper ring
14. Oil seal
15. Washer
16 Slider bushing
17. Oil lock piece
18. Fork slider
19. Clamp bolt
20. Gasket
21. Allen bolt
22. Nut

3. Temporarily install the fork spring, spring seat and spacer (**Figure 185**).

4. Install the top cap and using the same tool set-up used during disassembly, install the stopper ring in the fork tube.

5. Install the oil lock piece onto the damper rod (**Figure 186**).

6. Install the upper fork assembly into the slider (**Figure 187**).

7. Make sure the gasket (**Figure 188**) is on the Allen bolt.

8. Apply red Loctite (No. 271) to the threads of the Allen bolt prior to installation. Install it in the fork slider and tighten to the torque specification listed in **Table 11**.

9. Slide the fork slider bushing (A, **Figure 189**) and washer (B, **Figure 189**) down the fork tube and rest it on top of the fork slider.

10. Install the new oil seal as follows:

   a. Coat the new seal with SAE 10W fork oil.

   b. Position the seal with the open groove facing upward (**Figure 190**) and slide the oil seal (C, **Figure 189**) down onto the fork tube.

183

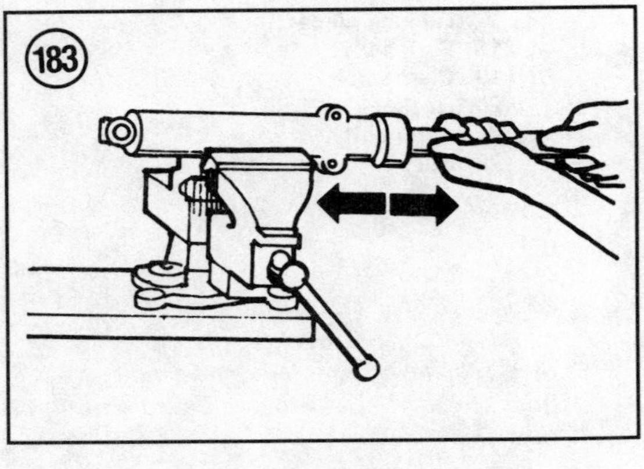

184

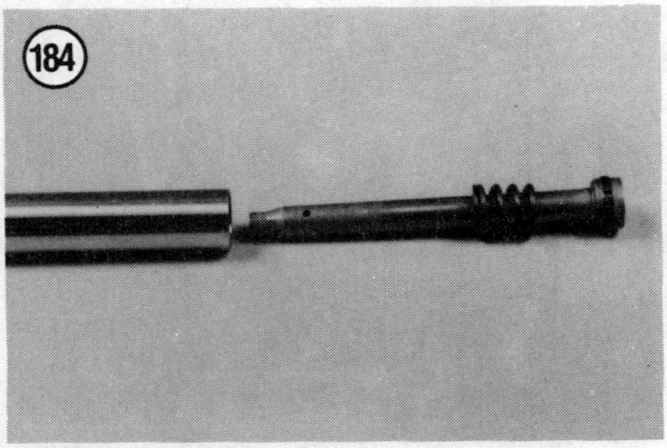

185

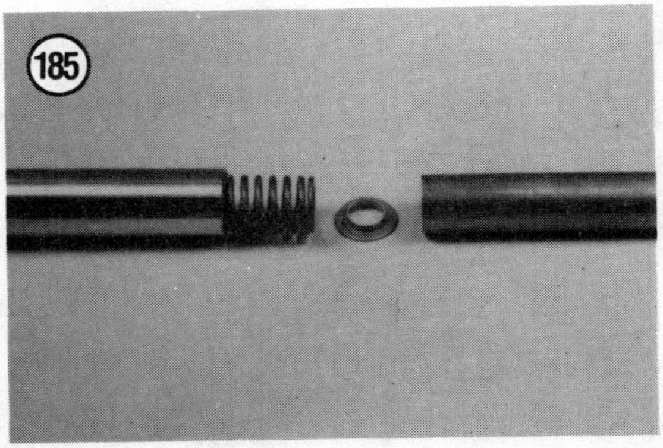

186

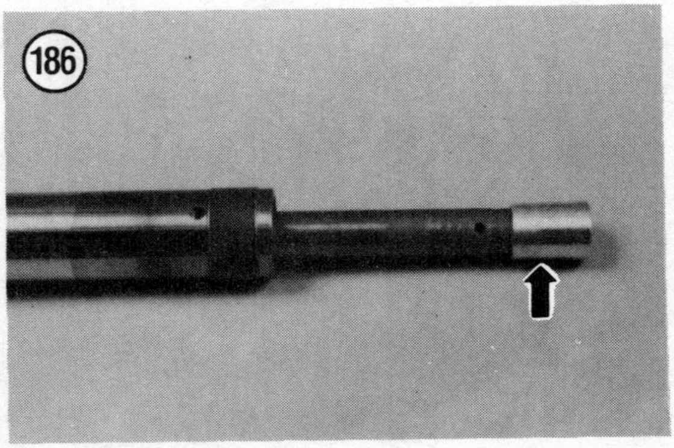

187

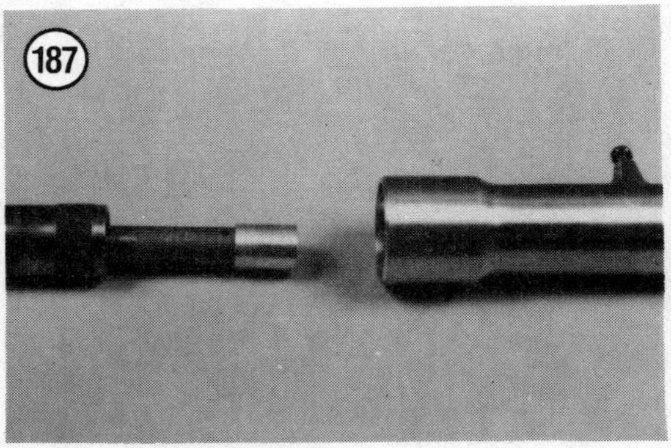

188

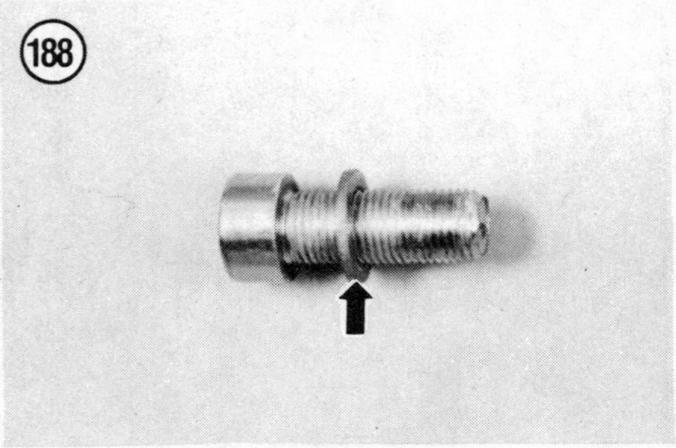

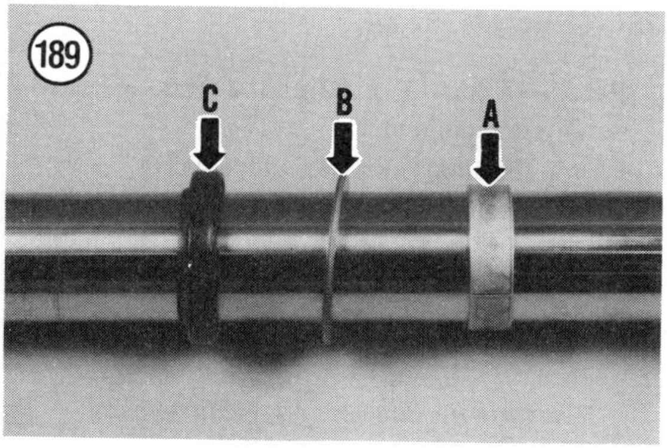

189

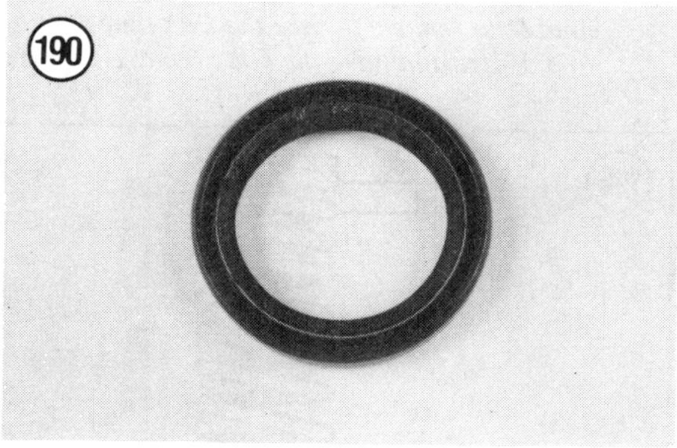
190

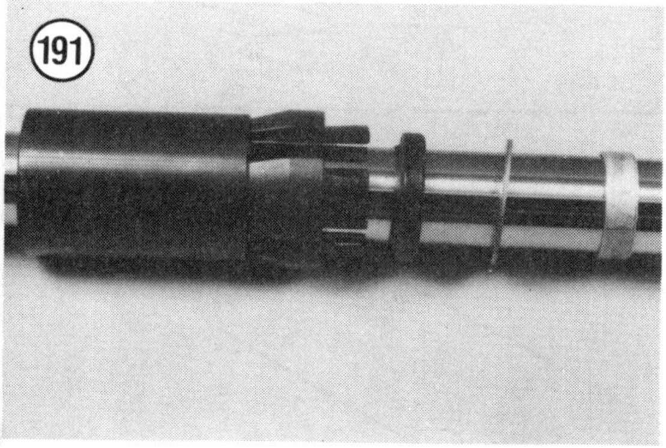
191

c. Drive the seal into the slider with Suzuki special tool Front Fork Oil Seal Installer (part No. 09940-50112) (**Figure 191**).

d. Drive the oil seal in until the groove in the slider can be seen above the top surface of the upper washer.

11. Install the stopper ring and make sure it is completely seated in the groove in the fork slider (**Figure 192**).

12. Install the dust seal (**Figure 193**) into the slider.

13. Use the same tool set-up and remove the fork cap and stopper ring. Remove the fork cap, spacer, spring seat and the fork spring.

14. Fill the fork tube with the correct quantity of SAE 10W fork oil. Refer to **Table 5** for specified quantity and oil level.

15. Check the fork oil level in each fork assembly as follows:

a. Hold the fork tube vertical and *completely* compress the fork tube into the slider.

b. Use an accurate ruler or the Suzuki Oil Level Gauge (part No. 09943-74111) and measure the distance from the top surface of the fork tube (**Figure 194**). Adjust the oil level as necessary.

NOTE

An oil level measuring device can be made as shown in ***Figure 195****. Position the lower edge of the hose clamp the specified oil level distance up from the small diameter hole. Fill the fork with a few cc's more than the required amount of oil. Position the hose clamp on the top edge of the fork tube and draw out the excess oil. Oil is sucked out until the level reaches the small diameter hole. A precise oil level can be achieved with this simple device.*

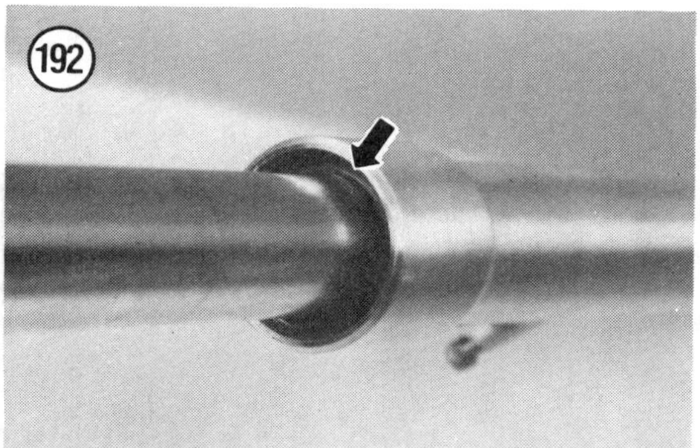
192

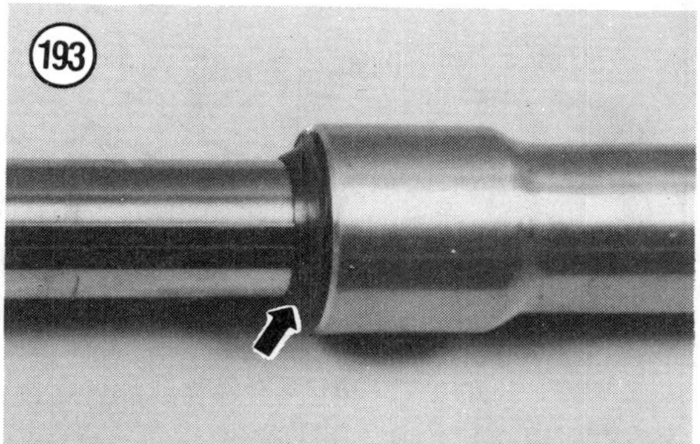
193

16. Install the fork spring with the narrow pitch coils (**Figure 196**) going in last.

17. Inspect the O-ring seal on the fork cap; replace if necessary.

18. Install the spring seat, spacer and the fork cap.

19. Install the top cap and, using the same tool set-up used during disassembly, install the stopper ring in the fork tube.

20. Repeat for the other fork assembly.

21. Install the fork assemblies as described in this chapter.

Disassembly (1989-on)

Refer to **Figure 197** during the disassembly and assembly procedures.

1. Clamp the slider in a vise with soft jaws.
2. If not loosened during the fork removal sequence, loosen the Allen bolt on the bottom of the slider.

NOTE

This bolt has been secured with Loctite and is often very difficult to remove because the damper rod will turn inside the slider. It sometimes can be removed with an air impact driver. If you are unable to remove it, take the fork tubes to a dealer and have the bolts removed.

194

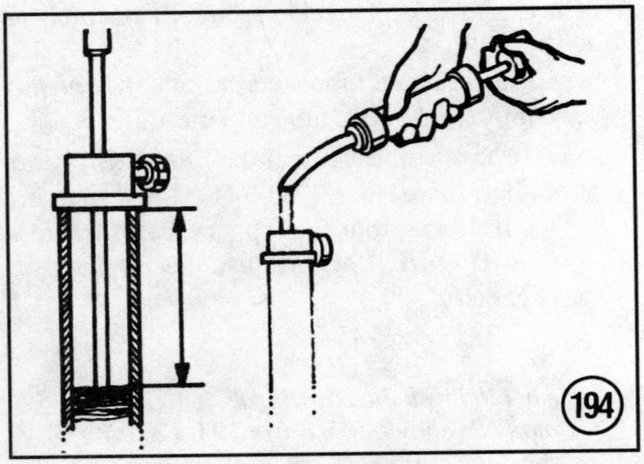

196

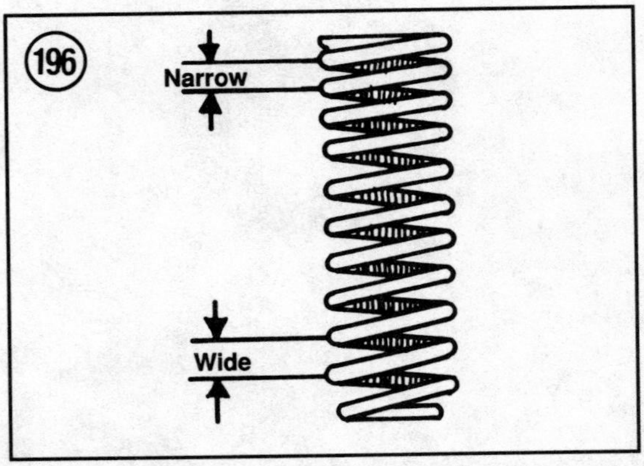

195

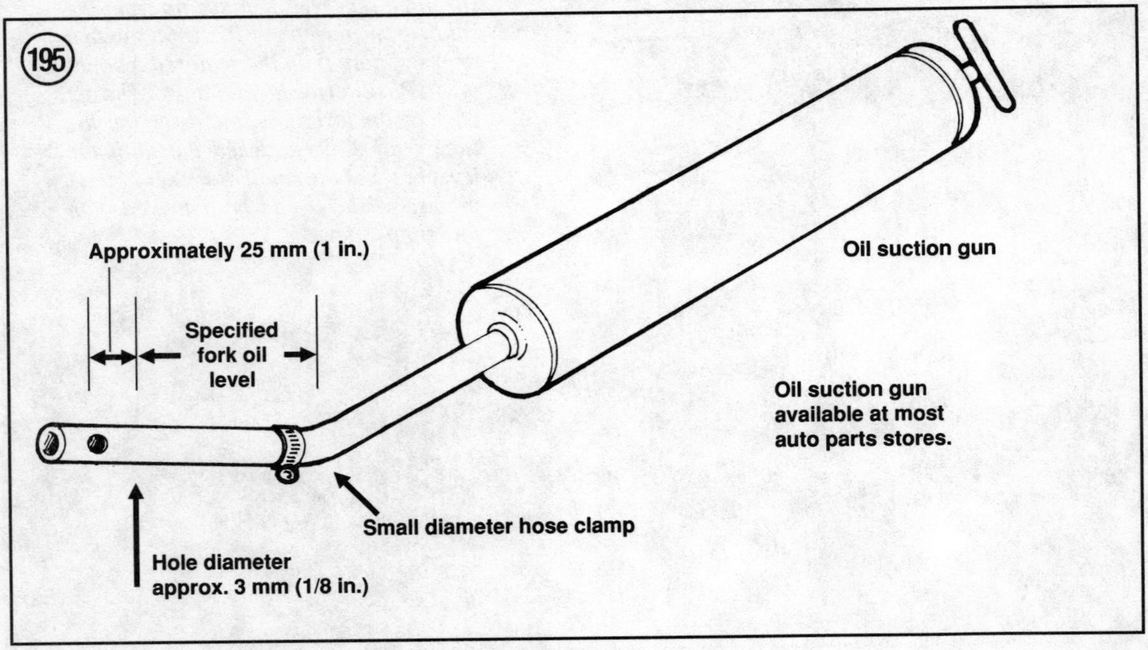

197

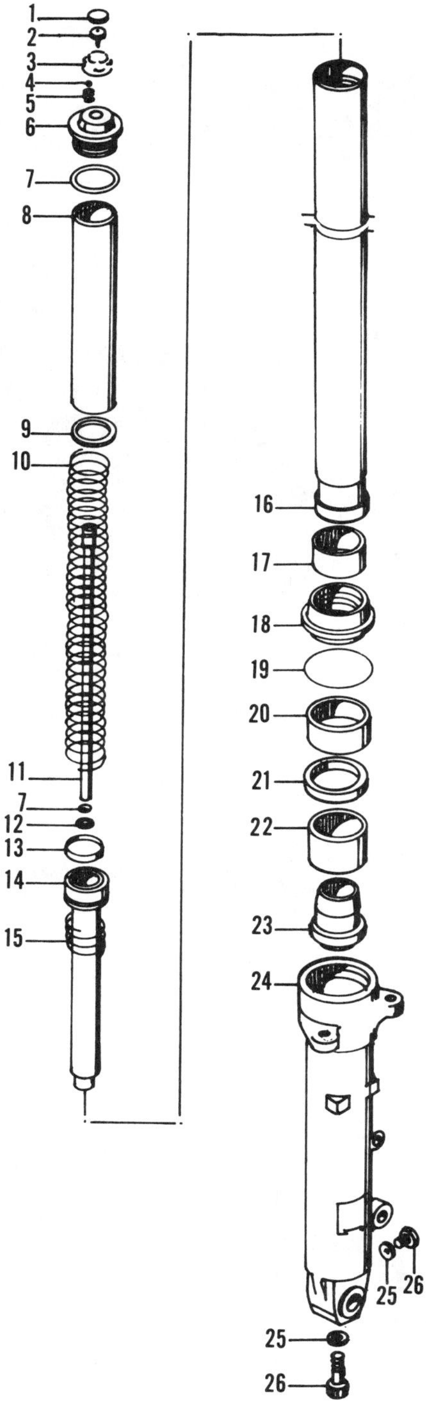

FRONT FORK ASSEMBLY (1989-ON KATANA 600)

1. Cap
2. Screw
3. Damping force adjuster
4. Steel ball
5. Spring
6. Fork cap bolt
7. O-ring
8. Spacer
9. Spring seat
10. Fork spring
11. Inner rod
12. Washer
13. Piston ring
14. Damper rod
15. Damper rod spring
16. Fork tube
17. Fork tube bushing
18. Dust seal
19. Stopper ring
20. Oil seal
21. Washer
22. Slider bushing
23. Oil lock piece
24. Fork slider
25. Gasket
26. Allen bolt

3. Remove the Allen bolt and gasket from the slider.
4. Hold the upper fork tube in a vise with soft jaws and loosen the fork cap bolt.

WARNING
Be careful when removing the fork cap bolt as the spring is under pressure. Protect your eyes accordingly.

5. Remove the upper fork cap bolt and rod from the fork leg.
6. Remove the spacer, spring seat and the fork spring.
7. Remove the fork from the vise, pour the fork oil out and discard it. Pump the fork several times by hand to expel most of the remaining oil.
8. Remove the dust seal from the slider.
9. Remove the stopper ring from the slider.

NOTE
On this type of fork, force is needed to remove the fork tube from the slider.

10. Install the fork tube in a vise with soft jaws.
11. There is an interference fit between the bushing in the fork slider and the bushing on the fork tube. In order to remove the fork tube from the slider, pull hard on the fork tube using quick in-and-out strokes (**Figure 183**). Doing so will withdraw the bushing washer and oil seal from the slider.

NOTE
It may be necessary to heat the area on the slider around the oil seal slightly prior to removal. Use a rag soaked in hot water; do not apply a flame directly to the fork slider.

12. Withdraw the fork tube from the slider.

NOTE
Do not remove the fork tube bushing unless it is going to be replaced. Inspect it as described in this chapter.

13. Remove the oil lock piece from the damper rod.
14. Remove the damper rod and rebound spring from the slider.
15. Inspect the components as described under *Inspection (All Models)* in this chapter.

Assembly (1989-on)

1. Coat all parts with fresh SAE 10W fork oil prior to installation.
2. If removed, install the drain screw and gasket. Tighten the screw securely.

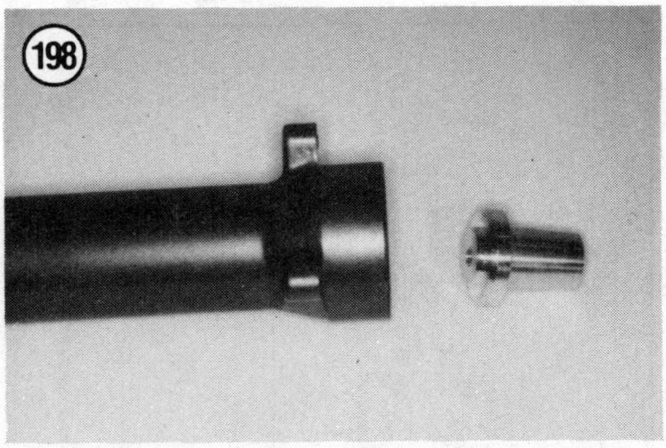

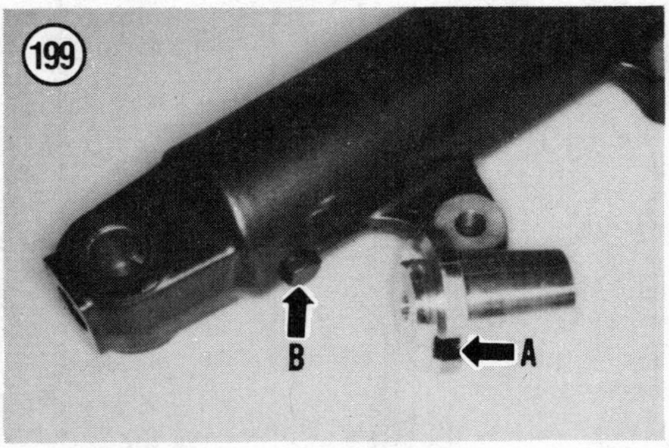

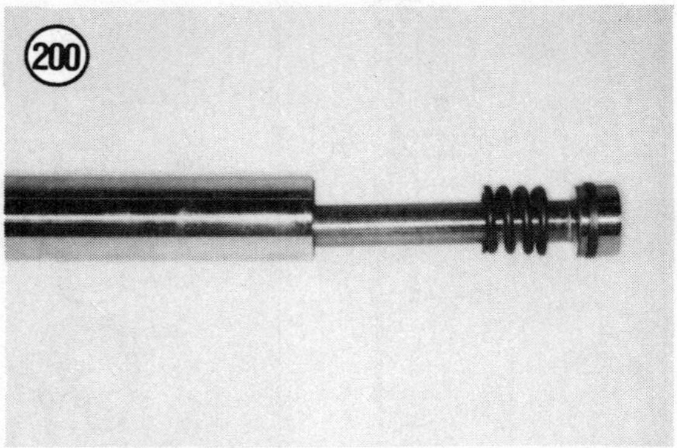

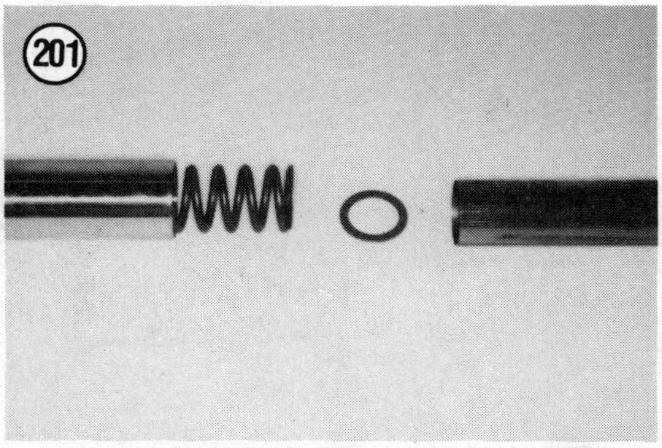

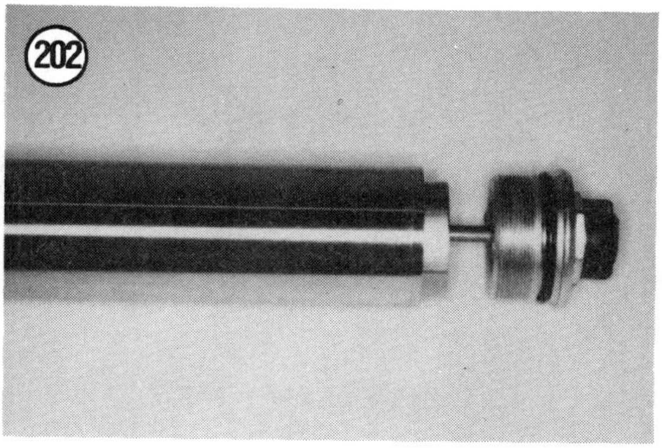

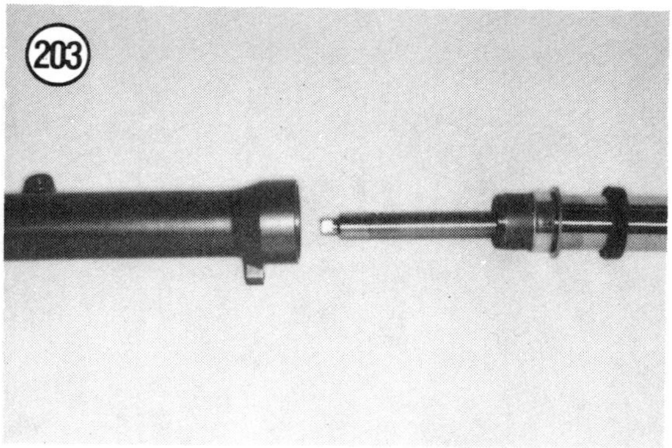

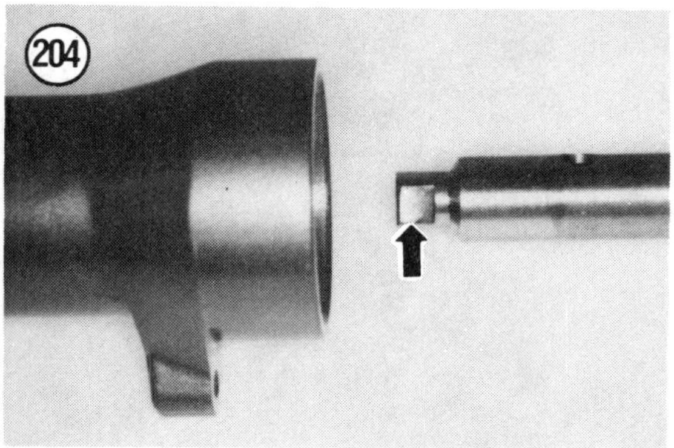

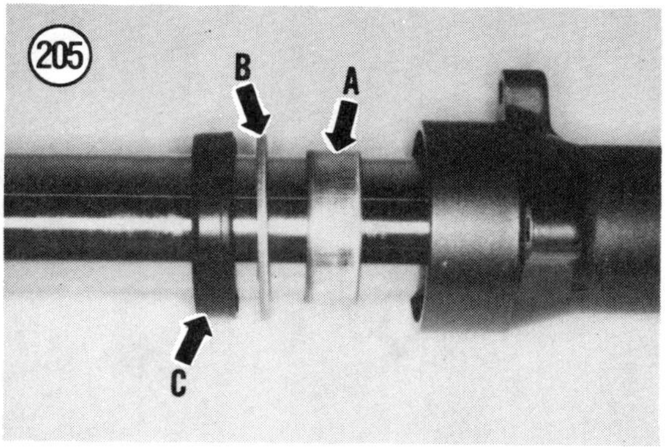

3. Install the oil lock piece (**Figure 198**) down into the slider and align the cutout (A, **Figure 199**) in the lock piece with the end of the drain screw (B, **Figure 199**). This alignment is necessary for proper fork operation.
4. Install the rebound spring onto the damper rod and insert this assembly into the fork tube (**Figure 200**).
5. Temporarily install the fork spring, spring seat and spacer (**Figure 201**).
6. Install the fork cap bolt (**Figure 202**) and tighten securely.
7. Install the upper fork assembly into the slider (**Figure 203**) and align the flat on the damper rod (**Figure 204**) with the flat in the top of the oil lock piece already installed in the slider.
8. Make sure the gasket is on the Allen bolt.
9. Apply red Loctite (No. 271) to the threads of the Allen bolt prior to installation. Install it in the fork slider and tighten to the torque specification listed in **Table 11**.
10. Slide the fork slider bushing (A, **Figure 205**) and washer (B, **Figure 205**) down the fork tube and rest it on top of the fork slider.
11. Install the new oil seal as follows:
   a. Coat the new seal with SAE 10W fork oil.
   b. Position the seal with the open groove facing upward (**Figure 190**) and slide the oil seal (C, **Figure 205**) down onto the fork tube.
   c. Drive the seal into the slider with Suzuki special tool Front Fork Oil Seal Installer (part No. 09940-50112) (**Figure 191**).
   d. Drive the oil seal in until the groove in the slider can be seen above the top surface of the upper washer.
12. Install the stopper ring and make sure it is completely seated in the groove in the fork slider (**Figure 206**).
13. Install the dust seal (**Figure 207**) into the slider.
14. Remove the upper fork cap bolt and rod from the fork leg.
15. Remove the spacer, spring seat and the fork spring.
16. Fill the fork tube with the correct quantity of SAE 10W fork oil. Refer to **Table 5** for specified quantity and oil level.
17. Check the fork oil level in each fork assembly as follows:
   a. Hold the fork tube vertical and *completely* compress the fork tube into the slider.
   b. Use an accurate ruler or the Suzuki Oil Level Gauge (part No. 09943-74111) and measure the distance from the top surface of the fork

13

tube (**Figure 194**). Adjust the oil level as necessary.

NOTE
*An oil level measuring device can be made as shown in **Figure 195**. Position the lower edge of the hose clamp the specified oil level distance up from the small diameter hole. Fill the fork with a few cc's more than the required amount of oil. Position the hose clamp on the top edge of the fork tube and draw out the excess oil. Oil is sucked out until the level reaches the small diameter hole. A precise oil level can be achieved with this simple device.*

18. Install the fork spring, spring seat and spacer (**Figure 201**). The spring is non-directional so either end can go in first.
19. Inspect the O-ring seal (**Figure 208**) on the fork cap bolt; replace if necessary.
20. Install the fork cap bolt (**Figure 202**). Align the flat on the rod with the flat in the top of the damper rod (**Figure 209**) and push the fork cap bolt into position in the fork tube. Start to tighten the fork cap bolt (**Figure 210**) and be careful not to cross thread it.
21. Place the slider in a vise with soft jaws and tighten the top fork cap bolt securely.
22. Repeat for the other fork assembly.
23. Install the fork assemblies as described in this chapter.

Inspection (All Models)

1. Thoroughly clean all parts in solvent and dry them. Check the fork tube for signs of wear or scratches.

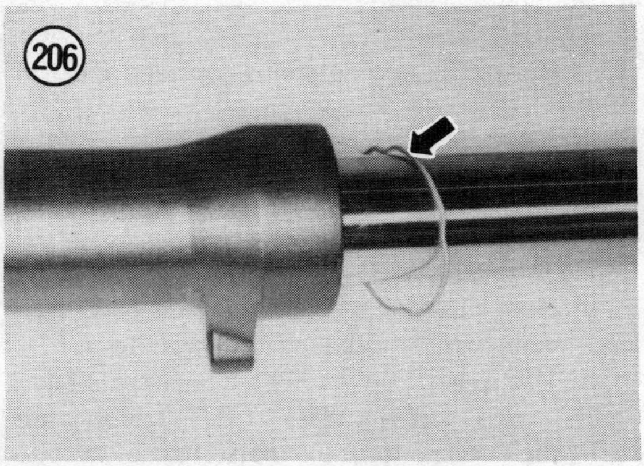

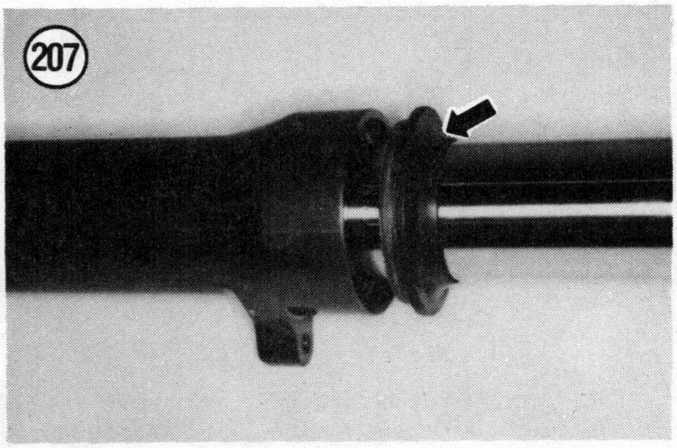

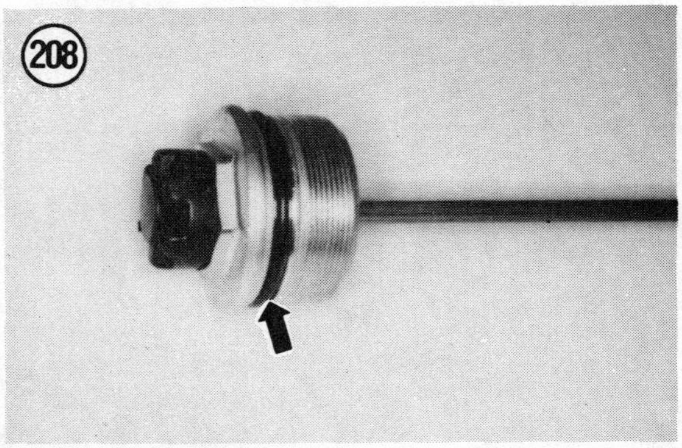

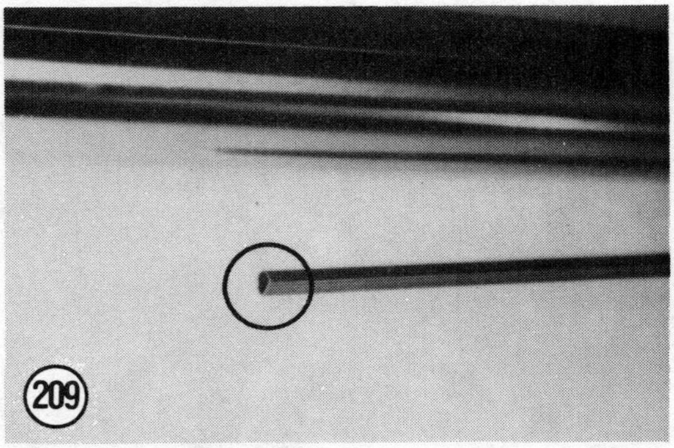

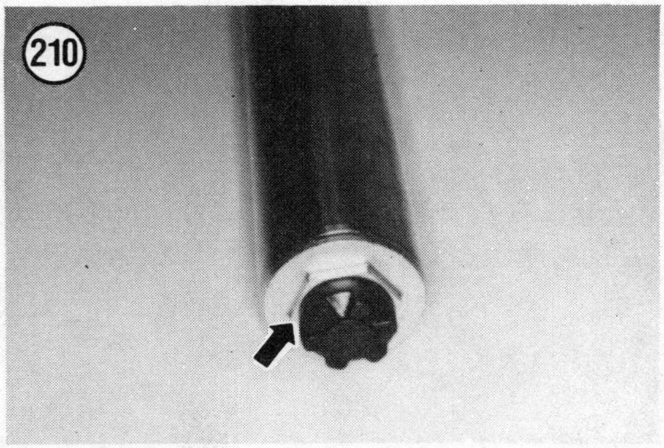

211

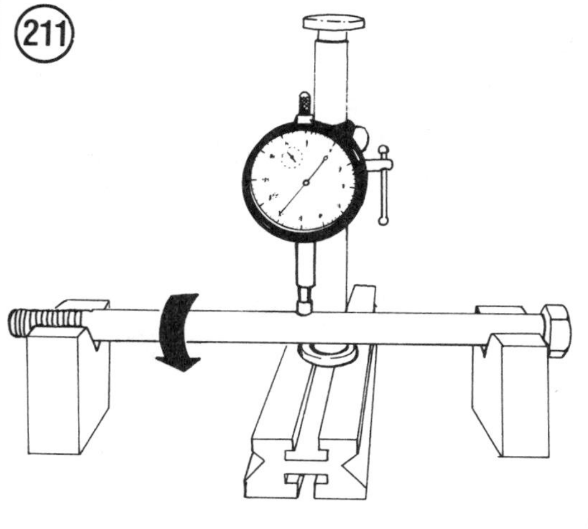

212

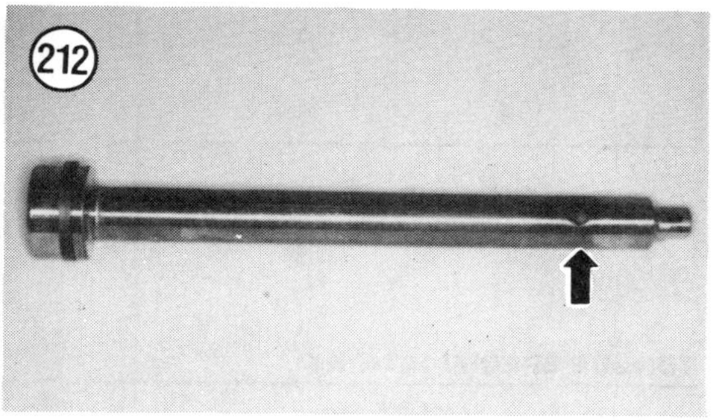

213

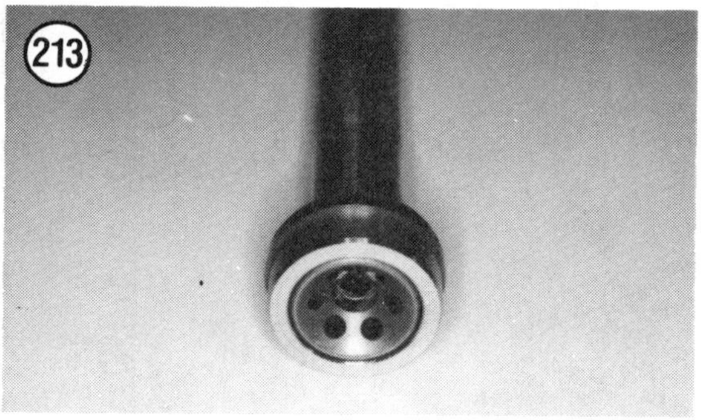

214

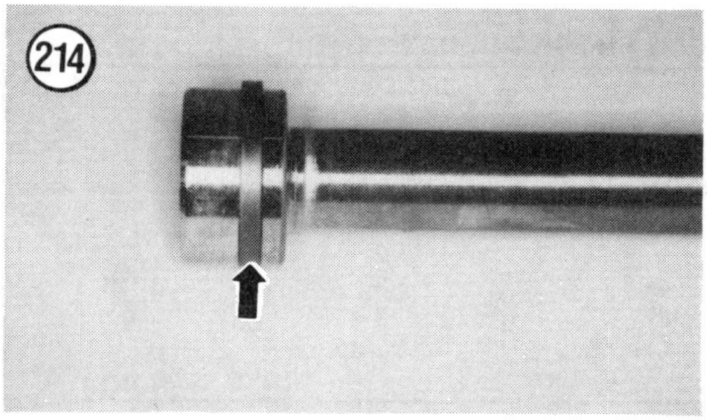

2. Check the damper rod for straightness. **Figure 211** shows one method. The damper rod should be replaced if the runout is 0.2 mm (0.008 in.) or greater.
3. Make sure the oil holes (**Figure 212**) in the damper rod are clear. Clean out if necessary.
4. On 1989-on models, make sure the oil control holes (**Figure 213**) on top of the damper rod are clear and open.
5. Inspect the damper rod and piston ring (**Figure 214**) for wear or damage. Replace as necessary.
6. Check the upper fork tube for straightness. If bent or severely scratched, it should be replaced.
7. Check the lower slider for dents or exterior damage that may cause the upper fork tube to hang up during riding. Replace if necessary.
8. Measure the uncompressed length of the fork spring (not rebound spring) as shown in **Figure 215**. If the spring has sagged to the following service limit dimensions, the spring must be replaced:
   a. 1988: 411.9 mm (16.2 in.).
   b. 1989-on: 299.4 mm (11.7 in.).
9. Inspect the slider and fork tube bushings (**Figure 216**). If either is scratched or scored, it must be replaced. If the Teflon coating is worn off so that the copper base material is showing on approximately 3/4 of the total surface, the bushing must be re-

215

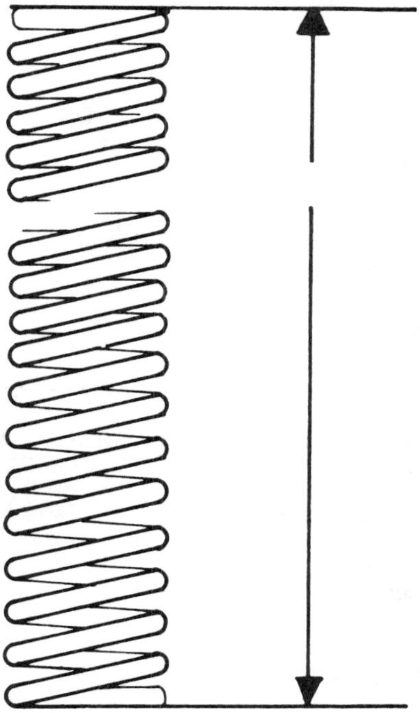

placed. Also check for distortion on the check points of the backup ring; replace as necessary. Refer to **Figure 217**.

10. Inspect the gasket on the Allen bolt, replace if damaged.

11. Any parts that are worn or damaged should be replaced. Simply cleaning and reinstalling unserviceable components will not improve performance of the front suspension.

216

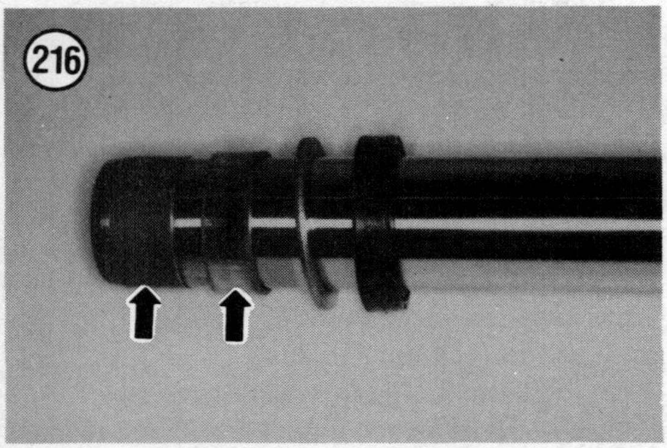

217

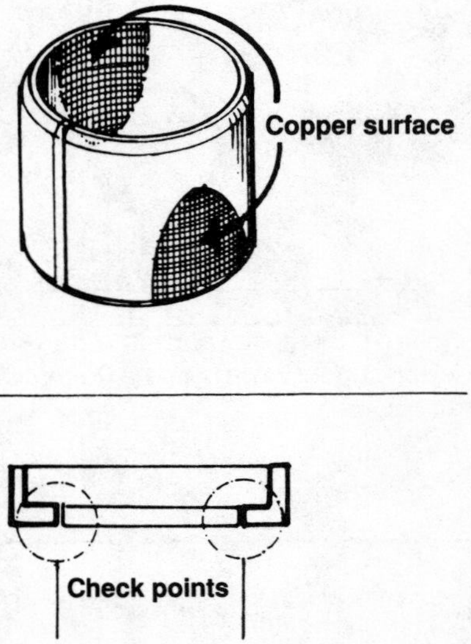

Table 11 FRONT SUSPENSION TORQUE SPECIFICATIONS

Item	N•m	ft.-lb.
Front axle nut	36-52	26-38
Front axle pinch bolt and nut	15-25	11-18
Brake disc bolts	15-25	11-18
Handlebar holder		
Allen bolt nut	20-30	14.5-21.5
Allen bolt	50-60	36-43.5
Fork bridge clamp bolts		
Upper	15-25	11-18
Lower	25-40	18-29
Steering stem bolt	35-55	25.5-40
Front fork Allen bolt	15-25	11-18
Front master cylinder clamp bolt	5-8	3.5-6

Table 12 FRONT FORK AND REAR SHOCK ADJUSTMENT

	Front	Rear	
	Damping force	Spring pre-load	Damping force
Solo riding			
Soft	1	4	2
Std.	2	4	3
Stiff	3	4	3-4
Dual riding	2-3	4-6	3-4

CHAPTER TEN

REAR SUSPENSION

REAR WHEEL

Removal/Installation

1. Remove the lower portion of the front fairing as described under *Front Fairing Removal/Installation* in this chapter.

2. Remove the cotter pin on the rear axle nut and discard the cotter pin.

3. Loosen the rear axle nut (A, **Figure 218**).

4. Loosen the drive chain adjuster nut (B, **Figure 218**) on each side of the swing arm so the wheel can be moved forward for maximum chain slack.

5. Place wood block(s) under the crankcase between the exhaust pipes to support the bike securely with the rear wheel off the ground.

6. Remove the cotter pin on the rear caliper torque link on the swing arm. Discard the cotter pin.

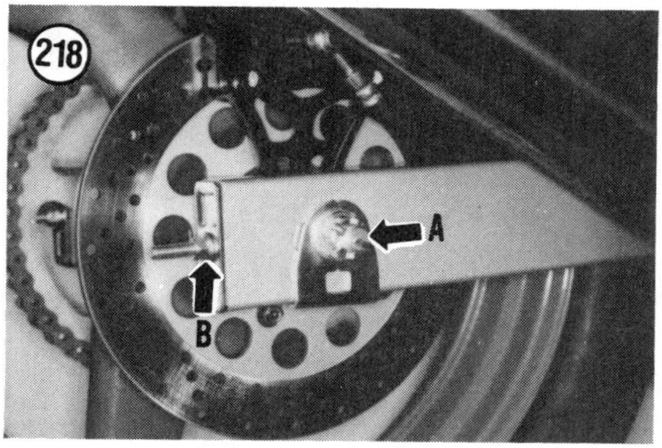

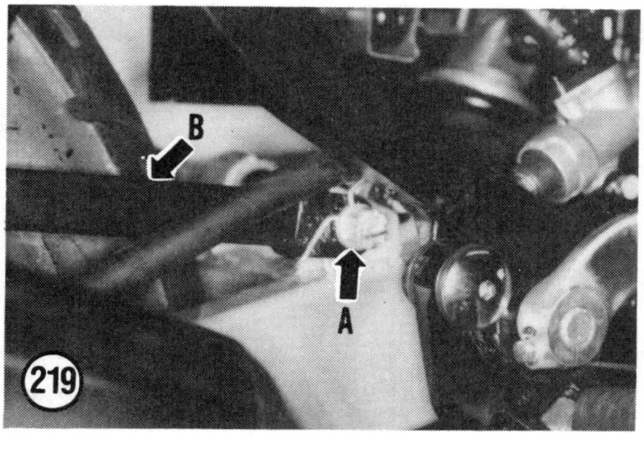

7. Remove the bolt, washer and nut (A, **Figure 219**) securing the torque link (B, **Figure 219**) to the swing arm.

8. Remove the rear axle nut, washer and special washer.

9. Withdraw the rear axle (A, **Figure 220**) and special washer (B, **Figure 220**) from the left-hand side.

10. Remove the drive chain adjuster assemblies from the rear of the swing arm.

11. Move the wheel forward, then rotate the rear wheel and derail the drive chain from the driven sprocket.

12. Carefully straighten the rear brake hose clamp on the swing arm and unhook the hose from the clamp.

NOTE

Insert a piece of vinyl tubing or wood in the caliper in place of the brake disc. That way if the brake lever is inadvertently squeezed, the piston will not be forced out of the cylinder. If this does happen, the caliper may have to be disassembled to reseat the piston and the system will have to be bled. By using the wood, bleeding the brake is not necessary when installing the wheel.

13. Tie the caliper and bracket assembly and the torque link to the frame with a Bunjee cord.

14. Slide the wheel to the rear and remove it. Don't lose the spacer on each side of the wheel hub.

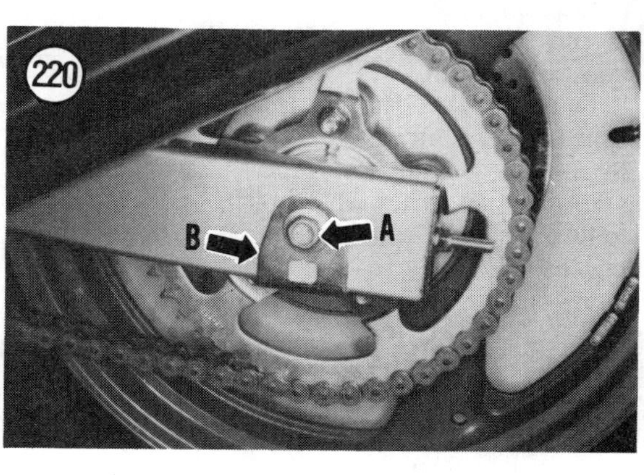

13

CAUTION
Do not set the wheel down on the disc surface as it may get scratched or warped. Set the sidewalls on 2 wood blocks.

15. Inspect the rear hub as described in this chapter.
16. Install by reversing these removal steps while noting the following:
    a. Position the right-hand spacer with the shoulder side facing in toward the bearing. This shoulder must be against the bearing inner race or the bearing will not spin properly. Install the right-hand spacer.
    b. Install the left-hand spacer into the hub.
    c. Adjust the drive chain as described in Chapter Three of the main body.
    d. Tighten the rear axle nut to the torque specification listed in **Table 13**.
    e. After the wheel is completely installed, rotate it several times to make sure that it rotates freely. Apply the rear brake as many times as necessary to make sure the brake pads are against the brake disc correctly.

REAR HUB

Inspection

Inspect each wheel bearing prior to removing it from the wheel hub.

CAUTION
Do not remove the wheel bearings for inspection purposes as they will be damaged during the removal process. Remove wheel bearings only if they are to be replaced.

1. Perform Steps 1-7 of *Disassembly* in Chapter Ten of the main body.
2. Turn each bearing by hand. Make sure the bearings turn smoothly.
3. On non-sealed bearings, check the balls for evidence of wear, pitting or excessive heat (bluish tint). Replace the bearings if necessary; always replace as a complete set. When replacing the bearings, be sure to take your old bearings along to ensure a perfect matchup.

NOTE
Fully sealed bearings are available from many bearing specialty shops. Fully sealed bearings provide better protection from dirt and moisture that may get into the hub.

4. Check the axle for wear and straightness. Use V-blocks and a dial indicator as shown in **Figure 221**. If the runout is 0.2 mm (0.01 in.) or greater, the axle should be replaced.
5. Inspect the raised webs (A, **Figure 222**) where the rubber dampers fit. Check for cracks or wear. If any damage is visible, replace the wheel.

Disassembly/Assembly

Refer to **Figure 223** for this procedure.

The disassembly and assembly of the rear hub are identical to the GSX-R750. Refer to the following illustrations that depict the components of the GSX600F Katana model:

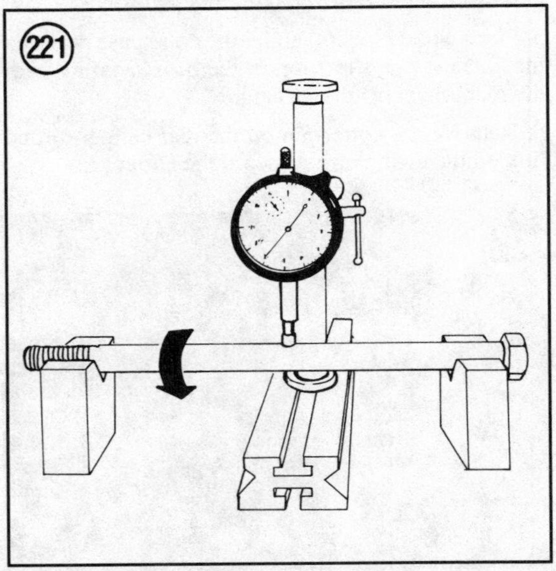

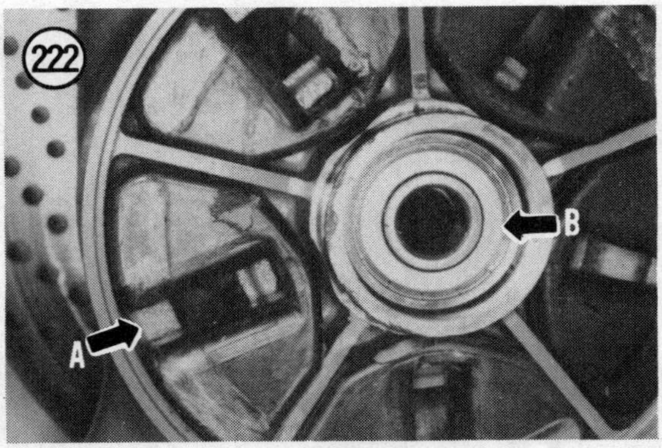

a. Brake disc bolts: A, **Figure 224**.

b. Left-hand bearing: B, **Figure 222**.

c. Right-hand bearing: B, **Figure 224**.

d. Rubber dampers: **Figure 225**.

e. Driven sprocket nuts: **Figure 226**.

SWING ARM, SHOCK ABSORBER AND SHOCK LEVER

In time, the needle bearings in the pivot points of these components will wear and will have to be replaced. The condition of the bearings can greatly

223

REAR WHEEL/HUB/DRIVEN SPROCKET (KATANA 600)

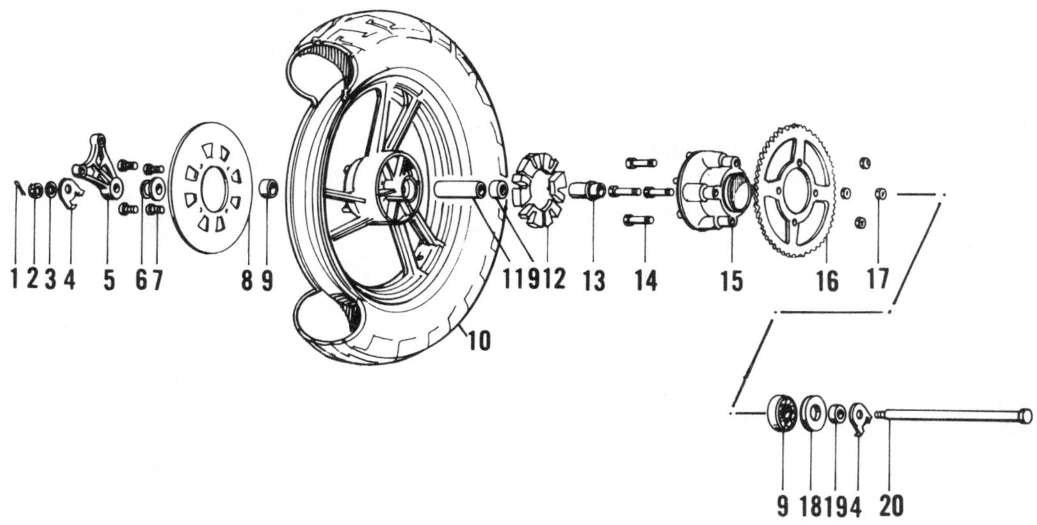

1. Cotter pin
2. Nut
3. Washer
4. Special washer
5. Caliper bracket
6. Right-hand spacer
7. Disc bolt
8. Brake disc
9. Bearing
10. Tire/rim
11. Distance collar
12. Rubber dampers
13. Spacer
14. Bolts
15. Driven sprocket hub
16. Driven sprocket
17. Nut
18. Grease seal
19. Left-hand spacer
20. Rear axle

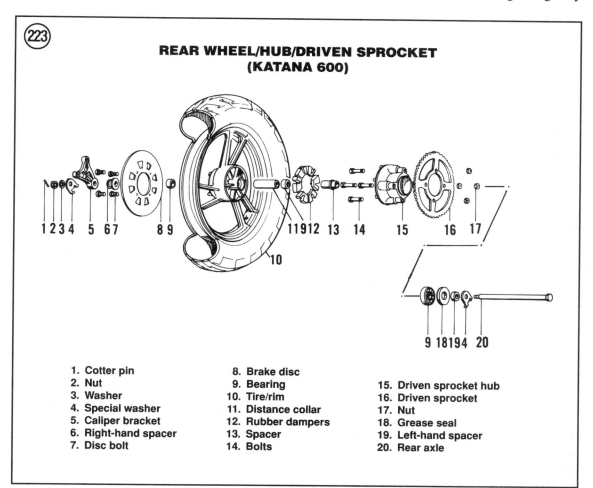

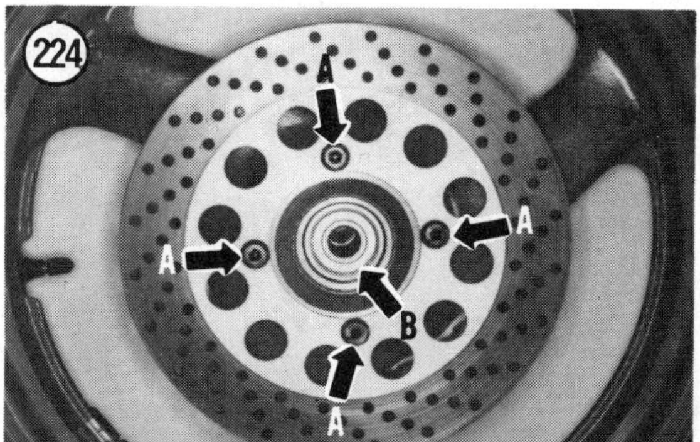

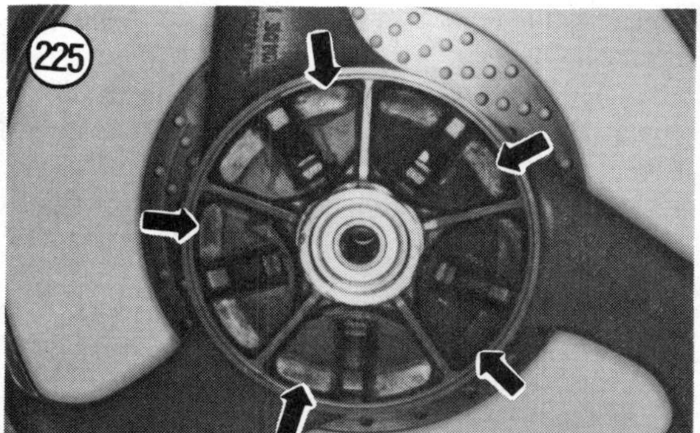

affect handling performance and if worn parts are not replaced, they can produce erratic and dangerous handling. Common symptoms are wheel hop, pulling to one side during acceleration and pulling to the other side during braking.

NOTE

All 3 components are removed from the bike's frame as an assembly and then separated on the work bench.

Removal

1. Remove the lower portion of the front fairing as described under *Front Fairing Removal/Installation* in this chapter.
2. Remove the seat as described under *Seat Removal/Installation* in this chapter.
3. Remove the side covers as described under *Side Cover Removal/Installation* in this chapter.
4. Place wood block(s) under the crankcase between the exhaust pipes to support the bike securely with the rear wheel off the ground.
5. Remove the cap from each side of the frame covering the swing arm pivot bolt and nut.
6. Remove the rear wheel as described under *Rear Wheel Removal/Installation* in this chapter.
7. Remove the screws and washers securing the drive chain cover and remove the cover.
8. Grasp the rear end of the swing arm (**Figure 227**) and try to move it from side to side in a horizontal arc. There should be no noticeable side play. If play is evident and the pivot bolt is tightened correctly, the needle bearings should be replaced.
9. Remove the shock absorber upper mounting bolt and nut (**Figure 228**).
10. Remove the bolt and nut (**Figure 229**) securing the shock lever to the frame.
11. Remove the self-locking nut and washer, then withdraw the pivot bolt (**Figure 230**) from the left-hand side.
12. Pull back on the swing arm, free it from the drive chain and remove the swing arm assembly from the frame.
13. Inspect the swing arm as described in this chapter.

NOTE

*Don't lose the dust seal and washer (**Figure 231**) on each side of the pivot points; they will usually fall off when the swing arm is removed.*

Installation

1. Correctly position the shock absorber within the swing arm (**Figure 232**).
2. Position the drive chain over the left-hand side of the swing arm.
3. Make sure the washer and dust seal (**Figure 231**) are correctly installed at each side of the swing arm.

226

227

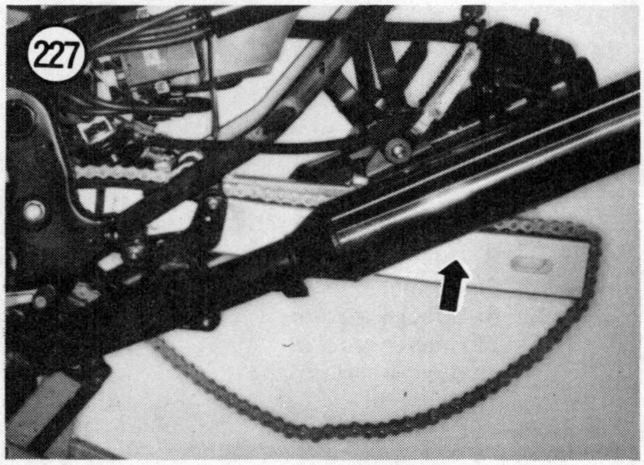

228

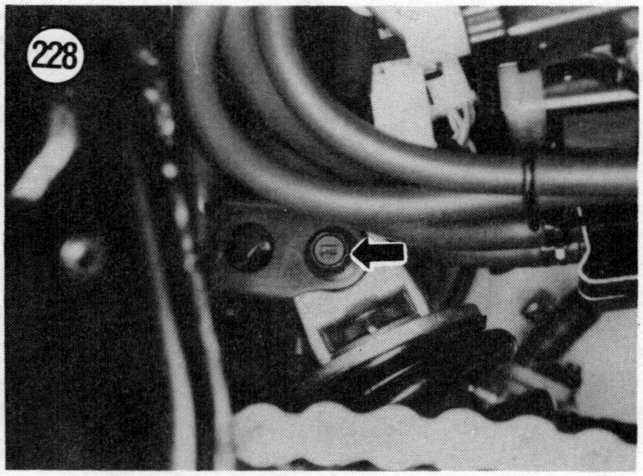

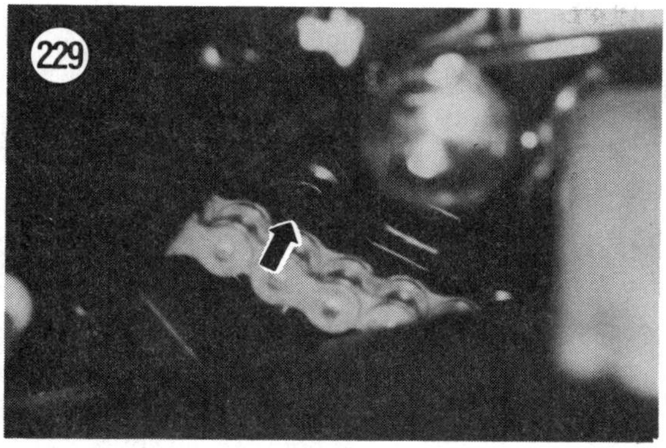
229

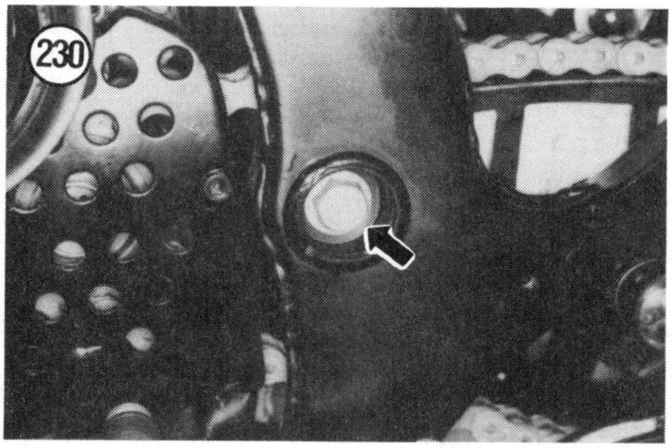
230

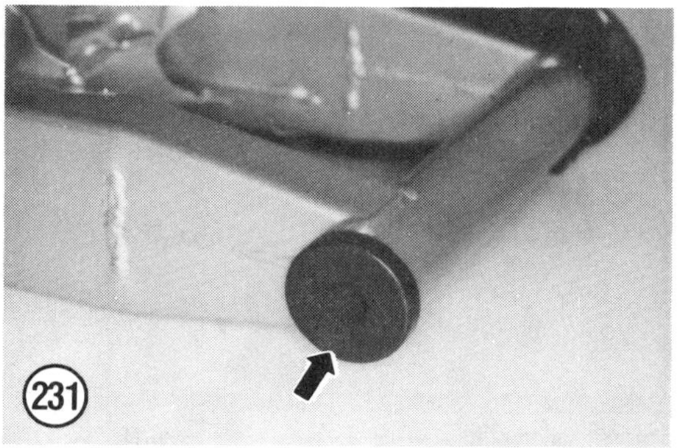
231

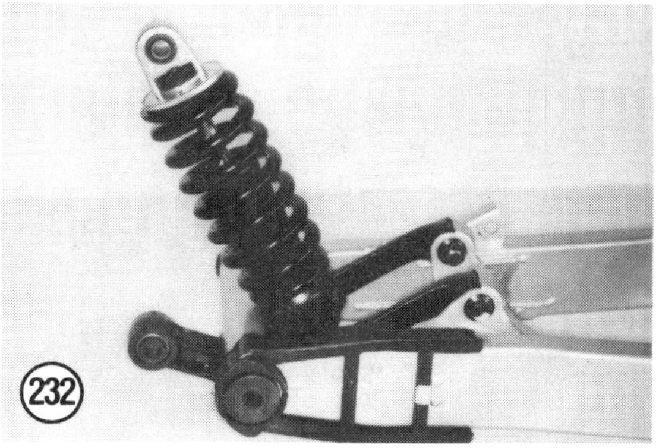
232

4. Position the swing arm into the mounting area of the frame while moving the shock absorber into position in the upper mounting bracket in the frame.
5. Align the swing arm mounting holes in the swing arm with the holes in the frame. To help align the holes, insert a drift in from the right-hand side.
6. Apply a light coat of molybdenum disulfide grease to the pivot bolt and install the pivot bolt from the left-hand side.
7. Install the upper mounting bolt (**Figure 228**) into the top of the shock absorber and install the nut.
8. Install the bolt and nut (**Figure 229**) securing the shock lever to the frame.
9. Install the swing arm pivot bolt self-locking nut and tighten to the torque specification listed in **Table 13**.
10. Tighten the shock absorber upper mounting bolt and nut to the torque specification listed in **Table 13**.
11. Tighten the bolt and nut securing the shock lever to the frame to the torque specification listed in **Table 13**.
12. Move the swing arm up and down several times to make sure all components are properly seated.
13. Insert the brake hose through the hose clamp on the swing arm.
14. Install the drive chain cover and tighten the screws securely.
15. Install the rear wheel as described in this chapter.
16. Install the cap on each side of the frame covering the pivot bolt and nut.
17. Install both side covers, seat and the lower portion of the front fairing as described in this chapter.

Disassembly/Inspection/Assembly

Refer to the following illustrations for this procedure:

a. Swing arm: **Figure 233**.
b. Shock absorber (1988): **Figure 234**.
c. Shock absorber (1989-on): **Figure 235**.
d. Shock lever: **Figure 236**.

1. Remove the swing arm assembly as described in this chapter.
2. Remove both dust seals and washers (**Figure 231**) if they have not already fallen off during the removal sequence.
3. Remove the bolts and nuts (**Figure 237**) securing the right- and left-hand shock rods to the swing arm.
4. Remove the shock arm and shock lever assembly from the swing arm.
5. Remove the bolt and nut (A, **Figure 238**) securing the shock absorber to the shock lever and remove the shock absorber.

6. Remove the bolt and nut (B, **Figure 238**) securing both shock rods to the shock lever and remove both shock rods.
7. Withdraw the spacers (**Figure 239**) from the shock lever.
8. Withdraw the spacer (**Figure 240**) from each shock rod.
9. Clean all parts in solvent and thoroughly dry.

NOTE
There are no factory specifications for the outside diameter of the spacers or pivot collar.

10. Inspect the spacers and the pivot collar for abnormal wear, scratches or score marks. Replace if necessary.

NOTE
If the spacers and the pivot collar are replaced, the needle bearing at each end must also be replaced at the same time.

11. Inspect the swing arm needle bearings as follows:

a. Wipe off any excess grease from the needle bearing at each end of the swing arm.

233

SWING ARM (KATANA 600)

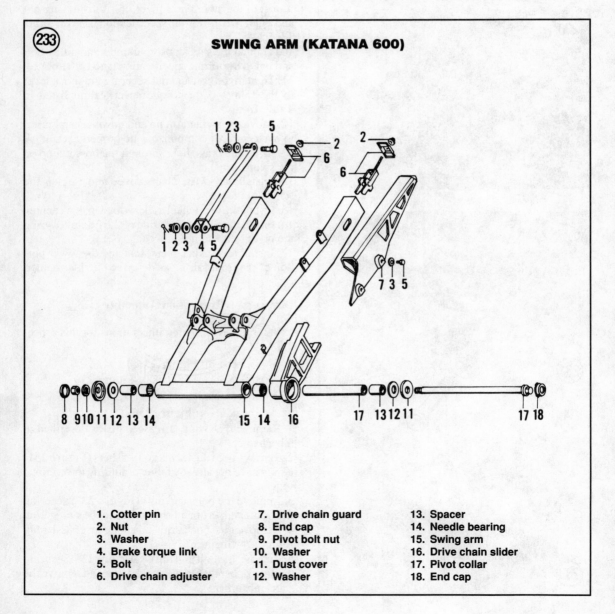

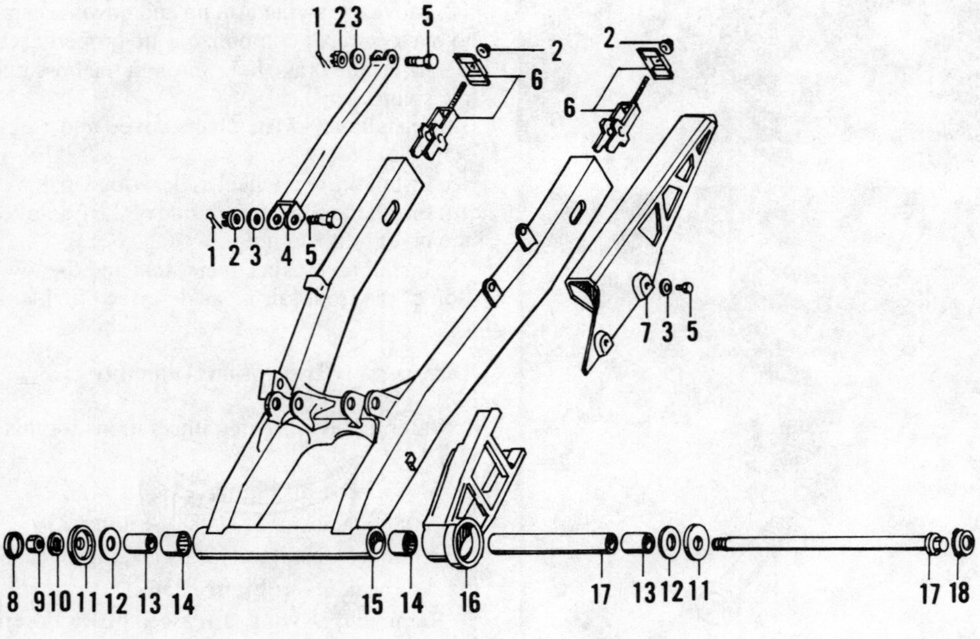

1. Cotter pin
2. Nut
3. Washer
4. Brake torque link
5. Bolt
6. Drive chain adjuster
7. Drive chain guard
8. End cap
9. Pivot bolt nut
10. Washer
11. Dust cover
12. Washer
13. Spacer
14. Needle bearing
15. Swing arm
16. Drive chain slider
17. Pivot collar
18. End cap

b. Turn each bearing with your fingers; make sure it rotates smoothly. The needle bearings wear very slowly and wear is very difficult to measure.

c. Check the rollers for evidence of wear, pitting or color change (bluish tint) indicating heat from lack of lubrication.

NOTE
Always replace both needle bearings even though only one may be worn.

12. Inspect the shock lever (**Figure 241**) and the shock rods (**Figure 242**) for wear or damage. Replace if necessary.

REAR SHOCK ABSORBER (1988 KATANA 600)

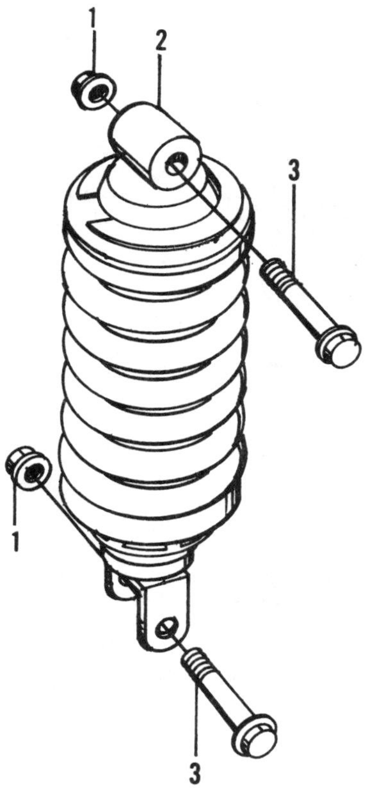

1. Nut
2. Shock absorber unit
3. Mounting bolt

234

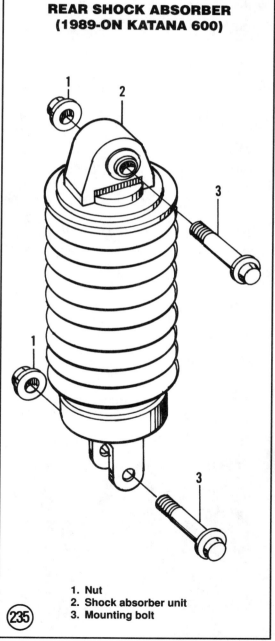

REAR SHOCK ABSORBER (1989-ON KATANA 600)

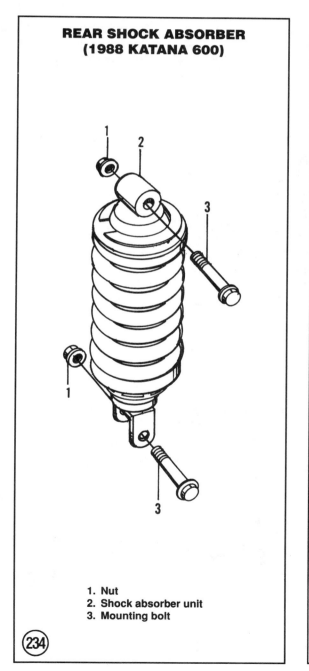

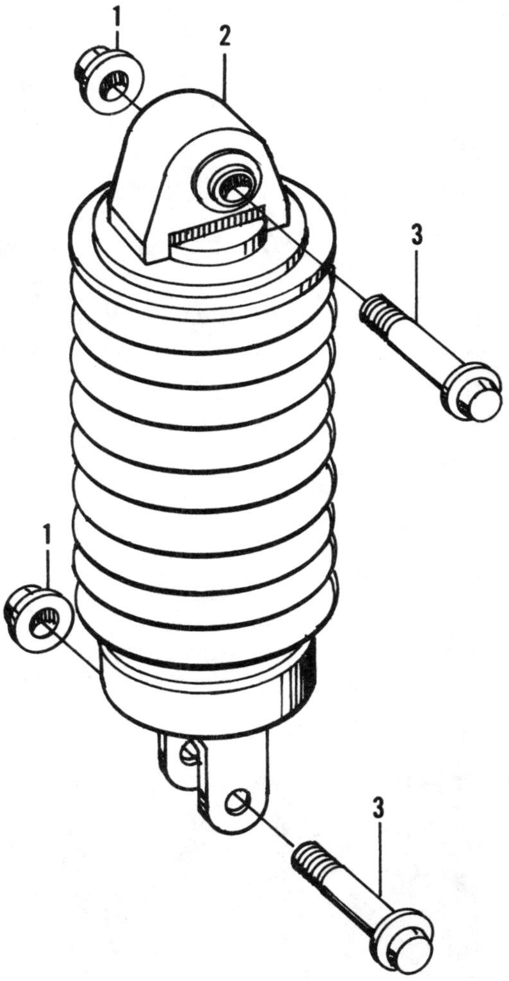

1. Nut
2. Shock absorber unit
3. Mounting bolt

235

13

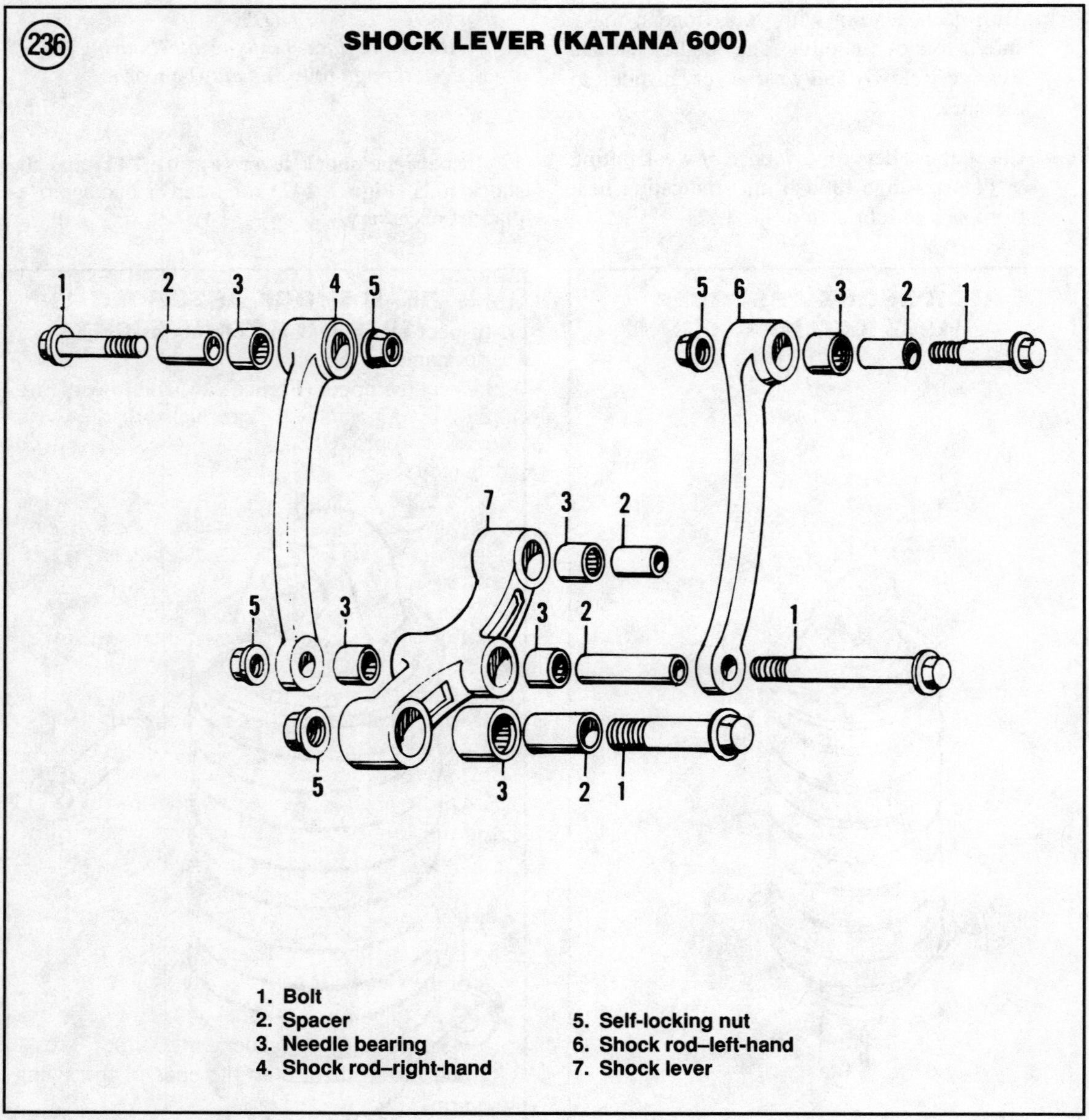
236
SHOCK LEVER (KATANA 600)
1
2
3
4
5
5
6
3
2
1
7
3
2
5
3
3
2
1
5
3
2
1
1. Bolt
2. Spacer
3. Needle bearing
4. Shock rod–right-hand
5. Self-locking nut
6. Shock rod–left-hand
7. Shock lever

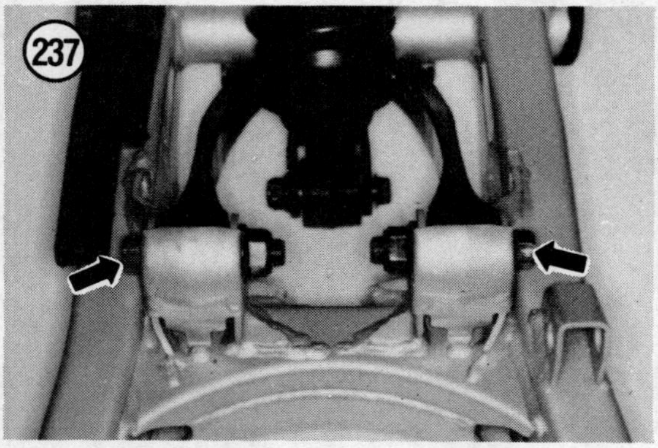
237

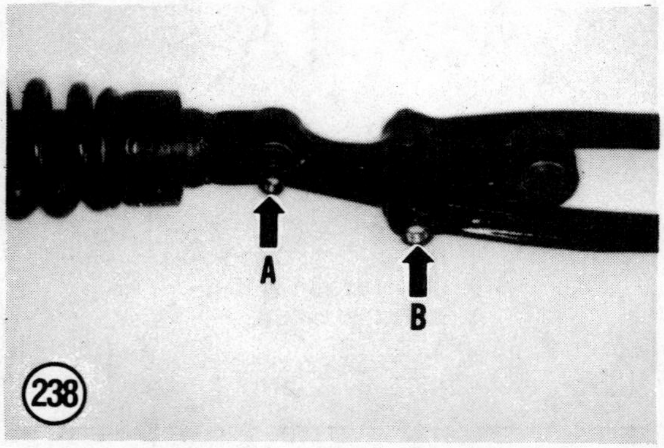
A
B
238

239

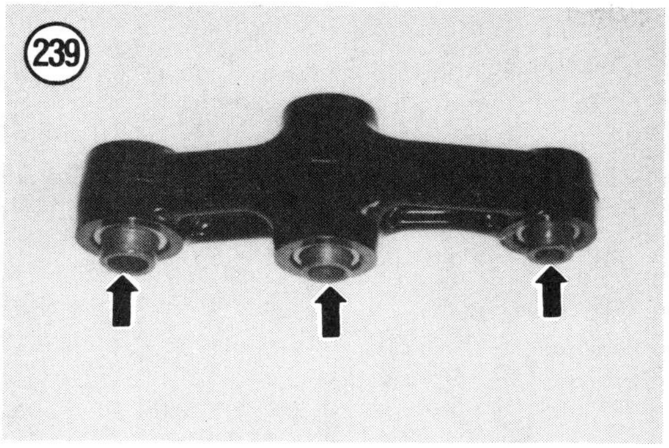

240

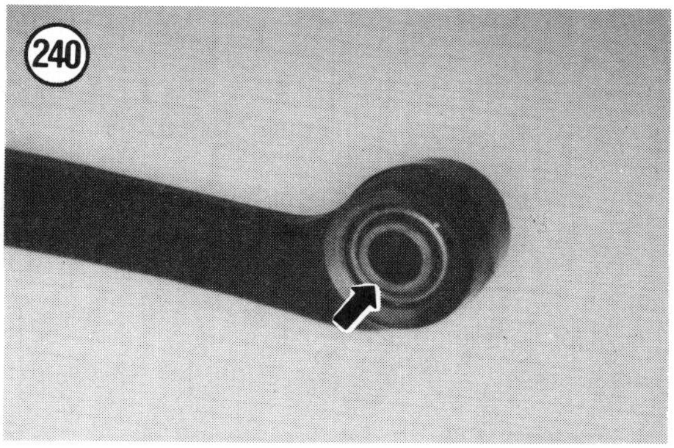

241

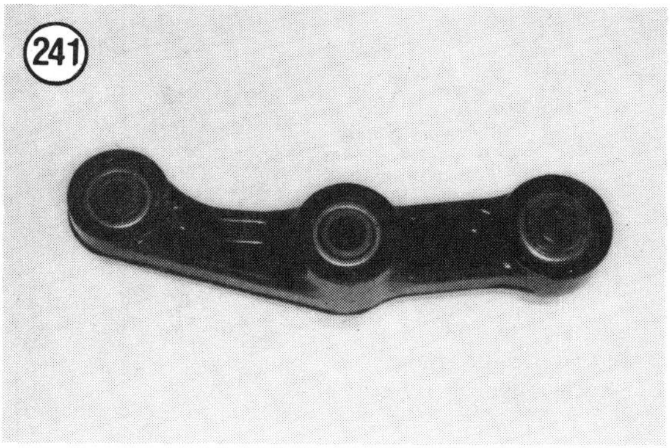

242

13. Inspect the spacer and needle bearing (**Figure 243**) on each side of the swing arm for wear or damage. Replace if necessary.

14. Inspect the shock absorber lever mounting bracket pivot holes (**Figure 244**) on the swing arm. If the holes are elongated or worn, replace the swing arm.

15. Check the welded sections on the swing arm for cracks or fractures.

16. Inspect the drive chain slider (**Figure 245**) for wear or damage, replace if necessary.

17. Inspect the drive chain adjuster assemblies for wear or damage, replace if necessary.

18. Inspect the upper (**Figure 246**) and lower (**Figure 247**) pivot points of the shock absorber for wear or damage. Replace the shock absorber if either end is damaged.

19. Check the damper unit (**Figure 248**) for dents, oil leakage or other damage. Make sure the damper rod is straight. If either is damaged, replace the shock absorber.

20. Prior to installing the shock absorber lever mounting bolt, coat it with molybdenum disulfide grease.

21. Position the shock absorber lever as shown in **Figure 232**. Install the mounting bolt from the left-hand side and install the nut. Tighten the bolt and nut to the torque specification listed in **Table 13**.

22. On the swing arm, perform the following:

   a. Prior to installing the swing arm pivot collar and spacers, coat the pivot collar, spacers and both needle bearings with molybdenum disulfide grease.

   b. Insert the pivot collar and spacer into each end of the swing arm.

   c. Coat the inside of both dust caps and the washers with molybdenum disulfide grease and install them onto the ends of the swing arm.

13

243

d. If removed, install the drive chain slider and tighten the screws securely.

23. Prior to installing the spacers into the shock lever and shock rods, coat the pivot collars with molybdenum disulfide grease.

24. Install the spacers (**Figure 239**) into the shock lever.

25. Install the spacer (**Figure 240**) onto each shock rod.

26. Install the bolt and nut (B, **Figure 238**) securing both shock rods to the shock lever. Tighten the bolt and nut to the torque specification listed in **Table 13**.

27. Install the bolt and nut (A, **Figure 238**) securing the shock absorber to the shock lever. Tighten the bolt and nut to the torque specification listed in **Table 13**.

28. Install the shock arm and shock lever assembly onto the swing arm. Tighten the bolt and nut to the torque specification listed in **Table 13**.

29. Install the bolts and nuts (**Figure 237**) securing the right- and left-hand shock rods to the swing arm. Tighten the bolt and nut to the torque specification listed in **Table 13**.

30. Install the swing arm as described under *Swing Arm Installation* in this chapter.

SHOCK ABSORBER

Spring Preload Adjustment (1988)

There must be pre-load on the spring at all times. Never ride the bike without spring preload as possible loss of control will result.

The spring length (pre-load) must be maintained within the following dimensions:

a. Standard length: 177.3 mm (6.98 in.).

b. Minimum length: 172.3 mm (6.78 in.).

c. Maximum length: 182.3 mm (7.18 in.).

1. Special Suzuki tools in the owner's tool kit are used to adjust the spring adjuster ring.

2. Loosen the adjuster locknut.

3. Turn the adjuster *counterclockwise* to increase spring pre-load and *clockwise* to decrease spring pre-load.

NOTE

Remember the spring length (pre-load) must be maintained within the previously listed dimensions.

4. Tighten the locknut securely.

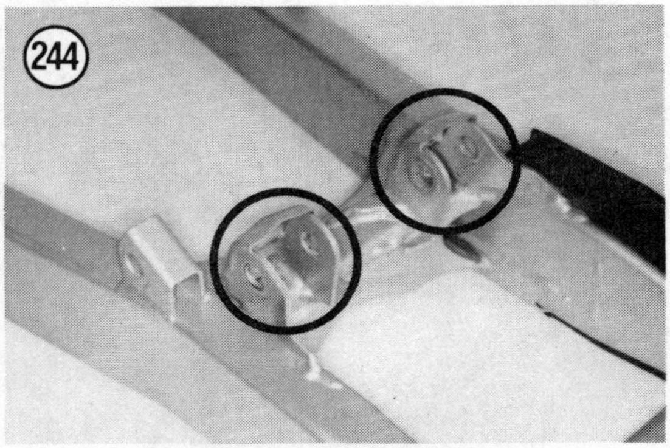

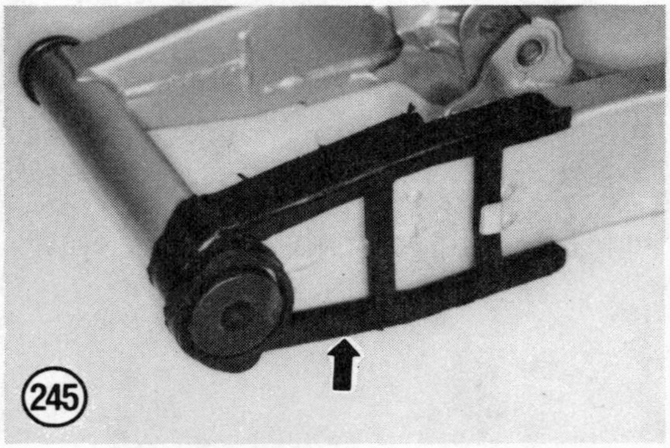

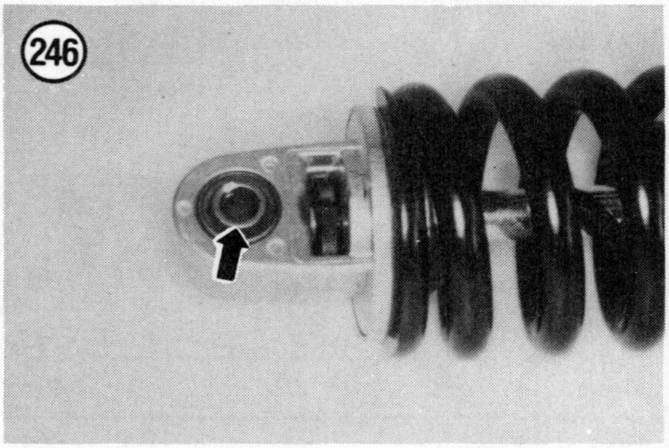

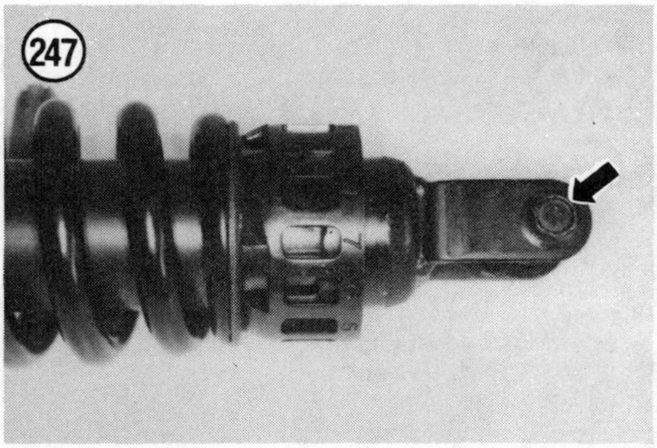

Spring Preload Adjustment (1989-on)

Spring preload can be adjusted by rotating the adjustment ring (**Figure 249**) on the base of the shock absorber. Suzuki recommends that the spring preload be set at the No. 4 position for solo riding or between No. 4 and No. 6 for dual riding. Refer to **Table 12**.

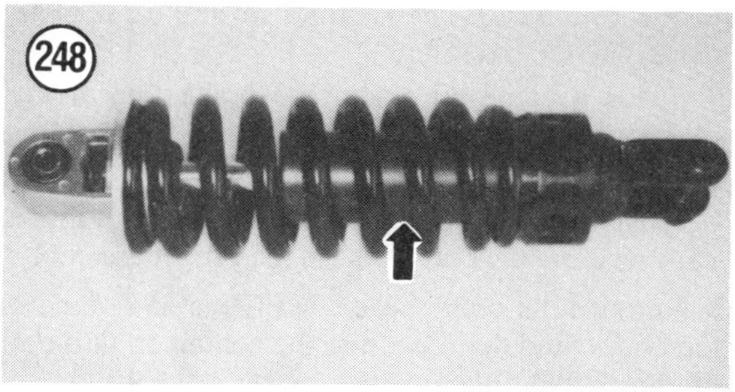

Damping Adjustment (1989-on)

Damping can be adjusted to 3 different settings (1, 2 and 3). Position 1 is the softest setting and position 3 is the stiffest setting. The adjuster knob is located at the top of the shock absorber (**Figure 250**). Rotate the adjuster to the desired setting. Make sure that the adjuster is located into one of the detents and not in between any 2 settings.

Table 13 REAR SUSPENSION TORQUE SPECIFICATIONS

Item	N•m	ft.-lb.
Rear axle nut	50-80	36-58
Rear caliper mounting bolt	15-25	11-18
Brake disc bolts	15-25	11-18
Driven sprocket nuts	48-72	35-52
Drive sprocket		
Nut	100-130	72.5-94
Bolt	8-12	6-9
Swing arm pivot bolt and nut	55-88	40-63.5
Shock absorber bolt and nut	48-72	34.5-52
Shock lever-to-frame bolt and nut	132-192	95.5-139
Shock rod		
To swing arm bolt and nut	84-120	60.5-87
To shock lever bolt and nut	84-120	60.5-87

CHAPTER ELEVEN

BRAKES

FRONT CALIPER

Removal/Installation

Refer to **Figure 251** for this procedure.

It is not necessary to remove the front wheel in order to remove the caliper assembly.

CAUTION
Do not spill any brake fluid on the front fork or front wheel. Wash off any spilled brake fluid immediately, as it will destroy the finish. Use soapy water and rinse completely.

1. Clean the top of the master cylinder of all dirt and foreign matter.
2. Loose the screws securing the master cylinder cover (**Figure 252**). Pull up and loosen the cover and the diaphragm. This will allow air to enter the reservoir and allow the brake fluid to drain out more quickly in the next step.
3. Place a container under the brake line at the caliper.
4. Hold onto the locknut (A, **Figure 253**) with an open end wrench. Loosen the nut adaptor (B, **Figure 253**) securing the brake hose to the caliper assembly.
5. Remove the brake hose (A, **Figure 254**) and let the brake fluid drain out into the container. Dispose of this brake fluid—never reuse brake fluid. To prevent the entry of moisture and dirt, cap the end of the brake hose and tie the loose end up to the forks.
6. Loosen the bolts (B, **Figure 254**) securing the brake caliper assembly to the front fork. Push in on the caliper while loosening the bolts to push the pistons back into the caliper bores.
7. Remove the bolts securing the brake caliper assembly to the front fork.
8. Remove the caliper assembly from the brake disc.

(251)

FRONT BRAKE CALIPER ASSEMBLY (KATANA 600)

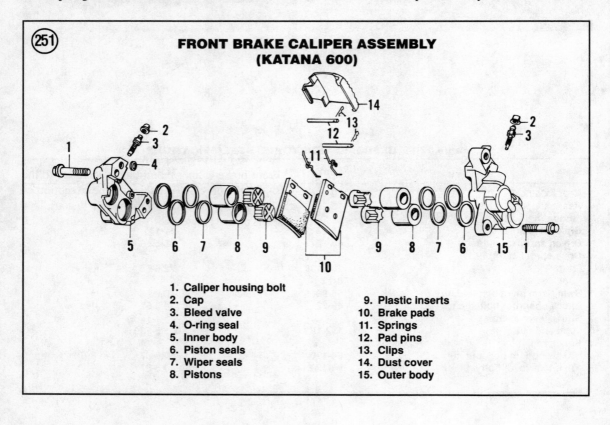

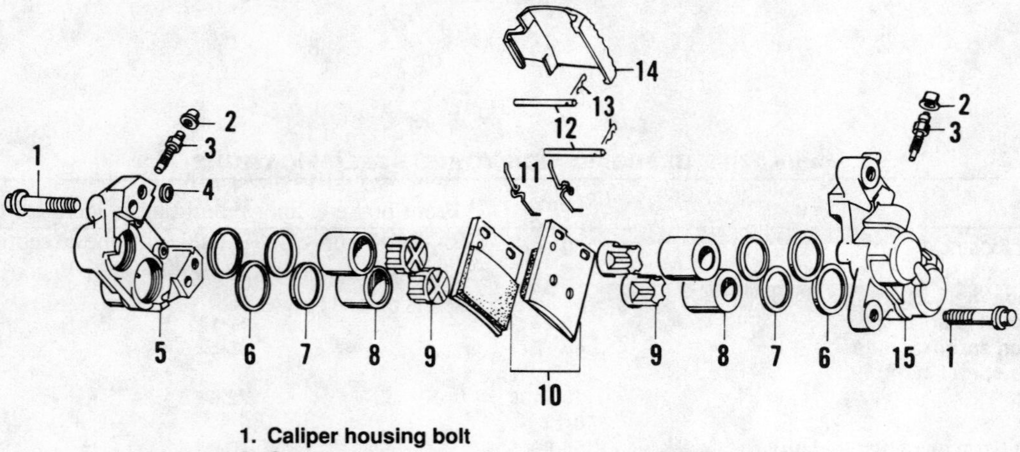

1. Caliper housing bolt
2. Cap
3. Bleed valve
4. O-ring seal
5. Inner body
6. Piston seals
7. Wiper seals
8. Pistons
9. Plastic inserts
10. Brake pads
11. Springs
12. Pad pins
13. Clips
14. Dust cover
15. Outer body

9. Install by reversing these removal steps while noting the following.

a. Carefully install the caliper assembly onto the disc being careful not to damage the leading edge of the brake pads.

b. Install the bolts securing the brake caliper assembly to the front fork and tighten to 15-25 N•m (11-18 ft.-lb.).

c. Install the brake hose onto the caliper.

d. Screw the brake hose into the caliper.

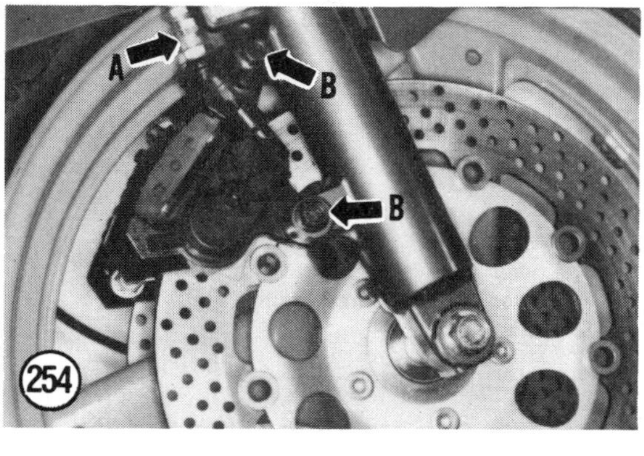

e. Hold onto the locknut (A, **Figure 253**) with an open end wrench. Tighten the nut adaptor (B, **Figure 253**) securing the brake hose to the caliper assembly to the torque specification listed in **Table 14**.

f. If necessary, repeat Steps 3-14 for the other caliper assembly.

g. Remove the master cylinder top cover and diaphragm.

WARNING

Use brake fluid clearly marked DOT 3 or DOT 4 from a sealed container. Other types may vaporize and cause brake failure. Always use the same brand name; do not intermix as many brands are not compatible. Do not intermix silicone-based (DOT 5) brake fluid as it can cause brake component damage leading to brake system failure.

h. Refill the master cylinder reservoir. Install the diaphragm and cover. Do not tighten the screws at this time.

i. Bleed the brake as described under *Bleeding the System* in Chapter Eleven of the main body.

WARNING

Do not ride the motorcycle until you are sure that the brakes are operating properly.

Caliper Rebuilding

Refer to **Figure 251** for this procedure.

Front brake caliper rebuilding is identical to the GSX-R750 and GSX-R1100 with the exception of the plastic insert installed into each piston. This insert is placed between the piston and the brake pad.

FRONT BRAKE HOSE REPLACEMENT

Suzuki recommends replacing all brake hoses every four years or when they show signs of cracking or damage.

Refer to **Figure 255** for this procedure.

1. Remove the front fairing as described under *Front Fairing Removal/Installation* in this chapter.

(255) FRONT BRAKE HOSES (KATANA 600)

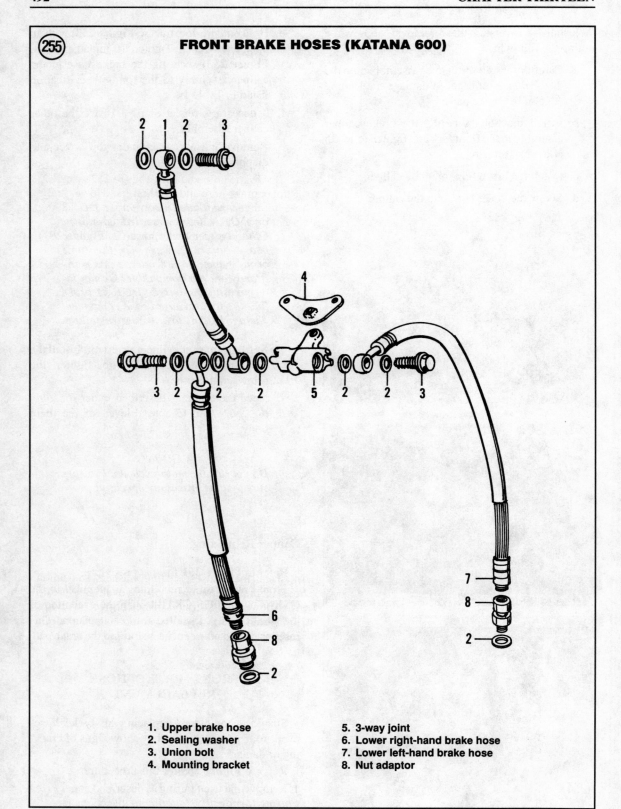

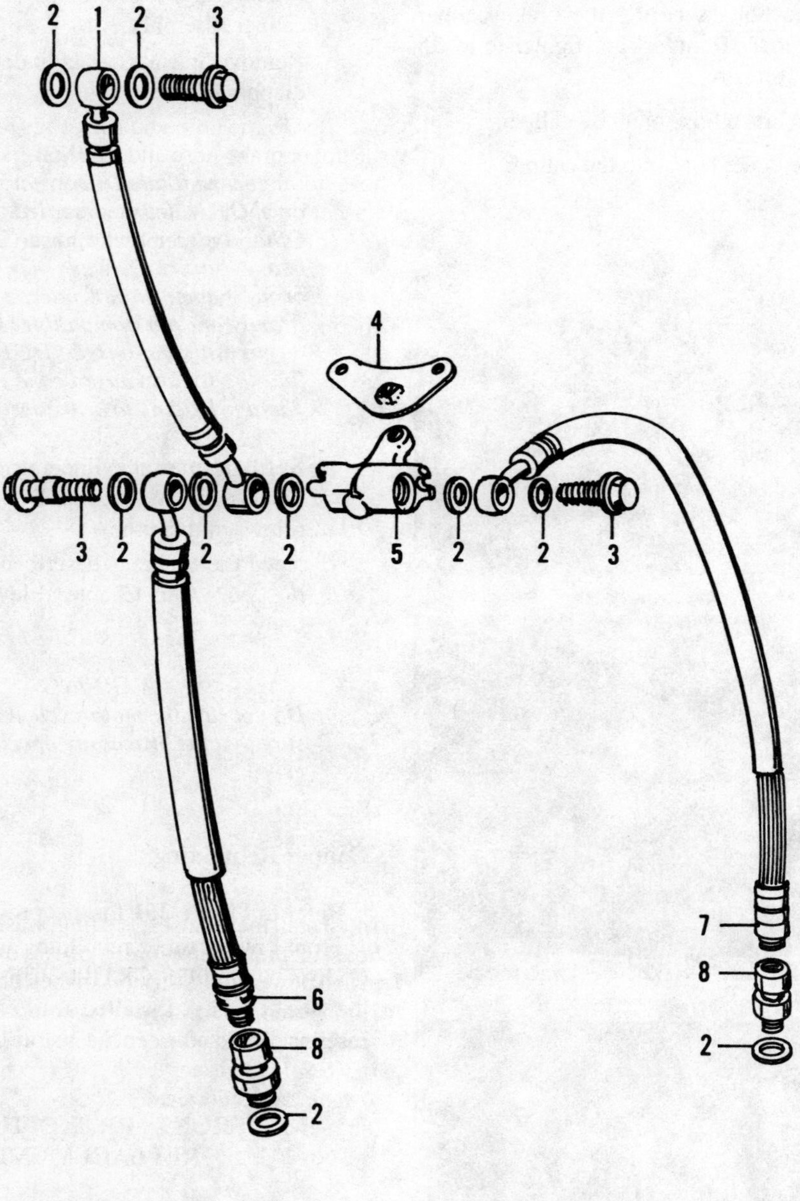

1. Upper brake hose
2. Sealing washer
3. Union bolt
4. Mounting bracket
5. 3-way joint
6. Lower right-hand brake hose
7. Lower left-hand brake hose
8. Nut adaptor

CAUTION
Cover the fuel tank, front fender and instrument cluster with a heavy cloth or plastic tarp to protect them from accidental brake fluid spills. Wash brake fluid off any painted or plated surfaces or plastic parts immediately, as it will destroy the finish. Use soapy water and rinse completely.

2. Clean the top of the master cylinder of all dirt and foreign matter.

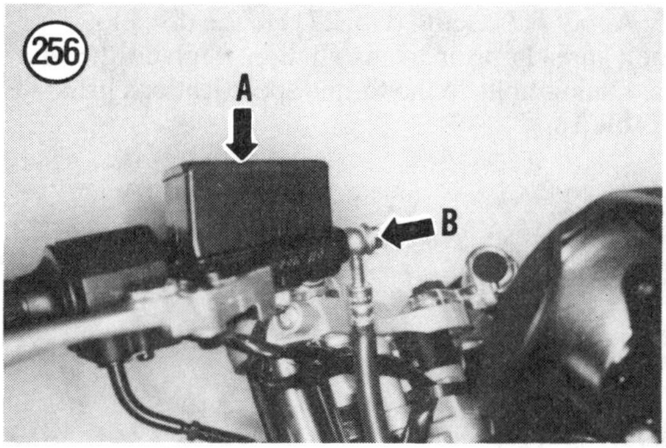

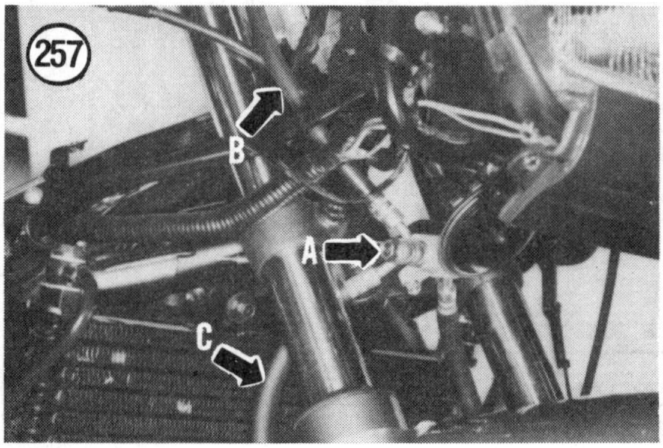

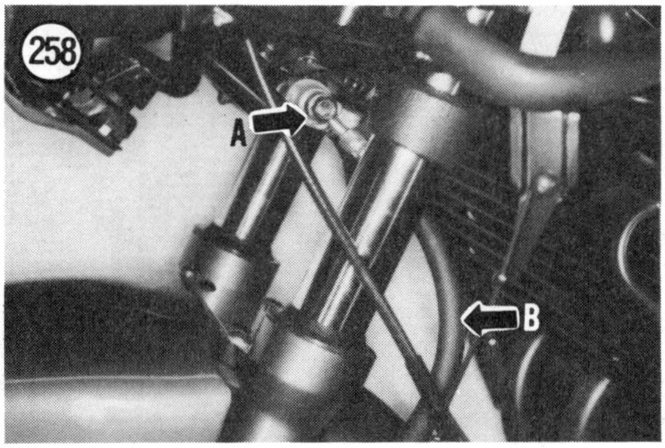

3. Loosen the screws securing the master cylinder cover (A, **Figure 256**). Pull up and loosen the cover and the diaphragm. This will allow air to enter the reservoir and allow the brake fluid to drain out more quickly in the next step.
4. Place a shop cloth under the union bolt (B, **Figure 256**) to catch any spilled brake fluid that will leak out.
5. Unscrew the union bolt securing the upper brake hose to the master cylinder. Don't lose the sealing washer on each side of the hose fitting.
6. Unscrew the union bolt (A, **Figure 257**) securing the upper brake hose and the right-hand lower brake hose to the 3-way joint. Don't lose the sealing washer on each side of the hose fittings.
7. Remove the upper brake hose (B, **Figure 257**) from the frame.
8. Hold onto the locknut (A, **Figure 253**) with an open end wrench. Loosen the nut adaptor (B, **Figure 253**) securing the right-hand lower brake hose to the caliper assembly.
9. Remove the right-hand lower brake hose (C, **Figure 257**) and let the brake fluid drain out into the container. Dispose of this brake fluid—never reuse brake fluid.
10. Unscrew the union bolt (A, **Figure 258**) securing the lower left-hand brake hose to the 3-way joint. Don't lose the sealing washer on each side of the hose fitting.
11. Hold onto the locknut with an open end wrench. Loosen the nut adaptor securing the left-hand brake hose to the caliper assembly.
12. Remove the left-hand lower brake hose (B, **Figure 258**) and let the brake fluid drain out into the container. Dispose of this brake fluid—never reuse brake fluid.
13. If necessary, remove the mounting bolt securing the 3-way joint to the frame and remove the 3-way joint.
14. Install new hoses, sealing washers and union bolts in the reverse order of removal. Be sure to install new sealing washers in their correct positions.
15. Tighten the fittings and union bolts to the torque specification listed in **Table 14**.
16. Refill the master cylinder reservoir, if necessary, to maintain the correct fluid level as seen through the viewing port on the side. Install the diaphragm and cover. Do not tighten the screws at this time.

WARNING
Use brake fluid clearly marked DOT 3 or DOT 4 from a sealed container. Other types may vaporize and cause brake failure. Always use the same brand name; do not intermix as many

13

brands are not compatible. Do not intermix silicone-based (DOT 5) brake fluid as it can cause brake component damage leading to brake system failure.

WARNING

Do not ride the motorcycle until you are sure that the brakes are operating properly.

17. Bleed the brake as described under *Bleeding the System* in Chapter Eleven of the main body.

FRONT BRAKE DISC

Removal/Installation

1. Remove the front wheel as described under *Front Wheel Removal* in this chapter.

NOTE

Place a piece of wood or vinyl tube in the caliper in place of the disc. This way, if the brake lever is inadvertently squeezed the pistons will not be forced out of the cylinders. If this does happen, the caliper might have to be disassembled to reseat the pistons and the system will have to be bled. By using the wood or vinyl tube, bleeding the system is not necessary when installing the wheel.

CAUTION

Do not set the wheel down on the disc surface, as it may get scratched or warped. Set the wheel on 2 blocks of wood.

2. Remove the bolts (**Figure 259**) securing the brake disc to the hub and remove the disc. Don't lose the shims between the brake disc and the wheel hub.
3. If necessary, repeat Step 2 for the brake disc on the other side.
4. Install by reversing these removal steps while noting the following.
5. Apply red Loctite (No. 271) to the disc mounting bolt threads prior to installation. Tighten the disc mounting bolts to the torque specifications listed in **Table 14**.

259

Table 14 BRAKE TORQUE SPECIFICATIONS

Item	N•m	ft.-lb.
Front master cylinder		
Clamping bolts	5-8	3-6
Union bolt	20-25	14-18
Front caliper		
Mounting bolts	15-25	11-18
Union bolt	15-20	11-14
Bleed valve	6-9	4-7
Housing bolts	30-36	21-26
Brake hose nut adaptor	15-20	11-14
Rear caliper		
Mounting bolts	15-25	11-18
Bleed valve	6-9	4-7
Union bolt	15-20	11-14
Housing bolts	30-36	21-26
Brake disc mounting bolt	15-25	11-18

CHAPTER TWELVE

BODY AND FRAME

SEATS

Rider Seat Removal/Installation

Refer to **Figure 260** for this procedure.

1. Insert the ignition key into the seat/helmet lock on the left-hand side cover.
2. Turn the ignition key *clockwise* until the seat lock is released.
3. Pull up on the rear of the seat and move the seat toward the rear.
4. Remove the seat assembly (**Figure 261**).
5. Install by reversing these removal steps while noting the following:

260

REAR SEAT (KATANA 600)

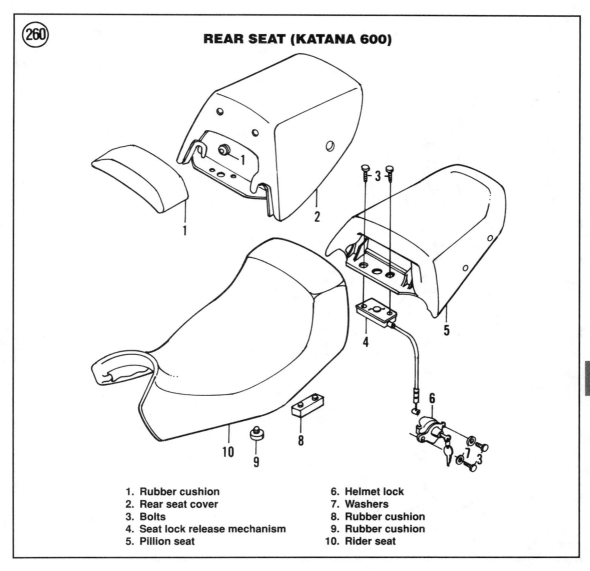

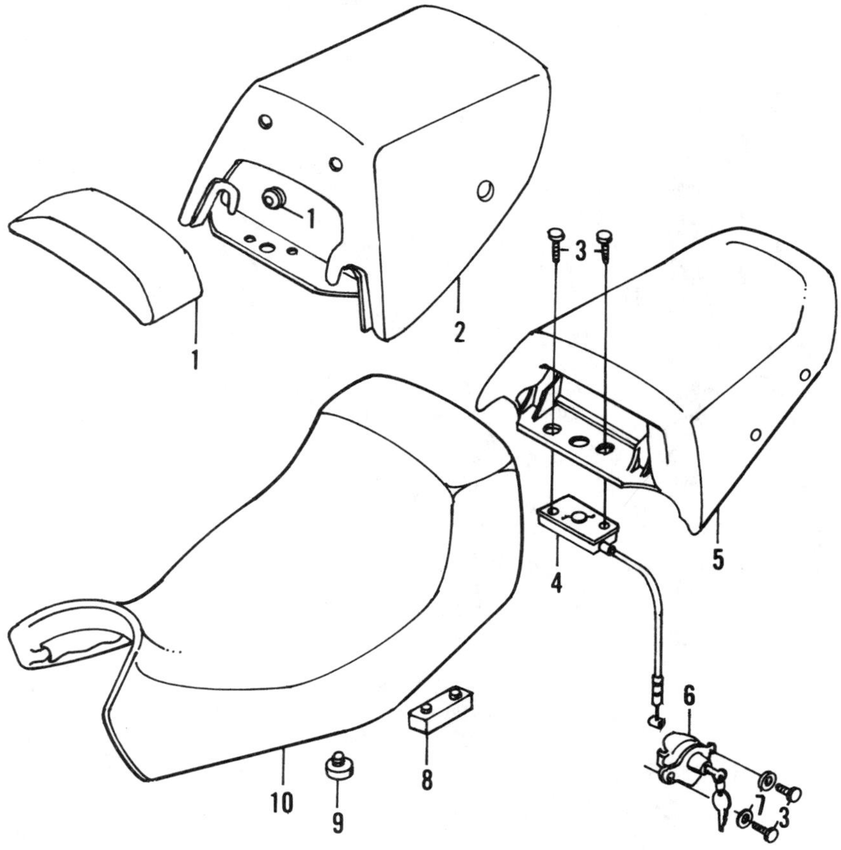

1. Rubber cushion
2. Rear seat cover
3. Bolts
4. Seat lock release mechanism
5. Pillion seat
6. Helmet lock
7. Washers
8. Rubber cushion
9. Rubber cushion
10. Rider seat

a. Make sure the locating tab on the front of the seat is correctly hooked onto the metal seat bracket on the frame.

WARNING

After the seat is installed, pull up on it firmly to make sure it is securely locked in place. If the seat is not correctly locked in place, it may slide to one side or the other when riding the bike. This

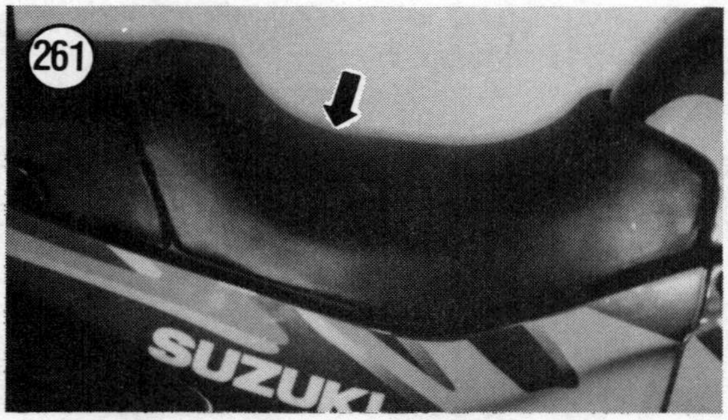

262

GRAB RAIL (KATANA 600)

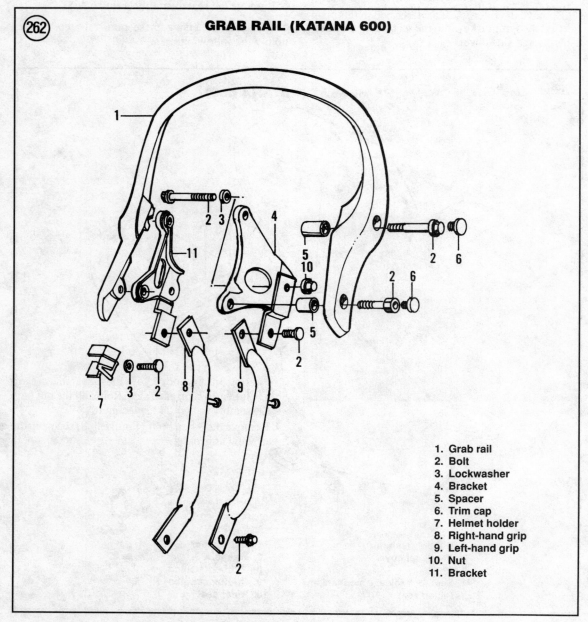

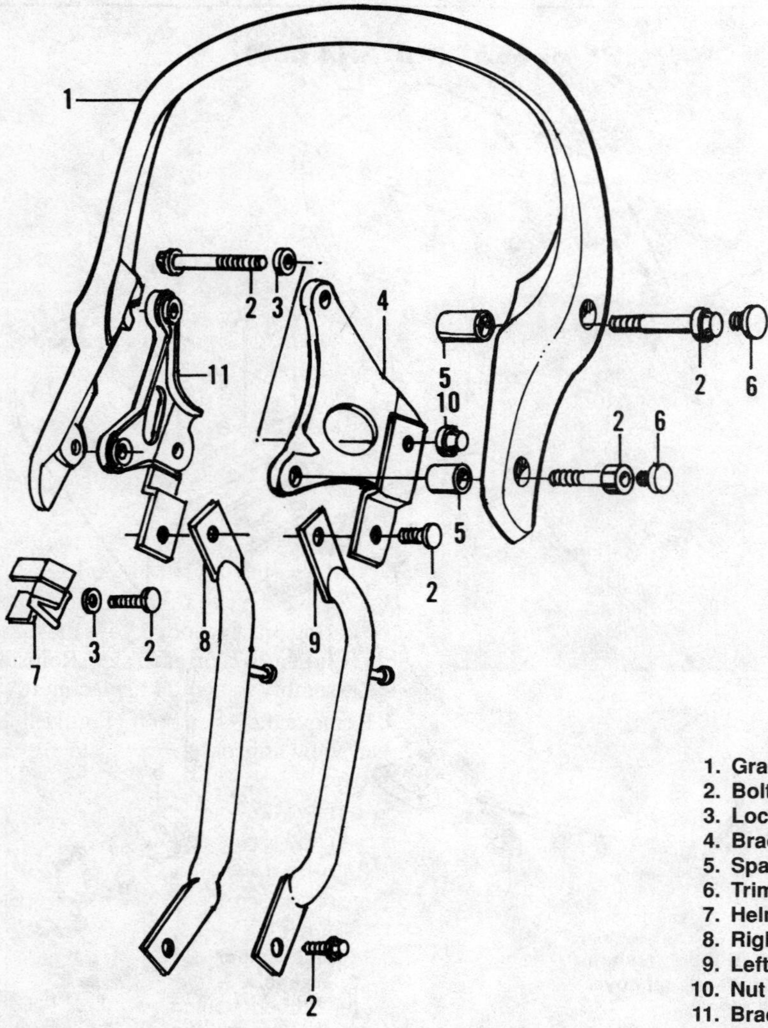

1. Grab rail
2. Bolt
3. Lockwasher
4. Bracket
5. Spacer
6. Trim cap
7. Helmet holder
8. Right-hand grip
9. Left-hand grip
10. Nut
11. Bracket

could lead to the loss of control and a possible accident.

b. Push the seat firmly down until the seat latch "snaps" into the locked position.

Pillion Seat and Grab Rail

Refer to **Figure 260** for the seat and **Figure 262** for the grab rail for this procedure.

1. Remove the rider's seat as described in this chapter.

2. Remove the screws securing the rider's seat release mechanism (**Figure 263**) and the pillion seat. Move the mechanism over to the side, it is not necessary to remove it completely.

3. Remove the trim caps and bolts (A, **Figure 264**) securing the grab bar and pillion seat.

4. Remove the grab bar (B, **Figure 264**) and pillion seat (C, **Figure 264**).

5. If necessary, remove the bolts and nuts securing the grip and bracket on each and remove them.

263

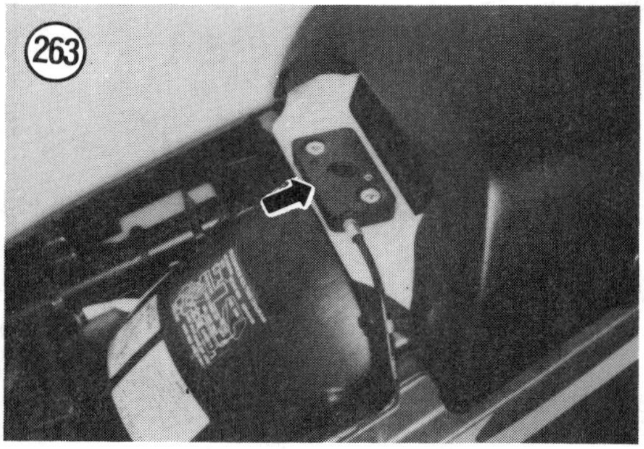

264

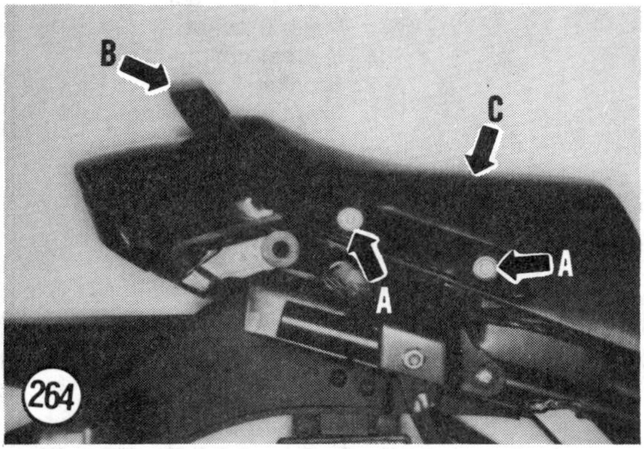

6. Install by reversing these removal steps making sure to tighten all bolts and nuts securely.

FRONT FAIRING, MOUNTING BRACKET AND SIDE COVERS

Removal/Installation

Refer to **Figure 265** for the front fairing and **Figure 266** for side covers for this procedure.

NOTE
At the rear of the bike some of the same fasteners secure the rear portion of the fairing as well as the front portion of the side cover to the frame.

CAUTION
Removal of the upper section requires the aid of a helper or some means to hold onto one side while the fasteners on the other side are removed. The fairing is not heavy, but it is bulky. Once the fasteners on one side are removed, you then have to remove the fasteners on the other side. After the fasteners on the first side are removed, ***do not allow the first side to "hang down"*** *by itself or part of the fairing or its fasteners will be damaged.*

1. Remove the rider's seat as described in this chapter.

2. Within the front of the fairing, disconnect the electrical connectors for both front turn signals.

3. Remove the nut securing the front turn signal to the fairing bracket and remove the turn signal assembly (**Figure 267**) on each side. Reinstall the nut onto the assembly to avoid misplacing it.

4. Remove the Allen bolts (**Figure 268**) securing the rear view mirror on each side and remove both mirrors.

5. Remove the screws and collars securing the windscreen and remove the windscreen.

6. Remove the screws securing the front under cover (**Figure 269**) and remove the cover.

7. Remove the bolts and nuts and the bracket securing the lower fairing panels together at the base (A, **Figure 270**). Remove the bracket.

8. Remove the bolts, washers and spacers (A, **Figure 271**) securing the lower fairing panels. Remove the lower fairing panel (B, **Figure 271**) from each side.

(265)

FRONT FAIRING AND MOUNTING BRACKET (KATANA 600)

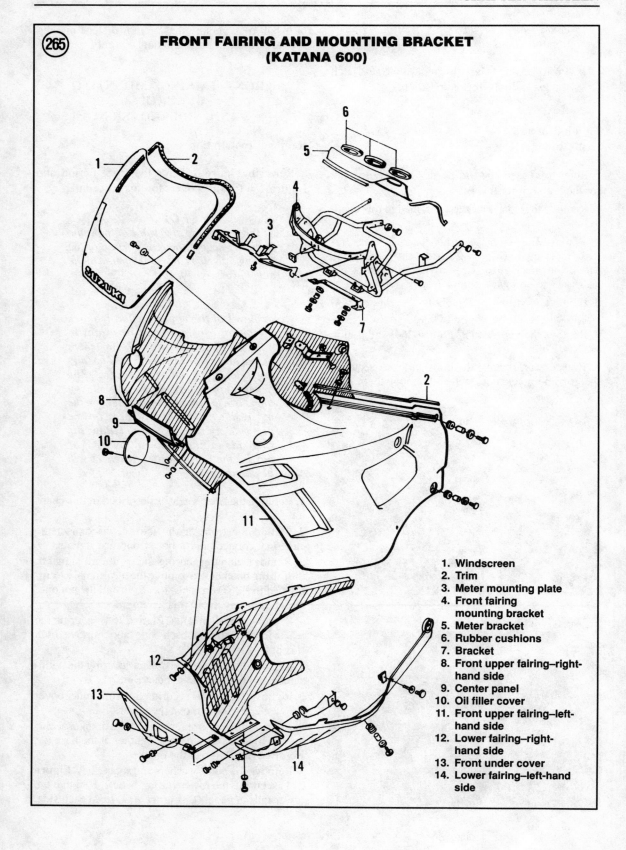

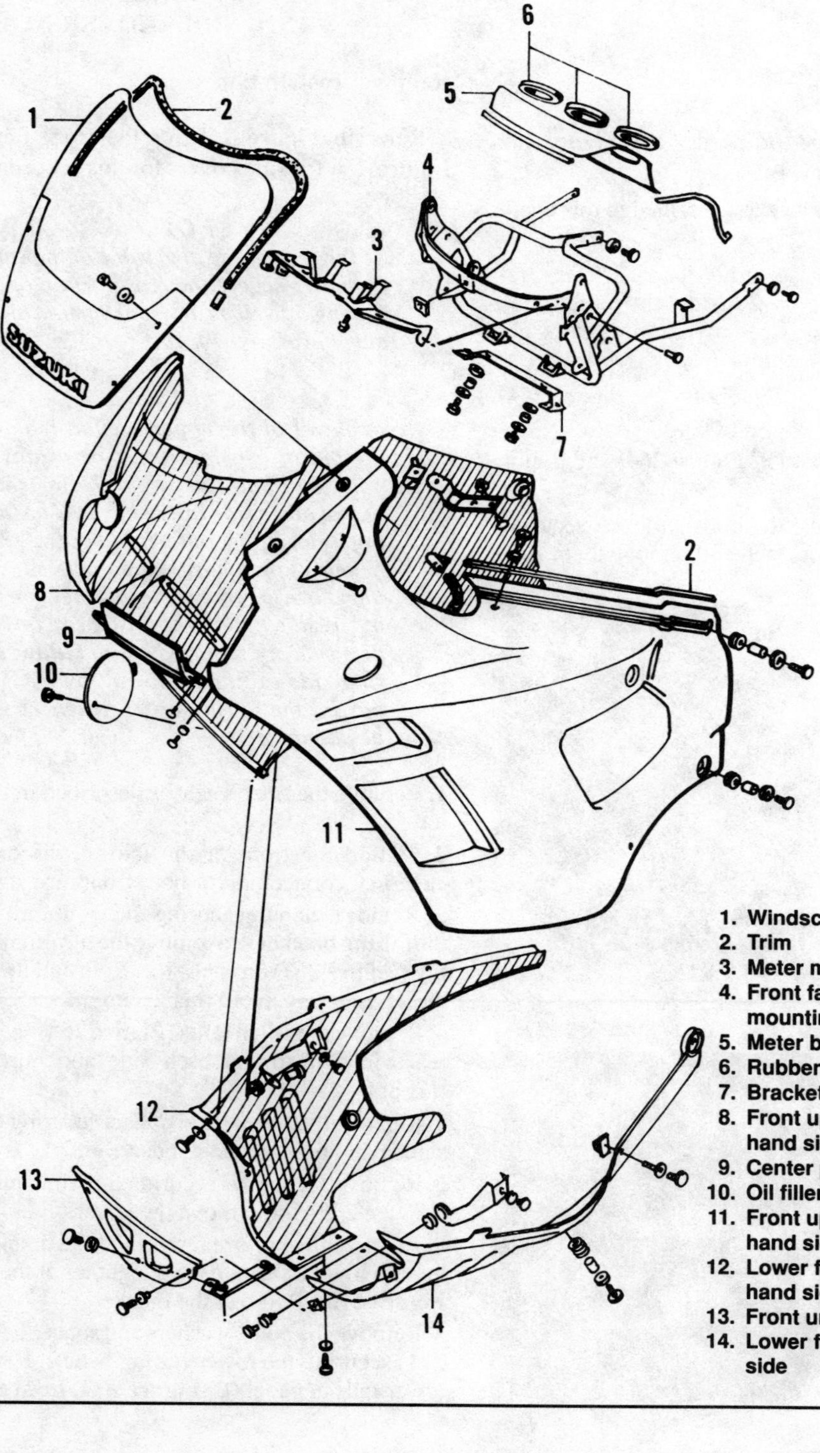

1. Windscreen
2. Trim
3. Meter mounting plate
4. Front fairing mounting bracket
5. Meter bracket
6. Rubber cushions
7. Bracket
8. Front upper fairing–right-hand side
9. Center panel
10. Oil filler cover
11. Front upper fairing–left-hand side
12. Lower fairing–right-hand side
13. Front under cover
14. Lower fairing–left-hand side

266

SIDE COVER (KATANA 600)

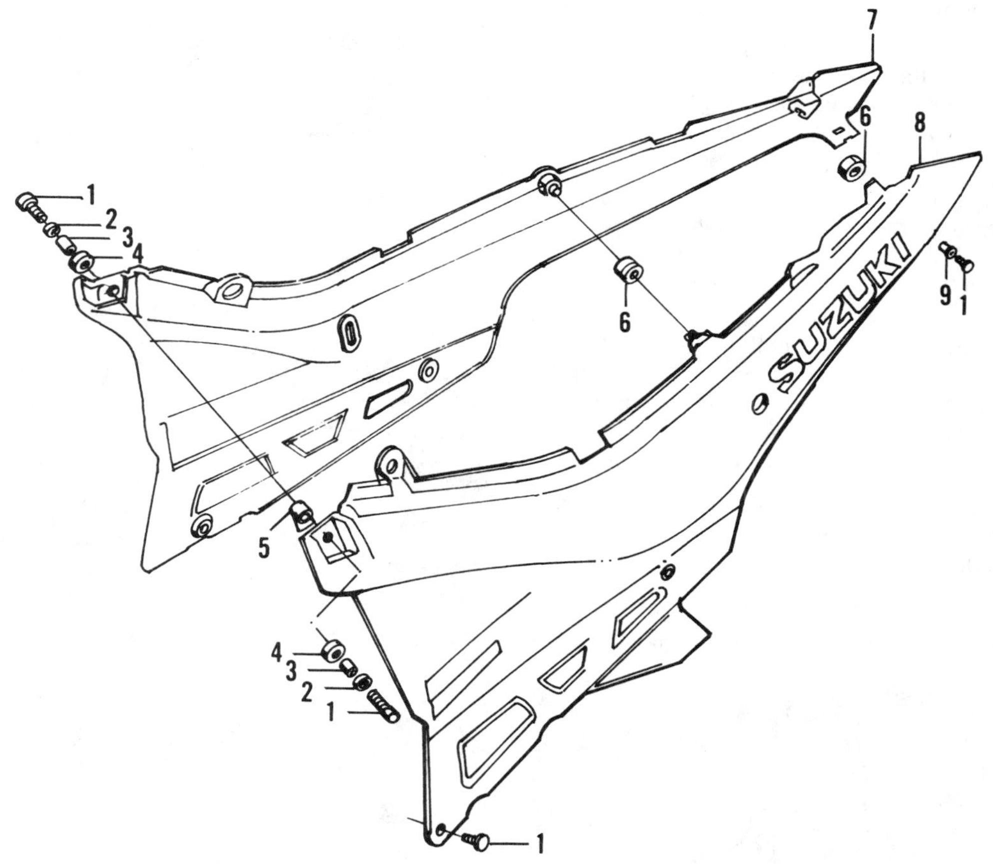

1. Bolt
2. Washer
3. Spacer
4. Rubber grommet
5. Spacer
6. Rubber cushion
7. Side cover–right-hand side
8. Side cover–left-hand side
9. Spacer

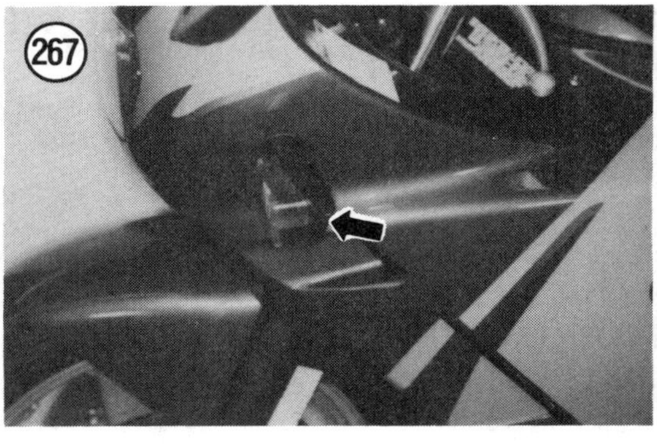

267

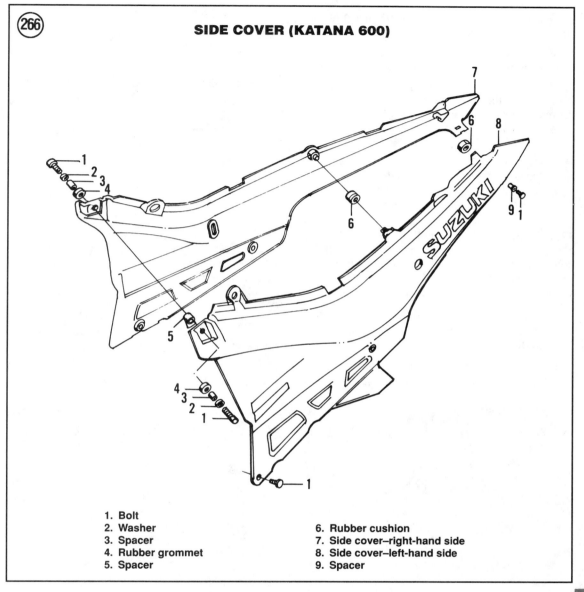

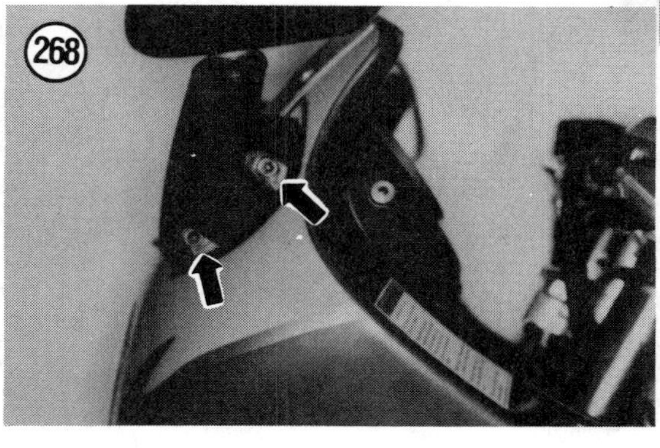

268

9. Remove the screw and washer (**Figure 272**) securing the side cover at the rear.

10. Remove the screws, washer and spacers (**Figure 273**) securing the lower portion of the side cover.

11. Remove the screws, washer and spacers (**Figure 274**) securing the upper portion of the side cover and the rear portion of the upper fairing.

NOTE

It is easier to remove the side cover after the upper fairing is removed, but if done carefully, the side cover can be removed with the upper fairing still in place.

12. If necessary, carefully pull the front of the side cover free from the front fairing and then carefully pull the rear locking tabs free from under the pillion seat and remove the side cover.

13. On one side of the bike, perform the following:

   a. Remove the lower fasteners (B, **Figure 270**) securing the front portion of the upper fairing to the frame.

   b. Remove the upper fasteners (**Figure 275**) securing the upper section to the frame.

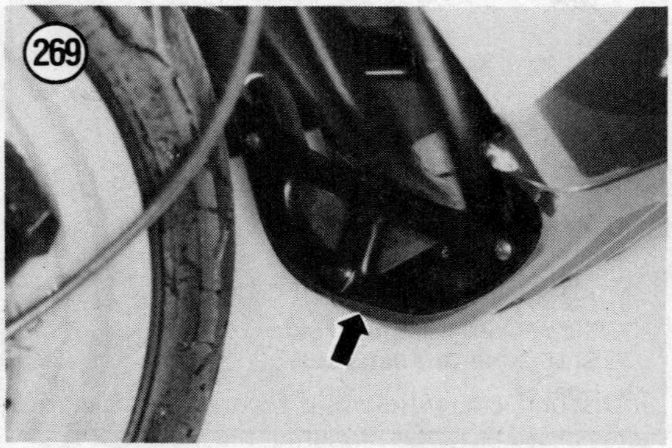

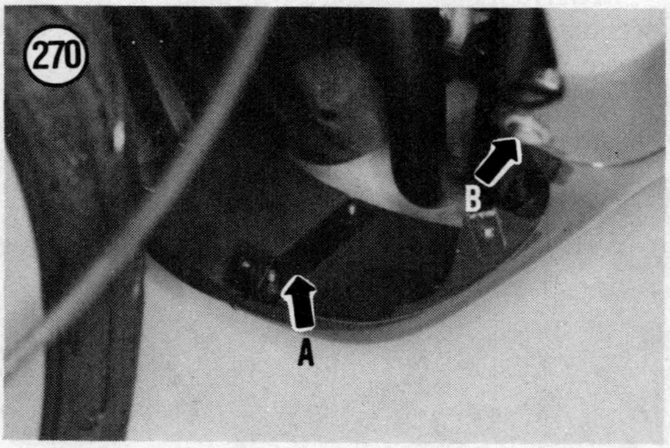

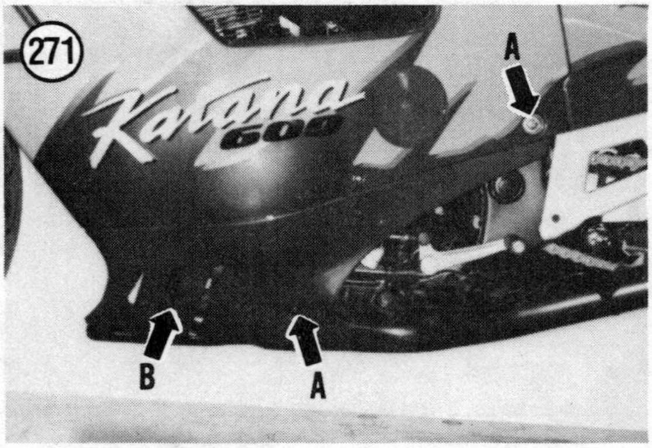

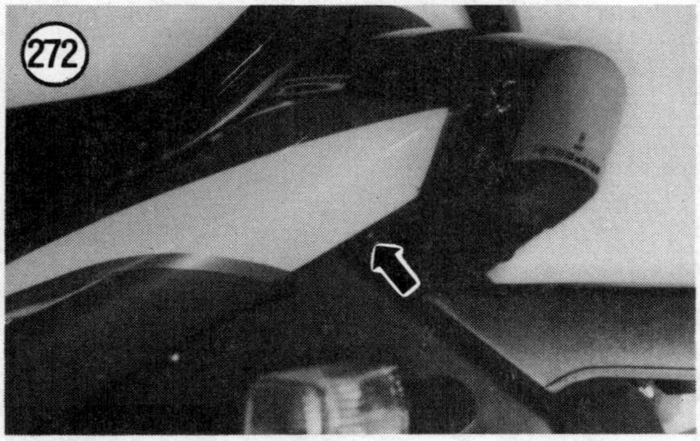

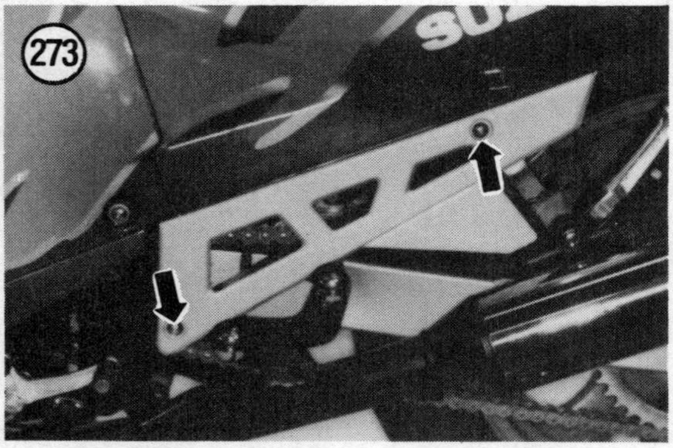

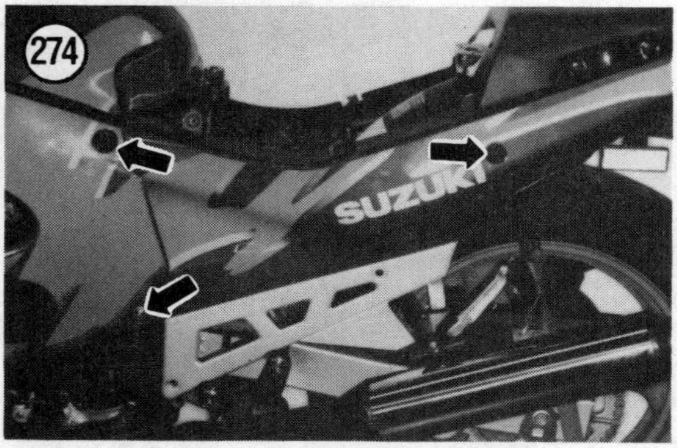

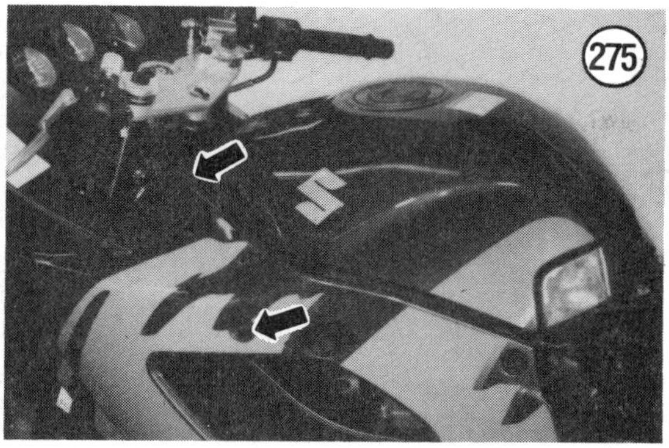

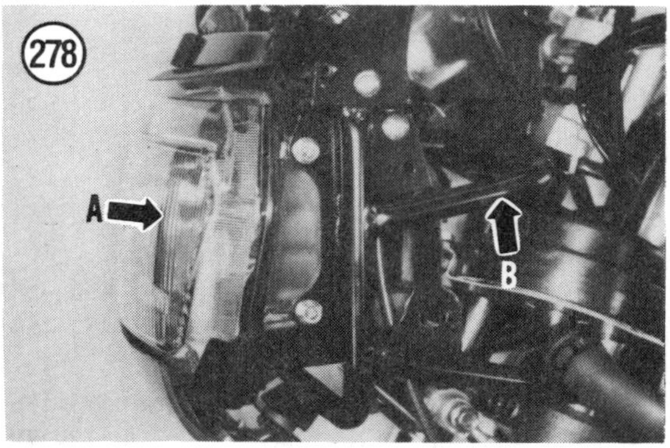

14. Either have an assistant hold onto the side where the fasteners were removed or place wood block(s) or a box under the lower section to hold it in position.

15. Repeat Step 13 for the other side of the bike.

NOTE

The following step is easier with the aid of a helper. It can be accomplished by one person but it is a little tricky.

16. Have an assistant hold onto that side of the upper section and repeat Step 14 for the other side of the bike.

17. Carefully pull the upper fairing assembly (**Figure 276**) forward and disengage it from the headlight housing area. The headlight assembly will stay with the front fairing mounting bracket.

18. Install by reversing these removal steps. Tighten all screws securely. Do not overtighten, as the plastic panels may fracture.

Front Fairing Mounting Bracket Removal/Installation

Refer to **Figure 265** for this procedure.

1. Remove the front fairing as described in this chapter.

2. Disconnect the speedometer cable from the base of the speedometer housing.

3. Disconnect all electrical connectors going to the instrument cluster.

4. Remove the rear bolt (**Figure 277**) on each side securing the mounting bracket to the frame.

5. Remove the headlight assembly (A, **Figure 278**) as described in this chapter.

6. Disconnect any tie-wraps securing any electrical wires or hoses to the mounting bracket.

7. Remove the bolt and washer securing the upper section of the mounting bracket to the steering head portion of the frame.

8. Carefully pull the front fairing bracket assembly (B, **Figure 278**) forward and make sure all electrical connectors are disconnected. Remove the bracket assembly.

9. Install by reversing these removal steps while noting the following:

   a. Make sure all electrical connectors are free of corrosion and are tight.

   b. Tighten all mounting bolts securely.

INDEX

14

V

W

14

1986 GSX-R750 (U.S.)
1986-1987 GSX-R750 (UK)

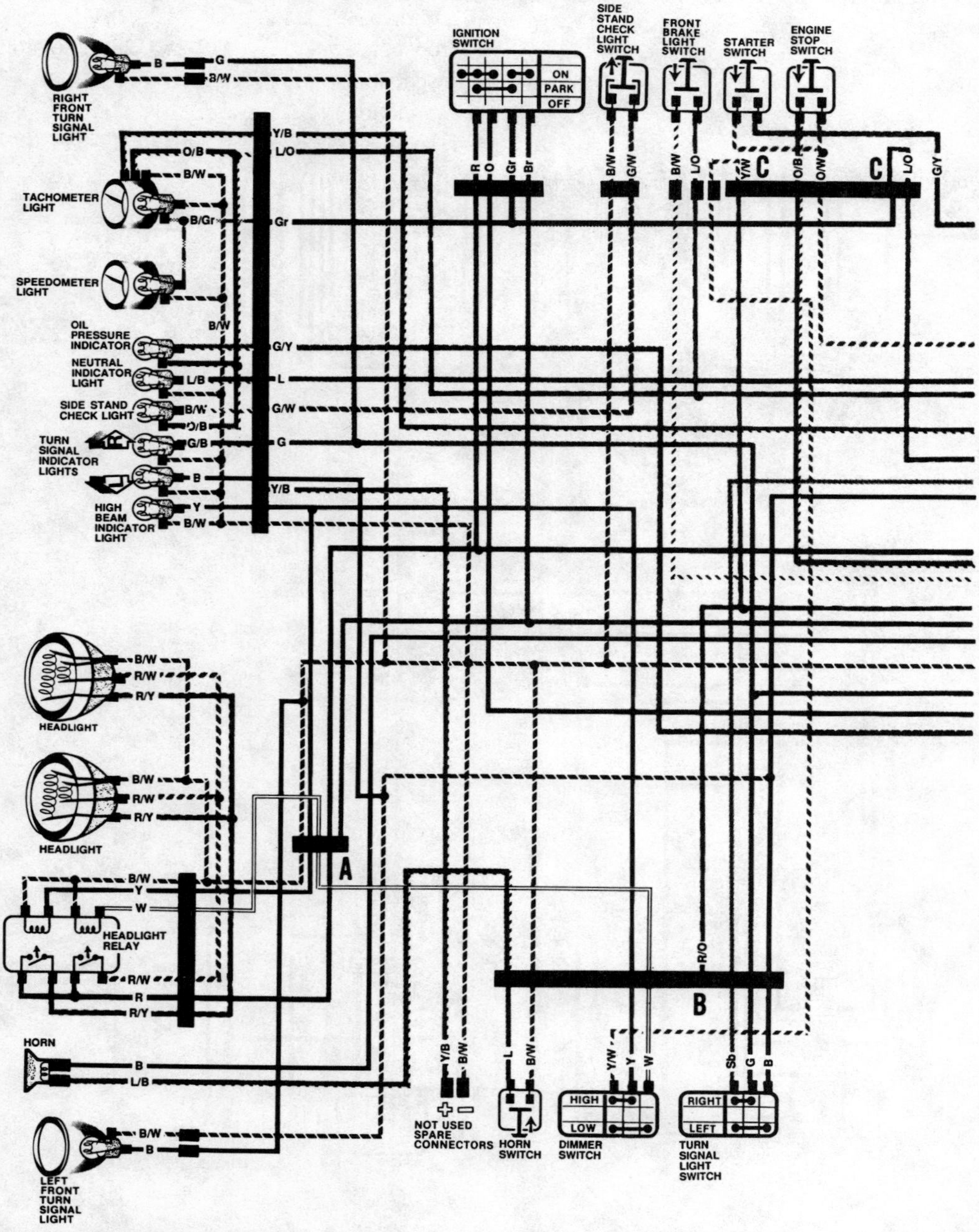

A. UK models are equipped with parking or city lights. A brown wire connects into the vacant brown wire within the connector and is routed to the left and right parking or city lights. A black/white wire leading from each parking or city light connects into the black/white ground circuit.

B. UK models are equipped with a passing light switch. A yellow wire connects into the yellow wire leading into the dimmer switch and an orange/red wire leading from the passing light switch connects into the vacant orange/red wire within the connector. Connection is made between the yellow and orange/red wires when the switch is depressed.

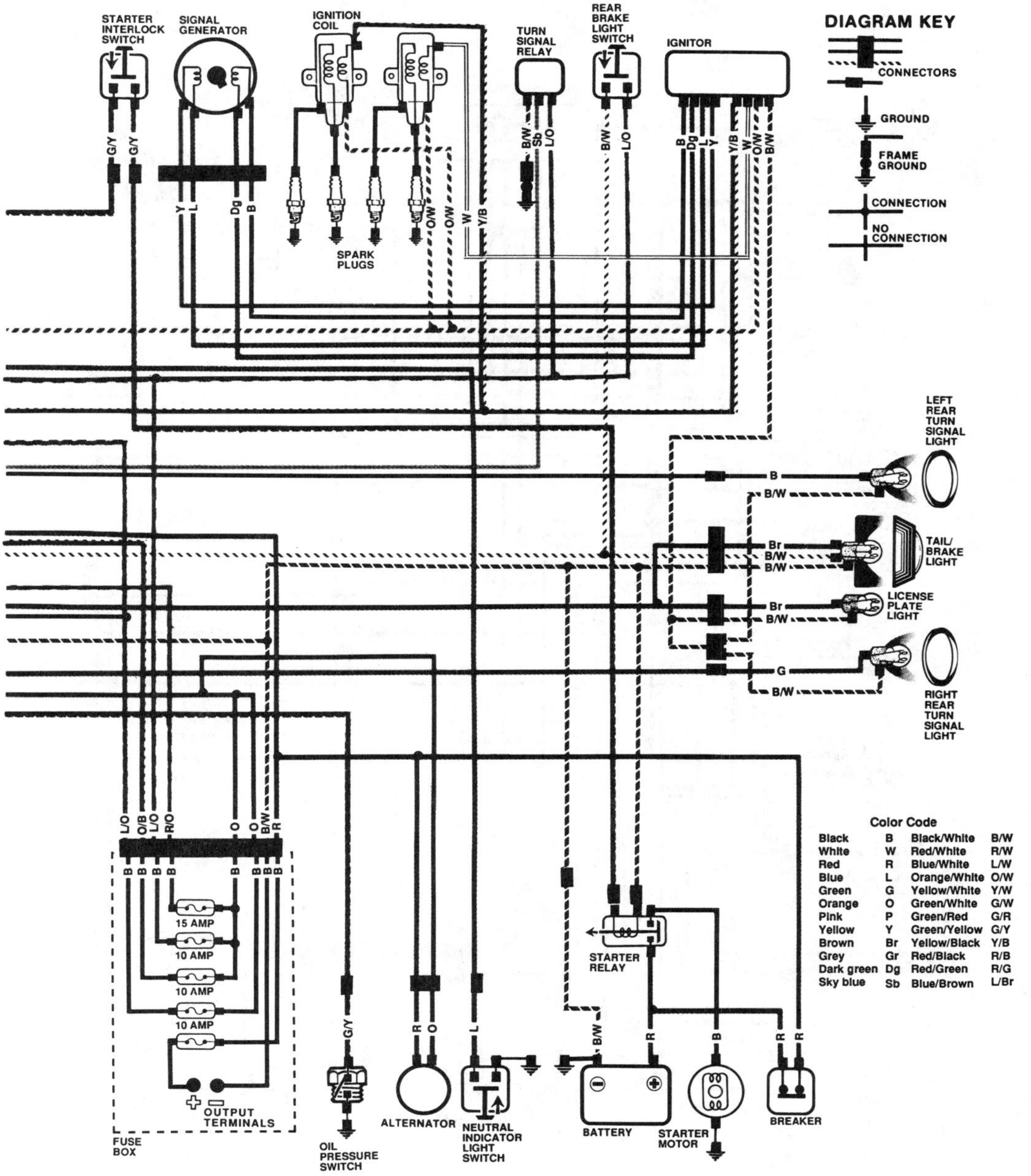

C. UK models are equipped with a manual control light switch. The light switch replaces the orange/blue and yellow/white bypass wires. No connection is made in the "OFF" position. In the "PO" position, connection is made between the grey and orange/blue wires. In the "ON" position, connection is made between the grey and orange/blue wires and the orange/red and yellow/white wires.

1986 GSX-R1100 (U.S.) & 1986 GSX-R750R LIMITED EDITION (U.S. & UK) 1986 & 1987 GSX-R1100 (UK)

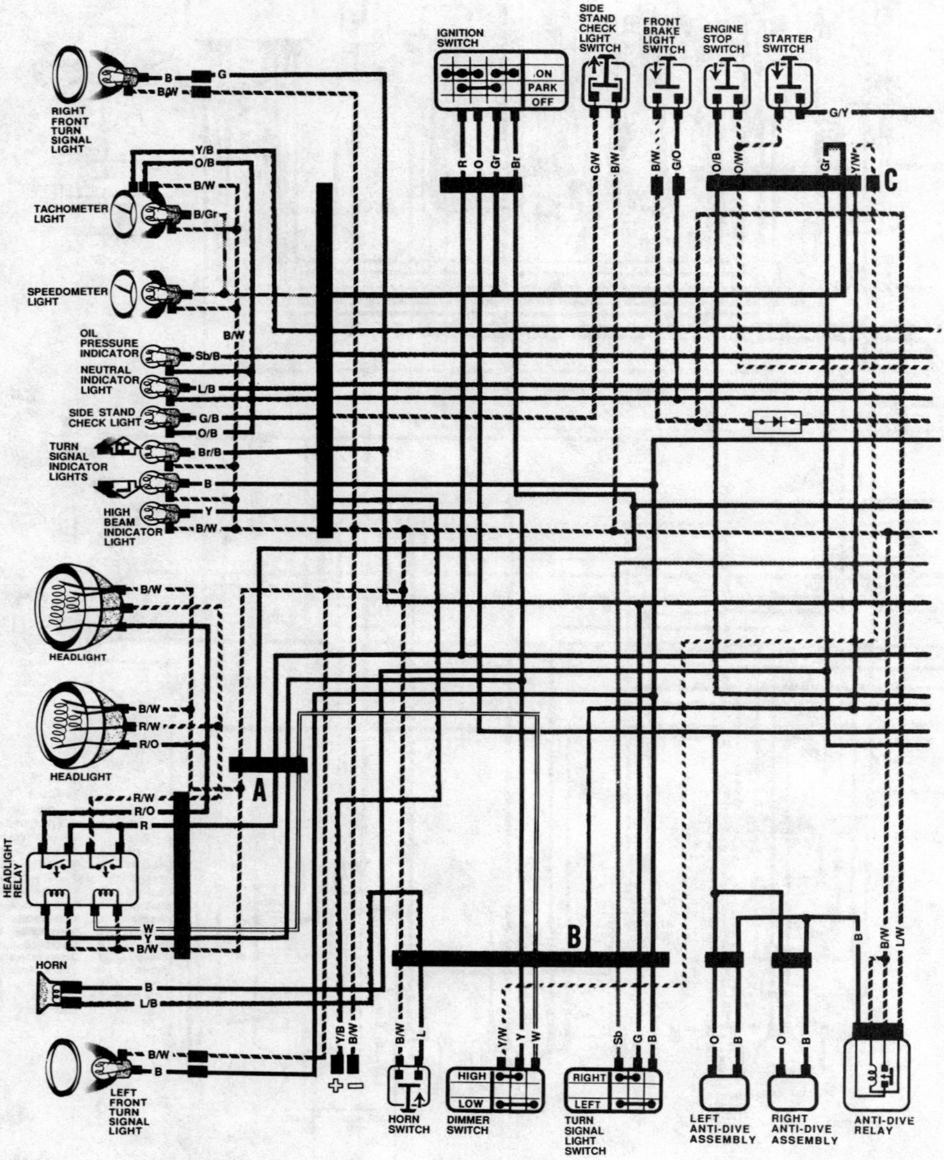

A. UK models are equipped with parking or city lights. A brown wire connects into the vacant brown wire within the connector and is routed to the left and right parking or city lights. A black/white wire leading from each parking or city light connects into the black/white ground circuit.

B. UK models are equipped with a passing light switch. A yellow wire connects into the yellow wire leading into the dimmer switch and an orange/red wire leading from the passing light switch connects into the vacant orange/red wire within the connector. Connection is made between the yellow and orange/red wires when the switch is depressed.

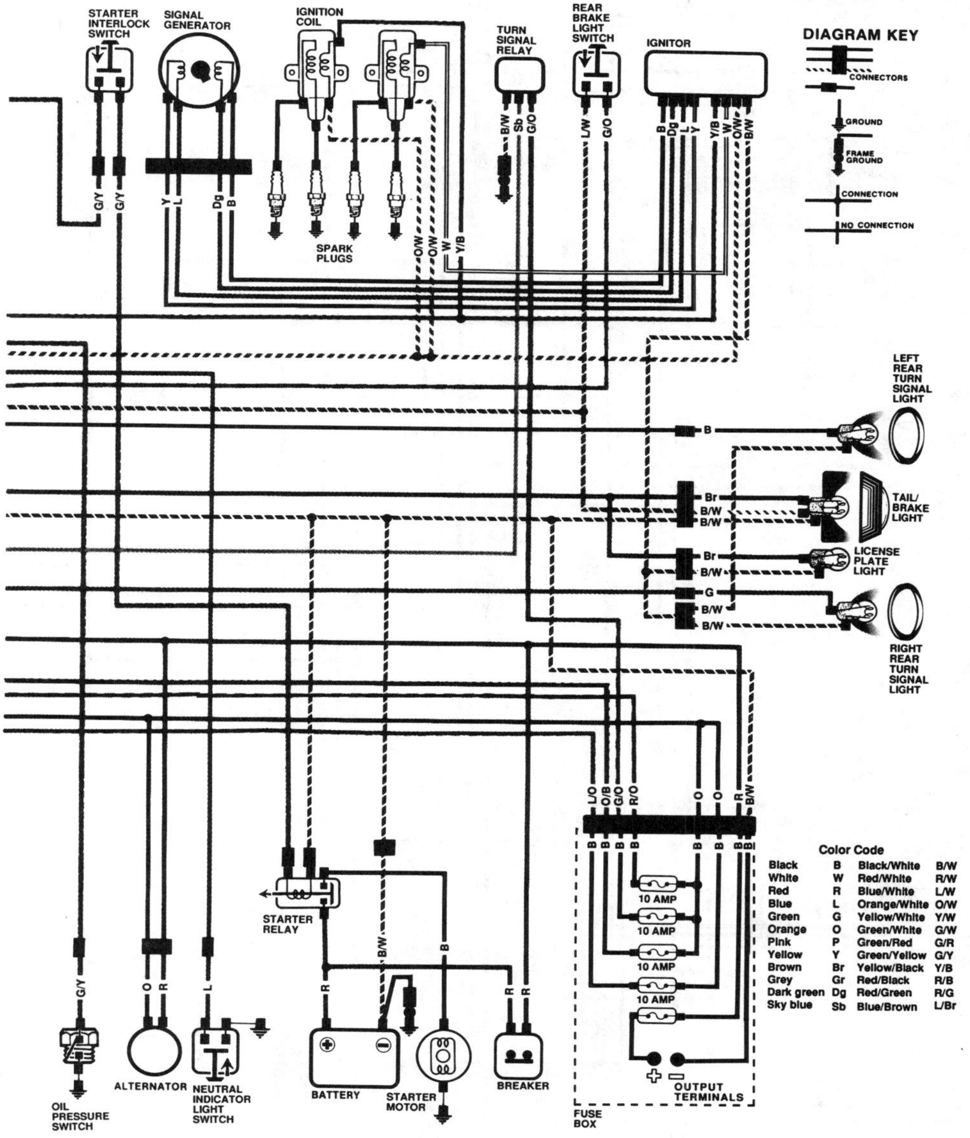

C. UK models are equipped with a manual control light switch. The light switch replaces the grey and yellow/white bypass wires. No connection is made in the "OFF" position. In the "PO" position, connection is made between the grey and orange/blue wires. In the "ON" position, connection is made between the grey and orange/blue wires and the orange/red and yellow/white wires.

1987 GSX-R750 (U.S.)

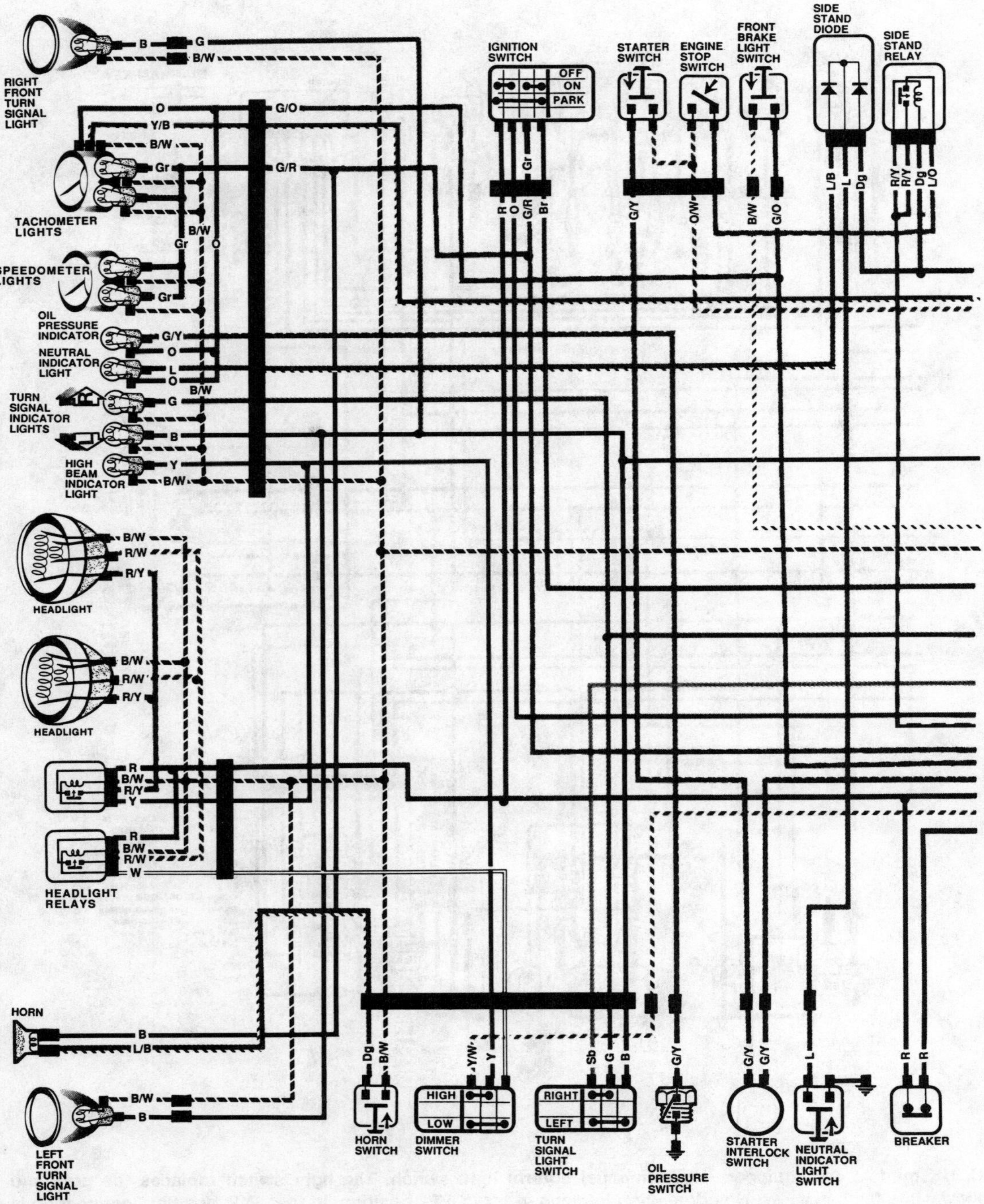

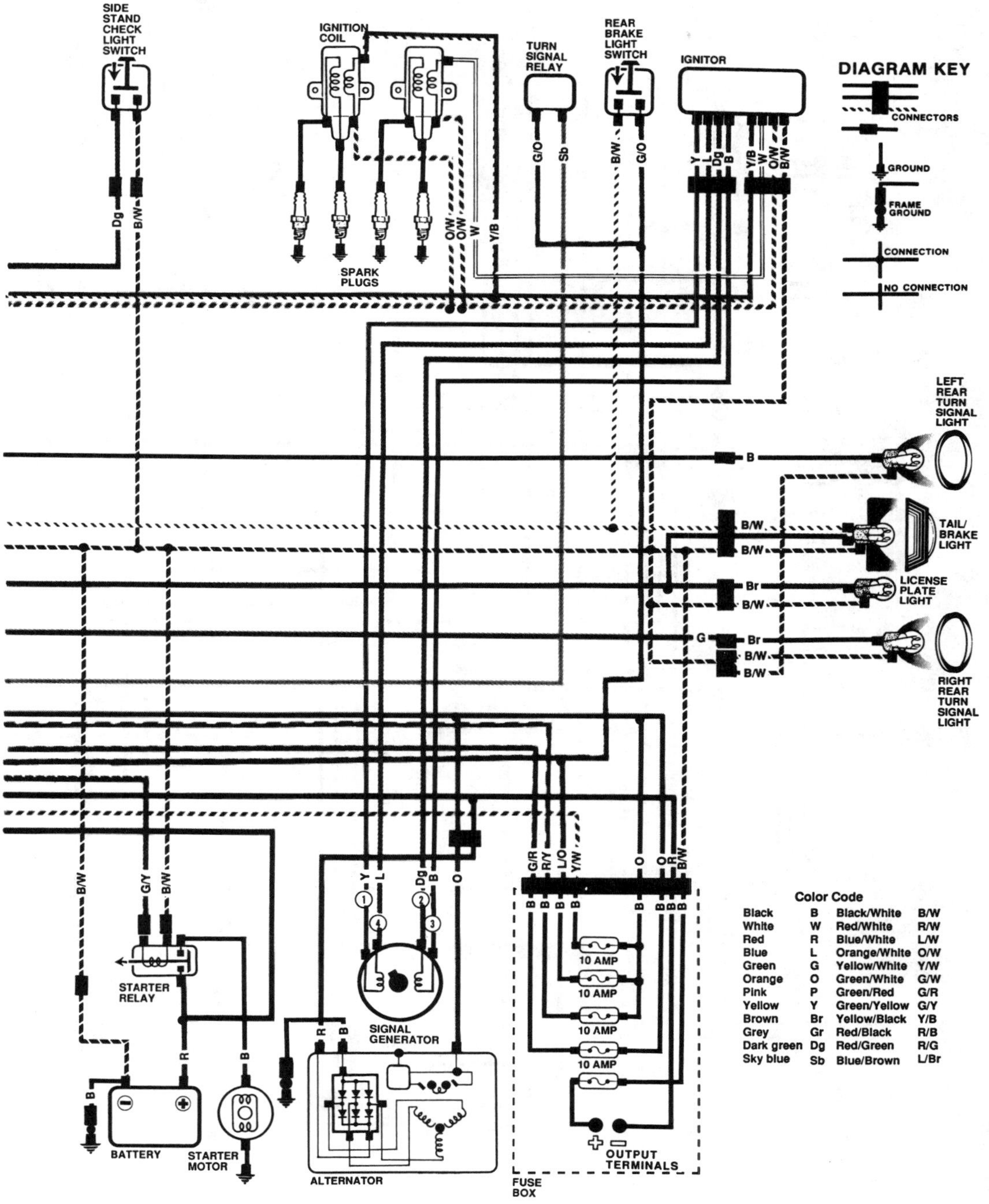

Color Code

Black	B	Black/White	B/W
White	W	Red/White	R/W
Red	R	Blue/White	L/W
Blue	L	Orange/White	O/W
Green	G	Yellow/White	Y/W
Orange	O	Green/White	G/W
Pink	P	Green/Red	G/R
Yellow	Y	Green/Yellow	G/Y
Brown	Br	Yellow/Black	Y/B
Grey	Gr	Red/Black	R/B
Dark green	Dg	Red/Green	R/G
Sky blue	Sb	Blue/Brown	L/Br

1987 GSX-R1100 (U.S.)

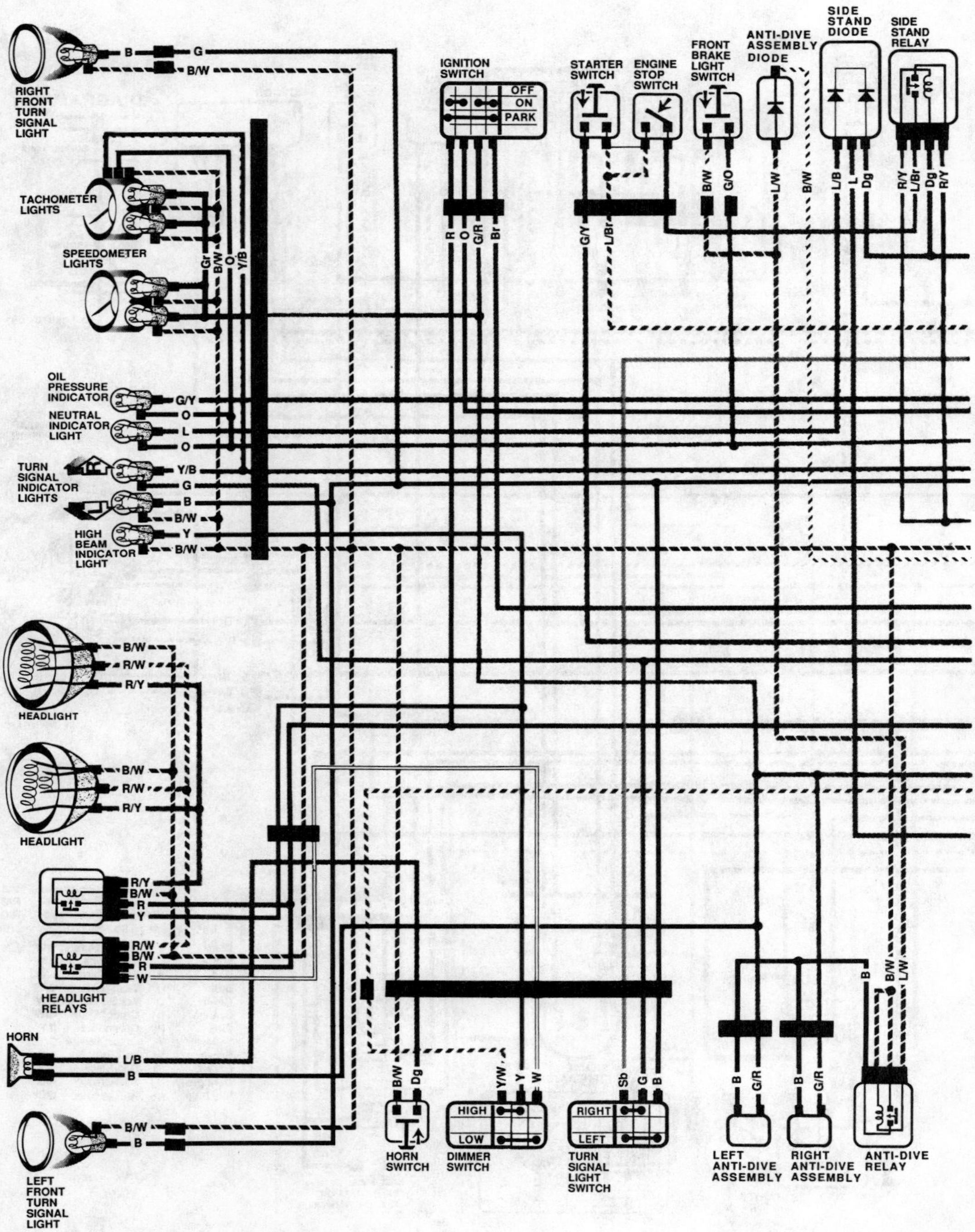

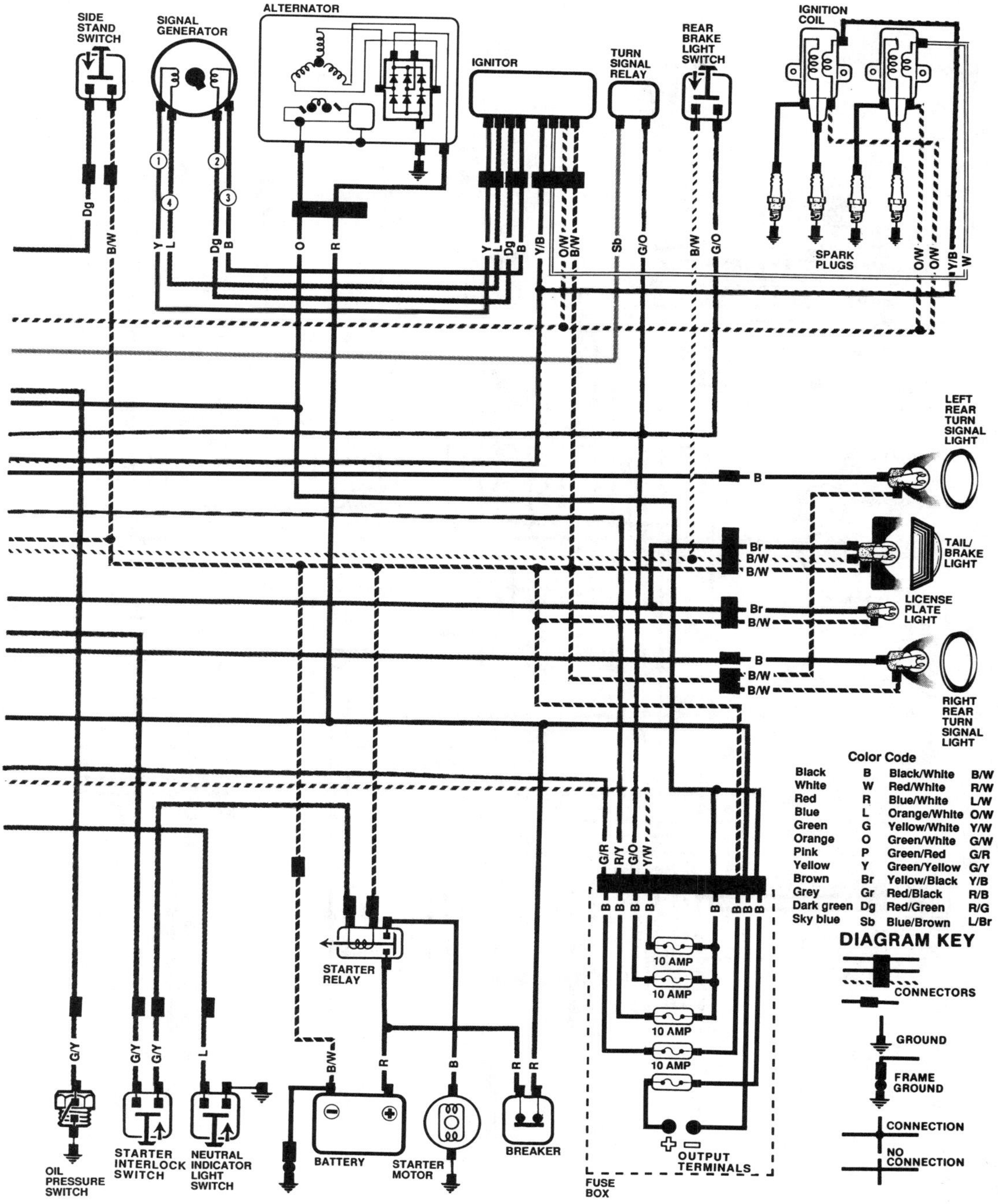
SIDE STAND SWITCH
SIGNAL GENERATOR
ALTERNATOR
IGNITOR
TURN SIGNAL RELAY
REAR BRAKE LIGHT SWITCH
IGNITION COIL
SPARK PLUGS
LEFT REAR TURN SIGNAL LIGHT
TAIL/ BRAKE LIGHT
LICENSE PLATE LIGHT
RIGHT REAR TURN SIGNAL LIGHT
STARTER RELAY
OIL PRESSURE SWITCH
STARTER INTERLOCK SWITCH
NEUTRAL INDICATOR LIGHT SWITCH
BATTERY
STARTER MOTOR
BREAKER
10 AMP
10 AMP
10 AMP
10 AMP
OUTPUT TERMINALS
FUSE BOX
Color Code
Black B Black/White B/W
White W Red/White R/W
Red R Blue/White L/W
Blue L Orange/White O/W
Green G Yellow/White Y/W
Orange O Green/White G/W
Pink P Green/Red G/R
Yellow Y Green/Yellow G/Y
Brown Br Yellow/Black Y/B
Grey Gr Red/Black R/B
Dark green Dg Red/Green R/G
Sky blue Sb Blue/Brown L/Br
DIAGRAM KEY
CONNECTORS
GROUND
FRAME GROUND
CONNECTION
NO CONNECTION

15

1988 GSX600F KATANA

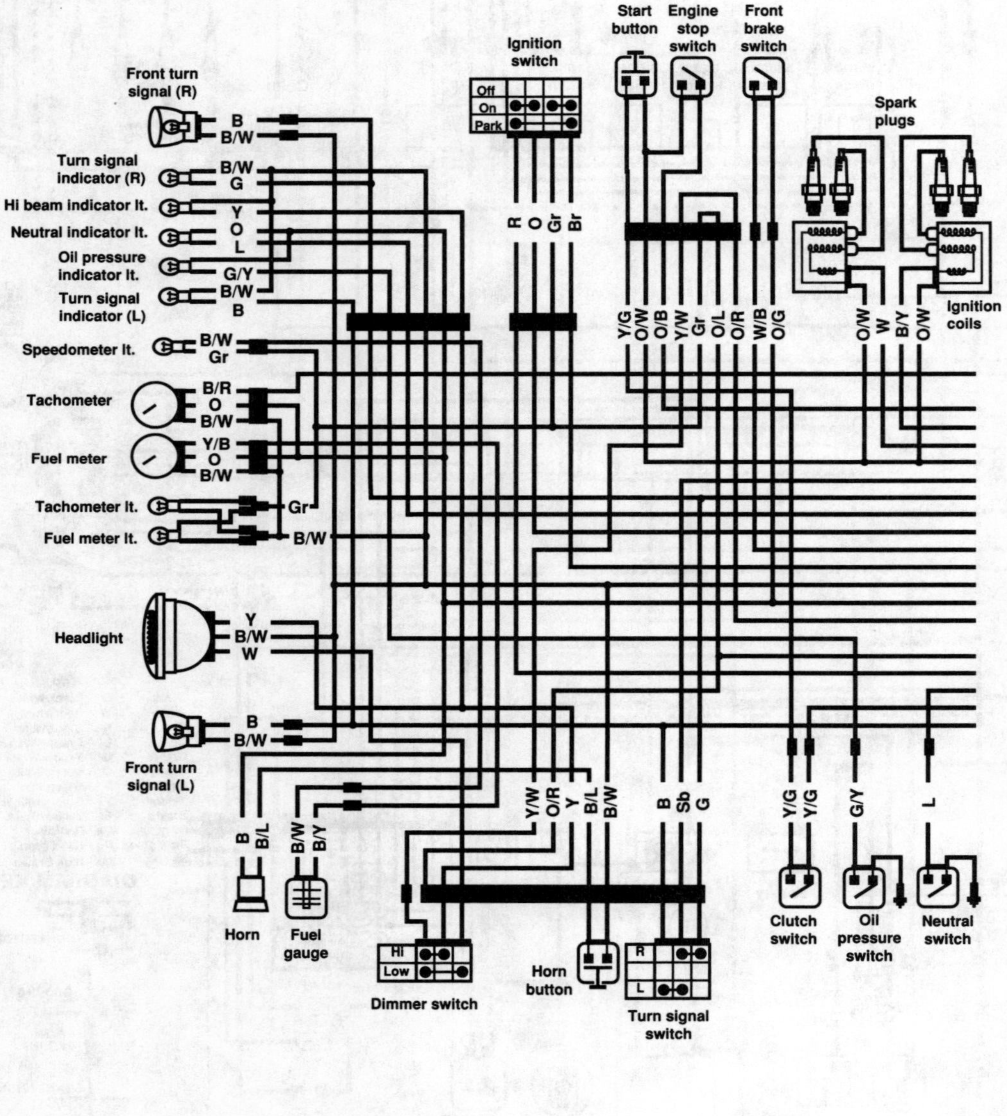

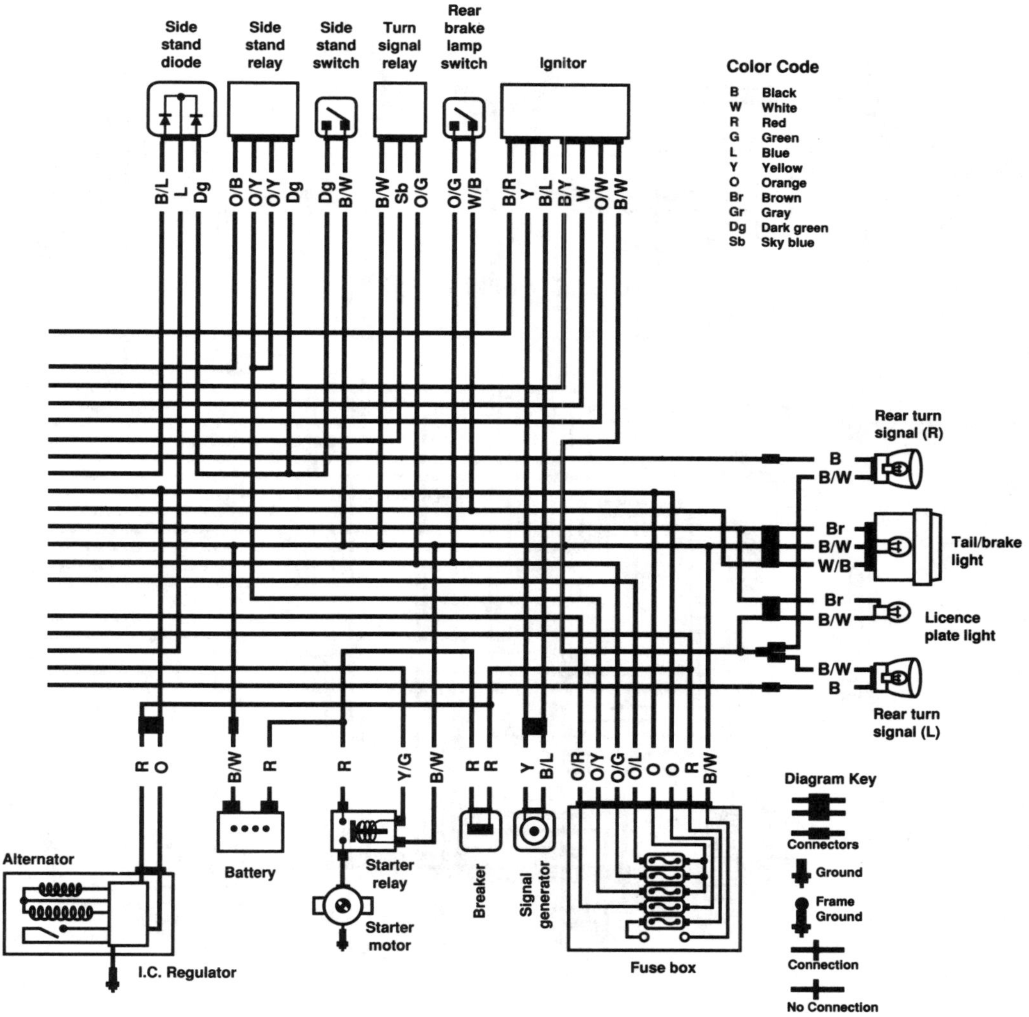

Side stand diode
Side stand relay
Side stand switch
Turn signal relay
Rear brake lamp switch
Ignitor
Color Code
B Black
W White
R Red
G Green
L Blue
Y Yellow
O Orange
Br Brown
Gr Gray
Dg Dark green
Sb Sky blue
B/L L Dg
O/B O/Y O/Y Dg
Dg B/W
B/W Sb O/G
O/G W/B
B/R Y B/L B/Y W O/W B/W
Rear turn signal (R)
B
B/W
Br
B/W
W/B
Tail/brake light
Br
B/W
Licence plate light
B/W
B
Rear turn signal (L)
R O
B/W R
R
Y/G
B/W
R R
Y B/L
O/R O/Y O/G O/L O O R B/W
Diagram Key
Connectors
Ground
Frame Ground
Connection
No Connection
Alternator
I.C. Regulator
Battery
Starter relay
Starter motor
Breaker
Signal generator
Fuse box

1989-1993 GSX600F KATANA

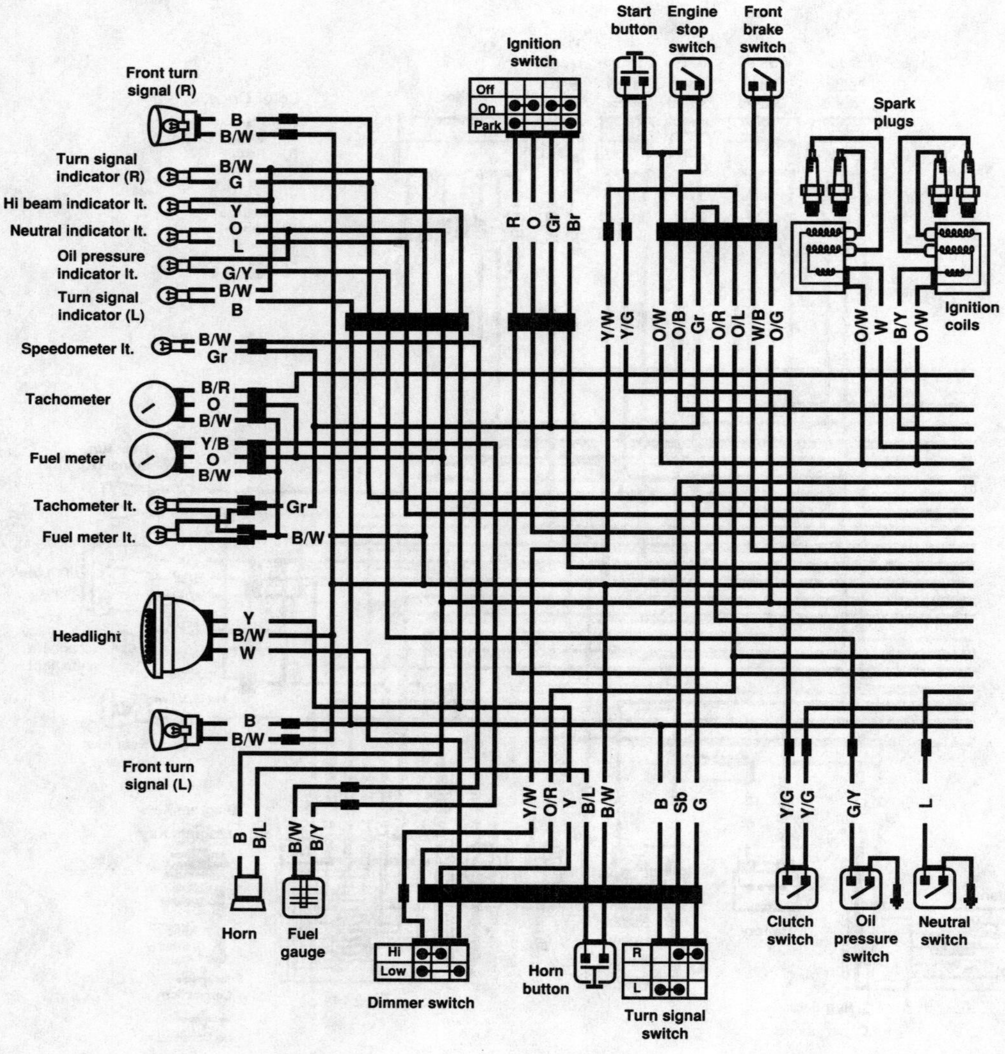

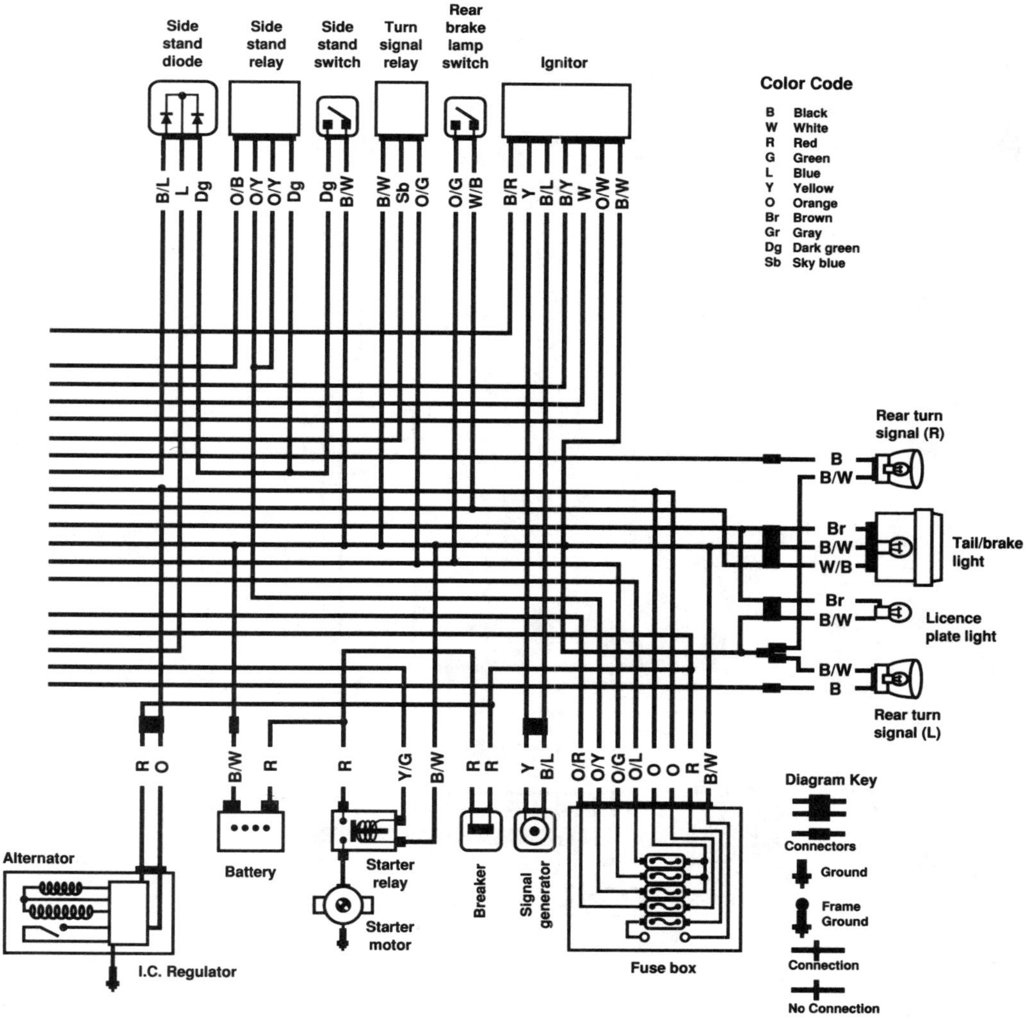
Side stand diode
Side stand relay
Side stand switch
Turn signal relay
Rear brake lamp switch
Ignitor
Color Code
B Black
W White
R Red
G Green
L Blue
Y Yellow
O Orange
Br Brown
Gr Gray
Dg Dark green
Sb Sky blue
Rear turn signal (R)
Tail/brake light
Licence plate light
Rear turn signal (L)
Alternator
I.C. Regulator
Battery
Starter relay
Starter motor
Breaker
Signal generator
Fuse box
Diagram Key
Connectors
Ground
Frame Ground
Connection
No Connection

15

NOTES

NOTES

NOTES

NOTES

NOTES

MAINTENANCE LOG

Date	Miles	Type of Service